PrincetonReview.com

THE BEST 386 COLLEGES
2021 Edition

**By Robert Franek, David Soto,
Stephen Koch, Aaron Riccio,
and The Staff of The Princeton Review**

Penguin
Random
House

The Princeton Review
110 East 42nd Street, 7th Floor
New York, NY 10017
E-mail: editorialsupport@review.com

Copyright © 2020 by TPR Education IP Holdings, LLC.
All rights reserved.

Published in the United States by Penguin Random House LLC,
New York, and in Canada by Random House of Canada, a division of Penguin Random House Ltd., Toronto.

All rankings, ratings, and listings are intellectual property
of TPR Education IP Holdings, LLC. No rankings, ratings,
listings, or other proprietary information in this book may be
repurposed, abridged, excerpted, combined with other data, or
altered for reproduction in any way without express permission
of The Princeton Review.

ISBN: 978-0-525-56972-5
eBook ISBN: 978-0-525-57007-3

The Princeton Review is not affiliated with Princeton University.

Editor: Aaron Riccio
Production Editor: Kathy Carter
Production Artist: Deborah Weber
Content Contributors: Jen Adams and Andrea Kornstein

Printed in the United States of America.

10 9 8 7 6 5 4 3 2 1

2021 Edition

Editorial
Rob Franek, Editor-in-Chief
David Soto, Director of Content Development
Stephen Koch, Survey Manager
Deborah Weber, Director of Production
Gabriel Berlin, Production Design Manager
Selena Coppock, Managing Editor
Aaron Riccio, Senior Editor
Meave Shelton, Senior Editor
Christopher Chimera, Editor
Eleanor Green, Editor
Orion McBean, Editor
Patricia Murphy, Editorial Assistant

Penguin Random House Publishing Team
Tom Russell, VP, Publisher
Alison Stoltzfus, Publishing Director
Amanda Yee, Associate Managing Editor
Ellen Reed, Production Manager
Suzanne Lee, Designer

Acknowledgments

Each year we assemble an awesomely talented group of colleagues who work together to produce our updated college profiles, and our 29th edition this year is no exception. Everyone involved in this effort—authors, editors, data managers, production specialists, and designers—goes above and beyond to make *The Best 386 Colleges* an exceptional student resource guide. For more than twenty-five years, we have worked to collect and publish what prospective college students really want: The most honest, accessible, and pertinent information about the colleges they are considering attending.

My sincere thanks go to everybody who has contributed to this tremendous project over the past quarter century. A special thank you goes to our authors, Jen Adams, Andrea Kornstein, Amanda Krupman, Hazel Schaeffer, Olivia Tejeda, and Tina Tuminaro for their dedication in poring through tens of thousands of surveys to produce the campus culture narratives of each school we profiled. Very special thanks goes to Aaron Riccio for his editorial commitment and vision, and to Stephen Koch, who continues to work in partnership with school administrators and students. My continued thanks go to our data guru, David Soto, for his successful efforts in collecting and accurately representing the statistical data that appear with each college profile. The scope of this project and its deadline constraints could not have been realized without the calm presence of our director of production, Deborah Weber, and production editor Kathy Carter—their dedication, focus, and attention to detail continue to impress and remind me of what a pleasure it is to work on this project each year. Special thanks also go to Jeanne Krier, my trusted colleague, media advisor, and friend, for the dedicated work she has done on this book and the overall series since its inception. Finally, I would like to make special mention of Tom Russell and Alison Stoltzfus, our Penguin Random House publishing team, for their continuous investment and faith in our ideas.

Robert Franek
Editor-in-Chief
Lead Author—*The Best 386 Colleges*

Contents

Get More (Free) Content
at PrincetonReview.com/guidebooks

As easy as 1·2·3

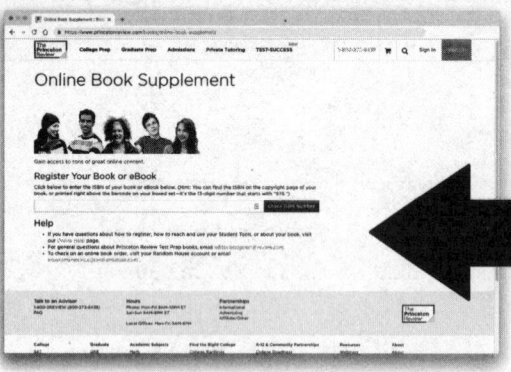

1 Go to PrincetonReview.com/guidebooks and enter the following ISBN for your book:
9780525569725

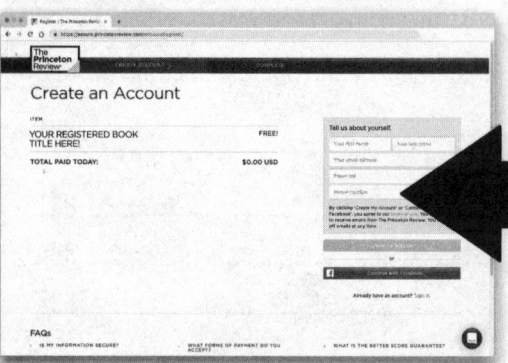

2 Answer a few simple questions to set up an exclusive Princeton Review account. *(If you already have one, you can just log in.)*

3 Enjoy access to your **FREE** content!

Once you've registered, you can...

- Take a full-length practice SAT and ACT

- Get valuable advice about applying to college

- Access a printable copy of the index for ease of use

- Check for any post-print updates or errata

Need to report a potential **content** issue?

Contact **EditorialSupport@review.com** and include:

- full title of the book
- ISBN
- page number

Need to report a **technical** issue?

Contact **TPRStudentTech@review.com** and provide:

- your full name
- email address used to register the book
- full book title and ISBN
- Operating system (Mac/PC) and browser (Firefox, Safari, etc.)

PART 1

Introduction

29 Years of The Princeton Review's College Rankings

1992	Edition	2021
250	Colleges profiled	386
30,000	Student surveys	143,000
120	Average surveys per campus	364
67	Survey questions	85

"There was a void in the college guide market and we have filled it with this book."

Twenty-nine years ago, The Princeton Review opened the first edition of *The Best Colleges* with this bold statement. In 1992, no other book provided in-depth descriptions of schools alongside statistics covering admissions, financial aid, and student body demographics.

Then, as now, no other guide was based on the input of so many students. Then, as now, we at The Princeton Review believe that current students are the real experts about life at a particular college or university—only they can give you the most candid and informed feedback on what life is really like on campus. More than a million students have participated in our surveys over the past quarter century, and we are pleased to continue to publish what we believe is the most substantive resource you need to find the college that will fit you best.

We've added (and dropped) schools from the book, we've exponentially increased our student survey results, and we've changed or renamed many of the categories in which we've used student feedback to rank 20 top colleges in each of 60+ fields. Our guiding conviction, however, remains the same: there is no single "best" college, only the best college for you. The profiles and ranking lists in this book can help you find the school that best fits your unique personality and goals.

What college is right for me?

We encourage students to consider their wants and needs across four categories: academics, campus culture, financial aid, and career services.

Academics

Does the college you're considering offer classes and learning opportunities that interest you? You don't need to declare a college major until your junior year of college—but you're more likely to succeed if you're excited about and engaged by the options available to you. Consider your learning style: Do you prefer informative lectures or lively discussions? Research and analysis, or hands-on experience and practice? Writing papers or working in small groups? Look for the academic experience you'll need to feel challenged and engaged, and what support you'll need for success—peer tutoring, accessible professors, mentorship, and career services are just some of the options you might find on campus. Check out course and program descriptions, reviews of professors, and sit in on some classes if you're able to visit campus.

Campus Culture

Do you want a big school or a small one? A hip urban campus or a verdant quad in the country? A college where everyone cheers on the basketball team, or one where every theater production gets a standing ovation? Every college has its own special vibe.

You can start narrowing down your list by making some decisions about the size of the student body and geographical location, and then move on to aspects you can identify by visiting campus, talking to current students, and trusting your gut instincts: the personalities, politics, and interests of the student body. Take quality of life into account, too, and try to check out the dorms, food, and recreational facilities on campus.

Financial Aid

The cost of college is one of the biggest concerns for students, parents, and counselors. We hear that from the students we work with and see it on our annual College Hopes & Worries Survey. It's important to be realistic about your family's finances and to avoid taking on unreasonable debts in the name of your education—but it's also important not to cross a school off your list because of a scary sticker price.

Many colleges and universities offer incredible financial aid packages (sometimes as a combination of grants and scholarships, which means no debt at all!). Raising your grades and your SAT® or ACT® scores will help you become more eligible for merit-based financial aid. And more and more data on college outcomes—that is, career placement rates and average starting salaries—is becoming available, which can help you assess the value of investing your tuition dollars in a particular college.

Check out our list of 200 "best value" schools on page 50, and read more about getting the most bang for your tuition buck in *The Best Value Colleges,* 13th Edition.

Career Development

Visit or contact the career development center at all the schools you're considering. Find out how each supports students in preparing for the professional world. Do they offer résumé writing workshops? Practice interviews? Networking events with alumni? If you foresee yourself in a particular field, location, or specific workplace, ask about past students' track records of finding internships, getting accepted to grad school, or landing entry-level jobs in those areas.

College admission officers and career counselors are more than happy to highlight their institutions' success stories—as well as the unique skill-building programs and experiences their campuses have to offer.

Our expert admission counselors will help you navigate the college process with less stress and submit stand-out applications to your top-choice schools. Learn more at PrincetonReview.com.

Getting into Selective Colleges: An Overview for High School Students

6 STEPS TO GETTING INTO COLLEGE

Putting some effort into your schoolwork and extracurricular experiences can make applying to your choice colleges a lot less stressful. Though they might sound obvious, the following steps are extremely important!

1. Work hard for good grades.

2. Enroll in challenging courses.

3. Spend time preparing for the ACT® or SAT® and SAT Subject™ Tests.

4. Polish your writing skills.

5. Establish relationships with teachers and advisors who can write strong letters of recommendation for you.

6. Get involved in some activities, community service, or work experiences that will enable you to show your values, talents, and skills.

College admission is all about compatibility. As an applicant, you are looking for an environment where you can thrive academically and personally, and it is the job of an admission officer to identify students who will make great additions to a unique campus community.

Your path to college begins your first year in high school. Grades and test scores are important factors in college admission, but admissions officers are also looking for curious and engaged candidates who will round out a diverse first-year class.

Grades

Most admissions officers report that your GPA and the rigor of your high school curriculum are the most important elements of your college application.

- Choose your high school classes carefully. Challenge yourself with honors, AP®, and IB® courses when they are available.

- Your grades count for all four years of high school. When colleges review your transcript, they often look at grade trends across subjects and course levels.

- Even if you had a rough first year of high school, there's still time to turn your grades around. Many schools will reward your upward trajectory.

Test Scores

SAT and/or ACT scores take the lead, but admissions officers consider your performance on other standardized tests as well.

- The PSAT® is optional your sophomore year, but your junior year PSAT scores can qualify you for scholarship programs such as the National Merit® Scholarship, which can help cover the cost of tuition and get you into a great college. It's also good practice for the SAT.

- Many selective colleges require you to submit SAT Subject Test scores, and some colleges grant course credit for excellent performance. It's a good idea to sit for the Subject Tests right after you finish the related classes in high school.

- Strong performances on AP Exams can indicate your potential for academic achievement to college admission officers. More than 1,400 colleges and universities accept high scores on AP Exams for course credits.

- Most schools view the ACT and SAT equally, so it's completely up to you which test you take (you can even take both!). Both the Essay section of the SAT and the Writing section of the ACT are optional, but some colleges may require them.

- Test optional schools: Schools that are test optional do not require standardized test scores as part of a complete application. Since your test scores could qualify you for merit scholarships even at test optional schools, it's still a smart idea to take (and prep for!) at least one standardized test.

Extracurriculars

What you do with your time shows colleges who you are and what qualities you'll bring to campus.

- Commitment to a sport, hobby, religious organization, or job over four years of high school is key. Colleges would much rather see you excited about a few worthwhile endeavors than marginally involved with a ton of clubs.

- If an after-school job is cutting into your extracurricular time, don't worry! Work experience demonstrates maturity and responsibility on your college application.

- Make your summer count! Some students enroll in university programs to start earning college credits. Others volunteer or find a summer job. Whatever you do, your experience can make your college application rise to the top of a competitive applicant pool.

What Should You Do This Summer?

Ahhh, summer. The possibilities seem endless. You can get a job, intern, travel, study, volunteer, or do nothing at all. Here are a few ideas to get you started:

- **Go to college:** No, not for real. However, you can participate in summer programs at colleges and universities at home and abroad. Programs can focus on anything from academics (stretch your brain by taking an intensive science or language course) to sports to admissions guidance. This is also a great opportunity to explore college life firsthand, especially if you get to stay in a dorm. Summer is also a time when families on vacations can squeeze in a college visit while they're in "the neighborhood." Even if classes aren't in session when you are able to tour a campus, the more colleges you can visit, the better informed your final college choice will be.

- **Prep for the PSAT, SAT, or ACT:** So maybe it's not quite as adventurous as trekking around Patagonia for the summer (it's also not as expensive!) or as cool as learning to slam dunk at basketball camp, but hey, there's nothing adventurous or cool about being rejected from your top-choice college because of unimpressive test scores. Plus, you'll be ahead of the game if you can return to school with much of your PSAT, SAT, and ACT preparation behind you.

- **Research scholarships:** College is expensive. While you should never rule out a school based on cost, the more scholarship money you can secure beforehand, the more college options you will have. You'll find loads of info on financial aid and scholarships on our site, PrincetonReview.com.

Applying for Financial Aid

The cost of college has been the biggest concern among respondents to our annual College Hopes & Worries survey for the past four years. Educate yourself on how financial aid works, so you can make the right choices for you and your family.

- Be aware that applying to college and applying for financial aid are two separate processes.

- Schools usually have their own net-price calculators so that families can get a sense of what their out-of-pocket costs would look like. Check out each prospective school's financial aid website as you research your college list.

- The Free Application for Federal Student Aid (FAFSA) is released on October 1 of every year. The form asks for information about your income and the size of your household to determine your expected family contribution (EFC) toward your college tuition.

- Schools may also use their own forms, or use the College Scholarship Service (CSS) Profile form for non-federal aid.

- Your financial aid package is intended to meet your need and will consist of:
  - o grants and scholarships
  - o federal work-study
  - o student loans

- Outside organizations offer scholarships tailored to academic interests, talents, extra-curricular activities, career goals, geographic location, and many more factors. Keep an eye on deadlines, which could fall as early as the summer before senior year.

Some of Our Other Helpful Books

The Princeton Review's *Paying for College* is the only annually updated guide to financial aid that has detailed, line-by-line strategies for completing the highly complicated FAFSA® for the upcoming school year (as well as the CSS Profile™ form) to one's best advantage. It explains how the financial aid process works and reveals strategies—all legal—for maximizing your eligibility for aid. Authored by Kal Chany, one of the nation's most widely sourced experts on college funding, it also includes annually updated information on education tax breaks, college savings programs, and student and parent loans. Check out Kal Chany's "26 Tips for Getting Financial Aid . . ." online in your student tools.

College Admission 101 presents simple answers to your toughest questions about the college admissions process, figuring out financial aid, and getting into the school of your choice.

K & W Guide to Colleges for Students with Learning Differences profiles 350+ schools highly recommended for such students. It includes strategies to help them successfully apply to the best programs for their needs, plus advice from specialists in the field of learning disabilities.

Great Schools for 20 of the Most Popular Undergraduate Majors

Worried about having to declare a major on your college application? Relax. Most colleges won't require you to declare a major until the end of your sophomore year, giving you plenty of time to explore your options. However, problems may arise if you are thinking about majoring in a program that limits its enrollment—meaning that if you don't declare that major early on, you might not get into that program at a later date.

On the flip side, some students declare a major on their application because they believe it will boost their chances of gaining admission. This can be problematic, however, if you later decide to change your major. It involves switching from one school within the college to another (e.g., from the school of arts and sciences to the school of business, for example), which can be difficult.

Never choose a college solely on the prestige of a particular program. College will expose you to new and exciting learning experiences. (Choosing a school based on program availability is a different story.) You may also want to investigate opportunities to design your own major. A commitment to a major would limit you in many ways.

How Did We Compile These Lists?

Each year we collect data from more than 2,000 colleges on the subject of—among many other things—undergraduate academic offerings. We ask colleges to report not only which undergraduate majors they offer, but also which of their majors have the highest enrollment and the number of bachelor's degrees each school awarded in these areas. The list below identifies (in alphabetical order) twenty of the forty "most popular" majors that the schools responding to our survey reported to us. We also conduct our own research on college majors. We look at institutional data, and we consult with our in-house college admissions experts as well as our National College Counselor Advisory Board (whom we list on pages 841–842) for their input on schools offering great programs in these majors. We thank them and all of the guidance counselors, college admissions counselors, and education experts across the country whose recommendations we considered in developing these lists. Of the nearly 3,000 four-year colleges across the United States, those on these lists represent only a snapshot of the many offering great programs in these majors. Use our lists as a starting point for further research.

Great Schools for Accounting Majors

- Agnes Scott College
- Alfred University
- Assumption University
- Auburn University
- Babson College
- Baylor University
- Bentley University
- Boston College
- Boston University
- Brigham Young University (UT)
- Bryant University
- Bucknell University
- Calvin College
- City University of New York—Baruch College
- City University of New York—Brooklyn College
- City University of New York—Hunter College
- City University of New York—Queens College
- Claremont McKenna College
- Clemson University
- College of Charleston
- Cornell University
- DePaul University
- Drexel University
- Duquesne University
- Elon University
- Emory University
- Fairfield University
- Fordham University
- George Mason University
- Georgetown University
- Hofstra University
- Illinois Wesleyan University
- Indiana University—Bloomington
- Iowa State University
- James Madison University
- Lehigh University
- Le Moyne College
- Marquette University
- Miami University (OH)
- New York University
- Northeastern University
- Pace University
- Penn State University Park
- Pepperdine University
- Rider University
- Rochester Institute of Technology
- St. Bonaventure University
- Seton Hall University
- Siena College
- Southern Methodist University
- Stonehill College
- Suffolk University
- Temple University
- Texas A&M University—College Station
- Transylvania University
- University of Alabama at Birmingham
- University of Houston
- University of Illinois at Urbana-Champaign
- University of Michigan—Ann Arbor
- University of Mississippi
- University of Oklahoma
- University of Pennsylvania
- University of Southern California
- The University of Texas at Austin
- The University of Texas at Dallas
- Washington & Jefferson College

Great Schools for Agriculture Majors

- Angelo State University
- Arizona State University
- Auburn University
- Berea College
- California State University, Stanislaus
- The Catholic University of America
- Clemson University
- College of the Atlantic
- College of the Ozarks
- Colorado State University
- The Cooper Union for the Advancement of Science and Art
- Cornell University
- Gettysburg College
- Illinois Institute of Technology
- Iowa State University
- Kansas State University
- Louisiana State University
- New Jersey Institute of Technology
- North Carolina State University
- Pennsylvania State University—University Park
- Purdue University—West Lafayette
- State University of New York—College of Environmental Science and Forestry
- Texas A&M University—College Station
- Texas Christian University
- Truman State University
- Tuskegee University
- University of Arizona
- University of Arkansas—Fayetteville
- University of California—Davis
- University of Florida
- University of Georgia
- University of Hawaii—Manoa
- University of Idaho
- University of Illinois at Urbana-Champaign
- University of Kentucky

- University of Maine
- University of Maryland—College Park
- University of Massachusetts Amherst
- University of Missouri—Columbia
- University of Nebraska—Lincoln

- University of Tennessee
- University of Vermont
- University of Wisconsin—Madison
- University of Wyoming
- West Virginia University

Great Schools for Biology Majors

- Agnes Scott College
- Albion College
- Amherst College
- Austin College
- Allegheny College
- Baylor University
- Berea College
- Berry College
- Brandeis University
- Brown University
- Bryn Mawr College
- Carleton College
- Case Western Reserve University
- Centenary College of Louisiana
- Christopher Newport University
- Clark University
- Clemson University
- Coe College
- Colby College
- College of Charleston
- The College of New Jersey
- College of Saint Benedict/Saint John's University
- Colorado College
- Colorado State University
- Connecticut College
- Cornell University
- Creighton University
- Davidson College
- Denison University
- Dickinson College
- Drexel University
- Drury University
- Duke University
- Earlham College
- Eckerd College
- Emory University
- Florida Southern College
- George Mason University
- Goucher College
- Grinnell College
- Guilford College
- Harvard College
- Haverford College
- Hillsdale College
- Hofstra University
- Howard University

- Illinois Wesleyan University
- Indiana University—Bloomington
- Johns Hopkins University
- Juniata College
- Lawrence University
- Le Moyne College
- Louisiana State University
- Loyola University—Chicago
- Lycoming College
- Massachusetts Institute of Technology
- Michigan State University
- Millsaps College
- Mount Holyoke College
- New College of Florida
- North Carolina State University
- The Ohio State University—Columbus
- Ohio University—Athens
- Ohio Wesleyan University
- Pomona College
- Randolph College
- Randolph-Macon College
- Reed College
- Rhodes College
- Rice University
- St. Bonaventure University
- Saint Louis University
- St. Olaf College
- Salisbury University
- Scripps College
- State University of New York—College of Environmental Science and Forestry
- State University of New York—Stony Brook University
- Swarthmore College
- Temple University
- Texas A&M University—College Station
- Transylvania University
- United States Coast Guard Academy
- University of Alabama at Birmingham
- University of California—Davis
- University of California—Los Angeles
- University of California—San Diego
- University of California—Santa Barbara
- University of California—Santa Cruz
- The University of Chicago
- University of Dallas
- University of Delaware

- University of Denver
- University of Georgia
- University of Hawaii—Manoa
- University of Houston
- University of Kansas
- University of Maryland, Baltimore County
- University of Miami
- University of New England
- University of New Mexico
- The University of North Carolina at Chapel Hill

- University of Scranton
- The University of Texas at Dallas
- Ursinus College
- Wabash College
- Washington University in St. Louis
- Wellesley College
- Wheaton College (MA)
- Whitman College
- Wofford College
- Xavier University of Louisiana

Great Schools for Business/Finance Majors

- Alfred University
- Arizona State University
- Babson College
- Bentley University
- Berea College
- Boston College
- Brigham Young University (UT)
- Bradley University
- Bryant University
- Butler University
- California State University, Stanislaus
- Calvin College
- Catawba College
- Carnegie Mellon University
- Champlain College
- Chapman University
- Christopher Newport University
- City University of New York—Baruch College
- City University of New York—Brooklyn College
- College of Charleston
- College of William and Mary
- Cornell University
- DePaul University
- Emory University
- Fairfield University
- Florida State University
- High Point University
- Indiana University—Bloomington
- Iowa State University
- Lehigh University
- Lycoming College
- Massachusetts Institute of Technology
- McDaniel College
- Mercer University
- Miami University (OH)
- Michigan State University
- Middle Tennessee State University
- New York University
- Northwestern University
- Ohio University—Athens
- Oregon State University

- Pace University
- Portland State University
- Rice University
- Roanoke College
- Rollins College
- Rutgers University—New Brunswick
- Seattle University
- San Diego State University
- Saint Joseph's University (PA)
- Saint Mary's College (CA)
- Saint Michael's College
- Santa Clara University
- Siena College
- Southwestern University
- Stetson University
- Suffolk University
- Texas State University
- University of Arkansas—Fayetteville
- University of California—Berkeley
- University of California—Los Angeles
- The University of Chicago
- University of Florida
- University of Houston
- University of Illinois at Urbana-Champaign
- University of Michigan—Ann Arbor
- University of New Orleans
- The University of North Carolina at Greensboro
- University of Notre Dame
- University of Pennsylvania
- University of Richmond
- University of San Diego
- University of San Francisco
- University of Southern California
- The University of Texas at Austin
- The University of Texas at Dallas
- The University of Tulsa
- University of Virginia
- Villanova University
- Washington University in St. Louis
- Wittenberg University

Great Schools for Communications Majors

- Baylor University
- Boston College
- Boston University
- Bradley University
- City University of New York—Hunter College
- Clemson University
- College of Charleston
- Cornell University
- Denison University
- DePaul University
- DePauw University
- Duquesne University
- Eckerd College
- Elon University
- Emerson College
- Fairfield University
- Fordham University
- Gonzaga University
- High Point University
- Hollins University
- Hofstra University
- Howard University
- Indiana University—Bloomington
- Iowa State University
- Ithaca College
- James Madison University
- Lake Forest College
- Loyola University—Maryland
- Loyola University—New Orleans
- Marist College
- Manhattanville College
- Muhlenberg College
- New York University
- Northwestern University
- Pepperdine University
- Quinnipiac University
- Ripon College
- Salisbury University
- Seton Hall University
- St. John's University (NY)
- Stanford University
- Suffolk University
- Susquehanna University
- Syracuse University
- Texas Christian University
- University of California—San Diego
- University of California—Santa Barbara
- University of Iowa
- University of Maryland—College Park
- University of San Diego
- University of Southern California
- University of Tampa
- The University of Texas at Austin
- University of Utah

Great Schools for Computer Science/Computer Engineering Majors

- Auburn University
- Boston University
- Bradley University
- Brown University
- California Institute of Technology
- Carleton College
- Carnegie Mellon University
- Champlain College
- Clemson University
- Drexel University
- Florida State University
- George Mason University
- Georgia Institute of Technology
- Gonzaga University
- Hampton University
- Harvey Mudd College
- Illinois Institute of Technology
- Iowa State University
- Johns Hopkins University
- Kettering University
- Lehigh University
- Massachusetts Institute of Technology
- Missouri University of Science and Technology
- New Jersey Institute of Technology
- Northeastern University
- Northwestern University
- Oregon State University
- Pennsylvania State University—University Park
- Princeton University
- Rice University
- Rensselaer Polytechnic Institute
- Roanoke College
- Rochester Institute of Technology
- Rose-Hulman Institute of Technology
- Seattle University
- Stanford University
- State University of New York at Binghamton
- Texas A&M University—College Station
- United States Air Force Academy
- University of Arizona
- University of California—Berkeley
- University of California—Los Angeles
- University of California—Riverside
- University of Illinois at Urbana-Champaign
- University of Maryland, Baltimore County
- University of Massachusetts Amherst
- University of Michigan—Ann Arbor
- University of Washington
- Worcester Polytechnic Institute

Great Schools for Criminology Majors

- American University
- Angelo State University
- Auburn University
- Becker College
- California State University, Stanislaus
- Champlain College
- Florida State University
- George Mason University
- Guilford College
- Indiana University of Pennsylvania
- North Carolina State University
- The Ohio State University—Columbus
- Ohio University—Athens
- Quinnipiac University
- St. John's University (NY)
- Suffolk University
- University of Delaware
- University of Denver
- University of Louisville
- University of Maryland—College Park
- University of Miami
- University of New Hampshire
- University of New Haven
- University of South Carolina—Columbia
- University of South Florida
- University of Tampa
- University of Utah
- Virginia Wesleyan College
- Whittier College

Great Schools for Education Majors

- Auburn University
- Barnard College
- Bucknell University
- Catawba College
- City University of New York—Brooklyn College
- City University of New York—Hunter College
- Colgate University
- The College of New Jersey
- College of the Ozarks
- College of William and Mary
- Columbia University
- Cornell College
- Cornell University
- Duquesne University
- East Carolina University
- Elmira College
- Elon University
- Gonzaga University
- Goucher College
- Hillsdale College
- Indiana University—Bloomington
- Knox College
- Loyola Marymount University
- Marquette University
- McGill University
- Miami University (OH)
- Monmouth University (NJ)
- Nazareth College
- New York University
- Northeastern University
- Northwestern University
- The Ohio State University—Columbus
- Simmons College
- Skidmore College
- Smith College
- Stephens College
- Trinity University (TX)
- University of Louisiana at Lafayette
- University of Maine
- University of Mississippi
- The University of Montana—Missoula
- Vanderbilt University
- Villanova University
- Wagner College
- Wellesley College
- William Jewell College
- Xavier University (OH)

Great Schools for Engineering Majors

- California Institute of Technology
- Carnegie Mellon University
- Case Western Reserve University
- Columbia University
- The Cooper Union for the Advancement of Science and Art
- Clarkson University
- Cornell University
- Drexel University
- Duke University
- Franklin W. Olin College of Engineering
- Georgia Institute of Technology
- Harvard College
- Harvey Mudd College
- Illinois Institute of Technology
- Johns Hopkins University
- Kettering University
- Lawrence Technological University
- Manhattan College

- Massachusetts Institute of Technology
- Michigan Technological University
- Missouri University of Science and Technology
- Montana Technological University
- Pennsylvania State University—University Park
- Princeton University
- Purdue University—West Lafayette
- Rensselaer Polytechnic Institute
- Rice University
- Rochester Institute of Technology
- Rose-Hulman Institute of Technology
- Stanford University
- Stevens Institute of Technology
- Texas A&M University—College Station
- United States Merchant Marine Academy
- United States Military Academy
- United States Naval Academy
- University of California—Berkeley
- University of California—Los Angeles
- University of Illinois at Urbana-Champaign
- University of Michigan—Ann Arbor
- The University of Texas at Austin
- University of Wisconsin—Madison
- Virginia Tech
- Webb Institute
- Worcester Polytechnic Institute

Great Schools for English Literature and Language Majors

- Amherst College
- Auburn University
- Bard College (NY)
- Barnard College
- Bates College
- Beloit College
- Bennington College
- Boston College
- Brown University
- Bryn Mawr College
- City University of New York—Hunter College
- Claremont McKenna College
- Clemson University
- Colby College
- Colgate University
- Columbia University
- Cornell University
- Dartmouth College
- Denison University
- Duke University
- Emerson College
- Emory University
- Fordham University
- George Mason University
- Gettysburg College
- Gordon College
- Grinnell College
- Harvard College
- Hollins University
- Johns Hopkins University
- Kalamazoo College
- Kenyon College
- Knox College
- Oberlin College
- Pitzer College
- Pomona College
- Princeton University
- Reed College
- Rice University
- Sewanee—The University of the South
- Smith College
- Stanford University
- St. Mary's College of Maryland
- Syracuse University
- Tufts University
- University of California—Berkeley
- The University of Chicago
- University of Michigan—Ann Arbor
- The University of North Carolina at Asheville
- University of Notre Dame
- University of Utah
- Vassar College
- Washington University in St. Louis
- Wellesley College
- Williams College
- Yale University

Great Schools for Environmental Studies Majors

- Allegheny College
- Bates College
- Bowdoin College
- Catawba College
- Colby College
- College of the Atlantic
- Colorado College
- Dickinson College
- Eckerd College
- Emory University
- The Evergreen State College
- Harvard College
- Hobart and William Smith Colleges
- Juniata College

- Middlebury College
- New College of Florida
- Northeastern University
- Occidental College
- Pitzer College
- Pomona College
- Portland State University
- Sewanee—The University of the South
- Sonoma State University
- State University of New York at Binghamton
- State University of New York—College of Environmental Science and Forestry
- University of California—Berkeley
- University of California—Santa Cruz
- University of Colorado Boulder
- University of Idaho
- The University of Montana—Missoula
- University of New Hampshire
- The University of North Carolina at Asheville
- The University of North Carolina at Chapel Hill
- University of Oregon
- University of Redlands
- University of Vermont
- Warren Wilson College
- Washington College

Great Schools for Health Services Majors

- Becker College
- Bellarmine University
- Boston University
- Clemson University
- College of the Ozarks
- Creighton University
- Drexel University
- Duquesne University
- East Carolina University
- Elmira College
- Fairfield University
- Gettysburg College
- Hampton University
- Howard University
- Ithaca College
- Johns Hopkins University
- Kalamazoo College
- Loyola University—Chicago
- Lynchburg College
- Monmouth University (NJ)
- Moravian College
- Nazareth College
- Northeastern University
- Ohio University—Athens
- Purdue University—West Lafayette
- Quinnipiac University
- Sacred Heart University
- St. Anselm College
- Saint Louis University
- Seton Hall University
- Simmons College
- State University of New York—Stony Brook University
- Stephens College
- Suffolk University
- Texas A&M University—College Station
- Texas Christian University
- Tulane University
- University of Alabama at Birmingham
- University of Central Florida
- University of Cincinnati
- University of Delaware
- University of Florida
- University of Houston
- University of Louisville
- University of Miami
- University of New England
- University of North Dakota
- University of Oklahoma
- University of Rhode Island
- The University of South Dakota
- University of South Florida
- University of Utah
- University of Wyoming
- Wagner College
- Washington University in St. Louis
- West Virginia University
- Westminster College (UT)
- Wheaton College (IL)
- William Jewell College
- Xavier University (OH)

Check out our list of Colleges That Create Futures—50 schools with compelling commitments to helping students segue to successful careers and post-graduate accomplishments—at https://www.princetonreview.com/college-rankings/colleges-that-create-futures.

Great Schools for History Majors

- Bates College
- Bowdoin College
- Brown University
- Centre College
- Colgate University
- College of the Holy Cross
- The College of Wooster
- Columbia University
- Davidson College
- Drew University
- Furman University
- Georgetown University
- Grinnell College
- Hampden-Sydney College
- Harvard College
- Haverford College
- Hillsdale College
- Kenyon College
- Oberlin College
- Princeton University
- Ripon College
- Trinity College (CT)
- Tulane University
- University of Dallas
- University of Virginia
- Wabash College
- Williams College
- Yale University

Great Schools for Journalism Majors

- American University
- Arizona State University
- Auburn University
- Boston University
- Carleton College
- Duke University
- Emerson College
- The George Washington University
- Hampton University
- Howard University
- Indiana University—Bloomington
- Iowa State University
- Ithaca College
- Kansas State University
- Loyola University—New Orleans
- Michigan State University
- New York University
- Northwestern University
- Ohio University—Athens
- Pennsylvania State University—University Park
- St. Bonaventure University
- State University of New York—Stony Brook University
- Syracuse University
- Temple University
- The University of Alabama—Tuscaloosa
- University of Arizona
- University of Arkansas—Fayetteville
- University of Florida
- University of Georgia
- University of Kansas
- University of Kentucky
- University of Idaho
- University of Illinois at Urbana-Champaign
- University of Iowa
- University of Maryland—College Park
- University of Minnesota—Twin Cities
- University of Mississippi
- University of Missouri—Columbia
- The University of Montana—Missoula
- University of Nebraska—Lincoln
- The University of North Carolina at Chapel Hill
- University of Oklahoma
- University of Oregon
- University of Southern California
- The University of Texas at Austin
- University of Wisconsin—Madison
- Washington State University

Great Schools for Marketing and Sales Majors

- Babson College
- Baylor University
- Bentley University
- Bryant University
- Butler University
- Drury University
- Duquesne University
- Fairfield University
- Hofstra University
- Indiana University—Bloomington
- Iowa State University
- James Madison University
- Loyola Marymount University
- Manhattan College
- Miami University (OH)
- Providence College
- Saint Joseph's University (PA)
- Seattle University

- Siena College
- Syracuse University
- Texas A&M University—College Station
- The University of Alabama—Tuscaloosa
- University of Central Florida
- University of Cincinnati
- University of Dayton
- University of Michigan—Ann Arbor
- University of Mississippi
- University of Pennsylvania
- University of South Florida
- The University of Texas at Austin

Great Schools for Mathematics & Statistics Majors

- Amherst College
- Agnes Scott College
- Bowdoin College
- Brown University
- Bryant University
- Bryn Mawr College
- California Institute of Technology
- Carleton College
- Carnegie Mellon University
- College of the Holy Cross
- Grinnell College
- Hamilton College
- Hampton University
- Harvard College
- Harvey Mudd College
- Haverford College
- Macalester College
- Massachusetts Institute of Technology
- Pomona College
- Randolph College
- Reed College
- Rice University
- St. Lawrence University
- St. Olaf College
- United States Coast Guard Academy
- The University of Chicago
- University of Rochester
- Wabash College
- Williams College

Great Schools for Mechanical Engineering Majors

- Auburn University
- Bradley University
- California Institute of Technology
- Clarkson University
- Colorado State University
- The Cooper Union for the Advancement of Science and Art
- Drexel University
- Franklin W. Olin College of Engineering
- Georgia Institute of Technology
- Grove City College
- Harvey Mudd College
- Illinois Institute of Technology
- Iowa State University
- Lafayette College
- Lehigh University
- Massachusetts Institute of Technology
- Michigan Technological University
- Missouri University of Science and Technology
- New Jersey Institute of Technology
- North Carolina State University
- Ohio Northern University
- Oregon State University
- Princeton University
- Purdue University—West Lafayette
- Rochester Institute of Technology
- Rose-Hulman Institute of Technology
- Stanford University
- Stevens Institute of Technology
- United States Military Academy
- University of California—Berkeley
- University of Illinois at Urbana-Champaign
- University of Maryland, Baltimore County
- University of Michigan—Ann Arbor
- Worcester Polytechnic Institute

Great Schools for Nursing Majors

- Angelo State University
- Baylor University
- Bellarmine University
- Creighton University
- Calvin College
- The Catholic University of America
- Drexel University
- Duquesne University
- Fairfield University
- Florida Southern College
- Indiana University of Pennsylvania
- Loyola University—Chicago

- Montana Technological University
- Ohio Northern University
- St. Anselm College
- Saint Louis University
- Texas Christian University
- The University of Alabama—Tuscaloosa
- University of Delaware
- University of Louisville

- University of North Dakota
- University of Pennsylvania
- University of Rhode Island
- University of Wyoming
- Villanova University
- Washington State University
- Xavier University (OH)

Great Schools for Political Science/Government Majors

- American University
- Amherst College
- Bard College (NY)
- Bates College
- Bowdoin College
- Brigham Young University (UT)
- Bryn Mawr College
- Carleton College
- Claremont McKenna College
- Clark University
- College of the Holy Cross
- Columbia University
- Connecticut College
- Davidson College
- Dickinson College
- Drew University
- Franklin & Marshall College
- Furman University
- George Mason University
- The George Washington University
- Georgetown University

- Gettysburg College
- Gonzaga University
- Grinnell College
- Harvard College
- Kenyon College
- Macalester College
- McGill University
- Princeton University
- Scripps College
- Stanford University
- Swarthmore College
- Syracuse University
- University of Arizona
- University of California—Berkeley
- University of California—Los Angeles
- University of Washington
- University of Wisconsin—Madison
- Vassar College
- Wake Forest University
- Yale University

Great Schools for Psychology Majors

- Agnes Scott College
- Albion College
- Allegheny College
- Assumption University
- Barnard College
- Bates College
- Bucknell University
- Carleton College
- Carnegie Mellon University
- Christopher Newport University
- City University of New York—Brooklyn College
- City University of New York—Hunter College
- City University of New York—Queens College
- Clark University
- Coe College
- College of the Holy Cross
- Colorado State University
- Columbia University
- Cornell University

- Dartmouth College
- DePaul University
- Duke University
- Earlham College
- Flagler College
- Florida State University
- Franklin & Marshall College
- George Mason University
- Gettysburg College
- Guilford College
- Hampton University
- Hanover College
- Harvard College
- James Madison University
- Lewis & Clark College
- Loyola University—New Orleans
- Loyola University—Chicago
- Mills College
- Moravian College

- Mount Holyoke College
- New York University
- The Ohio State University—Columbus
- Ohio Wesleyan University
- Pitzer College
- Portland State University
- Princeton University
- Quinnipiac University
- Randolph College
- Roanoke College
- St. Mary's College of Maryland
- Siena College
- Simmons College
- Smith College
- Spelman College
- Stanford University
- State University of New York at Geneseo
- Stetson University
- Stonehill College
- Temple University
- Texas A&M University—College Station
- Union College (NY)
- University of Arizona
- University of California—Davis
- University of California—Los Angeles
- University of California—Riverside
- University of California—Santa Barbara
- University of California—Santa Cruz
- University of Connecticut
- University of Florida
- University of Houston
- University of Idaho
- University of Mary Washington
- University of Maryland—College Park
- University of Massachusetts Amherst
- University of Michigan—Ann Arbor
- University of Minnesota—Twin Cities
- The University of Montana—Missoula
- University of Nebraska—Lincoln
- University of Pittsburgh—Pittsburgh Campus
- University of Puget Sound
- University of San Francisco
- The University of South Dakota
- University of South Florida
- University of Southern California
- University of Tennessee
- The University of Texas at Austin
- University of Utah
- Vassar College
- Washington & Jefferson College
- Washington College
- Washington University in St. Louis
- Wesleyan University
- Xavier University of Louisiana
- Yale University

How We Produce This Book

This Year's Edition

In the twenty-eight years since the first edition of this book, our *Best Colleges* guide has grown considerably. We've added more than 130 colleges to the guide and deleted several along the way. How we choose the schools for the book, and how we produce it, however, has not changed significantly over the years (with the exception of how we conduct our student survey—more on this follows).

To determine which schools will be in each edition, we don't use mathematical calculations or formulas. Instead we rely on a wide range of input, both quantitative and qualitative. Every year we collect data from more than 2,000 colleges that we use for *The Complete Book of Colleges* and *Best Value Colleges*, this book, and our online profiles of schools. We visit dozens of colleges and meet with their admissions officers, deans, presidents, and college students. We talk with hundreds of high school counselors, parents, and students. Colleges also submit information to us requesting consideration for inclusion in the book. As a result, we are able to maintain a constantly evolving list of colleges to consider adding to the book. Any college we add to the guide, however, must agree to support our efforts to survey its students via our anonymous student survey. (Sometimes a college's administrative protocols will not allow it to participate in our student survey; this has caused some academically outstanding schools to be absent from the guide.) Finally, we work to ensure that our roster of colleges in the book presents a wide representation of institutions by region, character, and type. Here you'll find profiles of public and private schools, Historically Black Colleges and Universities, men's and women's colleges, science- and technology-focused institutions, nontraditional colleges, highly selective schools, and some with virtually open-door admissions policies.

For this year's edition, we added two schools to the guide: Kettering University and Lawrence Technological University.

"We worked to create a guide that would help people who couldn't always get to the campus nonetheless get in-depth campus feedback to find the schools best for them."

Our ranking lists in this edition are based on our surveys of 143,000 students attending the 386 colleges in the book. We surveyed about 364 students per campus on average, though that number varies depending on the size of the student population. We've surveyed in schools like Deep Springs College (almost 100% of the 30-student campus) as well as those like University of Massachusetts—Amherst, Florida State University, and United States Air Force Academy (more than 1,000 collegians from each).

All of the institutions in this guide are academically terrific in our opinion. The 386 schools featured—our picks of the cream of the crop colleges and universities—comprise only the top 13 percent of the approximately 3,000 four-year colleges in the nation. These are all very different schools with many different and wonderful things to offer. We hope you will use this book as a starting point (it will certainly give you a snapshot of what life is like at these schools), but not as the final word on any one school. Check out other resources. Visit as many colleges as you can. Talk to students at those colleges—ask what they love and what bothers them most about their schools. Finally, form your own opinions about the colleges you are considering. At the end of the day, it's what YOU think about the schools that matters most, and that will enable you to answer that all-important question: "Which college is best for me?"

About Our Student Survey for Our *Best Colleges* Books

Surveying tens of thousands of students on hundreds of campuses is a large undertaking. In 1992, when we published the first edition of this book, we had surveyed an average of 120 students on each of the 250 campuses we profiled. We conducted that survey in person on the college campuses, setting up tables in central locations at which students filled out the surveys. Sometimes in order for us to collect surveys from a wide range of students, first years to seniors, this process took place over several days and at a variety of campus locations.

As you might imagine, today all of our surveys are completed online. The process is more efficient, secure, and representative, and we are able to gather opinions from far more students per college than we had reached previously. The average number of student surveys (per college) upon which our ranking lists are annually tallied is now 364 students per campus (and at some schools we hear from more than 5,000 students).

Our student survey is also now a continuous process. Students submit surveys online from all schools in the book and they can submit their surveys at any time during the academic year at http://survey.review.com. (Our site will accept only one survey from a student per academic year per school. We also officially conduct surveys of students at each school in the book once every three years on average, working with administrators to reach out to their students. We conduct these "official" surveys more often than once every three years if the colleges request that we do so (and we can accommodate their request) or if we deem it necessary to capture dramatic changes on a campus. And of course, surveys we receive from students outside of their schools' normal survey cycles are always factored into the subsequent year's ranking calculations, so our pool of student survey data is continuously refreshed.

The survey has more than 80 questions in four main sections: "About Yourself," "Your School's Academics/Administration," "Students," and "Life at Your School." We ask about all sorts of things, from "How many out-of-class hours do you spend studying each day?" to "How do you rate your campus food?" Most questions offer an answer choice on a five-point scale: students fill in one of five boxes on a grid with headers varying by topic (e.g., a range from "Excellent" to "Awful"). Once the surveys have been completed and responses stored in our database, every college is given a score (similar to a GPA) for its students' answers to each question. This score enables us to compare student opinion from college to college and to tally the ranking lists. Most of the lists are based on students' answers to one survey question; some lists are based on answers to several survey questions. But all of our 62 ranking lists are based entirely on our student survey results.

Once we have the student survey information in hand, we write the college profiles. Student quotations in each profile come from our surveys (eight survey questions invite the students to tell us in their own words what they think about various aspects of their student body and campus experiences). We chose quotations that represent sentiments expressed by the majority of survey respondents from the college, or that illustrate one side or another of a mixed bag of student opinion, in which case there will also appear a counterpoint within the text. We send draft profiles to administrative contacts at each school for comments and corrections. We take careful measures to review the school's suggestions against the student survey data we collected and make appropriate changes when warranted.

How This Book Is Organized

Each of the colleges and universities in this book has its own two-page profile. To make it easier to find and compare information about the schools, we've used the same profile format for every school. Look at the sample pages below: Each profile has nine major components. First, at the very top of the profile, you will see the school's address, telephone and fax numbers for the admissions office, the telephone number for the financial aid office, and the school's website and/or e-mail address. Second, there are two sidebars (the narrow columns on the outside of each page, which consist mainly of statistics) divided into the categories of Campus Life, Academics, Selectivity, and Financial Facts. Third, there are four sections in the narrative text: Students Say, Admissions, Financial Aid, and From the Admissions Office. Here's what you'll find in each part:

The Sidebars

The sidebars contain various statistics culled from our surveys of students attending the school and from questionnaires that school administrators complete at our request in the fall of each year.

Keep in mind that not every category will appear for every school—in some cases the information is not reported or not applicable. We compile the eight ratings—Quality of Life, Fire Safety, Green Rating, Academic, Profs Interesting, Profs Accessible, Admissions Selectivity, and Financial Aid—listed in the sidebars based on the results from our student surveys and/or institutional data we collect from school administrators.

These ratings are on a scale of 60–99. If a 60* (60 with an asterisk) appears as any rating for any school, it means that the school reported so few of the rating's underlying data points by our deadline that we were unable to calculate an accurate rating for it. (These measures are outlined in the ratings explanation below.) Be advised that because the Admissions Selectivity Rating is a factor in the computation that produces the Academic Rating, a school that has 60* (60 with an asterisk) as its Admissions Selectivity Rating will have an Academic Rating that is lower than it should be. Also bear in mind that each rating places each college on a continuum for purposes of comparing colleges within this edition only. Since our ratings computations may change from year to year, it is invalid to compare the ratings in this edition to those that appear in any prior or future edition.

Finally, these ratings are quite different from the ranking lists that appear in Part 2 of the book, "School Rankings and Lists." The ratings are numerical measures that show how a school "sizes up," if you will, on a fixed scale. Our sixty-two ranking lists report the top twenty (or in some cases bottom twenty) schools of the 386 in the book (not of all schools in the nation) in various categories. They are based on our surveys of students at the schools and/or institutional data. Here is what each heading in the sidebar tells you, in order of its appearance:

Quality of Life Rating

On a scale of 60–99, this rating is a measure of how happy students are with their campus experiences outside the classroom. To compile this rating, we weighed several factors, all based on students' answers to questions on our survey. They included the students' assessments of their overall happiness; the beauty, safety, and location of the campus; comfort of dorms; quality of food; ease of getting around campus and dealing with administrators; friendliness of fellow students; and the interaction of different student types on campus and within the greater community.

"Ratings are quite different from the ranking lists. The ratings are numerical measures that show how a school 'sizes up,' if you will, on a fixed scale. Our sixty-two ranking lists report the top twenty (or in some cases bottom twenty) schools of the 386 in the book (not of all schools in the nation) in various categories."

Fire Safety Rating

On a scale of 60–99, this rating measures how well prepared a school is to prevent or respond to campus fires, specifically in residence halls. We asked schools several questions about their efforts to ensure fire safety for campus residents. We developed the questions in consultation with the Center for Campus Fire Safety (www.campusfiresafety.org). Each school's responses to seven questions were considered when calculating its Fire Safety Rating. They cover:

1. The percentage of student housing sleeping rooms protected by an automatic fire sprinkler system with a fire sprinkler head located in the individual sleeping rooms

2. The percentage of student housing sleeping rooms equipped with a smoke detector connected to a supervised fire alarm system

3. The number of malicious fire alarms that occur in student housing per year

4. The number of unwanted fire alarms that occur in student housing per year

5. The banning of certain hazardous items and activities in residence halls, like candles, smoking, halogen lamps, etc.

6. The percentage of student housing fire alarm systems that, if activated, result in a signal being transmitted to a monitored location, where security investigates before notifying the fire department

7. The percentage of student housing fire alarm systems that, if activated, result in a signal being transmitted immediately to a continuously monitored location

Schools that did not report answers to a sufficient number of questions receive a Fire Safety Rating of 60* (60 with an asterisk). You can also find Fire Safety Ratings for our Best 386 Colleges (and hundreds of additional schools) in *The Complete Book of Colleges,* 2021 Edition. On page 49 of this book, you'll find a list of the schools with 99 (the highest score) Fire Safety Ratings.

Green Rating

We asked all the schools we collect data from annually to answer a number of questions that evaluate the comprehensive measure of their performance as an environmentally aware and responsible institution. The questions cover 1) whether students have a campus quality of life that is both healthy and sustainable; 2) how well a school is preparing students not only for employment in the clean energy economy of the 21st century, but also for citizenship in a world now defined by environmental challenges; and 3) how environmentally responsible a school's policies are.

Additionally, The Princeton Review, the Association for the Advancement of Sustainability in Higher Education (AASHE), and *Sierra* magazine, have collaborated on an effort to streamline the reporting process for institutions that choose to participate in various higher education sustainability assessments. The intent of this initiative is to reduce and streamline the amount of time campus staff spend tracking sustainability data and completing related surveys.

Please find more information here:

https://www.princetonreview.com/college-rankings/green-guide/data-partnership

School responses to the following questions were considered when calculating The Princeton Review's Green Rating:

1. What is the percentage of food expenditures that goes toward local, organic or otherwise environmentally preferable food?

2. Does the school offer programs including mass transit programs, bike sharing, facilities for bicyclists, bicycle and pedestrian plans, car sharing, a carpool discount, carpool/vanpool matching, cash-out of parking, prohibiting idling, local housing, telecommuting, and a condensed work week?

3. Does the school have a formal committee with participation from students that is devoted to advancing sustainability on campus?

4. Are school buildings that were constructed or underwent major renovations in the past three years LEED (Leadership in Energy and Environmental Design) certified?

5. What is the school's overall waste-diversion rate?

6. Does the school have an environmental studies major, minor, or concentration?

7. Do the school's students graduate from programs that include sustainability as a required learning outcome or include multiple sustainability learning outcomes?

8. Does the school have a formal plan to mitigate its greenhouse gas emissions?

9. What percentage of the school's energy consumption is derived from renewable resources?

10. Does the school employ a dedicated full-time (or full-time equivalent) sustainability officer?

Colleges that did not supply answers to a sufficient number of the green campus questions for us to fairly compare them to other colleges receive a Green Rating of 60*. On page 49 of this book and on our website at https://www.princetonreview.com/college-rankings/green-guide/green-honor-roll, you'll find a list of the schools with 99 (the highest score) Green Ratings.

Check out our free resource, The Princeton Review's Guide to Green Colleges at www.princetonreview.com/green-guide.

Type of school
Whether the school is public or private.

Affiliation
Any religious order with which the school is affiliated.

Environment

The type of school environment, based on population and setting.

- Rural (In or near a rural community, pop. under 5,000)
- Village (In a small town, pop. 5,000–24,999, or near a small town)
- Town (In a large town, pop. 25,000–74,999, or near a large town)
- City (In a small/medium city, pop. 75,000–299,999, or within its metropolitan area)
- Metropolis (In a major city, pop. 300,000 or more, or within its metropolitan area)

Total undergrad enrollment

The total number of undergraduates who attend the school.

"% male/female" through "# countries represented"

Demographic information about the full-time undergraduate student body, including male-to-female ratio, ethnicity, and the number of countries represented by the student body. Also included are the percentages of the student body who are from out of state, attended a public high school, first-year students living on campus, and belong to Greek organizations.

Survey Says . . .

A snapshot of key results of our student survey. This list names survey topics about which the body of students we surveyed at the school—as a group—showed a statistically higher consensus of opinion in their answers to our questions on those topics (as compared with their answers to questions on other topics). See the end of this section for a detailed explanation of items on the list.

Academic Rating

On a scale of 60–99, this rating is a measure of how hard students work at the school and how much they get back for their efforts. The rating is based on results from our surveys of students and data we collect from administrators. Factors weighed include the number of hours students reported that they study each day outside of class, students' assessments of their professors' teaching abilities and of their accessibility outside the classroom, and the quality of students the school attracts as measured by admissions statistics.

% of students returning for sophomore year

The percentage of degree-seeking first-year students returning for sophomore year.

% of students graduating within 4 years

The percentage of degree-seeking undergraduate students graduating in four years or less.

% of students graduating within 6 years

The percentage of degree-seeking undergraduate students graduating within six years.

Calendar

The school's schedule of academic terms. A "semester" schedule has two long terms, usually starting in September and January. A "trimester" schedule has three terms, one usually beginning before Christmas and two after. A "quarterly" schedule has four terms, which go by very quickly: the entire term, including exams, usually lasts only nine or ten weeks. A "4-1-4" schedule is like a semester schedule, but with a month-long term in between the fall and spring semesters. (Similarly, a "4-4-1" has a short term following two longer semesters.) It is always best to call the admissions office for details.

Student/faculty ratio

The ratio of full-time undergraduate instructional faculty members to all undergraduates.

Profs interesting rating

On a scale of 60–99, this rating is based on levels of surveyed students' agreement or disagreement with this statement: "Your instructors are good teachers."

Profs accessible rating

On a scale of 60–99, this rating is based on levels of surveyed students' agreement or disagreement with this statement: "Your instructors are accessible outside the classroom."

Most common regular class size; Most common lab size

The most commonly occurring class size for regular courses and for labs/discussion sections.

Most popular majors

The majors with the highest enrollments at the school.

Admissions Selectivity Rating

On a scale of 60–99, this rating is a measure of how competitive admission is at the school. This rating is determined by several factors, including the high school class rank of entering first-year students, test scores, and percentage of applicants accepted.

of applicants

The total number of students to apply.

% of applicants accepted

The percentage of applicants to whom the school offered admission.

% of acceptees attending

The percentage of accepted students who eventually enrolled at the school.

applicants offered a place on the wait list

Number of qualified applicants offered a place on waiting list.

% accepting a place on wait list

The percentage of students who decided to take a place on the wait list when offered this option.

% admitted from wait list

The percentage of applicants who opted to take a place on the wait list and were subsequently offered admission. These figures will vary tremendously from college to college, and should be a consideration when deciding whether to accept a place on a college's wait list.

of early decision applicants

The number of students who applied under the college's early decision or early action plan.

% accepted early decision

The percentage of early decision or early action applicants who were admitted under this plan. By the nature of these plans, the vast majority who are admitted ultimately enroll.

Range SAT EBRW, Range SAT Math, Range ACT Composite

The middle 50 percent range of test scores for entering first-year students.

We made the above information available to contacts at each school for review and approval. You may also cross-reference our print profiles with our online school profiles at PrincetonReview.com, which list the most up-to date data as reported by schools.

Don't be discouraged from applying to the school of your choice even if your combined SAT scores are 80 or even 120 points below the average, because you may still have a chance of getting in. Remember that many schools value other aspects of your application (e.g., your grades, how good a match you make with the school) more heavily than test scores.

Average HS GPA

The average grade point average of entering first-year students. The majority of schools report this on an unweighted scale of 1.0–4.0, but some have started to report using a weighted scale of 1.0–5.0, so please keep that in mind. (A few schools report averages on a 100 scale, in which case we report those figures.) This is one of the key factors in college admissions.

% graduated top 10%, top 25%, top 50% of class

Of those students for whom class rank was reported, the percentage of entering first-year students who ranked in the top tenth, quarter, and half of their high school classes.

Early decision, early action, priority, and regular admission deadlines

The dates by which all materials must be postmarked (we suggest "received in the office") in order to be considered for admission under each particular admissions option/cycle for matriculation in the fall term. This section also includes, where given, the expected dates for notifications about a decision on your application.

Nonfall registration

Some schools will allow incoming students to register and begin attending classes at times other than the fall term, which is the traditional beginning of the academic calendar year. Other schools will allow you to register for classes only if you can begin in the fall term. A simple "yes" or "no" in this category indicates the school's policy on nonfall registration.

Applicants also look at

These lists are based on information we receive directly from the colleges. Admissions officers are annually given the opportunity to review and suggest alterations to these lists for their schools, as most schools track as closely as they can other schools to which applicants they accepted applied, and whether the applicants chose their school over the other schools, or vice versa.

Financial Aid Rating

On a scale of 60–99, this rating is a measure of the financial aid the school awards and how satisfied students are with the aid they receive. It is based on school-reported data on financial aid and students' responses to the survey question, "If you receive financial aid, how satisfied are you with your financial aid package?" On page 49 of this book you'll find a list of the schools with 99 (the highest score) Financial Aid Ratings.

Annual tuition

The tuition at the school. For public colleges, the cost of tuition is provided for both residents of that school's state and for nonresidents. In-state tuition is typically much lower than out-of-state tuition.

Room and board

Estimated annual room and board costs.

Required fees

Any additional costs students must pay beyond tuition in order to attend the school. These often include fitness center fees and the like. A few state schools may not officially charge in-state students tuition, but those students are still responsible for hefty fees. In a few rare cases, this field may combine tuition and fees, or list a single comprehensive fee that accounts for the total cost of tuition, room and board, and fees. To see how these figures break down, we recommend contacting the school.

Books and supplies

Estimated annual cost of necessary textbooks and/or supplies.

Average frosh/undergraduate need-based scholarship

The average need-based scholarship and grant aid awarded to students with need.

% needy frosh receiving need-based scholarship or grant aid

The percentage of all degree-seeking first-year students who were determined to have need and received any need-based scholarship or grant.

% needy UG receiving need-based scholarship or grant aid

The percentage of all degree-seeking undergraduates who were determined to have need and received any need-based scholarship or grant.

% needy frosh receiving non-need-based scholarship or grant aid

The percentage of all degree-seeking first-year students, determined to have need, receiving any non-need based scholarship or grant aid.

% needy ugrads receiving non-need-based scholarship or grant aid

The percentage of all degree-seeking undergraduates, determined to have need, receiving any non-need based scholarship or grant aid.

% needy frosh receiving need-based self-help aid

The percentage of all degree-seeking first-year students, determined to have need, who received any need-based self-help aid.

% needy ugrads receiving need-based self-help aid

The percentage of all degree-seeking undergraduates, determined to have need, who received any need-based self-help aid.

% frosh receiving any financial aid

The percentage of all degree-seeking first-year students receiving any financial aid (need-based, merit-based, gift aid).

% UG receiving any financial aid

The percentage of all degree-seeking undergraduates receiving any financial aid (need-based, merit-based, gift aid).

% UG borrow to pay for school

The percentage who borrowed at any time through any loan programs (Institutional, state, Federal Perkins, Federal Subsidized and Unsubsidized, private loans that were certified by your institution, etc., excluding parent loans). Includes both Federal Direct Student Loans and Federal Family Education Loans.

Average Indebtedness

The average per-undergraduate borrower cumulative principal borrowed of those who borrowed at any time through any loan programs (Federal Perkins, Federal Subsidized and Unsubsidized, institutional, state, private loans that institution is aware of, etc. Includes both Federal Direct Student Loans and Federal Family Education Loans).

Nota Bene: The statistical data reported in this book, unless otherwise noted, was collected from the profiled colleges from the fall of 2019 through the winter of 2020. In some cases, we were unable to publish the most recent data because schools did not report the necessary statistics to us in time, despite our repeated outreach efforts. Because the enrollment and financial statistics, as well as application and financial aid deadlines, fluctuate from one year to another, we recommend that you check with the schools to make sure you have the most current information before applying.

% frosh and ugrad need fully met

The percentage of needy degree-seeking students whose needs were fully met (excludes PLUS loans, unsubsidized loans, and private alternative loans).

Average % of frosh and ugrad need met

On average, the percentage of need that was met of students who were awarded any need-based aid. Excludes any aid that was awarded in excess of need as well as any resources that were awarded to replace EFC (PLUS loans, unsubsidized loans, and private alternative loans).

Students Say

This section shares the straight-from-the-campus feedback we get from the school's most important customers: the students attending them. It summarizes the opinions of first-year students through seniors we've surveyed, and it includes direct quotes from scores of them. When appropriate, it also incorporates statistics provided by the schools. The Students Say section is divided into three subsections: Academics, Life, and Student Body. The Academics section describes how hard students work and how satisfied they are with the education they are getting. It also often tells you which programs or academic departments students rated most favorably and how professors interact with students. Student opinion regarding administrative departments also works its way into this section. The Life section describes life outside the classroom and addresses questions ranging from "How comfortable are the dorms?" to "How popular are fraternities and sororities?" In this section, students describe what they do for entertainment both on-campus and off, providing a clear picture of the social environment at their particular school. The Student Body section will give you the lowdown on the types of students the school attracts and how the students view the level of interaction among various groups, including those of different ethnic, socioeconomic, and religious backgrounds.

All quotations in these sections are from students' responses to open-ended questions on our survey. We select quotations based on the accuracy with which they reflect overall student opinion about the school as conveyed in the survey results.

Admissions

This section lets you know which aspects of your application are most important to the admissions officers at the school. It also lists the high school curricular prerequisites for applicants, which standardized tests (if any) are required, and special information about the school's admissions process (e.g., Do minority students and legacies, for example, receive special consideration? Are there any unusual application requirements for applicants to special programs?).

Financial Aid

Here you'll find out what you need to know about the financial aid process at the school, namely what forms you need and what types of merit-based aid and loans are available. Information about need-based aid is contained in the financial aid sidebar. This section includes specific deadline dates for submission of materials as reported by the colleges. We strongly encourage students seeking financial aid to file all forms—federal, state, and institutional—carefully, fully, and on time.

The Inside Word

This section gives you the inside scoop on what it takes to gain admission to the school. It reflects our own insights about each school's admissions process and acceptance trends. (We visit scores of colleges each year and talk with hundreds of admissions officers in order to glean this info.) It also incorporates information from institutional data we collect and our surveys over the years of students at the school.

From the Admissions Office

This section presents the key things the school's admissions office would like you to know about the institution. We have also encouraged schools to clarify their policies on ACT, SAT (especially the Writing portion of the exam), and SAT Subject Scores, but not every school has taken this opportunity.

Survey Says . . .

Our Survey Says list, located in the Campus Life sidebar on each school's two-page spread, is based entirely on the results of our student survey. In other words, the items on this list are based on the opinions of the students we surveyed at those schools (not on any quantitative analysis of library size, endowment, etc.). These items reveal popular or unpopular trends on campus for the purpose of providing a snapshot of life on that campus only. The appearance of a Survey Says item in the sidebar does not reflect the popularity of that item relative to its popularity among the student bodies at other schools. To ascertain the relative popularity of certain items/trends on campus, see the appropriate ranking (e.g., for the Survey Says item "Career Services are Great," see the "Best Career Services" ranking). Some of the terms that appear on the Survey Says list are not entirely self-explanatory. These terms are defined as follows:

Different types of students interact: We asked students whether students from different class and ethnic backgrounds interacted frequently and easily. When students' collective response is "yes," the heading "Different types of students interact" appears on the list. When the collective student response indicates there are not many interactions between students from different class and ethnic backgrounds, the phrase "Students are cliquish" appears on the list. Note: This topic is not based on demographic data about the student body.

No one cheats: We asked students how prevalent cheating is at their school. If students reported cheating to be rare, the term "No one cheats" shows up on the list.

Students are happy: This category reflects student responses to the question "Overall, how happy are you?"

Students are very religious or Students aren't religious: We asked students how religious students are at their school. Their responses are reflected in this category.

Diverse student types on campus: We asked students whether their student body is made up of a variety of ethnic groups. This category reflects their answers to this question. This heading shows up as "Diversity lacking on campus" or "Diverse student types on campus." It does not reflect any institutional data on this subject.

Students get along with local community: This category reflects student responses to a question concerning how well the student body gets along with residents of the college town or community.

Career services are great: This category reflects student opinion on the quality of career/job placement services on campus.

About Our College Ranking Lists

Finding a college that has terrific academics is easy. There are hundreds of academically great colleges out there. Their campus cultures, student bodies, and school offerings, however, differ widely. Finding the academically great school that is right for you is the tough part. Hence, we compile not one ranking list but sixty-three unique lists, each one reporting the top twenty (or in some cases bottom twenty) schools from our *Best Colleges* book in a specific category.

None of our lists are based on what we think of the schools (though members of the media, the public, and school administrators mistakenly credit or blame us for the results, saying "According to The Princeton Review, X school is the best in the nation for…" or "The Princeton Review ranks Y school the tenth most…."). In fact, the only thing we say is that all of the 386 colleges in this book are outstanding (hence, the "Best" designation). It's what students think of their schools—how they rate various aspects of their colleges' offerings and what they report to us about their campus experiences—that results in a school's appearance on our ranking lists.

You won't find the colleges in the book ranked hierarchically, 1 to 386. We think such lists—particularly those driven by and perpetuating a "best academics" mania—are not useful for the people they are supposed to serve (college applicants). More and more college administrators—including several at schools ranked high on these lists—agree. In fact, the primary reason we developed this book was to give applicants and parents better and broader information that will help them winnow a list of colleges right for them.

About 80 percent of the schools in our book end up on one or more of the lists in each edition. To college officials happy about the lists their schools are on, we say don't thank us, we're just the messengers. To college officials unhappy about the lists their schools are on, we say don't blame us, we're just the messengers.

All of these ranking lists are based entirely on students' answers to questions on our surveys (e.g., our "Best Campus Food" list and inverse list, "Is it Food?" are each based on the single survey question, "How do you rate your campus food?") or students' answers to a combination of survey questions (e.g., our "Party Schools" list and our inverse list, "Stone-Cold Sober Schools" are each based on students' answers to survey questions concerning the use of alcohol and drugs on their campuses, the popularity of the frat/sorority scene on their campuses, and the number of hours they say they study each day outside of class time).

Each list covers one of many aspects of a college's character that can be helpful in deciding if it's the right or wrong school for an individual student. The lists report on a wide range of issues that may be important, either singly or, more likely, in combination. Our ranking lists cover financial aid, campus facilities and amenities, extracurriculars, town-gown relations, the student body's political leanings, social life, race/class relations, LGBTQ-friendly (or not so friendly) atmosphere, career services, athletic facilities, and more.

"It's what students think of their schools—how they rate various aspects of their colleges' offerings and what they report to us about their campus experiences—that results in a school's appearance on our ranking lists."

Our newest ranking list was added in this edition: "Best Counseling Services."

The ranking categories that members of the media cover the most are our "Party Schools" and "Stone-cold Sober Schools" lists. These draw a wide range of reaction every year. Some students complain that their college didn't rank here. Others are irate because their college did.

Some people incorrectly assume that schools on our "Party Schools" list are not advisable to attend because they imagine that the social scene dominates over academic pursuits on those campuses. As we've noted, all the colleges and universities we profile in this book are academically excellent, and "work hard, play hard" is a favorite phrase of our survey respondents across many, many schools with a diverse array of social scenes.

Inversely, some people incorrectly assume that schools on our "Stone-cold Sober Schools" list are not advisable to attend because they imagine the social scene on those campuses is lacking. Skim each college's profile, however, and you'll find plenty of extracurricular activity: sports, games, clubs, and concerts.

We recommend all schools on these lists (and all 386 schools in this book) as outstanding institutions to earn one's college degree and have a fun time.

However, no one should assume that any one of these 386 outstanding colleges—regardless of which ranking list(s) it may (or may not) be on—is insulated from the influences of alcohol and drugs on its campus. An oft-quoted Harvard University School of Public Health 2002 study found that (then) 45 percent of undergraduates, in general, had engaged in binge drinking (consuming five or more alcoholic beverages in one sitting for men, four drinks or more for women).[1] These facts are alarming, as they should be. College administrators face tremendous challenges in creating and enforcing campus alcohol and drug use/abuse policies (and media have reported on how several institutions have toughed their

---

[1] Harvard University School of Public Health. "College Student Binge Drinking Rates Remain High Despite Efforts by School Administrations." http://archive.sph.harvard.edu/press-releases/archives/2000-releases/press03142000.html

---

policies subsequent to their appearances on our lists). Many colleges struggle with problems resulting from the prevalence of bars and liquor stores near their campuses; at some universities there are more than 100 such establishments within a few miles from the campus. "Dry campus" policies often exacerbate the problem, driving drinking off-campus, making it even more dangerous for students.

Over a decade ago, some administrators at colleges that had repeatedly made our "Party Schools" list claimed that our reporting this list promoted drinking on their campuses. (They were administrators at colleges receiving millions of dollars of funding through a program administrated within the American Medical Association to address their campuses' and communities' alcohol problems.) After these administrators (and their AMA program director) made news in 2002 with this claim, *USA TODAY* published an editorial that cited their unique affiliation and praised our reporting our ranking list as a "public service."

None of our lists promote behavior of any kind: they report what students on campuses told us about their opinions of their schools.

What our lists promote is information. What we say to college students is this: if you're going to drink, do it safely, responsibly, and (obviously) legally. If you're going off campus to drink, don't drive back—get a designated driver and never, ever drive drunk. Don't use alcohol or drugs as a badge of your coolness. Don't let any alcohol or drug-related situation put you in danger of getting hurt or hurting others—it's simply not worth it. Last, being responsible doesn't only apply to yourself—keep an eye on your friends, and never leave them passed out, alone, or at risk.

Finally, a grateful note to all the college officials, counselors, advisors, students, and parents who have made this annual guide possible by supporting us these past twenty-six years. Our ranking lists, rating scores, and profiles have factored in data from more than 2 million students and thousands of administrators. To all who have completed our past surveys and all who will do so this year: thanks. Your input is essential to our book. We know that it has helped students find "best fit" colleges ideal for them, and brought to the colleges in our book many outstanding applicants who otherwise may not have considered these "best" (in our opinion) colleges.

WE WANT TO HEAR FROM YOU

To all of our readers, we welcome your feedback on how we can continue to improve this guide. We hope you will share with us your comments, questions, and suggestions. Please contact us at editorialsupport@review.com. We welcome it.

To college applicants, we wish you all the best in your college search. And when you get to your campuses and settle in to your college life, come back to us online; participate in our survey for this book at https://www.princetonreview.com/college-rankings/student-survey. Let your honest comments about your schools guide prospective students who want your help answering the $64,000 question (goodness knows, the sticker price at some schools may be that high or even higher!): "Which is the best college for me?"

PART 2

School Rankings and Lists

We present our 62 "Top 20" ranking lists in eight categories.

Under each list heading, we tell you the survey question or assessment that we used to tabulate the list. We tally student responses to several questions on our survey for our lists "Best Classroom Experience," "Best Quality of Life," and the four lists in our Schools by Type rankings (including our "Party Schools" and "Stone-Cold Sober Schools" lists). Be aware that all of our 62 ranking lists are based entirely on our student surveys. They do not reflect our opinions of the schools. They are entirely the result of what students attending these schools tell us about them: It's how students rate their own schools and what they report to us about their campus experiences at them that make our ranking lists so unusual. After all, what better way is there to judge a school than by what its customers—its students—say about it?

ACADEMICS/ADMINISTRATION

Best Classroom Experience
Based on a combination of survey questions concerning teachers, classroom/lab facilities, classes attended, and amount of in-class discussion

1. Reed College
2. United States Military Academy
3. Franklin W. Olin College of Engineering
4. Williams College
5. St. John's College (MD)
6. Thomas Aquinas College
7. Grinnell College
8. Sarah Lawrence College
9. University of Richmond
10. Furman University
11. St. Olaf College
12. The College of Wooster
13. Mount Holyoke College
14. Hamilton College
15. Dickinson College
16. Earlham College
17. Bowdoin College
18. Agnes Scott College
19. Wabash College
20. Bucknell University

Students Study the Most
How many out-of-class hours do you spend studying each day?

1. Franklin W. Olin College of Engineering
2. California Institute of Technology
3. Reed College
4. Williams College
5. Rose-Hulman Institute of Technology
6. The College of Wooster
7. College of the Atlantic
8. United States Military Academy

9. Centre College
10. St. John's College (NM)
11. Wellesley College
12. Gettysburg College
13. Hillsdale College
14. Brown University
15. St. John's College (MD)
16. Grinnell College
17. Carnegie Mellon University
18. Bryn Mawr College
19. Bowdoin College
20. Lehigh University

Students Study the Least
How many out-of-class hours do you spend studying each day?

1. Emerson College
2. Becker College
3. Manhattanville College
4. Indiana University of Pennsylvania
5. Texas State University
6. West Virginia University
7. State University of New York—Purchase College
8. Champlain College
9. St. John's University (NY)
10. The University of Alabama—Tuscaloosa
11. Alfred University
12. Kansas State University
13. University of Rhode Island
14. DePaul University
15. Bryant University
16. Rider University
17. College of the Ozarks
18. University of South Carolina—Columbia
19. Middle Tennessee State University
20. East Carolina University

Professors Get High Marks
Are your instructors good teachers?

1. Mount Holyoke College
2. Reed College
3. Sarah Lawrence College
4. Franklin W. Olin College of Engineering
5. Grinnell College
6. St. John's College (MD)
7. Thomas Aquinas College
8. Wabash College
9. Hobart and William Smith Colleges
10. Hillsdale College
11. Wheaton College (IL)
12. United States Military Academy
13. Vanderbilt University
14. St. John's College (NM)
15. Williams College
16. Rose-Hulman Institute of Technology
17. University of Dallas
18. The College of Wooster
19. University of Richmond
20. Bowdoin College

Professors Get Low Marks
Are your instructors good teachers?

1. University of Hawaii—Manoa
2. Louisiana State University—Baton Rouge
3. Stevens Institute of Technology
4. State University of New York—Geneseo
5. University of Louisville
6. University of Kentucky
7. State University of New York—Stony Brook University
8. University of Connecticut
9. Illinois Institute of Technology
10. New Jersey Institute of Technology
11. Drexel University
12. University of Pittsburgh—Pittsburgh Campus
13. University of Cincinnati
14. St. John's University (NY)
15. University of Tennessee—Knoxville
16. East Carolina University
17. Elmira College
18. Pace University
19. George Mason University
20. University of Central Florida

Most Accessible Professors
Are your instructors accessible outside the classroom?

1. United States Military Academy
2. Williams College
3. Rose-Hulman Institute of Technology
4. Wabash College
5. Webb Institute
6. Union College (NY)
7. The College of Wooster
8. St. John's College (MD)
9. Thomas Aquinas College
10. Franklin W. Olin College of Engineering
11. Bowdoin College
12. Furman University
13. Centre College
14. Hillsdale College
15. University of Richmond
16. Randolph College
17. St. John's College (NM)
18. Reed College
19. Juniata College
20. United States Air Force Academy

Least Accessible Professors
Are your instructors accessible outside the classroom?

1. University of Kentucky
2. Pace University
3. Louisiana State University—Baton Rouge
4. University of Central Florida
5. University of Massachusetts Amherst
6. McGill University
7. University of Maine
8. New Jersey Institute of Technology
9. City University of New York—Hunter College
10. Oregon State University
11. State University of New York—Purchase College
12. University of Connecticut
13. Elmira College
14. Drexel University
15. Illinois Institute of Technology
16. St. John's University (NY)
17. University of Houston
18. University of Notre Dame
19. University of North Dakota
20. University of Cincinnati

Best Science Lab Facilities
Based on students' assessment of science lab facilities

1. California Institute of Technology
2. United States Military Academy
3. United States Naval Academy
4. Lake Forest College
5. Rose-Hulman Institute of Technology
6. St. Olaf College
7. Lehigh University
8. The University of Scranton
9. Loyola Marymount University
10. William & Mary
11. Emory University
12. Eckerd College
13. United States Air Force Academy
14. St. Lawrence University

15. Vanderbilt University
16. Grinnell College
17. Georgia Institute of Technology
18. Bucknell University
19. Williams College
20. Randolph-Macon College

Most Popular Study Abroad Program
How popular is studying abroad at your school?

1. Elon University
2. Dickinson College
3. University of Denver
4. University of Dallas
5. Goucher College
6. Centre College
7. St. Olaf College
8. William & Mary
9. Hobart and William Smith Colleges
10. University of Delaware
11. Pepperdine University
12. Juniata College
13. University of Richmond
14. University of San Diego
15. Wofford College
16. American University
17. St. Lawrence University
18. Hamilton College
19. Marist College
20. Tulane University

Best Health Services
Based on students' assessments of student health services/
facilities on campus

1. United States Air Force Academy
2. United States Military Academy
3. Kansas State University
4. University of Utah
5. Rice University
6. Georgia Institute of Technology
7. University of Wisconsin—Madison
8. Bowdoin College
9. Lake Forest College
10. Washington State University
11. University of Miami
12. Florida State University
13. Wabash College
14. University of Arizona
15. Calvin University
16. University of California—Santa Barbara
17. Southwestern University
18. University of Vermont
19. Indiana University of Pennsylvania
20. Auburn University

Best Counseling Services
Based on students' assessments of counseling services
available on campus

1. Virginia Tech
2. United States Military Academy
3. Vanderbilt University
4. United States Air Force Academy
5. Washington State University
6. Texas Christian University
7. Kansas State University
8. Rose-Hulman Institute of Technology
9. Lake Forest College
10. Calvin University
11. University of Richmond
12. Agnes Scott College
13. United States Naval Academy
14. Grove City College
15. University of Lynchburg
16. Franklin W. Olin College of Engineering
17. Saint Louis University
18. Loyola Marymount University
19. Florida State University
20. Southwestern University

Best Career Services
Based on students' rating of campus career/
job-placement services

1. Bentley University
2. Clemson University
3. Southwestern University
4. Elon University
5. Northeastern University
6. University of Richmond
7. Wabash College
8. Grove City College
9. Rose-Hulman Institute of Technology
10. Kansas State University
11. Texas Christian University
12. Franklin W. Olin College of Engineering
13. Randolph-Macon College
14. William & Mary
15. The University of the South
16. Stonehill College
17. Clarkson University
18. St. Lawrence University
19. High Point University
20. Florida State University

Best College Library
Based on students' assessment of library facilities

1. United States Military Academy
2. Brigham Young University (UT)
3. Columbia University
4. University of Denver
5. Hampden-Sydney College
6. Williams College

7. Loyola Marymount University
8. William & Mary
9. Mount Holyoke College
10. Emory University
11. University of Richmond
12. The College of Wooster
13. Texas Christian University
14. Cornell University
15. University of Wisconsin—Madison
16. Vanderbilt University
17. Franklin W. Olin College of Engineering
18. Reed College
19. Washington University in St. Louis
20. Salisbury University

This Is a Library?
Based on students' assessment of library facilities

1. Juniata College
2. University of Tampa
3. Clarkson University
4. Louisiana State University—Baton Rouge
5. Creighton University
6. University of Dallas
7. Drexel University
8. Elmira College
9. Pace University
10. Colorado College
11. City University of New York—Hunter College
12. The Cooper Union for the Advancement of Science and Art
13. Rider University
14. Montana Technological University
15. Transylvania University
16. State University of New York—College of Environmental Science and Forestry
17. State University of New York—Geneseo
18. University of Notre Dame
19. Bradley University
20. St. Mary's College of Maryland

Great Financial Aid
Based on students' assessments of how satisfied they are with their financial aid package

1. Vanderbilt University
2. Williams College
3. Grinnell College
4. Washington University in St. Louis
5. Bowdoin College
6. Reed College
7. Rice University
8. Thomas Aquinas College
9. College of the Atlantic
10. Denison University
11. California Institute of Technology
12. Skidmore College
13. Columbia University

14. Wellesley College
16. Emory University
16. St. Olaf College
17. Wabash College
18. Brown University
19. University of Wisconsin—Madison
20. Franklin W. Olin College of Engineering

Financial Aid Not So Great
Based on students' assessments of how satisfied they are with their financial aid package

1. State University of New York—Purchase College
2. The College of New Jersey
3. American University
4. Emerson College
5. University of Pittsburgh—Pittsburgh Campus
6. University of Massachusetts Amherst
7. Temple University
8. State University of New York—Geneseo
9. George Mason University
10. New York University
11. University of Cincinnati
12. Elon University
13. State University of New York—Binghamton University
14. High Point University
15. Duquesne University
16. Quinnipiac University
17. Colorado State University
18. Michigan State University
19. Stevens Institute of Technology
20. Oregon State University

Best-Run Colleges
Overall, how smoothly is your school run?

1. Elon University
2. Vanderbilt University
3. Rice University
4. University of Richmond
5. Texas Christian University
6. Rose-Hulman Institute of Technology
7. Washington University in St. Louis
8. Brigham Young University (UT)
9. Bowdoin College
10. The University of Alabama—Tuscaloosa
11. Kansas State University
12. Tulane University
13. University of Wisconsin—Madison
14. University of Dayton
15. Hillsdale College
16. Angelo State University
17. University of San Diego
18. St. Lawrence University
19. Emory University
20. Wabash College

Administrators Get Low Marks
Overall, how smoothly is your school run?

1. Earlham College
2. The Cooper Union for the Advancement of Science and Art
3. Stevens Institute of Technology
4. Illinois Institute of Technology
5. State University of New York—Purchase College
6. Xavier University of Louisiana
7. City University of New York—Queens College
8. Centenary College of Louisiana
9. Mills College
10. Simmons University
11. McGill University
12. Sarah Lawrence College
13. Seton Hall University
14. Rider University
15. Elmira College
16. St. Mary's College of Maryland
17. New Jersey Institute of Technology
18. Drexel University
19. Manhattanville College
20. Emerson College

Their Students Love These Colleges
Overall, how satisfied are you with your school?

1. Vanderbilt University
2. Kansas State University
3. Tulane University
4. University of Wisconsin—Madison
5. Clemson University
6. Brown University
7. Virginia Tech
8. Auburn University
9. Lehigh University
10. Thomas Aquinas College
11. Franklin W. Olin College of Engineering
12. University of Richmond
13. Bowdoin College
14. William & Mary
15. Emory University
16. Washington University in St. Louis
17. United States Military Academy
18. Rice University
19. Elon University
20. University of Vermont

QUALITY OF LIFE

Happiest Students
Overall, how happy are you?

1. Kansas State University
2. Vanderbilt University
3. Tulane University
4. William & Mary
5. University of Dallas
6. Thomas Aquinas College
7. Brown University
8. Texas Christian University
9. Rose-Hulman Institute of Technology
10. Auburn University
11. Clemson University
12. Rice University
13. Franklin W. Olin College of Engineering
14. University of Richmond
15. University of Dayton
16. Loyola Marymount University
17. Elon University
18. University of California—Santa Barbara
19. Hampden-Sydney College
20. Florida State University

Most Beautiful Campus
Based on students' rating of campus beauty

1. University of Richmond
2. Vanderbilt University
3. Bryn Mawr College
4. Elon University
5. The University of the South
6. University of San Diego
7. Rice University
8. Lehigh University
9. High Point University
10. Washington University in St. Louis
11. Loyola Marymount University
12. Berry College
13. Thomas Aquinas College
14. Scripps College
15. Bucknell University
16. Florida Southern College
17. Wellesley College
18. Mount Holyoke College
19. Pepperdine University
20. Texas Christian University

Least Beautiful Campus
Based on students' rating of campus beauty

1. City University of New York—Hunter College
2. Pace University
3. State University of New York—Purchase College
4. University of Dallas
5. Rochester Institute of Technology
6. State University of New York—Stony Brook University
7. University of Tennessee—Knoxville
8. Illinois Institute of Technology
9. George Mason University
10. University of Massachusetts Amherst
11. Montana Technological University
12. Drexel University
13. Middle Tennessee State University
14. The Cooper Union for the Advancement of Science and Art
15. New Jersey Institute of Technology
16. Xavier University of Louisiana
17. City University of New York—Baruch College
18. Brandeis University
19. Stevens Institute of Technology
20. Clarkson University

Is It Food?
Based on students' rating of campus food

1. Hampden-Sydney College
2. Centenary College of Louisiana
3. Clarkson University
4. Bentley University
5. Simmons University
6. Creighton University
7. Transylvania University
8. Providence College
9. Xavier University of Louisiana
10. State University of New York—Stony Brook University
11. Randolph-Macon College
12. Bryant University
13. Fordham University
14. Wagner College
15. Butler University
16. Stetson University
17. The Cooper Union for the Advancement of Science and Art
18. Saint Joseph's University (PA)
19. City University of New York—Hunter College
20. McDaniel College

Best Campus Food
Based on students' rating of campus food

1. University of Massachusetts Amherst
2. Bowdoin College
3. Washington University in St. Louis
4. Pitzer College
5. Cornell University
6. Vanderbilt University
7. The University of Scranton
8. Virginia Tech
9. Gettysburg College
10. College of the Atlantic
11. St. Olaf College
12. James Madison University
13. Kansas State University
14. University of Richmond
15. University of Dayton
16. Scripps College
17. Skidmore College
18. Bryn Mawr College
19. Wheaton College (IL)
20. University of Notre Dame

Best College Dorms
Based on students' rating of dorm comfort

1. High Point University
2. Washington University in St. Louis
3. Franklin W. Olin College of Engineering
4. Texas Christian University
5. Emory University
6. Rice University
7. Bryn Mawr College
8. Christopher Newport University
9. Bowdoin College
10. Mount Holyoke College
11. Rose-Hulman Institute of Technology
12. Elon University
13. State University of New York—College of Environmental Science and Forestry
14. Loyola University Maryland
15. Williams College
16. Scripps College
17. Vanderbilt University
18. University of Dayton
19. Pitzer College
20. Kansas State University

Is That a Dorm?
Based on students' rating of dorm comfort

1. United States Military Academy
2. Simmons University
3. The Cooper Union for the Advancement of Science and Art
4. Clarkson University
5. Wagner College
6. State University of New York—Purchase College
7. Stevens Institute of Technology
8. Rider University
9. Manhattanville College
10. Stetson University
11. Coe College
12. United States Naval Academy
13. Illinois Institute of Technology
14. Whittier College
15. Xavier University of Louisiana
16. University of Miami
17. Middle Tennessee State University
18. St. Mary's College of Maryland
19. University of Maine
20. City University of New York—Hunter College

Best Quality of Life
Based on The Princeton Review's Quality of Life Rating (page 21)

1. Rice University
2. Vanderbilt University
3. Kansas State University
4. Texas Christian University
5. Bowdoin College
6. Emory University
7. Washington University in St. Louis
8. University of San Diego
9. University of Richmond
10. Wheaton College (IL)
11. Washington State University
12. Tulane University
13. Bryn Mawr College
14. Brown University
15. William & Mary
16. University of Wisconsin—Madison
17. Clemson University
18. Franklin W. Olin College of Engineering
19. Auburn University
20. Christopher Newport University

POLITICS

Most Conservative Students
Based on students' assessment of their personal political views

1. College of the Ozarks
2. Baylor University
3. Hillsdale College
4. United States Air Force Academy
5. United States Military Academy
6. Grove City College
7. Hampden-Sydney College
8. Texas Christian University
9. Kansas State University
10. Clemson University
11. Wofford College
12. Wheaton College (IL)
13. Angelo State University
14. Auburn University
15. Montana Technological University
16. Fairfield University
17. University of North Dakota
18. University of Dallas
19. University of Dayton
20. University of South Carolina—Columbia

Most Liberal Students
Based on students' assessment of their personal political views

1. Sarah Lawrence College
2. Macalester College
3. Grinnell College
4. Bryn Mawr College
5. University of Puget Sound
6. Pitzer College
7. Earlham College
8. Reed College
9. University of Vermont
10. Wellesley College
11. Vassar College
12. Mount Holyoke College
13. Mills College
14. Skidmore College
15. Wesleyan University
16. College of the Atlantic
17. Brandeis University
18. Clark University
19. Brown University
20. Lawrence University

Most Politically Active Students
Based on students' assessment of their personal level of political awareness

1. Pitzer College
2. Furman University
3. Columbia University
4. Reed College
5. American University
6. Hollins University
7. Syracuse University
8. Grinnell College
9. Williams College
10. Brown University
11. Sarah Lawrence College
12. Hillsdale College
13. Emerson College
14. Hampden-Sydney College
15. Texas Christian University
16. University of North Carolina Asheville
17. Tulane University
18. University of Redlands
19. The University of Alabama—Tuscaloosa
20. Scripps College

Election? What Election?
Based on students' assessment of their personal level of political awareness

1. State University of New York—Geneseo
2. University of Denver
3. Sacred Heart University
4. Wagner College
5. University of Utah
6. Elon University
7. University of Nebraska—Lincoln
8. Brigham Young University (UT)
9. University of New England
10. Washington State University
11. Carnegie Mellon University
12. Moravian College
13. Rochester Institute of Technology
14. New Jersey Institute of Technology
15. St. John's University (NY)
16. Elmira College
17. Manhattan College
18. Worcester Polytechnic Institute
19. DePaul University
20. University of Louisiana at Lafayette

CAMPUS LIFE

Lots of Race/Class Interaction
Do different types of students (black/white, rich/poor) interact frequently and easily?

1. Rice University
2. United States Military Academy
3. William & Mary
4. St. John's College (MD)
5. United States Air Force Academy
6. Thomas Aquinas College
7. Loyola University New Orleans
8. Agnes Scott College
9. United States Naval Academy
10. University of Houston
11. Drew University
12. St. Bonaventure University
13. The College of Wooster
14. St. John's College (NM)
15. Drury University
16. Temple University
17. Emory University
18. Angelo State University
19. Hampden-Sydney College
20. College of the Atlantic

Little Race/Class Interaction
Do different types of students (black/white, rich/poor) interact frequently and easily?

1. Quinnipiac University
2. Providence College
3. Amherst College
4. University of Tennessee—Knoxville
5. University of Notre Dame
6. Simmons University
7. Gettysburg College
8. Monmouth University (NJ)
9. Stevens Institute of Technology
10. University of Richmond
11. Montana Technological University
12. Elmira College
13. Santa Clara University
14. Hobart and William Smith Colleges
15. Lehigh University
16. Colby College
17. Elon University
18. Auburn University
19. University of Virginia
20. Wagner College

LGBTQ-Friendly

Do students, faculty and administrators treat all persons equally, regardless of their sexual orientation and gender identity/expression?

1. Bryn Mawr College
2. Mount Holyoke College
3. Franklin W. Olin College of Engineering
4. Brown University
5. Agnes Scott College
6. College of the Atlantic
7. Reed College
8. Wellesley College
9. Rice University
10. University of North Carolina Asheville
11. Nazareth College
12. Scripps College
13. Pitzer College
14. Mills College
15. Columbia University
16. Macalester College
17. Emerson College
18. William & Mary
19. Wesleyan University
20. State University of New York—Purchase College

LGBTQ-Unfriendly

Do students, faculty and administrators treat all persons equally, regardless of their sexual orientation and gender identity/expression?

1. College of the Ozarks
2. University of Tennessee—Knoxville
3. Wheaton College (IL)
4. Brigham Young University (UT)
5. Grove City College
6. Auburn University
7. Gordon College
8. The University of Alabama—Tuscaloosa
9. University of Dallas
10. University of Notre Dame
11. Baylor University
12. Calvin University
13. Providence College
14. Louisiana State University—Baton Rouge
15. Montana Technological University
16. University of Wyoming
17. Gettysburg College
18. Hobart and William Smith Colleges
19. Texas State University
20. University of Arkansas—Fayetteville

Most Religious Students

Are students very religious?

1. University of Dallas
2. Brigham Young University (UT)
3. Thomas Aquinas College
4. College of the Ozarks
5. Wheaton College (IL)
6. Auburn University
7. Hillsdale College
8. Grove City College
9. Baylor University
10. University of Notre Dame
11. The Catholic University of America
12. Gordon College
13. Calvin University
14. Clemson University
15. The University of Scranton
16. Berry College
17. Pepperdine University
18. Sacred Heart University
19. University of Utah
20. Marquette University

Least Religious Students

Are students very religious?

1. Emerson College
2. Reed College
3. Grinnell College
4. Beloit College
5. Sarah Lawrence College
6. Pitzer College
7. Brown University
8. Franklin W. Olin College of Engineering
9. Scripps College
10. Wesleyan University
11. Bowdoin College
12. Macalester College
13. Columbia University
14. Kalamazoo College
15. University of North Carolina Asheville
16. College of the Atlantic
17. Colby College
18. University of Puget Sound
19. Eckerd College
20. Mills College

TOWN LIFE

College City Gets High Marks
Based on students' assessment of the surrounding
city or town

1. Columbia University
2. Vanderbilt University
3. Tulane University
4. American University
5. City University of New York—Baruch College
6. Stevens Institute of Technology
7. Northeastern University
8. Suffolk University
9. Emory University
10. Loyola University New Orleans
11. New York University
12. University of Arkansas—Fayetteville
13. The Cooper Union for the Advancement
    of Science and Art
14. University of Denver
15. Simmons University
16. University of Wisconsin—Madison
17. University of North Carolina Asheville
18. University of Vermont
19. DePaul University
20. Ithaca College

College City Gets Low Marks
Based on students' assessment of the surrounding
city or town

1. New Jersey Institute of Technology
2. United States Military Academy
3. Hofstra University
4. Elmira College
5. Earlham College
6. Colby College
7. Rose-Hulman Institute of Technology
8. Wabash College
9. Washington & Jefferson College
10. Hillsdale College
11. Allegheny College
12. The University of the South
13. Truman State University
14. University of California—Merced
15. Syracuse University
16. Hamilton College
17. High Point University
18. Mercer University
19. St. Mary's College of Maryland
20. University of Notre Dame

Town-Gown Relations Are Great
Do students get along well with members of the
local community?

1. Clemson University
2. Agnes Scott College
3. Vanderbilt University
4. Kansas State University
5. Brigham Young University (UT)
6. Wheaton College (IL)
7. United States Naval Academy
8. Loyola University New Orleans
9. Auburn University
10. United States Air Force Academy
11. Texas Christian University
12. College of the Ozarks
13. Nazareth College
14. Emory University
15. Virginia Tech
16. University of North Carolina Asheville
17. Grove City College
18. Rice University
19. William Jewell College
20. Stonehill College

Town-Gown Relations Are Strained
Do students get along well with members of the
local community?

1. Sarah Lawrence College
2. Lawrence University
3. Colby College
4. Providence College
5. Earlham College
6. Elmira College
7. Indiana University of Pennsylvania
8. Union College (NY)
9. Syracuse University
10. Colorado College
11. St. Mary's College of Maryland
12. Grinnell College
13. Lehigh University
14. University of Notre Dame
15. New Jersey Institute of Technology
16. Beloit College
17. State University of New York—Binghamton
    University
18. Quinnipiac University
19. Hofstra University
20. Elon University

EXTRACURRICULARS

Best Athletic Facilities
Based on students' rating of campus athletic facilities

1. Auburn University
2. Florida State University
3. The University of Alabama—Tuscaloosa
4. Vanderbilt University
5. University of Utah
6. Denison University
7. University of Richmond
8. Washington State University
9. Kansas State University
10. United States Air Force Academy
11. Louisiana State University—Baton Rouge
12. The Ohio State University—Columbus
13. Georgia Institute of Technology
14. Texas Christian University
15. University of Denver
16. Washington University in St. Louis
17. University of South Carolina—Columbia
18. Providence College
19. Tulane University
20. Clemson University

Students Pack the Stadiums
How popular are intercollegiate sports?

1. Arizona State University
2. Syracuse University
3. Auburn University
4. Clemson University
5. United States Air Force Academy
6. Xavier University (OH)
7. Marquette University
8. Creighton University
9. University of Connecticut
10. Brigham Young University (UT)
11. Providence College
12. The Ohio State University–Columbus
13. Florida State University
14. Michigan State University
15. Bowdoin College
16. Butler University
17. University of Wisconsin—Madison
18. University of Nebraska—Lincoln
19. University of Central Florida
20. University of Notre Dame

There's a Game?
How popular are intercollegiate sports?

1. Washington University in St. Louis
2. Hollins University
3. Brandeis University
4. Reed College
5. College of the Atlantic
5. McDaniel College

7. Thomas Aquinas College
8. McGill University
9. Skidmore College
10. Franklin W. Olin College of Engineering
11. Pitzer College
12. Suffolk University
13. State University of New York—Purchase College
14. Sarah Lawrence College
15. Bennington College
16. Carnegie Mellon University
17. University of South Florida
18. St. John's College (NM)
19. Pace University
20. The Cooper Union for the Advancement of Science and Art

Everyone Plays Intramural Sports
How popular are intramural sports?

1. Fordham University
2. Providence College
3. Clemson University
4. Saint Joseph's University (PA)
5. Grove City College
6. Wabash College
7. Mercer University
8. Brigham Young University (UT)
9. St. John's College (MD)
10. Florida State University
11. Michigan State University
12. Rose-Hulman Institute of Technology
13. Bryant University
14. Washington State University
15. University of Dayton
16. Iowa State University
17. Babson College
18. Syracuse University
19. University of Notre Dame
20. Kettering University

Nobody Plays Intramural Sports
How popular are intramural sports?

1. Drexel University
2. American University
3. Agnes Scott College
4. Sarah Lawrence College
5. Skidmore College
6. McDaniel College
7. The Cooper Union for the Advancement of Science and Art
8. Rice University
9. Denison University
10. Bryn Mawr College
11. State University of New York—Purchase College
12. Stephens College
13. Pace University
14. Gettysburg College

15. Reed College
16. Mills College
17. Emerson College
18. Wagner College
19. Franklin W. Olin College of Engineering
20. Simmons University

Best College Radio Station
How popular is the radio station?

1. University of South Florida
2. Emerson College
3. Arizona State University
4. St. Bonaventure University
5. Ithaca College
6. Syracuse University
7. McGill University
8. Reed College
9. Louisiana State University—Baton Rouge
10. Columbia University
11. Manhattanville College
12. Seton Hall University
13. Hofstra University
14. University of Puget Sound
15. Providence College
16. Denison University
17. Washington State University
18. Monmouth University (NJ)
19. University of Notre Dame
20. The University of the South

Best College Newspaper
How do you rate your campus newspaper?

1. Syracuse University
2. Ithaca College
3. Rice University
4. Columbia University
5. Hillsdale College
6. Bowdoin College
7. Wabash College
8. Grinnell College
9. Loyola University New Orleans
10. University of Wisconsin—Madison
11. University of North Carolina—Chapel Hill
12. Cornell University
13. Vanderbilt University
14. Elon University
15. Scripps College
16. The University of the South
17. University of Virginia
18. Eckerd College
19. American University
20. University of South Carolina—Columbia

Best College Theater
How do you rate college's theater productions?

1. Ithaca College
2. Carnegie Mellon University
3. Wagner College
4. State University of New York—Purchase College
5. Brown University
6. Elon University
7. Emerson College
8. Hollins University
9. Bard College
10. Wesleyan University
11. Wabash College
12. Furman University
13. Williams College
14. Grinnell College
15. Skidmore College
16. Sarah Lawrence College
17. Vanderbilt University
18. Florida State University
19. Drew University
20. Columbia University

Students Most Engaged in Community Service
Based on students' rating of their commitment to community service

1. Tulane University
2. Saint Louis University
3. Hillsdale College
4. Loyola Marymount University
5. University of Notre Dame
6. Brandeis University
7. William & Mary
8. United States Military Academy
9. The Catholic University of America
10. Sacred Heart University
11. Rhodes College
12. Vanderbilt University
13. Creighton University
14. Christopher Newport University
15. Xavier University of Louisiana
16. Marquette University
17. Berry College
18. University of Virginia
19. Brigham Young University (UT)
20. Elon University

Most Active Student Government

Based on a combination of survey questions concerning student run political groups, and the active and effective presence of student government on campus.

1. American University
2. Bryn Mawr College
3. College of the Atlantic
4. Reed College
5. Hampden-Sydney College
6. Mount Holyoke College
7. The University of Alabama—Tuscaloosa
8. Texas Christian University
9. Pitzer College
10. Wabash College
11. Eckerd College
12. Florida State University
13. Syracuse University
14. St. Lawrence University
15. Tulane University
16. Furman University
17. Kansas State University
18. Bucknell University
19. High Point University
20. Loyola University New Orleans

SOCIAL SCENE

Lots of Greek Life

How popular are fraternities/sororities?

1. The University of Alabama—Tuscaloosa
2. Washington University in St. Louis
3. Bucknell University
4. Wofford College
5. University of Delaware
6. Wabash College
7. Gettysburg College
8. Vanderbilt University
9. Transylvania University
10. Florida State University
11. Lehigh University
12. Tulane University
13. Elon University
14. The University of the South
15. University of Arkansas—Fayetteville
16. Worcester Polytechnic Institute
17. Auburn University
18. Texas Christian University
19. University of Richmond
20. Case Western Reserve University

Lots of Beer

How widely used is beer?

1. University of Wisconsin—Madison
2. University of Richmond
3. Eckerd College
4. Colgate University
5. Union College (NY)
6. The University of Alabama—Tuscaloosa
7. West Virginia University
8. Tulane University
9. University of Delaware
10. Syracuse University
11. Bucknell University
12. Wake Forest University
13. The University of the South
14. University of Dayton
15. Colby College
16. Providence College
17. Bowdoin College
18. University of Florida
19. Hobart and William Smith Colleges
20. University of Virginia

Got Milk?

How widely used is beer?

1. Brigham Young University (UT)
2. College of the Ozarks
3. City University of New York—Hunter College
4. City University of New York—Baruch College
5. Grove City College
6. Wheaton College (IL)
7. Calvin University
8. Xavier University of Louisiana
9. Thomas Aquinas College
10. Gordon College
11. United States Naval Academy
12. Baylor University
13. City University of New York—Queens College
14. Pepperdine University
15. University of California—Merced
16. United States Air Force Academy
17. Simmons University
18. Angelo State University
19. University of California—Riverside
20. Mills College

Lots of Hard Liquor

How widely used is hard liquor?

1. Syracuse University
2. Bentley University
3. Wake Forest University
4. Grinnell College
5. Tulane University
6. University of California—Santa Barbara
7. University of Maine
8. Union College (NY)

9. Elon University
10. Colgate University
11. West Virginia University
12. The University of the South
13. St. Lawrence University
14. University of Delaware
15. University of Wisconsin—Madison
16. Fairfield University
17. University of Connecticut
18. St. Bonaventure University
19. Denison University
20. Wesleyan University

Scotch and Soda, Hold the Scotch
How widely used is hard liquor?

1. College of the Ozarks
2. Brigham Young University (UT)
3. Thomas Aquinas College
4. City University of New York—Baruch College
5. City University of New York—Hunter College
6. United States Naval Academy
7. Wheaton College (IL)
8. United States Air Force Academy
9. Calvin University
10. Grove City College
11. Gordon College
12. Baylor University
13. City University of New York—Queens College
14. Pepperdine University
15. Angelo State University
16. University of California—Riverside
17. Illinois Institute of Technology
18. United States Military Academy
19. Mills College
20. University of California—Merced

Reefer Madness
How widely used is marijuana?

1. Skidmore College
2. Pitzer College
3. Wesleyan University
4. Reed College
5. University of Rhode Island
6. University of Maine
7. University of Vermont
8. Warren Wilson College
9. Sarah Lawrence College
10. State University of New York—Purchase College
11. Emerson College
12. Eckerd College
13. Goucher College
14. University of California—Santa Barbara
15. Syracuse University

16. Ithaca College
17. Clark University
18. Colby College
19. St. Lawrence University
20. Hamilton College

Don't Inhale
How widely used is marijuana?

1. United States Air Force Academy
2. United States Military Academy
3. United States Naval Academy
4. College of the Ozarks
5. Brigham Young University (UT)
6. Thomas Aquinas College
7. Wheaton College (IL)
8. City University of New York—Baruch College
9. Calvin University
10. Grove City College
11. City University of New York—Hunter College
12. Baylor University
13. Gordon College
14. Hillsdale College
15. Illinois Institute of Technology
16. University of Notre Dame
17. University of Dallas
18. Pepperdine University
19. Agnes Scott College
20. Rose-Hulman Institute of Technology

SCHOOLS BY TYPE

Party Schools
Based on a combination of survey questions concerning the use of alcohol and drugs, hours of study each day, and the popularity of the Greek system

1. The University of Alabama—Tuscaloosa
2. University of Delaware
3. Syracuse University
4. West Virginia University
5. Tulane University
6. University of Maine
7. Union College (NY)
8. Bucknell University
9. Colgate University
10. Wake Forest University
11. University of California—Santa Barbara
12. Elon University
13. University of Rhode Island
14. University of Wisconsin—Madison
15. The University of the South
16. St. Lawrence University
17. University of Dayton
18. University of Connecticut
19. Florida State University
20. Indiana University of Pennsylvania

Stone-Cold Sober Schools

Based on a combination of survey questions concerning the use of alcohol and drugs, hours of study each day, and the popularity of the Greek system

1. Brigham Young University (UT)
2. College of the Ozarks
3. Thomas Aquinas College
4. United States Naval Academy
5. Wheaton College (IL)
6. Calvin University
7. Gordon College
8. United States Air Force Academy
9. Grove City College
10. City University of New York—Baruch College
11. United States Military Academy
12. City University of New York—Hunter College
13. University of California–Merced
14. Agnes Scott College
15. Mills College
16. Baylor University
17. Berry College
18. Middle Tennessee State University
19. Simmons University
20. College of the Atlantic

Future Rotarians and Daughters of the American Revolution

Based on a combination of survey questions concerning the political persuasion, the use of drugs, the popularity of student government, and the level of acceptance of the LGBTQ community on campus

1. Grove City College
2. College of the Ozarks
3. Hillsdale College
4. Thomas Aquinas College
5. Wheaton College (IL)
6. Brigham Young University (UT)
7. United States Air Force Academy
8. Baylor University
9. Gordon College
10. University of Dallas
11. United States Military Academy
12. Auburn University
13. Calvin University
14. Berry College
15. Hampden-Sydney College
16. Angelo State University
17. Clemson University
18. Kansas State University
19. The Catholic University of America
20. United States Naval Academy

Birkenstock-Wearing, Tree-Hugging, Clove-Smoking Vegetarians

Based on a combination of survey questions concerning the political persuasion, the use of drugs, the popularity of student government, and the level of acceptance of the LGBTQ community on campus

1. Grinnell College
2. Reed College
3. Macalester College
4. University of Puget Sound
5. Pitzer College
6. Wesleyan University
7. Sarah Lawrence College
8. Wellesley College
9. University of Vermont
10. Emerson College
11. Brown University
12. Mount Holyoke College
13. College of the Atlantic
14. Eckerd College
15. State University of New York—Purchase College
16. Beloit College
17. Skidmore College
18. Warren Wilson College
19. Simmons University
20. Earlham College

THE PRINCETON REVIEW'S HONOR ROLLS

We salute theses schools that received a 99 (the highest score) in the tallies for our "Financial Aid," "Fire Safety," and "Green" Ratings—three of eight ratings on some of the school profiles in this book and at PrincetonReview.com. Our school ratings are numerical scores (Note: They are not ranking lists) that show how a school "sizes up" on a fixed scale. They are comparable to grades and based primarily on institutional data we collect directly from the colleges.

Financial Aid Honor Roll

Schools are listed in alphabetical order. See page 26 for information on how our "Financial Aid Rating" is determined.
Grinnell College
Pomona College
Princeton University
Vanderbilt University
Vassar College
Washington University in St. Louis
Williams College
Yale University

Fire Safety Honor Roll

Schools are listed in alphabetical order. See page 22 for information on how our "Fire Safety Rating" is determined.
Adelphi University*
Bay Path University*
Bentley University
Bloomfield College*
Brenau University*
Cazenovia College*
DePaul University
Emmanuel College*
Five Towns College*
Florida A&M University*
Franklin W. Olin College of Engineering
Georgia College & State University*
Hellenic College*
Holy Family University*
Husson University*
Indiana University South Bend*
Indiana University Southeast*
Johns Hopkins University
Monmouth University (NJ)
Mount St. Joseph University*
Mount St. Mary's University*
Mount Saint Mary's University (CA)*
New Jersey Institute of Technology*
Saint Mary-of-the-Woods College*
School of Visual Arts*
Southeastern University*
Stevens Institute of Technology
Suffolk University
Texas Woman's University*
Tufts University
United States Air Force Academy
University of Maine
University of Maine—Fort Kent*
University of Minnesota—Crookston*
University of New England
University of North Carolina—Greensboro
University of St. Francis*

Schools marked with an asterisk do not appear in the *Best 386 Colleges.* You can find those school profiles in *The Complete Book of Colleges*, 2021 Edition.

University of Saint Joseph*
University of South Florida—St. Petersburg*
Xavier University of Louisiana

Green Honor Roll

Schools are listed in alphabetical order. See page 22 for information on how our "Green Rating" is determined.
Carnegie Mellon University
Chatham University*
Colby College
Colgate University
College of the Atlantic
Colorado State University
Cornell University
Dickinson College
Emerson College
Iowa State University
Loyola Marymount University
Loyola University of Chicago
Middlebury College
Oberlin College
Pitzer College
Randolph College
St. Mary's College of Maryland
Seattle University
Stanford University
University of California—Berkeley
University of California—Irvine*
University of California—Merced
University of Colorado—Colorado Springs*
University of Connecticut
University of New Hampshire
University of San Diego
Vanderbilt University

Tuition-Free Schools Honor Roll

The following schools have been excluded from our ranking and ratings dealing with financial aid:
Berea College
College of the Ozarks
Deep Springs College
United States Air Force Academy
United States Coast Guard Academy
United States Merchant Marine Academy
United States Military Academy
United States Naval Academy
Webb Institute

We commend these schools on their ability to do the seemingly impossible: not charge tuition. While some charge students for room and board and other fees, the overall cost of attendance at these schools is very low, and at some schools: free! (Note: We do not include these schools in our ranking lists dealing with financial aid, since they would have an unfair advantage over schools that charge even a moderate tuition.)

THE PRINCETON REVIEW'S 200 BEST VALUE COLLEGES FOR 2020

The Princeton Review released its current list of the Best Value Colleges in February 2020. We selected the 200 schools based on forty weighted data points, including academics, cost, financial aid, and student debt to statistics on graduation rates, alumni salaries and job satisfaction. Alumni survey information was provided by PayScale.com. For detailed profiles of all these great schools, see our companion book, *The Best Value Colleges*.

Agnes Scott College
Allegheny College
Amherst College
Arizona State University
Auburn University
Babson College
Barnard College
Bates College
Baylor University
Beloit College
Bennington College
Bentley University
Berea College
Bowdoin College
Bradley University
Brandeis University
Brigham Young University
Brown University
Bryn Mawr College
Bucknell University
California Institute of Technology
California State University—Long Beach
Carleton College
Carnegie Mellon Universit
Case Western Reserve University
Centre College
Christopher Newport University
City University of New York—Baruch College
City University of New York—Brooklyn College
City University of New York—Hunter College
City University of New York—Queens College
Claremont McKenna College
Clark University
Clarkson University
Clemson University
Coe College
Colby College
Colgate University
College of the Atlantic
The College of New Jersey
College of the Ozarks
College of Wooster
Colorado College
Columbia University
The Cooper Union for the Advancement
of Science and Art
Cornell University
Creighton University
Dartmouth College

Davidson College
Deep Springs College
Denison University
Dickinson College
Drew University
Duke University
Earlham College
Emory University
Fairfield University
Florida State University
Franklin & Marshall College
Franklin W. Olin College of Engineering
Furman University
Georgetown University
Georgia Institute of Technology
Gettysburg College
Grinnell College
Grove City College
Hamilton College
Hampden-Sydney College
Harvard College
Harvey Mudd College
Haverford College
Hobart and William Smith Colleges
Hollins University
Illinois Institute of Technology
Iowa State University
Johns Hopkins University
Kalamazoo College
Kenyon College
Lafayette College
Lake Forest College
Lawrence University
Lehigh University
Macalester College
Marlboro College
Marquette University
Massachusetts Institute of Technology
McDaniel College
Miami University
Michigan Technological University
Middlebury College
Missouri University of Science and Technology
Montana Technological University
Mount Holyoke College
Muhlenberg College
New College of Florida
New Jersey Institute of Technology
North Carolina State University

Northeastern University
Northwestern University
Occidental College
Ohio State University—Columbus
Ohio Wesleyan University
Pennsylvania State University—University Park
Pepperdine University
Pitzer College
Pomona College
Princeton University
Purdue University—West Lafayette
Reed College
Rensselaer Polytechnic Institute
Rhodes College
Rice University
Rochester Institute of Technology
Rose-Hulman Institute of Technology
Saint Louis University
San Diego State University
Santa Clara University
Scripps College
Sewanee—The University of the South
Skidmore College
Smith College
Southwestern University
St. Anselm College
St. John's College (MD)
St. John's College (NM)
St. Lawrence University
St. Mary's College of Maryland
St. Olaf College
Stanford University
State University of New York at Binghamton
State University of New York—College of
Environmental Science and Forestry
State University of New York—Purchase College
State University of New York—Stony Brook University
Stevens Institute of Technology
Stonehill College
Swarthmore College
Texas A&M University—College Station
Texas Christian University
Thomas Aquinas College
Trinity University
Truman State University
Tufts University
Tulane University
Union College (NY)
United States Air Force Academy
United States Coast Guard Academy
United States Merchant Marine Academy
United States Military Academy
United States Naval Academy
The University of Alabama—Tuscaloosa
University of Arizona
University of California—Berkeley
University of California—Davis

University of California—Los Angeles
University of California—Riverside
University of California—San Diego
University of California—Santa Barbara
University of California—Santa Cruz
University of Central Florida
The University of Chicago
University of Colorado—Boulder
University of Connecticut
University of Dallas
University of Dayton
University of Denver
University of Florida
University of Georgia
University of Houston
University of Illinois at Urbana-Champaign
University of Massachusetts Amherst
University of Miami
University of Michigan—Ann Arbor
University of Minnesota—Twin Cities
The University of North Carolina at Chapel Hill
University of Notre Dame
University of Oklahoma
University of Pennsylvania
University of Pittsburgh—Pittsburgh Campus
University of Richmond
University of Rochester
University of South Florida
The University of Texas at Austin
The University of Texas at Dallas
University of Tulsa
University of Utah
University of Virginia
University of Washington
University of Wisconsin—Madison
Vanderbilt University
Vassar College
Virginia Tech
Wabash College
Wake Forest University
Washington College
Washington State University
Washington University in St. Louis
Webb Institute
Wellesley College
Wesleyan University
Wheaton College (IL)
Wheaton College (MA)
Whitman College
Willamette University
William & Mary
William Jewell College
Williams College
Wofford College
Worcester Polytechnic Institute
Yale University

The Best Value Colleges contains seven ranking lists, all of which focus on different aspects of financial aid and career preparation. Because this book already contains a Financial Aid Honors Roll, we've included six of those lists here.

Top 75 Best Value Colleges
The seventy-five schools that received the highest overall rating used to determine inclusion in *The Best Value Colleges, 13th Edition.*

1. Princeton University
2. Massachusetts Institute of Technology
3. Harvey Mudd College
4. Stanford University
5. California Institute of Technology
6. Yale University
7. Williams College
8. Harvard College
9. The Cooper Union for the Advancement of Science and Art
10. University of California—Berkeley
11. Georgia Institute of Technology
12. University of Virginia
13. Vanderbilt University
14. Rice University
15. Columbia University
16. Dartmouth College
17. Pomona College
18. Amherst College
19. Duke University
20. Rose-Hulman Institute of Technology
21. University of North Carolina—Chapel Hill
22. Claremont McKenna College
23. University of California—Santa Barbara
24. Brown University
25. Bowdoin College
26. Wabash College
27. Cornell University
28. University of Pennsylvania
29. University of Chicago
30. Swarthmore College
31. Lehigh University
32. Worcester Polytechnic Institute
33. Carleton College
34. Haverford College
35. Brigham Young University (UT)
36. University of California—Los Angeles
37. Johns Hopkins University
38. Carnegie Mellon University
39. University of California—San Diego
40. Grinnell College
41. Colgate University
42. University of Florida
43. William & Mary
44. Wellesley College
45. Hamilton College
46. Emory University
47. Middlebury College
48. Washington University in St. Louis
49. Purdue University—West Lafayette
50. Vassar College
51. North Carolina State University
52. Rhodes College
53. Lafayette College
54. Wesleyan University
55. Case Western Reserve University
56. City University of New York—Baruch College
57. University of Wisconsin-Madison
58. Babson College
59. University of Michigan—Ann Arbor
60. Trinity University
61. Union College (NY)
62. University of Richmond
63. Bates College
64. Denison University
65. Smith College
66. Rensselaer Polytechnic Institute
67. Florida State University
68. Tufts University
69. Bucknell University
70. St. Olaf College
71. University of Notre Dame
72. University of Texas at Austin
73. University of California—Davis
74. University of California—Riverside
75. Thomas Aquinas College

Top 25 Best Value Colleges for Students With No Demonstrated Need

To create this list, we used the same methodology for our ROI rating, but removed need-based aid information. If you don't qualify for financial aid, these are your twenty-five best value schools.

1. Harvey Mudd College
2. Georgia Institute of Technology
3. Massachusetts Institute of Technology
4. University of California—Berkeley
5. Stanford University
6. University of Virginia
7. California Institute of Technology
8. Princeton University
9. Brigham Young University (UT)
10. University of North Carolina at Chapel Hill
11. University of California—Santa Barbara
12. William & Mary
13. University of Florida
14. University of California—Los Angeles
15. Williams College
16. Worcester Polytechnic Institute
17. Yale University
18. Rose-Hulman Institute of Technology
19. Rice University
20. Dartmouth College
21. Purdue University—West Lafayette
22. Claremont McKenna College
23. North Carolina State University
24. Carnegie Mellon University
25. University of Michigan—Ann Arbor

Best Alumni Network

These twenty-five schools have the strongest and most active alumni networks, based on current students' ratings of alumni activity and visibility on campus.

1. Wabash College
2. Hampden-Sydney College
3. Pennsylvania State University Park
4. St. Lawrence University
5. Hollins University
6. University of Virginia
7. Texas Christian University
8. Georgia Institute of Technology
9. Agnes Scott College
10. Wellesley College
11. Clemson University
12. Worcester Polytechnic Institute
13. Mount Holyoke College
14. Bryn Mawr College
15. Williams College
16. Wheaton College (IL)
17. Emory University
18. Washington State University
19. Wofford College
20. The University of the South
21. The University of Alabama—Tuscaloosa
22. Tulane University
23. Florida State University
24. Clarkson University
25. William & Mary

Best Schools for Internships

This top twenty-five list is based on students' ratings of accessibility of internships at their school.

1. Wabash College
2. The University of Alabama—Tuscaloosa
3. Rose-Hulman Institute of Technology
4. Bentley University
5. Franklin W. Olin College of Engineering
6. University of Richmond
7. Northeastern University
8. Grove City College
9. Clemson University
10. Texas Christian University
11. University of Dayton
12. Stevens Institute of Technology
13. Southwestern University
14. Hampden-Sydney College
15. The University of the South
16. Coe College
17. William & Mary
18. College of Wooster
19. Marquette University
20. Worcester Polytechnic Institute
21. Hollins University
22. Vanderbilt University
23. Lake Forest College
24. Bradley University
25. Stonehill College

Best Career Placement

This top twenty-five list is based on students' ratings of career services at their school, and on PayScale.com's median starting and mid-career salary information.

1. Harvey Mudd College
2. Massachusetts Institute of Technology
3. Stanford University
4. California Institute of Technology
5. Princeton University
6. Worcester Polytechnic Institute
7. Rose-Hulman Institute of Technology
8. Harvard College
9. University of Pennsylvania
10. Carnegie Mellon University
11. Stevens Institute of Technology
12. Duke University
13. Dartmouth College
14. Babson College
15. Rensselaer Polytechnic Institute
16. Lehigh University
17. Yale University
18. Claremont McKenna College
19. Georgia Institute of Technology
20. Columbia University
21. Cornell University
22. University of California—Berkeley
23. Clarkson University
24. Colgate University
25. Franklin W. Olin College of Engineering

Best Schools for Making an Impact

These twenty-five schools were selected based on student ratings and responses to our survey questions covering community service opportunities at their school, student government, sustainability efforts, and on-campus student engagement. We also took into account PayScale.com's percentage of alumni from each school that reported that they had high job meaning.

1. Wesleyan University
2. Southwestern University
3. Lawrence University
4. Saint Louis University
5. Williams College
6. Brown University
7. Brandeis University
8. Dickinson College
9. Furman University
10. Whitman College
11. Mount Holyoke College
12. Wheaton College (IL)
13. Reed College
14. Union College (NY)
15. Hobart and William Smith Colleges
16. William & Mary
17. Emory University
18. Tulane University
19. Grinnell College
20. St. Olaf College
21. Clark University
22. Hampden-Sydney College
23. Allegheny College
24. Creighton University
25. Macalester College

PART 3

The Best 386 Colleges

AGNES SCOTT COLLEGE

141 E. College Avenue, Decatur, GA 30030-3770 • Admissions: 404-471-6285

CAMPUS LIFE

Quality of Life Rating	94
Fire Safety Rating	96
Green Rating	96
Type of school	Private
Affiliation	Presbyterian
Environment	Metropolis

STUDENTS

Total undergrad enrollment	974
% male/female	0/100
% from out of state	40
% frosh from public high school	75
% frosh live on campus	86
% ugrads live on campus	82
% African American	32
% Asian	8
% Caucasian	31
% Hispanic	14
% Native American	<1
% Pacific Islander	<1
% Two or more races	6
% Race and/or ethnicity unknown	3
% international	6
# of countries represented	28

SURVEY SAYS . . .

Students are happy
Lab facilities are great
Great library
Internships are widely available
Class discussions encouraged
No one cheats
Students are friendly
Diverse student types interact on campus
Students get along with local community
Students involved in community service
Students environmentally aware
Students love Decatur, GA
Easy to get around campus
Very little drug use
Alumni active on campus
Active student government
Active minority support groups
Active student-run political groups

ACADEMICS

Academic Rating	92
% students returning for sophomore year	85
% students graduating within 4 years	70
% students graduating within 6 years	73
Calendar	Semester
Student/faculty ratio	10:1
Profs interesting rating	92
Profs accessible rating	96

Most classes have 10–19 students.
Most lab/discussion sessions have 10–19 students.

MOST POPULAR MAJORS

Psychology, General; Public Health, General; Business Administration and Management, General

STUDENTS SAY "..."

Academics

Students lucky enough to attend Agnes Scott College, a small liberal arts school within the wide metropolitan Atlanta area, have the opportunity to join a "supportive community of strong women working to create change in the world." Indeed, undergrads here really respect the fact that the college truly "teach[es students] to engage in the social challenges of [their] time." And they love that Agnes Scott provides amazing "network[ing] connections" and "fantastic internship opportunities." What's more, the college is "great about providing financial support, especially to promising students that would not otherwise be able to attend such an institution." Students attend "small classes" which allow them to easily "get to know [their] professors." As one student boasts, "I've had professors write me letters of recommendation, let me know about global programs I'd be good for, and even send me job postings they saw that they know I'd be interested in." Of course, classes are "rigorous" and instructors "expect a lot" from their students. Nevertheless, these dedicated professors make it clear that they "care about you and your success." And more often than not, they are "willing to go that extra mile." As one incredulous student illustrates, "Some of my professors just asked if anyone needed a home to go to for Thanksgiving." All in all, they "want you to be the best you can be." It's really that simple.

Life

At Agnes Scott, academics often take top priority. New students soon discover that the student body is typically "busy with class assignments and reading materials." However, they also carve out time to become "heavily involved with different student organizations." A handful of students can also be found "playing music on the quad," attending "movie showings," or participating in "on-campus activities like trivia and crafts." Of course, the "college itself...invites important speakers—Janet Mock, for example—so we have the opportunity to go to those as well." Some undergrads here do bemoan the fact that the "campus [can be] dead on the weekends." Indeed, lots of students head to other schools like nearby "Georgia Tech...[to have some] fun." And, of course, many individuals love to take advantage of Agnes Scott's fabulous location. "Downtown Decatur...is [only] a quick walk from campus." In addition, Atlanta is quite accessible as well. Agnes Scott "provides a shuttle service" into the city, and is located "very close to a MARTA station," part of metro Atlanta's public transportation system.

Student Body

Students at Agnes Scott speak glowingly of their peers. Indeed, they describe their fellow Scotties as "ambitious" and "well-intentioned" women who hope to "make the world a... better [place]." As such, they are often interested "in a wide variety of social issues and take [any] opportunity...to enact the change they want to see." Undergrads here also proudly report that the student body is "a collection of intelligent and passionate women, trans... and [non-binary] individuals." Moreover, the students here represent "many different nationalities, religions, political opinions, and backgrounds." Students find the environment at Agnes Scott "welcoming" and boast that everyone [has the chance] to flourish in a safe-space feeling environment." As one undergrad further explains, "The uniqueness of this campus is mostly represented in the sense of community and sisterhood we have." Scotties also love that the school maintains a nice combination of "international students, first-generation college students, and a hardy mix of people from all over the United States." We'll give the last word to one Scottie who states, "Many words come to mind when I think about my peers, but the one that best embodies everyone is warmth.... Whenever I need help, my peers are continuously there for me, to answer questions and support the decisions I make. I never feel alone."

AGNES SCOTT COLLEGE

Financial Aid: 404-471-6395 • E-Mail: https://www.agnesscott.edu/admission/index.html • Website: www.agnesscott.edu

THE PRINCETON REVIEW SAYS

Admissions

Very important factors considered include: rigor of secondary school record, academic GPA, talent/ability, character/personal qualities. *Important factors considered include:* application essay, standardized test scores, recommendation(s), extracurricular activities. *Other factors considered include:* class rank, interview, first generation, alumni/ae relation, geographical residence, state residency, work experience, level of applicant's interest. High school diploma is required and GED is accepted. *Academic units recommended:* 4 English, 3 math, 2 science, 2 science labs, 2 foreign language, 2 social studies.

Financial Aid

Students should submit: FAFSA. Priority filing deadline is 1/15. The Princeton Review suggests that all financial aid forms be submitted as soon as possible after October 1. *Need-based scholarships/grants offered:* College/university scholarship or grant aid from institutional funds; Federal Pell; Private scholarships; SEOG; State scholarships/grants. *Loan aid offered:* Direct PLUS loans; Direct Subsidized Stafford Loans; Direct Unsubsidized Stafford Loans. Applicants will be notified of awards on a rolling basis beginning 2/1. Federal Work-Study Program available. Institutional employment available.

The Inside Word

Admissions officers at Agnes Scott College happily take a holistic approach to their process. They seek to create an incoming class that's diverse and reflective of a myriad of interests and ideas. They also realize that potential can be measured in a variety of ways. This college, which has long been test optional, allows applicants to submit SAT/ACT scores, a graded writing assignment, or to sit for an evaluative interview with an admissions counselor.

THE SCHOOL SAYS "..."

From the Admissions Office

"During four years at Agnes Scott, you'll grow as a person, discovering your strengths and building confidence. Through SUMMIT, a unique global learning and leadership development experience infused throughout the curriculum, you will choose a major, build your leadership skills, and gain global perspectives while guided by a four-person board of advisors. A SUMMIT advisor, peer advisor, faculty advisor, and career mentor will help you adjust to college, choose classes and activities, build connections to strengthen your academic experience, and boost your professional readiness.

"You'll spend four years with other brilliant individuals who won't stand for injustice or tolerate prejudice; who never settle, but question, confront, and debate. You will learn from professors who will push you to the limits—then challenge you again.

"You will explore your world, become immersed in other cultures and hone your leadership skills. You will also gain professional experience through research projects and internships with Fortune Global 500 companies or local, national, or international nonprofits.

"After four years at Agnes Scott, you will never be the same. You will be a better you: more reflective, more intelligent, more cultured, more prepared to lead. In other words, you'll be ready for the world.

"If you've read this far, why not give us a tour online or in person? We'd love to meet you, share more about our world and help plan your SUMMIT. Schedule your visit and see all of our in-person and virtual visit opportunities at agnesscott.edu/visit."

SELECTIVITY
Admissions Rating	86
# of applicants	1,751
% of applicants accepted	65
% of acceptees attending	26
# of early decision applicants	20
% accepted early decision	80

FRESHMAN PROFILE
Range SAT EBRW	590–690
Range SAT Math	540–650
Range SAT Composite	1140–1330
Range ACT Composite	24–30
# submitting SAT scores	150
% submitting SAT scores	50
# submitting ACT scores	108
% submitting ACT scores	36
Average HS GPA	3.8
% graduated top 10% of class	32
% graduated top 25% of class	67
% graduated top 50% of class	95

DEADLINES
Early decision	
Deadline	11/1
Notification	12/1
Early action	
Deadline	11/15
Notification	12/15
Regular	
Priority	1/15
Deadline	5/1
Notification	Rolling, 12/15
Nonfall registration?	No

APPLICANTS ALSO LOOK AT AND OFTEN PREFER
Georgia State University; Mt. Holyoke College

AND SOMETIMES PREFER
Georgia Institute of Technology

FINANCIAL FACTS
Financial Aid Rating	88
Annual tuition	$43,920
Room and board	$13,050
Required fees	$330
Books and supplies	$1,000
Average frosh need-based scholarship	$32,382
Average UG need-based scholarship	$31,975
% needy frosh rec. need-based scholarship or grant aid	100
% needy UG rec. need-based scholarship or grant aid	100
% needy frosh rec. non-need-based scholarship or grant aid	25
% needy UG rec. non-need-based scholarship or grant aid	21
% needy frosh rec. need-based self-help aid	75
% needy UG rec. need-based self-help aid	82
% frosh rec. any financial aid	100
% UG rec. any financial aid	99
% UG borrow to pay for school	64
Average cumulative indebtedness	$31,271
% frosh need fully met	25
% ugrads need fully met	22
Average % of frosh need met	86
Average % of ugrad need met	85

ALBION COLLEGE

611 East Porter, Albion, MI 49224 • Admissions: 517-629-0321 • Fax: 517-629-0569

CAMPUS LIFE

Quality of Life Rating	**83**
Fire Safety Rating	**86**
Green Rating	**70**
Type of school	Private
Affiliation	Methodist
Environment	Village

STUDENTS

Total undergrad enrollment	1,451
% male/female	47/53
% from out of state	28
% frosh live on campus	99
% ugrads live on campus	94
# of fraternities (% ugrad men join)	6 (35)
# of sororities (% ugrad women join)	6 (31)
% African American	16
% Asian	2
% Caucasian	59
% Hispanic	12
% Native American	0
% Pacific Islander	0
% Two or more races	3
% Race and/or ethnicity unknown	6
% international	2
# of countries represented	11

SURVEY SAYS . . .

Lab facilities are great
Lots of beer drinking
Very little drug use
Frats and sororities are popular

ACADEMICS

Academic Rating	**85**
% students returning for sophomore year	80
% students graduating within 4 years	61
% students graduating within 6 years	70
Calendar	Semester
Student/faculty ratio	11:1
Profs interesting rating	91
Profs accessible rating	97

Most classes have 10–19 students.
Most lab/discussion sessions have 10–19 students.

MOST POPULAR MAJORS

Biology/Biological Sciences, General; Psychology, General; Economics, General

STUDENTS SAY "..."

Academics

Armed with a "great reputation" and a "small-town feeling," Albion College provides undergraduates with a "rigorous but rewarding" academic experience replete with "huge opportunities." Students here truly appreciate that Albion works diligently to foster an environment that "encourages questions [and] thinking" all the while aiming to "provide personal attention to each student." While the college certainly offers a "great liberal arts education," undergrads are especially quick to highlight the strong science, premed, and business programs. Indeed, students like to boast that Albion "has a very high rate of students being accepted into medical school." And business majors point to the Gerstacker Institute for Business and Management, which allows students to "gain real-world experience" and even the potential to walk away with "a job offer." Of course, regardless of discipline or department, Albion undergrads are full of praise for their teachers. As one thrilled student eagerly shares, "The professors care about their students' success and are always there to help." Importantly, they are "very knowledgeable in their material and try to make sure you learn as much as possible." Further, they are "easily approachable," "extremely passionate about their work," and always "available for discussions." As one content undergrad sums up, "I would say that the overall experience has been great, and I couldn't be more pleased with my decision to attend Albion College."

Life

While Albion students are often quite "studious" during the week, once the weekend rolls around they certainly know how to get "crazy [and] exciting." Fortunately, there "is almost always something going on on campus." Indeed, the "Union Board plans lots of free activities, concerts, comedians, etc." Moreover, those interested in the party scene will be delighted to discover that fraternities and sororities are very popular at Albion. As one thrilled undergrad notes, "Greek life is fantastic. It really is the cornerstone of our campus. Every weekend there is a party or something going on at the fraternities. Whether you are into drinking or not, the guys there know how to have a good time." While students bemoan the fact that "there's not much to do in the city of Albion," they do take solace in finding other off campus options. As another satisfied student reveals, "Bigger cities like Jackson and Battle Creek are only a fifteen- or twenty-minute drive away, so if you're looking for a day at a mall, that's always an option. Plus, the college sponsors buses and vans to take students to places like Ann Arbor or Lansing. Generally you can find something to do."

Student Body

At first glance, Albion College appears to be "a microcosm of upper-class metro-Detroit and Chicago." Therefore, it's not surprising that a "slightly right-leaning, white, and Greek-loving [student body seems to be] the norm." However, those seeking more diversity should fear not! One student assures us, "I have met anarchists and proud communists. There is a mix, but you have to dig for it." Beyond race and political affiliation, undergrads here find their peers to be "serious about school but also very fun and friendly." Moreover, they are "bright individuals that want to succeed" and certainly people who "value their education." They also seem to have "a million interests," which they vigorously pursue through a number of extracurricular activities and programs. As one socially satisfied undergrad sums up, "I think there is a club or niche here where everyone can find a group of people they fit in with. I truthfully would feel comfortable sitting down at a table with any one of my classmates in the cafeteria and having lunch with them."

ALBION COLLEGE

Financial Aid: 517-629-0440 • E-Mail: admission@albion.edu • Website: www.albion.edu

THE PRINCETON REVIEW SAYS

Admissions

Very important factors considered include: rigor of secondary school record, academic GPA. *Important factors considered include:* class rank. *Other factors considered include:* application essay, recommendation(s), interview, extracurricular activities, talent/ability, character/personal qualities, alumni/ae relation, geographical residence, state residency, racial/ethnic status, volunteer work, work experience, standardized test scores. ACT with or without writing accepted. SAT with or without Essay component accepted. High school diploma is required and GED is accepted. *Academic units recommended:* 4 English, 5 math, 3 science, 2 science labs, 2 foreign language, 2 social studies.

Financial Aid

Students should submit: FAFSA. Priority filing deadline is 12/1. The Princeton Review suggests that all financial aid forms be submitted as soon as possible after October 1. *Need-based scholarships/grants offered:* College/university scholarship or grant aid from institutional funds; Federal Pell; Private scholarships; SEOG; State scholarships/grants. *Loan aid offered:* Direct PLUS loans; Direct Subsidized Stafford Loans; Direct Unsubsidized Stafford Loans. Applicants will be notified of awards on a rolling basis beginning 12/1. Federal Work-Study Program available. Institutional employment available.

The Inside Word

Albion's growing reputation means that earning a coveted acceptance letter is no easy feat. Academic success takes precedence, and applicants should have taken a challenging high school curriculum including a handful of honors and advanced placement courses. Of course, admissions officers are also concerned about maintaining a vibrant community, so careful attention will also be paid to essays and extracurricular activities.

THE SCHOOL SAYS "..."

From the Admissions Office

"As an Albion student, you'll be equipped to make an impact. You'll be prepared to go on to the nation's top graduate and professional schools and to assume leadership roles in the sciences and medicine, business, law, education, the arts, and social services. To do that, your education will take you beyond the classroom, beyond our campus, and beyond conventional thinking. It will help you discover what you're meant to do with your life. And it will prepare you to live it well.

"You'll identify your goals through a four-year individualized career plan and build a strong foundation in the liberal arts. You'll sharpen your career focus and develop skills through internships and other real-world, hands-on experiences like those in our prestigious institutes in business, public policy and service, sustainability and the environment, education, and pre-medicine and the sciences. Your creativity and curiosity may be satisfied through a multitude of research experiences available as early as your freshman year through our Foundation for Undergraduate Research, Scholarship and Creative Activity and the Prentiss M. Brown Honors Program.

"On our residential campus, you can choose from more than 100 campus organizations catering to a wide range of interests. Our athletic teams regularly head to NCAA Division III postseason play, and our equestrian team members compete regionally and nationally.

"Check us out online at www.albion.edu or visit us to learn if Albion will be right for you."

SELECTIVITY

Admissions Rating	80
# of applicants	4,043
% of applicants accepted	69
% of acceptees attending	15

FRESHMAN PROFILE

Range SAT EBRW	500–610
Range SAT Math	490–590
Range ACT Composite	21–27
# submitting SAT scores	315
% submitting SAT scores	76
# submitting ACT scores	102
% submitting ACT scores	25
Average HS GPA	3.5

DEADLINES

Early action	
Deadline	12/1
Regular	
Notification	Rolling, 10/15
Nonfall registration?	Yes

APPLICANTS ALSO LOOK AT AND OFTEN PREFER
Kalamazoo College; Michigan State University; University of Michigan—Ann Arbor

AND SOMETIMES PREFER
Central Michigan University; Grand Valley State University; Hope College

AND RARELY PREFER
Alma College

FINANCIAL FACTS

Financial Aid Rating	87
Annual tuition	$50,070
Room and board	$12,380
Required fees	$705
Books and supplies	$700
Average frosh need-based scholarship	$44,083
Average UG need-based scholarship	$40,700
% needy frosh rec. need-based scholarship or grant aid	100
% needy UG rec. need-based scholarship or grant aid	100
% needy frosh rec. non-need-based scholarship or grant aid	99
% needy UG rec. non-need-based scholarship or grant aid	99
% needy frosh rec. need-based self-help aid	86
% needy UG rec. need-based self-help aid	86
% frosh rec. any financial aid	100
% UG rec. any financial aid	100
% UG borrow to pay for school	69
Average cumulative indebtedness	$35,529
% frosh need fully met	32
% ugrads need fully met	22
Average % of frosh need met	94
Average % of ugrad need met	89

ALFRED UNIVERSITY

Alumni Hall, Alfred, NY 14802-1205 • Admissions: 607-871-2115 • Fax: 607-871-2198

STUDENTS SAY "..."

Academics

Alfred University is a small school with an impressive range of world-class majors. The school is known for its "excellent art program," particularly its ceramics and glass majors, as well as for its engineering and psychology programs. While some students at Alfred focus only on their majors, students happily report that there are a "variety of academic opportunities" and that it's "easy to take subjects outside your major." This is appreciated by many, including one art student who likes that Alfred offers "other majors versus a traditional art [school] setting. If I had decided to change majors, Alfred has almost every opportunity." Alfred's "outstanding, talented, dedicated" faculty is one of its biggest draws. An English writing student gushes that professors "bring a level of vibrancy and academic encouragement through enthusiasm to the classroom." "The professors are always pushing you to reach your full potential" and are "always willing to put time into student independent projects." Students also rave about the small classes sizes. "It is the closest to one-on-one teaching you can get," a clinical and counseling psychology major notes, and "the classroom size is perfect for a more personalized education."

Life

Alfred's "beautiful," "small" campus and its "somewhat rural location" are big draws for students looking for a quieter academic experience with a strong "sense of community." Of course, its location means the weather isn't exactly tropical. One student notes that it can feel like "it's basically winter here for about 80 percent of the school year, and it snows constantly." Luckily, "there is always something to do on weekends and week days," for distraction, such as "student club productions...and fundraisers and an excellent selection of movies shown on campus." On top of that, "there are so many clubs and options that you can find something to do," and "every sports team is supported, and superfans are at every event." "The facilities are amazing," particularly the "great" art buildings and the engineering facilities. Alfred's "strong equestrian program" and barn are also a big draw. Students find some of Alfred's dorms to be "pretty outdated," and there's a bit of grumbling about the "hit-or-miss" and "expensive" dining facilities.

Student Body

Alfred has a "warm" atmosphere, and "You can't go down the street without receiving a smile." Students are "friendly, outgoing, and involved," and many do community service work and are active in one of Alfred's many clubs or organizations. The prominent art school means that there's a large presence of creative types on campus, and the equally prominent engineering school ensures a good mix of personalities. One student notes there is "a pretty significant gap between the prevalent, spunky art students and the more reclusive engineers," but another adds that this means students are "well-acquainted with people from a variety of studies and backgrounds and with a variety of interests." Most people believe that "everyone finds their own little niche," but they appreciate that it "definitely does not mean they stay there—you are allowed to float between everything." In fact, "more often than not, you'll see engineers rubbing elbows with philosophy majors and artists chilling with math and chemistry majors."

Financial Aid: 607-871-2159 • E-Mail: admissions@alfred.edu • Website: www.alfred.edu

THE PRINCETON REVIEW SAYS

Admissions

Very important factors considered include: rigor of secondary school record, class rank, academic GPA, extracurricular activities, character/personal qualities. *Important factors considered include:* application essay, standardized test scores, recommendation(s), volunteer work, work experience. *Other factors considered include:* interview, talent/ability, first generation, racial/ethnic status, level of applicant's interest. ACT with or without writing accepted. High school diploma is required and GED is accepted. *Academic units required:* 4 English, 4 math, 3 science, 3 science labs, 3 social studies. *Academic units recommended:* 4 English, 4 math, 3 science, 3 science labs, 1 foreign language, 3 social studies.

Financial Aid

Students should submit: FAFSA; State aid form. Priority filing deadline is 3/15. The Princeton Review suggests that all financial aid forms be submitted as soon as possible after October 1. *Need-based scholarships/grants offered:* College/university scholarship or grant aid from institutional funds; Federal Pell; Private scholarships; SEOG; State scholarships/grants. *Loan aid offered:* Direct PLUS loans; Direct Subsidized Stafford Loans; Direct Unsubsidized Stafford Loans. Applicants will be notified of awards on a rolling basis beginning 2/15. Federal Work-Study Program available. Institutional employment available.

The Inside Word

Alfred is a fine university with a solid local reputation. The allure for arts students is obvious—Alfred's programs in the arts are especially well-regarded—and as a result, competition is fiercest among applicants for these programs. A killer portfolio, even more than great grades and standardized test scores, is your most likely ticket in. Competition for the engineering school is also tight. Applicants will need to have thrived in a rigorous high school program.

THE SCHOOL SAYS "..."

From the Admissions Office

"The admissions process at Alfred University is the foundation for the personal attention each student can expect during their time at AU. Each applicant is evaluated individually and receives genuine, individual care and consideration.

"The best way to discover all Alfred University has to offer is to come to campus. We truly have something for everyone with more than forty courses of study, twenty-one NCAA Division III sports and two IHSA sports and over eighty student-run clubs and organizations. You can tour campus; meet current students, faculty, coaches and staff; attend a class; and eat in our dining hall—experience firsthand what life at AU is like.

"Alfred University is a place where students are free to pursue their interests—all of them—no matter how varied or different. Academics, athletics, co-ops, study abroad, internships, special interests—they're all part of what makes you who you are and who you are going to become."

SELECTIVITY
Admissions Rating	82
# of applicants	4,485
% of applicants accepted	62
% of acceptees attending	16
# offered a place on the wait list	91
% accepting a place on wait list	36
% admitted from wait list	33
# of early decision applicants	49
% accepted early decision	92

FRESHMAN PROFILE
Range SAT EBRW	470–590
Range SAT Math	470–590
Range SAT Composite	940–1180
Range ACT Composite	19–26
# submitting SAT scores	396
% submitting SAT scores	86
# submitting ACT scores	105
% submitting ACT scores	23
Average HS GPA	3.1

DEADLINES
Early decision	
Deadline	12/1
Notification	12/15
Regular	
Priority	2/1
Deadline	8/1
Notification	Rolling, 11/15
Nonfall registration?	Yes

FINANCIAL FACTS
Financial Aid Rating	87
Annual tuition	$35,076
Room and board	$12,924
Required fees	$1,200
Books and supplies	$1,300
Average frosh need-based scholarship	$26,266
Average UG need-based scholarship	$23,184
% needy frosh rec. need-based scholarship or grant aid	99
% needy UG rec. need-based scholarship or grant aid	99
% needy frosh rec. non-need-based scholarship or grant aid	53
% needy UG rec. non-need-based scholarship or grant aid	55
% needy frosh rec. need-based self-help aid	89
% needy UG rec. need-based self-help aid	87
% frosh rec. any financial aid	96
% UG rec. any financial aid	92
% UG borrow to pay for school	86
Average cumulative indebtedness	$34,224
% frosh need fully met	14
% ugrads need fully met	17
Average % of frosh need met	85
Average % of ugrad need met	82

ALLEGHENY COLLEGE

Allegheny College, Meadville, PA 16335 • Admissions: 800-521-5293 • Fax: 814-337-0431

CAMPUS LIFE

Quality of Life Rating	**85**
Fire Safety Rating	**85**
Green Rating	**60***
Type of school	Private
Environment	Town

STUDENTS

Total undergrad enrollment	1,731
% male/female	44/56
% from out of state	48
% frosh from public high school	84
% frosh live on campus	96
% ugrads live on campus	95
# of fraternities (% ugrad men join)	6 (21)
# of sororities (% ugrad women join)	6 (22)
% African American	8
% Asian	4
% Caucasian	68
% Hispanic	9
% Native American	<1
% Pacific Islander	0
% Two or more races	4
% Race and/or ethnicity unknown	3
% international	3
# of countries represented	58

SURVEY SAYS . . .

Students environmentally aware
Students always studying
Active student government

ACADEMICS

Academic Rating	**86**
% students returning for sophomore year	86
% students graduating within 4 years	66
% students graduating within 6 years	74
Calendar	Semester
Student/faculty ratio	11:1
Profs interesting rating	90
Profs accessible rating	94
Most classes have 10–19 students.	
Most lab/discussion sessions have 10–19 students.	

MOST POPULAR MAJORS

Biology/Biological Sciences, General; Psychology, General; Economics, General

STUDENTS SAY "..."

Academics

Allegheny College, a small liberal arts school located in rural northwest Pennsylvania, has a campus "full of different interests, experiences and talents." Students highlight Allegheny's diversity and stress that they "are engaged in helping our campus community as well as the community of Meadville." In terms of a diverse educational experience, one of the college's draws is students' ability to mix and match majors and minors from different disciplines, leading to Allegheny's motto of "unusual combinations." This approach "toted by the Allegheny College curriculum board [resounds] not only in the academics but in the people and opportunities that are a part of this unique campus." Professors here are "dedicated to helping [students] succeed and they genuinely want to see [students] do well." With small class sizes and "classes taught by professors," students say the academics are rigorous at Allegheny but professors "go above and beyond to make themselves available to help them through [difficult times]." The mandatory independent senior research project is "challenging" but it "does a lot to bolster resumes and prep students for graduate schools."

Life

Though some say Allegheny is "the school that studies like an Ivy and parties like a state school," others contend that most students' weeks are full of books and weekends revolve around some sort of on-campus fun. (One point of contention is a recent ruling that students must live on campus all four years.) Meadville is a small town but with over 100 school-sponsored clubs and organizations, "everyone can find something [they're] passionate about at Allegheny." Greek life is "an important component of the school, but with only 25 percent of students involved, you'll never feel obligated to participate." The tight-knit school, with roughly 1,800 students, is "small enough that you will see a familiar face wherever you go, without feeling like you know everyone on campus." As one student puts it, Allegheny is "a school with traditions and weirdness" and during a pre-college campus visit it just "felt right." A very liberal campus, students note that while "there is always space for further diversity," the "majority of [the] student body prides itself on social justice and service work."

Student Body

Allegheny has a "very welcoming, judgment-free student body," with students who are "incredibly involved, engaged, and passionate about what they do." While students who hold more conservative viewpoints say that the school's generally liberal stance "may be alienating to conservative students," the majority of Allegheny students seem to applaud the college's emphasis on "welcoming students from different cultures and a general acceptance of varying creeds, sexual orientations, gender identities, and races." On the whole, students describe Allegheny as a "very active campus" and the "vast majority of people are involved with more than one organization on campus and are extremely invested in their studies and the school." Even though some say to "be prepared to have the majority of your life revolve just around what the school provides, which is a lot," adding that "the location is definitely a drawback," others add that students find plenty to do on campus and with off-campus trips to Pittsburgh and Erie, Pennsylvania, when Meadville gets too small.

Financial Aid: 800-835-7780 • E-Mail: admissions@allegheny.edu • Website: https://allegheny.edu

THE PRINCETON REVIEW SAYS

Admissions

Very important factors considered include: rigor of secondary school record, class rank, academic GPA. *Important factors considered include:* recommendation(s), interview, extracurricular activities, character/personal qualities, level of applicant's interest. *Other factors considered include:* application essay, standardized test scores, talent/ability, first generation, alumni/ae relation, geographical residence, racial/ethnic status, volunteer work, work experience. ACT with Writing recommended. SAT with Essay component recommended. High school diploma is required and GED is accepted. *Academic units required:* 4 English, 3 math, 3 science, 2 foreign language, 3 social studies, 1 academic elective.

Financial Aid

Students should submit: FAFSA. Priority filing deadline is 2/15. The Princeton Review suggests that all financial aid forms be submitted as soon as possible after October 1. *Need-based scholarships/grants offered:* College/university scholarship or grant aid from institutional funds; Federal Pell; Private scholarships; SEOG; State scholarships/grants. *Loan aid offered:* Direct PLUS loans; Direct Subsidized Stafford Loans; Direct Unsubsidized Stafford Loans; Allegheny Institutional Loan. Applicants will be notified of awards on a rolling basis beginning 12/1. Federal Work-Study Program available. Institutional employment available.

The Inside Word

Over a third of enrolled Allegheny students have a GPA of 3.75 or higher, with an average GPA of 3.53. In addition to grades, admission officers look hard at recommendation letters, essays, community involvement, and students' other talents that might not show up on a standardized test. The school is test-optional. The school has two early decision dates, in addition to a regular admissions date.

THE SCHOOL SAYS "..."

From the Admissions Office

"Allegheny College is one of the nation's most prestigious and dynamic institutions of higher education. Allegheny is one of the few colleges in the country that asks students to choose both a major and a minor, each of which is in a different academic division. Allegheny's distinctive major-minor combination and hands-on learning provide students with intellectual and personal growth, helping to cultivate the creative, big-picture thinking most desired by employers and graduate schools. Allegheny students don't have to wait behind graduate students for research positions on faculty-led projects but instead are actively engaged as research collaborators. Allegheny was the first baccalaureate college in the nation to receive the Award for Undergraduate Research Accomplishment from the Council on Undergraduate Research. Central to the College's focus on experiential learning is the Allegheny Gateway, which helps students connect classroom learning with real-world experience. Students can access career services, pre-professional and graduate school advising, internship and service opportunities, research fellowships, and more—all in one location. At Allegheny, opportunities to pursue one's passions are limited only by the imagination. A diverse campus life, with more than 130 student-led organizations, sets the stage for a vibrant college experience. Our residential campus includes historic architecture interspersed with facilities bristling with the latest communications and research technology. In the classroom, the community, and beyond, Allegheny provides opportunities that can lead students from hard work and dedication to extraordinary outcomes. Allegheny graduates are equipped to meet challenges and solve problems in a rapidly changing world."

SELECTIVITY

Admissions Rating	87
# of applicants	5,208
% of applicants accepted	62
% of acceptees attending	15
# offered a place on the wait list	255
% accepting a place on wait list	100
% admitted from wait list	4
# of early decision applicants	189
% accepted early decision	44

FRESHMAN PROFILE

Range SAT EBRW	590–680
Range SAT Math	580–680
Range SAT Composite	1170–1360
Range ACT Composite	24–30
# submitting SAT scores	280
% submitting SAT scores	56
# submitting ACT scores	136
% submitting ACT scores	27
Average HS GPA	3.5
% graduated top 10% of class	40
% graduated top 25% of class	63
% graduated top 50% of class	85

DEADLINES

Early decision	
Deadline	11/15
Notification	11/30
Other ED Deadline	2/1
Other ED Notification	2/15
Early action	
Deadline	12/1
Notification	1/1
Regular	
Deadline	2/15
Notification	3/15
Nonfall registration?	Yes

APPLICANTS ALSO LOOK AT AND OFTEN PREFER
Kenyon College; Oberlin College

AND SOMETIMES PREFER
Gettysburg College; Dickinson College

AND RARELY PREFER
Washington & Jefferson College; Juniata College

FINANCIAL FACTS

Financial Aid Rating	90
Annual tuition	$50,480
Room and board	$13,080
Required fees	$500
Books and supplies	$1,000
Average frosh need-based scholarship	$36,765
Average UG need-based scholarship	$37,471
% needy frosh rec. need-based scholarship or grant aid	100
% needy UG rec. need-based scholarship or grant aid	100
% needy frosh rec. non-need-based scholarship or grant aid	32
% needy UG rec. non-need-based scholarship or grant aid	19
% needy frosh rec. need-based self-help aid	71
% needy UG rec. need-based self-help aid	81
% frosh rec. any financial aid	100
% UG rec. any financial aid	99
% frosh need fully met	42
% ugrads need fully met	31
Average % of frosh need met	92
Average % of ugrad need met	90

AMERICAN UNIVERSITY

4400 Massachusetts Ave., NW, Washington, DC 20016-8001 • Admissions: 202-885-6000 • Fax: 202-885-1025

STUDENTS SAY "..."

Academics

"Tucked away in a beautiful part of Northwest D.C.," American University offers students a "campus [that] has a suburban feel." However, being near the nation's capital means they enjoy "the best of both worlds." Here, classes are structured "in a way that not only encourages, but nearly expects students to undertake internships in their field of study." Specifically, students tout the School of International Service (SIS) and the School of Public Affairs (SPA), "both [of which] are among the best in the nation and offer students opportunities to not just learn about but experience their studies." And inside the classroom, students are greeted by professors who are "passionate about [their] subject [matter]." Professors are "passionate about [their] subject [matter]" and tend to have "real-world experience which is helpful for bringing the material to life." Even better, they're "accessible and constantly reach out and encourage students to attend events." Finally, as one student sums it up, "So many of my classes have wound up being better than I ever could have expected, and have launched me down paths I didn't know existed."

Life

Undergrads at American lead busy and involved lives. Outside of class, students "fill their days with internships and extracurricular activities." This includes anything from "Greek life [to] tutoring to [being a] tour guide," or even singing with an a cappella group. Additionally, "there's always one event or another happening on campus, [whether it's] a concert, cultural event, or movie screening." There's a lot to do both on- and off-campus. Great local options include concerts, cultural events, and movie screenings, while in nearby D.C. you'll find undergrads "attending [a] music festival, visiting the National Mall, [or] going to a congressional hearing." In short, "there is always something going on." Students also love "checking out … museums [and] exploring new neighborhoods," which often sends them strolling through "Tenleytown, shopping in Georgetown … [or] walking around the waterfront." When the weather is nice, they also "love going [to] Rock Creek Park...or [the] farmer's markets on Sunday."

Student Body

Students at American are "truly passionate about what they are learning and are interested in exploring what both D.C. and the world have to offer." Indeed, "whenever you ask them what they are studying … they'll light up and talk for hours on end." Many are also "politically active," "knowledgeable about current events," and "convinced that they will save the world" someday. According to some, this mindset can be "pretty homogenous," as "the AU student body tends to be rather liberal-leaning and relatively affluent." However, another counters, "We have an incredibly diverse student body ranging from students from all across the U.S. to all across the world!" And many insist that "there is a place for everybody on campus." What's more, "everyone is friendly and so easy to strike up conversation with." AU undergrads "care about each other's successes and are there to build each other up, not tear each other down." As this grateful individual concludes, "No other student body both supports and challenges you to be the best student one could possibly be. I could not be more proud to call myself an AU student."

Financial Aid: 202-885-6500 • E-Mail: admissions@american.edu • Website: www.american.edu

THE PRINCETON REVIEW SAYS

Admissions

Very important factors considered include: rigor of secondary school record, academic GPA, level of applicant's interest. *Important factors considered include:* application essay, recommendation(s), extracurricular activities, talent/ability, character/personal qualities, volunteer work. *Other factors considered include:* standardized test scores, first generation, alumni/ae relation, geographical residence, racial/ethnic status, work experience. ACT with or without writing accepted. SAT with or without Essay component accepted. High school diploma is required and GED is accepted. *Academic units required:* 4 English, 3 math, 3 science, 2 science labs, 2 foreign language, 2 social studies, 3 academic electives. *Academic units recommended:* 4 English, 4 math, 4 science, 3 foreign language, 4 social studies, 4 academic electives.

Financial Aid

Students should submit: CSS/Financial Aid PROFILE; FAFSA. Priority filing deadline is 11/15. The Princeton Review suggests that all financial aid forms be submitted as soon as possible after October 1. *Need-based scholarships/grants offered:* College/university scholarship or grant aid from institutional funds; Federal Pell; Private scholarships; SEOG. *Loan aid offered:* Direct PLUS loans; Direct Subsidized Stafford Loans; Direct Unsubsidized Stafford Loans. Applicants will be notified of awards on or about 4/1. Federal Work-Study Program available. Institutional employment available.

The Inside Word

Admissions officers at American truly have an interest in getting to know each candidate. And they make a point of closely considering all facets of an application. So you can't slack on any aspect! Of course, your transcript will hold the most weight. And you'll need a challenging college prep curriculum to be a strong contender. Finally, if you loathe standardized tests you can rejoice: American is a test-optional school. Best of all, withholding your scores will not affect your consideration for merit awards or entrance to the Honors Program.

THE SCHOOL SAYS "..."

From the Admissions Office

"AU's undergraduate experience is built on the pillars of future-facing academics, active citizenship, and the power of our Washington, D.C., location. At AU, learning and discovery are enhanced when we embrace differences, elevate civil discourse, and collaborate with an open mind and heart. Our students, faculty, and staff are changemakers ready to address the challenges and opportunities of our rapidly changing world. An AU education is a launching pad for students who seek purposeful lives and want to achieve transformative outcomes for themselves and for society.

"AU's rigorous curriculum features high impact educational experiences that challenge students to combine serious theoretical study with meaningful real-world experiences. Regardless of their choice of major, AU students acquire a solid foundation in liberal arts while pursuing in-depth study in their chosen field without being limited to a single course of study.

"Our students, staff, and scholars are inspired and ambitious visionaries and practitioners who are hopeful about the world they live in and eager to champion what matters. At AU, our learning experience is shaped in the classroom, through experiences made possible in the world's most influential city, and as part of a dynamic community of changemakers. Our network of world-class faculty and visiting scholars with deep connections to businesses, government, and non-profits enhance the excellence of our programs, In short, AU is motivated to make a difference, determined to find solutions, and passionate about service. If that sounds like you, we invite you to apply to become a member of our unique community."

SELECTIVITY

Admissions Rating	92
# of applicants	18,545
% of applicants accepted	36
% of acceptees attending	26
# offered a place on the wait list	4,686
% accepting a place on wait list	21
% admitted from wait list	14
# of early decision applicants	983
% accepted early decision	85

FRESHMAN PROFILE

Range SAT EBRW	620–700
Range SAT Math	590–690
Range SAT Composite	1220–1380
Range ACT Composite	27–31
# submitting SAT scores	937
% submitting SAT scores	53
# submitting ACT scores	546
% submitting ACT scores	31

DEADLINES

Early decision	
Deadline	11/15
Notification	12/31
Other ED Deadline	1/15
Other ED Notification	2/15
Regular	
Deadline	1/15
Notification	4/1
Nonfall registration?	Yes

FINANCIAL FACTS

Financial Aid Rating	83
Annual tuition	$50,542
Room and board	$14,980
Required fees	$819
Books and supplies	$800
Average frosh need-based scholarship	$26,681
Average UG need-based scholarship	$29,427
% needy frosh rec. need-based scholarship or grant aid	95
% needy UG rec. need-based scholarship or grant aid	91
% needy frosh rec. non-need-based scholarship or grant aid	33
% needy UG rec. non-need-based scholarship or grant aid	26
% needy frosh rec. need-based self-help aid	89
% needy UG rec. need-based self-help aid	91
% frosh rec. any financial aid	74
% UG rec. any financial aid	67
% UG borrow to pay for school	63
Average cumulative indebtedness	$35,122
% frosh need fully met	24
% ugrads need fully met	16
Average % of frosh need met	87
Average % of ugrad need met	74

AMHERST COLLEGE

220 South Pleasant Street, Amherst, MA 01002 • Admissions: 413-542-2328 • Fax: 413-542-2040

STUDENTS SAY "..."

Academics

An open curriculum and a focus on undergraduates are the foundations of the Amherst College education, where approximately 1,850 students choose their own intellectual path from forty majors, numerous research opportunities, and additional classes and resources available from other members of the Five College Consortium. It's an "academically rigorous undergraduate education," but there are multiple resource centers to foster awareness and help students "continue and worship our identities" as well, including the Center for International Student Engagement, Women's and Gender Center, Multicultural Resource Center, Queer Resource Center, and Center for Diversity & Student Leadership. The "open curriculum offers the student a perfect level of curricular control over their own education," and students can supplement this with "fully-funded field trips or interesting guest lecturers" and a "plethora of research opportunities for undergraduates." Students still need to declare a major and fulfill the requirements, but they find the open curriculum "gives you so much space and freedom to take a variety of classes at this liberal arts college."

Faculty at Amherst "always leave their door open" with "ridiculously extensive and lenient office hours," and small class sizes further encourage "strong relationships with professors." They "help you think of paper topics, read drafts, and give active feedback." One student shares, "My professors have treated me like family—literally, I have been invited over for dinner … and academically and professionally pushed and helped to do my best." Classes are mainly "small group discussions that require students to teach other students," and students have the opportunity to engage in a variety of subjects with "different perspectives through collaboration."

Life

The packed weekdays at Amherst follow a pretty standard formula: "Go to class. Work. Generally participate in at least one activity a day. Study. Socialize. Repeat." That socializing takes many forms: "People see movies, bowl, and hike," but they also just hang out in the campus center. They also fill their time "cooking, spending time in town or in neighboring towns or cities," and going to recitals. Students here "are constantly moving and busy with packed schedules that encompass a variety of activities," and when the weather cooperates, "people will be found lounging in the grassy quads, playing Frisbee, [and] going out to nearby towns or ponds [and] mini-beaches." On the weekends, students attend "parties at night and events during the day, [including] sporting events." Most who attend call the campus home—98 percent of those enrolled live on campus.

Student Body

The people on this "fairly diverse campus" are "a collection of different ethnicities, gender identities, sexual preferences, and various background lives." Students find that "personalities and interests vary widely," but believe "everyone at Amherst has a story" and "everyone has a space." Amherst students are incredibly generous and "help each other because they want the best for one another." Overall, people are "academically and intellectually engaged and curious," and they "collaborate because they know that it's the best way to learn." The busy nature of the school and the "quite varied interests" of the student body naturally create peers who seek eclectic experiences: "No one is just a football player or a violinist, they are also a singer or an [on-campus organization's] senator," one student offers as an example.

Financial Aid: 413-542-2296 • E-Mail: admission@amherst.edu • Website: www.amherst.edu

THE PRINCETON REVIEW SAYS

Admissions

Very important factors considered include: rigor of secondary school record, academic GPA, application essay, standardized test scores (optional for fall 2021 entry), recommendation(s), extracurricular activities, talent/ability, character/personal qualities. *Important factors considered include:* class rank, first generation, volunteer work, work experience. *Other factors considered include:* alumni/ae relation, geographical residence, racial/ethnic status. ACT with or without writing accepted. SAT with or without Essay component accepted. High school diploma or equivalent is not required. *Academic units recommended:* 4 English, 4 math, 3 science, 1 science lab, 3 foreign language, 2 social studies, 2 history.

Financial Aid

Students should submit: CSS/Financial Aid PROFILE; FAFSA; Noncustodial PROFILE. Priority filing deadline is 1/4. The Princeton Review suggests that all financial aid forms be submitted as soon as possible after October 1. *Need-based scholarships/grants offered:* College/university scholarship or grant aid from institutional funds; Federal Pell; Private scholarships; SEOG; State scholarships/grants. *Loan aid offered:* Direct PLUS loans; Direct Subsidized Stafford Loans; Direct Unsubsidized Stafford Loans. Applicants will be notified of awards on or about 4/1. Federal Work-Study Program available. Institutional employment available.

The Inside Word

Membership certainly has its benefits at the highly selective Amherst College. For the price of entry to this school, students also gain entrance to the prestigious Five College Consortium, which allows enrolled students to take courses for credit at no additional cost at any of the four other participating consortium members (Hampshire College, Mount Holyoke College, Smith College, and the University of Massachusetts Amherst). And this deal isn't just confined to the classroom: Students can use other schools' libraries, eat meals at the other cafeterias, and participate in extracurricular activities offered at the other schools. And don't worry about how you'll get there—your bus fare is covered, too.

THE SCHOOL SAYS "..."

From the Admissions Office

"Founded in 1821, Amherst College is considered one of the premier liberal arts colleges in the nation, enrolling nearly 1,850 bright, talented and diverse students. A need-blind admission policy for all applicants (domestic and international) and generous, no-loan financial aid packages ensure that exceptional students from across the country and around the world are admitted to Amherst based on their accomplishments and promise, regardless of family income. Located in Amherst, Massachusetts, a town of 35,000 people in an area of great natural beauty in the western part of the state, the College's 1,000-acre campus includes top-notch academic, athletic and residential facilities. Our new state-of-the-art science center is designed to facilitate the interdisciplinary partnerships that are increasingly shaping scientific discoveries. Awarding the BA degree in forty different majors in the humanities, social sciences and natural sciences, Amherst offers an Open Curriculum, which allows students unusual independence and flexibility in the design of their educational programs, unconstrained by distribution or area requirements. Through the Five College Consortium, Amherst students can also take courses and participate in activities at Smith, Mount Holyoke and Hampshire Colleges and the University of Massachusetts Amherst, providing access to a remarkably broad and diverse collection of curricular and extracurricular options. Amherst's small classes and low student-faculty ratio foster one-on-one interactions with professors and fellow students, and provide exceptional opportunities for undergraduate research with highly talented, accomplished faculty, contributing to an uncommonly engaging intellectual and personal experience within a lively community."

SELECTIVITY

Admissions Rating	98
# of applicants	10,569
% of applicants accepted	11
% of acceptees attending	39
# offered a place on the wait list	1,447
% accepting a place on wait list	53
% admitted from wait list	6
# of early decision applicants	518
% accepted early decision	36

FRESHMAN PROFILE

Range SAT EBRW	690–760
Range SAT Math	720–790
Range SAT Composite	1420–1530
Range ACT Composite	31–34
# submitting SAT scores	276
% submitting SAT scores	59
# submitting ACT scores	240
% submitting ACT scores	51
% graduated top 10% of class	88
% graduated top 25% of class	98
% graduated top 50% of class	100

DEADLINES

Early decision	
Deadline	11/1
Notification	12/15
Regular	
Deadline	1/4
Notification	4/1
Nonfall registration?	No

FINANCIAL FACTS

Financial Aid Rating	97
Annual tuition	$57,640
Room and board	$15,310
Required fees	$1,000
Books and supplies	$1,000
Average frosh need-based scholarship	$58,697
Average UG need-based scholarship	$57,760
% needy frosh rec. need-based scholarship or grant aid	99
% needy UG rec. need-based scholarship or grant aid	99
% needy frosh rec. non-need-based scholarship or grant aid	0
% needy UG rec. non-need-based scholarship or grant aid	0
% needy frosh rec. need-based self-help aid	86
% needy UG rec. need-based self-help aid	88
% frosh rec. any financial aid	57
% UG rec. any financial aid	57
% UG borrow to pay for school	28
Average cumulative indebtedness	$22,629
% frosh need fully met	100
% ugrads need fully met	100
Average % of frosh need met	100
Average % of ugrad need met	100

ANGELO STATE UNIVERSITY

ASU Station #11014, San Angelo, TX 76909-1014 • Admissions: 325-942-2041 • Fax: 325-942-2078

CAMPUS LIFE
Quality of Life Rating	93
Fire Safety Rating	96
Green Rating	83
Type of school	Public
Environment	City

STUDENTS
Total undergrad enrollment	6,031
% male/female	43/57
% from out of state	3
% frosh live on campus	74
% ugrads live on campus	22
# of fraternities (% ugrad men join)	4 (4)
# of sororities (% ugrad women join)	2 (3)
% African American	7
% Asian	1
% Caucasian	46
% Hispanic	38
% Native American	<1
% Pacific Islander	<1
% Two or more races	3
% Race and/or ethnicity unknown	<1
% international	4
# of countries represented	26

SURVEY SAYS . . .
Lots of conservative students
Students are happy
School is well run
Diverse student types interact on campus
Students are very religious
Students get along with local community
Very little drug use
Intramural sports are popular

ACADEMICS
Academic Rating	79
% students returning for sophomore year	69
% students graduating within 4 years	31
% students graduating within 6 years	40
Calendar	Semester
Student/faculty ratio	20:1
Profs interesting rating	91
Profs accessible rating	93

Most classes have 20–29 students.
Most lab/discussion sessions have
20–29 students.

MOST POPULAR MAJORS
Multi-/Interdisciplinary Studies, Other; Business
Administration and Management, General;
Registered Nursing/Registered Nurse

STUDENTS SAY "..."

Academics

Angelo State University, located in San Angelo, Texas, puts forth an academic environment that is "small enough to foster a sense of family among its students, but large enough to carry out the usual dealings of universities that have many more students." Among these offerings are "outstanding instructors," "top-rated programs," and a low faculty-to-student ratio—one student says, "the small ... ratio is what really drew me to Angelo State." The university puts forth a variety of "resources available to enhance education." These include scholarship opportunities, ROTC programs, counseling services, and a dedicated Student Affairs office. Student advisory services are provided free of charge and make valuable additions to the overall academic experience. Angelo State students describe professors and other faculty members as "always willing to help" in a variety of ways. The university's professionals go above and beyond by "explaining concepts outside of class time, offering advice of which courses to take, or even offering career advice." They take the time to get to know individual students, "provide additional resources," and "encourage the next generation of scholars" by guiding students to think critically and "better understand multiple perspectives." One student raves, saying, "I have had several different majors in my college journey, and in every program ... I felt like the professors really cared about teaching."

Life

The average student at Angelo State tends to maintain a healthy balance between schoolwork and leisure. Students see their work as a priority but still find time to socialize with friends and participate in extracurricular activities. "Just hanging out is common," as students enjoy walking around campus, finding a place outdoors to simply relax, "studying around campus, [and talking] to their friends." Many students spend their time either at the library or at the University Center because both places are considered to be "the most calming." Other students use their personal time to visit the recreation center, which has a full gym, equipped with an inside track and a "weight room [that] is amazing," or they can participate in other recreational sports. "When it gets warm outside, the sand volleyball courts always have a good crowd at them," says a student. Those looking for entertainment off-campus will be pleased that the surrounding area of San Angelo includes restaurants, bars, a shopping mall, and other nearby stores, and "the nightlife is pretty solid around town."

Student Body

The students at Angelo State University offer an extraordinarily "friendly and welcoming" atmosphere on campus. It's also a large enough school that "you are constantly meeting new people, but at the same time you get to see the people you are well-acquainted with." Students at the school affectionately refer to fellow members of the university as the "Ram Fam," which "means that everyone is family at the school ... because everyone is out to help you." Most students say their peers are the type of people who are "polite," "uplifting," and "have your back." According to one undergraduate, "Everyone has the goals they want to achieve, and the students find support to achieve those goals within the community they build." Students go out of their way to make others feel comfortable and accepted, "offer to help you find your way to class," or even "open doors or greet you." One states, "I can't walk to class without receiving a 'hello' or 'what's up' from other students." And that crowd of friendly faces "seems to grow [in diversity] each year." Overall, students find the climate on campus to be "beyond amazing."

ANGELO STATE UNIVERSITY

Financial Aid: 325-942-2246 • E-Mail: admissions@angelo.edu • Website: www.angelo.edu

THE PRINCETON REVIEW SAYS

Admissions

Very important factors considered include: class rank, standardized test scores. *Important factors considered include:* rigor of secondary school record. *Other factors considered include:* academic GPA, extracurricular activities, talent/ability, character/personal qualities, first generation, geographical residence, state residency, volunteer work, work experience, level of applicant's interest. ACT with or without writing accepted. SAT with or without Essay component accepted. High school diploma is required and GED is accepted. *Academic units recommended:* 4 English, 4 math, 4 science, 2 foreign language, 3.5 social studies, 5.5 academic electives, 1 visual/performing arts.

Financial Aid

Students should submit: FAFSA. Priority filing deadline is 4/1. The Princeton Review suggests that all financial aid forms be submitted as soon as possible after October 1. *Need-based scholarships/grants offered:* College/university scholarship or grant aid from institutional funds; Federal Nursing Scholarships; Federal Pell; Private scholarships; SEOG; State scholarships/grants. *Loan aid offered:* Direct PLUS loans; Direct Subsidized Stafford Loans; Direct Unsubsidized Stafford Loans. Applicants will be notified of awards on a rolling basis beginning 4/1. Federal Work-Study Program available. Institutional employment available.

The Inside Word

When accepting new students to Angelo State University, the admissions department places a strong emphasis on academic achievement and the desire for students to "find what drives" them. The department takes into consideration the high school class rank and college entrance exam score of each of its prospective students. Students who have graduated in the top 25 percent of their class do not require a minimum SAT or ACT score. Students that fall into the next 25 percent of their class require either a minimum ACT score of 17 or a minimum SAT score of 920. Students in the third and fourth quarters of their graduating class are not assured admission but are still encouraged to apply for further review.

THE SCHOOL SAYS "..."

From the Admissions Office

"Undergraduate students at Angelo State University engage in faculty-mentored projects and research experiences. ASU also promotes community involvement through numerous organizations and outreach programs. ASU shines with superb records of graduates' acceptance into professional schools. Over 65 percent of pre-med students are accepted into medical school, well above the national average of 41 percent. Ninety percent of students who complete the pre-veterinary program, maintain a high GPA, complete the entrance requirements, and receive the highest recommendations from ASU faculty are accepted into veterinary school. Over 95 percent of agriculture, biology, chemistry, engineering, geology and physics majors who apply are accepted into graduate school. All graduates of ASU's Honors Program, who have applied to graduate programs or professional schools, including medicine and law, have been accepted. Additionally, since 1998, ASU students have maintained a 100 percent passing rate on the Texas Examination of Educator Standards (TExES) teacher certification test for secondary mathematics.

"Because of strong academics and a substantial gift aid program, including the Carr Academic Scholarship, which annually awards scholarships totaling approximately $7.5 million, ASU remains one of the top educational values in Texas. About 90 percent of ASU students receive some form of financial support and close to 40 percent graduate debt free. ASU also encourages healthy student lifestyles while fostering leadership development through 100-plus student organizations, a thriving intramurals program, and modern recreation and fitness facilities. ASU student-athletes just completed one of the most successful years in school history, competing in newly-renovated, state-of-the-art facilities."

SELECTIVITY

Admissions Rating	79
# of applicants	3,913
% of applicants accepted	77
% of acceptees attending	48

FRESHMAN PROFILE

Range SAT EBRW	470–570
Range SAT Math	460–550
Range SAT Composite	950–1130
Range ACT Composite	17–23
# submitting SAT scores	874
% submitting SAT scores	61
# submitting ACT scores	926
% submitting ACT scores	65
% graduated top 10% of class	13
% graduated top 25% of class	38
% graduated top 50% of class	72

DEADLINES

Regular	
Notification	Rolling, 9/1
Nonfall registration?	Yes

FINANCIAL FACTS

Financial Aid Rating	84
Annual in-state tuition	$5,516
Annual out-of-state tuition	$17,786
Room and board	$9,630
Required fees	$3,495
Books and supplies	$1,200
Average frosh need-based scholarship	$3,982
Average UG need-based scholarship	$3,607
% needy frosh rec. need-based scholarship or grant aid	90
% needy UG rec. need-based scholarship or grant aid	89
% needy frosh rec. non-need-based scholarship or grant aid	59
% needy UG rec. non-need-based scholarship or grant aid	54
% needy frosh rec. need-based self-help aid	61
% needy UG rec. need-based self-help aid	63
% frosh rec. any financial aid	71
% UG rec. any financial aid	64
% UG borrow to pay for school	58
Average cumulative indebtedness	$24,269
% frosh need fully met	14
% ugrads need fully met	14
Average % of frosh need met	71
Average % of ugrad need met	64

ARIZONA STATE UNIVERSITY

Admission Services, PO Box 871004, Tempe, AZ 85287-1004 • Admissions: 480-965-7788 • Fax: 480-965-3610

CAMPUS LIFE

Quality of Life Rating	87
Fire Safety Rating	84
Green Rating	98
Type of school	Public
Environment	Metropolis

STUDENTS

Total undergrad enrollment	61,693
% male/female	51/49
% from out of state	25
% frosh live on campus	73
% ugrads live on campus	25
# of fraternities (% ugrad men join)	42 (8)
# of sororities(% ugrad women join)	33 (10)
% African American	4
% Asian	8
% Caucasian	48
% Hispanic	25
% Native American	1
% Pacific Islander	<1
% Two or more races	5
% Race and/or ethnicity unknown	1
% International	7
# of countries represented	108

SURVEY SAYS . . .

Students love Tempe, AZ
Everyone loves the Sun Devils
College radio is popular

ACADEMICS

Academic Rating	74
% students returning for sophomore year	88
% students graduating within 4 years	55
% students graduating within 6 years	70
Calendar	Semester
Student/faculty Ratio	19
Profs interesting rating	83
Profs accessible rating	89

MOST POPULAR MAJORS

Business, Management, Marketing
Biology & Biological Sciences
Psychology

STUDENTS SAY "..."

Academics

Students report that Arizona State University's focus on "innovation" and its "abundance of resources" are major factors in their school choice. ASU is a large university, yet manages to "personalize every student's experience," and offers "endless...opportunities for success." The university has many strong academic departments and programs of study, and students are quick to brag that ASU has "one of the best journalism schools in the nation" as well as a "renowned business school" and "great engineering program." "Research opportunities" abound across academic disciplines.

ASU students praise their "enthusiastic, supportive and engaged" professors. Undergraduates report that most of the faculty is effective in incorporating "research interests and experiences" into coursework. "Most of my professors would bend over backward to help me out—even when the issue wasn't in their particular class," reports one enthusiastic undergraduate. It's "very easy to get help/make friends with professors." Another student admiringly tells us, "I had a professor who worked for the UN, as well as [one who was] a skateboarding punk music journalist."

Life

It's virtually impossible to be bored on the ASU campuses, as students are incredibly "active." "There are always people out at the pools, exercising in the gym, playing sports on the sand volleyball courts or soccer fields, or riding bikes or long boards." If you prefer indoor sports, don't worry: ASU has a "very strong gaming community." Undergraduates can also enjoy "really interesting lectures" and participate in "fun clubs." There is a "programming board which host[s] events every week, including free films and food." Many students "have jobs and internships" as well. Additionally, Greek life is pretty popular at ASU. Students say that it's "really fun [but] not as party-oriented as it used to be. Fraternities and sororities [now] get involved around campus, whether it be [through] community service, philanthropy, or intramural games." Downtown Tempe offers plenty of excitement as well. For example, "there is a thriving alternative music and DIY scene in the Maple-Ash district just off campus with ties to the local arts communities, political activism, and house shows where local bands play."

Student Body

Undergraduates at ASU love the "diversity" of the student body and describe meeting peers "from all different backgrounds, locations and cultures." There is a "large Greek life presence...along with a very serious academic body within Barrett, The Honors College, and a large section of international students." No matter where they come from, ASU undergraduates appreciate the student body's "unique blend of intelligence and fun." They also tend to be "nice and welcoming." One student sums it up: "Every person you meet has a smile on their face, ready to help with whatever problem there is." A number of undergraduates here also report that their peers "are excellent at getting involved in community activities and speaking up for what they believe in...[as well as] spread[ing] awareness about important issues." Thanks to the university's large size, many students insist that "everyone who comes to ASU is absolutely able to find other people with the same interests, passions, beliefs, and world views, as well as countless others who see the world very differently. No matter who you are, you can find a community of peers."

ARIZONA STATE UNIVERSITY

Financial Aid: 855-278-5080 • E-Mail: admissions@asu.edu • Website: www.asu.edu

THE PRINCETON REVIEW SAYS

Admissions

Very important factors considered include: class rank, academic GPA, standardized test scores. *Important factors considered include:* rigor of secondary school record. *Other factors considered include:* state residency. ACT with or without writing accepted. SAT with or without Essay component accepted. High school diploma is required and GED is accepted. *Academic units required:* 4 English, 4 math, 3 lab science, 2 foreign language, 2 social studies, 1 fine arts or CTE.

Financial Aid

Students should submit: FAFSA. Priority filing deadline is 1/15. The Princeton Review suggests that all financial aid forms be submitted as soon as possible after October 1. *Need-based scholarships/grants offered:* College/university scholarship or grant aid from institutional funds; Federal Pell; Private scholarships; SEOG; State scholarships/grants; United Negro College Fund. *Loan aid offered:* Direct PLUS loans; Direct Subsidized Stafford Loans; Direct Unsubsidized Stafford Loans. Applicants will be notified of awards on a rolling basis beginning 12/1. Federal Work-Study Program available. Institutional employment available.

The Inside Word

Admission officers at Arizona State University have built an incoming class that reflects diverse backgrounds and interests. The school takes a fairly straightforward approach to the admission process. Applicants must have or meet at least one of the following: minimum 3.00 GPA (based upon a 4.00 scale), be in the top 25 percent of their graduating class, or earned a minimum ACT score of 22 (residents) or 24 (nonresidents) or an SAT score of 1120 (residents) or 1180 (non-residents).

THE SCHOOL SAYS "..."

From the Admissions Office

"ASU is breaking down the walls of the traditional academic experience to increase the impact of education and research in local and global communities. As a New American University, ASU is committed to interdisciplinary connections, academic excellence, and societal impact. We are bold and forward-thinking, and we see challenges as opportunities. With 350+ undergraduate majors, ASU is a learning environment where personal expression is valued as much as research and discovery. ASU champions intellectual and cultural diversity and welcomes students from all 50 states and more than 130 countries. Our distinguished faculty receives prestigious honors including the Nobel Prize, the Pulitzer Prize, and membership in the National Academies. Student achievements include Rhodes, Fulbright, Marshall, Churchill and Goldwater scholars, National Merit Scholars, and National Hispanic Scholars.

"ASU has four unique campuses in metropolitan Phoenix, and a site in Lake Havasu City. All feature state-of-the-art living and learning facilities. The Downtown Phoenix campus creates strong learning and career connections for more than 11,400 students with media, health care, corporate, and government organizations. The Polytechnic campus, located in Mesa, Arizona, is home to 5,200 students who are exploring professional and technical programs. Thousands of square feet of laboratory space make way for project-based learning.

"ASU welcomes more than 53,000 students studying at the historic Tempe campus. The Sun Devils athletic complex, performing arts facilities, and high-tech research spaces create a dynamic and engaging learning environment.

"At the West campus in northwest Phoenix, ASU offers business, education, health, and interdisciplinary arts and science programs to more than 4,900 students. The campus's award-winning architecture and lush landscaping are designed to create a close-knit learning community."

SELECTIVITY

Admissions Rating	80
# of applicants	48,644
% of applicants accepted	85
% of acceptees attending	32

FRESHMAN PROFILE

Range SAT EBRW	560–660
Range SAT Math	550–680
Range SAT Composite	1120–1330
Range ACT Composite	21-28
# submitting SAT scores	7,355
% submitting SAT scores	56
# submitting ACT scores	7,904
% submitting ACT scores	60
Average HSGPA	3.5
% graduated top 10% of class	31
% graduated top 25% of class	62
% graduated top 50% of class	89

DEADLINES

Regular	
Priority	1/15
Notification	Rolling, 8/1
Nonfall registration?	Yes

FINANCIAL FACTS

Financial Aid Rating	85
Annual in-state tuition	$10,710
Annual out-of-state tuition	$28,800
Room and board	$13,267
Required fees	$628
Books and supplies	$1,171
Average frosh need-based scholarship	$13,893
Average UG need-based scholarship	$11,424
% needy frosh rec. need-based scholarship or grant aid	98
% needy UG rec. need-based scholarship or grant aid	94
% needy frosh rec non-need based scholarship or grant aid	15
% needy UG rec non-need-based scholarship or grant aid	9
% needy frosh rec need-based self-help aid	46
% needy UG rec need-based self-help aid	60
% frosh rec any financial aid	97
% UG rec any financial aid	87
% UG borrow to pay for school	47
Average cumulative indebtedness	$23,593
% frosh need fully met	22
% ugrads need fully met	19
Average % of frosh need met	70
Average % of ugrads need met	60

ASSUMPTION UNIVERSITY

The Office of Undergraduate Admissions, Assumption University, Worcester, MA 01609-1296 • Admissions: 508-767-7285 • Fax: 508-799-4412

CAMPUS LIFE
Quality of Life Rating	90
Fire Safety Rating	82
Green Rating	60*
Type of school	Private
Affiliation	Roman Catholic
Environment	City

STUDENTS
Total undergrad enrollment	1,955
% male/female	44/56
% from out of state	34
% frosh from public high school	68
% frosh live on campus	91
% ugrads live on campus	85
# of fraternities	0
# of sororities	0
% African American	5
% Asian	3
% Caucasian	77
% Hispanic	7
% Native American	<1
% Pacific Islander	<1
% Two or more races	3
% Race and/or ethnicity unknown	4
% international	1
# of countries represented	23

SURVEY SAYS . . .
Students are happy
Internships are widely available
Diverse student types interact on campus
Students get along with local community
Students involved in community service
Easy to get around campus
Everyone loves the Greyhounds
Active student government
Active minority support groups

ACADEMICS
Academic Rating	80
% students returning for sophomore year	85
% students graduating within 4 years	68
% students graduating within 6 years	70
Calendar	Semester
Student/faculty ratio	12:1
Profs interesting rating	88
Profs accessible rating	94

Most classes have 20–29 students.
Most lab/discussion sessions have
    10–19 students.

MOST POPULAR MAJORS
Human Services and Rehabilitation Studies;
Marketing; Management

STUDENTS SAY "..."

Academics

Located in the liberal arts college haven of Worcester, MA, Assumption University is "a tight knit, faith-based community where everyone is part of a family." The small school focuses on "educating aware and prospective young adults to become active and productive members of society while maintaining human core values" through "service, meaningful discussions, and liberal arts classes." Assumption is definitely all about education ("especially if you are a science major"), but there is also "a big push for sports" at this Division II school, and perhaps as a result the university's sense of community is "amazing." "We are one school, we are Assumption," says a student. The "beyond helpful" professors here are "engaging," "approachable," and "have a diversity of teaching styles," as well as being "willing to talk to you whenever you need it and [caring] about your well-being." They "bring their personal experiences into the classroom" to make studies "interesting and enjoyable," and the application of the liberal arts curriculum to small classes means that students "receive a greater impact" from their learning. "The professors here at Assumption all love what they do and it is obvious in the classroom," says a junior. However, some do admit that the school is "limited on the number of courses offered" which "can make getting into classes a little difficult." This "very welcoming and inclusive institution" focuses on giving its student every resource possible to help them succeed and be happy; tutoring is provided at the academic center, campus jobs are "abundant," and the Career and Internship Center admirably aids students in finding jobs after graduation. "Guidance counselors, teachers, [and] coaches are truly a blessing to have at this university," says a student. Overall, Assumption "helps foster well rounded, creative, intelligent and caring young adults to be successful and morally sound in their future endeavors."

Life

Life at Assumption is great. It's "easy to meet new people" and "there is a great sense of belonging." "Assumption does a great job of getting people involved one way or another," says a student. The "beautiful, diverse and secured campus" is "easily recognizable" from brochures, and those who get to take advantage of it "are very invested in academics, sports, extracurriculars, and social experiences." There is always an activity going on and "always something to do if you want to get off campus" in the college town of Worcester. Housing is guaranteed all four years and around 85 percent of students choose to take advantage of this, but "weekends can be dead sometimes" when students leave campus.

The school is "strict as far as drinking goes": Make no mistake, Assumption is "a VERY Catholic school" that "has a very conservative feel." This doesn't mean there's not fun to be had; though during the week "everyone is either in the library or involved in clubs/sports," once Thursday hits "upperclassmen flock to Leits off campus while underclassmen stick to their dorms." "Friday and Saturday are the go to nights for parties" for those that choose to so; however, a large majority go to the events the campus activities board puts on "like Bingo Nights, movie nights, trivia, [and] family feud." "They are really fun and have some amazing prizes like iPads, TV, etc." says a student.

Student Body

Though there's a lack of socioeconomic diversity—"generally middle-class Caucasians [who] are heterosexual"—students can be separated into "student-athletes and non-student-athletes." Most students "come from Catholic upbringings or have attended Catholic school but are not necessarily religious." New England preppy is a classic style; girls are usually seen in "leggings, Ugg boots, a North Face jacket." People here are "generally happy" and "very sociable and approachable" in all aspects of the university; everyone is "courteous and [will] hold doors open or lend you a calculator in class if your forgot yours." Overall, the student body "is like no other": People "genuinely care about each other and it makes for a wonderful experience."

Financial Aid: 508-767-7158 • E-Mail: admiss@assumption.edu • Website: http://www.assumption.edu

THE PRINCETON REVIEW SAYS

Admissions

Very important factors considered include: academic GPA, application essay. *Important factors considered include:* rigor of secondary school record, recommendation(s), interview, volunteer work. *Other factors considered include:* class rank, standardized test scores (optional), extracurricular activities, talent/ability, character/personal qualities, first generation, racial/ethnic status. ACT with or without writing accepted. SAT with or without Essay component accepted. High school diploma is required and GED is accepted. *Academic units required:* 4 English, 3 math, 2 science, 2 foreign language, 2 history, 5 academic electives.

Financial Aid

Students should submit: FAFSA. Priority filing deadline is 1/15. The Princeton Review suggests that all financial aid forms be submitted as soon as possible after October 1. *Need-based scholarships/grants offered:* College/university scholarship or grant aid from institutional funds; Federal Pell; Private scholarships; SEOG; State scholarships/grants. *Loan aid offered:* Federal Direct PLUS loans; Federal Direct Subsidized Loans; Federal Direct Stafford Loans. Applicants will be notified of awards on a rolling basis beginning mid-February. Federal Work-Study Program available. Institutional employment available.

The Inside Word

Around three-quarters of those who apply to Assumption are admitted; keeping in mind that the applicant pool is somewhat self-selective, average students shouldn't have a hard time getting in. Assumption uses the Common Application and submitting standardized test scores is optional.

THE SCHOOL SAYS "..."

From the Admissions Office

"Students flourish at Assumption especially during these exciting times of transitioning to Assumption University. The establishment of the College of Liberal Arts and Sciences, the Grenon School of Business, the School of Nursing, and the School of Health Professions offers students new opportunities including new programs in cybersecurity, neuroscience, nursing, physician assistant studies." Established in 1904 by the Augustinians of the Assumption, the University is a Catholic coeducational institution offering an educational experience that cultivates intellect and personal values and an academic atmosphere promoting individual attention and the quest for excellence. Approximately 2,000 undergraduates choose among 33 majors and 49 minors, gaining the depth and breadth of knowledge that is the foundation of lifelong success. Students engage with a highly credentialed faculty and staff in a community that fosters critical intelligence, thoughtful citizenship and compassionate service. With a student/faculty ratio of just 12:1, Assumption's professors challenge students to ask questions, find their answers and grow intellectually, socially and spiritually. Ninety-five percent of our Class of 2019 was employed, pursuing additional education, or engaged in community service within six months of graduation and 83 percent participated in at least one internship research or experiential learning opportunity.

"Assumption's beautiful 185-acre campus is situated in a residential neighborhood minutes from thriving downtown Worcester, Massachusetts. The campus is lively seven days a week with academic programming, activities sponsored by more than 60 student clubs and organizations, community service opportunities, campus ministry programs; and intercollegiate, intramural and club sports. The University's campus in Rome, Italy, which was recently ranked a Top 10 study abroad program in America, utilizes the city as the classroom and enriches students' academic and cultural pursuits."

SELECTIVITY

Admissions Rating	77
# of applicants	4,959
% of applicants accepted	81
% of acceptees attending	16
# offered a place on the wait list	95
% accepting a place on wait list	17
# of early decision applicants	33
% accepted early decision	94

FRESHMAN PROFILE

Range SAT EBRW	550–628
Range SAT Math	540–610
Range SAT Composite	1080–1240
Range ACT Composite	23–28
# submitting SAT scores	322
% submitting SAT scores	58
# submitting ACT scores	29
% submitting ACT scores	5
Average HS GPA	3.4
% graduated top 10% of class	14
% graduated top 25% of class	41
% graduated top 50% of class	76

DEADLINES

Early decision	
Deadline	11/1
Notification	12/1
Early action	
Deadline	11/1
Notification	12/15
Early action II	
Deadline	12/15
Notification	1/15
Regular	
Deadline	2/15
Notification	3/31
Nonfall registration?	Yes

FINANCIAL FACTS

Financial Aid Rating	88
Annual tuition	$43,178
Room and board	$13,590
Required fees	$800
Books and supplies	$1,000
Average frosh need-based scholarship	$26,390
Average UG need-based scholarship	$25,250
% needy frosh rec. need-based scholarship or grant aid	100
% needy UG rec. need-based scholarship or grant aid	100
% needy frosh rec. non-need-based scholarship or grant aid	24
% needy UG rec. non-need-based scholarship or grant aid	20
% needy frosh rec. need-based self-help aid	74
% needy UG rec. need-based self-help aid	79
% frosh rec. any financial aid	98.4
% UG rec. any financial aid	98
% frosh need fully met	31
% ugrads need fully met	30
Average % of frosh need met	79
Average % of ugrad need met	79

AUBURN UNIVERSITY

The Quad Center, Auburn, AL 36849-5149 • Admissions: 334-844-6425 • Fax: 334-844-6436

STUDENTS SAY "..."

Academics

Located in the heart of Alabama, Auburn University is called home by more than 20,000 undergraduates, making it one of the state's largest universities. Established before the Civil War, the school's environment is "challenging, captivating, unique and yet still timeless," and students say the university "provides you plenty of resources and opportunities to get a top-notch education." The school channels its efforts into developing young professionals through a "nurturing education, extracurricular involvement opportunities, and professional skill development." Classes may not be easy, "but the work pays off." Professors here are "approachable," "go out of their way to help you learn if you ask them," and "bring material to life." "My professors at Auburn University make it clear that they are there to teach me," says a student. While a few professors are difficult to follow or are more focused on research than on teaching, "graduate student assistants are helpful in assisting professors in understanding how to make material more exciting to learn." Along with "excellent diversity in courses/majors," students say that Auburn provides solid academic support and a faculty that is "always very intelligent on the subjects at hand." The science and the "very challenging engineering programs" benefit from updated facilities and classrooms (though some say that liberal arts programs "get less attention") with the added bonus of "many internship/co-op opportunities advertised and available." "I believe I have received a wonderful education from Auburn University," says a contented student.

Life

This "welcoming place" has "an Old South small town feeling," beautiful campus, and an "amazing new recreation center," where students can work out. There are more than 300 organizations for students to join, and "student involvement is high." Greek life is big here, but "it's definitely possible to fit in without being a part of Greek life." The city of Auburn "has a safe downtown area where students can go to bars" on weekends, and there is a nearby state park where people go for fun. There's also a "good food atmosphere in the community," and Birmingham and Atlanta are always doable options for travel and concerts. Sports (both watching and playing) "drive a ton of campus life and help unite the student body." "Football Saturdays at Auburn are second to none," says a student. "I was looking for a large school with an SEC football team but also a good academic program," says one student athlete within Auburn's famous athletic program. The student voice is also "very respected" among the administration and "can cause tangible change": the Student Government Association "is very strong at Auburn."

Student Body

Many here are "white," "Republican," and "tend to be conservative." The typical student is "friendly," an Alabama native, and "someone who would say 'hello' walking along the concourse to class" or "would lend a hand in a time of need." "There is so much school spirit" here (in no small part due to the football team) and almost everyone "is highly obsessed with football," which "has almost a religious following of fans." "Alabama students love Alabama football, Auburn students love Auburn," says one student of the communal loyalty in which one can rest assured that "the Auburn Family has your back."

Financial Aid: 334-844-4634 • E-Mail: admissions@auburn.edu • Website: www.auburn.edu

THE PRINCETON REVIEW SAYS

Admissions

Very important factors considered include: academic GPA, application essay, standardized test scores. *Important factors considered include:* rigor of secondary school record, extracurricular activities, talent/ability, character/personal qualities, first generation, alumni/ae relation, geographical residence, state residency, volunteer work. *Other factors considered include:* recommendation(s). ACT with or without writing accepted. SAT with or without Essay component accepted. High school diploma is required and GED is accepted. *Academic units required:* 4 English, 3 math, 2 science, 1 science lab, 3 social studies. *Academic units recommended:* 2 science labs, 1 foreign language, 4 social studies.

Financial Aid

Students should submit: FAFSA. Priority filing deadline is 2/1. The Princeton Review suggests that all financial aid forms be submitted as soon as possible after October 1. *Need-based scholarships/grants offered:* College/university scholarship or grant aid from institutional funds; Federal Pell; Private scholarships; SEOG; State scholarships/grants. *Loan aid offered:* Direct PLUS loans; Direct Subsidized Stafford Loans; Direct Unsubsidized Stafford Loans. Applicants will be notified of awards on a rolling basis beginning 10/2. Federal Work-Study Program available. Institutional employment available.

The Inside Word

Auburn admissions officers have nearly 21,000 applications to sort through each year, and admission here is somewhat selective. Applicants are evaluated as individuals, and those who fall short of the average GPA, curricular, and standardized test score standards for incoming freshmen should know that the admissions committee is also looking for those with unique talents and abilities that will contribute substantially to campus life. Letters of recommendation, essays, and extracurricular activities are the make-or-break point for borderline candidates. Applicants' test scores must be submitted directly from the testing agencies.

THE SCHOOL SAYS "..."

From the Admissions Office

"Auburn University is a comprehensive land, sea, and space-grant university serving Alabama and the nation. The university is especially charged with the responsibility of enhancing the economic, social, and cultural development of the state through its instruction, research, and extension programs. In all of these programs, the university is committed to the pursuit of excellence. The university assumes an obligation to provide an environment of learning in which the individual and society are enriched by the discovery, preservation, transmission, and application of knowledge; in which students grow intellectually as they study and do research under the guidance of competent faculty; and in which the faculty develop professionally and contribute fully to the intellectual life of the institution, community, and state. This obligation unites Auburn University's continuing commitment to its land-grant traditions and the institution's role as a dynamic and complex, comprehensive university."

SELECTIVITY

Admissions Rating	83
# of applicants	20,205
% of applicants accepted	81
% of acceptees attending	29

FRESHMAN PROFILE

Range SAT EBRW	580–650
Range SAT Math	570–670
Range ACT Composite	25–31
# submitting SAT scores	866
% submitting SAT scores	18
# submitting ACT scores	3,911
% submitting ACT scores	81
Average HS GPA	3.9
% graduated top 10% of class	33
% graduated top 25% of class	63
% graduated top 50% of class	89

DEADLINES

Early action	
Deadline	11/1
Notification	12/1
Regular	
Priority	11/1
Deadline	2/3
Nonfall registration?	Yes

APPLICANTS ALSO LOOK AT AND SOMETIMES PREFER

Clemson University; Georgia Institute of Technology; University of Florida ; University of Georgia; University of Tennessee, Knoxville; The University of Alabama—Tuscaloosa

FINANCIAL FACTS

Financial Aid Rating	81
Annual in-state tuition	$9,816
Annual out-of-state tuition	$29,448
Room and board	$13,600
Required fees	$1,676
Books and supplies	$1,200
Average frosh need-based scholarship	$9,040
Average UG need-based scholarship	$8,343
% needy frosh rec. need-based scholarship or grant aid	86
% needy UG rec. need-based scholarship or grant aid	75
% needy frosh rec. non-need-based scholarship or grant aid	13
% needy UG rec. non-need-based scholarship or grant aid	9
% needy frosh rec. need-based self-help aid	57
% needy UG rec. need-based self-help aid	74
% frosh rec. any financial aid	51
% UG rec. any financial aid	45
% UG borrow to pay for school	39
Average cumulative indebtedness	$31,732
% frosh need fully met	17
% ugrads need fully met	13
Average % of frosh need met	51
Average % of ugrad need met	45

AUSTIN COLLEGE

900 N. Grand Avenue, Sherman, TX 75090 • Admissions: 903-813-3000 • Fax: 903-813-3198

STUDENTS SAY "..."

Academics

"Individual attention" is the name of the game at Austin College. Indeed, the small size of the school allows for a lot of "one-on-one interaction" and provides students with "many opportunities to get involved on campus." Additionally, students are grateful that Austin seems to maintain a healthy financial aid office. A psychology major concurs stating, "This college was very generous in helping fund my education." Undergrads are also excited about Austin's "excellent study abroad program." As one thrilled biology major brags, "I have already traveled to Trinidad for three weeks and I am planning to study in Cuba for three weeks as well as a semester abroad in Australia." Students also rave about the college's "GREAT pre-medicine program," "strong Japanese program" and excellent five year education program. Importantly, undergrads find their professors to be "very accessible." They are generally "willing to help and give us opportunities to advance ourselves outside the classroom as well as inside the classroom." Moreover, professors are "devoted to teaching their students how to think, not memorize." Finally, they "encourage their students to engage the material and ask meaningful questions."

Life

Despite its small size, Austin College is certainly a hotbed of activity. Truly, there are a myriad of clubs and events from which to choose. As one amazed senior shares, "I have played in a woodwind ensemble, done swing dancing and English country dancing, [attended] theater performances, art displays, choir, band and symphony concerts." She continues gushing, "There [have even been] mini carnivals with rock walls, live music, food, and inflatable race courses." And undergrads here are quick to tip their (metaphorical) hats to the Campus Activities Board (CAB) which "[throws] events almost every day." These might include "making wax hands...[and] pumpkin painting." Additionally, "CAB also hosts bigger events such as Kangapalooza where the college brings in three bands to play for the student body." While there are plenty of school events, a handful of students feel that "house parties sponsored by Greek groups are usually what encompass social life at Austin." Some students itching to get off campus are dismayed by hometown Sherman which doesn't seem to offer much beyond "Target and a few book stores." However, others insist there is more than meets the eye. As an optimistic international relations major sums up, "At first, Sherman seemed really small to a big city girl like me. But it really grows on you and now I love it! There are lots of great little hole-in-the-wall restaurants with awesome food. And if you need some city time, Dallas is about an hour away!"

Student Body

Undergrads here emphatically insist that "there is no typical student at AC." As one biology major explains, "Personalities range from frat-tastic jock to the gothic president of the English Country Dancing club." Fortunately, most everyone is "very welcoming." Indeed, "the environment here is so warm and friendly that the students easily fit in." Nevertheless, despite the reported uniqueness of the student body, there are some commonalities to be found. For starters, most undergrads here are "motivated in their studies" as well as "engaged in other extracurricular activities." Many students also describe their peers as "laid back," "pretty liberal," and "open minded." Of course, Austin does net "a lot of local Texas kids." However, there are definitely "some foreign students thrown in [there]" and students appreciate the diversity they bring to campus. And if you're still wary, this junior is moved to assuage your fears: "After coming to campus it doesn't take long to realize that even though most of us call Texas home, we are in no way defined by the Texas stereotype. Don't be deceived; the differences in socio-economic status, religion, political beliefs, and general perspective on life could not be more varied."

AUSTIN COLLEGE

Financial Aid: 903-813-2900 • E-Mail: admission@austincollege.edu • Website: www.austincollege.edu

THE PRINCETON REVIEW SAYS

Admissions

Very important factors considered include: rigor of secondary school record, class rank, academic GPA, application essay, standardized test scores, recommendation(s). *Important factors considered include:* interview, talent/ability, character/personal qualities. *Other factors considered include:* extracurricular activities, first generation, alumni/ae relation, geographical residence, state residency, religious affiliation/commitment, volunteer work, work experience. ACT with Writing recommended. SAT with Essay component recommended. High school diploma is required and GED is accepted. *Academic units required:* 4 English, 3 math, 3 science, 1 science lab, 2 foreign language, 2 social studies, 1 history, 1 visual/performing arts. *Academic units recommended:* 4 English, 4 math, 4 science, 2 science labs, 4 foreign language, 3 social studies, 1 history, 2 visual/performing arts.

Financial Aid

Students should submit: FAFSA. Priority filing deadline is 3/1. The Princeton Review suggests that all financial aid forms be submitted as soon as possible after October 1. *Need-based scholarships/grants offered:* College/university scholarship or grant aid from institutional funds; Federal Pell; Private scholarships; SEOG; State scholarships/grants. *Loan aid offered:* Direct PLUS loans; Direct Subsidized Stafford Loans; Direct Unsubsidized Stafford Loans. Applicants will be notified of awards on a rolling basis beginning 12/1. Federal Work-Study Program available. Institutional employment available.

The Inside Word

Austin College takes a holistic approach to the admissions game. Indeed, the school does its best to get a feel for who each applicant is beyond his or her GPA and test scores. Therefore, expect your recommendations, extracurricular activities, and essay to be heavily vetted. Additionally, the college is impressed with students who challenge themselves academically. Admissions officers are frequently more impressed with a B in an honors course than an A in a standard college prep class.

THE SCHOOL SAYS "..."

From the Admissions Office

"If you want to be anonymous, choose a different school. But if you dream of connecting with others, exploring the world, and discovering more about yourself, then Austin College is exactly where you belong.

"Learning happens in classroom discussions led by talented professors, dedicated to teaching and passionate about their work, who act as partners in education with students. Faculty and students often work together in research projects and learning opportunities in which sometimes the answers discovered aren't as important as the process of inquiry and discovery.

"Students come to Austin College for exceptional academic offerings in more than 57 areas of study in the humanities, sciences, and social sciences. Over the past five years, 82 percent of graduates completed an internship as career preparation. 94 percent of our graduates are attending graduate or professional school or are employed within a year of graduation. The highest number of students enroll in medical and law schools. Many graduates receive prestigious honors like Fulbright grants or Teach for America positions."

From Deposit to Your Graduation in Four Years: Our Commitment to Your Success Is Guaranteed

"We are confident in our academic programs and personalized mentoring; we promise that any full-time student who meets the Finish in Four Guarantee requirements in effect at the time of their enrollment will graduate in four calendar years. And, if you don't, Austin College will waive tuition costs for any courses you need to complete your degree. Guaranteed."

SELECTIVITY

Admissions Rating	88
# of applicants	4,360
% of applicants accepted	51
% of acceptees attending	17
# of early decision applicants	14
% accepted early decision	100

FRESHMAN PROFILE

Range SAT EBRW	560–660
Range SAT Math	550–650
Range SAT Composite	1130–1300
Range ACT Composite	24–29
# submitting SAT scores	255
% submitting SAT scores	67
# submitting ACT scores	155
% submitting ACT scores	41
Average HS GPA	3.5
% graduated top 10% of class	29
% graduated top 25% of class	59
% graduated top 50% of class	90

DEADLINES

Early decision	
Deadline	11/1
Notification	12/4
Early action	
Deadline	12/1
Notification	1/15
Regular	
Priority	2/1
Deadline	3/1
Notification	4/1
Nonfall registration?	No

APPLICANTS ALSO LOOK AT AND SOMETIMES PREFER

Baylor University; Texas A&M University; Texas Christian University; Southwestern University

AND RARELY PREFER

University of Dallas; Trinity University; Hendrix College

FINANCIAL FACTS

Financial Aid Rating	89
Annual tuition	$42,405
Room and board	$12,752
Required fees	$210
Books and supplies	$1,250
Average frosh need-based scholarship	$35,872
Average UG need-based scholarship	$34,058
% needy frosh rec. need-based scholarship or grant aid	100
% needy UG rec. need-based scholarship or grant aid	100
% needy frosh rec. non-need-based scholarship or grant aid	18
% needy UG rec. non-need-based scholarship or grant aid	18
% needy frosh rec. need-based self-help aid	72
% needy UG rec. need-based self-help aid	70
% frosh rec. any financial aid	97
% UG rec. any financial aid	98
% frosh need fully met	25
% ugrads need fully met	27
Average % of frosh need met	88
Average % of ugrad need met	87

BABSON COLLEGE

Lunder Hall, Babson Park, MA 02457 • Admissions: 781-239-5522 • Fax: 781-239-4006

CAMPUS LIFE

Quality of Life Rating	87
Fire Safety Rating	95
Green Rating	91
Type of school	Private
Environment	Village

STUDENTS

Total undergrad enrollment	2,386
% male/female	53/47
% from out of state	75
% frosh live on campus	100
% ugrads live on campus	80
# of fraternities (% ugrad men join)	4 (13)
# of sororities (% ugrad women join)	3 (26)
% African American	4
% Asian	11
% Caucasian	34
% Hispanic	11
% Native American	<1
% Pacific Islander	<1
% Two or more races	2
% Race and/or ethnicity unknown	6
% international	30
# of countries represented	77

SURVEY SAYS . . .

Career services are great
Internships are widely available
School is well run

ACADEMICS

Academic Rating	82
% students returning for sophomore year	95
% students graduating within 4 years	90
% students graduating within 6 years	93
Calendar	Semester
Student/faculty ratio	14:1
Profs interesting rating	89
Profs accessible rating	93
Most classes have 20–29 students.	

MOST POPULAR MAJORS

Business Administration and Management, General

STUDENTS SAY "..."

Academics

Babson College in Wellesley, Massachusetts, has a straightforward goal: to create entrepreneurs through an integrated curriculum of business fundamentals and liberal arts. Students here "not only study innovation but learn to embody it," graduating with a Bachelor of Science degree. Each student can select one or two concentrations (similar to a major) in order to hone their degree more centrally to their interests, ranging from Statistical Modeling to Global Business Management, but all must participate in preset Core Experiences, including a First-Year Seminar and the year-long, "exciting [and] stimulating" Foundations of Management and Entrepreneurship (FME). FME puts students into small groups in which they develop and launch an actual business venture, innovations that then donate all proceeds to charity. Babson prides itself on this type of unique and innovative curriculum, which incorporates "project-based classes," "lots of out-of-classroom work," and "tons ... of funding opportunities" for travel, conferences, and research. Students love the sense of academic direction they are given from the start, as "the school has very specific learning goals and makes it clear as to what path you are heading down."

The core of academics at Babson are the "engaged professors with real-world experience" who call upon that experience to improve classroom learning: "They don't just pull everything from a textbook," says a student. In fact, faculty have achieved "great accomplishments in their respective fields" and are "really able to speak to things students will need in the workplace." Instructors will also meet with students "outside of the classroom to ... offer advice on ... business ventures," fostering entrepreneurial insight in students' free time. Extra help in that regard is offered by an alumni network that "is very responsive given how small and community-like Babson is." Plus, "the entrepreneurial education ... is particularly appealing to employers."

Life

Going hand-in-hand with the academic drive of students, class and work occupy most of the week, and "fun is something that is saved for weekends or late nights," explains one Babson Beaver. On those weekdays and nights not spent in class, students are "encouraged to take on some type of leadership position or at least be engaged in one or multiple clubs," so meetings flesh out the open hours. That might seem like a lot, but not for this motivated group— "because of the heavy emphasis on entrepreneurship, there is no 'I will do it later' attitude"— and it's not unusual for students "to be working on several other ventures and competitions outside of their classes and school-related extracurriculars." From a social perspective, "intelligence and achievement [are] valued," and "you would never hear someone boast about not doing their homework." Academics aside, Wellesley is "a beautiful place to explore, grab a bite to eat, and shop," and "since there is no class on Fridays, students will take weekend trips." For those willing to travel a little further, Boston is relatively close, and students often "spend ... days in the city visiting new places, restaurants, [and] museums."

Student Body

This is "a very tight-knit community among both students and professors," and people here are "active, involved, and love to get out of the classroom to be together." The student body has "many international students," which "gives it a real business setting." Better yet, students here are "humble but passionate about business." It's commonly said that you "need to be self-disciplined to survive here," and that holds true since all students seem to "have a certain ambition and drive" on campus. You won't have to worry much about entrepreneurial competition at Babson, though, as everyone is "very professional [and] focused on networking and making connections." And those connections are plentiful with the diversity of backgrounds brought to the school each year: There are "many extremely wealthy students along with many students who receive full financial aid." But regardless of background, "the business mentality is prominent in the entire student body." This is evidenced by the great lengths some will go to in order to promote their entrepreneurial efforts: "I don't think I've ever entered a bathroom stall without a link or poster for a start-up or FME venture posted on the wall," says one student.

BABSON COLLEGE

Financial Aid: 781-239-4219 • E-Mail: ugradadmission@babson.edu • Website: www.babson.edu

THE PRINCETON REVIEW SAYS

Admissions

Very important factors considered include: rigor of secondary school record, class rank, academic GPA, application essay, standardized test scores, recommendation(s), extracurricular activities, character/personal qualities. *Other factors considered include:* interview, talent/ability, first generation, alumni/ae relation, geographical residence, state residency, racial/ethnic status, volunteer work, work experience, level of applicant's interest. ACT with or without writing accepted. SAT with or without Essay component accepted. High school diploma is required and GED is accepted. *Academic units required:* 4 English, 4 math, 3 science, 4 social studies. *Academic units recommended:* 4 English, 4 math, 3 science, 4 foreign language, 4 social studies.

Financial Aid

Students should submit: CSS/Financial Aid PROFILE; FAFSA; Noncustodial PROFILE. Priority filing deadline is 2/1. The Princeton Review suggests that all financial aid forms be submitted as soon as possible after October 1. *Need-based scholarships/grants offered:* College/university scholarship or grant aid from institutional funds; Federal Pell; Private scholarships; SEOG; State scholarships/grants. *Loan aid offered:* Direct PLUS loans; Direct Subsidized Stafford Loans; Direct Unsubsidized Stafford Loans. Applicants will be notified of awards on or about 4/1. Federal Work-Study Program available. Institutional employment available.

The Inside Word

Babson's prominence as a noteworthy undergraduate business school continues to rise. Incoming students are evaluated on their academic performance (high school GPAs and standardized test scores) as well as nonacademic factors including leadership, involvement, and enthusiasm. Writing ability is a valued commodity, and prospective students should be ready for the supplemental writing section of the application. Besides Regular Decision application, Babson offers three fall application plans for first-years—Early Decision I, Early Decision II, and Early Action—in addition to January G.A.P. Enrollment, which allows students to apply for the spring semester.

THE SCHOOL SAYS "..."

From the Admissions Office

"Nationally recognized as the number one school in entrepreneurship for twenty-two years, Babson College is the premier institution for entrepreneurship education. Through our entrepreneurial thought & action methodology, we teach all of our students to think and act entrepreneurially to pursue their passions and create a path to success, no matter where that path might lead. As a result, Babson graduates are entrepreneurs of all kinds: startup founders, business leaders, corporate innovators, social changemakers, and so much more.

"Our immersive, hands-on curriculum provides students with the ability to adapt to ever-changing business environments, the experience to hit the ground running upon graduation, and the know-how to discover opportunities that will create economic and social value everywhere. As a business school where one-half of the classes are in liberal arts, Babson emphasizes creativity, innovation, and risk-taking as essential to learning the foundation of business.

"Babson's tight-knit community provides students with the opportunity to form close relationships with faculty and staff. An average class has twenty to twenty-nine students and a student/faculty ratio of 14:1 allows faculty to serve as role models and mentors committed to helping our students grow. With about 87 percent holding a doctoral degree, these accomplished business executives, authors, entrepreneurs, scholars, researchers, and artists bring intellectual diversity and real-world experiences that add depth to Babson's programs. Most importantly, faculty members teach 100 percent of the courses.

"At Babson, students receive a world-class education that is innovative and creative, yet practical. They study business, learn about leadership, and undertake a transformative life experience preparing them to create an authentic, powerful brand of success. Our students make friends, find mentors, and develop long-lasting relationships that will thrive long after graduation."

SELECTIVITY

Admissions Rating	95
# of applicants	6,362
% of applicants accepted	26
% of acceptees attending	36
# offered a place on the wait list	1,676
% accepting a place on wait list	39
% admitted from wait list	18
# of early decision applicants	584
% accepted early decision	35

FRESHMAN PROFILE

Range SAT EBRW	620–690
Range SAT Math	650–760
Range SAT Composite	1270–1450
Range ACT Composite	27–32
# submitting SAT scores	446
% submitting SAT scores	74
# submitting ACT scores	208
% submitting ACT scores	35

DEADLINES

Early decision	
Deadline	11/1
Notification	12/15
Other ED Deadline	1/2
Other ED Notification	2/15
Early action	
Deadline	11/1
Notification	1/1
Regular	
Priority	11/1
Deadline	1/2
Notification	4/1
Nonfall registration?	Yes

FINANCIAL FACTS

Financial Aid Rating	93
Annual tuition	$54,144
Room and board	$17,668
Books and supplies	$1,184
Average frosh need-based scholarship	$40,042
Average UG need-based scholarship	$42,389
% needy frosh rec. need-based scholarship or grant aid	95
% needy UG rec. need-based scholarship or grant aid	97
% needy frosh rec. non-need-based scholarship or grant aid	9
% needy UG rec. non-need-based scholarship or grant aid	14
% needy frosh rec. need-based self-help aid	87
% needy UG rec. need-based self-help aid	77
% frosh rec. any financial aid	42
% UG rec. any financial aid	42
% UG borrow to pay for school	42
Average cumulative indebtedness	$37,444
% frosh need fully met	100
% ugrads need fully met	77
Average % of frosh need met	100
Average % of ugrad need met	99

THE BEST 386 COLLEGES ■ 79

BARD COLLEGE

Office of Admissions, Annandale-on-Hudson, NY 12504 • Admissions: 845-758-7472 • Fax: 845-758-5208

STUDENTS SAY "..."

Academics

Bard College is "built on a very unique philosophy of the liberal arts," one that "truly values education for the sake of self-growth." To that end, every student's academic "experience is entirely customizable." Nevertheless, no matter their course load, all undergrads here are taught to think "critically, [to continually ask] questions...and [to follow through on] those questions." But these students wouldn't have it any other way! Certainly, prospective students should take note—the academics here are quite "rigorous." And virtually every major culminates in a massive "senior project" that requires "substantial independent work."

Inside the classroom, students are greeted by "incredible" professors who genuinely "care about teaching and mentoring." They are also "strong researchers as well" and make a concerted effort to "bring their research into [their classes] and into the community." They truly look to "involve students in almost everything they do." As one photography major boasts, "The classes are what make Bard an amazing school. I could not be happier academically."

Life

Though this is a small campus in a small town, there is no lack of engaging activity. For starters, the college itself sponsors "a multitude of cultural events, from having Edward Snowden speak [remotely]...to great bands playing at one of our venues." Bard also has a thriving performing arts scene. "There's probably a student production to see on average every other week or more. Students, [even] as non-majors, can easily produce their own shows. Plus, we have the Fisher Center, a Broadway-sized theatre that often hosts operas, dance troupes, and plays." Undergrads who tend to be more of the outdoorsy type will be thrilled to discover that "Bard is also surrounded by hiking trails, with easy access to our own private waterfall!" Of course, during those cold winter nights, "'Netflix and chill' is a reliable option." Even in inclement weather, "it's generally pretty easy to find people to go build snowmen with or go ice skating." Lastly, for those curious, Bard maintains a "very low-key party scene." A history major further explains, "Most of the larger parties happen at off-campus houses in Red Hook or Tivoli, the two surrounding towns where many students live. It can get repetitive, but I enjoy how you end up seeing/partying with similar people every weekend."

Student Body

When asked to describe their peers, undergrads here are quick to note that their fellow students are "unique, free-spirited, deviant, and epitomize critical thinking." Indeed, the average Bard student loves "intellectual conversations and enjoy[s] rehashing...topics [discussed in class]." An anthropology major further expounds, "We are always critiquing some aspect of the school, then relating this critique to one of the larger societal structures that we live in." Therefore, it's none too surprising when a sociology major tells us that "Bardians are [also] go-getters, self-motivated, driven, and thoughtful. We challenge authority and all social conventions." We've also been assured that "there isn't much competition between students when it comes to grades or classes. People are just supportive of the projects their peers are working on." Many undergrads here readily admit that they "felt in some way like outsiders in high school." Fortunately, once they arrive at Bard, "a lot of people seem to bond over their weirdness." Perhaps this supremely satisfied student puts it best, "I have been spoiled by my friendships here at Bard; I don't know where else I could find people this interesting and relationships this fulfilling."

Financial Aid: 845-758-7526 • E-Mail: admissions@bard.edu • Website: www.bard.edu

THE PRINCETON REVIEW SAYS

Admissions

Very important factors considered include: rigor of secondary school record, academic GPA, application essay, recommendation(s), extracurricular activities, talent/ability, character/personal qualities. *Other factors considered include:* class rank, standardized test scores, interview, first generation, alumni/ae relation, geographical residence, state residency, religious affiliation/commitment, racial/ethnic status, level of applicant's interest. High school diploma is required and GED is accepted. *Academic units recommended:* 4 English, 4 math, 4 science, 3 science labs, 4 foreign language, 4 social studies, 4 history.

Financial Aid

Students should submit: CSS/Financial Aid PROFILE; FAFSA; Noncustodial PROFILE. The Princeton Review suggests that all financial aid forms be submitted as soon as possible after October 1. *Need-based scholarships/grants offered:* College/university scholarship or grant aid from institutional funds; Federal Pell; Private scholarships; SEOG; State scholarships/grants. *Loan aid offered:* Direct PLUS loans; Direct Subsidized Stafford Loans; Direct Unsubsidized Stafford Loans. Applicants will be notified of awards on or about 4/1. Federal Work-Study Program available. Institutional employment available.

The Inside Word

We won't mince words; gaining admission to Bard is definitely competitive. Successful applicants tend to have high school transcripts rife with honors and advanced placement courses. And a strong college prep curriculum is clearly a must. Beyond that, admissions officers want students who appear to be independent thinkers with a thirst for knowledge. After all, those are the type of individuals who will likely take advantage of all Bard has to offer. Lastly, submitting ACT or SAT scores is optional.

THE SCHOOL SAYS "..."

From the Admissions Office

"An alliance with Rockefeller University, the renowned graduate scientific research institution, gives Bardians access to Rockefeller's professors and laboratories and to places in Rockefeller's Summer Research Fellows Program. Almost all our math and science graduates pursue graduate or professional studies; 90 percent of our applicants to medical and health professional schools are accepted.

"The Globalization and International Affairs (BGIA) Program is a residential program in the heart of New York City that offers undergraduates a unique opportunity to undertake specialized study with leading practitioners and scholars in international affairs and to gain internship experience with international-affairs organizations. Topics in the curriculum include human rights, international economics, global environmental issues, international justice, managing international risk, and writing on international affairs, among others. Internships/tutorials are tailored to students' particular fields of study.

"Civic engagement has become a large and growing part of student life at Bard, with a high percentage of students participating in a wide variety of local, national, and international programs sponsored by the college or initiated by students.

"Beyond the central campus, Bard has created global programs and satellite campuses from Berlin to the West Bank, offering students unique opportunities for study abroad and making Bard's student body strongly international."

SELECTIVITY

Admissions Rating	86
# of applicants	5,141
% of applicants accepted	65
% of acceptees attending	15
# of early decision applicants	46
% accepted early decision	89

FRESHMAN PROFILE

Range ACT Composite	27–31
# submitting ACT scores	83
% submitting ACT scores	17
% graduated top 10% of class	41
% graduated top 25% of class	69
% graduated top 50% of class	94

DEADLINES

Early decision	
Deadline	11/1
Notification	1/1
Early action	
Deadline	11/1
Notification	1/1
Regular	
Deadline	1/1
Notification	Rolling, 4/1
Nonfall registration?	No

APPLICANTS ALSO LOOK AT AND OFTEN PREFER

Barnard College; Boston University; Columbia University; Johns Hopkins University; New York University; Northeastern University; Oberlin College; Princeton University; Reed College; Sarah Lawrence College; Tufts University; University of California—Santa Cruz; The University of Chicago

AND SOMETIMES PREFER

Bates College; Bowdoin College; Brandeis University; Brown University; Connecticut College; Grinnell College; Haverford College; Kenyon College; Macalester College; Occidental College; Scripps College; Swarthmore College; Vassar College; Wesleyan University

AND RARELY PREFER

Bennington College; Bryn Mawr College; Colorado College; Hampshire College; Mount Holyoke College; Rhode Island School of Design; Smith College; University of Rochester

FINANCIAL FACTS

Financial Aid Rating	82
Annual tuition	$55,566
Room and board	$15,876
Required fees	$470
Books and supplies	$1,100
Average frosh need-based scholarship	$47,022
Average UG need-based scholarship	$44,444
% needy frosh rec. need-based scholarship or grant aid	97
% needy UG rec. need-based scholarship or grant aid	96
% needy frosh rec. non-need-based scholarship or grant aid	0
% needy UG rec. non-need-based scholarship or grant aid	0
% needy frosh rec. need-based self-help aid	82
% needy UG rec. need-based self-help aid	81
% frosh rec. any financial aid	69
% UG rec. any financial aid	68
% UG borrow to pay for school	57
Average cumulative indebtedness	$27,726
% frosh need fully met	25
% ugrads need fully met	22
Average % of frosh need met	81
Average % of ugrad need met	79

BARNARD COLLEGE

3009 Broadway, New York, NY 10027 • Admissions: 212-854-2014 • Fax: 212-280-8797

CAMPUS LIFE

Quality of Life Rating	**91**
Fire Safety Rating	**79**
Green Rating	**89**
Type of school	Private
Environment	Metropolis

STUDENTS

Total undergrad enrollment	2,557
% male/female	0/100
% from out of state	72
% frosh from public high school	45
% frosh live on campus	99
% ugrads live on campus	91
# of sororities	10
% African American	6
% Asian	15
% Caucasian	52
% Hispanic	12
% Native American	<1
% Pacific Islander	<1
% Two or more races	6
% Race and/or ethnicity unknown	<1
% international	10
# of countries represented	58

SURVEY SAYS . . .

Lots of liberal students
Great library
Career services are great
Students love New York, NY
Great off-campus food
Easy to get around campus

ACADEMICS

Academic Rating	**91**
% students returning for sophomore year	96
% students graduating within 4 years	87
% students graduating within 6 years	93
Calendar	Semester
Student/faculty ratio	9:1
Profs interesting rating	91
Profs accessible rating	94
Most classes have 10–19 students.	

MOST POPULAR MAJORS

English Language and Literature, General;
Economics, General; Psychology, General

STUDENTS SAY "..."

Academics

Barnard is a small school, an urban school, a resource-rich school, a school that "offers so many opportunities." In some ways, Barnard College combines all the desirable traits one would want from an all-women's liberal arts college. Located in New York City, here "you get the best of both worlds," both a "small academic setting" as well as having "full access to the Ivy League institution (Columbia University) right across the street." The school's size means it "provides a small, close community" where students will "see familiar faces often." Among those familiar faces are the professors themselves, who are "really engaging and make the material approachable and interesting." Classes are a mix between lectures and discussions, and even in the larger classes professors "definitely make time for students to come talk to them." Students say educators here are adept at "creating an environment to learn from and be inspired by classmates through the discussions held." The "phenomenal" education experience at Barnard may be "challenging and very stressful" at times, but students are "so grateful" for those challenges. And while the school itself may be small, "you can cross Broadway and feel that large, Ivy League University feel." Graduates from Barnard should expect to experience a "transition from a young female college student to an adjusted global citizen."

Life

Finding things to do at Barnard? "It's easy—we live in New York." When you live in "one of the greatest cities on Earth," you are "open to a wide range of things to do such as shows, film festivals, amazing restaurants, etc." As one student puts it, while there is a thriving party scene on campus, "put down your vodka and go to the Met." Students even enjoy free admission to many such attractions. But while the opportunities for entertainment and cultural activities are limitless in a city like New York—the museums, sports venues, book stores, music venues, cultural centers and more are too numerous to list—"a lot of fun events take place on campus." There are a number of clubs on campus, busy students often spend time "just chilling" because "everyone is working or going to office hours, or pursuing an internship, a personal job, etc.," and neighboring Columbia offers a "phenomenal Greek life" for those interested in that scene. No matter their chosen form of distraction from school work and extracurriculars, students here "are intensely dedicated to pursuing their interests, whether that be artistic, academic, pre-professional, or athletic ones."

Student Body

Finding a single trait to define a school full of "cool, creative, confident, well-spoken, and determined" women who are "aware that [they are] in the cosmopolitan NYC" may seem difficult, but the repeated refrain of students makes it clear that there is something that unites Barnard students: They are ambitious. These are "driven, intelligent" women who are "extremely interested, dedicated, and passionate about something." What that something may be varies—"biology, dance, theatre, architecture, economics, or international relations" and more—but the "strong, powerful, intelligent personalities" make them who they are. These "motivated individuals" sometimes "have a tendency to overload," but "all Barnard women are very proactive and use all resources available...to achieve their goals." That said, while students here are "ambitious, driven, and hard workers," it is "not at the cost of physical or mental health: they know how to have fun, too." Barnard women tend to be well-dressed and embrace the cosmopolitan side of New York City. One student comments, "I know of very few students here who feel they don't fit in or haven't found their niche," and maybe that is because a Barnard student is one who is "smart, independent, and ready to take on the world."

BARNARD COLLEGE

Financial Aid: 212-854-2154 • E-Mail: admissions@barnard.edu • Website: www.barnard.edu

THE PRINCETON REVIEW SAYS

Admissions

Very important factors considered include: rigor of secondary school record, academic GPA, application essay, recommendation(s), character/personal qualities. *Important factors considered include:* class rank, standardized test scores, extracurricular activities, talent/ability, volunteer work. *Other factors considered include:* interview, first generation, alumni/ae relation, geographical residence, racial/ethnic status, level of applicant's interest. ACT with or without writing accepted. SAT with or without Essay component accepted. High school diploma is required and GED is accepted. *Academic units recommended:* 4 English, 3 math, 3 science, 3 foreign language, 3 history.

Financial Aid

Students should submit: CSS/Financial Aid PROFILE; FAFSA; Noncustodial PROFILE; State aid form. The Princeton Review suggests that all financial aid forms be submitted as soon as possible after October 1. *Need-based scholarships/grants offered:* College/university scholarship or grant aid from institutional funds; Federal Pell; Private scholarships; SEOG; State scholarships/grants. *Loan aid offered:* Direct PLUS loans; Direct Subsidized Stafford Loans; Direct Unsubsidized Stafford Loans. Applicants will be notified of awards on or about 3/31. Federal Work-Study Program available. Institutional employment available.

The Inside Word

Barnard may have a highly competitive selection process—indeed, early decision applications have increased dramatically in recent years—but you wouldn't know it based on the admissions staff, who are surprisingly open and accessible. It comes as no surprise that the admission committee's expectations are high, given the school's long and impressive tradition of excellence, but those expectations reflect a genuine interest in who potential students are and what's on their minds.

THE SCHOOL SAYS "..."

From the Admissions Office

"Barnard College is a small, distinguished liberal arts college for women that is partnered with Columbia University and located in the heart of New York City. Barnard students are wide ranging in their interests and passions, but they also share in a distinctive experience that creates an enduring bond: they live and learn in an environment where women always come first, where they're surrounded by other smart and inspiring women, and where they have access to a wide array of opportunities, both on and off campus. The Barnard community thrives on high expectations. By setting rigorous academic standards and giving students the support they need to meet those standards, Barnard enables them to discover their own capabilities.

"The college enrolls women from all over the United States and around the world. More than forty countries, including Australia, Brazil, China, Denmark, France, India, Morocco, Russia, Turkey, and Zimbabwe are represented in the student body. Students pursue their academic studies in more than forty majors and are able to cross register at Columbia University. Students may participate in Division I Varsity Columbia University athletic teams, in more than thirty club sports, and in a wide variety of intramural sports, and have access to over 500 student clubs and organizations at Barnard and Columbia.

"Applicants for the entering class must submit scores from the SAT Reasoning test or the ACT."

SELECTIVITY

Admissions Rating	98
# of applicants	7,897
% of applicants accepted	14
% of acceptees attending	55
# offered a place on the wait list	1,608
% accepting a place on wait list	0
# of early decision applicants	993
% accepted early decision	30

FRESHMAN PROFILE

Range SAT EBRW	670–740
Range SAT Math	660–760
Range ACT Composite	30–33
# submitting SAT scores	352
% submitting SAT scores	58
# submitting ACT scores	309
% submitting ACT scores	51
% graduated top 10% of class	84
% graduated top 25% of class	97
% graduated top 50% of class	100

DEADLINES

Early decision	
Deadline	11/1
Notification	12/15
Regular	
Deadline	1/1
Notification	4/1
Nonfall registration?	No

FINANCIAL FACTS

Financial Aid Rating	90
Annual tuition	$53,252
Room and board	$17,525
Required fees	$1,780
Books and supplies	$1,150
% needy frosh rec. need-based scholarship or grant aid	0
% needy UG rec. need-based scholarship or grant aid	0
% needy frosh rec. non-need-based scholarship or grant aid	0
% needy UG rec. non-need-based scholarship or grant aid	0
% needy frosh rec. need-based self-help aid	0
% needy UG rec. need-based self-help aid	0
% frosh rec. any financial aid	51
% UG rec. any financial aid	47
% frosh need fully met	0
% ugrads need fully met	0
Average % of frosh need met	100
Average % of ugrad need met	100

BATES COLLEGE

23 Campus Avenue, Lewiston, ME 04240 • Admissions: 207-786-6000 • Fax: 207-786-6025

STUDENTS SAY "..."

Academics

Located in Lewiston, Maine, Bates College is a small liberal arts college that invites intellectual exploration and tailors every education to the individual student. This "unbelievably tight-knit community" thrives on an "everyone is welcome" atmosphere and an open classroom environment in which everyone is "challenged to express their opinions, try something new and stand up for a cause." "I've honestly never felt competitive in a class at Bates," says a student. Between academic studies, extracurriculars, volunteering, and employment, students here are known for being "well-rounded, curious, and supportive of all aspects of Bates life." Classes are small here which means that students can really take advantage of their professors' time and attention. The "dynamic" teachers here "make you think and come up with your own opinion about issues." They are "incredibly passionate people who are not afraid to stand on a desk, play devil's advocate, and urge you to think critically about the material you are learning." "The most important thing I've learned so far is how to come up with an intelligent stance on an issue or idea," says a student. A Short Term at the end of the year allows students to explore one subject in depth, and the "flexible calendar" also encourages studying abroad (which the majority of students do). The extensive and "helpful" alumni network demonstrates "a fundamental love for the school," and students are given plenty of additional support through "advising and residential life staff, student leadership opportunities, [and] fun and engaging school-wide traditions." "I couldn't ask for more helpful professors, a more helpful administration, or a variety of classes that suit the needs and requirements of my major," sums up a student.

Life

Bates students are a busy group, but they also appreciate the weekends and having fun with friends. There are "dances, theater productions, and a multitude of other events to go to any day of the week"; students also "really enjoy eating out and going to on-campus events like Wind Down Wednesdays," hosted by various student groups," and "the Village Club Series on Thursdays" when musical groups and performers play for campus. Students say that the Bates security plus a "pretty strict no-hard-alcohol policy" is "quite effective" at restricting underage alcohol consumption as well as maintaining a safe campus environment. The food and dining are "absolutely amazing at Bates": Fare here is "all extremely healthy, organic, and naturally sourced," plus "there's food for every dietary restriction." Opportunities to serve the community surrounding campus are abundant, and students take advantage of the outdoor activities Maine has to offer. The student-run Outing Club, in particular, "hosts events every weekend, from skiing at our nearby mountains to sunrise paddles to backpacking trips" and "has a room full of gear that's free to check out." The nights start early and end early here, mostly because "students want to get up early the next day to ski, hike, or just do something with their day." With Portland and Boston being so close, "you can always switch up your scenery when you need city life."

Student Body

Bates students have a range of interests and passions—"no student does just one thing"—and "are not a judgmental group." Everyone finds their niche, and there "is a ton of crossover and interaction between different people." In order to "fit in" here, a student "just has to be friendly and willing to make new friends." A normal lunch conversation "will span from the divine cheese quesadillas in Commons to the implications of language-use and its impact on creating a culture of apathy and ableism." Many here are New Englanders, so there are a fair number of "really preppy" students, and everyone "enjoys the great outdoors."

Financial Aid: 207-786-6096 • E-Mail: admission@bates.edu • Website: www.bates.edu

THE PRINCETON REVIEW SAYS

Admissions

Very important factors considered include: rigor of secondary school record, class rank, academic GPA, application essay, recommendation(s), extracurricular activities, talent/ability, character/personal qualities, level of applicant's interest. *Important factors considered include:* first generation, geographical residence, state residency. *Other factors considered include:* standardized test scores, interview, alumni/ae relation, racial/ethnic status, volunteer work, work experience. ACT with or without writing accepted. High school diploma is required and GED is not accepted. *Academic units required:* 4 English, 3 math, 3 science, 2 science labs, 2 foreign language, 3 social studies, 3 history. *Academic units recommended:* 4 English, 4 math, 4 science, 3 science labs, 4 foreign language, 4 social studies, 4 history.

Financial Aid

Students should submit: CSS/Financial Aid PROFILE; FAFSA; Noncustodial PROFILE. The Princeton Review suggests that all financial aid forms be submitted as soon as possible after October 1. *Need-based scholarships/grants offered:* College/university scholarship or grant aid from institutional funds; Federal Pell; Private scholarships; SEOG; State scholarships/grants. *Loan aid offered:* Direct PLUS loans; Direct Subsidized Stafford Loans; Direct Unsubsidized Stafford Loans. Applicants will be notified of awards on or about 4/1. Federal Work-Study Program available. Institutional employment available.

The Inside Word

Bates looks for students who challenge themselves in the classroom and beyond. A student's academic rigor, essays, and recommendations may be even more important than his or her GPA and test scores. The essay, in particular, is a chance to stand out—Bates is most interested in what has changed and inspired their applicants. Interviews are encouraged, and candidates who opt out of these face-to-face meetings may place themselves at a disadvantage.

THE SCHOOL SAYS "..."

From the Admissions Office

"Bates College is widely recognized as one of the finest liberal arts colleges in the nation. The curriculum and faculty challenge students to develop the essential skills of critical assessment, analysis, expression, aesthetic sensibility, and independent thought. Founded by abolitionists in 1855, Bates graduates have always included men and women from diverse ethnic and religious backgrounds. Bates highly values its study abroad programs, unique calendar (4-4-1), and the many opportunities available for one-on-one collaboration with faculty through seminars, research, service-learning, and the capstone experience of senior thesis. Co-curricular life at Bates is rich; most students participate in club or varsity sports; many participate in performing arts; and almost all students participate in one of more than 110 student-run clubs and organizations. More than two-thirds of alumni enroll in graduate study within ten years.

"The Bates College Admission Staff reads applications very carefully; the high school record and the quality of writing are of particular importance. Applicants are encouraged to have a personal interview, either on campus or with an alumni representative. Students who choose not to interview may place themselves at a disadvantage in the selection process. Bates offers tours, interviews, and information sessions throughout the summer and fall. Drop-ins are welcome for tours and information sessions. Please call ahead to schedule an interview. At Bates, the submission of standardized testing (the SAT, SAT Subject Tests, and the ACT) is not required for admission. After three decades of optional testing, our research shows no differences in academic performance and graduation rates between submitters and nonsubmitters."

SELECTIVITY

Admissions Rating	96
# of applicants	5,316
% of applicants accepted	22
% of acceptees attending	42
# offered a place on the wait list	1,640
% accepting a place on wait list	47
% admitted from wait list	1
# of early decision applicants	721
% accepted early decision	48

FRESHMAN PROFILE

Range SAT EBRW	640–730
Range SAT Math	630–720
Range ACT Composite	29–32
# submitting SAT scores	209
% submitting SAT scores	41
# submitting ACT scores	191
% submitting ACT scores	37
% graduated top 10% of class	63
% graduated top 25% of class	86
% graduated top 50% of class	97

DEADLINES

Early decision	
Deadline	11/15
Notification	12/20
Other ED Deadline	1/1
Other ED Notification	2/15
Regular	
Deadline	1/1
Notification	4/1

FINANCIAL FACTS

Financial Aid Rating	97
Annual tuition	$55,683
Room and board	$15,705
Books and supplies	$900
Average frosh need-based scholarship	$44,644
Average UG need-based scholarship	$44,590
% needy frosh rec. need-based scholarship or grant aid	100
% needy UG rec. need-based scholarship or grant aid	100
% needy frosh rec. non-need-based scholarship or grant aid	0
% needy UG rec. non-need-based scholarship or grant aid	0
% needy frosh rec. need-based self-help aid	98
% needy UG rec. need-based self-help aid	99
% frosh rec. any financial aid	41.6
% UG rec. any financial aid	42.4
% UG borrow to pay for school	35
Average cumulative indebtedness	$21,525
% frosh need fully met	100
% ugrads need fully met	100
Average % of frosh need met	100
Average % of ugrad need met	100

BAYLOR UNIVERSITY

One Bear Place #97056, Waco, TX 76798-7056 • Admissions: 254-710-3435 • Fax: 254-710-3436

CAMPUS LIFE

Quality of Life Rating	89
Fire Safety Rating	91
Green Rating	60*
Type of school	Private
Affiliation	Baptist
Environment	City

STUDENTS

Total undergrad enrollment	13,948
% male/female	40/60
% from out of state	33
% frosh live on campus	99
% ugrads live on campus	34
# of fraternities (% ugrad men join)	20 (20)
# of sororities (% ugrad women join)	23 (34)
% African American	6
% Asian	7
% Caucasian	62
% Hispanic	16
% Native American	<1
% Pacific Islander	<1
% Two or more races	5
% Race and/or ethnicity unknown	1
% international	4
# of countries represented	75

SURVEY SAYS . . .

Lots of conservative students
Students are happy
Lab facilities are great
Students are very religious
Recreation facilities are great
Very little drug use
Frats and sororities are popular

ACADEMICS

Academic Rating	85
% students returning for sophomore year	88
% students graduating within 4 years	63
% students graduating within 6 years	78
Calendar	Semester
Student/faculty ratio	13:1
Profs interesting rating	89
Profs accessible rating	93

Most classes have 10–19 students.
Most lab/discussion sessions have
10–19 students.

MOST POPULAR MAJORS

Biology/Biological Sciences, General; Registered
Nursing/Registered Nurse; Accounting

STUDENTS SAY "..."

Academics

The oldest continually operating university in Texas, Baylor University offers a "worldly view of academics ... [to] explore where cultures come from." Offering more than 125 undergraduate programs, the focus at Baylor is on critical thinking and analysis with the goal of contributing to the plentiful academic disciplines explored on campus. The school is strongly driven not only by academics but also by faith, "[prioritizing excellence] in school but [holding] faith to a very high standard as well." The school's history and mission statement encourage students to lead and serve worldwide by integrating academics with their Christian commitment. Although they are "pushed daily in studies," Baylor's students still "manage to participate in multiple clubs, have jobs, and stay active in the community."

Because Baylor's campus has "the perfect balance" of space and student population, professors are able to "show genuine care for students" both in terms of academics and personal well-being. Smaller class sizes mean "students can really get to know their professors" and build a professional and personal rapport that fosters the community and family-like feel present on the Baylor campus. In the classroom, students are given "hands-on experience working on real world projects" aimed at professional development. Innovations abound in Baylor's academics with students undergoing flipped classrooms—students lead a discussion rather than attending a traditional lecture—and field trips that take them to locations both near and far. These often take the form of visits to art museums, other religious institutions, and nonprofit organizations for added cultural exposure. The professors "believe we are the people who will change the world and make it a better place," one student says.

Life

With over 330 clubs and organizations, it's no wonder students balance their "rigorous course loads" with plenty of other activities. And with forty sororities and fraternities, that means Baylor's campus features a booming Greek life. Still, many students attend church every Sunday and are encouraged to take part in activities that will "enhance their religious view." Regardless of personal religious affiliations, the entire student body is "full of the Baylor spirit and open to interactions with everyone," and there are many opportunities for student involvement during the week, many of which include local community service.

The campus is located in Waco, Texas, and has bountiful options when it comes to good dining—a variety of food trucks even roll onto campus during larger events. Austin and Dallas are also nearby, and study breaks on weekends are normally spent taking trips to these larger cities. Baylor students seek "outdoorsy" activities, which is easy since the campus and nearby towns all have appealing options: hiking in Cameron Park, hammocking on campus, kayaking on the Brazos River. If they're not opting for outdoor forms of recreation or exercise, they can typically be found working out in the Student Life Center. With nineteen varsity sports, student claims that sports are huge on campus are also clearly true, and sporting events are often cause for the diverse student population to come together. In the fall, almost everyone attends football games; in the spring, almost everyone supports the basketball team.

Student Body

Despite the university's foundation in Christian ideals, students at Baylor have seen "a huge push toward diversity and learning about different cultures." While some students still find frustration in breaking past those traditional beliefs, Baylor has a "strong sense of community" and "everyone is still accepting of one another," a student says. "The campus and student body seem like the perfect size: big enough to where you don't know everyone, but small enough to where you can walk across campus knowing you will see at least one familiar face," says another. Baylor is home to a range of races, backgrounds, and religions, but above all else, the school "brings amazing people onto its campus."

Financial Aid: 254-710-2611 • E-Mail: admissions@baylor.edu • Website: www.baylor.edu

THE PRINCETON REVIEW SAYS

Admissions

Very important factors considered include: academic GPA, rigor of secondary school record, class rank and standardized test scores. *Other factors considered include:* application essay, recommendation(s), extracurricular activities, talent/ability, character/personal qualities, alumni/ae relation, volunteer work, work experience, level of applicant's interest. ACT with or without writing accepted. SAT with or without Essay component accepted. High school diploma is required and GED is accepted. *Academic units recommended:* 4 English, 4 math, 4 science, 2 science labs, 2 foreign language, 2 social studies, 1 history.

Financial Aid

Students should submit: CSS/Financial Aid PROFILE. Priority filing deadline is 2/1. The Princeton Review suggests that all financial aid forms be submitted as soon as possible after October 1. *Need-based scholarships/grants offered:* College/university scholarship or grant aid from institutional funds; Federal Pell; Private scholarships; SEOG; State scholarships/grants. *Loan aid offered:* Direct PLUS loans; Direct Subsidized Stafford Loans; Direct Unsubsidized Stafford Loans. Applicants will be notified of awards on a rolling basis beginning 12/15. Federal Work-Study Program available. Institutional employment available.

The Inside Word

Securing a spot on Baylor's campus doesn't just come down to GPA, class rank, and test scores—it's quite competitive outside of those factors. Prospective students' desire to be a part of a community valuing both faith and personal calling will also be assessed. Admissions officers will consider an essay, recommendation letters, short answer responses, and a résumé to determine which students are a good fit for their mission, also looking for those who express a true interest in becoming a Baylor Bear. Certain majors (such as Engineering and the Baylor Business Fellows program) have additional requirements, and those who plan to apply should investigate requirements thoroughly before doing so.

THE SCHOOL SAYS "..."

From the Admissions Office

"Baylor's mission is to education men and women for worldwide leadership and service by integrating academic excellence and Christian commitment within a caring community. Our professors share a commitment to research and teaching. That means Baylor faculty include some of the nation's foremost scholars who also have a passion for helping you succeed. What else makes Baylor unique? Our belief that the world needs a preeminent research university that is unambiguously Christian. This allows academics, research, and faith to work together. The outcome? Baylor students find both their career and calling in life. Many majors boast a 100% "success rate," meaning students find jobs or start graduate school within 90 days of graduation. When you become a student, you join the Baylor family. Professors and classmates become lifelong friends and your biggest cheerleaders. They will inspire you. Embolden you. Stretch you and walk with you. And you'll do the same for them because, after all, you're family. Traditions bind generations of Baylor students together by a shared experience that transcends culture, trends and time. That's why after graduation, you'll want to return "home" each fall for one of our favorite traditions: Baylor Homecoming."

SELECTIVITY

Admissions Rating	90
# of applicants	34,582
% of applicants accepted	45
% of acceptees attending	21
# offered a place on the wait list	6,884
% accepting a place on wait list	24
% admitted from wait list	49
# of early decision applicants	558
% accepted early decision	88

FRESHMAN PROFILE

Range SAT EBRW	600–680
Range SAT Math	600–700
Range SAT Composite	1210–1370
Range ACT Composite	26–32
# submitting SAT scores	1,599
% submitting SAT scores	49
# submitting ACT scores	1,696
% submitting ACT scores	51
% graduated top 10% of class	44
% graduated top 25% of class	76
% graduated top 50% of class	96

DEADLINES

Early decision	
Deadline	11/2
Notification	12/15
Other ED Deadline	2/1
Other ED Notification	2/15
Early action	
Deadline	11/2
Notification	1/15
Regular	
Deadline	2/1
Nonfall registration?	Yes

FINANCIAL FACTS

Financial Aid Rating	85
Annual tuition	$44,544
Room and board	$14,324
Required fees	$4,892
Books and supplies	$1,284
Average frosh need-based scholarship	$26,522
Average UG need-based scholarship	$26,384
% needy frosh rec. need-based scholarship or grant aid	98
% needy UG rec. need-based scholarship or grant aid	96
% needy frosh rec. non-need-based scholarship or grant aid	96
% needy UG rec. non-need-based scholarship or grant aid	93
% needy frosh rec. need-based self-help aid	75
% needy UG rec. need-based self-help aid	80
% UG borrow to pay for school	51
Average cumulative indebtedness	$49,610
% frosh need fully met	22
% ugrads need fully met	16
Average % of frosh need met	68
Average % of ugrad need met	66

BECKER COLLEGE

61 Sever Street, Worcester, MA 01609 • Admissions: 508-373-9400 • Fax: 508-890-1500

STUDENTS SAY "..."

Academics

At Becker College, a private institution founded in 1784 in the second largest city in New England, undergrads truly feel that their school is dedicated to "helping students achieve their dreams." Students say that the college prides itself on providing a "personal education," one that helps you "push yourself to do your best." And it offers a "small, close-knit community" where everybody can get to know their peers. Academically, Becker allows students the opportunity to pursue a number of great disciplines. Of course, we'd be remiss if we didn't highlight the "outstanding" nursing program and the "very well established and highly successful pre-veterinary program." In addition, the college has "one of the best game design programs in the country." Inside the classroom, undergrads love that so many of their courses involve "one-on-one interaction and class discussions." There's no fear of languishing through boring lectures here! And, certainly, that can be attributed to "great" professors who go out of their way to "include real life examples" in their teaching. Perhaps even more essential, the instructors at Becker "are all very nice and genuinely care about their students' success." An animal care major shares that "all of my professors are very thorough and answer all my questions and concerns. They are easy to meet up with outside of classes." And a fellow animal care student summarizes her classroom experience by stating, "The professors dedicate a lot of their time to make sure that we are studying and working to the best of our abilities."

Life

Becker maintains "a 50/50 split between commuters and residents." However, it's certainly possible to seek out some fun on the weekends. Given Becker's amazing game design and esports program—including a varsity team—it's no surprise that "everybody plays video games here." Beyond simply cozying up with an X-Box, undergrads can also be found playing "Magic: The Gathering," and some ingenious students have even "made their own card games." Even if you're not a gamer, you'll still be able to find activities. Many undergrads tend to congregate by "the pool tables in the student center." There are 14 Division III varsity sports and many activities, including plenty of clubs like the music club, Black Student Union, Ultimate Frisbee, and dance team. And Becker even "sponsors trips every weekend." Semester at Sea and College for Social Innovation Semester in the City programs are available. There is a moderate amount of alcohol consumption, but it doesn't seem to dominate campus life. A nursing student explains, "There are parties off campus, and I do enjoy going to them, but a lot of people choose not to drink." Finally, students enjoy taking advantage of the city of Worcester's many shopping and dining options.

Student Body

Becker undergrads tend to think very highly of their peers. And they assure us that anyone who chooses to attend can "make friends very quickly." This can certainly be attributed to the fact that "almost everyone is easy to talk to" as well as "easygoing." Even shy students can find their place here. The trick is simply to get involved. As one veterinarian science major explains, "Students fit in very well through sports teams and other activities and clubs outside the classroom." Despite having the adjective "nerd" bandied about, we're told that "the campus holds a diverse student body with many different interests." And, if "you play sports, video games, or share a love for animals, you'll fit in." Lastly, a nursing student shares, "what we all have in common is our dedication to our studies and our school. We all work hard in class."

Financial Aid: 508-373-9440 • E-Mail: admissions@becker.edu • Website: www.becker.edu

THE PRINCETON REVIEW SAYS

Admissions

Very important factors considered include: rigor of secondary school record, academic GPA. *Other factors considered include:* class rank, application essay, standardized test scores, recommendation(s), interview, extracurricular activities, first generation, alumni/ae relation, volunteer work, work experience, level of applicant's interest. ACT with or without writing accepted. SAT with or without Essay component accepted. High school diploma is required and GED is accepted. *Academic units recommended:* 4 English, 3 math, 3 science, 2 science labs, 2 foreign language, 2 social studies, 2 history.

Financial Aid

Students should submit: FAFSA. Priority filing deadline is 1/15. The Princeton Review suggests that all financial aid forms be submitted as soon as possible after October 1. *Need-based scholarships/grants offered:* College/university scholarship or grant aid from institutional funds; Federal Pell; Private scholarships; SEOG; State scholarships/grants. *Loan aid offered:* Direct PLUS loans; Direct Subsidized Stafford Loans; Direct Unsubsidized Stafford Loans. Applicants will be notified of awards on a rolling basis beginning 12/15. Federal Work-Study Program available. Institutional employment available.

The Inside Word

Applicants interested in attending Becker must have taken a college preparatory curriculum. And, to be considered strong candidates, they need to have earned a minimum GPA of 3.0. While the essay and letter of recommendation are optional, Becker says that if submitted they are useful in considering each applicant's personal strengths and achievements. A final note: Becker is test optional, but students are required to indicate at the time of application whether they will submit test scores. However, the College does require SAT or ACT scores to be admitted into specific majors, so visit Becker's website to ensure you supply them if necessary.

THE SCHOOL SAYS "..."

From the Admissions Office

"Becker College offers master's, bachelor's and select associate's degrees in a range of disciplines, and adult learning programs. Becker College students are engaged socially, academically, and athletically. Our students receive transformational learning experiences that prepare graduates to contribute to a global society that is increasingly focused on change. We emphasize The Agile Mindset, which encourages creative, divergent thinking, social responsibility, empathy, and cultivating skills to work collaboratively in cross-cultural environments. These skills are learned while engaging in all aspects of the college—from academics, community service, and student leadership, to campus activities, clubs, and social interaction. We also are committed to preparing students to be world ready for the rapidly changing and complex job market by offering unique, trans-disciplinary career pathways and learning experiences, and the development of the agile mindset in all graduates. We are proud of our placement rate for employment or further study, which averages over 90 percent.

"Our admissions process reflects the Becker College philosophy that each student is a unique individual. Because of this, our requirements allow you to put your best foot forward and provide as much information as possible about who you are, what you hope to accomplish during your time at Becker College, and what you hope to do upon graduation.

"The admissions process is personal and unique for each applicant. To be considered for admission, applicants must submit a completed application along with an official high school transcript and official SAT/ACT test score results. Transfer students must submit an official college transcript. Admission requirements vary by program.

"Due to the rigorous admission standards for many of our programs, the most academically qualified applicants will be selected for admission."

SELECTIVITY

Admissions Rating	77
# of applicants	2,902
% of applicants accepted	70
% of acceptees attending	13

FRESHMAN PROFILE

Range SAT EBRW	480–590
Range SAT Math	470–580
Range ACT Composite	17–24
# submitting SAT scores	214
% submitting SAT scores	83
# submitting ACT scores	16
% submitting ACT scores	6
Average HS GPA	3.2

DEADLINES

Early action	
Deadline	11/15
Notification	12/15
Regular	
Priority	2/15
Notification	Rolling, 11/15
Nonfall registration?	Yes

FINANCIAL FACTS

Financial Aid Rating	84
Annual tuition	$36,300
Room and board	$13,800
Required fees	$3,850
Books and supplies	$960
Average frosh need-based scholarship	$19,517
Average UG need-based scholarship	$17,856
% needy frosh rec. need-based scholarship or grant aid	100
% needy UG rec. need-based scholarship or grant aid	97
% needy frosh rec. non-need-based scholarship or grant aid	0
% needy UG rec. non-need-based scholarship or grant aid	9
% needy frosh rec. need-based self-help aid	100
% needy UG rec. need-based self-help aid	100
% frosh rec. any financial aid	99
% UG rec. any financial aid	99
% frosh need fully met	1
% ugrads need fully met	20
Average % of frosh need met	58
Average % of ugrad need met	55

BELLARMINE UNIVERSITY

2001 Newburg Road, Louisville, KY 40205 • Admissions: 502-272-8131 • Fax: 502-272-8002

STUDENTS SAY "..."

Academics

Located at the edge of Louisville, this small Catholic university offers fifty majors and "seeks to benefit the public interest, to help create the future, and to improve the human condition." A "superb teaching staff," a recently renovated library, and an Academic Resource Center with free tutoring cohere to deliver a "challenging but rewarding" academic experience for students. The nursing program is a big draw here, as are Bellarmine's study abroad programs in sixty-eight countries, which more than a third of students avail themselves of. Generous financial aid only sweetens the pot. In line with its mission, Bellarmine University "seeks to train its students in the love of truth and equips them with the skills and tools necessary (e.g., critical thinking, problem solving) to live an enriched life."

The "insightful and dedicated" professors are almost always available to answer questions or concerns, and "want their students to pass their class with as much knowledge as possible." Because of the small class sizes ("I have one class with seven students," reports an actuarial science major), students are able to have one-on-one discussions with their professors. Most professors at Bellarmine "even provide their personal cell phones to students on their syllabi." This access to professors "really [establishes] an ability to grow closer to future employers and be willing to open up with them about issues, concerns, or ideas." Material is often taught through real-world applications, and many teachers will even "help you find internships and jobs." Though students admit that some adjunct professors can be below par, "Bellarmine takes their course evaluations pretty seriously and assesses the situation quickly."

Life

People here are "very studious" during the week, but weekends offer plenty of options for socializing. A major hub of the city (Bardstown Road) is nearby, providing lots of little shops, restaurants, and bars, and the campus is close to the Louisville Zoological Garden, a park where students can often be found "playing and hanging out." The university also coordinates off-campus actives such as "Knight at the Movies" (the knight is Bellarmine's mascot), ice skating, and concerts, and students can take advantage of the Louisville Connections program, which offers "free tickets to events or places around Louisville, such as to Dracula at Actors Theatre, a day at Kentucky Kingdom, or a day horseback riding."

On campus, most people "hang around Cafe Ogle in between classes, sipping on coffee and working on their laptops." Bellarmine's men's basketball team draws huge crowds, and the school has "a niche, club or activity for everyone" (and "encourages and supports any club a student would like to create"). There are also events like "Late Knight Bingo, which is a huge Bingo party where students can win really awesome prizes," Homecoming, and "Ball on the Belle (a Halloween dance on the [steamboat] Belle of Louisville)." The campus itself is both beautiful and "small enough to be easily traversed if you only have 10 minutes between classes and need to be across campus."

Student Body

Though mostly white and from Kentucky and neighboring states, this is a socially wide-ranging group considering the small size of the student body, which naturally allows "blobbing of the social groups." The school is "welcoming to every single person and makes an effort to include everyone." "We are exposed to different cultures and customs from around the world seeing that our student body is so diverse," says a student. "I can't say I've ever met a stranger," says a student. Everyone is always willing to help and "comfort you with just a simple smile on their face." The strong athletic programs are never placed above academics, and "most all the athletes are also amazing students."

Financial Aid: 502-272-4723 • E-Mail: admissions@bellarmine.edu • Website: http://www.bellarmine.edu

THE PRINCETON REVIEW SAYS

Admissions

Very important factors considered include: rigor of secondary school record, academic GPA, standardized test scores, recommendation(s), character/personal qualities, level of applicant's interest. *Important factors considered include:* class rank, extracurricular activities. *Other factors considered include:* application essay, interview, talent/ability, first generation, alumni/ae relation, geographical residence, state residency, racial/ethnic status, volunteer work, work experience. ACT with or without writing accepted. SAT with or without Essay component accepted. High school diploma is required and GED is accepted. *Academic units required:* 4 English, 3 math, 3 science, 2 science labs, 2 foreign language, 2 social studies, 1 history, 5 academic electives. *Academic units recommended:* 4 English, 4 math, 4 science, 2 science labs, 2 foreign language, 3 social studies, 2 history, 7 academic electives.

Financial Aid

Students should submit: FAFSA. Priority filing deadline is 11/1. The Princeton Review suggests that all financial aid forms be submitted as soon as possible after October 1. *Need-based scholarships/grants offered:* College/university scholarship or grant aid from institutional funds; Federal Pell; Private scholarships; SEOG; State scholarships/grants. *Loan aid offered:* Direct PLUS loans; Direct Subsidized Stafford Loans; Direct Unsubsidized Stafford Loans. Applicants will be notified of awards on a rolling basis beginning 1/31. Federal Work-Study Program available. Institutional employment available.

The Inside Word

Admissions at Bellarmine University is relatively competitive. However, as you would expect from their mission statement, the admissions committee takes a holistic approach to applications, and is looking for a well-rounded candidate whose qualifications reflect more than the sum total of a GPA and test scores. Recommendations and personal statements—which should present a strong picture of the student's educational goals—volunteer experiences, and extracurricular commitments, hold significant weight. Candidates with strong grades and diverse interests are likely to earn acceptance.

THE SCHOOL SAYS "..."

From the Admissions Office

"Bellarmine University prepares students for success through a liberal arts education, combined with training for mastery in a specialized area. We offer more than fifty majors in the arts and sciences, humanities, education, communication, business, environmental studies, nursing and health science, plus graduate programs in nursing, education, physical therapy, business and communication. We engage students in state-of-the-art classrooms and expand their horizons through internship and study abroad opportunities. Bellarmine delivers this world-class education just five miles from downtown Louisville, the nation's sixteenth largest city. The 175-acre campus is set in a safe, historic and eclectic neighborhood, and features a fitness center, tennis courts, athletic fields and two new dining halls. With more than fifty clubs and organizations, twenty NCAA Division II athletic teams, plus Division I men's lacrosse, Bellarmine offers a variety of recreational opportunities for all students. Students who reside on campus also find a Bellarmine difference in the living arrangements. From traditional residence halls to apartment-style and suite living arrangements, students have many housing options to choose from; the newest residence halls surround a Tuscan-style piazza. As Bellarmine attracts more residential students, the university has created more gathering spaces for them, such as the café on the ground floor of the Siena Primo residence hall. New learning communities cater to residents and commuters alike, offering opportunities for focused, collaborative studies on topics such as leadership, healthcare, science and technology."

SELECTIVITY

Admissions Rating	75
# of applicants	5,535
% of applicants accepted	86
% of acceptees attending	14

FRESHMAN PROFILE

Range SAT EBRW	540–640
Range SAT Math	520–630
Range ACT Composite	22–28
# submitting SAT scores	121
% submitting SAT scores	19
# submitting ACT scores	595
% submitting ACT scores	91
Average HS GPA	3.6

DEADLINES

Early action	
Deadline	11/1
Notification	11/15
Regular	
Priority	2/1
Deadline	8/15
Notification	Rolling, 9/1
Nonfall registration?	Yes

FINANCIAL FACTS

Financial Aid Rating	86
Annual tuition	$40,880
Room and board	$9,420
Required fees	$1,950
Books and supplies	$752
Average frosh need-based scholarship	$30,751
Average UG need-based scholarship	$27,188
% needy frosh rec. need-based scholarship or grant aid	100
% needy UG rec. need-based scholarship or grant aid	98
% needy frosh rec. non-need-based scholarship or grant aid	32
% needy UG rec. non-need-based scholarship or grant aid	30
% needy frosh rec. need-based self-help aid	72
% needy UG rec. need-based self-help aid	69
% UG borrow to pay for school	71
Average cumulative indebtedness	$29,095
% frosh need fully met	25
% ugrads need fully met	22
Average % of frosh need met	82
Average % of ugrad need met	77

BELOIT COLLEGE

700 College St., Beloit, WI 53511 • Admissions: 608-363-2500 • Fax: 608-363-2075

STUDENTS SAY "..."

Academics

A small liberal arts college in southern Wisconsin, Beloit College offers students "small class sizes, [and] expansive study abroad opportunities" in an academic environment "that encourages debate and discovery." Beloit "embraces individuality" by giving students "freedom to study what they are passionate about." The student-designed "academic paths really can be customized to suit every student's needs, interests, and goals." One student explains that Beloit cultivates "critical thinkers who can put the liberal arts in practice." The college curriculum stresses "intensive essay writing and an emphasis on self-identity." One molecular biology major characterizes this approach by explaining, "There is no such thing as a one-sided problem—at Beloit we ask the hard questions and approach solutions in a multidisciplinary manner that requires critical thinking, collaboration, and creativity." Beloiters describe their academic experiences as "nothing short of phenomenal." As one student explains, "My first day of classes teachers already knew my name by the time I sat down at the desk." Students benefit from "many one-on-one experiences, hands-on classes, and project-based learning." Because of the low student-to-faculty ratio and "motivated student body, it is possible to have close relationships with faculty that make for a more enriching college experience." And students relish those relationships, describing their professors as "easily accessible," "dynamic and knowledgeable." "They have different ways of making us learn and are generally nice and open," one student notes. Beloit professors also prove to be "very good resources for helping you with research, internships, and graduate school applications and program decisions." Students appreciate that their professors "bring unique perspectives to class material, and the small class size allows them the flexibility to tailor the courses to their students."

Campus Life

Beloit is "decorated by its open, welcoming community." Students say that "there is a lot of freedom for students to learn from their mistakes while living on campus and to make their own decisions. Students at Beloit are responsible for taking initiative in their decisions to learn, both in the classroom and out." Students report that there is a fair amount of "drinking on the weekend" but that "it's usually done pretty safely." Even though it is a small school, there is plenty on campus to keep students occupied: "Whether it's a Greek event, Black Lives Matter panel, new movie screenings, school sponsored trip to a haunted house or musical, or our professors' band is playing in the quad, there is always something going on." Sports and extracurricular activities are also popular as "everyone is a part of at least one club, and usually several." As spring rolls around students look forward "to Spring Day," a day without classes when students enjoy "giant inflatable bouncy houses, caricature artists, free junk food, and the martial arts demonstration."

Student Body

Many students celebrate the "outstanding diversity of the student body," including "a large international student population on campus and domestic students [who] come from all over the United States." Others point out that, "while there is diversity on campus,...the campus is also overwhelmingly white." Beloiters are predominantly liberal and "very engaged students and citizens, who are passionate about various causes and their academics." Most agree that students aren't afraid to address tough subjects and seek out "different opinions, backgrounds, and ideas that allow [them] to explore things outside of [their] comfort zone socially, personally, and intellectually." Even for "students who have felt out of place before" arriving at college, Beloit provides "a safe space to learn." "Beloit College students are a mixed bunch." One student explains, "[We're] unafraid to be different, and aesthetically unmatched by any other student body."

BELOIT COLLEGE

Financial Aid: 608-363-2663 • E-Mail: admiss@beloit.edu • Website: www.beloit.edu

THE PRINCETON REVIEW SAYS

Admissions

Very important factors considered include: rigor of secondary school record, academic GPA, application essay, recommendation(s). *Important factors considered include:* extracurricular activities, talent/ability. *Other factors considered include:* class rank, standardized test scores, interview, character/personal qualities, first generation, alumni/ae relation, racial/ethnic status, volunteer work, work experience, level of applicant's interest. ACT with or without writing accepted. SAT with or without Essay component accepted. High school diploma is required and GED is accepted. *Academic units recommended:* 4 English, 3 math, 3 science, 3 science labs, 2 foreign language, 3 social studies.

Financial Aid

Students should submit: FAFSA. The Princeton Review suggests that all financial aid forms be submitted as soon as possible after October 1. *Need-based scholarships/grants offered:* College/university scholarship or grant aid from institutional funds; Federal Pell; Private scholarships; SEOG; State scholarships/grants. *Loan aid offered:* Direct PLUS loans; Direct Subsidized Stafford Loans; Direct Unsubsidized Stafford Loans. Federal Work-Study Program available. Institutional employment available.

The Inside Word

Beloit wants to see a rigorous academic transcript but also emphasizes a holistic approach that focuses on getting to know the student behind the application. The admission office prefers to receive a letter of recommendation from a teacher who taught you during your junior year, but it is most important to select someone who can provide the most insight to you as a student. Standardized test scores are optional for most applicants. Interviews can be arranged through Skype by contacting the school.

THE SCHOOL SAYS "..."

From the Admissions Office

"Beloiters spend four years challenged to explore their passions, excel in their studies, and apply the lessons of the classroom to the larger world, in their careers, and in service to others. That focus—putting the liberal arts into practice—has long set this college and its graduates apart. Study abroad, internships, research, service, and work opportunities are typical examples of the ways the Beloit experience extends beyond the classroom. Beloit students are more apt to value learning for its own sake and at the same time, understand the connection between college and the rest of their lives as citizens of the world.

"Beloit College accepts the Common Application, Beloit Application, Universal, or Coalition for Access, Affordability, and Success Application. Submission of ACT or SAT test scores is optional for most applicants; the college abides by a holistic review process and looks at the overall strength of an applicant's academic programs and performance, essays, and recommendations. Beloit offers two binding early decision plans with a deadline of either November 1 or January 15; notifications by December 1 or February 15, respectively. The college also has two nonbinding early action plans with deadlines of either November 1 or December 1; notifications by December 1 and January 1, respectively. The preferred deadline for regular decision applicants is January 15, with decision notification rolling through mid-March."

SELECTIVITY	
Admissions Rating	86
# of applicants	4,200
% of applicants accepted	56
% of acceptees attending	11
# offered a place on the wait list	69
% accepting a place on wait list	83
% admitted from wait list	26
# of early decision applicants	71
% accepted early decision	27

FRESHMAN PROFILE	
Range SAT EBRW	570–670
Range SAT Math	550–690
Range ACT Composite	21–29
# submitting SAT scores	81
% submitting SAT scores	30
# submitting ACT scores	79
% submitting ACT scores	30
Average HS GPA	3.3
% graduated top 10% of class	15
% graduated top 25% of class	56
% graduated top 50% of class	87

DEADLINES	
Early decision	
Deadline	11/1
Notification	12/1
Other ED Deadline	1/15
Other ED Notification	2/15
Early action	
Deadline	12/1
Notification	1/1
Regular	
Priority	1/15
Notification	4/1
Nonfall registration?	Yes

FINANCIAL FACTS	
Financial Aid Rating	91
Annual tuition	$51,050
Room and board	$9,360
Required fees	$482
Books and supplies	$1,000
Average frosh need-based scholarship	$38,277
Average UG need-based scholarship	$35,970
% needy frosh rec. need-based scholarship or grant aid	98
% needy UG rec. need-based scholarship or grant aid	98
% needy frosh rec. non-need-based scholarship or grant aid	54
% needy UG rec. non-need-based scholarship or grant aid	49
% needy frosh rec. need-based self-help aid	80
% needy UG rec. need-based self-help aid	83
% frosh rec. any financial aid	99
% UG rec. any financial aid	99
% UG borrow to pay for school	56
Average cumulative indebtedness	$31,675
% frosh need fully met	30
% ugrads need fully met	29
Average % of frosh need met	95
Average % of ugrad need met	95

BENNINGTON COLLEGE

One College Drive, Bennington, VT 05201 • Admissions: 802-440-4312 • Fax: 802-440-4320

CAMPUS LIFE

Quality of Life Rating	88
Fire Safety Rating	96
Green Rating	60*
Type of school	Private
Environment	Village

STUDENTS

Total undergrad enrollment	702
% male/female	35/65
% from out of state	96
% frosh from public high school	59
% frosh live on campus	99
% ugrads live on campus	98
# of fraternities	0
# of sororities	0
% African American	4
% Asian	1
% Caucasian	58
% Hispanic	10
% Native American	<1
% Pacific Islander	<1
% Two or more races	4
% Race and/or ethnicity unknown	3
% international	20
# of countries represented	60

SURVEY SAYS . . .

Lots of liberal students
Students always studying
Students are happy
Classroom facilities are great
Great library
Internships are widely available
Class discussions encouraged
No one cheats
Students aren't religious
Students environmentally aware
Dorms are like palaces
Easy to get around campus
Theater is popular
Active minority support groups

ACADEMICS

Academic Rating	96
% students returning for sophomore year	83
% students graduating within 4 years	66
% students graduating within 6 years	76
Calendar	Semester
Student/faculty ratio	10:1
Profs interesting rating	99
Profs accessible rating	97

Most classes have 10–19 students.

MOST POPULAR MAJORS

English Language and Literature, General; Visual and Performing Arts, General; Social Sciences, General

STUDENTS SAY "..."

Academics

A small, private liberal arts college tucked away in Southern Vermont, Bennington College maintains an academic philosophy that encourages a particularly high level of "independence," "creativity," and "critical thinking" among its student body. Bennington offers small, discussion-based classes, no core requirements, and individualized plans of study. Instead of majors and minors, students participate in a "Plan Process," where they design their own four-year curriculum with a strong "support system of advisors and committees." Faculty members are working practitioners in their field who are "driven and passionate," "highly accessible," "engaging," and "often feel like personal mentors." Students also note that their relationships with faculty feel less typically "hierarchal," with "transparent pedagogy," opportunities for midterm feedback, and student-professor relationships operating on a first-name basis. Coursework is generally "reading and writing-intensive," and it's far more common to see students working on a "project or essay" during finals than cramming for an exam. Students are also required to complete a "field work term"—each student spends seven weeks in an internship that can set them on a professional path and give them valuable connections that are useful after graduation.

Life

Bennington College students often have a "high workload in many disciplines, so a majority of time is spent studying or producing work." While some say that Bennington students "are very social...spend a lot of time together..." and "tend to work in communal spaces" instead of private rooms, others point out that students can be especially focused on their personal work and projects because they are so "passionate." Make no mistake: Bennington, Vermont is small-town living. With a car, you can go into town and see a movie, take mountain hikes, go on "runs through North Bennington," or "swim in Lake Paran when it's warm." But students have plenty of opportunities to socialize on campus. These might include Friday and Saturday night dance parties and "formal and informal" evening events spotlighting speakers, musicians, and other visiting performers. Other on-campus activities include "trivia nights and karaoke," and "film screenings and art shows." The residential houses at Bennington "are small and foster unique cultures and communities, so many students are comfortable relaxing with housemates in the house common rooms."

Student Body

Students at Bennington are by and large "passionate," "independent," "creative," "liberal," "hard-working and driven." "Students here are the very definition of unique," says one student. "There are many students who have interesting style, hobbies, and interests and it creates a really exciting atmosphere." While student's individualized academic plans are interdisciplinary in nature, providing opportunities for broad studies across the liberal arts and sciences, students report an emphasis on "niche work" by an "introspective" and "extremely eclectic group of students with a unifying sense of oddness." With just over 700 students, the small student body is "tight-knit." Some note that, given the self-directed nature of students' work and projects, students can "create a bubble," with work that can be overly "abstract." Yet "the community is very accepting, constructive, and there is little peer-pressure or competition." One student reports that "there's very little separation between social life and the classroom, in a way that can often feel intense." If issues related to "racial power dynamics" and "socio-economic class structures" arise, Bennington's small, "interconnected community" means "people have to work through these [issues] and understand them in different lights to move forward." "Bennington's students care as much about interpersonal and social relationships as they do work," says one student. "This isn't to the detriment of academia or the work itself but...an invigorator of collaboration and conversation."

Financial Aid: 800-833-6845 • E-Mail: admissions@bennington.edu • Website: www.bennington.edu

THE PRINCETON REVIEW SAYS

Admissions

Very important factors considered include: rigor of secondary school record, academic GPA, application essay, recommendation(s), interview, talent/ability, character/personal qualities. *Other factors considered include:* class rank, standardized test scores, extracurricular activities, first generation, racial/ethnic status, volunteer work, work experience. ACT with or without writing accepted. SAT with or without Essay component accepted. High school diploma is required and GED is accepted. *Academic units required:* 4 English. *Academic units recommended:* 4 math, 4 science, 3 science labs, 4 foreign language, 4 social studies.

Financial Aid

Students should submit: CSS/Financial Aid PROFILE; FAFSA; Institution's own financial aid form; Noncustodial PROFILE. Priority filing deadline is 1/3. The Princeton Review suggests that all financial aid forms be submitted as soon as possible after October 1. *Need-based scholarships/grants offered:* College/university scholarship or grant aid from institutional funds; Federal Pell; Private scholarships; SEOG; State scholarships/grants. *Loan aid offered:* Direct PLUS loans; Direct Subsidized Stafford Loans; Direct Unsubsidized Stafford Loans. Applicants will be notified of awards on or about 3/27. Federal Work-Study Program available. Institutional employment available.

The Inside Word

In addition to the Common Application, Bennington invites prospective students to submit "a collection of your work that reflects your capacities and demonstrates creativity, curiosity, and readiness to meet the demands of a Bennington education." Interviews and campus visits are recommended if possible, SAT and ACT test scores are optional to the application, and students who choose the open-form Dimensional Application are encouraged to submit thoughtful, creative supplemental materials. There are multiple early application deadlines in addition to regular admission—checking the website is recommended.

THE SCHOOL SAYS "..."

From the Admissions Office

"At Bennington, your education is unified and fueled by your intellect and imagination, guided by a rigorous and ongoing conversation with your faculty, and shaped by your experience working in the world each year. Bennington is the only college to require that its students spend a term—every year—at work in the world. And its new Center for the Advancement of Public Action provides a unique opportunity for students to explore how the questions that matter to them come together with the questions that matter to the world. Rooted in an abiding faith in the talent, imagination, and responsibility of the individual, Bennington invites students to pursue and shape their own intellectual inquiries and, in doing so, to discover the profound interconnection of things.

"Submission of standardized test scores (the SAT, SAT Subject Tests, or the ACT) is optional."

SELECTIVITY
Admissions Rating	88
# of applicants	1,344
% of applicants accepted	61
% of acceptees attending	22
# offered a place on the wait list	132
% accepting a place on wait list	57
% admitted from wait list	35
# of early decision applicants	59
% accepted early decision	51

FRESHMAN PROFILE
Range SAT EBRW	660–740
Range SAT Math	590–700
Range ACT Composite	29–32
# submitting SAT scores	58
% submitting SAT scores	34
# submitting ACT scores	23
% submitting ACT scores	13
Average HS GPA	3.5
% graduated top 10% of class	29
% graduated top 25% of class	69
% graduated top 50% of class	91

DEADLINES
Early decision	
Deadline	11/15
Notification	12/13
Other ED Deadline	1/15
Other ED Notification	2/7
Early action	
Deadline	12/1
Notification	1/31
Regular	
Deadline	1/15
Nonfall registration?	Yes

FINANCIAL FACTS
Financial Aid Rating	87
Annual tuition	$57,350
Room and board	$16,840
Required fees	$1,349
Books and supplies	$1,000
Average frosh need-based scholarship	$44,614
Average UG need-based scholarship	$41,440
% needy frosh rec. need-based scholarship or grant aid	93
% needy UG rec. need-based scholarship or grant aid	92
% needy frosh rec. non-need-based scholarship or grant aid	10
% needy UG rec. non-need-based scholarship or grant aid	8
% needy frosh rec. need-based self-help aid	80
% needy UG rec. need-based self-help aid	80
% frosh rec. any financial aid	93
% UG rec. any financial aid	91
% UG borrow to pay for school	61
Average cumulative indebtedness	$29,443
% frosh need fully met	25
% ugrads need fully met	14
Average % of frosh need met	86
Average % of ugrad need met	83

BENTLEY UNIVERSITY

175 Forest Street, Waltham, MA 02452 • Admissions: 781-891-2244 • Fax: 781-891-3414

CAMPUS LIFE

Quality of Life Rating	89
Fire Safety Rating	99
Green Rating	98
Type of school	Private
Environment	Town

STUDENTS

Total undergrad enrollment	4,157
% male/female	59/41
% from out of state	58
% frosh from public high school	64
% frosh live on campus	97
% ugrads live on campus	78
# of fraternities (% ugrad men join)	7 (5)
# of sororities (% ugrad women join)	4 (10)
% African American	4
% Asian	9
% Caucasian	58
% Hispanic	7
% Native American	<1
% Pacific Islander	0
% Two or more races	3
% Race and/or ethnicity unknown	4
% international	15
# of countries represented	68

SURVEY SAYS . . .
Lots of conservative students
Students are happy
Classroom facilities are great
Great library
Career services are great
Internships are widely available
Hard liquor is popular

ACADEMICS

Academic Rating	81
% students returning for sophomore year	92
% % students graduating within 4 years	85
% students graduating within 6 years	90
Calendar	Semester
Student/faculty ratio	11:1
Profs interesting rating	88
Profs accessible rating	91

Most classes have 20–29 students.

MOST POPULAR MAJORS
Finance, General; Business, Management,
Marketing, and Related Support Services, Other;
Business Administration and Management,
General

STUDENTS SAY "..."

Academics

Though Bentley University leads with its reputation as a business school, don't underestimate the breadth of its curriculum, which draws a comprehensive liberal arts element into its advanced business curriculum. The 4,200 undergraduates who attend this Massachusetts school gain "excellent technical knowledge and skills and [can choose from a] variety of business disciplines." The strong business curriculum (finance and accounting "are Bentley's bread and butter") is "dominated by relevant coursework," and it shows in the placement rates: more than 97 percent of students are employed or in graduate school within six months of graduation. Some classes run in conjunction with each other, "enhancing what students learn and take away from those courses," and many feature supplemental presentations outside of class in which students gain insights from working professionals. There's an academic program for everyone interested in business, with "niches for any unique students" and "plenty of opportunities for students to get involved."

Classrooms and teaching techniques take advantage of advanced technology, and in recent years, Bentley has "focused on growing students' soft skills by incorporating multiple group projects." Professors work hard to teach their subjects well and ensure students understand the topics, and many instructors "[have] industry experience and in-depth education prior to arriving at Bentley." The "above and beyond" Career Services office "does a great job of prepping students for life ahead," and classes are "relevant and feature real learning." To wit: "Even the General Education subjects are designed to be applicable in the corporate world."

Life

Everyone at Bentley has "a strong focus on jobs, internships, and résumé building," so much of students' free time goes to interest-based extracurriculars, which consist of clubs and activities (such as the student-run Bentley Investment Group) that "offer students an opportunity to explore their interests [and] acquire new knowledge and skills." Still, "students are able to prioritize work, but when we are finished up we have some fun." Most students are "part of an organization, whether it be Greek life or a club." On the weekends, there are usually some parties but "there is no pressure to go. They are fun but not a major part of life on campus." Fraternities are off-campus, and as such, "the frat-mosphere is not nearly as pronounced as the hyper-focus on where [you are] steering your career." "We hang out and discuss a lot of different ideas about business-related externalities.... It's the entire culture," says one student. The campus activities board "makes sure there are events throughout the week and weekends for people to attend that are school-sanctioned," and other fun activities around campus include attending Division 1 hockey games in the school's brand new sports complex, as well as "events that [the Campus Activities Board] constantly promotes."

Student Body

"Motivated" is the number one way to describe "driven yet collaborative" Bentley students, and most people "take academics extremely seriously" and "spend most of their time at the library or the stock trading room on campus." That said, people here are "very outgoing and involved in a range of activities on campus" and are "diverse in culture and educational experience, with broad perspectives from industries and countries across the world." Regardless of background, "everyone understands the language of business." There are a large number of international students, and "a lot more men than women." The student body is "a little bit cliquey, but alright in general," and there is "a sense of mutual respect among peers."

Financial Aid: 781-891-3441 • E-Mail: ugadmission@bentley.edu • Website: https://www.bentley.edu

THE PRINCETON REVIEW SAYS

Admissions

Very important factors considered include: rigor of secondary school record, academic GPA, standardized test scores. *Important factors considered include:* application essay, recommendation(s), extracurricular activities, talent/ability, character/personal qualities. *Other factors considered include:* class rank, interview, first generation, alumni/ae relation, geographical residence, state residency, racial/ethnic status, work experience. ACT with or without writing accepted. SAT with or without Essay component accepted. High school diploma is required and GED is accepted. *Academic units required:* 4 English, 4 math, 3 science, 2 science labs, 3 foreign language, 3 social studies. *Academic units recommended:* 4 English, 4 math, 3 science, 2 science labs, 3 foreign language, 4 social studies.

Financial Aid

Students should submit: Business/Farm Supplement; CSS/Financial Aid PROFILE; FAFSA; Noncustodial PROFILE. The Princeton Review suggests that all financial aid forms be submitted as soon as possible after October 1. *Need-based scholarships/grants offered:* College/university scholarship or grant aid from institutional funds; Federal Pell; Private scholarships; SEOG; State scholarships/grants; State loans. *Loan aid offered:* Direct PLUS loans; Direct Subsidized Stafford Loans; Direct Unsubsidized Stafford Loans. Applicants will be notified of awards on or about 4/1. Federal Work-Study Program available. Institutional employment available.

The Inside Word

If you're thinking about stacking your senior year electives with business classes in order to impress the Bentley admissions officers, think again. Taking a broad array of classes that challenge your skills, at AP level if possible, is your best approach. Whether in English, history/social sciences, math, lab sciences, and foreign language, the admissions committee wants to see academic diversity. And be sure your grades and test scores are up to snuff, because you'll have plenty of competition.

THE SCHOOL SAYS "..."

From the Admissions Office

"Bentley is an internationally recognized business university known for integrating business with the arts and sciences. Students learn in an unmatched collection of high-tech learning labs and benefit from close working relationships with faculty who collaborate across disciplines. Bentley students are highly sought after by today's leading organizations because of their classwork with corporate clients, service-learning projects and valuable internship experiences.

"More than 97 percent of 2019 graduates were employed or enrolled in graduate school within six months of commencement. Their success was recognized by The Princeton Review in 2019 as Bentley was ranked number one for 'Best Career Services.'

"Approximately 97 percent of freshmen live on campus. Students live and learn in a diverse environment that prepares them to thrive in today's diverse work world. International students representing nearly 100 countries are part of the Bentley community. There are more than 100 student organizations, as well as abundant intramurals, recreational sports, and 23 varsity teams in NCAA Divisions I and II. Bentley's location in Waltham, Massachusetts—minutes from Boston—puts the city's many resources within easy reach. Bentley's free shuttle makes regular trips to Harvard Square in Cambridge, just a subway ride from the heart of Boston. Boston also offers students many opportunities for internships and jobs after graduation."

SELECTIVITY

Admissions Rating	90
# of applicants	9,017
% of applicants accepted	47
% of acceptees attending	22
# offered a place on the wait list	1,460
% accepting a place on wait list	27
% admitted from wait list	23
# of early decision applicants	339
% accepted early decision	67

FRESHMAN PROFILE

Range SAT EBRW	600–680
Range SAT Math	630–730
Range SAT Composite	1250–1390
Range ACT Composite	27–31
# submitting SAT scores	807
% submitting SAT scores	85
# submitting ACT scores	226
% submitting ACT scores	24
% graduated top 10% of class	37
% graduated top 25% of class	73
% graduated top 50% of class	97

DEADLINES

Early decision	
Deadline	11/15
Notification	12/31
Other ED Deadline	1/7
Other ED Notification	2/1
Regular	
Priority	11/15
Deadline	1/7
Notification	3/31
Nonfall registration?	Yes

APPLICANTS ALSO LOOK AT AND SOMETIMES PREFER

Babson College; Boston College; Bryant University; Northeastern University; University of Massachusetts Amherst; Fordham University; State University of New York at Binghamton (Binghamton University); Fairfield University; Providence College; University of Connecticut

FINANCIAL FACTS

Financial Aid Rating	90
Annual tuition	$52,000
Room and board	$17,620
Required fees	$1,790
Books and supplies	$1,325
Average frosh need-based scholarship	$34,669
Average UG need-based scholarship	$34,395
% needy frosh rec. need-based scholarship or grant aid	97
% needy UG rec. need-based scholarship or grant aid	98
% needy frosh rec. non-need-based scholarship or grant aid	17
% needy UG rec. non-need-based scholarship or grant aid	14
% needy frosh rec. need-based self-help aid	94
% needy UG rec. need-based self-help aid	95
% frosh rec. any financial aid	79
% UG rec. any financial aid	73
% UG borrow to pay for school	55
Average cumulative indebtedness	$35,187
% frosh need fully met	29
% ugrads need fully met	36
Average % of frosh need met	89
Average % of ugrad need met	92

BEREA COLLEGE

CPO 2220, Berea, KY 40404 • Admissions: 859-985-3500 • Fax: 859-985-3512

CAMPUS LIFE

Quality of Life Rating	84
Fire Safety Rating	96
Green Rating	93
Type of school	Private
Environment	Village

STUDENTS

Total undergrad enrollment	1,630
% male/female	43/57
% from out of state	55
% frosh live on campus	100
% ugrads live on campus	87
% African American	16
% Asian	3
% Caucasian	54
% Hispanic	12
% Native American	<1
% Pacific Islander	<1
% Two or more races	7
% Race and/or ethnicity unknown	1
% international	8
# of countries represented	74

SURVEY SAYS . . .

Great financial aid
Diverse student types interact on campus
Students environmentally aware

ACADEMICS

Academic Rating	86
% students returning for sophomore year	83
% students graduating within 4 years	49
% students graduating within 6 years	66
Calendar	Semester
Student/faculty ratio	10:1
Profs interesting rating	88
Profs accessible rating	92
Most classes have 10–19 students.	

MOST POPULAR MAJORS

Biology/Biological Sciences, General; Business/
Commerce, General; Computer and Information
Sciences, General

STUDENTS SAY "..."

Academics

Kentucky's Berea College is one of the nation's few entirely tuition-free private colleges, providing a liberal arts education "to those who otherwise couldn't afford college but who are deserving of the opportunity." Berea is "truly a different world when it comes to the atmosphere of the college," and the "wonderful opportunity" offered to students is truly appreciated. The school takes a "holistic approach" to education and "expects a lot from students both in and outside of class," including labor (everyone is required to work at least ten hours per week) and convocations.

Professors take an active role in helping students learn: "If you miss a class, professors will email you to find out why." They "care about not just your learning but also about who you are as an individual" and "lively and passionate about their subjects, and it is very evident within their classrooms." "I've never felt more challenged than when I stepped foot in a Berea classroom," says a junior. The small student-to-faculty ratio gives professors the opportunity to get to know their students, and "[allows] them to adapt to their students' needs."

Dating back to 1855, the college is "very deeply rooted in Appalachian culture and history, but unafraid to address issues outside of that." The school gives low-income students the opportunity to pursue higher education while participating in a labor program, and so "produces well-rounded, hardworking students fully prepared for grad school or the workforce." "If the labor program is used to its fullest extent, each student has the opportunity to graduate with a fantastic résumé and many network connections," says a sophomore. It also offers "a huge scholarship to study abroad," of which many students take advantage.

Life

"Berea is a calm place" and "there isn't much going on unless you make something happen." Students are quite busy with studying and work, so "naps are rare" and "we usually don't sleep in because there is just so much to do." Most students are taking a full course load and then doing at least one or two extracurricular activities as well. "The town life is simply atrocious" but on campus, "student organizations are constantly holding events to keep Berea students occupied and having fun," including "movie nights, game nights, dances, [and] bowling." Heritage activities, such as Contra dancing, are big.

The town of Richmond is just a fifteen-minute drive away (there is also a campus shuttle, and Lexington is a bit further), so getting out of small town life for some shopping or restaurant dining "is a must" from time to time. It is illegal to sell alcohol in the town of Berea, and it is against school rules to have alcohol on campus, so "there isn't a big party scene." There also happen to be "a lot of couples on campus," and "people take relationships seriously" here.

Student Body

Berea students are "creative" and "incredibly resilient" and almost everyone "comes from the Appalachian region [and] limited resources." Many tend to be first-generation college students, and "most students' priorities are not in having the best material items or joining the best sorority." The most typical thing you'll see is "an overworked, but generally content student shuffling between classes and work." Also, "the one thing that ties us all together is the fact that we had to work so hard to get into Berea," says a freshman. ("You have to be either an outright nerd or a secret nerd to get [here].") As some have noticed, there "seems to be a great divide between traditional students and non-traditional."

BEREA COLLEGE

Financial Aid: 859-985-3310 • E-Mail: admissions@berea.edu • Website: www.berea.edu

THE PRINCETON REVIEW SAYS

Admissions

Very important factors considered include: interview. *Important factors considered include:* rigor of secondary school record, class rank, academic GPA, application essay, standardized test scores, character/personal qualities. *Other factors considered include:* recommendation(s), extracurricular activities, talent/ability, first generation, geographical residence, state residency, racial/ethnic status, volunteer work, work experience, level of applicant's interest. ACT with or without writing accepted. SAT with or without Essay component accepted. High school diploma is required and GED is accepted. *Academic units recommended:* 4 English, 3 math, 2 science, 2 science labs, 2 foreign language, 2 social studies.

Financial Aid

Students should submit: FAFSA. Priority filing deadline is 10/31. The Princeton Review suggests that all financial aid forms be submitted as soon as possible after October 1. *Need-based scholarships/grants offered:* College/university scholarship or grant aid from institutional funds; Federal Pell; Private scholarships; SEOG; State scholarships/grants. *Loan aid offered:* Direct PLUS loans; Direct Subsidized Stafford Loans; Direct Unsubsidized Stafford Loans. Applicants will be notified of awards on a rolling basis beginning 11/15. Federal Work-Study Program available.

The Inside Word

The Tuition Promise Scholarship that every student receives understandably attracts a lot of applicants. Competition among candidates is intense. It's also important to note, you may be too wealthy to get admitted here. Berea won't admit students whose parents can afford to send them elsewhere. Financially qualified applicants should apply as early as possible.

THE SCHOOL SAYS "..."

From the Admissions Office

"Since its founding in 1855, Berea College has provided a high quality, low-cost education to students of all races. As the first interracial and co-educational college in the South, Berea admits students with great academic promise but limited financial means. Over the past 150 years, Berea has evolved into one of the most distinctive colleges in the United States serving students primarily from the Appalachian region.

"All admitted students receive a Tuition Promise Scholarship, which completely covers the cost of tuition after other forms of grant & scholarship aid are applied. This leaves only minimal expenses for housing, meals, and other expenses. Students graduate with one of the lowest rates of student educational debt in the nation, and one in three students graduate debt free. In addition to the Scholarship, students receive a laptop computer and a paid on-campus job to assist with educational and personal expenses as well as gain valuable work experience before graduation.

"As a result of this combination of academic reputation and generous financial assistance, Berea attracts many more applicants than are able to be accepted, so admission is competitive. The best means of improving the chances for admission is to complete the application process as early as possible, preferably by October 31 of the senior year."

SELECTIVITY

Admissions Rating	94
# of applicants	1,576
% of applicants accepted	38
% of acceptees attending	73

FRESHMAN PROFILE

Range SAT EBRW	520–590
Range SAT Math	510–623
Range ACT Composite	22–27
# submitting SAT scores	68
% submitting SAT scores	16
# submitting ACT scores	362
% submitting ACT scores	83
Average HS GPA	3.5
% graduated top 10% of class	22
% graduated top 25% of class	69
% graduated top 50% of class	96

DEADLINES

Regular	
Priority	10/31
Deadline	3/31
Notification	Rolling, 11/15
Nonfall registration?	No

FINANCIAL FACTS

Financial Aid Rating	60
Annual tuition	$0
Room and board	$6,966
Required fees	$600
Books and supplies	$700
Average frosh need-based scholarship	$45,984
Average UG need-based scholarship	$45,083
% needy frosh rec. need-based scholarship or grant aid	100
% needy UG rec. need-based scholarship or grant aid	100
% needy frosh rec. non-need-based scholarship or grant aid	0
% needy UG rec. non-need-based scholarship or grant aid	0
% needy frosh rec. need-based self-help aid	100
% needy UG rec. need-based self-help aid	100
% frosh rec. any financial aid	100
% UG rec. any financial aid	100
% UG borrow to pay for school	56
Average cumulative indebtedness	$6,405
% frosh need fully met	0
% ugrads need fully met	0
Average % of frosh need met	96
Average % of ugrad need met	95

BERRY COLLEGE

P.O. Box 490159, Mount Berry, GA 30149-0159 • Admissions: 706-236-2215 • Fax: 706-290-2178

CAMPUS LIFE

Quality of Life Rating	91
Fire Safety Rating	95
Green Rating	89
Type of school	Private
Environment	Town

STUDENTS

Total undergrad enrollment	1,918
% male/female	39/61
% from out of state	30
% frosh from public high school	71
% frosh live on campus	95
% ugrads live on campus	89
% African American	7
% Asian	2
% Caucasian	78
% Hispanic	7
% Native American	<1
% Pacific Islander	0
% Two or more races	4
% Race and/or ethnicity unknown	1
% international	1
# of countries represented	18

SURVEY SAYS . . .

Lots of conservative students
Students are happy
Lab facilities are great
Internships are widely available
Students are friendly
Students are very religious
Students involved in community service
Recreation facilities are great
Theater is popular
Active student government

ACADEMICS

Academic Rating	84
% students returning for sophomore year	83
% students graduating within 4 years	63
% students graduating within 6 years	69
Calendar	Semester
Student/faculty ratio	11:1
Profs interesting rating	91
Profs accessible rating	95

Most classes have 10–19 students.
Most lab/discussion sessions have
10–19 students.

MOST POPULAR MAJORS

Zoology/Animal Biology; Exercise Science and
Kinesiology; Psychology, General

STUDENTS SAY "..."

Academics

A rigorous liberal arts school in northwest Georgia, Berry College offers undergraduates a "community" in which they can easily flourish. Student say Berry is well known for its Student Work Program, which provides valuable work experience and "enables students to earn money to contribute to [their] tuition or [for] personal spending." No matter what they do with their earnings, the program certainly provides valuable work experience. When it comes to academics, classroom standards are "high" though "not impossible" to meet. Of course, the college has many "renowned programs" including "business, animal science and nursing." Undergraduates also happily share that most professors at Berry "are invested in their students and care about their success." They are also "highly knowledgeable about their subjects and are able to convey that knowledge to their students." Even better, professors strive "to present the material in an engaging way and look to find new ways to help students do their best." And when undergrads do find themselves struggling, they can easily turn to the "incredible" Academic Success Center which "offers several different forms of tutoring." All in all, students find Berry to be a "community that is committed to developing the minds, hearts, and hands of students through impeccable faculty with a passion for learning...[and] incredible...programs [that provide] students [with] hands on experience in almost any area of study."

Life

Undergrads at Berry are hardworking. Indeed, "nearly everyone works on campus" so students say the majority of their time "is spent either in class or at our jobs." Nevertheless, this diligent bunch still manages to kick back and relax every now and again. For starters, many Berry undergrads are active and athletic. Therefore, a lot of people love to take advantage of the college's "rock wall and rock wall room, zip lining, indoor and outdoor pool, basketball courts, volleyball courts [and] hiking [trails]." "Intramural sports are very popular," as well. And students also "do a lot of outdoorsy things like camping and fishing deeper into campus and off campus." Fortunately, there are plenty of arts and culture options as well. For example, "the music department hosts a professional musician every Thursday." And a student organization called KCAB "plans multiple events every week [including activities like] pajama movie night, African storytelling, [a] welcome back dance, prayer breakfast [and] MLK Service Day." Finally, hometown Rome also offers a nice respite from academic stress. While it's "definitely a small town...it's [also] peaceful [and] fulfilling" with "a local theatre, a nice park, used bookstores [and] a nice selection of restaurants."

Student Body

All it takes is a few minutes with some Berry students to discover that they're "some of the nicest [individuals]" you'll ever meet. As one senior immediately boasts, "In all my four years of Berry I have yet to meet a single student who wasn't kind, compassionate, and eager to learn and make a difference." Additionally, most are "academically driven." Indeed, Berry undergrads are often "serious about their school work and tend to aim high in their goals." Students here also report that their peers are "slightly preppy" and that "longboards, Enos, Chacos, frisbees, L. L. Bean duck boots, and Patagonia sweaters are everywhere." Plus, "the majority of students are from Georgia and the surrounding states." However, fear not! You'll still find "people from various backgrounds, creeds, and religions." Perhaps most importantly, Berry undergrads describe their peers as "very trustworthy" and make a point of mentioning that they "value integrity." As this impressed student concludes, "While we do not have an official Berry honor code, we don't really find that our community needs one. Students can leave their computer or laptop or purse lying around the library or dining hall and it will be untouched thirty minutes later. It really is a special community."

Financial Aid: 706-236-1714 • E-Mail: admissions@berry.edu • Website: https://www.berry.edu/

THE PRINCETON REVIEW SAYS

Admissions

Very important factors considered include: rigor of secondary school record, academic GPA, standardized test scores. *Important factors considered include:* extracurricular activities. *Other factors considered include:* application essay, recommendation(s), interview, volunteer work, work experience. ACT with or without writing accepted. SAT with or without Essay component accepted. High school diploma is required and GED is accepted. *Academic units required:* 4 English, 4 math, 3 science, 2 foreign language, 3 social studies, 4 academic electives.

Financial Aid

Students should submit: CSS/Financial Aid PROFILE; FAFSA; State aid form. Priority filing deadline is 1/15. The Princeton Review suggests that all financial aid forms be submitted as soon as possible after October 1. *Need-based scholarships/grants offered:* College/university scholarship or grant aid from institutional funds; Federal Pell; Private scholarships; SEOG. *Loan aid offered:* Direct PLUS loans; Direct Subsidized Stafford Loans; Direct Unsubsidized Stafford Loans. Applicants will be notified of awards on a rolling basis beginning 11/1. Federal Work-Study Program available. Institutional employment available.

The Inside Word

Admissions officers at Berry College do their best to get to know and wholly consider each candidate. Of course, a solid college prep curriculum is a must. Students have the option of submitting either a Common App or using Berry's own application; both are given equal weight. Better yet, both are free. Finally, applicants who are sure that Berry is their top choice are encouraged to apply early decision.

SELECTIVITY

Admissions Rating	**83**
# of applicants	4,328
% of applicants accepted	71
% of acceptees attending	19
# of early decision applicants	80
% accepted early decision	34

FRESHMAN PROFILE

Range SAT EBRW	560–670
Range SAT Math	530–650
Range SAT Composite	1120–1300
Range ACT Composite	24–30
# submitting SAT scores	291
% submitting SAT scores	50
# submitting ACT scores	285
% submitting ACT scores	49
Average HS GPA	3.7
% graduated top 10% of class	32
% graduated top 25% of class	61
% graduated top 50% of class	87

DEADLINES

Early decision	
Deadline	11/1
Notification	12/1
Early action	
Deadline	11/1
Notification	12/15
Regular	
Priority	1/15
Deadline	7/24
Notification	Rolling, 11/1
Nonfall registration?	Yes

FINANCIAL FACTS

Financial Aid Rating	**89**
Annual tuition	$37,020
Room and board	$13,070
Required fees	$226
Books and supplies	$1,000
Average frosh need-based scholarship	$28,711
Average UG need-based scholarship	$27,857
% needy frosh rec. need-based scholarship or grant aid	100
% needy UG rec. need-based scholarship or grant aid	100
% needy frosh rec. non-need-based scholarship or grant aid	27
% needy UG rec. non-need-based scholarship or grant aid	23
% needy frosh rec. need-based self-help aid	60
% needy UG rec. need-based self-help aid	67
% frosh rec. any financial aid	100
% UG rec. any financial aid	99.5
% UG borrow to pay for school	61
Average cumulative indebtedness	$31,336
% frosh need fully met	34
% ugrads need fully met	30
Average % of frosh need met	86
Average % of ugrad need met	85

BOSTON COLLEGE

140 Commonwealth Avenue, Chestnut Hill, MA 02467-3809 • Admissions: 617-552-3100 • Fax: 617-552-0798

STUDENTS SAY "..."

Academics

Boston College, a small Jesuit school on the outskirts of Boston, "is all about educating the person as a whole." Its strong core curriculum ensures all students receive a "well-rounded" liberal arts education regardless of their chosen major. Boston College's well-respected education and business school attract a lot of students, and there are many other strong programs, including English and communication. Students think Boston College is a "great experience academically" and gush about their "phenomenal professors." A secondary education major student says, "Boston College's professors are truly exceptional and are devoted to undergraduate learning." They're "engaging, challenging, and understanding, [and] are genuinely interested in the student as a whole person." Boston College's "prestigious" academics come with "high expectations," but if students need help professors are "easily accessible outside of classes." Students "feel prepared for whatever is next" and note that their "well-connected" teachers and strong alumni network help with the job search. One student, who was drawn to Boston College because of its stellar reputation, finds it "even better than expected." Another adds, "I have always revered Boston College's academic and athletic reputation, and coming here, I have not been disappointed."

Life

Boston College's "gorgeous campus" and "perfect'" suburban location has created a very rich campus life and given the school a "strong community feel." There's "a superb sense of school spirit, which truly sets it apart." One student raves, "There is just so much school spirit and love for the university!" Boston College's "incredible sports teams" are well-supported by "superfans at every event." "There is also a large service component," to life at Boston College, which allows students "to serve the community in Boston and communities all around the world." Boston College offers a "plethora of extracurricular activities," and students think "there's a club or group for everyone here." The school has "great facilities" and "state-of-the-art resources." Dorms are generally well-reviewed, though students think the housing lottery could be more "fair." Students often go into Boston for all of its entertainment and cultural activities but are happy to return to their "close-knit college" where they "feel very at home."

Student Body

Boston College has gotten some flak for its "preppy," "white," and "homogenous" student body, and a communication student admits, "The school's nickname as 'J. Crew U' isn't entirely unwarranted." Boston College could definitely use "greater racial diversity," but one student says that each year "the student body becomes more and more diverse." A student double-majoring in economics and German says, "Once you've settled in you'll find that it's not at all difficult to find a group of friends" no matter who you are. "There is a large religious/spiritual community," because of the school's Jesuit affiliation, but "it is only one group of many." Boston College's Division I ranking means there are plenty of athletes and sports fans. Students warn that Boston College is "not the place to go to class in your pajamas." People, particularly women, are "very well-dressed" and "stylish." Students say their peers are "really ambitious" and "hardworking." "The majority of students seem intelligent and academically driven as well as dedicated to and passionate about one or more extracurricular activities." Though people at Boston College are "academically oriented," they're "also into having a good time, and "have a work hard, play hard mentality." There's a moderate amount of drinking on campus and off, but students say that no matter what, everyone "definitely [has] school as a top priority."

Financial Aid: 617-552-3300 • Website: www.bc.edu

THE PRINCETON REVIEW SAYS

Admissions

Very important factors considered include: rigor of secondary school record, academic GPA, standardized test scores. *Important factors considered include:* class rank, application essay, recommendation(s), extracurricular activities, talent/ability, character/personal qualities, alumni/ae relation, religious affiliation/commitment, volunteer work. *Other factors considered include:* first generation, racial/ethnic status, work experience. ACT with or without writing accepted. SAT with or without Essay component accepted. High school diploma is required and GED is accepted. *Academic units recommended:* 4 English, 4 math, 4 science, 4 science labs, 4 foreign language, 4 social studies, 4 history.

Financial Aid

Students should submit: Business/Farm Supplement; CSS/Financial Aid PROFILE; FAFSA; Noncustodial PROFILE. Priority filing deadline is 2/1. The Princeton Review suggests that all financial aid forms be submitted as soon as possible after October 1. *Need-based scholarships/grants offered:* College/university scholarship or grant aid from institutional funds; Federal Pell; Private scholarships; SEOG; State scholarships/grants. *Loan aid offered:* Direct PLUS loans; Direct Subsidized Stafford Loans; Direct Unsubsidized Stafford Loans. Applicants will be notified of awards on or about 4/1. Federal Work-Study Program available. Institutional employment available.

The Inside Word

Boston College is one of many selective schools that eschew set admissions formulae. While a challenging high school curriculum and strong test scores are essential for any serious candidate, the college seeks students who are passionate and make connections between academic pursuits and extracurricular activities. The application process should reveal a distinct, mature voice and a student whose interest in education goes beyond the simple desire to earn an A.

THE SCHOOL SAYS "…"

From the Admissions Office

"Boston College students achieve at the highest levels with honors in the past ten years including three Rhodes scholarship winners, 173 Fulbrights, four Marshalls, eight Goldwaters, ten Beckmans, and five Truman Postgraduate Fellowship Programs. Junior Year Abroad and Scholar of the College Program offer students flexibility within the curriculum. Facilities opened in the past ten years include: Stokes Hall, Cadigan Alumni Center, Thomas More Apartments, Fish Field House, Margot Connell Recreation Center, and the new Schiller Institute for Integrated Sciences and Society currently under construction slated to open in the Fall of 2021. Students enjoy the vibrant location in Chestnut Hill with easy access to the cultural and historical richness of Boston.

"Boston College requires freshman applicants to take the SAT with writing (or the ACT with the writing exam required). SAT Subject Tests are optional; but may be submitted if a student wishes to highlight a talent in a specific area."

SELECTIVITY

Admissions Rating	96
# of applicants	35,552
% of applicants accepted	27
% of acceptees attending	24
# offered a place on the wait list	6,438
% accepting a place on wait list	54
% admitted from wait list	5

FRESHMAN PROFILE

Range SAT EBRW	660–730
Range SAT Math	680–770
Range ACT Composite	31–34
# submitting SAT scores	1,532
% submitting SAT scores	67
# submitting ACT scores	951
% submitting ACT scores	41
% graduated top 10% of class	82
% graduated top 25% of class	93
% graduated top 50% of class	98

DEADLINES

Early decision	
Deadline	11/1
Notification	12/15
Other ED Deadline	1/1
Other ED Notification	2/15
Regular	
Deadline	1/1
Notification	4/1
Nonfall registration?	Yes

APPLICANTS ALSO LOOK AT AND OFTEN PREFER
Harvard College; Yale University; University of Notre Dame; Georgetown University; University of Southern California

AND SOMETIMES PREFER
Cornell University; University of Virginia; Vanderbilt University; New York University; William & Mary

AND RARELY PREFER
Fordham University; Northeastern University; Villanova University; Boston University; College of the Holy Cross

FINANCIAL FACTS

Financial Aid Rating	95
Annual tuition	$56,780
Room and board	$14,826
Required fees	$1,130
Books and supplies	$1,250
Average frosh need-based scholarship	$41,842
Average UG need-based scholarship	$42,240
% needy frosh rec. need-based scholarship or grant aid	87
% needy UG rec. need-based scholarship or grant aid	90
% needy frosh rec. non-need-based scholarship or grant aid	3
% needy UG rec. non-need-based scholarship or grant aid	2
% needy frosh rec. need-based self-help aid	91
% needy UG rec. need-based self-help aid	93
% UG rec. any financial aid	68
% UG borrow to pay for school	50
Average cumulative indebtedness	$21,421
% frosh need fully met	100
% ugrads need fully met	100
Average % of frosh need met	100
Average % of ugrad need met	100

BOSTON UNIVERSITY

233 Bay State Road, Boston, MA 02215 • Admissions: 617-353-2300

STUDENTS SAY "..."

Academics

Long recognized for offering both the breadth of a large research university and the depth of a private college, the "various schools and colleges within Boston University provide students with access to almost every imaginable program of study." In keeping with this, students report a wide variety of majors and concentrations, naming standout programs in engineering, education, and business administration. Professors are praised as much as is students' ability to choose them: BU professors are both "actively pursuing research in their field" and "engaging partners in my academic experience," and students find that professors' "interesting backgrounds...fuel class discussions in a variety of academic areas." Undergraduates also love the university's "location" as an "urban campus" in Boston's Back Bay, and benefit distinctly from BU's "opportunity access" when it comes to job placement. As a private university with a large student body, BU students also become the beneficiaries of the institution's "wealth," calling the experience one of "big campus resources with a small campus feel." The faculty and administration "are constantly striving to be better for the student's benefit" in delivering BU's unique curriculum, which is "equal parts liberal arts education and pre-professional experience." The university emphasizes "study abroad" and "research opportunities," which further broaden the possibilities of a BU education. Perhaps ideal for the student who desires a wide variety of choices in order to discover what comes next, "the range and diversity of opportunities at Boston University allows you to Be You."

Life

Continuing the theme of wide-ranging options, BU undergraduates divulge that student "life at BU is anything you want it to be." Because of BU's location in "the heart of Boston," "the city itself is like our campus," and BU undergrads can mingle freely with Boston's many other college students in nearby Cambridge, Somerville, Allston, and Brookline. Students are rarely bored because "there's always something interesting going on on- and off-campus": campus life boasts "a lot of clubs and activities to get involved in," as well as "house parties," "BU hockey games," and "frat parties," while students' access to Boston spans everything from "a run along the Charles River" to "shopping on Newbury or in Harvard Square" to frequenting "plays and ballets and museums" and the many local "clubs and bars." Students strive to maximize the best of both sides of BU life, "prid[ing] themselves on being able to find balance in living strong academic lives and exciting social lives as well." Students seem satisfied with the choices they do end up making, reporting that BU life is "wonderful" and that "there is more to do than you will be able to find the time for."

Student Body

"There is a great sense of diversity, yet an overwhelming feeling of unity" within BU's large but closely connected undergraduate population. Students strongly resist the idea of a "typical student," asserting that "originality is valued highly at BU," as is "diversity of thought." "Because we are an international university," many students point out, "the student body is vastly diverse." Students have "a wide range of interests both inside and outside the classroom," and characterize themselves as "motivated, culturally-aware, intelligent, adventurous," "driven and involved," and "very passionate." BU undergrads find their peers "intellectually stimulating in conversations" and tend to group, as in most college experiences, around shared interests and experiences. One student echoes many of her classmates this way: "My life at BU is quite packed because I chose to make it that way."

BOSTON UNIVERSITY

Financial Aid: 617-353-4176 • E-Mail: admissions@bu.edu; intadmis@bu.edu • Website: www.bu.edu

THE PRINCETON REVIEW SAYS

Admissions

Very important factors considered include: rigor of secondary school record. *Important factors considered include:* class rank, academic GPA, application essay, standardized test scores (optional for fall 2021/spring 2022 applicants), recommendation(s), extracurricular activities, character/personal qualities, alumni/ae relation. *Other factors considered include:* first generation, geographical residence, state residency, racial/ethnic status, volunteer work, work experience. ACT with or without writing accepted. SAT with or without Essay component accepted. High school diploma is required and GED is accepted. *Academic units required:* 4 English, 3 math, 3 science, 3 science labs, 2 foreign language, 3 social studies. *Academic units recommended:* 4 English, 4 math, 4 science, 4 science labs, 4 foreign language, 4 social studies.

Financial Aid

Students should submit: CSS/Financial Aid PROFILE; FAFSA; Noncustodial PROFILE. Priority filing deadline is 11/1. The Princeton Review suggests that all financial aid forms be submitted as soon as possible after October 1. *Need-based scholarships/grants offered:* College/university scholarship or grant aid from institutional funds; Federal Pell; Private scholarships; SEOG; State scholarships/grants. *Loan aid offered:* Direct PLUS loans; Direct Subsidized Stafford Loans; Direct Unsubsidized Stafford Loans. Applicants will be notified of awards on a rolling basis beginning 4/1. Federal Work-Study Program available. Institutional employment available.

The Inside Word

BU can afford to stay competitive, and they strongly emphasize high school academic performance as the key indicator of a student's admissibility to the university. BU values students who take on a challenging high school curriculum (especially AP and IB classes, or whatever the most challenging courseload available is). The personal essay, recommendations, extracurricular activities, and standardized test scores (SAT or ACT plus SAT Writing) are also important factors in assessing applicants. Several undergraduate courses of study (mostly in medicine and the arts) require specific standardized test supplements; prospective students are encouraged to read BU's admissions requirements carefully before applying.

THE SCHOOL SAYS "..."

From the Admissions Office

"Boston University is a world-recognized, private teaching and research university committed to excellence in undergraduate education. Students study with distinguished faculty that include Fulbright Scholars, Pulitzer Prize winners, a MacArthur Fellow, and a former Poet Laureate. In ten undergraduate schools and colleges, BU offers students more than 300 programs of study, cutting-edge research with faculty mentors, internships in the United States and abroad, and one of the nation's most extensive study abroad programs. Housing is guaranteed for four years in a variety of on-campus residences, including high-rise buildings and historic brownstones. BU students are engaged with their campus community through over 450 student organizations, club and intramural sports, and twenty-three NCAA Division I sports teams. Students experience the city of Boston as an extension of campus for study, internships, employment, and cultural and recreational activities.

"Students also benefit from research and internship opportunities in the United States and abroad and a network of almost 400,000 alumni in 177 countries around the world. With more than 90 study abroad opportunities and classmates from over 100 countries, BU is truly a global university."

SELECTIVITY

Admissions Rating	96
# of applicants	62,224
% of applicants accepted	19
% of acceptees attending	27
# offered a place on the wait list	5,235
% accepting a place on wait list	57
% admitted from wait list	11
# of early decision applicants	4,877
% accepted early decision	30

FRESHMAN PROFILE

Range SAT EBRW	650–720
Range SAT Math	690–790
Range SAT Composite	1360–1480
Range ACT Composite	30–34
# submitting SAT scores	2,313
% submitting SAT scores	73
# submitting ACT scores	1,024
% submitting ACT scores	32
Average HS GPA	3.7
% graduated top 10% of class	64
% graduated top 25% of class	92
% graduated top 50% of class	100

DEADLINES

Early decision	
Deadline	11/1
Notification	12/15
Other ED Deadline	1/1
Other ED Notification	2/15
Regular	
Deadline	1/1
Notification	4/1
Nonfall registration?	Yes

FINANCIAL FACTS

Financial Aid Rating	87
Annual tuition	$56,854
Room and board	$16,640
Required fees	$1,218
Books and supplies	$1,000
Average frosh need-based scholarship	$47,141
Average UG need-based scholarship	$40,969
% needy frosh rec. need-based scholarship or grant aid	99
% needy UG rec. need-based scholarship or grant aid	98
% needy frosh rec. non-need-based scholarship or grant aid	23
% needy UG rec. non-need-based scholarship or grant aid	21
% needy frosh rec. need-based self-help aid	75
% needy UG rec. need-based self-help aid	75
% frosh rec. any financial aid	53
% UG rec. any financial aid	55
% UG borrow to pay for school	46
Average cumulative indebtedness	$40,349
% frosh need fully met	34
% ugrads need fully met	25
Average % of frosh need met	93
Average % of ugrad need met	85

BOWDOIN COLLEGE

5000 College Station, Brunswick, ME 04011-8441 • Admissions: 207-725-3100 • Fax: 207-725-3101

STUDENTS SAY "..."

Academics

Bowdoin College is a small college in Brunswick, Maine, with faculty who are "passionate about their research and distributing their knowledge to hardworking students." Professors here "are absolutely fantastic" and "teach every class—[no teaching assistants]." They are "brilliant at leading discussions and pushing students to think deeper and, delightfully, stranger [in order] to consider new possibilities off of well-worn paths." Bowdoin's undergraduates also love the "small class sizes and the level of intimacy" they have access to with faculty members. This isn't a school for slackers. Says one student: "I soon learned that in order to do well here, you *must* give all your time and effort. There is no grade inflation at this institution." Students sum up their academics as "highly demanding but also highly rewarding." Bowdoin provides lots of hands-on opportunities, especially in environmental science, with instructors taking advantage of the college's coastal location. Other immersive courses that some describe as "engaging and challenging in the best possible way" include United Nations and Supreme Court simulations. Although students at Bowdoin "like to stay busy," they are never bored.

Life

You'd be forgiven for mistaking Bowdoin's cafeterias for Parisian cafés. "Every meal … is a [planned] social event," and it's "not abnormal for a meal to last two hours because you're deep in conversation with someone." And then there's the food: "Meals in the dining hall tend to be the centerpiece of social life during the week—it's fun to camp out [there]." Another student emphasizes that "every meal is significant because students socialize, expand their community, and engage with others." However, mealtimes buffer the demands of coursework, with students "spend[ing] the majority of their time doing schoolwork." On weekends, you'll find "a lot of outdoorsy people … kayaking, hiking," or camping in nearby Acadia National Park. In the winter, "a portion of the quad [is even transformed into] a makeshift ice rink."

Student Body

Bowdoin attracts "students who are excited to learn, challenge themselves and others, and engage beyond what is expected." The college "carries thirty-one varsity sports teams," which "leads to a large proportion of the student body being comprised of athletes" and "an increased sense of camaraderie between athletes and a large number of students that attend sporting events." The stereotypical divide between so-called nerds and jocks isn't present here: "Those same athletes might later converse about quantum physics and Russian literature in the dining hall." Bowdoin students "do it all when it comes to academics, athletics, and socializing." One student says, "the student body is thoughtful, outgoing, and dedicated, finding a … balance between life and work." Students describe their peers as being "often genuinely humble and friendly," "preppy," and "brilliant." Many are "drawn to Bowdoin because of the natural beauty of Maine, … and nature definitely influences campus culture and what students do in their free time."

BOWDOIN COLLEGE

Financial Aid: 207-725-3146 • E-Mail: admissions@bowdoin.edu • Website: www.bowdoin.edu

THE PRINCETON REVIEW SAYS

Admissions

Very important factors considered include: rigor of secondary school record, class rank, academic GPA, application essay, recommendation(s), extracurricular activities, talent/ability, character/personal qualities. *Important factors considered include:* standardized test scores. *Other factors considered include:* interview, first generation, alumni/ae relation, geographical residence, state residency, racial/ethnic status, volunteer work, work experience. ACT with or without writing accepted. SAT with or without Essay component accepted. High school diploma is required and GED is not accepted. *Academic units recommended:* 4 English, 4 math, 4 science, 3 science labs, 4 foreign language, 4 social studies.

Financial Aid

Students should submit: Business/Farm Supplement; CSS/Financial Aid PROFILE; FAFSA; Noncustodial PROFILE. The Princeton Review suggests that all financial aid forms be submitted as soon as possible after October 1. *Need-based scholarships/grants offered:* College/university scholarship or grant aid from institutional funds; Federal Pell; Private scholarships; SEOG; State scholarships/grants. *Loan aid offered:* Direct Subsidized Stafford Loans; Direct Unsubsidized Stafford Loans. Federal Work-Study Program available. Institutional employment available.

The Inside Word

Admissions officers at Bowdoin emphasize their search for students proving themselves to be curious, thoughtful, and engaged. Bowdoin looks at student grades relative to the respective school's level of difficulty, recommendations from teachers and counselors, writing samples, school and community involvement, character, personality, and overall academic potential. A personal interview isn't required but is recommended. Bowdoin has a test-optional policy and also provides the opportunity for students to submit a video response, which is optional but allows students to give a two-minute response to a randomly selected question.

THE SCHOOL SAYS "..."

From the Admissions Office

"Bowdoin is a welcoming and diverse community of students, faculty, and staff who care deeply about and support each other through four years of learning, exploration, and growth. We are dedicated to the liberal arts, to deep intellectual inquiry, and to discourse and debate on the toughest issues.

"Bowdoin offers a wide array of curricular and extracurricular opportunities combined with a 215-year tradition of serving the common good. Bowdoin also leads in the study and teaching of the environment, with a decades-long interdisciplinary approach, a dedication to placing the environment at the center of intellectual and social life, and a commitment to place-based research and teaching that train students to rigorously research, analyze, and communicate complex environmental problems across multiple angles: science, history, human behavior, the influence of politics and religion, the role of art, and the realities of economics and laws.

"The College makes a Bowdoin education affordable. We accept domestic students on a need-blind basis with a commitment to meet full demonstrated need for all four years. Nearly half of our students receive grant assistance from the College and Bowdoin stands firm in its decision to eliminate loans from aid packages.

"This all takes place in the easily accessible and vibrant town of Brunswick amid one of the most beautiful settings anywhere—the extraordinary coast of Maine. As Bowdoin's seventh president wrote in 'The Offer of the College' in 1906, the Bowdoin experience may very well be '... the best four years of your life.'"

SELECTIVITY

Admissions Rating	98
# of applicants	9,081
% of applicants accepted	10
% of acceptees attending	55
# of early decision applicants	1,093
% accepted early decision	23

FRESHMAN PROFILE

Range SAT EBRW	650–740
Range SAT Math	650–770
Range ACT Composite	30–34
# submitting SAT scores	304
% submitting SAT scores	60
# submitting ACT scores	234
% submitting ACT scores	46
% graduated top 10% of class	80
% graduated top 25% of class	96
% graduated top 50% of class	100

DEADLINES

Early decision	
Deadline	11/15
Notification	12/15
Other ED Deadline	1/1
Other ED Notification	2/15
Regular	
Deadline	1/1
Notification	4/1
Nonfall registration?	No

APPLICANTS ALSO LOOK AT AND OFTEN PREFER
Brown University; Dartmouth College; Yale University; Harvard College

AND SOMETIMES PREFER
Swarthmore College; Amherst College; Williams College; Cornell University

AND RARELY PREFER
Middlebury College; Wesleyan University

FINANCIAL FACTS

Financial Aid Rating	98
Annual tuition	$53,418
Room and board	$14,698
Required fees	$504
Books and supplies	$840
Average frosh need-based scholarship	$48,856
Average UG need-based scholarship	$47,522
% needy frosh rec. need-based scholarship or grant aid	100
% needy UG rec. need-based scholarship or grant aid	100
% needy frosh rec. non-need-based scholarship or grant aid	0
% needy UG rec. non-need-based scholarship or grant aid	0
% needy frosh rec. need-based self-help aid	98
% needy UG rec. need-based self-help aid	99
% frosh rec. any financial aid	52
% UG rec. any financial aid	50
% UG borrow to pay for school	27
Average cumulative indebtedness	$25,482
% frosh need fully met	100
% ugrads need fully met	100
Average % of frosh need met	100
Average % of ugrad need met	100

BRADLEY UNIVERSITY

1501 W. Bradley Avenue, Peoria, IL 61625 • Admissions: 309-677-1000 • Fax: 309-677-2797

STUDENTS SAY "..."

Academics

Bradley University, a mid-sized private university in Peoria, Illinois, offers more than 185 academic programs throughout its undergraduate and graduate schools, and "if there's not one that you like, you can make a hybrid degree." Students say that the university's biggest advantages are that it combines both large and small school benefits and is "super dedicated to getting all students real work experience before they graduate." Unique programs like the Hollywood Semester (where students live in Los Angeles for one semester and intern in all aspects of the entertainment business) and the engineering practicum come together with the curriculum in the service of "bettering you for your life after college" by "helping you develop the personal and professional skills you'll need after Bradley." Thanks to the school's size, first-years at Bradley are "able to be involved in hands-on learning... that at larger universities would be reserved for graduate students." The school "is set up for you to succeed," so there are resources (such as free tutoring) to support students.

The "challenging and rigorous" curriculum ("grades are earned, not given") is taught entirely by professors, who present students with lab research opportunities and internship connections. Faculty are "always willing to provide additional clarification and assistance" to help students gain a better understanding of materials. Each professor has office hours when students can ask questions and receive advisement, and "the content of teaching is always powerful and meaningful." These teachers are beloved across the board, and "are so genuinely caring" about not just students' education, but their personal health. "My professors regularly check up on me to make sure I am eating, sleeping, and happy," says one student of the "fantastic mentors" at Bradley.

Life

With so many organizations on campus, students tend to fill their time with "volunteering, going to meetings for different clubs, and hanging out with their Bradley family." Students rave about the "perfect size" of Bradley, which "feels like a small hometown in the middle of a big city." It is "large enough to have lots of major programs, extracurriculars, and internship connections," but not so large where one feels lost in the sea of students. Instead, "you are comfortable to go out of your comfort zone." The campus diversity is evident in the school's over 240 clubs and organizations, which include the American Sign Language club, the Association of Latin American Students, Jazz Ensemble, Swing Dance Society, Pinterest Club, and Greek life (which involves 30 percent of students). Off-campus, students "go on hikes," go to East Peoria for food, visit the Walmart, or frequent the very popular Ice Cream Shack. Many students here play intramural sports, and "partying is popular on the weekends" once work is done. However if that's not your scene, then there are "definitely other things to do." "People spend lots of time in the library and in the quad when the weather is nice."

Student Body

Bradley's student body is composed of "highly intellectual, diverse" students who push each other "to consider other viewpoints and considerations during classroom discussions." This "academically-driven" group is "aware of the importance of a good education" and "takes full advantage of the opportunities offered." "I have never been on a college campus where everyone is so genuinely happy to be where they are," says one student. Bradley's sense of campus camaraderie is strong, and "when one good thing happens, it trickles through the Bradley community." Because students count themselves as members of so many clubs, there are great networking opportunities, and "most students know one another or know someone who knows someone."

BRADLEY UNIVERSITY

Financial Aid: 309-677-3089 • E-Mail: admissions@bradley.edu • Website: www.bradley.edu

THE PRINCETON REVIEW SAYS

Admissions

Very important factors considered include: rigor of secondary school record, academic GPA. *Important factors considered include:* class rank, standardized test scores, if provided. *Other factors considered include:* application essay, recommendation(s), interview, extracurricular activities, talent/ability, character/personal qualities, first generation, alumni/ae relation, geographical residence, racial/ethnic status, volunteer work, work experience, level of applicant's interest. Admission is test-optional. ACT with or without writing accepted. SAT with or without Essay component accepted. High school diploma is required and GED is accepted. *Academic units required:* 4 English, 3 math, 2 science, 2 science labs, 2 social studies. *Academic units recommended:* 5 English, 4 math, 3 science, 3 science labs, 2 foreign language, 3 social studies, 2 history.

Financial Aid

Students should submit: FAFSA. Priority filing deadline is 12/1. The Princeton Review suggests that all financial aid forms be submitted as soon as possible after October 1. *Need-based scholarships/grants offered:* College/university scholarship or grant aid from institutional funds; Federal Pell; Private scholarships; SEOG; State scholarships/grants; United Negro College Fund. *Loan aid offered:* Direct PLUS loans; Direct Subsidized Stafford Loans; Direct Unsubsidized Stafford Loans. Applicants will be notified of awards on a rolling basis beginning 11/15. Federal Work-Study Program available. Institutional employment available.

The Inside Word

Due to Bradley's regional appeal, the vast majority of undergrads originate from Illinois. With an eye toward broadening the student body's geographic demographics, the school presents an opportunity for out-of-stater applicants seeking to attend an excellent university without having to endure the grueling admissions process of many private universities. Above-average students should find that gaining admission here is a relatively painless experience. There are three separate deadlines to apply (early action, regular, and extended).

THE SCHOOL SAYS "..."

From the Admissions Office

"Bradley offers nearly 6,000 students a broad range of academic programs enhanced by required experiential learning. The university prepares students for immediate and substantial career success by offering resources not found at small colleges and more personalized experiences than large universities. Great academic variety leads to choices of majors, minors and graduate programs that are uncommon at most private universities. More than 185 academic programs are available in business, communications, education, engineering, fine and performing arts, health sciences, liberal arts, science and technology. Unique programs include entrepreneurship, game design, sports communication and physical therapy. Located less than three hours from Chicago, St. Louis and Indianapolis, the eighty-five-acre residential campus is located in a historic neighborhood just one mile from downtown Peoria, the largest metropolitan area in downstate Illinois.

"Bradley students develop leadership skills in more than 240 student organizations, with more than 60 dedicated to student leadership and community service. Students may also participate in the nation's most winning speech team, fraternities and sororities, and NCAA Division I athletics.

"Bradley graduates are well prepared for a career or direct entry to graduate school with 93 percent employed, continuing their education or pursuing other postgraduate experiences within six months of graduation. Eighty-two percent of students reported having at least one career-related work experience before graduating, and 97 percent report having participated in an internship, practicum, undergraduate research, community service or study abroad.

"The Princeton Review rates Bradley's entrepreneurship program, internship opportunities and video game design programs as among the top in the nation."

SELECTIVITY
Admissions Rating	84
# of applicants	10,708
% of applicants accepted	70
% of acceptees attending	14

FRESHMAN PROFILE
Range SAT EBRW	540–630
Range SAT Math	530–640
Range SAT Composite	1090–1260
Range ACT Composite	22–28
# submitting SAT scores	736
% submitting SAT scores	70
# submitting ACT scores	542
% submitting ACT scores	52
Average HS GPA	3.8
% graduated top 10% of class	25
% graduated top 25% of class	60
% graduated top 50% of class	87

DEADLINES
Early action	
Deadline	10/15
Regular	
Priority	12/1
Notification	Rolling, 9/1
Nonfall registration?	Yes

APPLICANTS ALSO LOOK AT AND OFTEN PREFER
University of Illinois at Urbana-Champai

AND SOMETIMES PREFER
DePaul University; Marquette University

AND RARELY PREFER
Illinois State University; Augustana College (IL)

FINANCIAL FACTS
Financial Aid Rating	86
Annual tuition	$35,060
Room and board	$11,280
Required fees	$420
Books and supplies	$1,200
Average frosh need-based scholarship	$22,430
Average UG need-based scholarship	$20,854
% needy frosh rec. need-based scholarship or grant aid	100
% needy UG rec. need-based scholarship or grant aid	98
% needy frosh rec. non-need-based scholarship or grant aid	16
% needy UG rec. non-need-based scholarship or grant aid	12
% needy frosh rec. need-based self-help aid	77
% needy UG rec. need-based self-help aid	80
% frosh need fully met	20
% ugrads need fully met	17
Average % of frosh need met	77
Average % of ugrad need met	75

BRANDEIS UNIVERSITY

415 South St., Waltham, MA 02454-9110 • Admissions: 781-736-3500 • Fax: 781-736-3536

CAMPUS LIFE

Quality of Life Rating	86
Fire Safety Rating	98
Green Rating	80
Type of school	Private
Environment	Metropolis

STUDENTS

Total undergrad enrollment	3,678
% male/female	39/61
% from out of state	70
% frosh from public high school	65
% frosh live on campus	99
% ugrads live on campus	76
# of fraternities	0
# of sororities	0
% African American	5
% Asian	14
% Caucasian	46
% Hispanic	8
% Native American	<1
% Pacific Islander	<1
% Two or more races	4
% Race and/or ethnicity unknown	2
% international	20
# of countries represented	56

SURVEY SAYS . . .

Lots of liberal students
Lab facilities are great
Great financial aid
Students are friendly
Students involved in community service
Theater is popular
Campus newspaper is popular
Active minority support groups

ACADEMICS

Academic Rating	89
% students returning for sophomore year	93
% students graduating within 4 years	81
% students graduating within 6 years	87
Calendar	Semester
Student/faculty ratio	10:1
Profs interesting rating	91
Profs accessible rating	94

Most classes have 10–19 students.

MOST POPULAR MAJORS

Biology/Biological Sciences, General; Economics, General; Business/Commerce, General

STUDENTS SAY "..."

Academics

Situated just outside of Boston, Brandeis University is a phenomenal school that "teaches ... the value of hard work, cultivates curiosity and [an] interest in learning, and introduces one to various perspectives." Importantly, the university offers undergrads "the opportunity to explore every possible interest, from cupcakes to neuroscience, with the overwhelming support of faculty and peers." Because Brandeis embraces a policy of academic "flexibility," students feel free to "to study whatever they want." There's also an "abundance of undergraduate research opportunities in all majors." Overall, undergrads here find their coursework "challenging" and "rewarding." Inside the classroom they are greeted by "engaging, insightful, and responsive" professors who truly make an effort to "relate to students." As one delighted individual shares, "My current bio teacher is known for using memes in her lectures, and they're usually pretty funny." It's also quite evident that professors "care for their students and want them to be successful." To that end, they strive to make themselves "accessible" and "encourage students coming to talk to them." Perhaps that's why one highly contented undergrad asserts, "I strongly believe the professors are one of Brandeis's most appealing aspects."

Life

At Brandeis, academics often take top priority. And first-year students quickly discover that "on weeknights the library is the most social spot on campus." But fear not; undergrads here still manage to find plenty of time to step away from the books. In fact, we're told that "Brandeis thrives on its campus club and student activities culture," which makes sense given that there are over 200 clubs on campus to join. Many students can be found participating "in community service clubs, cultural clubs, electronics clubs, and religious organizations, do research in labs, perform in musicals and plays, participate in sport events, and play music in ensembles." Undergrads also simply "enjoy the green spaces on campus and have fun connecting [there] with other students." Once the weekend rolls around, "there are always shows going on, whether it's theatre, a cappella, or improv." Additionally, there tend to be "sports events and guest lecturers." Undergrads also frequently attend "Greek life events off campus." However, those gatherings are "not sanctioned by the university." Lastly, students love the school's "[close] proximity" to Cambridge and Boston. And since Brandeis has a commuter rail stop on campus and runs a free shuttle on weekends, both cities are wholly "accessible" and provide a great respite from campus life.

Student Body

It's safe to say that Brandeis students really care for their peers. After all, they rush to describe them as "intelligent, driven [and] kind-hearted." They also seem to maintain "a diverse range of interests (both academic and extracurricular) and are extremely passionate about everything they are involved in." Moreover, undergrads readily admit that they "do have the tendency to be a little more on the introverted and nerdy side." And they truly love that their classmates are often "quirky and a little weird in the best way possible." As one student explains, "There is no normal Brandeis. I love that I can wear whatever I want because I know there's nowhere where it will be a problem that I don't fit in or feel judged. Everyone's attitude is kind of 'do whatever you want to/need to do.'" Given that openness, it's not too surprising to learn that Brandeis students also report that their classmates are quite "friendly." Indeed, a student reports, "Everyone here is very welcoming and supportive and they push me to try a bit harder every day, while offering support whenever it is needed without even having to be asked to do so."

Financial Aid: 781-736-3700 • E-Mail: admissions@brandeis.edu • Website: http://www.brandeis.edu/

THE PRINCETON REVIEW SAYS

Admissions

Very important factors considered include: rigor of secondary school record, class rank, academic GPA, character/personal qualities. *Important factors considered include:* application essay, recommendation(s), extracurricular activities, talent/ability. *Other factors considered include:* standardized test scores, interview, first generation, alumni/ae relation, geographical residence, state residency, religious affiliation/commitment, racial/ethnic status, volunteer work, work experience, level of applicant's interest. ACT with or without writing accepted. SAT with or without Essay component accepted. High school diploma is required and GED is accepted. *Academic units recommended:* 4 English, 4 math, 4 science, 2 science labs, 4 foreign language, 4 social studies.

Financial Aid

Students should submit: CSS/Financial Aid PROFILE; FAFSA; Noncustodial PROFILE. The Princeton Review suggests that all financial aid forms be submitted as soon as possible after October 1. *Need-based scholarships/grants offered:* College/university scholarship or grant aid from institutional funds; Federal Pell; Private scholarships; SEOG; State scholarships/grants. *Loan aid offered:* Direct PLUS loans; Direct Subsidized Stafford Loans; Direct Unsubsidized Stafford Loans. Federal Work-Study Program available. Institutional employment available.

The Inside Word

Admissions to Brandeis is selective. Therefore, it's imperative that applicants have taken a challenging course load that includes a handful of honors, AP, or IB classes (if and when possible). However, admissions officers are also looking for students who will thrive in and contribute to campus life. Hence, personal statements, letters of recommendations, and extracurricular activities also hold some weight. Finally, Brandeis is a test-optional school. Students who opt not to submit SAT or ACT scores will have to send in a graded analytical paper or three different exams (from an approved list of AP, IB, and SAT Subject Tests) instead.

THE SCHOOL SAYS "..."

From the Admissions Office

"Brandeis University was founded in 1948 by the American Jewish community at a time when Jews and other marginalized groups faced discrimination in higher education. Today, Brandeis is a leading research university for anyone, regardless of background, who wants to use their knowledge, skills and experience to improve the world. Nearly 6,000 Brandeis students and 550 faculty members collaborate across disciplines, interests and perspectives on scholarship that has a positive impact throughout society.

At the core of our community are values rooted in Jewish history and experience: a reverence for academic excellence, a robust engagement in critical thinking, and a commitment to making the world a better place. Classes are taught by professors who value teaching undergraduates and serve as advisors and mentors. Our flexible curriculum lets students pursue their passions with the ability to double major, study abroad, and engage in research and internships in Waltham, Boston, and beyond.

"Brandeis is a vibrant, free-thinking, intellectual university that values community. Students are actively engaged on campus in pursuits ranging from the arts to athletics and student government to community service.

"Brandeis has an ideal location on the commuter rail right outside of downtown Boston, giving students access to internships, jobs, and research in law, medicine, government, finance, business, and the arts."

SELECTIVITY

Admissions Rating	95
# of applicants	11,343
% of applicants accepted	30
% of acceptees attending	25
# offered a place on the wait list	1,553
% accepting a place on wait list	41
% admitted from wait list	1
# of early decision applicants	953
% accepted early decision	37

FRESHMAN PROFILE

Range SAT EBRW	660–730
Range SAT Math	690–790
Range SAT Composite	1380–1490
Range ACT Composite	30–33
# submitting SAT scores	549
% submitting SAT scores	64
# submitting ACT scores	219
% submitting ACT scores	25
Average HS GPA	3.8
% graduated top 10% of class	56
% graduated top 25% of class	83
% graduated top 50% of class	97

DEADLINES

Early decision	
Deadline	11/1
Notification	12/15
Other ED Deadline	1/1
Other ED Notification	2/1
Regular	
Deadline	1/1
Notification	4/1
Nonfall registration?	Yes

FINANCIAL FACTS

Financial Aid Rating	95
Annual tuition	$55,340
Room and board	$16,080
Required fees	$2,596
Books and supplies	$1,000
Average frosh need-based scholarship	$44,006
Average UG need-based scholarship	$42,876
% needy frosh rec. need-based scholarship or grant aid	96
% needy UG rec. need-based scholarship or grant aid	95
% needy frosh rec. non-need-based scholarship or grant aid	10
% needy UG rec. non-need-based scholarship or grant aid	6
% needy frosh rec. need-based self-help aid	86
% needy UG rec. need-based self-help aid	92
% frosh rec. any financial aid	65
% UG rec. any financial aid	67
% UG borrow to pay for school	46
Average cumulative indebtedness	$32,158
% frosh need fully met	100
% ugrads need fully met	94
Average % of frosh need met	97
Average % of ugrad need met	97

BRIGHAM YOUNG UNIVERSITY (UT)

A-153 ASB, Provo, UT 84602-1110 • Admissions: 801-422-2507 • Fax: 801-422-0005

CAMPUS LIFE

Quality of Life Rating	**91**
Fire Safety Rating	**76**
Green Rating	**60***
Type of school	Private
Affiliation	Church of Jesus Christ
	of Latter-day Saints
Environment	City

STUDENTS

Total undergrad enrollment	31,292
% male/female	50/50
% from out of state	68
% frosh live on campus	63
% ugrads live on campus	16
# of fraternities	0
# of sororities	0
% African American	<1
% Asian	2
% Caucasian	80
% Hispanic	7
% Native American	<1
% Pacific Islander	1
% Two or more races	4
% Race and/or ethnicity unknown	1
% international	4
# of countries represented	121

SURVEY SAYS . . .

Great library
School is well run
No one cheats
Students are friendly
Students are very religious
Students get along with local community
Students involved in community service
Very little drug use
Everyone loves the Cougars
Intramural sports are popular
Theater is popular

ACADEMICS

Academic Rating	**85**
% students returning for sophomore year	90
% students graduating within 4 years	22
% students graduating within 6 years	78
Calendar	Semester
Student/faculty ratio	20:1
Profs interesting rating	89
Profs accessible rating	92
Most classes have 20–29 students.	

MOST POPULAR MAJORS

Business/Commerce, General; Elementary
Education and Teaching; Exercise Physiology and
Kinesiology

STUDENTS SAY "..."

Academics

Founded in 1875, Brigham Young University in Utah operates under the mission and support of The Church of Jesus Christ of Latter-day Saints, offering more than 30,000 undergraduates 187 majors at a low cost of tuition. Sixty-six percent of BYU students have served missions—"More than half also speak foreign languages"—and to add to that worldliness, "many professors bring in people from the field or other connections so that students can hear from more perspectives on their chosen careers." There are "so many internships and partner programs around the world thanks to university connections," and BYU "offers very enlightening religion courses that cover topics deeply but are sensitive to students not of the faith." Students can also avail themselves of "many opportunities for experimental learning and hands-on projects and experiences" and the "tons of beneficial real career experience right on campus."

BYU faculty are "great at structuring classes and lessons in a way that's engaging and non-traditional," and "actively work to adjust their classes and their teaching every year based on the feedback of students." They are "fair and willing to work with students if you approach them early with concerns," and can be proactive about helping others succeed. "Many of my professors have reached out to me personally when they noticed I was struggling and offered to help me," says a student. The variety of classes is both wide and deep thanks to the inclusion of "great programs in specific fields and a very moral environment." Moreover, professors are "always looking for better ways to educate with technology and other teaching techniques," such as an "integrated online learning and class experience."

Life

Whether you're full-time or part-time, on-campus or not, BYU "tries to involve everybody." In particular, "student activities are well-publicized," which can lead to high participation. "Lots of people make sporting events a priority," while others "do the same for things related to the school of music events." Overall, there's a sense that the community "fills their days with service and recreational activities," like theater, choir, and clubs, although they're especially fond of outdoors events that take advantage of the campus's proximity to "a number of lakes, reservoirs, ski resorts, and national parks." There's plenty to do indoors as well! For instance, the free International Cinema "shows different films every week that are all from different time periods and countries and in different languages," and for students who want to make use of free public transportation options, "Salt Lake is only one hour away." And for those looking to visit these various locales with a partner, students inform us that "Dating is huge at [BYU], and lots of people go on dates on the weekends or throughout the week."

Student Body

Students here are "hard-working and determined to succeed in all aspects of their life: academically, socially, emotionally, [and] spiritually." They are "held to a high standard" and hence "take academics very seriously, [and] the class discussions are always very stimulating." While "the majority of the student body is Caucasian, there still is a decent amount of diversity." Where most attendees are the same are in the values they share, a characteristic that students say make it "easy to connect with people." Furthermore, "the value system of the school provides a blanket level of honesty" from classmates and faculty that helps to facilitate trust and bonds. The community is also described as welcoming: "There is little judgment when it comes to hobbies or interests that are out of the ordinary," and "the students on this campus are some of the kindest, friendliest people."

BRIGHAM YOUNG UNIVERSITY (UT)

Financial Aid: 801-378-4104 • E-Mail: admissions@byu.edu • Website: www.byu.edu

THE PRINCETON REVIEW SAYS

Admissions

Very important factors considered include: rigor of secondary school record, academic GPA, application essay, standardized test scores, recommendation(s), extracurricular activities, talent/ability, character/personal qualities, religious affiliation/commitment, volunteer work, work experience. *Important factors considered include:* first generation, racial/ethnic status. *Other factors considered include:* level of applicant's interest. ACT with or without writing accepted. SAT with or without Essay component accepted. High school diploma is required and GED is accepted. *Academic units recommended:* 4 English, 4 math, 3 science, 2 foreign language, 2 history.

Financial Aid

Students should submit: FAFSA. Priority filing deadline is 2/1. The Princeton Review suggests that all financial aid forms be submitted as soon as possible after October 1. *Need-based scholarships/grants offered:* College/university scholarship or grant aid from institutional funds; Federal Pell; Private scholarships; State scholarships/grants. *Loan aid offered:* Direct PLUS loans; Direct Subsidized Stafford Loans; Direct Unsubsidized Stafford Loans.

The Inside Word

An applicant pool of more than 11,000 necessitates a reliance on numbers, especially during the first round of cuts. Much of the matchmaking done at other schools isn't necessary here, as a highly self-selecting applicant pool typically precludes those who would make a poor fit. Still, admissions officers want to see at least respect (if not reverence) for LDS principles, without which survival here would be difficult indeed.

THE SCHOOL SAYS "..."

From the Admissions Office

"The mission of Brigham Young University—founded, supported, and guided by The Church of Jesus Christ of Latter-day Saints—is to assist individuals in their quest for perfection and eternal life. That assistance should provide a period of intensive learning in a stimulating setting where a commitment to excellence is expected and the full realization of human potential is pursued. All instruction, programs, and services at BYU, including a wide variety of extracurricular experiences, should make their own contribution toward the balanced development of the total person. Such a broadly prepared individual will not only be capable of meeting personal challenge and change but will also bring strength to others in the tasks of home and family life, social relationships, civic duty, and service to mankind.

"Freshman applicants are required to take either the ACT (with the optional writing section) or the SAT. The highest composite score will be used in admissions decisions."

SELECTIVITY

Admissions Rating	91
# of applicants	10,500
% of applicants accepted	67
% of acceptees attending	81

FRESHMAN PROFILE

Range SAT EBRW	610–710
Range SAT Math	600–710
Range SAT Composite	1220–1410
Range ACT Composite	26–31
# submitting SAT scores	1,715
% submitting SAT scores	30
# submitting ACT scores	5,152
% submitting ACT scores	90
Average HS GPA	3.9

DEADLINES

Regular	
Deadline	12/15
Notification	2/18
Nonfall registration?	Yes

FINANCIAL FACTS

Financial Aid Rating	80
Annual tuition	$5,790
Room and board	$7,915
Books and supplies	$872
Average frosh need-based scholarship	$5,545
Average UG need-based scholarship	$5,712
% needy frosh rec. need-based scholarship or grant aid	51
% needy UG rec. need-based scholarship or grant aid	79
% needy frosh rec. non-need-based scholarship or grant aid	63
% needy UG rec. non-need-based scholarship or grant aid	53
% needy frosh rec. need-based self-help aid	25
% needy UG rec. need-based self-help aid	22
% frosh rec. any financial aid	53
% UG rec. any financial aid	64
% UG borrow to pay for school	24
Average cumulative indebtedness	$14,672
% frosh need fully met	2
% ugrads need fully met	3
Average % of frosh need met	32
Average % of ugrad need met	35

BROWN UNIVERSITY

Box 1876, Providence, RI 02912 • Admissions: 401-863-2378 • Fax: 401-863-9300

CAMPUS LIFE

Quality of Life Rating	94
Fire Safety Rating	90
Green Rating	89
Type of school	Private
Environment	City

STUDENTS

Total undergrad enrollment	6,834
% male/female	48/52
% from out of state	95
% frosh from public high school	55
% frosh live on campus	100
% ugrads live on campus	72
# of fraternities (% ugrad men join)	9 (11)
# of sororities (% ugrad women join)	5 (12)
% African American	7
% Asian	17
% Caucasian	43
% Hispanic	11
% Native American	<1
% Pacific Islander	<1
% Two or more races	6
% Race and/or ethnicity unknown	5
% international	11
# of countries represented	109

SURVEY SAYS . . .

Lots of liberal students
Students always studying
Students are happy
Lab facilities are great
Great library
Career services are great
Internships are widely available
Great financial aid
No one cheats
Students are friendly
Diverse student types interact on campus
Students aren't religious
Students involved in community service
Students environmentally aware
Students love Providence, RI
Easy to get around campus
Recreation facilities are great
Theater is popular
Campus newspaper is popular
Active student government
Active minority support groups
Active student-run political groups

ACADEMICS

Academic Rating	95
% students returning for sophomore year	98
% students graduating within 4 years	83
% students graduating within 6 years	96
Calendar	Semester
Student/faculty ratio	6:1
Profs interesting rating	94
Profs accessible rating	95

Most classes have 10–19 students.

MOST POPULAR MAJORS
Computer and Information Sciences, General;
Biology/Biological Sciences, General; Econometrics
and Quantitative Economics

STUDENTS SAY "..."

Academics

Interdisciplinary-focused Brown University in Providence, Rhode Island is dedicated to undergraduate freedom, meaning students must take responsibility for designing their own courses of study via the Open Curriculum. Students sing the praises of the academic flexibility at this Ivy League institution and the accompanying emphasis on social action. "We would not be...strong students and teachers without a proper system in place to encourage that," says one undergrad. Those who roam these hallowed halls are "constantly questioning what could make the world and our school a better place." Every person "has their own interests and pursues it without any push from others," which is why Brown can be a "very intense" place to go to school—not because students are competing academically with each other, but "because there are so many people doing so much and fighting so hard for it."

Brown's faculty "are at the top of their fields and are working on research that pushes those fields forward." The "engaging, personal, and incredibly dedicated" professors are "the heart and soul of our strongest departments." They "care so much about what they do and connect with students on a very human level." Undergraduates come first here, and Brown encourages students to "explore their academic interests independently in order to experience everything that academics have to offer." "No other school I had looked at allowed students to...build their own academic journey without any general requirements," says one student. Graduates tend to "not just go to the normative career options," and "career and internship placement has become a top priority of the new university administration."

Life

Life at Brown can be "exciting, but also filled with countless hours of study." Though academia reigns over the week, some people "go to house parties, sport parties, or downtown for the weekend," and there are "lectures, movie screenings, improv shows, dance performances, [and] a cappella showcases constantly." "Brown is generally a very happy place with many activities and events going on all the time," says a student. A great thing about these type of events is that "they are rarely exclusionary and the university is trusting of its students." Many here also do "intellectual activities or athletics over breaks," and "community clubs and special interest clubs (such as international student groups)" are extremely popular. Students also often go to the lounges in the dorms to watch movies with friends. The campus may be "beautiful," but when an off-campus breather is needed, students can easily walk one minute to Thayer Street and "enjoy restaurants and excellent dining" or walk twenty minutes to Providence Mall. Boston and New York are very close, but "Providence is busy enough that Brown never completely empties out."

Student Body

This "knowledgeable and inspiring" community is made up of people who are "very intelligent, care about global issues, and possess one or two quirks." The school "has a way of molding people into their best selves," and the most common trait is "a true zeal for whatever it is that we care most about." Although this is a liberal campus, there are "a handful of conservatives," and "the entire body has a general chilled-out vibe." There is "a prevailing intolerance of intolerance on campus," and the culture of activism "bespeaks an idealism and a strong moral code that drives a lot of the work students do on campus." "I've never experienced so many people willing to have a conversation about topics that usually make people uncomfortable or that people stray away," says one student.

BROWN UNIVERSITY

Financial Aid: 401-863-2721 • E-Mail: admission@brown.edu • Website: www.brown.edu

THE PRINCETON REVIEW SAYS

Admissions

Very important factors considered include: rigor of secondary school record, class rank, academic GPA, application essay, standardized test scores, recommendation(s), talent/ability, character/personal qualities. *Important factors considered include:* extracurricular activities. *Other factors considered include:* interview, first generation, alumni/ae relation, geographical residence, state residency, racial/ethnic status, volunteer work, work experience. ACT with or without writing accepted. SAT with or without Essay component accepted. High school diploma is required and GED is accepted. *Academic units required:* 4 English, 3 math, 3 science, 2 science labs, 3 foreign language, 2 history, 1 academic elective. *Academic units recommended:* 4 English, 4 math, 4 science, 3 science labs, 4 foreign language, 1 social studies, 2 history, 1 academic elective, 1 visual/performing arts.

Financial Aid

Students should submit: CSS/Financial Aid PROFILE; FAFSA; Noncustodial PROFILE. The Princeton Review suggests that all financial aid forms be submitted as soon as possible after October 1. *Need-based scholarships/grants offered:* College/university scholarship or grant aid from institutional funds; Federal Pell; Private scholarships; SEOG; State scholarships/grants. *Loan aid offered:* Direct PLUS loans; Direct Subsidized Stafford Loans; Direct Unsubsidized Stafford Loans. Applicants will be notified of awards on or about 4/1. Federal Work-Study Program available. Institutional employment available.

The Inside Word

The cream of just about every crop applies to Brown, and admission is competitive. Gaining admission requires more than just a superior academic profile from high school. Candidates from states that are overrepresented in the applicant pool, such as New York, have to be particularly distinguished in order to have the best chance at admission. Brown accepts the Common Application, with additional writing supplements for all first-year students, and requires some additional statements from students who apply to the Program in Liberal Medical Education or the Dual Degree Program with Rhode Island School of Design. Test scores (either SAT with or without essay component or the ACT with or without Writing) required. Two SAT Subject Tests of applicant's choice recommended but not required.

THE SCHOOL SAYS "..."

From the Admissions Office

Brown University is the nation's seventh oldest institution and one of eight members of the Ivy League. The University is known for its academic rigor rooted in its "Open Curriculum." Brown has no distribution requirements that students must complete to graduate, which attracts self-motivated students committed to being the architects of their own education. Our students like to say that only Brown gives them the absolute freedom to study what they love, and only what they love. Students sample courses in a wide range of subjects before immersing themselves in one of 80 academic concentrations in 44 different academic areas, with the option of independent study. Brown offers unparalleled opportunities for research collaboration directly with faculty who lead in their fields. Since 1764, Brown has offered the best in educational innovation, leading-edge scholarship and research, and opportunities for community-based service learning. This has contributed to a reputation for graduating creative, entrepreneurial, socially conscious students who make an impact in their communities and the world in areas of science and engineering, the arts, policy, medicine and many other fields. The Warren Alpert Medical School of Brown University, Rhode Island's only medical school, provides over 500 students with medical instruction and clinical training at seven Brown-affiliated hospitals in and around Providence.

SELECTIVITY

Admissions Rating	99
# of applicants	38,674
% of applicants accepted	7
% of acceptees attending	61
# of early decision applicants	4,230
% accepted early decision	18

FRESHMAN PROFILE

Range SAT EBRW	700–770
Range SAT Math	740–800
Range SAT Composite	1440–1550
Range ACT Composite	33–35
# submitting SAT scores	1,118
% submitting SAT scores	67
# submitting ACT scores	805
% submitting ACT scores	48
% graduated top 10% of class	94
% graduated top 25% of class	98
% graduated top 50% of class	100

DEADLINES

Early decision	
Deadline	11/1
Notification	12/15
Regular	
Deadline	1/1
Notification	3/31
Nonfall registration?	No

FINANCIAL FACTS

Financial Aid Rating	98
Annual tuition	$57,112
Room and board	$15,332
Required fees	$1,292
Books and supplies	$1,632
Average frosh need-based scholarship	$52,881
Average UG need-based scholarship	$52,057
% needy frosh rec. need-based scholarship or grant aid	100
% needy UG rec. need-based scholarship or grant aid	100
% needy frosh rec. non-need-based scholarship or grant aid	0
% needy UG rec. non-need-based scholarship or grant aid	0
% needy frosh rec. need-based self-help aid	84
% needy UG rec. need-based self-help aid	87
% frosh rec. any financial aid	58
% UG rec. any financial aid	49
% UG borrow to pay for school	31
Average cumulative indebtedness	$24,304
% frosh need fully met	100
% ugrads need fully met	100
Average % of frosh need met	100
Average % of ugrad need met	100

BRYANT UNIVERSITY

Office of Admission, 1150 Douglas Pike, Smithfield, RI 02917-1291 • Admissions: 401-232-6100 • Fax: 401-232-6731

STUDENTS SAY "..."

Academics

Bryant University in Rhode Island prides itself on doing things differently, and they stand by that by encouraging an integrated curriculum combining business and liberal arts fields. It's a tact that students don't seem to mind, citing "phenomenal job placement numbers." One student claims "it is very hard to *not* get a job within six months of graduating." That could be due, in part, to the fact that the school "excels in its ability to provide hands-on academic experiences" that "ensure all students are ready for what the real world will be like." One such initiative is the first-year Bryant IDEA Program, which is "a three-day intensive program that teaches design thinking." Those opportunities don't end on Bryant's campus, though, as students can also take advantage of programs like the one-to-two-week Sophomore International Experience abroad.

Regardless of where Bryant's students are, the "academic experience is always focused on learning rather than getting a grade." and everyone here is "very willing to offer extra help when it is needed," making it "hard [for a student] to fall through the cracks." To that end, faculty here are "professionals in their industry" and are "quite open … about their real-world experiences." Their words "bring great insight into various industries" and "allow students to get in touch with the latest information so they can catch up with the current [trends] in the business world." This also comes with the open style of teaching many classes employ, "which allows for a dialogue and expansion of thoughts and ideas in the classroom." That dialogue also reaches beyond the classroom thanks to an "incredible network of alumni who genuinely care and want to get Bryant students jobs."

Life

For Bryant Bulldogs, weekdays "are filled with class, homework, and group projects," so students are "always busy with group meetings." But when they're not in a meeting or in class, students "normally sit and do homework by the pond—if it is nice out." When they're ready to step away from their studies, sports offer an engaging distraction: "Everyone goes to … games … dressed in black and gold." Outside of intramurals, "various clubs attract a lot of students," with an assortment of options ranging from those that "promote mental health awareness [to those] that play video games every Friday night." On weekends, students will often "take a trip to Providence for dinner or go on a trip with the Student Programming Board to go bowling, to [see] a play, or to [watch] a Boston sports game." Whatever your tastes may be, this "extremely welcoming" community has the "perfect balance of academics, recreation, and extracurricular activities."

Student Body

At Bryant, "no one is simply looking for a job—everyone is searching for *the* job." This leads to "an air of professionalism here," although students can "be labelled as over-involved" as they do what they can to gain experience and stand out. It's not hard for students to recognize each other at Bryant, though, as it's a "relatively small school in land and in numbers." One student says, "That means we get to know our peers on a more personal level." This familiarity is also helped by the fact that "many choose to double major." Indeed, this group is "driven to succeed in their careers after college," and "almost everyone who can is employed in a summer internship." Overall, campus life is teeming with "different types of leaders who are each striving for their individual goals but are also devoted to maintaining a strong, cohesive student body."

Financial Aid: 401-232-6020 • E-Mail: http://www.bryant.edu/admissions/request • Website: http://www.bryant.edu/

THE PRINCETON REVIEW SAYS

Admissions

Very important factors considered include: rigor of secondary school record, academic GPA. *Important factors considered include:* class rank, application essay, standardized test scores, recommendation(s). *Other factors considered include:* interview, extracurricular activities, talent/ability, character/personal qualities, first generation, alumni/ae relation, geographical residence, state residency, racial/ethnic status, volunteer work, work experience, level of applicant's interest. ACT with or without writing accepted. SAT with or without Essay component accepted. High school diploma is required and GED is accepted. *Academic units required:* 4 English, 4 math, 2 science, 2 science labs, 2 foreign language, 2 history. *Academic units recommended:* 4 English, 4 math, 3 science, 2 science labs, 2 foreign language, 3 history.

Financial Aid

Students should submit: FAFSA. Priority filing deadline is 2/15. The Princeton Review suggests that all financial aid forms be submitted as soon as possible after October 1. *Need-based scholarships/grants offered:* College/university scholarship or grant aid from institutional funds; Federal Pell; Private scholarships; SEOG; State scholarships/grants. *Loan aid offered:* Direct PLUS loans; Direct Subsidized Stafford Loans; Direct Unsubsidized Stafford Loans. Applicants will be notified of awards on or about 3/24. Federal Work-Study Program available. Institutional employment available.

The Inside Word

The admissions process at Bryant University is wholly comprehensive. To begin, the school wants students who have taken a challenging college prep curriculum (including honors, AP, and IB courses when possible). Of course, letters of recommendation and extracurricular involvement are also important. Applicants wary of standardized tests will be delighted to learn that Bryant is a test-optional school. In lieu of submitting scores, students will have to respond to three short essay questions.

THE SCHOOL SAYS "..."

From the Admissions Office

"Bryant offers an innovative model of education that integrates business with the liberal arts and sciences, providing you with the world-ready experience and knowhow to stand out after graduation. It's an approach that prepares you for both personal fulfillment and professional success. Ninety-nine percent of the Class of 2019 was employed—or enrolled in graduate school—within six months of graduation. The median starting salary for graduates is $60,000.

"You'll graduate with either a major in business and a complementary minor in the liberal arts, or a liberal arts major and a business minor. With more than 195 major/minor combinations available, you'll design your studies to create the path that's right for you. The possibilities, and roads to success, are endless.

"Our faculty, whose expertise is sought after around the globe, will engage you in ways that educate the whole person. They'll be your mentors both in the classroom and beyond, and inspire you to reach your fullest potential. Our supportive culture will challenge you to achieve more than you ever thought possible.

"Bryant is a community that encourages different perspectives and celebrates racial, cultural, gender-based, and religious diversity. We put an emphasis on global immersion, both on-campus and abroad, so that when you graduate you can work effectively with anyone, anywhere.

"Our stunning, 435-acre campus in Smithfield, Rhode Island has a small town feel with easy access to major cities. Bryant is just fifteen minutes from downtown Providence, an hour from Boston, and three hours from New York City."

SELECTIVITY

Admissions Rating	81
# of applicants	7,632
% of applicants accepted	71
% of acceptees attending	16
# offered a place on the wait list	350
% accepting a place on wait list	31
% admitted from wait list	8
# of early decision applicants	174
% accepted early decision	78

FRESHMAN PROFILE

Range SAT EBRW	560–640
Range SAT Math	570–660
Range SAT Composite	1150–1280
Range ACT Composite	25–29
# submitting SAT scores	602
% submitting SAT scores	71
# submitting ACT scores	58
% submitting ACT scores	7
Average HS GPA	3.4
% graduated top 10% of class	20
% graduated top 25% of class	49
% graduated top 50% of class	88

DEADLINES

Early decision	
Deadline	11/1
Notification	12/1
Other ED Deadline	1/15
Other ED Notification	2/15
Early action	
Deadline	11/15
Notification	1/15
Regular	
Deadline	2/1
Notification	3/15
Nonfall registration?	Yes

APPLICANTS ALSO LOOK AT AND OFTEN PREFER
Babson College; Bentley University; Boston University; University of Connecticut; University of Massachusetts Amherst; Boston College

AND SOMETIMES PREFER
Fairfield University; Northeastern University; Providence College; University of Vermont; Fordham University; Loyola University Maryland; Marist College

AND RARELY PREFER
Quinnipiac University; Roger Williams University; Stonehill College; University of Rhode Island; Assumption University; Merrimack College; Sacred Heart University; Saint Joseph's University (PA); University of New Hampshire; Suffolk University

FINANCIAL FACTS

Financial Aid Rating	81
Annual tuition	$45,966
Room and board	$16,204
Required fees	$897
Books and supplies	$1,400
Average frosh need-based scholarship	$9,941
Average UG need-based scholarship	$9,760
% needy frosh rec. need-based scholarship or grant aid	61
% needy UG rec. need-based scholarship or grant aid	66
% needy frosh rec. non-need-based scholarship or grant aid	73
% needy UG rec. non-need-based scholarship or grant aid	76
% needy frosh rec. need-based self-help aid	70
% needy UG rec. need-based self-help aid	80
% frosh rec. any financial aid	94
% UG rec. any financial aid	89
% UG borrow to pay for school	65
Average cumulative indebtedness	$53,350
% frosh need fully met	22
% ugrads need fully met	47
Average % of frosh need met	47
Average % of ugrad need met	48

BRYN MAWR COLLEGE

101 North Merion Avenue, Bryn Mawr, PA 19010-2859 • Admissions: 610-526-5152 • Fax: 610-526-7471

STUDENTS SAY "..."

Academics

A women's liberal arts college founded in 1885 (and the first to offer the PhD), Bryn Mawr College in southeastern Pennsylvania is an "institution with a heart" that fosters "a close-knit community of empowered lifelong learners" who are "committed to striving for social equality and academic excellency." Students enjoy the relaxed and intimate atmosphere of a small college. One student describes "dinner parties in professors' homes, small reading groups that meet once a week, film screenings and weekend outings with my classmates" and shares, "I think I'm lucky to have such open and accessible professors and mentors." Bryn Mawr's low student-to-faculty ratio allows students to get plenty of face time with their professors and peers in during classes, which students describe as "laid back, in that everyone is working hard but does not feel the competitive pressure found at other schools." "It is easy to get a spot in most classes," one student tells us, "so your schedule truly reflects your interests." Bryn Mawr offers other ways for students to personalize their studies, even within the required coursework: "The freshman writing seminar has about twenty different classes, so students get to explore a topic that excites them." Bryn Mawr is also part of the Seven Sister Colleges and the Tri-College Consortium "with Haverford and Swarthmore [which] allows students to explore a range of fields without compromising on the small liberal arts college experience." Overall students are thrilled with their experience at Bryn Mawr and the support they receive, or, as one student puts it: "Bryn Mawr College represents hope and self-empowerment for every student who walks through Pem Arch."

Life

"Bryn Mawr students are serious about classes," but that doesn't mean they don't have a social life. While "most week days people do homework and study in the libraries," students use the weekends to "go into Philadelphia or just go around the area" for "restaurants, concerts, museums, and special events." And there is always something fun to do on campus as well. The "student activities office plans a lot of events like movie screenings, tie dye, concerts, [and] pumpkin decorating" and Bryn Mawr's many clubs and student groups host events as well, "like crafting nights, culture shows, [and] keynote speakers." These socially-minded students can also discuss, plan, and organize within the college's "activist groups with causes ranging from the environment to elder care." The college's rich and storied history means that there are a lot of "traditions and annual parties (e.g., 'East vs. West')" for students to take part in, and for off-campus parties, "We hop on the blue bus and head over to Haverford, which has a better music/party scene," students tell us.

Student Body

"Brilliantly smart, informed and active in the community," Bryn Mawr students show a high regard for one another and value the individual contributions each one of their peers makes. "While there are countless stereotypes about the sort of people who attend a women's college," one student explains, "there's really no one Bryn Mawr type." The college hosts "an incredibly talented and diverse group" of students who are united by "our love of Bryn Mawr and learning in general." Students say the student body is "quite political," and "while straight, cis women can certainly thrive at Bryn Mawr, you should come here prepared for an active and thriving LGBTQIA+ culture. It's a very special part of Bryn Mawr that I wouldn't trade for anything." These "intellectual, accepting, open, kind, inclusive and bright individuals" "are a part of dance groups, singing groups and just about any other activity," and they make sure to "attend each other's performances." Overall, students agree that the student body is a reflection of a BMC culture that thrives to "[help] people achieve their fullest potential without forcing them into a mould."

Financial Aid: 610-526-5245 • E-Mail: admissions@brynmawr.edu • Website: www.brynmawr.edu

THE PRINCETON REVIEW SAYS

Admissions

Very important factors considered include: rigor of secondary school record, recommendation(s). *Important factors considered include:* class rank, academic GPA, application essay, extracurricular activities, character/personal qualities. *Other factors considered include:* standardized test scores, interview, talent/ability, first generation, alumni/ae relation, geographical residence, state residency, racial/ethnic status, volunteer work, work experience. ACT with or without writing accepted. SAT with or without Essay component accepted. High school diploma is required and GED is accepted. *Academic units recommended:* 4 English, 4 math, 4 science, 1 science lab, 3 foreign language, 2 social studies, 2 history, 2 academic electives.

Financial Aid

Students should submit: CSS/Financial Aid PROFILE; FAFSA; Noncustodial PROFILE. The Princeton Review suggests that all financial aid forms be submitted as soon as possible after October 1. *Need-based scholarships/grants offered:* College/university scholarship or grant aid from institutional funds; Federal Pell; Private scholarships; SEOG; State scholarships/grants. *Loan aid offered:* Direct PLUS loans; Direct Subsidized Stafford Loans; Direct Unsubsidized Stafford Loans. Federal Work-Study Program available. Institutional employment available.

The Inside Word

Bryn Mawr College is among the most academically competitive in the nation. Incoming first-year students need to submit the Common Application or the Coalition Application, a writing supplement, two teacher evaluations, a mid-year report, standardized tests results (see test optional policy), and a final report. While not required, students are also encouraged to interview with an alum or admissions officer, and students can also submit art supplements through The Common App as well.

THE SCHOOL SAYS "..."

From the Admissions Office

"Bryn Mawr, a selective women's college with 1,350 undergraduates, is renowned for its academic excellence, diverse and close-knit community, and engagement with the world.

"On an historic campus just outside of Philadelphia, Bryn Mawr students find challenging courses and research; strong bonds with faculty, students, and alumnae/i; innovative programs that connect study with action; and top-tier partnerships that expand options.

"Critical, creative, and collaborative, Bryn Mawr alumnae/i are agents of change in every arena—and forever members of a community founded on respect for individuals.

"Minutes outside of Philadelphia and only two hours by train from New York City and Washington, D.C., Bryn Mawr is recognized by many as one of the most stunning college campuses in the United States.

"Standardized test scores for U.S. applicants or U.S. permanent residents are not required. Non-U.S. citizens and Non-U.S. permanent residents are required to submit standardized test scores (SAT or ACT) as well as either the TOEFL or IELTS if their primary language is not English and/or their language of instruction over the last four years has not been English."

SELECTIVITY

Admissions Rating	95
# of applicants	3,332
% of applicants accepted	33
% of acceptees attending	34
# offered a place on the wait list	627
% accepting a place on wait list	53
% admitted from wait list	11
# of early decision applicants	346
% accepted early decision	52

FRESHMAN PROFILE

Range SAT EBRW	640–740
Range SAT Math	650–770
Range ACT Composite	29–33
# submitting SAT scores	227
% submitting SAT scores	61
# submitting ACT scores	121
% submitting ACT scores	32
% graduated top 10% of class	67
% graduated top 25% of class	95
% graduated top 50% of class	99

DEADLINES

Early decision	
Deadline	11/15
Notification	12/15
Other ED Deadline	1/1
Other ED Notification	2/1
Regular	
Deadline	1/15
Notification	4/1
Nonfall registration?	No

FINANCIAL FACTS

Financial Aid Rating	97
Annual tuition	$53,180
Room and board	$17,100
Required fees	$1,260
Books and supplies	$1,000
Average frosh need-based scholarship	$43,829
Average UG need-based scholarship	$46,150
% needy frosh rec. need-based scholarship or grant aid	100
% needy UG rec. need-based scholarship or grant aid	100
% needy frosh rec. non-need-based scholarship or grant aid	16
% needy UG rec. non-need-based scholarship or grant aid	12
% needy frosh rec. need-based self-help aid	89
% needy UG rec. need-based self-help aid	92
% frosh rec. any financial aid	78
% UG rec. any financial aid	73
% UG borrow to pay for school	52
Average cumulative indebtedness	$28,772
% frosh need fully met	100
% ugrads need fully met	100
Average % of frosh need met	100
Average % of ugrad need met	100

BUCKNELL UNIVERSITY

Office of Admissions, 1 Dent Drive, Lewisburg, PA 17837 • Admissions: 570-577-3000 • Fax: 570-577-3538

CAMPUS LIFE

Quality of Life Rating	88
Fire Safety Rating	94
Green Rating	97
Type of school	Private
Environment	Village

STUDENTS

Total undergrad enrollment	3,608
% male/female	49/51
% from out of state	79
% frosh from public high school	54
% frosh live on campus	100
% ugrads live on campus	91
# of fraternities (% ugrad men join)	9 (35)
# of sororities (% ugrad women join)	9 (42)
% African American	3
% Asian	5
% Caucasian	74
% Hispanic	7
% Native American	<1
% Pacific Islander	0
% Two or more races	4
% Race and/or ethnicity unknown	<1
% international	6
# of countries represented	49

SURVEY SAYS . . .

Students are happy
Classroom facilities are great
Lab facilities are great
Great library
Career services are great
Internships are widely available
Easy to get around campus
Recreation facilities are great
Lots of beer drinking
Hard liquor is popular
Intramural sports are popular
Frats and sororities are popular
Alumni active on campus

ACADEMICS

Academic Rating	93
% students returning for sophomore year	92
% students graduating within 4 years	86
% students graduating within 6 years	90
Calendar	Semester
Student/faculty ratio	9:1
Profs interesting rating	93
Profs accessible rating	96

Most classes have 10–19 students.
Most lab/discussion sessions have
10–19 students.

MOST POPULAR MAJORS

Economics, General; Accounting and Finance;
Psychology, General

STUDENTS SAY "..."

Academics

Students choose Bucknell University, a private liberal arts school in central Pennsylvania, for its rep for "providing an excellent education, a small classroom setting with involved professors, and a close-knit community." The school packages a "great education and engineering school on a beautiful campus," where "the school spirit keeps students motivated to attend classes and try their hardest." Bucknell's academics provide "a well-rounded, interdisciplinary education" with a "strong focus on its undergraduates," who number over 3,600. The professors are "passionate about their area of study" and "truly care about us and encourage interaction outside of the classroom." They're "interesting, knowledgeable, and accessible." "The professors are at Bucknell because they want to work with students. It definitely shows in the classroom and during office hours." "There isn't one class where the professor doesn't know everyone's names within the first few weeks." Bucknell's culture fosters a "desire to develop its students as well-rounded, capable, intelligent and interesting individuals" who "are competent in both theory and practical application of coursework." The university's "well-respected engineering college" stands out among its academic offerings, as do Bucknell's small class sizes: "The ideal faculty to student ratio makes class time more meaningful and engaging. Our academics mean the perfect combination between challenging and fascinating." One student comments, "Unlike my friends at other universities, I honestly can't say that I have had a bad professor here." "The classes offered are extremely interesting and really instill a sense of passion and appreciation into what area you choose to study," and if you find an area of particular passion for you, "Bucknell offers many resources to its students that allow for success in whatever fields students would like to pursue." Indeed, Bucknell's undergrads are forward-looking, and many extol Bucknell's "unbelievable alumni network" and "retention rate," as well as its "research opportunities" and "high degree of job placement after school."

Life

If your ideal college experience includes "strong campus unity" with "opportunities for undergraduates, accessible professors, incredible athletic resources...engaging atmosphere," all on a "beautiful campus," Bucknell may deserve a close look. Students describe life at Bucknell as "a culture that fosters an eagerness to learn while simultaneously providing opportunities to engage and grow socially with an incredible student body." Students value both seriousness and fun, saying they "work hard play hard (and safe)," and that "everyone is very involved in various activities across campus. Students fit in well because everyone is part of many different groups." They feel "it's important to break out of your comfort zone, try new things, learn from your mistakes; you will be given opportunities of a lifetime at Bucknell, so take them." Bucknell's undergrads love "recreational sports of any kind" in the spaces between their ongoing "party, sleep, eat, study" cycle, and university-sponsored social highlights include "great events like cake decorating contests, canoe battleship, movie nights, and so many other fun events" on campus. "Bucknell has a reputation for being a party school, but there are plenty of students that do not party and live quite happily on this campus." "The school is good about getting artists and speakers here," so there's plenty to do besides drinking, but "house parties happen three to four times a week and the over twenty-one-year-olds go to the bars" as well. Overall, Bucknell is popular with its undergrads, who praise its "incredible opportunity, and incredible people."

Student Body

At Bucknell, "the way most students fit in is by joining Greek life." One student describes the student body as "very preppy, but all students are welcomed," and another as "a not very diverse but very open to diversity school!" "While most students may be geographically homogenous (tri-state area, Pennsylvania, Massachusetts)," one student believes that her school is distinctive "in that its people are extremely unique, and there is a lot of diversity of thought." Many students comment that the "white and wealthy" are prevalent at the university, and that the "campus looks like a country club."

Financial Aid: 570-577-1331 • E-Mail: admissions@bucknell.edu • Website: www.bucknell.edu

THE PRINCETON REVIEW SAYS

Admissions

Very important factors considered include: rigor of secondary school record, academic GPA, application essay, standardized test scores, talent/ability, character/personal qualities. *Important factors considered include:* recommendation(s), extracurricular activities, volunteer work. *Other factors considered include:* class rank, first generation, alumni/ae relation, geographical residence, religious affiliation/commitment, racial/ethnic status. ACT with or without writing accepted. SAT with or without Essay component accepted. High school diploma is required and GED is accepted. *Academic units required:* 4 English, 3 math, 2 science, 2 foreign language, 2 social studies, 2 history, 1 academic elective. *Academic units recommended:* 4 English, 4 math, 2 science, 2 science labs, 4 foreign language, 2 social studies, 2 history, 1 academic elective.

Financial Aid

Students should submit: CSS/Financial Aid PROFILE; FAFSA. The Princeton Review suggests that all financial aid forms be submitted as soon as possible after October 1. *Need-based scholarships/grants offered:* College/university scholarship or grant aid from institutional funds; Federal Pell; Private scholarships; SEOG; State scholarships/grants. *Loan aid offered:* Direct PLUS loans; Direct Subsidized Stafford Loans; Direct Unsubsidized Stafford Loans. Applicants will be notified of awards on or about 4/1. Federal Work-Study Program available. Institutional employment available.

The Inside Word

A well-rounded, extremely polished application is non-negotiable for the hopeful Bucknell applicant, as the school gets more competitive every year. Admissions officers strive to consider all facets of the applications they receive—test scores, essays, recommendations, transcripts—so make sure you consider all of them carefully. In particular, the admission committee is looking for applicants who can demonstrate how they are bold, thoughtful, and compassionate leaders. Bucknell accepts the Common Application.

THE SCHOOL SAYS "..."

From the Admissions Office

"Bucknell University offers more than 50 majors and 65 minors in the College of Arts & Sciences, College of Engineering and College of Management. Your professors will be mentors and innovators in their fields who will challenge you to think critically, develop your ideas thoughtfully and apply what you learn. Bucknell is a residential university, so most students live on campus, but learning, service, research and recreation extend off campus. You will have the opportunity to volunteer as close as the local nursing home, community center and sustainable farm, and as far away as New Orleans and Nicaragua. Every year, students also travel off campus to conduct research with faculty mentors. Destinations have included Alaska, Suriname and Australia.

"At Bucknell, you'll take advantage of career services such as advising, networking, mock interviews and employer fairs. You can explore your career options and network with alumni through summer internships with corporations, government organizations and non-profits locally, nationally and internationally. An externship program provides job-shadowing opportunities for sophomores.

"With its green spaces, brick buildings and striking vistas, Bucknell's 450-acre campus is a quintessential college environment in the heart of scenic central Pennsylvania. The restaurants and shops of downtown Lewisburg—including the Barnes & Noble at Bucknell University and the historic Campus Theatre—lie within walking distance of campus. The University is located within three- to four-hours' driving distance of Baltimore, New York City, Philadelphia, Pittsburgh and Washington, D.C."

SELECTIVITY

Admissions Rating	94
# of applicants	9,845
% of applicants accepted	34
% of acceptees attending	29
# offered a place on the wait list	3,149
% accepting a place on wait list	44
% admitted from wait list	9
# of early decision applicants	681
% accepted early decision	64

FRESHMAN PROFILE

Range SAT EBRW	620–700
Range SAT Math	635–730
Range SAT Composite	1280–1410
Range ACT Composite	28–32
# submitting SAT scores	695
% submitting SAT scores	72
# submitting ACT scores	350
% submitting ACT scores	36
Average HS GPA	3.6
% graduated top 10% of class	58
% graduated top 25% of class	83
% graduated top 50% of class	98

DEADLINES

Early decision	
Deadline	11/15
Notification	12/15
Other ED Deadline	1/15
Other ED Notification	2/15
Regular	
Deadline	1/15
Notification	4/1
Nonfall registration?	No

APPLICANTS ALSO LOOK AT AND OFTEN PREFER

Cornell University; Dartmouth College; Tufts University; University of Pennsylvania; University of Virginia

AND SOMETIMES PREFER

Boston College; Colgate University; Lehigh University; University of Richmond; Wake Forest University

AND RARELY PREFER

Elon University; Lafayette College; Northeastern University; Penn State University Park; Villanova University

FINANCIAL FACTS

Financial Aid Rating	89
Annual tuition	$57,882
Room and board	$14,670
Required fees	$320
Books and supplies	$900
Average frosh need-based scholarship	$33,700
Average UG need-based scholarship	$32,300
% needy frosh rec. need-based scholarship or grant aid	86
% needy UG rec. need-based scholarship or grant aid	87
% needy frosh rec. non-need-based scholarship or grant aid	33
% needy UG rec. non-need-based scholarship or grant aid	29
% needy frosh rec. need-based self-help aid	100
% needy UG rec. need-based self-help aid	100
% frosh rec. any financial aid	48
% UG rec. any financial aid	60
% UG borrow to pay for school	46
Average cumulative indebtedness	$31,000
% frosh need fully met	0
% ugrads need fully met	0
Average % of frosh need met	92
Average % of ugrad need met	92

BUTLER UNIVERSITY

Robertson Hall, 4600 Sunset Avenue, Indianapolis, IN 46208 • Admissions: 317-940-8100 • Fax: 317-940-8150

STUDENTS SAY ". . ."

Academics

Butler University in Indianapolis is a relatively small liberal arts school that prides itself on its established history of providing a quality education while doing things differently. With just under 5,000 students and more than sixty-five majors spread across six academic colleges, the "student to faculty ratio is excellent" and teachers "are open to collaboration with students on research and professional endeavors." The school is continually introducing "innovative technology into each of the classrooms" (such as wireless display devices and a Lightboard room), and its eight core course requirements "push students out of their comfort zones" and allow them to explore interests outside of their major, creating "an atmosphere of driven students."

Professors are willing "to support student ideas and make modifications to lectures to support student interests," and "always facilitate discussions in the classroom that create an intellectually stimulating experience." They are "engaging, fun, and extremely knowledgeable about their areas of expertise" and "bring life to learning." Students and teachers "interact multiple times a week and it is clear that both parties have a sincere desire to be there," and teachers "put in time and effort to developing relationships and getting to know their students closely."

As an added benefit, Butler offers more than 110 study abroad programs in seventy countries that "focus on the study abroad experience while keeping time and cost short." Students are expected to almost be "learning on the job," as much of the coursework provides real-life experiences and internships. Different majors have inventive requirements and classes: some science classes have "semester-long research projects"; one class participated in a "simulated village while studying modern China"; while the business school has a "Real Business Experience course," in which students must "develop a business and sell a product/service during a typical semester" that is funded by a loan from the university.

Life

Butler has an interesting campus in that "life is completely sustainable on-campus," which means that students typically stay there for studying, food, and socializing. On days with good weather, students can be found "out playing ball, Frisbee or hammocking around campus," and Butler has a nice park on campus as well. The school spirit at Butler is palpable and "Many people support athletics and the arts and there's a lot of fundraising for things"; "Basketball games are the best way to spend a weekend." Many students on campus are involved in Greek life, which is "a prominent social aspect of Butler's campus," and people at Butler are generally "very busy because they like to overcommit themselves." There "is always something going on," making it "just a really great environment to go to college." Downtown Indianapolis is only five miles away, and students like to go to Broad Ripple or take "other small trips around the area" for food and culture.

Student Body

It's a small campus, so "it's more close-knit than others," and there's definitely a community on campus "that cares and looks out for one another." Many students "would not consider the student body at Butler to have great ethnic/cultural diversity"; however, the student body is "welcoming and accepting." The campus is full of "incredibly friendly people who are more than willing to help or just smile at you"; it's "fairly Greek, but the Greek system is much more open and accepting than a lot of larger schools." The inclusive Butler culture is described as "The Butler Way," and "there is a camaraderie among everyone in the same class to help each other succeed." Most students here are involved in some sort of community service organization on or off campus, which "truly speaks to the character of the university and its students."

BUTLER UNIVERSITY

Financial Aid: 317-940-8200 • E-Mail: admission@butler.edu • Website: www.butler.edu

THE PRINCETON REVIEW SAYS

Admissions

Very important factors considered include: rigor of secondary school record, academic GPA, standardized test scores, character/personal qualities. *Important factors considered include:* application essay, recommendation(s), extracurricular activities, talent/ability. *Other factors considered include:* class rank, first generation, alumni/ae relation, geographical residence, racial/ethnic status, volunteer work, work experience. ACT with or without writing accepted. High school diploma is required and GED is accepted. *Academic units required:* 4 English, 3 math, 3 science, 3 science labs, 2 foreign language, 2 social studies, 2 history. *Academic units recommended:* 4 science, 4 science labs.

Financial Aid

Students should submit: FAFSA. Priority filing deadline is 12/1. The Princeton Review suggests that all financial aid forms be submitted as soon as possible after October 1. *Need-based scholarships/grants offered:* College/university scholarship or grant aid from institutional funds; Federal Pell; Private scholarships; SEOG; State scholarships/grants. *Loan aid offered:* Direct PLUS loans; Direct Subsidized Stafford Loans; Direct Unsubsidized Stafford Loans. Applicants will be notified of awards on a rolling basis beginning 1/15. Federal Work-Study Program available. Institutional employment available.

The Inside Word

Around 12,000 students apply to Butler each year for just around 1,000 slots, but don't let this fool you: solid students with the proper completed coursework will have no trouble gaining admission (over 65% are accepted). SAT or ACT scores are required for admission (writing test scores are not), and students are recommended to take both exams if possible. Students applying through the Butler specific application (instead of the Common App) must complete an essay based on a predetermined topic.

SELECTIVITY

Admissions Rating	87
# of applicants	16,418
% of applicants accepted	68
% of acceptees attending	12

FRESHMAN PROFILE

Range SAT EBRW	590–660
Range SAT Math	580–670
Range ACT Composite	25–30
# submitting SAT scores	873
% submitting SAT scores	66
# submitting ACT scores	951
% submitting ACT scores	72
Average HS GPA	3.9
% graduated top 10% of class	45
% graduated top 25% of class	76
% graduated top 50% of class	96

DEADLINES

Early action	
Deadline	11/1
Notification	12/15
Nonfall registration?	Yes

FINANCIAL FACTS

Financial Aid Rating	77
Annual tuition	$41,370
Room and board	$15,540
Required fees	$990
Books and supplies	$1,000
Average frosh need-based scholarship	$21,869
Average UG need-based scholarship	$21,842
% needy frosh rec. need-based scholarship or grant aid	99
% needy UG rec. need-based scholarship or grant aid	25
% needy frosh rec. non-need-based scholarship or grant aid	22
% needy UG rec. non-need-based scholarship or grant aid	16
% needy frosh rec. need-based self-help aid	64
% needy UG rec. need-based self-help aid	70
% frosh rec. any financial aid	97.4
% UG rec. any financial aid	94.9
% UG borrow to pay for school	58
Average cumulative indebtedness	$38,191
% frosh need fully met	14
% ugrads need fully met	12
Average % of frosh need met	64
Average % of ugrad need met	66

CALIFORNIA INSTITUTE OF TECHNOLOGY

Caltech Office of Undergrad Admissions, Pasadena, CA 91125 • Admissions: 626-395-6341 • Fax: 626-683-3026

CAMPUS LIFE
Quality of Life Rating	91
Fire Safety Rating	89
Green Rating	60*
Type of school	Private
Environment	City

STUDENTS
Total undergrad enrollment	938
% male/female	55/45
% from out of state	64
% frosh from public high school	74
% frosh live on campus	100
% ugrads live on campus	94
# of fraternities	0
# of sororities	0
% African American	2
% Asian	37
% Caucasian	27
% Hispanic	17
% Native American	<1
% Pacific Islander	<1
% Two or more races	9
% Race and/or ethnicity unknown	<1
% international	8
# of countries represented	25

SURVEY SAYS . . .
Students always studying
Lab facilities are great
Great financial aid
No one cheats
Students aren't religious
Students love Pasadena, CA
Dorms are like palaces
Easy to get around campus

ACADEMICS
Academic Rating	92
% students returning for sophomore year	98
% students graduating within 4 years	84
% students graduating within 6 years	94
Calendar	Quarter
Student/faculty ratio	3:1
Profs interesting rating	86
Profs accessible rating	89

Most classes have 10–19 students.
Most lab/discussion sessions have
  10–19 students.

MOST POPULAR MAJORS
Computer and Information Sciences, General;
Physics, General; Electrical and Electronics
Engineering

STUDENTS SAY "..."

Academics

Beyond arguably one of the most rigorous undergraduate educations in science out there, Caltech is a small, tight-knit community that is "geared towards training tomorrow's leaders and pioneers in the field of science." There may be a heavy emphasis on scientific learning and research, but "not to the point where students can do nothing else," as the core curriculum "exposes each student to a broad range of subjects" beyond the stereotypical fare. At Caltech, passionate researchers "work together to solve the problems of tomorrow, while enjoying great weather." Or to put it in the parlance of collegiate times: "Cross collaboration of ideas and ingenuity leads to epic-ness!" Academics are understandably "intense" at Caltech: "The work can be hell but you'll love what you learn." Fortunately, "classes are small and it's often easy to form tight bonds with the professors." The quality of teaching can vary—"just because they're Nobel Prize winners, does not make them good lecturers"—but the extremely low student-to-faculty ratio "makes it easier to interact on a personal basis with professors." "My academic experience here has been an extremely difficult whirlwind of humbling and fascinating knowledge," says a student. Much learning is done through the homework sets, on which students are encouraged to collaborate. The dedication Caltech has for training the researchers of tomorrow is renowned, and is evident in the accessibility to research for all students, even freshmen. The academic experience isn't just in the classroom; there are "lots of funding opportunities (for instance, the Housner and the MHF) for projects outside of the classroom." "One professor took me on for research after freshman year (we formulated an improved way to rank basketball players and teams), and I'm very good friends with him in what is now my junior year," says a mathematics major. Undergraduate student representation and self-government are happily welcomed here, and the school "really cares about the undergrads and wants to keep us happy." The school also does "a really good job of keeping students occupied and entertained while at the same time cramming a ridiculous amount of information into our heads."

Life

Modeled after the Oxford college system (and "very similar to Harry Potter"), the Caltech house system is the basis for undergraduate life, offering both a place to live and a social center for students. Freshmen are placed into one of eight houses after the first week of school, and "immediately are integrated into a close social network/safety net. Basically each student automatically gets ~100 friends." Each house has "a slightly different culture, and most people find that they identify strongly with at least one of the cultures"; as one student says, "My house has a tool room and turned down the housing office's offer to buy us a TV," says a senior electrical engineering major. In keeping with the one big happy family vibe, "undergraduates and grad students play Frisbee together, students and faculty play together in music groups, grad students go to undergraduate parties...and the students have a lot of unexploited trust from the faculty because of the Honor Code." Caltech has lots of fun traditions such as Halloween, when students "freeze pumpkins in liquid nitrogen and drop them off of Millikan library as a 'pumpkin-drop experiment.'" However, some feel that some of the new administrators "are trying to circumvent various student traditions and freedoms." The cherry on top of the Caltech sundae is "the fantastic SoCal weather, which is hard to beat anywhere in the world." Time is at a premium, but students "take trips to the beach and LA" over the weekend; during the week, "[problem] sets and extracurriculars keep us pretty close to campus."

Student Body

"Everyone knows each other" at this "beautiful, small campus," and there's "no way around it": students here are "smart" and "nerdier than average," but "there is a wide range in personality within the student body." Almost everyone has "an odd sense of humor and a serious hobby, whether it be Minecraft, building lasers, or rock climbing." There is "complete trust within the student body" at Caltech, and the house system provides "a family-like support network for students," which is a welcome respite from "extreme academic pressures."

CALIFORNIA INSTITUTE OF TECHNOLOGY

Financial Aid: 626-395-6280 • E-Mail: ugadmissions@caltech.edu • Website: www.caltech.edu

THE PRINCETON REVIEW SAYS

Admissions

Very important factors considered include: rigor of secondary school record, application essay, standardized test scores, recommendation(s), character/personal qualities. *Important factors considered include:* class rank, academic GPA, extracurricular activities. *Other factors considered include:* talent/ability, first generation, racial/ethnic status, volunteer work, work experience. ACT with or without writing accepted. SAT with or without Essay component accepted. High school diploma or equivalent is not required. *Academic units required:* 3 English, 4 math, 2 science, 1 science lab, 1 history. *Academic units recommended:* 4 English, 4 science.

Financial Aid

Students should submit: Business/Farm Supplement; CSS/Financial Aid PROFILE; FAFSA; Institution's own financial aid form; Noncustodial PROFILE; State aid form. Priority filing deadline is 3/2. The Princeton Review suggests that all financial aid forms be submitted as soon as possible after October 1. *Need-based scholarships/grants offered:* College/university scholarship or grant aid from institutional funds; Federal Pell; Private scholarships; SEOG; State scholarships/grants. *Loan aid offered:* Direct PLUS loans; Direct Subsidized Stafford Loans; Direct Unsubsidized Stafford Loans. Applicants will be notified of awards on or about 4/15. Federal Work-Study Program available. Institutional employment available.

The Inside Word

Each Caltech application receives more than one read before it's presented to the admissions committee. This ensures that all candidates receive a thorough evaluation. The school values the unique drive and energy of its current students and desires applicants who display a similar combination of creativity and intellect. Stellar academic credentials are a must, and prospective students must display an aptitude for math and science.

THE SCHOOL SAYS "..."

From the Admissions Office

"Admission to the freshman class is based on many factors—some quantifiable, some not. What you say in your application is important! We do not offer interviews as part of the application, meaning that your essays and recommendation letters are particularly substantial in our review, especially given that faculty serve on the admissions committee. High school academic performance is very important, as is a demonstrated interest in math, science, and/or engineering. We are also interested in your character, maturity, and motivation, and we're proud of a selection process that incorporates all these aspects into each individual and thorough review. If you have any questions about the process or about Caltech in general, send us an email or give us a call. We'd like to hear from you!

"Freshman applicants must submit scores from either the SAT or ACT. All applicants must submit the SAT Math II Subject exam, as well as one of the science subject exams (either biology, chemistry. or physics)."

SELECTIVITY

Admissions Rating	99
# of applicants	8,367
% of applicants accepted	6
% of acceptees attending	44
# offered a place on the wait list	501
% accepting a place on wait list	79
% admitted from wait list	1

FRESHMAN PROFILE

Range SAT EBRW	740–760
Range SAT Math	790–800
Range SAT Composite	1530–1570
Range ACT Composite	35–36
# submitting SAT scores	186
% submitting SAT scores	79
# submitting ACT scores	98
% submitting ACT scores	42
% graduated top 10% of class	99
% graduated top 25% of class	100

DEADLINES

Early action	
Deadline	11/1
Notification	12/15
Regular	
Deadline	1/3
Notification	3/15
Nonfall registration?	No

FINANCIAL FACTS

Financial Aid Rating	98
Annual tuition	$52,506
Room and board	$16,644
Required fees	$2,594
Books and supplies	$1,428
Average frosh need-based scholarship	$49,618
Average UG need-based scholarship	$50,058
% needy frosh rec. need-based scholarship or grant aid	100
% needy UG rec. need-based scholarship or grant aid	100
% needy frosh rec. non-need-based scholarship or grant aid	0
% needy UG rec. non-need-based scholarship or grant aid	0
% needy frosh rec. need-based self-help aid	46
% needy UG rec. need-based self-help aid	57
% frosh rec. any financial aid	57
% UG rec. any financial aid	50
% UG borrow to pay for school	30
Average cumulative indebtedness	$20,192
% frosh need fully met	100
% ugrads need fully met	100
Average % of frosh need met	100
Average % of ugrad need met	100

CALIFORNIA STATE UNIVERSITY, STANISLAUS

One University Circle, Turlock, CA 95382 • Admissions: 209-667-3070 • Fax: 209-667-3788

STUDENTS SAY "..."

Academics

One of the members of California's noted state university system, Stanislaus "provides affordable education" that focuses on helping students prepare for their careers with a "professional, yet laid-back demeanor." This is "a great environment to be a part of," and the school "wants you to succeed, and they give you the info you need to succeed." Many of the students here live nearby, and the in-state tuition offers "rigorous" academics and "a great place to meet mentors and learn different approaches to life." Professors get mixed but mainly positive reviews; "some are excellent...go above and beyond," and are "wonderful at helping the students as much as they can," but others are just "fair," and "some should not be teaching." Registration could use some rejiggering; students say that the registration priority needs to change each semester, and the more popular departments could use "more of the same classes offered every semester, with multiple sections." Still, for higher-level classes, "small class sizes where you are able to get a lot of help from professors" are a huge boon. Nursing and business are some of "the strongest subjects that come out of here," and it is "very inexpensive for a fully accredited business degree" relative to many other schools. In developing well-prepared students, Stanislaus personnel are "attentive" on all fronts. "Very rarely are any of your classes taught by a graduate student or someone without a PhD," says a student. The accessibility of departments and staff is "always very easy," and "they are very informative with upcoming changes or events." Job placement is a huge end goal for Stanislaus State, and "helping students (especially veterans) during these rough economic times is a priority at CSU Stanislaus."

Life

Though Stan State offers "scenery as beautiful and varied as the students" and "awesome" weather, popular complaints are that "buildings need updating" and "there are too many geese on the grounds." The university's efforts to provide "a ton of organizations on campus" give the commuter students "a college experience like that of any other student living on campus." "It's nice that the school recognizes that we need a break sometimes and promote being a healthy individual, both mind and body," says one student. Events are regularly held in the quad, "student-run shows [such] as dance-offs or karaoke," and "music concerts are regularly held throughout the semesters, usually featuring guest artists or students." Turlock is "not the biggest town," but there is "easy access to the freeway," and local events and great places "keep everyone occupied." On campus, "there are lounges that you can play pool, darts, video games, etc.," and "Greek life is well-supported." The many commuter students mean that resident community on campus is "small and tightly knit"; there are a fair number of nontraditional students here as well, and they have no problems getting by. "I am an older student, and life on campus is great; everybody accepts me as just another student working toward my degree," one says.

Student Body

Perhaps due to the focus on future careers here, students are "motivated and excited to be at school." "I think we all know that with every class session we are that much closer to graduation," says one. Because the campus is so small, "a big portion of the student life is also Greek." Diversity is "rich" here, and there are "many different ethnicities and cultures from all over." Though everyone is friendly and "easygoing," "typical students keep to themselves but do not hesitant to help another student if he or she asks for it," but even those who want to "can fit in almost anywhere, as most groups found around campus are very accepting."

CALIFORNIA STATE UNIVERSITY, STANISLAUS

Financial Aid: 209-667-3336 • E-Mail: Outreach_help_desk@csustan.edu • Website: www.csustan.edu

THE PRINCETON REVIEW SAYS

Admissions

Very important factors considered include: rigor of secondary school record, academic GPA, standardized test scores. *Important factors considered include:* class rank. ACT with or without writing accepted. SAT with or without Essay component accepted. Submission of scores from the SAT or ACT for admission in fall 2021 will not be required. High school diploma is required and GED is accepted. *Academic units required:* 4 English, 3 math, 2 science, 2 science labs, 2 foreign language, 1 social studies, 1 history, 1 academic elective, 1 visual/performing arts. *Academic units recommended:* 4 English, 3 math, 2 science, 2 science labs, 2 foreign language, 1 social studies, 1 history, 1 academic elective, 1 visual/performing arts.

Financial Aid

Students should submit: FAFSA; Institution's own financial aid form; State aid form. Priority filing deadline is 3/2. The Princeton Review suggests that all financial aid forms be submitted as soon as possible after October 1. *Need-based scholarships/grants offered:* College/university scholarship or grant aid from institutional funds; Federal Pell; Private scholarships; SEOG; State scholarships/grants. *Loan aid offered:* Direct PLUS loans; Direct Subsidized Stafford Loans; Direct Unsubsidized Stafford Loans; Federal Nursing Loans. Applicants will be notified of awards on a rolling basis beginning 4/1. Federal Work-Study Program available. Institutional employment available.

The Inside Word

Like most state schools, Stanislaus State admissions practices are fairly straightforward. The university adheres to the eligibility index as defined by the California state system, so applicants who meet GPA and standardized test score minimums are automatically granted admission. Out-of-state candidates face more stringent requirements, as do those applying for highly competitive majors and programs.

THE SCHOOL SAYS "..."

From the Admissions Office

"For sixty years, California State University, Stanislaus, has welcomed students from California's Central Valley and around the world. Stanislaus State continues to distinguish itself as an institution that provides top-quality degree programs with a high level of personal attention, offering forty-three majors, forty-one minors and more than 100 areas of concentration, along with sixteen master's degree programs, seven credential programs, and a doctorate in educational leadership. With a student-to-faculty ratio of 22:1, Stanislaus State demonstrates its commitment to individualized instruction over the more common lecture-hall style of many larger universities. The university enjoys an ideal location in the Northern San Joaquin Valley, a short distance from the San Francisco Bay Area, Monterey, Big Sur, the Sierra Nevada Mountains, and the state capital of Sacramento. The main campus is located in the city of Turlock, a community that prides itself on its small town atmosphere, clean living space, excellent schools, and low crime rate. Degree programs in these disciplines have earned specialized accreditation: art, business administration, education, genetic counseling, music, nursing, psychology, public administration, social work, and theater. The College of Business Administration and the College of Education, Kinesiology and Social Work have also earned prestigious state and national accreditation. Nearly $70 million in merit—and need-based grants and scholarships was awarded for the 2019–20 school year. Over 81 percent of undergraduates receive need-based aid, and more than $129 million in total financial assistance is awarded annually."

SELECTIVITY

Admissions Rating	73
# of applicants	8,764
% of applicants accepted	89
% of acceptees attending	20

FRESHMAN PROFILE

Range SAT EBRW	450–540
Range SAT Math	440–530
Range SAT Composite	900–1070
Range ACT Composite	15–21
# submitting SAT scores	1,295
% submitting SAT scores	83
# submitting ACT scores	300
% submitting ACT scores	19
Average HS GPA	3.4

DEADLINES

Regular	
Priority	11/30
Deadline	11/30
Notification	Rolling, 11/1
Nonfall registration?	Yes

FINANCIAL FACTS

Financial Aid Rating	71
Annual in-state tuition	$5,742
Annual out-of-state tuition	$19,464
Room and board	$10,950
Required fees	$1,842
Books and supplies	$1,160
Average frosh need-based scholarship	$10,798
Average UG need-based scholarship	$9,822
% needy frosh rec. need-based scholarship or grant aid	98
% needy UG rec. need-based scholarship or grant aid	97
% needy frosh rec. non-need-based scholarship or grant aid	7
% needy UG rec. non-need-based scholarship or grant aid	6
% needy frosh rec. need-based self-help aid	77
% needy UG rec. need-based self-help aid	87
% frosh rec. any financial aid	93
% UG rec. any financial aid	87
% UG borrow to pay for school	49
Average cumulative indebtedness	$17,952
% frosh need fully met	9
% ugrads need fully met	16
Average % of frosh need met	80
Average % of ugrad need met	78

CALVIN UNIVERSITY

3201 Burton Street S.E., Grand Rapids, MI 49546 • Admissions: 616-526-6106 • Fax: 616-526-6777

CAMPUS LIFE

Quality of Life Rating	92
Fire Safety Rating	83
Green Rating	85
Type of school	Private
Affiliation	Christian Reformed
Environment	Metropolis

STUDENTS

Total undergrad enrollment	3,382
% male/female	47/53
% from out of state	41
% frosh from public high school	52
% frosh live on campus	94
% ugrads live on campus	59
# of fraternities	0
# of sororities	0
% African American	3
% Asian	5
% Caucasian	70
% Hispanic	5
% Native American	<1
% Pacific Islander	<1
% Two or more races	3
% Race and/or ethnicity unknown	1
% international	13
# of countries represented	70

SURVEY SAYS . . .

Students are happy
Lab facilities are great
Internships are widely available
Students are very religious
Students environmentally aware
Students love Grand Rapids, MI
Easy to get around campus
Recreation facilities are great
Very little drug use

ACADEMICS

Academic Rating	82
% students returning for sophomore year	85
% students graduating within 4 years	64
% students graduating within 6 years	76
Calendar	4/1/4
Student/faculty ratio	13:1
Profs interesting rating	92
Profs accessible rating	95

Most classes have 20–29 students.
Most lab/discussion sessions have 10–19 students.

MOST POPULAR MAJORS

Engineering, General; Registered Nursing/
Registered Nurse; Business Administration and
Management, General

STUDENTS SAY "..."

Academics

Founded in 1876, Calvin University is a mid-sized Christian liberal arts institution located in Grand Rapids, Michigan that trains students "to think critically and live out their vocation in the world while working to advance God's Kingdom." The prestigious academics (the nursing and honors programs are standouts) feature a high level of integration of faith within the classroom, and "departments teach their specific content in the context of a Christian worldview." The coursework is "difficult and challenging," but faculty "make us feel welcomed and make sure they are available for all of our questions." Not only are their teaching methods stellar, they are "relatable and offer good advice, genuinely wishing the students a good future."

Professors have "a desire to share their wealth of experiences and passions with the students" and are "extremely talented, interesting, and connected in their specific fields." Instructors are also "masters at integration of education and Christianity," making the classes at Calvin less about teaching the requisites for getting a job and "more about how to continue to learn about the field and how Christianity should figure into it." Within courses, there is great opportunity to delve into complicated and often controversial topics "in a way that doesn't ignore culture, science, or social scientific data." Sharing ideas is encouraged between students. "I feel I can appropriately express my opinions and views without the condemnation of others," says one. No matter your passion or career choice, "you will be paired with advisors [who have] similar passions," which "allows freedom to express thoughts and talk openly with willing professors."

Life

"Dorm life is vibrant" at Calvin and "most of people's friends come from dorm life since that is such a big focus at Calvin." Within the dorms "there is plenty of opportunity for leadership, and everyone is encouraged to grow together." Floor events in the residential halls are huge bonding occasions. The Student Life Division does a good job of organizing events that many students attend, including movies, board game nights, and concerts, and there are also "lots of clubs on campus that you can get involved in." When people aren't studying (studying in the hammocks around campus is popular) or in class, they often go to coffee shops or to get food together. Most work part-time, and there are "many different opportunities for on campus jobs." Extracurriculars are big, and students "go backpacking, swing dancing...or hiking." There are also lots of things to do in the Grand Rapids area, and "people go out to meals, movies, bowling, sporting events, the downtown market, and other events in the city such as ArtPrize," or will go to Lake Michigan. Chapel is held daily but is not required, and there are a lot of "study groups and Bible studies to help each other grow toward academic and spiritual goals."

Student Body

Calvin's 3,700-strong student body includes a wide range of students and interests, including a significant number of international students, athletes, those with Dutch heritage, and "valedictorians everywhere." A large percentage of the students "are Christians and come from somewhere in the Midwest," and all are generally "friendly, helpful, outgoing, and hardworking." One student notes, "Some people feel that Calvin University is very diverse and others feel that it is not diverse at all, depending on where they came from." Diversity activities are highly emphasized and encouraged around campus, and the student body is "small enough that Calvin begins to feel like home, but large enough that you don't know everyone." "There is a niche for everyone in the social life of the school," says one student.

CALVIN UNIVERSITY

Financial Aid: 800-688-0122 • E-Mail: admissions@calvin.edu • Website: www.calvin.edu

THE PRINCETON REVIEW SAYS

Admissions

Very important factors considered include: rigor of secondary school record, academic GPA, standardized test scores, religious affiliation/commitment. *Important factors considered include:* application essay, recommendation(s), extracurricular activities, character/personal qualities. *Other factors considered include:* class rank, volunteer work, work experience, level of applicant's interest. ACT with or without writing accepted. SAT with or without Essay component accepted. High school diploma is required and GED is accepted. *Academic units required:* 3 English, 3 math, 2 science, 2 social studies, 3 academic electives. *Academic units recommended:* 4 English, 3 math, 2 science, 1 science lab, 2 foreign language, 3 social studies, 3 academic electives.

Financial Aid

Students should submit: FAFSA. Priority filing deadline is 11/15. The Princeton Review suggests that all financial aid forms be submitted as soon as possible after October 1. *Need-based scholarships/grants offered:* College/university scholarship or grant aid from institutional funds; Federal Pell; Private scholarships; SEOG; State scholarships/grants. *Loan aid offered:* Direct PLUS loans; Direct Subsidized Stafford Loans; Direct Unsubsidized Stafford Loans. Applicants will be notified of awards on a rolling basis beginning 12/15. Federal Work-Study Program available. Institutional employment available.

The Inside Word

Admissions officers at Calvin are interested in candidates who will flourish within the school's academic and social community. Just as importantly, they seek applicants who are looking to deepen and affirm their Christian faith. The college accepts roughly 75 percent of their applicant pool, so students who maintain solid transcripts should not have too much difficulty getting in. Bear in mind, though, that the high acceptance rate is partially due to the self-selecting nature of Calvin's applicant cohort.

THE SCHOOL SAYS "..."

From the Admissions Office

"Calvin University is a top-ranked Christian liberal arts college that prepares students to lead with courageous conviction. Through rigorous academic study and intentional Christian community, students learn to think deeply, act justly and live wholeheartedly.

"At Calvin, we dare to pursue excellence in everything we take on. We don't settle for good enough...not in a lab, not in an art show, not even in a jump shot. It's a bold college path, but thousands of alumni will tell you it's a path worth traveling, no matter what sparks your passion.

"Here we believe that no one major has the upper hand in uncovering truths about God and the world. All are invited into the discovery. In fact, Calvin has had a liberal arts bent—a desire to explore all things—since its beginnings in 1876.

"Today's multi-faceted core curriculum allows students to chase the wonderings of philosophy, the intricacies of languages foreign and familiar, and the beauty of the world at a molecular level. Calvin offers 100+ academic options, as well as a masters of education, and bachelor's-to-master's degree programs in accounting and speech pathology and audiology.

"You can start meaningful work in your area of interest right away during your Calvin experience: participate in the innovative career-and-life readiness program, Calvin LifeWork; conduct significant research, present and publish alongside world-class faculty; and make global connections by studying abroad through more than 40 faculty-led off-campus programs."

SELECTIVITY
Admissions Rating	81
# of applicants	3,401
% of applicants accepted	77
% of acceptees attending	30

FRESHMAN PROFILE
Range SAT EBRW	570–670
Range SAT Math	560–680
Range SAT Composite	1140–1340
Range ACT Composite	24–30
# submitting SAT scores	586
% submitting SAT scores	75
# submitting ACT scores	402
% submitting ACT scores	52
Average HS GPA	3.8
% graduated top 10% of class	35
% graduated top 25% of class	62
% graduated top 50% of class	87

DEADLINES
Regular	
Deadline	8/15
Notification	Rolling, 11/1
Nonfall registration?	Yes

APPLICANTS ALSO LOOK AT AND OFTEN PREFER
University of Michigan—Ann Arbor; Wheaton College (IL)

AND SOMETIMES PREFER
Cedarville University; Central Michigan University; Grand Valley State University; Hope College; Michigan State University; Purdue University—West Lafayette; Taylor University;

AND RARELY PREFER
Cornerstone University; Indiana Wesleyan University; Olivet Nazarene University; Spring Arbor University; Trinity Christian College; Western Michigan University

FINANCIAL FACTS
Financial Aid Rating	87
Annual tuition	$37,600
Room and board	$10,800
Required fees	$206
Books and supplies	$1,300
Average frosh need-based scholarship	$22,316
Average UG need-based scholarship	$20,082
% needy frosh rec. need-based scholarship or grant aid	100
% needy UG rec. need-based scholarship or grant aid	100
% needy frosh rec. non-need-based scholarship or grant aid	21
% needy UG rec. non-need-based scholarship or grant aid	14
% needy frosh rec. need-based self-help aid	76
% needy UG rec. need-based self-help aid	84
% frosh rec. any financial aid	100
% UG rec. any financial aid	97
% UG borrow to pay for school	55
Average cumulative indebtedness	$25,888
% frosh need fully met	31
% ugrads need fully met	23
Average % of frosh need met	80
Average % of ugrad need met	75

CARLETON COLLEGE

100 South College Street, Northfield, MN 55057 • Admissions: 507-222-4190 • Fax: 507-222-4526

CAMPUS LIFE
Quality of Life Rating	94
Fire Safety Rating	98
Green Rating	90
Type of school	Private
Environment	Village

STUDENTS
Total undergrad enrollment	2,069
% male/female	49/51
% from out of state	83
% frosh from public high school	60
% frosh live on campus	100
% ugrads live on campus	96
# of fraternities	0
# of sororities	0
% African American	5
% Asian	9
% Caucasian	58
% Hispanic	8
% Native American	<1
% Pacific Islander	0
% Two or more races	7
% Race and/or ethnicity unknown	2
% international	11
# of countries represented	42

SURVEY SAYS . . .
Lots of liberal students
Students always studying
Students are happy
Classroom facilities are great
Lab facilities are great
Great library
Internships are widely available
School is well run
Great financial aid
No one cheats
Students are friendly
Diverse student types interact on campus
Students environmentally aware
Easy to get around campus
Intramural sports are popular
College radio is popular
Active minority support groups

ACADEMICS
Academic Rating	98
% students returning for sophomore year	95
% students graduating within 4 years	88
% students graduating within 6 years	92
Calendar	Trimester
Student/faculty ratio	9:1
Profs interesting rating	97
Profs accessible rating	98

Most classes have 10–19 students.
Most lab/discussion sessions have 10–19 students.

MOST POPULAR MAJORS
Computer and Information Sciences, General; Biology/Biological Sciences, General; Economics, General

STUDENTS SAY "..."
Academics
Carleton College, with its low student-teacher ratio and small-town Minnesota setting, "is a rigorous school full of laid-back, outdoorsy students with a passion for learning and for developing strong community." With a trimester schedule and an emphasis on the liberal arts and interdisciplinary scholarship, Carleton also boasts strong programs in the sciences and social sciences. The school has a reputation for being "highly rigorous without the cut-throat competition that other elite institutions are known for"; many students use the words "challenging" and "collaborative" to describe this tight-knit, highly focused academic community. One student sums it up as an "Ivy League education without all the Ivy League pretensions." While academics are "challenging" and classes are "fairly fast-paced," the work is "worth every ounce of effort" and professors are almost universally praised as "friendly, accessible, supportive, and enthusiastic about teaching." Students "have no qualms about dropping in on office hours to chat" and have "been to many wonderful dinners at professors' homes." "Students help each other out a lot, too (even if it is just emotional support)." One student describes the school accurately with her reasons for choosing to attend: "I wanted to be at a place where I was challenged. I wanted to be surrounded by people who were smarter than me but also wanted to see me succeed." Finally, students report excellent resources for pursuing graduate study, and visible improvements within career services.

Life
Weekends at Carleton bustle with activity to help balance the intellectual challenges of weekday classes. As one student put it, "I often find myself attending a concert at the Cave, the student pub; going to a show one of my friends wrote at the Little Nourse Theater; taking a quick trip to the cities for Mall of America or an uptown excursion; or, most likely, having a surprisingly engaging and deep intellectual discussion with some friends at a party on a Friday night." Intramural sports such as broomball and ultimate Frisbee are "freakishly popular." Outdoor activities are very popular in the Arboretum, "an 800-acre forest where students go for runs, go snow-shoeing, or have camp fires." The campus even features Dacie Moses House, "a house for baking cookies 24/7." If you're looking to unwind with a less structured activity, "the drinking policy throughout Northfield is strict, but...it's relaxed here at Carleton," and most students report that while partying is an option, "there are just as many opportunities for substance-free activities. Even at parties, there is no pressure to drink." As Northfield is small and most students live in the dorms (a few wish for more off-campus living options), Carleton life tends to be campus-centric. "Carls" complain about very few things: the cold Minnesota weather, on-campus food options, and the accessibility of the health center. Overall, though, it's clear that students here feel well cared for.

Student Body
At Carleton, students are, "on the whole, pretty liberal" as well as "politically and environmentally aware," and "are highly interested in activism on the whole." Students note that they "spend the majority of the weekend studying but still find time for socializing and spending time on extracurriculars, but most students feel that they don't have enough 'down time.'" "Generally they are very welcoming, extremely kind (when walking around campus nearly everyone I pass will shoot me a smile), dedicated to their studies on weekdays but want to party on weekends, and kind of dorky." "There are so many clubs and organizations to get involved in, and so many people doing really interesting things outside of any structured class or club, that it is incredibly hard to not get involved in something or other." "Everyone loves to have meaningful conversations," "people are very self-aware, but not self-centered," and "the best part about that is that they all keep really open minds." Students feel that "Carleton has been ramping up diversity efforts in recent years," but could still stand a bit more improvement in that area.

Financial Aid: 507-222-4138 • E-Mail: admissions@carleton.edu • Website: www.carleton.edu

THE PRINCETON REVIEW SAYS

Admissions

Very important factors considered include: rigor of secondary school record, class rank, academic GPA. *Important factors considered include:* application essay, standardized test scores, recommendation(s), extracurricular activities, talent/ability, character/personal qualities, alumni/ae relation. *Other factors considered include:* interview, first generation, geographical residence, state residency. ACT with or without writing accepted. SAT with or without Essay component accepted. High school diploma is required and GED is accepted. *Academic units recommended:* 4 English, 3 math, 3 science, 1 science lab, 3 foreign language, 3 social studies.

Financial Aid

Students should submit: CSS/Financial Aid PROFILE; FAFSA; Noncustodial PROFILE. Priority filing deadline is 1/15. The Princeton Review suggests that all financial aid forms be submitted as soon as possible after October 1. *Need-based scholarships/grants offered:* College/university scholarship or grant aid from institutional funds; Federal Pell; Private scholarships; SEOG; State scholarships/grants. *Loan aid offered:* Direct PLUS loans; Direct Subsidized Stafford Loans; Direct Unsubsidized Stafford Loans. Applicants will be notified of awards on or about 3/31. Federal Work-Study Program available. Institutional employment available.

The Inside Word

Gaining admission to Carleton is highly competitive. While it is possible to get in without stellar high school grades and test scores if you show tremendous promise or have an exceptional talent, most successful applicants demonstrate all of these qualities. High school records are weighed most heavily here; standardized test scores are required, and your personal essay is also very important. Given the importance of community at Carleton, interviews are strongly recommended.

THE SCHOOL SAYS "..."

From the Admissions Office

"In an annual college freshmen survey, Carleton students identify themselves as everything from conservatives to liberals, with a majority of them falling in the moderate to liberal range. Although individualistic and energetic Carls take their academics seriously, they don't take themselves seriously. Participation in athletics, theater or music, religious events, or dining hall discussions marks the Carleton experience. The college recently opened two new LEED-certified, environmentally friendly residence halls and the new Weitz Center for Creativity, 134,000 square feet of performance, rehearsal, exhibition, teaching, and collaboration space as well as an integrated science complex. With nearly three-fifths of the student body receiving need-based grant aid, there is a broad socioeconomic representation across the student body. Eleven percent of all students are international, 28 percent come from traditionally underrepresented groups, and about 12 percent are first-generation students. A look at majors in the past decade shows that graduates cover all areas, with about 40 percent in math/science, a third in social sciences, and a fourth in humanities and arts. More than two-thirds of all students will spend time earning class credits off campus; Carleton participates in programs worldwide from Asia to Africa. You can scuba dive off the Great Barrier Reef or walk the Great Wall of China. Within ten years of graduating, about 80 percent of alumni pursue graduate or professional degrees. Carleton ranks second among liberal arts colleges in the number of PhDs earned by its alumni between 2000 and 2016."

SELECTIVITY

Admissions Rating	97
# of applicants	7,324
% of applicants accepted	19
% of acceptees attending	37
# offered a place on the wait list	1,521
% accepting a place on wait list	42
% admitted from wait list	0
# of early decision applicants	968
% accepted early decision	26

FRESHMAN PROFILE

Range SAT EBRW	670–750
Range SAT Math	690–790
Range SAT Composite	1380–1520
Range ACT Composite	31–34
# submitting SAT scores	301
% submitting SAT scores	57
# submitting ACT scores	281
% submitting ACT scores	54
% graduated top 10% of class	71
% graduated top 25% of class	93
% graduated top 50% of class	100

DEADLINES

Early decision	
Deadline	11/15
Notification	12/15
Other ED Deadline	1/15
Other ED Notification	2/15
Regular	
Deadline	1/15
Notification	3/31
Nonfall registration?	No

APPLICANTS ALSO LOOK AT AND OFTEN PREFER
Brown University; Pomona College; Williams College; Yale University

AND SOMETIMES PREFER
Swarthmore College; Bowdoin College

AND RARELY PREFER
Macalester College; Grinnell College

FINANCIAL FACTS

Financial Aid Rating	98
Annual tuition	$56,778
Room and board	$14,658
Required fees	$333
Books and supplies	$866
Average frosh need-based scholarship	$47,243
Average UG need-based scholarship	$44,774
% needy frosh rec. need-based scholarship or grant aid	100
% needy UG rec. need-based scholarship or grant aid	100
% needy frosh rec. non-need-based scholarship or grant aid	15
% needy UG rec. non-need-based scholarship or grant aid	14
% needy frosh rec. need-based self-help aid	98
% needy UG rec. need-based self-help aid	99
% frosh rec. any financial aid	55
% UG rec. any financial aid	55
% UG borrow to pay for school	40
Average cumulative indebtedness	$19,405
% frosh need fully met	100
% ugrads need fully met	100
Average % of frosh need met	100
Average % of ugrad need met	100

CARNEGIE MELLON UNIVERSITY

5000 Forbes Avenue, Pittsburgh, PA 15213 • Admissions: 412-268-2082 • Fax: 412-268-7838

STUDENTS SAY "..."

Academics

The dedicated students at Carnegie Mellon range from innovative engineering majors to the artsiest of drama students, making this research university "a breeding ground for interdisciplinary collaboration." The school's motto—"my heart is in the work"—rings true for all. Students say, "It is in our culture to stay up late, overload on classes, have more than one major, and to be extremely involved on campus." The university, founded by Andrew Carnegie in 1900, gives students the opportunity to become experts in their chosen field while also studying a broad range of coursework across disciplines. CMU's interdisciplinary environment is backed by the tremendous resources afforded students in whatever they choose, and the school "practically throws opportunities (internships, guidance)" at students. Though the course work is admittedly "stressful," the professors "are extremely knowledgeable and passionate about their subject[s]," and the "we're all in it together" mantra is a universal refrain. "Academically, you get challenged, but so does everyone else, so the work-heavy culture becomes a social thing," says a student. Though "there are some [professors] who are less reasonable grading-wise and/or are a bit boring in lecture," for the most part, they are "enthusiastic and very invested in the students' learning" and "will go as far as helping you pick out internships to apply for and giving advice on programs on campus and elsewhere." Much as its mission statement promises, CMU "provides excellent preparation for your future, especially [through] the career center." The residence life staff, RAs, and Housefellows are also "really committed to improving the social aspects of college." For those who know what they want, there are "unlimited opportunities to pursue your passions."

Life

Carnegie Mellon "students are unique for the amount of time they spend working on their studies," and most social activity "is based off of academics." "Carnegie Mellon offers endless opportunities for those who are willing to actively pursue it," and students find that there are "many clubs on campus that are constantly looking for new members." Despite the number of hours spent hitting the books, CMU has a decidedly collaborative atmosphere: "Carnegie Mellon is filled with a bunch of high-achieving, non-competitive students that want to help each other." Discussions "are just at a higher level," and if students have to work late into a Friday evening, then so be it. Some at CMU "enjoy complaining about how stressed out we are, but that doesn't stop us from overloading on classes, signing up for more activities, or taking on more leadership positions." "You get to pick two: sleep, good grades, or a social life," goes the student mantra, while CMU leadership is working to encourage balance. Recreation options include "a massive video game 'community,'" as well as "not your typical Greek Life," which "is a great way to open up lots of experiences." The Pittsburgh location offers a "safe campus...but it is still within a city that offers many things to do," including free entry into area museums, "great restaurants, and sports teams."

Student Body

At Carnegie Mellon, everybody is "quirky in an endearing way." Basically, "there isn't really a norm except for the fact that you can be yourself." The mix of student interests and majors provides a curious but totally harmonious balance at every turn: "There are engineering students who can belt out any song from a musical and art students who are great at tennis. CMU students are diverse and unique and still able to come together to...create an environment where success is encouraged without risk of judgment." "We're all weird in our own way—we're either a scientist or artist so we can seem a strange bunch...eventually the labels artist or scientist fades, and you become friends with people from all over campus," says a student. Students "love their work and work hard, but also tend to be very involved in side projects, whether it be playing quidditch or creating a startup." Basically, CMU is made up of "an incredibly diverse bunch of nerds—in the best way possible"; they're "insanely driven," and "all have hidden talents."

CARNEGIE MELLON UNIVERSITY

Financial Aid: 412-268-2082 • E-Mail: admission@andrew.cmu.edu • Website: www.cmu.edu

THE PRINCETON REVIEW SAYS

Admissions

Very important factors considered include: rigor of secondary school record, class rank, academic GPA, standardized test scores, extracurricular activities, volunteer work, work experience. *Important factors considered include:* application essay, recommendation(s), talent/ability, character/personal qualities, first generation, alumni/ae relation, racial/ethnic status. ACT with or without writing accepted. SAT with or without Essay component accepted. High school diploma is required and GED is accepted. *Academic units required:* varies by college/program. *Academic units recommended:* varies by college/program.

Financial Aid

Students should submit: FAFSA; CSS Profile, including Noncustodial profile if applicable. Priority filing deadline is 2/15. The Princeton Review suggests that all financial aid forms be submitted as soon as possible after October 1. *Need-based scholarships/grants offered:* College/university scholarship or grant aid from institutional funds; Federal Pell; Private scholarships; SEOG; State scholarships/grants. *Loan aid offered:* Direct PLUS loans; Direct Subsidized Stafford Loans; Direct Unsubsidized Stafford Loans. Applicants will be notified of awards on or about 4/1. Federal Work-Study Program available. Institutional employment available.

The Inside Word

While the university's overall acceptance rate is 15.4 percent, Carnegie Mellon considers students for a specific college/program in the admission process. Academic preparedness and demonstrated fit are very important to the admission committees. The university encourages students to pursue a rigorous high school curriculum that includes advanced coursework, especially if you're applying to some of Carnegie Mellon's more competitive academic colleges. The admissions office explicitly states that it doesn't use formulas when making decisions. That said, a record of strong academic performance in the area of your intended major is key. Each of the school's six undergraduate colleges has varying academic and testing recommendations. Applications to schools in the College of the Fine Arts also require an additional audition and/or portfolio.

THE SCHOOL SAYS "..."

From the Admissions Office

"Carnegie Mellon is a world-class, innovative university, rich with tradition and culture. Our interdisciplinary approach to education sharpens students' problem-solving, critical thinking, analytical and quantitative skills. With more than 90 majors and minors, our premier fine arts, business and humanities programs are equally matched by top-ranked technology, science and computer science programs. With our educational philosophy focused deeply on interdisciplinary knowledge, we develop world changers in problem-solving, leadership and communication. Our students leave Carnegie Mellon equipped with the skills to impact society in a transformative way.

"We take pride in our academics, but also realize the importance of life outside the classroom. Campus life at Carnegie Mellon is vibrant, with opportunities spanning Greek Life and service, clubs and organizations, and intramurals and athletics. Though we're in the midst of the city of Pittsburgh, we have a 148-acre campus bordered by 500-acre Schenley Park—there's plenty of green space in every direction. With hundreds of ways to spend a study break, students take advantage of our culturally rich residential-surrounding and get involved in the life of the Pittsburgh community. And with three of the best athletic teams around (the Penguins, Pirates and Steelers!) here in our city, we know you'll love being a Pittsburgher as much as we do."

SELECTIVITY

Admissions Rating	98
# of applicants	27,634
% of applicants accepted	15
% of acceptees attending	37
# offered a place on the wait list	5,761
% accepting a place on wait list	62
% admitted from wait list	4
# of early decision applicants	1,860
% accepted early decision	19

FRESHMAN PROFILE

Range SAT EBRW	700–760
Range SAT Math	760–800
Range ACT Composite	33–35
# submitting SAT scores	1,220
% submitting SAT scores	77
# submitting ACT scores	574
% submitting ACT scores	36
Average HS GPA	3.9
% graduated top 10% of class	88
% graduated top 25% of class	96
% graduated top 50% of class	99

DEADLINES

Early decision	
Deadline	11/1
Notification	12/15
Regular	
Deadline	1/1
Notification	4/1
Nonfall registration?	No

FINANCIAL FACTS

Financial Aid Rating	94
Annual tuition	$57,560
Room and board	$15,550
Required fees	$1,364
Books and supplies	$2,400
Average frosh need-based scholarship	$43,599
Average UG need-based scholarship	$43,475
% needy frosh rec. need-based scholarship or grant aid	96
% needy UG rec. need-based scholarship or grant aid	97
% needy frosh rec. non-need-based scholarship or grant aid	33
% needy UG rec. non-need-based scholarship or grant aid	27
% needy frosh rec. need-based self-help aid	95
% needy UG rec. need-based self-help aid	95
% frosh rec. any financial aid	55.6
% UG rec. any financial aid	52.5
% UG borrow to pay for school	52
Average cumulative indebtedness	$31,342
% frosh need fully met	93
% ugrads need fully met	76
Average % of frosh need met	99
Average % of ugrad need met	97

CASE WESTERN RESERVE UNIVERSITY

Wolstein Hall, Cleveland, OH 44106-7055 • Admissions: 216-368-4450 • Fax: 216-368-5111

STUDENTS SAY "..."

Academics

Located in Cleveland, Ohio, Case Western Reserve University is a mid-sized school that boasts "fantastic research opportunities," "an awesome environment," and "amazing financial aid." CWRU is "known as an outstanding engineering school" and "companies in the engineering field are aware of CWRU's excellence and rigor and are very eager to hire CWRU grads." "Our academics and academic reputation is phenomenal," one happy student boasts. The "well qualified and passionate" professors are "very involved in their fields" and "usually accessible and reasonable about their workload." "They all have connections within the research community or the private work sector." "Supplementary Instructors (past students who passed with an A) are also a great resource and host a variety of study sessions every week to go over material," one student brags. "We even get free tutoring (up to five hours a week). [The] academic load can be challenging, but if you take advantage of all the available resources around, it's definitely manageable!" "It is possible to do well in class and be involved in clubs and sports." If there's an area that academics could improve, it's the liberal arts, as students in these majors report feeling their departments are sometimes overlooked. "Administration and advising could still use some work," one student says. "It is not always clear what path you should be taking in order to graduate, but if you ask enough people, you can figure it out." Overall, CWRU "is very good at producing students prepared to excel in their career, especially within engineering, medicine, and business." In addition, a new university initiative works to pair up students with experts who can help them take full advantage of the campus resources that will help them reach their goals. The university "offers great scholarships and has fantastic research opportunities." A finance major reports she decided to attend because "it was affordable, prestigious, in an awesome environment, and the people here were all so genuine when I came to visit." All in all, students really feel that CWRU is a university on the rise. As a cognitive science and psychology student puts it, "If universities were stocks, I'd put all my money into Case Western."

Life

One student sums up the university as "nerdy but a lot of fun." Activities at Case reflect this "nerdy" nature. "One of our biggest campus events (which I help run) is a 10 day long game of tag known as Humans vs. Zombies," a sociology and theatre major says. On campus, "Case offers literally everything in the way of clubs, jobs, research, and things to do." Even though many students are "geeky," Greek life is also strong: "A lot of people are in fraternities or sororities (one-third of campus and rising)." Students do seem to feel that one area of campus life needs improvement: "school spirit." "Few students could tell you the football team's record or who the basketball team is facing this weekend," one student says, elaborating that it isn't a surprise since the school is "academically focused." Off campus, there's always the entire city of Cleveland. Students love the "beautiful" campus as well as its "fantastic" "location in uptown Cleveland" near that city's "cultural center." The area close to campus "offers great museums and downtown has lots of attractions to check out."

Student Body

"Case definitely has a 'nerd school' reputation" but students want everyone to know that "we are not a group of loners that spend all their time in a lab or playing D&D." "You can find all sorts of people" here and overall the student body is "a quirky mish-mosh of quirky students all engaging with one another and doing their best to advance society in one form or another." "The typical student at Case Western is focused, hard-working, clever, quirky, and probably a little bit nerdy, but in the best way," one student explains. Students are high achievers; a typical student "works hard [and] studies a lot" yet always makes sure to find "time to socialize and invest their time in numerous groups, activities, and other endeavors." The "best way to fit in" is to get active by "joining student organizations, doing community service, jamming out to music in the residence halls, or doing a group study session."

CASE WESTERN RESERVE UNIVERSITY

Financial Aid: 216-368-4530 • E-Mail: admission@case.edu • Website: www.case.edu

THE PRINCETON REVIEW SAYS

Admissions

Very important factors considered include: rigor of secondary school record, class rank, academic GPA, extracurricular activities. *Important factors considered include:* application essay, recommendation(s), interview, talent/ability, character/personal qualities, racial/ethnic status, volunteer work. *Other factors considered include:* first generation, alumni/ae relation, work experience, level of applicant's interest. ACT with or without writing accepted. SAT with or without Essay component accepted. High school diploma is required and GED is accepted. *Academic units required:* 4 English, 3 math, 3 science, 2 science labs, 2 foreign language, 3 social studies. *Academic units recommended:* 4 math, 3 science labs, 3 foreign language, 4 social studies.

Financial Aid

Students should submit: CSS Profile; FAFSA; Institution's own financial aid form; Noncustodial Profile. Priority filing deadline is 1/15. The Princeton Review suggests that all financial aid forms be submitted as soon as possible after October 1. *Need-based scholarships/grants offered:* College/university scholarship or grant aid from institutional funds; Federal Pell; Private scholarships; SEOG; State scholarships/grants. *Loan aid offered:* Direct PLUS loans; Direct Subsidized Stafford Loans; Direct Unsubsidized Stafford Loans. Applicants will be notified of awards upon admission. Federal Work-Study Program available. Institutional employment available.

The Inside Word

CWRU is a school with a growing profile, which means that the number of applications keeps increasing and competition is getting stiffer. CWRU uses a "single-door admission policy," meaning students apply to the whole school rather than individual departments. Once accepted, you can change majors without reapplying. CWRU accepts the Common Application and Coalition Application. Note that for the fall 2021 semester, there is a test-optional policy in place, and CWRU will determine policies for future classes in winter 2020–21.

THE SCHOOL SAYS "..."

From the Admissions Office

"Challenging and innovative academic programs, next-level technology, experiential learning, real-world environments, and faculty mentors are at the core of the Case Western Reserve University experience. CWRU's faculty challenges and supports motivated students, and its partnerships with world-class cultural, educational, and scientific institutions ensure that your education extends beyond the classroom. CWRU offers more than nearly 100 academic programs and a single-door admission policy; once admitted to CWRU, you can major in any of our programs, or double and even triple major in several of them. Our student/faculty ratio, among the best in the nation, allows students to have close interaction with professors. Co-ops, internships, research, creative endeavors, study abroad, and other opportunities bring theory to life in amazing settings, and 99 percent of students participate in these experiential learning opportunities. SAGES, CWRU's four-year undergraduate core curriculum, connects students with faculty, peers and the community through small seminars that explore effective communication and analytical skills, and culminates in a Senior Capstone project. With 80 percent of students living on campus, CWRU has a residential feel unique to urban universities. First-year students live together in one of four residential colleges. Each student has a 'navigator'—a professional with them for all four years who helps them learn about and access everything from post-graduate counseling to internships and study abroad."

SELECTIVITY

Admissions Rating	95
# of applicants	28,786
% of applicants accepted	27
% of acceptees attending	17
# offered a place on the wait list	10,375
% accepting a place on wait list	42
% admitted from wait list	14
# of early decision applicants	597
% accepted early decision	42

FRESHMAN PROFILE

Range SAT EBRW	640–720
Range SAT Math	700–790
Range ACT Composite	30–34
# submitting SAT scores	891
% submitting SAT scores	66
# submitting ACT scores	657
% submitting ACT scores	48
% graduated top 10% of class	70
% graduated top 25% of class	92
% graduated top 50% of class	99

DEADLINES

Early decision	
Deadline	11/1
Notification	12/15
Other ED Deadline	1/15
Other ED Notification	2/1
Early action	
Deadline	11/1
Notification	12/15
Regular	
Deadline	1/15
Notification	3/20
Nonfall registration?	Yes

APPLICANTS ALSO LOOK AT AND OFTEN PREFER
Carnegie Mellon University; Washington University in St. Louis

AND SOMETIMES PREFER
The Ohio State University--Columbus; University of Michigan—Ann Arbor; University of Pittsburgh—Pittsburgh Campus

FINANCIAL FACTS

Financial Aid Rating	92
Annual tuition	$50,450
Room and board	$16,874
Required fees	$1,049
Books and supplies	$1,200
Average frosh need-based scholarship	$37,456
Average UG need-based scholarship	$35,164
% needy frosh rec. need-based scholarship or grant aid	98
% needy UG rec. need-based scholarship or grant aid	97
% needy frosh rec. non-need-based scholarship or grant aid	32
% needy UG rec. non-need-based scholarship or grant aid	19
% needy frosh rec. need-based self-help aid	93
% needy UG rec. need-based self-help aid	95
% frosh rec. any financial aid	87
% UG rec. any financial aid	85
% UG borrow to pay for school	44
Average cumulative indebtedness	$33,946
% frosh need fully met	96
% ugrads need fully met	81
Average % of frosh need met	100
Average % of ugrad need met	95

CATAWBA COLLEGE

2300 West Innes Street, Salisbury, NC 28144 • Admissions: 704-637-4402 • Fax: 704-637-4222

STUDENTS SAY "..."

Academics

This small North Carolinian regional college (associated with the United Church of Christ) offers students a well-rounded education grounded in the liberal arts, a commitment to environmental sustainability, and classes structured around current events. Preparation for students entering their prospective fields is a focal point, and "professors go out of their way to make sure every student is involved in the learning process." Strong music, theatre, and environment and sustainability programs are standouts of the seventy available academic fields of study at Catawba, which students say is "a strong community of teachers, faculty, and students with a common goal of excellence in education." All professors have a genuine passion for their subject matter, "always make sure the students understand the material," and "enjoy conversing with interested, engaged students both in and out of class." "Each one was always there when I needed advice or one on one help," says a student of the faculty, which cultivates a "family-oriented feeling." Small class sizes allow for close relationships with professors: "I go to class knowing they want me to succeed," says one student. "The professors at Catawba are fantastic," says another. "They truly care for your success, not just in the classroom, but in life." Life at school is "very lively and uplifting," and Catawba is constantly increasing its offerings to compete with other regional colleges; the school recently added a Winter Term to allow students the option of taking a single class between the fall and spring semesters, often incorporating travel into the curriculum. The buildings are admittedly "getting a little worn down and old," but renovations and improvements have taken place and continue on an annual basis.

Life

The vibe at Catawba is extremely relaxed ("[the] school is small [so] you're always on time everywhere"), and the grounds make it evident that "there is time and effort put into this beautiful campus." The college provides a lot of activities and opportunities for student involvement, and these are well-taken advantage of. "The student activities group is always doing something," which gives all students the "opportunity to find a place where they can grow." There is a 189-acre preserve that "encourages students to get out and enjoy nature" (and is also used by professors as a living classroom), and "the college and the town are very active together." Downtown Salisbury is close enough that students can visit relatively easily (many local businesses offer discounts to Catawba students). Outside of club activities, laying low is the pastime of choice here, and many nights are spent playing board games or watching movies; "going to the entertainment center to play pool or ping pong is also popular."

Student Body

Many students here identify as "white, Christian, and southern," and around 85 percent of freshmen live on campus (though many will go on to live nearby as school progresses). There is an "equal mix of religious and sporty" among the roughly 1,300 students, who say that people tend to divide themselves by their primary field of study and "fit into their own groups but socialize outside of them." Closely related fields also have a tendency to form ties: "Biology and chemistry majors are often easy friends, as are theatre and English majors." Athletes are extremely well represented among the student population.

Financial Aid: 704-637-4416 • E-Mail: admission@catawba.edu • Website: www.catawba.edu

THE PRINCETON REVIEW SAYS

Admissions

Very important factors considered include: academic GPA, recommendation(s), extracurricular activities, talent/ability, character/personal qualities, geographical residence. *Important factors considered include:* rigor of secondary school record, standardized test scores. *Other factors considered include:* class rank, application essay, interview, first generation, alumni/ae relation, state residency, religious affiliation/commitment, racial/ethnic status, level of applicant's interest. ACT with or without writing accepted. High school diploma is required and GED is accepted. *Academic units required:* 4 English, 3 math, 3 science, 3 social studies. *Academic units recommended:* 2 foreign language.

Financial Aid

Students should submit: FAFSA; State aid form. Priority filing deadline is 3/15. The Princeton Review suggests that all financial aid forms be submitted as soon as possible after October 1. *Need-based scholarships/grants offered:* College/university scholarship or grant aid from institutional funds; Federal Pell; Private scholarships; SEOG; State scholarships/grants. *Loan aid offered:* Direct PLUS loans; Direct Subsidized Stafford Loans; Direct Unsubsidized Stafford Loans. Applicants will be notified of awards on a rolling basis beginning 1/15. Federal Work-Study Program available. Institutional employment available.

The Inside Word

Since Catawba competes for students with several top regional schools, students who may not have been the highest achievers in high school but are ready to excel at the college level should put Catawba on their list. Catawba's application is free for students who apply online via the school's own application or the Common Application, and offers a test-optional application option for students with a 3.25 GPA or higher.

THE SCHOOL SAYS "..."

From the Admissions Office

"Catawba College prepares students for rewarding lives and careers helping them reach their highest potential as individuals. This attractive campus is centrally located in Salisbury, North Carolina, a short drive away from the mountains and Atlantic beaches. The community possesses a rich past and commitment to preserving its cultural and historic charm. In contrast, just forty-five minutes away is the much faster pace of Charlotte, North Carolina where shopping, transportation, and entertainment of all kinds are readily available.

"On campus, students study and socialize in a small college setting that offers strong traditions, excellent facilities, and beautiful surroundings. The high standards of quality set by Catawba's academic programs are matched by equally demanding sports and co-curricular programs. Students describe the community as caring and personable. They are also highly involved in campus activities ranging from the performing arts to homecoming and travel abroad. Faculty and staff are described by students as being important mentors. Whether in a state-of-the-art environmental science facility, attractive music and theatrical performance center, classroom, or one of the college's first-class athletic facilities, students report they feel as if they are among family when on campus.

"Perhaps the most important testimony to the attractiveness of Catawba is found in the words of its graduates who report numerous successful careers and rich memories of their time at school. Students applying for admission to Catawba College can apply test optional if they have a cumulative grade point average of a 3.25 or higher. Students interested in this option and those who meet the GPA requirement, must submit an essay, letter of recommendation; and a co-curricular resume. For those students submitting test scores, Catawba accepts both ACT and SAT. Catawba does super score."

SELECTIVITY

Admissions Rating	87
# of applicants	3,125
% of applicants accepted	42
% of acceptees attending	25

FRESHMAN PROFILE

Range SAT EBRW	460–520
Range SAT Math	470–580
Range ACT Composite	18–23
# submitting SAT scores	190
% submitting SAT scores	57
# submitting ACT scores	191
% submitting ACT scores	57
Average HS GPA	3.8
% graduated top 10% of class	13
% graduated top 25% of class	44
% graduated top 50% of class	77

DEADLINES

Regular	
Notification	Rolling, 10/1
Nonfall registration?	Yes

FINANCIAL FACTS

Financial Aid Rating	85
Annual tuition	$30,520
Room and board	$10,488
Books and supplies	$1,400
Average frosh need-based scholarship	$7,347
Average UG need-based scholarship	$6,930
% needy frosh rec. need-based scholarship or grant aid	68
% needy UG rec. need-based scholarship or grant aid	75
% needy frosh rec. non-need-based scholarship or grant aid	99
% needy UG rec. non-need-based scholarship or grant aid	88
% needy frosh rec. need-based self-help aid	70
% needy UG rec. need-based self-help aid	78
% frosh rec. any financial aid	99
% UG rec. any financial aid	99
% UG borrow to pay for school	79
Average cumulative indebtedness	$31,471
% frosh need fully met	31
% ugrads need fully met	26
Average % of frosh need met	81
Average % of ugrad need met	78

THE CATHOLIC UNIVERSITY OF AMERICA

Office of Undergraduate Admissions, Washington, DC 20064 • Admissions: 202-319-5305 • Fax: 202-319-6533

STUDENTS SAY "..."

Academics

"D.C. is the perfect area for a university," and the students at Catholic University of America say "having a real campus just outside of Capitol Hill is fantastic," offering "tremendous perks," like "great access to internship and job opportunities." Students lament that their "stellar school...often gets lost among the power-players of Georgetown, GW, and American," but they argue that the opportunities for "collaborations with other universities" and "the numerous cultural offerings of the city" more than make up for it. Students praise "the small class sizes and individualized support from academic advisors," which "helps to foster a great working relationship" between students and faculty. These "world class researchers" "show a real interest in each student's success." "They are always willing to stay for a few minutes after class to talk" one student explains, "and are also always available at their office hours or via email and phone." Some professors even go as far as "[requiring] some sort of meeting with them outside of class to discuss course work and our progress in class." Attending a faith-based university where "Catholic Church teachings [are] ingrained throughout" is also important to some CUA students, who take pride in attending the "only school in the United States that is chartered by the Pope. Even so, "there is a wide variety of" religious sentiment at Catholic and "atheists...are tolerated quite well." Overall, students feel that "Catholic really strives to make our education as personal as possible."

Life

Washington, D.C., provides Catholic University students with "a surplus of activities, " and the school plans plenty of "events to keep students on campus entertained." For the school's "large athletic population," CUA offers "varsity, club, and intramural sports teams." As a "highly competitive Division III school" CUA sends many of its teams "to the final rounds of NCAA tournaments" and "even those who are not a part of athletics tend to attend the events." Students say that belonging to a religious university means that community service "is more popular here than on other campuses," but most find a balance between school work, service, and fun. An on-campus metro-stop means that "downtown D.C. is extremely accessible." This "wonderful city" "always offers new and exciting things to do. From going to the opera, ballet or symphony at the Kennedy Center, to a concert on U Street, to museums, to ice skating in the sculpture gardens," students always have something to fill their free time. Catholic isn't a dry campus and at some "events for upperclassmen (especially seniors), the university provides alcohol in moderation." Opinions are divided on the prevalence of drinking. Students who say that "there is a drinking culture on campus," also contend that they "don't feel any pressure" to partake if they don't want to. Others describe a student body where "a fair share enjoy some fun on the weekend, but it is not anything more than other colleges (in fact it is probably less)."

Student Body

Catholic University students are "largely white and Catholic" and are often "socially conservative," though there is "a small minority of liberal millennials." While some point to a lack of diversity, others argue that Catholic has "a good number of minority students for the size of our school." Most agree that the "student body seems to be very warm and welcoming." Many students identify a "big divide between the God Squad and the extreme party goers," but others say there is more overlap than meets the eye. "For example," one student told us, "I volunteer at Masses but also occasionally go to parties with my friends and have a little fun." "Certainly, some people are more religious than others," and the average Catholic University student "has a good mix of friends and a good balance on going out and doing school work."

THE CATHOLIC UNIVERSITY OF AMERICA

Financial Aid: 202-319-5307 • E-Mail: cua-admissions@cua.edu • Website: www.catholic.edu

THE PRINCETON REVIEW SAYS

Admissions

Very important factors considered include: rigor of secondary school record, academic GPA, character/personal qualities. *Important factors considered include:* application essay, recommendation(s), extracurricular activities, first generation. *Other factors considered include:* class rank, standardized test scores, interview, talent/ability, alumni/ae relation, geographical residence, racial/ethnic status, volunteer work, work experience, level of applicant's interest. ACT with or without writing accepted. SAT with or without Essay component accepted. High school diploma is required and GED is accepted. *Academic units recommended:* 4 English, 4 math, 3 science, 2 science labs, 3 foreign language, 4 social studies.

Financial Aid

Students should submit: CSS/Financial Aid PROFILE; FAFSA; Noncustodial PROFILE. Priority filing deadline is 2/1. The Princeton Review suggests that all financial aid forms be submitted as soon as possible after October 1. *Need-based scholarships/grants offered:* College/university scholarship or grant aid from institutional funds; Federal Pell; Private scholarships; SEOG; State scholarships/grants. *Loan aid offered:* Direct PLUS loans; Direct Subsidized Stafford Loans; Direct Unsubsidized Stafford Loans. Applicants will be notified of awards on a rolling basis beginning 2/15. Federal Work-Study Program available. Institutional employment available.

The Inside Word

The Catholic University of America's admission is fairly competitive. Certainly, the admission committee carefully assesses your GPA and the rigor of your course load, but standardized test scores are now optional. However, you must not slack on the other facets of your application as close attention is given to your personal statement and recommendations. Your extracurricular involvement is also vetted, and the university is especially on the lookout for candidates dedicated to community service.

THE SCHOOL SAYS "..."

From the Admissions Office

"Students at The Catholic University of America have opportunities and advantages unlike anywhere else. Our remarkable combination of outstanding academics, a vibrant residential student life, opportunities for meaningful undergraduate research, competitive athletics, and a rich array of student clubs and organizations is made even more distinctive by our location in Washington, D.C.—a world center for "big ideas" in business, science, politics and government, public policy, health care, the arts, and more. By the time they graduate, more than 75 percent of our students complete internships (more than 60 percent complete two or more) on Capitol Hill, at the Smithsonian, with NASA, the National Institutes of Health, Kennedy Center for the Performing Arts, or any of the hundreds of leading corporations and nonprofit organizations with headquarters in D.C. And when not studying or working, they and their classmates also get to enjoy the scores of museums and galleries, theaters, restaurants, monuments, markets, parks, and historic sites that make the U.S. capital one of the most interesting, dynamic, and influential cities in the world.

"Add to all of this having the largest and greenest campus in the District, our own University center in Rome (among nearly 100 international study programs we offer), rich opportunities for student leadership and community service, and the Office of Academic and Career Success, where dedicated professionals are ready to help guide and support students from the moment they enroll right through graduation and beyond, and you start to realize why the educational experience at Catholic University is unparalleled."

SELECTIVITY

Admissions Rating	77
# of applicants	5,668
% of applicants accepted	85
% of acceptees attending	17
# offered a place on the wait list	32
% accepting a place on wait list	81
% admitted from wait list	0
# of early decision applicants	90
% accepted early decision	81

FRESHMAN PROFILE

Range SAT EBRW	580–670
Range SAT Math	550–660
Range ACT Composite	24–29
# submitting SAT scores	523
% submitting SAT scores	63
# submitting ACT scores	168
% submitting ACT scores	21
Average HS GPA	3.5

DEADLINES

Early decision	
Deadline	11/15
Notification	12/17
Other ED Deadline	1/15
Other ED Notification	2/13
Early action	
Deadline	11/1
Notification	1/15
Regular	
Deadline	1/15
Nonfall registration?	Yes

APPLICANTS ALSO LOOK AT AND OFTEN PREFER
Villanova University

AND SOMETIMES PREFER
American University; Fordham University; Loyola University Maryland; The George Washington University

AND RARELY PREFER
St. Joseph's University

FINANCIAL FACTS

Financial Aid Rating	87
Annual tuition	$48,600
Room and board	$15,820
Required fees	$816
Books and supplies	$1,000
Average frosh need-based scholarship	$32,780
Average UG need-based scholarship	$30,418
% needy frosh rec. need-based scholarship or grant aid	98
% needy UG rec. need-based scholarship or grant aid	99
% needy frosh rec. non-need-based scholarship or grant aid	0
% needy UG rec. non-need-based scholarship or grant aid	0
% needy frosh rec. need-based self-help aid	78
% needy UG rec. need-based self-help aid	81
% frosh rec. any financial aid	94
% UG rec. any financial aid	90
Average cumulative indebtedness	$46,702
% frosh need fully met	43
% ugrads need fully met	42
Average % of frosh need met	82
Average % of ugrad need met	80

CENTENARY COLLEGE OF LOUISIANA

2911 Centenary Blvd, Shreveport, LA 71104 • Admissions: 318-869-5131 • Fax: 318-869-5005

CAMPUS LIFE

Quality of Life Rating	84
Fire Safety Rating	78
Green Rating	60*
Type of school	Private
Affiliation	United Methodist
Environment	Metropolis

STUDENTS

Total undergrad enrollment	544
% male/female	43/57
% from out of state	43
# of fraternities	4
# of sororities	2
% African American	14
% Asian	2
% Caucasian	65
% Hispanic	10
% Native American	<1
% Pacific Islander	<1
% Two or more races	6
% Race and/or ethnicity unknown	0
% international	1
# of countries represented	7

SURVEY SAYS . . .

Easy to get around campus
Theater is popular
Active student government

ACADEMICS

Academic Rating	86
% students returning for sophomore year	76
% students graduating within 6 years	48
Calendar	Semester
Student/faculty ratio	9:1
Profs interesting rating	92
Profs accessible rating	94

Most classes have fewer than 10 students.
Most lab/discussion sessions have
10–19 students.

MOST POPULAR MAJORS

Biology/Biological Sciences, General; Psychology,
General; Business Administration and
Management, General

STUDENTS SAY "..."

Academics

A private liberal arts school in Shreveport, Centenary College prides itself on fostering "global engagement" within students. Indeed, the school provides some "one of kind... opportunities [for undergrads] to immerse [themselves] in other cultures, both locally and internationally." As one excited student explains, "Their support for student travel through mission work and study abroad was a huge reason I chose to make my home here." Additionally, Centenary undergrads highlight the social sciences department which "offers really great student-faculty research collaboration and independent research opportunities." They are also quick to mention the "rigorous" biology department which boasts a "90 percent acceptance rate into medical school." Undergrads find that their professors at Centenary are "highly engaged" and "really nice." Their instructors strive "to connect" with students and to craft "assignments geared towards something we would understand or help us to understand the changing world." Undergrads here truly feel that their instructors are "invested in [their] education and success." As proof, one thrilled Centenary student reports that many professors "give out their cell phone numbers, eat at the cafeteria, and some even hold events for their students at their homes." And another satisfied student gushes, "[The professors] are one of my favorite parts of going to school here."

Life

It's quite easy to lead an active and fulfilled life at Centenary College. To begin with, "the Centenary Activities Board hosts events quite often to provide students with opportunities to get together and have fun." We're told that "karaoke night is very popular." Certainly, "there are a variety of clubs and organizations to get involved with," as well. For example, one student boasts that he's personally involved in "Student Government, the Christian Leadership Center, and I work on campus." Additionally, Greek life is strong here, and events are [thrown] regular[ly]." The many productions put on by the theater department are also well attended. "Students [like going] to the Robinson Film Center where we get in for free due to their partnership with the Centenary Film Society." The college also seems to attract a large number of athletes. Hence, "sports are a very big part of campus life." Finally, undergrads periodically head off-campus to "go out to eat, or go on trips and retreats with our [student] organizations." However, students do note that "other than that, we don't leave campus much; there's really no need. Everyone is so interlocked and connected, we're always hanging out with each other."

Student Body

Students at Centenary love that their peers "are all incredibly accepting." As they stroll through campus, students realize that "there's no pressure from others to act or present yourself in a certain way." And though the school is comprised of "predominately white middle-upper class" students, undergrads do mention that "for such a small, Southern school, there is actually a fair amount of racial, gender, and sexual diversity." Similarly, even though Centenary is located in a "traditionally conservative state," students assert that their classmates are "very open and progressively minded." They also continually prove themselves to be "very nice and hardworking." This helps to explain why the student body is so "tight knit." As one student exclaims, "Everyone knows everyone, and it's impossible to go on campus without seeing someone that you [are friendly with]." A fellow undergrad agrees, "You can always find someone who is there for you when you need someone to talk to. Since we are small we are also close to each other. We care for each other and make sure you are at your best." And a third classmate happily sums up, "Everyone makes this place feel like home. I'm from Texas, and everyone here gives me this homey Creole feeling."

CENTENARY COLLEGE OF LOUISIANA

Financial Aid: 318-869-5137 • E-Mail: admission@centenary.edu • Website: https://www.centenary.edu/

THE PRINCETON REVIEW SAYS

Admissions
Very important factors considered include: rigor of secondary school record, academic GPA, application essay, standardized test scores. *Important factors considered include:* class rank, extracurricular activities, volunteer work. *Other factors considered include:* recommendation(s), interview, talent/ability, character/personal qualities, alumni/ae relation, work experience. ACT with or without writing accepted. High school diploma is required and GED is accepted. *Academic units recommended:* 4 English, 3 math, 3 science, 2 foreign language, 3 social studies.

Financial Aid
Students should submit: FAFSA. Priority filing deadline is 2/15. The Princeton Review suggests that all financial aid forms be submitted as soon as possible after October 1. *Need-based scholarships/grants offered:* College/university scholarship or grant aid from institutional funds; Federal Pell; SEOG; State scholarships/grants. *Loan aid offered:* Direct PLUS loans; Direct Subsidized Stafford Loans; Direct Unsubsidized Stafford Loans. Applicants will be notified of awards on a rolling basis beginning 3/15. Federal Work-Study Program available. Institutional employment available.

The Inside Word
Centenary College takes a holistic yet straightforward approach to their admissions process. A selective institution, both high school curriculum and GPA will be closely evaluated. Successful students tend to have some Honors, accelerated, AP, or IB classes on their transcripts. Additionally, tests scores, application essays, letters of recommendation, extracurricular activities, and interviews will all hold some weight. Lastly, while candidates can submit applications past the regular 2/15 deadline, it's advantageous to apply earlier. More spaces will be available, and those applicants who apply by the regular deadline will have full consideration for scholarships.

THE SCHOOL SAYS "..."

From the Admissions Office
"Just as a student's four-year experience at Centenary will be very personalized, so too is the application process. We pride ourselves on treating each applicant as an individual. We encourage all interested students to visit us—not only so they can see our campus and get a sense of the atmosphere, but also to provide us the opportunity to meet and get to know them.

"Consider Centenary for a life-changing experience. Our professors value your ideas and contributions and are passionate about teaching. We consider the Centenary Experience to be more than just a degree. You will live in a comprehensive learning environment that features connections to your academic, social, personal, and residential lives.

"Our students work and live within a strong community to create personalized, distinctive experiences, and enjoy a vibrant college life and graduate from Centenary prepared for their professional and personal lives.

"First-year applicants may opt not to submit test scores; however, those students will be required to supply additional application materials to help the Admission Office's holistic approach to decision making."

SELECTIVITY

Admissions Rating	86
# of applicants	893
% of applicants accepted	60
% of acceptees attending	32

FRESHMAN PROFILE

Range SAT EBRW	530–610
Range SAT Math	520–610
Range ACT Composite	21–28
# submitting SAT scores	59
% submitting SAT scores	35
# submitting ACT scores	136
% submitting ACT scores	80
Average HS GPA	3.5

DEADLINES

Early action	
Deadline	11/15
Notification	1/15
Regular	
Priority	2/15
Deadline	8/1
Notification	4/1
Nonfall registration?	Yes

FINANCIAL FACTS

Financial Aid Rating	87
Annual tuition	$37,310
Room and board	$13,670
Average frosh need-based scholarship	$25,351
Average UG need-based scholarship	$26,816
% needy frosh rec. need-based scholarship or grant aid	100
% needy UG rec. need-based scholarship or grant aid	100
% needy frosh rec. non-need-based scholarship or grant aid	22
% needy UG rec. non-need-based scholarship or grant aid	19
% needy frosh rec. need-based self-help aid	62
% needy UG rec. need-based self-help aid	68
% UG borrow to pay for school	75
Average cumulative indebtedness	$32,900
% frosh need fully met	25
% ugrads need fully met	23
Average % of frosh need met	73
Average % of ugrad need met	75

CENTRE COLLEGE

600 West Walnut Street, Danville, KY 40422-1394 • Admissions: 859-238-5350 • Fax: 859-238-5373

STUDENTS SAY "..."

Academics

Centre College in Danville, Kentucky, swears by the Centre Commitment: all students will study abroad, have a research opportunity or internship, and graduate within four years, or else they're given an additional year at the college tuition-free. At this liberal arts school, about a quarter of students double-major, choosing from more than fifty majors, minors, and pre-professional programs. The school prides itself on "community-based learning initiatives through various service groups" and partnerships with community organizations, and there are "ample internship and career opportunities" as well as "a high level of student engagement in professor research." There is also the unique CentreTerm, which is a three-week period in January during which students can take classes abroad, complete internships or research, or take immersive courses that go beyond traditional lectures in order to expand one's knowledge and "engage in new and interesting, and often more applicable, curriculum."

"There is no greater support here than from the professors," who have an "intentionality in getting to know and teach students." They "make it really easy to get excited about learning" because "they really aren't here in Danville for any reason other than they love to teach and are incredibly good at it." Most of the faculty "maintain a difficult class curriculum and work load" but "are usually clear about what they are expecting from their students" and "offer office hours far beyond the required amount." The "academics here are unparalleled," and while Centre "is a hard school ... it is not competitive among students." As one student sums it up: "Your friends and classmates are there to support you."

Life

At Centre, 98 percent of students live on campus, so most "have some level of face recognition if not name recognition with each other." Students "are passionate about things they do," and during the week, "people are busy with homework, meetings for clubs/organizations, or sports practice." Come the weekend, "many people go out or find something fun to do [such as] midnight movies [or] hanging out with friends," and many "will go out to the fraternity parties or an event organized by the Student Activities Council." Greek life is a popular option, but "it is also very easy to be involved and have a great group of friends without it." Students "tend to eat off campus on the weekend," and will also go "bowling, play games outside, [play] card games, or just hang out in the campus center."

Student Body

"A lot of students come from Kentucky," and with more than 90 percent of the "very studious and mostly friendly" Centre students receiving some form of financial aid, this group comes from "diverse socioeconomic backgrounds." There is "a mindset of open communication and discussion which is facilitated in friend groups," which "makes the learning environment very collaborative." And since most students study abroad, "we also gain a diversity of perspectives from our experiences around the world." The Centre community—both on campus and through the alumni network—"is second to none," and since students run into each other all the time, these "frequent, often accidental, interactions strengthen the community atmosphere of Centre."

CENTRE COLLEGE

Financial Aid: 800-423-6236 • E-Mail: admission@centre.edu • Website: www.centre.edu

THE PRINCETON REVIEW SAYS

Admissions

Very important factors considered include: rigor of secondary school record, academic GPA. *Important factors considered include:* class rank, application essay, standardized test scores, recommendation(s). *Other factors considered include:* interview, extracurricular activities, talent/ability, character/personal qualities, first generation, alumni/ae relation, geographical residence, racial/ethnic status, volunteer work, work experience. ACT with or without writing accepted. SAT with or without Essay component accepted. High school diploma or equivalent is not required *Academic units required:* 4 English, 3 math, 2 science, 2 science labs, 2 foreign language, 2 history. *Academic units recommended:* 4 math, 4 science, 4 foreign language, 2 social studies, 2 history, 1 visual/performing arts.

Financial Aid

Students should submit: FAFSA; Institution's own financial aid form. The Princeton Review suggests that all financial aid forms be submitted as soon as possible after October 1. *Need-based scholarships/grants offered:* College/university scholarship or grant aid from institutional funds; Federal Pell; Private scholarships; SEOG; State scholarships/grants. *Loan aid offered:* Direct PLUS loans; Direct Subsidized Stafford Loans; Direct Unsubsidized Stafford Loans. Applicants will be notified of awards on or about 1/10. Federal Work-Study Program available. Institutional employment available.

The Inside Word

As Centre's reputation rises, earning a coveted acceptance becomes more and more competitive. A solid high school transcript full of challenging courses is a must. Standardized tests are also considered, though the school uses only the highest combination of scores if the student has taken either the ACT or SAT more than once (called a "superscore"). Make sure to include steady involvement in organizations and activities (including leadership roles), as well as work experience in your application. Lastly, students who are confident that Centre College is the school for them are highly encouraged to apply early admission.

THE SCHOOL SAYS "..."

From the Admissions Office

"Centre College offers its students a world of opportunities, highlighted by the nation's premier study abroad program. Approximately 85 percent of students study abroad at least once. CentreTerm programs explore an ever-increasing number of countries. Over the last several years, destinations have included Argentina, Austria, Barbados, Brazil, Costa Rica, Cuba, Ecuador, Egypt, England, Ghana, India, Israel, Italy, Japan, Malaysia, Mexico, Morocco, Myanmar, the Netherlands, New Zealand, Panama, Rwanda, Spain, and Uganda. In addition, there are nine permanent, semester-long residential programs: England, Scotland, Northern Ireland, France, Spain, Yucatan, China, and Japan. Centre's personalized approach means that most international study includes at least one Centre professor. Study abroad is so important that it is a component of the Centre Commitment: study abroad, an internship or research experience, and graduation in four years—guaranteed, or Centre will provide up to one more year of tuition for free. On average, 93 percent of graduates participated in either an internship and/or undergraduate research. Centre's stellar academic reputation and exceptional commitment to remaining affordable lead to extraordinary success for our students: entrance to top graduate and professional schools, prestigious undergraduate and postgraduate fellowships (Rhodes, Fulbright, Goldwater, Rotary, and Gates-Cambridge), and rewarding jobs. (On average, 97 percent are employed or in advanced study within one year of graduation.) Centre is a place where important conversations occur—in and out of the classroom. In 2012, for the second time in a dozen years, Centre's Norton Center for the Arts was the setting for the nation's only vice presidential debate. Annually, the Norton Center features an amazing array of high-profile arts performances and speakers, including the legendary Vienna Philharmonic and Yo-Yo Ma to rock legends Greg Allman and ZZ Top."

SELECTIVITY

Admissions Rating	87
# of applicants	2,212
% of applicants accepted	76
% of acceptees attending	21
# offered a place on the wait list	115
% accepting a place on wait list	15
% admitted from wait list	100
# of early decision applicants	73
% accepted early decision	88

FRESHMAN PROFILE

Range SAT EBRW	570–650
Range SAT Math	560–730
Range SAT Composite	1150–1380
Range ACT Composite	26–32
# submitting SAT scores	74
% submitting SAT scores	26
# submitting ACT scores	281
% submitting ACT scores	79
Average HS GPA	3.6
% graduated top 10% of class	52
% graduated top 25% of class	80
% graduated top 50% of class	97

DEADLINES

Early decision	
Deadline	11/15
Notification	12/15
Early action	
Deadline	12/1
Notification	1/15
Regular	
Deadline	1/15
Notification	3/15
Nonfall registration?	No

APPLICANTS ALSO LOOK AT AND OFTEN PREFER
Vanderbilt University

AND SOMETIMES PREFER
Furman University; Denison University

FINANCIAL FACTS

Financial Aid Rating	90
Annual tuition	$43,000
Room and board	$10,740
Required fees	$0
Books and supplies	$1,400
Average frosh need-based scholarship	$36,467
Average UG need-based scholarship	$33,652
% needy frosh rec. need-based scholarship or grant aid	100
% needy UG rec. need-based scholarship or grant aid	100
% needy frosh rec. non-need-based scholarship or grant aid	0
% needy UG rec. non-need-based scholarship or grant aid	0
% needy frosh rec. need-based self-help aid	62
% needy UG rec. need-based self-help aid	65
% frosh rec. any financial aid	97
% UG rec. any financial aid	96
% UG borrow to pay for school	51
Average cumulative indebtedness	$27,418
% frosh need fully met	36
% ugrads need fully met	32
Average % of frosh need met	90
Average % of ugrad need met	87

CHAMPLAIN COLLEGE

163 South Willard Street, Box 670, Burlington, VT 05402-0670 • Admissions: 802-860-2727 • Fax: 802-860-2767

STUDENTS SAY "..."

Academics

The students at Champlain College in Burlington, Vermont, are "professional" and "career-minded," and name Champlain's "career-focused curriculum" as a primary reason for choosing the college. "Networking and the emphasis on internships at Champlain lead to a great deal of job placements relevant to your chosen major after (or before!) graduation," extols one student. Students love the "small class sizes," which "allow your professors and classmates to know, contribute and follow your success." They're also crazy about Champlain's "upside-down curriculum," which uniquely allows undergraduates to "take major-specific courses [their] first semester": "I could begin major-related work on the first day." Game design, filmmaking, digital forensics, psychology, and marketing are all offered as majors, distinguishing Champlain's available courses of study to many applicants, with its "strong focus on major-specific skills, and field-applicable classwork." For the most part, students say the professors are "engaging, encouraging, and interesting" and "do all they can to help students understand the material and reach their full potential." Champlain works hard to produce graduates who know "how to survive and thrive in the business world" and "reach their highest level of satisfaction." Champlain is a "career-focused school that gives students the tools to succeed in the professional world." This career-conscious education is animated by Champlain's "engaging, encouraging, and interesting" professors, who "know your name," are "enthusiastic about the students' education," and "come from extremely professional backgrounds and add personal touches to their discussions that make students want to participate." In addition to academic curricula, Champlain's InSight program "readies students for outside life," teaching life skills such as "financial sophistication" and fostering a "strong sense of community." For those interested in the burgeoning gaming industry, "Champlain's game major is also rigorous and unique, bringing students from amateurs to developing a game in a seemingly short four years." Champlain's greatest academic strength lies in "excellent professors, innovative classes," and an "inviting small-classroom environment."

Life

The small liberal arts college in cozy Burlington, Vermont, has a heavy academic focus on the video game industry, and skiing and gaming figure prominently into Champlain's social life. "There is a lot to do in town and on campus there are often events put on by clubs or the SGA [Student Government Association]. Every Thursday, a bus also takes students from campus to free bowling or to see a free movie at the movie theater." Students love Burlington—"full of endless opportunities for both outside and indoor activities"—and enjoy the shops and nightlife of Church Street. Both Champlain and Burlington "heavily promote sustainable living," and as such, students learn "an incredible amount about how to help and be aware of my community and ecosystem." For the dedicated skier/student, Champlain IDs will nab you discounted ski passes in the area, and "snow dictates class attendance in the spring." Overall, the outdoorsy will find plenty to love about Champlain and the mantra seems to be, "Anything to be outside." Indoors, the "laid-back" social atmosphere tends toward "play[ing] video games rather often," and "there is an excellent music scene here in Burlington."

Student Body

Champlain's student population is summed up by one as "Champlain attracts a certain type: open, artistic, thoughtful, and intelligent," while another student is a little more blunt: "We are all nerdy in our own special way." It's a self-selective, "open-minded" population that's passionately adored by those who know what to expect: students "fit in well if they have researched the college before coming, as it is a small community within a larger community." There is "literally a bit of everything. Nerds, partiers, skiers, snowboarders, skateboarders and hippies." Another summarizes the Champlain student body as "everyone is incredibly friendly and supportive. I love that it's large enough not to know everyone but small enough that it still feels like family." As a whole, Champlain students are "motivated and engaged." They enjoy the social opportunities afforded by Burlington and Champlain, but "are also serious about doing big things and going far in life."

Financial Aid: 802-860-2730 • E-Mail: admission@champlain.edu • Website: www.champlain.edu/

THE PRINCETON REVIEW SAYS

Admissions

Very important factors considered include: rigor of secondary school record, academic GPA, talent/ability. *Important factors considered include:* application essay, recommendation(s), extracurricular activities, character/personal qualities, first generation, racial/ethnic status. *Other factors considered include:* class rank, standardized test scores, interview, alumni/ae relation, volunteer work, work experience. ACT with or without writing accepted. SAT with or without Essay component accepted. High school diploma is required and GED is accepted. *Academic units required:* 4 English, 3 math, 3 science, 2 science labs, 2 foreign language, 3 history, 5 academic electives. *Academic units recommended:* 4 math, 4 science, 4 foreign language, 4 history., 4 history.

Financial Aid

Students should submit: FAFSA. The Princeton Review suggests that all financial aid forms be submitted as soon as possible after October 1. *Need-based scholarships/grants offered:* College/university scholarship or grant aid from institutional funds; Federal Pell; Private scholarships; SEOG; State scholarships/grants; United Negro College Fund. *Loan aid offered:* Direct PLUS loans; Direct Subsidized Stafford Loans; Direct Unsubsidized Stafford Loans. Applicants will be notified of awards on a rolling basis beginning 3/1. Federal Work-Study Program available. Institutional employment available.

The Inside Word

For the BFA or BS programs in creative media, filmmaking, graphic design and digital media, game art and animation, and game design, prospective students must submit a portfolio of relevant creative work. Strong writing skills are important for all applicants.

THE SCHOOL SAYS "..."

From the Admissions Office

"Champlain's innovative, career-driven programs provide students with the academic, professional and practical knowledge they need to grow personally and thrive in an ever-changing world. Our distinctive Upside-Down Curriculum lets you start studying what matters most to you on day one. Even if you are undecided about your major, you can explore classes that interest you without losing ground toward graduation.

"Our liberal arts Core curriculum will teach you how to be a well-rounded intellectual leader by developing your critical thinking, communication and understanding of diverse perspectives. Along with Core, the InSight program is integrated with your major and teaches you career wisdom and financial savvy, so you'll be ready for the career and the life you want.

"The small classes here provide personal attention from our industry-expert faculty whose extensive professional networks can put you on the inside track to rewarding internships and career success.

"With two international campuses in Montreal, Canada, and Dublin, Ireland—and other study-abroad options in countries like New Zealand, Argentina, China, Italy and Scotland—you can see the world while learning how to change it for the better. In fact, 56 percent of Champlain's students study abroad.

"All first-year students live on campus in one of our 20 beautifully restored Victorian-era mansions. Champlain overlooks Lake Champlain and the Adirondack Mountains and is a short walk from downtown Burlington, Vermont, which is consistently ranked the best college town in the East. Schedule a visit and see what living and learning is like at Champlain: champlain.edu/visit."

SELECTIVITY

Admissions Rating	77
# of applicants	3,629
% of applicants accepted	85
% of acceptees attending	17
# of early decision applicants	274
% accepted early decision	84

FRESHMAN PROFILE

Range SAT EBRW	570–670
Range SAT Math	540–650
Range SAT Composite	1110–1310
Range ACT Composite	24–29
# submitting SAT scores	285
% submitting SAT scores	54
# submitting ACT scores	97
% submitting ACT scores	19
Average HS GPA	3.2
% graduated top 10% of class	14
% graduated top 25% of class	39
% graduated top 50% of class	74

DEADLINES

Early decision	
Deadline	11/15
Regular	
Priority	11/15
Deadline	1/15
Notification	Rolling, 12/1
Nonfall registration?	Yes

FINANCIAL FACTS

Financial Aid Rating	86
Annual tuition	$42,564
Room and board	$15,854
Required fees	$220
Books and supplies	$1,000
Average frosh need-based scholarship	$26,311
Average UG need-based scholarship	$25,089
% needy frosh rec. need-based scholarship or grant aid	99
% needy UG rec. need-based scholarship or grant aid	99
% needy frosh rec. non-need-based scholarship or grant aid	20
% needy UG rec. non-need-based scholarship or grant aid	14
% needy frosh rec. need-based self-help aid	80
% needy UG rec. need-based self-help aid	82
% UG borrow to pay for school	76
Average cumulative indebtedness	$36,976
% frosh need fully met	25
% ugrads need fully met	18
Average % of frosh need met	79
Average % of ugrad need met	75

CHAPMAN UNIVERSITY

One University Drive, Orange, CA 92866 • Admissions: 714-997-6711 • Fax: 714-997-6713

CAMPUS LIFE

Quality of Life Rating	90
Fire Safety Rating	79
Green Rating	63
Type of school	Private
Affiliation	Disciples of Christ
Environment	Metropolis

STUDENTS

Total undergrad enrollment	7,294
% male/female	39/61
% from out of state	30
% frosh live on campus	92
% ugrads live on campus	47
# of fraternities (% ugrad men join)	8 (30)
# of sororities (% ugrad women join)	8 (36)
% African American	2
% Asian	14
% Caucasian	52
% Hispanic	16
% Native American	<1
% Pacific Islander	<1
% Two or more races	8
% Race and/or ethnicity unknown	4
% international	4
# of countries represented	62

SURVEY SAYS . . .

Students are happy
Classroom facilities are great
Great library
Internships are widely available
Students aren't religious
Easy to get around campus
Frats and sororities are popular
College radio is popular

ACADEMICS

Academic Rating	83
% students returning for sophomore year	91
% students graduating within 4 years	72
% students graduating within 6 years	81
Calendar	4/1/4
Student/faculty ratio	13:1
Profs interesting rating	90
Profs accessible rating	94

Most classes have 10–19 students.
Most lab/discussion sessions have
    10–19 students.

MOST POPULAR MAJORS

Cinematography and Film/Video Production;
Business Administration and Management,
General; Public Relations/Image Management

STUDENTS SAY "..."

Academics

With its "small school" setting and So-Cal vibe, it's easy to see why students are charmed by Chapman. The university "truly emphasizes personal growth, campus involvement, and global citizenship," factors that undergrads here appreciate. There's also "great technology available" and a "gorgeous campus" to boot. Even better, "research and internship [opportunities]" abound. Chapman students also tend to rave about their "very engaging" professors, who make a concerted effort to "explain complex concepts in an understandable way." As a health sciences major shares, "These teachers aren't out to get you—they challenge you academically but are willing to help you if you're stuck or confused." It's quite obvious that "they're very dedicated and interested in the subject matters that they teach." Most importantly, they strive "to build meaningful relationships with students." And a biochemistry major boasts, "They offer so much help outside of the classroom and want to see you succeed. My overall academic experience has been wonderful."

Life

It's nearly impossible to not lead a "full and engaging" life here at Chapman. After all, there's simply too much of which to take advantage. To begin with, "the main campus provides concerts, plays, musical performances, art showings, and lectures, which are generally free for students." Additionally, "Dodge Film School has movie screenings...sometimes of movies that haven't come out yet." Chapman hosts plenty of "cool events like 'Yoga on the Lawn,' a winter festival or a chili cook off" as well. And we're also told that there's "a very large Greek presence." In fact, some undergrads insist that "Greek life can be instrumental in finding your group of friends." When the weekend rolls around, "there are usually house parties or people go to the local bars." However, many undergrads do complain that the parties tend to get shut down fairly early. Not surprisingly, students love attending school in Southern California. Chapman itself is located "right next to [Old Towne] Orange, which has many shops and restaurants where students love to walk around." Beyond that, "you can go to Disney, the beach, the Angels stadium, Los Angeles, San Diego, or wherever else tickles your fancy."

Student Body

When asked to describe their peers, many Chapman undergrads quickly resort to adjectives such as "affluent," "Caucasian," and "attractive." And while there is definitely some truth to that, these students also encompass far more. Yes, walking around campus you'll also encounter individuals who are "kind, respectful, artistic, intelligent, and adventurous." For the most part, Chapman undergrads are a "driven" lot as well. Fortunately, there's not much cutthroat competition here. Indeed, we're told that students "love to work together to understand the subject material." A digital art and television product major explains further, "The mood of the student body is very collaborative. Everyone wants to socialize and be friendly and meet new people." While students are generally "accepting [of] diversity," they do tend to be "more conservative in political matters." Lastly, a sociology major sums up her peers by stating, "No matter what the interest is, whether it be Greek life, community service, their major, or even their social life, [students here] are motivated to succeed in their endeavors."

Financial Aid: 714-997-6741 • E-Mail: admit@chapman.edu • Website: www.chapman.edu

THE PRINCETON REVIEW SAYS

Admissions

Very important factors considered include: rigor of secondary school record, class rank, academic GPA, application essay, standardized test scores, character/personal qualities. *Important factors considered include:* extracurricular activities, talent/ability. *Other factors considered include:* recommendation(s), interview, first generation, alumni/ae relation, geographical residence, state residency, racial/ethnic status, volunteer work, work experience, level of applicant's interest. ACT with or without writing accepted. SAT with or without Essay component accepted. High school diploma is required and GED is accepted. *Academic units required:* 4 English, 3 math, 2 science, 1 science lab, 2 foreign language, 2 social studies, 2 history. *Academic units recommended:* 4 English, 4 math, 4 science, 2 science labs, 4 foreign language, 2 social studies, 2 history, 2 academic electives.

Financial Aid

Students should submit: FAFSA; State aid form. Priority filing deadline is 3/2. The Princeton Review suggests that all financial aid forms be submitted as soon as possible after October 1. *Need-based scholarships/grants offered:* College/university scholarship or grant aid from institutional funds; Federal Pell; Private scholarships; SEOG; State scholarships/grants. *Loan aid offered:* Direct PLUS loans; Direct Subsidized Stafford Loans; Direct Unsubsidized Stafford Loans. Applicants will be notified of awards on a rolling basis beginning 3/15. Federal Work-Study Program available. Institutional employment available.

The Inside Word

Gaining admission to Chapman is certainly competitive. When reviewing applications, admissions officers tend to take a holistic approach. The rigor of an academic curriculum, grade trends, letters of recommendation, extracurricular activities and personal statements will all be closely evaluated. Chapman also considers an applicant's intended major and any academic or extracurricular experiences that reflect preparation (for that course of study). It should also be noted that certain majors have additional requirements. Applicants interested in studying in the arts or any major within Dodge College of Film & Media Arts will have additional application requirements. Students intending to pursue Film Production will need to apply by November 1, and those looking to pursue Dance, Pre-Pharmacy, Screen Acting, or Theatre Performance have a priority deadline of November 1.

THE SCHOOL SAYS "..."

From the Admissions Office

"Chapman University provides a personalized and interdisciplinary educational experience to highly qualified students. We offer more than 110 areas of study—options for nearly every interest and passion. Not sure what you want to do? No problem. Entering Undeclared is also a popular option. Our liberal arts education requires you to explore across subject areas—something that's supported inside and outside the classroom.

- Our average class size is 23; most of your classes will range from 10–19 students.
- There are more than 230 academic, professional, and special-interest clubs on campus.
- We offer 19 intercollegiate athletic teams (NCAA Division III) and 8 club teams.
- You can choose from over 90 semester and academic-year study abroad programs. (More than 40 percent of Chapman students study abroad.)

"With on-campus housing guaranteed for all first-year students and sophomores (more than 90 percent of them live on campus), our University is a vibrant community located in the heart of Orange County. From campus you can walk to downtown Orange, or drive to nearby attractions, including beaches, mountains, sporting venues, or Disneyland. We invite you to visit Chapman and see what's possible here. In the meantime, our website is a great resource to learn more about the University and schedule a campus tour."

SELECTIVITY
Admissions Rating	88
# of applicants	14,273
% of applicants accepted	56
% of acceptees attending	22

FRESHMAN PROFILE
Range SAT EBRW	600–680
Range SAT Math	590–700
Range SAT Composite	1210–1370
Range ACT Composite	25–31
# submitting SAT scores	1,225
% submitting SAT scores	69
# submitting ACT scores	737
% submitting ACT scores	42
% graduated top 10% of class	36
% graduated top 25% of class	75
% graduated top 50% of class	94

DEADLINES
Early decision	
Deadline	11/1
Notification	12/20
Early action	
Deadline	11/1
Notification	12/20
Regular	
Priority	11/1
Deadline	1/15
Nonfall registration?	Yes

FINANCIAL FACTS
Financial Aid Rating	85
Annual tuition	$56,830
Room and board	$18,530
Required fees	$384
Books and supplies	$1,600
Average frosh need-based scholarship	$20,910
Average UG need-based scholarship	$19,239
% needy frosh rec. need-based scholarship or grant aid	92
% needy UG rec. need-based scholarship or grant aid	91
% needy frosh rec. non-need-based scholarship or grant aid	78
% needy UG rec. non-need-based scholarship or grant aid	70
% needy frosh rec. need-based self-help aid	88
% needy UG rec. need-based self-help aid	90
% frosh rec. any financial aid	87
% UG rec. any financial aid	84
% UG borrow to pay for school	50
Average cumulative indebtedness	$27,117
% frosh need fully met	17
% ugrads need fully met	13
Average % of frosh need met	76
Average % of ugrad need met	70

CHRISTOPHER NEWPORT UNIVERSITY

1 Avenue of the Arts, Newport News, VA 23606-3072 • Admissions: 757-594-7015 • Fax: 757-594-7333

STUDENTS SAY ". . ."

Academics

Virginia's Christopher Newport University offers undergraduates "a private school atmosphere at a public school cost." And with a "beautiful" campus that has a "Disney World feel," it easy to understand why students clamor to attend. Current undergrads praise CNU's size, which is "small enough to know people of various majors and interests, but large enough to continue to meet new people every day." Many also report that the university's "biggest strengths are the academic tutor centers," which help ensure that all students can be successful in their classes despite the "rigor of the programs." Students are also eager to credit their professors who "push us to do our very best in any way they can, [by] meeting one-on-one, answering questions, and helping us figure out the answers to our own questions, too." Indeed, Christopher Newport instructors often take "an active interest in their students" and are great at connecting "classroom material to real-life situations, which [helps] make [learning] more interesting." All in all, CNU undergrads can anticipate a "very positive" academic experience that will surely "foster a lot of personal growth."

Life

Christopher Newport undergrads are a fairly active bunch. Students say that "the gym is often crowded," and "intramural sports fill up quickly." Additionally, when the weather is nice, a handful of students can often be found playing "Frisbee, soccer, or flag football on the Great Lawn." Of course, there's plenty to do beyond athletics. After all, "many student clubs and organizations put on fun events throughout the week and even on weekends." For example, "The Campus Activities Board will [frequently host] movie nights [and] on Thursdays there is a trivia night." A lot of students also enjoy attending all of the "plays, concerts [and] speakers [offered through] the Ferguson Center for the Arts." A "majority of students are [involved] in Greek life," but don't assume that that denotes a prominent drinking culture. On the contrary, the CNU campus itself is "dry." Therefore, "on the weekends, a lot of students go [to] off-campus… parties." And speaking of off-campus, undergrads have easy "access to multiple beaches along the mouth of the James River." They also love heading out to "Williamsburg, Busch Gardens, Norfolk, and Virginia Beach" all of which are only "a very short drive away."

Student Body

Undergrads at Christopher Newport have "great ... pride" in their peers, and it's easy to understand why. For starters, they continually prove themselves to be "kind" and "welcoming." As one student elaborates, "We will hold doors open for others, and we will smile and say hello." A fellow undergrad adds, "It isn't uncommon for someone you don't know on campus to acknowledge you and ask how you're doing that day." Therefore, it's not too surprising to learn that students here also tend to be "community and service driven." They're an "ambitious and inquisitive" bunch, and many seem to "possess an inherent [desire] to follow their passions." The one aspect a few students lament is the seeming "lack of diversity." We're told that "the majority of the students here come from wealthy families from the same region of northern Virginia, around the Washington D.C. area." Thankfully, we've been assured that CNU students are "very accepting of those who are different." And they're all united in their "goal to be successful and graduate with a degree." Most importantly, you can "expect everyone to treat one another with respect." We'll give this content undergrad the last word: "My peers are like my second family, and it is so easy to call this campus home."

CHRISTOPHER NEWPORT UNIVERSITY

Financial Aid: 757-594-7170 • E-Mail: admit@cnu.edu • Website: www.cnu.edu

THE PRINCETON REVIEW SAYS

Admissions

Very important factors considered include: rigor of secondary school record, academic GPA. *Important factors considered include:* class rank, application essay, standardized test scores, recommendation(s), interview, extracurricular activities, talent/ability, character/personal qualities. *Other factors considered include:* first generation, alumni/ae relation, geographical residence, state residency, volunteer work, work experience. ACT with or without writing accepted. SAT with or without Essay component accepted. High school diploma is required and GED is not accepted. *Academic units required:* 4 English, 4 math, 4 science, 4 science labs, 3 foreign language, 4 social studies, 2 academic electives, 1 visual/performing arts, 4 units from above areas or other academic areas. *Academic units recommended:* 4 English, 4 math, 4 science, 4 science labs, 3 foreign language, 4 social studies, 2 academic electives, 1 visual/performing arts, 4 additional units.

Financial Aid

Students should submit: FAFSA. Priority filing deadline is 3/1. The Princeton Review suggests that all financial aid forms be submitted as soon as possible after October 1. *Need-based scholarships/grants offered:* College/university scholarship or grant aid from institutional funds; Federal Pell; Private scholarships; SEOG; State scholarships/grants. *Loan aid offered:* Direct PLUS loans; Direct Subsidized Stafford Loans; Direct Unsubsidized Stafford Loans. Applicants will be notified of awards on a rolling basis beginning 3/1. Federal Work-Study Program available. Institutional employment available.

The Inside Word

Christopher Newport University takes a well-rounded approach to the admissions game. Certainly, your overall academic record is considered. And admissions officers pay close attention to grade trends—whether you remained consistent or had an upward or downward trend. The rigor of your high school curriculum will also be taken into account. Submitting SAT or ACT scores is optional for applicants who have maintained either a 3.5 GPA (in college prep courses) or who rank in the top 10 percent of their graduating class.

THE SCHOOL SAYS "..."

From the Admissions Office

"Christopher Newport University recruits future graduates who will thrive academically and socially on campus, and then go on to lead lives of significance. That's why our undergraduate experience—one that combines cutting-edge research and technology, innovative leadership opportunities, and high-impact service learning initiatives—inspires great leaders for the twenty-first century. Honoring the essential traditions of the liberal arts and sciences, our curriculum challenges hearts, as well as minds. We look for students of honor who will seek to make the world a better place. Fifty percent of our students score between 1130 and 1270 on the SAT (evidence-based reading and writing + math). Students are required to live on campus through their junior year. Our contemporary, state-of-the-art residential facilities win rave reviews from students and parents alike.

"Here you will study alongside distinguished professors, and over the last five years, we have added more than 100 tenure-track PhDs to our faculty. Outside the classroom, you will gain hands-on experience through internships with top organizations like NASA and the Thomas Jefferson National Accelerator Facility.

"At CNU, you will enjoy countless opportunities to develop leadership skills. Make an impact through the President's Leadership Program; design a challenging curriculum in the Honors Program; team with faculty on groundbreaking research; take your studies overseas by studying abroad; and share your talents through 200-plus student organizations. We are also home to one of the most successful NCAA Division III programs in the nation with student-athletes who excel both in the classroom and on the courts and fields of play. Check us out—we offer a truly distinctive student experience on a breathtakingly beautiful campus!"

SELECTIVITY
Admissions Rating	83
# of applicants	7,204
% of applicants accepted	72
% of acceptees attending	24
# offered a place on the wait list	1,001
% accepting a place on wait list	34
% admitted from wait list	30
# of early decision applicants	416
% accepted early decision	85

FRESHMAN PROFILE
Range SAT EBRW	570–650
Range SAT Math	540–630
Range SAT Composite	1130–1270
Range ACT Composite	22–27
# submitting SAT scores	1,112
% submitting SAT scores	90
# submitting ACT scores	320
% submitting ACT scores	26
Average HS GPA	3.8
% graduated top 10% of class	16
% graduated top 25% of class	48
% graduated top 50% of class	87

DEADLINES
Early decision	
Deadline	11/15
Notification	12/15
Early action	
Deadline	12/1
Notification	1/15
Regular	
Priority	2/1
Deadline	2/1
Notification	3/15
Nonfall registration?	Yes

APPLICANTS ALSO LOOK AT AND OFTEN PREFER
William & Mary; University of Virginia

AND SOMETIMES PREFER
George Mason University; James Madison University; Virginia Polytechnic Institute and State University

FINANCIAL FACTS
Financial Aid Rating	82
Annual in-state tuition	$14,924
Annual out-of-state tuition	$27,790
Room and board	$12,120
Average frosh need-based scholarship	$7,361
Average UG need-based scholarship	$7,839
% needy frosh rec. need-based scholarship or grant aid	72
% needy UG rec. need-based scholarship or grant aid	69
% needy frosh rec. non-need-based scholarship or grant aid	41
% needy UG rec. non-need-based scholarship or grant aid	34
% needy frosh rec. need-based self-help aid	69
% needy UG rec. need-based self-help aid	81
% frosh rec. any financial aid	74
% UG rec. any financial aid	69
% UG borrow to pay for school	61
Average cumulative indebtedness	$32,878
% frosh need fully met	21
% ugrads need fully met	22
Average % of frosh need met	67
Average % of ugrad need met	69

CITY UNIVERSITY OF NEW YORK—BARUCH COLLEGE

One Bernard Baruch Way, New York, NY 10010 • Admissions: 646-312-1400 • Fax: 646-312-1361

CAMPUS LIFE

Quality of Life Rating	90
Fire Safety Rating	60*
Green Rating	60*
Type of school	Public
Environment	Metropolis

STUDENTS

Total undergrad enrollment	15,066
% male/female	53/47
% from out of state	3
% frosh from public high school	90
% frosh live on campus	9
% ugrads live on campus	2
# of fraternities	0
# of sororities	0
% African American	9
% Asian	34
% Caucasian	20
% Hispanic	26
% Native American	<1
% Pacific Islander	<1
% Two or more races	2
% Race and/or ethnicity unknown	0
% international	10
# of countries represented	168

SURVEY SAYS . . .

Great library
Career services are great
Students love New York, NY
Very little drug use
Campus newspaper is popular
Active student government
Active minority support groups

ACADEMICS

Academic Rating	81
% students returning for sophomore year	89
% students graduating within 4 years	44
% students graduating within 6 years	70
Calendar	Semester
Student/faculty ratio	19:1
Profs interesting rating	89
Profs accessible rating	90

Most classes have 20–29 students.
Most lab/discussion sessions have
10–19 students.

MOST POPULAR MAJORS

Accounting; Finance, General

STUDENTS SAY "..."

Academics

One of the City University of New York's senior colleges, Baruch College's schools (Weissman School of Arts and Sciences, Marxe School of Public and International Affairs, and the Zicklin School of Business, which is the largest of the three) are located in Manhattan and take full advantage of being in "the greatest city of the world": Students here have access to "internships, big companies, and...Wall Street." Low in-state (as well as reasonable out-of-state) tuition means that many here "go to school while already working in interesting and impressive positions," and have come to Baruch purely "to improve themselves," which increases the level of maturity in the classroom. There is a wide variety of courses ("especially [for] those interested in business"), and the school offers ad-hoc majors, which allows students to design programs that will support their career goals.

Though this is not a research university, there are a "vast amount of resources" that are available to the students here. The education system is "well organized and up to date with the current world," and Baruch is tied with many companies in New York, which "creates even more opportunities for internships as well as job opportunities." "Some of my business professors came from leading huge corporations, and their anecdotes about their prior work help students internalize the material," says one student. There is "an impressive number of career-developing programs on campus that are free of charge and readily available to all students," and "it is clear that the professors at Baruch have first-hand experience in the material they are teaching to students."

Life

As a commuter school most students go to classes and go home, but "there are great clubs and events always happening" for those that do hang around, and the "lounges are usually packed." "It is all about how much time and effort you put into finding things to do," says a student. Most students are working part-time or full time while taking courses here, but find plenty to do in between classes, from "hanging out in the club area with the clubs, playing in the game room, working out in the gym, or taking classes in our trading floor." There is so much student activity around Baruch that it is often hard to contain, and "there is always something going on and always free food around campus."

Though most do not get the typical on-campus college experience, all agree that "for the price and the benefits associated with the school the tradeoff is worth it." This is New York City, which means "you can practically do ANYTHING with your day." Museums are free for students, and "of course the shopping and food are amazing." The school's Newman Vertical Campus on Lexington Ave is a hive of activity, and though elevator crowding is a problem, when a student's eyes look at the breathtaking view of the building, "It makes you feel proud to be a Baruchi!"

Student Body

Students come from all over the world and Baruch is "full of bright and ambitious minds"; being a student here "means you learn to interact with peers from all over the world." "My fellow peers have a good sense of where they want to steer their careers and exactly what they want to do after college," says one student. Baruch is "full of first generation college graduates," and the school is a real microcosm of NYC: "the hustle and bustle, crowds, everyone has somewhere to go, and everyone has a dream they hope will one day be fulfilled." This is a very unique commuter school in that "it has such an involved student body" where "there is a sense of community through clubs and extracurriculars."

CITY UNIVERSITY OF NEW YORK—BARUCH COLLEGE

Financial Aid: 646-312-1390 • E-Mail: admissions@baruch.cuny.edu • Website: www.baruch.cuny.edu

THE PRINCETON REVIEW SAYS

Admissions

Very important factors considered include: rigor of secondary school record, academic GPA, standardized test scores. *Important factors considered include:* application essay, recommendation(s). *Other factors considered include:* interview, extracurricular activities, talent/ability, character/personal qualities, work experience. ACT with or without writing accepted. High school diploma is required and GED is accepted. *Academic units required:* 4 English, 3 math, 2 science, 2 science labs, 2 foreign language, 4 social studies. *Academic units recommended:* 2 foreign language, 1 academic elective.

Financial Aid

Students should submit: FAFSA; State aid form. Priority filing deadline is 6/30. The Princeton Review suggests that all financial aid forms be submitted as soon as possible after October 1. *Need-based scholarships/grants offered:* College/university scholarship or grant aid from institutional funds; Federal Pell; Private scholarships; SEOG; State scholarships/grants. *Loan aid offered:* Direct PLUS loans; Direct Subsidized Stafford Loans; Direct Unsubsidized Stafford Loans. Applicants will be notified of awards on a rolling basis beginning 4/15. Federal Work-Study Program available. Institutional employment available.

The Inside Word

Admissions have grown steadily more competitive in recent years, especially for students seeking undergraduate business degrees. Today, Baruch receives nearly fifteen applications for every slot in its freshman class. Your math scores on standardized tests count more heavily here than verbal scores.

THE SCHOOL SAYS "..."

From the Admissions Office

"Baruch College is in the heart of New York City. As an undergraduate, you will join a vibrant learning community of students and scholars in the middle of an exhilarating city full of possibilities. Baruch is a place where theory meets practice. You can network with city leaders; secure business, cultural, and nonprofit internships; access the music, art, and business scene; and meet experts who visit our campus. You will take classes that bridge business, arts, science, government, political and international affairs, learning from professors who are among the best in their fields. One third of our freshmen participate in learning communities, which offer incoming students small, interdisciplinary classes and an opportunity to get to know our faculty through class room discussion and planned field trips throughout the city. Baruch offers 30 majors and 60 minors in three schools: the Marxe School of Public Affairs and International Affairs, the Weissman School of Arts and Science, and the Zicklin School of Business. Highly qualified undergraduates may apply to the Baruch College Honors program, which offers scholarships, small seminars and honors courses. Students may also study abroad through programs in more than 30 countries. Our 17-floor Newman Vertical Campus serves as the college's hub. Here you will find the atmosphere and resources of a traditional college campus, but in a lively urban setting. Our classrooms have state-of-the-art technology, and our library was named the top college library in the nation. Baruch also has a simulated trading floor for students who are interested in Wall Street. You can also enjoy a three-level athletics and recreation complex, which features a twenty-five-meter indoor pool as well as a performing arts complex. In 2013, Baruch College opened the 25th Street Pedestrian Plaza, providing outdoor space for major student actives like Freshmen Convocation, Winter Carnival and Spring Fling, as well as an informal setting for students to gather on a nice day. The college is now offering housing at 1760 3rd Avenue (in Manhattan, on the Upper East Side). The state-of-the-art residences are equipped with a concierge, high tech gym, laundry facility that texts when your clothes are dry, and a very chill lounge to study or relax with your friends. The building is just blocks away from Central Park, and Serendipity. Baruch's selective admission standards, strong academic programs, top national honors, as well as its internship and job-placement opportunities make it an exceptional educational value."

SELECTIVITY
Admissions Rating	91
# of applicants	20,303
% of applicants accepted	43
% of acceptees attending	26

FRESHMAN PROFILE
Range SAT EBRW	550–640
Range SAT Math	580–690
# submitting SAT scores	2,142
% submitting SAT scores	94
Average HS GPA	3.3
% graduated top 10% of class	41
% graduated top 25% of class	74
% graduated top 50% of class	92

DEADLINES
Early decision	
Deadline	12/13
Notification	1/7
Regular	
Priority	12/1
Deadline	2/1
Notification	12/1
Nonfall registration?	Yes

FINANCIAL FACTS
Financial Aid Rating	82
Annual in-state tuition	$6,930
Annual out-of-state tuition	$18,600
Room and board	$12,880
Required fees	$531
Books and supplies	$1,364
Average frosh need-based scholarship	$9,920
Average UG need-based scholarship	$8,248
% needy frosh rec. need-based scholarship or grant aid	96
% needy UG rec. need-based scholarship or grant aid	92
% needy frosh rec. non-need-based scholarship or grant aid	1
% needy UG rec. non-need-based scholarship or grant aid	2
% needy frosh rec. need-based self-help aid	13
% needy UG rec. need-based self-help aid	21
% frosh rec. any financial aid	64
% UG rec. any financial aid	62
% UG borrow to pay for school	13
Average cumulative indebtedness	$9,182
% frosh need fully met	5
% ugrads need fully met	3
Average % of frosh need met	51
Average % of ugrad need met	46

CITY UNIVERSITY OF NEW YORK—BROOKLYN COLLEGE

2900 Bedford Avenue, Brooklyn, NY 11210 • Admissions: 718-951-5001 • Fax: 718-951-4506

STUDENTS SAY "..."

Academics

Brooklyn College "is the perfect representative of Brooklyn as a borough and [of] success in the community," an institution that, like its home borough, "educates its students in an environment that reflects diversity, opportunity (study abroad, research, athletics, employment), and support." "Lauded as one of the best senior colleges in CUNY" and boasting "a beautiful campus," Brooklyn College entices a lot of bright students looking for an affordable, quality, undergraduate experience as well as some attracted by the school's relatively charitable admissions standards. It's easier to get in here than to stay in; Brooklyn College is "an academically challenging and rigorous school" that "feels a lot more competitive than one would anticipate." Professors "are fabulous" and "really passionate about the subjects that they teach and their students' career paths," although there are some "grumpy and nasty professors" that might best be avoided. Students are especially sanguine about special programs here, such as the various honors programs, in which "you will meet tons of highly intelligent people. Honors classes boast very good in-class discussions and highly vibrant, enthusiastic students. Non-honors classes are more run-of-the-mill but still very good academically." The school also works hard to provide "constant and innumerable job opportunities available to students and the Magner Center, which helps students find jobs and internships, and [to] help them prepare for the real world through résumé writing workshops [and] job interview workshops." There are also "many financial awards available."

Life

"Apart from all the clubs and athletics on campus, most people come for class and then leave" at Brooklyn College because "we are a commuter school, so it has to be this way. All social activities happen off campus." There are "pretty nice places to hang out around campus for the occasional coffee," and "there are a lot of student organizations and a lot of activities done to help enhance student life on campus," but the "immediate surroundings of the Brooklyn College campus are generally not where you would want to stay for hours," and "on weekends the campus usually is dead." That said, "the campus is quite beautiful, and the quad during spring time is usually a nice place to sit and relax." Furthermore, "New York City hotspots are a twenty- to forty-minute [subway] ride away," and Brooklyn itself is "a great place to live" where "there are always fun things happening."

Student Body

"The typical student at Brooklyn College is hardworking, from the NY metro area, and a commuter." Many "hold part-time jobs and pay at least part of their own tuition, so they are usually in a rush because they have a lot more responsibility on their shoulders than the average college student." Like Brooklyn itself, "the student body is very diversified," with everyone from "an aspiring opera singer to quirky film majors to single mothers looking for a better life for their children," and so "no student can be described as being typical. Everyone blends in as normal, and little segregation is noticed (if it exists)." Students here represent more than 100 nations and speak nearly as many languages. There are students who "come from Long Island to North Carolina, from Connecticut to even Hong Kong."

CITY UNIVERSITY OF NEW YORK—BROOKLYN COLLEGE

Financial Aid: 718-951-5051 • Website: www.brooklyn.cuny.edu

THE PRINCETON REVIEW SAYS

Admissions

Very important factors considered include: rigor of secondary school record, academic GPA, standardized test scores. High school diploma is required and GED is accepted. *Academic units recommended:* 4 English, 3 math, 3 science, 3 foreign language, 4 social studies, 4 academic electives.

Financial Aid

Students should submit: FAFSA; State TAP and Excelsior application. Priority filing deadline is 3/1. The Princeton Review suggests that all financial aid forms be submitted as soon as possible after October. *Need-based scholarships/grants offered:* College/university scholarship or grant aid from institutional funds; Federal Pell; Private scholarships; SEOG; State scholarships/grants. *Loan aid offered:* Direct PLUS loans; Direct Subsidized Stafford Loans; Direct Unsubsidized Stafford Loans. Applicants will be notified of awards on a rolling basis beginning 5/1. Federal Work-Study Program available. Institutional employment available.

The Inside Word

Brooklyn College doesn't set the bar inordinately high; students with less-than-stellar high school records can receive a chance to prove themselves here. Once they get in, though, they had better be prepared to work; Brooklyn College typically loses about 20 percent of its freshman class each year, and six-year graduation rates are just over 50 percent. Getting into Brooklyn College is one thing; surviving its academic challenges is a whole other thing entirely.

THE SCHOOL SAYS "..."

From the Admissions Office

"Brooklyn College is a premier public liberal arts college part of CUNY, consistently designated by The Princeton Review as one of America's Best Value Colleges (2019, 2009), as well as being named a Top College in NYS (2018); a Best College (2016); and a Best College in U.S. (2015). The College was also named the No.1 college among North Regional Universities for campus ethnic diversity by U.S. News and World Report (2019).

"Respected nationally for its rigorous academic standards, Brooklyn College takes pride in such innovative programs as its award-winning Freshman Year College; the Honors Academy, which houses six programs for high achievers; and its nationally recognized core curriculum. Its School of Education is ranked among the top twenty in the country for graduates who go on to be considered among the best teachers in New York City. The College's Murray Koppelman School of Business is the only business program in Brooklyn that is accredited by the Association to Advance Collegiate Schools of Business.

"Brooklyn College's strong academic reputation has attracted an outstanding faculty of nationally renowned teachers and scholars. Among the awards they have won are Pulitzers, Guggenheims, Fulbrights, and many National Institutes of Health grants.

"The student body consists of 17,811 student (14,970 undergraduate and 2,841 graduate) who represent the ethnic and cultural diversity of the borough. In recent years, student achievements have been acknowledged with Fulbright and Truman Scholarships and an Emmy Award. In 2010 the College received its third Rhodes Scholarship in eleven years.

"The college expanded its presence with the 2015 opening of the Feirstein Graduate School of Cinema, the only graduate film school housed on a working lot (Steiner Studios) and is the first public graduate film school in New York, dedicated to cultivating new and emerging voices in cinema.

"The most recent addition to campus, the Leonard & Claire Tow Center for the Performing Arts, opened in fall 2018, and is supported by a generous gift from the center's namesakes, Leonard '50 and Claire '52 Tow. The center is home to the Conservatory of Music and the Department of Theater. This building is the first LEED-certified, sustainable building on the campus."

SELECTIVITY

Admissions Rating	90
# of applicants	26,973
% of applicants accepted	45
% of acceptees attending	16
# offered a place on the wait list	1,001
% accepting a place on wait list	281
% admitted from wait list	275

FRESHMAN PROFILE

Range SAT EBRW	510–600
Range SAT Math	530–620
# submitting SAT scores	1,799
% submitting SAT scores	95
Average HS GPA	3.3

DEADLINES

Regular	
Priority	2/1
Notification	Rolling, 2/1
Nonfall registration?	Yes

FINANCIAL FACTS

Financial Aid Rating	86
Annual in-state tuition	$6,930
Annual out-of-state tuition	$18,600
Books and supplies	$1,364
Required fees	$510
Average frosh need-based scholarship	$9,842
Average UG need-based scholarship	$9,617
% needy frosh rec. need-based scholarship or grant aid	88
% needy UG rec. need-based scholarship or grant aid	88
% needy frosh rec. non-need-based scholarship or grant aid	68
% needy UG rec. non-need-based scholarship or grant aid	32
% needy frosh rec. need-based self-help aid	10
% needy UG rec. need-based self-help aid	20
% UG borrow to pay for school	12
Average cumulative indebtedness	$14,736
% frosh need fully met	50
% ugrads need fully met	42
Average % of frosh need met	74
Average % of ugrad need met	70

CITY UNIVERSITY OF NEW YORK—HUNTER COLLEGE

695 Park Ave, Room N203, New York, NY 10065 • Admissions: 212-272-4490

CAMPUS LIFE

Quality of Life Rating	81
Fire Safety Rating	93
Green Rating	81
Type of school	Public
Environment	Metropolis

STUDENTS

Total undergrad enrollment	16,081
% male/female	36/64
% from out of state	4
% frosh from public high school	78
# of fraternities	2
# of sororities	2
% African American	12
% Asian	32
% Caucasian	28
% Hispanic	24
% Native American	<1
% Pacific Islander	0
% Two or more races	0
% Race and/or ethnicity unknown	0
% international	5
# of countries represented	158

SURVEY SAYS . . .

Lots of liberal students
Students love New York, NY
Very little drug use
College radio is popular

ACADEMICS

Academic Rating	77
% students returning for sophomore year	87
% students graduating within 4 years	25
% students graduating within 6 years	57
Calendar	Semester
Student/faculty ratio	13:1
Profs interesting rating	83
Profs accessible rating	85
Most classes have 20–29 students.	

MOST POPULAR MAJORS

Computer Science; English Language and Literature, General; Psychology, General

STUDENTS SAY "..."

Academics

The crown jewel of the CUNY system, Hunter College is an institution teeming with "resources" and "endless...opportunities." Of course, many students are drawn to Hunter for its "very affordable" price tag and "prime location." Undergrads also love just how many "great" academic programs the college truly offers, including "nursing," "psychology," "political science," and "education." No matter what you want to study, you can rest assured Hunter will deliver. Students also benefit from the amazing "support systems" that Hunter maintains. Indeed, they can rely on the fact that numerous "advisors are always there to answer questions about careers, classes to take, and graduation needs." This care and concern can be found within the classroom as well. After all, Hunter professors tend to be "passionate about what they teach and prefer for students to be active in class." Moreover, "they are extremely willing to help outside the classroom" as well. And many undergrads simply find their instructors "very nice and knowledgeable." Finally, as this thrilled student boasts, "They keep challenging me to do better with my work and to never stop working at the idea that is in my head to make it a reality. They genuinely believe that the students at Hunter are above others which gives me a confidence that I chose the right school."

Life

Hunter College doesn't have a sprawling or self-contained campus. And, given that many undergrads here commute, it's quite common for people to pop in "just for classes and are running back to the train when classes are over." Of course, "if there's a break, people often join up with friends to eat, or study together in the library, by the halls, or the digital cafes." And, when time allows, "people often go to the gyms and workout downstairs." A large percentage of undergrads here hold "part-time jobs that offer flexible hours" as well. A decent number also carve out time to "volunteer." Additionally, the college itself "hosts many, many programs and activities all throughout the week." When the weather is nice, many students like to head to "nearby Central Park" to hang out and/or study. Students frequently "explore the city because there is always stuff to do in New York." For example, "there are tons of museums in the area that are free for Hunter students." And undergrads who are of age seem to love checking out the "bars and clubs" the city has to offer.

Student Body

Primarily a "commuter" school, Hunter's student body is dominated by New York City "locals who are trying to get their education in a cost efficient manner." Fortunately, they are also an extremely "diverse" lot. You can find undergrads of "every culture, religion, race, etc." And since "everyone comes from different walks of life," you will "never feel like an outcast." Indeed, Hunter students are extraordinarily "accepting." Some individuals lament, however, that their peers do tend to "keep to themselves." Others argue that if you take the time to talk to people, you quickly discover that most students are "friendly" and "welcoming." They can also be "very supportive and caring." As one undergrad explains, "We make sure that we help each other out in our studies and teach each other when there is something we do not understand." Additionally, the vast majority of Hunter students are "driven to succeed." They are often "found vigorously studying for their classes and forming networks with people that have similar interests as them." It's quite evident that everyone here really "wants to achieve something in life." And, as this wise undergrad succinctly states, "Being around people with that general same motivation is really good."

CITY UNIVERSITY OF NEW YORK—HUNTER COLLEGE

Financial Aid: 212-772-4820 • E-Mail: admissions@hunter.cuny.edu • Website: www.hunter.cuny.edu/main/

THE PRINCETON REVIEW SAYS

Admissions

Very important factors considered include: rigor of secondary school record, class rank, academic GPA. SAT with or without Essay component accepted. High school diploma is required and GED is accepted. *Academic units required:* 2 English, 2 math, 1 science, 1 science lab. *Academic units recommended:* 4 English, 3 math, 2 science, 2 foreign language, 4 social studies, 1 academic elective, 1 visual/performing arts.

Financial Aid

Students should submit: FAFSA; State aid form. The Princeton Review suggests that all financial aid forms be submitted as soon as possible after October 1. *Need-based scholarships/grants offered:* College/university scholarship or grant aid from institutional funds; Federal Pell; State scholarships/grants. *Loan aid offered:* Direct PLUS loans; Direct Subsidized Stafford Loans; Direct Unsubsidized Stafford Loans. Applicants will be notified of awards on a rolling basis beginning 5/15. Federal Work-Study Program available. Institutional employment available.

The Inside Word

The admissions process at Hunter College is rather straightforward. Admissions officers do their utmost to take a well-rounded approach, giving all application facets careful consideration. Of course, your high school transcript and GPA will hold the most weight. Hunter wants evidence that you're prepared for college-level courses after all. Your standardized test scores will speak to that as well. And, finally, the admissions committee relies on supplemental essays to assess what kind of impact you might have on life at Hunter.

THE SCHOOL SAYS "..."

From the Admissions Office

"Located in the heart of Manhattan, Hunter offers students the stimulating learning environment and career-building opportunities you might expect from a college that's been a part of the world's most exciting city since 1870. The largest senior college in the City University of New York, Hunter pulses with energy. Hunter's vitality stems from a large, highly diverse faculty and student body. Its schools—Arts and Sciences, Education, Nursing, Social Work and Public Health—provide an affordable first-rate education. Undergraduates have extraordinary opportunities to conduct high-level research with renowned faculty, and to participate in credit-bearing internships in media, the arts, government and many other fields. The college's high standards and special programs ensure a challenging education. Specialized programs for first-year students keep classmates together as they pursue courses in the liberal arts, pre–health science, pre-nursing, pre-med, or honors. A range of honors programs is available for students with strong academic records, including the highly competitive Macaulay Honors College for entering freshmen and the Thomas Hunter Honors Program for continuing students. There are also six different freshman scholar programs offered in the arts, sciences, humanities, computer science, public policy, and nursing. All honors programs are accompanied by significant merit scholarship opportunities and feature small classes with personalized mentoring by outstanding faculty members. Qualified students also benefit from Hunter's participation in minority science research and training programs, the prestigious Andrew W. Mellon Minority Undergraduate Program, and many other passports to professional success. Hunter College has four residence halls on Manhattan's east side, housing almost 1,000 students."

SELECTIVITY

Admissions Rating	92
# of applicants	33,750
% of applicants accepted	35
% of acceptees attending	22

FRESHMAN PROFILE

Range SAT EBRW	580–660
Range SAT Math	590–690
# submitting SAT scores	2,392
% submitting SAT scores	94
Average HS GPA	3.5

DEADLINES

Regular	
Deadline	2/1

FINANCIAL FACTS

Financial Aid Rating	90
Annual in-state tuition	$6,930
Annual out-of-state tuition	$18,000
Room and board	$4,857
Required fees	$450
Books and supplies	$1,364
Average frosh need-based scholarship	$8,892
Average UG need-based scholarship	$8,142
% needy frosh rec. need-based scholarship or grant aid	89
% needy UG rec. need-based scholarship or grant aid	88
% needy frosh rec. non-need-based scholarship or grant aid	76
% needy UG rec. non-need-based scholarship or grant aid	46
% needy frosh rec. need-based self-help aid	6
% needy UG rec. need-based self-help aid	11
% frosh rec. any financial aid	80
% UG rec. any financial aid	73
% UG borrow to pay for school	15
Average cumulative indebtedness	$16,272
% frosh need fully met	41
% ugrads need fully met	58
Average % of frosh need met	79
Average % of ugrad need met	82

CITY UNIVERSITY OF NEW YORK—QUEENS COLLEGE

6530 Kissena Blvd, Queens, NY 11367 • Admissions: 718-997-5600 • Fax: 718-997-5617

STUDENTS SAY "..."

Academics

Located in New York's "most diverse borough," Queens College "offers high quality academics for a very reasonable price." As one student puts it, "Queens is about getting a valuable and quality education that does not drain you financially for the future." In keeping with the fact that the majority of QC students live off campus in a variety of nearby communities, one of the school's strengths is helping students become "the best you can be so you can give back to the community." One student even goes as far as to say that QC is "considered the Harvard of CUNY." The Macaulay Honors College and the Aaron Copeland School of Music both get high marks, with students saying that QC as a whole "provides a strong liberal arts education to give [students] well-rounded knowledge and skills." Professors generally "genuinely care about [students'] grades and well-being"; as one student puts it, "They won't let me fall behind." But while "most professors genuinely care for [students'] success," it's inevitable that they will "vary in terms of quality." As one student puts it, "Many of my professors just lecture and don't interact too much, however, some are very involved and passionate." Students appreciate the "challenging yet interesting courses" but some lament that for the coveted courses, "you have to really run and register for those classes like it's a competition."

Life

Though the school opened the Summit Apartments, its first residence hall, in 2009, the majority of QC students still commute; as one student observes, "Even though the Summit Apartments can only house 500 students, it still remains pretty empty throughout the semesters." Since "most students come here to go to class and then head home or to their job afterwards," many QC students say that it's difficult to foster much sense of a school community—"the sense of community could use some work." But others counter, saying that, "I would not expect a school composed mostly of commuters to bond as much as we do." Outside of class, it's "very hard to be bored," especially "being so close to the city, there are a lot of activities to do around the area." Many students explore Queens, which is accessible via a free QC shuttle. For those who live on campus, or those commuters who stick around after class, as one student puts it, "We have clubs for everything, and if there isn't a club for something you like you could always start [one] up." One thing that students agree helps unite QC as a community is student government: "Student government provides us with events and carnivals during both the fall and spring semesters. It brings people together."

Student Body

Diversity is key at Queens College, where, as one student puts it, "We have a very diverse campus, so no minority is really ever a minority." "If one were to ask me to name every ethnicity, nationality, and religious group on campus, I would not even know where to begin," says another. QC "has a very friendly student body" and some says that "the friendships and bonds you make from taking transit together, or sharing stories is special in [its] own way." Others note that "there is not much of an established social life" and that "if you want to make friends here you really have to work for it." Many students "have part-time jobs," some students "are parents, and have to take care of their children"—"Of course, many people are straight out of high school [too], but even these people usually spend a lot of time off campus." Students describe their peers as "career-minded and focused"; they "love to have fun, but they [are] still focused on their studies and their futures."

CITY UNIVERSITY OF NEW YORK—QUEENS COLLEGE

Financial Aid: 718-997-5123 • E-Mail: vincent.angrisani@qc.cuny.edu • Website: www.qc.cuny.edu

THE PRINCETON REVIEW SAYS

Admissions

Very important factors considered include: rigor of secondary school record, academic GPA, standardized test scores. *Other factors considered include:* application essay, recommendation(s). ACT with or without writing accepted. SAT with or without Essay component accepted. High school diploma is required and GED is accepted. *Academic units required:* 4 English, 3 math, 2 science, 2 science labs, 3 foreign language, 4 social studies. *Academic units recommended:* 4 English, 3 math, 3 science, 3 science labs, 3 foreign language, 4 social studies.

Financial Aid

Students should submit: FAFSA; State aid form. The Princeton Review suggests that all financial aid forms be submitted as soon as possible after October 1. *Need-based scholarships/grants offered:* College/university scholarship or grant aid from institutional funds; Federal Pell; Private scholarships; SEOG; State scholarships/grants. *Loan aid offered:* Direct PLUS loans; Direct Subsidized Stafford Loans; Direct Unsubsidized Stafford Loans. Federal Work-Study Program available. Institutional employment available.

The Inside Word

Queens College looks for students with a B average (or better) or a GED score of at least 3500 to be a strong candidate for admission; the school encourages a high school education that includes a full range of language arts and science courses. Standardized test scores are also a requirement. Exceptional applicants should look into Macaulay Honors College, which provides free tuition and other benefits (including a study grant and a free laptop) to gifted students.

THE SCHOOL SAYS "..."

From the Admissions Office

"Queens College prepares students to become the leaders of tomorrow by offering a rigorous education in the liberal arts and sciences under the guidance of an outstanding faculty dedicated to teaching and scholarship. Our students graduate with the skills that employers and the best graduate schools are looking for: a critical, problem-solving intelligence, the ability to express ideas clearly, an aptitude for the latest technologies, and an appreciation of different cultures.

"Queens College has over 170 programs, and is recognized nationally for the excellence of its academic offerings. We have more computer science majors than any other university in New York City, and rank third in New York State for the number of accounting and business students we graduate. Our acclaimed Aaron Copland School of Music offers talented students a fine liberal arts education and conservatory-level training. We're the ideal choice for aspiring educators—no school in the metropolitan area has graduated more teachers, counselors, and principals than QC. Our tuition is among the most affordable in the nation.

"Located in the most exciting city in the world, QC provides a vibrant student life experience for students who live on or off campus. We have over 100 student clubs, 19 NCAA Division II teams, and numerous intramural and recreation programs. Our students represent 170 countries, which creates an extraordinarily diverse and welcoming campus community. With programs such as honors, internships, service-learning, and study abroad, QC offers countless opportunities for personal and professional growth."

SELECTIVITY

Admissions Rating	88
# of applicants	18,180
% of applicants accepted	43
% of acceptees attending	22

FRESHMAN PROFILE

Range SAT EBRW	520–600
Range SAT Math	540–620
# submitting SAT scores	945
% submitting SAT scores	83
Average HS GPA	3.5

DEADLINES

Regular	
Priority	2/1
Notification	Rolling, 2/1
Nonfall registration?	Yes

FINANCIAL FACTS

Financial Aid Rating	82
Annual in-state tuition	$6,930
Annual out-of-state tuition	$18,600
Room and board	$15,992
Required fees	$608
Books and supplies	$1,364
Average frosh need-based scholarship	$8,893
Average UG need-based scholarship	$8,244
% needy frosh rec. need-based scholarship or grant aid	88
% needy UG rec. need-based scholarship or grant aid	88
% needy frosh rec. non-need-based scholarship or grant aid	71
% needy UG rec. non-need-based scholarship or grant aid	32
% needy frosh rec. need-based self-help aid	7
% needy UG rec. need-based self-help aid	15
% frosh rec. any financial aid	76
% UG rec. any financial aid	51
% UG borrow to pay for school	15
Average cumulative indebtedness	$16,104
% frosh need fully met	5
% ugrads need fully met	4
Average % of frosh need met	59
Average % of ugrad need met	53

CLAREMONT MCKENNA COLLEGE

888 Columbia Avenue, Claremont, CA 91711 • Admissions: 909-621-8088 • Fax: 909-621-8516

CAMPUS LIFE

Quality of Life Rating	91
Fire Safety Rating	89
Green Rating	86
Type of school	Private
Environment	Town

STUDENTS

Total undergrad enrollment	1,335
% male/female	50/50
% from out of state	55
% frosh live on campus	100
% ugrads live on campus	96
# of fraternities	0
# of sororities	0
% African American	4
% Asian	12
% Caucasian	41
% Hispanic	15
% Native American	<1
% Pacific Islander	<1
% Two or more races	7
% Race and/or ethnicity unknown	5
% international	16
# of countries represented	46

SURVEY SAYS . . .

Great library
Career services are great
Internships are widely available
Class discussions encouraged
School is well run
Great financial aid
No one cheats
Diverse student types interact on campus
Great food on campus
Lots of beer drinking
Very little drug use
Alumni active on campus

ACADEMICS

Academic Rating	95
% students returning for sophomore year	95
% students graduating within 4 years	84
% students graduating within 6 years	91
Calendar	Semester
Student/faculty ratio	8:1
Profs interesting rating	96
Profs accessible rating	99
Most classes have 10–19 students.	

STUDENTS SAY "..."

Academics

Students at Claremont McKenna really love their school. With its "phenomenal academics," "brilliant professors," "amazing career services center," and "perfect weather," it's no wonder CMC students are "the happiest students in America." Claremont McKenna is known for its government and economics majors, but philosophy, international relations, and the Keck Science program also get high marks. CMC is a part of The Claremont Colleges, so if students are looking for something that CMC doesn't have, they can probably find it at one of the four sister schools. Students rave about Claremont's emphasis on "professionalism" and all of the "great research and internship opportunities." The workload is heavy, and professors set "high expectations," so "students spend their weeks [working on] their papers, books, readings, research projects, problem sets, etc." Despite the intense workload, students love their professors. "Professors are absolute geniuses in their field," one student gushes. They're "helpful and encouraging," "incredibly accessible," and even "willing to Skype on the weekends to answer questions." "This sounds corny," one student admits, "this really is a place where professors become like family." Students spend a "good deal of out-of-classroom time" with their teachers. "When you take both academics and quality of life into account," a cognitive neuroscience major says, "I can't believe I almost went to an Ivy over this place."

Life

Life is good at Claremont McKenna. The "constantly beaming California sun and the close vicinity to both mountains and beaches" mean students spend their time outdoors when they can. But even when students are lounging in the sun or playing Frisbee, they're not really taking a break. The "conversation doesn't end in the classroom," a student explains, and the "intellectual culture...really allows for twenty-four-hour learning." While Claremont McKenna has the campus and "community-life and identity of a small school" it "still [has] the resources of the other four C's." Even without the other schools students feel "completely pampered" because "the school cares about its students so much." A Spanish major says, "The relationship between the students and the administration is excellent here," and the "student government and Dean of Students Office...subsidize incredible off-campus trips and on-campus parties." One of the best things about Claremont McKenna is the Marian Miner Cook Athenaeum, which hosts prestigious guest lecturers four nights a week. One student wisely asks, "Where else could you have dinner with Jesse Jackson, Mitt Romney, etc.?" Students agree, "There's a niche for everyone, and the welcoming, accepting atmosphere makes fitting in easy."

Student Body

"Claremont McKenna doesn't accept students who aren't amazing." "Amazing" means a "really smart" person who's "incredibly motivated and career-driven." It's "a tight-knit community of driven, competitive, and intelligent people who know how to be successful and have a great time." "A lot of kids are political and well-informed"; most are "active on campus," very into sports, and involved with internships or clubs. Students are extremely well-rounded; they "know how to lead a discussion...clock hours in the library, play a varsity or club sport, and hold a leadership position in a club or organization," and they also know how to throw "a great party on Saturday night."

CLAREMONT MCKENNA COLLEGE

Financial Aid: 909-621-8356 • E-Mail: admission@cmc.edu • Website: www.claremontmckenna.edu

THE PRINCETON REVIEW SAYS

Admissions

Very important factors considered include: rigor of secondary school record, class rank, academic GPA, standardized test scores, recommendation(s), extracurricular activities, character/personal qualities. *Important factors considered include:* application essay, interview, talent/ability. *Other factors considered include:* first generation, alumni/ae relation, geographical residence, racial/ethnic status, volunteer work, work experience. ACT with or without writing accepted. SAT with or without Essay component accepted. High school diploma is required and GED is accepted. *Academic units required:* 4 English, 3 math, 2 science, 2 science labs, 3 foreign language, 1 social studies, 1 history. *Academic units recommended:* 4 English, 4 math, 3 science, 3 science labs, 3 foreign language, 1 social studies, 1 history.

Financial Aid

Students should submit: Business/Farm Supplement; CSS/Financial Aid PROFILE; FAFSA; Noncustodial PROFILE; State aid form. Priority filing deadline is 1/5. The Princeton Review suggests that all financial aid forms be submitted as soon as possible after October 1. *Need-based scholarships/grants offered:* College/university scholarship or grant aid from institutional funds; Federal Pell; Private scholarships; SEOG; State scholarships/grants. *Loan aid offered:* Direct PLUS loans; Direct Subsidized Stafford Loans; Direct Unsubsidized Stafford Loans. Applicants will be notified of awards on or about 4/1. Federal Work-Study Program available. Institutional employment available.

The Inside Word

Although applicants have to possess exemplary academic qualifications to gain admission to Claremont McKenna, the importance of making a good match shouldn't be underestimated. Colleges of such small size and selectivity devote much more energy to determining whether the candidate as an individual fits instead of whether a candidate has the appropriate test scores.

THE SCHOOL SAYS "..."

From the Admissions Office

"CMC offers a first-rate liberal arts education where students can acquire a broad experience across a range of disciplines from the humanities to the social sciences to the sciences, but where they can also pursue an unusually rich spectrum of courses in economics, public affairs, and international relations. CMC's mission is clear: To educate students for meaningful, productive, and responsible lives of leadership. By combining the intellectual breadth of liberal arts with the more pragmatic concerns of public affairs, CMC students gain the vision, skills, and values necessary for leadership in all sectors of society.

"Applicants must take the SAT Test or ACT both with writing. We will use the highest scores from the SAT or ACT. SAT Subject Tests are not required unless home-schooled."

SELECTIVITY

Admissions Rating	98
# of applicants	6,066
% of applicants accepted	10
% of acceptees attending	52
# offered a place on the wait list	578
% accepting a place on wait list	57
% admitted from wait list	13
# of early decision applicants	691
% accepted early decision	28

FRESHMAN PROFILE

Range SAT EBRW	670–730
Range SAT Math	690–780
Range SAT Composite	1380–1490
Range ACT Composite	31–34
# submitting SAT scores	185
% submitting SAT scores	56
# submitting ACT scores	173
% submitting ACT scores	53
% graduated top 10% of class	83
% graduated top 25% of class	100
% graduated top 50% of class	100

DEADLINES

Early decision	
Deadline	11/1
Notification	12/15
Other ED Deadline	1/5
Other ED Notification	2/15
Regular	
Deadline	1/5
Notification	4/1
Nonfall registration?	No

FINANCIAL FACTS

Financial Aid Rating	95
Annual tuition	$56,190
Room and board	$17,300
Average frosh need-based scholarship	$56,137
Average UG need-based scholarship	$51,838
% needy frosh rec. need-based scholarship or grant aid	98
% needy UG rec. need-based scholarship or grant aid	98
% needy frosh rec. non-need-based scholarship or grant aid	39
% needy UG rec. non-need-based scholarship or grant aid	44
% needy frosh rec. need-based self-help aid	92
% needy UG rec. need-based self-help aid	94
% frosh rec. any financial aid	43
% UG rec. any financial aid	42
% UG borrow to pay for school	36
Average cumulative indebtedness	$21,450
% frosh need fully met	100
% ugrads need fully met	100
Average % of frosh need met	100
Average % of ugrad need met	100

CLARKSON UNIVERSITY

8 Clarkson Ave, Box 5605, Potsdam, NY 13699 • Admissions: 315-268-6480 • Fax: 315-268-7647

CAMPUS LIFE

Quality of Life Rating	82
Fire Safety Rating	96
Green Rating	91
Type of school	Private
Environment	Village

STUDENTS

Total undergrad enrollment	2,982
% male/female	69/31
% from out of state	31
% frosh from public high school	86
% frosh live on campus	94
% ugrads live on campus	82
# of fraternities (% ugrad men join)	9 (14)
# of sororities (% ugrad women join)	4 (11)
% African American	3
% Asian	4
% Caucasian	79
% Hispanic	5
% Native American	<1
% Pacific Islander	0
% Two or more races	4
% Race and/or ethnicity unknown	2
% international	3
# of countries represented	30

SURVEY SAYS . . .

Career services are great
Intramural sports are popular
Alumni active on campus

ACADEMICS

Academic Rating	76
% students returning for sophomore year	91
% students graduating within 4 years	63
% students graduating within 6 years	81
Calendar	Semester
Student/faculty ratio	14:1
Profs interesting rating	83
Profs accessible rating	90

Most classes have 10–19 students.
Most lab/discussion sessions have
10–19 students.

MOST POPULAR MAJORS

Mechanical Engineering; Engineering/Industrial
Management; Civil Engineering, General

STUDENTS SAY "..."

Academics

Nestled at the northern reaches of New York state (with additional graduate and research facilities in Schenectady, Beacon, Saranac Lake, and New York City), Clarkson University is a science and engineering powerhouse that has consistently turned career-ready, "hard-working and determined" students out into the workforce. The school is known for its excellent job placement rate and "the large number of internship opportunities that Clarkson's connections bring"; "Everyone wants you to succeed and provides the resources for you to do so." One of Clarkson's greatest strengths is that all "come here with the understanding that engineering is one of our main concepts" and are encouraged to work with others. The administration "really stresses on how important your career is" and the curriculum and faculty drive home the fact that "you go to college to eventually one day get a career in what you love." Many courses here are project-based, so students receive "hands-on skills and real world experience that will immediately help in the workforce." Professors become "more engaging the higher level of class you take," and the majority of the harder science classes (such as biology and chemistry) pair each lecture with a lab and a discussion class where students "can get a more in-depth view of the material while working in a smaller classroom." "I have taken trips for my classes to visualize rather than just read," says a student.

Both "hard and soft skills have been developed and grown" at Clarkson, and are soon enough put to use; students rave about the Career Center, which holds two career fairs and "a myriad of workshops" to help students find and prepare for co-ops, internships, and jobs. Additionally, Clarkson SPEED (Student Projects for Engineering Experience and Design) teams like Design, Build, Fly "allow students to put their practical engineering knowledge to the test," and the Reh Center for Entrepreneurship and Shipley Center for Innovation offer business students "a chance to create their own companies."

Life

Potsdam is located close to the Adirondacks and near "some of the best skiing in the Northeast." During the long and very cold winters, "a lot of people go to local mountains to ski/snowboard on their days off." The atmosphere of the small campus is "very comforting" and like a "home away from home," and there are "ample things to do around campus, especially in the winter." The school "hosts numerous events to get students involved in campus life," and there is a wide spread of non-academic interests and clubs such as "The Outing Club [which] is the biggest club on campus." Schoolwork is "a large portion of any student's life" at Clarkson, but on the weekends students attend hockey games, go to parties, have movie nights, or "go fishing on the Raquette River, which is right next to the college."

Student Body

Clarkson truly acts as "a gathering place for like-minded individuals," where different personalities, ethnicities, majors, and cultures reside, but "no one is afraid of work." Everyone is friendly to each other: "You say hello to someone, and you will get a hello back." Clarkson has "a fair ratio of 'nerds' to 'jocks' due to the recruitment of athletes for teams," and the population also skews heavily male. "Diversity isn't huge at Clarkson, but it is something they are working on." In the end, everyone here "understands how difficult classes can be," and problem-solving together and "working in teams is a big part of being successful here." At Clarkson, "you constantly see students attempting to solve the same task in hundreds of different ways."

Financial Aid: 864-656-2280 • E-Mail: cuadmissions@clemson.edu • Website: www.clemson.edu

THE PRINCETON REVIEW SAYS

Admissions

Very important factors considered include: rigor of secondary school record, class rank, academic GPA, standardized test scores, state residency. *Other factors considered include:* application essay, recommendation(s), extracurricular activities, talent/ability, alumni/ae relation. ACT with or without writing accepted. SAT with or without Essay component accepted. High school diploma is required and GED is accepted. *Academic units required:* 4 English, 4 math, 3 science, 3 science labs, 2 foreign language, 1 social studies, 1 history, 2 academic electives, 1 computer science, 1 visual/performing arts, 1 unit from above areas or other academic areas. *Academic units recommended:* 4 science labs, 3 foreign language.

Financial Aid

Students should submit: FAFSA. Priority filing deadline is 1/2. The Princeton Review suggests that all financial aid forms be submitted as soon as possible after October 1. *Need-based scholarships/grants offered:* College/university scholarship or grant aid from institutional funds; Federal Pell; Private scholarships; SEOG; State scholarships/grants. *Loan aid offered:* Direct PLUS loans; Direct Subsidized Stafford Loans; Direct Unsubsidized Stafford Loans. Applicants will be notified of awards on a rolling basis beginning 3/1. Federal Work-Study Program available. Institutional employment available.

The Inside Word

The admissions game at Clemson is fairly by the book. The university typically gives most weight to your high school transcript and your standardized test scores. Applicants interested in studying music or theater will be required to audition. And individuals who want to study PGA Golf Management must demonstrate playing proficiency. It's also important to note that admission closes once all class spaces have been filled. Therefore, the earlier you apply, the better off you'll be. Finally, Clemson does not have an early admissions policy.

THE SCHOOL SAYS "..."

From the Admissions Office

"One of the country's most selective public research universities, Clemson University was founded with a mission to be a high seminary of learning dedicated to teaching, research, and service. Nearly 120 years later, these three concepts remain at the heart of this university and provide the framework for an exceptional educational experience for Clemson students.

"At Clemson, professors take the time to get to know students and to explore innovative ways of teaching. Exceptional teaching is one reason Clemson's retention and graduation rates rank among the highest in the country among public universities. Exceptional teaching is also why Clemson continues to attract an increasingly talented student body. The class rank and SAT scores of Clemson's incoming freshman are among the highest of the nation's public research universities.

"Clemson offers over 250 student clubs and organizations; the spirit that students show for this university is unparalleled.

"Midway between Charlotte, North Carolina, and Atlanta, Georgia, Clemson University is located on 1,400 acres of beautiful rolling hills within the foothills of the Blue Ridge Mountains and along the shores of Lake Hartwell.

"Applicants are required to take the SAT or the ACT with the writing section. The best combined scores from SAT test will be used in the admissions process. We do not, however, combine sub scores from the ACT in order to create a new composite score."

SELECTIVITY

Admissions Rating	91
# of applicants	28,845
% of applicants accepted	47
% of acceptees attending	28
# offered a place on the wait list	2,715
% accepting a place on wait list	42
% admitted from wait list	39

FRESHMAN PROFILE

Range SAT EBRW	610–690
Range SAT Math	610–710
Range ACT Composite	27–32
# submitting SAT scores	1,904
% submitting SAT scores	50
# submitting ACT scores	1,888
% submitting ACT scores	50
Average HS GPA	4.4
% graduated top 10% of class	56
% graduated top 25% of class	87
% graduated top 50% of class	98

DEADLINES

Regular	
Priority	12/1
Deadline	5/1
Notification	Rolling, 2/15
Nonfall registration?	Yes

FINANCIAL FACTS

Financial Aid Rating	82
Annual in-state tuition	$13,702
Annual out-of-state tuition	$35,056
Room and board	$10,832
Required fees	$1,268
Books and supplies	$1,392
Average frosh need-based scholarship	$10,967
Average UG need-based scholarship	$9,629
% needy frosh rec. need-based scholarship or grant aid	94
% needy UG rec. need-based scholarship or grant aid	82
% needy frosh rec. non-need-based scholarship or grant aid	94
% needy UG rec. non-need-based scholarship or grant aid	82
% needy frosh rec. need-based self-help aid	71
% needy UG rec. need-based self-help aid	74
% frosh rec. any financial aid	87
% UG rec. any financial aid	71
% UG borrow to pay for school	47
Average cumulative indebtedness	$32,285
% frosh need fully met	15
% ugrads need fully met	14
Average % of frosh need met	55
Average % of ugrad need met	52

COE COLLEGE

1220 First Avenue NE, Cedar Rapids, IA 52402 • Admissions: 319-399-8500 • Fax: 319-399-8816

STUDENTS SAY "..."

Academics

Tiny Coe College is truly a gem of the Midwest. This 1,400-student Cedar Rapids liberal arts college offers more than sixty areas of study and a nearly 100 percent employment (or graduate school) rate, with half of all students eventually going on to graduate studies. Every Coe student participates in an internship, student research, practicum, or off-campus study during their four years, fostering "an environment where student growth through leadership and responsibility is possible." Coe has been named one of the Top 25 Best Schools for Internships in the United States three years in a row. "We are equipped to make things happen for ourselves while we are here and once we leave," says one student. The Coe community is so close knit that "once one Kohawk goes and finds success somewhere, they make sure to bring others along with them."

Professors are "devoted to the understanding of course context and success of the students," and many of the classes are discussion-based, so "attendance is important." Students learn very quickly the dangers of falling behind, and academics can be "very difficult, but in a way that [is] enjoyable and strengthening." The school "has a great aptitude for raising the bar when it comes to [the] personal development of its students" and the Learning Commons provides guidance and help with class material for those who need it. Teachers here "love sharing knowledge and finding opportunities for students to achieve their fullest potential," and it is not unheard of that a professor "sometimes has to trim the syllabi to fit into our 16-week semester." Another big strength is the opportunities for undergraduate research and travel with professors, which allows students "to gain skill and knowledge that may not be available at a bigger college."

Life

Wellness is a huge part of Coe's culture, and students "see wellness as thriving only if all components of our life are cultivated." Many here attend on-campus events including athletics and Student Activities Committee events featuring comedians, singers, bowling, laser tag, and free movie Fridays. Blindspot is a popular event hosted one Friday each month by a student organization, where students can showcase their talent outside the classroom. "It's basically one big talent show, without winners or losers," says one happy student. The Office of Community & Civic Engagement provides students with ample opportunities to get off campus and volunteer within the community, and everyone makes it to Cedar Rapids "at least once a week."

Greek life has a surprisingly big following here, but it's not in the traditional sense, as the focus at Coe's fraternities and sororities is "on personal and professional development so that we can be exceptional contributors to society once we leave Coe." The library in particular is very welcoming, with easily reservable study rooms, and it often hosts events such as the "Long Night Against Procrastination." Coe also has strong multicultural organizations, which host a variety of events such as the International Club Banquet, Culture Show, and Cultural Appreciation Week.

Student Body

While some students come from small town Iowa, half of all students come from out of state, with a current growth in the international student population. This student body is "friendly, but opinionated." There is "a diversity of ideas, opinions, and leanings" and "people do not shy away from conversation no matter how difficult it may be." There "is little drama about getting the best grades or scholarships, just an appreciation of each other's strengths." Everyone is "helpful and considerate" and "most of the time people leave their stuff in the library and come back hours later." "If I am struggling with carrying something, don't know where I'm going, or need help with a class, people will go out of their way to help me regardless if I know them or not," says a student.

Financial Aid: 319-399-8540 • E-Mail: admission@coe.edu • Website: www.coe.edu

THE PRINCETON REVIEW SAYS

Admissions

Very important factors considered include: academic GPA, standardized test scores. *Important factors considered include:* class rank. *Other factors considered include:* rigor of secondary school record, application essay, recommendation(s), interview, extracurricular activities, talent/ ability, character/personal qualities, first generation, alumni/ae relation, volunteer work, level of applicant's interest. ACT with or without writing accepted. SAT with or without Essay component accepted. High school diploma is required and GED is accepted. *Academic units recommended:* 4 English, 3 math, 3 science, 1 science lab, 2 foreign language, 3 social studies, 2 academic electives.

Financial Aid

Students should submit: FAFSA. Priority filing deadline is 3/1. The Princeton Review suggests that all financial aid forms be submitted as soon as possible after October 1. *Need-based scholarships/grants offered:* College/university scholarship or grant aid from institutional funds; Federal Pell; Private scholarships; SEOG; State scholarships/grants. *Loan aid offered:* Direct PLUS loans; Direct Subsidized Stafford Loans; Direct Unsubsidized Stafford Loans. Applicants will be notified of awards on a rolling basis beginning 12/15. Federal Work-Study Program available. Institutional employment available.

The Inside Word

Over 400 new students begin their college journey at Coe College each fall, and it remains one of the most selective colleges in the state with an average high school GPA of 3.6. Despite its small size, Coe has the largest undergraduate writing center in the country, and many students benefit from its help. If you're seeking an intimate college experience with quality academics—Coe is one of the smallest colleges to contain a Phi Beta Kappa chapter and a Top Producer of U.S. Fulbright Students—you would do well to consider Coe. Under Coe's test-optional policy, ACT/SAT scores are not required for students applying for admission. Only students applying as first-year applicants with a 3.0 GPA or higher may choose to exclude their test score from the application process.

THE SCHOOL SAYS "..."

From the Admissions Office

"A Coe education begins to pay off right away. In fact, for many years, nearly 100 percent of reporting graduates have been either working or in graduate school within one year of graduation. Our graduates do so well because of our student-centered approach to learning and required hands-on experience which may be satisfied through an internship, research project, practicum experience or off-campus study. In recent years Coe students have interned at places like the Chicago Board of Trade, Google, Mayo Clinic and NASA. Others have completed research on Coe's campus through the National Science Foundation's Research Experiences for Undergraduates program or the Department of Business and Economics' Spellman Summer Research Program. Still others have combined travel with an internship in South Africa or student teaching in Tanzania for an unforgettable off-campus experience. Coe College is one of the few liberal arts institutions in the country to require hands-on learning for graduation."

SELECTIVITY

Admissions Rating	86
# of applicants	6,725
% of applicants accepted	50
% of acceptees attending	11

FRESHMAN PROFILE

Range SAT EBRW	510–620
Range SAT Math	510–650
Range ACT Composite	22–28
# submitting SAT scores	35
% submitting SAT scores	9
# submitting ACT scores	350
% submitting ACT scores	94
Average HS GPA	3.6
% graduated top 10% of class	30
% graduated top 25% of class	65
% graduated top 50% of class	89

DEADLINES

Early action	
Deadline	12/10
Notification	1/20
Regular	
Priority	12/10
Deadline	3/1
Notification	Rolling, 9/1
Nonfall registration?	Yes

FINANCIAL FACTS

Financial Aid Rating	88
Annual tuition	$42,090
Room and board	$9,140
Required fees	$340
Books and supplies	$1,000
Average frosh need-based scholarship	$31,524
Average UG need-based scholarship	$28,610
% needy frosh rec. need-based scholarship or grant aid	100
% needy UG rec. need-based scholarship or grant aid	100
% needy frosh rec. non-need-based scholarship or grant aid	14
% needy UG rec. non-need-based scholarship or grant aid	14
% needy frosh rec. need-based self-help aid	85
% needy UG rec. need-based self-help aid	82
% frosh rec. any financial aid	99
% UG rec. any financial aid	99
% UG borrow to pay for school	82
Average cumulative indebtedness	$35,782
% frosh need fully met	20
% ugrads need fully met	21
Average % of frosh need met	85
Average % of ugrad need met	83

COLBY COLLEGE

4000 Mayflower Hill, Waterville, ME 04901 • Admissions: 207-859-4828 • Fax: 207-859-4828

STUDENTS SAY "..."

Academics

Colby College boasts "extraordinarily strong" and "challenging" academics taught by "incredible," "brilliant," and "engaging," faculty. Students also praise the "many outlets of student support" ranging from "student led-peer groups," resources from the "Health Center, which includes free counseling services," and "tutoring and help centers for students who need support with their work." Professors often lead "Socratic-style" class discussions and professors utilize campus and other nearby assets in their teaching so that you are as likely to have a biology class held at Colby's Museum of Art as you are to venture on an art course within the beauteous Acadia National Park. "I've had an English professor bring us to the 3D printing lab to think of ideas about how to bring words to life physically," one student said. "Colby wants you to learn in a manner where you feel you'll be most interested in the material." The environmental science and policy classes are major at Colby, and make use of a campus arboretum in addition to local "lakes, ponds, and forests" for field research. And the new "Mule Works Innovation Lab" offers students access to "3D printing, lasers and much more," an example of how "Colby attempts to give all students the same opportunities with technology despite their major as well as keeping up to date with emerging advances in technology." Students note that even beyond facilities, Colby is staying ahead of the game by valuing faculty research into "emerging fields such as the digital humanities and environmental humanities." The school's "JanPlan" offers opportunities for students to take the January term and undertake "field study in Uganda," or experiment in classes like "Critical Race Feminisms and Tap Dance." Colby also provides "ample research opportunities to their students across all disciplines." Says one student, "If you want to really be engaged in learning and the production of knowledge, Colby is the place for you."

Life

Students uniformly praise the "great facilities," including a new, approximately 350,000 square-foot athletics and recreation center and "extremely comfortable dorms." Students put academics first: after class, most students study "in the libraries, rooms, or common spaces." There are plenty of special events and extracurricular activities on campus to fill the time, with "talks," "athletic events," and "student performances." Colby has a particularly strong outdoorsy and active student culture, with weekends bringing students into the surrounding areas for active adventures. The "beautiful" Maine location means it's "not uncommon for people to do day hikes or head to the beach if it's nice out." "Outing Club" runs trips every weekend, and in the winter many head to Sugarloaf for "skiing or snowboarding." Students less inclined to go camping or hiking can head into cities like Augusta, Portland, or Camden. During the spring, people "lounge on Miller lawn," and the "beautiful campus" allows students to "enjoy pleasant walks around campus."

Student Body

Colby students tend to be "high-achievers" with a "love of the outdoors," and are "gregarious," "preppy," and "adventurous." Many students are "politically active, and generally care about social issues." Students assess their peers as "smart but humble": "it's not a super competitive environment," but their peers are "definitely at an elite liberal arts college for a reason." Students are involved in a number of activities that "range from varsity sports to volunteering, to humanities clubs." Most students are described as coming from "WASP-y" and "wealthy" backgrounds. Others say that students as a whole are "very athletic," with "many of them on varsity sports teams."

COLBY COLLEGE

Financial Aid: 207-859-4124 • E-Mail: admissions@colby.edu • Website: www.colby.edu

THE PRINCETON REVIEW SAYS

Admissions

Very important factors considered include: rigor of secondary school record, academic GPA, recommendation(s), character/personal qualities. *Important factors considered include:* class rank, application essay, extracurricular activities, talent/ability. *Other factors considered include:* standardized test scores, first generation, alumni/ae relation, geographical residence, state residency, racial/ethnic status, volunteer work, work experience, level of applicant's interest. ACT with or without writing accepted. SAT with or without Essay component accepted. High school diploma is required and GED is not accepted. *Academic units recommended:* 4 English, 3 math, 2 science, 2 science labs, 3 foreign language, 2 social studies.

Financial Aid

Students should submit: Business/Farm Supplement; CSS/Financial Aid PROFILE; FAFSA. The Princeton Review suggests that all financial aid forms be submitted as soon as possible after October 1. *Need-based scholarships/grants offered:* College/university scholarship or grant aid from institutional funds; Federal Pell; SEOG; State scholarships/grants. *Loan aid offered:* Direct PLUS loans; Direct Subsidized Stafford Loans; Direct Unsubsidized Stafford Loans. Applicants will be notified of awards on or about 4/1. Federal Work-Study Program available. Institutional employment available.

The Inside Word

Colby continues to be both very selective and successful in converting admits to enrollees, which makes for a perpetually challenging admissions process. Currently, 10 percent of applicants are accepted, so hit those books and ace those exams to stand a fighting chance. One thing that could set you apart from the pack? An interest in other cultures. Approximately 60 percent of Colby students study abroad—in fact, for some degrees it's required. Students from low-income families should take note: combined total household income of $65k annually will mean $0 contribution from parents/guardians, and Colby pledges to meet "100 percent of demonstrated financial need" without loans.

THE SCHOOL SAYS "..."

From the Admissions Office

"Founded in 1813, Colby is one of America's most selective colleges. Serving only undergraduates, Colby's rigorous program is anchored to the world's most complex challenges and enriched by extraordinary access to faculty. Students pursue their intellectual passions by choosing among 58 majors and 35 minors, and have the option to design their own major. The College's partnerships with world-class research institutions provide transformative academic experiences rarely available to undergraduates. Colby's DavisConnects program guarantees access to global, research, or internship experiences for all students, regardless of their ability to pay. Upon graduation, students join a network of 25,000 alumni in over 90 countries who serve as leaders and influencers across all industries. The College's exceptional campus facilities, including one of the finest college art museums in the country and state-of-the-art academic buildings and labs, are enhanced by Maine's unique natural resources. A national leader in sustainability and environmental education, Colby was one of the first colleges in the country to achieve carbon neutrality. The College meets 100 percent of demonstrated financial need for all admitted students, without including loans in financial aid packages. Families with a total household income of $65,000 or less with typical assets should expect a parent or guardian contribution of $0. Families with a total household income of $150,000 and typical assets should expect a parent or guardian contribution of $15,000 or less. These initiatives position Colby as one of the most affordable four-year colleges in the country. Applying to Colby is straightforward: there is no fee to apply or extra essays to submit. Colby is test-optional, allowing applicants to choose whether to submit their standardized test scores."

SELECTIVITY

Admissions Rating	97
# of applicants	13,584
% of applicants accepted	10
% of acceptees attending	40
# offered a place on the wait list	3,668
% accepting a place on wait list	40
% admitted from wait list	1

FRESHMAN PROFILE

Range SAT EBRW	680–740
Range SAT Math	700–780
Range SAT Composite	1380–1520
Range ACT Composite	31–34
# submitting SAT scores	274
% submitting SAT scores	52
# submitting ACT scores	200
% submitting ACT scores	38
% graduated top 10% of class	68
% graduated top 25% of class	89
% graduated top 50% of class	99

DEADLINES

Early decision	
Deadline	11/15
Notification	12/15
Other ED Deadline	1/1
Other ED Notification	2/15
Regular	
Deadline	1/1
Notification	4/1
Nonfall registration?	Yes

APPLICANTS ALSO LOOK AT AND OFTEN PREFER

Bowdoin College, Brown University, Dartmouth College, Middlebury College

AND SOMETIMES PREFER

Amherst College, Cornell University, Williams College

AND RARELY PREFER

Carleton College, Hamilton College

FINANCIAL FACTS

Financial Aid Rating	97
Annual tuition	$54,870
Room and board	$14,720
Required fees	$2,410
Books and supplies	$800
Average frosh need-based scholarship	$55,650
Average UG need-based scholarship	$51,617
% needy frosh rec. need-based scholarship or grant aid	100
% needy UG rec. need-based scholarship or grant aid	100
% needy frosh rec. non-need-based scholarship or grant aid	0
% needy UG rec. non-need-based scholarship or grant aid	0
% needy frosh rec. need-based self-help aid	50
% needy UG rec. need-based self-help aid	46
% frosh rec. any financial aid	40
% UG rec. any financial aid	41
% UG borrow to pay for school	30
Average cumulative indebtedness	$24,380
% frosh need fully met	100
% ugrads need fully met	100
Average % of frosh need met	100
Average % of ugrad need met	100

COLGATE UNIVERSITY

13 Oak Drive, Hamilton, NY 13346 • Admissions: 315-228-7401 • Fax: 315-228-7524

CAMPUS LIFE

Quality of Life Rating	83
Fire Safety Rating	97
Green Rating	99
Type of school	Private
Environment	Rural

STUDENTS

Total undergrad enrollment	2,964
% male/female	45/55
% from out of state	74
% frosh from public high school	53
% frosh live on campus	100
% ugrads live on campus	92
# of fraternities	5
# of sororities	3
% African American	4
% Asian	5
% Caucasian	65
% Hispanic	9
% Native American	<1
% Pacific Islander	<1
% Two or more races	4
% Race and/or ethnicity unknown	3
% international	9
# of countries represented	48

SURVEY SAYS . . .

Classroom facilities are great
Lab facilities are great
Great library
Career services are great
Great financial aid
Recreation facilities are great
Lots of beer drinking
Hard liquor is popular
Alumni active on campus

ACADEMICS

Academic Rating	89
% students returning for sophomore year	94
% students graduating within 4 years	88
% students graduating within 6 years	91
Calendar	Semester
Student/faculty ratio	9:1
Profs interesting rating	93
Profs accessible rating	97

MOST POPULAR MAJORS
English Language and Literature, General;
Economics, General; Political Science and
Government, General

STUDENTS SAY "..."

Academics

Colgate University is known for its "very rigorous academic curriculum" and "invaluable" professors who "are the glue that hold the university together." Many students say they chose Colgate because they wanted "a small liberal arts school that had the opportunities and resources of a larger institution" combined with a "heavily involved alumni network" that "makes the Colgate connection a truly valuable resource." All agree that, at Colgate, you're "more than just a number" and that "there is no [shortage] of caring professors that are meaningfully invested in your academic success." As intimidating as it might seem to have, "internationally influential" professors, a history and political science double major assures that "classes are enjoyable and the professors are accessible." A junior adds, "One of the wonderful things about Colgate is that these relationships start as early as freshman year. Students do not have to wait until their senior year to build fantastic relationships with the faculty." However, another student grumbles, "Course selection is very stressful, and freshmen often get slighted." Any complaints about the faculty centered on "teaching styles" not meshing with individual students' "learning style." "However, there are a plethora of resources available to students to succeed despite any of their problems." "Colgate allowed me to become the person I always wanted to be, but didn't know I was capable of being," sings one senior whose sentiment is widely echoed.

Life

Colgate University "has an amazing campus with people who work hard and have goals but also know how to have a really fun time." Students say the campus is "breathtaking," and they value "its small size and intimate nature." A philosophy major says, "Colgate is great because you can't walk 200 feet without a professor, student, or faculty member acknowledging you by name, yet you're constantly meeting new people and having new experiences. There is never a dull moment at Colgate." Students say, "Colgate strives for the perfect combination of academics and extracurriculars," and they feel the university "does a great job at helping us balance those and gives us opportunities to get involved in all the groups and events around campus." In addition to a plethora of clubs, students are actively involved in Greek life and Division I athletics. A junior says, "I loved how Colgate was located in the middle of nowhere" because "everything revolved around the campus," but in case you're worried about isolation, another student adds, "Colgate brings a lot of interesting speakers to the campus, which helps provide for a more rounded liberal arts experience." Students praise the administration, saying, "It is easy for students to contact the administration and thus have their voices directly heard by the community. The president holds drop-in office hours for students every week and takes notes on what students say during the session."

Student Body

Colgate boasts a "happy and enthusiastic student body" with a typical student that "is athletic, smart, engaged, and down to earth." They "enjoy having fun, but spend time in the library as well." Many say "the typical Colgate student is a preppy New Englander, who can be found almost always wearing Patagonia and Sperrys." However, this stereotype seems to be becoming less apt as there is "great diversity under the surface." As long as students are "not afraid to do what they love, they will find their niche and fit in." Fraternities and sororities as well as partying in general are popular: "Greek life does have a huge presence in the social life at Colgate," but "it is not exclusive to just those who are members." Most students mentioned the recent changes in the school's alcohol policies. Some tout it as the impetus for "initiatives to expand the amount of alternatives to partying on weekends." Others cited it as "the biggest issue on campus right now" between the students and administration. Despite the "country club atmosphere," a computer science major says, "When you're stranded in Hamilton, New York, for four years you'll inevitably end up fitting in regardless whether you are the typical student or not."

Financial Aid: 315-228-7431 • E-Mail: admission@colgate.edu • Website: www.colgate.edu

THE PRINCETON REVIEW SAYS

Admissions

Very important factors considered include: rigor of secondary school record, class rank, academic GPA. *Important factors considered include:* application essay, standardized test scores, recommendation(s), extracurricular activities, talent/ability, character/personal qualities. *Other factors considered include:* first generation, alumni/ae relation, geographical residence, racial/ethnic status, volunteer work, work experience. ACT with or without writing accepted. SAT with or without Essay component accepted. High school diploma is required and GED is accepted. *Academic units required:* 4 English, 3 math, 3 science, 2 science labs, 3 foreign language, 3 social studies. *Academic units recommended:* 4 English, 4 math, 4 science, 4 science labs, 4 foreign language, 4 social studies.

Financial Aid

Students should submit: CSS/Financial Aid PROFILE; FAFSA; Noncustodial PROFILE. Priority filing deadline is 1/15. The Princeton Review suggests that all financial aid forms be submitted as soon as possible after October 1. *Need-based scholarships/grants offered:* College/university scholarship or grant aid from institutional funds; Federal Pell; SEOG. *Loan aid offered:* Direct PLUS loans; Direct Subsidized Stafford Loans; Direct Unsubsidized Stafford Loans. Applicants will be notified of awards on or about 3/25. Federal Work-Study Program available. Institutional employment available.

The Inside Word

Admission to this upstate New York gem is some of the most competitive around. You need to arm yourself with excellent grades, scores, recommendations, and extracurricular activities. However, Colgate is also looking for that extra ingredient which might not translate from the common app alone and is always seeking increased diversity across the board. Be aware that Colgate has adopted a test-optional policy for all fall 2021 applicants. Transfer admission also remains test-optional. Students who, at their own discretion, wish to submit SAT or ACT scores are welcome to do so, and these scores will be considered as part of the holistic review of the applicant.

THE SCHOOL SAYS "..."

From the Admissions Office

"Colgate provides an intellectually rigorous academic environment on a beautiful 575-acre campus in rural upstate New York. Of the Class of 2023, 22 percent self-identify as domestic students of color and 10 percent are international students. Colgate's student body includes students from 48 states and the District of Columbia, and represent 48 countries. Students and faculty alike are drawn to Colgate by the quality of its academic programs. Faculty initiative has given the university a broad mix of learning opportunities that includes a liberal arts core curriculum, 56 academic concentrations, and a wealth of chances for off-campus study abroad and within the United States, including Colgate faculty-led semester long and briefer programs, as well as approved programs offered by other institutions. The residential commons, Colgate's living and learning program, eases students' academic and social transition to college, and residential life in general includes an array of living options, on a campus described as one of the most beautiful in the country. The Trudy Fitness Center is a popular student destination, and the Shaw Wellness Institute fosters healthy, purposeful, and balanced lifestyles. The Max A. Shacknai Center for Outreach, Volunteerism, and Education builds upon the tradition of Colgate students interacting with the surrounding community in meaningful ways. Colgate students become extraordinarily devoted alumni, contributing significantly to career networking and exploration programs both on and off campus. Ten professional networks bring current students and alumni together for powerful career connections that last long after graduation. For students in search of a busy and varied campus life, Colgate is a place to learn and grow."

SELECTIVITY

Admissions Rating	**97**
# of applicants	9,951
% of applicants accepted	23
% of acceptees attending	35
# offered a place on the wait list	1,800
% accepting a place on wait list	47
% admitted from wait list	12
# of early decision applicants	941
% accepted early decision	47

FRESHMAN PROFILE

Range SAT EBRW	660–730
Range SAT Math	670–770
Range ACT Composite	31–34
# submitting SAT scores	438
% submitting SAT scores	56
# submitting ACT scores	348
% submitting ACT scores	44
Average HS GPA	3.7
% graduated top 10% of class	69
% graduated top 25% of class	92
% graduated top 50% of class	100

DEADLINES

Early decision	
Deadline	11/15
Notification	12/15
Other ED Deadline	1/15
Other ED Notification	Rolling
Regular	
Deadline	1/15
Notification	late-March
Nonfall registration?	No

FINANCIAL FACTS

Financial Aid Rating	**98**
Annual tuition	$57,695
Room and board	$14,540
Required fees	$350
Books and supplies	$2,065
Average frosh need-based scholarship	$55,553
Average UG need-based scholarship	$53,556
% needy frosh rec. need-based scholarship or grant aid	100
% needy UG rec. need-based scholarship or grant aid	100
% needy frosh rec. non-need-based scholarship or grant aid	0
% needy UG rec. non-need-based scholarship or grant aid	0
% needy frosh rec. need-based self-help aid	89
% needy UG rec. need-based self-help aid	81
% frosh rec. any financial aid	48
% UG rec. any financial aid	49
% UG borrow to pay for school	37
Average cumulative indebtedness	$25,044
% frosh need fully met	100
% ugrads need fully met	100
Average % of frosh need met	100
Average % of ugrad need met	100

COLLEGE OF CHARLESTON

66 George Street, Charleston, SC 29424 • Admissions: 843-953-5670 • Fax: 843-953-6322

STUDENTS SAY "..."

Academics

Founded in 1770, the College of Charleston provides its 10,000 undergraduates a mid-sized liberal arts experience within the boundaries of one of the south's most thriving cities. Good academic advising, a strong focus on writing skills and interdisciplinary studies, and a reputable business program are just some of the school's many perks, and many classes incorporate non-traditional types of learning such as "lots of field work and field trips around the city." "A tour of the city for my hospitality class really brought the material to life," says a student. The school "caters to everyone, not just a single department or major," and the quantity and breadth of courses offered is appreciated by students. Academic diversity is a huge boon at CofC, and within each major "there are plenty of students from different perspectives and the curriculum in class encourages the sharing of ideas from those perspectives."

Professors "care how well their students perform and help them find opportunities through networking and general encouragement." The ideal size of the school creates "a great student to professor ratio." Faculty are "engaged, knowledgeable, and passionate about the subject matter they teach," and they are "eager to engage with students that are excited to study and learn." The location and the school's reputation make for tons of internship and professional opportunities, and everything the school has to offer is available to all. If you need anything from academic advising to counseling or career planning, there are people here "with the passion and resources to help."

Life

The school has a "love of its own history," as well as one for the "booming" city of Charleston. People enjoy "shopping on King Street or going to events hosted by the city," and on weekends, "many people head to the beach or socialize at parties." "Restaurant culture is very popular here," and many students work in the food and beverage industry. In between classes, students are found "grabbing food, studying in the library, or working out," and they often gather at each other's dorms or apartments to relax and study together at night. There is something for everyone at the college with "tons of different groups on campus," and most students are "extremely involved" and "participate in multiple clubs."

Whether it means having the chance to work near campus or being close enough to walk to class every day, "the location is a perfect fit" for just about every student (particularly the many who surf). "Just going on a walk around town and seeing all of the beautiful houses and their history is extremely entertaining." The college "really does have a beautiful campus and we take pride in keeping it up," and students can just as easily live on-campus as rent nearby.

Student Body

While many people here are from "white," "middle to upper middle class backgrounds," "there are many diverse viewpoints and backgrounds," including students who identify as LGBTQ+. Students "can express themselves freely and openly with little to no judgement." Charleston may technically be an urban environment, but "the city lends to a cool sort of blending where every group overlaps and coexists." This is a "small school with large school energy," and everyone at the CofC "is welcoming to new students and freshmen." "People are always willing to help each other out and general class culture is very positive and uplifting."

Financial Aid: 843-953-5540 • E-Mail: admissions@cofc.edu • Website: http://cofc.edu

THE PRINCETON REVIEW SAYS

Admissions

Very important factors considered include: rigor of secondary school record, academic GPA, standardized test scores. *Important factors considered include:* class rank, talent/ability, character/personal qualities, first generation, state residency. *Other factors considered include:* application essay, recommendation(s), extracurricular activities, alumni/ae relation, geographical residence, volunteer work, work experience, level of applicant's interest. ACT with or without writing accepted. SAT with or without Essay component accepted. High school diploma is required and GED is accepted. *Academic units required:* 4 English, 4 math, 3 science, 3 science labs, 3 foreign language, 2 social studies, 1 history, 3 academic electives, 1 visual/performing arts, 1 unit from above areas or other academic areas. *Academic units recommended:* 4 English, 4 math, 2 history, 1 computer science.

Financial Aid

Students should submit: FAFSA. Priority filing deadline is 3/1. The Princeton Review suggests that all financial aid forms be submitted as soon as possible after October 1. *Need-based scholarships/grants offered:* College/university scholarship or grant aid from institutional funds; Federal Pell; Private scholarships; SEOG; State scholarships/grants. *Loan aid offered:* Direct PLUS loans; Direct Subsidized Stafford Loans; Direct Unsubsidized Stafford Loans. Applicants will be notified of awards on a rolling basis beginning 4/10. Federal Work-Study Program available. Institutional employment available.

The Inside Word

Typical first-year students at the College of Charleston had consistent academic achievement in the A/B range in high school. The admissions committee takes a hard look at high school performance, including the rigor of the pre-college workload, in addition to standardized test scores. High-performing high school seniors from South Carolina in traditionally underrepresented areas of the state may want to check out the college's Cougar Advantage program, open to students who achieve a certain class rank from a South Carolina public high school in a select group of counties.

THE SCHOOL SAYS "..."

From the Admissions Office

"To succeed in our increasingly complex world, college graduates must be able to think creatively, explore new ideas, compete, collaborate, and meet the challenges of our global society. At the College of Charleston, students find out about themselves, their lives and the lives of others. They discover how to shape their future, and they prepare to create change and opportunity. Founded in 1770, the College of Charleston's mission is to provide students with a first-class education in the arts and sciences, education and business. Students have 138 majors and minors from which to choose—and they often choose to combine several—and complement their academic courses with overseas study, research and internships for a truly customized education.

"Approximately 10,000 undergraduates choose the college for its small-college feel blended with the advantages and diversity of an urban, mid-sized university. The College, home to students from fifty-two U.S. states/territories and sixty-one countries, provides a creative and intellectually stimulating environment where students are challenged and guided by a committed and caring full-time faculty of distinguished teacher-scholars, all in an incomparable historic setting. The city of Charleston serves as a living and learning laboratory for student experiences in business, science, teaching, the humanities, languages and the arts. At the same time, students and faculty are engaged with the community in partnerships to improve education, enhance the business community and enrich the overall quality of life in the region. In the great liberal arts tradition, a College of Charleston education focuses on discovery and personal growth, as well as preparation for life, work and service to our society."

SELECTIVITY

Admissions Rating	78
# of applicants	11,675
% of applicants accepted	79
% of acceptees attending	24
# of early decision applicants	305
% accepted early decision	80

FRESHMAN PROFILE

Range SAT EBRW	550–640
Range SAT Math	520–610
Range ACT Composite	22–28
# submitting SAT scores	1,194
% submitting SAT scores	54
# submitting ACT scores	1,037
% submitting ACT scores	47
Average HS GPA	3.9
% graduated top 10% of class	20
% graduated top 25% of class	51
% graduated top 50% of class	87

DEADLINES

Early decision	
Deadline	11/1
Notification	12/1
Early action	
Deadline	12/1
Notification	1/15
Regular	
Priority	2/15
Deadline	2/15
Nonfall registration?	Yes

FINANCIAL FACTS

Financial Aid Rating	81
Annual in-state tuition	$12,418
Annual out-of-state tuition	$31,600
Room and board	$12,166
Required fees	$320
Books and supplies	$1,218
Average frosh need-based scholarship	$3,404
Average UG need-based scholarship	$3,184
% needy frosh rec. need-based scholarship or grant aid	76
% needy UG rec. need-based scholarship or grant aid	71
% needy frosh rec. non-need-based scholarship or grant aid	73
% needy UG rec. non-need-based scholarship or grant aid	47
% needy frosh rec. need-based self-help aid	69
% needy UG rec. need-based self-help aid	77
% frosh rec. any financial aid	53
% UG rec. any financial aid	49
% UG borrow to pay for school	51
Average cumulative indebtedness	$27,256
% frosh need fully met	17
% ugrads need fully met	15
Average % of frosh need met	53
Average % of ugrad need met	53

THE COLLEGE OF NEW JERSEY

PO Box 7718, Ewing, NJ 08628-0718 • Admissions: 609-771-2131 • Fax: 609-637-5174

STUDENTS SAY "..."

Academics

A strong liberal arts curriculum forms the core of an education at the beautiful College of New Jersey, where almost 7,000 undergraduates can choose from more than fifty programs spread across the college's seven schools. All courses take "a meticulous approach" to the subject at hand, and the small class sizes "foster close relationships between students and professors," contributing to the college's incredibly high retention rate. The programs here are well-respected and each major provides "a great foundation for people who may look for jobs right out of college." Professional development seminars are "typically packed," and "the competition for on-campus interviews for internships is incredible." TCNJ is a college where students can expect "academic rigor and opportunities to take part in multiple organizations, research, and to grow," but, ultimately, "the college is what a person can make of it."

The professors at TCNJ are "always welcoming and friendly" and "intend to help with any questions or problems a student has." They "put in the effort to help the student succeed," and "programs are very fleshed out and rigorous," as well as being "able to prepare us very well for our careers." Within majors like engineering, nursing, and the sciences, "there is little room to slack off," but all who go here find "a fair balance of academic life with socialness, athletics, or relaxing time." Students also "tend to engage fully in supplementary programs (i.e., lecture, awareness, volunteer, celebratory, or other campus events) often affiliated with their major."

Life

The TCNJ campus is "very beautiful and very unified," and students can walk everywhere (first-years aren't allowed to have cars). Students typically have Wednesdays off, during which time they schedule meetings with professors, attend a study group, or just relax. Students have plenty of activities to fill their day like "going to the gym, fishing, running, sleeping, watching a movie, ice cream party, [visiting] friends, [or] extra readings." Greek life is popular at TCNJ, and "there are always philanthropy events to go to." The College Union Board "does a lot of weekend and daily programming for students," including "Lions Latenight" which hosts weekly movies in the Student Center and "events for students to get free stuff." Though some facilities need a facelift or wrecking ball, the "housing has improved in some on-campus residential buildings and more will be renovated in the upcoming several years." The suburban setting means that "many people do go home during the weekend." Campus is only about thirty minutes away from Philadelphia, meaning that those who do stick around on weekends are close to "malls, restaurants, and movie theaters, which are all easily accessible through the highway nearby." Dorm living is popular, and students "often have movie and game board nights in their own dorms/apartments."

Student Body

For the most part, the students here are "very driven to do their work and get good grades." Although students' opinions on how diverse the campus is vary, everyone "still gets along and accepts each other." Students at TCNJ create "a community of support that allow each other to grow academically and socially." There's "a real sense of school spirit and camaraderie" and inclusivity, and "we don't have a cliquey feeling or vibe." The college features "several organizations dedicated to the LGBTQ+ community" as well as organizations supporting "multiple different ethnic communities." While the school has multiple sports teams, the student body is "generally not interested in sports," and "all games, with the exception of Homecoming, are sparsely attended."

Financial Aid: 609-771-2211 • E-Mail: tcnjinfo@tcnj.edu • Website: www.tcnj.edu

THE PRINCETON REVIEW SAYS

Admissions

Very important factors considered include: rigor of secondary school record, class rank, standardized test scores, extracurricular activities, volunteer work. *Important factors considered include:* application essay, recommendation(s), talent/ability, character/personal qualities, geographical residence, state residency. *Other factors considered include:* academic GPA, first generation, alumni/ae relation, racial/ethnic status, work experience, level of applicant's interest. ACT with or without writing accepted. SAT with or without Essay component accepted. High school diploma is required and GED is accepted. *Academic units required:* 4 English, 4 math, 4 science, 2 science labs, 2 foreign language, 2 social studies, 2 academic electives. *Academic units recommended:* 4 English, 4 math, 4 science, 2 science labs, 2 foreign language, 2 social studies, 4 academic electives.

Financial Aid

Students should submit: FAFSA. Priority filing deadline is 3/1. The Princeton Review suggests that all financial aid forms be submitted as soon as possible after October 1. *Need-based scholarships/grants offered:* College/university scholarship or grant aid from institutional funds; Federal Nursing Scholarships; Federal Pell; Private scholarships; SEOG; State scholarships/grants. *Loan aid offered:* Direct PLUS loans; Direct Subsidized Stafford Loans; Direct Unsubsidized Stafford Loans. Applicants will be notified of awards on a rolling basis beginning 6/1. Federal Work-Study Program available. Institutional employment available.

The Inside Word

TCNJ accepts a little under half of its 14,000 applicants, but that level of competition is what you might expect at a school that offers state residents a small-college experience and a highly respected degree at bargain prices. TCNJ's admissions staff examines every component of a student's application, but none more carefully than the high school transcript. Students should apply as soon as possible once the application becomes available.

THE SCHOOL SAYS "..."

From the Admissions Office

"The College of New Jersey is one of the United States' great higher education success stories. With a long history as New Jersey's preeminent teacher of teachers, the college has grown into a new role as educator of the nation's best students in a wide range of fields. The College of New Jersey has created a culture of constant questioning—a place where knowledge is not merely received but reconfigured. In small classes, students and faculty members collaborate in a rewarding process: As they seek to understand fundamental principles, apply key concepts, reveal new problems, and pursue new lines of inquiry, students gain a fluency of thought in their disciplines. The college's 289-acre tree-lined campus is a union of vision, engineering, beauty, and functionality. Neoclassical Georgian Colonial architecture, meticulous landscaping, and thoughtful design merge in a dynamic system, constantly evolving to meet the needs of TCNJ students. About half of TCNJ's entering class will be academic scholars, with large numbers of National Merit finalists and semifinalists. The College of New Jersey is bringing together the best ideas from around the nation and building a new model for public undergraduate education on one campus."

SELECTIVITY

Admissions Rating	89
# of applicants	13,824
% of applicants accepted	49
% of acceptees attending	24
# offered a place on the wait list	1,960
% accepting a place on wait list	27
% admitted from wait list	6
# of early decision applicants	659
% accepted early decision	65

FRESHMAN PROFILE

Range SAT EBRW	580–670
Range SAT Math	580–690
Range SAT Composite	1180–1340
Range ACT Composite	25–30
# submitting SAT scores	1,451
% submitting SAT scores	90
# submitting ACT scores	304
% submitting ACT scores	19
% graduated top 10% of class	36
% graduated top 25% of class	71
% graduated top 50% of class	97

DEADLINES

Early decision	
Deadline	11/1
Notification	12/1
Other ED Deadline	1/1
Other ED Notification	2/1
Regular	
Priority	11/1
Deadline	2/1
Notification	Rolling, 4/1
Nonfall registration?	Yes

APPLICANTS ALSO LOOK AT AND OFTEN PREFER

Rutgers University–New Brunswick; University of Delaware; Rowan University; Stevens Institute of Technology

AND SOMETIMES PREFER

Penn State University Park; Villanova University; New Jersey Institute of Technology; University of Maryland, College Park; Seton Hall University; Temple University

FINANCIAL FACTS

Financial Aid Rating	75
Annual in-state tuition	$13,239
Annual out-of-state tuition	$25,217
Room and board	$14,048
Required fees	$3,684
Books and supplies	$1,200
Average frosh need-based scholarship	$12,781
Average UG need-based scholarship	$11,609
% needy frosh rec. need-based scholarship or grant aid	46
% needy UG rec. need-based scholarship or grant aid	42
% needy frosh rec. non-need-based scholarship or grant aid	38
% needy UG rec. non-need-based scholarship or grant aid	29
% needy frosh rec. need-based self-help aid	67
% needy UG rec. need-based self-help aid	76
% frosh rec. any financial aid	70
% UG rec. any financial aid	62
% UG borrow to pay for school	62
Average cumulative indebtedness	$38,937
% frosh need fully met	8
% ugrads need fully met	11
Average % of frosh need met	38
Average % of ugrad need met	43

COLLEGE OF SAINT BENEDICT/SAINT JOHN'S UNIVERSITY

College of Saint Benedict/Saint John's University, St. Joseph, MN 56321-7155 • Admissions: 320-363-5060 • Fax: 320-363-5650

CAMPUS LIFE

Quality of Life Rating	90
Fire Safety Rating	98
Green Rating	89
Type of school	Private
Affiliation	Roman Catholic
Environment	Village

STUDENTS

Total undergrad enrollment	3,329
% male/female	48/52
% from out of state	18
% frosh from public high school	74
% frosh live on campus	100
% ugrads live on campus	91
# of fraternities	0
# of sororities	0
% African American	3
% Asian	4
% Caucasian	79
% Hispanic	8
% Native American	<1
% Pacific Islander	<1
% Two or more races	0
% Race and/or ethnicity unknown	0
% international	4
# of countries represented	18

SURVEY SAYS . . .

Students are happy
Great library
Career services are great
Students are friendly
Students are very religious
Great food on campus
Very little drug use
Campus newspaper is popular
Alumni active on campus

ACADEMICS

Academic Rating	85
% students returning for sophomore year	85
% students graduating within 4 years	72
% students graduating within 6 years	77
Calendar	Semester
Student/faculty ratio	11:1
Profs interesting rating	90
Profs accessible rating	95

MOST POPULAR MAJORS

Biology/Biological Sciences, General; Business Administration and Management, General; Accounting

STUDENTS SAY "..."

Academics

Minnesota's College of Saint Benedict (for women) and Saint John's University (for men) are two Catholic liberal arts colleges that share one academic program and classes, but retain separate dorms, campuses, and traditions. Students come to this "beautiful, friendly environment" and leave with "a well-rounded education...ready to take on the world." The Benedictine values "are upheld by every student in everyday life" and help breed graduates that are "all about service and making an impact in the world." "This school is a must for any student who wants to feel accepted and a part of a rich community, while at the same time receiving an education that is second to none," says one junior. Professors truly take to heart the feedback they receive from their students, are "extremely dedicated and passionate," and "are willing to work...on projects outside of class even if it means extra work for them." They "are interested in us figuring things out for ourselves" and are "big on [students] being prepared for class so more time can be spent discussing or practicing material instead of lecturing." The ultimate testament to faculty involvement: "At CSB/SJU, I have never had a professor that has struggled to know my name (besides the fact that I am a twin)." Discussion is "lively" (particularly in upper division courses), and students "are offered many great opportunities to further our experiences and education." The open environment "does what it can to help students feel comfortable and learn."

The school provides "excellent scientific and business opportunities" and "endless connections with not only other schools across the nation, but...across the world" that aid in post-undergraduate employment or continued education opportunities. The "incredible" study abroad program sees a large number of students take advantage of it at some point in their college careers.

Life

The school "really makes sure your transition into your first semester runs smoothly" and that students "have a lot of options for meeting new people." The Student Activities and Leadership Development Office plans "large campus events such as orientation and Thanksgiving dinners," and also has an "inspired leaders series" of after-hours classes taught by professors that promote leadership on campus. On weekends, students often take adventure trips (like "California Surfing trips, Boundary Waters canoe trips, and Colorado climbing trips") with the school's Peer Resource Program.

School pride is "ridiculous" at CSB/SJU and athletic events "are the high points for entertainment," especially against rival St. Thomas. For fun, students take advantage of the school's "rich recreational abilities" both in the arboretum and on nearby waterways, where "ice fishing, fishing, hiking, and hanging out at the beach are popular." "The warm months of the year are awesome with the lake/raft open. It feels like a summer camp," says a student. Many students "do go out on the weekends" to parties or bars, but there is an "outstanding campus programming board" that plans events every weekend on campus as an alternative to drinking. "As long as you can step out that door and make good use of your time, you'll have an amazing time," assures a sophomore.

Student Body

Most of the "Johnnies" and "Bennies" here are "from Minnesota or the surrounding states," are "hard-working, fun-loving," and "believe in the importance of education." Not surprisingly, the majority are Catholic and take "'Minnesota Nice' to a whole new level": "Expect to have doors open for you [and] people smile and greet you on occasion when you're passing by." People have no trouble finding a friend group with related interests via "the many clubs and activities that are offered." "Everyone fits like a puzzle piece" and students "commonly have social issues that they are passionate about, such as gender equality, sustainability, [or] health and wellness."

COLLEGE OF SAINT BENEDICT/SAINT JOHN'S UNIVERSITY

Financial Aid: 320-363-5388 • E-Mail: admissions@csbsju.edu • Website: www.csbsju.edu

THE PRINCETON REVIEW SAYS

Admissions

Very important factors considered include: rigor of secondary school record, academic GPA, standardized test scores, extracurricular activities. *Important factors considered include:* alumni/ae relation. *Other factors considered include:* application essay, recommendation(s), interview, talent/ability, character/personal qualities, first generation, geographical residence, volunteer work, work experience. ACT with or without writing accepted. SAT with or without Essay component accepted. High school diploma is required and GED is accepted. *Academic units required:* 4 English, 3 math, 2 science, 2 science labs, 2 social studies, 4 academic electives. *Academic units recommended:* 4 English, 3 math, 2 science, 2 science labs, 2 foreign language, 2 social studies, 4 academic electives.

Financial Aid

Students should submit: FAFSA. Priority filing deadline is 3/15. The Princeton Review suggests that all financial aid forms be submitted as soon as possible after October 1. *Need-based scholarships/grants offered:* College/university scholarship or grant aid from institutional funds; Federal Pell; Private scholarships; SEOG; State scholarships/grants. *Loan aid offered:* Direct PLUS loans; Direct Subsidized Stafford Loans; Direct Unsubsidized Stafford Loans. Applicants will be notified of awards on a rolling basis beginning 12/15. Federal Work-Study Program available. Institutional employment available.

The Inside Word

Students with decent grades and a few extracurricular activities that "show promise of community contribution" shouldn't have any problem getting into CSB/SJU. You may apply to CSB/SJU using the Common Application or by using the school's CSBSJU GET INspired application—the school doesn't have a preference.

THE SCHOOL SAYS "..."

From the Admissions Office

"The College of Saint Benedict (CSB), for women, and Saint John's University (SJU), for men, are nationally recognized Catholic liberal arts colleges and ranked as two of the top three Catholic colleges in the nation. They share one academic program, and students attend classes together on both campuses. This integrated learning experience combines a challenging academic program with extensive opportunities for international study, leadership, service learning, spiritual growth and cultural and athletic involvement. We provide students access to the resources of not one, but two nationally leading liberal arts colleges through a common undergraduate curriculum, identical degree requirements, and a single academic calendar. We are committed to the development of the whole person, meeting the unique needs of both women and men in single-gender and co-educational experiences—experiences that could not be provided by traditional single-sex colleges and would not typically be provided by co-educational colleges. The colleges are part of a centuries-old Benedictine tradition of faith, learning, and community. Hospitality, community, stewardship and service to the common good are bedrock Benedictine values expressed throughout the curriculum and the co-curriculum. We are part of a Catholic intellectual tradition committed to openness, intellectual inquiry, and the lively engagement of faith and reason. The colleges are committed to global learning and connection. We provide international study programs on six continents and are annually ranked among the top three baccalaureate colleges nationally in the number of students completing semester-long study abroad. Two-thirds of all students study abroad before they graduate—an international study participation rate significantly higher than the national average for liberal arts colleges. More than 200 academic courses have an international component or global emphasis. One-third of our faculty has led a study abroad program. We enroll nearly 160 students from more than twenty countries, creating an enriching and culturally diverse global experience on campus. CSB/SJU annually rank first or second among Minnesota's private colleges for the number of undergraduate international students."

SELECTIVITY

Admissions Rating	77
# of applicants	3,798
% of applicants accepted	79
% of acceptees attending	28

FRESHMAN PROFILE

Range SAT EBRW	520–620
Range SAT Math	510–610
Range ACT Composite	22–28
# submitting SAT scores	86
% submitting SAT scores	10
# submitting ACT scores	780
% submitting ACT scores	92
Average HS GPA	3.6
% graduated top 10% of class	26
% graduated top 25% of class	55
% graduated top 50% of class	84

DEADLINES

Early action	
Deadline	12/15
Notification	1/15
Regular	
Notification	Rolling, 10/1
Nonfall registration?	Yes

APPLICANTS ALSO LOOK AT AND OFTEN PREFER
University of Minnesota—Twin Cities Campus;
University of Saint Thomas (MN)

AND SOMETIMES PREFER
Minnesota State University, Mankato; North Dakota
State University; Saint Cloud State University;
Winona State University; Gustavus Adolphus
College; University of Minnesota Duluth

AND RARELY PREFER

FINANCIAL FACTS

Financial Aid Rating	89
Annual tuition	$45,730
Room and board	$11,684
Required fees	$1,090
Books and supplies	$1,000
Average frosh need-based scholarship	$33,661
Average UG need-based scholarship	$31,445
% needy frosh rec. need-based scholarship or grant aid	98
% needy UG rec. need-based scholarship or grant aid	97
% needy frosh rec. non-need-based scholarship or grant aid	95
% needy UG rec. non-need-based scholarship or grant aid	93
% needy frosh rec. need-based self-help aid	98
% needy UG rec. need-based self-help aid	95
% frosh rec. any financial aid	96
% UG rec. any financial aid	97
% UG borrow to pay for school	72
Average cumulative indebtedness	$40,434
% frosh need fully met	37
% ugrads need fully met	31
Average % of frosh need met	91
Average % of ugrad need met	89

COLLEGE OF THE ATLANTIC

105 Eden Street, Bar Harbor, ME 04609 • Admissions: 207-288-5015 • Fax: 207-288-4126

CAMPUS LIFE

Quality of Life Rating	92
Fire Safety Rating	97
Green Rating	99
Type of school	Private
Environment	Rural

STUDENTS

Total undergrad enrollment	327
% male/female	24/76
% from out of state	77
% frosh from public high school	43
% frosh live on campus	100
% ugrads live on campus	48
# of fraternities	0
# of sororities	0
% African American	2
% Asian	1
% Caucasian	65
% Hispanic	4
% Native American	<1
% Pacific Islander	0
% Two or more races	2
% Race and/or ethnicity unknown	3
% international	24
# of countries represented	47

SURVEY SAYS . . .

Lots of liberal students
Students always studying
Students are happy
Internships are widely available
Class discussions encouraged
Great financial aid
No one cheats
Students are friendly
Diverse student types interact on campus
Students aren't religious
Students environmentally aware
Great food on campus
Easy to get around campus
Active student government

ACADEMICS

Academic Rating	92
% students returning for sophomore year	81
% students graduating within 4 years	53
% students graduating within 6 years	66
Calendar	Trimester
Student/faculty ratio	9:1
Profs interesting rating	94
Profs accessible rating	95
Most classes have 10–19 students.	

MOST POPULAR MAJORS

Humanities/Humanistic Studies; Multi-/
Interdisciplinary Studies, Other; Ecology

STUDENTS SAY "..."

Academics

A hop, skip, and a jump from stunning Acadia National Park, with its campus on Maine's Frenchman Bay, College of the Atlantic (COA) offers undergraduates "an extreme degree of academic freedom." COA's "interdisciplinary structure" lets students create their own course of study with creative pedagogy from professors who regularly "provide immersive activities such as field work, class trips, and experiential opportunities." Students rave about faculty who have "big hearts" while upholding a "rigorous academic" standard. Students have a chance to take traditional classes, but there is also an "incredible amount of experiential learning opportunities," including hands-on projects like "working on a research boat" and building a "tiny house with other students" in a class dedicated to—yep—designing and building tiny houses. Furthermore, students say "the professors at COA foster a class environment that honors and values class discussion and a balanced student-teacher relationship." This is evidenced by "everyone go[ing] by their first name," and faculty "participating in every other aspect of life at COA" outside of the classroom. Independent students also noted that they were able to receive "substantial financial aid," and had "flexibility in shaping [their] own education." Students have numerous internship, residency, and study abroad opportunities, all of which complement the school's "culture of social responsibility and environmental sustainability." "Workshops," one student adds, "most notably, the Thoreau gatherings held once per term...on student skill-sets enable us to better organize and advocate for change."

Life

Students are drawn to COA's "small community with a commitment to sustainability." Many classes "move outdoors in good weather" to "explore Acadia National Park across the street or other sites on the coast of Maine." COA students also "play a large part in the governance and daily operation of the college, participating in work study positions and serving on committees." Between classes, students "often hang out at a cafeteria called TAB (Take-A-Break)," "a central location on campus," that "besides being used for meals, is a common study or social space." Hiking is popular year round, or playing water polo at the YMCA in town. Skiing and winter camping are go-to activities in the winter. Popular on weekends year round is the "movie theatre/pizza place in town, Reel Pizza." And "a lot of people go contra dancing once a month in a nearby city." Students are generally passionate about their coursework and fieldwork, and serve "on the school's research vessel, the MV Osprey," and at the "Peggy Rockefeller Farm."

Student Body

At the College of the Atlantic, you'll find a fascinating assortment of "geologists, guitarists, teachers, poets, fashionistas, sailors, rock climbers, film makers, and economists" among the student body, who are "curious about learning, especially in the field setting," "passionate about global climate change and social equality," and "overwhelmingly willing to contribute to projects and help out people in need even if there is no individual benefit to be claimed." Another student trait that "seems to be universal" is a "willingness for academic discussion on a range of topics, in settings like classrooms to the line in the dining hall, in which students are keen to take sides and find real depths of thought together in a safe way without coming to personal jabs." Proud COA students note that they have "few traditions" and are "experimental in the best sense of the word." Students are inspired by "the words of...former school president Ed Kaelber: 'Any college that is not constantly seeking new ways of doing things is only half alive.'" Students say their "tiny community is tied together much closer than most colleges get their students to be," and full of "self-directed learners who want to take charge of their learning rather than follow the general current."

COLLEGE OF THE ATLANTIC

Financial Aid: 207-801-5645 • E-Mail: inquiry@coa.edu • Website: www.coa.edu

THE PRINCETON REVIEW SAYS

Admissions

Very important factors considered include: rigor of secondary school record, application essay, recommendation(s). *Important factors considered include:* class rank, academic GPA, interview, extracurricular activities, talent/ability, character/personal qualities. *Other factors considered include:* standardized test scores, first generation, alumni/ae relation, geographical residence, state residency, racial/ethnic status, level of applicant's interest. ACT with or without writing accepted. High school diploma is required and GED is accepted. *Academic units required:* 4 English, 3 math, 2 science, 2 science labs, 2 social studies. *Academic units recommended:* 4 math, 3 science, 2 foreign language, 2 history, 1 academic elective.

Financial Aid

Students should submit: Business/Farm Supplement; FAFSA; Institution's own financial aid form; Noncustodial PROFILE. Priority filing deadline is 2/1. The Princeton Review suggests that all financial aid forms be submitted as soon as possible after October 1. *Need-based scholarships/grants offered:* College/university scholarship or grant aid from institutional funds; Federal Pell; Private scholarships; SEOG; State scholarships/grants. *Loan aid offered:* Direct PLUS loans; Direct Subsidized Stafford Loans; Direct Unsubsidized Stafford Loans. Applicants will be notified of awards on or about 4/1. Federal Work-Study Program available. Institutional employment available.

The Inside Word

Don't let COA's high acceptance rate fool you: the self-selecting applicant pool is comprised of dedicated and successful students. Standardized test scores are optional but encouraged for applicants from nontraditional programs or alternative grading systems. Admission interviews, while not required, are recommended and can take place on Skype or over the phone. Students are welcome to submit examples or a portfolio of writing, art, music, or another form of expression not easily conveyed through the Common App.

THE SCHOOL SAYS "..."

From the Admissions Office

"College of the Atlantic is a small, interdisciplinary college on Maine's Mount Desert Island. All students design their own major in human ecology—an educational approach that integrates knowledge from across academic disciplines and personal experience to investigate, and ultimately improve, the relationships between humans and our natural, social, and built environments. COA prepares students to become independent thinkers, challenge conventional wisdom, deal with pressing environmental and social issues, and engage passionately and thoughtfully to transform the world around them into a better place.

"Our campus is located on the shore of Frenchman Bay, a short walk from the mountains and trails of Acadia National Park—an ideal location for learning in the field. Many students spend time working or conducting research in the national park or on the college's organic farms and offshore island research stations on Mount Desert Rock and Great Duck Island. In addition to having numerous opportunities for research and field study, all COA students complete an internship and a capstone senior project.

"We look for students seeking a rigorous, hands-on, self-directed academic experience and meaningful engagement in a dynamic community of scholars. The best way to experience COA's unique approach to education, governance, and community life is to visit the campus. While you're here, make time to sit in on classes, connect with faculty and current students, sample a homemade meal in the dining hall, and explore the national park."

SELECTIVITY
Admissions Rating	87
# of applicants	459
% of applicants accepted	67
% of acceptees attending	27
# offered a place on the wait list	25
% accepting a place on wait list	36
% admitted from wait list	100
# of early decision applicants	33
% accepted early decision	76

FRESHMAN PROFILE
Range SAT EBRW	630–730
Range SAT Math	580–670
Range ACT Composite	30–33
# submitting SAT scores	28
% submitting SAT scores	34
# submitting ACT scores	11
% submitting ACT scores	13
Average HS GPA	3.6
% graduated top 10% of class	35
% graduated top 25% of class	59
% graduated top 50% of class	82

DEADLINES
Early decision	
Deadline	12/1
Notification	12/15
Other ED Deadline	1/15
Other ED Notification	1/30
Regular	
Deadline	2/1
Notification	4/1
Nonfall registration?	Yes

APPLICANTS ALSO LOOK AT AND SOMETIMES PREFER
Lewis & Clark College; Warren Wilson College; University of Vermont; Bennington College; University of Maine

AND RARELY PREFER
Unity College

FINANCIAL FACTS
Financial Aid Rating	91
Annual tuition	$42,993
Room and board	$9,747
Required fees	$549
Books and supplies	$600
Average frosh need-based scholarship	$41,454
Average UG need-based scholarship	$36,091
% needy frosh rec. need-based scholarship or grant aid	100
% needy UG rec. need-based scholarship or grant aid	100
% needy frosh rec. non-need-based scholarship or grant aid	2
% needy UG rec. non-need-based scholarship or grant aid	2
% needy frosh rec. need-based self-help aid	95
% needy UG rec. need-based self-help aid	95
% frosh rec. any financial aid	100
% UG rec. any financial aid	97
% UG borrow to pay for school	66
Average cumulative indebtedness	$24,496
% frosh need fully met	68
% ugrads need fully met	39
Average % of frosh need met	98
Average % of ugrad need met	94

COLLEGE OF THE HOLY CROSS

1 College Street, Worcester, MA 01610-2395 • Admissions: 508-793-2443 • Fax: 508-793-3888

STUDENTS SAY "..."

Academics

This small, Jesuit liberal arts school in Massachusetts operates under a selfless mission statement of "men and women for and with others." The school's strong academic tradition marries with "countless opportunities to learn through internships, speaker series," "strong student life," and "small classes" to focus on shaping the student as a whole person. Academics at Holy Cross are "rigorous, and the main priority of students on campus"; a caring faculty and administration foster "an incredible learning environment for students," and through their experiences, students receive "a broad-based foundation to be successful in variety of careers." "From the acceptance letter alone, I knew that my entire application was read thoroughly and that my character was closely examined," says one happy student. At Holy Cross, "you're more than just a number in the classroom and on the field." Professors here are "dedicated to creating an exciting learning environment." They are "always accessible and more than happy to help," and they "get to know you on an individual and personal level." Students are encouraged "to reflect on their experiences and continue to better himself/herself as a whole person." "There are endless opportunities despite the fact that it is a small college," one student says. "It is a place where like in the parable of the mustard seed one can grow." In addition to a "fantastic alumni network" spread across several fields in various industries, there is a strong science program that includes plenty of research opportunities. The college "demands enormous amounts of work from its students, but puts them in a great position to succeed." "Holy Cross equips their students with an intangible set of skills that not only prepares them for a job, but for life," says a student.

Life

Holy Cross has "a multitude" of groups and activities available to its students, as well as a plethora of community service opportunities. Everyone loves "going to sporting events, especially football and basketball." Though the "exceptionally beautiful" campus has a lot of fans, all agree that the college "could update some of the residence halls." Holy Cross has added new dining venues and was named among Bon Appetit's "healthiest dining halls" for its food fitting all kinds of dietary restrictions. The community among freshman dorms is "outstanding," and "many of the friends you make your first year will stay with you for years to come." During the week and on Sundays, "people take their work very seriously," and the library is generally pretty full, but parties are popular on weekends, and "that nerdy chem major you see working hard all week can turn into the girl riding the mechanical bull at a local bar." For those who choose to abstain from the party circuit, "SGA-sponsored events such as karaoke or dances are a blast." Worcester is a fun little town (and Boston a free weekend shuttle ride away), and the restaurants in the area are "amazing."

Student Body

Many students here are "preppy" and from New England, and most all of this "uncommonly friendly" lot is "studious with an activity or two that defines their interests and what they do during the weekend"; in fact, it is rare "to find someone with no extracurricular responsibilities." Everyone tends to be "very put together" and "generally articulate," and "there is a tremendous sense of community." There is "a diverse set of interests" among the whole student body. In general, "all love being here." "If you want to do well academically, have fun on the weekend...study hard and play hard, then you will fit in at Holy Cross."

COLLEGE OF THE HOLY CROSS

Financial Aid: 508-793-2265 • E-Mail: admissions@holycross.edu • Website: www.holycross.edu

THE PRINCETON REVIEW SAYS

Admissions

Very important factors considered include: rigor of secondary school record, academic GPA, application essay, recommendation(s), interview, character/personal qualities. *Important factors considered include:* extracurricular activities, talent/ability. *Other factors considered include:* class rank, standardized test scores, first generation, alumni/ae relation, geographical residence, state residency, religious affiliation/commitment, racial/ethnic status, volunteer work, work experience, level of applicant's interest. ACT with or without writing accepted. SAT with or without Essay component accepted. High school diploma is required and GED is accepted. *Academic units recommended:* 4 English, 4 math, 4 science, 2 science labs, 4 foreign language, 2 social studies, 2 history.

Financial Aid

Students should submit: Business/Farm Supplement; CSS/Financial Aid PROFILE; FAFSA; Noncustodial PROFILE. The Princeton Review suggests that all financial aid forms be submitted as soon as possible after October 1. *Need-based scholarships/grants offered:* College/university scholarship or grant aid from institutional funds; Federal Pell; Private scholarships; SEOG; State scholarships/grants. *Loan aid offered:* Direct PLUS loans; Direct Subsidized Stafford Loans; Direct Unsubsidized Stafford Loans. Federal Work-Study Program available. Institutional employment available.

The Inside Word

Admission to Holy Cross is competitive; therefore, a demanding high school course load is required to be a viable candidate. The college values effective communication skills—it thoroughly evaluates each applicant's personal statement and short essay responses. Interviews are important, especially for those applying early decision. Students who graduate from a Jesuit high school might find themselves at a slight advantage. Holy Cross meets 100% of an admitted student's demonstrated financial need.

THE SCHOOL SAYS "..."

From the Admissions Office

"When applying to Holy Cross, two areas deserve particular attention. First, the essay should be developed thoughtfully, with correct language and syntax in mind. That essay reflects for the Admissions Committee how you think and how you can express yourself. Second, activity beyond the classroom should be clearly defined. Since Holy Cross has only 3,000 students, the chance for involvement/participation is exceptional. The committee reviews many applications for academically qualified students. A key difference in being accepted is the extent to which a candidate participates in-depth beyond the classroom—don't be modest; define who you are. Interviews are highly recommended and are used as part of the evaluation process.

"Standardized test scores (i.e., SAT, SAT Subject Tests, and ACT) are optional. Students may submit their scores if they believe the results paint a fuller picture of their achievements and potential, but those students who don't submit scores will not be at a disadvantage in admissions decisions."

SELECTIVITY	
Admissions Rating	93
# of applicants	7,200
% of applicants accepted	34
% of acceptees attending	34
# offered a place on the wait list	1,875
% accepting a place on wait list	44
% admitted from wait list	1
# of early decision applicants	498
% accepted early decision	83

FRESHMAN PROFILE	
Range SAT EBRW	630–700
Range SAT Math	630–730
Range SAT Composite	1280–1410
Range ACT Composite	28–32
# submitting SAT scores	366
% submitting SAT scores	44
# submitting ACT scores	176
% submitting ACT scores	21
% graduated top 10% of class	53
% graduated top 25% of class	86
% graduated top 50% of class	100

DEADLINES	
Early decision	
Deadline	11/15
Notification	12/15
Other ED Deadline	1/15
Other ED Notification	Rolling
Regular	
Deadline	1/15
Notification	Mid-March
Nonfall registration?	No

FINANCIAL FACTS	
Financial Aid Rating	95
Annual tuition	$55,800
Room and board	$15,560
Required fees	$720
Books and supplies	$1,000
Average frosh need-based scholarship	$42,069
Average UG need-based scholarship	$40,064
% needy frosh rec. need-based scholarship or grant aid	77
% needy UG rec. need-based scholarship or grant aid	80
% needy frosh rec. non-need-based scholarship or grant aid	26
% needy UG rec. non-need-based scholarship or grant aid	16
% needy frosh rec. need-based self-help aid	78
% needy UG rec. need-based self-help aid	84
% frosh rec. any financial aid	67
% UG rec. any financial aid	63
% UG borrow to pay for school	60
Average cumulative indebtedness	$25,668
% frosh need fully met	100
% ugrads need fully met	100
Average % of frosh need met	100
Average % of ugrad need met	100

COLLEGE OF THE OZARKS

Office of Admissions, Point Lookout, MO 65726 • Admissions: 417-690-2636 • Fax: 417-690-2635

CAMPUS LIFE

Quality of Life Rating	89
Fire Safety Rating	83
Green Rating	68
Type of school	Private
Affiliation	Evangelical Christian
	Interdenominational
Environment	Rural

STUDENTS

Total undergrad enrollment	1,491
% male/female	45/55
% from out of state	24
% frosh from public high school	78
% frosh live on campus	93
% ugrads live on campus	90
# of fraternities	0
# of sororities	0
% African American	1
% Asian	1
% Caucasian	90
% Hispanic	2
% Native American	<1
% Pacific Islander	<1
% Two or more races	2
% Race and/or ethnicity unknown	2
% international	1
# of countries represented	17

SURVEY SAYS . . .

Lots of conservative students
Great financial aid
Students are very religious
Students get along with local community
Very little drug use
Theater is popular

ACADEMICS

Academic Rating	82
% students returning for sophomore year	73
% students graduating within 4 years	55
Calendar	Semester
Student/faculty ratio	14:1
Profs interesting rating	89
Profs accessible rating	91

Most classes have 10–19 students.
Most lab/discussion sessions have
10–19 students.

MOST POPULAR MAJORS

AGRICULTURAL/ANIMAL/PLANT/VETERINARY
SCIENCE AND RELATED FIELDS; Elementary
Education and Teaching; Business Administration
and Management, General

STUDENTS SAY "..."

Academics

A "private Christian college" in Missouri, College of the Ozarks is an institution where students quickly learn "the value of hard work." This is in large part due to the school's "work education program" which "allows student[s] to learn [a] trade or profession...[as they work] to pay off tuition." This enables undergrads to finish college debt free. Certainly, the focus at COFO isn't merely on the jobs students must hold; academics still take center stage here. And be forewarned that they are "rigorous." Luckily, undergrads report that their professors are "passionate about their subjects and genuinely want students to learn and excel in their classes." What's more, they "seek to have interaction in the classroom and highly encourage student participation." Even better, professors here "are always available after class and willing to help tutor a student if they need extra help." Aside from their regular coursework, COFO also offers students some really unique educational opportunities. For instance, "there is a program called the Patriotic Travel Program, and it [allows] students...to travel with a Veteran to a battle or war site, and learn [about] what happened there." Such programs truly bolster classroom learning and make for a richer educational experience.

Life

There's no denying that undergrads at COFO lead busy lives. To begin with, beyond attending classes, all students "work fifteen hours on campus each week." Additionally, undergrads are "required to attend convocations and chapel." Thankfully, despite all their obligations, these students still manage to find time to kick back, relax and enjoy campus life. And that's great because there's a lot of fun to be had. For example, the "Student Union [hosts] a lot of...activities, like the Sadie Hawkins dance, Homecoming festivities, and Coffee House events with live music." Undergrads also love participating in "Mud-fest (a game of tug-of-war), the Games (dormitory teams competing in fun athletic activities)...[and fall] bon-fire events." There are also plenty of great options for outdoor enthusiasts. Indeed, people frequently "go swimming at the lake when it's warm, cliff dive, and play volleyball. There are a lot of great trails around for students to walk and bike, as well." Many students are also "involved in intramural sports, such as ultimate frisbee and volleyball." And individuals passionate about performing will be delighted to learn that "the theatre department puts on plays every so often, and [the] concert band, jazz band, chapel choir and chorale perform regular concerts." However, those looking for a party scene—beware. COFO is "really strict about alcohol even if you are over 21."

Student Body

Given the "small campus environment," it's not surprising that College of the Ozarks is the kind of school where you see "a lot of familiar faces...every day." Fortunately, most students report that those very faces are quite "welcoming and supportive." Of course, it likely helps that many undergrads have similar upbringings. After all, a vast majority are "native to the Ozark region," "from an agricultural background," and "Republican." Many were also "homeschoolers and missionary kids before they attended COFO." Additionally, students here are united in their shared "Christian values and ethics [as well as their] determination to succeed in both work and school." It probably also doesn't hurt that many COFO students "are fans of country music and Kansas City or St. Louis sports teams." Perhaps more importantly, undergrads are eager to mention that their peers are very "driven" and extremely "busy." As one hardworking student shares, "It's not uncommon for students here, including myself, to work three jobs, adding up to well over 40 hours per week." Indeed, "they take their education seriously while still being able to enjoy their time at school." Finally, as one happy undergrad sums up, "You can pick out a CofO student from the crowd...because they stand out. [They're] always willing to go the extra mile, and accomplish their goals."

Financial Aid: 417-690-3292 • E-Mail: admissions@cofo.edu • Website: www.cofo.edu

THE PRINCETON REVIEW SAYS

Admissions

Very important factors considered include: rigor of secondary school record, class rank, interview, character/personal qualities. *Important factors considered include:* academic GPA, standardized test scores, recommendation(s), geographical residence. *Other factors considered include:* extracurricular activities, talent/ability, first generation, alumni/ae relation, state residency, religious affiliation/commitment. ACT with Writing required. SAT with or without Essay component accepted. High school diploma is required and GED is accepted. *Academic units required:* 4 English, 3 math, 2 science, 1 science lab, 3 history. *Academic units recommended:* 2 foreign language, 3 social studies.

Financial Aid

Students should submit: FAFSA. Priority filing deadline is 11/15. The Princeton Review suggests that all financial aid forms be submitted as soon as possible after October 1. *Need-based scholarships/grants offered:* College/university scholarship or grant aid from institutional funds; Federal Pell; Private scholarships; SEOG; State scholarships/grants. Applicants will be notified of awards on or about 7/1. Federal Work-Study Program available. Institutional employment available.

The Inside Word

Admissions officers at College of the Ozarks are generally looking to serve students hailing from the Ozark region. Indeed, they are on the hunt for local applicants in the top half of their class who lack the financial resources to pay for college. Applicants should also be individuals who are specifically looking for a Christian education. Finally, children of alumni in good standing will be given preferential consideration until December 31.

THE SCHOOL SAYS "..."

From the Admissions Office

"College of the Ozarks is unique because of its no-tuition, work-study program, but also because it strives to educate the head, the heart, and the hands. At C of O, there are high expectations of students—the college stresses character development as well as study and work. An education from 'Hard Work U.' offers many opportunities, not the least of which is the chance to graduate debt-free. Life at C of O isn't all hard work and no play, however. There are many opportunities for fun. The nearby resort town of Branson, Missouri, offers ample opportunities for recreation and summer employment, and Table Rock Lake, only a few miles away, is a terrific spot to swim, sun, and relax. Numerous on-campus activities such as Mudfest, Luau Night, dances, and holiday parties give students lots of chances for fun without leaving the college. At 'Hard Work U.,' we work hard, but we know how to have fun, too.

"Applicants are required to submit scores from the ACT or the SAT. We will use the student's best scores from either test. Writing scores are not required."

SELECTIVITY

Admissions Rating	97
# of applicants	2,879
% of applicants accepted	16
% of acceptees attending	84
# offered a place on the wait list	586
% accepting a place on wait list	100
% admitted from wait list	4

FRESHMAN PROFILE

Range SAT EBRW	560–625
Range SAT Math	543–605
Range ACT Composite	21–26
# submitting SAT scores	12
% submitting SAT scores	3
# submitting ACT scores	374
% submitting ACT scores	97
Average HS GPA	3.7
% graduated top 10% of class	25
% graduated top 25% of class	62
% graduated top 50% of class	96

DEADLINES

Regular	
Priority	12/31
Notification	2/15
Nonfall registration?	Yes

FINANCIAL FACTS

Financial Aid Rating	60
Annual tuition	$0
Room and board	$7,900
Required fees	$460
Books and supplies	$1,000
Average frosh need-based scholarship	$11,182
Average UG need-based scholarship	$11,182
% needy frosh rec. need-based scholarship or grant aid	100
% needy UG rec. need-based scholarship or grant aid	100
% needy frosh rec. non-need-based scholarship or grant aid	36
% needy UG rec. non-need-based scholarship or grant aid	94
% needy frosh rec. need-based self-help aid	64
% needy UG rec. need-based self-help aid	94
% frosh rec. any financial aid	100
% UG rec. any financial aid	100
% UG borrow to pay for school	0
% frosh need fully met	18
% ugrads need fully met	40
Average % of frosh need met	75
Average % of ugrad need met	81

THE COLLEGE OF WOOSTER

847 College Avenue, Wooster, OH 44691 • Admissions: 330-263-2322 • Fax: 330-263-2621

CAMPUS LIFE

Quality of Life Rating	92
Fire Safety Rating	64
Green Rating	78
Type of school	Private
Affiliation	Presbyterian
Environment	Town

STUDENTS

Total undergrad enrollment	1,942
% male/female	46/54
% from out of state	65
% frosh from public high school	61
% frosh live on campus	100
% ugrads live on campus	99
# of fraternities	4
# of sororities	7
% African American	9
% Asian	4
% Caucasian	61
% Hispanic	6
% Native American	<1
% Pacific Islander	0
% Two or more races	4
% Race and/or ethnicity unknown	1
% international	16
# of countries represented	58

SURVEY SAYS . . .

Students always studying
Students are happy
Classroom facilities are great
Great library
Career services are great
Internships are widely available
No one cheats
Students are friendly
Diverse student types interact on campus
Great off-campus food
Easy to get around campus
Recreation facilities are great
Campus newspaper is popular
Active minority support groups

ACADEMICS

Academic Rating	95
% students returning for sophomore year	86
% students graduating within 4 years	75
% students graduating within 6 years	77
Calendar	Semester
Student/faculty ratio	10:1
Profs interesting rating	95
Profs accessible rating	98

Most classes have fewer than 10 students.
Most lab/discussion sessions have
10–19 students.

MOST POPULAR MAJORS

Biological And Biomedical Sciences; Physical
Sciences; Social Sciences

STUDENTS SAY "..."

Academics

The College of Wooster in Ohio is a small, personable "tight-knit community" that offers "a truly stellar education" to those who attend. Mentoring is a huge focal point of Wooster's academics, and the "resources are endless" for those looking to take advantage of things like "numerous opportunities for research and internships." Independent study is a highlight of the undergraduate experience, and the school "teaches research and how to apply skills learned to the outside world." This "very open school" challenges its students to succeed both in and out of the classroom, and "the staff pushes [the college] to change with the times in the classroom and around the campus."

Professors at Wooster are "hidden gems" who are all "very passionate about their subjects" and their goal "to shape their students into lifelong learners." "It's as if your professor is your colleague on your quest for eternal knowledge," says a freshman. These intimate ties between student and professor are "what makes Wooster such an incredible place." "My professors, both past and present, know more than just my name," says a student. "My success is a product of my professors' enthusiasm towards their subject matter and our futures," says another. The work may be "challenging," but it "teaches students how to write exceptionally," and there is "plenty of help from professors, TAs, [and] peer tutoring." "Collaborative work and experience" are stressed, and classes are set up "in a way that allows people to learn from their peers as well as their professors."

Research plays a "huge" role at Wooster, especially with senior year Independent Study, when students are given the opportunity to work with a faculty mentor on a project in any topic they are passionate about—and "they can do so much with it." The institution is also aware of the effort that students must put in to have success and "is realistic in its expectations for students' learning." "Wooster is a community of learners working together to help one another reach their full potential and goals," says a sophomore chemistry major.

Life

"The character of the campus community is friendly beyond measure" at this "dazzling" campus. People are usually "busy in the library doing homework or working on their Independent Studies," but everyone finds time for (typically multiple) extracurriculars, which "run the gamut of recreational pastimes." "We have just as many students in our music ensembles as we do that play sports," says a student. People enjoy using the weekends to relieve the stress of a rigorous academic schedule, and the majority enjoy "social drinking" at the fraternity or program houses, or going to the on-campus club called "the Underground" on Friday nights.

For those who choose not to party, there are "many other recreational activities for those who are not in sports or who do not enjoy drinking," and the college "is very good at bringing in entertainment," such as "comedians, professional music artists, and forum speakers which are all free to students." A student run weekly flyer, *The Pot*, helps "keep students up to date on all of the campus events happening." A lot of the time, though, "students will just hang out together and relax."

Student Body

"The life force of this school is really our fantastic student body," says a student. This "unparalleled" community is made up of "quite a range of people," but most are "quirky," "friendly," "open-minded," and "liberal." It's also a "very involved" student body ("school spirit is huge at Wooster"), so a typical COW kid "tends to be in a hodgepodge of sports, clubs, music groups, etc. that suit their fancy." There are "very few social cliques" and everyone is friendly and "willing to interact with one another." Students here are "very accepting of different personalities, beliefs, and ways of life."

THE COLLEGE OF WOOSTER

Financial Aid: 330-263-2317 • E-Mail: admissions@wooster.edu • Website: www.wooster.edu

THE PRINCETON REVIEW SAYS

Admissions

Very important factors considered include: rigor of secondary school record, academic GPA. *Important factors considered include:* class rank, application essay, standardized test scores, recommendation(s), interview, extracurricular activities, character/personal qualities. *Other factors considered include:* talent/ability, first generation, alumni/ae relation, geographical residence, state residency, racial/ethnic status, volunteer work, work experience. ACT with Writing recommended. SAT with Essay component recommended. High school diploma is required and GED is accepted. *Academic units required:* 4 English, 3 math, 3 science, 2 science labs, 2 foreign language, 3 social studies, 1 academic elective.

Financial Aid

Students should submit: CSS/Financial Aid PROFILE; FAFSA; Institution's own financial aid form. Priority filing deadline is 2/15. The Princeton Review suggests that all financial aid forms be submitted as soon as possible after October 1. *Need-based scholarships/grants offered:* College/university scholarship or grant aid from institutional funds; Federal Pell; Private scholarships; SEOG; State scholarships/grants. *Loan aid offered:* Direct PLUS loans; Direct Subsidized Stafford Loans; Direct Unsubsidized Stafford Loans. Applicants will be notified of awards on a rolling basis beginning 1/1. Federal Work-Study Program available. Institutional employment available.

The Inside Word

The College of Wooster is a small, selective liberal arts school in a region of the country where there are quite a few small, selective liberal arts schools. For the most part, only solid students get past the gatekeepers here, and you should expect a thorough review of your application. Nevertheless, the admit rate is high. Stiff competition from similar institutions means the school will occasionally admit students who don't have stellar academic records.

THE SCHOOL SAYS "..."

From the Admissions Office

"The College of Wooster is America's premier college for mentored undergraduate research. Our mission is to graduate educated, not merely trained, people; to produce responsible, independent thinkers, rather than specialists in any given field. Our commitment to independence is especially evident in IS, the college's distinctive program in which every senior works one-to-one with a faculty mentor to complete a project in the major. IS comes from 'independent study,' but, in reality, it is an intellectual collaboration of the highest order and permits every student the freedom to pursue something in which he or she is passionately interested. IS is the centerpiece of an innovative curriculum. More than just the project itself, the culture that sustains IS—and, in turn, is sustained by IS—is an extraordinary college culture. The same attitudes of student initiative, openness, flexibility, and individual support enrich every aspect of Wooster's vital residential college life."

SELECTIVITY

Admissions Rating	**88**
# of applicants	6,352
% of applicants accepted	55
% of acceptees attending	16
# offered a place on the wait list	815
% accepting a place on wait list	23
% admitted from wait list	32
# of early decision applicants	201
% accepted early decision	100

FRESHMAN PROFILE

Range SAT EBRW	580–680
Range SAT Math	570–700
Range ACT Composite	24–31
# submitting SAT scores	320
% submitting SAT scores	59*
# submitting ACT scores	312
% submitting ACT scores	57
Average HS GPA	3.7
% graduated top 10% of class	46
% graduated top 25% of class	72
% graduated top 50% of class	92

DEADLINES

Early decision	
Deadline	11/1
Notification	11/15
Other ED Deadline	1/15
Other ED Notification	2/1
Early action	
Deadline	11/15
Notification	12/31
Regular	
Priority	2/15
Deadline	2/15
Notification	4/1
Nonfall registration?	Yes

FINANCIAL FACTS

Financial Aid Rating	**91**
Annual tuition	$49,810
Room and board	$11,850
Required fees	$440
Books and supplies	$1,000
Average frosh need-based scholarship	$37,249
Average UG need-based scholarship	$35,524
% needy frosh rec. need-based scholarship or grant aid	97
% needy UG rec. need-based scholarship or grant aid	97
% needy frosh rec. non-need-based scholarship or grant aid	34
% needy UG rec. non-need-based scholarship or grant aid	31
% needy frosh rec. need-based self-help aid	65
% needy UG rec. need-based self-help aid	67
% frosh rec. any financial aid	96
% UG rec. any financial aid	96
% UG borrow to pay for school	53
Average cumulative indebtedness	$32,194
% frosh need fully met	48
% ugrads need fully met	45
Average % of frosh need met	94
Average % of ugrad need met	93

COLORADO COLLEGE

14 East Cache la Poudre St., Colorado Springs, CO 80903 • Admissions: 719-389-6344 • Fax: 719-389-6816

STUDENTS SAY "..."

Academics

Students are drawn to Colorado College for its unique "Block Plan," in which students take one intensive class at a time. The academic year is structured as eight blocks of three to five weeks each, punctuated by five-day "block breaks." Students find the Block Plan empowers them to participate in "a strongly immersive approach to education," reporting that "the classes are very challenging, but after cramming in a semester's worth of calculus in four weeks, you basically feel like you can conquer anything." "Colorado College abhors mediocrity; either you succeed more than you ever thought possible, or fail in spectacular ways." Academically, students "love the class sizes and classes. I feel fully invested in each class I take here." The "intense and exhausting" pace of block classes bonds students and professors: "My professors have given me more opportunities for growth and cared more than I ever imagined they would. I have yet to have a professor whose home I haven't been to and family I haven't met." "In my last block the professor was spending the whole morning afternoon—and evening—with us!" "My professors appear to be geniuses in their respective fields...I have been amazed at the extent to which the block plan allows each student to delve into their course material." The "small classes" "do away with student anonymity" and "foster excellent discussion and intellectual growth." Students also appreciate the "internship opportunities" and "preparation for post-graduation" offered by the school, often in concert with the "ability to study off campus or abroad." Colorado College undergrads see their objective as "pursuing excellence through diverse and rich viewpoints" and "immersion in a dynamic array of intellectual endeavors." "My school emphasizes an attitude of working diligently, so that free time can be appreciated to its fullest." "They genuinely value the college's "great support system and connections," which make "opportunities to learn off campus" "accessible." "The shared values of intellectual engagement, physical and mental health, passion, and a sense of adventure define Colorado College's spirit."

Life

Students call the Colorado College experience one of "focused study in a Rocky Mountain environment." "Looking at Pikes Peak is a constant reminder about how beautiful of a state we are in." "Outdoor activities are a big thing here," and indeed, another student observes that "slacklining, doing homework in the sun, and playing guitar on the lawn all happen when it's nice out. Sledding and skiing down campus hills, snowball fights, and fire pits happen in the winter." Despite this athletic emphasis, "people are pretty accepting [of] what you like doing for fun" and "the common slang is 'you do you.' ... Another thing I like is there is no peer pressure to get involved with substances." "You really don't have to leave campus if you don't want to," but if you do, downtown Colorado Springs "is only about a ten minute walk from campus, and there are many interesting restaurants to dine at for special occasions or a fun night out." "Life at school is very busy," and CC students like it that way: "People think about how to have fun after intense weeks or blocks." In sum, a "Colorado College experience is" one of "non-competitive, non-judgmental, intellectual and physical adventure on the Block Plan in the little warm nest of the Rockies."

Student Body

Colorado College undergrads respect each other, saying that "everyone here is very intelligent" to the point at which it seems that "almost everyone was a valedictorian or salutatorian." In equal measure, "CC students have passion for academic and outdoor pursuits," as evidenced by one student's depiction of "intellectual discussion about our impact on nature while rock climbing." Students do say things like, "CC is great but there are rich hippies everywhere," and the school "is not very diverse, which is one of the main improvements I would like to see in the future." That said, students see well beyond themselves: "The typical student is well-traveled, intelligent...quirky, outdoorsy, and a bit of a hipster." CC students "are usually very accepting and friendly," as well as "largely involved with their community, environment and academics" and "very vocal about their opinions."

COLORADO COLLEGE

Financial Aid. 719 389 6779 • E-Mail: admission@coloradocollege.edu • Website: www.coloradocollege.edu

THE PRINCETON REVIEW SAYS

Admissions

Very important factors considered include: rigor of secondary school record. *Important factors considered include:* academic GPA, application essay, recommendation(s), interview, extracurricular activities. *Other factors considered include:* class rank, standardized test scores, talent/ability, character/personal qualities, first generation, alumni/ae relation, geographical residence, state residency, religious affiliation/commitment, racial/ethnic status, volunteer work, work experience, level of applicant's interest. ACT with or without writing accepted. SAT with or without Essay component accepted. High school diploma or equivalent is not required *Academic units required:* 4 English. *Academic units recommended:* 4 English.

Financial Aid

Students should submit: CSS/Financial Aid PROFILE; FAFSA; Noncustodial PROFILE; State aid form. Priority filing deadline is 11/1. The Princeton Review suggests that all financial aid forms be submitted as soon as possible after October 1. *Need-based scholarships/grants offered:* College/university scholarship or grant aid from institutional funds; Federal Pell; Private scholarships; SEOG; State scholarships/grants. *Loan aid offered:* Direct PLUS loans; Direct Subsidized Stafford Loans; Direct Unsubsidized Stafford Loans. Applicants will be notified of awards on or about 3/15. Federal Work-Study Program available. Institutional employment available.

The Inside Word

Admission at Colorado College is highly competitive, with over 98 percent of the student body accepted for fall 2014 graduated in the top quarter of their high school class. The rigor of the block program requires students to demonstrate self-motivation and commitment to both academics and extracurriculars, and strong writing skills are considered essential to the application. As of the 2020–2021 school year, CC will be going test optional. Interviews and arts supplements are non-required application options; students who feel their strengths will be showcased by these options should carefully consider them.

THE SCHOOL SAYS "..."

From the Admissions Office

"Students enter Colorado College for the opportunity to study intensely in small learning communities. Groups of students work closely with one another and faculty in discussion-based classes and hands-on labs. CC encourages a well-rounded education, combining the academic rigor of a traditional liberal arts college, with the focus and flexibility of the block plan. Rich programs in athletics, community service, student government, and the arts balance an engaged student life. The college encourages students to push themselves academically, and many continue their studies at the best graduate and professional schools in the nation. Because roughly 80 percent of students study abroad while at CC, the college has been recognized as a national leader in international education. The block plan allows classes to incorporate field study into the curriculum, whether studying winter field ecology at the CC Cabin or Dante and Michelangelo in Italy. Its location at the base of the Rockies makes CC a great choice for students who enjoy backpacking, hiking, climbing, and skiing."

SELECTIVITY

Admissions Rating	97
# of applicants	9,456
% of applicants accepted	14
% of acceptees attending	42
# offered a place on the wait list	1,052
% accepting a place on wait list	26
% admitted from wait list	8
# of early decision applicants	1,163
% accepted early decision	27

FRESHMAN PROFILE

Range SAT EBRW	650–730
Range SAT Math	650–750
Range ACT Composite	29–33
# submitting SAT scores	265
% submitting SAT scores	50
# submitting ACT scores	255
% submitting ACT scores	48
% graduated top 10% of class	82
% graduated top 25% of class	98
% graduated top 50% of class	100

DEADLINES

Early decision	
Deadline	11/1
Notification	12/15
Other ED Deadline	1/15
Other ED Notification	2/15
Early action	
Deadline	11/1
Notification	12/20
Regular	
Priority	1/15
Deadline	1/15
Notification	4/1
Nonfall registration?	Yes

FINANCIAL FACTS

Financial Aid Rating	97
Annual tuition	$60,390
Room and Board	$13,392
Required Fees	$474
Books and supplies	$1,240
Average frosh need-based scholarship	$53,720
Average UG need-based scholarship	$48,600
% needy frosh rec. need-based scholarship or grant aid	100
% needy UG rec. need-based scholarship or grant aid	90
% needy frosh rec. non-need-based scholarship or grant aid	5
% needy UG rec. non-need-based scholarship or grant aid	9
% needy frosh rec. need-based self-help aid	92
% needy UG rec. need-based self-help aid	73
% frosh rec. any financial aid	52
% UG rec. any financial aid	47
% UG borrow to pay for school	33
Average cumulative indebtedness	$23,579
% frosh need fully met	100
% ugrads need fully met	100
Average % of frosh need met	100
Average % of ugrad need met	100

COLORADO STATE UNIVERSITY

1062 Campus Delivery, Fort Collins, CO 80523-1062 • Admissions: 970-491-6909 • Fax: 970-491-7799

CAMPUS LIFE

Quality of Life Rating	91
Fire Safety Rating	65
Green Rating	99
Type of school	Public
Environment	City

STUDENTS

Total undergrad enrollment	25,542
% male/female	48/52
% from out of state	28
% frosh live on campus	94
% ugrads live on campus	24
# of fraternities (% ugrad men join)	31 (5)
# of sororities (% ugrad women join)	24 (7)
% African American	2
% Asian	3
% Caucasian	70
% Hispanic	15
% Native American	<1
% Pacific Islander	<1
% Two or more races	5
% Race and/or ethnicity unknown	1
% international	4
# of countries represented	76

SURVEY SAYS . . .
Students are happy
Students environmentally aware
Students love Fort Collins, CO
Great off-campus food
Recreation facilities are great
Campus newspaper is popular

ACADEMICS

Academic Rating	76
% students returning for sophomore year	86
% students graduating within 4 years	46
% students graduating within 6 years	70
Calendar	Semester
Student/faculty ratio	16:1
Profs interesting rating	86
Profs accessible rating	90

Most classes have 20–29 students.
Most lab/discussion sessions have
  20–29 students.

MOST POPULAR MAJORS
Mechanical Engineering; Biology/Biological
Sciences, General; Psychology, General

STUDENTS SAY "..."

Academics

Colorado State University is "an institution that is determined to engage and challenge its students, preparing them for post-graduate life beyond the university." Despite being a large public research university, CSU does a "phenomenal" job of fostering a "community feel." Students guarantee you won't "feel like just a number" here. Many students tell us that they are drawn to Colorado's "amazing" science and engineering programs and "outstanding" business school. And they really appreciate CSU's commitment to "sustainability." Undergrads here also note that the academics are "both challenging and fun." While you're likely to encounter "some good and some bad professors," the "vast majority are very interested in what they are teaching and very passionate." As one pleased student boasts, "My professors are fantastic, they make everything easy to learn, and teach [in] ways that make classes enjoyable even with large lectures." A fellow student concurs adding that "they bring the material to life and maintain a comfortable environment for discussion." Moreover, it's clear that not only do they care about each student's academic growth, professors here care about "their personal well-being" as well. All in all, Colorado State provides students with "the resources to succeed in academics, pursue hobbies and interests, and maintain good mental and physical health."

Life

Colorado State seems to attract a lot of outdoor enthusiasts. And with good reason. There are many "opportunities from volunteer cleanups to hiking and fishing all along the Poudre River." And, of course, "you have the Rocky Mountains at your doorstep." Therefore, "rock climbing" and "biking" are also popular activities. Further, many weekends are dedicated to "skiing and snowboarding." Of course, there's plenty happening on campus as well. A number of students participate in "intramural sports or [attend] rec center classes." Additionally, "there's always...a movie showing or a visiting professor lecture." And football games are well attended. Students can also join one of the "500 clubs and organizations at CSU." A handful of undergrads are active in Greek life too. Fraternities and sororities do tend to "throw parties on the weekend"; however, these typically "happen off campus." Students also love exploring downtown Fort Collins. After all, the "restaurants are amazing." Moreover, "there is always a buzz around the square, and often times a local band will be playing." And undergrads that are of age enjoy exploring and partaking in the city's "amazing craft beer culture." Finally, when CSU students are looking to get away, they can easily "travel to Denver or Boulder" for some fun!

Student Body

Colorado State students frequently describe their peers as "down to earth and energetic." They're also "respectful, kind, and full of CSU pride." And although undergrads here might appear "predominantly white" as you stroll through campus, many students assert that it's actually "a pretty diverse place." These undergrads also know how to carve out a good work/life balance. Indeed, "they understand when it is time to sit down and work really hard, but also know when a break from the work is needed." Even better, Colorado State undergrads are "extremely friendly." A pleased student shares, "I am always meeting new people and seeing warm faces." Another undergrad agrees adding, "No one ever hesitates to help out a fellow Ram." They are also highly intellectual and approach learning with "excitement and enthusiasm." Despite being a state school, CSU still manages to have a "good mix of out-of-state students." No matter where they hail from, most undergrads are "liberal and...environmentally focused." Finally, as one thankful student concludes, "It is a great, helpful community that I am so proud to be a part of."

COLORADO STATE UNIVERSITY

Financial Aid: 970-491-6321 • E-Mail: admissions@colostate.edu • Website: www.colostate.edu/

THE PRINCETON REVIEW SAYS

Admissions

Very important factors considered include: rigor of secondary school record, academic GPA. *Important factors considered include:* class rank, application essay, standardized test scores, recommendation(s). *Other factors considered include:* extracurricular activities, talent/ability, character/personal qualities, first generation, alumni/ae relation, geographical residence, volunteer work, work experience. ACT with or without writing accepted. SAT with or without Essay component accepted. High school diploma is required and GED is accepted. *Academic units required:* 4 English, 4 math, 3 science, 2 science labs, 1 foreign language, 3 social studies, 1 history, 2 academic electives. *Academic units recommended:* 4 English, 4 math, 3 science, 2 science labs, 2 foreign language, 3 social studies, 1 history, 2 academic electives.

Financial Aid

Students should submit: FAFSA; Institution's own financial aid form. Priority filing deadline is 3/1. The Princeton Review suggests that all financial aid forms be submitted as soon as possible after October 1. *Need-based scholarships/grants offered:* College/university scholarship or grant aid from institutional funds; Federal Pell; Private scholarships; SEOG; State scholarships/grants. *Loan aid offered:* Direct PLUS loans; Direct Subsidized Stafford Loans; Direct Unsubsidized Stafford Loans. Applicants will be notified of awards on a rolling basis beginning 3/1. Federal Work-Study Program available. Institutional employment available.

The Inside Word

When building their incoming class, Colorado State University seeks out students who will be able to meet the school's high academic standards. To do so, they closely examine the rigor of your high school curriculum. Admissions officers want to see that you've been successful in challenging college prep courses. Additionally, your standardized test scores will also hold weight. The university looks at your extracurricular involvement as well. Finally, the admissions office considers circumstances that might have impacted your course selection or academic performance.

THE SCHOOL SAYS "..."

From the Admissions Office

"As one of the nation's premier research universities, Colorado State offers more than 150 undergraduate programs of study in eight colleges. Students come here from fifty states and eighty-five countries, and they appreciate the quality and breadth of the university's academic offerings. But Colorado State is more than just a place where students can take their scholarship to the highest level. It's also a place where they can gain invaluable experience in the fields of their choice, whether they're immersing themselves in professional internships, studying on the other side of the globe or teaming up with faculty on groundbreaking research projects. In addition to an outstanding experiential learning environment, Colorado State students enjoy a sense of community that's unusual for a large university. They develop meaningful relationships with faculty members who bring out their best work, and they live and learn with diverse peers who value their ideas and expand their perspectives. These types of connections lead to countless opportunities for social networking and professional accomplishments. By the time our students graduate from Colorado State, they have the knowledge, practical experience, and interpersonal skills they need to make a significant contribution to their world.

"Although academic performance is a primary factor in admissions decisions, Colorado State's holistic review process also recognizes personal qualities and experiences that have the potential to enrich the university and the Fort Collins community. To apply, students may submit the Common Application or the Colorado State University application for admission."

SELECTIVITY

Admissions Rating	77
# of applicants	28,319
% of applicants accepted	81
% of acceptees attending	23

FRESHMAN PROFILE

Range SAT EBRW	540–650
Range SAT Math	530–640
Range SAT Composite	1090–1280
Range ACT Composite	23–29
# submitting SAT scores	4,153
% submitting SAT scores	80
# submitting ACT scores	2,228
% submitting ACT scores	43
Average HS GPA	3.7
% graduated top 10% of class	21
% graduated top 25% of class	48
% graduated top 50% of class	83

DEADLINES

Early action	
Deadline	12/1
Notification	1/1
Regular	
Priority	2/1
Deadline	7/1
Notification	Rolling, 9/1
Nonfall registration?	Yes

FINANCIAL FACTS

Financial Aid Rating	82
Annual in-state tuition	$9,426
Annual out-of-state tuition	$28,147
Room and board	$12,430
Required fees	$2,475
Books and supplies	$1,200
Average frosh need-based scholarship	$9,289
Average UG need-based scholarship	$8,892
% needy frosh rec. need-based scholarship or grant aid	73
% needy UG rec. need-based scholarship or grant aid	68
% needy frosh rec. non-need-based scholarship or grant aid	43
% needy UG rec. non-need-based scholarship or grant aid	29
% needy frosh rec. need-based self-help aid	62
% needy UG rec. need-based self-help aid	68
% frosh rec. any financial aid	77.8
% UG rec. any financial aid	72.26
% UG borrow to pay for school	53
Average cumulative indebtedness	$27,142
% frosh need fully met	25
% ugrads need fully met	18
Average % of frosh need met	66
Average % of ugrad need met	65

COLUMBIA UNIVERSITY

212 Hamilton Hall MC 2807, New York, NY 10027 • Admissions: 212-854-2522 • Fax: 212-854-1209

STUDENTS SAY "..."

Academics

Columbia University, the Ivy League's New York City office, has been around for more than 250 years, providing prestige, rigorous academics, a strong alumni network, and a multitude of opportunities to its students. As intimate spaces carved out of the larger university, Columbia College and The Fu Foundation School of Engineering and Applied Science throw a "vast amount of resources" at its students, with benefits that "extend from clubs to study abroad programs [to]...proximity to one of the greatest cities in the world." Columbia is "all about building intelligent [and] confident students who are ready for the workplace," and there are "many opportunities to satiate intellectual curiosity." The school's Core Curriculum ensures students leave with a breadth of knowledge, and "everyone is smart in some way."

Though some students have a bad teacher or two, Columbia professors are "fantastic in both their leadership in their field as well as in their interest in teaching students," and if "students carefully select which classes they will take they can find professors they like." The academics here "are truly great" and students "always know you're being taught by people at the forefront of their fields." Columbia attracts a very specific type of student "who is devoted to receiving a true liberal arts education in a variety of subjects," but those who go here shouldn't expect to have knowledge handed to them on a platter: "It is up to the student to get the most out of a class," says one.

Life

When it comes to free time, there's no question as to where students turn: New York City, where there are "countless things to do for fun." The "clubs downtown are always a late night option as are the Broadway shows and comedy clubs near Times Square"; and "from shopping in Soho to visiting museums to trying out a new restaurant in Midtown, there's literally nothing you can't do here." That's not to say that students don't stay on campus; people often hang out in dorms and sometimes this turns into a social event itself. "I can walk into my floor lounge at any moment for homework help on anything from Chinese to econometrics, and upon doing so I inevitably wind up having a mind-blowing intellectual discussion of some sort," says a student. The "Monday to Thursday grind is usually pretty tough": people go to classes, do homework and readings, and "try to fit in time with friends in between all the chaos." Weekends are more fun, and Columbia has "a great arts initiative which is perfect for getting [tickets] cheaper" as well as a World Leaders Forum where speakers historically have included "presidents and prime ministers from countries far and wide."

Student Body

This collection of "very ambitious" students is "not only extremely intelligent, but also passionate about everything they do." This group is "diverse in every sense of the word," from race to sexuality to age, and everyone has "a high awareness of the connections between academic, personal, and social issues." People "aren't afraid to speak out against what they think is wrong"; activism is "essential to the Columbia experience" and in fact, "it is encouraged by the school itself." This go-getting crowd tries to do it all, "taking on 5 to 6 classes per semester and holding multiple jobs and internships and leadership positions"; as a result, Columbia does have a bit of a "stress culture," due to the fact that "everyone here really wants to succeed." While it "can be competitive for programs," most students find people here "to be more kind than shrewd."

COLUMBIA UNIVERSITY

Financial Aid. 212 854 3711 • E-Mail: ugrad-ask@columbia.edu • Website: www.columbia.edu

THE PRINCETON REVIEW SAYS
Admissions
Very important factors considered include: rigor of secondary school record, class rank, academic GPA, application essay, standardized test scores, recommendation(s), extracurricular activities, character/personal qualities. *Important factors considered include:* talent/ability. *Other factors considered include:* interview, first generation, alumni/ae relation, geographical residence, racial/ethnic status, volunteer work, work experience. ACT with or without writing accepted. SAT with or without Essay component accepted. High school diploma is required and GED is accepted. *Academic units required:* 4 English, 3 math, 3 science, 3 science labs, 3 foreign language, 3 history, 3 academic electives. *Academic units recommended:* 4 English, 4 math, 4 science, 4 science labs, 4 foreign language, 4 history, 4 academic electives.

Financial Aid
Students should submit: CSS/Financial Aid PROFILE; FAFSA; Noncustodial PROFILE. Priority filing deadline is 2/15. The Princeton Review suggests that all financial aid forms be submitted as soon as possible after October 1. *Need-based scholarships/grants offered:* College/university scholarship or grant aid from institutional funds; Federal Pell; Private scholarships; SEOG; State scholarships/grants. *Loan aid offered:* Direct PLUS loans; Direct Subsidized Stafford Loans; Direct Unsubsidized Stafford Loans. Applicants will be notified of awards on or about 4/1. Federal Work-Study Program available. Institutional employment available.

The Inside Word
There's no magic formula or pattern to guide students who are seeking admission to Columbia University. Excellent grades in rigorous classes may not be enough, and many great candidates are rejected each year. Admissions officers take a holistic approach to evaluating applications, and they pay extra attention to personal accomplishments in non-academic activities as they look to build a diverse class that will greatly contribute to the university.

THE SCHOOL SAYS "..."
From the Admissions Office
"Columbia maintains an intimate college campus within one of the world's most vibrant cities. After a day exploring New York City you come home to a traditional college campus within an intimate neighborhood. Nobel Prize–winning professors will challenge you in class discussions and meet one-on-one afterward. The Core Curriculum attracts intensely free-minded scholars, and connects all undergraduates. Science and engineering students pursue cutting-edge research in world-class laboratories with faculty members at the forefront of scientific discovery. Classroom discussions are only the beginning of your education. Ideas spill out from the classrooms, electrifying the campus and Morningside Heights. Friendships formed in the residence halls solidify during a game of Frisbee on the South Lawn or over bagels on the steps of Low Library. From your first day on campus, you will be part of our diverse community.

"Columbia offers extensive need-based financial aid and meets the full need of every student admitted as a first-year with grants instead of loans. Parents with calculated incomes below $60,000 are not expected to contribute any income or assets to the cost of attendance, and families with calculated incomes between $60,000 and $100,000 have a significantly reduced contribution. Parents earning over $100,000 can still qualify for significant financial aid. To support students pursuing study abroad, research, internships and community service opportunities, Columbia offers the opportunity to apply for additional funding. A commitment to diversity—of every kind—is a long-standing Columbia hallmark. We believe cost should not be a barrier to pursuing your educational dreams."

SELECTIVITY
Admissions Rating	99
# of applicants	42,569
% of applicants accepted	5
% of acceptees attending	62
# of early decision applicants	4,461
% accepted early decision	16

FRESHMAN PROFILE
Range SAT EBRW	710–770
Range SAT Math	740–800
Range ACT Composite	33–35
# submitting SAT scores	913
% submitting SAT scores	66
# submitting ACT scores	630
% submitting ACT scores	45
% graduated top 10% of class	96
% graduated top 25% of class	99
% graduated top 50% of class	100

DEADLINES
Early decision	
Deadline	11/1
Notification	12/15
Regular	
Deadline	1/1
Notification	4/1
Nonfall registration?	No

FINANCIAL FACTS
Financial Aid Rating	97
Annual tuition	$58,920
Room and board	$14,490
Required fees	$3,510
Books and supplies	$1,294
Average frosh need-based scholarship	$61,365
Average UG need-based scholarship	$59,239
% needy frosh rec. need-based scholarship or grant aid	99
% needy UG rec. need-based scholarship or grant aid	99
% needy frosh rec. non-need-based scholarship or grant aid	7
% needy UG rec. non-need-based scholarship or grant aid	5
% needy frosh rec. need-based self-help aid	72
% needy UG rec. need-based self-help aid	78
% frosh rec. any financial aid	53
% UG rec. any financial aid	50
% UG borrow to pay for school	21
Average cumulative indebtedness	$27,595
% frosh need fully met	98
% ugrads need fully met	95
Average % of frosh need met	100
Average % of ugrad need met	100

THE BEST 386 COLLEGES ■ 191

CONNECTICUT COLLEGE

270 Mohegan Avenue, New London, CT 06320 • Admissions: 860-439-2200 • Fax: 860-439-4301

CAMPUS LIFE

Quality of Life Rating	85
Fire Safety Rating	62
Green Rating	91
Type of school	Private
Environment	Town

STUDENTS

Total undergrad enrollment	1,798
% male/female	38/62
% from out of state	81
% frosh from public high school	50
% frosh live on campus	100
% ugrads live on campus	99
# of fraternities	0
# of sororities	0
% African American	4
% Asian	5
% Caucasian	70
% Hispanic	9
% Native American	<1
% Pacific Islander	<1
% Two or more races	4
% Race and/or ethnicity unknown	2
% international	7
# of countries represented	42

SURVEY SAYS . . .

Internships are widely available
Great financial aid
No one cheats
Students environmentally aware
Active student government

ACADEMICS

Academic Rating	87
% students returning for sophomore year	91
% students graduating within 4 years	80
% students graduating within 6 years	85
Calendar	Semester
Student/faculty ratio	9:1
Profs interesting rating	89
Profs accessible rating	90

Most classes have 10–19 students.
Most lab/discussion sessions have 10–19 students.

MOST POPULAR MAJORS

Psychology, General; English Language and Literature, General; Economics, General

STUDENTS SAY "..."

Academics

Located in eastern Connecticut, the picturesque Connecticut College is a classic private New England liberal arts school that shows a "great commitment to being sustainable, to promoting community service, and to learning." The college provides "great academic, extracurricular, and athletic opportunities to all students," and the "beloved" honor code makes for "a close-knit, supportive community." A strong focus on interdisciplinary education, small classes, and self-scheduled exams gives students the autonomy to truly tailor their learning around their interests. The academics are "rigorous but continuously relevant, interesting, and enlightening." Most classes are discussion-based, which "allows students to express their own opinions while hearing from their fellow students and professors." Though there are a few bad apples, most professors are always accessible ("especially outside of their office hours") and are "constantly bringing learning outside of the classroom, whether it be within a residence hall, a restaurant, museum, or gallery downtown, or within their own homes." "All of my professors are incredibly engaging and obviously here to excite students about their studies," says a student. Other high points include the "approachability of the staff," excellent career office and internship opportunities, and strong residential programs and academic centers that "help students with a myriad of topics." Connecticut College assures that no student will go through school with "your typical major/minor pairing"; with certificate programs, tons of research opportunities, independent studies and more, every student "has a completely unique and entirely interdisciplinary experience here."

Life

"Life as a student is all about balancing your school work with your extracurricular activities and choosing which events you want to attend," says one. The residential programs lay a great groundwork for student life, and much of the fun on campus "is through social events through the dorms." It helps that "everyone knows one another—between offices, custodial staff, campus safety, and students." There are a wide range of activities to get involved with (everything from athletics, to arts, to activism, to community service, etc.), as well as "numerous faculty-led discussions and speakers every week." Most activities that take place on campus make it "lively and interesting." The campus as a whole is "very friendly, and you are always surrounded by familiar faces," though the relationship with the town of New London is "something that can always be improved upon." For fun, students "attend each other's events, attend social functions in the student center, grab some coffee at one of our coffee shops, and generally hang out with each other." The library is "a very social place during the week," and though students work very hard, they "know how to have a good time on the weekends"—every weekend there is a variety of on-campus social events (concerts, dances, spoken-word performances) put on by the Student Activities Council. Day trips to Boston and New York are also common.

Student Body

Many students at Conn are generally "smart, probably upper-class, well-dressed, and white," though the school "embraces diversity." The common theme among all Conn students is "their active involvement both on campus and off and their desire to be challenged in all aspects of their educations." Students fit in by "showing an interest in their studies, but also carrying on an active social life." It is fairly easy to find one's niche within the community, and "while it might take a semester to become adjusted, there are many groups, teams, and other resources...that help freshmen find a place here."

Financial Aid: 860-439-2058 • E-Mail: admission@conncoll.edu • Website: www.conncoll.edu

THE PRINCETON REVIEW SAYS

Admissions

Very important factors considered include: rigor of secondary school record, class rank, academic GPA, character/personal qualities. *Important factors considered include:* application essay, recommendation(s), interview, extracurricular activities, talent/ability. *Other factors considered include:* standardized test scores, first generation, alumni/ae relation, geographical residence, state residency, religious affiliation/commitment, level of applicant's interest. ACT with or without writing accepted. SAT with or without Essay component accepted. High school diploma is required and GED is accepted.

Financial Aid

Students should submit: CSS/Financial Aid PROFILE; FAFSA; Noncustodial PROFILE. Priority filing deadline is 1/15. The Princeton Review suggests that all financial aid forms be submitted as soon as possible after October 1. *Need-based scholarships/grants offered:* College/university scholarship or grant aid from institutional funds; Federal Pell; SEOG; State scholarships/grants. *Loan aid offered:* Direct PLUS loans; Direct Subsidized Stafford Loans; Direct Unsubsidized Stafford Loans. Applicants will be notified of awards on or about 4/1. Federal Work-Study Program available. Institutional employment available.

The Inside Word

Connecticut College is the archetypal selective New England college, and admissions officers are judicious in their decisions. Competitive applicants will have pursued a demanding course load in high school. Admissions officers look for students who are curious and who thrive in challenging academic environments. Since Connecticut College has a close-knit community, personal qualities are also closely evaluated, and interviews are important.

THE SCHOOL SAYS "..."

From the Admissions Office

"Connecticut College has all the hallmarks of the best liberal arts colleges: small classes; stellar teaching; close faculty-student relationships; more than 40 majors in the arts, sciences, humanities and social sciences; and plentiful co-curricular activities.

"A rigorous new curriculum, called Connections, gives students a chance to tailor their academic experiences around a problem they want to solve. It puts them in classes and conversations with people who are asking big questions similar to their own, and teaches them to look at the issues from many different angles. It demands that they understand what's going on in the world right outside their doors and across the globe. And it teaches them to grapple with and synthesize complex ideas in today's increasingly interconnected world.

"What sets this college apart is its active, outward-focused vision of 'liberal arts in action.' Interdisciplinary classes, programs, centers and majors foster critical think-ing and problem solving. Students connect theory to the real world via community service, community learning, student-faculty research, international experiences and campus leadership. More than half of students study away and more than 70 percent do a college-funded summer internship in the United States or abroad.

"Liberal arts in action also means living under a ninety-three-year-old Honor Code, with self-scheduled exams, a student-run Honor Council, and a student voice in campus decision making. The campus community is close and supportive; there is no Greek life. About 30 percent of students are varsity athletes competing in the New England Small College Athletic Conference (NCAA Division III)."

SELECTIVITY

Admissions Rating	93
# of applicants	6,433
% of applicants accepted	38
% of acceptees attending	21
# offered a place on the wait list	1,385
% accepting a place on wait list	41
% admitted from wait list	4
# of early decision applicants	362
% accepted early decision	62

FRESHMAN PROFILE

Range SAT EBRW	650–710
Range SAT Math	640–720
Range ACT Composite	30–32
# submitting SAT scores	147
% submitting SAT scores	29
# submitting ACT scores	99
% submitting ACT scores	19
% graduated top 10% of class	49
% graduated top 25% of class	80
% graduated top 50% of class	98

DEADLINES

Early decision	
Deadline	11/15
Notification	12/15
Other ED Deadline	1/1
Other ED Notification	2/15
Regular	
Deadline	1/1
Notification	3/31
Nonfall registration?	Yes

FINANCIAL FACTS

Financial Aid Rating	96
Annual tuition	$56,540
Room and board	$15,700
Required fees	$350
Books and supplies	$1,000
Average frosh need-based scholarship	$42,713
Average UG need-based scholarship	$41,921
% needy frosh rec. need-based scholarship or grant aid	97
% needy UG rec. need-based scholarship or grant aid	95
% needy frosh rec. non-need-based scholarship or grant aid	13
% needy UG rec. non-need-based scholarship or grant aid	9
% needy frosh rec. need-based self-help aid	82
% needy UG rec. need-based self-help aid	87
% frosh rec. any financial aid	93
% UG borrow to pay for school	45
Average cumulative indebtedness	$33,608
% frosh need fully met	100
% ugrads need fully met	100
Average % of frosh need met	100
Average % of ugrad need met	100

THE COOPER UNION FOR THE ADVANCEMENT OF SCIENCE AND ART

30 Cooper Square, 3rd Floor, New York, NY 10003 • Admissions: 212-353-4120 • Fax: 212-353-4342

STUDENTS SAY "..."

Academics

A truly unique New York City institution, Cooper Union provides grants covering more than half tuition to all students (as well as additional need-based aid). Degree programs focus in art, architecture, or engineering. Academics are "very rigorous, although consistent and achievable with the resources provided," and students are very driven in achieving their coursework, "especially with major projects that offer them a great deal of academic freedom to create their own content." Students are pushed "to achieve the most in a short amount of time" and are well aware of the value they are getting relative to "cost of tuition and good job placement after graduating."

Professors are "generally very knowledgeable in their subject area" and "you're not that likely to have the same professor over and over again," making for a diverse learning experience. The "very focused" engineering program "sets you up to be a functioning member of the engineering community and workforce": "Even as a sophomore I have had the opportunity to take (and understand) graduate level material," says one student. The art school "constructs an art curriculum around the individual practice," and the "caliber of art teachers is unbelievable," with professors that "have exhibited at the MOMA and Guggenheim, just to name a few." Students from all major programs mix in the required humanities courses. Though the school's 2009 addition of a new academic building (housing the engineering and art programs, and bringing the total up to two) increased visibility, the building is "chronically short on space due to its atrium," and the school "could use more classrooms to work with." The academic prestige of the school attracts a high standard all around, and art, architects, and engineers come together "to create a rich environment for scholarly thinking, problem solving, learning, and debate."

Life

Aside from classes, students have "ample opportunity to explore New York City" due to "the abundance of safe public transit and places of interest." The campus is in the heart of the East Village and accessible by two subway lines, so students "will often visit local off-campus businesses such as restaurants, stores, and gyms." The "limited on-campus food service," combined with the availability of stovetops in the residence hall, "encourages students to cook their own food when time permits." Meeting areas within the campus are utilized "for both group study and recreational uses," and the small campus (just two buildings) means students are "always near each other ready to chat and grab a coffee for a little break." The school "requires a lot of time to study in order to pass the courses" and "the life is packed"; many take to a bar on weekends or partake in "healthier activities like the gym; sports or video games (not as healthy) are also stress management mechanisms."

Student Body

Students at the Cooper Union are "generally stressed and hardworking, but high-spirited." Most are "socially and politically left"; "almost everyone is pretty friendly," and finds their niche within the "small but complex community." These "highly intelligent...and helpful" students are there to succeed, and "school work is valued over social interaction." Many students have part-time jobs, and "the level students are at and their work ethic makes you feel like the people here are destined for success." This "strange and ambitious" group "excels in their field doing extra activities that they don't need to because of the curiosity and fun." "Everyone has their own thing that makes them tick," says a student.

THE COOPER UNION FOR THE ADVANCEMENT OF SCIENCE AND ART

Financial Aid: 212-353-4113 • E-Mail: admissions@cooper.edu • Website: www.cooper.edu

THE PRINCETON REVIEW SAYS

Admissions

Very important factors considered include: academic GPA, talent/ability. *Important factors considered include:* rigor of secondary school record, application essay, recommendation(s), interview, character/personal qualities. *Other factors considered include:* class rank, extracurricular activities, volunteer work, work experience, level of applicant's interest. High school diploma is required and GED is accepted. *Academic units required:* 4 English, 1 math, 1 science, 1 social studies, 1 history, 8 academic electives. *Academic units recommended:* 4 English, 4 math, 4 science, 3 science labs, 2 foreign language, 4 social studies.

Financial Aid

Students should submit: FAFSA. Priority filing deadline is 3/1. The Princeton Review suggests that all financial aid forms be submitted as soon as possible after October 1. *Need-based scholarships/grants offered:* College/university scholarship or grant aid from institutional funds; Federal Pell; Private scholarships; SEOG; State scholarships/grants. *Loan aid offered:* Direct PLUS loans; Direct Subsidized Stafford Loans; Direct Unsubsidized Stafford Loans. Applicants will be notified of awards on a rolling basis beginning 12/20. Federal Work-Study Program available. Institutional employment available.

The Inside Word

The admission rate to Cooper Union is extremely competitive. All Cooper admits must be academically accomplished and top of their high school class. Depending on whether you plan to pursue engineering, art, or architecture, admissions requirements and application deadlines vary. Note that the Cooper Union undergraduate admission process will be test optional. This pilot program will be in effect for the Fall 2021 and 2022 entering classes.

THE SCHOOL SAYS "..."

From the Admissions Office

"Each of Cooper Union's three schools—architecture, art and engineering—adheres strongly to preparation for its profession and is committed to a problem-solving philosophy of education in a small, scholarship environment. A rigorous curriculum and group projects reinforce this unique atmosphere in higher education and contribute to a strong sense of community and identity in each school. With McSorley's Ale House and the Public Theatre nearby, Cooper Union remains at the heart of the city's tradition of free speech, enlightenment, and entertainment. Cooper's Great Hall has hosted national leaders, from Abraham Lincoln to Booker T. Washington, from Mark Twain to Samuel Gompers, from Susan B. Anthony to Betty Friedan, and more recently, President Bill Clinton and President Barack Obama. In fall of 2009, we opened the doors of our new academic building. Designed by Pritzker Prize–winning architect, Thom Mayne, the new building was designed to enhance and encourage more interaction between students in all three schools. We're seeking students who have a passion to study our professional programs. Cooper Union students are independent thinkers, following the beat of their own drum. Many of our graduates become world-class leaders in the disciplines of architecture, fine arts, design, and engineering.

"For art and architecture applicants, high school grades are considered after the home test and portfolio work. For engineering applicants, high school grades and the supplemental questions are the most important factors considered in admissions decisions."

SELECTIVITY

Admissions Rating	97
# of applicants	2,326
% of applicants accepted	16
% of acceptees attending	50
# offered a place on the wait list	177
% accepting a place on wait list	97
% admitted from wait list	15
# of early decision applicants	215
% accepted early decision	26

FRESHMAN PROFILE

Range SAT EBRW	650–740
Range SAT Math	655–790
Range SAT Composite	1340–1510
Range ACT Composite	30–35
# submitting SAT scores	151
% submitting SAT scores	81
# submitting ACT scores	49
% submitting ACT scores	26
Average HS GPA	3.8

DEADLINES

Early decision	
Deadline	12/2
Notification	2/1
Regular	
Deadline	1/6
Notification	4/1
Nonfall registration?	No

APPLICANTS ALSO LOOK AT AND OFTEN PREFER

Massachusetts Institute of Technology; Cornell University; New York University; University of California—Berkeley; California Institute of Technology; University of Pennsylvania; Princeton University; Carnegie Mellon University; Johns Hopkins University

AND SOMETIMES PREFER

Rensselaer Polytechnic Institute; Maryland Institute College of Art; Georgia Institute of Technology; Columbia University

AND RARELY PREFER

State University of New York—Stony Brook University; University at Albany—SUNY; Pratt Institute; Rhode Island School of Design

FINANCIAL FACTS

Financial Aid Rating	92
Annual tuition	$44,550
Required fees	$2,270
Books and supplies	$1,800
Average frosh need-based scholarship	$41,121
Average UG need-based scholarship	$39,165
% needy frosh rec. need-based scholarship or grant aid	100
% needy UG rec. need-based scholarship or grant aid	100
% needy frosh rec. non-need-based scholarship or grant aid	100
% needy UG rec. non-need-based scholarship or grant aid	100
% needy frosh rec. need-based self-help aid	23
% needy UG rec. need-based self-help aid	25
% frosh rec. any financial aid	100
% UG rec. any financial aid	100
% UG borrow to pay for school	53
Average cumulative indebtedness	$10,742
% frosh need fully met	64
% ugrads need fully met	52
Average % of frosh need met	99
Average % of ugrad need met	94

CORNELL COLLEGE

600 First Street South West, Mount Vernon, IA 52314-1098 • Admissions: 319-895-4215 • Fax: 319-895-4471

CAMPUS LIFE

Quality of Life Rating	85
Fire Safety Rating	83
Green Rating	60*
Type of school	Private
Affiliation	Methodist
Environment	Rural

STUDENTS

Total undergrad enrollment	1,017
% male/female	53/47
% from out of state	67
% frosh from public high school	85
% frosh live on campus	97
% ugrads live on campus	83
# of fraternities (% ugrad men join)	8 (24)
# of sororities (% ugrad women join)	7 (36)
% African American	6
% Asian	3
% Caucasian	71
% Hispanic	7
% Native American	1
% Pacific Islander	<1
% Two or more races	2
% Race and/or ethnicity unknown	3
% international	7
# of countries represented	19

SURVEY SAYS . . .

Class discussions encouraged
Easy to get around campus

ACADEMICS

Academic Rating	84
% students graduating within 4 years	69
% students graduating within 6 years	75
Calendar	Semester
Student/faculty ratio	12:1
Profs interesting rating	88
Profs accessible rating	94
Most classes have 10–19 students.	

MOST POPULAR MAJORS

Psychology, General; Economics, General

STUDENTS SAY "..."

Academics

Cornell College, a small liberal arts school in Iowa, employs a unique one-course-at-a-time program, allowing students to focus on just one course (or "block") each month, providing an "intense, thorough, and complete immersion." Though students agree that this "series of experiences" "doesn't give you any time to think about anything but the class you're in right then," it allows for personalized curricula design, and areas like the humanities "work perfectly with the block plan." Students also "always know when to find people," which makes it easy to get together. Some classes may not be the most challenging, but "upper-level courses are very engaging and fulfilling." "You could have hours and hours of homework one block and practically none the next," says a student. The block plan makes it very easy to gain off-campus field experience or do international study, and it's "easier to try off-campus opportunities." Administration is generally "excellent at taking a personal interest in each student," though some note, "There is not much transparency at the administrative level," which can be "out of touch" at times. On the classroom side, professors "know how to motivate and encourage their students," and though "you may get a bad apple maybe once a year," they're "not only knowledgeable but dedicated." "The personal attention you can receive from any given professor, if you seek them out, is especially rewarding," says a student. All in all, students love the block structure and the sense of community it creates, as "no matter what it is you may want to do, you can find someone to do it with you." One student claims he "cannot imagine learning any other way."

Life

Since Cornell is very campus-focused, the school makes sure there's a large variety of campus organizations and "many events going on almost every weekend." Though there's definitely a "small-town quiet," Cedar Rapids and Iowa City are both only a twenty-minute drive away, and "ice climbing, rock-climbing, paddling, and hiking" are popular outdoor pastimes. It's also "fairly easy to start up a new club or group." In addition, the school provides fall, winter, and spring breaks as well as "block breaks," which last four and a half days and give students the opportunity to travel, go skiing or camping, and so on. The cold weather can cause problems here, in both a locked-in feel and the possibility for accidents, and students are encouraged to "bring snow boots!" Many here tend to have a love-hate relationship with sports; while athletics are a huge boon, "the athletes and the non-athletes are seldom friends." Much like the curriculum, lunchtimes are pretty unique, and students all eat in a common cafeteria, naturally falling into a somewhat "high school" habit of eating at the same tables every day. Most people stay on campus for entertainment and socializing, "creating a cohesive community." Parties do take place on weekends, and "drinking is popular on campus but never forced," but in general, "people are more interested in just having a good conversation with their peers."

Student Body

There's "a great diversity of interests" in people who attend Cornell, and the "super busy" students have a hard time defining a more common characteristic than the fact that almost all are driven and involved. Some division into typical groups does occur—"the cafeteria design and Greek life are very conducive to this problem"—but "even group to group there is always mingling because you never know who will be in your next class." Since the classes are so small and "you see the same people four hours a day for three and a half weeks," people are generally accepting, and "you have to be really, really strange here to stick out." As one freshman says, "The only intolerance I've seen is toward the consistently indolent."

Financial Aid: 319-895-4216 • E-Mail: admission@cornellcollege.edu • Website: www.cornellcollege.edu

THE PRINCETON REVIEW SAYS

Admissions

Very important factors considered include: academic GPA. *Important factors considered include:* application essay, standardized test scores. *Other factors considered include:* rigor of secondary school record, class rank, recommendation(s), interview, extracurricular activities, character/personal qualities, first generation, alumni/ae relation, geographical residence, state residency, racial/ethnic status, volunteer work, work experience, level of applicant's interest. ACT with or without writing accepted. High school diploma is required and GED is accepted. *Academic units recommended:* 4 English, 3 math, 3 science, 1 science lab, 2 foreign language, 3 social studies.

Financial Aid

Students should submit: FAFSA. Priority filing deadline is 3/1. The Princeton Review suggests that all financial aid forms be submitted as soon as possible after October 1. *Need-based scholarships/grants offered:* College/university scholarship or grant aid from institutional funds; Federal Pell; SEOG; State scholarships/grants. *Loan aid offered:* Direct PLUS loans; Direct Subsidized Stafford Loans; Direct Unsubsidized Stafford Loans. Applicants will be notified of awards on a rolling basis beginning 1/1. Federal Work-Study Program available. Institutional employment available.

The Inside Word

Given Cornell's relatively unique approach to study, it's no surprise that the admissions committee here focuses attention on both academic and personal strengths. Cornell's small, highly self-selected applicant pool is chock-full of students with solid self-awareness, motivation, and discipline.

THE SCHOOL SAYS "..."

From the Admissions Office

"Cornell College, a selective liberal arts college in Mount Vernon, Iowa, is one of the colleges featured in *Colleges That Change Lives*. Characterized by the life-changing academic immersion of its One Course At A Time curriculum, this distinctive approach allows students to focus on a single academic subject per eighteen-day block. It lays the foundation for a student's entire Cornell education through transformative intellectual partnerships and close-knit learning communities that bring out the best in our ambitious students. The One Course curriculum mirrors the pace of most working environments where employees are expected to handle tight deadlines and high expectations on every project, every day. Since there is never more than one course to focus on, faculty can take entire classes on field trips for a day or an entire block. Cornell's residential campus attracts a student body from 45 states and 16 foreign countries. Together, they experience a vast array of off-campus opportunities designed to take them into the world to fulfill their academic and personal goals, as well as a lineup of speakers and entertainment options that brings the world to them. Cornell College is frequently cited as a 'Best Buy.' Ninety-three percent of Cornell graduates complete their degrees in four years, and 55 percent go on to complete an advanced degree."

SELECTIVITY

Admissions Rating	86
# of applicants	3,118
% of applicants accepted	62
% of acceptees attending	14

FRESHMAN PROFILE

Range SAT EBRW	540–675
Range SAT Math	560–670
Range ACT Composite	23–29
# submitting SAT scores	79
% submitting SAT scores	35
# submitting ACT scores	154
% submitting ACT scores	68
Average HS GPA	3.5
% graduated top 10% of class	17
% graduated top 25% of class	47
% graduated top 50% of class	83

DEADLINES

Early action	
Deadline	11/1
Notification	Rolling
Regular	
Deadline	Rolling
Notification	Rolling
Nonfall registration?	No

FINANCIAL FACTS

Financial Aid Rating	82
Annual tuition	$45,288
Room and board	$10,150
Required fees	$626
Books and supplies	$1,200
Average frosh need-based scholarship	$32,207
Average UG need-based scholarship	$30,116
% needy frosh rec. need-based scholarship or grant aid	100
% needy UG rec. need-based scholarship or grant aid	100
% needy frosh rec. non-need-based scholarship or grant aid	25
% needy UG rec. non-need-based scholarship or grant aid	20
% needy frosh rec. need-based self-help aid	68
% needy UG rec. need-based self-help aid	75
% frosh rec. any financial aid	100
% UG rec. any financial aid	99
% UG borrow to pay for school	79
Average cumulative indebtedness	$38,215
% frosh need fully met	26
% ugrads need fully met	24
Average % of frosh need met	84
Average % of ugrad need met	82

CORNELL UNIVERSITY

410 Thurston Avenue, Ithaca, NY 14850 • Admissions: 607-255-5241 • Fax: 607-255-0659

CAMPUS LIFE

Quality of Life Rating	91
Fire Safety Rating	96
Green Rating	99
Type of school	Private
Environment	Town

STUDENTS

Total undergrad enrollment	14,976
% male/female	46/54
# of fraternities (% ugrad men join)	37 (26)
# of sororities (% ugrad women join)	19 (24)
% African American	7
% Asian	20
% Caucasian	36
% Hispanic	14
% Native American	<1
% Pacific Islander	<1
% Two or more races	5
% Race and/or ethnicity unknown	8
% international	10
# of countries represented	90

SURVEY SAYS . . .

Students always studying
Students are happy
Classroom facilities are great
Lab facilities are great
Great library
Career services are great
Internships are widely available
Great financial aid
Students environmentally aware
Great food on campus
Great off-campus food
Lots of beer drinking
Campus newspaper is popular
Alumni active on campus

ACADEMICS

Academic Rating	92
% students returning for sophomore year	97
% students graduating within 4 years	87
% students graduating within 6 years	95
Calendar	Semester
Student/faculty ratio	9:1
Profs interesting rating	89
Profs accessible rating	92

Most classes have 10–19 students.
Most lab/discussion sessions have
10–19 students.

MOST POPULAR MAJORS

Biology/Biological Sciences, General

STUDENTS SAY "..."

Academics

The westernmost of the Ivies, Cornell University provides its students with a prestigious education, paired with "an unwavering commitment to leave a positive impact on the world." The school is "more than a bunch of books and exams—it's an experience that challenges students to break free from their comfort zones." Seven different undergraduate colleges (including the Cornell SC Johnson College of Business) "really make it feel small and specialized," and provide "top notch faculty." The university is "a place where any person can find instruction in any study (and it won't feel like work)," as it allows its students to explore any kind of interest they may have (ranging from Punk Rock as a literary genre to particle physics) while "also offering an incredible amount of depth within each department." There are endless opportunities to "pursue other topics, enhance your knowledge of things that you're already interested in, and try completely random things that you'd never even heard of before." Professors are "experts in their field, almost always conducting their own research, and are enthusiastic about passing their knowledge on to their students."

"[Since] being in Ithaca, you're kind of in the middle of nowhere," there are plenty of reasons to focus on your studies, but "Cornell as an administration keeps the faculty, research, and access to the most recent information so up-to-date that this campus is as connected as any place in the world." Between balancing those amazing resources and the community feel, the Cornell bigwigs get a lot of applause, as they have "proven time and time again that they care, both on an individual and system-wide level." Great internships, a strong alumni network, and "boundless opportunities after graduation" round out the "definition of amazing" that is Cornell University. "I was intimidated to go here, but now I will say that I cannot imagine going anywhere else," says a junior.

Life

As they say, "Ithaca is gorges," so hiking and outdoor activities are big pastimes. The "absolutely gorgeous campus" in the Finger Lakes region allows students to "truly, purely enjoy their time here" by "experiencing the natural beauties of Upstate New York, along with the eccentricity of surrounding town." "I think it sums up the Cornell experience to say that at dinner a few nights ago, our conversation included the presidential debate, Macbeth, sex, cantaloupes, sex WITH cantaloupes, drone strikes in Pakistan, the iPhones, and invasive parasitic species in Southeast Asia," says a freshman. The school's infrastructure is "intense"—"we have our own dairy so that we can make our own milk, for goodness sake"—and "there's just so much going on at every moment [that] the hard part is choosing what it is you want to do." Many admit that various aspects of Cornell life can cause stress—the upperclass housing lottery, course enrollment system, workload, and difficulty studying abroad all get singled out—but students are able to discern when to kick back and enjoy themselves. Fun can range anywhere from "an awesome party in Collegetown to a movie night in the dorm while ordering insomnia cookies," but "it's definitely acceptable to turn down weekend plans because you have too much work to do."

Student Body

With so many different colleges within Cornell, there is "a plethora of diverse students" here, but the underlying commonality between all students is "ambition and ability." "From farm kids and pre-med students to engineers and hoteltes, Cornell is home to all sorts of students," says one. "You'll find yourself with a roommate who was on Team USA, a friend who was a firefighter, and a classmate who's backpacked around the world." The integration of people with eclectic interests "[inspires] others to become active students," which is easily enough done at a university with hundreds upon hundreds of student organizations. "Everyone's smart and that's just accepted," but "a competitive environment isn't created." Cornellians are "very committed to academics but always know how to put books aside and relax." Most do research and volunteer work, and many "are involved in some form of Greek life."

CORNELL UNIVERSITY

Financial Aid: 607-255-5145 • E-Mail: admissions@cornell.edu • Website: www.cornell.edu

THE PRINCETON REVIEW SAYS

Admissions

Very important factors considered include: rigor of secondary school record, academic GPA, application essay, standardized test scores, recommendation(s), extracurricular activities, talent/ability, character/personal qualities. *Important factors considered include:* class rank. *Other factors considered include:* interview, first generation, alumni/ae relation, geographical residence, state residency, racial/ethnic status, volunteer work, work experience. ACT with or without writing accepted. SAT with or without Essay component accepted. High school diploma or equivalent is not required.

Financial Aid

Students should submit: CSS/Financial Aid PROFILE; FAFSA; Noncustodial PROFILE. The Princeton Review suggests that all financial aid forms be submitted as soon as possible after October 1. *Need-based scholarships/grants offered:* College/university scholarship or grant aid from institutional funds; Federal Pell; Private scholarships; SEOG; State scholarships/grants. *Loan aid offered:* Direct PLUS loans; Direct Subsidized Stafford Loans; Direct Unsubsidized Stafford Loans. Applicants will be notified of awards on or about 4/1. Federal Work-Study Program available. Institutional employment available.

The Inside Word

Gaining admission to Cornell is a tough coup regardless of your intended field of study, but some of the university's seven colleges are more competitive than others. If you're thinking of trying to "backdoor" your way into one of the most competitive schools—by gaining admission to a less competitive one, then transferring after one year—be aware that you will have to resubmit the entire application and provide a statement outlining your academic plans. It's not impossible to accomplish, but Cornell works hard to discourage this sort of maneuvering.

THE SCHOOL SAYS "..."

From the Admissions Office

"Cornell University, an Ivy League school and land-grant university located in the scenic Finger Lakes region of central New York, provides an outstanding education to students in seven small to midsize undergraduate colleges: Agriculture and Life Sciences; Architecture, Art, and Planning; Arts and Sciences; Engineering; Cornell SC Johnson College of Business; Human Ecology; and Industrial and Labor Relations. Cornellians come from all fifty states and more than 120 countries, and they pursue their academic goals in more than 100 departments. The College of Arts and Sciences, one of the smallest liberal arts schools in the Ivy League, offers more than forty majors, most of which rank near the top nationwide. Applied programs in the other six colleges also rank among the best in the world. Other special features of the university include a world-renowned faculty; over 4,000 courses available to all students; an extensive undergraduate research program; superb research, teaching, and library facilities; a large, diverse study abroad program; and more than 1,000 student organizations and thirty-six varsity sports. Cornell's campus is one of the most beautiful in the country; students pass streams, rocky gorges, and waterfalls on their way to class. First-year students make their home on North Campus, a living-learning community that features a special advising center, faculty-in-residence, a fitness center, and traditional residence halls as well as theme-centered buildings such as Ecology House. Cornell University invites applications from all interested students and uses the Common Application of the Universal College Application with a short required Cornell Supplement. Students applying for admissions will submit scores from the SAT or ACT (with writing). We also require SAT Subject Tests. Subject test requirements are college-specific."

SELECTIVITY
Admissions Rating	99
# of applicants	49,114
% of applicants accepted	11
% of acceptees attending	60
# offered a place on the wait list	4,948
% accepting a place on wait list	68
% admitted from wait list	4
# of early decision applicants	6,158
% accepted early decision	23

FRESHMAN PROFILE
Range SAT EBRW	680–760
Range SAT Math	720–800
Range SAT Composite	1420–1540
Range ACT Composite	32–35
# submitting SAT scores	2,257
% submitting SAT scores	71
# submitting ACT scores	1,298
% submitting ACT scores	41
% graduated top 10% of class	83
% graduated top 25% of class	96
% graduated top 50% of class	99

DEADLINES
Early decision	
Deadline	11/1
Notification	12/15
Regular	
Deadline	1/2
Notification	4/1
Nonfall registration?	Yes

FINANCIAL FACTS
Financial Aid Rating	97
Annual tuition	$56,550
Room and board	$14,816
Required fees	$604
Books and supplies	$970
Average frosh need-based scholarship	$44,767
Average UG need-based scholarship	$44,026
% needy frosh rec. need-based scholarship or grant aid	97
% needy UG rec. need-based scholarship or grant aid	96
% needy frosh rec. non-need-based scholarship or grant aid	0
% needy UG rec. non-need-based scholarship or grant aid	0
% needy frosh rec. need-based self-help aid	86
% needy UG rec. need-based self-help aid	91
% frosh rec. any financial aid	47
% UG rec. any financial aid	47
% UG borrow to pay for school	40
Average cumulative indebtedness	$27,094
% frosh need fully met	100
% ugrads need fully met	100
Average % of frosh need met	100
Average % of ugrad need met	100

CREIGHTON UNIVERSITY

2500 California Plaza, Omaha, NE 68178 • Admissions: 402-280-2703 • Fax: 402-280-2685

STUDENTS SAY "..."

Academics

Omaha's Creighton University is a Jesuit institution that prides itself on "shaping the whole person," which means that students find themselves "extremely involved in academic and extracurricular activities." As for the core class structure, all of its more than four thousand undergraduates must fulfill a set curriculum, with a variety of course options available for all requirements (other than a required one-hour oral communication course). By all accounts, this "sets you up very well for success," with students adding that the process "nearly holds your hand into your first job" and "prepares you for the next step, whether that is medical school, law school, or going out to work in the real world." Creighton "works so hard to make sure their students are successful learners and thinkers" by offering programs like EDGE, an all-inclusive tutoring, academic coaching, and academic counseling service that doubles as "a great platform for advisors to gear students to explore certain classes while remaining on track." All of this helps in "cultivating a safe community where we're encouraged to dive into what we believe, figure out what that is exactly, and serve others."

Creighton boasts an eleven-to-one student-faculty ratio, which leads to "really awesome relationships with faculty and many opportunities for things like undergraduate research." Professors go above and beyond in all ways, from doing their best "not to make lectures dry and boring" to being super receptive to students. Courses offered "are challenging to say the least," but because teachers are "willing to work on your terms and help at all hours of the day and night," both in and out of the classroom, it's a "very rewarding and manageable" process. Dialogue is also crucial: teachers "love when you ask questions" and many utilize a flipped classroom, where peers teach the rest of the class, which "provides a broken-down and simplified way of explaining difficult topics to provide clarification and insight." Adding to the variety and support offered, there are plenty of "field trips that [are] very interesting and insightful" and opportunities for "many upperclassmen [to] participate in research or internships."

Life

The pace at Creighton tends to be a busy one, and not just because of academic or school-related activities: "A lot of students work." That said, things get a bit more relaxed on weekends, which "consist of sporting events, parties, fraternity events, and the like." Creighton students are "very supportive of one another and go to all the home soccer, basketball, baseball, and volleyball games for both men and women's teams," and "people often take part in sports or group exercise programs on campus." The city setting also means that the "campus is a few blocks away from Old Market and Midtown which are full of activities, shops, and restaurants," and there are "also gorgeous outdoor places to go running/walking near downtown when the weather is nice." Students "are encouraged to form clubs and join organizations," and "the resources available to students are absolutely endless."

Student Body

There's a sense of togetherness at Creighton, to the extent that, because there's an "expectation that you go to class every day and on time . . . if you don't, people will reach out." In short, the community is "very goal-oriented toward their careers," although not in an oppressive sense. If anything, students describe the atmosphere as "fun and light-hearted" and note that "wherever you go you will find a welcoming environment." (This applies across all grades, with students noting that senior students "work hard to make [first-years] feel at home during the first couple weeks at school.") Students are in it together, according to those who list "service and giving back" as a core value, and there's an eagerness described for all activities: "When it comes to getting involved with student organizations and other things on campus, students will jump at the chance to do so."

Financial Aid: 402-280-2731 • E-Mail: admissions@creighton.edu • Website: www.creighton.edu

THE PRINCETON REVIEW SAYS

Admissions

Very important factors considered include: rigor of secondary school record, academic GPA. *Important factors considered include:* application essay, standardized test scores. *Other factors considered include:* class rank, recommendation(s), extracurricular activities, talent/ability, character/personal qualities, first generation, racial/ethnic status, volunteer work, level of applicant's interest. ACT with or without writing accepted. SAT with or without Essay component accepted. High school diploma is required and GED is accepted. *Academic units required:* 4 English, 3 math, 2 science, 1 science lab, 2 foreign language, 2 social studies, 3 academic electives. *Academic units recommended:* 4 English, 4 math, 3 science, 2 science labs, 3 foreign language, 4 social studies, 3 academic electives.

Financial Aid

Students should submit: FAFSA; Institution's own financial aid form. Priority filing deadline is 1/15. The Princeton Review suggests that all financial aid forms be submitted as soon as possible after October 1. *Need-based scholarships/grants offered:* College/university scholarship or grant aid from institutional funds; Federal Pell; Private scholarships; SEOG; State scholarships/grants. *Loan aid offered:* Direct PLUS loans; Direct Subsidized Stafford Loans; Direct Unsubsidized Stafford Loans. Applicants will be notified of awards on a rolling basis beginning 2/15. Federal Work-Study Program available. Institutional employment available.

The Inside Word

Creighton University proudly takes a holistic approach to the admissions game. The school doesn't maintain any strict standardized test score or GPA minimums. However, the committee does scour transcripts for evidence of academic rigor and intellectual curiosity. Applicants who have taken multiple advanced placement, honors, or IB classes will have a leg up; the school also considers superscores for both the SAT and ACT. Moreover, as a Jesuit university, Creighton is partial to students who are committed to making the world a better place. Candidates with a passion for social justice issues will be noted.

THE SCHOOL SAYS "..."

From the Admissions Office

Students come to Creighton University for the opportunities of a lifetime. Our 9 schools and colleges deliver a powerful education that connects renowned programs in arts and sciences, law and business with 9 health professions programs (dentistry, medicine, nursing, pharmacy, occupational and physical therapy, public health, physician assistant, and emergency medical services). We are expanding opportunities for medical and health sciences to our new Phoenix campus, which will become home to 900 students, including medical, nursing, occupational and physical therapy, pharmacy, and physician assistant. Creighton's rigorous academics and commitment to Jesuit, Catholic values creates an environment that fosters academic excellence, social justice and personal growth. Our 4,000+ undergraduates find new possibilities through personalized advising, a strong focus on leadership skills and undergraduate research. The Center for Undergraduate Research and Scholarship (CURAS) ensures that undergraduates work directly with faculty researchers, present at national conferences and publish in scholarly journals. And not all learning takes place in the classroom or lab. With 4 Fortune 500 company headquarters located close to campus, Creighton business students find more paid internship opportunties than there are students to fill them. Students find life-changing experiences through community service opportunities, contributing more than 1 million hours of service locally, regionally, nationally and internationally each year.

"At Creighton, you get it all—a 99% success rate (graduates employed, enrolled in graduate/professional school or in volunteer programs within 6 months of graduation); an 11:1 student-to-faculty ratio; 60+ undergraduate majors; honors programs; abundant service opportunities; study abroad, including our 4-year educational and professional development Global Scholars Program; BIG EAST athletic competition; 200+ clubs and organizations and more—because Creighton University is the complete package."

SELECTIVITY

Admissions Rating	86
# of applicants	9,381
% of applicants accepted	74
% of acceptees attending	16
# offered a place on the wait list	244
% accepting a place on wait list	19
% admitted from wait list	60

FRESHMAN PROFILE

Range SAT EBRW	590–670
Range SAT Math	580–680
Range SAT Composite	1170–1330
Range ACT Composite	23–29
# submitting SAT scores	319
% submitting SAT scores	30
# submitting ACT scores	874
% submitting ACT scores	81
Average HS GPA	3.8
% graduated top 10% of class	35
% graduated top 25% of class	66
% graduated top 50% of class	91

DEADLINES

Early action	
Deadline	11/1
Regular	
Priority	12/1
Notification	Rolling, 11/1
Nonfall registration?	Yes

APPLICANTS ALSO LOOK AT AND OFTEN PREFER
University of Notre Dame

AND SOMETIMES PREFER
University of Wisconsin-Madison; University of Minnesota—Twin Cities Campus

AND RARELY PREFER
Marquette University; Loyola University of Chicago; University of Kansas; University of Portland; Fordham University

FINANCIAL FACTS

Financial Aid Rating	87
Annual tuition	$41,176
Room and board	$11,600
Required fees	$1,842
Books and supplies	$1,200
Average frosh need-based scholarship	$22,856
Average UG need-based scholarship	$22,255
% needy frosh rec. need-based scholarship or grant aid	99
% needy UG rec. need-based scholarship or grant aid	94
% needy frosh rec. non-need-based scholarship or grant aid	30
% needy UG rec. non-need-based scholarship or grant aid	22
% needy frosh rec. need-based self-help aid	72
% needy UG rec. need-based self-help aid	78
% frosh rec. any financial aid	99.7
% UG rec. any financial aid	96.6
% UG borrow to pay for school	59
Average cumulative indebtedness	$38,042
% frosh need fully met	33
% ugrads need fully met	25
Average % of frosh need met	84
Average % of ugrad need met	78

DARTMOUTH COLLEGE

6016 McNutt Hall, Hanover, NH 03755 • Admissions: 603-646-2875 • Fax: 603-646-1216

CAMPUS LIFE

Quality of Life Rating	93
Fire Safety Rating	89
Green Rating	91
Type of school	Private
Environment	Village

STUDENTS

Total undergrad enrollment	4,365
% male/female	51/49
% from out of state	97
% frosh from public high school	57
% frosh live on campus	100
% ugrads live on campus	85
# of fraternities (% ugrad men join)	13 (27)
# of sororities (% ugrad women join)	10 (31)
% African American	6
% Asian	15
% Caucasian	51
% Hispanic	11
% Native American	1
% Pacific Islander	<1
% Two or more races	6
% Race and/or ethnicity unknown	1
% international	10
# of countries represented	99

SURVEY SAYS . . .

Classroom facilities are great
Lab facilities are great
Great library
Internships are widely available
Great financial aid
Recreation facilities are great
Lots of beer drinking
Frats and sororities are popular
Alumni active on campus

ACADEMICS

Academic Rating	94
% students returning for sophomore year	97
% students graduating within 4 years	87
% students graduating within 6 years	95
Calendar	Quarter
Student/faculty ratio	7:1
Profs interesting rating	91
Profs accessible rating	97
Most classes have 10–19 students.	

MOST POPULAR MAJORS

Economics, General; Political Science and Government, General; Psychology, General

STUDENTS SAY "..."

Academics

Tucked away in bucolic New Hampshire, Dartmouth College manages to strike a nice "balance between the intimacy of a college [and] the opportunity of a university." Students feel fortunate that the administration places an "emphasis on pursuing passions, and making the college experience your own." And while Dartmouth certainly maintains a "competitive" atmosphere, students here truly appreciate that "no one really talks about their grades openly." Indeed, it's "generally understood that everyone is smart." A neuroscience major tells us that academically, "Dartmouth puts a huge focus on the undergraduate students, and I have found my professors to be available and engaging in nearly every instance. My classes are all challenging, but they are very discussion based and tend to be small, which keeps me working hard and interested in the material." And an impressed Middle Eastern studies major interjects, "I came to Dartmouth for the professors, but they were far beyond anything I could have hoped for. Not only are they great lecturers and accomplished scholars, they go out of their way to be available outside of the classroom, and to forge relationships beyond what is expected or necessary." When it comes down to it, "Dartmouth is considered to be a combination of Hogwarts and Disney World because it is known for its community and intelligent students and faculty, who also are personable and know how to have fun."

Life

There's no getting around it; at Dartmouth, the "Greek system is the main source of social activity." However, if you're wary of fraternities and sororities, fret not. A biology major reveals that a "very large percentage of students are involved which makes the Greek houses quite diverse and representative of the student body as a whole." Indeed, fraternities "are very inclusive" and while students definitely drink "there really isn't any pressure to." Further, plenty of social options exist beyond the party scene. "On any given night, you can do anything from see a hockey game to the early premiere of some cool new movie at the Hop[kins Center for the Arts], you can go to a dance party or just play cards or jam out on guitar or something... there are so many options to do whatever you're interested in doing." Dartmouth undergrads also love convening with nature. "Outdoorsy activities are huge here. The Appalachian Trail literally runs right through our campus. The Dartmouth Outing Club is the oldest and largest college outing club, and many students (even students who never did so before college) get involved with hiking, canoeing, rock climbing, and so forth." And a philosophy major concludes, "Whether it's skating on Occom Pond, going on a hike, going kayaking, apple picking, thrift shopping... there are boundless opportunities to do anything that interests you, and it means that whatever you're doing in your free time is always something really awesome."

Student Body

Undergrads here emphatically insist that it's "hard to define a typical student because at Dartmouth literally every type of person is represented." Of course, if pressed, they might reluctantly admit that the average student comes across as "preppy, academically goal oriented but also extremely social." And, as you might expect, undergrads also report that their peers are certainly very "smart." Fortunately, they "do not boast about their intellectual capacity." A happy senior tells us that "the common denominator is that Dartmouth students are very involved." Indeed, "whether it's with a club sports team, a cappella group, community service project, academic research, or a Greek house, Dartmouth students manage to do a lot of things in the course of the day." One incredulous sophomore concurs, adding that his friends "are always studying and participating in some extracurricular activity and you wonder how they have time to sleep and then you will see them out at a frat too. Then they show up at class the next morning with all of the work completed and they seem like a magician." Finally a junior concludes, "It's a small enough school that there is a sense of community that's always present, but large enough that everyone can find their own niche and their own area of the school and the community that caters to them perfectly."

Financial Aid: 800-443-3605 • E-Mail: admissions.office@dartmouth.edu • Website: www.dartmouth.edu

THE PRINCETON REVIEW SAYS

Admissions

Very important factors considered include: rigor of secondary school record, class rank, academic GPA, application essay, standardized test scores, recommendation(s), extracurricular activities, character/personal qualities. *Important factors considered include:* talent/ability, volunteer work. *Other factors considered include:* interview, first generation, alumni/ae relation, geographical residence, racial/ethnic status. ACT with or without Writing required. SAT with or without Essay component required. High school diploma or equivalent is not required *Academic units recommended:* 4 English, 4 math, 4 science, 4 foreign language, 4 social studies.

Financial Aid

Students should submit: Business/Farm Supplement; CSS/Financial Aid PROFILE; FAFSA; Noncustodial PROFILE. The Princeton Review suggests that all financial aid forms be submitted as soon as possible after October 1. *Need-based scholarships/grants offered:* College/university scholarship or grant aid from institutional funds; Federal Pell; Private scholarships; SEOG; State scholarships/grants. *Loan aid offered:* Direct PLUS loans; Direct Subsidized Stafford Loans; Direct Unsubsidized Stafford Loans. Applicants will be notified of awards on or about 4/2. Federal Work-Study Program available. Institutional employment available.

The Inside Word

Competition to secure a coveted acceptance letter from Dartmouth is fierce. After all, the majority of admitted students are in the top of their respective high school classes. Therefore, academic success is mandatory for any serious contender as is a schedule chock-full of honors, AP and/or IB courses. Of course, admissions officers are looking for well-rounded students so extracurricular activities, personal statements and recommendations will also be closely assessed. Finally, it's important to know that Dartmouth is a need-blind institution.

THE SCHOOL SAYS "..."

From the Admissions Office

"Dartmouth College is a fusion of renowned liberal arts college and robust research university, where our faculty are scholars who teach, and where students partner with them to take on the world's challenges. All classes are taught by professors who are advancing the frontiers of knowledge while mentoring and collaborating with undergraduates.

"Think of Dartmouth as a base camp to the world, where the boundaries of the traditional study abroad model have been erased. The curriculum and structure of our ten-week terms and our revolutionary language-learning model, the Rassias Method, allow students to follow their research and passions around the world while staying on track with their academic aspirations. Dartmouth graduates emerge equipped with experience, connections, and opportunities on a global scale.

"With a profound sense of place and powerful sense of community developed over two and a half centuries, Dartmouth is home to many beloved traditions, from Winter Carnival to the Homecoming Bonfire. Each season brings a new energy and set of events to campus. The adventuresome spirit of the College permeates our nearly 400 student groups, from the country's oldest outing club to our 35 Division I varsity teams to our vibrant arts scene.

"Dartmouth's holistic, need-blind admissions process is designed to identify students who will thrive in this intimate environment of curiosity and creativity. There is no 'typical' Dartmouth student, but our students all share a passion for intellectual inquiry, a willingness to embrace adventure, and a desire to build a close-knit community."

SELECTIVITY

Admissions Rating	99
# of applicants	23,650
% of applicants accepted	8
% of acceptees attending	64
# offered a place on the wait list	2,151
% accepting a place on wait list	64
% admitted from wait list	0
# of early decision applicants	2,474
% accepted early decision	23

FRESHMAN PROFILE

Range SAT EBRW	710–770
Range SAT Math	730–790
Range SAT Composite	1450–1550
Range ACT Composite	32–35
# submitting SAT scores	659
% submitting SAT scores	57
# submitting ACT scores	493
% submitting ACT scores	43
% graduated top 10% of class	95
% graduated top 25% of class	99
% graduated top 50% of class	99

DEADLINES

Early decision	
Deadline	11/1
Notification	12/15
Regular	
Deadline	1/2
Notification	3/30

APPLICANTS ALSO LOOK AT AND OFTEN PREFER
Harvard College; Stanford University; Yale University; Princeton University

AND SOMETIMES PREFER
Brown University; Columbia University; Massachusetts Institute of Technology; Duke University; University of Pennsylvania

AND RARELY PREFER
Cornell University; The University of Chicago; Johns Hopkins University; University of California—Berkeley

FINANCIAL FACTS

Financial Aid Rating	97
Annual tuition	$57,796
Room and board	$17,022
Required fees	$2,313
Books and supplies	$1,105
Average frosh need-based scholarship	$57,562
Average UG need-based scholarship	$53,952
% needy frosh rec. need-based scholarship or grant aid	92
% needy UG rec. need-based scholarship or grant aid	95
% needy frosh rec. non-need-based scholarship or grant aid	0
% needy UG rec. non-need-based scholarship or grant aid	0
% needy frosh rec. need-based self-help aid	87
% needy UG rec. need-based self-help aid	92
% frosh rec. any financial aid	58
% UG rec. any financial aid	54
% UG borrow to pay for school	40
Average cumulative indebtedness	$25,071
% frosh need fully met	100
% ugrads need fully met	100
Average % of frosh need met	100
Average % of ugrad need met	100

DAVIDSON COLLEGE

PO Box 7156, Davidson, NC 28035-7156 • Admissions: 704-894-2230 • Fax: 704-894-2016

STUDENTS SAY "..."

Academics

This small school north of Charlotte, North Carolina, cultivates an environment "that is very open to change and improvement" and empowers students to "be better people and make a difference in the world." The administration works hard to create an on-campus community and constantly makes efforts "to support and improve Davidson," all while keeping students happy and their minds full. "I have never witnessed people so eager to come do their job every day. [Professors] are almost too willing to help," says a student. There is also a trickle-down effect because even the student body is supportive and "eager to watch you succeed." The school offers a classic liberal arts education, encouraging students to take classes in all areas, and "all of these people come out smarter than they came in." "If I could spend twenty years being educated by this administration and these professors, I would," says a very happy junior. School is the number one priority for all of the students here, and while academics are all-consuming, time-wise, they are also "fascinating and rewarding." Without a doubt, Davidson is a tough school—"99 percent of us left our 4.0 GPAs back in high school," claims a student—and professors don't believe in grade inflation or curving grades, but they do readily make themselves available outside of class for help or discussion. There is a lot of work, but it "is accompanied by even more resources with which it can be successfully managed." One student testimonial: "My calculus teacher last semester had office hours in the student union, and he invited the whole class over to his house for chicken dinner—twice!" The dedication of the staff is contagious, and "though the work is rigorous, time spent in school never feels wasted."

Life

Davidson "possesses an intense study culture, and people hit the books regularly; it's cool to be smart." One of the many wonderful things about Davidson "is that academics voluntarily leave the classroom." "It's not uncommon to hear people discussing their current academic topics at lunch or in the gym." Basketball is a huge common ground for the student body at large; "Everyone enjoys being a part of the underdog/Cinderella story." Weeks are devoted to study, as well as extracurricular activities—"you see your friends because you are doing homework together or eating meals together, not because you're vegging out." Of course, even Davidson students need to kick back, and there are always plenty of parties to be found on the weekends. Fraternities and eating houses (the Davidson version of sororities) are popular. Fortunately, "there really is no pressure to drink. You can go out and dance and have a great time or have movie nights with friends," says a student. The combination of the idyllic atmosphere and the workload "can make it hard to stay up-to-date on current events, yet most students remain well-informed."

Student Body

Davidson is "an amalgamation of all types of people, religiously, ethnically, politically, economically, etc.," all "united under the umbrella of intellectual curiosity" and their devotion to the school as a community. The typical Davidson student is "probably white," but in the past few years, admissions has been making progress in racially diversifying the campus, which students agree upon as necessary. Though there are plenty of Southern, preppy, athletic types to fit the brochure examples, there are many niches for every type of "atypical" student. "There are enough people that one can find a similar group to connect with, and there are few enough people that one ends up connecting with dissimilar [people] anyway," says a student. Everyone here is smart and well-rounded; admissions "does a good job...so if you're in you'll probably make the cut all the way through the four years." Most students have several extracurriculars to round out their free time, and they have a healthy desire to enjoy themselves when the books shut. "During the week we work hard. On the weekends we play hard. We don't do anything halfway," says a senior. Though the majority of students lean to the left, there's a strong conservative contingent, and there are no real problems between the two.

DAVIDSON COLLEGE

E-Mail: admission@davidson.edu • Website: www.davidson.edu

THE PRINCETON REVIEW SAYS

Admissions

Very important factors considered include: rigor of secondary school record, recommendation(s), character/personal qualities, volunteer work. *Important factors considered include:* application essay, extracurricular activities, talent/ability. *Other factors considered include:* class rank, academic GPA, alumni/ae relation. Davidson is test-optional for students applying for admission beginning with the 2020–21 cycle. High school diploma is required and GED is not accepted. *Academic units required:* 4 English, 3 math, 2 science, 2 foreign language, 2 units from above areas or other academic areas. *Academic units recommended:* 4 math, 4 science, 4 foreign language.

Financial Aid

Students should submit: Business/Farm Supplement; CSS/Financial Aid PROFILE; FAFSA; Noncustodial PROFILE. Priority filing deadline is 2/15. The Princeton Review suggests that all financial aid forms be submitted as soon as possible after October 1. *Need-based scholarships/grants offered:* College/university scholarship or grant aid from institutional funds; Federal Pell; Private scholarships; SEOG; State scholarships/grants. *Loan aid offered:* Direct PLUS loans; Direct Subsidized Stafford Loans; Direct Unsubsidized Stafford Loans. Applicants will be notified of awards on or about 4/1. Federal Work-Study Program available. Institutional employment available.

The Inside Word

The combination of Davidson's low acceptance rate and high yield really packs a punch. Prospective applicants beware: Securing admission at this prestigious school is no easy feat. Admitted students are typically at the top of their high school classes and have strong standardized test scores. Candidates with leadership experience generally garner the favor of admissions officers. The college takes its honor code seriously and, as a result, seeks out students of demonstrated reputable character.

THE SCHOOL SAYS "..."

From the Admissions Office

"Davidson is a community defined by smart, driven and kind people. The relationships and experiences here cultivate the qualities needed in the world today: curiosity, empathy, integrity and courage. The college merges challenging academics with a distinctly supportive community. Mentors push and counsel. Classmates challenge and collaborate. Davidson students are encouraged to think critically, communicate with audiences from all backgrounds and navigate the unfamiliar through research, internships, a campus-based innovation and entrepreneurship hub, and international experience. A strong honor code means doing right when no one is watching. The Davidson community supports student artists and cheers for Division I athletes who are roommates, classmates and friends. Through The Davidson Trust, the college meets 100 percent of calculated financial need for domestic applicants through grants and student employment. Our financial aid packages do not include student loans."

SELECTIVITY
Admissions Rating	97
# of applicants	5,982
% of applicants accepted	18
% of acceptees attending	49

FRESHMAN PROFILE
Range SAT EBRW	650–730
Range SAT Math	660–755
Range SAT Composite	1320–1470
Range ACT Composite	30–33
# submitting SAT scores	331
% submitting SAT scores	63
# submitting ACT scores	243
% submitting ACT scores	46
Average HS GPA	3.8
% graduated top 10% of class	72
% graduated top 25% of class	95
% graduated top 50% of class	100

DEADLINES
Early decision	
Deadline	11/15
Notification	12/15
Other ED Deadline	1/2
Other ED Notification	2/1
Regular	
Deadline	1/7
Notification	4/1
Nonfall registration?	Yes

FINANCIAL FACTS
Financial Aid Rating	95
Annual tuition	$54,520
Room and board	$15,225
Required fees	$540
Books and supplies	$1,000
Average frosh need-based scholarship	$47,531
Average UG need-based scholarship	$47,233
% needy frosh rec. need-based scholarship or grant aid	100
% needy UG rec. need-based scholarship or grant aid	100
% needy frosh rec. non-need-based scholarship or grant aid	44
% needy UG rec. non-need-based scholarship or grant aid	29
% needy frosh rec. need-based self-help aid	61
% needy UG rec. need-based self-help aid	66
% frosh rec. any financial aid	65
% UG rec. any financial aid	64
% UG borrow to pay for school	30
Average cumulative indebtedness	$23,535
% frosh need fully met	100
% ugrads need fully met	100
Average % of frosh need met	100
Average % of ugrad need met	100

THE BEST 386 COLLEGES ■ 205

Deep Springs College

Applications Committee, Dyer, NV 89010 • Admissions: 760-872-2000 • Fax: 760-872-4466

CAMPUS LIFE

Quality of Life Rating	91
Fire Safety Rating	88
Green Rating	60*
Type of school	Private
Environment	Rural

STUDENTS

Total undergrad enrollment	30
% male/female	67/33
% from out of state	82
% frosh from public high school	67
% frosh live on campus	100
% ugrads live on campus	100
# of fraternities	0
# of sororities	0
% African American	0
% Asian	14
% Caucasian	64
% Hispanic	4
% Native American	<1
% Pacific Islander	0
% Two or more races	4
% Race and/or ethnicity unknown	0
% international	14
# of countries represented	5

SURVEY SAYS . . .

Lots of liberal students
Students always studying
Students are happy
Internships are widely available
Class discussions encouraged
School is well run
Great financial aid
No one cheats
Students are friendly
Diverse student types interact on campus
Students aren't religious
Students get along with local community
Students environmentally aware
Great food on campus
Dorms are like palaces
Easy to get around campus
Very little drug use
Intramural sports are popular

ACADEMICS

Academic Rating	99
% students returning for sophomore year	92
Calendar	Continuous
Student/faculty ratio	4:1
Profs interesting rating	99
Profs accessible rating	99
Most classes have 10–19 students.	

MOST POPULAR MAJORS

Liberal Arts and Sciences, General Studies and Humanities, Other

STUDENTS SAY "..."

Academics

The "three pillars" of a Deep Springs education—"labor, academics, and self-governance"—combine to produce "unparalleled challenges" that run the gamut "from fixing a hay baler in the middle of the night to puzzling over a particularly difficult passage of Hegel." That's what those who attend Deep Springs tell us. These unique undergraduates basically run their own school, work the ranch where it is located, and complete a rigorous curriculum, an itinerary that "creates an environment of intense growth and responsibility." Class work occurs in a seminar format in which "teachers participate similarly to students." Classes "aren't so much a transfer of information from professor to student as they are a time for the entire class to push the boundaries of collective thought as far as possible." Composition and public speaking are the only required courses; all others are chosen by the student body and taught by a faculty of three long-term professors (one each in the humanities, social sciences, and natural sciences) and one to three visiting scholars or artists. The system relies on a commitment to self-determination, which means "how successful Deep Springs is as an institution depends upon the manner in which its students are engaging with its project." While the size of the school inevitably means that "lab and library facilities are not what they might be," students tell us that the overall Deep Springs experience compensates for any shortcomings. A student explains: "Mistakes and flaws are seen as pedagogy in action. See a broken fence or heater? Fix it, or learn to fix it. The mechanical skills we pick up during the process of taking responsibility for our livelihood are surely valuable, but the self-confidence and that emerges from learning to do things one never could have thought possible is the essence of a Deep Springer's education."

Life

At Deep Springs, where "the desert sun rises slowly," everyday student life is totally unlike other colleges because "no one drinks, everyone helps run the ranch in some way, and no one can be totally self-absorbed (unless he's out hiking in the desert)." Instead, students immerse themselves in the Deep Springs way. As one student explains, "Life is very intellectual but also in constant relationship to the natural beauty of the desert and the operation of the College's farm and ranch." Conversations tend to revolve around "what work needs to be done, what decisions need to be made, [and] which classes are most interesting," or, as one student puts it, "Sunsets. Hegel. Welding. Jane Austen." Fun at Deep Springs, where days are "marked by an extreme busyness," is "self-generated": "'Fun' is hard to come by, and one has to learn how to enjoy people, work, and engagement." Students do occasionally take a break, however: "Fun just means something a little different...Half-naked dances to Miley Cyrus, fully naked soccer, or fully clothed conversations on anything from Kierkegaard to Kanye West ensure that there really isn't a dull moment in the Valley." Also, occasionally "there are 'boojies'," a kind of hectic dance party in the Rumpus Room of the dorm, " or students will "go to the dunes a valley over for a bit of late-night naked surfing down the sand." Undergrads concede that Deep Springs "life can be intense": There is "a whirlwind of activity from labor to class to meals to labor again to meetings to a few precious hours of sleep. But where many students would find such a lifestyle stressful and unsustainable, we find it meaningful and valuable" and that keeps undergrads energized and motivated."

Student Body

"It is impossible to characterize a 'typical' student," students understandably warn, but they add that "we all are hardworking and are committed to a life of service." Undergrads are also predictably "outdoorsy," "interested in the arts," "motivated, and responsible," as "it takes a unique type of person to even consider Deep Springs, much less succeed and thrive in such an environment." As one student puts it, "The typical student at Deep Springs is committed to the life of the intellect and committed to finding education in our labor program. Most of the students here believe that a life of service, informed by discourse and labor, is a necessary notion to understand in today's world."

DEEP SPRINGS COLLEGE

Financial Aid: 760-872-2000 • E-Mail: apcom@deepsprings.edu • Website: www.deepsprings.edu

THE PRINCETON REVIEW SAYS

Admissions

Very important factors considered include: application essay, interview, character/personal qualities, level of applicant's interest. *Important factors considered include:* rigor of secondary school record, academic GPA, extracurricular activities, volunteer work, work experience. *Other factors considered include:* class rank, standardized test scores, recommendation(s), talent/ability, first generation, racial/ethnic status. ACT with or without writing accepted. High school diploma or equivalent is not required.

Financial Aid

The Princeton Review suggests that all financial aid forms be submitted as soon as possible after October 1.

The Inside Word

Students will be hard-pressed to find a school with a more personal or thorough application process than Deep Springs. Given the intimate and collegial atmosphere of the school, matchmaking is the top priority. Candidates are evaluated by a body composed of students, faculty, and staff members. The application is writing intensive; finalists are expected to spend several days on campus, during which they will undergo a lengthy interview.

THE SCHOOL SAYS "..."

From the Admissions Office

"Founded in 1917, Deep Springs College lies isolated in a high desert valley of eastern California, thirty miles from the nearest town. Its enrollment is limited to twenty-eight students, each of whom receives a full scholarship that covers tuition and room and board, and is valued at more than $50,000 per year. Students engage in rigorous academics, govern themselves, and participate in the operation of our ranch and farm.

"Given our small size, statistics must be viewed with context. Nonetheless, we have compiled data from the past five years to give some perspective on the characteristics of our students.

"The Applications Committee (ApCom) receives between 180 and 250 applications each year. Between thirteen and fifteen applicants are invited to enroll; ten are added to a waitlist. After two years at Deep Springs, students generally transfer to other schools to complete their studies. Students regularly attend Yale, University of Chicago, and Brown, and also have recently chosen several other schools including Cornell, Evergreen, Harvard, Reed, Stanford, Swarthmore, and UC Berkeley.

"Despite its small size, Deep Springs is a diverse community. In the past five years, 30 percent of Deep Springs students have been people of color. More than 11 percent of students have identified as LGBT. International students have made up about 20 percent of the Student Body. In each year, at least one student has spent between one semester and two years enrolled at another college before attending Deep Springs."

SELECTIVITY

Admissions Rating	99
# of applicants	200
% of applicants accepted	10
% of acceptees attending	84
# offered a place on the wait list	5
% accepting a place on wait list	100
% admitted from wait list	100

FRESHMAN PROFILE

Range SAT EBRW	740–800
Range SAT Math	670–740
# submitting SAT scores	12
% submitting SAT scores	80
# submitting ACT scores	3
% submitting ACT scores	20
% graduated top 10% of class	100
% graduated top 25% of class	100
% graduated top 50% of class	100

DEADLINES

Regular	
Deadline	11/7
Notification	4/15
Nonfall registration?	No

FINANCIAL FACTS

Financial Aid Rating	60
Annual tuition	$0
Books and supplies	$1,200
% frosh rec. any financial aid	100
% UG rec. any financial aid	100

DENISON UNIVERSITY

100 West College Street, Granville, OH 43023 • Admissions: 740-587-6276 • Fax: 740-587-6306

CAMPUS LIFE

Quality of Life Rating	90
Fire Safety Rating	96
Green Rating	96
Type of school	Private
Environment	Village

STUDENTS

Total undergrad enrollment	2,368
% male/female	46/54
% from out of state	74
% frosh from public high school	67
% frosh live on campus	100
% ugrads live on campus	99
# of fraternities (% ugrad men join)	9 (48)
# of sororities (% ugrad women join)	9 (27)
% African American	6
% Asian	4
% Caucasian	63
% Hispanic	9
% Native American	<1
% Pacific Islander	0
% Two or more races	3
% Race and/or ethnicity unknown	2
% international	12
# of countries represented	37

SURVEY SAYS . . .

Students are happy
Lab facilities are great
Great library
Career services are great
Internships are widely available
Great financial aid
Recreation facilities are great
Lots of beer drinking
Everyone loves the Big Red
Theater is popular
College radio is popular

ACADEMICS

Academic Rating	91
% students returning for sophomore year	89
% students graduating within 4 years	84
% students graduating within 6 years	87
Calendar	Semester
Student/faculty ratio	10:1
Profs interesting rating	93
Profs accessible rating	96
Most classes have 10–19 students.	

MOST POPULAR MAJORS

Economics, General; Biology, General; Psychology, General

STUDENTS SAY "..."

Academics

Ohio's Denison University is a small private liberal arts university that "makes people able to critically think and attack any task that they are confronted with," so it follows that the school listens to its students, and "if there is something you want to add to or change about the school, it is easy to do if you put in the effort." Support networks abound, from the Austin E. Knowlton Center for Career Exploration (which offers "a variety of help with career decisions: practice interviews, career coaching, resume building, and more") to the Writing Center and the library, which offers help to students in classes with lots of research- ing and writing. Academically, students "often are involved in multiple departments" either though double majors, minors, or concentrations, and "conducting research is very common for undergraduate students...during the school year or over the summer." All classes are taught by "intelligent, thought-provoking professors," and there are "a multitude of unique class options."

At Denison, "one will find professors who are completely committed to their job: teaching their students." Small classes mean students "really get to know their professors and can learn a lot outside of a traditional classroom setting," and "a student is bound to form a great relationship, if not a friendship," with many professors during their education at Denison. They are "almost always accessible outside of class time" and "have a knack for making students appreciate the interconnectedness of concepts and disciplines." Professors are even helpful when connecting students to professionals in fields related to their majors, and alumni are a great boon to the school. The network is "very diverse in occupation and found all around the world," and alumni "love Denison and are willing to help any graduate seeking advice, internships, or any job-related detail."

Life

Located east of Columbus, Denison "sits atop the hill overlooking the village of Granville and is surrounded by beautiful forest." "One easily feels at home here," and although it may be somewhat isolated, "the community makes up for that." Denison has an active student body regarding co-curricular and extracurricular activities, and "most students hold at least one leadership position on campus." The average schedule of a Denison student is packed with "classes, meetings, rehearsals, practices, volunteer work, and much more." This is an entirely residential campus which "encourages students to engage with each other in multiple settings," and students congregate in common rooms to hang out regularly. "Everyone stays on campus during the weekends regardless of where they're from," and while some students drink and go out to parties, others watch movies or go to concerts. For people that don't want to party, Denison has a large amount of programming—so much so that "students sometimes com- plain that the school is actually over-programmed." "There's so much to do on campus that people rarely leave," says a student.

Student Body

Since Denison is a small university, students know or recognize most of their peers. "I can comfortably sit with most fellow students during any meal at the dining hall or in the class- room," says a student. Within the "extremely diverse" student body, there are many different interests on campus, "from sports to film, from math to poetry, and from theatre to science," and this "creates dialogue between [students]." In fact, the university has "an East Coast liberal arts feeling," except in central Ohio. Denison students are "always very engaged," and there's "a high expectation of involvement on campus." They "are passionate about their futures and the futures of those around them" and are "heavily engaged in current events and take politics a little too seriously." There are a fair number of international students here, and Denison has "people who have traveled from the other side of Earth, to students who live in Granville themselves." "Although we are all very different, we all come together," says one.

Financial Aid: 740-587-6279 • E-Mail: admissions@denison.edu • Website: denison.edu

THE PRINCETON REVIEW SAYS

Admissions

Very important factors considered include: rigor of secondary school record, academic GPA, application essay, recommendation(s). *Important factors considered include:* interview, extra-curricular activities, talent/ability. *Other factors considered include:* class rank, standardized test scores, character/personal qualities, first generation, alumni/ae relation, geographical residence, state residency, racial/ethnic status, volunteer work, work experience, level of applicant's interest. ACT with or without writing accepted. SAT with or without Essay component accepted. High school diploma is required and GED is accepted. *Academic units recommended:* 4 English, 4 math, 4 science, 4 foreign language, 4 social studies.

Financial Aid

Students should submit: CSS/Financial Aid PROFILE; FAFSA; Noncustodial PROFILE. Priority filing deadline is 1/15. The Princeton Review suggests that all financial aid forms be submitted as soon as possible after October 1. *Need-based scholarships/grants offered:* College/university scholarship or grant aid from institutional funds; Federal Pell; Private scholarships; SEOG; State scholarships/grants. *Loan aid offered:* Direct PLUS loans; Direct Subsidized Stafford Loans; Direct Unsubsidized Stafford Loans. Applicants will be notified of awards on or about 3/15. Federal Work-Study Program available. Institutional employment available.

The Inside Word

Admission to Denison is pretty straightforward. The school "suggests" an interview, meaning you should do one if at all possible. It's a great way to demonstrate your interest in the school, which improves your chances of admission, especially if your grades, test scores, and overall profile put you on the admit/reject borderline. Students may apply using either The Common Application or the Coalition Application.

THE SCHOOL SAYS "..."

From the Admissions Office

"Denison University is a leading national residential liberal arts college located just outside Columbus, Ohio. The college balances a rigorous and relevant academic experience founded on perceptive mentorship by dedicated faculty at the cutting edge of their research, with robust co-curricular and extra-curricular programming, which includes athletics, performing and fine arts, and more than 170 student-run organizations, providing abundant opportunities for students to develop leadership qualities and nurture friendships that will last throughout their lives. Wellness and academic support programs serve the whole student, promoting academic accomplishment as well as resilience, balance and well-being.

"Denison students are comprehensively prepared for lifetimes of civic and personal success, expanding their skills and expertise through extensive research opportunities and innovative career programming. The college is creating the gold standard in supporting students transitioning to life after college, through meaningful alumni networking, innovative programs that establish discrete capabilities related to vocations, and well-paid summer internships in their field of interest, which help them to establish relationships and forge skills directly related to their future careers. Proof of our student success is provided on an interactive webpage, 'The Denison Difference,' which reports graduate placement in careers, graduate schools and service opportunities. Denison students have been granted more than 150 Fulbright and other international post-graduate scholarships, and in recent years have garnered 100 percent acceptance rates to both medical and law school programs. The college's distinguished alumni claim both Rhodes Scholar and a Gates Cambridge Scholar honors."

SELECTIVITY

Admissions Rating	93
# of applicants	8,042
% of applicants accepted	34
% of acceptees attending	24
# offered a place on the wait list	1,555
% accepting a place on wait list	14
% admitted from wait list	11
# of early decision applicants	506
% accepted early decision	65

FRESHMAN PROFILE

Range SAT EBRW	600–670
Range SAT Math	610–710
Range ACT Composite	28–31
# submitting SAT scores	297
% submitting SAT scores	45
# submitting ACT scores	202
% submitting ACT scores	31
% graduated top 10% of class	64
% graduated top 25% of class	85
% graduated top 50% of class	100

DEADLINES

Early decision	
Deadline	11/15
Notification	12/15
Other ED Deadline	1/15
Other ED Notification	2/15
Regular	
Priority	1/15
Deadline	1/15
Notification	4/1
Nonfall registration?	No

APPLICANTS ALSO LOOK AT AND OFTEN PREFER

Carleton College; Colby College; Colgate University; Hamilton College

AND SOMETIMES PREFER

Case Western Reserve University; Miami University; Bucknell University; Dickinson College; Franklin and Marshall College; Grinnell College; Kenyon College; Macalester College; Oberlin College; University of Michigan—Ann Arbor; Connecticut College; Bates College; Colorado College

AND RARELY PREFER

The College of Wooster; The Ohio State University—Columbus; Centre College; DePauw University; The University of North Carolina at Chapel Hill; Occidental College; Skidmore College; Smith College; Gettysburg College; Lafayette College

FINANCIAL FACTS

Financial Aid Rating	94
Annual tuition	$52,620
Room and board	$13,050
Required fees	$1,210
Books and supplies	$1,000
Average frosh need-based scholarship	$41,158
Average UG need-based scholarship	$41,138
% needy frosh rec. need-based scholarship or grant aid	100
% needy UG rec. need-based scholarship or grant aid	100
% needy frosh rec. non-need-based scholarship or grant aid	17
% needy UG rec. non-need-based scholarship or grant aid	15
% needy frosh rec. need-based self-help aid	80
% needy UG rec. need-based self-help aid	84
% frosh rec. any financial aid	93
% UG rec. any financial aid	95
% UG borrow to pay for school	53
Average cumulative indebtedness	$31,551
% frosh need fully met	89
% ugrads need fully met	63
Average % of frosh need met	100
Average % of ugrad need met	96

DePaul University

1 East Jackson Boulevard, Chicago, IL 60604-2287 • Admissions: 312-362-8300 • Fax: 312-362-5749

CAMPUS LIFE

Quality of Life Rating	90
Fire Safety Rating	99
Green Rating	60*
Type of school	Private
Affiliation	Roman Catholic
Environment	Metropolis

STUDENTS

Total undergrad enrollment	14,009
% male/female	47/53
% from out of state	25
% frosh from public high school	81
% frosh live on campus	66
% ugrads live on campus	19
# of fraternities (% ugrad men join)	12 (6)
# of sororities (% ugrad women join)	16 (11)
% African American	8
% Asian	11
% Caucasian	52
% Hispanic	20
% Native American	<1
% Pacific Islander	<1
% Two or more races	4
% Race and/or ethnicity unknown	2
% international	3
# of countries represented	113

SURVEY SAYS . . .

Students love Chicago, IL
Great off-campus food
Recreation facilities are great

ACADEMICS

Academic Rating	79
% students returning for sophomore year	85
% students graduating within 4 years	61
% students graduating within 6 years	74
Calendar	Differs By Program
Student/faculty ratio	16:1
Profs interesting rating	88
Profs accessible rating	92

Most classes have 20–29 students.
Most lab/discussion sessions have 20–29 students.

MOST POPULAR MAJORS

Public Relations, Advertising, and Applied
Communication, Other; Accounting; Finance,
General

STUDENTS SAY "..."

Academics

DePaul University is the nation's largest Catholic university, offering its 14,500 undergraduate students over 130 majors across two campuses, including the option for combined Bachelor's and Master's degrees. These various programs are anchored by a core curriculum that features over 1,400 course options and a Focal Point Seminar, in which students must investigate a significant person, place, event or idea. Further supplementing that core is an ever-expanding series of options, as "each year [DePaul] strives to improve and add new programs to suit different future career paths of its students." Such offerings are only enhanced by the school's heart-of-Chicago location, which puts it "close to so many educational and vocational opportunities." There are thousands of internships available, as well as "peer-to-peer study groups" and study abroad programs. The administration rises to the task of "keeping the school's environment safe, clean, and well-educated," and "there are plenty of resources specifically set up to help students with pretty much anything," including "tutoring sessions every day, a writing center to help improve papers, a counseling center, [and] financial aid advisers."

Ninety-eight percent of classes are taught by the "highly professional" faculty, so "instead of only learning from a textbook, I am able to gain real experience from professors who have worked in the field for decades at a time." There's a maximum to each class size as well, which guarantees that "teachers actually get to know the students that are in the class." This also lends itself to an accessibility "like no other and it really helps the students that need extra help outside of the classroom." All in all, professors have so "many years of experience behind them, they are able to transfer all their knowledge to students in an effective and fun way." There "are museums, parks, guest speakers in the city that professors will often take advantage of by taking the class to them allowing us to learn the subject from a real-world perspective."

Life

DePaul has "lots of organizations that cater to different causes and a lot of extracurricular activities," as well as fifteen Division I athletic teams that students enjoy watching. The Chicago-based campus also ensures that there's not only a lot to do, but plenty of opportunity to put what's being learned to the test. In particular, students complete "a lot of community service in the neighborhood as well as throughout the USA," but many also just "enjoy going out into the city and trying out new restaurants around the city." That doesn't mean DePaul skimps out on campus offerings! There are "always events happening to increase student interaction," and these are "really creative and interesting." And even though DePaul is spread across two campuses, students note that activities are always planned in such a way "that there is enough time to catch a train to get to the other campus."

Student Body

One in three people at DePaul is a first-generation college student, and the student body as a whole "is pretty diverse when it comes to race, gender, religion, and orientation of each student." Attendees find this to be a bonus, because not only are they learning from the professors, but they're also "gain[ing] considerable knowledge from [their] peers." This is especially true given the warm atmosphere, where it is both "easy to make friends and easy to get engaged with events going on around campus," regardless of socioeconomic background. "The campus is pretty liberal," students observe, but stress that everyone has "freedom and respect of choice for views [and] religion." This ultimately results in "a large sense of belonging in any classroom between all the students," and helps to ensure that everyone remains "very focused."

DePaul University

Financial Aid: 312-362-8610 • E-Mail: admission@depaul.edu • Website: www.depaul.edu

THE PRINCETON REVIEW SAYS

Admissions

Very important factors considered include: rigor of secondary school record, academic GPA, standardized test scores. *Important factors considered include:* class rank, recommendation(s), extracurricular activities, talent/ability, character/personal qualities. *Other factors considered include:* application essay, interview, first generation, alumni/ae relation, geographical residence, state residency, religious affiliation/commitment, racial/ethnic status. ACT with or without writing accepted. SAT with or without Essay component accepted. High school diploma is required and GED is accepted. *Academic units required:* 4 English, 3 math, 3 science, 2 science labs, 2 units from above areas or other academic areas. *Academic units recommended:* 4 English, 3 math, 3 science, 2 science labs, 2 foreign language.

Financial Aid

Students should submit: FAFSA. Priority filing deadline is 12/1. The Princeton Review suggests that all financial aid forms be submitted as soon as possible after October 1. *Need-based scholarships/grants offered:* College/university scholarship or grant aid from institutional funds; Federal Pell; Private scholarships; SEOG; State scholarships/grants. *Loan aid offered:* Direct PLUS loans; Direct Subsidized Stafford Loans; Direct Unsubsidized Stafford Loans. Applicants will be notified of awards on a rolling basis beginning 12/15. Federal Work-Study Program available. Institutional employment available.

The Inside Word

DePaul's reputation as one of the most diverse schools in the country is not mere hyperbole, it's a truth expressed by student after student, and by the actions of the administration itself. The school actively seeks out minority students both as freshmen and transfers, and in an effort to surmount tuition-related obstacles works with local community colleges so students can meet their requirements at a lower cost before transferring to DePaul. Based on research and DePaul's student-centered approach to education, DePaul has adopted a test-optional alternative for freshman admission. Students applying for freshman admission can choose whether or not to submit ACT or SAT scores as part of the application.

THE SCHOOL SAYS "..."

From the Admissions Office

"The nation's largest Catholic university, DePaul University is nationally recognized for its innovative academic programs that embrace a comprehensive learn-by-doing approach. DePaul has two residential locations. The Lincoln Park Campus is home to the College of Liberal Arts and Social Sciences, the College of Science and Health, the College of Education, the School of Music, The Theatre School and the extensive John T. Richardson Library. The Loop location, located in Chicago's downtown—a world-class center for business, government, law, and culture—is home to DePaul's Driehaus College of Business, College of Communication, College of Law, College of Computing and Digital Media, and School of Continuing & Professional Studies."

SELECTIVITY

Admissions Rating	81
# of applicants	26,895
% of applicants accepted	68
% of acceptees attending	14

FRESHMAN PROFILE

Range SAT EBRW	540–650
Range SAT Math	530–640
Range SAT Composite	1080–1280
# submitting SAT scores	1,694
% submitting SAT scores	64
Average HS GPA	3.7

DEADLINES

Early action	
Deadline	11/15
Notification	1/15
Regular	
Priority	11/15
Deadline	2/1
Notification	3/15
Nonfall registration?	Yes

FINANCIAL FACTS

Financial Aid Rating	84
Annual tuition	$40,551
Room and board	$14,736
Required fees	$651
Books and supplies	$1,104
Average frosh need-based scholarship	$24,581
Average UG need-based scholarship	$21,739
% needy frosh rec. need-based scholarship or grant aid	99
% needy UG rec. need-based scholarship or grant aid	96
% needy frosh rec. non-need-based scholarship or grant aid	11
% needy UG rec. non-need-based scholarship or grant aid	7
% needy frosh rec. need-based self-help aid	67
% needy UG rec. need-based self-help aid	74
% frosh rec. any financial aid	97
% UG rec. any financial aid	86
% UG borrow to pay for school	64
Average cumulative indebtedness	$29,621
% frosh need fully met	12
% ugrads need fully met	8
Average % of frosh need met	70
Average % of ugrad need met	65

DePauw University

204 E. Seminary Street, Greencastle, IN 46135 • Admissions: 765-658-4006 • Fax: 765-658-4007

STUDENTS SAY "..."

Academics

Serious-minded students are drawn to DePauw University for its "small classes," "encouraging" professors, and the "individual academic attention" they can expect to receive. Academically, DePauw is "demanding but rewarding," and "requires a lot of outside studying and discipline" in order to keep up. Professors' "expectations are very high," which means "you can't slack off and get good grades." Be prepared to pull your "fair share of all-nighters." Fortunately, DePauw professors are more than just stern taskmasters. Though they pile on the work, they "are always helpful and available" to students in need. When things get overwhelming, "they are very understanding and will cut you a break if you really deserve" it. As a result, students come to know their professors "on a personal level," making DePauw the kind of school where it is "common [for students] to have dinner at a professor's house." Beyond stellar professors, DePauw's other academic draws include "extraordinary" study abroad opportunities and a "wonderful" alumni network great for "connections and networking opportunities." Alums also "keep our endowment pretty high, making it easy for the school to give out merit scholarships," which undergraduates appreciate. Student opinion regarding the administration ranges from ambivalent to slightly negative. One especially thorny issue is class registration; you "rarely" get into all the classes you want.

Life

Few schools are as Greek as DePauw, but students are quick to point out that "it is by no means *Animal House*." The Greek system here is more holistic than that. It "promotes not only social activities but also philanthropic events." That's not to say there aren't lots of frat parties here. There are. But "the administration has cracked down big time" on the larger frat parties, and "now there are just small parties in apartments and dorms." One recently issued rule is that freshmen "will not be allowed on Greek property until after rush, which is the first week of second semester." In addition to administrative regulation, students exercise their own self-restraint; for the typical undergraduate, "the week is mostly reserved for studying." Beyond the frats and sororities, "there is always a theater production, athletic event, or organization-sponsored event going on," and popular bands occasionally perform on campus. It's a good thing so much is happening at the school because off-campus entertainment options are scarce: "If there is really any fun to be had, it's not in Greencastle." The situation could be greatly improved if there were just a few "more restaurants and stores in the town or a nearby town." As things stand, however, students "have to go to Indianapolis (forty-five miles) to go shopping, watch a good movie, eat at a good restaurant, etc."

Student Body

Students feel their typical classmates are "upper middle class," "a little preppy, a little athletic," and "hardworking"; students "[party] hard on weekend," and "usually become involved with the Greek system." Students describe their peers as "driven" and wearing "polos and pearls." They "have all had multiple internships, international experience, and [have held] some type of leadership position." Though these folks may seem "overcommitted," they "always get their work done." For those who don't fit this mold, don't fret; most students seem to be "accepting of the different types" of people on campus. Diversity on campus is augmented through the school's partnership with the Posse Foundation, which brings in urban (though not necessarily minority) "students from Chicago and NYC every year." These students are described as "leaders on campus" and "take real initiative to hold their communities together."

Financial Aid: 765-658-4030 • E-Mail: admission@depauw.edu • Website: www.depauw.edu

THE PRINCETON REVIEW SAYS

Admissions

Very important factors considered include: rigor of secondary school record, academic GPA, standardized test scores. *Important factors considered include:* class rank, application essay, recommendation(s). *Other factors considered include:* interview, extracurricular activities, talent/ability, character/personal qualities, first generation, alumni/ae relation, geographical residence, state residency, volunteer work, work experience, level of applicant's interest. ACT with or without writing accepted. SAT with or without Essay component accepted. High school diploma is required and GED is accepted. *Academic units recommended:* 4 English, 4 math, 3 science, 2 science labs, 2 foreign language, 2 social studies.

Financial Aid

Students should submit: FAFSA; Institution's own financial aid form. Priority filing deadline is 12/15. The Princeton Review suggests that all financial aid forms be submitted as soon as possible after October 1. *Need-based scholarships/grants offered:* College/university scholarship or grant aid from institutional funds; Federal Pell; Private scholarships; SEOG; State scholarships/grants. *Loan aid offered:* Direct Subsidized Stafford Loans; Direct Unsubsidized Stafford Loans. Applicants will be notified of awards on a rolling basis beginning 2/1. Federal Work-Study Program available. Institutional employment available.

The Inside Word

Prospective applicants should not be deceived by DePauw's high acceptance rate. The students who are accepted and choose to enroll here have the academic goods to justify their admission. Many of them are accepted by more "competitive" schools and still choose DePauw. DePauw's generous financial aid packages have a lot to do with students' choice to enroll.

THE SCHOOL SAYS "..."

From the Admissions Office

"DePauw University is a nationally recognized liberal arts university that is so confident in the outcomes of our distinct education that we are the first university to guarantee it through the Gold Commitment. Committed to both the rigorous academics and co-curricular opportunities available to students, DePauw encourages all its students to find and explore their passions, confident that they will find success post graduation regardless of what those are. Our graduates experience uncommon success among their peers, leading to careers as CEOs, Pulitzer Prize winners, humanitarian leaders, congressmen and women, entrepreneurs, and a Nobel Laureate scientist. Our students demonstrate academic curiosity, a willingness to explore new avenues not yet discovered and the courage to question previously held assumptions. With more than 65% of students having an international experience, our students have a unique ability to connect with individuals from all backgrounds and bring a worldly perspective to solving difficult issues."

SELECTIVITY

Admissions Rating	86
# of applicants	5,173
% of applicants accepted	67
% of acceptees attending	17

FRESHMAN PROFILE

Range SAT EBRW	560–650
Range SAT Math	550–680
Range ACT Composite	24–29
# submitting SAT scores	333
% submitting SAT scores	56
# submitting ACT scores	407
% submitting ACT scores	68
Average HS GPA	3.8
% graduated top 10% of class	40
% graduated top 25% of class	70
% graduated top 50% of class	95

DEADLINES

Early decision	
Deadline	11/1
Notification	12/1
Early action	
Deadline	12/1
Notification	1/15
Regular	
Deadline	2/1
Notification	Rolling, 12/15
Nonfall registration?	Yes

FINANCIAL FACTS

Financial Aid Rating	89
Annual tuition	$50,278
Room and board	$13,400
Required fees	$868
Books and supplies	$1,000
Average frosh need-based scholarship	$40,869
Average UG need-based scholarship	$39,150
% needy frosh rec. need-based scholarship or grant aid	100
% needy UG rec. need-based scholarship or grant aid	100
% needy frosh rec. non-need-based scholarship or grant aid	18
% needy UG rec. non-need-based scholarship or grant aid	17
% needy frosh rec. need-based self-help aid	79
% needy UG rec. need-based self-help aid	81
% UG borrow to pay for school	80
Average cumulative indebtedness	$25,813
% frosh need fully met	27
% ugrads need fully met	26
Average % of frosh need met	90
Average % of ugrad need met	90

DICKINSON COLLEGE

P.O. Box 1773, Carlisle, PA 17013-2896 • Admissions: 717-245-1231 • Fax: 717-245-1442

STUDENTS SAY "..."

Academics

Founded just days after the conclusion of the American Revolution by a signer of the Declaration of Independence, Dickinson College was borne with the mission of preparing young people to be active and engaged leaders in society via a "global, sustainable, and pragmatic liberal arts education." This Pennsylvania college's serious focus on global engagement and service seeps into every crevice of its "outstanding," interdisciplinary academics, and it has a support system and "infinite amount of resources and facilities" on offer. For instance, there is "a makery for students to use containing craft supplies and a media center" available to all. There are "ample opportunities to keep your mind engaged" (more than half of all students study abroad at some point), and Dickinson gives students incredible freedom to study under different disciplines. Even students with a focus on one specific major "are able and required to experience classes in other academic areas." Professors at Dickinson are "incredibly accessible and eager to reach out," and "all have very impressive credentials and connections." They "help students see things from various perspectives and not just their own" and encourage students to keep an open mind. Every course is "elaborately prepared by the department" and deans and advisors are helpful when trying to figure out a major. There's no easy ride at Dickinson; faculty "expect a lot from you, [and] outside work can be 1 to 3 hours per class per day." The school encourages students to be educated in all fields of study, and Dickinson students "are always seeking a new answer, discovery, or understanding in every field." A tight 9:1 student-to-faculty ratio and a wide course selection help make students diverse in background and interests, and these interests "many times overlap in seemingly opposite majors."

Life

Although a small school, students here are involved in the many different available extracurricular organizations, and "most take leadership roles in at least one if not several." They "take their schoolwork seriously, but they take their other roles at least equally as seriously." Many people have jobs on campus, and "when the weather is nice, most students are outside." The college's student activities board, MOB, is the largest organizer of events, which range "from food- to music- to entertainment-related," and the Clarke Forum regularly brings in guest speakers who talk on a variety of topics. Dickinson's food "is not great," but it does a good job of making sure there are kosher and vegan options at meals, and the town has great restaurants and shops. The weekend party scene is "very inclusive and energetic," but "it's definitely possible to enjoy oneself without drinking." Carlisle, the small town that surrounds the school, "has enough to do that you will be entertained." The local movie theater is a popular attraction (especially for the $6 matinees on Saturday and Sunday afternoons) and during the spring, students also attend Harrisburg Senators games, the local minor-league affiliate of the Washington Nationals.

Student Body

This is an "interesting bunch for sure." "We have people who are ardent defenders of social justice, people concerned with community service, artists, musicians, as well as people who can speak six languages...[or] who came to Dickinson from Carlisle itself." Although the student body "isn't the most diverse" from an ethnic standpoint, everyone here "seems to have an open mind and heart" and is "friendly and involved." "Students' voices are heard" here, and "everyone feels welcome" in this "safe and trustworthy community," which also has a fair number of international students. There is also "a strong activist strain" among Dickinson students, and "most people on campus are very attuned to issues of class, race, sexual orientation, gender, and many other identities."

DICKINSON COLLEGE

Financial Aid: 717-245-1308 • E-Mail: admissions@dickinson.edu • Website: www.dickinson.edu/

THE PRINCETON REVIEW SAYS

Admissions

Very important factors considered include: rigor of secondary school record, academic GPA, application essay, recommendation(s), extracurricular activities, talent/ability, character/personal qualities, volunteer work, level of applicant's interest. *Important factors considered include:* class rank, standardized test scores, interview, alumni/ae relation, geographical residence, state residency, racial/ethnic status. *Other factors considered include:* first generation. ACT with or without writing accepted. SAT with or without Essay component accepted. High school diploma is required and GED is accepted. *Academic units required:* 4 English, 3 math, 3 science, 2 science labs, 2 foreign language, 2 social studies, 2 academic electives. *Academic units recommended:* 3 foreign language.

Financial Aid

Students should submit: CSS/Financial Aid PROFILE; FAFSA; Noncustodial PROFILE; State aid form. Priority filing deadline is 11/15. The Princeton Review suggests that all financial aid forms be submitted as soon as possible after October 1. *Need-based scholarships/grants offered:* College/university scholarship or grant aid from institutional funds; Federal Pell; Private scholarships; SEOG; State scholarships/grants. *Loan aid offered:* Direct PLUS loans; Direct Subsidized Stafford Loans; Direct Unsubsidized Stafford Loans. Federal Work-Study Program available. Institutional employment available.

The Inside Word

The applicant pool for small liberal arts colleges has become increasingly competitive in recent years, and Dickinson is no exception. For admission here, you'll want to be the stereotypical well-rounded student, with a solid GPA in challenging classes, and broad extracurricular involvement.

THE SCHOOL SAYS "..."

From the Admissions Office

"Dickinson is a nationally recognized liberal arts college chartered in 1783 in Carlisle, Pennsylvania. Devoted to its revolutionary roots, the college maintains the mission of founder Benjamin Rush—to provide a useful education for the common good in the liberal arts and sciences. Dickinson has a robust academic program, offering forty-five majors plus minors, certificates, independent research, and internships. Our innovative programs range from neuroscience to security studies and develop intellectual independence by actively engaging in research, fieldwork, lab work in state-of-the-art science programs, and other experiential opportunities. The newest additions to our curriculum—certificates in health studies, food studies, and social innovation & entrepreneurship—are evidence of our emphasis on being responsive in today's ever-changing economy. Dickinson's global curriculum includes international business & management, international studies, thirteen languages, and many globally oriented courses. Dickinson offers one of the world's most respected study-abroad programs, and about two-thirds of Dickinson's students study in thirty-nine programs in twenty-four countries on six continents. Dickinson is recognized as a leader among educational institutions committed to sustainability and green initiatives. The Center for Sustainability Education integrates sustainability into its academics, facilities, operations, and campus culture. Dickinson has received the highest awards from the Association for the Advancement of Sustainability in Higher Education, Sierra Club, Sustainable Endowments Institute, The Princeton Review, and Second Nature. Dickinson alumni are at the top of their fields as business leaders, professional artists and writers, sports agents and athletes, doctors and researchers. And many of them used their liberal arts foundation to forge their own paths. Our graduate school partnerships enable our students to enter top programs with greater ease and reflect the high regard in which Dickinson is held."

SELECTIVITY

Admissions Rating	91
# of applicants	6,426
% of applicants accepted	40
% of acceptees attending	18
# offered a place on the wait list	762
% accepting a place on wait list	31
% admitted from wait list	11
# of early decision applicants	309
% accepted early decision	62

FRESHMAN PROFILE

Range SAT EBRW	600–690
Range SAT Math	590–700
Range ACT Composite	26–32
# submitting SAT scores	267
% submitting SAT scores	59
# submitting ACT scores	119
% submitting ACT scores	26
% graduated top 10% of class	43
% graduated top 25% of class	73
% graduated top 50% of class	96

DEADLINES

Early decision	
Deadline	11/15
Notification	12/15
Other ED Deadline	1/15
Other ED Notification	2/15
Regular	
Deadline	1/15
Notification	3/31
Nonfall registration?	No

FINANCIAL FACTS

Financial Aid Rating	95
Annual tuition	$56,498
Room and board	$14,672
Books and supplies	$1,324
Average frosh need-based scholarship	$41,571
Average UG need-based scholarship	$43,188
% needy frosh rec. need-based scholarship or grant aid	97
% needy UG rec. need-based scholarship or grant aid	98
% needy frosh rec. non-need-based scholarship or grant aid	7
% needy UG rec. non-need-based scholarship or grant aid	7
% needy frosh rec. need-based self-help aid	91
% needy UG rec. need-based self-help aid	90
% frosh rec. any financial aid	85
% UG rec. any financial aid	82
% UG borrow to pay for school	55
Average cumulative indebtedness	$27,030
% frosh need fully met	93
% ugrads need fully met	74
Average % of frosh need met	99
Average % of ugrad need met	98

DREW UNIVERSITY

Office of Undergraduate Admissions, Madison, NJ 07940-1493 • Admissions: 973-408-3739 • Fax: 973-408-3068

STUDENTS SAY "..."

Academics

Located in Madison, New Jersey, Drew University is just a hop-and-a-skip away from the New York City universe, and the school takes full advantage of its proximity to industry hubs. The 1,500 undergraduates have access to more than fifty majors and minors and thousands of related internships, as well as lots of study abroad options. Drew's seven unique NYC semesters allow students to do coursework with professors and then commute into New York City to learn in the field (for example, on Wall Street, at the United Nations, or in the art, communications, social entrepreneurship and theatre scene). The science departments are standouts—one of its fellows won the Nobel Prize for Medicine in 2015—and its top-ranked theatre program is "comprehensive in such a way that every graduate of the program will have at least tried every single part of the theatrical process."

The "incredibly engaging" professors go "above and beyond the role of just...teacher" and are "very much willing to assist in any way." They "facilitate conversations so that you learn in a way that's not just your average PowerPoint [presentation]" and "invest time in you academically and as a young adult looking for a career." The university does an excellent job of fostering undergraduate student research, and professors "require a level of accountability that motivates a student to perform" both in and out of the classroom. Far and away the things that students appreciate the most about Drew are its small class sizes, which bolster the personal attention from teachers, almost all of whom have PhDs. ("There are no classes taught by TAs, which makes for better quality learning.") This "mentorship with professors" is a lasting benefit to students, who say that "you really get to know your professors in an impactful way."

Life

While the small, wooded town of Madison isn't exactly hopping, students make the most of the "gorgeous" campus (where housing is guaranteed all four years; currently 87 percent of the student body lives on campus) and "tend to be proactive in creating their own recreational experiences." People "are very involved in sports and activities, such as clubs and organizations," and many have jobs or internships. New York City is a short 50-minute train ride away, and nearby Morristown also provides some flavor. Academics "take up a good amount of daytime, but life at school is "always manageable"; "classes are challenging enough and the workload isn't overbearing" so "there is always time to relax if you're responsible and manage your time well." Tuesdays and Thursdays are dollar beer nights, so "many students take time out of studying to go out for a little," but "most free time is spent in friends' rooms, playing video games or watching shows." Though school events aren't terribly well-attended from time to time there are things which students make sure to have fun at, "such as Bingo night, the holiday ball, and Drewchella (a live music festival)." All in all, "there is a good balance of leisure and education."

Student Body

While about half of the students are from New Jersey, the student body is diverse and includes a growing international student population. As a small school, "Everyone at least knows of everyone else and is friendly with them." "Drew students are the type that see a $50 bill in the street and find the person who dropped it," says one student of this group that is "attractive inside and out." There's a large percentage of people actively involved in both the arts and sciences, and the regular cliques—"jocks, theatre kids, science nerds"—all "blend together and overlap so that there are no definite lines separating people." Drew is an eco-friendly campus, and "there is a fairly large number of gluten free/vegetarian students."

Financial Aid: 973-408-3112 • E-Mail: cadm@drew.edu • Website: www.drew.edu

THE PRINCETON REVIEW SAYS

Admissions

Very important factors considered include: rigor of secondary school record, academic GPA, interview. *Important factors considered include:* application essay, recommendation(s), extra-curricular activities, talent/ability, character/personal qualities. *Other factors considered include:* class rank, standardized test scores, first generation, alumni/ae relation, racial/ethnic status, volunteer work, work experience, level of applicant's interest. ACT with or without writing accepted. SAT with or without Essay component accepted. High school diploma is required and GED is accepted. *Academic units recommended:* 4 English, 3 math, 2 science, 2 foreign language, 2 social studies, 2 history, 3 academic electives.

Financial Aid

Students should submit: FAFSA. Priority filing deadline is 1/1. The Princeton Review suggests that all financial aid forms be submitted as soon as possible after October 1. *Need-based scholarships/grants offered:* College/university scholarship or grant aid from institutional funds; Federal Pell; Private scholarships; SEOG; State scholarships/grants. *Loan aid offered:* Direct PLUS loans; Direct Subsidized Stafford Loans; Direct Unsubsidized Stafford Loans. Applicants will be notified of awards on or about 3/25. Federal Work-Study Program available. Institutional employment available.

The Inside Word

Drew takes a holistic approach to evaluating applications, so you definitely want to showcase more than just your GPA (though that's also important). Drew's applicant pool has grown significantly in recent years, so presenting yourself as not only a great student but also a great fit with the school will help you stand out from the pack. The university is test optional.

THE SCHOOL SAYS "..."

From the Admissions Office

"Our Launch undergraduate experience ensures that every student graduates with a purpose, sought-after transferable skills, a network of mentors, and an experience-based résumé. Launch is universal to all students—we make sure that every Drew student cultivates a support network of personal, academic and professional mentors. In and out of the classroom, every Drew student develops the transferable workplace skills most sought by employers and graduate programs, from creative thinking and collaboration to problem solving and ethical thinking. And every Drew student is guaranteed at least two immersive experiences (like our seven NYC Semesters) that are résumé ready—an essential part of a Drew degree.

"We are affordable and work to provide great access to the benefits of a Drew education to even more families. In 2018–19, Drew offered $32 million in grants and scholarships and 80 percent of students received merit or need-based aid. The Princeton Review named Drew among their 200 *Best Value Colleges* and twice saluted it as one of fifty *Colleges that Create Futures*.

"Drew's beautiful campus is located in a charming small town twenty miles from New York City, a region full of leading organizations. Drew students recently interned at employers such as CNN, Goldman Sachs, Michael Kors, the Red Sox, and the United Nations, among others. Ninety-four percent of recent graduates were working or in graduate school within six months of graduation. They are employed at places such as Google, Bank of America, Lincoln Center, the U.S. Department of State, Morgan Stanley, and Prudential, and they attend graduate programs at Harvard, Stanford, Princeton, Oxford, and Columbia, among others.

"Drew students are part of a powerful community on a lively and diverse campus. Ninety percent live on campus, and housing is guaranteed for four years. Students are active in 100+ student-run clubs and 25 percent are Drew Ranger student-athletes. Community traditions include Halloweekend, 99 Nights, Drewchella, and Junior Senior Semiformal. Located within one hour are a wildlife refuge, ski resorts, beaches, the Meadowlands (home of the Giants and Jets), and the museums, concert venues, sports arenas, clubs, galleries, theaters, etc. of New York City."

SELECTIVITY

Admissions Rating	81
# of applicants	3,928
% of applicants accepted	71
% of acceptees attending	14
# offered a place on the wait list	147
% accepting a place on wait list	32
% admitted from wait list	70
# of early decision applicants	104
% accepted early decision	80

FRESHMAN PROFILE

Range SAT EBRW	570–650
Range SAT Math	535–650
Range SAT Composite	1110–1270
Range ACT Composite	23–29
# submitting SAT scores	259
% submitting SAT scores	65
# submitting ACT scores	82
% submitting ACT scores	21
Average HS GPA	3.5
% graduated top 10% of class	23
% graduated top 25% of class	49
% graduated top 50% of class	86

DEADLINES

Early decision	
Deadline	11/15
Notification	12/15
Other ED Deadline	1/15
Other ED Notification	2/15
Early action	
Deadline	12/15
Notification	1/25
Regular	
Priority	11/15
Deadline	2/1
Notification	3/18
Nonfall registration?	Yes

FINANCIAL FACTS

Financial Aid Rating	87
Annual tuition	$39,828
Room and board	$14,672
Required fees	$1,132
Books and supplies	$1,200
Average frosh need-based scholarship	$32,964
Average UG need-based scholarship	$31,510
% needy frosh rec. need-based scholarship or grant aid	100
% needy UG rec. need-based scholarship or grant aid	100
% needy frosh rec. non-need-based scholarship or grant aid	9
% needy UG rec. non-need-based scholarship or grant aid	8
% needy frosh rec. need-based self-help aid	82
% needy UG rec. need-based self-help aid	82
% frosh rec. any financial aid	99
% UG rec. any financial aid	96
% UG borrow to pay for school	62
Average cumulative indebtedness	$25,049
% frosh need fully met	15
% ugrads need fully met	15
Average % of frosh need met	83
Average % of ugrad need met	83

DREXEL UNIVERSITY

3141 Chestnut Street, Main Building, Philadelphia, PA 19104 • Admissions: 215-895-2400 • Fax: 215 895-1207

CAMPUS LIFE

Quality of Life Rating	82
Fire Safety Rating	97
Green Rating	88
Type of school	Private
Environment	Metropolis

STUDENTS

Total undergrad enrollment	15,500
% male/female	52/48
% from out of state	49
% frosh live on campus	87
% ugrads live on campus	22
# of fraternities (% ugrad men join)	20 (11)
# of sororities (% ugrad women join)	11 (10)
% African American	7
% Asian	18
% Caucasian	52
% Hispanic	7
% Native American	<1
% Pacific Islander	<1
% Two or more races	4
% Race and/or ethnicity unknown	2
% international	11
# of countries represented	115

SURVEY SAYS ...

Career services are great
Internships are widely available
Students love Philadelphia, PA

ACADEMICS

Academic Rating	78
% students returning for sophomore year	89
% students graduating within 6 years	71
Calendar	Quarter
Student/faculty ratio	11:1
Profs interesting rating	82
Profs accessible rating	85

Most classes have 10–19 students.

MOST POPULAR MAJORS

Business/Commerce, General; Registered Nursing/
Registered Nurse; Mechanical Engineering

STUDENTS SAY "..."

Academics

A large private research university, Philadelphia's Drexel University draws many students through its cooperative education ("co-op") program, in which students take major-oriented classes in their first year and then alternate six-month studies with six-month full-time employment. Drexel "moves fast," and students love the feeling that "our work makes an impact in real companies." As a research-driven university, the school has found a "really strong area within the sciences" and also does very well in challenging students with "a fast-paced curriculum" that prepares them for a working environment and helps them to get "a hands-on look at what [they] can do with [their] degree." Though students find the schedule "very different compared to the normal college experience," they are well-aware of the track they've signed up for: "a lot more challenging and a lot less down time." One student explains, "If you are not a very self-motivated, hard-working student, you'll fall behind."

Most Drexel professors work in the industry that they're teaching and "are beyond knowledgeable on the subject" (a good number of professors are also Drexel alumni). Professors are all "extremely intelligent," but many students admit that "sometimes there is a language barrier." Still, teachers here are "resourceful and ready to help solve a problem or redirect to someone who can." The quarter system keeps students on their toes academically, but it "makes the year go by faster." "I was skeptical at first, but it was worth it," says one quarter-system fan. At the end of the day, students say that you "can't beat 21 months' worth of full-time experiences," and the school succeeds in giving students "a rigorous, great education that almost guarantees a job or place in grad school after graduation."

Life

Students generally spend their days "in class, in our gym, or working on co-op." Everyone here "works extremely hard"; due to the quarter system, "there is never a time where students aren't hitting the library or studying with friends." There are plenty of open areas of the campus that you can find students studying ("especially the quad in the spring or summer"), and though students are "not big on structured extracurricular activities," they "do occasionally party." Food trucks are a very popular source of grub, particularly "the Food Truck Alley" behind the Main Building. For fun, Center City Philadelphia is just a short walk or subway ride away, and has everything from the Philadelphia Orchestra and Pennsylvania Ballet to "a variety of clubs, theaters, and bars." The campus is perfectly placed so that "all the conveniences and exciting things about city life are in your backyard, but all the comforts of being on a college campus (security, familiarity) are also there." In those rare periods without midterms or finals, people also "go to the gym frequently and play intramural sports."

Student Body

This work-oriented university is filled with highly-motivated individuals that "consistently challenge themselves and are willing to push themselves so that they can tap their full potential." Most people at Drexel are pretty transparent about their reasons for being there: They're "looking for a good job." Since the "very stressful" curriculum keeps the pedal to the metal, students "rely on one another to ensure they understand and complete the tasks that are assigned." Everyone here is "generally in a state of caffeination or exhaustion (or both)," depending on their schedule for that day. The student body is very diverse (with a large number of international students), with "lots of colorful and unique characters on campus." The community can be fairly "clique-y," but the suite-style rooming "really helps with making friends."

Financial Aid: 215-895-2537 • E-Mail: enroll@drexel.edu • Website: www.drexel.edu

THE PRINCETON REVIEW SAYS

Admissions

Very important factors considered include: rigor of secondary school record, class rank, academic GPA, standardized test scores. *Important factors considered include:* application essay, recommendation(s), character/personal qualities. *Other factors considered include:* interview, extracurricular activities, talent/ability, first generation, alumni/ae relation, volunteer work, work experience, level of applicant's interest. ACT with or without writing accepted. SAT with or without Essay component accepted. High school diploma is required and GED is accepted. *Academic units required:* 3 math, 1 science, 1 science lab. *Academic units recommended:* 1 foreign language.

Financial Aid

Students should submit: CSS/Financial Aid PROFILE; FAFSA. The Princeton Review suggests that all financial aid forms be submitted as soon as possible after October 1. *Need-based scholarships/grants offered:* College/university scholarship or grant aid from institutional funds; Federal Pell; Private scholarships; SEOG; State scholarships/grants. *Loan aid offered:* Direct PLUS loans; Direct Subsidized Stafford Loans; Direct Unsubsidized Stafford Loans. Applicants will be notified of awards on or about 4/1. Federal Work-Study Program available. Institutional employment available.

The Inside Word

Drexel University's nationally recognized co-op program provides unique hands-on experience for students with companies in and around Philadelphia to help them in their post-college employment. Given the current state of the economy, that's a huge boost for prospective applicants, especially in the engineering fields that Drexel still specializes in. Drexel accepts the Common Application for most programs, and takes into consideration a number of criteria when determining admission, including high school performance, letters of recommendation, standardized test scores, and the essay.

THE SCHOOL SAYS "..."

From the Admissions Office

"Drexel University has maintained a reputation for academic excellence since its founding in 1891. Through Drexel Co-op, students have the opportunity to test-drive their degree in paid full-time positions where they can earn up to 18 months of workplace experience before graduation with employers such as *Fortune* 500 companies, major pharmaceutical companies, and top design firms, as well as nonprofit agencies and government organizations. More than 1,600 employers in thirty-two states and forty-six international locations participate in the Drexel Co-op program. The average six-month paid co-op salary is more than $16,000.

"Drexel offers more than 80 undergraduate majors and over twenty accelerated degree programs. Accelerated degree options include the BA/BS/JD in law; BA/BS+MD in medicine; BS/DPT in physical therapy; BS/MS in computing and informatics; and BS/MBA in business.

"Qualified students can apply to the Honors program, which is open to students in every academic discipline. The Honors program offers special living communities designed for the exceptional student and opportunities for social activities, traveling, and independent projects. The STAR (Students Tackling Advanced Research) Scholars program invites qualified students to participate in faculty-mentored research projects in their chosen fields as early as the freshman year. Drexel also has an active Study Abroad program in more than two dozen countries around the world."

SELECTIVITY

Admissions Rating	83
# of applicants	30,242
% of applicants accepted	77
% of acceptees attending	14
# offered a place on the wait list	1,215
% accepting a place on wait list	0
# of early decision applicants	313
% accepted early decision	86

FRESHMAN PROFILE

Range SAT EBRW	580–670
Range SAT Math	590–710
Range ACT Composite	25–30
# submitting SAT scores	2,903
% submitting SAT scores	86
# submitting ACT scores	867
% submitting ACT scores	26
Average HS GPA	3.7
% graduated top 10% of class	33
% graduated top 25% of class	64
% graduated top 50% of class	90

DEADLINES

Early decision	
Deadline	11/1
Notification	12/15
Early action	
Deadline	11/1
Notification	12/15
Regular	
Deadline	1/15
Notification	4/1
Nonfall registration?	Yes

FINANCIAL FACTS

Financial Aid Rating	86
Annual tuition	$52,146
Room and board	$14,241
Required fees	$2,370
Books and supplies	$1,200
Average frosh need-based scholarship	$33,305
Average UG need-based scholarship	$29,091
% needy frosh rec. need-based scholarship or grant aid	100
% needy UG rec. need-based scholarship or grant aid	96
% needy frosh rec. non-need-based scholarship or grant aid	15
% needy UG rec. non-need-based scholarship or grant aid	11
% needy frosh rec. need-based self-help aid	66
% needy UG rec. need-based self-help aid	73
% frosh rec. any financial aid	99.8
% UG rec. any financial aid	94.2
% frosh need fully met	30
% ugrads need fully met	23
Average % of frosh need met	81
Average % of ugrad need met	74

DRURY UNIVERSITY

900 North Benton Avenue, Springfield, MO 65802-3712 • Admissions: 417-873-7205 • Fax: 417-866-3873

STUDENTS SAY ". . ."

Academics

There is a lot to admire about "the atmosphere that Drury creates," a "truly beautiful and unique" college in Springfield, Missouri. After all, it provides students with a "well-rounded" education, "close community," and numerous "opportunities [for] leadership." Many undergrads also appreciate Drury's course "flexibility," which allows students to "be involved in non-major-specific courses/organizations." Of course, while the university offers a wide range of disciplines, many students highlight the "pre-health" and "architecture" departments as especially strong. Fortunately, no matter the major, Drury's "small size" lends itself to a "personalized [academic] experience." Indeed, since the "average class...is 12 students," everyone has a "better opportunity to communicate with professors on a one-on-one level." Though this doesn't negate the fact that classes here are rather "rigorous." Nevertheless, "the faculty works closely with students to help them be...successful." One grateful student agrees adding, "[Professors] are always available outside of class and really work with me on topics that I am struggling with." They make it evident that "they really care about what they are teaching." Best of all, Drury professors are "very personable, and always willing to go the extra mile to ensure the best learning experience for their students." Therefore, it comes as no surprise that undergrads here are able to develop "last[ing] relationships" with their professors.

Life

There's plenty of fun to be had at Drury. To begin with, "during the fall semester you can find a lot of activity outside and on the campus green spaces, mostly sporting activities sprinkled with friendly gatherings and discussions." Additionally, a large number of students "volunteer in the community on a weekly basis." And most people "participate in at least one organization on campus." "Greek life is really big here" as are "intramural sports... such as basketball and volleyball." If those activities aren't your thing, fear not. The Student Union Board hosts "a lot of events" and those are typically well attended. Undergrads do note that "there is a party scene," as well, although mostly off-campus. Drury students are also rather adept at making their own fun. As one individual shares, "The students on my hall love to have board game nights, and we also have access to a projector room where we watch movies together." Lastly, the Springfield area offers "plenty of bars and clubs" that become quite popular on the weekends. And there are plenty of "coffee shops, restaurants, bookstores, bakeries, movie theatres, etc." too.

Student Body

When asked to describe their peers, undergrads at Drury immediately boast that they are "very engaging and friendly." One student quickly illustrates, "Walking down Drury Lane you say hello to at least five people, some you may not even really know; however, people are so nice and welcoming here that you don't have to...know [them] to say [hi]." Aside from this gregariousness, Drury undergrads are "bright and ambitious" and filled with "awesome school spirit." Moreover, many students desire to become "informed global citizens." As another undergrad proudly states, "I am surrounded by students who take every opportunity and experience to learn about themselves, their community, and the world." Hence, these undergrads love that the university draws students "from all around the world." In fact, it's not unusual for a person to find himself "sitting next to someone from Springfield (a local) or someone from Germany or Kenya." Perhaps this explains why "acceptance is a big part of [Drury's] campus." Indeed, "everyone tries to be as unified as possible." It helps that Drury's "small" size means that there's "so much room for building friendships and the possibility of knowing a good majority of the students here is most certainly possible." As this satisfied undergrad concludes, "I never imagined a college campus could feel so supportive and connected until I came to Drury."

Financial Aid: 417-873-7312 • E-Mail: druryad@drury.edu • Website: www.drury.edu

THE PRINCETON REVIEW SAYS

Admissions

Very important factors considered include: academic GPA, rigor of secondary school record. *Important factors considered include:* standardized test scores, talent/ability. *Other factors considered include:* application essay, recommendation(s), interview, extracurricular activities, character/personal qualities, first generation, alumni/ae relation, religious affiliation/commitment, racial/ethnic status, volunteer work, work experience, level of applicant's interest. ACT with or without writing accepted. SAT with or without Essay component accepted. High school diploma is required and GED is accepted. *Academic units required:* 3 math. *Academic units recommended:* 4 English, 3 math, 3 science, 2 foreign language, 3 social studies.

Financial Aid

The Princeton Review suggests that all financial aid forms be submitted as soon as possible after October 1. *Need-based scholarships/grants offered:* College/university scholarship or grant aid from institutional funds; Federal Pell; Private scholarships; SEOG; State scholarships/grants. *Loan aid offered:* Direct PLUS loans; Direct Subsidized Stafford Loans; Direct Unsubsidized Stafford Loans. Applicants will be notified of awards on a rolling basis beginning 2/15. Federal Work-Study Program available. Institutional employment available.

The Inside Word

The admissions process at Drury is fairly selective. Admissions officers look for applicants who have taken a challenging college prep curriculum. They also closely evaluate personal statements and each student's extracurricular participation. Standardized test scores hold some weight as well, though the university has no preference between the SAT or ACT. Finally, Drury operates on a basis of rolling admission. If you're really interested in attending, consider submitting your application as early as possible.

THE SCHOOL SAYS "..."

From the Admissions Office

"From day one, Drury students are engaged in real research and scholarship with faculty mentors. This is a rare advantage; one that speaks to Drury's singular approach to equipping students for leadership in the 21st century. Through its distinctive *Your Drury Fusion* program, the University provides students with an opportunity to blend career, calling, life, community, self and service to gain a broader perspective on the world. It also is a place where students get to really know their professors as well as their classmates, creating a strong sense of culture and community that transcends the classroom.

"Established in 1873, Drury University sits on 90 acres in the heart of Springfield, Missouri. A designated "Tree Campus" by the Arbor Day Foundation, it is an oasis within the city where students are engaged in highly interactive, intellectual exercises that teach them to be flexible, innovative and creative problem solvers.

"The university offers competitive and innovative degree programs, like music therapy, a nationally recognized architecture program and a pre-med program, that are unmatched by most other colleges and universities of its size.

"More than 30% of students have multiple majors and minors. This is the essence of Your Drury Fusion, a unique program that blends career and intellectual passions that are credentialed and for which students gain real-world experience that can be highlighted on their resume. In fact, 98% of graduates were employed, in graduate school or not seeking employment/education within six months of graduation."

SELECTIVITY

Admissions Rating	85
# of applicants	1,664
% of applicants accepted	64
% of acceptees attending	32

FRESHMAN PROFILE

Range SAT EBRW	520–620
Range SAT Math	525–605
Range SAT Composite	1080–1205
Range ACT Composite	22–28
# submitting SAT scores	43
% submitting SAT scores	13
# submitting ACT scores	309
% submitting ACT scores	90
Average HS GPA	3.8
% graduated top 10% of class	29
% graduated top 25% of class	60
% graduated top 50% of class	87

DEADLINES

Regular	
Deadline	8/30
Notification	Rolling, 9/1
Nonfall registration?	Yes

FINANCIAL FACTS

Financial Aid Rating	87
Annual tuition	$29,900
Room and board	$9,172
Required fees	$1,315
Books and supplies	$1,200
Average frosh need-based scholarship	$21,735
Average UG need-based scholarship	$20,513
% needy frosh rec. need-based scholarship or grant aid	100
% needy UG rec. need-based scholarship or grant aid	100
% needy frosh rec. non-need-based scholarship or grant aid	18
% needy UG rec. non-need-based scholarship or grant aid	20
% needy frosh rec. need-based self-help aid	66
% needy UG rec. need-based self-help aid	66
% frosh rec. any financial aid	100
% UG rec. any financial aid	98
% UG borrow to pay for school	62
Average cumulative indebtedness	$37,144
% frosh need fully met	22
% ugrads need fully met	25
Average % of frosh need met	78
Average % of ugrad need met	76

DUKE UNIVERSITY

2138 Campus Drive, Durham, NC 27708 • Admissions: 919-684-3214 • Fax: 919-668-1661

CAMPUS LIFE

Quality of Life Rating	**86**
Fire Safety Rating	**60***
Green Rating	**60***
Type of school	Private
Affiliation	Methodist
Environment	Metropolis

STUDENTS

Total undergrad enrollment	6,596
% male/female	50/50
% from out of state	85
% frosh from public high school	65
% frosh live on campus	100
% ugrads live on campus	85
# of fraternities (% ugrad men join)	21 (29)
# of sororities (% ugrad women join)	14 (42)
% African American	10
% Asian	22
% Caucasian	42
% Hispanic	9
% Native American	<1
% Pacific Islander	<1
% Two or more races	2
% Race and/or ethnicity unknown	4
% international	10
# of countries represented	89

SURVEY SAYS . . .

Classroom facilities are great
Lab facilities are great
Great library
Internships are widely available
Great financial aid
No one cheats
Recreation facilities are great
Lots of beer drinking
Hard liquor is popular
Very little drug use
Everyone loves the Blue Devils
Active student government

ACADEMICS

Academic Rating	**92**
% students returning for sophomore year	98
% students graduating within 4 years	87
% students graduating within 6 years	96
Calendar	Semester
Student/faculty ratio	6:1
Profs interesting rating	89
Profs accessible rating	93

Most classes have 10–19 students.
Most lab/discussion sessions have
 10–19 students.

MOST POPULAR MAJORS

Public Policy Analysis, General; Economics,
General; Psychology, General

STUDENTS SAY "..."

Academics

Duke University is "all about academic excellence complemented by highly competitive Division I sports and an enriching array of extracurricular activities," making the university "an exciting, challenging, and enjoyable place to be." Undergraduates choose Duke because they "are passionate about a wide range of things, including academics, sports, community service, research, and fun." And because the school seems equally committed to accommodating all of those pursuits, as one student puts it, "Duke is for the Ivy League candidate who is a little bit more laid-back about school and overachieving (but just a bit)." There's an "across-the-board excellence in all departments from humanities to engineering." In all areas, there's a "supportive environment in which the faculty, staff, and students are willing to look out for the other person and help them succeed." It's the norm to have large study groups, and "the review sessions, peer tutoring system, writing center, and academic support center are always helpful when students are struggling with anything from math homework to creating a résumé." Professors' "number-one priority is teaching undergraduates," and their love of discussion means they "would rather that the students lead the class as opposed to them leading the class." "There are a few who make me want to stay at Duke forever," says a student. Because "the school has a lot of confidence in its students," it offers them "seemingly limitless opportunities."

Life

Life at Duke "is very relaxed," and "you can either be a part of nothing, or you can be so over-committed that it's not even funny." Because "the student union and other organizations provide entertainment all the time, from movies to shows to campus-wide parties," there's "a wealth of on-campus opportunities to get involved." Indeed, weekends are for relaxing, and "people usually stay on campus for fun," because hometown Durham "has a few quirky streets and squares with restaurants, shops, clubs, etc." Undergrads' fervor for Blue Devils sports, on the other hand, can be boundless; sports, "especially basketball, are a huge deal here," and undergrads "will paint themselves completely blue and wait in line on the sidewalk in K-ville for three days to jump up and down in Cameron Indoor Stadium." Greek life "plays a big role in the social scene here," but "almost all the parties are open, so it definitely isn't hard to get into a party." A lot of people "just do their own thing—have a movie night, go exploring, go skiing or to the beach for a weekend." Still, the social scene can be "a little too intense" at times.

Student Body

The student body "is surprisingly ethnically diverse, with a number of students of Asian, African, and Hispanic descent," and "every type of person finds a welcoming group where he or she fits in." The typical Duke student "is someone who cares a lot about his or her education but at the same time won't sacrifice a social life for it." Life involves "getting a ton of work done first and then finding time to play and have fun." The typical student here is studious but social, athletic but can never be seen in the gym, job hunting but not worrying, and so on and so forth." Everyone is "incredibly focused," but "that includes social success as well." Students tend to be "focused on graduating and obtaining a lucrative and prosperous career," and although they "go out two to three times a week," they're "always looking polished." An "overwhelming number" are athletes, "not just varsity athletes...but athletes in high school or generally active people. Duke's athletic pride attracts this kind of person."

E-Mail: undergrad-admissions@duke.edu • Website: www.duke.edu

THE PRINCETON REVIEW SAYS

Admissions

Very important factors considered include: rigor of secondary school record, academic GPA, application essay, standardized test scores, recommendation(s), extracurricular activities, talent/ability, character/personal qualities. *Other factors considered include:* interview, first generation, alumni/ae relation, geographical residence, state residency, religious affiliation/ commitment, racial/ethnic status, volunteer work, work experience, level of applicant's interest. ACT or SAT (with or without writing) required. High school diploma is required and GED is not accepted. *Academic units recommended:* 4 English, 3 math, 3 science, 3 foreign language, 3 social studies.

Financial Aid

Students should submit: Business/Farm Supplement; CSS/Financial Aid PROFILE; FAFSA; Noncustodial PROFILE. The Princeton Review suggests that all financial aid forms be submitted as soon as possible after October 1. *Need-based scholarships/grants offered:* College/ university scholarship or grant aid from institutional funds; Federal Pell; Private scholarships; SEOG; State scholarships/grants. *Loan aid offered:* Direct PLUS loans; Direct Subsidized Stafford Loans; Direct Unsubsidized Stafford Loans. Federal Work-Study Program available. Institutional employment available.

The Inside Word

Duke is an extremely selective undergraduate institution, which affords the school the luxury of rejecting many qualified applicants. You'll have to present an exceptional record just to be considered; to make the cut, you'll have to impress the admissions office that you can contribute something unique and valuable to the incoming class. Being one of the best basketball players in the nation (male or female) helps a lot, but even athletes have to show academic excellence to get in the door here.

THE SCHOOL SAYS "..."

From the Admissions Office

"From the Admissions Office "Duke University offers a blend of tradition and innovation, undergraduate college and major research university, academic excellence and athletic achievement, and global presence and regional charm. Students come to Duke from all over the United States and the world and from a range of racial, ethnic, and socioeconomic backgrounds. They enjoy contact with a world-class faculty through small classes and independent study. More than forty majors are available in the arts and sciences and engineering; arts and sciences students may also design their own curriculum through Program II. Certificate programs are available in a number of interdisciplinary areas. Special academic opportunities include the Focus Program and seminars for first-year students DukeImmerse, study abroad, domestic study away programs in New York, Los Angeles, Washington, DC, Chicago, Silicon Valley, and Alaska, Bass Connections research programs, and DukeEngage summer service opportunities. While admission to Duke is highly selective, applications of U.S. citizens, Permanent Residents, and undocumented students are evaluated without regard to financial need and the university pledges to meet 100 percent of the demonstrated need of all admitted U.S. students and permanent residents. A limited amount of financial aid is also available for foreign citizens, and the university will meet the full demonstrated financial need for those admitted students as well.

"Applicants must take either the ACT or the SAT. When possible, students taking only the SAT should also take two Subject Tests."

SELECTIVITY

Admissions Rating	99
# of applicants	35,767
% of applicants accepted	9
% of acceptees attending	55
# of early decision applicants	4,070
% accepted early decision	22

FRESHMAN PROFILE

Range SAT EBRW	710–770
Range SAT Math	740–800
Range ACT Composite	33–35
# submitting SAT scores	928
% submitting SAT scores	53
# submitting ACT scores	1,252
% submitting ACT scores	72
% graduated top 10% of class	95
% graduated top 25% of class	98
% graduated top 50% of class	100

DEADLINES

Early decision	
Deadline	11/1
Notification	12/15
Regular	
Priority	12/20
Deadline	1/3
Notification	4/1
Nonfall registration?	No

FINANCIAL FACTS

Financial Aid Rating	96
Annual tuition	$55,880
Room and board	$15,588
Required fees	$2,051
Books and supplies	$1,434
Average frosh need-based scholarship	$82,265
Average UG need-based scholarship	$53,214
% needy frosh rec. need-based scholarship or grant aid	94
% needy UG rec. need-based scholarship or grant aid	95
% needy frosh rec. non-need-based scholarship or grant aid	16
% needy UG rec. non-need-based scholarship or grant aid	10
% needy frosh rec. need-based self-help aid	73
% needy UG rec. need-based self-help aid	81
% UG borrow to pay for school	32
Average cumulative indebtedness	$21,525
% frosh need fully met	100
% ugrads need fully met	100
Average % of frosh need met	100
Average % of ugrad need met	100

DUQUESNE UNIVERSITY

600 Forbes Avenue, Pittsburgh, PA 15282-0201 • Admissions: 412-396-6222 • Fax: 412-396-6223

CAMPUS LIFE

Quality of Life Rating	**88**
Fire Safety Rating	**98**
Green Rating	**86**
Type of school	Private
Affiliation	Roman Catholic
Environment	Metropolis

STUDENTS

Total undergrad enrollment	5,837
% male/female	36/64
% from out of state	28
% frosh live on campus	94
% ugrads live on campus	61
# of fraternities (% ugrad men join)	9 (18)
# of sororities (% ugrad women join)	11 (24)
% African American	5
% Asian	3
% Caucasian	81
% Hispanic	4
% Native American	<1
% Pacific Islander	<1
% Two or more races	3
% Race and/or ethnicity unknown	1
% international	2
# of countries represented	42

SURVEY SAYS . . .

Lots of conservative students
Students love Pittsburgh, PA
Frats and sororities are popular

ACADEMICS

Academic Rating	**77**
% students returning for sophomore year	85
% students graduating within 4 years	71
% students graduating within 6 years	80
Calendar	Semester
Student/faculty ratio	14:1
Profs interesting rating	85
Profs accessible rating	90
Most classes have 20–29 students.	
Most lab/discussion sessions have 20–29 students.	

MOST POPULAR MAJORS

Biology/Biological Sciences, General; Pharmacy; Nursing Science

STUDENTS SAY "..."

Academics

A modestly-sized Catholic university in the heart of Pittsburgh, Duquesne offers students "small class sizes [and a] welcoming staff" along with good "financial aid and scholarship opportunities." The university is especially renowned for its "strong health profession programs," and we're told that the "Nursing, Physician's Assistant, and Pharmacy Programs are all very well developed" in particular. Additionally, the nearby "hospital system provides ... a quality learning and clinical environment for students." Fortunately, most departments, by and large, offer students "great research opportunities." Undergrads also appreciate the fact that it's rather easy to "make strong connections [with their professors]." As one student explains, "My professors all seem to *love* Duquesne, and [they] love to share their research ... with the class." The vast majority of professors "are very open to questions and will do anything to help their students, in and out of the classroom." Indeed, they make it quite evident that "[they] care about ... the well-being of their students" beyond academics. Finally, as another student concludes, "I ... feel as if I've been given unbelievable opportunities by attending Duquesne."

Life

There's no denying that academics take top priority at Duquesne. And on any given weekday you'll find most students "in the library ... study[ing]." However, these industrious undergrads still manage to carve out some time for fun. For starters, many students are "involved in Greek life, whether it be a professional or social [type of organization]." Additionally, every Friday the school hosts events ranging from "epic bingo" to movies on the waterfront. Of course, the weather dictates activities as well. "In the winter we head to Market Square to go skating," one student says. Once the temperature starts rising, you can often find undergrads "playing with a frisbee or playing catch" or they simply "bring [out] the hammock[s] and ... hang out on the lawn." We should note that Duquesne "is not a party school." Students looking for a more partying experience often "go to [nearby] Pitt." Finally, Pittsburgh proper provides ample social and cultural opportunities. For example, students love to head "to the South Side on the weekends where there are a lot of restaurant and shopping options to choose from." And, of course, they love attending "a lot of sporting events [to cheer on the] Penguins, Steelers, and Pirates."

Student Body

At first glance, Duquesne undergrads appear to be largely "white, middle/upper-middle class Christian" with a "heavy majority of female students" to boot. However, others insist that you will find "a very diverse group of people," noting that the university has a "fair amount of international students." Regardless of background, the school tends to attract students who are "driven and have a desire to work and learn." Just as important, undergrads are quick to mention that their peers are "very friendly." And you are sure to always find a "familiar face when walking to class/dining halls." One student even goes a step further, describing classmates as "the type of people who do basic things like hold the elevators for you, but if they overhear you stressing about an exam in the library ... [they'll] help you out and give you some pointers." Another student boasts, "I personally found my life-long friends on the first day, and my friend group only grows with each passing day. Duquesne is a place where I feel I belong and I am welcomed."

DUQUESNE UNIVERSITY

Financial Aid: 412-396-6607 • E-Mail: admissions@duq.edu • Website: www.duq.edu

THE PRINCETON REVIEW SAYS

Admissions

Very important factors considered include: rigor of secondary school record, academic GPA. *Important factors considered include:* standardized test scores. *Other factors considered include:* class rank, application essay, recommendation(s), interview, extracurricular activities, talent/ability, character/personal qualities, first generation, alumni/ae relation, racial/ethnic status, volunteer work, work experience, level of applicant's interest. ACT with or without writing accepted. SAT with or without Essay component accepted. High school diploma is required and GED is accepted. *Academic units recommended:* 4 English, 2 math, 2 science, 2 foreign language, 2 social studies, 4 academic electives.

Financial Aid

Students should submit: FAFSA; Institution's own financial aid form. Priority filing deadline is 5/1. The Princeton Review suggests that all financial aid forms be submitted as soon as possible after October 1. *Need-based scholarships/grants offered:* College/university scholarship or grant aid from institutional funds; Federal Pell; Private scholarships; SEOG; State scholarships/grants; United Negro College Fund. *Loan aid offered:* Direct PLUS loans; Direct Subsidized Stafford Loans; Direct Unsubsidized Stafford Loans. Applicants will be notified of awards on a rolling basis beginning 1/31. Federal Work-Study Program available. Institutional employment available.

The Inside Word

Duquesne takes a relatively straightforward approach to the admissions process. That means that your GPA and the rigor of your high school curriculum will be the two most important factors. However, the application process is a little more stringent for individuals applying for health sciences. Academic recommendations, standardized test scores, and personal statements will also play a role. The university is test optional for students interested in music, liberal arts, or business. However, those individuals will need a minimum 3.0 GPA for their candidacy to be considered.

THE SCHOOL SAYS "..."

From the Admissions Office

"Duquesne is one of the nation's top Catholic universities. Over our 140+ year history, we've developed a national reputation for academic excellence, including praise for innovation, continued high quality and affordability, accolades of 'first-tier university,' 'top 100 undergraduate school,' and among the top fifty in the 'Great Schools, Great Prices' list. 99 percent of freshmen receive some form of financial assistance. Choose from eighty majors in business, education, health sciences, liberal arts, music, natural and environmental sciences, nursing and pharmacy. Take classes on a fifty-acre park-like campus centrally located in Pittsburgh—one of America's most livable cities. Learn with and from students of diverse cultural, socioeconomic and religious backgrounds from every state and forty-five countries. Our faculty are among the best in their fields, and, with an average student-faculty ratio of 14:1, your professors will know you by name. Choose from more than thirty-five semester and short-term study abroad programs. Duquesne's central location provides a perfect laboratory for off-campus learning and community engagement. Students gain practical experience through fieldwork, research projects and internships at Pittsburgh's major corporations, healthcare systems, schools and other organizations. Students also enjoy walking to Pittsburgh's cultural district, sports stadiums, shopping and dining. There are more than 250 student organizations in areas such as academics, social, service, governance, spiritual, political, performing arts, media and sports. Duquesne also offers plenty of opportunities for sports: seventeen NCAA Division I men's and women's teams as well as club and intramural sports. Over 10,000 undergraduate and graduate students attend Duquesne annually."

SELECTIVITY

Admissions Rating	82
# of applicants	7,231
% of applicants accepted	74
% of acceptees attending	24

FRESHMAN PROFILE

Range SAT EBRW	570–650
Range SAT Math	560–650
Range ACT Composite	23–28
# submitting SAT scores	955
% submitting SAT scores	73
# submitting ACT scores	402
% submitting ACT scores	31
Average HS GPA	3.7
% graduated top 10% of class	25
% graduated top 25% of class	55
% graduated top 50% of class	85

DEADLINES

Regular	
Priority	11/1
Deadline	7/1
Notification	Rolling, 10/1
Nonfall registration?	Yes

FINANCIAL FACTS

Financial Aid Rating	85
Annual tuition	$41,892
Room and board	$13,612
Books and supplies	$1,400
Average frosh need-based scholarship	$25,353
Average UG need-based scholarship	$23,681
% needy frosh rec. need-based scholarship or grant aid	100
% needy UG rec. need-based scholarship or grant aid	98
% needy frosh rec. non-need-based scholarship or grant aid	100
% needy UG rec. non-need-based scholarship or grant aid	97
% needy frosh rec. need-based self-help aid	81
% needy UG rec. need-based self-help aid	85
% frosh rec. any financial aid	99
% UG rec. any financial aid	99
% UG borrow to pay for school	58
Average cumulative indebtedness	$44,243
% frosh need fully met	22
% ugrads need fully met	19
Average % of frosh need met	75
Average % of ugrad need met	71

EARLHAM COLLEGE

801 National Road West, Richmond, IN 47374-4095 • Admissions: 765-983-1600 • Fax: 765-983-1560

STUDENTS SAY "..."

Academics
A small school with Quaker roots, Earlham College offers "small class sizes [that allow] faculty to easily connect with students." This is a result of a low student-faculty ratio which means students have plenty of opportunity to "have a strong and close connection with professors." Additionally, faculty are "extremely available and willing to connect" to help their students really understand the subjects they "are passionate in teaching." Those professors are "amazing to work with," says a student. Another gushes, "They are like incredibly knowledgeable friends who have [a] strong interest in your future and helping you succeed." Overall, their courses are described as "rigorous," "interesting," and "engaging," and students also find they can "get the help [they] need" without much trouble. Students here cite the unique academic programs which include Peace and Global Studies as well as a program called EPIC, "which [allots] students funds to … research [or intern] in any place or country of their liking." One student sums up the academic experience at Earlham: "Each professor … has made me care about the subject of their class in a way I never would have expected—whether that's opening up a field I already love or finding ways to connect new material to the subjects that are close to me."

Life
Many undergrads proudly proclaim that the "possibilities are endless" at Earlham when it comes to campus activities. Indeed, it's "a wonderful environment for passionate and self-driven students" who thrive on having "back-to-back commitments." As one enthusiastic individual explains, "I run a club, direct and act in plays, sing in the choir, go to the gym, and still take nineteen credits." It's hard to resist the many school-sponsored activities "such as concerts, bowling, movie night, [and] roller skating." Another popular activity is Dance Alloy, which is a "bi-yearly student choreographed dance performance" that many students join and "spend multiple nights a week practicing and preparing" to get just right. Moreover, "every other Friday night there is an open mic event … [where] everyone is welcome to perform." And when the weekend fully rolls around, you can "usually [find some] house parties or people just [hanging] out with their friends." Those hang-out sessions can include "talking about literature, playing cards, [or having] occasional nights of drinking and video games." And a good number simply love exploring the "large chunk of undeveloped woods behind [the] campus."

Student Body
Despite being a small school, Earlham manages to yield a "diverse population." Indeed, you can find students "from all over the world" who enrich the campus with their "interesting stories and backgrounds." Undergrads seem to mesh well as everyone treats each other "with kindness and compassion." Moreover, many students here are "concerned about social issues and justice" and a large number "seem to be inclined to left-wing policies." Or, as another undergrad puts it, "Earlham is hippies. Earlham is bare feet and climbing trees. Earlhamites are activists. They are earth lovers, peace lovers, and lovers of learning." Therefore, it's not too shocking to learn that many students also describe their peers as "collaborative and encouraging" because of the "close-knit bonds [they have] to the people around them." They "care a lot about [their] community" and "make sure everyone feels welcomed." As one undergrad concludes, "After being on campus for so long, it is easy to realize that everyone here is weird in their own ways, and the great part is that the community is very accepting and less judgmental than most other places."

EARLHAM COLLEGE

Financial Aid: 765-983-1217 • E-Mail: admissions@earlham.edu • Website: www.earlham.edu

THE PRINCETON REVIEW SAYS

Admissions

Very important factors considered include: rigor of secondary school record, academic GPA. *Important factors considered include:* application essay, extracurricular activities, character/personal qualities. *Other factors considered include:* class rank, standardized test scores, recommendation(s), interview, talent/ability, racial/ethnic status, volunteer work, work experience. ACT with Writing recommended. SAT with Essay component recommended. High school diploma is required and GED is accepted. *Academic units required:* 4 English, 3 math, 3 science, 2 science labs, 2 foreign language, 2 social studies, 2 history. *Academic units recommended:* 4 English, 4 math, 4 science, 2 science labs, 2 foreign language, 2 social studies, 2 history.

Financial Aid

Students should submit: FAFSA. Priority filing deadline is 11/1. The Princeton Review suggests that all financial aid forms be submitted as soon as possible after October 1. *Need-based scholarships/grants offered:* College/university scholarship or grant aid from institutional funds; Federal Pell; Private scholarships; SEOG; State scholarships/grants. *Loan aid offered:* Direct PLUS loans; Direct Subsidized Stafford Loans; Direct Unsubsidized Stafford Loans. Applicants will be notified of awards on or about 3/15. Federal Work-Study Program available. Institutional employment available.

The Inside Word

Earning admission to Earlham is no easy feat. The application process is competitive, and students must demonstrate that that they are academically prepared and intellectually curious. Therefore, you can expect admissions officers to pay close attention to the rigor of your high school curriculum. Of secondary importance will be your personal statement, recommendations, and extracurricular activities. Lastly, we should mention that Earlham is a test-optional school. You don't need to submit your scores unless you're an international student, home-schooled, or you earned a GED.

THE SCHOOL SAYS "..."

From the Admissions Office

"Earlham is an academically distinguished liberal arts college that uniquely equips students for the 21st century. In addition to its programs of study, the College emphasizes hands-on and collaborative learning through the Earlham Advantage Grant, a central feature of the Earlham experience. Thanks to a generous gift from an alumnus, the College funds high-impact, immersive experiences like internships and student-faculty research for all students, making these experiences possible to students regardless of family income. These powerful experiences take place across the United States and the world. The result is transformative and leads to compelling opportunities for graduates. Earlham ranks among the top percent of all colleges for graduates who earn a Ph.D., and acceptance rates to medical, law, and other professional schools are exceptionally high. Earlham has recently invested more than $60 million in academic facilities, and its professors are known for both their scholarship and innovative teaching. Earlham is renowned as a distinctively welcoming community, embracing both individual and cultural differences. Shaped by Quaker perspectives, Earlham prepares its students to be catalysts for good in a changing world. Earlham enrolls students from almost all fifty states and sixty nations. Students compete in nineteen intercollegiate sports and in an equestrian program. The College's diverse and multi-talented student body brings positive energy to campus life, community service, and a drive to make a difference."

SELECTIVITY

Admissions Rating	87
# of applicants	2,070
% of applicants accepted	63
% of acceptees attending	13
# offered a place on the wait list	166
% accepting a place on wait list	93
% admitted from wait list	40
# of early decision applicants	43
% accepted early decision	74

FRESHMAN PROFILE

Range SAT EBRW	550–680
Range SAT Math	550–690
Range ACT Composite	23–30
# submitting SAT scores	107
% submitting SAT scores	62
# submitting ACT scores	58
% submitting ACT scores	34
Average HS GPA	3.6
% graduated top 10% of class	42
% graduated top 25% of class	71
% graduated top 50% of class	93

DEADLINES

Early action	
Deadline	1/1
Notification	2/1
Regular	
Priority	12/1
Deadline	2/1
Notification	Rolling, 10/1
Nonfall registration?	Yes

APPLICANTS ALSO LOOK AT AND SOMETIMES PREFER

DePauw University; Indiana University Bloomington; Kalamazoo College; The College of Wooster; Oberlin College; Hanover College

FINANCIAL FACTS

Financial Aid Rating	92
Annual tuition	$47,106
Room and board	$11,347
Required fees	$985
Books and supplies	$1,050
Average frosh need-based scholarship	$34,196
Average UG need-based scholarship	$34,312
% needy frosh rec. need-based scholarship or grant aid	100
% needy UG rec. need-based scholarship or grant aid	100
% needy frosh rec. non-need-based scholarship or grant aid	18
% needy UG rec. non-need-based scholarship or grant aid	21
% needy frosh rec. need-based self-help aid	90
% needy UG rec. need-based self-help aid	96
% frosh rec. any financial aid	92
% UG rec. any financial aid	93
% UG borrow to pay for school	44
Average cumulative indebtedness	$26,103
% frosh need fully met	62
% ugrads need fully met	52
Average % of frosh need met	92
Average % of ugrad need met	93

EAST CAROLINA UNIVERSITY

Office of Undergraduate Admissions, Greenville, NC 27858-4353 • Admissions: 252-328-6640 • Fax: 252-328-6945

STUDENTS SAY "..."

Academic

East Carolina University is a growing public research university in North Carolina that gives students the chance to participate in cutting-edge research, hybrid online and classroom courses, and hands-on learning. Of particular note are the engineering program, which "offers students an unlimited number of opportunities," and "the nursing school, [which] is second to none." Regardless of the chosen program, professors help students "consider all aspects of the material when learning" so they can gain a deeper understanding, and they will often "come in on Saturday or Sunday to help." One student says, "The passion and enthusiasm they show reflects onto the students," describing teaching methods that include scenario-based learning and an "avoidance of reading PowerPoints word-by-word." Most professors "are very interactive and make a great school environment," but there are "a couple that just lecture the whole time."

Both in and out of the classroom, the number of people at East Carolina "make it possible to make a lot of connections for everything," and there are "endless resources here on campus to utilize and use to your advantage to be advanced in your curriculum and personal life." Those resources include a "huge library, writing center, multiple computer labs and study lounges, career center, organization start up lessons, [and] counseling center." There are "so many different services provided for students to help them succeed" and "the Pirate Academic Success Center is always open for tutoring to give a helping hand."

Life

ECU students are physically active: some "will go to the gym and play basketball after class," and "the rec center provides plenty of things to do in terms of working out and swimming." In all, the "Pirate Nation loves to hang out and support ECU athletics." After, they'll quite often "spend time at home with roommates" or find "a comedy night or karaoke night at some of the restaurants, bars or breweries downtown." There are plenty of on-campus activities too, like talent shows and game nights. In all, students "like to turn up and party," and as a result "pack their class schedule to be in the middle of the day" so they have "time to sleep in not too late but [don't have] to get to those dreadful eight or nine AM classes." The campus itself is "sprawling but well-organized" in terms of the main academic buildings and dorms, and "everything is close together." Plus, Greenville is "really a college town" where "you feel like you are with people who are in the same mindset."

Student Body

This "very diverse and unique group of students" primarily hails from North Carolina, and despite the large number of students, "it is a very small and family-oriented campus that does not make you feel small." Extracurriculars help build that community on campus, with many taking part in "at least one extracurricular group or activity, and they wear the shirt to prove it." As one East Carolina Pirate puts it, "the library's group study rooms are always full," because "most students try very hard." That said, there is definitely a range "from the typical hardworking motivated student to the atypical Greek life individual who flunks out after a year or two." Overall, these are "great people," and "there is a crowd for whatever type of experience you are looking for."

EAST CAROLINA UNIVERSITY

Financial Aid: 252-328-4347 • E-mail: admis@ecu.edu • Website: www.ecu.edu

THE PRINCETON REVIEW SAYS

Admissions

Very important factors considered include: rigor of secondary school record, academic GPA, standardized test scores, state residency. *Important factors considered include:* class rank. *Other factors considered include:* application essay, extracurricular activities, talent/ability, character/personal qualities, first generation, alumni/ae relation, volunteer work, work experience, level of applicant's interest. ACT with or without writing accepted. SAT with or without Essay component accepted. High school diploma is required and GED is accepted. *Academic units required:* 4 English, 4 math, 3 science, 1 science lab, 2 foreign language, 1 social studies, 1 history. *Academic units recommended:* 4 English, 4 math, 3 science, 1 science lab, 2 foreign language, 2 social studies, 1 history, 1 visual/performing arts.

Financial Aid

Students should submit: FAFSA. Priority filing deadline is 3/1. The Princeton Review suggests that all financial aid forms be submitted as soon as possible after October 1. *Need-based scholarships/grants offered:* College/university scholarship or grant aid from institutional funds; Federal Nursing Scholarships; Federal Pell; Private scholarships; SEOG; State scholarships/grants. *Loan aid offered:* Direct PLUS loans; Direct Subsidized Stafford Loans; Direct Unsubsidized Stafford Loans. Applicants will be notified of awards on a rolling basis beginning 4/1. Federal Work-Study Program available. Institutional employment available.

The Inside Word

Admissions shouldn't be a problem for B students who have taken a solid roster of college preparatory classes, including four years of math and English, three years of natural sciences, and two years of social studies and a foreign language (a foreign language is also strongly recommended during senior year). If you are applying for in-state tuition, you must visit NCresidency.org and verify your residency first.

SELECTIVITY

Admissions Rating	**77**
# of applicants	19,234
% of applicants accepted	79
% of acceptees attending	29

FRESHMAN PROFILE

Range SAT EBRW	520–600
Range SAT Math	510–590
Range SAT Composite	1030–1180
Range ACT Composite	19–24
# submitting SAT scores	3,027
% submitting SAT scores	69
# submitting ACT scores	2,854
% submitting ACT scores	65
Average HS GPA	3.3
% graduated top 10% of class	13
% graduated top 25% of class	36
% graduated top 50% of class	71

DEADLINES

Regular	
Deadline	3/1
Notification	Rolling, 8/1
Nonfall registration?	Yes

APPLICANTS ALSO LOOK AT AND OFTEN PREFER
The University of North Carolina at Chapel Hill; North Carolina State University; University of North Carolina at Charlotte

AND SOMETIMES PREFER
University of North Carolina Wilmington; Appalachian State University; Western Carolina University

FINANCIAL FACTS

Financial Aid Rating	**81**
Annual in-state tuition	$4,452
Annual out-of-state tuition	$20,729
Room and board	$10,354
Required fees	$2,736
Books and supplies	$1,432
Average frosh need-based scholarship	$7,468
Average UG need-based scholarship	$7,918
% needy frosh rec. need-based scholarship or grant aid	68
% needy UG rec. need-based scholarship or grant aid	73
% needy frosh rec. non-need-based scholarship or grant aid	29
% needy UG rec. non-need-based scholarship or grant aid	21
% needy frosh rec. need-based self-help aid	88
% needy UG rec. need-based self-help aid	86
% frosh rec. any financial aid	70
% UG rec. any financial aid	66
% UG borrow to pay for school	68
Average cumulative indebtedness	$23,709
% frosh need fully met	7
% ugrads need fully met	9
Average % of frosh need met	56
Average % of ugrad need met	62

ECKERD COLLEGE

4200 54th Avenue South, St. Petersburg, FL 33711 • Admissions: 727-864-8331 • Fax: 727-866-2304

STUDENTS SAY "..."

Academics

Located on Florida's Gulf Coast in St. Petersburg, Eckerd College is a small liberal arts college that prepares students to be "well-rounded, educated people for the 'real world,' rather than for just one job." Indeed, 45 percent of all students will go on to pursue advanced degrees, and the school's "academics are top notch and continue to impress," particularly the constantly expanding, "hands-on" science and art departments. Also of note is the study abroad program, of which most students take advantage.

Eckerd is "all about having small class sizes in order to maximize learning and personal connections to professors." Professors are "always approachable on an academic and personal level" and "make the classes fun and interesting." There is a "level of genuine care" from the teachers; according to a senior, "If I have a question, it gets answered, simple as that." "Not once has an email been ignored that I have sent to a professor," echoes a junior. Class discussion is very important (many classes have a sizeable participation grade), and faculty encourages opposing views, creating "an environment where it is easy for everybody to openly express their opinions without judgment."

The Mentor program assigns students to professors of their major(s), their job being "to help guide the student through choosing classes and registration, or anything else." The "quirky" liberal arts curriculum turns out graduates that "are not pigeonholed into the skills associated with their major, but [who] have developed a wide range of abilities which make them attractive to employers."

Life

The school's heartstoppingly beautiful location on the waterfront gives it a feel of being "like summer camp with an enriching academic experience"; as a senior asks (rhetorically): "How can you beat a dorm that overlooks the bay?" The residence halls "are beautiful so there is no need to live off campus," and the school's Community Bike program allows students to "just pick up the yellow bikes and ride wherever you need" (though some students think there should be "more dedication through internal action to the environmental principles it espouses").

There are "eclectic options of student activities" at Eckerd, and with no Greek life, the Campus Activities crew is allotted "a crazy amount of money to have fun events on campus, such as cookouts, dances, casino nights, and an actual carnival brought onto campus." Obviously marine activities are popular, and for fun, people "go to the beach, go downtown, [and borrow] paddleboards/kayaks at the Waterfront." People love exploring downtown St. Pete, and there are many famous restaurants nearby (good thing, as the cafeteria food is "definitely our weakest point," according to many students).

There's a definite party streak here, and "pot and beer are not strangers to Eckerd parties," which typically take place outdoors. Still, it's "a very no-pressure environment" for those who choose not to partake, and "there is a very 'free as a bird' mentality" here so "people rarely feel trapped." Life at this school is generally relaxed but busy. It matches the atmosphere of the location," says a first-year student.

Student Body

This "barefooted and brainy" brood "has a wide variety of students who all fit different niches." "It isn't unheard of to see people in three-piece suits sitting with what we might call modern-day hippies," says a student. The "very relaxed" crowd adopts a "laid-back Florida attitude," and every student is "friendly, approachable and has a general positive attitude about being here at Eckerd." Almost everyone is "pretty liberal" and "has a strong interest in environmental sustainability."

Financial Aid: 727-864-8854 • E-Mail: admissions@eckerd.edu • Website: www.eckerd.edu

THE PRINCETON REVIEW SAYS

Admissions

Very important factors considered include: rigor of secondary school record, academic GPA. *Important factors considered include:* application essay, standardized test scores, recommendation(s), interview, extracurricular activities, talent/ability, character/personal qualities, volunteer work. *Other factors considered include:* class rank, first generation, alumni/ae relation. ACT with or without writing accepted but not required for students seeking admission for 2021 or 2022. SAT with or without Essay component accepted but not required for students seeking admission for 2021 or 2022. High school diploma is required and GED is accepted. *Academic units recommended:* 4 English, 3 math, 3 science, 2 science labs, 2 foreign language, 2 social studies, 1 history, 3 academic electives.

Financial Aid

Students should submit: FAFSA. Priority filing deadline is 2/1. The Princeton Review suggests that all financial aid forms be submitted as soon as possible after October 1. *Need-based scholarships/grants offered:* College/university scholarship or grant aid from institutional funds; Federal Pell; SEOG; State scholarships/grants. *Loan aid offered:* Direct PLUS loans; Direct Subsidized Stafford Loans; Direct Unsubsidized Stafford Loans. Federal Work-Study Program available. Institutional employment available.

The Inside Word

Most of the applicants Eckerd admits come from the top quarter of their high school classes. However, competition from other small liberal arts schools of roughly the same caliber or better is stiff. As a result, Eckerd is a relatively easy admit for B-plus students with decent standardized test scores (the school gives more weight in its decisions to courses and grades than to SAT and ACT scores, however). In fact, students applying to Eckerd for 2021 or 2022 will not be required to submit SAT or ACT scores for consideration. The admissions process here is rolling, which means that applying early will help your chances. Eckerd can afford to be more selective later on in the admissions cycle, especially for candidates who profess an interest in its most esteemed programs (for example, Marine Science), so those with serious interest should consider Eckerd's early admission policy.

THE SCHOOL SAYS "..."

From the Admissions Office

"Students from 48 states and territories and 36 countries take advantage of our spectacular mile of campus waterfront near the Gulf of Mexico for outdoor laboratories in biology, marine science and environmental studies along with an array of intramural, club and intercollegiate sports and water recreation. Offerings in the arts and humanities inspire creativity and foster critical thinking and self-awareness. Eckerd is dedicated to minimizing its operational footprint and maximizing sustainable practices, and our students are service-oriented—donating over 12,000 hours of service outside of graduation requirements annually. With more than 180 Eckerd grads having served in the Peace Corps, we're a top producer of volunteers among small colleges in the U.S. and recently joined the nationally recognized Peace Corps Prep undergraduate certificate program. Eckerd's innovative 4-1-4 calendar gives students the opportunity to study abroad during the January Winter Term or semester-long programs. Nearly 70 percent of our graduates have taken classes overseas, many at our London Study Centre. In addition to recently building the 55,000-square-foot James Center for Molecular and Life Sciences, the college significantly upgraded equipment, labs and classrooms for the environmental studies, math, physics, computer science and behavioral sciences departments and in 2018 opened the Nielsen Center for Visual Arts. This state-of-the-art facility provides space and equipment for studying, creating and exhibiting visual art—with student studios for ceramics and sculpture, printmaking, painting, drawing, digital arts and more. We venture together in the Eckerd experience to think beyond the conventional questions, methods and solutions. At Eckerd College, we ThinkOUTside."

SELECTIVITY	
Admissions Rating	83
# of applicants	4,644
% of applicants accepted	67
% of acceptees attending	17
# offered a place on the wait list	186
% accepting a place on wait list	10
% admitted from wait list	17

FRESHMAN PROFILE	
Range SAT EBRW	560–650
Range SAT Math	530–630
Range SAT Composite	1093–1270
Range ACT Composite	23–29
# submitting SAT scores	390
% submitting SAT scores	72
# submitting ACT scores	240
% submitting ACT scores	45
Average HS GPA	3.5

DEADLINES	
Early action	
Deadline	11/15
Notification	12/15
Regular	
Notification	Rolling, 12/1
Nonfall registration?	Yes

FINANCIAL FACTS	
Financial Aid Rating	88
Annual tuition	$45,452
Room and board	$13,026
Required fees	$644
Books and supplies	$1,350
Average frosh need-based scholarship	$27,507
Average UG need-based scholarship	$27,705
% needy frosh rec. need-based scholarship or grant aid	99
% needy UG rec. need-based scholarship or grant aid	100
% needy frosh rec. non-need-based scholarship or grant aid	0
% needy UG rec. non-need-based scholarship or grant aid	0
% needy frosh rec. need-based self-help aid	87
% needy UG rec. need-based self-help aid	86
% frosh rec. any financial aid	99
% UG rec. any financial aid	86
% UG borrow to pay for school	58
Average cumulative indebtedness	$33,661
% frosh need fully met	18
% ugrads need fully met	21
Average % of frosh need met	84
Average % of ugrad need met	85

ELMIRA COLLEGE

One Park Place, Elmira, NY 14901 • Admissions: 607-735-1724 • Fax: 607-735-1718

STUDENTS SAY "..."

Academic

Situated in upstate New York, Elmira College was established in 1855 and has long brought its nearly 1,000 undergraduates a solid liberal arts education grounded in critical thinking and reading. Class sizes are low, "so you are guaranteed a shot at success and a connection with your professors." Terms are also shorter, with the academic year broken up into two twelve-week terms, followed by a third six-week term of special, immersive classes. Not only does this structure give students the opportunity to study abroad—about 40 percent of students choose to do so—but it keeps courses "rigorous and challenging because ... the shortened amount of time requires each class to be fast-paced and stimulating."

Those challenges are easily faced, as Elmira professors "are dead-set on providing their students with quality information" and are "engaged and willing to help any student with anything." And thanks to the faculty's different perspectives and backgrounds, "students really do experience a wide span of different people with different ideas and passions." This occurs in the classroom as well: though most classes are in lecture format, professors "make an effort to provide us with interactive activities, videos, and hands-on activities." Many also "use alternative assessments, such as a radio broadcast, creative writing, a debate, or a project of choice for a final," and are often "willing to offer independent and directed study courses if students are looking for different classes to take that are not offered."

Life

Elmira is truly a "picturesque college campus" where "the ground is cobblestone with octagon-shaped bricks" and "the buildings are beautiful ... and in a Gothic revival style." As one student describes, "It has an air of elegance and beauty founded on tradition while being fun and quirky as well." That fun is evident since students at Elmira "always find something to do, whether on campus or off," and despite the small size of the campus, "everyone is encouraged to cultivate their interests and be as involved and outgoing as possible." This means that while most students eat in the dining halls, some "may drive to nearby Horseheads to go shopping at local stores and eat at name-brand restaurants" or visit nearby Corning and Ithaca on weekends. On this communal campus, students can often be found "in the lounges of the dorms by the fire [telling] stories" and "campus events are brought in regularly" by the college. There is "a good variety in the social scene, so students can partake in what they like best," and "some students hang out and watch movies [while] some students party."

Student Body

Here you'll find a "generous and welcoming" group that "makes the college community a comfortable place to be." Elmira "is its own little bubble" and the "mostly white" student body is "similar to that of a small town high school" in terms of a social breakdown, with athletes, "NARPs (non-athletic regular people)," and "thought-leader" students all involved in many extracurricular activities. A big part of that comes in the form of inter-collegiate athletics, with around one-third of the student body devoting "a huge part of [their] days" to practice and games. That's met with school spirit that pervades even outside of sports: "Elmira College may be small, but we are very proud of our college." One student says, "Just walking through campus you can sense the traditions and how the college values its students."

Financial Aid: 607-735-1728 • E-Mail: admissions@elmira.edu • Website: www.elmira.edu

THE PRINCETON REVIEW SAYS

Admissions

Very important factors considered include: rigor of secondary school record, academic GPA, application essay, character/personal qualities. *Important factors considered include:* class rank, recommendation(s), interview, extracurricular activities. *Other factors considered include:* standardized test scores, talent/ability, alumni/ae relation, geographical residence, state residency, racial/ethnic status, volunteer work, work experience. ACT with or without writing accepted. SAT with or without Essay component accepted. High school diploma is required and GED is not accepted. *Academic units required:* 4 English, 3 math, 3 science, 2 science labs, 3 social studies, 1 history, 2 academic electives. *Academic units recommended:* 2 foreign language.

Financial Aid

Students should submit: FAFSA; State aid form. Priority filing deadline is 2/1. The Princeton Review suggests that all financial aid forms be submitted as soon as possible after October 1. *Need-based scholarships/grants offered:* College/university scholarship or grant aid from institutional funds; Federal Pell; Private scholarships; SEOG; State scholarships/grants. *Loan aid offered:* Direct PLUS loans; Direct Subsidized Stafford Loans; Direct Unsubsidized Stafford Loans. Applicants will be notified of awards on a rolling basis beginning 12/1. Federal Work-Study Program available. Institutional employment available.

The Inside Word

Elmira offers two options for students wishing to apply: Early Action and Regular (rolling) Admission. The school doesn't leave students hanging, with the Early Action decision issued just two weeks after the November 1 deadline, whereas Regular admission takes about a month. Test scores and interviews are optional, but both are encouraged if the student believes it will improve their application. With its fairly high acceptance rate, students without any major blemishes on their record have a good shot at admission.

THE SCHOOL SAYS "..."

From the Admissions Office

"Founded in 1855, Elmira College is a private, residential, liberal arts college offering 30-plus majors, an honors program, 17 academic societies, and 20 Division III varsity teams. Located in the Southern Finger Lakes Region of New York, Elmira's undergraduate and graduate student population hails from more than 30 states and nine countries. Elmira is a Phi Beta Kappa College and has been ranked a top college, nationally, for student internships.

"Elmira College has a tradition of offering hands-on, immersive learning experiences with small classes. Alumni report the opportunity to complete research, the development of relationships with faculty, and the lifelong friendships with classmates among their most impactful experiences at Elmira.

"The College offers several opportunities for post-graduate work through partnerships with various graduate schools including Lake Erie College of Osteopathic Medicine. Elmira College students already enjoy reserved, early acceptance spots at LECOM sites for those who meet the LECOM acceptance requirements. The addition of LECOM at Elmira College expands the number of reserved medical spots for EC students to 25, the number of reserved pharmacy spots to 20 and the number of reserved dentistry spots to 5, and provides a seamless transition from undergraduate coursework to medical school.

"The College is also home to the Center for Mark Twain Studies, one of four historically significant Twain heritage sites in the U.S., which attracts Twain scholars and educators from around the world. Proud of its history and tradition, the College is committed to the ideals of community service and intellectual growth."

SELECTIVITY

Admissions Rating	75
# of applicants	2,110
% of applicants accepted	84
% of acceptees attending	12

FRESHMAN PROFILE

Range SAT EBRW	510–610
Range SAT Math	510–610
Range ACT Composite	21–25
# submitting SAT scores	127
% submitting SAT scores	58
# submitting ACT scores	40
% submitting ACT scores	18
Average HS GPA	3.3

DEADLINES

Early action	
Deadline	11/1
Notification	11/15
Regular	
Priority	2/1
Notification	Rolling, 11/15
Nonfall registration?	Yes

APPLICANTS ALSO LOOK AT AND OFTEN PREFER

St John Fisher College; The College at Brockport— SUNY; Hartwick College

AND SOMETIMES PREFER

Ithaca College; Le Moyne College; State University of New York at Geneseo

AND RARELY PREFER

Alfred University; Houghton College

FINANCIAL FACTS

Financial Aid Rating	87
Annual tuition	$34,578
Room and board	$13,125
Required fees	$1,650
Books and supplies	$600
Average frosh need-based scholarship	$30,508
Average UG need-based scholarship	$29,638
% needy frosh rec. need-based scholarship or grant aid	80
% needy UG rec. need-based scholarship or grant aid	80
% needy frosh rec. non-need-based scholarship or grant aid	14
% needy UG rec. non-need-based scholarship or grant aid	16
% needy frosh rec. need-based self-help aid	77
% needy UG rec. need-based self-help aid	80
% UG rec. any financial aid	99
% UG borrow to pay for school	82
Average cumulative indebtedness	$30,084
% frosh need fully met	24
% ugrads need fully met	20
Average % of frosh need met	80
Average % of ugrad need met	79

ELON UNIVERSITY

50 Campus Drive, Elon, NC 27244-2010 • Admissions: 336-278-3566 • Fax: 336-278-7699

STUDENTS SAY "..."

Academics

Located in central North Carolina, Elon University offers a "visually stunning" campus and a "focus for learning [that] is very hands on." One student shares, "Many of my classes actually introduced real life clients that we worked with," like "the NAACP, Habitat for Humanity International, … and numerous local businesses." This reach beyond the classroom is perfect for Elon students, as many "are intent on becoming global citizens." Options to "study abroad for a semester, summer, or winter term are all very popular," and those who remain local will find a curriculum that encourages experiential learning through "internships, research, service, and leadership." The campus is packed with "amazing resources, such as the SPDC [Student Professional Development Center], and [the] Maker Hub," but the classes themselves remain intentionally small, which "allows for connections and questions between faculty and students." Professors, too, earn high marks for being "extremely student focused" and "engaged, caring, and smart," and this connection fosters an atmosphere where "every student is a person, not just a number."

Life

Since Elon was "founded on the basis of community engagement and participation," student schedules outside of class are full at Elon. Here, it's known "that everyone is too busy, overly involved, and loving it." Still, school work is a priority, and students "have a passion for knowledge, as seen through their exceptional academic efforts." When they do want a break, students spend time at the campus movie theatre, sporting events, student organizations, and social events—Elon Phoenix love their "trivia or bingo." There is live entertainment, too, with "many talented student groups/bands, and the music theatre department … puts on a spectacular show every semester." There's also no question that students "definitely love to party," and "Greek life is a dominant force" on campus. While one student notes, "It does get hard at times … not being in Greek life," another assures that "there are plenty of other opportunities for students." As for the town of Elon itself, students admit "the surrounding area can be a little barren," but "hiking in the mountains, beach trips, and mini adventures to nearby small towns" are all available options. In all, Elon is "a campus that inspires and collaborates," and as one student says: "Everyone at Elon misses it when we go back home."

Student Body

At Elon University "students are driven go-getters" who thrive in the "sense of community on campus." They appreciate that their classmates "are very motivated and want a bright future." It's nearly universally accepted that they "over involve themselves in outside activities, but all in an effort to better themselves." It's also fairly agreed-upon that Elon is "striving for a racially diverse campus," and some cite a "growing international student population" as evidence. The demographic, however, still skews "predominantly white" with "a great deal of wealthy students." Others go on to add that, while they may prefer more ethnic diversity, "Elon students are diverse in their perspectives, experiences, interests, and passions." As one happy undergrad reports, "The sense of community is truly unbelievable .... It is unlike anything I have ever experienced."

Financial Aid: 336-278-7640 • E-Mail: admissions@elon.edu • Website: www.elon.edu

THE PRINCETON REVIEW SAYS

Admissions

Very important factors considered include: rigor of secondary school record, academic GPA, application essay, recommendation(s). *Important factors considered include:* extracurricular activities, talent/ability, alumni/ae relation. *Other factors considered include:* class rank, character/personal qualities, first generation, geographical residence, state residency, racial/ethnic status, level of applicant's interest. ACT with or without writing accepted. SAT with or without Essay component accepted. High school diploma is required and GED is accepted. *Academic units required:* 4 English, 3 math, 3 science, 1 science lab, 2 foreign language, 2 social studies, 1 history. *Academic units recommended:* 4 English, 4 math, 3 science, 1 science lab, 3 foreign language, 2 social studies, 1 history.

Financial Aid

Students should submit: CSS/Financial Aid PROFILE; FAFSA. Priority filing deadline is 3/15. The Princeton Review suggests that all financial aid forms be submitted as soon as possible after October 1. *Need-based scholarships/grants offered:* College/university scholarship or grant aid from institutional funds; Federal Pell; Private scholarships; SEOG; State scholarships/grants; United Negro College Fund. *Loan aid offered:* Direct PLUS loans; Direct Subsidized Stafford Loans; Direct Unsubsidized Stafford Loans. Applicants will be notified of awards on a rolling basis beginning 1/31. Federal Work-Study Program available. Institutional employment available.

The Inside Word

Admission is competitive at Elon. In their search for the right fit, admissions officers pay close attention to a student's high school record and favor a course of academic study with exemplary grades and high class standing. The admissions essay is also a top consideration. Extracurricular activities and community involvement help demonstrate a student's potential to contribute to the Elon campus. Merit-based opportunities are available here, so it is recommended that you review application criteria carefully before submitting. Elon offers test-optional admission. While the ACT or SAT will not be used for admission or scholarship consideration, all enrolling students must submit a standardized test prior to enrollment.

THE SCHOOL SAYS "..."

From the Admissions Office

"Elon offers the resources of a large university in a close-knit community atmosphere. The university's more than 6,000 undergraduates choose from more than 60 majors. Graduate programs are offered in business administration, law, business analytics, accounting, education, higher education, interactive media, physical therapy and physician assistant studies. The National Survey of Student Engagement recognizes Elon among the nation's most effective universities in promoting hands-on learning. Academic and co-curricular activities are seamlessly blended, especially in the Elon Experiences: study abroad, internships, service, leadership and undergraduate research. Participation is among the highest in the nation; 78 percent of graduating seniors have studied abroad; 88 percent have internship experiences and 87 percent have participated in service. Elon's 4-1-4 academic calendar allows students to devote January to global study or to explore innovative on-campus courses. Elon's historic 656-acre campus is recognized as one of the most beautiful in the country. New additions include expansion of the School of Communications to a three-building quad with a 220-seat theater, two digital TV studios, a student newsroom and more; Schar Center, a 5,100-seat athletics arena and venue for campus events; East Neighborhood, three new three-story residence halls; Richard W. Sankey Hall, designed to promote Elon's entrepreneurship and design thinking programs across all majors; the Koenigsberger Learning Center for academic advising, tutoring and disabilities resources; and a South Campus gym."

SELECTIVITY

Admissions Rating	84
# of applicants	10,500
% of applicants accepted	78
% of acceptees attending	20
# offered a place on the wait list	948
% accepting a place on wait list	21
% admitted from wait list	6
# of early decision applicants	374
% accepted early decision	88

FRESHMAN PROFILE

Range SAT EBRW	590–660
Range SAT Math	570–660
Range ACT Composite	25–30
# submitting SAT scores	1,070
% submitting SAT scores	65
# submitting ACT scores	760
% submitting ACT scores	46
Average HS GPA	4.0
% graduated top 10% of class	25
% graduated top 25% of class	56
% graduated top 50% of class	84

DEADLINES

Early decision	
Deadline	11/1
Notification	12/1
Early action	
Deadline	11/1
Notification	12/20
Regular	
Priority	11/1
Deadline	1/10
Notification	3/20
Nonfall registration?	Yes

APPLICANTS ALSO LOOK AT AND OFTEN PREFER

Boston College; University of Maryland, College Park; The University of North Carolina at Chapel Hill; University of Richmond; University of Virginia; Wake Forest University; Bucknell University; Villanova University; James Madison University

AND SOMETIMES PREFER

North Carolina State University; Syracuse University; Furman University; Clemson University; Tulane University

FINANCIAL FACTS

Financial Aid Rating	83
Annual tuition	$36,082
Room and board	$12,685
Required fees	$489
Books and supplies	$900
Average frosh need-based scholarship	$15,187
Average UG need-based scholarship	$16,206
% needy frosh rec. need-based scholarship or grant aid	88
% needy UG rec. need-based scholarship or grant aid	90
% needy frosh rec. non-need-based scholarship or grant aid	63
% needy UG rec. non-need-based scholarship or grant aid	55
% needy frosh rec. need-based self-help aid	81
% needy UG rec. need-based self-help aid	80
% frosh rec. any financial aid	69
% UG rec. any financial aid	66
% UG borrow to pay for school	34
Average cumulative indebtedness	$32,028
% frosh need fully met	14
% ugrads need fully met	17
Average % of frosh need met	58
Average % of ugrad need met	61

EMERSON COLLEGE

120 Boylston Street, Boston, MA 02116-4624 • Admissions: 617-824-8600 • Fax: 617-824-8609

STUDENTS SAY "..."

Academics

Emerson College boasts its "urban" Boston location as a solid locus for "networking and career-preparation," including the "amazing alumni network," lovingly referred to as the "Emerson Mafia." In particular, "journalism, writing, film, marketing, and theater programs" are especially "strong," and classes are "taught by industry professionals" who "never fail to enlighten." Most of the classes are focused on job readiness: "You do work with actual organizations rather than discuss theories." There are "impressive" facilities and resources, including "film and TV studio facilities and equipment" with broad "availability to students," and "small class sizes with easy-to-reach professors, specific course material, and no meaningless busy work," that "often work more like collaborations than lectures." "We aren't test takers at Emerson," one student says, "so we don't study. We create projects, videos, presentations, [and so on]." Professors are "passionate about the learning material," and "are in constant discourse with the class," "keen on showcasing global perspectives." Emerson stresses "hands on activities, volunteer opportunities, real-time demonstrations, and frequent class discussions," and classes "integrated with external organizations," means students are often out in the community, "working with local nonprofits," or navigating "creative opportunities through internships in the Boston area." Emerson offers a "wealth of resources" on campus, including the "ArtsEmerson productions," "Bright Lights Film series," "Emerson Channel," and the "EVVY Award" give "media creators" all the immersive experience they need to prepare for post-college professions. The study abroad trips are "phenomenal," with students raving about trips to Cuba, Colombia, and the Netherlands.

Life

Students report that while Boston gives them everything they can hope for in terms of entertainment and culture, the on-campus extracurricular activities at Emerson "are innumerable and invaluable." Emerson provides "enough resources that you can do pretty much anything you want to do": clubs are "largely student run and provide a good amount of field experience for whatever it is you want to do." The campus is located "right on the Boston Common," so students enjoy "taking walks," visiting museums, many with "free entry," and trying out "lots of good food." Many students "work part-time" in the city, and otherwise students "hang out in the common rooms," "spend time working with a number of student organizations," exploring "wonderful Common Park," which is located close to campus. Other students like "watching NCAA games" or "attending interesting plays at the Emerson theatre." "Emerson students are known to overcommit themselves to activities," says one student. Another says, "It is not unusual to hear of students working on…several different shows and organizations while always taking challenging courses. Students, however, rarely complain that this affects the "quality of their lives or academic experience."

Student Body

The student body is described as "small, open-minded, artsy, but with a distinct student-athlete crowd." Emerson students "usually enter the school with a career already in mind" with some having "prior experience." It is "rare to find people who are undeclared." Students describe Emerson as "an art school without the label," attracting "creative forces" who are "ambitious, driven, and self-starters." Students "can be a little pretentious and business oriented" and "casual conversations can sometimes feel like a networking event." Yet others stress that their "peers are collaborative and kind," with most "extremely kind and willing to work with each other." Everybody is generally "open to new ideas and perspectives, very accepting and friendly," and "all very committed to their art." One student comments on diversity: "It's a diverse campus in sexual and gender identity, however racial diversity is limited. There's a range of interests, but the majority of students at Emerson are here to study some aspect of film, and so life is somewhat dominated by that." The campus tends to be "pro-social justice," with a "great activism community" that is "highly involved in Black Lives Matter," "climate change," and other hot-button political issues.

EMERSON COLLEGE

Financial Aid: 617-824-8655 • E-Mail: admission@emerson.edu • Website: www.emerson.edu

THE PRINCETON REVIEW SAYS

Admissions

Very important factors considered include: academic GPA, application essay. *Important factors considered include:* rigor of secondary school record, class rank, recommendation(s), extracurricular activities, talent/ability, character/personal qualities. *Other factors considered include:* standardized test scores, first generation, alumni/ae relation, geographical residence, racial/ethnic status, volunteer work, work experience. ACT with or without writing accepted. SAT with or without Essay component accepted. High school diploma is required and GED is accepted. *Academic units required:* 4 English, 3 math, 3 science, 3 foreign language, 3 social studies. *Academic units recommended:* 4 English, 3 math, 3 science, 3 foreign language, 3 social studies, 4 academic electives.

Financial Aid

Students should submit: Business/Farm Supplement; CSS/Financial Aid PROFILE; FAFSA; Noncustodial PROFILE. Priority filing deadline is 11/15. The Princeton Review suggests that all financial aid forms be submitted as soon as possible after October 1. *Need-based scholarships/grants offered:* College/university scholarship or grant aid from institutional funds; Federal Pell; Private scholarships; SEOG; State scholarships/grants. *Loan aid offered:* Direct PLUS loans; Direct Subsidized Stafford Loans; Direct Unsubsidized Stafford Loans. Applicants will be notified of awards on or about 4/1. Federal Work-Study Program available. Institutional employment available.

The Inside Word

From its location in Boston's theatre district to its large alumni network, Emerson is the perfect school for students interested in communications, theater, and television, among other academic offerings. Jobs and internship opportunities abound in those fields, helping students jumpstart their careers upon graduation. If you are applying in cinematography or the performing arts, be prepared to complete an artistic review with your application. In Fall 2017, the college moved to test-optional applications: students who choose not to submit standardized test scores will be required to submit either a "contemplative essay responding to a topic related to communication and the arts" or a "creative sample or portfolio that relates specifically to their chosen major."

THE SCHOOL SAYS "..."

From the Admissions Office

"Emerson College is the nation's only four-year, liberal arts institution devoted exclusively to the study of communication and the arts. For over 130 years Emerson has educated the most innovative and creative minds in the fields of marketing, visual and media arts, entrepreneurship, publishing and writing, journalism, performing arts, and speech pathology and audiology. Guided by an award-winning faculty, Emerson students are provided with the real-world experience, professional-grade facilities, and foundational liberal arts knowledge they need to be at the cutting edge of their ever-changing industries. Located in the heart of Boston's Theatre District, Emerson's main campus is home to award-winning literary journals, sound treated television studios, and several digital editing and audio post-production suites. The Tufte Performance and Production Center houses a theater design/technology center, makeup lab, and costume shop. There are several programs to observe speech and hearing therapy, a professional marketing focus group room, digital newsroom, and the Paramount Center, which includes a sound stage, scene shop, rehearsal studios, black box theatre, and film screening room. Emerson has nearly eighty student organizations and performance groups as well as fourteen NCAA Division III teams. The college also sponsors programs in Los Angeles and Washington, D.C.; study abroad in the Netherlands, Taiwan, and Czech Republic; and course cross-registration with the six-member Boston ProArts Consortium. The tightly-knit network of 28,000 alumni and the connections that Emerson students make on campus follow them into their post-graduate life, paving the way to collaborative projects, internships, and career opportunities across the globe."

SELECTIVITY

Admissions Rating	92
# of applicants	15,353
% of applicants accepted	33
% of acceptees attending	18
# offered a place on the wait list	1,611
% accepting a place on wait list	50
% admitted from wait list	6

FRESHMAN PROFILE

Range SAT EBRW	610–700
Range SAT Math	590–710
Range SAT Composite	1230–1380
Range ACT Composite	27–31
# submitting SAT scores	626
% submitting SAT scores	67
# submitting ACT scores	246
% submitting ACT scores	26
Average HS GPA	3.7
% graduated top 10% of class	27
% graduated top 25% of class	65
% graduated top 50% of class	93

DEADLINES

Early decision	
Deadline	11/1
Notification	12/15
Early action	
Deadline	11/1
Notification	12/15
Regular	
Deadline	1/15
Notification	4/1
Nonfall registration?	Yes

APPLICANTS ALSO LOOK AT AND OFTEN PREFER

New York University; Boston University; Chapman University; University of Southern California

AND SOMETIMES PREFER

Northeastern University; Ithaca College; Syracuse University; Fordham University; American University

AND RARELY PREFER

Pace University

FINANCIAL FACTS

Financial Aid Rating	80
Annual tuition	$48,560
Room and board	$18,400
Required fees	$872
Books and supplies	$1,150
Average frosh need-based scholarship	$23,198
Average UG need-based scholarship	$20,223
% needy frosh rec. need-based scholarship or grant aid	94
% needy UG rec. need-based scholarship or grant aid	90
% needy frosh rec. non-need-based scholarship or grant aid	13
% needy UG rec. non-need-based scholarship or grant aid	6
% needy frosh rec. need-based self-help aid	89
% needy UG rec. need-based self-help aid	88
% UG borrow to pay for school	61
Average cumulative indebtedness	$24,193
% frosh need fully met	11
% ugrads need fully met	6
Average % of frosh need met	55
Average % of ugrad need met	46

EMORY UNIVERSITY

Emory University, Boiseuillet Jones Center, Atlanta, GA 30322 • Admissions: 404-727-6036 • Fax: 404-727-4303

STUDENTS SAY "..."

Academics

This top research university in Atlanta offers more than eighty undergraduate programs spread across nine schools, and affords students the academic freedom to customize their own curriculum and pursue multiple programs of study, no matter how strange the combination might be. "Intramural basketball and intro to theater? Sure. History of the human world and advanced mathematics? Go ahead," says a student. In allowing students the room to create their own experience, Emory is also "constantly testing out new programs that may one day benefit future students" and strengthening the community. Most here are "involved in the real world in some aspect," whether through an internship during the summer, or an actual job during the year, and students "are encouraged to pursue their interests" both in and out of the classroom. All in all, Emory cultivates an atmosphere of "bold, courageous inquiry facilitated by world-renowned professors, state-of-the-art facilities, and an omnipresent desire to learn."

Professors at Emory are "incredibly successful in their fields but believe that you can be too," and "are willing to invest time and effort" into seeing this come true. All have open office hours, are "very feedback-oriented," and "respect what students have to say." There is an emphasis on a collaborative environment here, and the "amazing, smart people who bring their brains to class and help educate us" make sure that this permeates every inch of the classroom. There is a lack of competition on campus, which is "actually really heartening and refreshing because students are being pushed to learn and do well in classes and on their topics of interest." Additionally, the school's status as a pre-eminent research university allows students to perform "some of the most cutting-edge research in disciplines ranging from the humanities to the social sciences to the natural and physical sciences." "As a whole, I know that I am graduating with a support system behind me and endless opportunities in front of me," says a student.

Life

Emory is in the suburbs, but just a scant 15 minutes from downtown Atlanta, and the school's popular "Experience Shuttles" take students out to various attractions in the city on a weekly basis. Much of life at Emory revolves around extracurriculars, and the opportunities to get involved on campus abound, with "many volunteer, Greek, arts, and sports organizations." Outside of these activities, many students "hang out at coffee shops on campus, explore the Atlanta area, hike in Emory's large nature preserve, or go to social events on Greek Row." Greek life is very prominent here, so "there is always something going on, whether it is an open social event, a philanthropy event, or commitments within your organization." While many people go to parties or club meetings during the majority of their free time, everyone is perfectly happy to "just chill in the dorm rooms and watch a movie on the free television Emory provides."

Student Body

The diversity within the student body is a huge draw; not only are students "from all over the United States and from around the globe," but the perspectives represented on this campus are "truly astounding." Many students come here with friends from high school, and a fair number of students are in the business school or are pre-med (due to the noted Emory Healthcare system). Everyone at Emory is "extremely curious about the world around them" and passionate about both their areas of study as well as their extracurricular involvements. There's "a niche for literally anything and everything," and "the mood on campus is overall happy and light-hearted." The spirit of Emory encompasses "a community of care, embracing diversity, and providing a learning environment conducive to academic success."

Financial Aid: 404-727-6039 • E-Mail: admiss@emory.edu • Website: www.emory.edu

THE PRINCETON REVIEW SAYS

Admissions

Very important factors considered include: rigor of secondary school record, academic GPA, recommendation(s), extracurricular activities, talent/ability, character/personal qualities. *Important factors considered include:* application essay, standardized test scores. *Other factors considered include:* class rank, interview, first generation, alumni/ae relation, geographical residence, state residency, racial/ethnic status, work experience. ACT with or without writing accepted. SAT with or without Essay component accepted. High school diploma is required and GED is not accepted. *Academic units recommended:* 4 English, 4 math, 4 science, 2 science labs, 4 foreign language, 2 social studies, 2 history, 1 computer science, 1 visual/performing arts.

Financial Aid

Students should submit: CSS/Financial Aid PROFILE; FAFSA; Noncustodial PROFILE. Priority filing deadline is 2/15. The Princeton Review suggests that all financial aid forms be submitted as soon as possible after October 1. *Need-based scholarships/grants offered:* College/university scholarship or grant aid from institutional funds; Federal Pell; Private scholarships; SEOG; State scholarships/grants. *Loan aid offered:* Direct PLUS loans; Direct Subsidized Stafford Loans; Direct Unsubsidized Stafford Loans. Applicants will be notified of awards on or about 4/1. Federal Work-Study Program available. Institutional employment available.

The Inside Word

Early decision applications to Emory have surged in the past several years, leading students to question whether they want to join the early word crowd—perhaps increasing the likelihood of admission—or take their chances with regular admission. Those hoping for admission should aim for a 3.75 (or better) GPA and polish up their writing skills and extracurricular activities.

THE SCHOOL SAYS "..."

From the Admissions Office

"Emory is an inquiry-driven, ethically engaged, and diverse community whose members work collaboratively for positive transformation in the world through courageous leadership in teaching, research scholarship, health care, and social action. The university is internationally recognized for its outstanding liberal arts colleges, superb professional schools, and leading health care system. Emory is noted as one of the most diverse selective universities in the country.

"Emory offers a distinctive undergraduate experience with programs in the humanities, sciences, business, and nursing allowing students to explore their interests and talents in the classroom and in the field. Entering freshman may apply to Emory College, a four-year liberal arts education within the heart of a major research university. Students may also apply to Oxford College where students spend the first two years on Emory's original campus thirty-eight miles east of Atlanta. Emory provides a rich setting for learning from excellent teaching in small classes to lectures from prominent scholars to opportunities for study abroad, research, and internships.

"Emory students balance hard work with having fun. With 63 percent of students living on campus, the community is enhanced by a close-knit living environment. The campus life thrives on constant activity, and students are encouraged to get involved, share opinions, and flourish. Emory is a dynamic place that is constantly in a state of sustainable growth and improvement. Take a look at all Emory has to offer—you'll see why Emory students feel inspired to do more with what they learn here."

SELECTIVITY

Admissions Rating	98
# of applicants	30,017
% of applicants accepted	16
% of acceptees attending	29
# offered a place on the wait list	4,679
% accepting a place on wait list	80
% admitted from wait list	5
# of early decision applicants	3,125
% accepted early decision	23

FRESHMAN PROFILE

Range SAT EBRW	670–740
Range SAT Math	690–790
Range SAT Composite	1390–1510
Range ACT Composite	31–34
# submitting SAT scores	816
% submitting SAT scores	59
# submitting ACT scores	558
% submitting ACT scores	41
Average HS GPA	3.8
% graduated top 10% of class	84
% graduated top 25% of class	97
% graduated top 50% of class	100

DEADLINES

Early decision	
Deadline	11/1
Notification	12/15
Other ED Deadline	1/1
Other ED Notification	2/15
Regular	
Deadline	1/1
Notification	4/1
Nonfall registration?	No

FINANCIAL FACTS

Financial Aid Rating	97
Annual tuition	$55,200
Room and board	$15,572
Required fees	$798
Books and supplies	$1,224
Average frosh need-based scholarship	$48,738
Average UG need-based scholarship	$43,659
% needy frosh rec. need-based scholarship or grant aid	94
% needy UG rec. need-based scholarship or grant aid	96
% needy frosh rec. non-need-based scholarship or grant aid	34
% needy UG rec. non-need-based scholarship or grant aid	22
% needy frosh rec. need-based self-help aid	89
% needy UG rec. need-based self-help aid	90
% frosh rec. any financial aid	62
% UG rec. any financial aid	61
% UG borrow to pay for school	35
Average cumulative indebtedness	$24,889
% frosh need fully met	100
% ugrads need fully met	98
Average % of frosh need met	100
Average % of ugrad need met	100

THE EVERGREEN STATE COLLEGE

2700 Evergreen Pkwy NW, Olympia, WA 98505 • Admissions: 360-867-6170 • Fax: 360-867-5114

STUDENTS SAY "..."

Academics

"Keeping education in its purest form alive and well in the heart of the Northwest," The Evergreen State College offers "a unique approach" to academics. The school provides an "interactive environment—with a diverse, enriching learning method," which allows students "to focus on [their] passions and explore them in detail." Everyone creates their own educational paths and directs the pace of their own learning. As a few students say admiringly, "I feel a sense of freedom with the academics at Evergreen." "I have more power as a student." Greatly appreciated is the flexibility found within the curriculum. "I was excited about building my own major." "No self-motivated student will leave Evergreen unsatisfied." Students work collaboratively here and support one another in their endeavors. "It's not about grades or competition; it's about self-improvement and personal fulfillment." Evaluations are used to view student progress, with "interdisciplinary education over declared majors" being the focus. "Your classes are all interconnected, so it's easy to link what you're doing into a defined path." "My transcript says more about me than A's, B's, and C's possibly could." "The philosophy...definitely lowers the stress I experience around academics." Professors assist students in innumerable ways and are "very intimately involved in the education of their students." "At Evergreen, in order to have a great experience you need to be able to talk to your professors and engage with them." "I have not met a professor yet who was not willing to rework their mode of teaching to better serve the class." The educational atmosphere is highly interactive. Almost every student "actively engages the material with field work, undergraduate research, and extended trips." "Class time is spent doing workshops, seminars, or a led discussion where everyone participates." "Even the science programs involve large portions of discussion and peer collaboration." As one undergraduate describes slyly, "My professors have been A++, if Evergreen assigned grades."

Life

Evergreen has a "booming extracurricular life"; students enjoy the "thriving local art and music scene, very hip and fresh," in Olympia as well as easily accessible Seattle or Portland. "The Flaming Eggplant, the student-run cafe, is simply the cheapest and most delicious place on the planet," as well as a very popular hangout. The Student Activities office has no shortage of options for undergraduates here, with "more than fifty different clubs and student groups." Physical activity is popular, and the recreational center has racquetball, a pool, a rock-climbing wall, and various places to exercise. There is "no shortage of local hiking, backpacking, and biking opportunities." "Hikes in the woods, down to the beach, or up to the bluff are very common as well as late-night stargazing." The physical surroundings are viewed with much admiration at Evergreen. "Our campus is set back in this magical forest with these winding paths down to the beach. There are tree forts, giant sculptures, dream catchers in the trees, hidden drum circles, and music everywhere." As one student describes fondly, "To me, it is reminiscent of Thoreau's solitude in nature."

Student Life

The "kindness and awareness of the community" is frequently said by students to be one of the most valued aspects of their experience here. "Articulate" and "inquisitive" undergraduates are evident in large numbers. "Students tend to be very politically aware and active with very liberal points of view" and are "mostly peaceful relaxed people" amidst an "open-minded social environment." The dorms are divided into different themes, and "the residential staff is professional and keeps the housing community functioning and safe." "The campus police are pretty awesome people," as well. Evergreen is respected by students throughout the college for its "forward-thinking" administration and faculty, with a "dedication to sustainability" being clearly evident around the campus.

Financial Aid: 360-867-6205 • E-Mail: admissions@evergreen.edu • Website: www.evergreen.edu

THE PRINCETON REVIEW SAYS

Admissions
Very important factors considered include: rigor of secondary school record, academic GPA. *Important factors considered include:* standardized test scores, level of applicant's interest. *Other factors considered include:* application essay, recommendation(s), interview, extracurricular activities, volunteer work, work experience. ACT with or without writing accepted. SAT with or without Essay component accepted. High school diploma is required and GED is accepted. *Academic units required:* 4 English, 3 math, 2 science, 2 science labs, 2 foreign language, 3 social studies, 1 academic elective, 1 unit from above areas or other academic areas.

Financial Aid
Students should submit: FAFSA. Priority filing deadline is 2/1. The Princeton Review suggests that all financial aid forms be submitted as soon as possible after October 1. *Need-based scholarships/grants offered:* College/university scholarship or grant aid from institutional funds; Federal Pell; Private scholarships; SEOG; State scholarships/grants. *Loan aid offered:* Direct PLUS loans; Direct Subsidized Stafford Loans; Direct Unsubsidized Stafford Loans. Applicants will be notified of awards on a rolling basis beginning 4/1. Federal Work-Study Program available. Institutional employment available.

The Inside Word
Students at Evergreen are commonly some of the strongest performers from their high schools, although the admissions department considers a variety of traits from applicants (including strength of character) when considering prospective undergraduates. The school's unique and self-directed academic curriculum favors those students who can adequately handle the responsibility of creating and developing their own educational path.

THE SCHOOL SAYS "..."

From the Admissions Office
"The Evergreen State College is a public liberal arts college located in Olympia, Washington, between Seattle and Portland. As a public college, Evergreen offers unsurpassed value—the academic and campus environment typical of a private college, for lower tuition.

"Evergreen attracts students inspired by the complexity of the world and those that want to take charge of their education. Rather than checking off lists created by someone else, students create their own path to a Bachelor degree, choosing from among 60 academic fields.

"Evergreen has embraced a different model of liberal arts education since its inception in 1967. Students don't take several unrelated classes each term, instead they register for a single, team-taught, full-time course (a program) that incorporates multiple fields of study and focuses on real-life problems and experiences. Students learn in a truly integrated and interdisciplinary way from faculty with experience in multiple academic fields.

"Evergreen graduates go on to careers ranging from public service and non-profit leadership, business, and the creative arts. They're valued in the workplace for their ability to lead diverse teams, meld together ideas and form divergent points of view, and adapt at the speed of today's world.

"Aligning with our belief that each student is an individual defined by much more than a single letter or number, Evergreen offers test-optional admission beginning with fall 2020 admissions.

"Evergreen is a proud member of Colleges That Changes Lives, The Common Application, Consortium for Innovative Environments in Learning, and Western Undergraduate Exchange."

SELECTIVITY
Admissions Rating	73
# of applicants	1,303
% of applicants accepted	98
% of acceptees attending	20

FRESHMAN PROFILE
Range SAT EBRW	530–640
Range SAT Math	470–580
Range ACT Composite	20–27
# submitting SAT scores	219
% submitting SAT scores	71
# submitting ACT scores	97
% submitting ACT scores	31
Average HS GPA	3.1
% graduated top 10% of class	19
% graduated top 25% of class	24
% graduated top 50% of class	60

DEADLINES
Regular	
Priority	2/1
Notification	Rolling, 11/1
Nonfall registration?	Yes

APPLICANTS ALSO LOOK AT AND OFTEN PREFER
Western Washington University; University of Washington; University of California—Santa Cruz; Washington State University; Portland State University

AND SOMETIMES PREFER
Hampshire College; University of Puget Sound; Willamette University; University of Oregon; Central Washington University; Humboldt State University

AND RARELY PREFER
Colorado State University; Eastern Washington University; Pacific Lutheran University; Seattle University; Lewis & Clark College; University of Colorado Boulder

FINANCIAL FACTS
Financial Aid Rating	80
Annual in-state tuition	$7,005
Annual out-of-state tuition	$26,325
Room and board	$12,363
Required fees	$1,203
Books and supplies	$900
Average frosh need-based scholarship	$10,756
Average UG need-based scholarship	$10,923
% needy frosh rec. need-based scholarship or grant aid	92
% needy UG rec. need-based scholarship or grant aid	87
% needy frosh rec. non-need-based scholarship or grant aid	3
% needy UG rec. non-need-based scholarship or grant aid	1
% needy frosh rec. need-based self-help aid	69
% needy UG rec. need-based self-help aid	73
% frosh rec. any financial aid	67
% UG rec. any financial aid	67
% UG borrow to pay for school	58
Average cumulative indebtedness	$20,488
% frosh need fully met	5
% ugrads need fully met	5
Average % of frosh need met	56
Average % of ugrad need met	63

FAIRFIELD UNIVERSITY

1073 North Benson Road, Fairfield, CT 06824 • Admissions: 203-254-4100 • Fax: 203-254-4199

CAMPUS LIFE

Quality of Life Rating	**92**
Fire Safety Rating	**98**
Green Rating	**77**
Type of school	Private
Affiliation	Roman Catholic-Jesuit
Environment	Town

STUDENTS

Total undergrad enrollment	4,303
% male/female	41/59
% from out of state	73
% frosh from public high school	60
% frosh live on campus	95
% ugrads live on campus	73
# of fraternities	0
# of sororities	0
% African American	2
% Asian	3
% Caucasian	77
% Hispanic	7
% Native American	<1
% Pacific Islander	0
% Two or more races	2
% Race and/or ethnicity unknown	6
% international	4
# of countries represented	49

SURVEY SAYS . . .

Lots of conservative students
Students are happy
Great library
Internships are widely available
Students love Fairfield, CT
Great off-campus food
Recreation facilities are great
Everyone loves the Stags
Intramural sports are popular

ACADEMICS

Academic Rating	**84**
% students returning for sophomore year	90
% students graduating within 4 years	80
% students graduating within 6 years	83
Calendar	Semester
Student/faculty ratio	12:1
Profs interesting rating	90
Profs accessible rating	94

Most classes have 20–29 students.
Most lab/discussion sessions have fewer than 10 students.

MOST POPULAR MAJORS

Registered Nursing/Registered Nurse; Finance, General; Marketing/Marketing Management, General

STUDENTS SAY "..."

Academics

It's easy to fall in love with Fairfield University. After all, the school offers a "strong and accepting community [that] strive[s] to make everyone feel at home." Plus, it doesn't hurt that the campus is "beautiful." Perhaps more importantly, undergrads are privy to "small class [sizes] where professors really get to know you" and "lots of internship opportunities." Students also tout the "outstanding" business and nursing programs, both of which are "nationally ranked." And all undergrads, regardless of chosen discipline, learn from professors who tend to prioritize "teaching [over] their own research." The professors are also extraordinarily "engaging [and] passionate" and often "have real-world experience [to] bring into the classroom." Moreover, Fairfield professors challenge students to "think outside the box." And "if you show an interest in [a particular] subject, most of the professors here will [work] with you for as long as necessary to make sure you are getting everything you want out of the class." They truly are committed to the "success of their students," and they work diligently to ensure that the academics at Fairfield are "tough but manageable." In other words, "if you put in the time and focus in class, you will do well."

Life

Students gush that "every day is different at Fairfield." After all, "there is always something happening that students are able to participate in." This could be anything from "a concert [or] food trucks" to "bingo and sporting events." And one student excitedly shares, "Recently we had a Stuff a Stag [event where students created their own stuffed animals and] almost a quarter of the university attended." Aside from school-sponsored events, Fairfield undergrads can join a wide variety of clubs ranging from the campus radio station to the student-run competitive dance group, Fairfield Dance Fusion. Intramural sports and going to the gym are also pretty popular. Additionally, "community service is very prominent" and a number of students pursue "campus jobs [or] internships" as well. Once the weekend arrives, you can frequently "find students partying, ... and in the nicer weather, [they do so] on the nearby beach." Undergrads also like heading into downtown Fairfield, which has "lots of opportunities to eat out." Even better, "NYC is very accessible and [the university] offers very cheap Broadway trips that include tickets and transportation." All in all, Fairfield makes it relatively easy to find a "good balance between doing school work and [socializing]."

Student Body

The student body at Fairfield University is an "extremely close-knit" community. Undergrads do readily admit that the school is mostly "comprised of white, middle-upper class kids." However, they also adamantly insist that there is plenty of diversity in terms of "ideals, personalities and interests." And they note that "everyone can find their people here." Moreover, Fairfield students highlight the fact that their peers are "hard-working individuals with an unwavering dedication to learning as much as possible." They are also "welcoming and happy to get to know everyone." As one student further explains, "Fairfield has the type of student body that each student holds the door for the person behind them even if they are not necessarily close behind." Another agrees: "Fairfield is unique in the sense that all the students genuinely want to get to know each other. Being a smaller school, everyone is super friendly and interested in creating new friendships." With all this good feeling permeating campus, it's no wonder that students here are imbued with "lots of school spirit."

FAIRFIELD UNIVERSITY

Financial Aid: 203-254-4125 • E-Mail: admis@fairfield.edu • Website: www.fairfield.edu

THE PRINCETON REVIEW SAYS

Admissions

Very important factors considered include: rigor of secondary school record, academic GPA, application essay, recommendation(s). *Important factors considered include:* interview, extra-curricular activities, talent/ability, character/personal qualities, first generation, volunteer work. *Other factors considered include:* class rank, standardized test scores, alumni/ae relation, geographical residence, racial/ethnic status. ACT with or without writing accepted. SAT with or without Essay component accepted. High school diploma is required and GED is accepted. *Academic units required:* 4 English, 3 math, 3 science, 2 science labs, 2 foreign language, 2 social studies, 2 history. *Academic units recommended:* 4 English, 4 math, 4 science, 4 foreign language, 2 social studies, 2 history.

Financial Aid

Students should submit: Business/Farm Supplement; CSS/Financial Aid PROFILE; FAFSA; Noncustodial PROFILE. Priority filing deadline is 12/1. The Princeton Review suggests that all financial aid forms be submitted as soon as possible after October 1. *Need-based scholarships/grants offered:* College/university scholarship or grant aid from institutional funds; Federal Pell; Private scholarships; SEOG; State scholarships/grants. *Loan aid offered:* Direct PLUS loans; Direct Subsidized Stafford Loans; Direct Unsubsidized Stafford Loans. Applicants will be notified of awards on or about 4/1. Federal Work-Study Program available. Institutional employment available.

The Inside Word

When it comes to making admissions decisions, Fairfield University takes a well-rounded approach. The school wants to ensure that it admits students who will be successful and reflect their Jesuit ideals. While all facets of the application are critical, there's no denying academic records will be of primary importance. Expect admissions officers to closely assess both grades and the rigor of your curriculum. And if you panic at the thought of standardized tests, you can breathe a sigh of relief: Fairfield is test-optional. However, if you choose not to submit, it's highly recommended you sit for an interview.

THE SCHOOL SAYS "..."

From the Admissions Office

"Fairfield University welcomes students into a learning and living community that will give them a solid intellectual foundation and the confidence they need to reach their individual goals. Students at Fairfield benefit from the deep-rooted Jesuit commitment to education of the whole person—mind, body, and spirit, and our admission policies are consistent with that mission. When considering an applicant, Fairfield looks at measures of academic achievement, students' curricular and extracurricular activities, their life skills and accomplishments, and the degree to which they have an appreciation for Fairfield's mission and outlook. In keeping with its holistic review process, Fairfield is a test optional institution. Students choosing not to submit test scores do not have to submit any additional documents, but are encouraged to schedule a campus interview. Fairfield University students are challenged to be creative and active members of a community in which diversity is encouraged and honored. The university community is committed to excellence in educating, serving, inspiring and training students in a wide variety of disciplines and fields. Students can complement their classroom performance with a rich array of study abroad, internship and research opportunities. Our location is ideal, offering a picturesque 200-acre campus in the coastal community of Fairfield, Connecticut, just an hour away from the cultural, intellectual and economic opportunities of New York City. On campus, students participate in a vast array of activities, including varsity and intramural athletics, performing arts groups and an extremely active student government. All of this prepares our graduates for a rich and fulfilling future, whether students pursue a career, service opportunities or graduate study. In our most recent survey of graduates of the Class of 2017 six months after graduation, 98 percent of students were employed full time, in graduate school or pursuing a service opportunity."

SELECTIVITY

Admissions Rating	89
# of applicants	12,315
% of applicants accepted	57
% of acceptees attending	17
# offered a place on the wait list	3,750
% accepting a place on wait list	32
% admitted from wait list	1
# of early decision applicants	223
% accepted early decision	78

FRESHMAN PROFILE

Range SAT EBRW	610–670
Range SAT Math	600–680
Range SAT Composite	1220–1340
Range ACT Composite	26–30
# submitting SAT scores	680
% submitting SAT scores	58
# submitting ACT scores	191
% submitting ACT scores	16
Average HS GPA	3.6
% graduated top 10% of class	41
% graduated top 25% of class	73
% graduated top 50% of class	97

DEADLINES

Early decision	
Deadline	11/15
Notification	12/15
Other ED Deadline	1/15
Other ED Notification	2/15
Early action	
Deadline	11/1
Notification	12/20
Regular	
Deadline	1/15
Notification	4/1
Nonfall registration?	Yes

APPLICANTS ALSO LOOK AT AND OFTEN PREFER
Boston College; Villanova University

AND SOMETIMES PREFER
Fordham University; Providence College

AND RARELY PREFER
Loyola University Maryland; University of Connecticut; Quinnipiac University

FINANCIAL FACTS

Financial Aid Rating	87
Annual tuition	$50,550
Room and board	$15,610
Required fees	$775
Books and supplies	$1,150
Average frosh need-based scholarship	$32,441
Average UG need-based scholarship	$31,843
% needy frosh rec. need-based scholarship or grant aid	75
% needy UG rec. need-based scholarship or grant aid	81
% needy frosh rec. non-need-based scholarship or grant aid	93
% needy UG rec. non-need-based scholarship or grant aid	90
% needy frosh rec. need-based self-help aid	74
% needy UG rec. need-based self-help aid	78
% frosh rec. any financial aid	97
% UG rec. any financial aid	90
% UG borrow to pay for school	61
Average cumulative indebtedness	$39,214
% frosh need fully met	33
% ugrads need fully met	31
Average % of frosh need met	89
Average % of ugrad need met	87

FLAGLER COLLEGE

74 King Street, St. Augustine, FL 32085-1027 • Admissions: 904-819-6220 • Fax: 904-819-6466

STUDENTS SAY "..."

Academics

For those seeking "an excellent education in a beautiful location," Flagler College is a small comprehensive liberal arts school in Florida that offers a "comfortable atmosphere," "tons of history and culture," and "a perfect ratio of professors to student." The school's strong education program is a huge draw here, but there are plenty of other strong programs in Flagler's twenty-five available majors. Hard workers get noticed, and there are plenty of opportunities to excel outside of the classroom, which "has been the most valuable aspect," according to one student.

The faculty here is "extremely enthusiastic about their jobs" and "very knowledgeable in their fields," though "there are a few that I don't think have real direction," says a student. Nevertheless, most are "always willing to meet and discuss work outside of the classroom," and the fact that "it is pretty easy to get to know the professors within your major on a personal basis makes things a lot easier and comfortable." This close-knit community breeds an environment where every person actively wants "to share experiences and knowledge with the faculty and other students." Class time is treated as an "intellectual journey," wherein one main question or discussion topic is introduced, and students explore every aspect of it using the professor as the tour guide. "This system the professors at Flagler College have evokes curiosity from all students, leaving very little room for confusion."

Aside from the "ample help from teachers," the "personable" administration is "good at communicating to all students via school e-mail." The best classes are the ones with eight or so people in them, as "you really lean on each other throughout the semester."

Life

Life is "pretty chill at Flagler," where "homework usually isn't too bad most of the time." As far as making friends, this "relaxed," happy lot has no problems. "Attend a few of the many social activities that Flagler College offers. It's really easy to make friends there!" suggests one student. On the first Friday of the month, all the art galleries "throw their doors wide open and serve treats," and the "casual and quaint" tourist-centric town of St. Augustine "is an awesome place to spend your time, walking around, going out to eat, and doing a little bit of shopping." Campus activities tend to "die around 7:00 P.M.," and many students tend to live nearby off campus.

Sunny days mean "the pool and West lawn are the places to be," and on weekends, "many times we drive to Jacksonville and go out at night there." Biking, beach volleyball, and walking along the sand dunes are just some of the beachy pastimes here, where "the beach mentality triumphs, including surfer culture." The campus itself "is beautiful, we sometimes even compare it to Hogwarts," says a student.

Student Body

Your typical Flagler student is "easygoing and very laid-back" ("How can you not be with the beach five miles away?" asks a student) as well as "super nice and friendly." It's not difficult to fit in at Flagler College, because "there is a crowd for everybody, despite the small size of the student body," even if this student body as a whole is a bit "homogenous." All students provide different viewpoints and "seem to be very respectful of others' views." There are quite a few surfers and artistic types, and even these groups are "very motivated and ready to broaden their education."

FLAGLER COLLEGE

Financial Aid: 904-819-6225 • E-Mail: admissions@flagler.edu • Website: www.flagler.edu

THE PRINCETON REVIEW SAYS

Admissions

Very important factors considered include: academic GPA, standardized test scores. *Important factors considered include:* rigor of secondary school record, application essay, recommendation(s), first generation, geographical residence. *Other factors considered include:* extracurricular activities, character/personal qualities, alumni/ae relation, volunteer work, work experience, level of applicant's interest. ACT with or without writing accepted. SAT with or without Essay component accepted. High school diploma is required and GED is accepted. *Academic units recommended:* 4 English, 4 math, 3 science, 1 science lab, 2 foreign language, 1 social studies, 3 history.

Financial Aid

Students should submit: FAFSA; State aid form. Priority filing deadline is 3/1. The Princeton Review suggests that all financial aid forms be submitted as soon as possible after October 1. *Need-based scholarships/grants offered:* College/university scholarship or grant aid from institutional funds; Federal Pell; Private scholarships; SEOG; State scholarships/grants. *Loan aid offered:* Direct PLUS loans; Direct Subsidized Stafford Loans; Direct Unsubsidized Stafford Loans. Applicants will be notified of awards on a rolling basis beginning 11/1. Federal Work-Study Program available. Institutional employment available.

The Inside Word

Several high-profile programs, a desirable location, and a small, incoming freshman class all conspire to drive down Flagler's admissions rate. Still, Flagler is not top-tier when it comes to selectivity, and strong candidates should meet little resistance from the admissions office. About half of the incoming freshmen graduated in the top quarter of their classes, so make sure you build a strong application with harder courses and strong grades.

THE SCHOOL SAYS "..."

From the Admissions Office

"Flagler College is an independent, four-year, coeducational, residential institution located in picturesque St. Augustine. A famous historic tourist center in northeast Florida, it is located to the south of Jacksonville and north of Daytona Beach. Flagler students have ample opportunity to explore the rich cultural heritage and international flavor of St. Augustine, and there's always time for a relaxing day at the beach, about four miles from campus. The annual cost for tuition, room, and board at Flagler is about the same as state universities. The small student body helps to keep one from becoming 'just a number.' Flagler serves a predominately full-time student body and seeks to enroll students who can benefit from the type of educational experience the college offers. Because of the college's mission and distinctive characteristics, some students may benefit more from an educational experience at Flagler than others. The college's admission standards and procedures are designed to select from among the applicants those students most likely to succeed academically, to contribute significantly to the student life program at Flagler, and to become graduates of the college. Flagler College provides an exceptional opportunity for a private education at an extremely affordable cost."

SELECTIVITY

Admissions Rating	84
# of applicants	4,569
% of applicants accepted	65
% of acceptees attending	22
# of early decision applicants	335
% accepted early decision	68

FRESHMAN PROFILE

Range SAT EBRW	530–630
Range SAT Math	500–580
Range SAT Composite	1045–1200
Range ACT Composite	21–26
# submitting SAT scores	309
% submitting SAT scores	48
# submitting ACT scores	202
% submitting ACT scores	32
Average HS GPA	3.5

DEADLINES

Early decision	
Deadline	11/1
Regular	
Deadline	3/1
Notification	Rolling, 10/1
Nonfall registration?	Yes

APPLICANTS ALSO LOOK AT AND OFTEN PREFER
Florida State University; University of Central Florida; University of North Florida; University of South Florida

AND SOMETIMES PREFER
Florida Gulf Coast University; Florida Southern College; Florida Atlantic University; Rollins College; Stetson University; University of Florida ; University of Tampa

AND RARELY PREFER
College of Charleston; Coastal Carolina University; Eckerd College; Florida International University; High Point University; Jacksonville University; New College of Florida; Palm Beach Atlantic University; University of West Florida

FINANCIAL FACTS

Financial Aid Rating	84
Annual tuition	$19,940
Room and board	$12,540
Required fees	$100
Books and supplies	$1,100
Average frosh need-based scholarship	$11,458
Average UG need-based scholarship	$10,444
% needy frosh rec. need-based scholarship or grant aid	98
% needy UG rec. need-based scholarship or grant aid	97
% needy frosh rec. non-need-based scholarship or grant aid	8
% needy UG rec. non-need-based scholarship or grant aid	8
% needy frosh rec. need-based self-help aid	76
% needy UG rec. need-based self-help aid	76
% frosh rec. any financial aid	94
% UG rec. any financial aid	91
% UG borrow to pay for school	67
Average cumulative indebtedness	$29,837
% frosh need fully met	13
% ugrads need fully met	14
Average % of frosh need met	55
Average % of ugrad need met	57

FLORIDA SOUTHERN COLLEGE

111 Lake Hollingsworth Drive, Lakeland, FL 33801-5698 • Admissions: 863-680-4131 • Fax: 863-680-4120

CAMPUS LIFE

Quality of Life Rating	87
Fire Safety Rating	90
Green Rating	65
Type of school	Private
Affiliation	Methodist
Environment	City

STUDENTS

Total undergrad enrollment	2,665
% male/female	37/63
% from out of state	32
% frosh from public high school	75
% frosh live on campus	94
% ugrads live on campus	80
# of fraternities (% ugrad men join)	7 (29)
# of sororities (% ugrad women join)	7 (35)
% African American	7
% Asian	3
% Caucasian	71
% Hispanic	13
% Native American	<1
% Pacific Islander	<1
% Two or more races	0
% Race and/or ethnicity unknown	1
% international	3
# of countries represented	37

SURVEY SAYS . . .

Lots of conservative students
Class discussions encouraged
Frats and sororities are popular
Theater is popular

ACADEMICS

Academic Rating	82
% students returning for sophomore year	82
% students graduating within 4 years	57
Calendar	Semester
Student/faculty ratio	14:1
Profs interesting rating	88
Profs accessible rating	90

Most classes have 10–19 students.
Most lab/discussion sessions have
10–19 students.

MOST POPULAR MAJORS

Biology/Biological Sciences, General; Registered
Nursing/Registered Nurse; Business
Administration and Management, General

STUDENTS SAY "..."

Academics

This small private college in Lakeland, Florida, is "an educational institution with a small campus and big opportunities." Home to the world's largest single-site collection of Frank Lloyd Wright architecture, this beautiful campus offers over seventy undergraduate majors, small class sizes, a guaranteed internship, and the "Junior Journey," in which every new student is guaranteed domestic or foreign travel experience. "Going through the program with a consistent core group of peers has helped me to grow so much as a person," says one student. Resources (such as the Wellness Center, chaplain's office, and advising services) are definitely plentiful here, but "if students want more opportunit[ies] then they need to go out for them." "Faculty...aren't going to just place them in the laps of students without effort on their end." The business school is housed in a new building, and there are lots of groups and speakers brought on campus to help students "develop leadership and organizational skills."

Thanks to the small student body, professors are able to devote individual attention all around, and engaging the students in class and calling on quieter or unfocused students "to ensure we are all learning." All teachers "bring a wealth of knowledge to the classroom" and "encourage [students] to become the best we can be and do nothing but try to guide us." Students readily admit that the FSC academic experience is what one makes of it: Florida Southern "is all about the student taking charge of his or her education, [and] enhancing it through the many roles they take on in addition to being a student."

Life

Since this "very student-centered" campus is so small, students here see people they know everywhere they go, which "makes a really neat sense of community." There's plenty to do between studying, including "great intramural sports and people getting together and playing soccer, volleyball, [and] basketball," as well as a modern gym (this is a Division II school) and a running trail right off campus that wraps around a lake. Students are "incredibly involved on campus"; there is "a vibrant Greek community" and so many "clubs that include people of all areas and majors [that] cliques don't really exist." The theater department puts on three plays and two musicals each year; the improv comedy team puts on shows nearly every Friday night; and "the Association of Campus Entertainment brings music artists and comedy acts to campus on a regular basis, even recruiting student talent to be opening acts."

Lakeland itself is an up-and-coming city with a central downtown within walking distance to campus that boasts craft coffee shops, museums, restaurants, shops, and weekly farmer's markets and food trucks. Tampa, Orlando, and of course, the beach are all accessible, and this adds to the general sunshine of the school: "It's Florida and the weather is usually gorgeous, so most people are happy," sums up a student.

Student Body

The campus "is small enough that you'll quickly recognize others' faces even if you've never had a class with them," and though it "may seem pretty homogeneous on the surface," Florida Southern College places a high value on individuality. People come from all of the United States (primarily Florida and the northeast), and this forms a group of "outgoing peers who you can get to know pretty well." Athletes and Greek lifers are the two main groups at play here, and "there is an extremely high level of school spirit and enthusiasm for everything that happens on our campus." "Every day I am greeted with a smile by everyone I walk by," says one student of this welcoming bunch.

Financial Aid: 863-680-4140 • E-Mail: fscadm@flsouthern.edu • Website: www.flsouthern.edu

THE PRINCETON REVIEW SAYS

Admissions

Very important factors considered include: rigor of secondary school record, academic GPA. *Important factors considered include:* application essay, standardized test scores, recommendation(s), extracurricular activities, talent/ability, character/personal qualities. *Other factors considered include:* class rank, interview, first generation, alumni/ae relation, religious affiliation/commitment, racial/ethnic status, volunteer work, work experience. ACT with or without writing accepted. SAT with or without Essay component accepted. High school diploma is required and GED is accepted. *Academic units required:* 4 English, 3 math, 2 science, 2 science labs, 3 social studies, 3 history, 1 academic elective. *Academic units recommended:* 4 English, 3 math, 2 science, 2 science labs, 2 foreign language, 3 social studies, 3 history, 1 academic elective.

Financial Aid

Students should submit: FAFSA; Institution's own financial aid form. Priority filing deadline is 3/1. The Princeton Review suggests that all financial aid forms be submitted as soon as possible after October 1. *Need-based scholarships/grants offered:* College/university scholarship or grant aid from institutional funds; Federal Nursing Scholarships; Federal Pell; Private scholarships; SEOG; State scholarships/grants. *Loan aid offered:* Direct PLUS loans; Direct Subsidized Stafford Loans; Direct Unsubsidized Stafford Loans. Applicants will be notified of awards on a rolling basis beginning 3/1. Federal Work-Study Program available. Institutional employment available.

The Inside Word

Grades and test scores are the most important admission criteria here, but extracurricular activities, community service, and leadership experience also count for a lot. Admissions officers are on the lookout for applicants who demonstrate intellectual curiosity and a desire to succeed. Without a doubt, the strongest candidates are those who have challenged themselves by taking honors, advanced placement, AICE, or IB courses.

THE SCHOOL SAYS "..."

From the Admissions Office

"Florida Southern is a national leader in engaged learning, offering dynamic opportunities that include guaranteed internships, student-faculty collaborative research and performance, service learning, and study abroad. The Junior Journey is an innovative travel program that guarantees all students the opportunity to study overseas or domestically—often at no additional cost.

"FSC offers more than seventy majors in fields such as art, biology, business, chemistry, communication, computer science, education, marine biology, music and theater performance, nursing, and psychology.

"Outstanding pre-professional programs are offered in dentistry, engineering, law, medicine, occupational therapy, optometry, pharmacy, physical therapy, physician assistant, theology, and veterinary medicine.

"The college is known for its friendly, vibrant, and energetic campus. Our involved student population enjoys rich and varied student life programming that includes 20 championship NCAA Division II athletic programs, intramurals, more than 100 clubs and organizations, and 14 national fraternities and sororities. The college's popular lakefront allows for weekend activities like kayaking, canoeing, and paddle-boating.

"The college has a state-of-the-art technology center, as well as contemporary residence halls with scenic views of Lake Hollingsworth. FSC is home to the world's largest single-site collection of Frank Lloyd Wright structures, which provides a stunning setting for living and learning.

"Within a year of graduation, 97 percent of students report having achieved their post-baccalaureate degree goals by securing employment or beginning an advanced degree program."

SELECTIVITY

Admissions Rating	83
# of applicants	5,914
% of applicants accepted	71
% of acceptees attending	16
# of early decision applicants	92
% accepted early decision	76

FRESHMAN PROFILE

Range SAT EBRW	570–645
Range SAT Math	550–620
Range SAT Composite	1120–1260
Range ACT Composite	24–29
# submitting SAT scores	439
% submitting SAT scores	64
# submitting ACT scores	242
% submitting ACT scores	35
Average HS GPA	3.7
% graduated top 10% of class	25
% graduated top 25% of class	58
% graduated top 50% of class	87

DEADLINES

Early decision	
Deadline	11/1
Notification	12/1
Regular	
Priority	3/1
Deadline	5/1
Notification	Rolling, 8/1
Nonfall registration?	Yes

APPLICANTS ALSO LOOK AT AND SOMETIMES PREFER
University of Florida; Florida State University

AND RARELY PREFER
Rollins College; University of Tampa; Stetson University

FINANCIAL FACTS

Financial Aid Rating	88
Annual tuition	$36,860
Room and board	$11,880
Required fees	$780
Books and supplies	$1,250
Average frosh need-based scholarship	$27,949
Average UG need-based scholarship	$25,663
% needy frosh rec. need-based scholarship or grant aid	100
% needy UG rec. need-based scholarship or grant aid	99
% needy frosh rec. non-need-based scholarship or grant aid	68
% needy UG rec. non-need-based scholarship or grant aid	72
% needy frosh rec. need-based self-help aid	1
% needy UG rec. need-based self-help aid	6
% frosh rec. any financial aid	100
% UG rec. any financial aid	92.31
% UG borrow to pay for school	89
Average cumulative indebtedness	$25,576
% frosh need fully met	31
% ugrads need fully met	29
Average % of frosh need met	79
Average % of ugrad need met	77

FLORIDA STATE UNIVERSITY

PO Box 3062400, Tallahassee, FL 32306-2400 • Admissions: 850-644-6200 • Fax: 850-644-0197

CAMPUS LIFE

Quality of Life Rating	91
Fire Safety Rating	90
Green Rating	96
Type of school	Public
Environment	City

STUDENTS

Total undergrad enrollment	32,881
% male/female	43/57
% from out of state	11
% frosh from public high school	79
% frosh live on campus	76
% ugrads live on campus	20
# of fraternities (% ugrad men join)	23 (13)
# of sororities (% ugrad women join)	24 (23)
% African American	9
% Asian	3
% Caucasian	60
% Hispanic	22
% Native American	<1
% Pacific Islander	<1
% Two or more races	4
% Race and/or ethnicity unknown	1
% international	2
# of countries represented	107

SURVEY SAYS . . .

Students are happy
Great library
Career services are great
Internships are widely available
Recreation facilities are great
Everyone loves the Seminoles
Intramural sports are popular
Frats and sororities are popular
Theater is popular
Alumni active on campus
Active student government
Active minority support groups
Active student-run political groups

ACADEMICS

Academic Rating	82
% students returning for sophomore year	93
% students graduating within 4 years	68
% students graduating within 6 years	83
Calendar	Semester
Student/faculty ratio	21:1
Profs interesting rating	88
Profs accessible rating	92

Most classes have 10–19 students.
Most lab/discussion sessions have
20–29 students.

MOST POPULAR MAJORS

Psychology, General; Criminal Justice/Safety
Studies; Finance, General

STUDENTS SAY "..."

Academics

"Research, service, scholarship, and extracurricular opportunities" are abundant at the "large campus" of Florida State University in Tallahassee. It's rather easy to understand why students are drawn to Florida State. After all, the "campus is gorgeous," "the weather is always nice" and there are an abundance "of resources at your fingertips." What's more, "despite its large size...the community is welcoming and [undergrads] don't feel like an anonymous face in the student body." Incredibly, it's still "easy to feel at home." Much of that can be credited to faculty who "are very willing to help undergraduate students with classes, research, career prospects, and everything in between." Florida State professors also excel at bringing their "courses to life and mak[ing] them interesting enough that [students truly] want to learn." Many are also "experts in their field." And "they make it known that they want students to succeed." To that end, "in addition to making themselves available...for office hours, they [continually] offer to make time for students [beyond those hours]." Perhaps this grateful undergrad says it best, "Their advice has pushed me to be a better student and pushed me to find a great future."

Life

Life at Florida State offers a great "mix of academics, socializing, [and] extracurricular [activities]." To begin with, athletics are fairly popular and you can frequently spot "basketball games and volleyball games" popping up around campus. And during the fall, weekends "are spent [at] football games and tailgates." Aside from sports, we've been informed that the "Student Life Cinema always has cool events going on" and "there are always free concerts at Club Down Under on campus" as well. FSU also has "many organizations that are focused on philanthropy." For example, "Dance Marathon is the largest student run organization on campus and we have one of the largest Dance Marathons in the entire country. We also have a large Relay for Life organization." Moreover, a number of undergrads enjoy FSU's reservation, an "off campus [spot] where students can go swimming, paddle boarding, relaxing, or even [try out a] ropes course." Of course, it's also important to mention that some students feel as though "Greek life dominates" the social scene, even though "less than 50% of the student population [participates]." Finally, undergrads greatly appreciate hometown Tallahassee. The city offers "endless" nightlife along with "many great clubs and places for social events as well as pretty landscapes and historical sites."

Student Body

Florida State manages to attract a student body that's a "unique mixture of south Floridians, crunchy granolas, Northern snowbirds, sorority girls, and good ole boys, with a nice international population mixed in there." Despite these diverse personalities, the university still seems to cultivate a "strong sense of community." Of course, it definitely helps that students are "very friendly and always willing to [strike] up conversation." Even better, "everyone you see seems genuinely happy" and everyone "is pushing for you." People here want to see their peers "succeed." As one impressed student shares, "Everyone is so kind. No one is afraid to ask for help, and if they do most would be more than willing to help you out." Undergrads also applaud FSU for doing "a great job in creating or allowing students to create spaces for all communities, particularly those that are historically marginalized/typically first gen students." And no matter what else, students here come together in their shared "love for FSU." As this satisfied student sums up, "I have never been on a campus with such school spirit, excitement, and motivation to improve."

FLORIDA STATE UNIVERSITY

Financial Aid: 850-644-5716 • E-Mail: admissions@fsu.edu • Website: www.fsu.edu

THE PRINCETON REVIEW SAYS

Admissions

Very important factors considered include: rigor of secondary school record. *Important factors considered include:* academic GPA, standardized test scores, talent/ability, state residency. *Other factors considered include:* class rank, application essay, extracurricular activities, character/personal qualities, first generation, geographical residence, volunteer work, work experience. ACT with or without writing accepted. SAT with or without Essay component accepted. High school diploma is required and GED is accepted. *Academic units required:* 4 English, 4 math, 3 science, 2 science labs, 2 foreign language, 1 social studies, 2 history, 3 academic electives. *Academic units recommended:* 4 English, 4 math, 4 science, 2 science labs, 4 foreign language, 2 social studies, 2 history, 3 academic electives.

Financial Aid

Students should submit: FAFSA; State aid form. The Princeton Review suggests that all financial aid forms be submitted as soon as possible after October 1. *Need-based scholarships/grants offered:* College/university scholarship or grant aid from institutional funds; Federal Pell; Private scholarships; SEOG; State scholarships/grants; United Negro College Fund. *Loan aid offered:* Direct PLUS loans; Direct Subsidized Stafford Loans; Direct Unsubsidized Stafford Loans. Applicants will be notified of awards on a rolling basis beginning 4/5. Federal Work-Study Program available. Institutional employment available.

The Inside Word

Aspiring FSU students should be forewarned that admission here is selective. Fortunately, the university does take a holistic approach to the process. And candidates should expect that all facets of their application will be thoroughly reviewed. Of course, admissions officers favor students who have taken a rigorous course-load throughout high school. A solid GPA is also a must. Finally, though the essay section of the application is not required, submission is highly recommended. Students who don't write one may be putting themselves at a disadvantage.

THE SCHOOL SAYS "..."

From the Admissions Office

"Florida State University is one of the top public universities in the world and is proud to be recognized as a Preeminent University by the State of Florida. Designated as a Carnegie Research University (with very high research activity), Florida State offers more than 320 undergraduate, graduate, and professional degree programs, including medicine and law. Our diverse and highly talented student body includes students from all fifty states and more than 130 countries. The university is committed to student success for all students as evidenced by impressive retention and graduation rates that place us it at the highest levels nationally. World class faculty, including Nobel laureates, Pulitzer Prize winners, Guggenheim Fellows, members of the National Academy of Sciences and American Academy of Arts and Sciences, and other globally recognized teachers and researchers, are actively creating the knowledge you will be studying in class. You will be encouraged to become engaged in research, internships, entrepreneurial initiatives and other creative activities. You will be supported by comprehensive and innovative student services. And you will be enriched by the extensive variety of cultural, athletic, and recreational offerings available outside the classroom. Our singular goal is make you better than when you arrived, so that you can make a difference in your community and the world."

SELECTIVITY
Admissions Rating	93
# of applicants	58,936
% of applicants accepted	36
% of acceptees attending	34

FRESHMAN PROFILE
Range SAT EBRW	610–670
Range SAT Math	590–670
Range SAT Composite	1220–1330
Range ACT Composite	26–30
# submitting SAT scores	4,967
% submitting SAT scores	70
# submitting ACT scores	2,139
% submitting ACT scores	30
Average HS GPA	4.1
% graduated top 10% of class	47
% graduated top 25% of class	73
% graduated top 50% of class	95

DEADLINES
Regular	
Priority	11/1
Deadline	3/1
Notification	Rolling, 1/27
Nonfall registration?	Yes

FINANCIAL FACTS
Financial Aid Rating	92
Annual in-state tuition	$4,640
Annual out-of-state tuition	$19,806
Room and board	$10,666
Required fees	$1,877
Books and supplies	$1,000
Average frosh need-based scholarship	$13,401
Average UG need-based scholarship	$13,033
% needy frosh rec. need-based scholarship or grant aid	93
% needy UG rec. need-based scholarship or grant aid	87
% needy frosh rec. non-need-based scholarship or grant aid	85
% needy UG rec. non-need-based scholarship or grant aid	63
% needy frosh rec. need-based self-help aid	35
% needy UG rec. need-based self-help aid	50
% frosh rec. any financial aid	97
% UG rec. any financial aid	89
% UG borrow to pay for school	42
Average cumulative indebtedness	$25,013
% frosh need fully met	69
% ugrads need fully met	65
Average % of frosh need met	95
Average % of ugrad need met	93

FORDHAM UNIVERSITY

441 East Fordham Road, Bronx, NY 10458 • Admissions: 718-817-4000 • Fax: 718-817-0549

STUDENTS SAY "..."

Academics

Sure, Fordham is a midsize university located in one of the world's most dazzling cities. Nevertheless, the school still manages to "really [care] about individual students" and foster a "big sense of community." As one thankful undergrad shares, "There are many people willing to help … and I never feel like I am alone." And while the "curriculum is challenging," students report that "overall … the workload [is] manageable." And with a core that includes philosophy, theology, and history classes, "every student is intellectually well-rounded by graduation regardless of major." Nonetheless, many undergrads love to highlight Fordham's "exceptional business program" and remark that the university's "arts programs are an asset" as well. The effusive praise doesn't end there! Indeed, these undergrads speak glowingly of their "lively and engaging" professors who continually "[push students] to do [their] best work." Another hallmark of Fordham faculty? Accessibility. As one student shares, "Office hours are held regularly, but all my professors were available to meet at other times as well, even holding Skype calls, to make sure that I understood the topics." Given all these factors, it's quite easy to understand why students declare Fordham to be a "great academic experience."

Life

It's virtually impossible to be bored at Fordham. After all, there are numerous "clubs, guest speakers, panels … and networking events" along with activities like "bingo nights [and] movie screenings." Students here are also a fairly active lot, so "intramurals are really popular" as well. One undergrad also boldly proclaims that Fordham has "the best college [radio] station in the world." Of course, once Friday hits, "many people go to local bars … and attend off-campus house parties." However, rest assured that while "party culture is present … it is by no means oppressive." As described by another student, "You could also comfortably go all four years at Fordham without partying and you wouldn't feel shunned."

One aspect of Fordham life that virtually all students embrace? The opportunity to explore New York City. The university itself "sponsors a lot of [city] activities," including "ice skating in Bryant Park, [going to] Broadway shows, [and taking] food outings." Moreover, "Central park is two blocks away" from the Lincoln Center campus and "museums like the Natural History Museum [and] the Met … are almost free with a student ID." Not to be outdone, the Rose Hill campus offers opportunities to "hang out … at the green areas or go to the Botanical Gardens and the Bronx Zoo."

Student Body

Undergrads at Fordham emphasize that the student body is "highly diverse." Of course, perhaps this should be expected given that the university attracts "students from all around the world." "In addition to being diverse in background, students at Fordham are diverse in their ideas and perspectives," says a student. As another impressed undergrad adds, "My peers are all unique with different passions and experiences that would be hard to find anywhere else." Nonetheless, another student explains, "There is a relaxed attitude that almost everyone shares, so sometimes you can forget that the people around you are involved in multiple clubs, internships, have a YouTube channel, and go running every morning." Indeed, almost everyone here is "extremely hard-working … and [has] a drive to perform very well academically." Even better, Fordham undergrads steadfastly assert that their peers are "very friendly and always willing to help." Finally, as one thrilled Ram concludes, "From empathetic to just outright hilarious and relatable, my peers here at Fordham have made my first semester as a college student nothing short of memorable."

Financial Aid: 718-817-3800 • E-Mail: enroll@fordham.edu • Website: www.fordham.edu

THE PRINCETON REVIEW SAYS

Admissions

Very important factors considered include: rigor of secondary school record, academic GPA, trend in grades, character/personal qualities. *Important factors considered include:* application essay, recommendation(s), extracurricular activities, leadership and engagement, talent/ability, internships/work and community service. *Other factors considered include:* standardized test scores (if submitted), class rank, first generation, alumni/ae relation, geographical residence, racial/ethnic status, work experience, level of applicant's interest and/or knowledge of the university. ACT with or without writing accepted. SAT with or without Essay component accepted. High school diploma is required and GED is accepted. *Academic units required:* 4 English, 3 math, 3 science, 2 foreign language, 3 social studies. *Academic units recommended:* 4 English, 4 math, 4 science, 4 foreign language, 4 social studies.

Financial Aid

Students should submit: Business/Farm Supplement; CSS/Financial Aid PROFILE; FAFSA; Noncustodial PROFILE; State aid form. Priority filing deadline is 11/15. The Princeton Review suggests that all financial aid forms be submitted as soon as possible after October 1. *Need-based scholarships/grants offered:* College/university scholarship or grant aid from institutional funds; Federal Pell; Private scholarships; SEOG; State scholarships/grants. *Loan aid offered:* Direct PLUS loans; Direct Subsidized Stafford Loans; Direct Unsubsidized Stafford Loans. Applicants will be notified of awards on or about 4/1. Federal Work-Study Program available. Institutional employment available.

The Inside Word

Admissions officers at Fordham are on the hunt for candidates who would be a good match for the school. And in order to find them, they closely consider all facets of student applications. Demonstrated interest such as online engagement or regional programming goes a long way, and a student's inability to visit would never be a barrier to admission. The application review is holistic, which means that the university seeks evidence of leadership, integrity, and academic excellence. The strongest applicants will have taken a challenging course load in high school. You'll definitely want a transcript laden with honors and AP classes, if possible. Fordham only requires one letter of recommendation, but be sure it comes from an individual who can really speak to who you are as a person and as a student. Beginning with the entering class of Fall 2021, Fordham will be piloting a test-optional policy for two years, during which time the ACT and SAT, both with or without writing/essay components, will be accepted, but not required.

THE SCHOOL SAYS "..."

From the Admissions Office

"Fordham University offers a distinctive, values-centered educational experience that is rooted in the Jesuit tradition of intellectual rigor and personal attention. Located in New York City, Fordham offers to students the unparalleled educational, cultural and recreational advantages of one of the world's greatest cities. Fordham has two residential campuses in New York—the tree-lined, eighty-five-acre Rose Hill campus in the Bronx, and the cosmopolitan Lincoln Center campus in the heart of Manhattan's performing arts center. The university's state-of-the-art facilities and buildings include one of the most technologically advanced libraries in the country. Fordham offers a variety of majors, concentrations and programs that can be combined with an extensive career planning and placement program. More than 3,500 organizations in the New York metropolitan area offer students internships that provide hands-on experience and valuable networking opportunities in fields such as business, communications, medicine, law and education."

SELECTIVITY

Admissions Rating	91
# of applicants	47,930
% of applicants accepted	46
% of acceptees attending	10
# offered a place on the wait list	8,603
% accepting a place on wait list	26
% admitted from wait list	48
# of early decision applicants	357
% accepted early decision	59

FRESHMAN PROFILE

Range SAT EBRW	620–710
Range SAT Math	620–740
Range ACT Composite	28–32
# submitting SAT scores	1,689
% submitting SAT scores	74
# submitting ACT scores	727
% submitting ACT scores	32
Average HS GPA	3.6
% graduated top 10% of class	46
% graduated top 25% of class	80
% graduated top 50% of class	97

DEADLINES

Early decision	
Deadline	11/1
Notification	12/20
Early action	
Deadline	11/1
Notification	12/20
Regular	
Priority	11/1
Deadline	1/1
Nonfall registration?	Yes

APPLICANTS ALSO LOOK AT AND OFTEN PREFER

New York University; Boston University; Boston College; Villanova University; The George Washington University

AND SOMETIMES PREFER

Northeastern University; Rutgers University–New Brunswick; University of Connecticut; Penn State University Park; State University of New York—Stony Brook University; State University of New York at Binghamton (Binghamton University)

FINANCIAL FACTS

Financial Aid Rating	87
Annual tuition	$52,980
Room and board	$18,510
Required fees	$1,413
Books and supplies	$1,039
Average frosh need-based scholarship	$32,045
Average UG need-based scholarship	$29,814
% needy frosh rec. need-based scholarship or grant aid	95
% needy UG rec. need-based scholarship or grant aid	96
% needy frosh rec. non-need-based scholarship or grant aid	62
% needy UG rec. non-need-based scholarship or grant aid	22
% needy frosh rec. need-based self-help aid	69
% needy UG rec. need-based self-help aid	71
% frosh rec. any financial aid	91
% UG rec. any financial aid	85.5
% UG borrow to pay for school	62
Average cumulative indebtedness	$37,429
% frosh need fully met	28
% ugrads need fully met	27
Average % of frosh need met	80
Average % of ugrad need met	77

FRANKLIN & MARSHALL COLLEGE

P.O. Box 3003, Lancaster, PA 17604-3003 • Admissions: 717-358-3953 • Fax: 717-358-4389

CAMPUS LIFE

Quality of Life Rating	87
Fire Safety Rating	97
Green Rating	95
Type of school	Private
Environment	Town

STUDENTS

Total undergrad enrollment	2,315
% male/female	45/55
% from out of state	70
% frosh from public high school	60
% frosh live on campus	100
% ugrads live on campus	99
# of fraternities (% ugrad men join)	7 (13)
# of sororities (% ugrad women join)	4 (19)
% African American	6
% Asian	5
% Caucasian	55
% Hispanic	11
% Native American	<1
% Pacific Islander	0
% Two or more races	3
% Race and/or ethnicity unknown	3
% international	19
# of countries represented	44

SURVEY SAYS . . .

Students always studying
Lab facilities are great
Great financial aid
Easy to get around campus
Frats and sororities are popular
College radio is popular

ACADEMICS

Academic Rating	92
% students returning for sophomore year	90
% students graduating within 4 years	78
% students graduating within 6 years	85
Calendar	Semester
Student/faculty ratio	9:1
Profs interesting rating	92
Profs accessible rating	97

Most classes have 10–19 students.
Most lab/discussion sessions have
    10–19 students.

MOST POPULAR MAJORS

Psychology, General; Political Science and
Government, General; Business Administration,
Management and Operations

STUDENTS SAY "..."

Academics

Established in 1787, Franklin & Marshall College is a little liberal arts gem located in south central Pennsylvania. With around 2,300 students, F&M offers numerous opportunities for academic exploration and expansion, and there is "a great balance between a strong and competitive academic culture, talented and successful athletic teams, and a vibrant social life." The school offers numerous interdisciplinary majors and minors, "does an excellent job of making sure you know how to write," and a collaborative learning experience that extends beyond the classroom through research opportunities, the College Houses (residential communities), and multiple affiliated study abroad programs.

The rigorous academics are "demanding and challenging" gauntlets thrown down by professors that are "esteemed published scholars in their respective fields." "You'll work hard but you'll learn a lot," says a student. Small classes offer plenty of face and advice time with these scholars: "Whether it be for class selection or post graduate paths, they are always there to help." "The support for a student here is absolutely astonishing," says another. The classroom setting at F&M is completely different from the traditional lecture halls of bigger schools, and students "often have round tables for close discussion with...professors." Students love the fact that academic and personal growth are equally important, and the environment is shaped by "people who are active both in school and extracurriculars, and who get excited about both." "Someone said to me the other week that you're not taking advantage of what F&M has to offer if you haven't been to a professor's office and discussed something other than class," says a student. The professors at F&M all have "a certain level of uniqueness" in them, but students appreciate that they all possess a great level of understanding. "My professors have managed to get me engaged in areas that have always seemed like a bore to me."

Life

Athletic teams are "highly competitive and are very active in the local community," and there is a "large emphasis" on fraternity and sorority life and sports teams at F&M. There is always something to do on weekends, between "[staying] in or [going] to the cinemas to watch movies with your roommates, [hanging] out in frat parties or [attending] events run by an organization for alternative options for frat parties." Club organizations are wildly popular, and "campus is not big, so getting around takes about ten minutes no matter where you are." "We all really get into our extracurricular activities," says a student.

Off-campus, downtown Lancaster, dubbed by Forbes in 2018 as a "newly hip Victorian city" and among its top 10 "coolest places to visit," offers plenty of entertainment and dining options (such as the Central Market), and a mall is just fifteen minutes away.

Student Body

These "smart overachievers who work hard" are also "some of the nicest people you'll ever meet." Though a modest majority are white, there is an "amazing diversity" on campus, with a bent towards "slightly preppy, but very open-minded." Many F&M students are on a varsity sports team as well as a member of a sorority or fraternity, and a typical student "is probably involved in three to five clubs and is trying out for theater, an a capella group, or another organization." Students categorically study hard, and "fill our free time with fun and meaningful clubs and community service."

FRANKLIN & MARSHALL COLLEGE

Financial Aid: 717-358-3991 • E-Mail: admission@fandm.edu • Website: www.fandm.edu

THE PRINCETON REVIEW SAYS

Admissions

Very important factors considered include: rigor of secondary school record, class rank, academic GPA, character/personal qualities. *Important factors considered include:* application essay, standardized test scores, recommendation(s), interview, extracurricular activities, talent/ability, volunteer work. *Other factors considered include:* alumni/ae relation, geographical residence, racial/ethnic status, work experience, level of applicant's interest. ACT with or without writing accepted. SAT with or without Essay component accepted. High school diploma is required and GED is accepted. *Academic units required:* 4 English, 3 math, 2 science, 2 science labs, 2 foreign language, 1 social studies, 2 history, 1 visual/performing arts. *Academic units recommended:* 4 math, 3 science, 3 science labs, 4 foreign language, 3 social studies, 3 history.

Financial Aid

Students should submit: CSS/Financial Aid PROFILE; FAFSA; Noncustodial PROFILE. Priority filing deadline is 2/1. The Princeton Review suggests that all financial aid forms be submitted as soon as possible after October 1. *Need-based scholarships/grants offered:* College/university scholarship or grant aid from institutional funds; Federal Pell; Private scholarships; SEOG; State scholarships/grants. *Loan aid offered:* Direct PLUS loans; Direct Subsidized Stafford Loans; Direct Unsubsidized Stafford Loans. Applicants will be notified of awards on or about 4/1. Federal Work-Study Program available.

The Inside Word

While admission at F&M is competitive, the admissions committee does show some flexibility. The college allows students who feel that standardized test scores don't reflect their true academic capacity to submit two graded writing samples to replace the test scores. Applicants are also encouraged to include nontraditional materials, such as art portfolios or recordings of musical performances, in their applications.

THE SCHOOL SAYS "..."

From the Admissions Office

"The hallmarks of a Franklin & Marshall education are individual attention and a supportive community. Our faculty members challenge you to achieve your best and engage you personally on a level you will not find at other institutions. We have one professor for every nine students, and two-thirds of our students collaborate on a research project or other directed study directly with a faculty member. Here are four more things you should know about F&M: 1) Our professors do not confine learning to classrooms and labs. They take you into the field and the local community to teach you how to *do* what students at other institutions may only read about. 2) We have College Houses, not dorms. Our five College Houses, which bring together first-year students into smaller groups, are student-governed spaces where you socialize, learn, and stretch your intellect. Based in each house are a faculty mentor and an administrative counselor to guide you. 3) No one gets lost. The depth and breadth of student activities and experiences provide everyone with a place to belong. Our students find a strong sense of self, and they find their 'homes' in clubs, athletic teams, their College Houses, fraternities and sororities, the performing and musical arts, and the other strong communities they have the freedom to create for themselves. 4) Our Office of Student and Post-Graduate Development is committed to your success. Ninety-seven percent of 2018 graduates were employed or pursuing further education six months after graduating."

SELECTIVITY

Admissions Rating	94
# of applicants	9,502
% of applicants accepted	30
% of acceptees attending	22
# offered a place on the wait list	2,196
% accepting a place on wait list	0
# of early decision applicants	555
% accepted early decision	68

FRESHMAN PROFILE

Range SAT EBRW	610–700
Range SAT Math	640–760
Range ACT Composite	28–32
# submitting SAT scores	386
% submitting SAT scores	62
# submitting ACT scores	149
% submitting ACT scores	23
% graduated top 10% of class	71
% graduated top 25% of class	88
% graduated top 50% of class	99

DEADLINES

Early decision	
Deadline	11/15
Notification	12/15
Other ED Deadline	1/15
Other ED Notification	2/15
Regular	
Deadline	1/15
Notification	4/1
Nonfall registration?	Yes

FINANCIAL FACTS

Financial Aid Rating	97
Annual tuition	$58,615
Room and board	$14,450
Required fees	$385
Books and supplies	$1,200
Average frosh need-based scholarship	$55,102
Average UG need-based scholarship	$54,166
% needy frosh rec. need-based scholarship or grant aid	100
% needy UG rec. need-based scholarship or grant aid	100
% needy frosh rec. non-need-based scholarship or grant aid	23
% needy UG rec. non-need-based scholarship or grant aid	22
% needy frosh rec. need-based self-help aid	91
% needy UG rec. need-based self-help aid	91
% frosh rec. any financial aid	54
% UG rec. any financial aid	55
% UG borrow to pay for school	54
Average cumulative indebtedness	$27,928
% frosh need fully met	100
% ugrads need fully met	100
Average % of frosh need met	100
Average % of ugrad need met	100

FRANKLIN W. OLIN COLLEGE OF ENGINEERING

1000 Olin Way, Needham, MA 02492-1200 • Admissions: 781-292-2222 • Fax: 781-292-2210

STUDENTS SAY "..."

Academics

Franklin W. Olin College of Engineering in Massachusetts just graduated its fifteenth class in 2020, but it's already taking the engineering world by storm with its rigorous hands-on program on the "bleeding edge of engineering education." Olin stresses creating one's own academic path to its 350 undergraduates: The curriculum weaves independent studies and co-curriculars seamlessly throughout four years of "learning skills through project-based learning in order to use engineering and design for the good of the world." At the end of their time at Olin, students emerge as engineers with "fantastic and practical technical skill-sets" that they are able to wield in a variety of settings. Classes are "hard, but interesting and worthwhile," and students are also able to take courses at nearby Babson, Wellesley, and Brandeis. Classes traditionally involve breaking into small groups, and "most problems dividing work in teams have to do with students getting too excited about the work and doing more than their fair share rather than shirking group duties," says one student. Self-directed study is important here, and Olin encourages students to design their own semester-long project on a topic that interests them through the college's Passionate Pursuits program.

Professors are "extremely dedicated" to the work they are doing at Olin. "I have had professors come to campus at 10 pm because they heard that students were struggling with homework assignments, and stay until well after midnight," says one. Uniqueness is everywhere: There is a tremendous amount of flexibility in the classroom, with almost no lectures; TAs are referred to as NINJAs (Need Information Now Just Ask); and most semesters offer at least one new experimental course ("and the classes that aren't new are better than they were last semester"). Faculty are "interested in how their teaching works," and there is "constant improvement in the curriculum and learning styles." At the end of the day, "Olin doesn't create engineers—it prepares them."

Life

There are "lots of things happening for such a small school." For starters, people "work...a lot." Students work all day every day and "all the rest of the time seems to get filled by working on random interests." This quirky and innovative group makes time to go on a quick adventure and "explore the local forest, make a code that does something stupid, or eat chips and watch YouTube videos" in the "hotel-room-sized dorms."

For first-years and sophomores, lounge culture is really big in the dorms, and "if you ever want something to do, just explore the lounges and you will find something." It's easy for students to get to Boston, and "there are always students up for spontaneous fun things" like sudden dodgeball in the dining hall or a random dance party. There's even a mailing list called Carpe Diem in which "people randomly send out info on fun things they are doing all the time so others can join." A lot of the things students do in their spare time are the same things they do for school, because "what we're doing in class is genuinely fun."

Student Body

Olin College hosts an "incredibly intelligent and very motivated" body of individuals that are "not your typical engineer." Because of the nature of the student body, you can join any group of people at any time and know that they will be having an interesting discussion. "If one wants to have a conversation on middle eighteenth-century philosophy or if the earth suddenly stopped would we go flying off into space, both are easily found in the dining hall," says a student. With 80 or so new students flipping each year, some qualities of the student body are "easily changeable" (athleticism, for instance), but this remains a fun group in which "everybody has something that gets them so excited they could stay up all night working on it."

FRANKLIN W. OLIN COLLEGE OF ENGINEERING

Financial Aid: 781-292-2215 • E-Mail: info@olin.edu • Website: www.olin.edu

THE PRINCETON REVIEW SAYS

Admissions

Very important factors considered include: rigor of secondary school record, academic GPA, application essay, recommendation(s), interview, extracurricular activities, talent/ability, character/personal qualities, level of applicant's interest. *Important factors considered include:* class rank, standardized test scores. *Other factors considered include:* first generation, alumni/ae relation, geographical residence, state residency. ACT with or without writing accepted. SAT with or without Essay component accepted. High school diploma is required and GED is accepted. *Academic units recommended:* 4 English, 4 math, 4 science, 3 science labs, 2 foreign language, 2 social studies, 2 history.

Financial Aid

Students should submit: FAFSA. Priority filing deadline is 2/15. The Princeton Review suggests that all financial aid forms be submitted as soon as possible after October 1. *Need-based scholarships/grants offered:* College/university scholarship or grant aid from institutional funds; Federal Pell; SEOG. *Loan aid offered:* Direct PLUS loans; Direct Subsidized Stafford Loans; Direct Unsubsidized Stafford Loans. Applicants will be notified of awards on or about 4/1. Institutional employment available.

The Inside Word

Brains alone are not enough to get into Olin. Social skills, depth, and the ability to communicate are taken seriously by admissions. Olin boasts many students who have turned down offers from schools like MIT and Caltech for just this reason. It is a unique school that looks for passion, creativity, and a spirit of adventure in its students. If you're a reclusive genius, you will be at a disadvantage in this pool of applicants.

THE SCHOOL SAYS "..."

From the Admissions Office

"We are a vibrant community of talented, empathetic, energetic students and faculty and we are looking for students who are not only academically accomplished but also like adventure, thrive on creativity and have an entrepreneurial streak—and come from every kind of cultural, economic and geographic background imaginable. The Olin Tuition Scholarship, valued at more than $100,000, is awarded to every enrolled student to recognize their achievements and is complemented by our policy of meeting full demonstrated need—meaning finances should never stand in the way of an Olin education.

"Our admission process is, like Olin, unique. It's done in two stages; first students apply using the Common Application or the Coalition Application; then from our exceptionally talented and academically gifted applicant pool we invite about 225 students to attend one of three Candidates' Weekends. We seek to get to know our applicants' personal qualities (like risk-taking, creativity, passion and team spirit) during these weekends of getting acquainted through group activities and interviews. Admission is then offered to candidates who possess the greatest promise of contributing to—and benefiting from—the Olin experience. Following the Candidates' Weekends admission is offered to approximately 125 students.

"Olin is not your typical engineering school. We are a creative, collaborative community of team players who want to work hard to solve problems and have some serious fun along the way!"

SELECTIVITY

Admissions Rating	98
# of applicants	905
% of applicants accepted	16
% of acceptees attending	60
# offered a place on the wait list	39
% accepting a place on wait list	77
% admitted from wait list	0

FRESHMAN PROFILE

Range SAT EBRW	700–760
Range SAT Math	760–800
Range SAT Composite	1450–1540
Range ACT Composite	34–35
# submitting SAT scores	57
% submitting SAT scores	67
# submitting ACT scores	38
% submitting ACT scores	45
Average HS GPA	3.9

DEADLINES

Regular	
Deadline	1/1
Notification	4/1
Nonfall registration?	No

FINANCIAL FACTS

Financial Aid Rating	97
Annual tuition	$52,164
Room and board	$16,872
Required fees	$3,336
Books and supplies	$200
Average frosh need-based scholarship	$52,376
Average UG need-based scholarship	$48,901
% needy frosh rec. need-based scholarship or grant aid	100
% needy UG rec. need-based scholarship or grant aid	100
% needy frosh rec. non-need-based scholarship or grant aid	100
% needy UG rec. non-need-based scholarship or grant aid	99
% needy frosh rec. need-based self-help aid	63
% needy UG rec. need-based self-help aid	63
% frosh rec. any financial aid	100
% UG rec. any financial aid	100
% UG borrow to pay for school	28
Average cumulative indebtedness	$13,480
% frosh need fully met	100
% ugrads need fully met	99
Average % of frosh need met	99
Average % of ugrad need met	99

FURMAN UNIVERSITY

3300 Poinsett Highway, Greenville, SC 29613 • Admissions: 864-294-2034 • Fax: 864-294-2018

STUDENTS SAY "..."

Academics

Students can't stop talking about Furman University's "beautiful campus" and "warm, but challenging, academic community." This combination of brains and beauty is what makes Furman "an ideal choice" for four years. "Furman is about academic excellence through engaged learning," says one undergrad. Expect to hear "engaged" used "ad nauseum" on campus, but students claim that such a term "truly describes the kind of personal education available" thanks to "small class sizes," professors "who love to teach and enjoy getting to know their students," and "numerous" academic and extracurricular opportunities. Furman's science programs are "especially" challenging. Professors here are "very qualified (sometimes overqualified), passionate about what they teach, and are not easy graders." That said, they're "very willing to help their students." Students praise the administration, which is "really accessible." In the words of one undergrad, "They work with students to solve problems and genuinely care about making Furman a better school and not just a higher-ranking institution." However, some students find that the administration can be "very conservative in their thinking about student on-campus social life." Ultimately, while "Furman is not for the academically faint-of-heart," there's pride in knowing that "you're receiving a great education that will help you after you graduate."

Life

With so many students reporting that Furman's campus is "absolutely gorgeous," it's a wonder they ever leave it. However, "the surrounding city of Greenville is great," and its "thriving, small-town feel" brings in plenty of students on the weekends. Life at school is "busy, but so much fun." Students here spend "a lot of time thinking about academics, classes, and their future," but they also "invest a lot of time in their relationships with their friends." The school's "inclusive, close-knit community" is complemented with "lots of interesting things to do on campus, from music concerts to improv shows to sports games." "Weeknights are mostly spent studying," says one undergrad, which makes the library "a popular social spot." However, once the weekend rolls around, students spend their nights "out on the town." "There are tons of bars, restaurants, and clubs for people to go to" in Greenville. While the university "is not as crazy party-wise as larger schools," students "can find a party if they want to." Mostly though, students are happy to "meet up with friends for meals, coffee, or just to hang out."

Student Body

Many find that Furman is something of a "country club" when it comes to its student body, not just "because it is private and somewhat expensive," but also because the "typical" student is "wealthy, white, conservative, and preppy." Some find that "the majority of the student body is obsessed with being as 'generic' and 'normal' as possible, so that any student who does not fit the norm, be it due to a difference in religion or clothing style, will find it harder to fit in." However, others have found that there's more to the student body than first meets the eye. As one undergrad says, "The longer I stay at Furman, the more I realize that many students don't fit the stereotype." One thing that everyone seems to agree on is that everyone is "very accepting" and "very committed to their academic pursuits." That said, some wouldn't mind seeing the school "improve by attracting a more diverse student body, as well as lowering the cost of tuition."

FURMAN UNIVERSITY

Financial Aid: 864-294-2030 • E-Mail: admissions@furman.edu • Website: www.furman.edu

THE PRINCETON REVIEW SAYS

Admissions

Very important factors considered include: rigor of secondary school record. *Important factors considered include:* class rank, academic GPA, application essay, extracurricular activities, character/personal qualities. *Other factors considered include:* standardized test scores, recommendation(s), interview, talent/ability, first generation, alumni/ae relation, racial/ethnic status, volunteer work, work experience, level of applicant's interest. ACT with or without writing accepted. SAT with or without Essay component accepted. High school diploma is required and GED is accepted. *Academic units required:* 4 English, 3 math, 2 science, 2 science labs, 2 foreign language, 3 social studies. *Academic units recommended:* 4 English, 4 math, 3 science, 2 science labs, 3 foreign language, 4 social studies.

Financial Aid

Students should submit: Business/Farm Supplement; CSS/Financial Aid PROFILE; FAFSA; Noncustodial PROFILE. Priority filing deadline is 3/1. The Princeton Review suggests that all financial aid forms be submitted as soon as possible after October 1. *Need-based scholarships/grants offered:* College/university scholarship or grant aid from institutional funds; Federal Pell; Private scholarships; SEOG; State scholarships/grants. *Loan aid offered:* Direct PLUS loans; Direct Subsidized Stafford Loans; Direct Unsubsidized Stafford Loans. Applicants will be notified of awards on or about 4/1. Federal Work-Study Program available. Institutional employment available.

The Inside Word

Chances are, if you're applying to Furman, you already have a good idea if you can get in or not. Furman's applicant pool is highly self-selected, meaning that the university's high acceptance rate doesn't equate to easy admission; in fact, it's the direct opposite, as applicants are typically very strong. Looking for a way to stand out from the crowd? Let the admissions committee know how valuable you are through your extracurriculars—sports, community service, and artistic endeavors will go a long way in making your case.

THE SCHOOL SAYS "..."

From the Admissions Office

"At Furman, your experience is your education. Through stimulating coursework, combined with relevant, real-world experiences, you will explore your interests and passions to discover what drives you. Guaranteed for every Furman student are opportunities to get involved in internships, study away, research, and community-centered learning experiences that will empower you to apply your classroom learning in a variety of settings and prepare you for success. Furman's highly-qualified faculty and dedicated mentors will provide the knowledge, skills, and support you need to achieve your personal and professional goals. Your experience will take place on a stunningly beautiful 750-acre, residential campus at the foothills of the Blue Ridge Mountains, in one of the country's fastest growing and most vibrant cities, Greenville, South Carolina. There will be endless opportunities for outdoor excursions and urban adventures. We strive to give you a well-rounded, once-in-a-lifetime college experience that will prepare you for anything. That's The Furman Advantage.

"Our holistic application review is based on an evaluation of your grades, rigor of curriculum, test scores (optional), essay, extracurricular involvement, and potential contribution to campus. Beyond your application, we value personally connecting with each applicant to learn more about you and your interest in Furman. We invite you to visit campus, connect with students and faculty, and learn more about The Furman Advantage that is awaiting you."

SELECTIVITY
Admissions Rating	90
# of applicants	5,258
% of applicants accepted	57
% of acceptees attending	22
# offered a place on the wait list	1,035
% accepting a place on wait list	95
% admitted from wait list	4
# of early decision applicants	152
% accepted early decision	85

FRESHMAN PROFILE
Range SAT EBRW	630–710
Range SAT Math	610–710
Range SAT Composite	1255–1400
Range ACT Composite	28–32
# submitting SAT scores	267
% submitting SAT scores	41
# submitting ACT scores	284
% submitting ACT scores	43
Average HS GPA	3.6
% graduated top 10% of class	55
% graduated top 25% of class	75
% graduated top 50% of class	96

DEADLINES
Early decision	
Deadline	11/15
Notification	12/1
Other ED Deadline	1/6
Other ED Notification	1/15
Early action	
Deadline	12/1
Notification	2/15
Regular	
Priority	1/15
Deadline	1/15
Notification	3/1
Nonfall registration?	No

APPLICANTS ALSO LOOK AT AND OFTEN PREFER
The University of North Carolina at Chapel Hill

FINANCIAL FACTS
Financial Aid Rating	89
Annual tuition	$50,464
Room and board	$13,776
Required fees	$380
Books and supplies	$810
Average frosh need-based scholarship	$35,154
Average UG need-based scholarship	$37,440
% needy frosh rec. need-based scholarship or grant aid	100
% needy UG rec. need-based scholarship or grant aid	100
% needy frosh rec. non-need-based scholarship or grant aid	43
% needy UG rec. non-need-based scholarship or grant aid	51
% needy frosh rec. need-based self-help aid	63
% needy UG rec. need-based self-help aid	63
% UG borrow to pay for school	41
Average cumulative indebtedness	$30,388
% frosh need fully met	27
% ugrads need fully met	34
Average % of frosh need met	79
Average % of ugrad need met	82

GEORGE MASON UNIVERSITY

4400 University Drive, FairFax, VA 22030-4444 • Admissions: 703-993-2400 • Fax: 703-993-4622

STUDENTS SAY "..."

Academics

With the "nation's capital in its backyard," George Mason University in Fairfax, Virginia offers "strong academics" combined with proximity to a bustling center of industry and innovation. Mason prepares its students to enter by offering a "large variety of academic programs" and providing a solid infrastructure that is "constantly growing" and "providing many excellent opportunities for students," including research opportunities for undergraduates. The "humanities and economics draw on the local Washington D.C. talent" "and the engineering school has an "advanced" IT program that "Is developed with concentrations in information security, healthcare, networking, and more." Students note that "jobs in all the fields that Mason provides are just within a 10-mile radius of campus," including "top tech companies," which "come to Mason because there is a huge Mason alumni community in the Northern Virginia area." One grateful student notes "it was easy to transfer to with NOVA's Pathway Program" because they had an "easy outline of what classes I needed to take at NOVA to transfer over and pursue a certain degree."

Life

With Washington, D.C. just "a metro ride away," "the majority of students at Mason are commuters," meaning "many of them are not very involved." Even in the "close-knit layout of the main campus," in fact, even for on-campus residents, most campus life happens off campus, including the partying, since fraternities are off-campus. There are many social clubs and organizations, however, with "most students taking part in several." Examples include the "acapella group" and "swing dancing." Many also "meet to practice for competitions, including the Indian dance troupe." Mason has a "free shuttle bus that takes students to the metro" for activities in D.C. The Johnson Center is another "major place that students spend time: there is a food court, a library, meeting rooms, kiosks, the cinema, and huge study areas." Students will also "go to one of the three gyms on campus and work out, a lot of people bike around campus."

Student Body

This is one school where "diversity" is truly an accurate term in all its breadth. Students choose Mason for this wide representation of culture and experience. "As a first-generation student of color," one student says, "I think representation is integral to creating a sense of belonging. Because I could see myself reflected in the students, I chose Mason because I knew that I wouldn't be bothered or feel like I was the minority." There is a "large population of immigrant-heritage students, international students, and students from almost every state in the United States." and the "littlest differences like different name spellings, accents, dress, and more importantly, different political ideas and perspectives are respected and acknowledged, and even more so, celebrated here at Mason." While there are "many students who entered straight from high school...there are also many students who are already working and are returning to school as well as many international students." The "campus keeps growing, housing over 6,000 residents,"—of the 37,000 or so total students. "Due to the enormous and intimidating physical size of GMU, the school offers many ways for students to feel included and engage themselves in extracurricular activities should they choose to do so," one student offers.

GEORGE MASON UNIVERSITY

Financial Aid: 703-993-2353 • E-Mail: admissions@gmu.edu • Website: https://www2.gmu.edu

THE PRINCETON REVIEW SAYS

Admissions

Very important factors considered include: rigor of secondary school record, academic GPA. *Important factors considered include:* standardized test scores, talent/ability. *Other factors considered include:* class rank, application essay, recommendation(s), extracurricular activities, character/personal qualities, first generation, geographical residence, state residency, volunteer work, work experience, level of applicant's interest. ACT with or without writing accepted. SAT with or without Essay component accepted. High school diploma is required and GED is accepted. *Academic units required:* 4 English, 3 math, 2 science, 2 science labs, 2 foreign language, 3 social studies, 3 academic electives. *Academic units recommended:* 4 English, 4 math, 3 science, 3 science labs, 3 foreign language, 4 social studies, 5 academic electives.

Financial Aid

Students should submit: FAFSA. Priority filing deadline is 1/15. The Princeton Review suggests that all financial aid forms be submitted as soon as possible after October 1. *Need-based scholarships/grants offered:* College/university scholarship or grant aid from institutional funds; Federal Pell; Private scholarships; SEOG; State scholarships/grants. *Loan aid offered:* Direct PLUS loans; Direct Subsidized Stafford Loans; Direct Unsubsidized Stafford Loans. Applicants will be notified of awards on a rolling basis beginning 4/1. Federal Work-Study Program available. Institutional employment available.

The Inside Word

GMU is a popular college choice for two key reasons: its proximity to Washington, D.C., and the fact that its applicant pool isn't as competitive as other universities in the Virginia state system. GMU's quality faculty and impressive facilities make it worth consideration, especially if you're looking for a school in the D.C. area and affordability is a factor.

THE SCHOOL SAYS "..."

From the Admissions Office

"George Mason University is an entrepreneurial Tier I research institution with global distinction in a range of academic fields. Located just outside Washington, D.C., our beautiful 677-acre residential campus boasts a diverse student population. Over 6,200 students live on campus in over 40 residence halls.

"As the largest public research institution in Virginia, Mason enrolls more than 37,000 students in over 210 degree programs at the undergraduate, master's, doctoral, and professional levels. Students at all levels are routinely recognized with national and international scholarships and awards. Faculty members have received some of academia's highest honors, including twice winning the Nobel Prize in Economics.

"Our connection to the D.C. area results in engaged and dedicated faculty members who are at the top of their respective fields. This connectivity extends to our students, who take advantage of our unparalleled internship and research opportunities, and who secure careers at national and international companies and organizations, ranging from National Geographic and the Smithsonian Institution to the CIA and the White House. Many of our innovative degree programs are the first of their kind, including the first PhD program in biodefense, the first D.C.-based undergraduate program in Conflict Analysis and Resolution, the first dedicated Cybersecurity Engineering program in the region, and one of the most innovative performing arts management programs in the United States. Mason is at the forefront of the emerging field of biotechnology, is a leader in the performing arts, and holds a preeminent position in the fields of economics, electronic journalism, and history."

SELECTIVITY

Admissions Rating	76
# of applicants	19,554
% of applicants accepted	87
% of acceptees attending	22
# offered a place on the wait list	1,379
% accepting a place on wait list	63
% admitted from wait list	35

FRESHMAN PROFILE

Range SAT EBRW	560–660
Range SAT Math	550–660
Range ACT Composite	24–30
# submitting SAT scores	2,720
% submitting SAT scores	72
# submitting ACT scores	301
% submitting ACT scores	8
Average HS GPA	3.7
% graduated top 10% of class	15
% graduated top 25% of class	44
% graduated top 50% of class	81

DEADLINES

Early action	
Deadline	11/1
Notification	12/15
Regular	
Priority	11/1
Deadline	1/15
Nonfall registration?	Yes

APPLICANTS ALSO LOOK AT AND SOMETIMES PREFER

James Madison University; Old Dominion University; The George Washington University; University of Maryland, College Park; University of Virginia; Virginia Polytechnic Institute and State University; Penn State University Park; Virginia Commonwealth University

FINANCIAL FACTS

Financial Aid Rating	80
Annual in-state tuition	$9,060
Annual out-of-state tuition	$32,520
Room and board	$11,705
Required fees	$3,504
Books and supplies	$1,278
Average frosh need-based scholarship	$7,507
Average UG need-based scholarship	$6,932
% needy frosh rec. need-based scholarship or grant aid	84
% needy UG rec. need-based scholarship or grant aid	85
% needy frosh rec. non-need-based scholarship or grant aid	39
% needy UG rec. non-need-based scholarship or grant aid	21
% needy frosh rec. need-based self-help aid	75
% needy UG rec. need-based self-help aid	72
% frosh rec. any financial aid	74
% UG rec. any financial aid	65
% UG borrow to pay for school	58
Average cumulative indebtedness	$33,362
% frosh need fully met	3
% ugrads need fully met	2
Average % of frosh need met	61
Average % of ugrad need met	53

GEORGETOWN UNIVERSITY

Room 103 White Gravenor Hall, Washington, DC 20057 • Admissions: 202-687-3600 • Fax: 202-687-5084

CAMPUS LIFE

Quality of Life Rating	65
Fire Safety Rating	88
Green Rating	60*
Type of school	Private
Affiliation	Roman Catholic
Environment	Metropolis

STUDENTS

Total undergrad enrollment	7,083
% male/female	44/56
% from out of state	98
% frosh from public high school	49
% frosh live on campus	100
% ugrads live on campus	77
# of fraternities	0
# of sororities	0
% African American	7
% Asian	10
% Caucasian	52
% Hispanic	10
% Native American	<1
% Pacific Islander	0
% Two or more races	5
% Race and/or ethnicity unknown	2
% international	14
# of countries represented	138

SURVEY SAYS . . .

Great financial aid
Alumni active on campus
Students politically aware
Easy to get around campus

ACADEMICS

Academic Rating	75
% students returning for sophomore year	96
% students graduating within 4 years	90
% students graduating within 6 years	95
Calendar	Semester
Student/faculty ratio	11:1
Profs interesting rating	65
Profs accessible rating	63

Most classes have 10–19 students.
Most lab/discussion sessions have 10–19 students.

MOST POPULAR MAJORS

English Language and Literature, General;
International Relations and Affairs; Political
Science and Government, General

STUDENTS SAY "..."

Academics

This moderately sized elite academic establishment stays true to its Jesuit foundations by educating its students with the idea of "cura personalis," or "care for the whole person." The "well-informed" student body perpetuates upon itself, creating an atmosphere full of vibrant intellectual life, that is "also balanced with extracurricular learning and development." "Georgetown is...a place where people work very, very hard without feeling like they are in direct competition," says an international politics major. Located in Washington, D.C., there's a noted School of Foreign Service here, and the access to internships is a huge perk for those in political or government programs. In addition, the proximity to the nation's capital fetches "high-profile guest speakers," with many of the most powerful people in global politics speaking regularly, as well as a large number of adjunct professors who, either are currently working in government, or have retired from high-level positions.

Georgetown offers a "great selection of very knowledgeable professors, split with a good proportion of those who are experienced in realms outside of academia (such as former government officials) and career academics," though there are a few superstars who might be "somewhat less than totally collegial." Professors tend to be "fantastic scholars and teachers" and are "generally available to students," as well as often being "interested in getting to know you as a person (if you put forth the effort to talk to them and go to office hours)." Though Georgetown has a policy of grade deflation, meaning "A's are hard to come by," there are "a ton of interesting courses available," and TAs are used only for optional discussion sessions and help with grading. The academics "can be challenging or they can be not so much (not that they are ever really easy, just easier)"; it all depends on the courses you choose and how much you actually do the work. The school administration is well-meaning and "usually willing to talk and compromise with students," but the process of planning activities can be full of headaches and bureaucracy, and the administration itself "sometimes is overstretched or has trouble transmitting its message." Nevertheless, "a motivated student can get done what he or she wants."

Life

Students are "extremely well aware of the world around them," from government to environment, social to economic, and "Georgetown is the only place where an argument over politics, history, or philosophy is preceded by a keg stand." Hoyas like to have a good time on weekends, and parties at campus and off-campus apartments and townhouses "are generally open to all comers and tend to have a somewhat networking atmosphere; meeting people you don't know is a constant theme." With such a motivated group on such a high-energy campus, "people are always headed somewhere, it seems—to rehearsal, athletic practice, a guest speaker, [or] the gym." Community service and political activism are particularly popular, as is basketball. Everything near Georgetown is in walking distance, including the world of D.C.'s museums, restaurants, and stores, and "grabbing or ordering late night food is a popular option."

Student Body

There are "a lot of wealthy students on campus," and preppy-casual is the fashion de rigueur; this is "definitely not a 'granola' school," but students from diverse backgrounds are typically welcomed by people wanting to learn about different experiences. Indeed, everyone here is well-traveled and well-educated, and there are "a ton of international students." "You better have at least some interest in politics or you will feel out-of-place," says a student. The school can also be "a bit cliquish, with athletes at the top," but there are "plenty of groups for everybody to fit into and find their niche," and "there is much crossover between groups."

GEORGETOWN UNIVERSITY

Financial Aid: 202-687-4547 • E-Mail: guadmiss@georgetown.edu • Website: www.georgetown.edu

THE PRINCETON REVIEW SAYS

Admissions

Very important factors considered include: rigor of secondary school record, class rank, academic GPA, application essay, standardized test scores, recommendation(s), talent/ability, character/personal qualities, first generation. *Important factors considered include:* interview, extracurricular activities. *Other factors considered include:* alumni/ae relation, geographical residence, state residency, racial/ethnic status, work experience. ACT with or without writing accepted. SAT with or without Essay component accepted. High school diploma is required and GED is accepted. *Academic units required:* 4 English, 2 math, 1 science, 2 foreign language, 2 social studies, 2 history.

Financial Aid

Students should submit: Business/Farm Supplement; CSS/Financial Aid PROFILE; FAFSA. Priority filing deadline is 2/1. The Princeton Review suggests that all financial aid forms be submitted as soon as possible after October 1. *Need-based scholarships/grants offered:* Federal Pell; Private scholarships; SEOG; State scholarships/grants. *Loan aid offered:* Direct PLUS loans; Direct Subsidized Stafford Loans; Direct Unsubsidized Stafford Loans. Federal Work-Study Program available. Institutional employment available.

The Inside Word

It was always tough to get admitted to Georgetown, but in the early 1980s Patrick Ewing and the Hoyas created a basketball sensation that catapulted the place into position as one of the most selective universities in the nation. There has been no turning back since. GU receives over twelve applications for every space in the entering class, and the academic strength of the pool is impressive. Virtually 80 percent of the entire student body took AP courses in high school. Candidates who are wait-listed should hold little hope for an offer of admission; over the past several years Georgetown has taken very few off their lists.

THE SCHOOL SAYS "..."

From the Admissions Office

"Georgetown was founded in 1789 by John Carroll, who concurred with his contemporaries Benjamin Franklin and Thomas Jefferson in believing that the success of the young democracy depended upon an educated and virtuous citizenry. Carroll founded the school with the dynamic Jesuit tradition of education, characterized by humanism and committed to the assumption of responsibility and action. Georgetown is a national and international university, enrolling students from all fifty states and over 100 foreign countries. Undergraduate students are enrolled in one of four undergraduate schools: the College of Arts and Sciences, School of Foreign Service, Georgetown School of Business, and Georgetown School of Nursing and Health Studies. All students share a common liberal arts core and have access to the entire university curriculum.

"Applicants must submit scores from SAT or the ACT. Three SAT Subject Tests are highly recommended."

SELECTIVITY

Admissions Rating	98
# of applicants	22,872
% of applicants accepted	15
% of acceptees attending	49
# offered a place on the wait list	1,753
% accepting a place on wait list	1
% admitted from wait list	75

FRESHMAN PROFILE

Range SAT EBRW	680–750
Range SAT Math	690–780
Range ACT Composite	31–34
# submitting SAT scores	1,192
% submitting SAT scores	75
# submitting ACT scores	789
% submitting ACT scores	50
Average HS GPA	3.9
% graduated top 10% of class	89
% graduated top 25% of class	97
% graduated top 50% of class	99

DEADLINES

Early action	
Deadline	11/1
Notification	12/15
Regular	
Deadline	1/10
Notification	4/1
Nonfall registration?	No

FINANCIAL FACTS

Financial Aid Rating	95
Annual tuition	$55,440
Room and board	$18,218
Required fees	$618
Average frosh need-based scholarship	$45,572
Average UG need-based scholarship	$45,585
% needy frosh rec. need-based scholarship or grant aid	93
% needy UG rec. need-based scholarship or grant aid	93
% needy frosh rec. non-need-based scholarship or grant aid	34
% needy UG rec. non-need-based scholarship or grant aid	30
% needy frosh rec. need-based self-help aid	83
% needy UG rec. need-based self-help aid	83
% UG borrow to pay for school	37
Average cumulative indebtedness	$25,726
% frosh need fully met	100
% ugrads need fully met	100
Average % of frosh need met	100
Average % of ugrad need met	100

THE GEORGE WASHINGTON UNIVERSITY

800 21st St. NW, Suite 100, Washington, DC 20052 • Admissions: 202-994-6040 • Fax: 202-994-0325

CAMPUS LIFE

Quality of Life Rating	84
Fire Safety Rating	60*
Green Rating	92
Type of school	Private
Environment	Metropolis

STUDENTS

Total undergrad enrollment	12,161
% male/female	39/61
% from out of state	96
% frosh from public high school	70
% frosh live on campus	98
% ugrads live on campus	60
# of fraternities (% ugrad men join)	12 (15)
# of sororities (% ugrad women join)	9 (19)
% African American	7
% Asian	11
% Caucasian	51
% Hispanic	10
% Native American	<1
% Pacific Islander	<1
% Two or more races	4
% Race and/or ethnicity unknown	6
% international	11
# of countries represented	122

SURVEY SAYS . . .

Students love Washington, DC
Lots of beer drinking
Hard liquor is popular
Active student government

ACADEMICS

Academic Rating	82
% students returning for sophomore year	93
% students graduating within 4 years	73
% students graduating within 6 years	81
Calendar	Semester
Student/faculty ratio	13:1
Profs interesting rating	90
Profs accessible rating	91

Most classes have 10–19 students.
Most lab/discussion sessions have 20–29 students.

MOST POPULAR MAJORS

International Relations and Affairs; Business Administration and Management, General; Psychology, General

STUDENTS SAY "..."

Academics

Get ready for "hands-on learning in an environment unlike any other" at George Washington University, where a location "four blocks away from the White House, down the street from the State Department, and near nearly all world headquarters" means "connections and opportunity" for undergraduates. Students call it "the perfect place to study international affairs" and praise the "amazing journalism program," the excellent political communications major, the political science program ("What political science major would pass up the chance to go toe-to-toe with protestors every week at the rallies outside the White House and Congress?"), the sciences (benefiting from the region's many research operations), and other departments too numerous to name. As one student puts it, "GW is a place where everyone can find their niche. Whether you are a politically active campaign volunteer, a hip-hop dancer, or a future Broadway actor, there is a place for you at GW." The school places a premium on hiring "professors of practice," teachers who "are either currently working in their field or just retired to teach." The faculty includes "former ambassadors, governors on the Federal Reserve Board, and CNN correspondents." These instructors emphasize "a balance between theory and practice that provides a foundation of knowledge and pragmatism from which students can feel prepared to enter any sector of work after school." The resulting education "gets students prepared for post-college life through an emphasis on internships and career-focused classes," putting "a lot of emphasis on acclimation to the real world." GWU has a new Science and Engineering Hall, the largest science facility at a university in D.C.

Life

"Life at GW is about independence," students report. "There are no real cafeterias" on campus, "you have to rely on your own feet for transportation, and there is very little regulation in dorms." As a result, "there is little school spirit, but that fact alone seems to tie everyone together." The campus isn't entirely dead; there are frat parties ("which are hard to attend for non-member males and easy to attend for women"), the "occasional dorm-room party, which is usually small," and "apartment parties off campus" for upperclassmen. Campus organizations offer all sorts of events, and the school hosts a veritable who's who of guest speakers on a regular basis. Students love the school's Midnight Monument Tour, held "during the warmer parts of the year," during which "students walk the five blocks to the National Mall at 2:00 A.M. and tour the monuments. It is an awesome experience." Still, most students prefer to spend free time exploring D.C. on their own. The city provides "so much to do... it's overwhelming: monuments, free museums, fairs, every major sports franchise, and lots of student specials on the above things." D.C.'s upscale Georgetown neighborhood is nearby for "shopping, dining, seeing movies, etc.," while culturally diverse Adams Morgan is great for shopping, ethnic dining, and live music. Students have access to all of D.C. with a metro stop on campus.

Student Body

Though "GW students are often stereotyped as spoiled and wealthy Northeastern kids," and a few students here concede that there's some basis for the stereotype, most would also add that "white, preppy, fraternity/sorority members" who "like nice labels on their clothing" neither define nor dominate the campus population. "The reality is that there's tremendous diversity here of all stripes—geographic, religious, political, racial, and intellectual," with "students from dozens of countries and all fifty states." "GW is truly a national and even international school," one student writes. "I love walking out of the library and hearing conversations happening in a half-dozen languages." The school has always been a popular destination for Jewish students. There is also "a huge LGBT group on campus, with very little discrimination." Nearly everyone here is "incredibly driven," "combining classes with an internship, maybe a sport, and usually a few extracurriculars."

THE GEORGE WASHINGTON UNIVERSITY

E-Mail: gwadm@gwu.edu • Website: www.gwu.edu

THE PRINCETON REVIEW SAYS

Admissions

Very important factors considered include: rigor of secondary school record, academic GPA. *Important factors considered include:* application essay, recommendation(s), extracurricular activities, talent/ability, volunteer work. *Other factors considered include:* standardized test scores, character/personal qualities, first generation, alumni/ae relation, geographical residence, racial/ethnic status, work experience, level of applicant's interest. ACT with Writing recommended. SAT with Essay component recommended. High school diploma is required and GED is accepted. *Academic units required:* 4 English, 2 math, 2 science, 1 science lab, 2 foreign language, 2 social studies. *Academic units recommended:* 4 English, 4 math, 4 science, 4 foreign language, 4 social studies.

Financial Aid

Students should submit: CSS/Financial Aid PROFILE; FAFSA; Noncustodial PROFILE. Priority filing deadline is 1/5. The Princeton Review suggests that all financial aid forms be submitted as soon as possible after October 1. *Need-based scholarships/grants offered:* College/university scholarship or grant aid from institutional funds; Federal Pell; SEOG; State scholarships/grants. *Loan aid offered:* Direct PLUS loans; Direct Subsidized Stafford Loans; Direct Unsubsidized Stafford Loans. Applicants will be notified of awards on a rolling basis following decision release. Federal Work-Study Program available. Institutional employment available.

The Inside Word

With more than 25,000 applications to process annually, GW could be forgiven if it gave student essays only a perfunctory glance. The school insists, however, that essays are carefully reviewed. Take note and proceed accordingly. Application rates have surged throughout the past decade. This school is only getting more popular, so applicants should be prepared to bring their A-game.

THE SCHOOL SAYS "..."

From the Admissions Office

"Located in the heart of Washington, D.C., the George Washington University enrolls a diverse, motivated, and active student body from all 50 states and 130 countries. Our students study, learn, and grow on two fully integrated D.C. campuses—Foggy Bottom, blocks from the National Mall, and Mount Vernon, in a residential neighborhood.

"As a comprehensive global research university, GW offers more than 75 majors in the arts, business, engineering, international affairs, public health, and social and physical sciences —all taught mere blocks from the White House and amid D.C.'s business and high-tech sectors. Students work closely with well-connected faculty to utilize the many academic and cultural resources of the District. Some classes take field trips to museums to study collections while others welcome guest speakers who are experts in their fields. In addition to dynamic classroom experiences, a GW education allows students the ability to put knowledge in action. Through research, internships, community service, and study abroad, GW students implement classroom learning to change the world and improve the human experience.

"We look for bright and diverse students who are ambitious, energetic, and self-motivated. As a test-optional school, we believe that the best indicator of success at GW is a student's high school performance. Our holistic review takes all pieces of a student's admission application into consideration. We aim to make a GW education affordable to all admitted students, offering generous scholarships and financial aid."

SELECTIVITY

Admissions Rating	93
# of applicants	26,510
% of applicants accepted	42
% of acceptees attending	26
# offered a place on the wait list	4,963
% accepting a place on wait list	42
% admitted from wait list	1
# of early decision applicants	1,292
% accepted early decision	70

FRESHMAN PROFILE

Range SAT EBRW	640–720
Range SAT Math	640–740
Range ACT Composite	29–32
# submitting SAT scores	1,419
% submitting SAT scores	50
# submitting ACT scores	955
% submitting ACT scores	34
% graduated top 10% of class	61
% graduated top 25% of class	88
% graduated top 50% of class	99

DEADLINES

Early decision	
Deadline	11/1
Notification	12/15
Other ED Deadline	1/5
Other ED Notification	2/1
Regular	
Priority	11/1
Deadline	1/5
Notification	4/1
Nonfall registration?	Yes

FINANCIAL FACTS

Financial Aid Rating	90
Annual tuition	$56,845
Room and board	$18,000
Required fees	$90
Books and supplies	$1,400
Average frosh need-based scholarship	$33,447
Average UG need-based scholarship	$31,471
% needy frosh rec. need-based scholarship or grant aid	97
% needy UG rec. need-based scholarship or grant aid	91
% needy frosh rec. non-need-based scholarship or grant aid	76
% needy UG rec. non-need-based scholarship or grant aid	59
% needy frosh rec. need-based self-help aid	75
% needy UG rec. need-based self-help aid	77
% UG borrow to pay for school	49
Average cumulative indebtedness	$32,482
% frosh need fully met	49
% ugrads need fully met	44
Average % of frosh need met	89
Average % of ugrad need met	85

GEORGIA INSTITUTE OF TECHNOLOGY

Office of Undergraduate Admissions, Atlanta, GA 30332-0320 • Admissions: 404-894-4154 • Fax: 404-894-9511

CAMPUS LIFE

Quality of Life Rating	**90**
Fire Safety Rating	**96**
Green Rating	**96**
Type of school	Public
Environment	Metropolis

STUDENTS

Total undergrad enrollment	15,212
% male/female	62/38
% from out of state	34
% frosh live on campus	97
% ugrads live on campus	43
# of fraternities (% ugrad men join)	40 (28)
# of sororities (% ugrad women join)	15 (33)
% African American	7
% Asian	22
% Caucasian	48
% Hispanic	7
% Native American	<1
% Pacific Islander	0
% Two or more races	4
% Race and/or ethnicity unknown	4
% international	8
# of countries represented	113

SURVEY SAYS . . .
Students are happy
Lab facilities are great
Internships are widely available
Students love Atlanta, GA
Recreation facilities are great
College radio is popular
Alumni active on campus

ACADEMICS

Academic Rating	**83**
% students returning for sophomore year	97
% students graduating within 4 years	39
% students graduating within 6 years	85
Calendar	Semester
Student/faculty ratio	21:1
Profs interesting rating	86
Profs accessible rating	90
Most classes have 20–29 students.	
Most lab/discussion sessions have 10–19 students.	

MOST POPULAR MAJORS
Computer and Information Sciences, General;
Mechanical Engineering; Industrial Engineering

STUDENTS SAY "..."

Academics

A world-renowned public research university, Georgia Institute of Technology has a reputations that "opens many doors" for its students. Undergrads here are quick to sing the praises of the university's "rigorous" and "challenging" engineering, science, and business programs. Students also love Georgia Tech's focus on "innovation and hands-on learning" which leaves them well prepared to face the job market come graduation. For example, "throughout the school year there are plenty of competitions to create startup companies, flesh out innovative ideas, and show off prototypes." As if that wasn't enough, many courses have "a project built-in to force you to apply the material you've been studying." Inside the classroom, undergrads are greeted by professors who are "truly passionate about what they are teaching." One student further explains, "Most of the professors do research and continue learning themselves. This is the sort of environment that they foster." Undergrads further appreciate that their instructors "try and stimulate thinking rather than just letting you regurgitate facts." Another undergrad concurs remarking that her professors "challenge me to grow as an intellectual." Best of all, they frequently demonstrate themselves to be "invested in your success and making their classes interesting and applicable to real life."

Life

Given the academic rigors at Georgia Tech, many students will tell you that "studying" is the number one activity. However, even these hard working undergrads need a break every now and then. And thankfully "there is almost always something going on somewhere on campus." For starters, "there are an abundance of clubs...covering a huge variety of interests, and the majority of students are involved in at least one." Additionally, "during the fall, large numbers of students spend their weekends tailgating and attending football games." Undergrads here also enjoy attending "plays and musical events at the arts center." Moreover, Greek life is extremely popular at Georgia Tech. Fortunately, if you choose not join a sorority or fraternity, your social life won't take a hit. After all, we've been informed that "fraternity parties are generally very welcome...even [to] students who choose not to drink" or "people who are not members." Finally, students also love to take advantage of Georgia Tech's prime Atlanta location. The city offers many things to do "from museums, to concerts, festivals, restaurants, clubs, and every other sort of attraction in between!"

Student Body

When asked about their peers, Georgia Tech students immediately describe them as "smart," "driven, and ambitious." Indeed, it's rare to find an undergrad here who is "slacking off." Fortunately, "there isn't a sense of cut-throat academic rivalry; everyone is much more helpful and supportive of one another." As one relieved student shares, "People will help you if you're struggling on a math problem, or if you can't get your program to function correctly, instead of letting you suffer so that they can get a better grade." Undergrads also report that their fellow students are often quite "passionate." Unsurprisingly, that passion is "usually [connected to something] in the technology field." Indeed, "You walk to campus and you hear kids debating which programming language is better." Another student agrees explaining, "Most of the jokes exchanged seem to be science-related, and every now and then you see remote-controlled drones flying in the air." Aside from the "nerd" exterior, you'll find undergrads that are "witty" and "quirky" as well as "sleep deprived." There's also "a very large foreign component to the student body" which many here appreciate. Finally, we'd be remiss if we didn't mention that Georgia Tech is "not just a bunch of computer geeks sitting in their room all day but a group of people who are out there making a difference."

GEORGIA INSTITUTE OF TECHNOLOGY

Financial Aid: 404-894-4160 • E-Mail: admission@gatech.edu • Website: www.gatech.edu

THE PRINCETON REVIEW SAYS

Admissions

Very important factors considered include: rigor of secondary school record, academic GPA, extracurricular activities. *Important factors considered include:* application essay, standardized test scores, talent/ability, character/personal qualities, geographical residence, state residency, volunteer work. *Other factors considered include:* recommendation(s), first generation, alumni/ae relation, racial/ethnic status, level of applicant's interest. ACT with or without writing accepted. SAT with Essay component recommended. High school diploma is required and GED is not accepted. *Academic units required:* 4 English, 4 math, 4 science, 2 science labs, 2 foreign language, 3 social studies.

Financial Aid

Students should submit: CSS/Financial Aid PROFILE; FAFSA; Institution's own financial aid form. Priority filing deadline is 1/31. The Princeton Review suggests that all financial aid forms be submitted as soon as possible after October 1. *Need-based scholarships/grants offered:* College/university scholarship or grant aid from institutional funds; Federal Pell; Private scholarships; SEOG; State scholarships/grants; United Negro College Fund. *Loan aid offered:* Direct PLUS loans; Direct Subsidized Stafford Loans; Direct Unsubsidized Stafford Loans. Applicants will be notified of awards on or about 4/1. Federal Work-Study Program available. Institutional employment available.

The Inside Word

Gaining admission to Georgia Tech is extremely competitive. Admissions officers here are looking to see how much candidates have pushed and stretched themselves academically throughout high school. They want intellectually curious students who aren't afraid of a challenge. Hence, it's imperative to have taken honors, advanced placement and/or international baccalaureate classes (assuming your high school offers them). Beyond academics, the university is also looking for applicants who are involved in their communities. And most of all, it wants students who will be a good fit for Georgia Tech.

THE SCHOOL SAYS "..."

From the Admissions Office

"Georgia Tech consistently ranks among the nation's top public universities producing leaders in engineering, computing, business, architecture, and the sciences while remaining one of the best college buys in the country. The 400-acre campus is nestled in the heart of the fun, dynamic and progressive city of Atlanta. Recent campus improvements yielded new state-of-the art academic and research buildings, apartment-style housing, phenomenal social and recreational facilities, and the most extension fiber-optic cable system on any college campus.

"Georgia Tech has a great academic reputation, and our graduates are well-prepared to meet today's challenges. A unique advantage many students find is Georgia Tech's strong emphasis on undergraduate students. Undergraduates can gain practical work experience through our co-op and internship programs and can begin doing research as early as their freshman year. Students can also gain an international perspective through study abroad, work abroad, or the international plan. In addition, Georgia Tech has the Clough Undergraduate Center, a state-of-the-art facility that includes forty-one classrooms, two 300-plus seat auditoriums, group study rooms, presentation rehearsal studios, a rooftop garden, and a café.

"With a Division I ACC sports program and access to Atlanta's music, theater, and other cultural venues, Georgia Tech offers its diverse and passionate student body a unique combination of top academics in a thriving and vibrant setting. We encourage you to come visit campus and see why Georgia Tech continues to attract the nation's most motivated, interesting, and creative students."

SELECTIVITY
Admissions Rating	97
# of applicants	35,611
% of applicants accepted	23
% of acceptees attending	39
# offered a place on the wait list	3,511
% accepting a place on wait list	65
% admitted from wait list	3

FRESHMAN PROFILE
Range SAT EBRW	640–730
Range SAT Math	690–790
Range ACT Composite	30–34
# submitting SAT scores	2,282
% submitting SAT scores	73
# submitting ACT scores	1,813
% submitting ACT scores	58
Average HS GPA	3.8
% graduated top 10% of class	89
% graduated top 25% of class	97
% graduated top 50% of class	99

DEADLINES
Early action	
Deadline	10/15
Notification	1/12
Regular	
Priority	10/15
Deadline	1/1
Notification	3/15
Nonfall registration?	Yes

APPLICANTS ALSO LOOK AT AND OFTEN PREFER
University of Georgia

FINANCIAL FACTS
Financial Aid Rating	84
Annual in-state tuition	$10,258
Annual out-of-state tuition	$31,370
Room and board	$12,090
Required fees	$2,424
Books and supplies	$800
Average frosh need-based scholarship	$14,630
Average UG need-based scholarship	$12,581
% needy frosh rec. need-based scholarship or grant aid	90
% needy UG rec. need-based scholarship or grant aid	88
% needy frosh rec. non-need-based scholarship or grant aid	68
% needy UG rec. non-need-based scholarship or grant aid	42
% needy frosh rec. need-based self-help aid	46
% needy UG rec. need-based self-help aid	54
% frosh rec. any financial aid	46
% UG rec. any financial aid	45
% UG borrow to pay for school	36
Average cumulative indebtedness	$32,760
% frosh need fully met	29
% ugrads need fully met	24
Average % of frosh need met	66
Average % of ugrad need met	57

THE BEST 386 COLLEGES ■ 265

GETTYSBURG COLLEGE

Admissions Office, Gettysburg, PA 17325-1484 • Admissions: 717-337-6100 • Fax: 717-337-6145

CAMPUS LIFE

Quality of Life Rating	88
Fire Safety Rating	98
Green Rating	86
Type of school	Private
Affiliation	Lutheran
Environment	Village

STUDENTS

Total undergrad enrollment	2,371
% male/female	48/52
% from out of state	72
% frosh live on campus	100
% ugrads live on campus	95
# of fraternities (% ugrad men join)	9 (31)
# of sororities (% ugrad women join)	7 (33)
% African American	4
% Asian	2
% Caucasian	74
% Hispanic	9
% Native American	<1
% Pacific Islander	0
% Two or more races	3
% Race and/or ethnicity unknown	2
% international	6
# of countries represented	33

SURVEY SAYS . . .

Students always studying
Students are happy
Lab facilities are great
Great library
Internships are widely available
Great financial aid
Great food on campus
Easy to get around campus
Recreation facilities are great
Lots of beer drinking
Frats and sororities are popular
Active student government
Active student-run political groups

ACADEMICS

Academic Rating	93
% students returning for sophomore year	91
% students graduating within 4 years	77
% students graduating within 6 years	81
Calendar	Semester
Student/faculty ratio	9:1
Profs interesting rating	91
Profs accessible rating	95
Most classes have 10–19 students.	

MOST POPULAR MAJORS

Psychology, General; Political Science and Government, General; Business/Commerce, General

STUDENTS SAY "..."

Academics

Established in 1832, Pennsylvania's Gettysburg College is a selective college of the liberal arts and sciences that focuses on interdisciplinary study and advanced scholarship. To facilitate this, the school often utilizes distinctive programs, such as its Civil War Institute (dedicated to academic research and historic preservation) and Center for Public Service. To "support intellectual curiosity" for the school's 2,400 students, Gettysburg also provides an individualized major option. This is backed up by programs like the Cross-Disciplinary Science Institute that allow interested students to weave other interests into their academic schedule, and hundreds of students may receive funding for various research projects under the guidance of a faculty mentor. "There are a lot of research opportunities for us even though we are undergraduate students," says one. There are also tons of "opportunities to present research, field trips, hands-on learning experiences, [and] immersion trips."

Small class sizes—there's a nine-to-one student-faculty ratio—provide students with further opportunities to "form close relationships with professors, which makes the education experience personalized and thorough." Professors also take point in encouraging "leadership and involvement in academics through research and presentations," and utilize "discussion-based classes [to] foster a greater sense of investment." In turn, the inquisitive minds at Gettysburg "feel comfortable sharing their perspectives and opinions, which makes classes and discussions on campus much more interesting and eye-opening." Experiential learning also keeps things fresh and active, like "community service, going to see movies pertinent to a course's topic, field trips" or, for example, a German class that "used the rock wall in our gym as a trust exercise and to practice giving commands in German." Whatever the situation, professors "are always willing to help and make time to meet outside of class."

Life

The work week is, in fact, a work week here. "Almost everyone is studying or doing work at their favorite study space," says one student. But while there's a lot of agreement that "Mondays to Fridays are rigorous," there's also consensus that "then the weekend rolls around." With more than ninety percent of the student body living on campus, there are lots of ways to stay active, "whether it be in a Greek organization, clubs, athletics, or working on-campus." Sports and Greek life may "dominate the social scene," but there are plenty of other entertainment outlets, from "cool reenactment options" to "events the Campus Activities Board plans." Gettysburg also boasts "all the advantages other more rural schools have, like plenty of space to run, bike, and walk, and a quaint town too."

Student Body

Students describe their "very interconnected" community as "unmatched," thanks largely to the smaller size and high levels of sociability. "Everybody knows most of the other students from a class taken together, or a club they both attend, or maybe they just go to the gym at the same time." Diversity is important to both students and the school, and there's a lot of appreciation voiced for how the community is "open to different opinions" and "able to have healthy conversations about hard topics." Perhaps that's because students are all "eager to learn about the world beyond their academic area" or because they're "diligent with work and extracurriculars." Whatever the case, "we all click very well."

GETTYSBURG COLLEGE

Financial Aid: 717-337-6611 • E-Mail: admiss@gettysburg.edu • Website: www.gettysburg.edu

THE PRINCETON REVIEW SAYS

Admissions

Very important factors considered include: rigor of secondary school record, academic GPA, application essay, recommendation(s). *Important factors considered include:* class rank, standardized test scores, interview, extracurricular activities, talent/ability, character/personal qualities, volunteer work. *Other factors considered include:* first generation, alumni/ae relation, geographical residence, racial/ethnic status, work experience, level of applicant's interest. ACT with or without writing accepted. SAT with or without Essay component accepted. High school diploma is required and GED is accepted. *Academic units required:* 4 English, 3 math, 3 science, 3 science labs, 3 foreign language, 3 social studies, 3 history. *Academic units recommended:* 4 English, 4 math, 4 science, 4 science labs, 4 foreign language, 4 social studies, 4 history.

Financial Aid

Students should submit: CSS/Financial Aid PROFILE; FAFSA. Priority filing deadline is 1/15. The Princeton Review suggests that all financial aid forms be submitted as soon as possible after October 1. *Need-based scholarships/grants offered:* College/university scholarship or grant aid from institutional funds; Federal Pell; Private scholarships; SEOG; State scholarships/grants. *Loan aid offered:* Direct PLUS loans; Direct Subsidized Stafford Loans; Direct Unsubsidized Stafford Loans. Applicants will be notified of awards on or about 3/18. Federal Work-Study Program available. Institutional employment available.

The Inside Word

To really get a feel for Gettysburg, many students say a campus visit is a must. Test scores are optional here, and the school strongly emphasizes its desire for extracurricular involvement and positive contributions to the community, as well as students who have made the most of the academic offerings of their high school.

THE SCHOOL SAYS "..."

From the Admissions Office

"Founded in 1832, Gettysburg College is a highly selective, four-year residential college of the liberal arts and sciences offering students the opportunity to choose from 65 majors, minors, and academic programs. At Gettysburg, our curriculum and learning environment are designed to foster critical and inquisitive thinking. Our students' intellectual growth extends beyond the classroom. Students conduct research alongside faculty, study abroad through our Center for Global Education, and engage in our distinctive programs: the Eisenhower Institute, Center for Public Service, Garthwait Leadership Center, Civil War Institute, and Sunderman Conservatory of Music.

"Starting in the first-year, students connect every experience they have on campus to an individualized career plan and build their professional network. We encourage students to be open to new possibilities so that they may fully unleash their potential. Our students tap into our global and active network of 30,000 alumni and utilize the services of the Center for Career Engagement. We see the return on investment as 98 percent of our most recent alums are either employed or enrolled in graduate school one year after graduation.

"As a community, we share a contagious enthusiasm for collaboration and forward-thinking. As a result, our students are prepared to make a difference—here at Gettysburg and in the world after they graduate."

SELECTIVITY

Admissions Rating	92
# of applicants	5,916
% of applicants accepted	48
% of acceptees attending	24
% admitted from wait list	0
# of early decision applicants	419
% accepted early decision	64

FRESHMAN PROFILE

Range SAT EBRW	630–700
Range SAT Math	620–700
Range ACT Composite	27–31
% graduated top 10% of class	60
% graduated top 25% of class	85
% graduated top 50% of class	99

DEADLINES

Early decision	
Deadline	11/15
Notification	12/15
Other ED Deadline	1/15
Other ED Notification	2/15
Regular	
Priority	1/15
Deadline	1/15
Notification	3/18
Nonfall registration?	No

FINANCIAL FACTS

Financial Aid Rating	95
Annual tuition	$56,390
Room and board	$13,460
Books and supplies	$1,000
Average frosh need-based scholarship	$43,235
Average UG need-based scholarship	$40,404
% needy frosh rec. need-based scholarship or grant aid	98
% needy UG rec. need-based scholarship or grant aid	98
% needy frosh rec. non-need-based scholarship or grant aid	62
% needy UG rec. non-need-based scholarship or grant aid	58
% needy frosh rec. need-based self-help aid	85
% needy UG rec. need-based self-help aid	83
% frosh rec. any financial aid	67
% UG rec. any financial aid	61
% UG borrow to pay for school	60
Average cumulative indebtedness	$34,630
% frosh need fully met	90
% ugrads need fully met	89
Average % of frosh need met	90
Average % of ugrad need met	90

GONZAGA UNIVERSITY

502 E Boone Avenue, Spokane, WA 99258 • Admissions: 509-313-6572 • Fax: 509-313-5780

STUDENTS SAY "..."

Academics

Gonzaga University "has a strong Jesuit Catholic tradition and has sustained an environment of academic excellence." By far, the two most commonly cited strengths are the basketball team and the "awesome community!" Gonzaga is a "close-knit community." "At Gonzaga, we are one big family," one student says. "Everyone is incredibly friendly," and there's "a great sense of school spirit and a family-like environment." "Not to mention being able to cheer in one of the most intimidating basketball stadiums in the United States." "It is a family here, and you really get to know your professors," one student explains. "Everyone here is interconnected, and basketball is wonderful too! It's a way we all come together." Students also believe "the Jesuit mission of Gonzaga sets it apart from other schools." Gonzaga "is a socially competent, caring institution" where you'll "be constantly challenged to be your best, make lifelong relationships, and develop a critical understanding of the world around you." The professors get mixed reviews: "It is about a 50 percent chance of getting a good professor." "Professors are good in general, but adjunct faculty is typically hired at the last minute and not good," one student explains. "Many of the professors for the core requirements are very religious and not especially open to new ideas." "Gonzaga tries to get students to think about the world in a holistic way—understanding how everything is interrelated—and finding our purpose in that." Students think the "registration processes" and "cafeteria food" could "use some improvement," and "because Gonzaga is a smaller school, it is at times difficult to arrange your schedule due to limited availability of classes and time constraints."

Life

Students at Gonzaga are "devoted equally to...academics and social life." "People generally just want to socialize," one student explains. "Everyone for the most part does do their work, but there is definitely an emphasis on developing relationships." "The party scene is lively" at Gonzaga although students caution "we're not *that* big of a party school." During basketball season, Gonzaga basketball becomes "a way of life," and "basketball games and waiting in line for tickets are the largest social experience on campus." "*Everyone* goes to the basketball games. It's practically required to graduate." This leads some students to wish there was "less focus on men's basketball." Because the school is located in rainy Spokane, Washington, "the worst thing about Gonzaga is the weather, which the school can't really do anything about." Still, many students "stay active through sports" and enjoy the outdoors, "whether that's skiing, hiking, rafting, climbing, wake boarding, or just soaking up some rays." "People often snowboard at Mount Spokane, or if they are feeling adventurous, they drive the hour to Canada or hour to Montana." At Gonzaga, students "Read, Rage, Repent, Repeat. We wake up, work out, eat, and make memories."

Student Body

Although Gonzaga students stress the college's tight-knit community, many feel that while "the university claims to be accepting of all beliefs, opinions, and lifestyles," "in reality that's just not the case." "It is a community for sure, but really only if you're white and upper middle class, and the Jesuit Catholic mission can sometimes be troublesome for those of us with liberal and non-mainstream Catholic beliefs," explains one student. "Even feminism is kind of seen as taboo here." Others insist that "everyone here seems to blend well together," and "no matter your background, you are accepted here." Students study "hard through the week" but have "a lot of fun on weekends." Students describe themselves as "friendly, very open," "mostly preppy," "conventionally minded," "well-mannered," "religious," and tending to come "from a good family." Gonzaga has "a mostly Caucasian population," and "diversity is a huge issue, and Gonzaga could definitely improve how it treats students of diverse backgrounds." It should be no shock that "the typical student is a huge basketball fan" with "extreme school spirit."

GONZAGA UNIVERSITY

Financial Aid: 509-313-6582 • E-Mail: admissions@gonzaga.edu • Website: www.gonzaga.edu

THE PRINCETON REVIEW SAYS

Admissions

Very important factors considered include: rigor of secondary school record, academic GPA, character/personal qualities, first generation. *Important factors considered include:* application essay, recommendation(s), extracurricular activities, talent/ability. *Other factors considered include:* optional standardized test scores, interview (optional), alumni/ae relation, racial/ethnic status, volunteer work, work experience, level of applicant's interest. If test scores are submitted, the ACT with or without writing is accepted. Similarly, the SAT with or without the Essay component is accepted. High school diploma is required and GED is not accepted. *Academic units required:* 4 English, 3 math, 3 science, 3 science labs, 2 foreign language, 2 social studies, 2 history, 2 academic electives. *Academic units recommended:* 4 English, 4 math, 4 science, 4 science labs, 3 foreign language, 3 social studies, 3 history, 3 academic electives.

Financial Aid

Students should submit: FAFSA. The Princeton Review suggests that all financial aid forms be submitted as soon as possible after October 1. *Need-based scholarships/grants offered:* College/university scholarship or grant aid from institutional funds; Federal Pell; Private scholarships; SEOG; State scholarships/grants. *Loan aid offered:* Direct PLUS loans; Direct Subsidized Stafford Loans; Direct Unsubsidized Stafford Loans; Federal Nursing Loans; College/University Loans from Institutional Funds. Applicants will be notified of awards on a rolling basis beginning 3/1. Federal Work-Study Program available. Institutional employment available.

The Inside Word

Gonzaga is a great example of how a high-profile athletic program can transform a competitive school into a highly competitive one. During the past decade, Gonzaga's admit rate has decreased substantially while class rank, standardized test scores, and high school GPA have all increased measurably. Nursing and Engineering programs are considered "direct entry" programs, for which a student must declare the major on the application to be considered for that program, and there are additional curricular and academic qualifications.

THE SCHOOL SAYS "..."

From the Admissions Office

"Gonzaga educates students for lives of leadership and service for the common good. We seek motivated students who will benefit from the University's challenging academic programs and will positively contribute to our campus with extracurricular achievement, community involvement, unique experiences, and diverse personal interests. In the application, let us know about your experiences thus far and your goals and hopes for the future. Please note that we will be test optional for the entering class of fall 2021. Please check Gonzaga's website for announcements concerning future classes.

SELECTIVITY

Admissions Rating	**88**
# of applicants	9,279
% of applicants accepted	62
% of acceptees attending	22
# offered a place on the wait list	807
% accepting a place on wait list	23
% admitted from wait list	29

FRESHMAN PROFILE

Range SAT EBRW	600–670
Range SAT Math	600–690
Range SAT Composite	1210–1358
Range ACT Composite	25–30
# submitting SAT scores	919
% submitting SAT scores	72
# submitting ACT scores	590
% submitting ACT scores	46
Average HS GPA	3.8
% graduated top 10% of class	40
% graduated top 25% of class	75
% graduated top 50% of class	95

DEADLINES

Regular	
Priority	12/1
Deadline	2/1
Notification	3/15
Nonfall registration?	Yes

APPLICANTS ALSO LOOK AT AND OFTEN PREFER
University of Washington

AND SOMETIMES PREFER
University of Portland; Santa Clara University; Seattle University

AND RARELY PREFER
Washington State University

FINANCIAL FACTS

Financial Aid Rating	**87**
Annual tuition	$46,060
Room and board	$12,951
Required fees	$860
Books and supplies	$1,196
Average frosh need-based scholarship	$8,432
Average UG need-based scholarship	$7,435
% needy frosh rec. need-based scholarship or grant aid	94
% needy UG rec. need-based scholarship or grant aid	93
% needy frosh rec. non-need-based scholarship or grant aid	99
% needy UG rec. non-need-based scholarship or grant aid	98
% needy frosh rec. need-based self-help aid	70
% needy UG rec. need-based self-help aid	70
% frosh rec. any financial aid	99
% UG rec. any financial aid	98
% UG borrow to pay for school	54
Average cumulative indebtedness	$29,685
% frosh need fully met	21
% ugrads need fully met	23
Average % of frosh need met	78
Average % of ugrad need met	78

GORDON COLLEGE

255 Grapevine Road, Wenham, MA 01984-1899 • Admissions: 978-867-4218 • Fax: 978-867-4682

STUDENTS SAY "..."

Academics

Tucked away in beautiful, bucolic Massachusetts, Gordon College is a liberal-arts institution that's built on "Christian values without being unnecessarily strict." Here, students receive a "well-rounded education" that encourages them "to make interdisciplinary connections." There's also an appreciated "emphasis on servant leadership through opportunities like the outdoor education requirement." And while there's no denying that "the school is academically rigorous," students note that "there's so much here for support, so it's hard to do poorly in a course." The faculty is described both as "accomplished" and "extremely passionate about the subjects that they teach." and the majority are "very involved and want to know you personally." Students are proud to share their own relationships: "I'm actually friends with my English professor and I've only been in class with him for a semester so far." Another divulges, "I was struggling financially and had professors email me over the summer to help me find a way to get back." This isn't just an "enjoyable [academic] environment" either; there's a sense that "when people leave here, they are prepared to get a job and do well."

Life

Gordon is a school that's always humming with some sort of activity, especially on Mondays, Wednesdays, and Fridays, where "you can find a good portion of [the] student body in chapel." Outside of that, the college sponsors numerous events like "waffle nights, student hosted dinners, coffeehouses, parties [and] game nights," and "sports are pretty popular on campus." (We've been told that "the quad is great for playing spikeball.") There's also a music department that "is very strong and holds a lot of performances," though it's not uncommon to stumble upon unofficial "chill house concerts or jam sessions." Of course, New England weather plays a fairly big role in dictating the activity schedule. "When it's warm everyone hammocks [and] when it snows everyone has snowball fights and builds snowmen." When the opportunity presents itself, undergrads enjoy exploring the "quaint New England coastal towns" that surround the campus, whether that's "to hike or spend a day at the beach," and of course nearby Boston makes for a good weekend getaway for those seeking out things like "museums or concerts." Overall, though, students note that campus life is "pretty tame": there are "some off-campus parties," but people "who drink [and] do drugs . . . are the exception and are in the minority."

Student Body

When asked about their peers, many individuals at Gordon gush that their classmates are "genuine and kind people" who really "care about how you are doing socially, academically, and spiritually." According to one undergrad, "I could pull aside any random person, tell them I'm having a bad day, and they would listen to me and care about me." Students also value that many of their peers "have a real, lived-out relationship with God." And though it frequently feels as though most students come from "Massachusetts or New England" and are "majority white, majority Christian," you'll also discover that "there are many countries and nationalities represented" among the student body as well. And while there's "not a lot of middle ground" between the very liberal and conservative points of view on campus, students take pride in everyone's ability to "enter into a curious and respectful conversation" when encountering someone who disagrees with them. Perhaps that's because at the end of the day, students find unity in being "committed to their education and goals" and gladly help "one another achieve academic success." Or maybe it's as simple as a shared desire to "work hard and Netflix hard."

GORDON COLLEGE

Financial Aid: 978-867-4246 • E-Mail: admissions@gordon.edu • Website: www.gordon.edu

THE PRINCETON REVIEW SAYS

Admissions

Very important factors considered include: rigor of secondary school record, academic GPA, application essay, standardized test scores, recommendation(s), interview, talent/ability, character/personal qualities, religious affiliation/commitment. *Important factors considered include:* class rank, extracurricular activities, volunteer work. *Other factors considered include:* alumni/ae relation, racial/ethnic status. ACT with or without writing accepted. SAT with or without Essay component accepted. High school diploma is required and GED is accepted. *Academic units required:* 4 English, 2 math, 2 science, 1 science lab, 2 foreign language, 2 social studies, 5 academic electives. *Academic units recommended:* 4 English, 3 math, 3 science, 1 science lab, 4 foreign language, 2 social studies, 5 academic electives.

Financial Aid

Students should submit: FAFSA. Priority filing deadline is 3/1. The Princeton Review suggests that all financial aid forms be submitted as soon as possible after October 1. *Need-based scholarships/grants offered:* College/university scholarship or grant aid from institutional funds; Federal Pell; Private scholarships; SEOG; State scholarships/grants. *Loan aid offered:* Direct PLUS loans; Direct Subsidized Stafford Loans; Direct Unsubsidized Stafford Loans. Applicants will be notified of awards on a rolling basis beginning 1/15. Federal Work-Study Program available. Institutional employment available.

The Inside Word

Admissions officers at Gordon College are on the hunt for applicants who display an intellectual curiosity and excitement for learning. You'll need to have earned solid grades and taken a strong college prep curriculum if you want to be a contender. Successful students also demonstrate commitment to Christian values. Finally, it's recommended that you sit for an interview if at all possible. This allows the college to get a better sense of who you are and provides you with the opportunity to see if the school is a good fit for you.

THE SCHOOL SAYS "..."

From the Admissions Office

"There are three core distinctions that—taken together—set Gordon College apart as a place that better prepares students for a greater purpose:

"Gordon's mission. Gordon graduates men and women distinguished by intellectual maturity and Christian character, committed to lives of service, and prepared for leadership worldwide. With a liberal arts education in the tradition of New England's best colleges, our students gain the qualities most sought by employers—the ability to think critically, reason analytically, communicate persuasively and—even more importantly—to act morally.

"The Gordon Commission. This is the essence of our experience—to stretch the mind, deepen the faith and elevate the contribution Gordon students and graduates make to the world around us. We stretch the mind through a challenging education that is both broad and deep, and one that offers the freedom to ask and explore tough questions. We deepen the faith by integrating Christian beliefs and practice into all aspects of our educational experience. We elevate the contribution—to the common good, to our communities, to developing the next generation of thoughtful Christian leaders—through programs and outreach that emphasize service over self and that span the globe.

"Gordon's Location. Boston is the global 'hub' of higher education—this is where the world comes to study. We are strategically located in the proximity of the cultural centers of education (Boston), finance (New York) and politics (Washington). Boston also has a reputation as a leader in developing talent—which means greater opportunity for students who study here."

SELECTIVITY

Admissions Rating	81
# of applicants	2,624
% of applicants accepted	74
% of acceptees attending	18

FRESHMAN PROFILE

Range SAT EBRW	540–660
Range SAT Math	520–650
Range SAT Composite	1070–1300
Range ACT Composite	21–30
# submitting SAT scores	310
% submitting SAT scores	87
# submitting ACT scores	81
% submitting ACT scores	23
Average HS GPA	3.6
% graduated top 10% of class	25
% graduated top 25% of class	51
% graduated top 50% of class	80

DEADLINES

Early action	
Deadline	12/1
Notification	12/15
Regular	
Priority	12/1
Deadline	8/1
Notification	Rolling, 8/15
Nonfall registration?	Yes

FINANCIAL FACTS

Financial Aid Rating	86
Annual tuition	$37,560
Room and board	$11,420
Required fees	$1,670
Books and supplies	$950
Average frosh need-based scholarship	$25,568
Average UG need-based scholarship	$23,073
% needy frosh rec. need-based scholarship or grant aid	100
% needy UG rec. need-based scholarship or grant aid	100
% needy frosh rec. non-need-based scholarship or grant aid	18
% needy UG rec. non-need-based scholarship or grant aid	15
% needy frosh rec. need-based self-help aid	80
% needy UG rec. need-based self-help aid	81
% frosh rec. any financial aid	99
% UG rec. any financial aid	98
% UG borrow to pay for school	66
Average cumulative indebtedness	$35,210
% frosh need fully met	22
% ugrads need fully met	19
Average % of frosh need met	77
Average % of ugrad need met	73

GOUCHER COLLEGE

Admissions Office, 2021 Dulaney Valley Road, Baltimore, MD 21204-2794 • Admissions: 410-337-6100 • Fax: 410-337-6354

CAMPUS LIFE

Quality of Life Rating	86
Fire Safety Rating	95
Green Rating	93
Type of school	Private
Environment	City

STUDENTS

Total undergrad enrollment	1,444
% male/female	31/69
% from out of state	65
% frosh from public high school	62
% frosh live on campus	94
% ugrads live on campus	93
# of fraternities	0
# of sororities	0
% African American	14
% Asian	4
% Caucasian	59
% Hispanic	9
% Native American	<1
% Pacific Islander	<1
% Two or more races	5
% Race and/or ethnicity unknown	4
% international	3
# of countries represented	27

SURVEY SAYS . . .

Lots of liberal students
Great library
Class discussions encouraged
Students environmentally aware
Active minority support groups

ACADEMICS

Academic Rating	83
% students graduating within 4 years	53
% students graduating within 6 years	62
Calendar	Semester
Student/faculty ratio	10:1
Profs interesting rating	90
Profs accessible rating	94
Most classes have 10–19 students.	

MOST POPULAR MAJORS

English Language and Literature, General;
Business Administration and Management,
General; Psychology, General

STUDENTS SAY ". . ."

Academics

The tiny and innovative Goucher College, located just outside of Baltimore, boasts a welcoming, collaborative learning environment, a 100 percent study abroad rate/requirement, and a liberal arts curriculum that focuses on the 3Rs of the Goucher education: strong student-faculty-peer Relationships, encouraging Resilience, and teaching students to Reflect. The school encourages its students "to be mindful of diverse perspectives" and to live outside of their comfort zones "so as to learn from those diverse perspectives." Students here are "curious to learn" and "thrive on engaging in deep conversation, and are not afraid to speak their minds." Small class sizes and a tight student-to-faculty ratio promote these conversations, and "discussion and critical thinking skills are built into every class so you learn or formulate an argument around a wide variety of issues."

As a way of easing the transition into college, Goucher also provides a course called First Year Experience (FYE) that every first-year student is required to take. During FYE, first-year students "meet with their mentor who was with them during orientation to talk about certain resources provided [at] Goucher for safety, and other subjects about racial identity and how we're getting acquainted with our new environment." As for regular classes, there are a ton of "very interesting" classes, and "it is easy to enroll in a class that is either full or that you don't have the prerequisites for." Professors receive high marks across the board; they get to know students on a personal level and are "invested in [their] unique reasoning for being a part of the department." They "want everyone to share their opinions and certain personal experiences that go along with the topic" at hand. "I know they see me first as a person, second as a student," says one happy student.

Life

The Goucher campus is "beautiful." When it's sunny, "a lot of students are outside doing homework, socializing, playing Frisbee, or doing various other physical activities." The school is full of "liberal, outspoken, quirky students" and dinners "can start out with you arriving with a friend, but you end up sitting with many different people and are stuck there for two hours." During the week, most people work and study ("lots of people use the library as a common place"), so the weekend "is when people hang out." Not a lot of students go off campus, so a lot of small groups and open mics form. Parties "aren't all that common."

Students subscribe to the idea that "a rising tide lifts all boats." One student explains, "There is no internal competition at Goucher, we all work together." There is also no Greek life and sports teams are not emphasized, but there are 20 Division III athletic teams, and one co-ed equestrian team. Activism is huge on campus, and if you are passionate about a cause, "there is usually a club or student union that is already organized, or students who are more than willing to start a club."

Student Body

The Goucher student body comprises "a symposium [of students] to do Socrates proud." Goucher students are "engaged, trust each other, and are brave enough to dialogue in a way most campuses don't seem to be anymore." The degree of political openness here is "only left-looking," and this "delightfully weird" group tends to include "alternative, creative, artistic people who aren't afraid to express themselves." Most students are middle to upper-middle class and from the East Coast. There's an active community on campus and the Center for Race, Equity, and Identity supports people of color (POC) movements and LGBTQAI events. Keeping it in their own backyard, students love to help and "do their best to give back to their Baltimore and local community."

GOUCHER COLLEGE

Financial Aid: 410-337-6141 • E-Mail: admissions@goucher.edu • Website: www.goucher.edu

THE PRINCETON REVIEW SAYS

Admissions

Very important factors considered include: rigor of secondary school record, academic GPA. *Important factors considered include:* application essay, recommendation(s), extracurricular activities, talent/ability. *Other factors considered include:* class rank, standardized test scores, interview, character/personal qualities, first generation, alumni/ae relation, geographical residence, state residency, racial/ethnic status, work experience, level of applicant's interest. ACT with or without writing accepted. SAT with or without Essay component accepted. High school diploma is required and GED is accepted. *Academic units required:* 4 English, 3 math, 2 science, 2 science labs, 2 foreign language, 3 social studies, 2 academic electives. *Academic units recommended:* 4 English, 4 math, 3 science, 3 science labs, 4 foreign language, 3 social studies, 2 academic electives.

Financial Aid

Students should submit: FAFSA. Priority filing deadline is 2/1. The Princeton Review suggests that all financial aid forms be submitted as soon as possible after October 1. *Need-based scholarships/grants offered:* College/university scholarship or grant aid from institutional funds; Federal Pell; Private scholarships; SEOG; State scholarships/grants. *Loan aid offered:* Direct PLUS loans; Direct Subsidized Stafford Loans; Direct Unsubsidized Stafford Loans. Applicants will be notified of awards on a rolling basis beginning 12/15. Federal Work-Study Program available. Institutional employment available.

The Inside Word

Goucher College is the first college in the nation to create an application option requesting student-submitted videos as the decisive factor for admission. Students may choose not to submit transcripts, standardized test scores, and other traditional application materials. Instead, applicants can send Goucher a straightforward, two-minute video about how they see themselves flourishing at the college.

THE SCHOOL SAYS "..."

From the Admissions Office

"Goucher College, a leader in the liberal arts, is dedicated to providing a multidisciplinary, international education, and preparing students for the jobs of the future. A Goucher education focuses on the 3Rs: helping students develop strong faculty and peer relationships, encouraging resilience, and teaching students to reflect upon their cognitive styles so they can become true lifelong learners.

"The selection process at Goucher is individualized, and members of the admissions committee pay particularly close attention not only to students' academic development, but also to their personal qualities, talents, interests, and extracurricular involvement—qualifications that may not be reflected in standardized test scores, which are optional in Goucher's admissions process.

"The application process differs for traditional first-year students, transfer students, international students, homeschoolers, students eligible for the Maryland Scholars Program, and non-traditional undergraduates, so be sure to check what you need to include in your complete application to be considered for admission.

"If you don't think the traditional application process enables you to fully tell your story, consider the Goucher Video Application (GVA). The GVA components include: a short video (no more than two minutes), a digital application, a signed statement of academic integrity, and two works from your high school years (one of which must be a graded writing assignment)."

SELECTIVITY
Admissions Rating	77
# of applicants	3,474
% of applicants accepted	79
% of acceptees attending	15
# offered a place on the wait list	69
% accepting a place on wait list	78
% admitted from wait list	20
# of early decision applicants	33
% accepted early decision	76

FRESHMAN PROFILE
Range SAT EBRW	550–660
Range SAT Math	500–600
Range ACT Composite	23–29
# submitting SAT scores	279
% submitting SAT scores	66
# submitting ACT scores	144
% submitting ACT scores	34
Average HS GPA	3.1
% graduated top 10% of class	28
% graduated top 25% of class	54
% graduated top 50% of class	78

DEADLINES
Early decision	
Deadline	11/15
Notification	12/15
Early action	
Deadline	12/1
Notification	2/1
Nonfall registration?	No

FINANCIAL FACTS
Financial Aid Rating	87
Annual tuition	$43,412
Room and board	$14,506
Required fees	$888
Books and supplies	$1,200
Average frosh need-based scholarship	$36,284
Average UG need-based scholarship	$34,719
% needy frosh rec. need-based scholarship or grant aid	100
% needy UG rec. need-based scholarship or grant aid	100
% needy frosh rec. non-need-based scholarship or grant aid	16
% needy UG rec. non-need-based scholarship or grant aid	13
% needy frosh rec. need-based self-help aid	82
% needy UG rec. need-based self-help aid	86
% frosh rec. any financial aid	100
% UG rec. any financial aid	95
% UG borrow to pay for school	59
Average cumulative indebtedness	$28,321
% frosh need fully met	27
% ugrads need fully met	22
Average % of frosh need met	85
Average % of ugrad need met	82

GRINNELL COLLEGE

1227 Park Street, Grinnell, IA 50112-1690 • Admissions: 641-269-3600 • Fax: 641-269-4800

STUDENTS SAY "..."

Academics

A commitment to the common good is the overarching theme of Grinnell College, a private liberal arts school in Iowa. With "an articulated commitment to social responsibility," students can choose from more than five hundred courses each year and more than eighty study abroad options. "Academics here are difficult," but "classes are also in-depth and engaging" and "Grinnell has great support systems" should you find any course to be too challenging. And while professors "may make you work hard, they are just as committed to helping you as you are to trying." They have "a deep understanding of both their subject material and how to teach it" and are "willing to take substantial time to make sure individual students are keeping up." Many classes are based on "engaging, thought-provoking discussion" (including language classes) and professors "know how to pivot any student response for productive discussion," often incorporating creative learning methods to do so. "My political science class featured extensive political theory games run by the professor [such as] designing nations, playing as competing social movements, [and] trying to keep others from polluting common resources," says a student. Each professor "lets their personality shine through lectures and class discussion," and "you will [quickly] learn which professors speak to your interests, and you will likely stick with them."

Life

There are "lots of niche interests" here and there's a club for almost every one of them—there's even "Nerf at Noyce, which is the club dedicated to spending Friday nights in the enormous science building playing giant games with Nerf guns." With options like that, "basically every student is involved in some extracurricular activities." However, "studying will take a good portion of the weekdays" at this "always busy" school, so "fun is usually reserved for the weekends, which are full of socializing and club activities." Students note that when it's warmer out, "students can be seen LARPing [live action role-playing] outside on the field, or playing Frisbee with a group of friends." Outside of those on-campus activities, "you better be creative and active in searching for/creating your own fun, because Grinnell is no metropolis." And while there aren't a lot of events in Grinnell, "there are a variety of locations off campus (pubs, bars, bowling alleys, farms, restaurants, and parks)" where students can also decompress.

Student Body

This is a "motivated, vibrant, interesting and interested, and ... very, very smart" group of students. On top of being "unpretentious and down-to-earth," they also tend "to be passionately [in favor of] social justice." In pursuit of that, Grinnellians are "very curious people" and "are usually busy and working on some combination of academic and extracurricular projects." With a "common interest of learning and being intellectually stimulated as well as being critical of societal practices and other big picture problems occurring today," this is a "very inclusive environment" where "resistance to unique expression is often looked down upon." To that extent, "all students are invited to any on-campus or off-campus event." One student says, "Everyone can find their tribe here." Another puts the student body in perspective: "There [must] be something different about you if you're willing to trek to rural Iowa for your undergrad education."

Financial Aid: 641-269-3250 • E-Mail: admission@grinnell.edu • Website: www.grinnell.edu

THE PRINCETON REVIEW SAYS

Admissions

Very important factors considered include: rigor of secondary school record, class rank, academic GPA, recommendation(s). *Important factors considered include:* application essay, standardized test scores, extracurricular activities, talent/ability. *Other factors considered include:* interview, character/personal qualities, first generation, alumni/ae relation, geographical residence, state residency, racial/ethnic status, volunteer work, work experience, level of applicant's interest. ACT with or without writing accepted. SAT with or without Essay component accepted. High school diploma is required and GED is accepted. *Academic units recommended:* 4 English, 4 math, 3 science, 3 science labs, 3 foreign language, 3 social studies, 3 history.

Financial Aid

Students should submit: CSS/Financial Aid PROFILE; FAFSA; Noncustodial PROFILE. Priority filing deadline is 1/15. The Princeton Review suggests that all financial aid forms be submitted as soon as possible after October 1. *Need-based scholarships/grants offered:* College/university scholarship or grant aid from institutional funds; Federal Pell; Private scholarships; SEOG; State scholarships/grants. *Loan aid offered:* Direct PLUS loans; Direct Subsidized Stafford Loans; Direct Unsubsidized Stafford Loans. Applicants will be notified of awards on or about 4/1. Federal Work-Study Program available. Institutional employment available.

The Inside Word

Grinnell's admissions process is quite straightforward. Students must be able to thrive academically as well as demonstrate an ability to take an active role in their education because you will be responsible for co-creating your curriculum with an advisor, and you'll have to find your voice in a self-governing residential community. Grinnell is extremely selective, so you'll have to give it your all. An interview isn't required, but it is highly recommended to complete one anyway.

THE SCHOOL SAYS "..."

From the Admissions Office

"Grinnell College is a place where independence of thought and social conscience are instilled. Grinnell is a college with the resources of a school ten times its size, a faculty that reads like a Who's Who of Teaching, and a learning environment where debate does not end in the classroom and often begins in the dining hall.

"Grinnellians are committed to learning, respect for themselves and others, contributing to global social good, willing collaboration, and the courage to try.

"We look for students who show strong potential, have the courage to try new things, demonstrate a willingness to speak out and share their opinions, and bring different perspectives to our international campus in the middle of Iowa. Grinnell College is filled with students who are serious about learning but are not always serious."

SELECTIVITY

Admissions Rating	96
# of applicants	8,004
% of applicants accepted	23
% of acceptees attending	25
# offered a place on the wait list	1,633
% accepting a place on wait list	48
% admitted from wait list	1
# of early decision applicants	348
% accepted early decision	57

FRESHMAN PROFILE

Range SAT EBRW	670–740
Range SAT Math	700–790
Range ACT Composite	31–34
# submitting SAT scores	252
% submitting SAT scores	55
# submitting ACT scores	207
% submitting ACT scores	45
% graduated top 10% of class	62
% graduated top 25% of class	87
% graduated top 50% of class	98

DEADLINES

Early decision	
Deadline	11/15
Notification	12/15
Other ED Deadline	1/1
Other ED Notification	1/31
Regular	
Deadline	1/15
Notification	Rolling, 4/1
Nonfall registration?	No

FINANCIAL FACTS

Financial Aid Rating	99
Annual tuition	$56,188
Room and board	$13,864
Required fees	$492
Books and supplies	$900
Average frosh need-based scholarship	$46,609
Average UG need-based scholarship	$45,482
% needy frosh rec. need-based scholarship or grant aid	100
% needy UG rec. need-based scholarship or grant aid	100
% needy frosh rec. non-need-based scholarship or grant aid	17
% needy UG rec. non-need-based scholarship or grant aid	14
% needy frosh rec. need-based self-help aid	83
% needy UG rec. need-based self-help aid	86
% frosh rec. any financial aid	86
% UG rec. any financial aid	86
% UG borrow to pay for school	61
Average cumulative indebtedness	$20,093
% frosh need fully met	100
% ugrads need fully met	100
Average % of frosh need met	100
Average % of ugrad need met	100

GROVE CITY COLLEGE

100 Campus Drive, Grove City, PA 16127-2104 • Admissions: 724-458-2100 • Fax: 724-458-3395

CAMPUS LIFE

Quality of Life Rating	**89**
Fire Safety Rating	**94**
Green Rating	**63**
Type of school	Private
Environment	Village

STUDENTS

Total undergrad enrollment	2,186
% male/female	53/47
% from out of state	44
% frosh from public high school	60
% frosh live on campus	98
% ugrads live on campus	95
# of fraternities (% ugrad men join)	10 (17)
# of sororities (% ugrad women join)	8 (20)
% African American	1
% Asian	2
% Caucasian	92
% Hispanic	1
% Native American	<1
% Pacific Islander	0
% Two or more races	3
% Race and/or ethnicity unknown	<1
% international	1
# of countries represented	11

SURVEY SAYS . . .

Lots of conservative students
Students are happy
Classroom facilities are great
Lab facilities are great
Career services are great
Internships are widely available
Students are friendly
Students are very religious
Easy to get around campus
Very little drug use
Intramural sports are popular
Theater is popular
Active student government

ACADEMICS

Academic Rating	**85**
% students returning for sophomore year	90
% students graduating within 4 years	82
% students graduating within 6 years	1
Calendar	Semester
Student/faculty ratio	13:1
Profs interesting rating	91
Profs accessible rating	96
Most classes have 10–19 students.	
Most lab/discussion sessions have 10–19 students.	

MOST POPULAR MAJORS

Computer Science; Mechanical Engineering; Accounting

STUDENTS SAY "..."

Academics

Located an hour north of Pittsburgh, Pennsylvania, Grove City College provides a Christ-centered, non-sectarian environment in which students and faculty "create a vibrant and uplifting community that encourages one another to live to the fullest in a Christ-like manner." The school desires to see students excel inside and outside the classroom, integrating Christ "into all aspects of education and a career for the future," and it "challenges ... students to grow in all aspects—intellectually, spiritually, emotionally, and athletically." And, this philosophy works: "The majority of the students here apply their spiritual relationship with God to all activities on campus, whether it be academic or social." The low cost of tuition is just gravy, as is the strong alumni network and "really good reputation with employers."

The professors at Grove City "vary from department to department" but on the whole they are "engaging, approachable, and very knowledgeable about the course material" and "willing to personally invest in the students." Many expect a lot from their students and assign a heavy workload, but people find the academics to be "challenging, but not suffocating." The "very intelligent, friendly, and available" faculty usually "have extensive office hours and are more than willing to help [students]." Current students say their instructors maintain "a very open dialogue about various beliefs," and "challenge [students] to ask hard questions" both in an area of study and on a more personal level.

Life

Since Grove City College is located in a relatively remote area of Western Pennsylvania, most activities are done on-campus, but "for a small town, there's lots to do," including plenty of places to eat, a movie theater, and ice cream shops. Days at Grove City are pretty typical, spent "going to class, studying, catching up with friends over meals, movie and game nights on the weekends, dances, campus ministries, [and] club activities." Many are also on sports teams, especially "intramural sports teams like volleyball, basketball, Frisbee, [and] soccer," plus students also "like to hang out in our recreational room or go bowling." Forget about Footloose: there is actually "a great deal of dancing and singing here," and people like to "go for walks when the weather is nice, play games, watch movies, do sports, and simply talk together." Indeed, many lunches "devolve into an ideological, theological, or philosophical discussion." Grove City students are proud of their involvement in the world around them through "various academic lectures, Warriors (an hour-long worship service), and screenings of political debates"; these events, though not required, are "extremely well-attended." Likewise, there "are many great groups on campus that provide community service or benefit for a good cause." Intervisitation between male and female dorms is "limited," and this is in no way a party school.

Student Body

As might be expected, those who come to Grove City are "largely Christian kids," who are "generally polite and law-abiding," and the student body tends to swing conservative or moderate politically. According to students, the college "avoids being ... restrictive or closed-minded." "Grove City students know what they believe, but are open to discussion," a student explains. These students collectively provide "the most friendly atmosphere" many have ever been a part of. "Peers I've never even met smile at me as I pass them on the sidewalk," describes one happy student. The college as a whole "welcomes students with open arms," and it is very easy to find "a community that encourages and inspires one another." There are a fair number of type A personalities here: Grove City students are "hardworking and highly motivated to do well," and "many people over-commit themselves to the various on-campus groups."

Financial Aid: 724-458-3300 • E-Mail: admissions@gcc.edu • Website: www.gcc.edu

THE PRINCETON REVIEW SAYS

Admissions

Very important factors considered include: rigor of secondary school record, academic GPA, application essay, standardized test scores, interview, character/personal qualities, level of applicant's interest. *Important factors considered include:* recommendation(s), extracurricular activities. *Other factors considered include:* class rank, talent/ability, first generation, alumni/ae relation, geographical residence, state residency, religious affiliation/commitment, racial/ethnic status, volunteer work, work experience. ACT with or without writing accepted. SAT with or without Essay component accepted. High school diploma is required and GED is accepted. *Academic units required:* 4 English, 3 math, 3 science, 2 history. *Academic units recommended:* 4 English, 3 math, 3 science, 2 science labs, 2 foreign language, 3 social studies, 2 history.

Financial Aid

Students should submit: Institution's own financial aid form. The Princeton Review suggests that all financial aid forms be submitted as soon as possible after October 1. *Need-based scholarships/grants offered:* College/university scholarship or grant aid from institutional funds; Private scholarships; State scholarships/grants. Applicants will be notified of awards on a rolling basis beginning 3/1. Institutional employment available.

The Inside Word

Gaining entrance to Grove City College is difficult and highly competitive. Students must have outstanding personal characteristics, and they need to be prepared for a strenuous but workable course load. Christian values are of utmost importance at Grove City College, and the school values students who seek out surroundings based on those principles. Interviews and letters of recommendation are highly valued as components of the admission process.

THE SCHOOL SAYS "..."

From the Admissions Office

"Students flourish at Grove City College because faith is its foundation. From the classroom to the practice fields, from the dining halls to the dormitories, students seek to understand how faith influences their daily activities and ultimately how they might use their abilities to serve others. The College equips students to discover and pursue their unique callings through an academically excellent and Christ-centered learning and living experience.

"The cornerstone of our excellent education is our incredible community of learners—students, faculty and staff who are committed to pursuing knowledge and truth for the advancement of the common good. Surrounded by peers and mentors who sharpen them, students develop into leaders of the highest proficiency guided by these core values: faithfulness, excellence, community, stewardship, and independence.

"We offer students and families an amazing value. Tuition and costs run about half the national average before scholarships and financial aid. Unlike the vast majority of colleges and universities, we do not practice tuition discounting—tuition price is the same for every student and no student unwittingly subsidizes another student's tuition through artificial scholarships.

"Our nationally ranked Career Services Office begins working with students before they arrive as freshmen, ensuring that by the time they graduate, they will be prepared not only to pursue a fulfilling career but for a lifetime of professional success."

SELECTIVITY

Admissions Rating	86
# of applicants	1,697
% of applicants accepted	79
% of acceptees attending	36
# offered a place on the wait list	56
% accepting a place on wait list	95
% admitted from wait list	38
# of early decision applicants	249
% accepted early decision	96

FRESHMAN PROFILE

Range SAT EBRW	576–691
Range SAT Math	554–693
Range ACT Composite	23–30
# submitting SAT scores	410
% submitting SAT scores	84
# submitting ACT scores	182
% submitting ACT scores	37
Average HS GPA	3.7
% graduated top 10% of class	39
% graduated top 25% of class	84
% graduated top 50% of class	93

DEADLINES

Early decision	
Deadline	11/1
Notification	12/15
Other ED Deadline	12/1
Other ED Notification	1/15
Regular	
Deadline	3/20
Notification	4/15
Nonfall registration?	Yes

APPLICANTS ALSO LOOK AT AND OFTEN PREFER

Calvin College; Cedarville University; Geneva College; Liberty University; Messiah College; Penn State University Park; Wheaton College (IL); University of Pittsburgh—Pittsburgh Campus; Westminster College (PA); Saint Vincent College

AND SOMETIMES PREFER

Duquesne University; Gordon College; Slippery Rock University of Pennsylvania; Houghton College; Youngstown State University; Covenant College; John Carroll University; Allegheny College; Robert Morris University

FINANCIAL FACTS

Financial Aid Rating	82
Annual tuition	$18,930
Room and board	$10,310
Books and supplies	$1,000
Average frosh need-based scholarship	$8,385
Average UG need-based scholarship	$7,999
% needy frosh rec. need-based scholarship or grant aid	100
% needy UG rec. need-based scholarship or grant aid	100
% needy frosh rec. non-need-based scholarship or grant aid	14
% needy UG rec. non-need-based scholarship or grant aid	7
% needy frosh rec. need-based self-help aid	60
% needy UG rec. need-based self-help aid	63
% frosh rec. any financial aid	79
% UG rec. any financial aid	80
% UG borrow to pay for school	57
Average cumulative indebtedness	$41,690
% frosh need fully met	14
% ugrads need fully met	8
Average % of frosh need met	52
Average % of ugrad need met	49

GUILFORD COLLEGE

5800 West Friendly Avenue, Greensboro, NC 27410 • Admissions: 336-316-2100 • Fax: 336-316-2954

CAMPUS LIFE
Quality of Life Rating	89
Fire Safety Rating	94
Green Rating	95
Type of school	Private
Affiliation	Quaker
Environment	City

STUDENTS
Total undergrad enrollment	1,493
% male/female	46/54
% from out of state	29
% frosh from public high school	75
% frosh live on campus	89
% ugrads live on campus	74
# of fraternities	0
# of sororities	0
% African American	25
% Asian	3
% Caucasian	56
% Hispanic	9
% Native American	<1
% Pacific Islander	<1
% Two or more races	4
% Race and/or ethnicity unknown	1
% international	1
# of countries represented	10

SURVEY SAYS . . .
Students are happy
Lab facilities are great
Career services are great
Class discussions encouraged
Students are friendly
Diverse student types interact on campus
Students get along with local community
Students environmentally aware
Easy to get around campus
College radio is popular

ACADEMICS
Academic Rating	85
% students returning for sophomore year	66
% students graduating within 4 years	47
% students graduating within 6 years	61
Calendar	Semester
Student/faculty ratio	12:1
Profs interesting rating	93
Profs accessible rating	95

Most classes have 10–19 students.
Most lab/discussion sessions have 10–19 students.

STUDENTS SAY "..."

Academics

Guilford's legendarily "accepting culture" arises through the incorporation of a number of core tenets that include "diversity, equality, community, stewardship, etc." The school is "a place where you can express yourself free from judgment," and "impacts every aspect of your life and continues to carry you as part of its family even after you graduate." Students are given the opportunity to make all of their own choices, and the school works at "providing support for those decisions," and heavily promotes the idea "that doing things the hard way is usually worth it."

The Quaker college is known for being green (to put it mildly), and the administration works to raise "student and individual awareness of the environment and everyday life through education and service learning." The level of engagement of the students is matched only by the school's willingness to listen; student involvement is in everything from policy changes to food options, and "can be one person's efforts or many." "I know someone who campaigned for getting coffee in the cafeteria's ice cream selection, and this year we had a trial run that seems to have gone over well," says a sophomore. Still, a few students do think the administration could let up on "parenting the students."

Professors are able to "create an environment that invites discussion of materials from different perspectives" that "[pushes] and [supports] you at the same time." The "intensity of academic learning" means that "your absence in a class does not go unnoticed," unsurprising at a place where teachers are called by their first name ("which is really awesome"). The small scale class sizes "really allow for individual attention and academic growth." Most classrooms are arranged with the desks in a circle and the classes are "highly interactive"; every class "is filled with questions for the class to answer, even simple questions."

Life

Fun at this "socially intriguing" college comes in many forms: walking in the woods, hiking, community service, the local art and music scene. "It's always felt like more of a village than an institution," says one student. Relaxation is taken very seriously after a week of hard work (Guilford is "writing heavy" and "the library and its resources are used a great deal"), and "lying down by the lake and playing music or watching movies with friends is almost mandatory." Bars in Greensboro are also an option, but if students can't get there "the school does a good job at hosting activities around campus, which can help the slower weekends." There is admittedly "a lot of weed, but it's totally fine if you aren't into smoking or drinking."

People on this "beautiful" campus are very socially and politically aware, and "someone … is always planning protests or creating petitions." Food options are a sore spot for Guilford students, and "there's also sometimes an athletic divide." Students are "really active" in groups and organizations, and there is "lots of talk of oppression, gender issues, and race in the social sciences and humanities."

Student Body

This is one "funky community of diverse people," all of whom "seem to share some appreciation for the outdoors and nuttier aspects of life." "Hippies or athletes" covers the majority of the student body (as does "liberal"), and there are many "refreshingly weird individuals" who've "taken their time at Guilford as an opportunity to redefine themselves." "We color outside of the lines in innovative and interesting ways," says one student. Friend groups tend to be in cliques, but are "still very friendly with other groups"; as one junior puts it, "There's a lot of varying interests but some wires tend to be the same across the board … like being culturally aware, or fighting against the oppression of minorities."

Financial Aid: 336-316-2410 • E-Mail: admission@guilford.edu • Website: https://www.guilford.edu

THE PRINCETON REVIEW SAYS

Admissions

Important factors considered include: rigor of secondary school record, class rank, academic GPA, application essay, standardized test scores, character/personal qualities. *Other factors considered include:* recommendation(s), interview, extracurricular activities, talent/ability, first generation, alumni/ae relation, geographical residence, state residency, religious affiliation/commitment, racial/ethnic status, work experience. ACT with or without writing accepted. SAT with or without Essay component accepted. High school diploma is required and GED is accepted. *Academic units recommended:* 4 English, 3 math, 3 science, 2 foreign language, 3 social studies.

Financial Aid

Students should submit: FAFSA; Institution's own financial aid form. Priority filing deadline is 2/15. The Princeton Review suggests that all financial aid forms be submitted as soon as possible after October 1. *Need-based scholarships/grants offered:* College/university scholarship or grant aid from institutional funds; Federal Pell; Private scholarships; SEOG; State scholarships/grants. *Loan aid offered:* Direct PLUS loans; Direct Subsidized Stafford Loans; Direct Unsubsidized Stafford Loans. Applicants will be notified of awards on a rolling basis beginning 3/1. Federal Work-Study Program available. Institutional employment available.

The Inside Word

Getting into Guilford College goes beyond the numbers. Guilford is looking for students who demonstrate strong drive and personal motivation. Applicants to the school should have a solid high school record and good extracurricular activities (preferably of the tree-hugging and/or varsity sports variety). While a Quaker connection couldn't hurt, the school is more interested in your character and personal qualities and level of interest in the school. The admissions essay is your chance to make your case.

THE SCHOOL SAYS "..."

From the Admissions Office

"Guilford is proud to be included for the twenty-eighth consecutive year in The Princeton Review's *Best Colleges* edition. Guilford can best be described by its academic rigor, preparation for graduate school and careers, and its commitment to service in a caring, socially aware and supportive community.

"This is a campus that celebrates all walks of life. Guilford brings together students from many different religious, socioeconomic, geographic, and ethnic backgrounds. You can be yourself here and that's a great feeling. Open-mindedness is embraced, especially in the classrooms, living spaces, and social settings on campus where you will challenge others and be challenged yourself.

"There is no stereotypical Guilford student. Our students have many passions including athletics and intramurals, community service, social justice and multiculturalism. However the bond that ties them together is the academic curriculum that prepares them for life and a career. The Guilford experience is truly a transformative one."

SELECTIVITY

Admissions Rating	73
# of applicants	1,865
% of applicants accepted	91
% of acceptees attending	20
# of early decision applicants	18
% accepted early decision	89

FRESHMAN PROFILE

Range SAT EBRW	440–585
Range SAT Math	463–558
Range ACT Composite	19–25
# submitting SAT scores	22
% submitting SAT scores	6
# submitting ACT scores	131
% submitting ACT scores	38
Average HS GPA	3.2
% graduated top 10% of class	13
% graduated top 25% of class	32
% graduated top 50% of class	66

DEADLINES

Early decision	
Deadline	11/1
Other ED Deadline	1/15
Early action	
Deadline	12/1
Notification	12/15
Regular	
Priority	11/15
Notification	Rolling, 1/1
Nonfall registration?	Yes

FINANCIAL FACTS

Financial Aid Rating	89
Annual tuition	$37,920
Room and board	$11,800
Required fees	$830
Books and supplies	$1,650
Average frosh need-based scholarship	$13,608
Average UG need-based scholarship	$11,289
% needy frosh rec. need-based scholarship or grant aid	100
% needy UG rec. need-based scholarship or grant aid	97
% needy frosh rec. non-need-based scholarship or grant aid	100
% needy UG rec. non-need-based scholarship or grant aid	83
% needy frosh rec. need-based self-help aid	95
% needy UG rec. need-based self-help aid	94
% frosh rec. any financial aid	98
% UG rec. any financial aid	86
% UG borrow to pay for school	70
Average cumulative indebtedness	$39,658
% frosh need fully met	32
% ugrads need fully met	34
Average % of frosh need met	88
Average % of ugrad need met	91

HAMILTON COLLEGE

Office of Admission, Clinton, NY 13323 • Admissions: 315-859-4421 • Fax: 315-859-4457

CAMPUS LIFE

Quality of Life Rating	87
Fire Safety Rating	92
Green Rating	60*
Type of school	Private
Environment	Rural

STUDENTS

Total undergrad enrollment	1,913
% male/female	47/53
% from out of state	72
% frosh from public high school	60
% frosh live on campus	100
% ugrads live on campus	100
# of fraternities (% ugrad men join)	8 (21)
# of sororities (% ugrad women join)	4 (15)
% African American	4
% Asian	7
% Caucasian	64
% Hispanic	10
% Native American	<1
% Pacific Islander	0
% Two or more races	5
% Race and/or ethnicity unknown	4
% international	7
# of countries represented	49

SURVEY SAYS . . .

Students always studying
Students are happy
Classroom facilities are great
Lab facilities are great
Great library
Great financial aid
Students aren't religious
Lots of beer drinking
Campus newspaper is popular
College radio is popular

ACADEMICS

Academic Rating	94
% students returning for sophomore year	94
% students graduating within 4 years	89
% students graduating within 6 years	93
Calendar	Semester
Student/faculty ratio	9:1
Profs interesting rating	94
Profs accessible rating	96

Most classes have 10–19 students.
Most lab/discussion sessions have 10–19 students.

MOST POPULAR MAJORS

Mathematics; Economics; Political Science and Government

STUDENTS SAY "..."

Academics

Hamilton College in upstate New York is steeped in the ideals of intellectual pursuit, allowing students to plot their course of study through an open curriculum under the guidance of an academic advisor. Critical thinking is one core skill developed, though, and that's accomplished through classroom projects and methods like "writing a mock grant proposal for biology" or "student-led discussions where we bring in a topic … and tie it in to the theories being taught in class." Finding topics that are personal draws is a crucial element that makes Hamilton tick, and students often "pursue interests that don't seem traditionally compatible" on the surface. However, this allows students "to enjoy [their] major while being able to supplement [it] with other classes" of interest. "The open curriculum gives you freedom and responsibility over what and how you want to learn," boasts one student. Others say "the ability to mix and match your interests to create your major is incredibly liberating." Hamilton is truly "a living and learning community where learning happens outside the classroom."

The academics at Hamilton would be nothing without professors who are "highly invested in their field and … bring that energy to their classrooms." They "make their expectations clear," "will challenge students to produce reasonable yet impassioned results," and "are open to new opinions and discussions, but obviously have a plan for discussion-based classes." Those discussions are still manageable due to Hamilton's small class sizes—which also means "it's almost impossible to slide under the radar." And there are even more positives to those small classes: They "[give] you such an advantage when taking difficult classes" because students can "get one-on-one interaction during office hours or even during class."

Life

Hamilton's campus is separated into what students call "a Light Side and a Dark Side," and students tend to socially segregate to one or the other. "The Light Side is where the athletes and Greek life participants" can be found, and the Dark Side is where the "artsy, hipster, and alternative" students will hang out. There is "no animosity between lightsiders and darksiders, except for a few jokes here and there," and "most of the time students utilize this dynamic to explore new classes and friends." Opportunities for those new experiences abound here since the school features "an incredible array of student clubs and organizations"—there are "lots of activities happening all the time." On weekends, different student clubs will typically have an all-campus event—"a dance club might have a night where they teach people how to salsa, a Harry Potter club might host a Yule Ball"—and students definitely enjoy a party, although attendance is "pretty optional."

Many students "love the outdoors and that is a huge culture here." When the weather is favorable, students "often sit outside for meals or in Adirondack chairs scattered around campus doing work." Those looking for things to do off campus can rest easy: Students (only those sophomore year and above are permitted to have vehicles on campus) who have cars can "go off campus to local restaurants, to see movies, or to go bowling or shopping," whereas those without "can use the jitney [shuttle service] which drives on a loop to all of these places."

Student Body

Hamilton has a "quintessential small, communal, and progressive liberal arts feel" that its students seek out and adore. The "weirdly nice" group here is "predominantly white and from the northeastern area" and has "a healthy sense of irreverence." The open curriculum tends to "attract a diverse set of interests and values among its student body," which makes this a "perpetually stimulating environment" where "everyone wants to contribute to campus." The social aspects of that contribution mean "everyone is looking to make friends" and is "very inclusive and welcoming." Life here is "very balanced" and students "generally know how to take a joke and make a joke." As one student sums it up: People here are "friendly and academic, but not cut-throat or competitive in any way."

Financial Aid: 800-859-4413 • E-Mail: admission@hamilton.edu • Website: www.hamilton.edu

THE PRINCETON REVIEW SAYS

Admissions

Very important factors considered include: rigor of secondary school record, class rank, academic GPA. *Important factors considered include:* application essay, standardized test scores (waived for 2021–22 entrance), recommendation(s), interview, character/personal qualities. *Other factors considered include:* extracurricular activities, talent/ability, first generation, alumni/ae relation, geographical residence, state residency, racial/ethnic status, volunteer work, work experience, level of applicant's interest. SAT, ACT, SAT Subject test, AP exams will be considered if submitted. High school diploma is required and GED is accepted. *Academic units recommended:* 4 English, 3 math, 3 science, 3 foreign language, 3 social studies.

Financial Aid

Students should submit: Business/Farm Supplement; CSS/Financial Aid PROFILE; FAFSA; Institution's own financial aid form; Noncustodial PROFILE. Priority filing deadline is 1/15. The Princeton Review suggests that all financial aid forms be submitted as soon as possible after October 1. *Need-based scholarships/grants offered:* College/university scholarship or grant aid from institutional funds; Federal Pell; Private scholarships; SEOG; State scholarships/grants. *Loan aid offered:* Direct PLUS loans; Direct Subsidized Stafford Loans; Direct Unsubsidized Stafford Loans. Applicants will be notified of awards on or about 4/1. Federal Work-Study Program available. Institutional employment available.

The Inside Word

Similar to any prestigious liberal arts schools, Hamilton takes a well-rounded, personal approach to admissions. They rely heavily on academic achievement and intellectual curiosity, but in a mission to create a talented and diverse incoming class, admissions officers also strive to attain a complete, accurate profile of each candidate. Standardized tests are required *(though waived for applicants for 2021–22 entrance due to COVID-19 pandemic)*, but students may choose which scores to submit from an approved menu that includes the ACT, SAT, and SAT Subject Tests (scores can even be submitted from sections across different tests). Relationships and fit matter a great deal at Hamilton, so the admission team strongly recommends that students interview either on or off campus, when possible. Also, all candidates have the opportunity to enhance their candidacy by submitting optional materials available to them in their personalized application portal.

THE SCHOOL SAYS "..."

From the Admissions Office

"There is no one Hamilton student, just as there is no one Hamilton experience, but the promise we make to our students is the same: At Hamilton, our open curriculum enables you to study what interests you, our welcoming and unpretentious student body will accept you for who you are and what you believe, and our devoted network of alumni and career center professionals will help you find your future. Our faculty will expect your full attention and participation academically, and you will learn to expect a lot from yourself.

"We are also committed to ensuring that a Hamilton education is available to all deserving students, so for those unable to pay our fees, we make an additional promise: We will review your application without considering your financial circumstances (which is known as 'need-blind' admission) and then, once you are admitted, we will meet your full demonstrated need for all four years.

"We ask you for a pledge in return: We expect you to work to your ability, be open to new ideas, and contribute your talents to our community."

SELECTIVITY

Admissions Rating	97
# of applicants	8,339
% of applicants accepted	16
% of acceptees attending	35
# offered a place on the wait list	1,934
% accepting a place on wait list	55
% admitted from wait list	2
# of early decision applicants	582
% accepted early decision	41

FRESHMAN PROFILE

Range SAT EBRW	670–740
Range SAT Math	700–780
Range SAT Composite	1410–1510
Range ACT Composite	32–34
# submitting SAT scores	196
% submitting SAT scores	41
# submitting ACT scores	187
% submitting ACT scores	40
% graduated top 10% of class	83
% graduated top 25% of class	96
% graduated top 50% of class	100

DEADLINES

Early decision	
Deadline	11/15
Notification	12/15
Other ED Deadline	1/1
Other ED Notification	2/15
Regular	
Deadline	1/1
Notification	4/1
Nonfall registration?	Yes

APPLICANTS ALSO LOOK AT AND OFTEN PREFER

Amherst College; Bowdoin College; Brown University; Dartmouth College; Middlebury College; Princeton University; Williams College

AND SOMETIMES PREFER

Colby College; Colgate University; Wesleyan University; Tufts University; Vassar College

FINANCIAL FACTS

Financial Aid Rating	97
Annual tuition	$57,930
Room and board	$14,860
Required fees	$580
Books and supplies	$1,000
Average frosh need-based scholarship	$50,238
Average UG need-based scholarship	$47,345
% needy frosh rec. need-based scholarship or grant aid	100
% needy UG rec. need-based scholarship or grant aid	100
% needy frosh rec. non-need-based scholarship or grant aid	0
% needy UG rec. non-need-based scholarship or grant aid	0
% needy frosh rec. need-based self-help aid	89
% needy UG rec. need-based self-help aid	80
% frosh rec. any financial aid	55
% UG rec. any financial aid	52
% UG borrow to pay for school	44
Average cumulative indebtedness	$17,292
% frosh need fully met	100
% ugrads need fully met	100
Average % of frosh need met	100
Average % of ugrad need met	100

HAMPDEN-SYDNEY COLLEGE

PO Box 667, Hampden-Sydney, VA 23943-0667 • Admissions: 434-223-6120 • Fax: 434-223-6346

STUDENTS SAY ". . ."

Academics

A storied men's college with the oldest private charter in the South, Hampden-Sydney College broadly states its intentions on the front gate: "Come here as youths so that you may leave as men." The academic offerings may be streamlined—there are just twenty-seven majors and twenty-five minors available to the 1,100 men who come here—but the college's required Rhetoric Program provides Olympic-level training in writing and speech, and the interdisciplinary Core Cultures program ensures students learn about the past from both a Western and a global cultures perspective. "My school is an academic power-house while at the same time having a guys' weekend all the time," sums up a student concisely. There is "an incredible alumni network" and the school's Honor Code allows the campus "to be a safe and secure place where we can learn and become better men and citizens." The "dynamic yet traditional" curriculum encourages students to challenge themselves "and to look deeper [rather than] just reading a text," and the college "excels in imparting [to] its students the ability to think critically." "There is no stupid argument; however, this is a properly supported and uninformed argument."

Hampden-Sydney College professors are "nothing short of excellent"; they are "eager to teach and they keep the class engaged." Classes are small, and professors "know all their students fairly well"; many live near or on campus and so "are easily accessible," and all "want to teach you all you can learn." Teachers "care deeply about each of their students," and recognize when someone is not present and "offer help repeatedly when they see that one is falling behind." If a student "is willing to accept a challenging road, he will be rewarded." Many professors operate their classes through the means of discussion or the Socratic method, and thanks to the faculty and staff, students "are provided with every opportunity to succeed and reach our potential." Hampden-Sydney College "really is unlike any other school out there and any student here will back that up."

Life

During most of the week and during the day, almost all students are attending classes or studying, but "on many Thursday, Friday, and Saturday nights, the parties are easy to find." "The social scene at this school is darn near ubiquitous," says one student. Academics take main priority, but there are many activities to do throughout the day "whether it be just throwing football outside the dorms or playing ping pong at the Tiger Inn." "No matter what you decide to do in your downtime, you definitely won't be bored," says a student. Many students are active in fraternity life on campus, and the school is also located in close proximity to other colleges and universities, which provides "opportunities for students to mix-up their routines and visit friends at other places." A large percentage of the school is active in outdoors programs on campus "such as fly fishing, skeet shooting, hunting, and the Outsiders Club."

Student Body

The young men that make up the Hampden-Sydney student body are "a brotherhood rather than a group of peers." These are "well-educated gentlemen" that are knowledgeable in the fields of "rhetoric, mathematics, economics, debate, history, politics, foreign language, sports, and partying." Everyone is "clean cut, normal, [has] manners," and "both honesty and politeness are not hard to come across." There is only one type of person who may feel left out here at Hampden-Sydney, and "that is someone who isn't willing to buy in and be for the boys." With such a close group, "there is little to no drama on campus." This "extraor-dinary" student body is "driven internally to attain their goals" but are not self-interested, instead holding each other accountable for their actions and "always moving forward by pushing our peers and ourselves."

Financial Aid: 434-223-6119 • E-Mail: hsapp@hsc.edu • Website: www.hsc.edu

THE PRINCETON REVIEW SAYS

Admissions

Very important factors considered include: rigor of secondary school record, academic GPA, application essay, standardized test scores, recommendation(s), character/personal qualities. *Important factors considered include:* class rank, extracurricular activities. *Other factors considered include:* interview, talent/ability, first generation, alumni/ae relation, volunteer work, work experience, level of applicant's interest. ACT with or without writing accepted. SAT with or without Essay component accepted. High school diploma is required and GED is accepted. *Academic units required:* 4 English, 3 math, 2 science, 1 science lab, 2 foreign language, 1 social studies, 1 history, 3 academic electives. *Academic units recommended:* 4 math, 3 science, 3 foreign language.

Financial Aid

Students should submit: FAFSA; State aid form. Priority filing deadline is 3/1. The Princeton Review suggests that all financial aid forms be submitted as soon as possible after October 1. *Need-based scholarships/grants offered:* College/university scholarship or grant aid from institutional funds; Federal Pell; Private scholarships; SEOG; State scholarships/grants. *Loan aid offered:* Direct PLUS loans; Direct Subsidized Stafford Loans; Direct Unsubsidized Stafford Loans. Applicants will be notified of awards on a rolling basis beginning 12/15. Federal Work-Study Program available. Institutional employment available.

The Inside Word

Hampden-Sydney provides undergrads with a competitive academic environment. Therefore, admissions officers are looking for students who enrolled in demanding college prep courses and earned solid grades. Moreover, on-campus interviews are highly encouraged; we recommend scheduling one if at all possible. Finally, those applicants who are convinced that Hampden-Sydney is their top choice should consider applying early.

THE SCHOOL SAYS "..."

From the Admissions Office

"Of the colleges you're considering, this one stands apart. Hampden-Sydney is a close-knit brotherhood of young men on a mission—not simply to get a great college education, but to have a coming-of-age experience that can lead them to more successful, more rewarding, and more joyful lives.

As a result, our men do well in the world, in a wide range of career fields. In recent years, this small school in Virginia has produced alumni with far-reaching impact, including the director of an Oscar-winning film, a U.S. ambassador, executives with YETI and the Denver Broncos, a leading hedge fund manager and part-owner of the Pittsburgh Steelers, a James Beard Award-winning chef, and many leaders, public servants, and innovators across every industry and field you can imagine.

How does this happen? Our Rhetoric Program teaches you the art of effective communication. Our expert faculty and experiential-focused liberal arts curriculum instill a wealth of knowledge and skills that make you more competitive for top jobs and graduate programs. And our renowned commitment to honor and character means that others know you're a man to be trusted.

This is a college for young men searching for something different, an experience that stands apart. They are looking for a richer experience than the usual because they are interested in a richer life than the usual. Through a combination of better learning, stronger character, and a lasting brotherhood, Hampden-Sydney enables young men to emerge more confident and capable than they could have ever dreamed."

SELECTIVITY

Admissions Rating	85
# of applicants	3,240
% of applicants accepted	59
% of acceptees attending	18
# of early decision applicants	166
% accepted early decision	45

FRESHMAN PROFILE

Range SAT EBRW	530–630
Range SAT Math	520–620
Range ACT Composite	21–27
# submitting SAT scores	302
% submitting SAT scores	88
# submitting ACT scores	102
% submitting ACT scores	30
Average HS GPA	3.5
% graduated top 10% of class	11
% graduated top 25% of class	22
% graduated top 50% of class	64

DEADLINES

Early decision	
Deadline	11/1
Notification	12/1
Early action	
Deadline	1/15
Notification	2/15
Regular	
Deadline	3/1
Notification	4/15
Nonfall registration?	Yes

APPLICANTS ALSO LOOK AT AND OFTEN PREFER
Virginia Polytechnic Institute and State University

AND SOMETIMES PREFER
The University of North Carolina at Chapel Hill; University of South Carolina—Columbia; James Madison University; North Carolina State University; Virginia Military Institute; University of Virginia

AND RARELY PREFER
Christopher Newport University; Randolph-Macon College; Virginia Commonwealth University

FINANCIAL FACTS

Financial Aid Rating	88
Annual tuition	$44,532
Room and board	$13,712
Required fees	$2,358
Books and supplies	$1,000
Average frosh need-based scholarship	$30,345
Average UG need-based scholarship	$30,385
% needy frosh rec. need-based scholarship or grant aid	100
% needy UG rec. need-based scholarship or grant aid	100
% needy frosh rec. non-need-based scholarship or grant aid	24
% needy UG rec. non-need-based scholarship or grant aid	20
% needy frosh rec. need-based self-help aid	75
% needy UG rec. need-based self-help aid	74
% frosh rec. any financial aid	99.4
% UG rec. any financial aid	99.6
% UG borrow to pay for school	67
Average cumulative indebtedness	$33,777
% frosh need fully met	29
% ugrads need fully met	26
Average % of frosh need met	80
Average % of ugrad need met	80

HAMPTON UNIVERSITY

Office of Admissions, Hampton, VA 23668 • Admissions: 757-727-5328 • Fax: 757-727-5095

CAMPUS LIFE

Quality of Life Rating	80
Fire Safety Rating	72
Green Rating	60*
Type of school	Private
Environment	City

STUDENTS

Total undergrad enrollment	3,714
% male/female	34/66
% from out of state	73
% frosh from public high school	90
% frosh live on campus	82
% ugrads live on campus	57
# of fraternities (% ugrad men join)	5 (5)
# of sororities (% ugrad women join)	4 (4)
% African American	95
% Asian	<1
% Caucasian	1
% Hispanic	1
% Native American	<1
% Pacific Islander	<1
% Two or more races	0
% Race and/or ethnicity unknown	<1
% international	0
# of countries represented	21

SURVEY SAYS . . .

Lots of liberal students
Students are very religious
Campus newspaper is popular

ACADEMICS

Academic Rating	75
% students returning for sophomore year	75
% students graduating within 4 years	40
% students graduating within 6 years	57
Calendar	Semester
Student/faculty ratio	14:1
Profs interesting rating	79
Profs accessible rating	85

Most classes have 50-99 students.
Most lab/discussion sessions have
10–19 students.

MOST POPULAR MAJORS

Biology, General; Psychology, General;
Journalism; Kinesiology

STUDENTS SAY "..."

Academics

Virginia's Hampton University is one of the world's top historically black universities, offering students a progressive education in business, the sciences, and the liberal arts. This "school of tradition, family values, and excellent education" is well-known for its focus on STEM programs and its five-year MBA program, and proudly forces its students to be at the top of their game. "My school exudes and strives for a standard of excellence in any and every aspect," says a junior political science major of the oft-quoted motto "The Standard of Excellence."

Professors "are at the top of their field," and the majority of the faculty members provide office hours "where students can have more one-to-one assistance" on lecture topics on which they may need more clarification. "My professors have not only been teachers in the classroom, but in my personal life as well," says a student. "I have been taught how to use the communication and research skills that I have obtained outside of the classroom." In addition, the university provides "a plethora of outside resources" such as paid internships, undergraduate research, and job shadowing opportunities.

The "historically rich" institution is "supportive of its legacy being upheld by all that pass through" while at the same time making individuals aware of their own legacies and "supporting them in their professional and academic endeavors through all available resources." Alumni connections abound in such an environment, and there are plenty of "excellent career planning tools," internships, and careers available to students "during and after their tenure at Hampton." There is "an immense amount of clout and history behind Hampton University's walls." Though the campus is undoubtedly "beautiful" (and sits right on the water), many agree that some of the facilities (especially the dorms) could use renovation. In recent years, three new dorms were constructed and historic halls were modernized.

Life

Hampton does an excellent job of "blending past traditions with modern times," and Homecoming and Spring Fest are two important events for Hampton. On the "closed" campus, there is an "unlimited [number] of activities for students to participate in." During Organization Week, the student center has a two hour "12–2" period, during which "students are able to be social during the day," and many students love to "catch a Friday movie" night there as well, or hang out with friends in the new waterfront dining hall.

Hampton is small and "not a college town," and since "the University is really the only thing around," having a car is useful. Monday through Friday campus life is "mostly academic and extracurricular," with students mostly focused on class and the various clubs that they may be involved in. On the weekends students attend on- and off-campus parties, or go to "kickbacks," which are "a more low key version of a party." "Student life is lacking as far as dorm life," so many students "often interact with the students from NSU, ODU, and William & Mary." For the most part, "everyone on campus has the same mindset, a unanimous goal, and that's to graduate and strive for a successful life."

Student Body

The typical student here is an African-American "go-getter" who is "trying to make something of themselves." He or she is "poised, considerate, and self-sufficient" and "knows how to act and dress in the appropriate setting and time." "Hampton students have a certain attitude about themselves, you can always tell a Hamptonian. Once you have been Hamptonized, there is no going back," explains one student cryptically. This "driven," "hardworking" crowd gets along fairly well, and there are no issues of isolation "unless one chooses that lifestyle." Students are almost without fail "outgoing and involved in many organizations within the school and the community."

Financial Aid: 757-727-5332 • E-Mail: admit@hamptonu.edu • Website: www.hamptonu.edu

THE PRINCETON REVIEW SAYS

Admissions

Very important factors considered include: rigor of secondary school record, academic GPA, application essay, character/personal qualities. *Important factors considered include:* class rank, recommendation(s). *Other factors considered include:* interview, extracurricular activities, talent/ability, volunteer work, work experience, level of applicant's interest. ACT with or without writing accepted. SAT with or without Essay component accepted. High school diploma is required and GED is accepted. *Academic units required:* 4 English, 3 math, 2 science, 2 science labs, 2 social studies, 6 academic electives. *Academic units recommended:* 2 foreign language.

Financial Aid

Students should submit: FAFSA. Priority filing deadline is 2/15. The Princeton Review suggests that all financial aid forms be submitted as soon as possible after October 1. *Need-based scholarships/grants offered:* College/university scholarship or grant aid from institutional funds; Federal Nursing Scholarships; Federal Pell; Private scholarships; SEOG; State scholarships/grants. *Loan aid offered:* Direct PLUS loans; Direct Subsidized Stafford Loans; Direct Unsubsidized Stafford Loans. Applicants will be notified of awards on a rolling basis beginning 2/1. Federal Work-Study Program available.

The Inside Word

Hampton University allows for early action admissions, meaning that students can receive an early decision without having to commit to attending the school. Around a quarter of HU's applicant pool pursues this option. You would be wise to follow suit; the school is bound to be more lenient early in the process than later, when it has already admitted many qualified students.

THE SCHOOL SAYS "..."

From the Admissions Office

"Hampton attempts to provide the environment and structures most conducive to the intellectual, emotional, and aesthetic enlargement of the lives of its members. The university gives priority to effective teaching and scholarly research while placing the student at the center of its planning. Hampton will ask you to look inwardly at your own history and culture and examine your relationship to the aspirations and development of the world."

SELECTIVITY

Admissions Rating	90
# of applicants	9,551
% of applicants accepted	36
% of acceptees attending	27

FRESHMAN PROFILE

Range SAT EBRW	480–720
Range SAT Math	450–720
Range ACT Composite	18–36
# submitting SAT scores	115
% submitting SAT scores	12
# submitting ACT scores	242
% submitting ACT scores	26
Average HS GPA	3.4
% graduated top 10% of class	12
% graduated top 25% of class	25
% graduated top 50% of class	74

DEADLINES

Early action	
Deadline	11/1
Notification	12/31
Regular	
Priority	3/1
Nonfall registration?	Yes

APPLICANTS ALSO LOOK AT AND OFTEN PREFER

Howard University; North Carolina A&T State University; University of Richmond; Radford University

AND SOMETIMES PREFER

Old Dominion University; Virginia State University; Virginia Commonwealth University

FINANCIAL FACTS

Financial Aid Rating	84
Annual tuition	$26,198
Room and board	$12,986
Required fees	$2,964
Books and supplies	$1,100
Average frosh need-based scholarship	$7,336
Average UG need-based scholarship	$7,115
% needy frosh rec. need-based scholarship or grant aid	96
% needy UG rec. need-based scholarship or grant aid	95
% needy frosh rec. non-need-based scholarship or grant aid	73
% needy UG rec. non-need-based scholarship or grant aid	59
% needy frosh rec. need-based self-help aid	76
% needy UG rec. need-based self-help aid	82
% frosh rec. any financial aid	42
% UG rec. any financial aid	50.5
% UG borrow to pay for school	84
Average cumulative indebtedness	$33,680
% frosh need fully met	38
% ugrads need fully met	41
Average % of frosh need met	39
Average % of ugrad need met	43

HANOVER COLLEGE

P.O. Box 108, Hanover, IN 47243-0108 • Admissions: 800-213-2178 • Fax: 812-866-7098

STUDENTS SAY "..."

Academics

Hanover College is a school that is brimming with opportunity. And with its "beautiful" campus and emphasis on "gaining real-life skills and making lifelong connections," it's easy to understand why students are drawn here. The vast majority of classes at Hanover are "small and discussion based," and many also place "a heavy focus on writing." While the academics can be challenging, students eagerly report that "many of the harder classes have tutors for that specific class." Additionally, the Learning Center is always "willing to go over things with you, edit papers and more." Importantly, it's evident that Hanover professors "love what they teach…and that excitement often carries over to the student." Indeed, they excel at "bring[ing] the material to life…and easily keep the attention of the class." Just as essential, Hanover professors are also known to be "caring and down to earth" and "devoted to their students." And, as this ecstatic art history major concludes, "Most of the professors on staff are part of the best people you will ever meet in life."

Life

While some undergrads grumble that "life at Hanover is pretty slow," others steadfastly argue that "there are SO many things [with which] to be involved." For starters, students can participate in "over sixty organizations" including "Adopt A Grandparent, Circle K Community Service, Best Buddies, and so many more." Additionally, individuals who enjoy the arts will be delighted to hear that both "the theater department and the improv group…never disappoint [and] the choir and band concerts [are] always very enjoyable [as well]." For those that are more athletically inclined, we're told that "when it's warm out, students go hiking, play wiffleball, or…sand volleyball." Many undergrads also gravitate to the Student Activities Center which offers "game tables, [a] theater room, televisions [and] study spots." And, in the evenings, "chances are some club always has something planned—be it a movie showing [or] a poetry night!" Hanover also has a relatively robust party scene. Indeed, undergrads inform us that "Greek life is big on… campus." And while there "are only four frats…they are a [major] part of [the] social life." Finally, when students are looking for a break from the campus routine, they often head to nearby Madison or Louisville, which is a mere "forty-minute drive [away]" and the closest major city.

Student Body

Hanover is home to a "small, pretty laid back and surprising[ly] interesting community." Indeed, while undergrads here admit that ethnic diversity "is still an issue," they happily point out that you'll find a wide array of personality types. Of course, the "majority of the students are committed to their academics and [strive to find] a balance between work and play." Many Hanover undergrads "are also extremely passionate about the things in which they invest their time, whatever that may be, and encourage that passion in others." It's important to note that the college's small size does make it "[easy] for cliques…to form." However, we're assured "it is also quite easy to break into the cliques if you are really interested in hanging out with certain groups of people." This social ease can be attributed to the fact that Hanover features some of the "friendliest individuals that Indiana has to offer." In fact, you are virtually guaranteed "to see a smiling face or to get a hello anywhere you walk on campus, whether it be from a fellow student or a faculty member." As one satisfied economics major sums up, "We are all about making everyone feel welcome and making Hanover College home."

Financial Aid: 812-866-7029 • E-Mail: admission@hanover.edu • Website: www.hanover.edu

THE PRINCETON REVIEW SAYS

Admissions

Very important factors considered include: rigor of secondary school record, class rank, academic GPA. *Important factors considered include:* standardized test scores, talent/ability, character/personal qualities. *Other factors considered include:* application essay, recommendation(s), interview, extracurricular activities, first generation, alumni/ae relation, geographical residence, state residency, racial/ethnic status, volunteer work, work experience, level of applicant's interest. ACT with Writing recommended. SAT with Essay component recommended. High school diploma is required and GED is not accepted. *Academic units required:* 4 English, 3 math, 3 science, 2 science labs, 2 foreign language, 2 social studies, 2 history, 2 academic electives. *Academic units recommended:* 4 English, 4 math, 4 science, 3 science labs, 4 foreign language, 3 social studies, 3 history, 3 academic electives, 1 visual/performing arts.

Financial Aid

Students should submit: FAFSA. The Princeton Review suggests that all financial aid forms be submitted as soon as possible after October 1. *Need-based scholarships/grants offered:* College/university scholarship or grant aid from institutional funds; Federal Pell; Private scholarships; SEOG; State scholarships/grants. *Loan aid offered:* Direct PLUS loans; Direct Subsidized Stafford Loans; Direct Unsubsidized Stafford Loans. Applicants will be notified of awards on or about 3/1. Federal Work-Study Program available. Institutional employment available.

The Inside Word

Similar to many liberal arts college, Hanover takes a holistic approach to the admissions process. Certainly, the school closely evaluates your high school curriculum as well as your GPA. Standardized test scores are also considered, though they hold less weight than your transcript. Beyond academics, admissions officers look at your extracurricular participation and community activities. Letters of recommendation and a writing sample will also be important. Further, expect Hanover to assess the strength of your high school. And, lastly, ethnic, cultural and geographic diversity will likely come into play.

THE SCHOOL SAYS "..."

From the Admissions Office

"Since our founding in 1827, we have been committed to providing students with a personal, rigorous, and well-rounded liberal arts education. Part of the college search process is finding that school that proves to be a good match. For those who see the value in an education that demands engagement and who see college as a time for exploration and involvement, they will find that Hanover is all they could hope for and more.

"The admission process serves as an introduction to the personal education that students receive at Hanover College. Every application is considered individually with emphasis being placed on a student's high school curriculum and the student's academic performance in that curriculum. While we realize that not every high school has the same course offerings, we expect students to have selected a college preparatory curriculum as challenging as possible within his or her particular high school or academic setting.

"Hanover College accepts both the SAT and ACT. Students taking the ACT are required to take the optional writing section. For students who have taken one or both of the tests multiple times, we will use the highest sub scores when calculating a student's score on either test for admission and scholarship purposes."

SELECTIVITY

Admissions Rating	77
# of applicants	2,757
% of applicants accepted	84
% of acceptees attending	15

FRESHMAN PROFILE

Range SAT EBRW	540–640
Range SAT Math	530–620
Range ACT Composite	22–27
# submitting SAT scores	154
% submitting SAT scores	45
# submitting ACT scores	188
% submitting ACT scores	55
Average HS GPA	3.6
% graduated top 10% of class	32
% graduated top 25% of class	60
% graduated top 50% of class	90

DEADLINES

Early action	
Deadline	12/1
Notification	12/20
Regular	
Notification	Rolling, 9/15
Nonfall registration?	Yes

FINANCIAL FACTS

Financial Aid Rating	89
Annual tuition	$36,900
Room and board	$11,580
Required fees	$770
Books and supplies	$1,200
Average frosh need-based scholarship	$26,222
Average UG need-based scholarship	$25,419
% needy frosh rec. need-based scholarship or grant aid	100
% needy UG rec. need-based scholarship or grant aid	100
% needy frosh rec. non-need-based scholarship or grant aid	31
% needy UG rec. non-need-based scholarship or grant aid	20
% needy frosh rec. need-based self-help aid	66
% needy UG rec. need-based self-help aid	78
% frosh rec. any financial aid	100
% UG rec. any financial aid	100
% UG borrow to pay for school	72
Average cumulative indebtedness	$30,835
% frosh need fully met	36
% ugrads need fully met	27
Average % of frosh need met	86
Average % of ugrad need met	82

HARVARD COLLEGE

86 Brattle Street, Cambridge, MA 02138 • Admissions: 617-495-1551 • Fax: 617-495-8821

CAMPUS LIFE

Quality of Life Rating	**80**
Fire Safety Rating	**60***
Green Rating	**60***
Type of school	Private
Environment	City

STUDENTS

Total undergrad enrollment	6,695
% male/female	51/49
% from out of state	84
% frosh from public high school	59
% frosh live on campus	100
% ugrads live on campus	98
# of fraternities	0
# of sororities	0
% African American	9
% Asian	21
% Caucasian	37
% Hispanic	11
% Native American	<1
% Pacific Islander	<1
% Two or more races	8
% Race and/or ethnicity unknown	1
% international	12
# of countries represented	109

SURVEY SAYS . . .

Great financial aid
Campus newspaper is popular
Students politically aware
Students love Cambridge, MA

ACADEMICS

Academic Rating	**84**
% students returning for sophomore year	97
% students graduating within 4 years	85
% students graduating within 6 years	97
Calendar	Semester
Student/faculty ratio	6:1
Profs interesting rating	78
Profs accessible rating	81

Most classes have fewer than 10 students.
Most lab/discussion sessions have
  fewer than 10 students.

MOST POPULAR MAJORS

Social Sciences, General; Economics, General;
Computer Science

STUDENTS SAY ". . ."

Academics

Harvard College students describe the school as a "dynamic universe" and an "amazing irresistible hell" that pushes them to the extremes of their intellect and ability. Unsurprisingly, the legendarily "very difficult" school attracts some of the country's most promising youth, who rise to the occasion in almost every aspect of their life on campus, not just the classroom. Harvard's recent financial aid enhancements have increased the number of applications by a landslide, but even after getting past the admissions hurdle, "people find ways to make everything (especially clubs and even partying) competitive." Happily, this streak is more of a "latent competition," as there are more than enough opportunity and resources to go around. "It is impossible to 'get the most out of Harvard' because Harvard offers so much," says one student. Much like the students, the professors at this "beautiful, fun, historic, and academically alive place" in Cambridge, Massachusetts, are among "the brightest minds in the world," and "the level of achievement is unbelievable." Some of the larger introductory classes are taught by teaching fellows (TFs), meaning "you do have to go to office hours to get to know your big lecture class professors on a personal level," but once your figurative underclass dues are paid, the access to "incredible" and "every so often, fantastic" professors is perfectly within reach. Top it off with Grade-A internship and employment opportunities, a good old alumni network, and a crimson pedigree for your résumé, and you may just end up agreeing with the Harvard student who refers to his experience as "rewarding beyond anything else I've ever done." Though the administration can be "waaaaay out of touch with students" and "reticent to change," it at least "does a good job of watching over its freshmen through extensive advising programs," and students all have faith that their best interests are being kept in mind.

Life

Cambridge and Boston are nothing if not college towns, and students never lack for options if they just want to "go see a play, a concert, hit up a party, go to the movies, or dine out." Students quickly learn when to hit the books and when to hit the streets, so "studying becomes routine." "There is a vibrant social atmosphere on campus and between students and the local community." As one student puts it, "Boredom does not exist here. There are endless opportunities and endless passionate people to do them with." "Basically, if you want to do it, Harvard either has it or has the money to give to you so you can start it." "Partying in a more traditional setting is available at Harvard, but is not a prevalent aspect of the school's social life. While there is a pub on campus that provides an excellent venue to hang out and play a game of pool or have a reasonably priced drink," and parties happen on weekends at Harvard's finals clubs, there's no real pressure for students to partake if they're not interested.

Student Body

Much as you might expect, ambition and achievement are the ties that bind at Harvard, and "Everyone is great for one reason or another," says a student. Almost every student can be summed up with the same statement: "Works really hard. Doesn't sleep. Involved in a million extracurriculars." Diversity is found in all aspects of life, from ethnicities to religion to ideology, and "there is a lot of tolerance and acceptance at Harvard for individuals of all races, religions, socioeconomic backgrounds, life styles, etc."

HARVARD COLLEGE

Financial Aid: 617-495-1581 • E-Mail: college@fas.harvard.edu • Website: www.college.harvard.edu

THE PRINCETON REVIEW SAYS

Admissions

Other factors considered include: rigor of secondary school record, academic GPA, application essay, standardized test scores, recommendation(s), interview, extracurricular activities, talent/ability, character/personal qualities, first generation, alumni/ae relation, geographical residence, racial/ethnic status, volunteer work, work experience. ACT with or without writing accepted. SAT with or without Essay component accepted. High school diploma or equivalent is not required. *Academic units recommended:* 4 English, 4 math, 4 science, 4 foreign language, 3 social studies, 2 history.

Financial Aid

Students should submit: Business/Farm Supplement; CSS/Financial Aid PROFILE; FAFSA; Noncustodial PROFILE. Priority filing deadline is 2/1. The Princeton Review suggests that all financial aid forms be submitted as soon as possible after October 1. *Need-based scholarships/grants offered:* College/university scholarship or grant aid from institutional funds; Federal Pell; Private scholarships; SEOG; State scholarships/grants. *Loan aid offered:* Direct PLUS loans; Direct Subsidized Stafford Loans; Direct Unsubsidized Stafford Loans. Applicants will be notified of awards on or about 4/1. Federal Work-Study Program available. Institutional employment available.

The Inside Word

It just doesn't get any tougher than this. Candidates to Harvard face dual obstacles—an awe-inspiring applicant pool and, as a result, admissions standards that defy explanation in quantifiable terms. Harvard denies admission to the vast majority, and virtually all of them are top students. It all boils down to splitting hairs, which is quite hard to explain and even harder for candidates to understand. Rather than being as detailed and direct as possible about the selection process and criteria, Harvard keeps things close to the vest—before, during, and after. They even refuse to admit that being from lesser populated states like South Dakota is an advantage. Thus the admissions process does more to intimidate candidates than to empower them. Moving to a common application seemed to be a small step in the right direction, but with the current explosion of early decision applicants and a super-high yield of enrollees, things aren't likely to change dramatically.

THE SCHOOL SAYS "..."

From the Admissions Office

"The admissions committee looks for energy, ambition, and the capacity to make the most of opportunities. Academic ability and preparation are important, and so is intellectual curiosity—but many of the strongest applicants have significant, non-academic interests and accomplishments, as well. There is no formula for admission, and applicants are considered carefully, with attention to future promise.

"Freshman applicants may submit the SAT. The ACT with writing component is also accepted. All students must also submit three SAT Subject Tests of their choosing."

SELECTIVITY

Admissions Rating	99
# of applicants	43,330
% of applicants accepted	5
% of acceptees attending	82

FRESHMAN PROFILE

Range SAT EBRW	710–770
Range SAT Math	750–800
Range ACT Composite	33–35
# submitting SAT scores	1,172
% submitting SAT scores	71
# submitting ACT scores	743
% submitting ACT scores	45
Average HS GPA	4.2
% graduated top 10% of class	93
% graduated top 25% of class	98
% graduated top 50% of class	100

DEADLINES

Early action	
Deadline	11/1
Notification	12/16
Regular	
Deadline	1/1
Notification	4/1
Nonfall registration?	No

FINANCIAL FACTS

Financial Aid Rating	95
Annual tuition	$49,653
Room and board	$18,389
Required fees	$4,349
Books and supplies	$1,000
Average frosh need-based scholarship	$58,643
Average UG need-based scholarship	$55,709
% needy frosh rec. need-based scholarship or grant aid	99
% needy UG rec. need-based scholarship or grant aid	100
% needy frosh rec. non-need-based scholarship or grant aid	0
% needy UG rec. non-need-based scholarship or grant aid	0
% needy frosh rec. need-based self-help aid	0
% needy UG rec. need-based self-help aid	0
% frosh rec. any financial aid	76
% UG rec. any financial aid	68
% UG borrow to pay for school	7
Average cumulative indebtedness	$6,170
% frosh need fully met	100
% ugrads need fully met	100
Average % of frosh need met	100
Average % of ugrad need met	100

HARVEY MUDD COLLEGE

301 Platt Boulevard, Claremont, CA 91711 • Admissions: 909-621-8011 • Fax: 909-607-7046

STUDENTS SAY "..."

Academics
Harvey Mudd College, according to its mission statement, "seeks to educate engineers, scientists, and mathematicians well versed in all of these areas and in the humanities and the social sciences so that they may assume leadership in their fields with a clear understanding of the impact of their work on society." As a result, its students "really understand their impact on both their global and campus communities." Breadth is also instilled in a Harvey Mudd education through its membership in the "Claremont Colleges," a five-college consortium that includes Pomona and Claremont McKenna, and because of this, its "students are more well-rounded than most in the sciences and get to pursue their passions outside of the STEM fields." Students also praise the "broad core curriculum at Harvey Mudd," which "produces scientists who can rise to meet interdisciplinary challenges within the sciences" and facilitates "great post-grad opportunities." Classes are hard but rewarding: "The brutal work fosters an extremely collaborative environment where people focus not on the grade they get but the learning behind it." "Academics are perfect. Could not ask for more rigorous and interesting learning." HMC undergrads demonstrate a "commitment to" Harvey Mudd's "honor code," which requires students "to conduct themselves with honesty and integrity both personally and academically and to respect the rights of others." This ethic, as well as support systems like "the proctor mentor system in the dorms," which positions RAs to act as resources to students "without all of the policing," creates a "tight community" on campus. "There is no segregation based on class year, major, race, academic ability, dorm or anything. Everyone is respectful, smart, aware, supportive, and unique." Professors are almost universally reported to be "incredible," "truly dedicated to undergraduate teaching," and "always willing to spend hours outside of class answering questions." HMC's small classes and lack of graduate programs focuses faculty attention on undergrads: "My only 'large' class as a freshman is an intro to CS Class of 100 students and by the fifth day the professor knew all 100 names." Overall, "the work at HMC is very challenging, but I have had the best support system; from the Academic Excellence tutors providing help for all required core classes to the professors who are readily accessible and enthusiastic helpers."

Life
Students agree that Harvey Mudd enables tremendous growth, which isn't always easy: "You feel really smart before Mudd, you feel really stupid during Mudd, and after Mudd you feel like a genius." Socially speaking, "conversations at dinner are probably really weird and nerdy from an outsiders point of view," and "people care about ...lots of other serious issues along with more frivolous ones." Many appreciate that "campus-wide parties are funded by the college, ensuring that they are safe and well-funded," and these include "a foam party, where a dorm courtyard is filled with soap foam," and "a holiday party where (literally) tons of snow are trucked in." There's plenty to do on campus, but "Claremont Village is within a 20-minute walk," and "it takes about an hour and a half to get to LA's Union Station from Mudd, and downtown LA and Little Tokyo are both accessible from there." "A lot of students do drink, but there is honestly never any pressure. I don't drink at all and I have never felt any pressure to do anything I wasn't comfortable with." One student sums up the HMC life this way: "Work really, really hard, play hard."

Student Body
"Harvey Mudd has a strong community of talented students that build each other up." Many HMC students offer similar praise for the college's "small, tight knit community in which everyone looks after one another." The "typical student is friendly, outgoing, and passionate about their (sometimes slightly weird) interests," and "it's really easy to form close friendships, whether in your dorm or through study groups." "Everyone at the school is extremely enthusiastic about learning," and the college's culture promotes lots of intellectual bonding amongst "nerds, but the kind that can hold conversations." "Most people are top of their class from high school, so freshman year, everyone is a bit cocky (but Mudd humbles you really quickly)." Undergrads value that "the honor code works very well, and students are pretty much always eager to help one another."

HARVEY MUDD COLLEGE

Financial Aid: 909-621-8055 • E-Mail: admission@hmc.edu • Website: https://www.hmc.edu/

THE PRINCETON REVIEW SAYS

Admissions

Very important factors considered include: rigor of secondary school record, academic GPA, application essay, recommendation(s). *Important factors considered include:* standardized test scores, extracurricular activities, character/personal qualities. *Other factors considered include:* class rank, interview, talent/ability, first generation, alumni/ae relation, geographical residence, state residency, racial/ethnic status, volunteer work, work experience. ACT with or without writing accepted. SAT with or without Essay component accepted. High school diploma or equivalent is not required. *Academic units required:* 4 English, 4 math, 3 science, 1 history. *Academic units recommended:* 4 English, 4 math, 4 science, 2 science labs, 2 foreign language, 2 social studies, 2 history, 2 academic electives.

Financial Aid

Students should submit: Business/Farm Supplement; CSS/Financial Aid PROFILE; FAFSA; Noncustodial PROFILE; State aid form. Priority filing deadline is 2/1. The Princeton Review suggests that all financial aid forms be submitted as soon as possible after October 1. *Need-based scholarships/grants offered:* College/university scholarship or grant aid from institutional funds; Federal Pell; Private scholarships; SEOG; State scholarships/grants. *Loan aid offered:* Direct PLUS loans; Direct Subsidized Stafford Loans; Direct Unsubsidized Stafford Loans. Applicants will be notified of awards on or about 4/1. Federal Work-Study Program available. Institutional employment available.

The Inside Word

Harvey Mudd is as rigorous in admissions as it is in its education, so serious applicants are well advised to demonstrate big chops in their high school STEM courseload, without sacrificing attention to humanities and extracurriculars. Applicants should carefully review HMC's eligibility requirements for high school transcripts, as well as its standardized testing requirements, and remember that the college is competitive enough that admission is no guarantee even for highly qualified applicants.

THE SCHOOL SAYS "..."

From the Admissions Office

"HMC is a wonderfully unusual combination of a liberal arts college and research institute. Our students love math and science, want to live and learn deeply in an intimate climate of cooperation and trust, thrive on innovation and discovery, and enjoy rigorous coursework in arts, humanities, and social sciences in addition to a technical curriculum. At least a year of research or our innovative clinic program is required (or guaranteed, if you prefer). The resources at HMC are astounding, and all are accessible to undergraduates: labs, shops, work areas, and most importantly, faculty. You'll find the professors and student body stimulating and supportive—they'll challenge you inside and outside the classroom, and share your love of learning and collaboration. They'll also share your love of fun and sense of humor (math jokes and all). In addition, we benefit from the unique consortium that is the Claremont Colleges.

"In the final analysis, our graduates are prepared well for whatever their next steps will be. They can see relationships between disparate fields of study and investigation, are resourceful, know how to work in teams, and are able to articulate their ideas to both lay-people and specialized experts. A wide range of companies are eager to hire our seniors, and HMC sends the highest proportion of graduates to PhD programs of any undergraduate college in the country."

SELECTIVITY

Admissions Rating	98
# of applicants	4,045
% of applicants accepted	14
% of acceptees attending	41
# offered a place on the wait list	500
% accepting a place on wait list	68
% admitted from wait list	3
# of early decision applicants	437
% accepted early decision	19

FRESHMAN PROFILE

Range SAT EBRW	710–770
Range SAT Math	780–800
Range SAT Composite	1490–1550
Range ACT Composite	33–35
# submitting SAT scores	165
% submitting SAT scores	74
# submitting ACT scores	98
% submitting ACT scores	44

DEADLINES

Early decision	
Deadline	11/15
Notification	12/15
Other ED Deadline	1/5
Other ED Notification	2/15
Regular	
Deadline	1/5
Notification	4/1
Nonfall registration?	No

APPLICANTS ALSO LOOK AT AND OFTEN PREFER
California Institute of Technology; Massachusetts Institute of Technology; Stanford University

AND SOMETIMES PREFER
University of California—Berkeley; Brown University; Carnegie Mellon University

AND RARELY PREFER
University of California, Los Angeles; The University of Chicago; Rose-Hulman Institute of Technology

FINANCIAL FACTS

Financial Aid Rating	97
Annual tuition	$58,359
Room and board	$18,679
Required fees	$551
Books and supplies	$800
Average frosh need-based scholarship	$48,474
Average UG need-based scholarship	$45,010
% needy frosh rec. need-based scholarship or grant aid	97
% needy UG rec. need-based scholarship or grant aid	97
% needy frosh rec. non-need-based scholarship or grant aid	37
% needy UG rec. non-need-based scholarship or grant aid	43
% needy frosh rec. need-based self-help aid	61
% needy UG rec. need-based self-help aid	66
% frosh rec. any financial aid	74
% UG rec. any financial aid	71
% UG borrow to pay for school	47
Average cumulative indebtedness	$29,139
% frosh need fully met	100
% ugrads need fully met	100
Average % of frosh need met	100
Average % of ugrad need met	100

HAVERFORD COLLEGE

370 Lancaster Avenue, Haverford, PA 19041 • Admissions: 610-896-1350 • Fax: 610-896-1338

STUDENTS SAY ". . ."

Academics

Founded in 1833, Haverford College in Pennsylvania is "small, but exceptionally vibrant and engaging," offering a "solid academic experience" under one of the country's oldest honor codes. Though founded by Quakers, the school is nonsectarian, but the community aspect of its founders remains, creating what one student calls "a challenging, interesting environment with the best people I know." The real love affair is with Haverford's "awesome, invested" professors, who "lead a group of idealistic students to point—but never force—us into a better way of thinking." They want to put in the time to get to know you, and the small size of the school "allows for plenty of opportunities for collaborating with faculty and staff and building a relationship." "You are more than just a face in a classroom of many; you are a unique person that has something to offer," says a student. "My 'big intro lecture course' has forty-one students," says another. "My professor still knows me by name, and we have long conversations when we pass on Founder's Green." The school's learning environment stresses "engaging in hard and honest conversations with your peers," and "students have a lot of power" through their roles in the administration of the college. "I love the amount of independence and autonomy [the school] gives to its students," says a student. Because of the kind of student this attracts, "we wind up with a really conscientious student body invested in the school." The resources available to students here are incredible, as well. You can get "credit for research" (there is plenty of research here in every department), and if you want to go off campus for research, "you can get funding for that as well."

Life

The culture of "trust, concern, and respect" created by the honor code carries over into the rest of this "awesome, at times idiosyncratic, place where community thrives and cliques are very loose if existent at all." "The honor code unifies everyone." "Being able to take an exam in your own room, sitting relaxed on your bed because your professor trusts you not to look at your books is one of the luxuries of being here," says a student. People study hard here, but they take a break over the weekend at a party or two "before cracking the books again. Athletics are also "really important" for much of the student body—most here are athletic, even if it's not at a varsity level—and some of the male sports teams "function like fraternities" (which do not exist at HC). Because it's a small place, "sometimes it feels like everyone knows your business," but everyone is so insanely nice that "the social scene is great." Students govern themselves and the happenings at the school through the "Plenaries" that happen twice a year, when the majority of the student body must be present. New York and Philadelphia are both easily accessible by train, and "Suburban Square (the local outdoor shopping center) is a great place to hang out, get coffee, or even go shopping."

Student Body

Everyone is "passionate," "people are always up for intellectual discussion," and "everyone works very hard." Students here were all motivated enough to get in and "want to succeed for themselves and not to appease others." Students describe other students as having "hearts of gold and giant brains that they put to use to change the world for the better." "It's a small school full of nice kids—not naive (well, sometimes naive), just genuinely compassionate and interested in other people, whether or not that's 'cool,'" says a student. Though all are bound by "intellectual passion and interests outside of academics," diversity otherwise on campus "lacks a little." Still, "the great thing about Haverford is that, although we have a variety of students from all different social circles, everyone is a touch awkward." This is a fact that the "nerdy and ridiculously friendly" students embrace. "I feel like I could potentially become friends with anyone on campus," says a student.

HAVERFORD COLLEGE

Financial Aid: 610-896-1350 • E-Mail: http://www.haverford.edu/admission/ • Website: www.haverford.edu

THE PRINCETON REVIEW SAYS

Admissions

Very important factors considered include: rigor of secondary school record, academic GPA, application essay, recommendation(s), extracurricular activities, character/personal qualities. *Important factors considered include:* class rank, standardized test scores, talent/ability, volunteer work. *Other factors considered include:* interview, first generation, alumni/ae relation, geographical residence, racial/ethnic status, level of applicant's interest. Haverford is test-optional: Candidates for admission may choose whether or not to submit the results of the SAT and/or the ACT as a part of their application. High school diploma is required and GED is accepted. *Academic units recommended:* 4 English, 3 math, 3 science, 3 science labs, 3 foreign language, 3 social studies.

Financial Aid

Students should submit: Business/Farm Supplement; CSS/Financial Aid PROFILE; FAFSA; Noncustodial PROFILE. The Princeton Review suggests that all financial aid forms be submitted as soon as possible after October 1. *Need-based scholarships/grants offered:* College/university scholarship or grant aid from institutional funds; Federal Pell; Private scholarships; SEOG; State scholarships/grants. *Loan aid offered:* Direct PLUS loans; Direct Subsidized Stafford Loans; Direct Unsubsidized Stafford Loans. Applicants will be notified of awards on or about 3/25. Federal Work-Study Program available. Institutional employment available.

The Inside Word

Haverford's applicant pool is an impressive and competitive lot (only about 20 percent of applicants get in). Intellectual curiosity is paramount, and applicants are expected to keep a demanding academic schedule in high school. Additionally, the college places a high value on ethics, as evidenced by its honor code. The admissions office seeks students who will reflect and promote Haverford's ideals.

THE SCHOOL SAYS "..."

From the Admissions Office

"Haverford College offers one of the finest liberal arts educations in the world and attracts incredibly bright and dedicated students from nearly every state and 36 foreign countries. Haverford students reap the many benefits of attending an all-undergraduate institution, where all courses are taught by professors, and all resources and facilities are available to undergraduates. Haverford provides a rigorous and intensely personal undergraduate education inspired by intellectual depth, integrity, collaboration, and dedication to improving the human condition.

"Our campus culture engenders an immediate sense of colleagueship between students and faculty and creates a relaxed, personal atmosphere. A philosophy of trust, concern, and respect for every individual guides our community and serves as the basis of our completely student-governed honor code. In addition to governing the honor code, students serve on hiring committees, manage budgets, and run more than 145 clubs and organizations.

"Haverford College meets 100 percent of the demonstrated need of all admitted students and seeks to minimize debt for our graduates. Students with family income below $60,000 will not have any loans included in their financial aid package; students with family income above this level will have loans ranging from $1,500 to $3,000 per year. The Haverford Student Loan Debt Relief Fund, an innovative program to help students who do graduate from Haverford with debt, provides funds to young alumni who are employed in jobs of high social value with low remuneration or who are in transition at some point following graduation."

SELECTIVITY

Admissions Rating	98
# of applicants	4,672
% of applicants accepted	19
% of acceptees attending	41
# offered a place on the wait list	1,349
% accepting a place on wait list	45
% admitted from wait list	2
# of early decision applicants	444
% accepted early decision	44

FRESHMAN PROFILE

Range SAT EBRW	680–750
Range SAT Math	690–780
Range ACT Composite	32–34
# submitting SAT scores	240
% submitting SAT scores	67
# submitting ACT scores	149
% submitting ACT scores	42
% graduated top 10% of class	95
% graduated top 25% of class	97
% graduated top 50% of class	100

DEADLINES

Early decision	
Deadline	11/15
Notification	12/15
Other ED Deadline	1/1
Other ED Notification	2/15
Regular	
Deadline	1/15
Notification	4/1
Nonfall registration?	No

FINANCIAL FACTS

Financial Aid Rating	98
Annual tuition	$58,402
Room and board	$17,066
Required fees	$738
Books and supplies	$1,194
Average frosh need-based scholarship	$51,777
Average UG need-based scholarship	$51,198
% needy frosh rec. need-based scholarship or grant aid	100
% needy UG rec. need-based scholarship or grant aid	100
% needy frosh rec. non-need-based scholarship or grant aid	0
% needy UG rec. non-need-based scholarship or grant aid	0
% needy frosh rec. need-based self-help aid	92
% needy UG rec. need-based self-help aid	93
% frosh rec. any financial.aid	47
% UG rec. any financial aid	46
% UG borrow to pay for school	36
Average cumulative indebtedness	$11,000
% frosh need fully met	100
% ugrads need fully met	100
Average % of frosh need met	100
Average % of ugrad need met	100

HIGH POINT UNIVERSITY

One University Parkway, High Point, NC 27268 • Admissions: 336-841-9216 • Fax: 336-888-6382

STUDENTS SAY "..."

Academics

North Carolina's High Point University is a private liberal arts college with an emphasis on professional development. "It is designed for a student to be able to work, live, and thrive as if they were in an actual urban city," which means that the academic experience is geared toward providing a ton of experience. From the moment students first set foot on campus, they can take advantage of opportunities such as job shadowing, an entrepreneurship center, and learning labs that teach intangibles like business dining etiquette. The university president even leads a life skills seminar for first-years, while the faculty offer "various workshops and discussions ... about different topics that affect the world today." Students find life skills such as "knowing how to dress and present while being mobile" to be of great help in the job search, and the Entrepreneur Center sparks connections thanks to "biannual pitch competitions, the ability to be connected with start-ups in the area, and two dedicated entrepreneur professors that spend most of their time meeting with students and brainstorming ideas."

The professors are carefully selected for their "great industry knowledge" and the passion they bring for helping the next generation. Small class sizes ensure that they can focus on caring "for their students' well-being," especially important given the "very rigorous courses," and forming "more personal relationships." Beyond the accessibility of the staff, the president included, High Point University also "has innovation in their DNA, and is always looking for the best ways to teach students outside of the classroom." Thanks to them, at least according to one student, "my world has become a much bigger and brighter place."

Life

Students confess that "Life at school is busy for most ... but in the best way." Beyond the coursework, there's a lot to do, whether that's "socializing on campus dining areas and being involved in different types of clubs" or "soaking up all the social events the campus has to offer." There's a lot of open-to-all academic opportunity as well, like the way that "the school of business holds a wonderful speaker series throughout the whole year" or how the new planetarium "offers free showings to anyone on campus every Friday." For those looking to get away from it all, "cities like Asheville, Raleigh, and Charlotte aren't far at all." And of course, for those wanting to stay local, there are plenty of popular outdoor activities: "When the weather is nice outside there are always people playing beach volleyball or spike ball" and "there are a lot of hiking areas nearby."

Student Body

Nearly four-fifths of students come from out-of-state, and these "open-minded, creative students [are] able to think of possible solutions to solve current problems of our generations." HPU students are "friendly and helpful" and most "hold multiple leadership positions in organizations across campus." Whether you're actively involved or just contemplating joining a group, "the atmosphere here is encouraging," and enrollees "all work together to help inspire each other every day." Some of that, surely, is the result of the common bond students share with the career-focused attitudes, the way in which "many take advantage of the career and professional development opportunities on campus." But according to students, it seems to be true for all walks of life. If you look, you're likely to "find a group of people that like doing the same things you do."

HIGH POINT UNIVERSITY

Financial Aid: 336-841-9032 • E-Mail: admiss@highpoint.edu • Website: www.highpoint.edu

THE PRINCETON REVIEW SAYS

Admissions

Very important factors considered include: academic GPA. *Important factors considered include:* rigor of secondary school record, application essay, standardized test scores, recommendation(s), interview, extracurricular activities, talent/ability, character/personal qualities, volunteer work. *Other factors considered include:* class rank, first generation, alumni/ae relation. ACT with or without writing accepted. SAT with or without Essay component accepted. High school diploma is required and GED is accepted. *Academic units required:* 4 English, 3 math, 3 science, 1 science lab, 2 foreign language, 3 social studies. *Academic units recommended:* 4 English, 4 math, 3 science, 1 science lab, 3 foreign language, 3 social studies.

Financial Aid

Students should submit: FAFSA; State aid form. Priority filing deadline is 3/1. The Princeton Review suggests that all financial aid forms be submitted as soon as possible after October 1. *Need-based scholarships/grants offered:* College/university scholarship or grant aid from institutional funds; Federal Pell; Private scholarships; SEOG; State scholarships/grants. *Loan aid offered:* Direct PLUS loans; Direct Subsidized Stafford Loans; Direct Unsubsidized Stafford Loans. Applicants will be notified of awards on a rolling basis beginning 4/1. Federal Work-Study Program available. Institutional employment available.

The Inside Word

The admissions committee at High Point strives to take a well-rounded approach to their decisions. While your high school transcript certainly holds the most weight, the school will also closely consider your recommendations and extracurriculars. Additionally, High Point is a test-optional school. However, you will have to submit either your SAT or ACT scores if you want to be considered for the Honors Scholar Program or Presidential Scholarship Programs. Finally, it should be known that early decision and early decision II candidates are given priority in terms of housing, class selection, and move-in dates.

THE SCHOOL SAYS "..."

From the Admissions Office

"High Point University is invested in creating an immersive learning environment where character and careers are crafted in unison. At HPU, you won't just be asked to question the world around you—you'll be expected to become an active citizen in it. It's through this journey that you'll develop the tools and intellectual know-how to thrive in an ever-changing global marketplace. You will constantly be given the opportunity to combine classroom content with real-world context as experiential learning is woven into every major. You will be exposed to undergraduate research opportunities and a wide range of learning labs that extend well beyond traditional classroom walls. At High Point University, you will receive an education that inspires greatness, instills purpose, cultivates life-long learning, promotes service and stimulates the desire to live a life of both success and significance.

"Nationally recognized for innovation, HPU's academic model is based on four pillars: academic excellence, experiential learning, modeling values and building character, and the four-year development of each student's life skills. This educating of the entire person coupled with our four year Career Development plan best positions our students for success. Ninety-seven percent of High Point graduates are either continuing their education in graduate school or working in the field within 6 months of graduation.

"At High Point University, every student receives an extraordinary education in an inspiring environment with caring people."

SELECTIVITY	
Admissions Rating	80
# of applicants	11,298
% of applicants accepted	75
% of acceptees attending	17
# offered a place on the wait list	931
% accepting a place on wait list	100
% admitted from wait list	14
# of early decision applicants	748
% accepted early decision	76

FRESHMAN PROFILE	
Range SAT EBRW	550–630
Range SAT Math	540–630
Range SAT Composite	1090–1260
Range ACT Composite	22–28
# submitting SAT scores	806
% submitting SAT scores	58
# submitting ACT scores	541
% submitting ACT scores	39
Average HS GPA	3.3
% graduated top 10% of class	17
% graduated top 25% of class	43
% graduated top 50% of class	73

DEADLINES	
Early decision	
Deadline	11/1
Notification	11/22
Other ED Deadline	2/1
Other ED Notification	2/1
Early action	
Deadline	11/15
Notification	12/16
Regular	
Priority	2/1
Deadline	3/1
Notification	Rolling, 2/1
Nonfall registration?	Yes

FINANCIAL FACTS	
Financial Aid Rating	83
Annual tuition	$33,358
Room and board	$15,438
Required fees	$4,722
Books and supplies	$1,500
Average frosh need-based scholarship	$16,662
Average UG need-based scholarship	$14,388
% needy frosh rec. need-based scholarship or grant aid	100
% needy UG rec. need-based scholarship or grant aid	99
% needy frosh rec. non-need-based scholarship or grant aid	90
% needy UG rec. non-need-based scholarship or grant aid	84
% needy frosh rec. need-based self-help aid	69
% needy UG rec. need-based self-help aid	75
% frosh rec. any financial aid	89
% UG rec. any financial aid	84
% UG borrow to pay for school	47
Average cumulative indebtedness	$34,079
% frosh need fully met	15
% ugrads need fully met	12
Average % of frosh need met	62
Average % of ugrad need met	55

HILLSDALE COLLEGE

33 East College Street, Hillsdale, MI 49242 • Admissions: 517-607-2327 • Fax: 517-607-2223

CAMPUS LIFE

Quality of Life Rating	90
Fire Safety Rating	91
Green Rating	62
Type of school	Private
Affiliation	Christian (Nondenominational)
Environment	Village

STUDENTS

Total undergrad enrollment	1,454
% male/female	51/49
% from out of state	69
% frosh from public high school	45
% frosh live on campus	99
% ugrads live on campus	74
# of fraternities (% ugrad men join)	4 (22)
# of sororities (% ugrad women join)	3 (33)
% African American	0
% Asian	0
% Caucasian	0
% Hispanic	0
% Native American	<1
% Pacific Islander	0
% Two or more races	0
% Race and/or ethnicity unknown	100
% international	0
# of countries represented	10

SURVEY SAYS . . .

Lots of conservative students
Students always studying
Students are happy
Classroom facilities are great
Internships are widely available
School is well run
No one cheats
Students are friendly
Students are very religious
Students involved in community service
Easy to get around campus
Very little drug use
Intramural sports are popular
Frats and sororities are popular
Theater is popular
Campus newspaper is popular
College radio is popular
Active student government
Active student-run political groups

ACADEMICS

Academic Rating	92
% students returning for sophomore year	96
% students graduating within 4 years	74
% students graduating within 6 years	86
Calendar	Semester
Student/faculty ratio	9:1
Profs interesting rating	97
Profs accessible rating	98

Most classes have fewer than 10 students.
Most lab/discussion sessions have
   10–19 students.

MOST POPULAR MAJORS

Economics, General; History, General; English
Language and Literature, General

STUDENTS SAY "..."

Academics

"If you come to Hillsdale College, be prepared to work," students say about this "academically intense" liberal arts college in Michigan. The Hillsdale College motto is "strength rejoices in the challenge," and Hillsdale students clearly take great pride in rising to the occasion. They praise Hillsdale's "rigorous and diverse core curriculum," "small class size," and "dedicated faculty." Philosophically and pedagogically, the college focuses on developing "self-government and leadership" skills. Students appear to be uniformly attracted to the "classically liberal" and "traditional" approach to education, which they praise as distinctive among liberal arts colleges in the 21st century; this sentiment is reflected in the words of one student: "Hillsdale does not conform to society, liberalism, fads, or mainstream media." Faculty members are "extraordinarily tough graders" but "fair" and generally "accessible." Students describe their professors as being "incredibly patient, kind, and willing to go out of their way to help students learn and understand the material." Most offer classes that dig into "deeply interesting questions" with assignments that one student describes to be "driving us to fight for ideas that matter to us, rather than just being summaries of the reading."

Life

Weekends at Hillsdale College provide ample opportunity for socializing and engaging in special activities. In addition to intramural sports and Greek life, the "student activities board puts out a lot of fantastic events, from big semester events (such as an end-of-the-year music party modeled after Lollapalooza) to small weekly events (coffee and painting in the Union and Friday night cookouts)." Students also spend a lot of time in the student union, where they can play indoor games or watch TV. Popular organized activities on campus include various film clubs and dance clubs: "swing club is very popular, and ballroom dance is catching on." Hillsdale lies in a rural area of Southern Michigan, so students note that food options off-campus are "limited," but "meal times in the cafeteria are a major social event." Hayden Park and Baw Beese Lake "provide great outdoor recreation." Many students "are very religiously and politically involved. Hillsdale students are "more often than not over committed." Each day, "most people attend a Bible Study and/or do a devotional." In the warmer months, "kayaking, hiking, and volleyball" are popular outdoor activities. Many students "leave campus and go home to Detroit, Lansing, or Toledo to get back to a bigger city" or travel to nearby Jackson, Coldwater, or Ann Arbor to see concerts.

Student Body

Greek life is popular at Hillsdale with one student estimating that nearly one third of the students participate. The other half of this small student body is the "prototypical Hillsdale student"—"fundamental Christians" who tend to "stay in the dorms," and "love to talk about politics [and] philosophy." Students note that groups do overlap, and there is a solid sense of community across campus. "Hillsdale College attracts authentic people," says one student, "and promotes authenticity among students through the Honor Code and Mission Statement, both of which most students take seriously." The majority of students, faculty, and the administration are "morally conservative." Many students argue that they "respectfully disagree with the LGBT lifestyle" while remaining "accepting." Nevertheless, some students report "discomfort and anxiety" with the administration's "openly anti-LGBT stance" that "prohibits engaging in same-sex relationships." Demographic and political diversity is limited ("a clash of ideologies is a debate between a Libertarian and a Republican"), but students are also "intellectually diverse and curious" and "near[ly] impossible to offend."

Financial Aid: 517-607-2350 • E-Mail: admissions@hillsdale.edu • Website: www.hillsdale.edu

THE PRINCETON REVIEW SAYS

Admissions

Very important factors considered include: rigor of secondary school record, academic GPA, application essay, standardized test scores, interview, extracurricular activities, character/personal qualities, level of applicant's interest. *Important factors considered include:* recommendation(s), volunteer work. *Other factors considered include:* talent/ability, alumni/ae relation. ACT with or without writing accepted. SAT with or without Essay component accepted. High school diploma is required and GED is accepted. *Academic units required:* 4 English, 3 math, 3 science, 2 social studies, 3 history. *Academic units recommended:* 4 English, 4 math, 4 science, 2 science labs, 3 foreign language, 4 social studies, 4 history.

Financial Aid

Students should submit: Institution's own financial aid form. Priority filing deadline is 5/1. The Princeton Review suggests that all financial aid forms be submitted as soon as possible after October 1. *Need-based scholarships/grants offered:* College/university scholarship or grant aid from institutional funds; Private scholarships. Institutional employment available.

The Inside Word

While the academic profile of incoming students is impressive, the College strongly considers a student's extracurricular activities, character, and ambition as well. In addition to the SAT and ACT, Hillsdale also accepts the Classic Learning Test (CLT). Applicants are encouraged to submit a resume of their extracurricular, leadership, and work experiences along with their applications. Interviews are highly recommended, especially for those seeking a scholarship.

THE SCHOOL SAYS "..."

From the Admissions Office

"The College's strength is found in its mission and curriculum. The core curriculum at Hillsdale contains the essence of the classical liberal arts education. Through it, students are introduced to the history, the philosophical and theological ideas, the works of literature, and the scientific discoveries that set Western Civilization apart. As explained in its mission statement, 'the College also considers itself a trustee of our Western philosophical and theological inheritance tracing to Athens and Jerusalem, a heritage finding its clearest expression in the American experiment of self-government under law.'

"Personal attention is a hallmark at Hillsdale. Small classes are combined with teaching professors who make their students a priority. The academic environment at Hillsdale will actively engage you as a student. Extracurricular activities abound at Hillsdale with more than 100 clubs and organizations that offer excellent leadership opportunities. From athletics and the fine arts, to Greek life and community volunteer programs, you will find it difficult not to be involved in our thriving campus community. In addition, numerous study abroad programs, a 685-acre biological station in northern Michigan, and an internship program in Washington, D.C., are just a few of the unique off-campus opportunities available to students at Hillsdale.

"We seek students who are ambitious, intellectually active and who are ready to become leaders worthy of this heritage in their personal as well as professional lives.

"All students sign and abide by the Honor Code, which says: 'A Hillsdale College student is honorable in conduct, honest in word and deed, dutiful in study and service, and respectful of the rights of other. Through education, the student rises to self-government.'"

SELECTIVITY

Admissions Rating	92
# of applicants	1,593
% of applicants accepted	48
% of acceptees attending	45
# offered a place on the wait list	154
% accepting a place on wait list	26
% admitted from wait list	30
# of early decision applicants	188
% accepted early decision	62

FRESHMAN PROFILE

Range SAT EBRW	660–740
Range SAT Math	640–730
Range SAT Composite	1310–1450
Range ACT Composite	29–33
# submitting SAT scores	138
% submitting SAT scores	40
# submitting ACT scores	198
% submitting ACT scores	58
Average HS GPA	3.9

DEADLINES

Early decision	
Deadline	11/1
Notification	12/1
Regular	
Priority	1/1
Deadline	4/1
Notification	Rolling, 12/1
Nonfall registration?	Yes

APPLICANTS ALSO LOOK AT AND OFTEN PREFER

Case Western Reserve University; Eastern Michigan University; King's College (PA); Princeton University; Valparaiso University; The Ohio State University—Columbus; Patrick Henry College

AND SOMETIMES PREFER

Cedarville University; Cornerstone University; Creighton University; Davidson College; University of Dayton; United States Naval Academy; University of Toledo; William & Mary; The Catholic University of America

AND RARELY PREFER

Dartmouth College; Kenyon College; Knox College; Oberlin College; Reed College; Swarthmore College; Colorado College

FINANCIAL FACTS

Financial Aid Rating	84
Annual tuition	$27,090
Room and board	$11,390
Required fees	$1,278
Books and supplies	$1,200
Average frosh need-based scholarship	$8,388
Average UG need-based scholarship	$8,184
% needy frosh rec. need-based scholarship or grant aid	59
% needy UG rec. need-based scholarship or grant aid	66
% needy frosh rec. non-need-based scholarship or grant aid	86
% needy UG rec. non-need-based scholarship or grant aid	83
% needy frosh rec. need-based self-help aid	55
% needy UG rec. need-based self-help aid	65
% frosh rec. any financial aid	99
% UG rec. any financial aid	96
% UG borrow to pay for school	45
Average cumulative indebtedness	$32,198
% frosh need fully met	35
% ugrads need fully met	41
Average % of frosh need met	67
Average % of ugrad need met	60

HOBART AND WILLIAM SMITH COLLEGES

629 South Main Street, Geneva, NY 14456 • Admissions: 315-781-3622 • Fax: 315-781-3914

CAMPUS LIFE

Quality of Life Rating	85
Fire Safety Rating	96
Green Rating	91
Type of school	Private
Environment	Village

STUDENTS

Total undergrad enrollment	2,036
% male/female	48/52
% from out of state	61
% frosh from public high school	65
% frosh live on campus	100
% ugrads live on campus	90
# of fraternities (% ugrad men join)	6 (18)
# of sororities (% ugrad women join)	1 (2)
% African American	6
% Asian	3
% Caucasian	73
% Hispanic	6
% Native American	<1
% Pacific Islander	<1
% Two or more races	2
% Race and/or ethnicity unknown	4
% international	5
# of countries represented	34

SURVEY SAYS . . .

Students always studying
Students are happy
Career services are great
Internships are widely available
Class discussions encouraged
Lots of beer drinking
Intramural sports are popular

ACADEMICS

Academic Rating	87
% students returning for sophomore year	88
% students graduating within 4 years	73
% students graduating within 6 years	77
Calendar	Semester
Student/faculty ratio	10:1
Profs interesting rating	92
Profs accessible rating	95

Most classes have 10–19 students.
Most lab/discussion sessions have
 fewer than 10 students.

MOST POPULAR MAJORS

Mass Communication/Media Studies; Biology/
Biological Sciences, General; Economics, General

STUDENTS SAY "..."

Academics

Though the idyllic Seneca Lake setting of Hobart and William Smith Colleges can at times feel like a beautiful fantasy, undergrads can't stop talking about how "The school really uses all of its resources to ensure the student body is not only ready to face the 'real world,' but have experiences to back up their job search." There are a ton of options packed into this two-school institution, and many agree that it shows a "commitment to providing opportunities" to its body of just over 2,000 students. "Our study abroad program, community service department, and alumni network are some of the best in the nation." Just as critically, the school offers "merit-based scholarships [to] students who might not otherwise be able to attend HWS."

That same choice and opportunity applies to day-to-day classes as well. "The extensive list of majors and ability to create an individual major allows students to have a certain sense of freedom while studying their passions." Of course, the real secret sauce, so to speak, comes from the faculty experience. Not only do "small classes make it really easy for professors to know who you are," but teachers also "work hard to facilitate meaningful discussions and provide thought-provoking and challenging questions." The overall consensus is that the staff are "engaging, dynamic and truly interested in fostering the next generation." As one undergrad puts it, "My professors believe in me, support me, and share their passion in pursuit of me finding my own."

Life

The campus of Hobart and William Smith Colleges is best described as "very physically active," so there's always something going on, particularly for popular intramural sports like soccer and volleyball. "When the weather is nice, the lake and surrounding area are very scenic and excellent for running/biking," and you'll often find people "playing catch or frisbee on the quad." Depending on the time of year, students may take a boat out on the lake, or take note of how "ski areas are accessible by car from campus, and trips are often run there." Now, when it comes to nightlife, students stress that while you can definitely find "some decent parties on the weekend," the campus itself can be somewhat "overbearing" with its rules, which means that many head "downtown to the bars" instead. To its credit, "the student activities board always has events that occur during the weekend." This can range from funhouses and bubble tea to free movie screenings, which presents a fairly varied alternative.

Student Body

Undergrads at Hobart and William Smith admit that at first glance, their peers might not seem incredibly diverse. After all, many students are "from [the] Northeast/mid-Atlantic region, (relatively) upper-middle and upper class," but filled with varying passions and personalities, such as "playing the bagpipes, opera, tall ships sailing, and writing lyric essays, just to name a few." To its credit, the school fully acknowledges the socioeconomic homogeneity that sometimes arises, and has "initiatives in place to attempt to identify and balance" this. At worst, students note that the campus can get a bit clique-y, but most phrase it as an "interesting dynamic of wealth," with the overall attitude leaning toward "very inclusive and friendly." As one undergrad puts it, "There is a culture of problem solving, of community, and of collaboration," and another describes the overall class as filled with "some of the nicest human beings, who go out of the way to help." Whatever their background, the majority of HWS undergrads are united by the fact that they're "very intellectually curious, self-motivated people looking to take advantage of the many opportunities the school has to offer."

HOBART AND WILLIAM SMITH COLLEGES

Financial Aid: 315-781-3315 • E-Mail: admissions@hws.edu • Website: www.hws.edu

THE PRINCETON REVIEW SAYS

Admissions

Very important factors considered include: rigor of secondary school record, academic GPA. *Important factors considered include:* application essay, recommendation(s), interview, extracurricular activities. *Other factors considered include:* class rank, character/personal qualities, alumni/ae relation, geographical residence, state residency, religious affiliation/commitment, racial/ethnic status, level of applicant's interest. ACT with or without writing accepted. SAT with or without Essay component accepted. High school diploma is required and GED is accepted. *Academic units required:* 4 English, 3 math, 3 science, 2 science labs, 2 foreign language, 2 social studies, 2 academic electives. *Academic units recommended:* 3 foreign language, 3 social studies, 4 academic electives.

Financial Aid

Students should submit: CSS/Financial Aid PROFILE; FAFSA; Noncustodial PROFILE; State aid form. Priority filing deadline is 2/1. The Princeton Review suggests that all financial aid forms be submitted as soon as possible after October 1. *Need-based scholarships/grants offered:* College/university scholarship or grant aid from institutional funds; Federal Pell; Private scholarships; SEOG; State scholarships/grants. *Loan aid offered:* Direct PLUS loans; Direct Subsidized Stafford Loans; Direct Unsubsidized Stafford Loans. Applicants will be notified of awards on or about 4/1. Federal Work-Study Program available. Institutional employment available.

The Inside Word

Hobart and William Smith seeks applicants who want to be challenged both inside and outside the classroom. To find such students, the school takes a holistic approach to the admissions process. Therefore, you can expect that all facets of your application will be carefully assessed. And if you're truly gunning for an acceptance letter, you'll want to make sure you've taken a rigorous curriculum throughout high school. The college also typically favors students who have actively worked to better their community and demonstrate great character.

THE SCHOOL SAYS "..."

From the Admissions Office

"Hobart and William Smith Colleges seek students with a sense of adventure and a commitment to the life of the mind. In our vibrant intellectual community, students engage in a rigorous academic environment guided by dedicated professors who are deeply committed to teaching and to partnering with students on scholarship and research. With a flexible curriculum, students design an academic plan that matches their interests, strengths and goals. At HWS, students are welcomed into a supportive community focused on academic excellence and enhanced by study abroad opportunities, career preparation, leadership programs, service and civic engagement, and athletics. Hobart and William Smith are committed to equity, inclusion and diversity.

"Hobart and William Smith Colleges are test optional. Students may submit the SAT, ACT or no standardized tests at all."

SELECTIVITY

Admissions Rating	86
# of applicants	3,439
% of applicants accepted	66
% of acceptees attending	20
# offered a place on the wait list	445
% accepting a place on wait list	32
% admitted from wait list	6
# of early decision applicants	242
% accepted early decision	86

FRESHMAN PROFILE

Range SAT EBRW	590–670
Range SAT Math	590–690
Range SAT Composite	1190–1350
Range ACT Composite	26–30
# submitting SAT scores	251
% submitting SAT scores	55
# submitting ACT scores	89
% submitting ACT scores	19
Average HS GPA	3.5
% graduated top 10% of class	33
% graduated top 25% of class	63
% graduated top 50% of class	90

DEADLINES

Early decision	
Deadline	11/15
Notification	12/15
Other ED Deadline	1/15
Other ED Notification	2/15
Regular	
Deadline	2/1
Notification	4/1
Nonfall registration?	Yes

APPLICANTS ALSO LOOK AT AND OFTEN PREFER

Colgate University; Hamilton College; Cornell University; University of Rochester

AND SOMETIMES PREFER

Dickinson College; St. Lawrence University; Union College; University of Vermont

AND RARELY PREFER

State University of New York—Binghamton University; State University of New York—Geneseo; Rochester Institute of Technology

FINANCIAL FACTS

Financial Aid Rating	88
Annual tuition	$55,835
Room and board	$14,570
Books and supplies	$1,300
Average frosh need-based scholarship	$40,317
Average UG need-based scholarship	$37,831
% needy frosh rec. need-based scholarship or grant aid	100
% needy UG rec. need-based scholarship or grant aid	100
% needy frosh rec. non-need-based scholarship or grant aid	19
% needy UG rec. non-need-based scholarship or grant aid	18
% needy frosh rec. need-based self-help aid	79
% needy UG rec. need-based self-help aid	80
% frosh rec. any financial aid	89
% UG rec. any financial aid	86.5
% UG borrow to pay for school	72
Average cumulative indebtedness	$36,561
% frosh need fully met	26
% ugrads need fully met	24
Average % of frosh need met	84
Average % of ugrad need met	81

HOFSTRA UNIVERSITY

100 Hofstra University, Hempstead, NY 11549 • Admissions: 516-463-6700 • Fax: 516-463-5100

STUDENTS SAY "..."

Academics

From the instant you set foot on Hofstra University's "beautiful" campus, you can sense the "comforting and welcoming" vibe that permeates the school. Undergrads here happily report that their college is "full of opportunities" to develop "socially as well as intellectually." Many are also quick to note that the university provides "really great services for people with disabilities." And students value Hofstra's "proximity to New York City, [which] makes it ideal for [landing]…internships and [jobs]."

Academically, undergrads especially love to highlight the "impressive" Lawrence Herbert School of Communications, which is flush with some rather unique opportunities. For example, as one amazed students explains, Hofstra's radio station—WRHU—"is the ONLY college radio station to be a flagship station for a professional sports team. We are the radio home for the New York Islanders." Across all courses of study, Hofstra undergrads benefit from "small" class sizes. In turn, this gives students "a better opportunity to connect with their professors and advisors" than they'd have in large lectures. And, speaking of professors, the university consistently hires instructors who are "very knowledgeable and passionate about their subjects." It's also quite evident that they "really care about their students and want them to succeed." Finally, as one thrilled dance major sums up, "I could not put together a better university if I tried."

Life

It's not uncommon for Hofstra students to spend the majority of their week hitting the books. Fortunately, when they need a distraction from studying, there is plenty of fun to be had! To begin with, the student body is fairly athletic. As one psychology major shares, "Our sports team[s] have dedicated followings, from quidditch to volleyball." Moreover, "there are so many amazing clubs that offer so much to their members and provide community outreach and volunteer opportunities." Undergrads also love partaking in events such as "trivia night, [and] coffee house, which presents student-based music and comedy performances." "A lot of students also participate in Hofstra Versus Zombies…once every semester." When undergrads truly need a break, they often consider heading to the beach, which is a mere "ten miles [away]." And, of course, undergrads here absolutely love that New York City is so accessible. A physician assistant student explains, "there is…a direct train to NYC only fifteen minutes away and Hofstra provides a shuttle to the train station." All in all, you have to work pretty hard to be bored here.

Student Body

The "student body at Hofstra is a unique mixture of commuters and residential students." The school manages to attract both individuals from the surrounding Long Island area as well as undergrads who come all the way from China. No matter where they hail from, Hofstra students gladly report that, for the most part, their peers are "very friendly." As an English major further explains, "I can walk up to just about anyone and start a conversation on anything from the weather to Plato and Socrates." An industrial engineering student concurs, assuring us that students "are really helpful; whenever you need anything, they [are] there for you even if they haven't gotten to know you yet." And, perhaps most importantly, undergrads here "are notorious for their work ethic and ability to juggle internships, academics, and getting involved on campus." Finally, one confident psych student assures us that, "with over 200 clubs, everyone is able to find their niche and join a friend group."

Financial Aid: 516-463-8000 • E-Mail: admission@hofstra.edu • Website: http://www.hofstra.edu

THE PRINCETON REVIEW SAYS

Admissions

Very important factors considered include: rigor of secondary school record, class rank, academic GPA, application essay, recommendation(s). *Important factors considered include:* interview, extracurricular activities, talent/ability, character/personal qualities. *Other factors considered include:* standardized test scores, first generation, alumni/ae relation, geographical residence, racial/ethnic status, volunteer work, work experience, level of applicant's interest. ACT with Writing recommended. SAT with Essay component recommended. High school diploma is required and GED is accepted. *Academic units required:* 4 English, 3 math, 3 science, 1 science lab, 2 foreign language, 3 social studies. *Academic units recommended:* 4 math, 4 science, 2 science labs, 3 foreign language, 4 social studies.

Financial Aid

Students should submit: FAFSA; State aid form. Priority filing deadline is 11/15. The Princeton Review suggests that all financial aid forms be submitted as soon as possible after October 1. *Need-based scholarships/grants offered:* College/university scholarship or grant aid from institutional funds; Federal Pell; Private scholarships; SEOG; State scholarships/grants; United Negro College Fund. *Loan aid offered:* Direct PLUS loans; Direct Subsidized Stafford Loans; Direct Unsubsidized Stafford Loans. Applicants will be notified of awards on a rolling basis beginning 1/15. Federal Work-Study Program available. Institutional employment available.

The Inside Word

Hofstra admissions officers take a comprehensive look at each applicant's transcript to assess academic ability and potential. ACT or SAT scores are required for home-schooled students, individuals applying for Hofstra's Trustee Scholarship, and candidates interested in dual degree programs—but standardized tests are optional for everyone else.

THE SCHOOL SAYS "..."

From the Admissions Office

"Hofstra is a dynamic private institution that is internationally recognized for academic excellence, civic engagement and community service.

"We provide you with the resources of a large university, but the personal attention of a small college. Our average undergraduate class size is just 20, and our student:faculty ratio is 13:1. Undergraduate students, who come from 47 U.S. states and 77 countries, choose from 160 program options. Hofstra is home to schools of engineering, business, communication, education, nursing, medicine and law, as well as 17 Division I sports and 35 residence halls.

"Our 244-acre suburban campus, which is a nationally recognized arboretum, is just 25 miles east of New York City, opening the door to prestigious internships at world-class corporations.

"You'll also benefit from experiential learning on campus in our state-of-the-art facilities, including an academic trading room with 34 Bloomberg terminals; advanced engineering labs; and a cutting-edge converged newsroom and multimedia classroom. More than 200 pre-professional, social and academic clubs provide leadership and community service opportunities. Hofstra also values bringing exclusive learning opportunities to campus, most notably by hosting U.S. presidential debates in 2008, 2012 and 2016—the only school to ever host 3 consecutive debates.

"Our faculty are entrepreneurs, scholars, artists, and scientists who are pioneers in their disciplines and mentors in the classroom. They'll invite you to collaborate on research projects and connect you with industry veterans.

"At Hofstra, you will pursue your passion and find your purpose."

SELECTIVITY

Admissions Rating	85
# of applicants	24,425
% of applicants accepted	68
% of acceptees attending	9
# offered a place on the wait list	51
% accepting a place on wait list	12
% admitted from wait list	67

FRESHMAN PROFILE

Range SAT EBRW	580–660
Range SAT Math	580–680
Range ACT Composite	25–30
# submitting SAT scores	1,048
% submitting SAT scores	69
# submitting ACT scores	325
% submitting ACT scores	21
Average HS GPA	3.7
% graduated top 10% of class	32
% graduated top 25% of class	60
% graduated top 50% of class	91

DEADLINES

Early action	
Deadline	11/15
Notification	12/15
Nonfall registration?	Yes

APPLICANTS ALSO LOOK AT AND OFTEN PREFER

Boston University; New York University; Syracuse University; Northeastern University

AND SOMETIMES PREFER

Drexel University; Fordham University; Penn State University Park; State University of New York at Binghamton (Binghamton University); State University of New York—Stony Brook University; University of Delaware; Rutgers University–New Brunswick

AND RARELY PREFER

Quinnipiac University; St. John's University; University of Connecticut

FINANCIAL FACTS

Financial Aid Rating	86
Annual tuition	$46,450
Room and board	$16,428
Required fees	$1,060
Books and supplies	$1,000
Average frosh need-based scholarship	$23,883
Average UG need-based scholarship	$21,778
% needy frosh rec. need-based scholarship or grant aid	99
% needy UG rec. need-based scholarship or grant aid	96
% needy frosh rec. non-need-based scholarship or grant aid	21
% needy UG rec. non-need-based scholarship or grant aid	17
% needy frosh rec. need-based self-help aid	79
% needy UG rec. need-based self-help aid	72
% frosh rec. any financial aid	97
% UG rec. any financial aid	91
% UG borrow to pay for school	60
% frosh need fully met	25
% ugrads need fully met	23
Average % of frosh need met	71
Average % of ugrad need met	65

HOLLINS UNIVERSITY

7916 Williamson Road, Box 9707, Roanoke, VA 24020-1707 • Admissions: 540-362-6401 • Fax: 540-362-6218

STUDENTS SAY ". . ."

Academics
This small, private women's college in Roanoke, Virginia celebrated its 175th birthday during the 2016–17 academic year, and is a place for unique individuals to thrive, empowering each other and forming a supportive community for women. The school offers twenty-nine degrees with fourteen concentrations (including large English and Psychology departments), has extended campuses in London and more than twenty other study abroad destinations ("The internship and study abroad opportunities for students of this school are exceptional"), and all are required to take a collaborative First-Year Seminar. Hollins is "a great place for people who want life experience," whether in their field of study or in the world in general, and the institution offers "a lot of incredible opportunities for anyone willing to take them." Traditions abound, such as Tinker Day, when classes are randomly canceled and students and faculty hike up nearby Tinker Mountain in costume. The alumni network is similarly solid, and many students land jobs and internships through previous graduates.

Hollins professors are "amazing, talented, dedicated, and compassionate." They know their courses and "can walk you through something front to back and blindfolded." Students often "get invited out to dinner with professors or to parties and readings at their houses," and "we have professors [who go] around campus singing Christmas songs to cheer students during finals" and take students with them to the Women's March. Students "get to interact almost daily with our president, and she knows our names." Most classes here will have fewer than twenty students (even 100 level courses) so "the line of communication is direct and open," and "opportunities for involvement on campus are extremely high."

Life
Life at Hollins usually starts with "breakfast around a small table with too many people" and "really bad puns." Ladies here just love hanging out with each other, and often "play board games, go to the mall, work out together, watch movies," or "go to the music building for impromptu jam sessions." "We've also hooked our laptops up to projectors in different class-rooms to stream Netflix and various music competition live streams," says one. Arts and crafts are everywhere, and students take regular breaks to knit, crochet, and embroider, and "the hiking opportunities are endless" thanks to the nearby Blue Ridge Mountains. "Every day I am surrounded by mountains. It's a vacation view in every direction," says a student. "Hollins is its own little bubble," so many find it "nice to go out into the city every once in a while" (particularly to avoid the "less than impressive" cafeteria food) and hop a shuttle into Roanoke or to Walmart. There are also "numerous campus-wide activities put on by HAB (Hollins Activity Board)" around the year to give students the chance to meet new people or "mix with groups you usually don't have a chance to talk to."

Student Body
Many Hollins students identify as non-binary and are in the LGBTQ+ community, and the Gender Studies program is quite popular in "really [getting] students involved with what women can do and have done." This "trustworthy" bunch makes the campus "a place where you don't have to lock up your bike or worry about leaving your laptop unattended." Hollins women [aren't afraid to speak up when something they don't agree [with] pops up," and this "normally quite liberal" (as well as "predominantly white") crew is open to learning about others' different experiences. The atmosphere here can sometimes "be gossipy or clique-like, though people are usually open to lots of others."

Financial Aid: 540-362-6332 • E-Mail: huadm@hollins.edu • Website: www.hollins.edu

THE PRINCETON REVIEW SAYS

Admissions

Very important factors considered include: academic GPA, standardized test scores. *Important factors considered include:* rigor of secondary school record, application essay, recommendation(s). *Other factors considered include:* class rank, interview, extracurricular activities, talent/ability, character/personal qualities, first generation, alumni/ae relation, volunteer work, work experience, level of applicant's interest. ACT with or without writing accepted. SAT with or without Essay component accepted. High school diploma is required and GED is accepted. *Academic units required:* 4 English, 3 math, 3 science, 3 social studies. *Academic units recommended:* 3 foreign language.

Financial Aid

Students should submit: FAFSA; State aid form. Priority filing deadline is 2/1. The Princeton Review suggests that all financial aid forms be submitted as soon as possible after October 1. *Need-based scholarships/grants offered:* College/university scholarship or grant aid from institutional funds; Federal Pell; Private scholarships; SEOG; State scholarships/grants. *Loan aid offered:* Direct PLUS loans; Direct Subsidized Stafford Loans; Direct Unsubsidized Stafford Loans. Applicants will be notified of awards on a rolling basis beginning 3/1. Federal Work-Study Program available. Institutional employment available.

The Inside Word

The admit rate at Hollins University is high and gaining admission won't be terribly difficult if you have decent test scores and above-average grades. Keep in mind, though, that the applicants here are a highly self-selecting group and the admissions staff is able to take a long look at everyone who applies. Consequently, your best bet is to demonstrate a sincere desire to be a part of the unique milieu of the campus.

THE SCHOOL SAYS "..."

From the Admissions Office

"Empowering women since 1842, Hollins University unites excellence in liberal arts education with experiential learning opportunities and career preparation to help our students lead lives of consequence.

"Our broad liberal arts curriculum offers strong academic programs and superior teaching that emphasize critical thinking, problem solving, creativity, and collaboration—skills that employers seek. Our top five majors (English, business, biology, psychology, and art) underscore the breadth and scope of the Hollins experience in the physical sciences, social sciences, arts, and humanities. The university's athletic program is dedicated to the pursuit of academic achievement and athletic excellence, and is committed to the overall success of the student-athlete.

"Experiential learning opportunities include a January Short Term, where students can test drive a career with an internship, take a travel/study course, or conduct research through opportunities supported by the Rutherford Center for Experiential Learning; the Batten Leadership Institute, which teaches students how to understand and navigate feedback, conflict, and negotiation; and the Entrepreneurial Learning Institute, which provides students with the resources needed to develop an entrepreneurial outlook across all fields, including the social sciences, business, humanities, fine arts, and STEM.

"Career preparation is also a hallmark: 80% of Hollins students complete at least one internship during their undergraduate careers, and more than half participate in two or more internships. The university places students in companies, nonprofits, museums, law firms, and hospitals, both in the U.S. and abroad. One year after graduation, 95% of our students are employed or in graduate school."

SELECTIVITY

Admissions Rating	83
# of applicants	3,244
% of applicants accepted	71
% of acceptees attending	8
# of early decision applicants	11
% accepted early decision	91

FRESHMAN PROFILE

Range SAT EBRW	560–670
Range SAT Math	510–630
Range SAT Composite	1090–1280
Range ACT Composite	22–30
# submitting SAT scores	156
% submitting SAT scores	84
# submitting ACT scores	47
% submitting ACT scores	25
Average HS GPA	3.7
% graduated top 10% of class	29
% graduated top 25% of class	56
% graduated top 50% of class	86

DEADLINES

Early decision	
Deadline	11/1
Notification	11/15
Early action	
Deadline	11/15
Notification	12/1
Regular	
Priority	2/1
Deadline	Rolling
Notification	Rolling, 11/1
Nonfall registration?	Yes

FINANCIAL FACTS

Financial Aid Rating	89
Annual tuition	$39,360
Room and board	$14,300
Required fees	$750
Books and supplies	$800
Average frosh need-based scholarship	$32,963
Average UG need-based scholarship	$32,163
% needy frosh rec. need-based scholarship or grant aid	100
% needy UG rec. need-based scholarship or grant aid	100
% needy frosh rec. non-need-based scholarship or grant aid	100
% needy UG rec. non-need-based scholarship or grant aid	100
% needy frosh rec. need-based self-help aid	71
% needy UG rec. need-based self-help aid	74
% frosh rec. any financial aid	100
% UG rec. any financial aid	100
% UG borrow to pay for school	74
Average cumulative indebtedness	$33,691
% frosh need fully met	26
% ugrads need fully met	24
Average % of frosh need met	86
Average % of ugrad need met	85

HOWARD UNIVERSITY

2400 Sixth Street, NW, Suite 111, Washington, DC 20059 • Admissions: 202-806-2755 • Fax: 202-806-4465

STUDENTS SAY ". . ."

Academics

Noted for "outstanding achievements as an institution as well as the accomplishments of a great majority of its alumni," Howard University takes great pride in preparing students "to compete on a local and global level." With "inspiring faculty and a perspective that cannot be found anywhere else," the school "breeds pride and excellence" and is a "formidable force in producing African American intellectuals." "Howard University is more than a place to get an education, it is a once-in-a-lifetime experience that not only strengthens your mind, but also your spirit and pride in who you are as a person and who you have the potential to become," says an appreciative student. Other undergrads add, "I wanted the experience of attending a Historically Black College," with a rich tradition and history. "Once you become a Bison," you experience "the sense of being a part of such a tremendous legacy." Students here believe that a Howard education is wonderful preparation for life in today's competitive employment environment. "Howard pushes you and teaches patience." Professors are admired for being able to "bridge the gap between the real world and the textbook"; "it is up to you to apply information outside of class through internships and supplementary experiences." They are "supportive and helpful," have "a genuine interest in their subject," and they make sure "course material is appropriate." Discussions are encouraged, which "helps to solidify understanding.... I am able to have a voice in the class and share my opinion." Networking opportunities are abundant, and job placement upon graduation is high.

Life

A common theme heard throughout Howard University is how "students are very tight-knit and supportive of one another." "Dormitories are lively," and "life is fast-paced." School events are normally a "major part of the social calendar," and there is great encouragement for students "to be involved in campus organizations and student government." While there are many Greeks on campus, "the main focus of our Greek Life is community service. Any social event or gathering that is hosted by the Greeks normally has most or all of the proceeds going to a charity or community service project." There are also "student-run organizations that work in the community," providing "opportunities to be a part of something bigger than you." Students obviously love taking advantage of all of the opportunities the Washington, D.C., area provides. The Metro is a popular form of transportation, with the station "very easily accessible from the main Howard University campus." Many locations are Metro-accessible, but you must be cognizant of operating hours.

Student Body

At Howard University, there is at least one commonality everyone can agree on: Students are busy. "At any given time a student at Howard can be found taking a full course load, working, and interning." Extracurricular activities and community service are also on the plate of many Howard undergraduates. Students are often described as "friendly, outgoing, stylish, and fashionable." The campus exudes "a culture of achievement and encouragement"; "most students are very goal-oriented and driven." "A Howardite is very career-oriented and knows what he or she wants to do after graduation." Students here are also "very socially conscious." Geographic diversity is prevalent, and "Howard students are educated to think on a global scale." "Students are very accepting of each other and their backgrounds"; "we are an ever-changing, comprehensive, innovative, and supportive community." Meaningful conversation is prevalent, with many "discussions surrounding social and political issues." "Howard represents the best of the educated and progressive African American community."

Financial Aid: 202-806-2840 • E-Mail: admission@howard.edu • Website: www.howard.edu

THE PRINCETON REVIEW SAYS

Admissions

Very important factors considered include: rigor of secondary school record, class rank, academic GPA, standardized test scores. *Other factors considered include:* application essay, recommendation(s), extracurricular activities, talent/ability, first generation, alumni/ae relation, volunteer work, work experience, level of applicant's interest. ACT with Writing required. SAT with Essay component required. High school diploma is required and GED is accepted. *Academic units required:* 4 English, 3 math, 2 science, 2 science labs, 2 foreign language, 2 social studies, 4 academic electives.

Financial Aid

Students should submit: FAFSA. Priority filing deadline is 2/1. The Princeton Review suggests that all financial aid forms be submitted as soon as possible after October 1. *Need-based scholarships/grants offered:* College/university scholarship or grant aid from institutional funds; Federal Nursing Scholarships; Federal Pell; Private scholarships; SEOG; State scholarships/grants; United Negro College Fund. *Loan aid offered:* Direct PLUS loans; Direct Subsidized Stafford Loans; Direct Unsubsidized Stafford Loans. Applicants will be notified of awards on a rolling basis beginning 4/1. Federal Work-Study Program available. Institutional employment available.

The Inside Word

Howard attracts quite a significant number of applicants, and the school maintains a high rate of graduation for those who do gain admittance. While standardized testing is certainly a primary part of evaluating those looking to enroll, this does not preclude other students from seeking entrance; proven ability from high school and the capacity to handle higher learning in a diligent, responsible manner is also highly valued.

THE SCHOOL SAYS "..."

From the Admissions Office

"Since its founding, Howard has stood among the few institutions of higher learning where blacks and other minorities have participated freely in a truly comprehensive university experience. Thus, Howard has assumed a special responsibility in preparing its students to exercise leadership wherever their interests and commitments take them. Howard has issued approximately 111,233 degrees, diplomas, and certificates to men and women in the professions, the arts and sciences, and the humanities. The university has produced and continues to produce a high percentage of the nation's African American professionals in the fields of medicine, dentistry, pharmacy, engineering, nursing, architecture, religion, law, music, social work, education, and business. There are more than 10,036 students from across the nation and approximately eighty-six countries and territories attending the university. Their varied customs, cultures, ideas, and interests contribute to Howard's international character and vitality. More than 1,598 faculty members represent the largest concentration of black scholars in any single institution of higher education.

"All applicants who have never been to college are required to submit scores from either the SAT or the ACT (with the writing component)."

SELECTIVITY

Admissions Rating	92
# of applicants	20,946
% of applicants accepted	32
% of acceptees attending	23

FRESHMAN PROFILE

Range SAT EBRW	590–650
Range SAT Math	550–635
Range ACT Composite	22–27
# submitting SAT scores	1,123
% submitting SAT scores	75
# submitting ACT scores	625
% submitting ACT scores	42
Average HS GPA	3.6
% graduated top 10% of class	27
% graduated top 25% of class	58
% graduated top 50% of class	89

DEADLINES

Early action	
Deadline	11/1
Notification	12/20
Regular	
Priority	2/15
Deadline	2/15
Notification	Rolling, 12/20
Nonfall registration?	Yes

FINANCIAL FACTS

Financial Aid Rating	78
Annual tuition	$24,966
Room and board	$13,895
Required fees	$1,790
Books and supplies	$1,500
Average frosh need-based scholarship	$9,510
Average UG need-based scholarship	$9,833
% needy frosh rec. need-based scholarship or grant aid	61
% needy UG rec. need-based scholarship or grant aid	63
% needy frosh rec. non-need-based scholarship or grant aid	41
% needy UG rec. non-need-based scholarship or grant aid	41
% needy frosh rec. need-based self-help aid	64
% needy UG rec. need-based self-help aid	72
% frosh rec. any financial aid	96
% UG rec. any financial aid	96
% UG borrow to pay for school	78
Average cumulative indebtedness	$25,090
% frosh need fully met	6
% ugrads need fully met	7
Average % of frosh need met	64
Average % of ugrad need met	63

ILLINOIS INSTITUTE OF TECHNOLOGY

10 West 33rd Street, Chicago, IL 60616 • Admissions: 312-567-3025 • Fax: 312-567-6939

CAMPUS LIFE

Quality of Life Rating	**80**
Fire Safety Rating	**83**
Green Rating	**78**
Type of school	Private
Environment	Metropolis

STUDENTS

Total undergrad enrollment	2,722
% male/female	69/31
% from out of state	26
% frosh from public high school	87
% frosh live on campus	77
% ugrads live on campus	39
# of fraternities (% ugrad men join)	7 (10)
# of sororities (% ugrad women join)	3 (13)
% African American	6
% Asian	14
% Caucasian	33
% Hispanic	16
% Native American	<1
% Pacific Islander	0
% Two or more races	3
% Race and/or ethnicity unknown	7
% international	21
# of countries represented	94

SURVEY SAYS . . .

Very little drug use
Students love Chicago, IL
College radio is popular

ACADEMICS

Academic Rating	**77**
% students returning for sophomore year	93
% students graduating within 4 years	36
% students graduating within 6 years	71
Calendar	Semester
Student/faculty ratio	12:1
Profs interesting rating	82
Profs accessible rating	87

Most classes have 10–19 students.
Most lab/discussion sessions have fewer than 10 students.

MOST POPULAR MAJORS

Architecture; Computer and Information Sciences, General; Mechanical Engineering

STUDENTS SAY "..."

Academics

Minutes from downtown Chicago, Illinois Institute of Technology is a "beautiful green oasis in a bustling city." This career-oriented university prepares students to "[make] the jump from student to professional" with a curriculum "strongly based on applied learning" and access "to student research at all levels." But IIT "caters to those individuals that want to pursue careers in areas of STEM," the curriculum "puts an equal emphasis on the life sciences and doesn't discount humanities." And while most come for the school's "historic reputation," particularly in engineering and architecture, students don't dismiss the value of the school's diversity. "The size and diversity of Illinois Tech is perfect," one student argues, "small enough for individual attention, but large enough for various resources to be available. Working with students from around the world gives you a unique perspective that is useful after college as well." Many students offer hot and cold reviews of the faculty. "I have had some really fantastic professors who are engaging and make the material genuinely interesting," one student explains. "However, I've had the exact opposite too." Others say that their "professors are very willing to help... but [they] want you to think for yourself." Most agree that IIT "is a very academic-based institution with mostly excellent professors, especially in upper-level classes. Academics here are challenging but rewarding." Others are quick to point out that many of IIT professors "also work in the field" and, therefore, they "apply topics studied in the lectures to the real world," and "their lectures are very current with the solutions and technologies that are actually being used."

Life

Students enjoy "playing chess," "video/tabletop gaming, movie watching," but many report that "life at school is work and study every day with a few breaks in between." Or as one student appreciatively and jokingly puts it, "This school is nerd school." While some prefer a lifestyle that is "simple and sorted," these academically driven students also enjoy playing intramural sports and exploring the many museums, restaurants, and cultural attractions of the city. Between the workload, the "very strict" on-campus alcohol policies and "mostly small apartments" in Chicago "that get packed quickly," students say "there doesn't seem to be much partying going on at this school." But many students emphasize the important role that Greek life plays in their lives. "The brotherhoods and sisterhoods on campus can be a serious lifesaver," one student explains, "for those struggling socially, mentally, emotionally, and academically. Most people who go Greek refer to it as the best decision they made while at school, and those who don't join immediately often wish they did. Yes, it's that good."

Student Body

"The students at IIT are absolute nerds, and we all say that with pride." IIT "students study hard, focus for the future, bathe in the diversity of campus life, and are able to enjoy all events/programs that IIT and Chicago have to offer." Many students highlight an interest in "innovation and in aspiring creativity." IIT has "a very heavily male demographic" of "quiet introverts" who value teamwork and hail from around the world. Roughly half of the total IIT student body are international students, which "provides a variety of perspectives" and cultures present in classroom discussions and clubs. Students largely describe one another as "warm, accepting, welcoming, and friendly." Overwhelmingly, "Illinois Tech students are serious about their studies, have a great eye for design and architecture, and love to have a good time especially when there is free food involved, which is often the case."

ILLINOIS INSTITUTE OF TECHNOLOGY

Financial Aid: 312-567-7219 • E-Mail: admission@iit.edu • Website: http://www.iit.edu/

THE PRINCETON REVIEW SAYS

Admissions

Very important factors considered include: rigor of secondary school record, academic GPA, standardized test scores. *Important factors considered include:* class rank, recommendation(s). *Other factors considered include:* application essay, interview, extracurricular activities, talent/ability, character/personal qualities, first generation, alumni/ae relations, volunteer work, work experience, level of applicant's interest. ACT with or without writing accepted. High school diploma is required and GED is accepted. *Academic units required:* 4 English, 4 math, 3 science, 2 science labs. *Academic units recommended:* 4 English, 4 math, 3 science, 2 science labs, 2 foreign language, 2 social studies, 2 history, 1 computer science, 1 visual/performing arts.

Financial Aid

Students should submit: FAFSA. Priority filing deadline is 1/1. The Princeton Review suggests that all financial aid forms be submitted as soon as possible after October 1. *Need-based scholarships/grants offered:* College/university scholarship or grant aid from institutional funds; Federal Pell; Private scholarships; SEOG; State scholarships/grants. *Loan aid offered:* Direct PLUS loans; Direct Subsidized Stafford Loans; Direct Unsubsidized Stafford Loans. Applicants will be notified of awards on a rolling basis beginning 2/15. Federal Work-Study Program available. Institutional employment available.

The Inside Word

Competition to get in includes students worthy of top tech schools like MIT and CalTech, so only those who feel confident they can handle the rigorous curriculum bother applying, making the admissions pools self-selecting. It would be smart to emphasize work ethic and career goals to win over admission officers at this academically demanding and career-driven school. Extracurriculars and leadership roles always look good, but you should especially highlight any STEM-based activities outside the classroom.

THE SCHOOL SAYS "..."

From the Admissions Office

"Illinois Tech is committed to providing students a distinctive and relevant education through hands-on learning, dedicated teachers, small class sizes, and undergraduate research opportunities. From our signature Interprofessional Projects (IPRO) Program to high-tech maker spaces to cutting-edge research, we prepare students to think big and lead big like no other university can.

Classes are taught by senior faculty—not teaching assistants—who foster our culture of innovation with their own firsthand research experience. Our IPRO Program joins students from various majors to work together to solve real-world problems, often on behalf of sponsor companies and nonprofits. IPRO teaches leadership, creativity, teamwork, design thinking, and project management—uniquely preparing students to succeed in a professional work environment.

Our Elevate program connects undergraduates with experiential opportunities that allow them to learn valuable skills that will enable their upward trajectory. These opportunities include on-campus research in professors' labs, off-campus research with national and international funded programs, internships and co-ops, and study abroad. Our location in the world-class city of Chicago gives students priceless access to the professional world through internships and employment.

Illinois Tech's Accelerated Master's Program allows students to complete both a bachelor's and master's degree in as few as five years. Undergraduate scholarships apply to the fifth year of study, meaning students pay the lower undergraduate tuition rate for graduate courses.

Illinois Tech strives to make higher education accessible for all. Ninety-eight percent of undergraduates receive some form of financial aid, including merit-based scholarships ranging from $10,000 to full tuition."

SELECTIVITY

Admissions Rating	88
# of applicants	4,708
% of applicants accepted	54
% of acceptees attending	19

FRESHMAN PROFILE

Range SAT EBRW	580–680
Range SAT Math	650–730
Range ACT Composite	25–31
# submitting SAT scores	156
% submitting SAT scores	33
# submitting ACT scores	361
% submitting ACT scores	77

DEADLINES

Regular	
Priority	11/15
Deadline	8/1
Notification	Rolling, 12/1
Nonfall registration?	Yes

FINANCIAL FACTS

Financial Aid Rating	86
Annual tuition	$48,670
Room and board	$15,328
Required fees	$1,820
Books and supplies	$1,250
Average frosh need-based scholarship	$35,496
Average UG need-based scholarship	$33,045
% needy frosh rec. need-based scholarship or grant aid	99
% needy UG rec. need-based scholarship or grant aid	100
% needy frosh rec. non-need-based scholarship or grant aid	20
% needy UG rec. non-need-based scholarship or grant aid	12
% needy frosh rec. need-based self-help aid	65
% needy UG rec. need-based self-help aid	71
% frosh rec. any financial aid	99
% UG rec. any financial aid	97
% UG borrow to pay for school	54
Average cumulative indebtedness	$32,671
% frosh need fully met	22
% ugrads need fully met	13
Average % of frosh need met	85
Average % of ugrad need met	77

ILLINOIS WESLEYAN UNIVERSITY

P.O. Box 2900, Bloomington, IL 61702-2900 • Admissions: 309-556-3031 • Fax: 309-556-3820

STUDENTS SAY "..."

Academics

Located in Bloomington, Illinois Wesleyan University is a community that "invites you to make the most of your education and is ready to bend over backwards to ensure you enjoy your experience." Though the school doesn't have that big of a reputation outside the Midwest "despite its excellent education," it is an underrated gem that is "always trying to give students opportunities that are beyond what most schools can give." It truly is "a small school that oozes big opportunities."

Professors are "brilliant and accessible" "insightful" individuals who are "the best in their field." "The exuberance they have for their subject area and their students is very evident." Many of them are involved in research and "often include students in helping them," while others are involved in other ways; for example, "the mayor of Bloomington is also a political science professor—how cool is that!" "There have been a few life-changing professors who I am so grateful to have taken their class," says a business administration major.

Facilities and the career center are excellent, there are numerous opportunities for community engagement and research, and "there are so many resources and programs that help students who are seeking any type of support, whether it be academic, moral, or health." Wesleyan also "does a great job getting students ready for graduate school," and faculty "put [a lot of] effort into the information being taught, and really try and relate it to real life."

The school has a reputation for "overinvolved students who travel abroad, are the president of three clubs, and still maintain excellent grades." "IWU pushes us to excel academically while encouraging us to pursue our passions outside of our schoolwork," says a student. Overall, IWU is "a friendly community where your professors become mentors, your classmates become lifelong friends, and you graduate prepared to make a real difference in the world."

Life

As with many colleges, there's a strong weekday-weekend divide: "There is a fair trade of work and play." Sunday through Wednesday nights, "people are studying, going to meetings for clubs, maybe going to an event or two," but come the weekend, students "will go to parties at fraternity houses or off-campus houses, or go to the bars." Bloomington-Normal also has a variety of "great restaurants" and shopping venues which "are fun places to go to on the weekends," and neighboring ISU offers "some of that big college town culture [that] can be found in the area."

The Office of Student Activities "does a great job having entertainment available for students" and almost every weekend a free event is held in the student center, "whether that be a concert, comedian, movie, or other entertainment." There is a "plethora of study groups" ("People are very receptive to getting work done together"), "great opportunities for intellectual discussions" at the coffee shop, and "students are always in food areas discussing, reading, or doing homework." "We have a weird obsession with the Game Show network as well here," confesses a student. "Buncha dorks. We know it and we own it!"

Student Body

The typical Wesleyan student "has a major that they take great pride in studying" and "often compare workloads to bond." Students here are "very academically focused" ("it's very rare to find students who don't try") but are also aware that "having a social life is important as well." Almost everyone is "very liberal and rather artistic" and "very involved with many different activities." While there are noticeable groups such as "athletes, Greek life, and theater kids" which mainly stick together, "everyone has friends in other departments and organizations." There is "lots of competition on campus for internships and research opportunities," but "everyone is very helpful when it comes to informing others of opportunities." A "large percentage" of the campus is Greek life-affiliated.

ILLINOIS WESLEYAN UNIVERSITY

Financial Aid: 309-556-3096 • E-Mail: iwuadmit@iwu.edu • Website: www.iwu.edu

THE PRINCETON REVIEW SAYS

Admissions

Very important factors considered include: rigor of secondary school record, academic GPA, interview. *Important factors considered include:* class rank, application essay, standardized test scores, extracurricular activities, talent/ability, character/personal qualities. *Other factors considered include:* recommendation(s), first generation, alumni/ae relation, geographical residence, state residency, racial/ethnic status, volunteer work, work experience, level of applicant's interest. ACT with or without writing accepted. SAT with or without Essay component accepted. High school diploma is required and GED is accepted. *Academic units recommended:* 4 English, 3 math, 3 science, 2 science labs, 3 foreign language, 2 social studies.

Financial Aid

Students should submit: FAFSA; Institution's own financial aid form. Priority filing deadline is 3/1. The Princeton Review suggests that all financial aid forms be submitted as soon as possible after October 1. *Need-based scholarships/grants offered:* College/university scholarship or grant aid from institutional funds; Federal Pell; Private scholarships; SEOG; State scholarships/grants. *Loan aid offered:* Direct PLUS loans; Direct Subsidized Stafford Loans; Direct Unsubsidized Stafford Loans. Applicants will be notified of awards on a rolling basis beginning 3/1. Federal Work-Study Program available. Institutional employment available.

The Inside Word

There's no application fee at IWU, and the school accepts the Common Application, so there are few reasons not to apply to IWU if you're even slightly interested in attending. Those applying to any of the creative arts school may be required to submit additional materials such as a portfolio. Don't expect to breeze through, though. You won't get into this highly selective college without a solid academic profile or a compelling story.

THE SCHOOL SAYS "..."

From the Admissions Office

"Illinois Wesleyan University attracts a wide variety of students who are interested in pursuing diverse fields such as vocal performance, biology, psychology, political science, physics, or business administration. At IWU, students are not forced into either/or choices. Rather, they are encouraged to pursue multiple interests simultaneously—a philosophy that is in keeping with the spirit and value of a liberal arts education. The distinctive 4-4-1 calendar allows students to follow their interests each school year in two semesters followed by an optional month-long class in May. May term opportunities include classes on campus; research collaboration with faculty; travel and study in such places as Australia, China, South Africa, and Europe; as well as local, national, and international internships. Study abroad is very popular, with one out of every two students enjoying a travel experience.

"The IWU mission statement reads in part: 'A liberal education at Illinois Wesleyan fosters creativity, critical thinking, effective communication, strength of character, and a spirit of inquiry; it deepens the specialized knowledge of a discipline with a comprehensive world view. It affords the greatest possibilities for realizing individual potential while preparing students for democratic citizenship and life in a global society...The university, through its policies, programs, and practices, is committed to diversity, social justice, and environmental sustainability. A tightly knit, supportive university community, together with a variety of opportunities for close interaction with excellent faculty, both challenges and supports students in their personal and intellectual development.'"

SELECTIVITY
Admissions Rating	86
# of applicants	3,785
% of applicants accepted	59
% of acceptees attending	22

FRESHMAN PROFILE
Range SAT EBRW	570–660
Range SAT Math	550–665
Range ACT Composite	24–29
# submitting SAT scores	295
% submitting SAT scores	60
# submitting ACT scores	325
% submitting ACT scores	66
Average HS GPA	3.8
% graduated top 10% of class	34
% graduated top 25% of class	63
% graduated top 50% of class	95

DEADLINES
Early action	
Deadline	11/15
Notification	12/15
Regular	
Notification	Rolling, 1/15
Nonfall registration?	Yes

APPLICANTS ALSO LOOK AT AND OFTEN PREFER
Illinois State University; Northwestern University

AND SOMETIMES PREFER
University of Illinois at Urbana-Champaign;
Washington University in St. Louis

AND RARELY PREFER
Augustana College (IL); DePaul University

FINANCIAL FACTS
Financial Aid Rating	87
Annual tuition	$49,284
Room and board	$11,412
Required fees	$204
Books and supplies	$800
Average frosh need-based scholarship	$33,749
Average UG need-based scholarship	$30,077
% needy frosh rec. need-based scholarship or grant aid	100
% needy UG rec. need-based scholarship or grant aid	100
% needy frosh rec. non-need-based scholarship or grant aid	17
% needy UG rec. non-need-based scholarship or grant aid	11
% needy frosh rec. need-based self-help aid	79
% needy UG rec. need-based self-help aid	74
% frosh rec. any financial aid	100
% UG rec. any financial aid	99
% UG borrow to pay for school	68
Average cumulative indebtedness	$35,077
% frosh need fully met	24
% ugrads need fully met	18
Average % of frosh need met	87
Average % of ugrad need met	84

INDIANA UNIVERSITY—BLOOMINGTON

940 E. Seventh Street, Bloomington, IN 47405 • Admissions: 812-855-0661 • Fax: 812-855-5102

CAMPUS LIFE

Quality of Life Rating	92
Fire Safety Rating	94
Green Rating	86
Type of school	Public
Environment	City

STUDENTS

Total undergrad enrollment	32,794
% male/female	51/49
% from out of state	36
% frosh live on campus	98
% ugrads live on campus	33
# of fraternities (% ugrad men join)	35 (19)
# of sororities (% ugrad women join)	33 (24)
% African American	5
% Asian	6
% Caucasian	69
% Hispanic	7
% Native American	<1
% Pacific Islander	0
% Two or more races	5
% Race and/or ethnicity unknown	<1
% international	8
# of countries represented	116

SURVEY SAYS . . .

Great library
Internships are widely available
Students love Bloomington, IN
Recreation facilities are great
Lots of beer drinking
Hard liquor is popular
Everyone loves the Hoosiers
Intramural sports are popular
Theater is popular
Active student government

ACADEMICS

Academic Rating	82
% students returning for sophomore year	90
% students graduating within 4 years	67
% students graduating within 6 years	79
Calendar	Semester
Student/faculty ratio	16:1
Profs interesting rating	88
Profs accessible rating	94

Most classes have 20–29 students.
Most lab/discussion sessions have
20–29 students.

MOST POPULAR MAJORS

Public Administration; Business/Commerce,
General

STUDENTS SAY " . . ."

Academics

Indiana University Bloomington focuses on creating well-rounded students who will be successful in and after college. This large state school challenges its students academically, but it "creates a fun collegiate environment, as well." "Academics and school spirit are its specialties!" says one student. The institution offers excellent financial aid and numerous opportunities for graduate and undergraduate students across all departments to conduct research, adding to "the perfect combination of excellent undergraduate teaching, Division I athletic teams backed by a passionate sense of school spirit, and a lively social scene." The "many excellent professors" here "really care about what they do," and they really "know what they're talking about." They "clearly want what's best for their students," and "the learning environment they create is excellent." "I have been very impressed with the individual attention I have received—mostly due to the level of commitment by professors to their students," says one student. The "rigorous and competitive classroom environment" gives students "the knowledge to be successful in our futures through great faculty, facilities, and tradition." Most professors at IU have professional experiences, and therefore "can bring their subjects to life." The "world-renowned business program" and the education and media schools are standouts here, but students say that all of the "school systems are great and easy to access," which makes "communicating with students/professors easy." Even with 50,000 people on campus, the administration gives student groups "much freedom of planning," and this warm environment allows students to "collaborate academically and non-academically as one community." This autonomy grants students the chance to explore "anything we want, whenever, but [find] the key thing we'll love through many opportunities and great programs."

Life

This "best-kept secret of the Midwest" is located in "the vibrant city of Bloomington," where "the restaurants off campus are amazing," with "many options to choose from." During the week, people "work really hard," and the campus is very active, with "a good number of students working out or running." There is "always something going on and something to do on campus that will fit the need of any student." Weekends generally start on Thursday night and go through Saturday night, when "house parties are popular," and the Greek system, although it only encompasses roughly 20 percent of the campus, "provides a strong social scene." The legendary IU basketball team is "starting to really rebuild its legacy," and attending games is common. There are also "free movies at the Union on weekends," and just "a very fun social scene" in general. Looking around the "beautiful" campus, you can see people jogging, and if the weather's really nice, you can find people lying outside on the grass and on benches snoozing."

Student Body

With such a large student body, "You are destined to find someone who you 'click' with." "It's unheard of that a student won't be able to fit in somewhere," says one. Typical is hard to nail down with tens of thousands of people, but many here are "very respectful of one another and ready to help out a fellow Hoosier" and "very lively and fun," and each student manages to have "an equal balance of school and social life." International students (often attracted by the business and music schools) are "accepted and encouraged to attend IU." Most students can be called "hard workers who also know how to have fun on the weekends."

Financial Aid: 812-855-6500 • E-Mail: admissions@indiana.edu • Website: https://www.indiana.edu/

THE PRINCETON REVIEW SAYS

Admissions

Very important factors considered include: rigor of secondary school record, class rank, academic GPA, standardized test scores (optional). *Important factors considered include:* application essay, *Other factors considered include:* recommendation(s), interview, extracurricular activities, talent/ability, character/personal qualities, first generation, alumni/ae relation, geographical residence, state residency, racial/ethnic status, volunteer work, work experience. ACT with or without writing accepted. SAT with or without Essay component accepted. High school diploma is required and GED is accepted. *Academic units required:* 4 English, 3.5 math, 3 science, 2 science labs, 2 foreign language, 3 social studies, 1.5 academic electives.

Financial Aid

Students should submit: FAFSA. Priority filing deadline is 4/15. The Princeton Review suggests that all financial aid forms be submitted as soon as possible after October 1. *Need-based scholarships/grants offered:* College/university scholarship or grant aid from institutional funds; Federal Pell; Private scholarships; SEOG; State scholarships/grants. *Loan aid offered:* Direct PLUS loans; Direct Subsidized Stafford Loans; Direct Unsubsidized Stafford Loans. Applicants will be notified of awards on a rolling basis beginning 2/15. Federal Work-Study Program available. Institutional employment available.

The Inside Word

Above-average high school performers (defined by both grade point average and test scores) should meet little resistance from the IU admissions office. Students will have the opportunity to meet admissions representatives at numerous recruiting events held in many locations throughout the country or during a campus visit. Rolling admission favors those who apply early in the process. IU's music program is highly competitive; admission hinges upon a successful audition.

THE SCHOOL SAYS "..."

From the Admissions Office

"Indiana University Bloomington, one of America's great teaching and research universities, extends learning and teaching beyond the traditional classroom. When visiting campus, students and parents typically describe IU as 'what college should be like.' Students bring diverse experiences, beliefs, and backgrounds from all fifty states and more than 100 countries to a campus often cited as one of the most beautiful in the nation. IU offers a quintessential college experience. Students enjoy the advantages, opportunities, and resources of a large school, while still receiving personal attention and support. Because of the outstanding academic and cultural resources, students have the best of both worlds.

"Indiana University offers more than 4,000 courses and 200+ undergraduate majors—many nationally and internationally known—including programs in the arts, sciences, humanities, and social sciences as well as highly rated Schools of Business, Music, Education, Media, Public and Environmental Affairs, and Public Health. Students customize academic programs with double and individualized majors, internships, and research opportunities, utilizing state-of-the-art technology. Representatives from more than 1,300 businesses, government agencies, and not-for-profit organizations come to campus yearly to recruit IU students.

"Applicants must submit a complete application for admission, including official transcript, IU-specific essay, and SAT/ACT scores (if applicable) by November 1 to receive highest consideration for IU Academic Scholarships and the Selective Scholarship Application."

SELECTIVITY

Admissions Rating	85
# of applicants	42,902
% of applicants accepted	78
% of acceptees attending	25
# offered a place on the wait list	1,945
% accepting a place on wait list	21
% admitted from wait list	1

FRESHMAN PROFILE

Range SAT EBRW	580–670
Range SAT Math	570–690
Range SAT Composite	1160–1350
Range ACT Composite	24–31
# submitting SAT scores	6,292
% submitting SAT scores	76
# submitting ACT scores	4,689
% submitting ACT scores	57
Average HS GPA	3.7
% graduated top 10% of class	35
% graduated top 25% of class	69
% graduated top 50% of class	95

DEADLINES

Early action	
Deadline	11/1
Notification	1/15
Regular	
Priority	2/1
Notification	1/15
Nonfall registration?	Yes

FINANCIAL FACTS

Financial Aid Rating	84
Annual in-state tuition	$9,575
Annual out-of-state tuition	$35,140
Room and board	$10,830
Required fees	$1,372
Books and supplies	$1,110
Average frosh need-based scholarship	$12,490
Average UG need-based scholarship	$12,679
% needy frosh rec. need-based scholarship or grant aid	87
% needy UG rec. need-based scholarship or grant aid	81
% needy frosh rec. non-need-based scholarship or grant aid	24
% needy UG rec. non-need-based scholarship or grant aid	19
% needy frosh rec. need-based self-help aid	51
% needy UG rec. need-based self-help aid	56
% frosh rec. any financial aid	84.7
% UG rec. any financial aid	74.6
% UG borrow to pay for school	44
Average cumulative indebtedness	$27,555
% frosh need fully met	31
% ugrads need fully met	29
Average % of frosh need met	71
Average % of ugrad need met	71

INDIANA UNIVERSITY OF PENNSYLVANIA

1011 South Drive, Indiana, PA 15705-1085 • Admissions: 724-357-2230 • Fax: 724-357-6281

STUDENTS SAY ". . ."

Academics

Indiana University of Pennsylvania maintains a simple way of doing things—provide students with an "inexpensive" education replete with "respected" programs. And the university has certainly delivered on those promises. Indeed, from the "good business school" to the "great writing program," undergrads have their pick of some truly stellar academic departments. Special praise is reserved for IUP's "fantastic" communications media program in which students have access to "a full-fledged commercial radio station (WIUP-FM), television studio (IUP-TV), two photography studios, a print studio, a full audio lab, a full motion capture/video game lab, and a huge center dedicated for media production and research (CMPR)." Beyond amazing facilities, undergrads at IUP have the privilege of learning from "great," "knowledgeable" professors. Most instructors here work to ensure that "discussion[s are] a big part of [the classroom]...experience." Moreover, it's clearly evident that they're "passionate about what they do." As a journalism and public relations major explains, "My professors really care about their subjects and take the time to thoroughly explain concepts and ideas to students." And a thrilled nursing major sums it up: "[Professors] feel like family and express that they genuinely care about the students outside of just the classroom situation. They see [us] as more than just students and aim to help us get the most out of IUP resources and time."

Life

It's quite easy to lead a full (and busy!) life at IUP. After all, "there are many opportunities to get involved on campus." Students can participate in "everything from National Honors Societies to sports teams, and everything in between." While some students admit that "drinking is a large part of [social life]" at IUP, others insist that there "are great alternatives to partying." These include "bingo on Friday nights, the incredible theatre productions, as well as multiple art galleries on campus." We're also told that "Indiana, PA is very much a college town." And when students want to take a break from campus life, they often head to Philadelphia Street, "a bustling center of bars and restaurants...almost all of the businesses on Philly Street are very welcoming to students." Many undergrads love taking advantage of "dollar bowling night" as well. And students yearning to get a little farther away can take advantage of IUP's "really great entertainment network," which frequently organizes trips to "Pirates games, Penguins games, Steeler[s'] games, museums, [and] concerts." All in all, it's easy to get out and about and Pittsburgh is only about an hour's drive away.

Student Body

Many undergrads at Indiana University of Pennsylvania steadfastly assert that there's "no typical student here." As a geology and applied math double-major explains, "The variety of majors offered here attracts many different people with different interests and goals in life. Whatever you are looking for here, you will most likely find it." A nutrition major concurs adding, "There is [a] large mix of personalities on campus. From jock, preppy, intellectual, band member, religious etc. Because of this, everyone can fit in with at least one type of group." That being said, it can often feel as though the vast majority of students are "white, Christian, straight, and from an upper-middle class family in central or western PA." A premed student bemoans, "IUP has very little diversity, and the towns these students come from also have very little diversity. It can be tough being different sometimes." Thankfully, however, the majority of undergrads here are "friendly" and "helpful" and "open to meeting new people."

INDIANA UNIVERSITY OF PENNSYLVANIA

Financial Aid: 724-357-2218 • E-Mail: admissions-inquiry@iup.edu • Website: www.iup.edu

THE PRINCETON REVIEW SAYS

Admissions

Very important factors considered include: academic GPA. *Important factors considered include:* rigor of secondary school record, standardized test scores. *Other factors considered include:* class rank, application essay, recommendation(s), interview, extracurricular activities, talent/ability, character/personal qualities, first generation. ACT with or without writing accepted. SAT with or without Essay component accepted. High school diploma is required and GED is accepted. *Academic units required:* 4 English, 3 math, 3 science, 2 science labs. *Academic units recommended:* 2 foreign language, 3 social studies.

Financial Aid

Students should submit: FAFSA; State aid form. Priority filing deadline is 5/1. The Princeton Review suggests that all financial aid forms be submitted as soon as possible after October 1. *Need-based scholarships/grants offered:* College/university scholarship or grant aid from institutional funds; Federal Pell; Private scholarships; SEOG; State scholarships/grants; United Negro College Fund. *Loan aid offered:* Direct PLUS loans; Direct Subsidized Stafford Loans; Direct Unsubsidized Stafford Loans. Applicants will be notified of awards on a rolling basis beginning 12/15. Federal Work-Study Program available. Institutional employment available.

The Inside Word

Admissions officers at Indiana University of Pennsylvania pay closest attention to academic preparation and performance when considering applications. Officers typically only consider personal statements, recommendations and extracurricular participation for applicants on the border of eligibility. Finally, IUP operates on the basis of rolling admissions. Therefore, it is advantageous to apply as early as possible.

THE SCHOOL SAYS "..."

From the Admissions Office

"At IUP, we look at each applicant as an individual, not as a number. That means we'll review your application materials very carefully. When reviewing applications, the admissions committee's primary focus is on the student's high school record and SAT or ACT scores. We're always happy to speak with prospective students. E-mail us at admissions-inquiry@iup.edu.

"Students applying for admission are required to take the SAT or ACT."

SELECTIVITY

Admissions Rating	73
# of applicants	10,061
% of applicants accepted	93
% of acceptees attending	19

FRESHMAN PROFILE

Range SAT EBRW	460–570
Range SAT Math	450–550
Range SAT Composite	920–1110
Range ACT Composite	16–23
# submitting SAT scores	1,575
% submitting SAT scores	89
# submitting ACT scores	225
% submitting ACT scores	13
Average HS GPA	3.3
% graduated top 10% of class	9
% graduated top 25% of class	27
% graduated top 50% of class	59

DEADLINES

Regular	
Notification	Rolling, 9/1
Nonfall registration?	Yes

APPLICANTS ALSO LOOK AT AND OFTEN PREFER

Penn State University Park; West Chester University of Pennsylvania; University of Pittsburgh—Pittsburgh Campus; Bloomsburg University of Pennsylvania; Slippery Rock University of Pennsylvania

FINANCIAL FACTS

Financial Aid Rating	79
Annual in-state tuition	$9,570
Annual out-of-state tuition	$13,890
Room and board	$12,744
Required fees	$3,784
Books and supplies	$1,100
Average frosh need-based scholarship	$6,904
Average UG need-based scholarship	$6,341
% needy frosh rec. need-based scholarship or grant aid	68
% needy UG rec. need-based scholarship or grant aid	66
% needy frosh rec. non-need-based scholarship or grant aid	57
% needy UG rec. non-need-based scholarship or grant aid	61
% needy frosh rec. need-based self-help aid	93
% needy UG rec. need-based self-help aid	90
% frosh rec. any financial aid	84
% UG rec. any financial aid	84
% UG borrow to pay for school	84
Average cumulative indebtedness	$41,222
% frosh need fully met	4
% ugrads need fully met	5
Average % of frosh need met	52
Average % of ugrad need met	53

IOWA STATE UNIVERSITY

100 Enrollment Services Center, Ames, IA 50011-2011 • Admissions: 515-294-5836 • Fax: 515-294-2592

CAMPUS LIFE

Quality of Life Rating	91
Fire Safety Rating	89
Green Rating	99
Type of school	Public
Environment	Town

STUDENTS

Total undergrad enrollment	27,936
% male/female	57/43
% from out of state	37
% frosh live on campus	93
% ugrads live on campus	20
# of fraternities (% ugrad men join)	44 (13)
# of sororities (% ugrad women join)	36 (21)
% African American	3
% Asian	4
% Caucasian	76
% Hispanic	6
% Native American	<1
% Pacific Islander	<1
% Two or more races	3
% Race and/or ethnicity unknown	4
% international	5
# of countries represented	118

SURVEY SAYS . . .

Students are happy
Recreation facilities are great
Everyone loves the Cyclones
Intramural sports are popular
Frats and sororities are popular

ACADEMICS

Academic Rating	76
% students returning for sophomore year	87
% students graduating within 4 years	47
% students graduating within 6 years	74
Calendar	Semester
Student/faculty ratio	18:1
Profs interesting rating	85
Profs accessible rating	90

Most classes have 20–29 students.
Most lab/discussion sessions have
  20–29 students.

STUDENTS SAY "..."

Academics

Iowa State University is the state's largest research university, offering more than one hundred majors, most notably in the science and technical fields, including an engineering program which is "practically unrivaled." Other standouts include the aerospace program and the journalism and design schools. The school is "quick to add new courses on developing technology" and even make some courses available online, and an excellent job placement rate means "if you're looking to not just get a job but build a career, you're in the right place." Due to the size of the university, there are a lot of opportunities (such as "getting to tour and even work at some of the cutting edge research locations in the world"), and teachers will bring in people who work in the field "to talk to you about what their job is like so you can network and learn about your opportunities." In addition to all the classroom and professional resources, there is a largely popular campus lecture series on various topics, and the university is also currently building a student innovation center. "If you are willing to work hard, you can accomplish a lot."

The faculty at the school are "outstanding" and "represent some of the best instructors in the country." Professors "have so much knowledge to share" and include "innovative approaches" in which students "use technology and applications to do assignments." "Not only are they great teachers, but they're great people," says one student. Classes are hands-on and coursework is "challenging in a way that helps [students] know that [they] will be prepared to perform well" in their future careers, but for anyone struggling with their work, "there's a lot of help if you look for it." Overall, students find that Iowa State "offers everything a student needs to succeed" and strives to ensure that every student "succeeds and performs at a high level academically, professionally, and in their personal lives."

Life

Ames is "the perfect college town." Since Iowa State is the main focus, "everyone that lives here cheers for the Cyclones." The school as a whole has "Midwest values," as well as "a plethora of extracurricular opportunities to be involved as a leader or for fun." All of the classes and buildings are located in the same area or near each other to help students avoid being late to class and "a walk across campus is usually only ten minutes." The fun usually happens on the weekends, with students heading to parties, bars, or sporting events, and there are also "great places to go for dinner, movie theaters, and lots of volunteering opportunities" to keep busy. Clubs (over 800!) "are huge here" and "everyone has their niche." One student says, "Living in a dorm is the best choice" you can make as a first-year student. Dorms often host game tournaments, movie nights, and other events. There's a "state of the art" recreation center (and other facilities), and during nice times of the year, people around campus hammock in the trees and go hiking.

Student Body

According to some students, Iowa State University "lacks diversity as a student body." But students consistently feel that their peers are "very kind, hardworking, and smart," and tend to be "generally a mix of engineering, design, and agriculture students," all of whom comprise "a good mix of people having fun and studying." There is a sizable number of international students at Iowa State, and the entire student body "looks after one another and are always very helpful towards newcomers." The "Iowa Nice" idea is "clearly embodied by the students of Iowa State," and this is "a special breed of people displaying hospitality and kindness in any situation."

IOWA STATE UNIVERSITY

Financial Aid: 515-294-2223 • E-Mail: admissions@iastate.edu • Website: www.iastate.edu

THE PRINCETON REVIEW SAYS

Admissions

Very important factors considered include: rigor of secondary school record, class rank, academic GPA, standardized test scores. *Other factors considered include:* application essay, recommendation(s), interview, extracurricular activities, talent/ability, character/personal qualities, geographical residence, state residency, volunteer work, work experience. ACT with or without writing accepted. SAT with or without Essay component accepted. High school diploma is required and GED is accepted. *Academic units required:* 4 English, 3 math, 3 science, 2 science labs, 2 foreign language, 2 social studies. *Academic units recommended:* 4 English, 4 math, 4 science, 3 science labs, 3 foreign language, 4 social studies.

Financial Aid

Students should submit: FAFSA. Priority filing deadline is 12/1. The Princeton Review suggests that all financial aid forms be submitted as soon as possible after October 1. *Need-based scholarships/grants offered:* College/university scholarship or grant aid from institutional funds; Federal Pell; SEOG; State scholarships/grants. *Loan aid offered:* Direct PLUS loans; Direct Subsidized Stafford Loans; Direct Unsubsidized Stafford Loans. Applicants will be notified of awards on a rolling basis beginning 1/30. Federal Work-Study Program available. Institutional employment available.

The Inside Word

Admission to Iowa State University is formula driven and based on: ACT composite score; high school GPA; high school percentile rank; and number of high school courses completed in core subject areas. The formula, known as the Regent Admission Index (RAI), is as follows: RAI = (2 × ACT composite score) + (1 × percentile high school rank) + (20 × high school grade point average) + (5 × number of years of high school courses completed in the core subject areas). Anyone earning an RAI score of at least 245 is automatically admitted. The admissions office reviews applicants scoring below 245 individually to determine whom among them will also be admitted. An alternate RAI is calculated for schools that do not use class rank.

THE SCHOOL SAYS " . . . "

From the Admissions Office

"Iowa State University offers all the advantages of a major university along with the friendliness and warmth of a residential campus. There are more than 100 undergraduate programs of study in the Colleges of Agriculture and Life Sciences, Business, Design, Human Sciences, Engineering, Liberal Arts and Sciences, and Veterinary Medicine. Our 1,800 faculty members include Rhodes Scholars, Fulbright Scholars, and National Academy of Sciences and National Academy of Engineering members. Recognized for its high quality of life, Iowa State has taken practical steps to make the university a place where students feel like they belong. Iowa State has been recognized for the high quality of campus life and the exemplary out-of-class experiences offered to its students. Along with a strong academic experience, students also have opportunities for further developing their leadership skills and interpersonal relationships through any of the more than 800 student organizations, sixty intramural sports, and a multitude of arts and recreational activities."

SELECTIVITY

Admissions Rating	**79**
# of applicants	18,246
% of applicants accepted	92
% of acceptees attending	33

FRESHMAN PROFILE

Range SAT EBRW	540–650
Range SAT Math	560–690
Range ACT Composite	22–28
# submitting SAT scores	965
% submitting SAT scores	17
# submitting ACT scores	4,860
% submitting ACT scores	87
Average HS GPA	3.7
% graduated top 10% of class	28
% graduated top 25% of class	62
% graduated top 50% of class	93

DEADLINES

Regular	
Priority	3/1
Nonfall registration?	Yes

FINANCIAL FACTS

Financial Aid Rating	**87**
Annual in-state tuition	$8,042
Annual out-of-state tuition	$23,230
Room and board	$9,149
Required fees	$1,278
Books and supplies	$1,041
Average frosh need-based scholarship	$9,264
Average UG need-based scholarship	$8,499
% needy frosh rec. need-based scholarship or grant aid	98
% needy UG rec. need-based scholarship or grant aid	97
% needy frosh rec. non-need-based scholarship or grant aid	47
% needy UG rec. non-need-based scholarship or grant aid	44
% needy frosh rec. need-based self-help aid	66
% needy UG rec. need-based self-help aid	70
% frosh rec. any financial aid	90.6
% UG rec. any financial aid	81.6
% UG borrow to pay for school	56
Average cumulative indebtedness	$28,097
% frosh need fully met	20
% ugrads need fully met	21
Average % of frosh need met	82
Average % of ugrad need met	78

ITHACA COLLEGE

Ithaca College, Office of Admission, Ithaca, NY 14850-7002 • Admissions: 800-429-4274

STUDENTS SAY ". . ."

Academics

"Small class sizes" that afford plenty of "personal attention," "outstanding" scholarships, and cross-registration with nearby Cornell University are a few great reasons to choose Ithaca College, a smallish school in central New York that offers many of the resources you would expect to find at a much larger university. "You are able to be a part of a community and get the chance to pursue interests that are not necessarily a part of your chosen course of study," relates an English major. "We have loads of opportunities to do and try a wide variety of things." The vast multitude of academic offerings includes "one of the best communication schools in the country." Also notable are "strong" majors in music, business, and drama; a "highly competitive" six-year doctorate program in physical therapy; and the cinema and photography program. Professors are "really engaging and understand how to present the material so that it is relevant and meaningful." On the whole, faculty members are "really passionate about their fields and have a genuine interest in getting students excited about their passions." By far, the most common academic complaint about academics at Ithaca concerns registration, which can be trying. Some say, "the buildings—inside and out—are a bit outdated." Overall the campus is known for its picturesque beauty. "People aren't kidding when they say 'Ithaca is Gorges (gorgeous),'" promises one student.

Life

The number of extracurricular choices is "considerable" at Ithaca College. At the same time, "the school is small enough for anyone to get involved." There are "speakers and events offered on campus." There's also a nearly professional-quality college radio station. Many students "are part of an athletic team or participate in intramural athletics." For relaxation, students often "hang out on the quad," throwing Frisbees or "playing music on the lawns on tie-dye sheets." The social situation at Ithaca is "nothing like the party scene you'd find at a larger university," but "there are some good parties" now and then. While the campus is a little "isolated," students also frequently manage to attend frat parties at Cornell and generally "enjoy the social scene" the nearby Ivy offers. "The town of Ithaca is quaint but lively." There's "a good music scene and a lot of cool stores." When the weather is nice, "there's always some festival," or at least it seems that way. "If you're an outdoorsy person," the wooded and rocky surrounding area is a wonderland of activity. "The hiking here is unbelievable," and few other schools offer the opportunity to "go cliff jumping on a hot Saturday." On the negative side, winters are cold as a matter of course, and "the cold and rain do hinder activities." Students joke, be prepared to get your exercise walking between classes; "the hills here will kill you."

Student Body

The typical undergrad here is "genuine," "easygoing," "always busy," "well-dressed," and has a "sunny disposition despite the gray skies." Beyond those qualities, the population is "a wide mix of hipsters, jocks, theater kids, music students," and "crunchy granola hippies." "People of all kinds fit in here." "Everyone finds their niche." Cliques are often based loosely on academics. "Ithaca is not so much one community as a whole," explains one student. "Instead, each school (music, communications, business, etc.) is its own community." Ethnic diversity and other kinds of diversity are "not entirely unheard of." However, people are "usually from the Northeast," and "the population of students that fit into the typical suburban, upper-middle-class family is definitely significant." Politically, "students at Ithaca tend to be liberal." Some students tell us that you'll find "a lot of people are environmentally and socially conscious" here who want "to change the world."

Financial Aid: 607-274-3131 • E-Mail: admission@ithaca.edu • Website: www.ithaca.edu

THE PRINCETON REVIEW SAYS

Admissions

Very important factors considered include: rigor of secondary school record, academic GPA, level of applicant's interest. *Important factors considered include:* application essay, recommendation(s), extracurricular activities, talent/ability, character/personal qualities. *Other factors considered include:* class rank, standardized test scores, interview, first generation, alumni/ae relation, volunteer work, work experience. ACT with or without writing accepted. SAT with or without Essay component accepted. High school diploma is required and GED is accepted. *Academic units required:* 4 English, 3 math, 3 science, 2 foreign language, 3 social studies, 1 academic elective. *Academic units recommended:* 4 English, 4 math, 4 science, 3 foreign language, 4 social studies, 1 academic elective.

Financial Aid

Students should submit: CSS/Financial Aid PROFILE; FAFSA. Priority filing deadline is 2/1. The Princeton Review suggests that all financial aid forms be submitted as soon as possible after October 1. *Need-based scholarships/grants offered:* College/university scholarship or grant aid from institutional funds; Federal Pell; Private scholarships; SEOG; State scholarships/grants. *Loan aid offered:* Direct PLUS loans; Direct Subsidized Stafford Loans; Direct Unsubsidized Stafford Loans. Applicants will be notified of awards on a rolling basis beginning 2/15. Federal Work-Study Program available. Institutional employment available.

The Inside Word

Ithaca's admissions profile continues to be on the rise with a good deal of highly competitive applicants. Programs requiring an audition (for example, music) are among Ithaca's most demanding for admission. If you want to pursue the six-year clinical doctorate in physical therapy, focus on completing substantial math and science coursework in high school.

THE SCHOOL SAYS "..."

From the Admissions Office

"Located in central New York's Finger Lakes region, Ithaca College offers almost 100 majors in its Schools of Business, Communications, Health Sciences and Human Performance, Humanities and Sciences, and Music.

"Whether you dream of becoming a media mogul, nonprofit hero, groundbreaking scientist, or brilliant composer—Ithaca College will prepare you for a successful future. Our dedicated professors are experts in their fields and will make you an expert in yours by providing hands-on experience from day one. Experiment in a lab, light up the stage, take risks in the stock market—whatever your interests, you'll dive in right away to turn classroom theory into well-practiced skill.

"From our vibrant campus community to the world beyond, you'll find exciting opportunities to expand your mind and enhance your education. Nearly 200 student organizations provide the perfect place to create award-winning projects, volunteer, philosophize, and connect. Add more valuable skills with a fast-paced internship or enlightening study-abroad program, including our semester-long options in New York City, L.A., and London. From campus life to life experience, Ithaca College will prepare you for your career and anything that comes your way.

"To learn more, visit ithaca.edu/life."

SELECTIVITY

Admissions Rating	84
# of applicants	14,192
% of applicants accepted	73
% of acceptees attending	15
# offered a place on the wait list	278
% accepting a place on wait list	108
% admitted from wait list	43
# of early decision applicants	144
% accepted early decision	135

FRESHMAN PROFILE

Range SAT EBRW	590–680
Range SAT Math	570–670
Range SAT Composite	1170–1340
Range ACT Composite	26–30
# submitting SAT scores	752
% submitting SAT scores	50
# submitting ACT scores	254
% submitting ACT scores	17
% graduated top 10% of class	23
% graduated top 25% of class	57
% graduated top 50% of class	88

DEADLINES

Early decision	
Deadline	11/1
Notification	12/15
Early action	
Deadline	12/1
Notification	2/1
Regular	
Deadline	2/1
Notification	4/15
Nonfall registration?	Yes

APPLICANTS ALSO LOOK AT AND OFTEN PREFER
Boston University; New York University; Northeastern University; Syracuse University

AND SOMETIMES PREFER
Penn State University Park; University of Vermont

FINANCIAL FACTS

Financial Aid Rating	86
Annual tuition	$45,274
Room and board	$15,570
Books and supplies	$1,200
Average frosh need-based scholarship	$29,394
Average UG need-based scholarship	$29,930
% needy frosh rec. need-based scholarship or grant aid	97
% needy UG rec. need-based scholarship or grant aid	99
% needy frosh rec. non-need-based scholarship or grant aid	40
% needy UG rec. non-need-based scholarship or grant aid	19
% needy frosh rec. need-based self-help aid	90
% needy UG rec. need-based self-help aid	89
% frosh rec. any financial aid	98.5
% UG rec. any financial aid	96.4
% UG borrow to pay for school	69
Average cumulative indebtedness	$42,000
% frosh need fully met	59
% ugrads need fully met	46
Average % of frosh need met	92
Average % of ugrad need met	88

JAMES MADISON UNIVERSITY

Sonner Hall, Harrisonburg, VA 22807 • Admissions: 540-568-5681 • Fax: 540-568-3332

STUDENTS SAY "..."

Academics

James Madison University has a reputation as "a school that values education, respect, and integrity." The university boasts "one of the best BA programs for musical theater on the East Coast," and an "amazing" business school. A communication major says, "James Madison offered a positive, enriching, and supportive learning environment," and most students agree that JMU is an "inspiring environment filled with students striving to be productive members of society." A senior says, "I found the JMU environment to be comfortable and conducive to learning," and it seems clear that "JMU is all about taking your academics seriously." Professors get consistently high marks for being "available to help" and "interested in student achievement." Although they're often described as "challenging," students say professors are "willing to facilitate your education in any way possible" and "are very down to earth, approachable, and huge supporters of discussion-based classes." Like any large university, there are "some professors you want to avoid," and students grumble that "registering for classes, if you don't have priority, is a pain." It's worth noting, however, that "classrooms and facilities are always well kept and very up-to-date with all the best teaching technology."

Life

Located in Virginia's Shenandoah Valley, JMU is known for its "beautiful" campus, and students rave about the "benefits of walking in the mountains." An English major says, "The moment I walked on campus I was captured by the student spirit and how beautiful it is." School spirit is generally high, and students say, "There's a huge sense of JMU pride, everyone loves the Dukes!" A senior adds, "We have so much pride for our school. There is a friendly, collaborative ambiance here that is unparalleled anywhere else." The university is known for its Southern hospitality, and one student describes the student body as "the 'door-holding freaks of America' because even when people are several feet away, we stand there to hold the door for them." There are numerous ways to get involved on campus, and the "sheer number of student activities is stellar." Students rave about the "personal involvement that JMU offer(s)," and say, "They make you feel like a part of the campus, not just another number." Food services and facilities get high marks across the board, and most agree that the "administration and faculty are always willing to talk to students and point them in the right direction," noting that one of "the greatest strengths of the school is the ability to get any sort of assistance when needed." Regardless, there are complaints about traffic on campus, and many feel, "the school could improve on parking, by a long shot."

Student Body

At JMU, "the typical student is friendly, smart, open-minded, and fun." Students describe themselves as "excellent [at] maintaining a round, balanced life," and say, "Everyone seems relaxed and knows how to have fun but keep their school work a priority." One student jokes that the typical student is "probably a girl considering our ratio seems like eighty to twenty at times," and another concurs, "more males would be nice." Students tend to be "white from the upper- to middle-class," and an International Affairs major says, "Although we do have all types here, most people consist of your typical prep wearing Uggs and a North Face." Some complain, "There is party atmosphere here that can seem dominating," and say, "If you do not go out and party you stand out." Others note, however, "Greek life is small," and parties "are usually open to everyone," adding that partying isn't "all students here think about. People will get together and drink for fun, but it isn't a necessity." A sophomore says, "On the weekends, students can go to downtown Harrisonburg to the various restaurants and shops," or enjoy on-campus movies at a reduced rate. Still others take advantage of the "great places to hike and spend time outdoors" and JMU's easy accessibility to nearby ski resorts.

JAMES MADISON UNIVERSITY

Financial Aid: 540-568-7820 • E-Mail: admissions@jmu.edu • Website: www.jmu.edu

THE PRINCETON REVIEW SAYS

Admissions

Very important factors considered include: rigor of secondary school record, academic GPA. *Other factors considered include:* application essay, standardized test scores, recommendation(s), extracurricular activities, talent/ability, character/personal qualities, first generation, alumni/ae relation, geographical residence, state residency, racial/ethnic status, volunteer work, work experience. High school diploma is required and GED is accepted. *Academic units required:* 4 English, 4 math, 3 science, 3 foreign language, 2 social studies, 3 history. *Academic units recommended:* 4 English, 4 math, 3 science, 3 foreign language, 2 social studies, 3 history.

Financial Aid

Students should submit: FAFSA. Priority filing deadline is 3/1. The Princeton Review suggests that all financial aid forms be submitted as soon as possible after October 1. *Need-based scholarships/grants offered:* College/university scholarship or grant aid from institutional funds; Federal Pell; Private scholarships; SEOG; State scholarships/grants. *Loan aid offered:* Direct PLUS loans; Direct Subsidized Stafford Loans; Direct Unsubsidized Stafford Loans. Applicants will be notified of awards on a rolling basis beginning 4/1. Federal Work-Study Program available. Institutional employment available.

The Inside Word

At JMU admissions are competitive, but the admissions staff insists that they're not searching for a "magic combination" of test scores and GPA. Admissions officers review each application individually and are most interested in the quality of an applicant's secondary school education, followed by performance and test scores. The personal statement is a vehicle for conveying information an applicant deems important but doesn't appear elsewhere in the application, as such it's optional.

THE SCHOOL SAYS "..."

From the Admissions Office

"James Madison University's philosophy of inclusiveness—known as 'all together one'—means that students become a part of a real community that nurtures its own to learn, grow, and succeed. Our professors, many of whom have a wealth of real-world experience, pride themselves on making teaching their top priority. We take seriously the responsibility to maintain an environment that fosters learning and encourages students to excel in and out of the classroom. Our rich variety of educational, social, and extracurricular activities includes more than 100 innovative and traditional undergraduate majors and programs, a well-established study abroad program, a cutting-edge information security program, more than 350 student clubs and organizations, and an expanded 280,000-square-foot, state-of-the-art recreation center. The university's picturesque, self-contained campus is located in the heart of the Shenandoah Valley, a four-season area that's easy to call home. Great food, fun times, exciting intercollegiate athletics, and rigorous academics all combine to create the unique James Madison experience. From the library to the residence halls and from our outstanding Honors College to our highly successful career placement program, the university is committed to equipping our students with the tools they need to achieve their dreams."

SELECTIVITY

Admissions Rating	82
# of applicants	21,099
% of applicants accepted	75
% of acceptees attending	29
# offered a place on the wait list	2,500
% accepting a place on wait list	57
% admitted from wait list	16

FRESHMAN PROFILE

Range SAT EBRW	560–640
Range SAT Math	540–620
Range ACT Composite	23–28
# submitting SAT scores	4,064
% submitting SAT scores	87
# submitting ACT scores	1,629
% submitting ACT scores	35
% graduated top 10% of class	16
% graduated top 25% of class	51
% graduated top 50% of class	94

DEADLINES

Early action	
Deadline	11/1
Notification	1/15
Regular	
Deadline	1/15
Notification	4/1
Nonfall registration?	No

FINANCIAL FACTS

Financial Aid Rating	82
Annual in-state tuition	$7,250
Annual out-of-state tuition	$24,100
Room and board	$10,740
Required fees	$4,956
Books and supplies	$1,038
Average frosh need-based scholarship	$8,076
Average UG need-based scholarship	$6,908
% needy frosh rec. need-based scholarship or grant aid	56
% needy UG rec. need-based scholarship or grant aid	55
% needy frosh rec. non-need-based scholarship or grant aid	7
% needy UG rec. non-need-based scholarship or grant aid	7
% needy frosh rec. need-based self-help aid	72
% needy UG rec. need-based self-help aid	65
% frosh rec. any financial aid	62
% UG rec. any financial aid	58
% UG borrow to pay for school	51
Average cumulative indebtedness	$29,189
% frosh need fully met	77
% ugrads need fully met	67
Average % of frosh need met	34
Average % of ugrad need met	37

JOHNS HOPKINS UNIVERSITY

3400 North Charles Street, Baltimore, MD 21218 • Admissions: 410-516-8171 • Fax: 410-516-6025

STUDENTS SAY "..."

Academics

Johns Hopkins University in Baltimore might have a rep for STEM, but undergrads say JHU offers a diversity of strong programs, including in music and political science, in which students "[can] study anything and still be taught by the highest of experts." Students say that the academics here are "beyond compare" and rave about the interdisciplinary studies, hands-on engagement, and an "availability of resources, research, internship, and job opportunities [that] are unmatched." With 5,300 undergrads, Hopkins is "small enough for strong interactions among students" and large enough for "unparalleled opportunities to pursue research, form strong relationships with professors, and learn from an outstanding group of peers." While most students major in STEM fields, they "come from various backgrounds and have vastly different experiences," and every student here is "overwhelmingly passionate about what they do and aspires to make an impact in their field." Students have the ability to design their own curriculum, and professors "make themselves very accessible to their students for coffee chats, career advice or even just to give life advice." Though there are a few duds in the bunch (and "some TAs sometimes don't speak the best English"), most instructors are "more than willing to push class topics beyond the confines of the textbook to expose us to the implications of the topics discussed in class." Students appreciate that Hopkins posts what other students think of courses so each person "can see what classes appear 'better' and so professors can gain feedback and improve." Classes are "rigorous but very cooperative" and teach you "how to approach any problem fearlessly." The strong alumni network helps with job placement, and the school "gives out a lot of money to undergrads with good ideas through the Wilson Fellowship." Professors are eager ("almost giddy even") to take undergraduates under their wings and show them how to do research, and these opportunities are available regardless of your major: "One of my art history major friends curated his own exhibit in a gallery downtown (with work from several world-renowned artists) as his research project," says a student.

Life

There's a saying about the "Hopkins 500"—that "it's the same 500 people who are social and go out to parties and bars." In reality, "it's probably closer to one thousand but it's always the same people you see out," and the library doesn't necessarily die down just because it's a weekend night; "some of the students prefer to study all the time." Though life can get stressful, "most students at Hopkins are the type that thrive under pressure." The majority of student life "revolves around clubs and organizations," and throughout the week (as well as on weekends), students will also attend "concerts, symposiums with famous guest speakers or explore what Baltimore has to offer, such as its "a great music and food scene." Nearby Mount Vernon "has fantastic culture and food," and Fells Point and Federal Hill are known for their nightlife; Orioles and Ravens games are also popular. Thanks to the city's relatively low cost of living, students "tend to go out and eat at nice restaurants without paying too much money." During lacrosse season, some people will go the games and "get really involved in the season."

Student Body

This group of "ambitious workhorses" are "very intellectually curious and smart" and "want to be on the forefront of innovation." The typical Hopkins student "works really hard, and knows how to cut loose as well." Though many students are interested in the sciences, everyone at Johns Hopkins "brings something unique to the school whether it is their love for art, school spirit at sporting events or their desire to find a cure for cancer." The demographics include "a lot of international people and people from various backgrounds." There may be "a lot of introverts," but "people are very nice and helpful," and everyone is "invested in the livelihood of the Hopkins community."

JOHNS HOPKINS UNIVERSITY

Financial Aid: 410-516-8028 • E-Mail: gotojhu@jhu.edu • Website: apply.jhu.edu

THE PRINCETON REVIEW SAYS

Admissions

Very important factors considered include: rigor of secondary school record, academic GPA, application essay, standardized test scores, recommendation(s), character/personal qualities. *Important factors considered include:* class rank, extracurricular activities, talent/ability. *Other factors considered include:* first generation, geographical residence, state residency, racial/ethnic status, volunteer work, work experience. ACT with or without writing accepted. SAT with or without Essay component accepted. High school diploma or equivalent is not required. *Academic units recommended:* 4 English, 4 math, 4 science, 4 foreign language, 2 social studies, 2 history.

Financial Aid

Students should submit: CSS/Financial Aid PROFILE; FAFSA; Noncustodial PROFILE. Priority filing deadline is 1/15. The Princeton Review suggests that all financial aid forms be submitted as soon as possible after October 1. *Need-based scholarships/grants offered:* College/university scholarship or grant aid from institutional funds; Federal Pell; Private scholarships; SEOG; State scholarships/grants. *Loan aid offered:* Direct PLUS loans; Direct Subsidized Stafford Loans; Direct Unsubsidized Stafford Loans. Applicants will be notified of awards on or about 4/1. Federal Work-Study Program available. Institutional employment available.

The Inside Word

Top schools like Hopkins receive more and more applications every year and, as a result, grow harder and harder to get into. With nearly 30,000 applicants, Hopkins can be highly selective and looks for individuals who will thrive in the Hopkins community. Counselors utilize a holistic approach to admissions and in particular are looking for applicants who can demonstrate their academic character, their impact outside of the classroom, and how they engage with their communities. Hopkins is need-blind, meets 100 percent of demonstrated need, and funds financial aid packages with grants instead of loans.

THE SCHOOL SAYS "..."

From the Admissions Office

"Johns Hopkins University is a place where ambitious, talented, and creative students thrive. We offer students the freedom to pursue their intellectual curiosities, the opportunity to learn from academic leaders, and the chance to make an impact right away. With a flexible curriculum, students are able—and encouraged—to build the academic path that is right for them, with guidance from staff and administrators to help them find their way. Our students combine their interests—academic and otherwise—in ways that are meaningful to them and often discover new passions. More than 60 percent double major or minor, establishing a dynamic, engaging learning environment where students from various backgrounds bring different perspectives to class discussions. Students also encounter real-world experiences—like implementing marketing plans for local companies and heading startup businesses on campus—through FastForward (an entrepreneurial hub for students) and the Center for Leadership Education and classes in business, marketing and communications, accounting and financial management, and entrepreneurship and management. Eighty percent of students across all disciplines participate in research, which takes place in labs, museums, and unconventional places throughout campus and in the city of Baltimore. Studying abroad is also a common option, with one third of students studying abroad annually in nearly 50 countries all over the globe. Outside of the classroom, students are active and engaged on a lively campus, involved in activities from dance or singing groups to international service organizations. The admissions committee approaches applications from a holistic perspective, evaluating the 'whole student.' In addition to looking at a student's academic achievement, intellectual curiosity, and community impact, we seek to admit students who are excited about learning and living at Johns Hopkins. We look for students who will bring something to the campus community while taking advantage of all Johns Hopkins has to offer."

SELECTIVITY

Admissions Rating	99
# of applicants	30,164
% of applicants accepted	10
% of acceptees attending	46
# offered a place on the wait list	2,108
% accepting a place on wait list	67
% admitted from wait list	0
# of early decision applicants	2,047
% accepted early decision	31

FRESHMAN PROFILE

Range SAT EBRW	710–770
Range SAT Math	760–800
Range SAT Composite	1480–1550
Range ACT Composite	33–35
# submitting SAT scores	851
% submitting SAT scores	63
# submitting ACT scores	503
% submitting ACT scores	37
Average HS GPA	3.9
% graduated top 10% of class	98
% graduated top 25% of class	99
% graduated top 50% of class	100

DEADLINES

Early decision	
Deadline	11/1
Notification	12/15
Regular	
Deadline	1/1
Notification	3/15
Nonfall registration?	No

FINANCIAL FACTS

Financial Aid Rating	96
Annual tuition	$57,010
Room and board	$16,800
Required fees	$500
Books and supplies	$1,260
Average frosh need-based scholarship	$52,523
Average UG need-based scholarship	$47,843
% needy frosh rec. need-based scholarship or grant aid	96
% needy UG rec. need-based scholarship or grant aid	97
% needy frosh rec. non-need-based scholarship or grant aid	7
% needy UG rec. non-need-based scholarship or grant aid	6
% needy frosh rec. need-based self-help aid	76
% needy UG rec. need-based self-help aid	80
% frosh rec. any financial aid	56
% UG rec. any financial aid	55
% UG borrow to pay for school	41
Average cumulative indebtedness	$24,107
% frosh need fully met	97
% ugrads need fully met	99
Average % of frosh need met	100
Average % of ugrad need met	100

JUNIATA COLLEGE

1700 Moore Street, Huntingdon, PA 16652-2119 • Admissions: 814-641-3420 • Fax: 814-641-3100

STUDENTS SAY "..."

Academics

Juniata College is a private liberal arts college located in Huntingdon, Pennsylvania. The college is named after the Juniata River. The school has "excellent science programs," and a few students say that there need to be "more resources [for] non-science programs." However, even students not majoring in science get access to some great facilities, with theater students exclaiming, "The theater program is unlike any other in country" and praising their new Halbritter Center for the Performing Arts. At Juniata, students can design their educational plan with the college's Program of Emphasis. Many students do so, about 30 percent. Those interested in a specific established program—something like accounting or chemistry—can use an existing designated Program of Emphasis. All students have the option of working with two faculty advisors. The "outstanding education" is built on a bedrock of strong faculty members who offer "superior education through meaningful personal interaction." Most class sizes tend to be fairly small, and though some classes are "tough to get in to because there is only one professor for a certain subject," many agree that they love the attention that each professor gives and that the teachers "really go out of their way" to help students succeed and "value student success as much as the student does." Success, however, doesn't come without a price at Juniata, with a large amount of the students agreeing that their "good grades do not come without effort," but that the class load is "challenging, but not overwhelming."

Life

Students seem to agree that there "isn't much to do in the town" of Huntingdon, but Juniata College makes up for it by making sure there is "always something to do" on campus. There are so many activities and groups on campus that some say, "It feels like you're missing out if you go home for the weekend." There are a "lot of traditions such as Storming of the Arch, Mountain Day, and Madrigal" that have been around the campus for decades and help bring students together. For instance, during Mountain Day, classes are canceled, and students and faculty are shuttled to a state park near the school where there are lunches, nature walks, and various games being played, and neither group knows when exactly it is going to be until the morning of the event. While there might be a lot of activities to do on campus, "if you want to party you can find one." If you want to just relax with your fellow students, "Raystown Lake is only twenty minutes away," where many students like to go and relax. Back on campus, many students seem to think that the "dorms and food" need improvement, but believe that the academic experience they receive outweighs those drawbacks.

Student Body

Students tend to describe themselves as "driven" and "passionately interested in their subjects," though they also take pride in their "laid-back" attitudes, saying they "know how to balance fun and work." During the week students "tend to buckle down and get their work done." A lot of "exchange students from around the world" come to Juniata College to pursue their education. Students agree that "everyone fits in somewhere" at Juniata College because "people are accepted not despite their differences, but because of them."

Financial Aid: 814-641-3144 • E-Mail: admissions@juniata.edu • Website: www.juniata.edu

THE PRINCETON REVIEW SAYS

Admissions

Very important factors considered include: rigor of secondary school record, academic GPA, application essay, recommendation(s), character/personal qualities. *Important factors considered include:* extracurricular activities, talent/ability, first generation. *Other factors considered include:* class rank, standardized test scores, interview, alumni/ae relation, geographical residence, state residency, racial/ethnic status, work experience, level of applicant's interest. ACT with or without writing accepted. SAT with or without Essay component accepted. High school diploma is required and GED is accepted. *Academic units required:* 4 English, 3 math, 3 science, 2 science labs, 1 social studies, 3 history. *Academic units recommended:* 4 English, 3 math, 3 science, 2 science labs, 2 foreign language, 1 social studies, 3 history.

Financial Aid

Students should submit: FAFSA. Priority filing deadline is 3/15. The Princeton Review suggests that all financial aid forms be submitted as soon as possible after October 1. *Need-based scholarships/grants offered:* College/university scholarship or grant aid from institutional funds; Federal Pell; Private scholarships; SEOG; State scholarships/grants. *Loan aid offered:* Direct PLUS loans; Direct Subsidized Stafford Loans; Direct Unsubsidized Stafford Loans. Federal Work-Study Program available. Institutional employment available.

The Inside Word

High school seniors who are interested in Juniata must apply either by November 15 for early decision, January 5 for early action, or March 15 for regular decision. Interested applicants can submit their SAT or ACT scores, but standardized test scores are not required. This is in addition to the required essays that are part of the application process. For those looking to save some money, there is no application fee for anyone who applies to Juniata via the website. They also provide incoming freshman with Inbound Retreats each August, which allows them to sign up for one of thirty-eight different retreats and get an idea of what college life is like, but without having to go to class.

THE SCHOOL SAYS "..."

From the Admissions Office

"Surrounded by stunning natural beauty, Juniata College welcomes inquisitive, talented, and hardworking students who do the work of becoming broadly educated, effective citizens of the world. Students can write their own academic programs based on their interests, talents, and goals. They contribute to a close-knit community of people who support, celebrate, and enjoy one another. Highly focused scholars, Juniata students conduct research, engage in meaningful service, intern on or near campus and across the globe, compete as athletes, and collaborate as artists. All of this happens in a modern oasis seemingly reserved for the purpose of fostering exploration and reflection.

"We firmly believe college years are the time to contemplate individual goals and explore options while enjoying the journey. We encourage students to consider new ideas and perspectives, take risks, push themselves to new experiences. As a result, our students graduate in four years not only with a useful college degree, but also with self-reliance, intellectual dexterity, courage of heart, and a collaborative, compassionate spirit.

"In discussions with their advisers, students choose a single discipline POE or write one that is customized to their interests. Still others become the authors of a POE no student has done before. The POE system at Juniata helps students act upon their deepening understanding of themselves and complete an undergraduate education that prepares them for success as they choose to define it. The true power of the POE, however, is that it provides a foundation upon which layers of experiences and opportunities can be added. The result is meaningful outcomes for individuals of consequence."

SELECTIVITY

Admissions Rating	85
# of applicants	2,437
% of applicants accepted	70
% of acceptees attending	20

FRESHMAN PROFILE

Range SAT EBRW	540–660
Range SAT Math	540–660
Range ACT Composite	27–32
# submitting SAT scores	284
% submitting SAT scores	80
# submitting ACT scores	71
% submitting ACT scores	20
Average HS GPA	3.8
% graduated top 10% of class	31
% graduated top 25% of class	67
% graduated top 50% of class	93

DEADLINES

Early decision	
Deadline	11/15
Notification	12/1
Early action	
Deadline	1/5
Notification	2/15
Regular	
Priority	11/15
Deadline	3/15
Notification	2/1
Nonfall registration?	Yes

APPLICANTS ALSO LOOK AT AND SOMETIMES PREFER

Penn State University Park; Allegheny College; Susquehanna University

FINANCIAL FACTS

Financial Aid Rating	88
Annual tuition	$46,250
Room and board	$12,800
Required fees	$825
Books and supplies	$1,000
Average frosh need-based scholarship	$33,956
Average UG need-based scholarship	$32,148
% needy frosh rec. need-based scholarship or grant aid	99
% needy UG rec. need-based scholarship or grant aid	99
% needy frosh rec. non-need-based scholarship or grant aid	19
% needy UG rec. non-need-based scholarship or grant aid	13
% needy frosh rec. need-based self-help aid	83
% needy UG rec. need-based self-help aid	87
% frosh rec. any financial aid	99
% UG rec. any financial aid	98
% UG borrow to pay for school	77
Average cumulative indebtedness	$31,156
% frosh need fully met	24
% ugrads need fully met	19
Average % of frosh need met	87
Average % of ugrad need met	84

KALAMAZOO COLLEGE

1200 Academy Street, Kalamazoo, MI 49006 • Admissions: 269-337-7166 • Fax: 269-552-5083

STUDENTS SAY " . . . "

Academics

Kalamazoo College, a private liberal arts college in Michigan, brings a personalized approach to education through a flexible, open curriculum featuring real-world experience, service learning, study abroad, and an independent senior year project. This small, nationally-recognized institution "allows students to really develop personal relationships with their peers and professors" and is "a campus run by and for the students." The open curriculum means "students have more time to explore exactly what they want to learn, rather than being required to take classes in which they have no interest," and the school motto of "More in Four" not only describes how much students will learn in their time at Kalamazoo, but "also that this institution will try as hard as possible to get you to graduate in four years." As for post-graduate plans, alumni are "very easy to contact and willing to help." "Through alumni interaction and my experiences at Kalamazoo, there is a huge culture of giving back to the school and being there for each other," says a student.

Full-time professors here, 96 percent of whom hold a PhD or the highest degree in their field, "present challenging information and generally work to achieve camaraderie with students." They "definitely understand that classes may be difficult and really, truly want to help students learn the best they can," and also view students "as equals and peers, and are open to listening to everyone's ideas in classes." Professors "demand quite a lot, but only from a desire to teach the material effectively"; they also "message their departments with internship opportunities quite regularly." Most students have only three classes at a time (the school is on a quarter system) "because each class here tends to be more intense."

Life

Academics are a universal student priority at Kalamazoo, and "missing classes or letting work slack for social lives and hangovers doesn't happen often." Many times residence halls will host community building events that provide "good food and fun activities," and the school puts on numerous events for the students such as Friday night movies and "Zoo After Dark," and offers a wide variety of programs and clubs to join, and "all are accessible to students who want to pursue them." There "isn't a lot to do' in the surrounding area, but those that are twenty-one can hit a few bars or clubs and those with access to a car can drive to nearby malls and cities. There "is not a lot of time to have fun on weekdays since things move quickly," but people make time for good old Netflix, room hangs, and coffee breaks. Athletics are popular and "easy to get into"; some teams are more competitive than others, "but for the most part if you played in high school you can play in college." Most students study abroad at some point in their Kalamazoo career (typically junior year).

Student Body

Kalamazoo College students are generally "very open-minded, unique, liberal, and quirky," and "you will never find any two students that are the same here." This is mostly a campus of "socially conscious liberals who are predominantly white," though there are a fair number of people with conservative ideologies. While many admit Kalamazoo "needs more diversity in race," students say it is a "very open campus community for people of different gender identities and sexualities." Each student is able to find their niche quickly due to the small-school environment, thus "everyone is always engaged in some kind of work they truly care about."

KALAMAZOO COLLEGE

Financial Aid: 269-337-7192 • E-Mail: admission@kzoo.edu • Website: www.kzoo.edu

THE PRINCETON REVIEW SAYS

Admissions

Very important factors considered include: rigor of secondary school record, academic GPA, extracurricular activities. *Important factors considered include:* application essay, recommendation(s). *Other factors considered include:* standardized test scores, interview, talent/ability, character/personal qualities, first generation, alumni/ae relation, geographical residence, state residency, racial/ethnic status, volunteer work, work experience, level of applicant's interest. ACT with or without writing accepted. SAT with or without Essay component accepted. High school diploma is required and GED is accepted. *Academic units required:* 4 English, 3 math, 3 science, 3 foreign language, 2 social studies, 2 history. *Academic units recommended:* 4 English, 4 math, 4 science, 4 foreign language, 2 social studies, 2 history.

Financial Aid

Students should submit: FAFSA. Priority filing deadline is 11/15. The Princeton Review suggests that all financial aid forms be submitted as soon as possible after October 1. *Need-based scholarships/grants offered:* College/university scholarship or grant aid from institutional funds; Federal Pell; Private scholarships; SEOG; State scholarships/grants. *Loan aid offered:* Direct PLUS loans; Direct Subsidized Stafford Loans; Direct Unsubsidized Stafford Loans. Applicants will be notified of awards on a rolling basis beginning 1/15. Federal Work-Study Program available. Institutional employment available.

The Inside Word

The "K-Plan," which focuses on a broad liberal arts education and engagement with other cultures, is central to the Kalamazoo education. Consequently, college admissions officers are on the lookout for students that show the creativity, ambition, and motivation to thrive at Kalamazoo. Students with artistic backgrounds will want to emphasize that in their application. Admissions are competitive here, so applicants will be expected to have strong standardized test scores and high school grades.

THE SCHOOL SAYS "..."

From the Admissions Office

"The *K-Plan* at Kalamazoo College offers an integrated approach to experiential education that is comprehensive and customizable. Seventy percent of students participate in a meaningful, immersive study abroad program; 71 percent participate in career development programs such as internships, externships, and career treks; and 100 percent complete a senior project. Our students often pursue international internships and senior project experiences, in addition to their planned study abroad terms. Also, Kalamazoo College is one of the few selective liberal arts colleges to be found in a city—the Kalamazoo metro area has a population of nearly 335,000 with the advantage of being near a university of nearly 25,000 students. It is a diverse and vibrant community with wonderful access to the arts, athletics, service-learning, and social activism opportunities. We do more in four years so students can do more in a lifetime.

"Emphasis in admission is placed on a student's high school experience, including GPA, course selection, application essay, and co-curricular involvement."

SELECTIVITY

Admissions Rating	87
# of applicants	3,371
% of applicants accepted	73
% of acceptees attending	17
# offered a place on the wait list	291
% accepting a place on wait list	51
% admitted from wait list	91
# of early decision applicants	59
% accepted early decision	85

FRESHMAN PROFILE

Range SAT EBRW	590–690
Range SAT Math	550–680
Range ACT Composite	24–31
# submitting SAT scores	163
% submitting SAT scores	40
# submitting ACT scores	112
% submitting ACT scores	27
Average HS GPA	3.8
% graduated top 10% of class	54
% graduated top 25% of class	84
% graduated top 50% of class	99

DEADLINES

Early decision	
Deadline	11/1
Notification	12/1
Other ED Deadline	2/1
Other ED Notification	2/15
Early action	
Deadline	11/1
Notification	12/20
Regular	
Priority	11/15
Deadline	1/15
Notification	4/1
Nonfall registration?	No

FINANCIAL FACTS

Financial Aid Rating	90
Annual tuition	$50,046
Room and board	$10,134
Required fees	$516
Books and supplies	$825
Average frosh need-based scholarship	$37,082
Average UG need-based scholarship	$34,817
% needy frosh rec. need-based scholarship or grant aid	97
% needy UG rec. need-based scholarship or grant aid	98
% needy frosh rec. non-need-based scholarship or grant aid	23
% needy UG rec. non-need-based scholarship or grant aid	18
% needy frosh rec. need-based self-help aid	76
% needy UG rec. need-based self-help aid	79
% frosh rec. any financial aid	98
% UG rec. any financial aid	97
% UG borrow to pay for school	61
Average cumulative indebtedness	$32,226
% frosh need fully met	39
% ugrads need fully met	36
Average % of frosh need met	94
Average % of ugrad need met	91

KANSAS STATE UNIVERSITY

119 Anderson Hall, Manhattan, KS 66506 • Admissions: 785-532-6250 • Fax: 785-532-6393

STUDENTS SAY ". . ."

Academics

Kansas State is a large institution, but despite its size, the university manages to feel "very personable and really [focused] on the student," offering a "welcoming environment and atmosphere." When it comes to academics, "K-State's are top notch." Students particularly call out the programs at the school's "great College of Agriculture, College of Engineering, and College of Veterinary Medicine." Additionally, professors from across all disciplines receive glowing reviews: the faculty "truly cares about teaching," and the "engaging" professors provide "stimulating discussion and work" by "encouraging discussion and in-class participation." It's also common for instructors to "go above and beyond to make sure students learn and enjoy their classes." Lastly, undergrads here truly value the fact that K-State professors are typically "very willing to meet you outside of class to help with any questions or further explain concepts."

Life

It's virtually impossible to be bored at Kansas State. Activities on-campus truly run the gamut, ranging from a "Greek community [with] strong participation" to "the Steel Bridge team where [you can learn] to weld." Students also note that "sports are a big part of life here." As one undergrad adds, "The lead-up to [games] is celebrated days out and dominates much of [the] culture." You can also always find a handful of undergrads "playing basketball at the Rec or playing sand volleyball." Beyond team sports, you'll discover that "a lot of students use the recreational complex to work out individually or with a class." For those looking for a milder form of relaxation, many K-State Wildcats simply like to "hang up hammocks on campus in the spring." Moreover, a number of undergrads rave about Manhattan, Kansas, which is "a small town [that has] so much to do and experience." Students also love to head to Aggieville, a neighborhood that has tons of "shopping [and a] bar and restaurant district." And the more outdoorsy types enjoy taking advantage of bike rides along Linear Trail as well as "hiking the Konza or visiting Turtle Creek Reservoir."

Student Body

Undergraduates at K-State share sentiments about the "helpful, polite, and friendly" nature that permeates the student body. As one student explains, "Wherever I go on campus, people are always willing to hold the door open for me, and I … am always willing to do the same." A fellow classmate adds, "As a K-State Family, we help each other out, whether that be … forming study groups, carpooling, or walking someone to a building that they are looking for." This is truly a "genuinely kind" student body. They're also a "hardworking," "passionate," and "driven" lot, a sentiment highlighted by the many students who "spend hours upon hours in the … library studying." K-State students are also united by their deep ties to the school, finding it is "often … a generational thing [in which] parents, grandparents, and great parents have gone here and continue to instill a passion" for the university. When it comes down to it, one student sums it up nicely: "At Kansas State, we live for each other, we work for each other, and most importantly, we succeed together." As another explains, "The … reason that I chose K-State was that I felt at home when I visited the campus."

Financial Aid: 785-532-6420 • E-Mail: k-state@k-state.edu • Website: www.k-state.edu

THE PRINCETON REVIEW SAYS

Admissions

Very important factors considered include: rigor of secondary school record, class rank, academic GPA, standardized test scores. *Important factors considered include:* level of applicant's interest. *Other factors considered include:* recommendation(s). ACT with or without writing accepted. SAT with or without Essay component accepted. High school diploma is required and GED is accepted. *Academic units required:* 4 English, 3 math, 3 science, 3 social studies, 3 academic electives.

Financial Aid

Students should submit: FAFSA. Priority filing deadline is 3/1. The Princeton Review suggests that all financial aid forms be submitted as soon as possible after October 1. *Need-based scholarships/grants offered:* College/university scholarship or grant aid from institutional funds; Federal Pell; Private scholarships; SEOG; State scholarships/grants. *Loan aid offered:* Direct PLUS loans; Direct Subsidized Stafford Loans; Direct Unsubsidized Stafford Loans. Applicants will be notified of awards on a rolling basis beginning 4/1. Federal Work-Study Program available. Institutional employment available.

The Inside Word

Kansas State is pretty transparent about their admission requirements. Students must take a pre-college curriculum and earn a minimum 2.0 GPA. Applicants applying from out-of-state must have at least a 2.5 GPA. Additionally, all candidates need to earn a minimum of 21 on the ACT, 1060 on the SAT (assuming it was taken after March 2016), or be in the top third of their graduating class. Students who don't meet these standards may appeal and have their application considered on a case-by-case basis, but be aware that this might entail sending in additional documentation or information.

THE SCHOOL SAYS "..."

From the Admissions Office

"Kansas State University is synonymous with community, and its family-like environment is hailed by students past and present. The land-grant university also is home to some of the nation's top academic programs, world-renowned researchers, and unparalleled student support. K-State students have access to first-year programs, free tutoring, research opportunities, career exploration, and much more.

"K-State is rooted in diversity and inclusion with students from all 50 states and 100-plus countries. There are numerous opportunities to explore other cultures through student groups and events, and our Black Student Union has been named No. 1 in the Big 12 almost every year in the last decade. Academic experiences can easily be customized for individual goals with 250-plus majors and options alongside faculty who are committed to helping students find success. Our student experience is one of the best in the nation thanks to programs like K-State First, a first-year experience program helping freshmen connect with the university, and K-State Proud, a student-led philanthropy that has raised more than $1 million for fellow students in need.

"The university awards $38 million in scholarships each year, as well as $248 million in financial aid. Whatever it takes to help students succeed both today and in the future, the K-State family is committed to making it happen."

SELECTIVITY

Admissions Rating	75
# of applicants	8,310
% of applicants accepted	95
% of acceptees attending	43

FRESHMAN PROFILE

Range ACT Composite	22–28
# submitting SAT scores	38
% submitting SAT scores	1
# submitting ACT scores	3,136
% submitting ACT scores	94
Average HS GPA	3.5
% graduated top 10% of class	25
% graduated top 25% of class	51
% graduated top 50% of class	80

DEADLINES

Regular	
Priority	12/1
Nonfall registration?	Yes

FINANCIAL FACTS

Financial Aid Rating	83
Annual in-state tuition	$9,375
Annual out-of-state tuition	$25,251
Room and board	$13,540
Required fees	$1,065
Books and supplies	$924
Average frosh need-based scholarship	$4,468
Average UG need-based scholarship	$4,329
% needy frosh rec. need-based scholarship or grant aid	53
% needy UG rec. need-based scholarship or grant aid	56
% needy frosh rec. non-need-based scholarship or grant aid	75
% needy UG rec. non-need-based scholarship or grant aid	51
% needy frosh rec. need-based self-help aid	65
% needy UG rec. need-based self-help aid	74
% frosh rec. any financial aid	70
% UG rec. any financial aid	59
% UG borrow to pay for school	57
Average cumulative indebtedness	$27,198
% frosh need fully met	22
% ugrads need fully met	19
Average % of frosh need met	80
Average % of ugrad need met	78

KENYON COLLEGE

Kenyon College, Admissions Office, Gambier, OH 43022-9623 • Admissions: 740-427-5776 • Fax: 740-427-5770

STUDENTS SAY "..."

Academics

This tiny midwestern liberal arts mainstay is Ohio's oldest private college, and is filled with "uniquely quirky and motivated" students and faculty alike. The school's "academic vigor" and intense focus on writing (it is known as "The Writers' College") are two of Kenyon's hallmarks, and the curriculum provides "a well-rounded liberal arts education in which emphasis [is] placed on critical thinking and class discussion." "Even though I don't want to be an English major, I think any college that values writing as much as Kenyon does has its priorities straight," says a student of the highly valued workforce skill.

The school "really knows how to offer a huge diversity of programs and activities to a very small campus," and "it is honestly hard to find a professor who is not thrilled by the content that they are teaching." The faculty is a deeply caring bunch who "love learning just as much as the students" and challenge them to succeed, and they make it known that "your voice is valued in class discussion." "I once met with a professor for an hour every day leading up to the final because I was so nervous about it, and he hardly batted an eye at taking that much time out of his day for only one student," says a sophomore.

"Small, individualized class sizes" make it so that classes are "terrifically interesting," and "out of class work is always meaningful." Students don't compete with each other when it comes to grades so "the cooperative learning environment makes it less stressful," and though "you will spend the vast majority of your time studying ... it is also extremely rewarding." The "relatively" open curriculum allows students to take courses that they are truly interested in, and "there is a wide variety of options available in terms of classes" for students to develop new passions.

Life

People come to this "small campus with a big sense of community" because they know it will be a good fit, and it shows in the satisfaction levels here. "I stepped on campus and noticed two things: everyone was happy and the campus was gorgeous," says one of many happy students. The school is a place for "smart, forward-thinking students who study hard but also understand the necessity of taking breaks and having a good time on weekends." People at Kenyon are taught "to see, discuss, and connect the dots"; "Even though I'm not a philosophy major, I feel just as at home in those conversations as I do when I discuss Mahler or the next big party," says a student.

The "utterly pastoral" campus is "absolutely lovely"; "It's like going to school in a Marlowe poem—and with all of the English majors running around, most people know who Marlowe is," says a student. The town of Gambier is "in the middle of nowhere, so campus can get to be claustrophobic at times," but it provides its fair share of entertainment. "Greeks throw great parties [and] intramurals are popular, as are activist groups for everything from gender awareness to Palestine," and the nearby Kokosing Gap Trail is oft-used. The KAC (Kenyon Athletic Center) is unparalleled for a Division III school, and the "dining hall has an amazing commitment to local food." Partying on Wednesdays and the weekends "is a typical activity to unwind after a challenging week of academics."

Student Body

The word most often used to describe Kenyon students in "quirky." There are a variety of types, but "most people have a quirk or five." There are "a lot of hipster students and then a good selection of athletes" at Kenyon, but everyone "tends to be extremely friendly, well-rounded, and smart." Everyone is seriously involved in academics and extracurriculars, and "you're either a jack of all trades here or a master of four." There aren't really many cliques; "someone on the football team could just as easily be in the community choir or quiz bowl club."

KENYON COLLEGE

Financial Aid: 740-427-5240 • E-Mail: admissions@kenyon.edu • Website: www.kenyon.edu

THE PRINCETON REVIEW SAYS

Admissions

Very important factors considered include: rigor of secondary school record, academic GPA, application essay, recommendation(s). *Important factors considered include:* class rank, standardized test scores, interview, extracurricular activities, talent/ability, character/personal qualities. *Other factors considered include:* first generation, alumni/ae relation, geographical residence, state residency, racial/ethnic status, volunteer work, work experience. ACT with or without writing accepted. SAT with or without Essay component accepted. High school diploma is required and GED is accepted. *Academic units required:* 4 English, 4 math, 3 science, 3 science labs, 3 foreign language, 3 social studies, 3 academic electives. *Academic units recommended:* 4 English, 4 math, 4 science, 3 science labs, 4 foreign language, 3 social studies, 3 academic electives.

Financial Aid

Students should submit: CSS/Financial Aid PROFILE; FAFSA; Noncustodial PROFILE. Priority filing deadline is 1/15. The Princeton Review suggests that all financial aid forms be submitted as soon as possible after October 1. *Need-based scholarships/grants offered:* College/university scholarship or grant aid from institutional funds; Federal Pell; Private scholarships; SEOG; State scholarships/grants. *Loan aid offered:* Direct PLUS loans; Direct Subsidized Stafford Loans; Direct Unsubsidized Stafford Loans. Federal Work-Study Program available. Institutional employment available.

The Inside Word

In terms of admissions selectivity, Kenyon is of the first order of selective, small, Midwestern, liberal arts schools. Kenyon shares a lot of application and admit overlap with other schools in this niche, and the choice for many students comes down to "best fit." As Kenyon is a writing-intensive institution, applicants should expect that all written material submitted to the school in the admissions process will be scrutinized. Revise and proofread accordingly.

THE SCHOOL SAYS "..."

From the Admissions Office

"Students and alumni alike think of Kenyon as a place that fosters 'learning in the company of friends.' While faculty expectations are rigorous and the work challenging, the academic atmosphere is cooperative, not competitive. Indications of intellectual curiosity and passion for learning, more than just high grades and test scores, are what we look for in applications. Important as well are demonstrated interests in non-academic pursuits, whether in athletics, the arts, writing, or another passion. Life in this small college community is fueled by the talents and enthusiasm of our students, so the admission staff seeks students who have a range of talents and interests.

"The high school transcript, recommendations, and the personal statement are of primary importance in reviewing preparedness and fit. Standardized tests (SAT or ACT) are of secondary importance."

SELECTIVITY

Admissions Rating	93
# of applicants	6,152
% of applicants accepted	36
% of acceptees attending	24
# offered a place on the wait list	1,857
% accepting a place on wait list	49
% admitted from wait list	0
# of early decision applicants	334
% accepted early decision	70

FRESHMAN PROFILE

Range SAT EBRW	640–730
Range SAT Math	640–740
Range ACT Composite	29–33
# submitting SAT scores	287
% submitting SAT scores	49
# submitting ACT scores	311
% submitting ACT scores	87
Average HS GPA	3.9
% graduated top 10% of class	55
% graduated top 25% of class	79
% graduated top 50% of class	96

DEADLINES

Early decision	
Deadline	11/15
Notification	12/15
Other ED Deadline	1/15
Other ED Notification	2/1
Regular	
Priority	1/15
Deadline	1/15
Notification	4/1
Nonfall registration?	No

FINANCIAL FACTS

Financial Aid Rating	98
Annual tuition	$56,430
Room and board	$12,580
Books and supplies	$1,900
Average frosh need-based scholarship	$41,461
Average UG need-based scholarship	$42,001
% needy frosh rec. need-based scholarship or grant aid	100
% needy UG rec. need-based scholarship or grant aid	100
% needy frosh rec. non-need-based scholarship or grant aid	40
% needy UG rec. non-need-based scholarship or grant aid	31
% needy frosh rec. need-based self-help aid	80
% needy UG rec. need-based self-help aid	88
% frosh rec. any financial aid	42
% UG rec. any financial aid	42
% UG borrow to pay for school	46
Average cumulative indebtedness	$26,271
% frosh need fully met	100
% ugrads need fully met	100
Average % of frosh need met	100
Average % of ugrad need met	100

KETTERING UNIVERSITY

1700 University Ave., Flint, MI 48504-6214 • Admissions: 810-762-9500

STUDENTS SAY "..."

Academics

Students with an interest in business or STEM subjects will be pleased with the offerings of Kettering University, which has a focus not just on those disciplines, but in fostering the next generation of industry leaders. Students attribute some of their success to the institution's "awesome" co-op program which is "unparalleled in preparing students." The way co-op works is by splitting the academic calendar into four approximately 11-week terms, two of which are for school, and two of which are for work. This means that from their first year on, undergrads "get to make money during school while also getting experience and making industry connections."

A word of warning from students, though: this type of scheduling is quite demanding. "Course loads are high and there is often a lot of homework." This can be compounded by what current enrollees feel is an all-or-nothing split between instructor styles: some "care deeply about the subject and the students" and others who are just plain prickly, or as one puts it, "I have had many professors gladly tell me how many students have failed their class." There are plenty of students who share happy stories of faculty members who are "available almost whenever you need them" or who are "very understanding" and "always willing to help," but "there isn't really an in-between."

Life

Kettering may have an unconventional calendar, and some busy students may quip that "We're all engineers, so we're studying all the time," and yet we heard at length about all the fun activities that students found time to squeeze in. "There is a club for anything and everyone," shares one student, and that doesn't seem to be an exaggeration. In addition to the school's SAE teams, which are among "the best in the country," interest-driven activities like the Financial Club, and popular options like the student-run newspaper or radio station, there's even a blacksmithing club. Students also list a variety of intramural sports like flag football and basketball as a great way to escape academic stress. "We may go out bowling, to play top golf, to catch a movie, [to go] skiing or off-roading." Nearby Detroit and Ann Arbor offer even more events, as does the university itself. Undergrads also share that "Greek life is very popular," although here, too, note that some describe the Greek scene as "completely different at Kettering than it is at other campuses."

Student Body

The "very bright" students at Kettering, despite sometimes feeling "overworked, stressed out, and sleep deprived," overall find themselves "bonded by our struggles in our rigorous coursework." Students stay in good humor and find the silver lining in every experience, or as one colorfully puts it, "We are all ... caffeine-fueled sarcasm machines that pump out math and science equations at the drop of a hat." The "personable" atmosphere of this "relatively small" school may help to liven everyone's mood. "Even if you do not know someone's name, you recognize a face in the hallway or in a lecture that you can share a smile with." More importantly, students say that their classmates are "very helpful" and note that "it is easy to join a group who is studying and get to know them." Easy, at least, if you're male—the "vast majority is white male engineering students," and some find that to create "a culture of masculinity" that sometimes offers "very little support for the women." Then again, other enrollees dispute this, suggesting that Kettering is "a very inclusive school" where students "accept and accommodate each other's differences." At the end of the day, all undergrads are "technically minded people" who "want to push boundaries and go further than anyone else," and one notes that "if you love cars, engineering, and the automotive industry there probably is no better school."

KETTERING UNIVERSITY

Financial Aid: 810-762-7859 • Website: www.kettering.edu

THE PRINCETON REVIEW SAYS

Admissions

Very important factors considered include: rigor of secondary school record, academic GPA, standardized test scores. *Important factors considered include:* extracurricular activities. *Other factors considered include:* class rank, application essay, recommendation(s), talent/ability, racial/ethnic status, volunteer work, work experience, level of applicant's interest. ACT with or without writing accepted. SAT with or without Essay component accepted. High school diploma is required and GED is accepted. *Academic units required:* 3 English, 3.5 math, 2 science, 2 science labs. *Academic units recommended:* 4 English, 4 math, 3 science, 3 science labs, 2 social studies, 2 history, 1 academic elective.

Financial Aid

Students should submit: FAFSA. Priority filing deadline is 3/1. The Princeton Review suggests that all financial aid forms be submitted as soon as possible after October 1. *Need-based scholarships/grants offered:* College/university scholarship or grant aid from institutional funds; Federal Pell; Private scholarships; SEOG; State scholarships/grants; United Negro College Fund. *Loan aid offered:* Direct PLUS loans; Direct Subsidized Stafford Loans; Direct Unsubsidized Stafford Loans. Applicants will be notified of awards on or about 3/1. Federal Work-Study Program available. Institutional employment available.

The Inside Word

Kettering aims to find students who will be able to handle the university's demanding curriculum. Given that it's a STEM school, the grades you earned in your math and science classes will need to be high. It's also strongly recommended that you take calculus and any computer or drafting courses available. If for any reason you think your GPA or test scores don't accurately reflect your abilities, you are invited to call the admissions office to discuss your application with one of the school's counselors.

THE SCHOOL SAYS "..."

From the Admissions Office

"Kettering University is recognized as a leader in Engineering, Computer and Laboratory Sciences, Math and Business Management. Students can expect small classes featuring technical curricula and hands-on learning in workshops and labs. The balance of their time is spent gaining paid professional work experience with our 500+ corporate partners: our focus is on real-world application. Kettering students are passionate problem solvers and entrepreneurs, and are changing the world in a million innovative, collaborative ways. 98% of grads are employed *in their field* or pursuing a grad degree within 6 months. Starting salaries of last year's graduating seniors averaged over $78,000.

"Kettering degree programs generally require 4-1/2 years to complete, including up to nine rotations of progressively-advancing co-op employment. Most seniors receive full time employment offers before they even graduate due to the reputation of their degree, tremendous professional experience, and considerable professional networking.

"Freshmen live in Thompson Hall, just a few steps from the Connie and Jim John Recreation Center and main academic buildings, and students are welcome to have cars on campus. Almost 30% of the student body has participated in competitive robotics at some point. Many volunteer in the FIRST Robotics Community Center: home to nine teams, machining space, programming labs, multiple annual events, and Kettering's BattleBot team. Intramurals, music, community service and Greek Life are among many other popular endeavors."

SELECTIVITY

Admissions Rating	86
# of applicants	2,262
% of applicants accepted	73
% of acceptees attending	21
# of early decision applicants	1,561
% accepted early decision	81

FRESHMAN PROFILE

Range SAT EBRW	580–660
Range SAT Math	610–700
Range ACT Composite	24–30
# submitting SAT scores	308
% submitting SAT scores	89
# submitting ACT scores	110
% submitting ACT scores	32
Average HS GPA	3.8
% graduated top 10% of class	46
% graduated top 25% of class	76
% graduated top 50% of class	95

DEADLINES

Early action	
Deadline	11/15
Notification	12/15

APPLICANTS ALSO LOOK AT AND OFTEN PREFER
University of Michigan—Ann Arbor

AND SOMETIMES PREFER
Michigan State University; Michigan Technological University

AND RARELY PREFER
Lawrence Technological University; Oakland University

FINANCIAL FACTS

Financial Aid Rating	83
Annual tuition	$44,380
Room and board	$8,400
Books and supplies	$1,100
Average frosh need-based scholarship	$24,281
Average UG need-based scholarship	$20,840
% needy frosh rec. need-based scholarship or grant aid	100
% needy UG rec. need-based scholarship or grant aid	99
% needy frosh rec. non-need-based scholarship or grant aid	13
% needy UG rec. non-need-based scholarship or grant aid	12
% needy frosh rec. need-based self-help aid	55
% needy UG rec. need-based self-help aid	61
% frosh rec. any financial aid	100
% UG rec. any financial aid	86
% frosh need fully met	16
% ugrads need fully met	14
Average % of frosh need met	69
Average % of ugrad need met	66

KNOX COLLEGE

2 East South Street, Campus Box 148, Galesburg, IL 61401 • Admissions: 309-341-7100 • Fax: 309-341-7070

CAMPUS LIFE

Quality of Life Rating	87
Fire Safety Rating	96
Green Rating	92
Type of school	Private
Environment	Town

STUDENTS

Total undergrad enrollment	1,229
% male/female	43/57
% from out of state	46
% frosh from public high school	70
% frosh live on campus	97
% ugrads live on campus	82
# of fraternities (% ugrad men join)	6 (28)
# of sororities (% ugrad women join)	4 (16)
% African American	8
% Asian	5
% Caucasian	46
% Hispanic	14
% Native American	<1
% Pacific Islander	<1
% Two or more races	6
% Race and/or ethnicity unknown	2
% international	19
# of countries represented	48

SURVEY SAYS . . .

Lots of liberal students
Great library
Internships are widely available
Class discussions encouraged
No one cheats
Diverse student types interact on campus
Students environmentally aware

ACADEMICS

Academic Rating	89
% students returning for sophomore year	81
% students graduating within 4 years	65
% students graduating within 6 years	74
Calendar	Quarter
Student/faculty ratio	10:1
Profs interesting rating	94
Profs accessible rating	97

Most classes have 10–19 students.
Most lab/discussion sessions have
10–19 students.

MOST POPULAR MAJORS

Creative Writing; Biology/Biological Sciences,
General; Research and Experimental Psychology,
Other

STUDENTS SAY "..."

Academics

Students say that Knox College enjoys a "great academic reputation" for its dedication to providing a "well-rounded liberal arts program" that "values independent initiative," while "staying in tune with its roots as a progressive and accessible institution." The college has a saying about students having "the freedom to flourish." The institution gives everyone "the appropriate space to grow on their own." "I knew that I would be allowed to be myself, choose the classes that I felt would have the most influence on my education and prepare me for the future." Students are highly encouraged to take classes outside of their majors. Undergraduates are "commonly studying two vastly different subjects and allowing them to merge into one interdisciplinary interest." Knox does have "one of the best creative writing programs in the country," as well as the Peace Corps Preparatory Program—Knox is the first college or university in the country to host the contemporary Peace Corps Preparatory Program. The academic trimester system, comprised of three classes each term, provides students with "a semester's worth of course work in a ten-week period." Many in the student body believe that this arrangement "promotes better study habits and more attention focused on each class," which are "tough and require a lot of time studying, reading, writing, and thinking." "You don't come to Knox if you want to shy away from class discussion," and professors "concentrate on the student having good critical thinking skills." Students are pleased to find that "you are academically challenged without fierce competition." "I've never had an easy professor, but I've always had reasonable ones." Projects and presentations are common; if tests are given, there is an honor code, and "they trust you not to cheat." The faculty and administration are spoken of highly, and they "not only encourage the students to take charge and make change, but they listen and act on the student body's opinions."

Life

Popular manners of relaxation and recreation include intramural sports, campus organizations, and "artistic expression, be it poetry, visual art, performance art, music." Students "go to parties, play games, dance, etc., just like any other college campus. The difference is, our fraternity parties are open to the entire campus and do not serve alcohol." Parties here "are places where you generally know everyone there, you have a good time and no one steals your coat or purse." Undergrads here are also very creative. "When we want to do something fun we typically organize it ourselves." A much-anticipated event is "Flunk Day, a day every spring when classes are canceled and the entire campus goes out on the lawn and plays games, eats great food and enjoys free entertainment." Union Board "brings films, entertainers, concerts, and other groups to campus, including Second City," and the Gizmo is "one of the best places to socialize and eat some late night food." Wandering off-campus a bit is also fun. Undergrads say "Galesburg is a charming town...you just have to look a little bit," for fun affairs such as The Knox Jazz Night, hosted at Fat Fish Pub in the downtown area. Students enjoy the town's intimate, relaxing atmosphere: "Good coffee shops, a really nice park with a lake, and many beautiful old historic buildings," and "an annual Chocolate Festival." A twenty-four-hour diner is nearby, and "students can also drive to Peoria or take the train to Chicago."

Student Body

Knox is praised throughout the campus for its "support for first-generation college students, which really reflects Knox's history and values." "You'll meet a lot of people very fast, and by the end of your first term you'll already be good friends with a pretty big portion of the student body." Many undergrads portray themselves as "weird," with variations on a common theme: "We call it the "Knox awkward." "The smart but sort of socially awkward kids in high school," what they describe as their social "Knoxwardness." "Everyone at Knox is a little eccentric, but we embrace each other's differences." "Students fit in by being themselves, no matter who they are." As one student perceptively notes, there is a "highly diverse combination of creative, intellectual minds here. It's as if every person here is some highly distinctive character from an artsy film." Another puts it a bit more succinctly: "Thank you college admission gods."

Financial Aid: 309-341-7149 • E-Mail: admission@knox.edu • Website: www.knox.edu

THE PRINCETON REVIEW SAYS

Admissions

Very important factors considered include: rigor of secondary school record, academic GPA. *Important factors considered include:* class rank, application essay, recommendation(s). *Other factors considered include:* standardized test scores, interview, extracurricular activities, talent/ability, character/personal qualities, first generation, alumni/ae relation, geographical residence, state residency, racial/ethnic status, volunteer work, work experience, level of applicant's interest. ACT with or without writing accepted. SAT with or without Essay component accepted. High school diploma is required and GED is accepted. *Academic units recommended:* 4 English, 4 math, 3 science, 2 science labs, 3 foreign language, 2 social studies, 1 history.

Financial Aid

Students should submit: FAFSA; Institution's own financial aid form. Priority filing deadline is 11/1. The Princeton Review suggests that all financial aid forms be submitted as soon as possible after October 1. *Need-based scholarships/grants offered:* College/university scholarship or grant aid from institutional funds; Federal Pell; Private scholarships; SEOG; State scholarships/grants. *Loan aid offered:* Direct PLUS loans; Direct Subsidized Stafford Loans; Direct Unsubsidized Stafford Loans. Applicants will be notified of awards on a rolling basis beginning 12/1. Federal Work-Study Program available. Institutional employment available.

The Inside Word

Knox draws students from nearly fifty countries and almost fifty states—with a student body of only 1,400, diversity is hugely important here. Admission standards are high, and prospective students are viewed both qualitatively and quantitatively. Three out of every four freshman were ranked in the top quarter of their high school classes.

THE SCHOOL SAYS "..."

From the Admissions Office

"We believe that every experience is an education, that every new venture, every fantastic idea, every great journey, is human-powered. We also believe you learn the most from the people least like you. Knox is one of the 50 most diverse campuses in America, with a campus community of 1,400 students from nearly every state and 51 countries, including a wide array of races, ethnicities, ages, cultures, backgrounds, genders and gender identities, sexual orientations, and beliefs. A Knox education is not something you sit and watch—it's something you do. Our students test their knowledge by applying theory to practice both in and out of the classroom. That can take the form of advanced research and creative work, internships, off-campus (sometimes way off-campus) programs, community service, or some combination of your own devising. We help make these experiences possible with a $2,000 Power of Experience Grant available to all incoming students during their junior and senior years. These experiences, combined with opportunities to live and learn with students from different backgrounds and to develop leadership skills in clubs and organizations, all empower graduates to find success after Knox. Our students become engaged, innovative, and productive global citizens, ready to lead lives of purpose and prepared to work in fields that don't even exist yet. They run Fortune 500 companies and grassroots nonprofits, they conduct major research at sites around the world, they found startups and music festivals, they see a human need and they meet it."

SELECTIVITY

Admissions Rating	85
# of applicants	3,397
% of applicants accepted	68
% of acceptees attending	14
# offered a place on the wait list	82
% accepting a place on wait list	11
% admitted from wait list	44
# of early decision applicants	32
% accepted early decision	47

FRESHMAN PROFILE

Range SAT EBRW	550–670
Range SAT Math	540–680
Range SAT Composite	1150–1350
Range ACT Composite	24–31
# submitting SAT scores	171
% submitting SAT scores	54
# submitting ACT scores	130
% submitting ACT scores	41
% graduated top 10% of class	35
% graduated top 25% of class	69
% graduated top 50% of class	97

DEADLINES

Early decision	
Deadline	11/1
Notification	11/15
Early action	
Deadline	11/1
Notification	12/15
Regular	
Priority	11/1
Deadline	1/15
Notification	3/15
Nonfall registration?	Yes

APPLICANTS ALSO LOOK AT AND SOMETIMES PREFER

DePaul University; Lawrence University; St. Olaf College; The University of Chicago; University of Illinois at Urbana-Champaign

AND RARELY PREFER

Augustana College (IL); Bradley University; The College of Wooster; Denison University; DePauw University; Illinois State University; Marquette University

FINANCIAL FACTS

Financial Aid Rating	90
Annual tuition	$49,815
Room and board	$10,170
Required fees	$789
Books and supplies	$900
Average frosh need-based scholarship	$39,286
Average UG need-based scholarship	$38,128
% needy frosh rec. need-based scholarship or grant aid	100
% needy UG rec. need-based scholarship or grant aid	98
% needy frosh rec. non-need-based scholarship or grant aid	29
% needy UG rec. non-need-based scholarship or grant aid	20
% needy frosh rec. need-based self-help aid	100
% needy UG rec. need-based self-help aid	87
% frosh rec. any financial aid	99
% UG rec. any financial aid	98
% UG borrow to pay for school	61
Average cumulative indebtedness	$29,988
% frosh need fully met	33
% ugrads need fully met	30
Average % of frosh need met	95
Average % of ugrad need met	93

LAFAYETTE COLLEGE

730 High Street, Easton, PA 18042 • Admissions: 610-330-5100 • Fax: 610-330-5355

STUDENTS SAY "..."

Academics

Lafayette College is "a small, prestigious liberal arts school" that offers a "warm, community feel." Even before you decide to attend, "walking around campus left me with a cozy, at-home feeling," one psychology major gushes. Thanks to the "top-quality engineering education," many students say, "Lafayette is your classic liberal arts college with a twist" and point to the "vast array of research" and "study abroad opportunities" available to undergrads. The college "prides itself on student/faculty relationships." A geology major proclaims when professors are "good, they're great. Even the 'bad' professors, however, take the time to know each student and are usually available outside of class." An international affairs major says, "Whether you're an engineer, a premed student, or an art major, there is a great academic program and an embracing group of people waiting for you at Lafayette." Overall the professors get high marks because "their office doors are always open," and "are invested in seeing [students] not only graduate but also do well." The focus on undergraduate education provides "maximum opportunities and makes resumes and applications for graduate school and jobs look fierce!" Students go so far as to claim, "It's not very common to hear that someone doesn't like one of their professors at Lafayette." Generally, "classes are challenging but manageable, if you put in the time."

Life

At Lafayette, the "campus is gorgeous," and students say you feel the "close atmosphere of the school" after "immediately walking onto the campus." Overall students feel, "the campus community is very supportive," and a civil engineering major says, "The family atmosphere adds to the education and makes Lafayette feel more like home than school." With "over 200 clubs and organizations on campus," there "is something that will fit everyone's lifestyle and hobbies," and when it comes to their Division I athletics, "students radiate school pride." Lafayette boasts a "great career center due to the close ties alumni have with the college," and career services are offered to students during all four years of their undergraduate study. The administration actively requests "student forums and opinions when decisions need to be made." Some say "the facilities are first rate" and improving. A new arts campus opened in 2016, including facilities for the theatre, film, and media studies departments, and a new five-story sciences center opened in 2019.

Student Body

Lafayette students are "passionate and driven" and "tend to be athletic, very preppy, and serious about their education." A sophomore says the typical student is "white middle to upper-middle class students from the tri-state area," but another adds, "Recent years have brought in a number of different types of people." "More lower income, international, and non-white students have joined" the Lafayette community. Regardless, some students point out that it can be "a very self-segregated campus." "These cliques are not unique to Lafayette, but they are present." Just under 30 percent of the student body is "involved with Greek life," and some feel that those "not involved in Greek life or sports can be isolated"; however, many students have felt a change occurring in recent years with Lafayette "trying to add more living learning communities (LLCs) to create a social living space outside the Greek system." On weekends, most students stay on campus, and "very rarely is there a weekend where something isn't going on." Organizations are always "sponsoring fun events, including Condom Bingo, which is a fan favorite. And if you're into the party scene, it isn't too hard to stumble into one."

LAFAYETTE COLLEGE

Financial Aid: 610 330-5055 • E-Mail: admissions@lafayette.edu • Website: http://www.lafayette.edu/

THE PRINCETON REVIEW SAYS

Admissions

Very important factors considered include: rigor of secondary school record, academic GPA. *Important factors considered include:* class rank, application essay, standardized test scores, recommendation(s), interview, extracurricular activities, talent/ability, character/personal qualities. *Other factors considered include:* first generation, alumni/ae relation, geographical residence, racial/ethnic status, volunteer work, work experience, level of applicant's interest. ACT with or without writing accepted. SAT with or without Essay component accepted. High school diploma or equivalent is not required. *Academic units recommended:* 4 English, 3 math, 2 science, 2 science labs, 2 foreign language, 5 academic electives.

Financial Aid

Students should submit: CSS/Financial Aid PROFILE; FAFSA; Noncustodial PROFILE. Priority filing deadline is 1/15. The Princeton Review suggests that all financial aid forms be submitted as soon as possible after October 1. *Need-based scholarships/grants offered:* College/university scholarship or grant aid from institutional funds; Federal Pell; Private scholarships; SEOG; State scholarships/grants. *Loan aid offered:* Direct PLUS loans; Direct Subsidized Stafford Loans; Direct Unsubsidized Stafford Loans. Applicants will be notified of awards on or about 4/1. Federal Work-Study Program available. Institutional employment available.

The Inside Word

Like all elite institutions, Lafayette College takes into account a variety of factors when evaluating prospective students. While emphasis is placed on scores, high school record, rigor of courses, and other numbers, the admissions committee also values a commitment to social awareness and potential for leadership as exhibited through extracurricular activities such as community service. In fact, service is a big part of the Lafayette community.

THE SCHOOL SAYS "..."

From the Admissions Office

"The Marquis de Lafayette, our namesake, was 19 years old when he crossed an ocean to a new world, fought for American independence, forged lasting connections, and altered the course of history.

"Like him, you have choices to make that rely on practical thinking, tactical maneuvers, and sheer brilliance. You stand at the helm, turning a wheel that will direct the first major decision of your adult life. What is your course?

"Cur Non, the motto for the Marquis, means Why Not. His example demonstrates what young people are capable of accomplishing when they dare to ask Why Not. Cur Non is our rally cry. It means anything is possible here.

"Why not have the courage and confidence to take risks? Why not engage in every aspect of learning? Why not use your intellect, energy, and talent to find your place in the world?

"You want an international community where you will learn alongside and from students with different backgrounds and experiences. You want a rigorous curriculum that blends the best of the liberal arts tradition with the latest in technological innovation. You also want a place where a strong career services team and dedicated alumni network will help set you on a path to future success.

"Lafayette is that place. Your journey awaits."

SELECTIVITY
Admissions Rating	94
# of applicants	8,521
% of applicants accepted	31
% of acceptees attending	26
# offered a place on the wait list	2,190
% accepting a place on wait list	40
% admitted from wait list	6
# of early decision applicants	716
% accepted early decision	51

FRESHMAN PROFILE
Range SAT EBRW	620–700
Range SAT Math	630–740
Range SAT Composite	1280–1430
Range ACT Composite	28–33
# submitting SAT scores	493
% submitting SAT scores	71
# submitting ACT scores	247
% submitting ACT scores	35
Average HS GPA	3.5
% graduated top 10% of class	54
% graduated top 25% of class	81
% graduated top 50% of class	97

DEADLINES
Early decision	
Deadline	11/15
Notification	12/15
Other ED Deadline	2/1
Other ED Notification	2/15
Regular	
Deadline	1/15
Notification	4/1
Nonfall registration?	No

APPLICANTS ALSO LOOK AT AND OFTEN PREFER
Cornell College; Princeton University; Tufts University

AND SOMETIMES PREFER
Lehigh University; Villanova University; Bucknell University; Northeastern University; Fordham University; Boston College; Colgate University; Dickinson College; Brown University

FINANCIAL FACTS
Financial Aid Rating	97
Annual tuition	$56,556
Room and board	$16,874
Required fees	$496
Books and supplies	$1,000
Average frosh need-based scholarship	$47,148
Average UG need-based scholarship	$46,031
% needy frosh rec. need-based scholarship or grant aid	98
% needy UG rec. need-based scholarship or grant aid	98
% needy frosh rec. non-need-based scholarship or grant aid	18
% needy UG rec. non-need-based scholarship or grant aid	13
% needy frosh rec. need-based self-help aid	79
% needy UG rec. need-based self-help aid	85
% frosh rec. any financial aid	59
% UG rec. any financial aid	57
% UG borrow to pay for school	39
Average cumulative indebtedness	$30,863
% frosh need fully met	100
% ugrads need fully met	100
Average % of frosh need met	100
Average % of ugrad need met	100

LAKE FOREST COLLEGE

555 North Sheridan Road, Lake Forest, IL 60045 • Admissions: 847-735-5000 • Fax: 847-735-6271

STUDENTS SAY "..."

Academics

With its "small campus and welcoming community," Lake Forest is a college that understands how to "accommodate ... students very well" and how to "set [them] up for success." Undergrads here love that they can capitalize on Lake Forest's "breadth of study abroad options" as well as numerous "opportunities for internships and service learning." Additionally, the "small class sizes" truly allow students to "build personal relationships with [their] professors." As one undergrad gushes, "Not only will your professors know you by name here, but they will know your interests, aspirations, strengths, and weaknesses." On top of that, professors are described as "passionate," "amazing," and "very accessible": those who "love teaching and actually *teach*." This makes most students eager to attend their courses—which is good, because "if you aren't in class, your professors will notice." The faculty works hard to ensure their classes are both "challenging [and] rewarding." And, best of all, "their door is always open for any student to come and ask questions."

Life

Rest assured that when students at Lake Forest need a study break, "there is always something fun to do." To begin with, undergrads flock to the Student Center to "play pool, video games, [or] Cards Against Humanity." Additionally, every Saturday students can attend "all-campus programs, which are basically big parties put on by the school." Many people are also "highly involved in athletics" and "everyone shows up to games" regardless of whether or not they play a sport. As far as the drinking culture, we're told you can certainly "find parties at night, but nothing too crazy." It's also common to hit the local bars. And of course, students can always take a trip to nearby Chicago, should they want to "explore the nightlife or museums" there. A "gorgeous" beach is also in the area, which makes for a good "change of scenery to do homework or enjoy the water and sun." As one student puts it: "I can get the best of both worlds by going to school in a nice suburb with the ability to travel into Chicago at any time I want."

Student Body

Even with its small size, Lake Forest is "extremely diverse, drawing in students ... from across the country and the world." A student underscores this by noting, "A lot of my close friends are from places [like] ... Lebanon ... and Costa Rica." But no matter their background, undergrads report that peers are "warm and welcoming." As one student explains, "It's easy to make friends because people are genuinely interested in who you are and what you're interested in." Another classmate agrees adding, "You will always see someone you know at any given spot on campus and everyone greets each other with a smile." Beyond their friendly vibes, Lake Forest students also tend to be "hardworking and caring" and the type of individuals who are "always willing to find the positive in any situation." Of course, they're driven as well and "the library is always filled to the brim with students of all majors." In short, "The Lake Forest College community is tightly knit, inviting, authentic, and provides you with the necessary tools and support to grow into the best version of yourself."

Financial Aid: 847-725-5103 • E-Mail: admissions@lakeforest.edu • Website: www.lakeforest.edu

THE PRINCETON REVIEW SAYS

Admissions

Very important factors considered include: rigor of secondary school record, application essay, interview, extracurricular activities, talent/ability, character/personal qualities. *Important factors considered include:* academic GPA. *Other factors considered include:* class rank, standardized test scores, recommendation(s), first generation, alumni/ae relation, geographical residence, volunteer work, work experience, level of applicant's interest. ACT with or without writing accepted. SAT with or without Essay component accepted. High school diploma is required and GED is accepted. *Academic units required:* 4 English, 3 math, 3 science, 3 science labs, 2 foreign language, 2 social studies, 2 history, 3 academic electives. *Academic units recommended:* 4 English, 4 math, 4 science, 4 science labs, 4 foreign language, 2 social studies, 2 history, 3 academic electives.

Financial Aid

Students should submit: FAFSA. Priority filing deadline is 1/1. The Princeton Review suggests that all financial aid forms be submitted as soon as possible after October 1. *Need-based scholarships/grants offered:* College/university scholarship or grant aid from institutional funds; Federal Pell; Private scholarships; SEOG; State scholarships/grants. *Loan aid offered:* Direct PLUS loans; Direct Subsidized Stafford Loans; Direct Unsubsidized Stafford Loans. Applicants will be notified of awards on a rolling basis beginning 12/15. Federal Work-Study Program available. Institutional employment available.

The Inside Word

When admissions officers at Lake Forest review applications, they're looking for candidates who would be a good fit for the school. Expect the committee to closely examine your high school transcript for evidence of a strong college prep curriculum. If you've taken a handful of honors, AP, and/or IB classes you'll be in good stead. Additionally, your letter of recommendation will hold some weight, so be sure to ask someone who can truly speak to your talents. And while interviews are not required, it's highly recommended that you schedule one.

THE SCHOOL SAYS "..."

From the Admissions Office

"Our beautiful 107-acre campus is ideally located on Chicago's North Shore near Lake Michigan. Lake Forest College gives every student direct access to superb faculty and a powerful network of alumni who help our graduates begin careers. This access provides every student with a valuable edge on a bright future.

"Our flexible curriculum supports double majors and minors, and students are also offered unparalleled internships in Chicago, great lab research experiences, championship athletics, and study-abroad opportunities. Students learn in a rigorous academic environment in small class settings where professors do all of the teaching and advising. Career-building internships are plentiful in the Chicago area, and students can pursue up to three for credit. Study abroad is encouraged, and students can also spend a semester living and interning in Chicago.

"The student body is comprised of students from nearly every state and seventy-two countries around the world and together they form a diverse learning community that prepares them to succeed in today's global society.

"Developing career goals—and a plan of action to achieve them—is a fundamental goal of the Career Advancement Center and the College community as a whole. Students have access to programs, resources, career advisors, and a powerful network of alumni throughout their four years.

"Our outcomes are hard to match: Ninety-seven percent of recent graduates had jobs, graduate school, or other opportunities secured within six months of graduation, well above the national average."

SELECTIVITY

Admissions Rating	87
# of applicants	4,739
% of applicants accepted	55
% of acceptees attending	14
# offered a place on the wait list	6
% accepting a place on wait list	0
# of early decision applicants	26
% accepted early decision	73

FRESHMAN PROFILE

Range SAT EBRW	540–640
Range SAT Math	540–640
Range SAT Composite	1100–1270
Range ACT Composite	23–29
# submitting SAT scores	216
% submitting SAT scores	57
# submitting ACT scores	167
% submitting ACT scores	44
Average HS GPA	3.7
% graduated top 10% of class	40
% graduated top 25% of class	63
% graduated top 50% of class	87

DEADLINES

Early decision	
Deadline	11/1
Notification	12/15
Other ED Deadline	1/15
Other ED Notification	2/1
Early action	
Deadline	11/1
Notification	12/15
Regular	
Deadline	2/15
Notification	Rolling, 11/1
Nonfall registration?	Yes

FINANCIAL FACTS

Financial Aid Rating	91
Annual tuition	$48,920
Room and board	$10,954
Books and supplies	$1,000
Average frosh need-based scholarship	$39,501
Average UG need-based scholarship	$35,925
% needy frosh rec. need-based scholarship or grant aid	100
% needy UG rec. need-based scholarship or grant aid	100
% needy frosh rec. non-need-based scholarship or grant aid	0
% needy UG rec. non-need-based scholarship or grant aid	0
% needy frosh rec. need-based self-help aid	88
% needy UG rec. need-based self-help aid	85
% frosh rec. any financial aid	98
% UG rec. any financial aid	95
% UG borrow to pay for school	72
Average cumulative indebtedness	$33,440
% frosh need fully met	31
% ugrads need fully met	46
Average % of frosh need met	88
Average % of ugrad need met	88

LAWRENCE TECHNOLOGICAL UNIVERSITY

21000 West Ten Mile Rd., Southfield, MI 48075-1058 • Admissions: 248-204-3160 • Fax: 248-204-2228

STUDENTS SAY "..."

Academics

Students don't often discuss a school's motto, but with Lawrence Technological University's, "Theory and Practice," they're eager to share how they feel the school's "greatest strength is how involved you become in your major." Sure, the numerous scholarship opportunities don't hurt, but at the end of the day, it's all praise for the "exceptional" academics across all programs from industrial design to biomedical engineering, and, accordingly, a post-graduation job rate that is "nearly 100%, which is a plus." Undergrads love that their coursework often has a "hands-on aspect; it isn't all about hitting the books!" They also appreciate that professors are not only "technologically advanced," but "still in the industries they teach in," or as one enrollee puts it, "My CAD professor has a day job working at Ford doing CAD and teaches class Monday nights after work." Not only does this help to provide additional tools and connections to the real world, but because classes are already "relatively small," there's more opportunity for students to interact with faculty. Professors really "make themselves available for and encourage office hour visits." And while they definitely hold undergrads to a "high standard," this "extremely helpful and caring staff" consists of those who are "always willing to go out of their way to help you."

Life

The workload at Lawrence Tech is fairly demanding and undergrads say that "a lot of time is spent studying." Additionally, given that there's a sizable commuter population, a number of students simply "go home at the end of their day." However, individuals that make a point of sticking around insist you can find lots of activities and excitement. For instance, one resident shares that in their dorm's community area, "Most nights we play pool or ping pong and listen to music. In addition to the fairly robust Greek scene, the campus itself offers "many different sports" and great facilities "that can be used all year round for working out," and the schools is understandably keen about "academic-based activities like Formula 1 racing or concrete canoe." Students also stay busy by finding ways to give back: "There's a big focus on community service as well, and a lot of students contribute to the [surrounding] area in some way." The local "Southfield area doesn't have a lot of activities, but Detroit is only a 20 minute drive away," and that city is filled with everything from "ice skating to fun bars, biking, or art exhibits."

Student Body

If forced to categorize their peers, students at Lawrence Tech might say that there "are the nerds of the nerds and then some student athletes" for good measure. Of course, deep down nearly "everyone is a techie." Indeed, "they all love some form of technology and are extremely good at working with it." Undergrads here also emphasize that their classmates are "hard working, dedicated and determined." The majority are "extremely friendly" as well. One student further explains, "As you walk from the atrium to class, you can't help but have someone say hello and ask how you are doing." Undergrads appreciate that their peers tend to be "very intelligent" noting that "you can learn a lot from everyone." Moreover, undergrads pride themselves on the fact that the university attracts "people from all over the world." You'll discover a "large population of students from Middle Eastern countries, as well as a significant population of students from China." Ultimately, no matter where they grew up, "students at LTU get to know each other fast and form a family. We help each other in courses and lift each other up."

LAWRENCE TECHNOLOGICAL UNIVERSITY

Financial Aid: 248-204-2280 • E-Mail: admissions@ltu.edu • Website: www.ltu.edu

THE PRINCETON REVIEW SAYS

Admissions

Very important factors considered include: rigor of secondary school record, academic GPA, standardized test scores. *Other factors considered include:* application essay, recommendation(s). ACT with or without writing accepted. High school diploma is required and GED is accepted. *Academic units required:* 4 English, 3 math, 2 science, 3 social studies. *Academic units recommended:* 4 English, 4 math, 4 science, 2 science labs, 2 history.

Financial Aid

Students should submit: FAFSA. Priority filing deadline is 4/1. The Princeton Review suggests that all financial aid forms be submitted as soon as possible after October 1. *Need-based scholarships/grants offered:* College/university scholarship or grant aid from institutional funds; Federal Pell; Private scholarships; SEOG; State scholarships/grants. *Loan aid offered:* Direct PLUS loans; Direct Subsidized Stafford Loans; Direct Unsubsidized Stafford Loans. Applicants will be notified of awards on a rolling basis beginning 4/1. Federal Work-Study Program available. Institutional employment available.

The Inside Word

The admissions process at Lawrence Tech is fairly selective. After all, the university works really hard to find the candidates that they think will have the most academic success. You'll need a strong GPA and test scores to earn acceptance. The school also asks applicants to write an essay about their educational career and goals. Therefore, having a solid sense of who you are and where you want to go is important. Lastly, Lawrence operates on the basis of rolling admissions so the earlier you apply, the better your chances.

THE SCHOOL SAYS "..."

From the Admissions Office

"Lawrence Technological University is a private, 3,000-student university that offers more than 100 innovative programs in Colleges of Architecture and Design, Arts and Sciences, Business and Information Technology, and Engineering.

"At LTU, you will benefit from small class sizes, taught by faculty with industry savvy, and an exceptional focus on theory and practice, with a hands-on education that begins on day one in programs such as design, engineering, nursing, and business. You will also have access to LTU's well-connected career placement services on a high-tech, wireless 107-acre campus. Lawrence Tech produces leaders with an entrepreneurial spirit and global view—helping LTU grads earn some of the highest alumni salaries in the nation.

"Lawrence Tech's unique Southfield, Michigan location also provides you with opportunities for co-ops, internships, and professional development in a region with one of the largest concentrations of engineering, architecture, and technology jobs in the world. Not only that – you will gain exposure to architecture and design, the sciences, and engineering through interdisciplinary projects, giving you a distinct advantage in today's technologically driven global job market.

"You will also be provided with your own high-end laptop loaded with industry standard software—retailing on average over $75,000—a benefit you'll only get at LTU. And there are plenty of opportunities to get involved with on campus including fraternities, sororities, honor societies and student chapters of professional groups; men's and women's athletics; and residential living."

SELECTIVITY

Admissions Rating	**86**
# of applicants	2,398
% of applicants accepted	79
% of acceptees attending	19

FRESHMAN PROFILE

Range SAT EBRW	510–620
Range SAT Math	510–650
Range ACT Composite	21–27
# submitting SAT scores	300
% submitting SAT scores	83
# submitting ACT scores	110
% submitting ACT scores	30
Average HS GPA	3.5
% graduated top 10% of class	0
% graduated top 25% of class	40
% graduated top 50% of class	80

DEADLINES

Nonfall registration?	Yes

FINANCIAL FACTS

Financial Aid Rating	**84**
Annual tuition	$35,430
Room and board	$10,900
Required fees	$1,200
Books and supplies	$1,567
Average frosh need-based scholarship	$16,204
Average UG need-based scholarship	$15,506
% needy frosh rec. need-based scholarship or grant aid	97
% needy UG rec. need-based scholarship or grant aid	93
% needy frosh rec. non-need-based scholarship or grant aid	86
% needy UG rec. non-need-based scholarship or grant aid	82
% needy frosh rec. need-based self-help aid	83
% needy UG rec. need-based self-help aid	82
% frosh rec. any financial aid	75
% UG rec. any financial aid	65
% UG borrow to pay for school	56
Average cumulative indebtedness	$34,547
% frosh need fully met	19
% ugrads need fully met	12
Average % of frosh need met	71
Average % of ugrad need met	67

LAWRENCE UNIVERSITY

711 East Boldt Way, Appleton, WI 54911-5699 • Admissions: 920-832-6500 • Fax: 920-832-6782

STUDENTS SAY "..."

Academics

Lawrence University is a small liberal arts college in Appleton, Wisconsin, centered entirely around the ethos of Engaged Learning, in which students learn by doing. Beginning with the cornerstone Freshman Studies program, these "crazy smart" students are grouped into course sections of about fifteen students, and commence the reading and discussion of great works. Exploration of the mind is stressed, and "even the smallest idea is considered on a grand scale." Tutoring is readily available, and the school "places an incredible focus on mental health issues and counseling." Professors "have great opportunities for help and discussion outside of class," and "there are many opportunities for experiential learning (off-campus study, visits, field trips, grants) that are available to those that work for them, without being too hard to get." Lawrence is especially good at "providing a creative and explorative atmosphere within the college," and structuring itself in a manner that allows for student flexibility, so students "are able to explore and study whatever we are interested in and we are encouraged to do so." A stunning 8:1 student-to-faculty ratio means students have access to their professors at all times, all of whom "are excited to transfer their knowledge to us through various kind of ways." Professors are "upfront with us and treat us more like academic peers," and make time to help students outside of class and connect the course to larger ideas. "To the professors, you are a person and they make sure that they know your name and what you're about," says a student.

Life

One student sums up Lawrentian life: "cheese curds, high stress, ten weeks, snow, repeat." "Study takes big part of people's life," but most are also on many different clubs or committees "whether for the student government, towards our major, or just for fun like long boarding club or painting club." "People are always hoping for more time in a day here," says a student. Admittedly, "there isn't much to do in Appleton," so this entirely residential campus is able "to cultivate a fantastic atmosphere within the college," but "outside of the Lawrence bubble is a mystery to most of us." Many people take advantage of the school's offered activities like dances, comedians, musicians, speakers who are brought to campus, and movies shown in the cinema, and every term has a big event, such as the Fall Festival, Trivia, Winter Carnival, Cabaret and LU-aroo. On weekends, partying is a popular pastime; underclassmen spend their time at the cafe on campus while upperclassmen "flock to our on-campus bar, where we often see our professors during happy hour." As the university houses a popular music conservatory, "there is ALWAYS a type of concert going on (Monday jazz sessions are highlight)."

Student Body

There's a surprisingly large number of international students at Lawrence University, and people embrace the opportunity to learn about different cultures and topics in general: they are all "exceptionally curious and eager to explore fields outside their own major." "Not only do we yearn for experiences that take us outside what is comfortable and known, it is safe to do so," says one. Students here "are not afraid to show who they really are" and "truly just love expressing how every person is their own and that we all accept it." This "healthy and excellent" social atmosphere is due to the chemistry of the student body, which is a "combination of odd, quirky kids, who are dedicated to music or the arts, but also dedicated student athletes." More than anything, the students here "are kind, funny, intelligent and a little bit wacko—in the best way."

Financial Aid: 920-832-6584 • E-Mail: admissions@lawrence.edu • Website: www.lawrence.edu

THE PRINCETON REVIEW SAYS

Admissions

Very important factors considered include: rigor of secondary school record, class rank, academic GPA, talent/ability, character/personal qualities. *Important factors considered include:* application essay, recommendation(s), interview, extracurricular activities. *Other factors considered include:* standardized test scores, first generation, alumni/ae relation, geographical residence, racial/ethnic status, volunteer work, work experience, level of applicant's interest. ACT with or without writing accepted. SAT with or without Essay component accepted. High school diploma is required and GED is accepted. *Academic units recommended:* 4 English, 3 math, 3 science, 2 foreign language, 2 social studies, 2 history.

Financial Aid

Students should submit: CSS/Financial Aid PROFILE; FAFSA; Noncustodial PROFILE. Priority filing deadline is 1/15. The Princeton Review suggests that all financial aid forms be submitted as soon as possible after October 1. *Need-based scholarships/grants offered:* College/university scholarship or grant aid from institutional funds; Federal Pell; Private scholarships; SEOG; State scholarships/grants. *Loan aid offered:* Direct PLUS loans; Direct Subsidized Stafford Loans; Direct Unsubsidized Stafford Loans. Applicants will be notified of awards on or about 1/15. Federal Work-Study Program available. Institutional employment available.

The Inside Word

Lawrence University takes a holistic approach to the admissions game. The school does its best to look beyond numbers and get a full sense of each applicant. Admissions officers pay close attention to the types of classes candidates have taken and the activities pursued. They also consider a student's background. Interviews are highly important so it would behoove applicants to sit for one. Finally, those who are test-taking averse can breathe a sigh of relief; submitting SAT or ACT scores is optional.

THE SCHOOL SAYS "..."

From the Admissions Office

"Lawrence believes college should not be a one-size-fits-all experience, and that you'll learn best when you're educated as a unique individual. Within our college of liberal arts and sciences and our conservatory of music—both devoted exclusively to undergraduate education—you'll have unparalleled opportunities to collaborate closely with your professors. With one of the smallest student-faculty ratios in the country (8:1) and an average class size of 15, Lawrence is built to deliver a highly individualized, interactive (and challenging) academic experience. Our 1,500 students come from nearly every state and about fifty countries to enjoy the distinctive benefits of this engaged—and engaging—community. It's a welcoming and supportive, residential, 24/7 campus filled with smart and talented people who are pursuing an astonishing variety of academic and extracurricular interests in a collaborative rather than competitive way. Our picturesque, residential campus is nestled on the banks of the Fox River in Appleton, Wisconsin, (metro population: 250,000), one of the fastest growing metropolitan areas in the Midwest. Björklunden, our 441-acre estate on more than one mile of pristine Lake Michigan shoreline (two hours north of campus), provides educational and recreational opportunities for students to enhance their on-campus learning experiences. Lawrentians enjoy 99 percent placement within six months of graduation (73 percent working; 23 percent in graduate/professional school; 4 percent traveling/volunteering)."

SELECTIVITY

Admissions Rating	87
# of applicants	3,612
% of applicants accepted	61
% of acceptees attending	16
# offered a place on the wait list	176
% accepting a place on wait list	26
% admitted from wait list	2

FRESHMAN PROFILE

Range SAT EBRW	620–730
Range SAT Math	600–730
Range ACT Composite	25–32
# submitting SAT scores	99
% submitting SAT scores	28
# submitting ACT scores	202
% submitting ACT scores	57
Average HS GPA	3.5
% graduated top 10% of class	38
% graduated top 25% of class	68
% graduated top 50% of class	94

DEADLINES

Early decision	
Deadline	10/31
Notification	12/1
Other ED Deadline	11/1
Other ED Notification	12/15
Early action	
Deadline	12/1
Notification	1/25
Regular	
Deadline	1/15
Nonfall registration?	Yes

APPLICANTS ALSO LOOK AT AND SOMETIMES PREFER

St. Olaf College; University of Wisconsin-Madison

AND RARELY PREFER

Denison University; Macalester College

FINANCIAL FACTS

Financial Aid Rating	91
Annual tuition	$47,175
Room and board	$10,341
Required fees	$300
Books and supplies	$900
Average frosh need-based scholarship	$36,619
Average UG need-based scholarship	$33,921
% needy frosh rec. need-based scholarship or grant aid	98
% needy UG rec. need-based scholarship or grant aid	98
% needy frosh rec. non-need-based scholarship or grant aid	0
% needy UG rec. non-need-based scholarship or grant aid	0
% needy frosh rec. need-based self-help aid	79
% needy UG rec. need-based self-help aid	82
% frosh rec. any financial aid	100
% UG rec. any financial aid	99
% UG borrow to pay for school	60
Average cumulative indebtedness	$32,488
% frosh need fully met	58
% ugrads need fully met	47
Average % of frosh need met	96
Average % of ugrad need met	94

LEHIGH UNIVERSITY

27 Memorial Drive West, Bethlehem, PA 18015 • Admissions: 610-758-3100 • Fax: 610-758-4361

STUDENTS SAY "..."

Academics

Located in Pennsylvania's Lehigh Valley, Lehigh University offers students a long history of traditions, more than 100 majors and programs, and "the ability to collaborate with other students across different fields of study." The coursework here is difficult—"keeping even the brightest students on their toes"—but "the kinship formed through the struggle and triumph are irreplaceable." Research opportunities are abundant, study abroad is wildly popular, and a strong engineering school and business school do "an amazing job making sure everyone gets high-paying internships junior year and jobs after college" (in fact, 95 percent of students are employed or in graduate school within six months of graduation).

The professors are "very intellectual beings who are also very interesting as people": "knowledgeable, available, and some are even awakening." They are incredibly accessible, and "always give students their emails, mail boxes, phone numbers, and sometimes even cell phone numbers." "Make sure to get to know them outside of the classroom since they often give out career advice," advises a student. The cross-disciplinary programs that Lehigh offers (such as the IDEAS program, which integrates arts and engineering) are "beyond what many other institutions provide." Resources are in good supply at Lehigh; for example, there are tutors "consistently available to assist students in any subject they are struggling with." In addition to having world-class facilities, students are "encouraged by those around them to become involved in research," which is just one component in the awesome "return on investment" that so many speak of as the great perk of attending Lehigh.

Life

This is a truly beautiful school and "a great compact campus that you can walk." There is "never a dull moment" because everyone here is "always working on a project or a class or something they're independently creating." Over 200 different clubs and organizations make it easy to get involved, and Lehigh is "big into Greek life." There are "so many events, guest speakers, athletic competitions, student groups, and alcohol-free/drug-free After Dark events" that students can't even conceive of doing it all. It's also not unusual for groups of friends to plan activities at this collaborative school: "In the past few weeks, I've had snowball fights, gone hiking, eaten dinner with friends, and gone ice skating."

Lehigh is a both-ends-of-the candle school, and typically students spend "countless hours" in the library and then relax by going out at night; "even the kids who are in the hardest classes and wake up at 7:00 A.M. to study are going hard at these parties." "Everyone gets a true college experience," says a student. Not only are students double and sometimes triple majors in various fields, but "many are also varsity athletes, have multiple minors, and are heavily involved in some type of organization or club on campus."

Student Body

The student body at Lehigh is "extremely hard-working, both academically and socially." "We work hard and have fun doing it," says a student. This group is "fairly affluent" and a majority of the students are from New Jersey, New York, and Pennsylvania, but "Lehigh prides itself on its search for diversity." The utter respect that Mountain Hawks have for their fellow students is admirable: "The best part about the people around me is the common bond of intelligence," says a student. "No matter what another student is doing, whether it be marching band, or joining a fraternity or a sorority, I know that every student on this campus is an intellectual."

LEHIGH UNIVERSITY

Financial Aid: 610-758-3181 • E-Mail: admissions@lehigh.edu • Website: www.lehigh.edu

THE PRINCETON REVIEW SAYS

Admissions

Very important factors considered include: rigor of secondary school record, class rank, academic GPA, standardized test scores, talent/ability, character/personal qualities. *Important factors considered include:* application essay, recommendation(s), extracurricular activities, first generation, geographical residence, racial/ethnic status, volunteer work. *Other factors considered include:* interview, alumni/ae relation, work experience. ACT with Writing recommended. SAT with Essay component recommended. High school diploma is required and GED is accepted. *Academic units required:* 4 English, 3 math, 2 science, 2 science labs, 2 foreign language, 2 social studies, 2 history, 2 academic electives. *Academic units recommended:* 4 English, 4 math, 4 science, 3 science labs, 3 foreign language, 3 social studies, 2 history, 2 academic electives, 1 computer science, 1 visual/performing arts.

Financial Aid

Students should submit: CSS/Financial Aid PROFILE; FAFSA; Noncustodial PROFILE. The Princeton Review suggests that all financial aid forms be submitted as soon as possible after October 1. *Need-based scholarships/grants offered:* College/university scholarship or grant aid from institutional funds; Federal Pell; Private scholarships; State scholarships/grants. *Loan aid offered:* Direct PLUS loans; Direct Subsidized Stafford Loans; Direct Unsubsidized Stafford Loans. Applicants will be notified of awards on or about 3/30. Federal Work-Study Program available. Institutional employment available.

The Inside Word

Competition for spots in Lehigh's freshmen class is perennially increasing. Students should be sure to start their applications early, be well prepared with scores and grades, as well as demonstrate their talents and passions through volunteer opportunities, work experience, or extracurricular activities. Prospective students should visit the campus and make contact with the admissions staff. Interviews are recommended but not required.

THE SCHOOL SAYS "..."

From the Admissions Office

"Lehigh is a premier private residential research university. The majority of our students—undergraduate and graduate—live on campus, allowing research and discovery to happen almost anywhere. We are a top tier national research university and have earned a reputation for an entrepreneurial and interdisciplinary approach to learning. This learning is connected to real-world applications and reinforced with cutting edge academic research and hands–on experiences. Lehigh's beautifully wooded campus spans 2,358 acres, making it one of the largest private campuses in the country. More than 6,849 students call this hillside university 'home.' With three distinguished undergraduate colleges (Arts & Sciences, Business, Engineering, and Health), Lehigh strikes the perfect balance: students can expect a personalized experience while benefiting from the resources, opportunities and environment of an internationally recognized research university. The Lehigh community is guided by a common set of core values: integrity, equitable community, academic freedom, intellectual curiosity and leadership.

"Today, our global alumni community includes more than 80,000 loyal graduates. Nearly 95 percent of last year's graduates are employed or in graduate school just six months after leaving campus.

"Located in Pennsylvania's scenic Lehigh Valley, home to about 800,000 people, the campus is in close proximity to both New York City and Philadelphia. Our campus is on South Mountain in Bethlehem and consists of three contiguous areas: Asa Packer Campus (most academic and residential buildings), Mountaintop Campus and the Murray H. Goodman Campus (Division I athletic complex)."

SELECTIVITY

Admissions Rating	94
# of applicants	15,649
% of applicants accepted	32
% of acceptees attending	28
# offered a place on the wait list	6,212
% accepting a place on wait list	40
% admitted from wait list	53
# of early decision applicants	1,154
% accepted early decision	66

FRESHMAN PROFILE

Range SAT EBRW	620–690
Range SAT Math	660–760
Range SAT Composite	1300–1430
Range ACT Composite	29–33
# submitting SAT scores	981
% submitting SAT scores	70
# submitting ACT scores	425
% submitting ACT scores	30
% graduated top 10% of class	58
% graduated top 25% of class	85
% graduated top 50% of class	97

DEADLINES

Early decision	
Deadline	11/1
Notification	12/15
Other ED Deadline	1/1
Other ED Notification	2/8
Regular	
Deadline	1/1
Notification	3/27
Nonfall registration?	Yes

APPLICANTS ALSO LOOK AT AND OFTEN PREFER
University of Pennsylvania; Johns Hopkins University; Cornell University; Boston College

AND SOMETIMES PREFER
Tufts University; Bucknell University; Penn State University Park; Villanova University; Northeastern University

AND RARELY PREFER
Drexel University; Boston University; Lafayette College

FINANCIAL FACTS

Financial Aid Rating	96
Annual tuition	$56,980
Room and board	$14,740
Required fees	$720
Average frosh need-based scholarship	$48,666
Average UG need-based scholarship	$47,745
% needy frosh rec. need-based scholarship or grant aid	99
% needy UG rec. need-based scholarship or grant aid	99
% needy frosh rec. non-need-based scholarship or grant aid	15
% needy UG rec. non-need-based scholarship or grant aid	18
% needy frosh rec. need-based self-help aid	96
% needy UG rec. need-based self-help aid	95
% frosh rec. any financial aid	57.5
% UG rec. any financial aid	57.7
% UG borrow to pay for school	50
Average cumulative indebtedness	$39,609
% frosh need fully met	88
% ugrads need fully met	89
Average % of frosh need met	98
Average % of ugrad need met	99

LE MOYNE COLLEGE

1419 Salt Springs Rd., Syracuse, NY 13214-1301 • Admissions: 315-445-4300 • Fax: 315-445-4711

STUDENTS SAY ". . ."

Academics

Founded in 1946, Syracuse's Le Moyne College is a 3,500-student private college that "combines Jesuit teachings and traditions while engaging all students into their own development as an individual, part of the community and the world as a whole." Those who go to Le Moyne cite the "unparalleled" feeling of community and that the constant sense that the "personable and endearing administrators" "actually care about you" as the best part of their time here, and the "focus on community service" helps drive the foundational Jesuit principles home.

One of Le Moyne's greatest strengths is the amount of help available to students. "Between office hours, the Academic Support Center and friendly upperclassmen, your questions will be answered!" promises a student. "Small intimate class sizes" mean that "professors are always willing to help students," and nothing is taught by TAs so "it is easy to foster a personal connection with your professors." Classes are "intellectually challenging," the honors program is "very worthwhile," and the majority of professors really "try to bring the material to life." They "bring in outside information that connects with the material we are learning, which I find helps spark discussions with every person in the class." "I have learned so much in so little time. And I have evolved a thirst for more," says a freshman chemistry major.

Strong nursing and business programs stand out in this "active learning community," as does the desire to keep the college "a place of high moral values." Some of the facilities on school such as the science labs or library "could be renovated," but luckily nearly all the classrooms are accessible within buildings connected by tunnels and hallways, eliminating the need to travel outside from class to class (a huge benefit in the freezing, and long, Central NY winters).

Life

Life in Syracuse "offers so many opportunities," and students revel in their four years in a "perfect community—small, generous, and service oriented." Almost all students are required to live on campus all four years, which creates "a cozy campus with a homey atmosphere" (not to mention beautiful). Parking is definitely on students' wish lists, but the dining facilities receive rare high marks: "The food is great and there is a good variety."

The school keeps students pleasantly busy, and "offers a lot of activities around the campus [so] you will never get bored." Le Moyne offers "free tickets to concerts and SU basketball games" and "puts on a lot of fun events such as movie nights…comedy improv groups, and other performers." "Partying is a big factor here," and students often head up to Syracuse or to the campus bar on weekends. However, there is "a pretty sizable portion of students who don't like to go out" and there are always programs going on at night, such as "a snow tubing trip, bowling trip, and an on-campus Pinterest Live! Event…in addition to Trivia Night at the on-campus pub, of course!"

Student Body

Many students come from cities and small towns in New York State, are "family-oriented," "Catholic," and "most likely white." Everyone is "extremely friendly," though Le Moyne has a great deal of cliques, although "one can create friends easily" and said cliques "interact far more fluidly" than in high school. Most are "usually dressed nicely and seem prepared for class," and do the standard work during the week, go out on weekends routine. "A lot of students here are athletes as well," and many "bond over sports, or the performing arts." The "wide range" of people on campus means there are "many who are up all night partying non-stop from Thursday until Sunday, then there are those who still grab coloring books and sit down to watch Disney movies for fun."

Financial Aid: 315-445-4400 • E-Mail: admission@lemoyne.edu • Website: www.lemoyne.edu

THE PRINCETON REVIEW SAYS

Admissions

Very important factors considered include: rigor of secondary school record, academic GPA. *Important factors considered include:* class rank, application essay, recommendation(s), interview, extracurricular activities, talent/ability. *Other factors considered include:* standardized test scores, character/personal qualities, alumni/ae relation, geographical residence, state residency, volunteer work, level of applicant's interest. ACT with or without writing accepted. SAT with or without Essay component accepted. High school diploma is required and GED is accepted. *Academic units required:* 4 English, 3 math, 3 science, 3 foreign language, 4 social studies. *Academic units recommended:* 4 math, 4 science, 3 science labs.

Financial Aid

Students should submit: FAFSA; State aid form. Priority filing deadline is 1/15. The Princeton Review suggests that all financial aid forms be submitted as soon as possible after October 1. *Need-based scholarships/grants offered:* College/university scholarship or grant aid from institutional funds; Federal Pell; Private scholarships; SEOG; State scholarships/grants. *Loan aid offered:* Direct PLUS loans; Direct Subsidized Stafford Loans; Direct Unsubsidized Stafford Loans. Applicants will be notified of awards on or about 2/15. Federal Work-Study Program available. Institutional employment available.

The Inside Word

As a younger college, Le Moyne sees slightly lower application numbers than many other small private colleges in the Northeast. While a strong college prep record and good SAT or ACT scores are required (as well as one letter of recommendation from a guidance/college counselor or three letters of recommendation from clergy, coaches, employers, teachers, etc.), those who have decent academic record should have no trouble getting in.

THE SCHOOL SAYS "..."

From the Admissions Office

"Learning, leadership and service are the hallmarks of a Le Moyne College education. Those values are evident in the College's recently reconfigured Core Curriculum, a series of courses steeped in the Jesuit tradition and designed to develop the intellectual skills that are critical for success in the 21st century. The intent of the Core Curriculum is to do more than provide knowledge in specific disciplines, though. It was created to stretch the minds of our students, to remove barriers to their ways of thinking, and to help them discover new approaches to life's challenges. At the center of the Le Moyne experience is a commitment to social justice and to providing students with the best possible preparation for life and work.

"Le Moyne students can choose from more than thirty undergraduate majors as well as pre-professional studies and graduate programs in business administration, education, nursing and physician assistant studies. Whatever field they choose to pursue, Le Moyne graduates are prepared to lead successful lives of leadership and service to others.

"Beyond the academics, Le Moyne students have the opportunity to grow and explore on a campus with dynamic new academic, athletic and social spaces at a cost that is remarkably affordable. (More than 90 percent of undergrads receive some form of financial aid.). With over eighty clubs and organizations, students are sure to find an activity that interests them while forming life-long friendships. Our picturesque 160-acre campus in the heart of New York state enhances Le Moyne's outstanding programs."

SELECTIVITY

Admissions Rating	78
# of applicants	7,323
% of applicants accepted	74
% of acceptees attending	12
# offered a place on the wait list	191
% accepting a place on wait list	18
% admitted from wait list	31

FRESHMAN PROFILE

Range SAT EBRW	533–640
Range SAT Math	540–640
Range SAT Composite	1090–1270
Range ACT Composite	22–28
# submitting SAT scores	418
% submitting SAT scores	64
# submitting ACT scores	112
% submitting ACT scores	17
Average HS GPA	3.5
% graduated top 10% of class	21
% graduated top 25% of class	53
% graduated top 50% of class	87

DEADLINES

Early action	
Deadline	11/15
Notification	12/15
Regular	
Priority	2/1
Notification	Rolling, 1/1
Nonfall registration?	Yes

APPLICANTS ALSO LOOK AT AND SOMETIMES PREFER

Ithaca College; State University of New York—University at Buffalo; St John Fisher College; Siena College; State University of New York at Cortland; State University of New York—Oswego; University at Albany—SUNY; State University of New York—Binghamton University; State University of New York—Geneseo; Syracuse University; Nazareth College

FINANCIAL FACTS

Financial Aid Rating	87
Annual tuition	$34,230
Room and board	$14,120
Required fees	$1,000
Books and supplies	$1,300
Average frosh need-based scholarship	$24,374
Average UG need-based scholarship	$22,964
% needy frosh rec. need-based scholarship or grant aid	100
% needy UG rec. need-based scholarship or grant aid	100
% needy frosh rec. non-need-based scholarship or grant aid	21
% needy UG rec. non-need-based scholarship or grant aid	19
% needy frosh rec. need-based self-help aid	76
% needy UG rec. need-based self-help aid	76
% frosh rec. any financial aid	89
% UG rec. any financial aid	91
% UG borrow to pay for school	88
Average cumulative indebtedness	$40,522
% frosh need fully met	28
% ugrads need fully met	28
Average % of frosh need met	81
Average % of ugrad need met	79

LEWIS & CLARK COLLEGE

0615 SW Palatine Hill Road, Portland, OR 97219-7899 • Admissions: 503-768-7040 • Fax: 503-768-7055

STUDENTS SAY "..."

Academics

While living in Portland, Oregon, you may "get rained on a lot," that doesn't stop many students from extolling about the otherwise "wonderful," "perfect," "ideal," and "exciting" location. This "suburban-hilltop liberal arts college" sits in an "absolutely beautiful" spot "next to a huge forest, [with] downtown only twenty minutes away." Besides the setting, students are lured by the school's "strong outdoors program," "great study abroad opportunities," as well as the promise of "a very green and liberal school." "Lewis & Clark is a utopia for thinkers and outdoors lovers alike. While challenging academically, the emphasis on a holistic education means that students are encouraged to explore all that Portland and the beautiful Northwest has to offer." Professors are noted for their support and "are devoted to their students in a way that wouldn't be possible in a larger school." "Lewis & Clark has professors that care so much, and if you want to put the effort into building relationships with them you will get so much from the education." Students give excellent marks for the "seasoned professors in upper-level classes." However, one student feels that "some of the temporary staff are less excellent."

Life

Life is full, and friends are plentiful at Lewis & Clark. "It's beautiful, small, and an overall friendly place with students who really take education seriously." Community supported agriculture (CSA) is taken seriously here, too. "Many are very concerned about living a healthy and sustainable life style" and are "very active gardeners and composters." The small campus is "beautiful and enjoyable to study and live in." "It feels intimate without feeling claustrophobic." When the weather is nice, "people try to find every excuse to be outside." "They generally enjoy hiking, skiing, camping, and many other activities that bring them closer to nature." Although partying exists, it is not at the forefront here. "Parties are frequent, but hardly out of control." "A lot of students are involved in student-run organizations such as a cappella, theatrical improv, open mic nights, and their own bands. Many people are advocates, and lots of students give significant amounts of their time to assist their communities." With Portland easily accessible using the school's "free shuttle that goes from campus to downtown," escaping campus is "extremely easy." "There are so many fun things to do downtown—concerts, coffee shops, restaurants, and a ton of funky antique shops that are perfect to explore on a nice day. The Pearl District, Hawthorne Boulevard, and of course the Saturday Market are all fun places to go check out." Athletics are popular at Lewis & Clark, and students speak proudly of their teams. Although some students point out a lack of fans cheering them on at games and meets, one classmate puts it into perspective. "L&C was one of the only colleges to really support me being [a part] of the athletic department as a varsity basketball player and the music department as a classical double bass player. I didn't want to go to a college that would force me to choose between my two passions. L&C has allowed me to grow as an athlete, musician, and as a student; not a lot of colleges can do that."

Student Body

To generalize, "students are usually athletes or hippies." There seems to be some divide between the two groups, but almost everyone is "very liberal, engaged in a variety of issues, and smart." One student describes the school as being "full of people that you'd actually want to make friends with." Another says classmates are "genuine" and "really independent." "Most kids are more than willing to try something adventurous, and most take advantage of the fact that our student body has students coming from all over the country and world." Students tend to value "freedom of expression and thought, and an open environment in which to discuss differences." The fact that many students have traveled or lived in another country enriches the classroom experience. Classmates "constantly have stories about their time abroad," and "it is also very difficult to find someone who has never traveled abroad."

LEWIS & CLARK COLLEGE

Financial Aid: 503-768-7090 • E-Mail: admissions@lclark.edu • Website: www.lclark.edu

THE PRINCETON REVIEW SAYS

Admissions

Very important factors considered include: rigor of secondary school record, academic GPA. *Important factors considered include:* application essay, recommendation(s), extracurricular activities, talent/ability, character/personal qualities, volunteer work. *Other factors considered include:* standardized test scores (when submitted), class rank, interview, first generation, alumni/ae relation, geographical residence, racial/ethnic status, level of applicant's interest. ACT with or without writing accepted. SAT with or without Essay component accepted. High school diploma is required and GED is accepted. *Academic units recommended:* 4 English, 4 math, 3 science, 2 science labs, 2 foreign language, 3 social studies, 1 visual/performing arts.

Financial Aid

Students should submit: CSS/Financial Aid PROFILE; FAFSA. Priority filing deadline is 1/15. The Princeton Review suggests that all financial aid forms be submitted as soon as possible after October 1. *Need-based scholarships/grants offered:* College/university scholarship or grant aid from institutional funds; Federal Pell; Private scholarships; SEOG; State scholarships/grants. *Loan aid offered:* Direct PLUS loans; Direct Subsidized Stafford Loans; Direct Unsubsidized Stafford Loans. Applicants will be notified of awards on a rolling basis beginning 1/30. Federal Work-Study Program available. Institutional employment available.

The Inside Word

If you have your heart set on L&C, make sure you tell that to the admissions committee, because the college is interested in students who will take advantage of the school's unique philosophy and educational environment. So make sure your application essay and interview emphasizes why L&C is the right fit for both you and the school. L&C is a test-optional school, which means that applicants indicate whether they want their scores to be considered as part of the holistic admissions review. Note, however, that these scores play no role in the awarding of merit-based or need-based financial aid.

THE SCHOOL SAYS "..."

From the Admissions Office

"At Lewis & Clark, you will explore the liberal arts in small classes with an average size of 18. No matter which of our 29 majors and 30 minors you choose, you will learn to see connections others miss, creatively pursue the ideas you find most intriguing, and solve complex problems across disciplines. Entering first-year students benefit from our 4-5-6 Commitment, in which professors and professional academic advisors guide you through to a BA in four years, or we pay for your ninth semester. If you want to stay for five years, we have a pathway to our Graduate School of Teaching and Counseling that will get you an MAT + licensure in five years. Or in six years, you can earn your BA + a JD from our School of Law. Our location, just six miles from downtown Portland, offers access to internship and employment opportunities that you can explore with help from our Career Center and Bates Center for Entrepreneurship. Sixty percent of our students participate in our distinctive overseas study programs, the majority of which are led by our faculty and take place in countries outside of Western Europe. Our academics will challenge you. Our professors will mentor you. You'll graduate from Lewis & Clark ready to take on the world!"

SELECTIVITY	
Admissions Rating	83
# of applicants	6,139
% of applicants accepted	74
% of acceptees attending	12
# offered a place on the wait list	390
% accepting a place on wait list	31
% admitted from wait list	6
# of early decision applicants	53
% accepted early decision	74

FRESHMAN PROFILE	
Range SAT EBRW	640–710
Range SAT Math	590–680
Range ACT Composite	27–31
# submitting SAT scores	298
% submitting SAT scores	53
# submitting ACT scores	223
% submitting ACT scores	39
Average HS GPA	3.9

DEADLINES	
Early decision	
Deadline	11/1
Notification	12/5
Early action	
Deadline	11/1
Notification	12/31
Regular	
Priority	1/15
Deadline	1/15
Notification	4/1
Nonfall registration?	Yes

FINANCIAL FACTS	
Financial Aid Rating	89
Annual tuition	$50,574
Room and board	$12,490
Required fees	$360
Books and supplies	$1,050
Average frosh need-based scholarship	$35,207
Average UG need-based scholarship	$35,666
% needy frosh rec. need-based scholarship or grant aid	99
% needy UG rec. need-based scholarship or grant aid	99
% needy frosh rec. non-need-based scholarship or grant aid	19
% needy UG rec. non-need-based scholarship or grant aid	11
% needy frosh rec. need-based self-help aid	89
% needy UG rec. need-based self-help aid	90
% frosh rec. any financial aid	94
% UG rec. any financial aid	93
% UG borrow to pay for school	59
Average cumulative indebtedness	$32,379
% frosh need fully met	36
% ugrads need fully met	38
Average % of frosh need met	84
Average % of ugrad need met	85

LOUISIANA STATE UNIVERSITY—BATON ROUGE

Pleasant Hall, Baton Rouge, LA 70803 • Admissions: 225-578-1175 • Fax: 225-578-4433

STUDENTS SAY "..."

Academics

Louisiana State University is heralded by its students for having "tons of different programs to choose from" and "stellar academics." A few that students mention are the strong engineering and mass communications programs. Students also appreciate that they're not just abandoned under a variety of classes and programs. "No matter what issue you're having, there is [someone] whose entire job is to help you deal with it," says a student. "The tutoring centers are beyond helpful," if you need assistance with your studies, and faculty is "always available to help students" outside of class. This extra scaffolding keeps the rigor of academic programs "challenging but not unbearable." Some students recall lectures that are "extremely boring," and cite language barriers they've encountered with a few professors. But undergrads are impressed overall, stating, "Professors at LSU ... are passionate about their fields of study" and are "accessible, accommodating, and well-informed."

Life

This "beautiful southern university" offers "the best of both worlds," combining its academics with "so many clubs and groups ... for students to join." For fun and fitness, "the weather is beautiful here and [the] campus is located next to large lakes where a lot of people run or walk." If you want to take it indoors, the recreation center is an "amazing facility" that "is great for group classes and working out during the day or relaxing at the pool." Socially, "Greek life is prominent," but if that's not your thing, "there are so many different subgroups, and there's really a place for everyone." No matter where you fit in, "tailgating and football are central to the school." As one student says, "It is [an] absolutely amazing environment [in which] everyone comes together to support the teams." Another adds, "When 'Calling Baton Rouge' gets played at an event you end up singing it and dancing to it with someone new, whoever is next to you, no matter where they are from." That love for Baton Rouge extends off-campus as well, to the city itself, which students call "underrated [and] cool."

Student Body

"Southern hospitality shines through in most" here, as "many students are clearly Louisianans first and students second." While many may be state natives, students frequently comment that "the student body at LSU is very diverse." One adds, "I love being able to walk around campus and see people of all cultures speaking different languages and engaging with one another." Along with cultures, interests vary, too: "You have people that are party animals, Christian loyalists, sports enthusiasts, [and] academic maniacs." While students appreciate the diversity, some note that the population "continues to be predominated by white, cisgender, and mostly heterosexual people." Nonetheless, a community atmosphere prevails, allowing students to "really feel like they are a part of something bigger." This camaraderie extends all across campus because "people here care about smiles and friendliness," giving it "a smaller and more intimate atmosphere." As one student puts it, as long as "you're a Tiger, then you're family." As another student observes, "When you mix Louisiana culture with 30,000 students who love their school, you get an amazing combination."

LOUISIANA STATE UNIVERSITY—BATON ROUGE

Financial Aid: 225-578-3103 • E-Mail: admissions@lsu.edu • Website: www.lsu.edu

THE PRINCETON REVIEW SAYS

Admissions

Very important factors considered include: rigor of secondary school record, academic GPA, standardized test scores. *Important factors considered include:* talent/ability. *Other factors considered include:* class rank, application essay, recommendation(s), interview, extracurricular activities, first generation, alumni/ae relation, level of applicant's interest. ACT with or without writing accepted. SAT with or without Essay component accepted. High school diploma is required and GED is accepted. *Academic units required:* 4 English, 4 math, 4 science, 2 foreign language, 3 social studies, 1 history, 1 visual/performing arts.

Financial Aid

Students should submit: FAFSA; Institution's own financial aid form. Priority filing deadline is 4/1. The Princeton Review suggests that all financial aid forms be submitted as soon as possible after October 1. *Need-based scholarships/grants offered:* College/university scholarship or grant aid from institutional funds; Federal Pell; Private scholarships; SEOG; State scholarships/grants. *Loan aid offered:* Direct PLUS loans; Direct Subsidized Stafford Loans; Direct Unsubsidized Stafford Loans. Applicants will be notified of awards on a rolling basis beginning 11/15. Federal Work-Study Program available. Institutional employment available.

The Inside Word

When assessing applications, LSU looks at the big picture of a student's educational history. With a 74 percent acceptance rate, admissions officers consider previous curriculum, grades, and courses. Test scores are factors, as well, with half of admitted freshman achieving a 23–28 on the ACT or 1100–1270 on the SAT. LSU notes, however, that they consider students who fall above and below these scores, and that demonstrated academic potential is an important consideration.

THE SCHOOL SAYS "..."

From the Admissions Office

"LSU, one of only twenty-one universities nationwide designated as a land-grant, sea-grant, and space-grant institution, also holds the Carnegie Foundation's 'very high research activity' university designation.

"LSU's instructional programs include around 200 undergraduate and graduate or professional degrees. Outside of the classroom, residential colleges, service-learning opportunities, and more than 300 registered student organizations contribute to an exciting and meaningful college experience.

"Louisiana State University offers the Southern hospitality of a small community while providing the benefits of a large, technologically advanced institution.

"Freshman applicants are required to take the SAT or ACT; ACT with writing component required for Honors College applicants. LSU will use the best scores from either SAT or ACT, when making admission decisions."

SELECTIVITY

Admissions Rating	83
# of applicants	24,501
% of applicants accepted	75
% of acceptees attending	34

FRESHMAN PROFILE

Range SAT EBRW	550–650
Range SAT Math	530–660
Range SAT Composite	1090–1280
Range ACT Composite	23–29
# submitting SAT scores	838
% submitting SAT scores	14
# submitting ACT scores	5,272
% submitting ACT scores	86
Average HS GPA	3.42
% graduated top 10% of class	24
% graduated top 25% of class	48
% graduated top 50% of class	76

DEADLINES

Regular	
Priority	11/15
Deadline	4/15
Notification	Rolling, 10/1
Nonfall registration?	Yes

FINANCIAL FACTS

Financial Aid Rating	83
Annual in-state tuition	$8,038
Annual out-of-state tuition	$24,715
Room and board	$12,276
Required fees	$3,924
Books and supplies	$1,038
Average frosh need-based scholarship	$14,106
Average UG need-based scholarship	$12,782
% needy frosh rec. need-based scholarship or grant aid	97
% needy UG rec. need-based scholarship or grant aid	93
% needy frosh rec. non-need-based scholarship or grant aid	5
% needy UG rec. non-need-based scholarship or grant aid	3
% needy frosh rec. need-based self-help aid	57
% needy UG rec. need-based self-help aid	65
% frosh rec. any financial aid	96
% UG rec. any financial aid	77.9
% UG borrow to pay for school	44
Average cumulative indebtedness	$24,851
% frosh need fully met	15
% ugrads need fully met	14
Average % of frosh need met	65
Average % of ugrad need met	61

LOYOLA MARYMOUNT UNIVERSITY

1 LMU Drive, Los Angeles, CA 90045-2659 • Admissions: 310-338-2750

STUDENTS SAY "..."

Academics

Armed with a "strong Jesuit" tradition, Loyola Marymount University on the Westside of Los Angeles places an emphasis on both "social justice" as well as "the education of the whole person." Importantly, the school also offers interested students the "ability to [participate in] research," something not always afforded to undergraduates. In addition, LMU's fabulous L.A. location is "amazing for networking opportunities [as well as potential] future employment." Students also greatly benefit from an "academic program [that] promotes learning in multiple...fields rather than just the major you choose." Hence, "an engineering major will be proficient in writing. An English major will understand higher level math. [And] a business student will be experience[d] in art history."

Loyola Marymount's "small size" is certainly a boon to the academic experience as well. After all its 10:1 student-to-faculty ratio makes "it...really easy to get to know your professors and advisors." As one insightful undergrad explains, "All my professors know my name, which makes it really easy to find someone to write recommendations for internships, jobs, and grad school." And speaking of professors, students find the majority of their instructors to be "passionate...about [their] subject matter." Professors generally "encourage students to participate in discussions." Even better, they're "very understanding," and they make it known that they truly "care...about your success."

Life

You can rest assured that there "is always something going on at LMU." For starters, "there are tons of campus-wide events that are coordinated by students, although first-years are most likely to go than [upperclassmen]." Community service is also incredibly popular here. In fact, "there are [ten] service organizations: Gryphons, Marians, Ignatians, Sursum Corda, Creare, Belles, Crimson, Magis, Esperer, [and Agape]. Each is amazing in [its] own way." A large number of LMU undergrads also "hold internships [or]...have on-campus jobs." And "Greek life" is somewhat prevalent as well (though there are no fraternity or sorority houses on campus). Further, students here tend to be "active" and health conscious. And we're told that "most of the time, the gym is packed." Additionally, you better believe that undergrads here love to take advantage of LMU's prime Southern California location and weather. After all, the beach is a mere "ten minutes away." The "sand volleyball court on campus" is a popular spot to gather, and plenty of students can be found relaxing at "the Bluff with a hammock or slack line." Finally, hometown Los Angeles, a "beautiful city," offers tons of excitement as well. LMU students love that they have the opportunity to enjoy L.A.'s "many sports teams, museums, beaches, malls, mountains, [and] restaurants."

Student Body

Loyola Marymount does a great job of attracting "a passionate group of people who are driven towards the promotion of social justice and the service of faith." Indeed, many students are "very giving" and "participate in some kind of community service." They also tend to be "hardworking" and "compassionate." What's more, undergrads here love the fact that "the community is the perfect size to be able to walk on campus and see a friendly face every day, but also have the opportunity to meet someone new." LMU students are also pretty gregarious. According to one undergrad, "People I have had only one class with will still smile and start up a conversation if I see them around campus." "The student body is very diverse." As one undergrad observes, "There are many races and religions that coexist on this campus." Fortunately, no matter the ethnic makeup, students do agree that it's "really a very welcoming...community." Another undergrad explains, "there is a great sense of...unity among LMU [classmates] and I love it!" One content student sums it up: "The students at LMU are people I consider my family. You can feel the warm presence in the air as soon as you step onto campus, and it doesn't go away."

Financial Aid: 310-338-2753 • E-Mail: admissions@lmu.edu • Website: www.lmu.edu

THE PRINCETON REVIEW SAYS

Admissions

Very important factors considered include: academic GPA. *Important factors considered include:* rigor of secondary school record, application essay, talent/ability, character/personal qualities. *Other factors considered include:* class rank, recommendation(s), extracurricular activities, first generation, alumni/ae relation, volunteer work, work experience. High school diploma is required and GED is accepted. *Academic units recommended:* 4 English, 3 math, 2 science, 2 science labs, 3 foreign language, 3 social studies, 1 academic elective.

Financial Aid

Students should submit: FAFSA. Priority filing deadline is 2/1. The Princeton Review suggests that all financial aid forms be submitted as soon as possible after October 1. *Need-based scholarships/grants offered:* College/university scholarship or grant aid from institutional funds; Federal Pell; Private scholarships; SEOG; State scholarships/grants. *Loan aid offered:* Direct PLUS loans; Direct Subsidized Stafford Loans; Direct Unsubsidized Stafford Loans; College/university loans from institutional funds. Federal Work-Study Program available. Institutional employment available.

The Inside Word

A selective institution, Loyola Marymount University takes a well-rounded approach to admissions. While each applicant's academic record is of primary importance, LMU also considers everything from writing ability and service-related endeavors to letters of recommendation, artistic and athletic prowess, and even an individual's relationship to the university. It should be noted that requirements can vary depending on the program. For example, business students must have taken elementary algebra, geometry and intermediate algebra/trigonometry. Arts applicants must audition or submit a portfolio. Please note that LMU will be test optional for 2021 applicants.

THE SCHOOL SAYS "..."

From the Admissions Office

"Loyola Marymount University (LMU) is a nationally ranked, Jesuit university devoted to undergraduate and graduate academic excellence and *cura personalis*, "care for the whole person". LMU strives to develop the whole person in mind, body and spirit. We commit to providing a launching pad for students to be agile problem solvers and creative thinkers who become passionate leaders ready to ignite change in the world.

"Curiosity and intellectual exploration are encouraged at LMU. We offer more than 150 undergraduate degrees, certificates, and credentials; along with 4+1 master's degrees and over 90 graduate programs, to prepare each individual for lives of meaning, purpose, and professional success. LMU's small-size classes taught by dedicated, award-winning professors result in personal attention and deep intellectual engagement that are the hallmarks of Jesuit education. Nationally-ranked programs in a broad range of areas—including the liberal arts, entrepreneurship, film, finance, theatre, science, engineering,—are paired with a vibrant campus life and innovative career and professional development programs.

"LMU welcomes students to our diverse, scenic, and vibrant campus, which is adjacent to the tech hub of Silicon Beach and in the epicenter of Los Angeles' vibrant art, culture, and business communities. Our LMU Career and Professional development programs help connect you to our impressive alumni and business partners for internships, job opportunities, and special events ensuring you have the chance to build upon your personal interests and professional network."

SELECTIVITY

Admissions Rating	91
# of applicants	18,592
% of applicants accepted	44
% of acceptees attending	18
# offered a place on the wait list	3,596
% admitted from wait list	<1
# of early decision applicants	382
% accepted early decision	44

FRESHMAN PROFILE

Range SAT EBRW	620–700
Range SAT Math	610–710
Range SAT Composite	1250–1400
Range ACT Composite	27–31
# submitting SAT scores	1,016
% submitting SAT scores	69
# submitting ACT scores	596
% submitting ACT scores	41
Average HS GPA	3.9
% graduated top 10% of class	47
% graduated top 25% of class	79
% graduated top 50% of class	98

DEADLINES

Early decision	
Deadline	11/1
Notification	12/1
Early action	
Deadline	11/1
Notification	12/20
Regular	
Deadline	1/15
Notification	Rolling, 11/1
Nonfall registration?	Yes

APPLICANTS ALSO LOOK AT AND OFTEN PREFER

University of California—Berkeley; University of California, Los Angeles; University of Southern California

AND SOMETIMES PREFER

Santa Clara University; California Polytechnic State University; New York University; University of California—Santa Barbara

AND RARELY PREFER

Pepperdine University; University of California, Irvine; University of California—San Diego; University of San Diego; Chapman University

FINANCIAL FACTS

Financial Aid Rating	86
Annual tuition	$52,553
Room and Board	$16,165
Required Fees	$757
Books and Supplies	$1,080
Average frosh need-based scholarship	$23,161
Average UG need-based scholarship	$23,162
% needy frosh rec. need-based scholarship or grant aid	97
% needy UG rec. need-based scholarship or grant aid	96
% needy frosh rec. non-need-based scholarship or grant aid	19
% needy UG rec. non-need-based scholarship or grant aid	17
% needy frosh rec. need-based self-help aid	66
% needy UG rec. need-based self-help aid	71
% frosh rec. any financial aid	92
% UG rec. any financial aid	85
% UG borrow to pay for school	49
Average cumulative indebtedness	$33,742
% frosh need fully met	23
% ugrads need fully met	24
Average % of frosh need met	68
Average % of ugrad need met	66

LOYOLA UNIVERSITY OF CHICAGO

820 North Michigan Avenue, Chicago, IL 60611 • Admissions: 312-915-6500 • Fax: 312-915-7216

STUDENTS SAY " . . ."

Academics

With its main campus standing tall alongside the shore of Lake Michigan and eight miles north of downtown Chicago, Loyola University Chicago "provides the best of both worlds: an integrated campus and a taste of the city life." The Lake Shore Campus and the surrounding area are "gorgeous." The academic programs are "rigorous and fascinating," and the school offers "significant financial assistance and plenty of scholarships." The school's location "allows Loyola to attract top-notch faculty while giving students of all disciplines the opportunity to find something that interests them." Built on strong Jesuit values, Loyola cares deeply about social justice ("Go forth and set the world on fire" is a common credo) and "developing intellectual and socially responsible students." "My school is about preparing students for careers and being aware of problems around us," says a student.

"The majority of the professors [are] excellent." The professors "find a good balance in their teaching methods that allows students to engage the material and engage other students in the classroom." "They are the kind of teachers that one remembers for a long time," says a student. "Many bring in business professionals to relate our classroom material to the real world," and "the work is challenging, but not overbearing." "I've had several professors who I would go out of my way to take again," says a student. "The academics make everyone work hard, regardless of natural ability, but it pays off every time."

The "well-known academic integrity of the school" provides a great reputation in Chicago, and the "connections and opportunities" the school provides to students seeking jobs and internships are numerous. Because the curriculum is centered on being well rounded, "students can build an education that will serve them well in the future." "Loyola challenges its students to be the best they can be, no matter what their major or background is."

Life

"What's great about Loyola is that it is very future focused, but it never forgets about the present either," says a student. Students at this school are quite involved, and they "find a good core group of people that they work together with in classes, clubs, organizations, and/or athletics." "Community service opportunities" abound, as do plenty of study abroad opportunities, and students "go on trips that involve doing out-of-the-ordinary activities," including skiing and skydiving.

Chicago is "a gold mine" of recreational opportunities, though students admit that the "social atmosphere of the campus is very dull." "Basically, the biggest hobby around here is exploring Chicago. We go out every weekend, just looking for things to do and always finding them," says a student. "Many students drink, but not all." The campus itself is "very relaxed, a sort of oasis in a bustling city," and there is even a beach right off campus on Lake Michigan, so "clearly, it does not feel much like a city most of the time."

Student Body

This group of "witty, hardworking, smart, and outgoing" people are all "studious and fairly involved but able to have fun." The typical student "comes from an upper-middle-class family, has some faith background, and balances school with social life well." Many are from local suburbs of Chicago ("being in the city, many Loyola students are fashionable and like to experiment with clothing") and care about "enjoying the city." "It is very easy to fit in because of how accepting people are," and "there is a real feel of family." Students "normally fit in the best in activities or the freshmen residence halls." Many students comment that there seems to be a lot of pre-med students here. Almost everyone is "involved in some extracurricular or another," and many students have a job as well.

LOYOLA UNIVERSITY CHICAGO

Financial Aid: 773-508-7704 • E-Mail: admission@luc.edu • Website: www.luc.edu/

THE PRINCETON REVIEW SAYS

Admissions

Very important factors considered include: rigor of secondary school record, academic GPA, standardized test scores. *Important factors considered include:* application essay, recommendation(s), extracurricular activities, character/personal qualities. *Other factors considered include:* class rank, interview, talent/ability, first generation, alumni/ae relation, geographical residence, state residency. ACT with or without writing accepted. SAT with or without Essay component accepted. High school diploma is required and GED is accepted. *Academic units required:* 4 English, 3 math, 3 science, 2 foreign language, 2 social studies, 1 history. *Academic units recommended:* 4 English, 4 math, 3 science, 2 foreign language, 2 social studies, 2 history, 3 academic electives.

Financial Aid

Students should submit: FAFSA. Priority filing deadline is 3/1. The Princeton Review suggests that all financial aid forms be submitted as soon as possible after October 1. *Need-based scholarships/grants offered:* College/university scholarship or grant aid from institutional funds; Federal Pell; Private scholarships; SEOG; State scholarships/grants. *Loan aid offered:* Direct PLUS loans; Direct Subsidized Stafford Loans; Direct Unsubsidized Stafford Loans. Applicants will be notified of awards on a rolling basis beginning 2/15. Institutional employment available.

The Inside Word

Loyola is fairly conventional when it comes to admissions policies. Successful candidates usually have a combination of strong grades, success in a tough college preparatory curriculum, and solid extracurricular activities. The school adheres to Jesuit teaching, so applicants with significant volunteer work should impress admissions officers.

THE SCHOOL SAYS "..."

From the Admissions Office

"As a Jesuit, Catholic university, Loyola University Chicago provides a strong liberal arts education, one that stresses the importance of knowledge, curiosity, global perspectives, and *cura personalis,* which translates to "care for the whole person." Loyola offers more than 80 majors and minors, with extensive program options that allow students to explore and develop their unique talents in a vibrant, urban atmosphere. The core curriculum provides a rich selection of courses with a diverse focus, emphasizing lifelong skills and values. The University continues to enhance its undergraduate academic programming by modifying and adding majors in emerging fields.

"For example, Loyola's new Parkinson School of Health Sciences and Public Health is dedicated to improving patient and population health and minimizing inequities—with degrees in exercise science, health systems management, and dietetics. Loyola's Institute for Environmental Sustainability offers degree program options in environmental studies, environmental policy, and environmental science with concentrations such as conservation and restoration. Housed in a state-of-the-art and LEED-certified facility, the institute features a greenhouse, a biodiesel lab, collaborative research labs, and one of the largest geothermal facilities in the Chicago region. Loyola continues to open new facilities and renovate existing buildings, including a new freshman residence hall, athletics facility, and engineering lab. Between Loyola's two lakeside campuses, students benefit from a traditional campus feel as well as a downtown that's home to Fortune 500 companies. For more information about undergraduate academics, housing, student life, financial aid, scholarship opportunities, and more, visit LUC.edu/undergrad."

SELECTIVITY

Admissions Rating	86
# of applicants	25,583
% of applicants accepted	67
% of acceptees attending	15

FRESHMAN PROFILE

Range SAT EBRW	570–660
Range SAT Math	560–660
Range SAT Composite	1140–1310
Range ACT Composite	25–30
# submitting SAT scores	1,541
% submitting SAT scores	59
# submitting ACT scores	1,583
% submitting ACT scores	60
Average HS GPA	3.7
% graduated top 10% of class	35
% graduated top 25% of class	68
% graduated top 50% of class	93

DEADLINES

Regular	
Priority	12/1
Notification	Rolling, 10/15
Nonfall registration?	Yes

APPLICANTS ALSO LOOK AT AND OFTEN PREFER

DePaul University; University of Illinois at Chicago; Marquette University; University of Illinois at Urbana-Champaign; Indiana University Bloomington

AND SOMETIMES PREFER

Michigan State University; Saint Louis University; University of Wisconsin-Madison; Purdue University—West Lafayette; University of Michigan—Ann Arbor

AND RARELY PREFER

University of Oregon; University of Minnesota—Twin Cities Campus; Illinois State University; University of Kentucky; Hope College

FINANCIAL FACTS

Financial Aid Rating	84
Annual tuition	$45,500
Room and board	$15,020
Required fees	$1,398
Books and supplies	$1,200
Average frosh need-based scholarship	$23,642
Average UG need-based scholarship	$22,358
% needy frosh rec. need-based scholarship or grant aid	99
% needy UG rec. need-based scholarship or grant aid	95
% needy frosh rec. non-need-based scholarship or grant aid	15
% needy UG rec. non-need-based scholarship or grant aid	11
% needy frosh rec. need-based self-help aid	80
% needy UG rec. need-based self-help aid	80
% frosh rec. any financial aid	99.5
% UG rec. any financial aid	91.2
% UG borrow to pay for school	65
Average cumulative indebtedness	$35,509
% frosh need fully met	18
% ugrads need fully met	15
Average % of frosh need met	84
Average % of ugrad need met	83

LOYOLA UNIVERSITY MARYLAND

4501 North Charles Street, Baltimore, MD 21212 • Admissions: 410-617-5012 • Fax: 410-617-2176

STUDENTS SAY ". . ."

Academics

The Jesuits have a long history of excellence in higher education, and that tradition is richly reflected in the academic programs at Loyola University in Maryland. The undergraduate experience is built around Loyola's "fantastic core curriculum," which ensures "a solid foundation in the natural sciences, English, history, philosophy, and theology." Through the core, students across disciplines "take some awesome classes that will completely change your perspective on the world." Jesuit values and philosophy are emphasized in the coursework, yet the school strikes the "right balance between religion, spirituality, and the everyday life of college students." No matter what field you choose to study, "the academics are outstanding and the coursework is challenging." A true teaching university, Loyola professors use "different learning techniques to cater to everyone's different learning styles." Professors "actually know each of their students by name." Serving as both personal and academic mentors, Loyola professors "get to know you personally, take time out of their office hours to have intellectual discussions, show you how to learn and how to teach, and help you out when you are having difficulties." The relationship can even extend off campus, as it's "fairly common for professors to give out their personal cell phone numbers or to even invite the class to their home for dinner." There's extensive "academic support" and tutoring for students in every discipline, and the "Career Center is open for students starting at day one." Though some would like to see a "larger variety of classes" for undergraduates, many praise the "excellent study abroad program," which offers the opportunity to spend a year in one of fourteen countries.

Life

Loyola students juggle school, service, spirituality, and social life with extraordinary flair. Monday through Friday, most undergraduates are "insanely busy doing loads of homework, projects, reading, community service, clubs, lectures, [and] sports." Of particular note, Loyola offers "amazing opportunities to get involved in the Baltimore community through service." In fact, the school uses "Baltimore city as an extension of the classroom," where students learn about real life, rather than living in a college bubble. On the weekends, things slow down around campus, though students can partake of the "numerous speakers, movies, events, or sporting events" hosted by the university. In addition, "a lot of people go out to bars on Fridays and Saturdays," because "there is no Greek life" on campus and Loyola's strict alcohol policies make it difficult to throw parties. Loyola students can be found out and about in Baltimore, "going out to eat, catching an Orioles game, attending a concert at the BSO, [or] walking around the harbor." "Most students live on campus" during the school year, enjoying a surprisingly comfortable lifestyle in Loyola's cushy dormitories. If you score a spot in one of the suites, you and your roommates will "have full kitchens in your dorm by sophomore year."

Student Body

In addition to being predominantly Catholic, "many of the students are white, from New York or New Jersey, and come from private high schools." You'll see plenty of "Uggs, North Face, pearls, and J. Crew" around campus. Although "the student body may appear homogenous," students insist that "everyone can fit in well if you get past the initial stereotypes and immerse yourself in the opportunities Loyola has to offer." On that note, students "try to live out the core values of the university and enjoy being a contributing member of school community." Here, students "care about their academics and do well in school, but they also try to balance that with extracurriculars and their spiritual life." On the whole, the campus is "really welcoming and trustworthy," with a "great sense of community." With so many ways to get involved, most students "find their niche at Loyola very quickly."

LOYOLA UNIVERSITY MARYLAND

Financial Aid: 410-617-2576 • E-Mail: admissions@loyola.edu • Website: www.loyola.edu

THE PRINCETON REVIEW SAYS

Admissions

Very important factors considered include: rigor of secondary school record, academic GPA, application essay, recommendation(s), character/personal qualities. *Important factors considered include:* extracurricular activities, talent/ability, volunteer work. *Other factors considered include:* class rank, standardized test scores, first generation, alumni/ae relation, geographical residence, racial/ethnic status, work experience, level of applicant's interest. ACT with or without writing accepted. High school diploma is required and GED is accepted. *Academic units required:* 4 English, 3 math, 3 science, 3 foreign language, 2 social studies, 2 history. *Academic units recommended:* 4 English, 4 math, 4 science, 4 foreign language, 3 social studies, 3 history, 1 computer science, 1 visual/performing arts.

Financial Aid

The Princeton Review suggests that all financial aid forms be submitted as soon as possible after October 1. Federal Work-Study Program available. Institutional employment available.

The Inside Word

Loyola University in Maryland considers a student's academic record to be among the most important factors in an admissions decision. Successful students usually rank in the top quarter of their classes. Although Loyola will consider standardized test scores if you submit them, the SAT or ACT are optional for all first-year applicants. If you decide to apply without taking the SAT, Loyola asks that you submit an additional personal essay or recommendation.

THE SCHOOL SAYS "..."

From the Admissions Office

"To make a wise choice about your college plans, you will need to find out more. We extend to you these invitations. Question-and-answer periods with an admissions counselor are helpful to prospective students. An appointment should be made in advance. Admission office hours are 9:00 A.M. to 5:00 P.M., Monday through Friday. College day programs and Saturday information programs are scheduled during the academic year. These programs include a video about Loyola, a general information session, a discussion of various majors, a campus tour, and lunch. Summer information programs can help high school juniors to get a head start on investigating colleges. These programs feature an introductory presentation about the university and a campus tour."

SELECTIVITY

Admissions Rating	80
# of applicants	10,251
% of applicants accepted	85
% of acceptees attending	12
# offered a place on the wait list	1,037
% accepting a place on wait list	6
% admitted from wait list	88

FRESHMAN PROFILE

Range SAT EBRW	580–660
Range SAT Math	560–650
Range ACT Composite	25–30
# submitting SAT scores	680
% submitting SAT scores	63
# submitting ACT scores	270
% submitting ACT scores	25
Average HS GPA	3.5
% graduated top 10% of class	28
% graduated top 25% of class	61
% graduated top 50% of class	90

DEADLINES

Early action	
Deadline	11/15
Notification	1/15
Regular	
Priority	11/15
Deadline	1/15
Notification	4/1
Nonfall registration?	Yes

FINANCIAL FACTS

Financial Aid Rating	92
Annual tuition	$48,700
Room and board	$16,040
Required fees	$1,565
Books and supplies	$1,250
Average frosh need-based scholarship	$18,861
Average UG need-based scholarship	$21,273
% needy frosh rec. need-based scholarship or grant aid	60
% needy UG rec. need-based scholarship or grant aid	69
% needy frosh rec. non-need-based scholarship or grant aid	74
% needy UG rec. non-need-based scholarship or grant aid	65
% needy frosh rec. need-based self-help aid	81
% needy UG rec. need-based self-help aid	88
% frosh rec. any financial aid	74.9
% UG rec. any financial aid	70.1
% frosh need fully met	86
% ugrads need fully met	88
Average % of frosh need met	88
Average % of ugrad need met	90

LOYOLA UNIVERSITY NEW ORLEANS

6363 St. Charles Avenue, New Orleans, LA 70118-6195 • Admissions: 504-865-3240 • Fax: 504-865-3383

CAMPUS LIFE

Quality of Life Rating	**92**
Fire Safety Rating	**98**
Green Rating	**86**
Type of school	Private
Affiliation	Roman Catholic-Jesuit
Environment	Metropolis

STUDENTS

Total undergrad enrollment	3,043
% male/female	34/66
% from out of state	57
% frosh from public high school	58
% frosh live on campus	82
% ugrads live on campus	50
# of fraternities (% ugrad men join)	5 (7)
# of sororities (% ugrad women join)	7 (15)
% African American	17
% Asian	3
% Caucasian	46
% Hispanic	19
% Native American	<1
% Pacific Islander	<1
% Two or more races	5
% Race and/or ethnicity unknown	6
% international	3
# of countries represented	37

SURVEY SAYS . . .

Students are happy
Great library
Diverse student types interact on campus
Students get along with local community
Students love New Orleans, LA
Great off-campus food
Easy to get around campus
Theater is popular
Campus newspaper is popular
Active student government

ACADEMICS

Academic Rating	**79**
% students returning for sophomore year	79
% students graduating within 4 years	51
% students graduating within 6 years	62
Calendar	Semester
Student/faculty ratio	12:1
Profs interesting rating	88
Profs accessible rating	91
Most classes have 10–19 students.	
Most lab/discussion sessions have 10–19 students.	

MOST POPULAR MAJORS

Psychology, General; Music Management; Business Administration and Management, General

STUDENTS SAY "..."

Academics

Loyola University New Orleans is a prominent Catholic university located in the heart of one of the country's most dynamic cities. Students love its "small size" which translates into "a lot of one-on-one attention." For example, as one Loyola undergrad elaborates, "Personal attention from mentors in the business school helps us prepare for MBA[s] and the [future] job [market alike]. Everyone has a success coach, so no question goes unanswered." Many students are also attracted to Loyola for its amazing "music industry program" as well. Fortunately, no matter what you choose to study, there are "opportunities in every [discipline] to work...with professors and older students who...[conduct] research in your field [starting] from your freshman semester." Students also love that most classes here tend to be "discussion-based." As another undergrad explains, "While professors will chime in with tidbits of knowledge, their hope is that the students are leading the discussion." Nevertheless, undergrads find their professors to be "super caring, kind and knowledgeable." And they are always there to help "whenever we struggle with something in class." All in all, it's quite evident that "Loyola cares about its students and is invested in making sure we succeed, are fulfilled, and challenged."

Life

There's no denying that Loyola undergrads "study hard every day and spend a...sufficient amount of time in the library." That being said, these kids are also "very social" and join "lots of clubs" and "academic societies." You can find Loyola students participating in everything from "the Quidditch team" to hitting up "the Rec center for intramural games" or watching "fellow students perform at a local music venue." Many undergrads also like to head to nearby Audubon Park to "feed...the ducks [or] jog...after class." Of course, while "campus life is fun," these students do have the wonderful city of New Orleans as their playground too. For starters, "you can get on the streetcar and go downtown and hang out in the French Quarter (which is beautiful if you get out of Bourbon St.)." And of course, "during Mardi Gras season, people will go watch parades a lot on the weekends." Moreover, "there are bars that are within walking distance from campus that are 18+, so partying is a huge aspect of our culture." However, even if you don't drink "there is always something to do in this city...whether it is uptown, downtown, mid-city, there is no chance of getting bored."

Student Body

Loyola undergrads all manage to tap into the "great spirit of inclusion" that seemingly permeates this campus. Indeed, students are quick to define their peers as "welcoming" and rather "friendly." As one grateful undergrad further explains, "I am never afraid to start talking to the person next to me, even if I have never formally met them before." Many people also love that their classmates are usually "very passionate about social issues and social justice, meaning that we are very open to having dialogue with one another." And they brag that their friends are "progressive and innovative [and] always looking for a way to improve daily life on campus and around the world." Loyola students pride themselves on being "artsy" and "alternative" as well. And they celebrate how "unique" and "diverse" their peers truly are. "We all come from different backgrounds, different economic upbringings, different cultures, but yet we all come together at Loyola in unity and harmony. Everyone at Loyola has their own story, and my university gives many chances for us to share them."

LOYOLA UNIVERSITY NEW ORLEANS

Financial Aid: 504-865-3231 • E-Mail: admit@loyno.edu • Website: www.loyno.edu

THE PRINCETON REVIEW SAYS

Admissions

Very important factors considered include: rigor of secondary school record, academic GPA, standardized test scores. *Important factors considered include:* application essay, recommendation(s), extracurricular activities, talent/ability. *Other factors considered include:* class rank, interview, character/personal qualities, alumni/ae relation, geographical residence, volunteer work, work experience, level of applicant's interest. ACT with or without writing accepted. SAT with or without Essay component accepted. High school diploma is required and GED is accepted. *Academic units required:* 4 English, 2 math, 2 science, 2 social studies. *Academic units recommended:* 4 English, 3 math, 3 science, 1 science lab, 2 foreign language, 2 social studies, 2 history.

Financial Aid

Students should submit: FAFSA. Priority filing deadline is 2/15. The Princeton Review suggests that all financial aid forms be submitted as soon as possible after October 1. *Need-based scholarships/grants offered:* College/university scholarship or grant aid from institutional funds; Federal Pell; Private scholarships; SEOG; State scholarships/grants; United Negro College Fund. *Loan aid offered:* Direct PLUS loans; Direct Subsidized Stafford Loans; Direct Unsubsidized Stafford Loans. Applicants will be notified of awards on a rolling basis beginning 3/1. Federal Work-Study Program available. Institutional employment available.

The Inside Word

Admissions officers at Loyola don't mince words. They're seeking candidates who demonstrate intellectual curiosity and look to challenge themselves academically. Therefore, successful applicants typically have a transcript replete with honors, advanced placement or IB courses. Beyond coursework, Loyola wants students who have proven themselves to be active in their communities and leaders in their schools. Finally, when it comes to standardized tests, the admissions committee will only consider the highest score(s) earned. There's no penalty for taking the test multiple times.

THE SCHOOL SAYS "..."

From the Admissions Office

"Nationally recognized for diversity and inclusion, Loyola University New Orleans celebrates the rich history of a Jesuit education, including the commitment to social justice and education of the whole person—body, mind, and spirit. In 2020, in recognition that students are more than their scores, Loyola became a test-blind institution.

"Loyola is home to three undergraduate colleges, a College of Law, and a College of Nursing and Health. Home to aspiring journalists, filmmakers, musicians, designers, artists, producers and music industry executives, the College of Music and Media fosters cross-collaborative learning and innovative storytelling of all kinds. The College of Business capitalizes on New Orleans' entrepreneurial spirit and burgeoning tech and creativity hubs; its Center for Entrepreneurship provides vital links to the business community. The College of Arts and Sciences is home to the Center for Editing and Publishing, which provides opportunities for students to engage in the creation of books and articles. In 2020, the college created two exciting new programs in neuroscience and cybersecurity.

"All first-year students at Loyola receive personalized student success coaching and enjoy a wealth of mentoring, advising and tutoring services in the brand-new Pan-American Student Success Center. In the last five years, Loyola New Orleans has twice been named a Top Producer of Fulbright Students and Scholars, as well as a Top Producer of Peace Corps Volunteers and Top Producer of Teach for America Volunteers, demonstrating the school's commitment to academic excellence and service. The Maroon, Loyola's 96-year-old student newspaper routinely wins top awards in the field."

SELECTIVITY
Admissions Rating	75
# of applicants	4,857
% of applicants accepted	75
% of acceptees attending	19

FRESHMAN PROFILE
Range SAT EBRW	540–650
Range SAT Math	510–610
Range ACT Composite	22–28
# submitting SAT scores	346
% submitting SAT scores	42
# submitting ACT scores	531
% submitting ACT scores	65
Average HS GPA	3.5
% graduated top 10% of class	20
% graduated top 25% of class	41
% graduated top 50% of class	78

DEADLINES
Early action	
Deadline	11/15
Notification	12/1
Regular	
Priority	11/15
Notification	Rolling
Nonfall registration?	Yes

FINANCIAL FACTS
Financial Aid Rating	86
Annual tuition	$40,288
Room and board	$13,606
Required fees	$1,742
Books and supplies	$1,276
Average frosh need-based scholarship	$33,447
Average UG need-based scholarship	$30,629
% needy frosh rec. need-based scholarship or grant aid	100
% needy UG rec. need-based scholarship or grant aid	99
% needy frosh rec. non-need-based scholarship or grant aid	15
% needy UG rec. non-need-based scholarship or grant aid	13
% needy frosh rec. need-based self-help aid	74
% needy UG rec. need-based self-help aid	75
% frosh rec. any financial aid	88
% UG rec. any financial aid	88
% UG borrow to pay for school	71
Average cumulative indebtedness	$27,049
% frosh need fully met	16
% ugrads need fully met	17
Average % of frosh need met	80
Average % of ugrad need met	76

LYCOMING COLLEGE

700 College Place, Williamsport, PA 17701-5192 • Admissions: 570-321-4026 • Fax: 570-321-4317

STUDENTS SAY "..."

Academics

Pennsylvania's Lycoming College is truly a school that allows all students to "realize [their] potential." This can certainly be attributed to the fact that the "faculty and administration work hard to customize the...college experience to each student's needs." Additionally, the "small" campus at this liberal arts college fosters a "close-knit community." And there's a "wide array of interdisciplinary classes and programs that help develop well-rounded students." Students appreciate that Lycoming provides "great opportunities to do hands-on research with your professors" as well as excellent "undergraduate internship...[and] study abroad opportunities." What's more, "small class sizes" virtually guarantee that all of your professors will "know you by name." Speaking of professors, Lycoming students typically find their instructors to be "engaging" and "really passionate about what they are teaching." A student explains, "Classes are not just boring lectures, but the professors bring in their own personal experiences and stories to keep class interesting." They're also "very understanding" and "always prepared," and they "actively encourage student participation." Accessibility is another important hallmark of the faculty, "willing to help [out] all students" who are struggling even by "staying late into the evening for office hours and tutoring [assistance]." Best of all, professors frequently "become close mentors in and outside of the classroom."

Life

Life at Lycoming is active and exciting. "Students [may] involve themselves...in [the] student senate or the campus activities board, [as] officers in Greek organizations or other...clubs [and] members of choir, band, and other ensembles." Moreover, there are a myriad of "volunteer opportunities, employment opportunities [and] events with speakers on relevant societal topics [as well as] programs to develop leadership [skills]." Additionally, undergrads can enjoy numerous entertainment options "such as plays, operas, dance shows, concerts, magicians, and comedians." It's also worth noting that "campus movie night is another popular activity." Undergrads do admit that once the weekend arrives, "there are parties" to be found. However, they insist that no one is ever pressured to participate. Further, when the weather allows, lots of students "spend time relaxing on the quad and play some pickup games of Frisbee and soccer." Outdoors enthusiasts can be found biking "around the Susquehanna River Walk" as well. In fact, athletics are fairly popular at Lycoming. Go Warriors! A good portion of the student body (if they're not playing), attend "sporting events to cheer on the teams."

Student Body

Thanks to Lycoming's "small and intimate campus," the student body often feels "like a family." Indeed, undergrads here describe their peers as "friendly," "nice," and "open." Some students caution that "there are different cliques like the athletic teams and the different fraternities," but, for the most part, everyone "come[s] together to help one another in [their] time of need." Fortunately, "Nobody judges you because you do your own thing or dress differently [than] others." And while a large percentage of students "are white and from the Northeast," undergrads quickly mention that there's been a huge push at Lycoming to increase diversity in recent years. An excited student explains, "We boast high numbers of international students, from at least ten countries. We also have partner schools in urban areas like Houston and Philadelphia, bringing in students who would normally struggle to secure a place in a liberal arts college. Our international program is expanding, and we have students from various places like Vietnam, Argentina, and Rwanda." Of course, many students find common ground given the fact that most are "hard workers and very involved on campus." As one undergrad concludes, "Lycoming College students are passionate about their education and are committed to bettering themselves and preparing for graduation."

Financial Aid: 570-321-4040 • E-Mail: admissions@lycoming.edu • Website: www.lycoming.edu

THE PRINCETON REVIEW SAYS

Admissions

Very important factors considered include: rigor of secondary school record, recommendation(s). *Important factors considered include:* class rank, academic GPA, application essay, standardized test scores, interview. *Other factors considered include:* extracurricular activities, talent/ability, character/personal qualities, first generation, alumni/ae relation, geographical residence, state residency, racial/ethnic status, volunteer work, work experience, level of applicant's interest. ACT with or without writing accepted. SAT with or without Essay component accepted. High school diploma is required and GED is accepted. *Academic units required:* 4 English, 3 math, 3 science, 2 foreign language, 3 social studies, 2 academic electives. *Academic units recommended:* 4 English, 4 math, 3 science, 3 foreign language, 4 social studies, 3 academic electives.

Financial Aid

Students should submit: FAFSA. Priority filing deadline is 5/1. The Princeton Review suggests that all financial aid forms be submitted as soon as possible after October 1. *Need-based scholarships/grants offered:* College/university scholarship or grant aid from institutional funds; Federal Pell; Private scholarships; SEOG; State scholarships/grants; United Negro College Fund. *Loan aid offered:* Direct PLUS loans; Direct Subsidized Stafford Loans; Direct Unsubsidized Stafford Loans. Applicants will be notified of awards on a rolling basis beginning 2/1. Federal Work-Study Program available. Institutional employment available.

The Inside Word

Admissions officers at Lycoming College consider the whole applicant. To that end, everything from GPA and rigor of your course load to recommendations and personal essays will be closely evaluated. Further, some applicants will be delighted to learn that Lycoming is also a test-optional school (with exceptions). To be eligible, candidates must be in the top half of their graduating class and submit two graded writing samples that are analytical in nature.

THE SCHOOL SAYS "..."

From the Admissions Office

"Lycoming College takes traditional liberal arts to the next level with cutting-edge programs, experiential learning, and extracurriculars that let students think deeply and act boldly. Students are encouraged to craft customized, cross-disciplinary academic pathways tailored to their unique interests and career goals. Lycoming offers more than forty majors and sixty-six minors, with programs that seek to answer 21st century questions, such as neuroscience, astrophysics, energy studies, and entrepreneurship.

"As a solely undergraduate institution, Lycoming is able to give students access to advanced equipment, research opportunities, and fieldwork starting freshman year. Professors are both scholars in their field as well as mentors and regularly include students in their personal research projects. Small class sizes foster workshops, hands-on labs, and discussion-based learning. Professors know students by name and have even been known to invite students to their homes for dinner.

"Unique to Lycoming is the Center for Enhanced Academic Experiences—a gateway for students to acquire experiential learning via internships, research, fellowships, and study abroad opportunities as well as receive subject-specific career advising and pre-professional/graduate school guidance.

"Nestled in the Susquehanna River Valley, the city of Williamsport offers something for everyone: a vibrant entertainment, shopping, and arts scene and a rich, natural landscape that beckons outdoor adventure. On campus, the already tight-knit community is strengthened through a variety of clubs, organizations, and programming. It is often said that at Lycoming, it's not a matter of if you'll get involved, but how much."

SELECTIVITY

Admissions Rating	83
# of applicants	2,433
% of applicants accepted	66
% of acceptees attending	20
# of early decision applicants	27
% accepted early decision	81

FRESHMAN PROFILE

Range SAT EBRW	510–600
Range SAT Math	500–598
Range ACT Composite	19–24
# submitting SAT scores	250
% submitting SAT scores	77
# submitting ACT scores	68
% submitting ACT scores	21
Average HS GPA	3.5
% graduated top 10% of class	21
% graduated top 25% of class	46
% graduated top 50% of class	79

DEADLINES

Early decision	
Deadline	11/15
Notification	12/1
Early action	
Deadline	12/1
Notification	12/15
Regular	
Priority	12/1
Notification	Rolling, 12/15
Nonfall registration?	Yes

FINANCIAL FACTS

Financial Aid Rating	89
Annual tuition	$39,360
Room and board	$12,568
Required fees	$955
Books and supplies	$1,200
Average frosh need-based scholarship	$36,514
Average UG need-based scholarship	$33,028
% needy frosh rec. need-based scholarship or grant aid	100
% needy UG rec. need-based scholarship or grant aid	100
% needy frosh rec. non-need-based scholarship or grant aid	9
% needy UG rec. non-need-based scholarship or grant aid	11
% needy frosh rec. need-based self-help aid	75
% needy UG rec. need-based self-help aid	88
% frosh rec. any financial aid	100
% UG rec. any financial aid	100
% frosh need fully met	17
% ugrads need fully met	26
Average % of frosh need met	86
Average % of ugrad need met	85

MACALESTER COLLEGE

1600 Grand Avenue, St. Paul, MN 55105-1899 • Admissions: 651-696-6357 • Fax: 651-696-6724

STUDENTS SAY "..."

Academics

Students looking for the best of both worlds—a small college in a metropolitan location—will be keen on Macalester College in St. Paul, Minnesota. It's a "tough school [where] professors take material seriously." They "have high expectations and can assign a lot of work," but they are also "sensitive to student needs, … funny, warm, and highly intelligent." They want their students "to not only think critically about the world, but also to engage with … problems in community projects." "The classroom environment is generally fairly chill," says a student, "and the small class sizes make for interesting and meaningful discussion and individualized support." Classes on your schedule might include "trips into the community, community-service dimensions, and unique assignments."

The Twin Cities make it "easy for a class to assign first-hand learning experiences" that require tasks like "visiting certain neighborhoods, analyzing architecture, [and] going to museums." "Geology overnight camping trips to Wisconsin and the Boundary Waters" are also class highlights students mention. Macalester's Idea Lab offers a "creative space to play with ideas in a non-traditional format," or as one student puts it, "an upscale, college version of an arts-and-crafts area."

Life

The location doesn't just offer enriching academic experiences. St. Paul and Minneapolis provide Macalester's student body a variety of distractions from their intense workloads. Students frequent nearby museums for class assignments and for fun. Other weekend day trips include visiting the Mall of America, just "an hour away by bus," or the Science Museum of Minnesota. There are "plenty of restaurants and local bars" surrounding campus and "people will often go to coffee shops either around campus or around the Twin Cities to study or just hang out." But make no mistake: folks are happy to stay on campus to socialize and unwind. "The program board runs events all the time," one student says, citing trivia nights and student concerts as ongoing occasions. Meals are "very social times," and "parties at upperclassmen houses are common." In the warmer months, "you can walk between classes and see students sitting all over campus on the lawns studying, listening to music, doing yoga, slacklining, and playing frisbee…." Film buffs can "rent a projector from the library and have movie nights" in their dorms. "It's a great place to have a routine," says one student who details their typical day: "Wake up at 6 o'clock, have a nice swim in the pool, refresh yourself in the sauna, have breakfast, and then go to class…." Macalester students are "pretty active," and "Macalester's campus is perfect for those who like running," which you can do by the Mississippi River.

Student Body

Macalester has "many different characters on campus," the majority of whom are "incredibly accepting, intelligent, and socially conscious." Students "are certainly very occupied with the demanding workload," but the campus "retains a fun, lighthearted vibe even in the thick of finals." A student stresses that while everyone is for the most part "highly intelligent and hardworking," they have found "very little competition between students [and instead find] mostly cooperation," which students note "fosters a welcoming community." The "robust community of international students" on campus means "there is a large amount of different perspectives represented." One student sums it up: "Macalester is comprised of a special coalescence of intellectuals, artists, athletes, question-askers, and question-answerers; We're nerdy, but in a cool way."

MACALESTER COLLEGE

Financial Aid: 651-696-6214 • E-Mail: admissions@macalester.edu • Website: www.macalester.edu

THE PRINCETON REVIEW SAYS

Admissions

Very important factors considered include: rigor of secondary school record, academic GPA. *Important factors considered include:* application essay, recommendation(s), extracurricular activities, character/personal qualities. *Other factors considered include:* class rank, interview, talent/ability, first generation, alumni/ae relation, racial/ethnic status, volunteer work, work experience. Beginning with the fall 2021 admissions cycle, submission of ACT or SAT results is optional. High school diploma or equivalent is not required. *Academic units recommended:* 4 English, 3 math, 3 science, 3 science labs, 3 foreign language, 3 social studies.

Financial Aid

Students should submit: CSS/Financial Aid PROFILE; FAFSA; Noncustodial PROFILE. Priority filing deadline is 1/15. The Princeton Review suggests that all financial aid forms be submitted as soon as possible after October 1. *Need-based scholarships/grants offered:* College/university scholarship or grant aid from institutional funds; Federal Pell; Private scholarships; SEOG; State scholarships/grants. *Loan aid offered:* Direct PLUS loans; Direct Subsidized Stafford Loans; Direct Unsubsidized Stafford Loans. Applicants will be notified of awards on or about 4/1. Federal Work-Study Program available. Institutional employment available.

The Inside Word

To say that Macalester's star is on the rise is to put it very mildly. The number of applicants to the school continues to increase. Accordingly, it has grown substantially more difficult to gain admission here within a very short period of time. Candidates need to put their best foot forward in their applications; 63 percent of the current first-year class ranked in the top 10 percent of their high school classes.

THE SCHOOL SAYS "..."

From the Admissions Office

"Macalester College is one of very few selective liberal arts colleges located in the heart of a major metropolitan area. The campus sits within a friendly residential neighborhood, surrounded by restaurants, coffee houses, bike paths, and bookstores. Students who thrive at Macalester are curious, highly motivated, serious about their academic pursuits, and supportive of each other; choosing collective success over competition. The demanding academic program and commitments to internationalism, multiculturalism, and service to society are amplified by Macalester's location in the Twin Cities of Saint Paul and Minneapolis. Being in a metropolitan area allows for over 60 courses and the internship program to partner with organizations including nonprofits, government agencies, and Fortune 500 companies. Small class sizes allow for a rich experience with strong faculty partnerships, individual attention, and meaningful connections with classmates from more than 90 countries and all 50 states. Contributing to lasting friendships and a sense of community, there are over 100 student organizations available. These groups reflect the diverse interests of students, ranging from outdoor adventures, gaming, politics, and Quiz Bowl, to rocketry, slam poetry, and ultimate frisbee. Macalester has 19 varsity athletic teams as well as club and intramural sports. More than 60% of students study abroad for 15 weeks or longer, immersing themselves in another culture and widening their global perspective. Macalester provides a financial aid package meeting 100% of demonstrated financial need for every student. The United Nations flag has flown over campus since 1950, symbolizing Macalester's commitment to world peace and understanding. "

SELECTIVITY

Admissions Rating	94
# of applicants	6,598
% of applicants accepted	32
% of acceptees attending	24
# offered a place on the wait list	801
% accepting a place on wait list	52
% admitted from wait list	13
# of early decision applicants	287
% accepted early decision	58

FRESHMAN PROFILE

Range SAT EBRW	660–740
Range SAT Math	660–770
Range ACT Composite	29–33
# submitting SAT scores	285
% submitting SAT scores	57
# submitting ACT scores	252
% submitting ACT scores	50
% graduated top 10% of class	64
% graduated top 25% of class	88
% graduated top 50% of class	99

DEADLINES

Early decision	
Deadline	11/15
Notification	12/15
Other ED Deadline	1/1
Other ED Notification	2/1
Regular	
Deadline	1/15
Notification	3/30
Nonfall registration?	No

FINANCIAL FACTS

Financial Aid Rating	94
Annual tuition	$58,248
Room and board	$13,084
Required fees	$230
Books and supplies	$1,213
Average frosh need-based scholarship	$43,693
Average UG need-based scholarship	$42,774
% needy frosh rec. need-based scholarship or grant aid	100
% needy UG rec. need-based scholarship or grant aid	100
% needy frosh rec. non-need-based scholarship or grant aid	11
% needy UG rec. non-need-based scholarship or grant aid	6
% needy frosh rec. need-based self-help aid	83
% needy UG rec. need-based self-help aid	90
% frosh rec. any financial aid	85
% UG rec. any financial aid	82
% UG borrow to pay for school	59
Average cumulative indebtedness	$23,060
% frosh need fully met	76
% ugrads need fully met	64
Average % of frosh need met	100
Average % of ugrad need met	100

MANHATTAN COLLEGE

Manhattan College Parkway, Riverdale, NY 10471 • Admissions: 718-862-7200 • Fax: 718-862-8019

CAMPUS LIFE

Quality of Life Rating	86
Fire Safety Rating	83
Green Rating	65
Type of school	Private
Affiliation	Roman Catholic
Environment	Metropolis

STUDENTS

Total undergrad enrollment	3,654
% male/female	55/45
% from out of state	31
% frosh from public high school	57
% frosh live on campus	70
% ugrads live on campus	51
# of fraternities (% ugrad men join)	2 (1)
# of sororities (% ugrad women join)	2 (1)
% African American	6
% Asian	5
% Caucasian	55
% Hispanic	23
% Native American	<1
% Pacific Islander	0
% Two or more races	2
% Race and/or ethnicity unknown	6
% international	3
# of countries represented	46

SURVEY SAYS . . .
Everyone loves the Jaspers

ACADEMICS

Academic Rating	77
% students returning for sophomore year	82
% students graduating within 4 years	58
% students graduating within 6 years	75
Calendar	Semester
Student/faculty ratio	13:1
Profs interesting rating	86
Profs accessible rating	91

Most classes have 20–29 students.
Most lab/discussion sessions have 20–29 students.

MOST POPULAR MAJORS
Marketing/Marketing Management, General;
Special Education and Teaching, Other; Civil
Engineering, General

STUDENTS SAY "..."

Academics

Manhattan College in New York, isn't actually in Manhattan, but is close enough—a quick 30-minute subway trip from the Riverdale section of the Bronx. A Catholic university, Manhattan honors the "five LaSallian values" ("promoting faith, respect, education, community and social justice"), which shape the culture on campus, primarily in its commitment to "service," but also apparent in the presence of Catholic brothers, who teach some of the courses. Students overwhelmingly praise "outstanding" professors who are "not only outstanding in fields they teach, but they also care very deeply for their students." Most "are industry professionals, or PhDs that have a lot of experience in the subject matter that they are teaching," providing "an academic experience where one is able to connect the theory behind a certain subject to practical real world applications." Small classes offer a "12:1 student-faculty ratio." The school "carries prestige" and has "a lot of connections," in the "public sector and private industry," so students have a "greater chance of being placed/connected with an internship that closely relates to their field of choice." This is "especially true for the engineering and education departments." Manhattan "gives you room to take initiative, but also does a good job of keeping students on track." Manhattan has "an outstanding internship program," and "good rates at helping students finding jobs after college," especially with the help of past Jaspers [the college mascot] in the strong alumni network.

Life

Students say Manhattan College's location—last stop on the 1 train—can't be beat for ease into the more bustling parts of the city, but if you stay on campus, "the size of the school is large enough that there are plenty of people to meet and activities to participate in." In nice weather, "everyone hangs out outside on the Quad" or at "Kelly Commons." "Van Cortlandt Park is also very close so people will hike and just hang out" in the "green spaces" there. Manhattan College "isn't considered a party school; however, most people do party and go out on the weekends," including those thrown by "frats" or a sport's team's house, or they head over to Fordham's college bars. At the end of the night, however, "everyone always ends up at Fenwick's (the only bar at Manhattan College). Dorms are "a pleasure," though students point out that "the campus itself is fairly spread out, with the Engineering building being separated from what is called Main Campus," which effectively "separates the student population." Yet "you seem to meet everyone, whether it's in the small classes or sitting next to them in the student section during an insane basketball game."

Student Body

Manhattan has "an eclectic mix of students, typical of an institution within...New York City." Many students are "relatives of alumni that have gone here, usually their parents," and many are also "first-generation college students, which is something LaSallian institutions pride themselves on." Students boast of the campus's true diversity and familiarity: "Coming back to school at Manhattan after a break is like going to a family reunion," a student says. "You meet people from NY to Alaska" and "all over the world." Students are "generally engaged in class discussions and are passionate about their studies and extracurricular activities." Students get a chance to "make a ton of friends and build relationships that will last a lifetime." One comment sums up the general student body sentiment: "I am very lucky to call myself a Jasper."

Financial Aid: 718-862-7100 • E-Mail: admit@manhattan.edu • Website: www.manhattan.edu

THE PRINCETON REVIEW SAYS

Admissions

Very important factors considered include: rigor of secondary school record, class rank, academic GPA, standardized test scores. *Important factors considered include:* application essay, recommendation(s). *Other factors considered include:* talent/ability, character/personal qualities, first generation, alumni/ae relation, geographical residence, volunteer work, work experience, level of applicant's interest. ACT with Writing recommended. SAT with Essay component recommended. High school diploma is required and GED is accepted. *Academic units required:* 4 English, 3 math, 2 science, 2 science labs, 2 foreign language, 3 social studies, 2 academic electives. *Academic units recommended:* 4 English, 4 math, 4 science, 4 science labs, 3 foreign language, 4 social studies.

Financial Aid

Students should submit: FAFSA. Priority filing deadline is 3/1. The Princeton Review suggests that all financial aid forms be submitted as soon as possible after October 1. *Need-based scholarships/grants offered:* College/university scholarship or grant aid from institutional funds; Federal Pell; Private scholarships; SEOG; State scholarships/grants. *Loan aid offered:* Direct PLUS loans; Direct Subsidized Stafford Loans; Direct Unsubsidized Stafford Loans. Applicants will be notified of awards on a rolling basis beginning 2/15. Federal Work-Study Program available. Institutional employment available.

The Inside Word

Manhattan College admission is all done on a rolling basis, though priority is given to those who apply before March 1. With nearly two-thirds of applicants gaining admission, students with a solid academic background (emphasis on rigorous courses) and decent SAT scores shouldn't find any problems getting in.

THE SCHOOL SAYS "..."

From the Admissions Office

"We are a Lasallian Catholic college offering a transformative education that touches your mind and heart. We strive to promote faith, respect, education, community and social action. Manhattan College promises great value by consistently ranking among schools with the best return on investment and highest graduate salaries. In Riverdale, the greatest city in the world is at the doorstep of campus. In a quiet neighborhood in the Bronx, located ten miles from the bustling streets of midtown Manhattan, students enjoy a traditional college campus that's just a short subway ride from the endless opportunities available in NYC. Our professors often use the city as a classroom with field trips to Wall Street, museums and other world-famous locations.

"We have 3,500 students and a student-to-faculty ratio of 12:1, so our students enjoy the benefits of a small college with close faculty interaction. With more than forty majors and twenty graduate programs across six distinct schools, Manhattan College has big academic opportunities. Our students take what they learn in the classroom and apply it to the real world through internships, service-learning projects and study abroad.

"Founded on the principles of John Baptist de La Salle, patron saint of teachers, the College strives to promote faith, respect, quality education, community and social justice in all that we do. One example, The Lasallian Outreach Volunteer Experience (L.O.V.E.), provides service and social-justice travel experiences. Some offer immersion experiences: the chance to live in solidarity with the poor, experience an unfamiliar culture and learn about issues of social justice. Others involve more hands-on service work, such as helping rebuild in New Orleans post-Hurricane Katrina."

SELECTIVITY

Admissions Rating	79
# of applicants	7,882
% of applicants accepted	75
% of acceptees attending	13

FRESHMAN PROFILE

Range SAT EBRW	540–630
Range SAT Math	530–630
Range ACT Composite	23–28
% submitting SAT scores	83
% submitting ACT scores	16
% graduated top 10% of class	23
% graduated top 25% of class	54
% graduated top 50% of class	79

DEADLINES

Early decision	
Deadline	11/15
Notification	12/15
Regular	
Priority	3/1
Notification	Rolling, 12/15
Nonfall registration?	Yes

FINANCIAL FACTS

Financial Aid Rating	78
Annual tuition	$40,400
Room and board	$16,870
Required fees	$1,964
Books and supplies	$1,200
Average frosh need-based scholarship	$19,365
Average UG need-based scholarship	$14,027
% needy frosh rec. need-based scholarship or grant aid	0
% needy UG rec. need-based scholarship or grant aid	0
% needy frosh rec. non-need-based scholarship or grant aid	12
% needy UG rec. non-need-based scholarship or grant aid	14
% needy frosh rec. need-based self-help aid	64
% needy UG rec. need-based self-help aid	59
% frosh rec. any financial aid	88
% UG rec. any financial aid	86
% UG borrow to pay for school	97
Average cumulative indebtedness	$46,498
% frosh need fully met	34
% ugrads need fully met	14
Average % of frosh need met	80
Average % of ugrad need met	70

MANHATTANVILLE COLLEGE

2900 Purchase Street, Purchase, NY 10577 • Admissions: 914-323-5464 • Fax: 914-694-1732

STUDENTS SAY ". . ."

Academics

For students who don't like to limit themselves, Manhattanville College provides "endless opportunities to find your passion and get involved." Undergraduates take comfort from the institution's carefully fostered "communal environment" and the "close-knit relationships" this leads to. They also freely capitalize on the college's "diverse course selection," and the way both the academics and school provide "many connections for internships and jobs" while also serving to "help you build your portfolio as a young professional." Students are fairly quick to give credit where it's due, praising professors who often act as "amazing resources" and generally "bring a lot of expertise into their classrooms." In particular, those at Manhattanville appreciate that professors strive to "teach in a way that makes learning interesting and fun." It's no wonder, then, that while students here actually seem eager to take difficult courses, knowing that they'll be backed up by a faculty is "very personable and clearly communicates that they are here to help their students and facilitate their success." Based on the feedback we've seen, it's clear that "no matter what the students need, there is always an office, a person, or department ready, willing, and able to help out." Considering all that, it's no wonder that one undergrad describes time spent at Manhattanville as a "challenging but stressless experience."

Life

At Manhattanville, there's tons of fun to be had both in and out of the classroom. To begin with, sports are certainly very popular and you'll find that the "majority of students attend athletic events to support their fellow Valiants." Many people also participate in intramurals for rugby, volleyball and dodgeball (among others). But don't fret if you're not particularly sporty; there are plenty of other ways to get involved, whether that's participating in the active student government, joining the Finance Society, working on the Manhattanville Video Project, or joining a cultural institution like the Asian American Student Association. One particular highlight is the Mary T. Clark Community Service Program, "where students often will go just to be around the positive energy." Additionally, "acapella and performance opportunities [abound]" and the college sponsors numerous events such as Fall Fest, a family weekend "with rides, food, and plenty of entertainment" as well as Quad Jam, a music festival with "food trucks, student performances, and a headliner performance such as We The Kings and Lupe Fiasco." Once the weekend rolls around, it's fairly common for undergrads to head off campus—free transportation both to White Plains and New York City doesn't hurt. "There's something for everyone, you just have to be ambitious enough to find exactly what it is you like to do."

Student Body

Manhattanville undergrads seem to pride themselves on the school's "very diverse" community. As one student immediately explains, "I have made friends from all different backgrounds, states, and countries." Just as critically, people here are "willing to embrace different cultures, ethnicities, sexualities and personality types." While a few individuals do note that the "student body is somewhat divided into athletes and non-athletes," others insist that "it's easy to meet people and make friends." By and large, students say their classmates "genuinely care about everyone's well being" and are "willing to help you when you need." And it's certainly common to encounter a "friendly face" as you walk across campus. The vast majority of students are also "very hardworking" and extremely "passionate about their education and extracurriculars." Indeed, "they know the fields they want to be in and strive to achieve their goals." One individual further elaborates, "I also describe them as warriors who don't give up once they reach a failure; they keep on going no matter the road ahead." As this undergrad concludes, "Everyone I've met is so kind and passionate and talented, it's a great environment to be in."

MANHATTANVILLE COLLEGE

Financial Aid: 914-323-5357 • E-Mail: admissions@mville.edu • Website: www.mville.edu

THE PRINCETON REVIEW SAYS

Admissions

Very important factors considered include: rigor of secondary school record, academic GPA, application essay, recommendation(s), extracurricular activities, talent/ability, character/personal qualities, alumni/ae relation, level of applicant's interest. *Important factors considered include:* geographical residence. *Other factors considered include:* class rank, standardized test scores, interview, first generation, state residency, work experience. ACT with or without writing accepted. SAT with or without Essay component accepted. High school diploma is required and GED is accepted. *Academic units required:* 4 English, 3 math, 2 science, 2 social studies, 5 academic electives.

Financial Aid

Students should submit: FAFSA; State aid form. Priority filing deadline is 3/1. The Princeton Review suggests that all financial aid forms be submitted as soon as possible after October 1. *Need-based scholarships/grants offered:* College/university scholarship or grant aid from institutional funds; Federal Pell; Private scholarships; SEOG; State scholarships/grants; United Negro College Fund. *Loan aid offered:* Direct PLUS loans; Direct Subsidized Stafford Loans; Direct Unsubsidized Stafford Loans. Applicants will be notified of awards on a rolling basis beginning 11/15. Federal Work-Study Program available. Institutional employment available.

The Inside Word

Earning admission to Manhattanville is certainly competitive. Fortunately, the college takes a straightforward approach when assessing applicants. You can expect your high school transcripts and test scores will be carefully considered along with your personal statement and letters of recommendation. While you are not required to sit for an interview, it is strongly recommended. It's also important to note that Manhattanville operates on the basis of rolling admissions. Therefore, the earlier you apply the better your chances.

THE SCHOOL SAYS "..."

From the Admissions Office

"At Manhattanville College, we believe higher education elevates students' knowledge both academically and practically. That's why we offer 50+ undergraduate areas of study reinforced by internships, career counseling, mentors, and networking opportunities. We call it outcomes-based learning. The college's strongest offerings include education, business (particularly management and finance), and psychology, while communication studies and performing arts are also popular. Manhattanville's School of Education, which offers nineteen five-year Bachelor's-Master's programs, boasts a near-perfect pass rate for the New York State Teaching Exam. Manhattanville recently opened the School of Nursing and Health Sciences, which offers two degrees: Bachelor of Science in Nursing for traditional 4-year and transfer students and an accelerated second degree Bachelor of Science in Nursing for students who already hold a Bachelor's degree. 84 percent of our full time faculty hold the highest degree in their field. There are ample opportunities for service to the College and to the outside community through the Sister Mary T. Clark Center for Religion and Social Justice, the Connie Hogarth Center for Social Action, the Center for Inclusion, and the more than 50 various student organizations on campus. There are more than 60 outlets for community service available on campus and more than 600 Manhattanville College students give their time to service projects. With a wide range of academic programs, diverse student population, and community service found at Manhattanville College, we are committed to fulfilling our mission to educate students to be ethical and socially responsible leaders in a global community."

SELECTIVITY

Admissions Rating	74
# of applicants	3,435
% of applicants accepted	90
% of acceptees attending	13

FRESHMAN PROFILE

Range SAT EBRW	490–580
Range SAT Math	490–590
Range ACT Composite	19–27
# submitting SAT scores	165
% submitting SAT scores	42
# submitting ACT scores	31
% submitting ACT scores	8
Average HS GPA	3.2
% graduated top 10% of class	14
% graduated top 25% of class	19
% graduated top 50% of class	75

DEADLINES

Early action	
Deadline	12/1
Notification	1/1
Regular	
Priority	3/1
Notification	Rolling, 12/1
Nonfall registration?	Yes

APPLICANTS ALSO LOOK AT AND SOMETIMES PREFER

Sacred Heart University; St. John's University; Mercy College; Marist College; Manhattan College; Iona College

FINANCIAL FACTS

Financial Aid Rating	84
Annual tuition	$38,880
Room and board	$14,810
Required fees	$1,450
Books and supplies	$800
Average frosh need-based scholarship	$7,941
Average UG need-based scholarship	$6,116
% needy frosh rec. need-based scholarship or grant aid	81
% needy UG rec. need-based scholarship or grant aid	84
% needy frosh rec. non-need-based scholarship or grant aid	99
% needy UG rec. non-need-based scholarship or grant aid	95
% needy frosh rec. need-based self-help aid	100
% needy UG rec. need-based self-help aid	84
% frosh rec. any financial aid	98.21
% UG rec. any financial aid	94.23
% UG borrow to pay for school	68
Average cumulative indebtedness	$35,092
% frosh need fully met	19
% ugrads need fully met	16
Average % of frosh need met	70
Average % of ugrad need met	73

MARIST COLLEGE

3399 North Road, Poughkeepsie, NY 12601-1387 • Admissions: 845-575-3226 • Fax: 845-575-3215

CAMPUS LIFE

Quality of Life Rating	89
Fire Safety Rating	65
Green Rating	84
Type of school	Private
Environment	Town

STUDENTS

Total undergrad enrollment	5,460
% male/female	42/58
% from out of state	48
% frosh live on campus	98
% ugrads live on campus	64
# of fraternities (% ugrad men join)	3 (3)
# of sororities (% ugrad women join)	4 (3)
% African American	4
% Asian	3
% Caucasian	74
% Hispanic	12
% Native American	<1
% Pacific Islander	<1
% Two or more races	3
% Race and/or ethnicity unknown	1
% international	3
# of countries represented	50

SURVEY SAYS . . .

Students are happy
Great library
Internships are widely available
Intramural sports are popular
Theater is popular

ACADEMICS

Academic Rating	82
% students returning for sophomore year	88
% students graduating within 4 years	77
% students graduating within 6 years	84
Calendar	Semester
Student/faculty ratio	16:1
Profs interesting rating	89
Profs accessible rating	92

Most classes have 20–29 students.
Most lab/discussion sessions have
10–19 students.

MOST POPULAR MAJORS

Communication and Media Studies; Psychology,
General; Business Administration and
Management, General

STUDENTS SAY "..."

Academics

At Marist College, faculty "like to make classes interactive yet challenging in a positive aspect." They also value real-life experience and connections in their classrooms. "I have had faculty ... [in contact with] a finance firm ... within minutes of me mentioning interest in working there," says a student. Professors are "highly qualified," "diverse in the way they teach," and "always willing to help," both in and out of class. "The academics are the best thing about Marist," says another student. Support staff and advisors are also highly praised for being "some of the most supportive people." The Honors program at Marist is "a huge strength because it unlocks many advantages" by "[exploring] unique perspectives on topics related to all sorts of majors." Honors courses include "a class on the ethical implications of emerging technology [and] an economics course focused on why nations fail." One course even involves "riding a boat up and down the Hudson River" in order to examine the environment of the area.

Life

Marist is near the Hudson River, so students often "fill their days by walking along and laying out ... when [the weather] is nice." In the winter, "students may be sledding on snow days or getting together with friends" elsewhere. "A big tradition is jumping into the Hudson River before you graduate," says a student. Indeed, Marist's beauty, which "never fails to amaze" students, offers nearby Rhinebeck and New Paltz for hiking and access to the Walkway Over the Hudson, as well as the chance to just walk around the "rich community." For study time, there are campus cafés, and "there are a lot of cute [off-campus cafés] around Poughkeepsie," too. The library "is a very popular hub for studying, group work, or just [hanging] out." Clubs and intramurals "[give] the campus life after dark." Students also mention that "the student center often holds events like bingo nights, stand-up [comedy nights], and more." Outside of participating either in sports or clubs, many students "intern in NYC several times a week while also maintaining a social life."

Student Body

Students identify the community at Marist as "incredibly friendly," and they point out that students have an unspoken "policy to hold the door open for people," "no matter the weather condition." One student commented: "I've never met so many friendly strangers in New York in my life." Another observes that "nearly everyone ... is Catholic, but the majority are not religious." While many students herald Marist for its diversity, others claim that appears more "on paper" than on campus. The dominant groups on campus appear to be "athletes," "in the fashion department," or those "studying computers/technology." "I find that students are very hungry for knowledge," says a student. A large portion of the student body also likes to give back: it's common for students to "participate in two hours of weekly community service ... [or] help with one-time community-service events."

Financial Aid: 845-575-3230 • E-Mail: Admission@Marist.edu • Website: http://www.Marist.edu/

THE PRINCETON REVIEW SAYS
Admissions
Very important factors considered include: rigor of secondary school record, academic GPA. *Important factors considered include:* class rank, application essay, recommendation(s), extracurricular activities, talent/ability, character/personal qualities, geographical residence, state residency, volunteer work. *Other factors considered include:* standardized test scores, first generation, alumni/ae relation, racial/ethnic status, level of applicant's interest. ACT with or without writing accepted. SAT with or without Essay component accepted. High school diploma is required and GED is accepted. *Academic units required:* 4 English, 3 math, 3 science, 2 science labs, 2 foreign language, 2 social studies, 1 history, 2 academic electives. *Academic units recommended:* 4 math, 4 science, 3 science labs, 3 foreign language.

Financial Aid
Students should submit: FAFSA. Priority filing deadline is 11/15. The Princeton Review suggests that all financial aid forms be submitted as soon as possible after October 1. *Need-based scholarships/grants offered:* College/university scholarship or grant aid from institutional funds; Federal Pell; Private scholarships; SEOG; State scholarships/grants. *Loan aid offered:* Direct PLUS loans; Direct Subsidized Stafford Loans; Direct Unsubsidized Stafford Loans. Applicants will be notified of awards on or about 3/31. Federal Work-Study Program available. Institutional employment available.

The Inside Word
Marist College has a 42 percent acceptance rate of about 11,000 applications they received in 2017. The school does not require SAT/ACT scores. However, average scores from students who submit are 1200–1340 for the SAT and 26–30 for the ACT. Marist takes all other typical aspects of applications into consideration—essay, extracurriculars, leadership accomplishments, and recommendation letters—but emphasizes academic performance via GPA and the difficulty of a student's high school course load.

THE SCHOOL SAYS "..."
From the Admissions Office
"Applications to Marist are up over 50 percent in the last few years. Meanwhile, the number of seats available for the first-year class remains at about 1,100, making for a competitive admission process. Our recommendations: keep your grades up, participate in community service, and exercise leadership in the classroom, extracurricular endeavors, and your community. We encourage a campus visit. When prospective students see Marist—our beautiful location on the Hudson River, top-notch facilities, the close interaction between students and faculty, and the fact that students enjoy their time here—they want to become a part of the Marist community. We'll help you in the transition to college through an innovative first-year program that provides mentors for every student. Whatever field you pursue, Marist's emphasis on industry-specific technology gives students a competitive edge. Marist invests in the student experience. New academic buildings (music, science, art, and fashion) and new residence halls have dramatically improved both academic and social space. Students call the dining hall 'Hogwarts on the Hudson.' Marist main goals are ensuring student success, promoting innovation, and advancing the social good. The College is home to the nationally recognized Marist Poll, which employs hundreds of students each year, offering valuable experience into polling, politics, journalism, and interpretation of data. At Marist, you'll get a premium education, develop skills, have fun and make lifelong friends, have the opportunity to gain valuable experience through internship and study abroad programs, including at our branch campus in Florence, Italy, and be ahead of the competition for graduate school or a career."

SELECTIVITY
Admissions Rating	89
# of applicants	11,260
% of applicants accepted	49
% of acceptees attending	24
# offered a place on the wait list	4,404
% accepting a place on wait list	20
% admitted from wait list	20
# of early decision applicants	269
% accepted early decision	86

FRESHMAN PROFILE
Range SAT EBRW	580–660
Range SAT Math	580–670
Range ACT Composite	25–30
# submitting SAT scores	702
% submitting SAT scores	52
# submitting ACT scores	216
% submitting ACT scores	16
Average HS GPA	3.3
% graduated top 10% of class	24
% graduated top 25% of class	51
% graduated top 50% of class	84

DEADLINES
Early decision	
Deadline	11/15
Notification	12/15
Other ED Deadline	2/1
Other ED Notification	2/15
Early action	
Deadline	11/15
Notification	1/15
Regular	
Deadline	2/1
Notification	4/1
Nonfall registration?	Yes

APPLICANTS ALSO LOOK AT AND OFTEN PREFER
Boston College; New York University; Villanova University; Quinnipiac University; University of Connecticut; University of Delaware; Syracuse University; State University of New York at Binghamton (Binghamton University); State University of New York—Stony Brook University; Loyola University Maryland; Ithaca College; Fordham University; Fairfield University; University of Massachusetts Amherst

AND SOMETIMES PREFER
Northeastern University; State University of New York—Geneseo

FINANCIAL FACTS
Financial Aid Rating	85
Annual tuition	$44,800
Room and board	$18,530
Required fees	$730
Books and supplies	$1,125
Average frosh need-based scholarship	$24,087
Average UG need-based scholarship	$20,112
% needy frosh rec. need-based scholarship or grant aid	98
% needy UG rec. need-based scholarship or grant aid	96
% needy frosh rec. non-need-based scholarship or grant aid	14
% needy UG rec. non-need-based scholarship or grant aid	11
% needy frosh rec. need-based self-help aid	83
% needy UG rec. need-based self-help aid	84
% UG borrow to pay for school	65
Average cumulative indebtedness	$40,007
% frosh need fully met	20
% ugrads need fully met	19
Average % of frosh need met	75
Average % of ugrad need met	69

MARQUETTE UNIVERSITY

PO Box 1881, Milwaukee, WI 53201-1881 • Admissions: 414-288-7302 • Fax: 414-288-3764

STUDENTS SAY "..."

Academics

A highly regarded Jesuit school, Marquette University "seeks to provide a well-rounded education based upon excellence, faith, leadership and service." Undergrads here truly value how the university is able to seamlessly integrate "the classroom [with] the greater Milwaukee area through applied programs, service learning and social activities." Marquette also manages to foster "great relationships with many companies in the area (and in other states) and those companies come [here when] looking for interns to hire." As if that wasn't enough, the university's size is also a fantastic asset. A biomedical science major explains, "There's a real sense of community. It's a big enough school so you don't know everyone, but small enough so that you feel important."

Academically, the school's physical therapy, physician's assistant and business programs are all quite "strong" and very "highly" regarded. Fortunately, no matter your major, Marquette undergrads are privy to "enthusiastic" professors who seem to "genuinely care about [their] students." A nursing student agrees adding, "I've seen professors send students home to rest when they are sick, offer study sessions outside of class, lend students a book if they bought the wrong one, etc." Many professors also have ample professional experience. Therefore, they're able to bring "real world" insight directly into classroom. Overall, though "classes are difficult," professors "push you to do your best and you definitely come out learning a lot."

Life

If there's one notion that undergrads here make abundantly clear, it's that there is never a shortage of fun to be had at Marquette. Whether it's "a sorority or fraternity event, a get-together at your friend's, a concert at the Rave...a school sponsored event such as discounted tickets to the Broadway musical showing downtown, or free admission to the Olympic training ice rink off campus (skates included!)—there is ALWAYS something to do." Naturally, given that Marquette is part of the Big East Conference, the campus maintains a healthy "basketball culture." Students also love the fact that there are "a multitude of opportunities to get involved with community service." Additionally, Marquette offers groups "for everything from knitting to dancing to sailing...[as well as] club sports...[and] various martial arts and Quidditch." During the warmer months, it's not uncommon to see students simply "studying [outside] or playing catch/Frisbee [on] the quad." Finally, undergrads love the fact that the campus is a mere "five minutes away from downtown [Milwaukee]." This makes it easy for students to explore all the city has to offer from restaurants and shops to museums and cultural festivals.

Student Body

Given Marquette's location, it's not surprising that the majority of students hail "from the Midwest" with "a [hefty] number...from the Chicago area" in particular. And though "many students come from wealthy families, there are a large portion of people that attend Marquette due to generous scholarships." Thankfully, no matter your geographic heritage or economic status, undergrads assure us that you'll find a "friendly" student body. And though it's a Jesuit university, "Marquette welcomes students of all backgrounds [and] promotes unity among students of all faiths and cultural communities." More importantly, when pressed to describe and define their peers, undergrads assert that their fellow students are "down to earth, kind, funny [and] hardworking." They are also extremely "concerned about others and about social issues [as well]." Additionally, most students tend to be "very upbeat and passionate about everything that has to do with Marquette." Lastly, a political science major gushes, "This place felt like home right away because of how many genuine people are here."

MARQUETTE UNIVERSITY

Financial Aid: 414-288-7390 • E-Mail: admissions@Marquette.edu • Website: www.marquette.edu

THE PRINCETON REVIEW SAYS

Admissions

Very important factors considered include: rigor of secondary school record, academic GPA. *Important factors considered include:* application essay, standardized test scores, extracurricular activities, volunteer work. *Other factors considered include:* class rank (when available), recommendation(s), talent/ability, character/personal qualities, first generation, alumni/ae relation, racial/ethnic status, work experience. ACT with or without writing is optional. SAT with or without Essay component is optional. High school diploma is required and GED is accepted. *Academic units required:* 4 English, 2 math, 2 science, 2 science labs, 2 social studies, 2 academic electives. *Academic units recommended:* 4 English, 4 math, 4 science, 3 science labs, 2 foreign language, 3 social studies, 2 history, 5 academic electives.

Financial Aid

Students should submit: FAFSA. The Princeton Review suggests that all financial aid forms be submitted as soon as possible after October 1. *Need-based scholarships/grants offered:* College/university scholarship or grant aid from institutional funds; Federal Pell; Private scholarships; SEOG; State scholarships/grants. *Loan aid offered:* Direct PLUS loans; Direct Subsidized Stafford Loans; Direct Unsubsidized Stafford Loans. Applicants will be notified of awards on a rolling basis beginning 1/9. Federal Work-Study Program available. Institutional employment available.

The Inside Word

Marquette's admissions officers do not take their job lightly. Each application is read by at least two individuals before any decisions are made. When evaluating a candidate, officers first look to assess the high school transcript. They make a note of grade trends and pay close attention to how challenging an applicant's course load was. There is a new test optional policy, and those not submitting a test score will not be penalized for making this choice. However, if a student chooses to submit an ACT or SAT score, the counselor will consider it as part of the review. Next, they take into account an applicant's personal statement along with his/her extracurricular activities. Finally, the school weighs the evaluation submitted by the guidance counselor.

SELECTIVITY

Admissions Rating	80
# of applicants	15,078
% of applicants accepted	83
% of acceptees attending	16
# offered a place on the wait list	609
% accepting a place on wait list	100
% admitted from wait list	38

FRESHMAN PROFILE

Range SAT EBRW	560–650
Range SAT Math	560–670
Range ACT Composite	24–29
# submitting SAT scores	639
% submitting SAT scores	32
# submitting ACT scores	1,556
% submitting ACT scores	79
% graduated top 10% of class	33
% graduated top 25% of class	63
% graduated top 50% of class	94

DEADLINES

Regular	
Priority	12/1
Deadline	12/1
Notification	Rolling, 12/23
Nonfall registration?	Yes

FINANCIAL FACTS

Financial Aid Rating	87
Annual tuition	$44,970
Room and board	$13,656
Required fees	$696
Books and supplies	$816
Average frosh need-based scholarship	$29,527
Average UG need-based scholarship	$25,967
% needy frosh rec. need-based scholarship or grant aid	99
% needy UG rec. need-based scholarship or grant aid	98
% needy frosh rec. non-need-based scholarship or grant aid	10
% needy UG rec. non-need-based scholarship or grant aid	10
% needy frosh rec. need-based self-help aid	81
% needy UG rec. need-based self-help aid	82
% UG borrow to pay for school	59
Average cumulative indebtedness	$38,173
% frosh need fully met	23
% ugrads need fully met	25
Average % of frosh need met	80
Average % of ugrad need met	78

MASSACHUSETTS INSTITUTE OF TECHNOLOGY

77 Massachusetts Avenue, Cambridge, MA 02139 • Admissions: 617-253-3400 • Fax: 617-258-8304

STUDENTS SAY "..."

Academics

Massachusetts Institute of Technology, the East Coast mecca of engineering, science, and mathematics, "is the ultimate place for information overload, endless possibilities, and expanding your horizons." The "amazing collection of creative minds" includes enough Nobel laureates to fill a jury box as well as brilliant students who are given substantial control of their educations; one explains, "The administration's attitude toward students is one of respect. As soon as you come on campus, you are bombarded with choices." Students need to be able to manage a workload that "definitely push[es you] beyond your comfort level." A chemical engineering major elaborates: "MIT is different from many schools in that its goal is not to teach you specific facts in each subject. MIT teaches you how to think, not about opinions but about problem solving. Facts and memorization are useless unless you know how to approach a tough problem." Professors here range from "excellent teachers who make lectures fun and exciting" to "dull and soporific" ones, but most "make a serious effort to make the material they teach interesting by throwing in jokes and cool demonstrations." "Access to an amazing number of resources, both academic and recreational," "research opportunities for undergrads with some of the nation's leading professors," and a rock-solid alumni network complete the picture. If you ask "MIT alumni where they went to college, most will immediately stick out their hand and show you their 'brass rat' (the MIT ring, the second most recognized ring in the world)."

Life

At MIT, "it may seem…like there's no life outside problem sets and studying for exams," but "there's always time for extracurricular activities or just relaxing" for those "with good time-management skills" or the "ability to survive on [a] lack of sleep." Options range from "building rides" (recent projects have included a motorized couch and a human-sized hamster wheel) "to partying at fraternities to enjoying the largest collection of science fiction novels in the United States at the MIT Science Fiction Library." Students occasionally find time to "pull a hack," which is an prank, "like the life-size Wright brothers' plane that appeared on top of the Great Dome for the one-hundredth anniversary of flight." Undergrads tell us, "MIT has great parties—a lot of Wellesley, Harvard, and BU students come to them," but also that "there are tons of things to do other than party" here. "Movies, shopping, museums, and plays are all possible with our location near Boston. There are great restaurants only [blocks] away from campus too.... From what I can tell, MIT students have way more fun on the weekends than their Cambridge counterparts [at] Harvard."

Student Body

"There actually isn't one typical student at MIT," students here assure us, explaining that "hobbies range from building robots and hacking to getting wasted and partying every weekend. The one thing students all have in common is that they are insanely smart and love to learn. Pretty much anyone can find the perfect group of friends to hang out with at MIT." "Most students do have some form of 'nerdiness'" (like telling nerdy jokes, being an avid fan of Star Wars, etc.), but "contrary to MIT's stereotype, most MIT students are not geeks who study all the time and have no social skills. The majority of the students here are actually quite 'normal.'" The "stereotypical student [who] looks techy and unkempt…only represents about 25 percent of the school." The rest include "multiple-sport standouts, political activists, fraternity and sorority members, hippies, clean-cut business types, LARPers, hackers, musicians, and artisans. There are people who look like they stepped out of an Abercrombie & Fitch catalog and people who dress in all black and carry flashlights and multi-tools. Not everyone relates to everyone else, but most people get along, and it's almost a guarantee that you'll fit in somewhere."

MASSACHUSETTS INSTITUTE OF TECHNOLOGY

Financial Aid: 617-258-8600 • E-Mail: admissions@mit.edu • Website: web.mit.edu

THE PRINCETON REVIEW SAYS

Admissions

Very important factors considered include: character/personal qualities. *Important factors considered include:* rigor of secondary school record, academic GPA, application essay, standardized test scores, recommendation(s), interview, extracurricular activities, talent/ability. *Other factors considered include:* class rank, first generation, geographical residence, racial/ethnic status, volunteer work, work experience. ACT with or without writing accepted. SAT with or without Essay component accepted. High school diploma or equivalent is not required. *Academic units recommended:* 4 English, 4 math, 4 science, 2 foreign language, 2 social studies.

Financial Aid

Students should submit: CSS/Financial Aid PROFILE; FAFSA; Noncustodial PROFILE. Priority filing deadline is 2/15. The Princeton Review suggests that all financial aid forms be submitted as soon as possible after October 1. *Need-based scholarships/grants offered:* College/university scholarship or grant aid from institutional funds; Federal Pell; Private scholarships; SEOG; State scholarships/grants; United Negro College Fund. *Loan aid offered:* Direct PLUS loans; Direct Subsidized Stafford Loans; Direct Unsubsidized Stafford Loans. Applicants will be notified of awards on or about 3/15. Federal Work-Study Program available. Institutional employment available.

The Inside Word

MIT has one of the nation's most competitive admissions processes. The school's applicant pool is so rich it turns away numerous qualified candidates each year. Put your best foot forward and take consolation in the fact that rejection doesn't necessarily mean that you don't belong at MIT, but only that there wasn't enough room for you the year you applied. Your best chance to get an edge: Find ways to stress your creativity, a quality that MIT's admissions director told *USA TODAY* is lacking in many prospective college students.

THE SCHOOL SAYS "..."

From the Admissions Office

"The students who come to the Massachusetts Institute of Technology are some of America's—and the world's—best and most creative. As graduates, they leave here to make real contributions—in science, technology, business, education, politics, architecture, and the arts. From any class, many will go on to do work that is historically significant. These young men and women are leaders, achievers, and producers. Helping such students make the most of their talents and dreams would challenge any educational institution. MIT gives them its best advantages: a world-class faculty, unparalleled facilities, and remarkable opportunities. In turn, these students help to make the institute the vital place it is. They bring fresh viewpoints to faculty research: More than three-quarters participate in the Undergraduate Research Opportunities Program, developing solutions for the world's problems in areas such as energy, the environment, cancer, and poverty. They play on MIT's thirty-three intercollegiate teams as well as in its fifty-plus music, theater, and dance groups. To their classes and to their out-of-class activities, they bring enthusiasm, energy, and individual style."

SELECTIVITY

Admissions Rating	99
# of applicants	21,706
% of applicants accepted	7
% of acceptees attending	76
# offered a place on the wait list	460
% accepting a place on wait list	83
% admitted from wait list	0

FRESHMAN PROFILE

Range SAT EBRW	720–770
Range SAT Math	780–800
Range ACT Composite	34–36
# submitting SAT scores	837
% submitting SAT scores	75
# submitting ACT scores	531
% submitting ACT scores	48
% graduated top 10% of class	97
% graduated top 25% of class	100
% graduated top 50% of class	100

DEADLINES

Early action	
Deadline	11/1
Notification	12/20
Regular	
Deadline	1/1
Notification	3/22
Nonfall registration?	No

APPLICANTS ALSO LOOK AT AND SOMETIMES PREFER

Harvard College; Princeton University; Stanford University; Yale University

AND RARELY PREFER

California Institute of Technology; Columbia University; Cornell University; Duke University; University of Pennsylvania

FINANCIAL FACTS

Financial Aid Rating	97
Annual tuition	$53,450
Room and board	$16,390
Required fees	$340
Books and supplies	$820
Average frosh need-based scholarship	$49,010
Average UG need-based scholarship	$48,562
% needy frosh rec. need-based scholarship or grant aid	98
% needy UG rec. need-based scholarship or grant aid	98
% needy frosh rec. non-need-based scholarship or grant aid	3
% needy UG rec. non-need-based scholarship or grant aid	3
% needy frosh rec. need-based self-help aid	63
% needy UG rec. need-based self-help aid	70
% frosh rec. any financial aid	83
% UG rec. any financial aid	70
% UG borrow to pay for school	29
Average cumulative indebtedness	$22,696
% frosh need fully met	100
% ugrads need fully met	100
Average % of frosh need met	100
Average % of ugrad need met	100

McDaniel College

2 College Hill, Westminster, MD 21157 • Admissions: 410-857-2230

CAMPUS LIFE

Quality of Life Rating	84
Fire Safety Rating	88
Green Rating	60*
Type of school	Private
Environment	Town

STUDENTS

Total undergrad enrollment	1,669
% male/female	48/52
% from out of state	32
% frosh live on campus	95
% ugrads live on campus	86
# of fraternities (% ugrad men join)	5 (14)
# of sororities (% ugrad women join)	6 (15)
% African American	21
% Asian	2
% Caucasian	57
% Hispanic	6
% Native American	<1
% Pacific Islander	0
% Two or more races	3
% Race and/or ethnicity unknown	7
% international	3
# of countries represented	30

SURVEY SAYS . . .

Everyone loves the Green Terror
Great library
Easy to get around campus
Frats and sororities are popular

ACADEMICS

Academic Rating	81
% students returning for sophomore year	77
% students graduating within 4 years	60
% students graduating within 6 years	68
Calendar	4/1/4
Student/faculty ratio	12:1
Profs interesting rating	91
Profs accessible rating	93
Most classes have 10–19 students.	

STUDENTS SAY ". . ."

Academics

Located in quiet Westminster, Maryland, McDaniel College is a small, student-centered liberal arts college of just 1,600 undergraduate students, which makes it the perfect place for enrollees "to really get to know their professors and participate in class without feeling like they are drowning in a sea of students." The academic program is made up of 33 degrees, but allows students to design their own interdisciplinary major, and while that may feel overwhelming, the first-year experience also features flex classes to help ease students into the collegiate experience. A twelve-to-one student-faculty ratio and an average class size of just fifteen to give each student a chance to stand out and establish themselves: "The campus is ripe with opportunities—you just have to be there to take them."

Classes at McDaniel stress critical thinking and a creative approach, which means that there are plenty of "field trips to experience topics firsthand" and opportunities for students to "take the floor and share their ideas" through Socratic discussion. You may find novel approaches to grading as well, like how "my entrepreneurship professor allows us to make the core of our grade trying to create a small business from scratch" or how one student "took a class about Viking literature in which we had a 'Viking feast' day." Make no mistake, though: students work hard to earn their grades. Classes are "challenging but not overwhelming," thanks to a faculty that serves as "a great support system for both academic life and personal life."

Life

Eighty-five percent of students happily live on campus, taking advantage of the "variety of different foods" in the dining hall, or the layout of the college, as "academic buildings are convenient when walking from anywhere." Students say that there isn't that much to do in the area, but they praise the beautiful campus and note that "it is what you make of it." If anything, that's a creative challenge that most students seem to overcome by using the recreation lounge to "play games with friends or just hang out with doing anything" or by joining the "many clubs and organizations on campus" or being "strongly involved in on-campus academic and social groups," which includes Greek life. During the week, students tend to be "about their business in the classroom," but nice weekends are particularly bustling, as "a ton of people go outside and play cornhole, spike ball, throw frisbees and footballs, or hammock." Those in the mood for getaways "love when [McDaniel] offers weekend Blitz trips," which are $10–$15 events that include "football games, hockey games, Hershey Park, etc."

Student Body

"Because we're a small school, I think there is a unique sense of community," explains one student who notes that "people I barely know will stop to ask how I am or wave at me from across the quad just because we've had a class together." Though "a majority of the students are either part of a sports team or a sorority/fraternity," they come with "a wide range of backgrounds and views on the world." Furthermore, regardless of affiliation, undergrads claim that "there are no defined groupings that people are stuck in and the entire campus feels like a big family." Those relationships are further established "through classes, sports, clubs, and social events [where] people get to know each other and build positive relationships."

Financial Aid: 410-857-2233 • E-Mail: admissions@mcdaniel.edu • Website: www.mcdaniel.edu

THE PRINCETON REVIEW SAYS

Admissions

Very important factors considered include: rigor of secondary school record, academic GPA. *Important factors considered include:* application essay, recommendation(s). *Other factors considered include:* class rank, interview, extracurricular activities, talent/ability, character/personal qualities, first generation, alumni/ae relation, volunteer work, work experience. High school diploma is required and GED is accepted. *Academic units required:* 4 English, 3 math, 3 science, 3 science labs, 3 foreign language, 3 social studies. *Academic units recommended:* 4 English, 4 math, 4 science, 4 foreign language, 3 social studies.

Financial Aid

Students should submit: FAFSA. Priority filing deadline is 11/15. The Princeton Review suggests that all financial aid forms be submitted as soon as possible after October 1. *Need-based scholarships/grants offered:* College/university scholarship or grant aid from institutional funds; Federal Pell; Private scholarships; SEOG; State scholarships/grants. *Loan aid offered:* Direct PLUS loans; Direct Subsidized Stafford Loans; Direct Unsubsidized Stafford Loans. Applicants will be notified of awards on a rolling basis beginning 12/15. Federal Work-Study Program available. Institutional employment available.

The Inside Word

McDaniel prides itself on taking the time to get to know applicants, so each student has their own admissions counselor who can help plan a campus visit and ensure applications are complete. The school looks at the applicant as an entire picture, meaning grades, recommendations, extracurriculars, and writing abilities on an essay—students will respond to one of four pre-selected questions—are all seriously considered. There are no guarantees, but those with at least average grades and who show a commitment to attending McDaniel stand a good chance of getting in.

THE SCHOOL SAYS "..."

From the Admissions Office

"McDaniel College is a four-year, independent college of the liberal arts and sciences. Founded in 1867 as one of the first coeducational colleges in the nation and the first south of the Mason-Dixon Line, McDaniel is a diverse, student-centered community of 1,600 undergraduates and 1,400 graduate students. As one of 40 "Colleges That Change Lives," McDaniel is committed to access and affordability. More than 90 percent of students receive some type of financial assistance and McDaniel invests over $40 million annually in grants and scholarships. Students can choose from more than 70 undergraduate programs of study, including pre-professional specializations and student-designed majors, plus over 20 graduate programs. Academics center on the McDaniel Plan, a customized, interdisciplinary curriculum that emphasizes experiential learning and student-faculty collaboration to develop the unique potential in every student. The McDaniel Commitment guarantees every student two experiential learning opportunities, including service learning, study abroad, student-faculty collaborative research, credit-based internship or independent study. Students also enroll in first-year seminars and senior capstone projects. Special opportunities abound through McDaniel's Center for Experience and Opportunity, The Encompass Distinction program in innovation and entrepreneurship, the Honors Program, and Global Initiatives including the Global Fellows program. Represented by the Green Terror, its 24 athletic teams compete in the NCAA Division III Centennial Conference. Additionally, students are involved in over 90 student organizations, intramural sports, and fraternities and sororities. McDaniel offers access to both Baltimore and Washington, D.C., plus a European campus in Budapest, Hungary. McDaniel is proudly test optional."

SELECTIVITY

Admissions Rating	75
# of applicants	3,761
% of applicants accepted	92
% of acceptees attending	17

FRESHMAN PROFILE

Range SAT EBRW	500–600
Range SAT Math	488–590
Range SAT Composite	990–1190
Range ACT Composite	19–25
# submitting SAT scores	300
% submitting SAT scores	52
# submitting ACT scores	59
% submitting ACT scores	16
Average HS GPA	3.5
% graduated top 10% of class	20
% graduated top 25% of class	44
% graduated top 50% of class	75

DEADLINES

Early decision	
Deadline	11/1
Notification	12/1
Other ED Deadline	1/15
Other ED Notification	2/1
Early action	
Deadline	12/15
Notification	1/15
Regular	
Priority	2/1
Nonfall registration?	Yes

FINANCIAL FACTS

Financial Aid Rating	88
Annual tuition	$44,540
Room and board	$11,772
Books and supplies	$1,200
Average frosh need-based scholarship	$38,636
Average UG need-based scholarship	$36,238
% needy frosh rec. need-based scholarship or grant aid	100
% needy UG rec. need-based scholarship or grant aid	100
% needy frosh rec. non-need-based scholarship or grant aid	13
% needy UG rec. non-need-based scholarship or grant aid	22
% needy frosh rec. need-based self-help aid	77
% needy UG rec. need-based self-help aid	70
% UG borrow to pay for school	67
Average cumulative indebtedness	$16,622
% frosh need fully met	1
% ugrads need fully met	21
Average % of frosh need met	85
Average % of ugrad need met	84

McGILL UNIVERSITY

3415 McTavish St., Montreal, QC H3A 0C8 • Admissions: 514-398-7878 • Fax: 514-398-5544

CAMPUS LIFE

Quality of Life Rating	88
Fire Safety Rating	79
Green Rating	60*
Type of school	Public
Environment	Metropolis

STUDENTS

Total undergrad enrollment	25,081
% male/female	40/60
% from out of state	37
% frosh live on campus	51
% ugrads live on campus	12
# of fraternities	8
# of sororities	4
% African American	0
% Asian	0
% Caucasian	0
% Hispanic	0
% Pacific Islander	0
% Two or more races	0
% Race and/or ethnicity unknown	0
% international	0
# of countries represented	136

SURVEY SAYS . . .
Lots of liberal students
Students love Montreal, QC
College radio is popular

ACADEMICS

Academic Rating	79
Calendar	Semester
Student/faculty ratio	16:1
Profs interesting rating	86
Profs accessible rating	88

Most classes have 10–19 students.
Most lab/discussion sessions have
20–29 students.

MOST POPULAR MAJORS
Business/Commerce, General; Political Science
and Government, General; Psychology, General

STUDENTS SAY ". . ."

Academics
Montreal's McGill University is a public research institution teeming with "international recognition" and amazing "academic and research opportunities." Students fortunate enough to attend have "access to world-class resources and professors" as well as a "beautiful campus"—all at a "low cost." They also benefit from "an atmosphere that cultivates critical thinking and broadens your perspective of the world." Though a few individuals do complain that first-year classes can be "huge and [comprised of] impersonal lectures," they also reveal that "the higher you get in courses, the better they become." Further, "smaller class sizes" are the norm in departments such as "English, History, and Languages, Literatures, and Cultures (LLC)." Regardless of what you ultimately choose to study, McGill undergrads generally find their professors to be "very well-versed in their subjects and...passionate." Importantly, they're also "dedicated" and "accessible." But they won't let their students slack. As one undergrad shares, "The amount of work is a little excessive during some stretches, and the grading is by no means easy." Fortunately, instructors do "encourage students to come to conferences and office hours." And it's clearly evident that "the faculty truly love what they teach."

Life
McGill University undergrads are pretty honest about the fact that they "mostly spend their time studying." After all, classes can be very demanding and "time consuming." Nevertheless, even these intellectually-minded students need to kick back every now and again. When they're looking for a break, undergrads can turn to the "on-campus...pubs [which frequently host] events." McGill undergrads also tend to be "very active in the community" and often carve out some "time for volunteering." It's also quite common for students to organize and stage "music shows...themselves." For students looking to enjoy the outdoors, the Macdonald campus has a [great] area to hike in, an arboretum, and a bird observatory just half an hour away by walk." Or, as one ecstatic student sees it, "We have a magical forest to escape to in any season!" Once the weekend arrives, it is "party time." One knowing student explains, "First-year students often party [in] residence or go to local bars, while upperclassmen go to clubs more often." Lastly, hometown Montreal offers plenty of excitement. Students can explore everything from the newest cafes to museums and cutting edge art galleries. This city has something for everyone, no matter your interests.

Student Body
Undergrads at McGill University take pride in the fact that their peers are "highly diverse" and hail from a number of countries. Of course, there are plenty of Montreal natives as well. And many suggest that the "bilingualism of local students...adds to the cultural experience" as well. Looking beyond geography, undergrads here also reveal that their peers are "very hardworking and committed to school, spending many hours a day studying." They also tend to be quite "inclusive." One student shares, "All of the students are open-minded and appreciative of the differences that make our school [unique]." A fellow undergrad adds, "I haven't met a rude student yet. Everyone is kind and willing to collaborate or help." This attitude could be attributed to the fact that undergrads here "are always working on personally developing themselves, academically, and culturally." McGill also boasts that its peers are "motivated to do well and be successful and help as many people in the world as they can." When it comes to politics, students are "mostly liberal or left leaning." And perhaps most importantly, "Despite having a large student body with nearly 40,000 individuals, the McGill community will never let you feel insignificant as an individual."

Financial Aid: 514-398-6013 • Website: http://www.mcgill.ca/admissions/

THE PRINCETON REVIEW SAYS

Admissions

Very important factors considered include: rigor of secondary school record, academic GPA, standardized test scores. *Important factors considered include:* class rank. *Other factors considered include:* recommendation(s). ACT with Writing required. High school diploma is required and GED is not accepted. *Academic units recommended:* 4 English, 4 math, 3 science, 3 science labs, 3 foreign language, 2 social studies, 2 history.

Financial Aid

Students should submit: Institution's own financial aid form. The Princeton Review suggests that all financial aid forms be submitted as soon as possible after October 1. *Need-based scholarships/grants offered:* College/university scholarship or grant aid from institutional funds; Private scholarships. Applicants will be notified of awards on a rolling basis beginning 3/1. Institutional employment available.

The Inside Word

As one of Canada's top universities, you can rest assured that admission to McGill is highly competitive. The university places the most emphasis on your grades and high school transcript. However, different schools/programs require different grade minimums. For example, the School of Arts and Sciences requires at least a B+ average overall and an A– for English courses. The School of Architecture requires an overall A– minimum and at least a B+ in math and science prerequisites. Be sure to check the requirements for the specific school you are interested in attending.

THE SCHOOL SAYS "..."

From the Admissions Office

"McGill processes more than 30,000 online applications a year. Very few programs are available to non-Quebec students for January admission; consult the website for details.

"Applicants may submit results from the SAT (plus at least two appropriate SAT Subject Tests). The ACT is accepted in lieu of the SAT and SAT Subject Test combination. Please note that certain programs can require specific SAT Subject Tests."

SELECTIVITY

Admissions Rating	87
# of applicants	24,901
% of applicants accepted	56
% of acceptees attending	0

FRESHMAN PROFILE

Range SAT EBRW	640–740
Range SAT Math	650–720
Range ACT Composite	29–32
# submitting SAT scores	441
% submitting SAT scores	73
# submitting ACT scores	238
% submitting ACT scores	39

DEADLINES

Regular	
Deadline	1/15
Notification	Rolling, 1/30
Nonfall registration?	Yes

FINANCIAL FACTS

Financial Aid Rating	75
Annual in-state tuition	$2,294
Annual out-of-state tuition	$7,031
Required fees	$2,552
Books and supplies	$1,000
Average UG need-based scholarship	$3,715
% needy frosh rec. need-based scholarship or grant aid	0
% needy UG rec. need-based scholarship or grant aid	63
% needy frosh rec. non-need-based scholarship or grant aid	0
% needy UG rec. non-need-based scholarship or grant aid	31
% needy frosh rec. need-based self-help aid	0
% needy UG rec. need-based self-help aid	89
% UG rec. any financial aid	28
% frosh need fully met	0
% ugrads need fully met	0

MERCER UNIVERSITY

1501 Mercer University Drive, Macon, GA 31207-0001 • Admissions: 478-301-2650 • Fax: 478-301-2828

STUDENTS SAY "..."

Academics

As the oldest private university in Georgia, Mercer University is a school that provides boundless opportunities for its undergraduates. Indeed, its "small size and focus on research and leadership enables students to quickly get involved in both academic pursuits with professors, as well as leadership positions in the extracurricular of their choice." Moreover, service is central to its educational mission, and Mercer aims to produce graduates who will endeavor to "make positive changes in their local community and the world [at large]." While the academics here are challenging, it's obvious that the university wants to see its students succeed. Hence, the school maintains an "academic resource center on campus that is open until 3 A.M. and has tutors for almost every subject, people willing to help edit and revise papers, etc."

Undergrads also happily report that their professors all seem "genuinely invested in their students." One pleased individual elaborates, "Professors WANT students to come to their office hours, and make it easy through appointments or regular office hours." And a fellow student boasts, "All my professors have absolutely floored me with their enthusiasm, intelligence, and willingness to help." They've also been known to "incorporate videos, activities, and discussions into the class" to stimulate students and keep courses interesting. Perhaps this satisfied student explains it best, "Our professors are not simply in the classroom for fifty minutes Monday, Wednesday, and Friday. They are [there for us] throughout our entire four years at Mercer."

Life

Mercer has done an outstanding job creating "an inviting, stimulating atmosphere for its students." After all, there's always an activity or event to attend. To begin with, the university "has one of the best, if not the best, intramural sports programs in the country." And everyone from first-years through seniors are keen to get in on the action. Beyond that, "two of our major student-led organizations, QuadWorks and Mercer Maniacs, put on events all of the time for students. QuadWorks plans about eighty events each semester doing things like riding camels on hump day, having movie nights out on the lawn, or even attending our annual music festival, Bearstock, for free!" Fraternities and sororities do have a presence at Mercer. However, Greek life doesn't wholly dominate campus life. We've also been informed that "there is also a vibrant party scene if you know where to look." Lastly, students report that hometown Macon is "a nice city" that offers many exciting options and activities including "hiking at the Indian Mounds," along with "trampoline parks, movie theaters, [and] fine dining." It's quite common to see undergrads heading "downtown on weekend nights."

Student Body

Undergrads at Mercer are quick to sing the praises of their "absolutely amazing" peers. To begin with, students here tend to be "full of energy, enthusiasm, and drive." As one proud undergrad explains, "We have a running joke that everyone is involved in at least three student organizations, has at least one job, and regularly participates in some off-campus organization." Even better, they're also extremely welcoming and friendly." Another ecstatic student chimes in, "Everyone's...ready and willing to offer assistance or check up on you if you seem to be having a bad day, even students...you've never met before are quick to make sure you know they're there for you." A third undergrad agrees sharing, "When I...came to visit Mercer for the first time, EVERYONE was so kind, and I honestly thought [it] was a facade. Come to find out that everyone really is kind here." Importantly, though the university does have "a large white population," students assure us that "diversity does exist on campus." Indeed, "Mercer is attractive to international students of all sorts, minority students, and students of all types from different regions of the country and world." And, the "best part about it is that everybody here is so accepting of people's differences and so open-minded." What more could you ask for from your fellow students?

MERCER UNIVERSITY

Financial Aid: 478-301-2670 • E-Mail: admissions@mercer.edu • Website: www.mercer.edu

THE PRINCETON REVIEW SAYS

Admissions

Very important factors considered include: rigor of secondary school record, academic GPA, standardized test scores, level of applicant's interest. *Important factors considered include:* application essay, recommendation(s), extracurricular activities, talent/ability, character/personal qualities, volunteer work. *Other factors considered include:* class rank, interview, work experience. ACT with or without writing accepted. SAT with or without Essay component accepted. High school diploma is required and GED is accepted. *Academic units required:* 4 English, 4 math, 4 science, 3 science labs, 2 foreign language, 1 social studies, 2 history.

Financial Aid

Students should submit: FAFSA. Priority filing deadline is 2/1. The Princeton Review suggests that all financial aid forms be submitted as soon as possible after October 1. *Need-based scholarships/grants offered:* College/university scholarship or grant aid from institutional funds; Federal Pell; Private scholarships; SEOG; State scholarships/grants. *Loan aid offered:* Direct PLUS loans; Direct Subsidized Stafford Loans; Direct Unsubsidized Stafford Loans. Applicants will be notified of awards on a rolling basis beginning 1/15. Federal Work-Study Program available.

The Inside Word

Admissions officers at Mercer seek individuals who will both add to the university's vibrant campus life as well as benefit from the myriad of academic opportunities provided. To that end, they carefully consider the rigor of each applicant's high school curriculum and GPA. Standardized test scores, personal statements and teacher recommendations are also heavily weighed. Lastly, officers evaluate extracurricular involvement, paying close attention to any leadership roles attained.

THE SCHOOL SAYS "..."

From the Admissions Office

"Mercer's Office of University Admissions strives to make the college admissions process as clear and easy to navigate as possible. As an admissions counseling team, we are committed to helping each and every student that we meet to identify their best personal 'fit' for a college or university. During this process, many find that Mercer is the right place for their higher education journey. At Mercer, each student is matched with a personal admissions counselor. This counselor remains his or her primary point of contact from application through enrollment. We get to know our applicants through personal contact, high school visits, regional receptions, college fairs, and a variety of campus visit opportunities. Our counselors work closely with students and their families through the application, financial aid, housing, orientation, and other enrollment processes to ensure that students make a smooth transition from high school to college. This makes for a truly enjoyable and informed admissions experience for all involved.

"Mercer University begins accepting applications for undergraduate admission on August 1. We encourage high school seniors to submit their completed applications (including official transcripts, letter of recommendation, and test scores; IELTS or TOEFL for international students) before our Early Action deadline of October 15 to be considered for the University's most prestigious scholarships. Our regular decision deadline is February 1. Following the release of Early Action decisions in early November, we begin evaluating applications on a rolling basis throughout the academic year."

SELECTIVITY

Admissions Rating	85
# of applicants	5,034
% of applicants accepted	74
% of acceptees attending	24

FRESHMAN PROFILE

Range SAT EBRW	590–670
Range SAT Math	580–670
Range SAT Composite	1170–1340
Range ACT Composite	25–30
# submitting SAT scores	527
% submitting SAT scores	59
# submitting ACT scores	372
% submitting ACT scores	41
Average HS GPA	3.9
% graduated top 10% of class	36
% graduated top 25% of class	68
% graduated top 50% of class	92

DEADLINES

Early action	
Deadline	10/15
Notification	11/5
Regular	
Priority	2/1
Deadline	7/1
Notification	Rolling, 11/18
Nonfall registration?	Yes

FINANCIAL FACTS

Financial Aid Rating	90
Annual tuition	$37,508
Room and board	$12,968
Required fees	$300
Books and supplies	$1,200
Average frosh need-based scholarship	$29,043
Average UG need-based scholarship	$26,745
% needy frosh rec. need-based scholarship or grant aid	99
% needy UG rec. need-based scholarship or grant aid	99
% needy frosh rec. non-need-based scholarship or grant aid	27
% needy UG rec. non-need-based scholarship or grant aid	26
% needy frosh rec. need-based self-help aid	60
% needy UG rec. need-based self-help aid	63
% frosh rec. any financial aid	99
% UG rec. any financial aid	98
% UG borrow to pay for school	59
Average cumulative indebtedness	$27,949
% frosh need fully met	43
% ugrads need fully met	41
Average % of frosh need met	89
Average % of ugrad need met	85

MIAMI UNIVERSITY

301 S. Campus Ave., Oxford, OH 45056 • Admissions: 513-529-2531 • Fax: 513-529-1550

STUDENTS SAY " . . ."

Academics

Attending school at Miami University may be "the iconic college experience." Located in Oxford, Ohio, "a quaint college town" with a "beautiful red brick campus," which students describe as "gorgeous" and "astoundingly beautiful," the school "has a rich tradition and history" that "is committed to its image as a premier undergraduate institution." The "prestige" of the business school affords many promising opportunities both during school and after graduation. Students agree, "Miami really prepares students for the real world after college." "A degree from Miami is worth a lot to many employers." "Miami University students are recruited by companies, and that provides great leverage when looking for internships and jobs." The curriculum as a whole offers "a challenging academic workload" that truly tests a student's abilities as well as "prepares students for the workplace after graduation while also giving them the opportunity to thrive while on campus." This "devotion to excellent undergraduate instruction" is backed by "an extremely strong orientation program, a dedicated student affairs department, and an overwhelming amount of student involvement in co-curricular activities." Smaller classrooms that allow for "engaging" discussion are more highly valued than large lectures, which may be "hard to sit through." Professors are a "mixed bag." "If you get the right ones, it makes all the difference." A student in the Honors Program calls the experience "phenomenal. It offers the ability to grow as a student and person through both in and out of class experiences."

Life

Miami University offers "a vibrant social atmosphere." With more than 17,000 undergraduate students on campus Miami may be "the perfect size," where you "can see everyone…but still meet many new people." With a "plethora of student activities," "Miami makes it possible to find groups or organizations that can fit any student's interest, and many tend to help in propelling graduates into jobs or programs once they leave the campus." "Greek life is everywhere you look," according to one student who posits "it often seems as though everyone is [Greek affiliated] because of how visible they are on campus," though statistics indicate only about one-third of undergraduates go Greek. On the partying front, "if you are looking to drink, you will certainly find it here if you want." "Miami students can find a wealth of great bars and clubs uptown—many of which are eighteen-plus, allowing freshmen and sophomores to enjoy the dance floors and bars that make up almost all of the nightlife." The campus also "offers a lot of alternative programs for students who wish to avoid alcohol." "Late night programming is offered through Miami, as well as athletic events and other cultural events." Among sports, "hockey is really popular." Students tend to be happy with life at Miami. "There is a ton to do on and off campus. The town is quaint, but it is mainly a college town, so it's like an extension of the school. Nightlife is pretty big here, but so are academics and activities. Students definitely are actively thinking about their futures, and they take academics seriously."

Student Body

The typical student is "very involved on campus, is concerned about his or her academics, and wants to make a good impression on others. We care about how we present ourselves, but in a good way." Another student says, "The typical student is very academically focused, challenge-driven, competitive, extraverted, and demonstrates a preference for dressing well." Several students commented that students tend to "look and dress alike." "It can be very cliquish, especially in the Greek community." Anyone can fit in though, it's "all about finding your niche on campus which is generally done through people in your major, and especially student organizations." Miami tends to attract students who are "white, upper-middle-class, and Christian. The campus lacks diversity socioeconomically, ethnically, and religiously; however, the student body is generally accepting of all students no matter the background." One student relishes the challenge "to find diversity even in people who look similar and [has] grown because of it."

MIAMI UNIVERSITY

Financial Aid: 513-529-0001 • E-Mail: admission@miamioh.edu • Website: http://www.miamioh.edu/

THE PRINCETON REVIEW SAYS

Admissions

Very important factors considered include: rigor of secondary school record, class rank, academic GPA, application essay, standardized test scores, recommendation(s), talent/ability, character/personal qualities. *Other factors considered include:* extracurricular activities, first generation, alumni/ae relation, geographical residence, state residency, volunteer work, work experience. ACT with or without writing accepted. SAT with or without Essay component accepted. High school diploma is required and GED is accepted. *Academic units recommended:* 4 English, 4 math, 3 science, 2 foreign language, 2 social studies, 1 history, 1 visual/performing arts.

Financial Aid

Students should submit: FAFSA. Priority filing deadline is 2/15. The Princeton Review suggests that all financial aid forms be submitted as soon as possible after October 1. *Need-based scholarships/grants offered:* College/university scholarship or grant aid from institutional funds; Federal Pell; Private scholarships; SEOG; State scholarships/grants. *Loan aid offered:* Direct PLUS loans; Direct Subsidized Stafford Loans; Direct Unsubsidized Stafford Loans. Applicants will be notified of awards on a rolling basis beginning 3/20. Federal Work-Study Program available. Institutional employment available.

The Inside Word

Getting into Miami University isn't easy. High grades and ACT scores are a good start, and there is more you can do to better your odds. Admissions officers favor students who have challenged themselves academically, are active in their schools, lead student organizations or other activities, and volunteer in their community.

THE SCHOOL SAYS "..."

From the Admissions Office

"At Miami, you'll find a level of involvement—in your classes, in your research, in your extracurricular activities—that you won't find at other schools. What sets Miami apart as a Public Ivy is the ability to give students a personalized small-college experience within the reputation, experiences, and opportunities of a large research university, all at a public school cost. With more than 100 majors to choose from, and a liberal arts foundation that allows students to explore different areas of interest, finding your true passion—in and out of the classroom—is at the heart of what the Miami University experience is all about. This deep level of engagement is reflected in the 92 percent freshman to sophomore retention rate and Miami's 78 percent graduation rate, which is among the top for public universities across the country. Miami's reputation for producing outstanding leaders with real-world experience makes us a target school for top global firms, leads to acceptance rates into law and medical school which far exceed the national averages, and result in impressive placement rates for graduates. According to surveys and national data, 97 percent of Miami University students who graduated in 2016–2017 were employed or in school by fall 2017. Students also benefit from small class sizes—66 percent of undergraduate classes have fewer than thirty students—and personal attention from faculty members in the classroom, through research opportunities, and through faculty mentoring programs. Outside of the classroom, students can participate in over 500 student organizations, attend social and cultural events, or get involved with one of the most extensive intramural and club sports program in the country."

SELECTIVITY

Admissions Rating	**84**
# of applicants	30,126
% of applicants accepted	75
% of acceptees attending	18
# offered a place on the wait list	1,527
% accepting a place on wait list	22
% admitted from wait list	22
# of early decision applicants	852
% accepted early decision	81

FRESHMAN PROFILE

Range SAT EBRW	590–670
Range SAT Math	610–710
Range ACT Composite	25–30
# submitting SAT scores	1,102
% submitting SAT scores	28
# submitting ACT scores	3,245
% submitting ACT scores	82
Average HS GPA	3.8
% graduated top 10% of class	34
% graduated top 25% of class	66
% graduated top 50% of class	92

DEADLINES

Early decision	
Deadline	11/15
Notification	12/15
Early action	
Deadline	12/1
Notification	2/1
Regular	
Deadline	2/1
Notification	3/15
Nonfall registration?	Yes

APPLICANTS ALSO LOOK AT AND OFTEN PREFER

Case Western Reserve University; Northwestern University; University of Illinois at Urbana-Champaign; University of Michigan—Ann Arbor; Vanderbilt University; Washington University in St. Louis

AND SOMETIMES PREFER

Indiana University Bloomington; Purdue University—West Lafayette; The Ohio State University—Columbus; Penn State University Park; Southern Methodist University; University of Wisconsin-Madison

FINANCIAL FACTS

Financial Aid Rating	**84**
Annual in-state tuition	$14,315
Annual out-of-state tuition	$33,832
Room and board	$13,860
Required fees	$1,063
Books and supplies	$1,234
Average frosh need-based scholarship	$12,867
Average UG need-based scholarship	$11,276
% needy frosh rec. need-based scholarship or grant aid	85
% needy UG rec. need-based scholarship or grant aid	86
% needy frosh rec. non-need-based scholarship or grant aid	21
% needy UG rec. non-need-based scholarship or grant aid	16
% needy frosh rec. need-based self-help aid	72
% needy UG rec. need-based self-help aid	78
% UG borrow to pay for school	49
Average cumulative indebtedness	$29,434
% frosh need fully met	28
% ugrads need fully met	23
Average % of frosh need met	64
Average % of ugrad need met	64

MICHIGAN STATE UNIVERSITY

250 Administration Building, East Lansing, MI 48824 • Admissions: 517-355-8332 • Fax: 517-353-1647

STUDENTS SAY "..."

Academics

Michigan State University in East Lansing, Michigan is a "research intensive school, meaning there are a lot of opportunities to pursue undergraduate research." As a "top-tier research university, many students involved in undergraduate research can participate in meaningful studies that yield publications, " and students say that "through [their] professors, [they] have been able to secure paid international internships and research positions." One student says that during their first year, "I participated on a panel for entrepreneurship with the dean of the business school, the director of entrepreneurship, two other students and an alum." Professors in schools such as James Madison and Lyman Briggs, and the Honors College, "which prides itself on offering course flexibility and customization," have "some of the best professors in the country." A transfer student says that professors largely "understand that teaching a class not only means spewing out information, but also means teaching students how to learn and be successful in and beyond class." They can "teach flexibly, meaning they can adjust their techniques to cater to the students and they can also explain the subject matter in multiple ways so that it gets across to all of the different learners." The college offers generous scholarships and "professor assistantships to incoming freshmen," which provide "the opportunity to do paid research." Top programs include the "Veterinary Medicine, teaching, and business schools that attract people from all over the world," and the nationally renowned nuclear physics and agriculture programs."

Life

"The greatest strength of this school, for me, is the beauty of the campus," says one student. The large campus and its surroundings offer "a lot of options, from museums, gardens, fountains, the famous Rock, where people paint to promote events and clubs, and a river in the middle of campus." Boasts another student, "Some schools have terrible cafeteria food, but MSU has some of the best in the country," with "a variety of choices as well as healthy options and meals for those with special dietary needs." The dining plans have unlimited access to the dozen or so dining halls across campus, so it is "always easy to get good food when living on campus." Sports are popular too, with "huge campus-wide spirit on football game days." Broadcast "in almost every residence hall on the TVs and certainly in every recreational facility, the sports here are what make MSU, MSU!" Most students "enjoy tailgating, as well as basketball and hockey games." The campus bus route "takes students to MSU/East Lansing and surrounding town locations, including shopping malls." The Wharton Center "gives student discounts for most shows," and "people go out to eat on Grand River, which has a lot of great restaurants." Students also "chill" at large parties "with loud music and alcohol." Many students are concerned that Michigan State hasn't dealt with high-profile and troubling sexual assault cases in a pro-active way, and strongly urge administration to establish better policies.

Student Body

MSU "fosters an environment of laid-back, yet urgent creativity," says one student. "You won't find an air of pompous prestige anywhere on campus (maybe some frats) but you will find extremely driven people." Another says "We're Spartan strong and we're here to support and encourage one another: It's a big family here." The student body at Michigan State is "diverse and massive." The student body certainly shares a sense of camaraderie "epitomized by the popular slogan 'Spartans Will.'" While the student body is "academically oriented" and "can provide their peers an intellectual challenge," the student body at MSU is "not overly competitive, and generally seems to work towards intellectual cooperation rather than cut-throat competition." "It is hard to paint one picture of a student body that hosts more than 50,000 people," says one student, "especially one as diverse as the one we have at Michigan State." Yet everyone at MSU "never misses a beat to yell Go White! in response to Go Green!"

MICHIGAN STATE UNIVERSITY

Financial Aid: 517-353-5940 • E-Mail: admis@msu.edu • Website: www.msu.edu

THE PRINCETON REVIEW SAYS

Admissions

Very important factors considered include: academic GPA, application essay, standardized test scores. *Important factors considered include:* rigor of secondary school record. *Other factors considered include:* class rank, recommendation(s), interview, extracurricular activities, talent/ability, character/personal qualities, first generation, alumni/ae relation, geographical residence, state residency, volunteer work, work experience, level of applicant's interest. ACT with Writing recommended. SAT with Essay component recommended. High school diploma is required and GED is accepted. *Academic units required:* 4 English, 3 math, 3 science, 1 science lab, 2 foreign language, 3 social studies. *Academic units recommended:* 4 English, 3 math, 3 science, 2 foreign language, 3 social studies.

Financial Aid

Students should submit: FAFSA. The Princeton Review suggests that all financial aid forms be submitted as soon as possible after October 1. *Need-based scholarships/grants offered:* College/university scholarship or grant aid from institutional funds; Federal Pell; Private scholarships; SEOG; State scholarships/grants; United Negro College Fund. *Loan aid offered:* Direct PLUS loans; Direct Subsidized Stafford Loans; Direct Unsubsidized Stafford Loans. Applicants will be notified of awards on a rolling basis beginning 1/1. Federal Work-Study Program available. Institutional employment available.

The Inside Word

Michigan State takes a traditional approach to evaluation: Your academic performance in high school, strength and quality of your curriculum, recent trends in your academic performance, class rank, ACT or SAT results (the writing score isn't required, but recommended), and your leadership, talents, conduct, and diversity of experience are all factors in admission.

THE SCHOOL SAYS "..."

From the Admissions Office

"It's not just what we do that makes us Spartans—but also why and how we do it.

"It's the will to think bigger, work harder, and never give up. It's pushing ourselves to achieve our personal best, while pushing the boundaries of what's possible to make a better world.

"Believing we are strong as one and extraordinary together.

"Michigan State University got its start more than 160 years ago when we pioneered a new kind of higher education that opened doors and expanded opportunities.

"Today, we continue to blaze trails with a spirit that runs within students and faculty, driving us to work together, crossing disciplines and time zones to make a lasting impact.

"More than half a million strong worldwide, we proudly call ourselves Spartans. Join us."

SELECTIVITY

Admissions Rating	84
# of applicants	44,322
% of applicants accepted	71
% of acceptees attending	28

FRESHMAN PROFILE

Range SAT EBRW	550–650
Range SAT Math	550–670
Range SAT Composite	1120–1310
Range ACT Composite	23–29
# submitting SAT scores	6,882
% submitting SAT scores	78
# submitting ACT scores	3,336
% submitting ACT scores	38
Average HS GPA	3.8
% graduated top 10% of class	28
% graduated top 25% of class	65
% graduated top 50% of class	93

DEADLINES

Early action	
Deadline	11/1
Notification	1/15
Regular	
Priority	11/1
Notification	Rolling, 10/1
Nonfall registration?	Yes

FINANCIAL FACTS

Financial Aid Rating	80
Annual in-state tuition	$16,650
Annual out-of-state tuition	$41,002
Room and board	$10,522
Books and supplies	$1,134
Average frosh need-based scholarship	$12,069
Average UG need-based scholarship	$11,628
% needy frosh rec. need-based scholarship or grant aid	72
% needy UG rec. need-based scholarship or grant aid	74
% needy frosh rec. non-need-based scholarship or grant aid	48
% needy UG rec. non-need-based scholarship or grant aid	37
% needy frosh rec. need-based self-help aid	69
% needy UG rec. need-based self-help aid	73
% frosh rec. any financial aid	69
% UG rec. any financial aid	65
% UG borrow to pay for school	51
Average cumulative indebtedness	$31,393
% frosh need fully met	11
% ugrads need fully met	11
Average % of frosh need met	53
Average % of ugrad need met	53

MICHIGAN TECHNOLOGICAL UNIVERSITY

1400 Townsend Drive, Houghton, MI 49931 • Admissions: 906-487-2335 • Fax: 906-487-2125

STUDENTS SAY "..."

Academics

Michigan Technological University has "very high standards when it comes to education" and offers "serious study in a beautiful (often snowy) environment." It boasts a "really good reputation as an engineering school," and it's no secret that "engineering is a part of everybody's life." All agree, "Michigan Tech provides an atmosphere that nurtures learning" and "puts students first when it comes to their learning experience by providing hands-on experience." The university offers "lots of internship and co-op opportunities" and "pathways for career development and professional advancement." Students say that the courses are "challenging" and that the university "pushes students to excel academically." Professors are "generally interesting and helpful," but some can be "dull." A junior says, "Concentrated courses are great, but [general education courses] are huge, impersonal, and just plain awful," and another student adds, "The experience gets better with more time you put into your program, the professors become more interactive, and the experience becomes more meaningful."

Life

Michigan Tech "is in a small town in the middle of the deep North woods," which makes "the sense of community remarkable." Students say that campus is "incredibly safe," that "the atmosphere is very friendly," and that "there are a lot of opportunities to get involved." A physics major notes, "You start to see people you know everywhere on campus. It is really easy to find a friend and talk to someone." Enhancing the "strong student community" are "over 200 clubs" and a variety of "winter activities to be a part of." Many students take advantage of "free access to Mont Ripley," the university's own ski hill and the oldest one in Michigan. A freshman says, "We have broomball, Winter Carnival, and lots of campus-wide events!" Many students agree, "The administration in every department works hard to answer questions and help out as much as possible, which is really great when you're a freshman," but some feel there's a "gap between [the] administration and students," particularly when it comes to spending. There are complaints about dorm food, leading a junior to say, "I would like to see some more selection and variation between dining halls," and students feel there's a need for "more parking spots close to campus." While "the library is a great place to study," some "of the classrooms are dated" and could use technological updating.

Student Body

At Michigan Tech, the typical student "is smart and a little more introspective than average," but still "great at balancing school and hanging out." Most students "are looking to get a good education and are fairly laid-back," and the student body consists of "down-to-earth friendly people," who "work hard during the week and look forward to relaxing and having fun on the weekends." It's no secret that "the ratio is a little guy-heavy" and that, because of this, "girls get doors opened for them across campus." Students tend to be "white and male," and a junior acknowledges, "There's little diversity ethnically, but everyone feels welcome." A chemical engineering major says, "You have to be a little bit of a nerd to fit in," and another student agrees, "I think most people think about classes first, hanging out second." It's common for students to "stay in and play video games," but there's also a large contingent of "outdoorsy people." A sophomore says, "Winters are long and cold up here," and students take advantage of the plentiful snow by "hiking, biking, four-wheeling, skiing, [and] snowmobiling." Students look forward to Winter Carnival, "a long weekend off from classes where students build giant, impressive snow sculptures, play broomball, [and] stay out all night," and for fun they enjoy "house parties and moderate drinking/merrymaking [to] warm up the cold winters."

MICHIGAN TECHNOLOGICAL UNIVERSITY

Financial Aid: 906-487-2622 • E-Mail: mtu4u@mtu.edu • Website: www.mtu.edu

THE PRINCETON REVIEW SAYS

Admissions

Very important factors considered include: academic GPA, standardized test scores. *Important factors considered include:* rigor of secondary school record. *Other factors considered include:* application essay, recommendation(s), extracurricular activities, talent/ability, character/ personal qualities. ACT with or without writing accepted. SAT with or without Essay component accepted. High school diploma is required and GED is accepted. *Academic units required:* 3 English, 3 math, 2 science. *Academic units recommended:* 4 English, 4 math, 3 science, 2 foreign language, 3 social studies, 2 academic electives, 1 computer science.

Financial Aid

Students should submit: FAFSA. Priority filing deadline is 3/1. The Princeton Review suggests that all financial aid forms be submitted as soon as possible after October 1. *Need-based scholarships/grants offered:* College/university scholarship or grant aid from institutional funds; Federal Pell; Private scholarships; SEOG; State scholarships/grants. *Loan aid offered:* Direct PLUS loans; Direct Subsidized Stafford Loans; Direct Unsubsidized Stafford Loans. Applicants will be notified of awards on a rolling basis beginning 1/1. Federal Work-Study Program available. Institutional employment available.

The Inside Word

Michigan Tech strives to enroll bright, adventurous students. Students aren't required to submit recommendations from teachers, although they may submit a "High School Counselor Information Page" if they would like their counselor to share information regarding their high school performance. Applicants to the Visual and Performing Arts Department degree programs are required to submit supplemental materials, including an essay.

THE SCHOOL SAYS "..."

From the Admissions Office

"At Michigan Tech, our students know that tomorrow needs talented visionaries and new solutions. They are ready. Our unique Enterprise Program lets students work on real industry projects, from building and launching spacecraft for NASA to designing advanced robotics systems, developing better alternative fuels, and inventing water-rescue devices at our Great Lakes Research Center.

"Students can choose from more than 120 degree programs in engineering; forest resources; technology; business and economics; mathematics; natural, physical and environmental sciences; arts; humanities; health professions and pre-health preparation; and social sciences. We offer degree opportunities in growing fields such as biomedical engineering and wildlife ecology and management, as well as cybersecurity and mechatronics in our College of Computing, the first college of its kind in the state of Michigan.

"Outside of classrooms and labs, students enjoy our golf course, ski hill, recreational trails, and 5,000+ acres of University forests, along with a safe, friendly, small-town atmosphere in beautiful Upper Michigan. Situated on the Keweenaw Waterway, the campus is minutes from Lake Superior. During Winter Carnival, students build huge snow statues and play broomball, the most popular of many intramural sports on campus. The varsity sports line-up includes the first varsity-level esports team at a public university in Michigan, along with football, men's and women's basketball, tennis, cross-country, Nordic skiing, track and field, soccer, volleyball, and NCAA Division I hockey.

"Ready to build, design, code, and lead with Lake Superior all around you? Applying to Michigan Tech is free and easy—and there's no deadline."

SELECTIVITY

Admissions Rating	85
# of applicants	5,978
% of applicants accepted	74
% of acceptees attending	29

FRESHMAN PROFILE

Range SAT EBRW	580–680
Range SAT Math	590–690
Range SAT Composite	1170–1360
Range ACT Composite	25–30
# submitting SAT scores	1,048
% submitting SAT scores	81
# submitting ACT scores	528
% submitting ACT scores	41
Average HS GPA	3.8
% graduated top 10% of class	31
% graduated top 25% of class	65
% graduated top 50% of class	91

DEADLINES

Regular	
Priority	1/15
Notification	Rolling, 6/15
Nonfall registration?	Yes

APPLICANTS ALSO LOOK AT AND SOMETIMES PREFER

Grand Valley State University; Michigan State University; Milwaukee School of Engineering; Northern Michigan University; Purdue University—West Lafayette; University of Illinois at Urbana-Champai; University of Michigan—Ann Arbor; University of Minnesota—Twin Cities Campus; University of Wisconsin-Madison; Western Michigan University

FINANCIAL FACTS

Financial Aid Rating	85
Annual in-state tuition	$16,312
Annual out-of-state tuition	$36,432
Room and board	$11,314
Required fees	$306
Books and supplies	$1,200
Average frosh need-based scholarship	$8,708
Average UG need-based scholarship	$8,088
% needy frosh rec. need-based scholarship or grant aid	86
% needy UG rec. need-based scholarship or grant aid	77
% needy frosh rec. non-need-based scholarship or grant aid	93
% needy UG rec. non-need-based scholarship or grant aid	85
% needy frosh rec. need-based self-help aid	74
% needy UG rec. need-based self-help aid	82
% frosh rec. any financial aid	99
% UG rec. any financial aid	92
% UG borrow to pay for school	70
Average cumulative indebtedness	$37,903
% frosh need fully met	28
% ugrads need fully met	20
Average % of frosh need met	84
Average % of ugrad need met	72

MIDDLEBURY COLLEGE

The Emma Willard House, Middlebury, VT 05753-6002 • Admissions: 802-443-3000 • Fax: 802-443-2056

CAMPUS LIFE

Quality of Life Rating	91
Fire Safety Rating	65
Green Rating	99
Type of school	Private
Environment	Village

STUDENTS

Total undergrad enrollment	2,555
% male/female	47/53
% from out of state	95
% frosh live on campus	100
% ugrads live on campus	95
# of fraternities	0
# of sororities	0
% African American	4
% Asian	7
% Caucasian	62
% Hispanic	10
% Native American	<1
% Pacific Islander	0
% Two or more races	5
% Race and/or ethnicity unknown	1
% international	10
# of countries represented	65

SURVEY SAYS . . .

Lots of liberal students
Students always studying
Classroom facilities are great
Lab facilities are great
School is well run
Great financial aid
No one cheats
Students aren't religious
Students environmentally aware
Great food on campus
Recreation facilities are great
Lots of beer drinking
Hard liquor is popular

ACADEMICS

Academic Rating	98
% students returning for sophomore year	94
% students graduating within 4 years	85
% students graduating within 6 years	93
Calendar	4/1/4
Student/faculty ratio	8:1
Profs interesting rating	96
Profs accessible rating	97
Most classes have 10–19 students.	

MOST POPULAR MAJORS

Economics, General; Psychology, General;
Environmental Studies

STUDENTS SAY " . . ."

Academics

One of the most highly regarded liberal arts colleges in the United States, Middlebury College in Vermont is about "creating a person both socially and intellectually prepared for the world." The school has "a high level of global thinking and language acquisition in such a rural place," and there is an "emerging focus on creativity and entrepreneurship." When teaching students to develop communication, writing, creativity, and critical thinking skills, the school "allows you to develop these skills in whatever subject or subjects that one is most passionate about." Students' needs and choices are "of very high priority" to the administration, and there is "institutional support for whatever absurd idea might strike you." Professors are, on the whole, "truly top-notch"; not only are they "brilliant academics, but they are also adept teachers and classroom leaders." They come here because they want to teach undergraduates and conduct research; "Middlebury expects both; most professors deliver." "Several of my professors have given out their cell phone numbers after particularly difficult lectures to make sure that students can figure things out," says one. "It's almost impossible to actually be 'invisible.'" The overall academic experience is "very intense" ("If you haven't done the reading, prepare to be called out for it"), but "students reliably enjoy their classes."

Life

Empty hours at Middlebury are in short supply: "If you've got free time in your day at Middlebury, you're doing something wrong," says a student. However, after all that reading, "at the end of the day, we all just like to get together and hit up the Snow Bowl to go skiing." "Vermont does make a difference," says one student of Middlebury's location near mountains, lakes, and ski trails, and its focus on "how important the outdoor experience is for the school." Drinking is "fairly prevalent" on Fridays and Saturdays, but "not during the week." It's a healthy culture, and "public safety does a good job of keeping things safe while not being overly intrusive." The dorms are "gorgeous," and there is even one called the Chateau, modeled after the largest chateau in Fontainebleau, France. The number of activities available are admirable, and "most people actually choose not to go into cities on weekends because they would hate to miss what's going on on-campus that weekend."

Student Body

The pervasive atmosphere at Middlebury is "super friendly and caring," and there is not only the pressure to work hard, but "also the encouragement to make sure students succeed." Students "compete with themselves, not their classmates." With a happy population, beautiful environs, and not a single student going unchallenged, the school encompasses "a perfect blend of intellectual curiosity, responsible living, and fun." As one student eloquently puts it, it's a bunch of "bright kids doing too many things—all of them good, none related to sleep." This "engaged, active," "preppy" student body "doesn't take themselves too seriously but do take serious initiative." A typical go-getter student "pursues at least one major, a minor, and is the star of at least one sports team or special interest group, but usually more." Social life can be "very centered around athletic teams," but these "well-read, outgoing," and "well-rounded students from stable backgrounds" always end up connecting with people they can relate with easily. "You will struggle to find time to spend with all the different friends you will make," says a student. Social ease is a common trait among MiddKids, and most students "know how to hold a conversation and [are] open to new experiences."

MIDDLEBURY COLLEGE

Financial Aid: 802-443-5158 • E-Mail: admissions@middlebury.edu • Website: www.middlebury.edu

THE PRINCETON REVIEW SAYS

Admissions

Very important factors considered include: rigor of secondary school record, class rank, academic GPA, extracurricular activities, talent/ability, character/personal qualities. *Important factors considered include:* application essay, standardized test scores, recommendation(s), racial/ethnic status. *Other factors considered include:* interview, first generation, alumni/ae relation, geographical residence, volunteer work, work experience, level of applicant's interest. ACT with or without writing accepted. SAT with or without Essay component accepted. High school diploma or equivalent is not required. *Academic units recommended:* 4 English, 4 math, 3 science, 3 science labs, 4 foreign language, 3 social studies.

Financial Aid

Students should submit: CSS/Financial Aid PROFILE; FAFSA; Institution's own financial aid form; Noncustodial PROFILE. Priority filing deadline is 11/15. The Princeton Review suggests that all financial aid forms be submitted as soon as possible after October 1. *Need-based scholarships/grants offered:* College/university scholarship or grant aid from institutional funds; Federal Pell; Private scholarships; SEOG; State scholarships/grants. *Loan aid offered:* Direct PLUS loans; Direct Subsidized Stafford Loans; Direct Unsubsidized Stafford Loans. Applicants will be notified of awards on or about 4/1. Federal Work-Study Program available. Institutional employment available.

The Inside Word

Middlebury gives you options in standardized testing. The school will accept either the ACT or the SAT or three SAT Subject Tests (the tests must be in three different subject areas, however). Middlebury is extremely competitive; improve your chances of admission by crafting a standardized test profile that shows you in the best possible light.

THE SCHOOL SAYS "..."

From the Admissions Office

"The successful Middlebury candidate excels in a variety of areas including academics, athletics, the arts, leadership, and service to others. These strengths and interests permit students to grow beyond their traditional 'comfort zones' and conventional limits. Our classrooms are as varied as the Green Mountains, the Metropolitan Museum of Art, or the great cities of Russia and Japan. Outside the classroom, students informally interact with professors in activities such as intramural basketball games and community service. At Middlebury, students develop critical-thinking skills, enduring bonds of friendship, and the ability to challenge themselves.

"Middlebury's Commons system is the backbone of student residential life at the College. The residence halls are grouped into 'living-learning communities,' or Commons, which combine the academic, social, and residential components of college life. They also foster close relationships between the student residents and the faculty and staff who are part of their Commons.

"Middlebury offers majors and programs in forty-six different fields, with particular strengths in languages, international studies, environmental studies, literature and creative writing, and the sciences. Opportunities for engaging in individual research with faculty abound at Middlebury."

SELECTIVITY
Admissions Rating	97
# of applicants	9,754
% of applicants accepted	15
% of acceptees attending	40
# offered a place on the wait list	1,576
% accepting a place on wait list	37
% admitted from wait list	4
# of early decision applicants	831
% accepted early decision	45

FRESHMAN PROFILE
Range SAT EBRW	670–750
Range SAT Math	690–780
Range ACT Composite	32–34
# submitting SAT scores	372
% submitting SAT scores	62
# submitting ACT scores	273
% submitting ACT scores	45

DEADLINES
Early decision	
Deadline	11/1
Notification	12/15
Other ED Deadline	1/1
Other ED Notification	2/1
Regular	
Deadline	1/1
Notification	3/31
Nonfall registration?	Yes

FINANCIAL FACTS
Financial Aid Rating	98
Annual tuition	$55,790
Room and board	$16,630
Books and supplies	$1,000
Average frosh need-based scholarship	$49,740
Average UG need-based scholarship	$49,992
% needy frosh rec. need-based scholarship or grant aid	98
% needy UG rec. need-based scholarship or grant aid	96
% needy frosh rec. non-need-based scholarship or grant aid	0
% needy UG rec. non-need-based scholarship or grant aid	0
% needy frosh rec. need-based self-help aid	89
% needy UG rec. need-based self-help aid	89
% frosh rec. any financial aid	42
% UG rec. any financial aid	45
% UG borrow to pay for school	50
Average cumulative indebtedness	$19,838
% frosh need fully met	100
% ugrads need fully met	100
Average % of frosh need met	100
Average % of ugrad need met	100

MIDDLE TENNESSEE STATE UNIVERSITY

1301 East Main Street, Murfreesboro, TN 37132 • Admissions: 615-898-2111 • Fax: 615-898-5478

STUDENTS SAY "..."

Academics

Middle Tennessee State University has become a go-to choice for those wishing to receive a quality and affordable education close to home. The school offers more than 140 degree programs for undergraduates—some "that are not seen in other universities, like animation." One student says, "You can literally major in fermentation and learn about the process of brewing beer." Students find these "highly specialized programs are closely tied to their industry, which means really good job placement." The on-campus growth doesn't stop there: "A staggering amount of resources [are] available to students, [ranging] from research programs to counseling services to 3D printing." Furthermore, students cite "pretty good technology [being] available for students to use or borrow, with updated versions of most programs."

As far as professors go, they "like to be on a first name basis" with students and often "make it a point to get to know you." Students call faculty "very helpful and fair" and "thorough in every aspect of the subject matter." One student shares, "A professor of mine teaches by walking around to every individual student and making sure they understand the subject matter." They're also "willing to circle back around if anyone in the class gets off track." Students who do find themselves needing extra assistance with coursework or concepts can rest easy: "There are a lot of programs in place to help you, such as free tutoring," and students also have "plenty of opportunities to gain a mentor" for more focused guidance during their college careers. Many say this "advising is top notch," and that MTSU takes the time to "foster an environment of care for each and every student." Overall, students agree: "This school is amazing, and it is such a hidden gem."

Life

"The campus is big" but feels like a "comfortable and home-like school" environment where people "sit on the quad by the library and talk with their friends, play music, and skateboard." This type of campus takes advantage of the other outdoor areas of campus too, and students like to "hang hammocks on trees to sit and read and study." One student comments, "There are also many different parks and greenways that we enjoy visiting." For on-campus events, the school is always offering things "like art classes, study groups, or simply a movie showing." Those looking to spend a little time elsewhere, though, will turn to nearby Murfreesboro, where they can hang out at the "plethora of restaurants and bars." Nashville isn't far, either, and students will often "go out to ... clubs or arcades" there on weekends. Overall, students find themselves to be quite busy, but the good kind of busy—as one student puts it: "Despite how busy I am, I am happy doing it."

Student Body

"At a school as large as MTSU, you see all types [of students] from different ends of the spectrum" as everyone "is very open to whoever comes into the school." Here you'll find "a mixed bag of fresh-out-of-high-school students, ... parents, ... returning military veterans, and foreign students." No matter who they are, people at Middle Tennessee are "extremely friendly and inclusive," "pretty laid back," and "nice, courteous and really helpful." "Though everyone is different here, it is still easy to find people like yourself [who are] studying the same things or taking similar classes," says a student.

MIDDLE TENNESSEE STATE UNIVERSITY

Financial Aid: 615-898-2111 • E-Mail: admissions@mtsu.edu • Website: www.mtsu.edu

THE PRINCETON REVIEW SAYS

Admissions

Very important factors considered include: academic GPA, standardized test scores. *Other factors considered include:* rigor of secondary school record, application essay only required for conditional admission, letters of recommendation not needed, extracurricular activities, talent/ability, character/personal qualities, volunteer work, work experience, level of applicant's interest. ACT with or without writing accepted. SAT with or without Essay component accepted. High school diploma is required and GED is accepted. *Academic units required:* 4 English, 4 math, 3 science, 1 science lab, 2 foreign language, 1 social studies, 1 history, 1 visual/performing arts.

Financial Aid

Students should submit: FAFSA. Priority filing deadline is 2/1. The Princeton Review suggests that all financial aid forms be submitted as soon as possible after October 1. *Need-based scholarships/grants offered:* College/university scholarship or grant aid from institutional funds; Federal Pell; Private scholarships; SEOG; State scholarships/grants. *Loan aid offered:* Direct PLUS loans; Direct Subsidized Stafford Loans; Direct Unsubsidized Stafford Loans. Applicants will be notified of awards on a rolling basis beginning 2/15. Federal Work-Study Program available. Institutional employment available.

The Inside Word

Middle Tennessee State University is very transparent about what guarantees admission for first-year students: Anyone who has completed the recommended college prep classes with a 3.0 GPA will be admitted, as will anyone with a minimum composite ACT score of 22. Additionally, a combination of a 19 composite ACT score and a 2.7 GPA or higher will be admitted. Students who do not meet any these requirements can still be considered for conditional admission, but they must submit a personal statement and are subjected to an individual review process.

SELECTIVITY

Admissions Rating	75
# of applicants	8,973
% of applicants accepted	94
% of acceptees attending	39

FRESHMAN PROFILE

Range SAT EBRW	510–640
Range SAT Math	500–620
Range SAT Composite	1030–1260
Range ACT Composite	20–26
# submitting SAT scores	71
% submitting SAT scores	2
# submitting ACT scores	3,033
% submitting ACT scores	93
Average HS GPA	3.5

DEADLINES

Regular	
Priority	12/1
Nonfall registration?	Yes

FINANCIAL FACTS

Financial Aid Rating	81
Annual in-state tuition	$7,554
Annual out-of-state tuition	$27,168
Room and board	$8,976
Required fees	$1,870
Books and supplies	$1,260
Average frosh need-based scholarship	$6,717
Average UG need-based scholarship	$6,088
% needy frosh rec. need-based scholarship or grant aid	65
% needy UG rec. need-based scholarship or grant aid	63
% needy frosh rec. non-need-based scholarship or grant aid	88
% needy UG rec. non-need-based scholarship or grant aid	64
% needy frosh rec. need-based self-help aid	50
% needy UG rec. need-based self-help aid	59
% frosh rec. any financial aid	94
% UG rec. any financial aid	80
% UG borrow to pay for school	59
% frosh rec. any financial aid	94
% UG rec. any financial aid	80
Average cumulative indebtedness	$25,328
% frosh need fully met	12
% ugrads need fully met	11
Average % of frosh need met	65
Average % of ugrad need met	62

MILLS COLLEGE

5000 MacArthur Boulevard, Oakland, CA 94613 • Admissions: 510-430-2135

STUDENTS SAY "..."

Academics

Mills College, a small Oakland college for women and gender non-binary students, delivers a top-quality liberal arts education to its just 700 undergraduates at a great price; the school recently reduced its tuition for new and continuing undergraduate students by 36%. This school provides a cooperative learning environment, and "even lecture-based classes have opportunities for engagement and discussion." The college's small size gives students the advantage of "getting to connect with professors who encourage us to speak our minds to advocate for ourselves"; students "know that someone is listening to what we have to say." This is truly a hidden gem, and the support from fellow peers and strong academics "are constantly underestimated by" those who haven't experienced Mills.

The professors at Mills "are so passionate for their material"; they "know what they're doing and they do it very right." They are able to connect students to mentors or other faculty that could "help you on your journey to fellowships, internships, or even job opportunities." The faculty "always have research opportunities that are open for students to join in and help with," and constantly encourage students "to step out of [their] comfort zone in order to critically think and problem solve." If extra help is needed, professors are "very accessible and creative," and make learning in the classroom "interesting and understandable while still making the course subject matter challenging." They "actually care about you," and will "call you by your first name and remember you had a job interview the week before."

Life

The Mills College 135-acre campus is "beautiful," and when students visit, it is "easy to fall in love with the campus and the overall Mills vibe." There is a "strong residential community" here and the school creates an environment where "all students, potential, undergraduate, graduate, or alum, can take pride in their connection to Mills." "I...feel like my academic experience at Mills has caused me to be a better advocate for causes that I feel passionate about," says a student.

Work is the dominant activity here, and students use the campus to study throughout the day, "in the Tea Shop cafe, the dining hall, the library, the lawns, Mills Hall, and other places." If students have extra time outside of their classes, they are "often working on projects or community events," and there are "many science talks, art collectives, and spoken word events throughout the year" that students will organize and orchestrate. "We are all very busy people but still happy people," says a student. Oakland itself is a "diverse and culturally rich city," and there are many street fairs and farmers markets around "which are fun to go to." Off campus, students picnic at Lake Merritt, "go out for food at one of the many incredible restaurants in nearby Laurel [District]," or visit Jack London Square, the Oakland Zoo, or Tilden Regional Park. San Francisco is also just 20 minutes across the bay, and "it is very easy for students to access the many things the city has to offer."

Student Body

While Mills College is historically female, there are some men enrolled in its graduate programs. There is a sizeable LGBTQ+ population, and the people here are "accepting and brilliant."

A good portion of Mills students are "resumers" (over the age of 23) and "there is an independent living community that helps with older students." Forty-three percent of undergraduates are first-generation college students, and sixty-three percent are students of color. "Social justice is very important to the student body" at Mills, and students here are "unafraid to share their opinions and are active in their community." Most here are "liberal/progressive" and "never take anything at face value," instead taking "every aspect of things into close consideration."

Financial Aid: 510-430-2039 • E-Mail: admission@mills.edu • Website: www.mills.edu

THE PRINCETON REVIEW SAYS

Admissions

Very important factors considered include: rigor of secondary school record. *Important factors considered include:* class rank, academic GPA, application essay, recommendation(s), extra-curricular activities, character/personal qualities. *Other factors considered include:* interview, talent/ability, first generation, geographical residence, state residency, racial/ethnic status, volunteer work, work experience. ACT with or without writing accepted. SAT with or without Essay component accepted. High school diploma is required and GED is accepted. *Academic units required:* 4 English, 3 math, 2 science, 2 science labs, 2 foreign language, 2 social studies, 2 history. *Academic units recommended:* 4 English, 4 math, 4 science, 2 science labs, 4 foreign language, 4 social studies, 4 history, 2 visual/performing arts.

Financial Aid

Students should submit: FAFSA; Noncustodial PROFILE. Priority filing deadline is 2/15. The Princeton Review suggests that all financial aid forms be submitted as soon as possible after October 1. *Need-based scholarships/grants offered:* College/university scholarship or grant aid from institutional funds; Federal Pell; Private scholarships; SEOG; State scholarships/grants. *Loan aid offered:* Direct PLUS loans; Direct Subsidized Stafford Loans; Direct Unsubsidized Stafford Loans. Applicants will be notified of awards on a rolling basis beginning 2/15. Federal Work-Study Program available. Institutional employment available.

The Inside Word

Mills strives to create a diverse community of students and has shown its commitment to welcoming diverse students beyond its resumer students. Transgender students and students who do not identify with the gender binary, first-generation college students, and students of color are all welcome to become part of the Mills community. Though not required, admissions interviews are highly encouraged and conducted via Skype or FaceTime.

THE SCHOOL SAYS "..."

From the Admissions Office

"Mills offers a challenging liberal arts curriculum that encourages you to think creatively, prepares you to take well-calculated risks, and equips you to put your passions into practice. We are driven by our determination to improve ourselves and the world around us and to work smarter by working together. Here you will be emboldened to think big and empowered to make a statement—in your life, in your career, and in your community.

"At Mills, you'll ask thoughtful questions, generate new ideas, and share your opinions in an inclusive community that welcomes women and gender non-binary students from all ages and backgrounds. With mentoring from accomplished professors and an 10:1 student-faculty ratio, you will learn how to examine every side of an argument so that you can succeed in every type of situation. Where most people see problems, you'll see possibilities as you gain the confidence to speak up and the power to create your own path.

"Mills has been educating creative, independent thinkers since 1852, two years after California became a state. Since then, we have been ranked as one of the top colleges in the West. Our 135-acre campus in the heart of the San Francisco Bay Area has been home to more than 25,000 alumnae who have gone on to excel as authors, composers, scientists, lawyers, professors, ambassadors, news anchors, governors, congresswomen, and activists."

SELECTIVITY

Admissions Rating	75
# of applicants	1,003
% of applicants accepted	86
% of acceptees attending	19

FRESHMAN PROFILE

Range SAT EBRW	513–640
Range SAT Math	495–600
Range ACT Composite	21–29
# submitting SAT scores	61
% submitting SAT scores	37
# submitting ACT scores	33
% submitting ACT scores	20
Average HS GPA	3.6

DEADLINES

Early action	
Deadline	11/15
Notification	12/1
Regular	
Priority	1/15
Notification	Rolling, 11/15
Nonfall registration?	Yes

APPLICANTS ALSO LOOK AT AND OFTEN PREFER

University of California—Berkeley; University of California—Santa Cruz; Smith College; University of California, Los Angeles; University of San Francisco; University of California, Irvine; Saint Mary's College of California; University of California—Santa Barbara; University of California, Riverside; University of California, Davis; University of California—San Diego

AND SOMETIMES PREFER

Santa Clara University; California Polytechnic State University; San Diego State University; Wellesley College; Reed College; San Jose State University; Mount Holyoke College; University of Redlands; Hampshire College; Loyola Marymount University; Scripps College; University of Washington; Willamette University; Dominican University of California; San Francisco State University; Sonoma State University; University of Puget Sound

FINANCIAL FACTS

Financial Aid Rating	85
Annual tuition	$29,340
Room and board	$13,883
Required fees	$1,537
Books and supplies	$1,611
Average frosh need-based scholarship	$26,408
Average UG need-based scholarship	$22,495
% needy frosh rec. need-based scholarship or grant aid	95
% needy UG rec. need-based scholarship or grant aid	96
% needy frosh rec. non-need-based scholarship or grant aid	99
% needy UG rec. non-need-based scholarship or grant aid	91
% needy frosh rec. need-based self-help aid	70
% needy UG rec. need-based self-help aid	75
% frosh rec. any financial aid	100
% UG rec. any financial aid	99
% UG borrow to pay for school	85
Average cumulative indebtedness	$29,693
% frosh need fully met	7
% ugrads need fully met	10
Average % of frosh need met	71
Average % of ugrad need met	70

MILLSAPS COLLEGE

1701 North State Street, Jackson, MS 39210 • Admissions: 601-974-1050 • Fax: 601-974-1059

CAMPUS LIFE
Quality of Life Rating	88
Fire Safety Rating	90
Green Rating	68
Type of school	Private
Affiliation	Methodist
Environment	Metropolis

STUDENTS
Total undergrad enrollment	793
% male/female	48/52
% from out of state	55
% frosh from public high school	55
% frosh live on campus	98
% ugrads live on campus	89
# of fraternities (% ugrad men join)	6 (58)
# of sororities (% ugrad women join)	6 (55)
% African American	20
% Asian	4
% Caucasian	63
% Hispanic	5
% Native American	<1
% Pacific Islander	0
% Two or more races	0
% Race and/or ethnicity unknown	2
% international	5
# of countries represented	31

SURVEY SAYS . . .
Class discussions encouraged
No one cheats
Diverse student types interact on campus
Lots of beer drinking
Frats and sororities are popular

ACADEMICS
Academic Rating	88
% students returning for sophomore year	79
% students graduating within 4 years	62
% students graduating within 6 years	67
Calendar	Semester
Student/faculty ratio	9:1
Profs interesting rating	93
Profs accessible rating	97

Most classes have 10–19 students.
Most lab/discussion sessions have fewer than 10 students.

MOST POPULAR MAJORS
Business Administration, Management and Operations; Biology/Biological Sciences, General; Psychology, General

STUDENTS SAY "..."

Academics

Millsaps is a small college, so students "get a lot of personal attention." It is a "school where everybody knows your name," as well as "a place where every student has to work hard to stay above water; excellence is the norm, not the exception." What makes Millsaps unique is how it "breaks the mold by providing superb education as well as fun, combining the two in ways so subtle that a student may not even realize they're learning!" The school "offers great courses taught by charismatic professors" who "bring the material to life...through their innovative teaching methods." "Classes are not easy but the quality of learning is top notch." "Professors always encourage students to discuss class material and voice their opinions and questions about it. They encourage you to form your own ideas." These "friendly and approachable" professors "continue to teach outside of the classroom." "They welcome one-on-one time...to further develop understanding." Students have praise for the education they are receiving saying, "coming out of Millsaps I will be fully prepared for grad school. My professors not only lecture, but they turn the material into hands-on learning opportunities," and "I seriously respect my school's standard of excellence in hiring people who are wonderful at their jobs." Besides "great professors," the school offers "a prestigious business school," "abundant study abroad programs," and "strong Southern hospitality and heritage." The school's small size provides opportunities to receive "a top-notch education, while also getting to play sports and be in clubs." Although Millsaps may not be affordable for everyone, it "strives to be generous with scholarships." One student was pleased to report, "They offered the most financial assistance by far." Although student surveys were mostly positive, like this one: "Millsaps College provides the ideal learning atmosphere for liberal arts studies where they teach us how to think and not what to think," there were complaints about "the internet and networking capabilities," and "the cafeteria is an area where great improvement is needed."

Life

"Students at Millsaps think about their classwork first and foremost. After that, we think about hanging out with friends and having fun." The campus is "so beautiful and filled with cozy spots that many students spend a lot of their time outside." "While most schools have 'the quad' where students hang out between classes, Millsaps has 'The Bowl.' It is a beautiful area of grass and trees in the center of campus." But one student notes that there is still room for improvement. "The campus is beautiful, but the insides of the buildings need a serious upgrade. Every time I walk into a building, I feel like I've been transported back to the seventies." Although "most of the upperclassmen dorms are amazing," the "freshman dorms are a little sketchy." On campus "there are concerts and fun days all throughout the semester." "There are parties at the fraternity houses, and...some really cool things to do from concerts to oxygen bars to laser tag." "I would definitely call it a 'party school,' despite the tough academics." "There is a lot of partying on the weekends but almost everyone still manages to get studying finished." Students also point out, "We don't have to drink to have fun at Millsaps, though. You can always find a friend to hang out with, go to the movies, shop, or find a new great place to eat. The Millsaps curriculum even makes study groups fun (for the most part), believe it or not." Off campus, students venture into Jackson where "there are great restaurants."

Student Body

Is there a typical Millsaps student? Some students think so: "The typical student at Millsaps was an over-involved, cool nerd in high school. We throw ourselves into sports, clubs, Greek life, and community service like it's our job. It's how we thrive." "Students fit in by being involved in Greek life and other organizations." "A typical student is involved in many activities from sports to community service clubs. Student interests are diverse, and the student body in general is very friendly and interactive." Another student disagrees, "There is no 'typical student' really—the most common thread is a desire to change the world (usually, with a stop at graduate school)."

MILLSAPS COLLEGE

Financial Aid: 800-352-1050 • E-Mail: admissions@millsaps.edu • Website: www.millsaps.edu

THE PRINCETON REVIEW SAYS

Admissions

Very important factors considered include: rigor of secondary school record, academic GPA, standardized test scores, character/personal qualities. *Important factors considered include:* class rank, application essay, recommendation(s), extracurricular activities, talent/ability. *Other factors considered include:* interview, volunteer work, work experience. ACT with or without writing accepted. SAT with or without Essay component accepted. High school diploma is required and GED is accepted. *Academic units required:* 4 English, 3 math, 3 science, 2 science labs, 1 foreign language, 2 social studies, 2 history, 1 academic elective. *Academic units recommended:* 4 English, 4 math, 4 science, 2 science labs, 2 foreign language, 2 social studies, 2 history, 2 academic electives.

Financial Aid

Students should submit: FAFSA. Priority filing deadline is 3/1. The Princeton Review suggests that all financial aid forms be submitted as soon as possible after October 1. *Need-based scholarships/grants offered:* College/university scholarship or grant aid from institutional funds; Federal Pell; Private scholarships; SEOG; State scholarships/grants. *Loan aid offered:* Direct PLUS loans; Direct Subsidized Stafford Loans; Direct Unsubsidized Stafford Loans. Applicants will be notified of awards on a rolling basis beginning 3/15. Federal Work-Study Program available. Institutional employment available.

The Inside Word

Millsaps' trademark friendliness begins during the admissions process. The school encourages prospective students to get in touch with an admissions counselor to ask questions, arrange a visit, or connect you with a current student. For early action admission or scholarships, students need to apply in January. After that, the school admits students on a rolling basis.

THE SCHOOL SAYS "..."

From the Admissions Office

"Students at Millsaps College choose their own paths, propelled by individual interests and goals. Guided by teachers and mentors who know them well, Millsaps students are elevated by countless opportunities to put ideas into motion. Through broad exploration of the humanities, sciences, socials sciences, and business, students pursue individualized academic programs, gaining exposure to new disciplines, new points of view, and new possibilities. At Millsaps, every course is taught at the honors level. Of the faculty members, 94 percent hold the highest degree attainable in their discipline. And, with a student-teacher ratio of 9:1 and an average class size of fourteen, professors expect students to actively participate in their educations. Millsaps College is one of the few liberal arts colleges in the country with both a Phi Beta Kappa Chapter (the first in Mississippi) and an AACSB-accredited business program at the Else School of Management. Millsaps' new Compass Curriculum will guide the course planning for all incoming first-year students to find their best path to graduation and beyond. The Compass Curriculum will challenge students and engage them in the exploration of knowledge domains focused on four key Student Learning Outcomes: Thinking and Reasoning, Communication, Integrative and Collaborative Learning, and Problem Solving and Creative Practice."

SELECTIVITY

Admissions Rating	85
# of applicants	4,161
% of applicants accepted	59
% of acceptees attending	10

FRESHMAN PROFILE

Range SAT EBRW	550–630
Range SAT Math	530–630
Range ACT Composite	22–28
# submitting SAT scores	45
% submitting SAT scores	18
# submitting ACT scores	228
% submitting ACT scores	89
Average HS GPA	3.7
% graduated top 10% of class	0
% graduated top 25% of class	100
% graduated top 50% of class	100

DEADLINES

Early action	
Deadline	11/15
Notification	1/15
Regular	
Priority	2/1
Deadline	7/1
Notification	Rolling, 10/15
Nonfall registration?	Yes

FINANCIAL FACTS

Financial Aid Rating	87
Annual tuition	$38,600
Room and board	$14,210
Required fees	$2,714
Books and supplies	$1,200
Average frosh need-based scholarship	$30,284
Average UG need-based scholarship	$29,435
% needy frosh rec. need-based scholarship or grant aid	99
% needy UG rec. need-based scholarship or grant aid	99
% needy frosh rec. non-need-based scholarship or grant aid	25
% needy UG rec. non-need-based scholarship or grant aid	18
% needy frosh rec. need-based self-help aid	72
% needy UG rec. need-based self-help aid	78
% frosh rec. any financial aid	100
% UG rec. any financial aid	98
% UG borrow to pay for school	65
Average cumulative indebtedness	$34,619
% frosh need fully met	32
% ugrads need fully met	23
Average % of frosh need met	80
Average % of ugrad need met	78

MISSOURI UNIVERSITY OF SCIENCE AND TECHNOLOGY

106 Parker Hall, 300 W. 13th Street, Rolla, MO 65409-1060 • Admissions: 573-341-4165 • Fax: 573-341-4082

STUDENTS SAY "..."

Academics

Top performers in science and technology will find a home at Missouri S&T, because here "students are exposed to just about every different type of engineering," making it "one of the best universities that prepares engineers for industry." Unsurprisingly, this does not come without challenge. Classes can be "very tough and intimidating," where "it's not uncommon to have a 55 percent or less average on a test." Students ready for the rigorous academics should "not expect to be babied at all" because "the professors are there to challenge you." The aim is to "prepare students to find a job in the real world and help us to get the experience to succeed in it." Students who have run the gauntlet say "the quality of education and availability of resources here is second to none." That education comes via "hands-on learning, small class sizes, and caring professors" who are "some of the smartest professors in the world." Though they challenge their students, they don't leave them out to dry. "All of the professors have office hours, whether open or by appointment," students note. Indeed, "the accessibility of instructors and other faculty/staff" at this small school is seen as a strength. Yes, "this school definitely is willing to challenge their students," but numbers-crunching engineers will find value in their education, because S&T "comes in the top three schools in average starting salary for graduates, and won't guarantee a huge debt burden."

Life

Missouri University of Science and Technology may be "a small school in the middle of Missouri," but "our range of student organizations is mind-boggling." You name the club and it probably exists, as well as school activities ranging from "scavenger hunts, video game nights, cooking classes, viewing parties, dance lessons, and much more." Of course, in a school where "all of the students are always worrying about that next exam in calculus or dreading their lab in the afternoon," it is not surprising that studying is as big a pastime as hanging out. Here, "academics are everyone's top priority." When not studying, "drinking is pretty big on weekends." Other activities include "playing sports, video games, and working out." Downtown Rolla isn't a thriving Mecca of activity because "there's not so much to do in the town"; however, "someone always has something going on." St. Louis is close enough for day trips, and there are a slew of student organizations to occupy downtime. "Virtually every student is either heavily involved in a diverse group of these student organizations or devotes much of their time to design teams or research." Generally, if you're at S&T and are not kept busy, it's probably because you don't want to be busy.

Student Body

Imagine a less stereotypical Big Bang Theory and you're close to the mark. The typical student may be "a little nerdy," "those kids that didn't fit in during high school" but who "now can be themselves." A typical S&T student "is someone who never really had to study in high school to get good grades, but they are working hard here to maintain that standard." While most S&T students are smart—"we came here primarily to learn," one attendee notes—they are not introverted or antisocial. The "very friendly" people on campus "live together in harmony." Indeed, "everyone can find a place to fit in" thanks to the "over 212 student organizations." While about half of the students here are from Missouri or nearby states, the others "are from the edges of the nation and even some foreign countries, which is astounding considering our small enrollment size." Education is the priority for those who attend, so meeting people is simple because "it is really easy just to strike up a conversation with someone." The like-minded atmosphere makes socializing easy. "We are all nerds, so we adapt to the social environment once we are introduced."

MISSOURI UNIVERSITY OF SCIENCE AND TECHNOLOGY

Financial Aid: 573-341-4282 • E-Mail: admissions@mst.edu • Website: www.mst.edu

THE PRINCETON REVIEW SAYS

Admissions

Very important factors considered include: rigor of secondary school record, class rank, academic GPA, standardized test scores. ACT with or without writing accepted. SAT with or without Essay component accepted. High school diploma is required and GED is accepted. *Academic units required:* 4 English, 4 math, 3 science, including 1 science lab, 2 single foreign language, 3 social studies, 1 fine arts.

Financial Aid

Students should submit: FAFSA. Priority filing deadline is 2/1. The Princeton Review suggests that all financial aid forms be submitted as soon as possible after October 1. *Need-based scholarships/grants offered:* College/university scholarship or grant aid from institutional funds; Federal Pell; Private scholarships; SEOG; State scholarships/grants. Applicants will be notified of awards on a rolling basis beginning 4/1. Federal Work-Study Program available. Institutional employment available.

The Inside Word

Winning admission to Missouri University of Science and Technology is largely a numbers game, as it often is with other leading public universities. Expect to have to meet class rank and standardized test cutoffs, along with general education requirements, in order to be granted admission. And apply early if possible. The pool of applicants is competitive, and is made up of students of similar caliber. Get off to an early start and you'll have an advantage.

THE SCHOOL SAYS " . . ."

From the Admissions Office

"Missouri University of Science and Technology is one of the nation's top technological universities and offers strong academics in humanities, social sciences, education, business and other degree programs. Our fifteen engineering programs and computing and science programs are nationally and internationally renowned. With 8,096 students from the US and globe, Missouri S&T provides a 'big campus' feel of diversity and student engagement on a medium-sized campus.

"S&T offers rigorous academics, exceptional graduation and placement rates, excellent access to co-ops and internships, experiential learning for all undergraduates, affordable tuition combined with generous scholarship programs, and a 3.4 percent loan default rate as a result of superior career outcomes for our students.

"S&T students are successful due to a combination of outstanding academics and easy access to personal and professional growth. The vast majority of courses are taught by tenured professors engaged in cutting-edge research and scholarship, in a faculty culture that values undergraduate education and 'hands-on' learning and personal attention, which extends back to our founding in 1870. S&T sponsors over 250 student clubs, and students enjoy outdoor activities among the area's scenic parks, lakes and riverways.

"Widely recognized as one of the nation's best universities, Missouri S&T provides an outstanding education, at a reasonable cost with exceptional student outcomes."

SELECTIVITY

Admissions Rating	83
# of applicants	5,107
% of applicants accepted	79
% of acceptees attending	28

FRESHMAN PROFILE

Range SAT EBRW	600–700
Range SAT Math	590–730
Range SAT Composite	1210–1420
Range ACT Composite	26–32
# submitting SAT scores	58
% submitting SAT scores	5
# submitting ACT scores	1,047
% submitting ACT scores	82
Average HS GPA	3.765
% graduated top 10% of class	41
% graduated top 25% of class	73
% graduated top 50% of class	94

DEADLINES

Regular	
Priority	12/1
Deadline	7/1
Notification	Rolling, 8/1

FINANCIAL FACTS

Financial Aid Rating	84
Annual in-state tuition	$8,376
Annual out-of-state tuition	$26,060
Room and board	$10,402
Required fees	$1,680
Books and supplies	$1,200
Average frosh need-based scholarship	$11,453
Average UG need-based scholarship	$9,070
% needy frosh rec. need-based scholarship or grant aid	97
% needy UG rec. need-based scholarship or grant aid	92
% needy frosh rec. non-need-based scholarship or grant aid	52
% needy UG rec. non-need-based scholarship or grant aid	34
% needy frosh rec. need-based self-help aid	83
% needy UG rec. need-based self-help aid	90
% frosh rec. any financial aid	97
% UG rec. any financial aid	87
% UG borrow to pay for school	62
Average cumulative indebtedness	$30,168
% frosh need fully met	53
% ugrads need fully met	37
Average % of frosh need met	88
Average % of ugrad need met	77

MONMOUTH UNIVERSITY (NJ)

Admission, Monmouth University, West Long Branch, NJ 07764-1898 • Admissions: 732-571-3456 • Fax: 732-263-5166

CAMPUS LIFE
Quality of Life Rating	84
Fire Safety Rating	99
Green Rating	77
Type of school	Private
Environment	Village

STUDENTS
Total undergrad enrollment	4,429
% male/female	41/59
% from out of state	18
% frosh from public high school	85
% frosh live on campus	79
% ugrads live on campus	40
# of fraternities (% ugrad men join)	6 (7)
# of sororities (% ugrad women join)	8 (17)
% African American	5
% Asian	3
% Caucasian	70
% Hispanic	14
% Native American	<1
% Pacific Islander	0
% Two or more races	3
% Race and/or ethnicity unknown	4
% international	1
# of countries represented	27

SURVEY SAYS . . .
Frats and sororities are popular
Students are happy
Great off-campus food

ACADEMICS
Academic Rating	75
% students returning for sophomore year	81
% students graduating within 4 years	60
% students graduating within 6 years	73
Calendar	Semester
Student/faculty ratio	12:1
Profs interesting rating	84
Profs accessible rating	91

Most classes have 20–29 students.
Most lab/discussion sessions have 2–9 students.

MOST POPULAR MAJORS
Speech Communication and Rhetoric; Business Administration and Management, General; Education, General

STUDENTS SAY ". . ."

Academics

Monmouth University, just an hour or so away from both New York City and Philadelphia, wants to be your future home away from home. It's far more than a "beautiful" campus—though that's the way many attendees happily describe it—it's also "great at opening new doors for students." That comes from the institution's responsiveness, such that "if there is a problem, Monmouth staff is quick to resolve it and come to your aid." It also comes from their foresight, with numerous career- and success-minded initiatives and resources, particularly when it comes to tutoring or writing services. There are also a lot of popular volunteering opportunities, with "service trips to Haiti and Guatemala."

The meat-and-potatoes coursework is also praised by undergrads, who note there's a "great variety of course offerings and programs" many of which prioritize "hands-on experience." Additionally, students say that "small class sizes help the learning experience" and "allow you to develop a good rapport with your professors." Don't underestimate the small things either: "Teachers actually knowing your name means a lot." While "some professors are more dedicated than others," many are "wonderful and truly invested in helping you do well." They tend to be "passionate about the subject they teach and make it interesting for the students." Overall, "they're here to push you, but also make it clear that they will be more than willing to meet with you outside of class." Perhaps best of all, professors often strive "to connect what we learn in class to the real world."

Life

If you're into the Greek scene or athletics, Monmouth may be the perfect place for you, as students say that the scene is "dominated" by those two factions. Students mean this in the most fun and flattering light: "Greek Life is the best experience of my college career. I was able to make amazing connections and develop leadership skills." There's plenty of opportunity to connect with students outside of the classroom given that "people work out a lot" at facilities like "basketball courts, a swimming pool, and a bowling alley," or just plain attend the athletic events, where there "is always a great, energized student crowd." Of course, there's far more than just athletics here, and as examples of how you can find "a club for most interests," students list things from debate and model UN to the 5678 Dance Club, psychology club, and even a "student-run record label." The school also sponsors a variety of events, from "craft fairs and bonfires" as do the individual residence halls, which have things like "painting night." And should you need a breather from campus life, the surrounding area offers many options. "We are right near the beach, and [an] hour's drive from [New York City]."

Student Body

Undergrads note that at Monmouth University, the "student body is heavily white and rich," and a place where "diversity only exists in small pockets" because most "tend to be from New Jersey." And yet, there's far more beneath the surface, because peers are overall described as "motivated and creative people" and one attendee notes that "the community at Monmouth is more inclusive than any I have ever seen." Friendliness abounds, such that "everyone is always saying hello to each other on their ways to class" and it's rather commonplace to have someone "hold the doors open for you." In short, there's a "very chill beach vibe," which can be refreshing during one's downtime, given the general bustle of those who are "academically driven and work hard to be involved in many things on campus." All in all, "Everyone at Monmouth has something unique to offer, and everyone has their own interests and beliefs which makes it exciting to meet new people."

MONMOUTH UNIVERSITY (NJ)

Financial Aid: 732-571-3463 • E-Mail: admission@monmouth.edu • Website: www.monmouth.edu

THE PRINCETON REVIEW SAYS

Admissions

Very important factors considered include: rigor of secondary school record, academic GPA, standardized test scores. *Important factors considered include:* application essay, recommendation(s), extracurricular activities, volunteer work. *Other factors considered include:* character/personal qualities, alumni/ae relation. ACT with or without writing accepted. SAT with or without Essay component accepted. High school diploma is required and GED is accepted. *Academic units required:* 4 English, 3 math, 2 science, 1 science lab, 2 history, 5 academic electives. *Academic units recommended:* 4 English, 3 math, 2 science, 1 science lab, 2 foreign language, 2 social studies, 2 history, 5 academic electives.

Financial Aid

Students should submit: FAFSA. Priority filing deadline is 12/15. The Princeton Review suggests that all financial aid forms be submitted as soon as possible after October 1. *Need-based scholarships/grants offered:* College/university scholarship or grant aid from institutional funds; Federal Pell; Private scholarships; SEOG; State scholarships/grants. *Loan aid offered:* Direct PLUS loans; Direct Subsidized Stafford Loans; Direct Unsubsidized Stafford Loans. Applicants will be notified of awards on a rolling basis beginning 2/1. Federal Work-Study Program available. Institutional employment available.

The Inside Word

Monmouth University takes a fairly standard approach to the admissions process: your cumulative GPA and your SAT or ACT scores are the two most critical factors. Letters of recommendation and extracurricular activities will be of secondary importance. Undergrads interested in transferring to Monmouth can take advantage of Instant Decision Tuesdays wherein they meet with an admissions counselor to discuss enrollment potential, the university experience, and scholarship opportunities.

THE SCHOOL SAYS "..."

From the Admissions Office

"As the region's premier private coastal university, Monmouth University attracts students looking for a personalized learning environment that will ignite their curiosity and prepare them for life after graduation.

"Students benefit from an intellectually challenging academic experience built on a strong liberal arts foundation and learning experiences that are both high impact and immersive, extending beyond the classroom. Small class sizes foster collaborative learning and research opportunities with faculty and peers who know you by name. Our breathtaking campus provides a safe, suburban setting in one of the world's largest metropolitan regions, ideally positioned to help our students develop and pursue their career interests while enjoying rich cultural opportunities.

"Monmouth's student life features active student clubs and organizations, including eight sororities and eight fraternities, and dozens of academic/leadership honor societies. Monmouth's 23 NCAA Division I athletic teams attract lively support from students and other members of the campus and local communities while instilling university pride.

"There is a real spirit of entrepreneurship on campus that comes to life through activities like Blue Hawk Records, our student-run record label, and the student-managed investment fund, Hawk Capital. For those adventurers interested in extending their experiences beyond campus, Monmouth encourages students to take part in service projects, study abroad programs, and community-building activities in locales around the globe. Monmouth University is committed to graduating people of purpose with the critical thinking skills required for global relevance and impact."

SELECTIVITY

Admissions Rating	77
# of applicants	8,984
% of applicants accepted	77
% of acceptees attending	14

FRESHMAN PROFILE

Range SAT EBRW	520–610
Range SAT Math	510–600
Range SAT Composite	1030–1200
Range ACT Composite	21–27
# submitting SAT scores	890
% submitting SAT scores	90
# submitting ACT scores	103
% submitting ACT scores	10
Average HS GPA	3.5
% graduated top 10% of class	15
% graduated top 25% of class	42
% graduated top 50% of class	78

DEADLINES

Early action	
Deadline	12/1
Notification	1/15
Regular	
Priority	12/1
Deadline	3/1
Notification	Rolling, 4/1
Nonfall registration?	Yes

FINANCIAL FACTS

Financial Aid Rating	81
Annual tuition	$38,880
Room and board	$14,534
Required fees	$712
Books and supplies	$996
Average frosh need-based scholarship	$14,703
Average UG need-based scholarship	$13,822
% needy frosh rec. need-based scholarship or grant aid	75
% needy UG rec. need-based scholarship or grant aid	66
% needy frosh rec. non-need-based scholarship or grant aid	97
% needy UG rec. non-need-based scholarship or grant aid	98
% needy frosh rec. need-based self-help aid	84
% needy UG rec. need-based self-help aid	84
% frosh rec. any financial aid	99
% UG rec. any financial aid	97
% UG borrow to pay for school	78
Average cumulative indebtedness	$26,012
% frosh need fully met	17
% ugrads need fully met	14
Average % of frosh need met	71
Average % of ugrad need met	68

MONTANA TECHNOLOGICAL UNIVERSITY

1300 West Park Street, Butte, MT 59701 • Admissions: 406-496-4256 • Fax: 406-496-4710

STUDENTS SAY ". . ."

Academics

Located in the foothills of the Rocky Mountains, Montana Technological University is about "science," "engineering," and "getting students ready for a career in high-paying fields." With its "strong STEM programs," the focus is certainly on the technical side of education, and students praise Tech's engineering program and "connection to industry." The relatively small campus creates a "home-like atmosphere where everyone has a sense of community," as well as "the opportunity to really get to know professors." Looking beyond college, "Montana Tech's Career Fair almost guarantees an internship to anyone who is serious about their career." Several students who choose majors outside the popular STEM degrees do wish that the school would "[treat] our non-engineering degrees as part of the school and not [as] second-rate." Tech's nursing program is growing in popularity, and the school is known to "produce compassionate, intelligent nurses." Professors generally earn high marks, as "most of them come from industry backgrounds before they started teaching; therefore, the quality of the material brought to the classroom is top notch." Many professors are "actual engineers with real world experience," and while "Tech is not an easy school," students say that with "the help provided by the professors and the other facilities available on campus," it is possible for "anyone with the work ethic [to] meet their goals."

Life

Life in Montana Tech's hometown of Butte is oriented around the outdoors, and students flock to activities like " skiing, biking, camping, [and] fishing" when they're not buried in schoolwork. Beyond the great outdoors, students say that Butte is "pretty quiet with mostly bars and churches around town," so a lot of time is spent on campus or at off-campus residences (only roughly 12 percent of undergraduates live on campus). The rigorous curriculum means most students study during the week and let loose during the weekend. As one student puts it, "You have to be willing to search for things to do outside of class, [other than] drinking." There are intramural sports and Tech-sponsored events, and "sporting events are very popular activities at Montana Tech."

Student Body

There's no question that men outnumber women at Montana Tech, though the ratio is improving. While some say, "It isn't a problem being a woman here," others counter that Tech "is an unfriendly place for women." In general, the student body "is extremely focused and pushes each other to do better. With such a small campus, the students know each other quite well and want to see their classmates succeed." While some describe their fellow students as "lots of Canadians and cowboys," others say that there is "a very diverse population here at Montana Tech, everyone from transfer students to international students from Saudi Arabia." Even with a competitive atmosphere, students say that at Montana Tech the "clubs are active, the Student Senate genuinely cares about the happiness of their students, and the faculty [do] whatever they can to bring a smile to your face, especially during difficult days of midterms, flu season, and cold weather."

MONTANA TECHNOLOGICAL UNIVERSITY

Financial Aid: 406-496-4213 • E-Mail: enrollment@mtech.edu • Website: www.mtech.edu

THE PRINCETON REVIEW SAYS

Admissions

Very important factors considered include: class rank, academic GPA, standardized test scores. ACT with Writing recommended. High school diploma is required and GED is accepted. *Academic units required:* 4 English, 3 math, 2 science, 2 science labs, 3 social studies, 2 units from above areas or other academic areas. *Academic units recommended:* 4 math.

Financial Aid

Students should submit: FAFSA. Priority filing deadline is 12/1. The Princeton Review suggests that all financial aid forms be submitted as soon as possible after October 1. *Need-based scholarships/grants offered:* College/university scholarship or grant aid from institutional funds; Federal Pell; Private scholarships; SEOG; State scholarships/grants. *Loan aid offered:* Direct PLUS loans; Direct Subsidized Stafford Loans; Direct Unsubsidized Stafford Loans. Applicants will be notified of awards on a rolling basis beginning 2/15. Federal Work-Study Program available. Institutional employment available.

The Inside Word

For those leaning towards a technical career, Montana Tech is the place to go. Strong academics are important, but the school can be a place for students that may not be offered a spot at one of the country's larger tech schools. The acceptance rate is high, and admitted students generally having a high school GPA around 3.48. Transcripts are important as well as prospective students' standardized test scores and high school class rank. There are a variety of math and writing proficiency requirements students must meet, either through minimum ACT/SAT testing or AP and IB scores, and the school looks for a high school course load that includes a full range of college prep classes.

THE SCHOOL SAYS "..."

From the Admissions Office

"Characterize Montana Tech by listening to what employers say. They tell us Tech graduates stand out with an incredible work ethic and top-notch technical skills. Last year, 68 organizations held on-campus interviews and 120 companies attended Montana Tech career fairs competing for our students and graduates. The beneficiaries: the students! Montana Tech has a five-year average career outcomes rate of 91 percent and a 92 percent acceptance into professional and graduate programs. Learning takes place in a personalized environment, in first-class academic facilities, and in the heart of the Rocky Mountains. Outdoor recreation provides a great balance to the rigors of the course work at Montana Tech. We are a small school where our students receive a terrific education, and in the end, get great jobs! The SAT (or the ACT with the writing section) is recommended for all students applying for admission. Students who do not take the tests with the writing component may be required to take an additional English placement test from college before they enroll."

SELECTIVITY

Admissions Rating	77
# of applicants	1,307
% of applicants accepted	92
% of acceptees attending	34

FRESHMAN PROFILE

Range SAT EBRW	540–630
Range SAT Math	575–670
Range ACT Composite	22–27
# submitting SAT scores	37
% submitting SAT scores	16
# submitting ACT scores	193
% submitting ACT scores	84
Average HS GPA	3.6
% graduated top 10% of class	25
% graduated top 25% of class	56
% graduated top 50% of class	87

DEADLINES

Nonfall registration?	Yes

FINANCIAL FACTS

Financial Aid Rating	83
Annual in-state tuition	$7,431
Annual out-of-state tuition	$22,595
Room and board	$9,996
Books and supplies	$1,350
Average frosh need-based scholarship	$5,777
Average UG need-based scholarship	$5,768
% needy frosh rec. need-based scholarship or grant aid	90
% needy UG rec. need-based scholarship or grant aid	84
% needy frosh rec. non-need-based scholarship or grant aid	17
% needy UG rec. non-need-based scholarship or grant aid	7
% needy frosh rec. need-based self-help aid	60
% needy UG rec. need-based self-help aid	70
% frosh rec. any financial aid	87
% UG rec. any financial aid	62
% UG borrow to pay for school	54
Average cumulative indebtedness	$23,632
% frosh need fully met	22
% ugrads need fully met	13
Average % of frosh need met	66
Average % of ugrad need met	58

MORAVIAN COLLEGE

1200 Main Street, Bethlehem, PA 18018 • Admissions: 610-861-1320 • Fax: 610-625-7930

STUDENTS SAY ". . ."

Academics

One of the standout features of Moravian College isn't just that it's a "close knit community" filled with those who "support each other and give back to the community in many ways," but that it puts its money where its mouth is. Here, it's "one of the few schools in the nation [that] allow students and faculty [to] have a full vote on their Board of Trustees," which makes appreciative students feel as if they actually have a voice. Consequently, undergrads agree that the school "really does look after its students and makes sure that they succeed here."

A handful of students specifically note that, among the many great academic departments, the "nursing and education programs are what stand out to students when applying." But regardless of your major, the college "really strives for all academic courses to integrate critical thinking in order to better prepare students for their future careers." The incorporation of technology is also praised, with undergrads observing that "it is amazing that each incoming student is provided with a laptop and iPad so that everyone coming in is on the same level." Further backing up both the structure and accessories are Moravian's best aspect—"It's a small school so you get close with your professors and build connections easily." This especially true at the higher academic levels, where professors are uniformly cited as being "stellar," though most are described as "extremely friendly" and as having "lots of passion for their subject, and they're happy to explain things to you when you have difficulty understanding the material."

Life

Moravian students lead fairly busy lives both academically and socially and they wouldn't have it any other way. There's a wide variety of clubs, which "people are really passionate about." For example, "One of my favorite activities on campus is Board Game Club, where we meet every week and play board and card games." Things can get very niche, as with the Brain Club, which is always "reaching out to the Lehigh Valley to educate the public on neuroscience." There's plenty of broad appeal as well when it comes to the "many sporting events that students can get into and go support their friends." And when it comes to events, Moravian once again allows its students more involvement than usual, thanks to the Moravian Activities Council (MAC), which promotes extracurriculars "programmed by a handful of our very own students," and which include numerous free activities "like movie nights, trivia nights, painting, scavenger hunts, and bingo nights" as well as off-campus trips to "Broadway [shows], rock-climbing, ice skating, goat yoga, top golf, and much more." Additionally, "Greek life is pretty big on campus and is very involved." Speaking of fraternities and sororities, students note that there's "a good party culture on campus: present and safe enough to enjoy, but easy enough to avoid if you'd prefer." Lastly, should anyone tire of dining on campus, hometown Bethlehem has "lots of great restaurants" right on Main Street.

Student Body

Those fearing a difficult transition from high school to college, worry not. Everyone at Moravian is reported to be "approachable and friendly," so much so that "All the upperclassmen helped the freshmen learn the campus and made them feel welcomed. It's like one big family." The overall composition of the student body leans towards being "predominantly white," but there is "a significant international student population. Many share a common denominator, too, when it comes to their activity levels: "Nearly every student is in multiple clubs, organizations, or sports teams." This helps to explain why one undergrad notes that "athletes, nerds, and theater kids mix together and do not isolate," and why overall almost everyone maintains "a strong amount of respect for each other." As one student puts it, "Whenever I want to eat, I can always find someone to chat with at whatever dining spot I'm in on campus," and another notes that "We're always smiling or saying hello to one another when we pass each other on campus."

Financial Aid: 610-861-1330 • E-Mail: admission@moravian.edu • Website: www.moravian.edu

THE PRINCETON REVIEW SAYS

Admissions

Very important factors considered include: rigor of secondary school record, extracurricular activities, character/personal qualities. *Important factors considered include:* class rank, academic GPA, application essay, standardized test scores, recommendation(s), talent/ability, volunteer work. *Other factors considered include:* interview, first generation, alumni/ae relation, work experience. ACT with or without writing accepted. SAT with or without Essay component accepted. High school diploma is required and GED is accepted. *Academic units required:* 4 English, 3 math, 3 science, 2 science labs, 2 foreign language, 4 social studies.

Financial Aid

Students should submit: FAFSA. The Princeton Review suggests that all financial aid forms be submitted as soon as possible after October 1. *Need-based scholarships/grants offered:* College/university scholarship or grant aid from institutional funds; Federal Nursing Scholarships; Federal Pell; Private scholarships; SEOG; State scholarships/grants; United Negro College Fund. *Loan aid offered:* Direct PLUS loans; Direct Subsidized Stafford Loans; Direct Unsubsidized Stafford Loans. Applicants will be notified of awards on a rolling basis beginning 11/30. Federal Work-Study Program available. Institutional employment available.

The Inside Word

Admissions officers seek applicants who will best complement life at Moravian. The school is looking for students who have taken a challenging college prep curriculum and have demonstrated that they're ready for collegiate level coursework. Importantly, Moravian is test-optional and you will not be at a disadvantage if you choose not to submit scores. However, it is highly recommended that you schedule an interview with an admissions counselor if at all possible.

THE SCHOOL SAYS ". . ."

From the Admissions Office

"America's sixth-oldest college, Moravian College emphasizes the deliberate integration of a broad-based liberal arts curriculum with hands-on learning experiences to effectively prepare its students, not just for jobs, but for successful careers. Moravian College excels at transforming good students into highly competent graduates that are ready to enter the workplace with confidence or shine in graduate school. Students benefit from Moravian College's strong academic majors, opportunities for internships, undergraduate research and scholarship, and programs that foster a deeper enjoyment of life. The 11:1 student-faculty ratio means students get personal attention from a scholarly and dedicated faculty who ensure their success. The proof is in the results, 97 percent of students who earn a bachelor's degree, do so in four years. Moravian College issues a MacBook Pro laptop and an iPad to all incoming freshmen to enhance learning and help students gain the 21st-century knowledge and skills that will be transferrable over numerous careers. The College offers fifty programs of study; business, education, health professions, social and biological sciences are among the most popular. Moravian College's strong athletics, music, and art programs, and more than eighty clubs and organizations offer healthy physical and creative outlets for every student.

"Located in historic Bethlehem, Pa., Moravian College has long history of educating and developing leaders in many fields. Students leave Moravian College with the skills, knowledge, and support necessary to more deeply enjoy life, work, and their role in the world. More than 95 percent of its graduates are employed or attending graduate school within ten months of graduation."

SELECTIVITY
Admissions Rating	81
# of applicants	2,127
% of applicants accepted	75
% of acceptees attending	27

FRESHMAN PROFILE
Range SAT EBRW	530–610
Range SAT Math	510–600
Range SAT Composite	1040–1210
Range ACT Composite	21–26
# submitting SAT scores	376
% submitting SAT scores	88
# submitting ACT scores	64
% submitting ACT scores	15
Average HS GPA	3.6
% graduated top 10% of class	15
% graduated top 25% of class	51
% graduated top 50% of class	83

DEADLINES
Regular	
Priority	3/1
Deadline	3/1
Notification	Rolling, 11/15
Nonfall registration?	Yes

APPLICANTS ALSO LOOK AT AND OFTEN PREFER
Penn State University Park; Temple University; Lehigh University; Dickinson College

AND SOMETIMES PREFER
Kutztown University of Pennsylvania; The College of New Jersey; The University of Scranton

AND RARELY PREFER
Albright College; Ramapo College of New Jersey; Rowan University; Misericordia University

FINANCIAL FACTS
Financial Aid Rating	85
Annual tuition	$45,321
Room and board	$14,471
Required fees	$2,046
Books and supplies	$1,200
Average frosh need-based scholarship	$29,847
Average UG need-based scholarship	$27,678
% needy frosh rec. need-based scholarship or grant aid	100
% needy UG rec. need-based scholarship or grant aid	96
% needy frosh rec. non-need-based scholarship or grant aid	15
% needy UG rec. non-need-based scholarship or grant aid	13
% needy frosh rec. need-based self-help aid	82
% needy UG rec. need-based self-help aid	84
% frosh rec. any financial aid	99
% UG rec. any financial aid	98
% UG borrow to pay for school	80
Average cumulative indebtedness	$38,514
% frosh need fully met	18
% ugrads need fully met	16
Average % of frosh need met	78
Average % of ugrad need met	73

MOUNT HOLYOKE COLLEGE

Newhall Center, South Hadley, MA 01075 • Admissions: 413-538-2023 • Fax: 413-538-2409

CAMPUS LIFE

Quality of Life Rating	91
Fire Safety Rating	85
Green Rating	91
Type of school	Private
Environment	Town

STUDENTS

Total undergrad enrollment	2,175
% male/female	0/100
% from out of state	81
% frosh from public high school	62
% frosh live on campus	99
% ugrads live on campus	96
# of sororities	0
% African American	5
% Asian	8
% Caucasian	47
% Hispanic	7
% Native American	<1
% Pacific Islander	<1
% Two or more races	4
% Race and/or ethnicity unknown	2
% international	27
# of countries represented	76

SURVEY SAYS . . .

Lots of liberal students
Students always studying
Students are happy
Classroom facilities are great
Lab facilities are great
Great library
Internships are widely available
Great financial aid
No one cheats
Students are friendly
Diverse student types interact on campus
Students environmentally aware
Great food on campus
Dorms are like palaces
Theater is popular
Campus newspaper is popular
Alumni active on campus
Active student government
Active minority support groups
Active student-run political groups

ACADEMICS

Academic Rating	93
% students returning for sophomore year	93
% students graduating within 4 years	79
% students graduating within 6 years	83
Calendar	Semester
Student/faculty ratio	9:1
Profs interesting rating	95
Profs accessible rating	96
Most classes have 10–19 students.	
Most lab/discussion sessions have 10–19 students.	

MOST POPULAR MAJORS
Biology/Biological Sciences, General; Psychology, General

STUDENTS SAY ". . ."

Academics

Massachusetts' Mount Holyoke College is a small women's-only research liberal arts school that stresses interdisciplinary study, offering more than fifty departmental and interdepartmental majors (30 percent of all majors are cross-departmental). Students even have the option to design their own major. As a member of the Five Colleges Consortium, students here are also able to take advantage of the courses and resources of four nearby schools: Amherst College, Hampshire College, Smith College, and the University of Massachusetts at Amherst. There's "a lot of flexibility" and the academic rigor is "challenging but encourages learning." One student says, "I feel like I'm pushed to be a smarter person here." With such resources as "a Makerspace lab, archives, and an art museum, [students] are always using campus resources to enhance … learning beyond the classroom."

Professors at Mount Holyoke are "wonderful scholars and wonderful people" who are "caring and receptive to concerns" and "incredibly accessible and helpful in and out of office hours." Courses offer "hands-on lab experience, real-world scenarios outside of the classroom, and creative teaching exercises," and when not on field visits, students take part in "a vibrant, excited classroom experience that inspires students to go above and beyond." Mount Holyoke "is the true definition of a liberal arts experience," and many professors "are careful to set up the room so that the seating lends itself to open discussion and thought." This makes for classes that are "intimate and intersectional with professors who prioritize their students above all else."

Life

Weekday life is all about the books and staying "very busy with club activities," but many people spend their non-classroom time "in the student center, the art facilities, and in common rooms." There is a "large on-campus culture" and most here "are content to stay on campus and attend cultural events and parties," though students will "frequently go to the Village Commons, which are right across the street from the college." Most simply like to "spend a long time at meals, just chatting with friends" or in the campus pub. When South Hadley can't do the trick, they'll go to the "neighboring towns of Amherst and Northampton for food and shopping" since the local buses "[make] travel to these towns easy and cheap." When the weather allows, people take part in club outing events such as "trips to the rock gym [and] trips to Boston or New York City." Others generally "just enjoy the sunshine or go apple picking in the fall or find somewhere to go for a hike."

Student Body

This is a "very intellectually driven" group that still manages to be "continually supportive of other students" and is "incredibly open-minded and accepting." The environment at Mount Holyoke "[makes] it clear that being an institution full of bright, ambitious thinkers does not mean that this environment has to be a cutthroat one." There is a "large international population as well as LGBTQ presence" (Mount Holyoke "is easily one of the best colleges out there for trans, non-binary, and gender nonconforming folks") and the school is "very successful in embracing diversity in many contexts." Thanks to the makeup of the student body, students here are "exposed to different cultures and viewpoints," are "very much dedicated to sustainability," and "love debates and learning new things." "Being unique and quirky is welcomed, if not encouraged," and almost everyone is "very liberal" and values "relaxation and engagement with the world." Most here join a "wide variety of clubs" but still make time "to join … student government meetings or local political protests."

MOUNT HOLYOKE COLLEGE

Financial Aid: 413-538-2291 • E-Mail: admission@mtholyoke.edu • Website: www.mtholyoke.edu

THE PRINCETON REVIEW SAYS

Admissions

Very important factors considered include: rigor of secondary school record, academic GPA, application essay, recommendation(s). *Important factors considered include:* class rank, interview, extracurricular activities, talent/ability, character/personal qualities, volunteer work. *Other factors considered include:* standardized test scores, first generation, alumni/ae relation, geographical residence, racial/ethnic status, level of applicant's interest. ACT with or without writing accepted. SAT with or without Essay component accepted. High school diploma is required and GED is accepted. *Academic units recommended:* 4 English, 3 math, 3 science, 3 science labs, 3 foreign language, 3 history, 1 academic elective.

Financial Aid

Students should submit: CSS/Financial Aid PROFILE; FAFSA; Noncustodial PROFILE. Priority filing deadline is 2/1. The Princeton Review suggests that all financial aid forms be submitted as soon as possible after October 1. *Need-based scholarships/grants offered:* College/university scholarship or grant aid from institutional funds; Federal Pell; Private scholarships; SEOG; State scholarships/grants. *Loan aid offered:* Direct PLUS loans; Direct Subsidized Stafford Loans; Direct Unsubsidized Stafford Loans. Applicants will be notified of awards on or about 4/1. Federal Work-Study Program available. Institutional employment available.

The Inside Word

Competition to gain admission to Mount Holyoke is tight but there are no defined cut-offs or scores; therefore, a strong academic record is a must. Transcripts are evaluated first for performance over time, and candidates should have taken a rigorous course load, complete with honors, AP, and/or IB classes. The college also values strong writing skills, so expect essays/personal statements and short answers to be closely assessed. While interviews are not required they are strongly recommended. Standardized tests are optional, but homeschooled and other students who feel that their application may need more traditional measurements are encouraged to submit scores.

THE SCHOOL SAYS "..."

From the Admissions Office

"The majority of students who choose Mount Holyoke do so because it is an outstanding research liberal arts college. After a semester or two, they start to appreciate the distinctive advantages of a women's college, even though most never thought they'd attend a women's college when they started their college search. They appreciate the remarkable array of opportunities that are available—for academic achievement, career exploration, internships, study abroad, and leadership—and the impressive, creative accomplishments of their peers. If you're looking for a college that will challenge you to be your best, most powerful self and to fulfill your potential, Mount Holyoke should be at the top of your list.

"Submission of standardized test scores is optional for most applicants to Mount Holyoke College. However, the TOEFL is required of students whose primary language is not English, and the SAT Subject Tests are required for home-schooled students."

SELECTIVITY

Admissions Rating	94
# of applicants	3,908
% of applicants accepted	38
% of acceptees attending	33
# offered a place on the wait list	769
% accepting a place on wait list	57
% admitted from wait list	13
# of early decision applicants	397
% accepted early decision	57

FRESHMAN PROFILE

Range SAT EBRW	630–720
Range SAT Math	640–770
Range SAT Composite	1320–1450
Range ACT Composite	27–32
# submitting SAT scores	247
% submitting SAT scores	50
# submitting ACT scores	134
% submitting ACT scores	27
Average HS GPA	3.8
% graduated top 10% of class	52
% graduated top 25% of class	82
% graduated top 50% of class	97

DEADLINES

Early decision	
Deadline	11/15
Notification	1/1
Other ED Deadline	1/1
Other ED Notification	2/1
Regular	
Deadline	1/15
Notification	4/1
Nonfall registration?	Yes

APPLICANTS ALSO LOOK AT AND OFTEN PREFER

Brown University; Barnard College; University of California—Berkeley; Amherst College

AND SOMETIMES PREFER

Skidmore College; Clark University; Northeastern University; Brandeis University; Bryn Mawr College; Vassar College; Wellesley College; Wesleyan University; Smith College; New York University

AND RARELY PREFER

University of Massachusetts Amherst; Fordham University; Simmons University; University of Vermont; Boston University

FINANCIAL FACTS

Financial Aid Rating	97
Annual tuition	$52,040
Room and board	$15,320
Required fees	$218
Books and supplies	$2,000
Average frosh need-based scholarship	$40,492
Average UG need-based scholarship	$37,322
% needy frosh rec. need-based scholarship or grant aid	98
% needy UG rec. need-based scholarship or grant aid	100
% needy frosh rec. non-need-based scholarship or grant aid	16
% needy UG rec. non-need-based scholarship or grant aid	15
% needy frosh rec. need-based self-help aid	84
% needy UG rec. need-based self-help aid	87
% frosh rec. any financial aid	73
% UG rec. any financial aid	74
% UG borrow to pay for school	67
Average cumulative indebtedness	$25,811
% frosh need fully met	100
% ugrads need fully met	100
Average % of frosh need met	100
Average % of ugrad need met	100

MUHLENBERG COLLEGE

2400 West Chew Street, Allentown, PA 18104-5596 • Admissions: 484-664-3200 • Fax: 484-664-3032

CAMPUS LIFE

Quality of Life Rating	**90**
Fire Safety Rating	**97**
Green Rating	**95**
Type of school	Private
Affiliation	Lutheran
Environment	City

STUDENTS

Total undergrad enrollment	2,190
% male/female	39/61
% from out of state	73
% frosh from public high school	69
% frosh live on campus	97
% ugrads live on campus	91
# of fraternities (% ugrad men join)	3 (15)
# of sororities (% ugrad women join)	5 (18)
% African American	4
% Asian	3
% Caucasian	74
% Hispanic	9
% Native American	<1
% Pacific Islander	0
% Two or more races	2
% Race and/or ethnicity unknown	4
% international	3
# of countries represented	20

SURVEY SAYS . . .

Students are happy
Lab facilities are great
Class discussions encouraged
Students are friendly
Students are very religious
Great food on campus
Easy to get around campus
Recreation facilities are great
Theater is popular

ACADEMICS

Academic Rating	**87**
% students returning for sophomore year	88
% students graduating within 4 years	81
% students graduating within 6 years	85
Calendar	Semester
Student/faculty ratio	9:1
Profs interesting rating	91
Profs accessible rating	95

Most classes have 10–19 students.
Most lab/discussion sessions have
10–19 students.

MOST POPULAR MAJORS

Psychology, General; Drama and Dramatics/
Theatre Arts, General; Business/Commerce,
General

STUDENTS SAY "..."

Academics

Students who attend Muhlenberg College in Allentown, Pennsylvania are welcomed into a "close-knit" community and are privy to "a well-rounded liberal arts education." And while the academics are certainly "rigorous," undergraduates here love the fact it's "[not] a cutthroat atmosphere." Importantly, students have their pick of many terrific disciplines, from the "amazing theater department" to the "extremely strong" business and science programs. Undergrads are also happy to champion their "dedicated" professors who understand how to create and foster "engaging courses." They also value the fact that Muhlenberg instructors "really take the time to get to know you and answer your questions." As one satisfied student interjects, "My professors so far have all been amazing and truly want me to succeed." Finally, as an international studies and Spanish double major sums up, "Muhlenberg is a place where someone can pursue theater AND chemistry, play a varsity sport AND lead a volunteer organization, work individually with a professor AND befriend a dining services worker."

Life

It's quite easy to lead a full and fulfilling life at Muhlenberg. To begin with, the "school offers tons of free activities over the weekends, from movie showings to Stuff-A-Plush." Undergrads here also love to take advantage of the college's strong performing arts scene. Indeed, "a cappella groups are very popular at Muhlenberg." Additionally, given "the large theater department," it's virtually guaranteed that "there's always a show in production." Sports are equally popular and we're told that "football and basketball games have good attendance records." While there's a modest amount of drinking, the college doesn't have a crazy party scene. As a biology major shares, "There's a few bars and clubs in the area that offer college nights on Thursdays which is fun. Every now and then the fraternities will host parties. A lot of people frequent the sports houses' parties on the weekends. But a lot of people also just chill and watch a movie." From time to time, the school hosts theme parties "like flapper-era zombies or a speakeasy (with a live jazz band!)" as well. Lastly, undergrads enjoy Allentown's public parks which provide "great areas to hike, explore, bird-watch, read or take a jog." And they periodically capitalize on Muhlenberg's relatively close proximity to both Philadelphia and New York.

Student Body

Strolling around the Muhlenberg campus, you'll probably pass by a number of students who are "white, upper-middle class [and] from New Jersey." Thankfully, though that might seem to define the typical undergrad here, there's much more to these students. Indeed, many individuals assert that their peers are extremely "hardworking" and "friendly." A French and education double-major explains, "Most people are involved with many different aspects of campus life, and these aspects tend not to be 'cliquey' because of the crossover. For example, there are many football players who are members of a cappella groups or who take dance." Importantly, we're also told that "being nice is kind of important" at Muhlenberg. An English major somewhat sarcastically qualifies, "If someone doesn't hold the door open for the person behind them, they're basically made to wear a scarlet letter and deemed a pariah." And, finally, a biology major sums up his peers by stating, "There is a place for everyone on campus. We have a huge theater program, yet almost 30 percent of our school participates in athletics, so you can see there are all extremes and everything in between."

Financial Aid: 484-664-3175 • E-Mail: admissions@muhlenberg.edu • Website: www.muhlenberg.edu

THE PRINCETON REVIEW SAYS

Admissions

Very important factors considered include: rigor of secondary school record, academic GPA, character/personal qualities. *Important factors considered include:* application essay, standardized test scores (if submitted), recommendation(s), interview, extracurricular activities, talent/ability, volunteer work. *Other factors considered include:* class rank, first generation, alumni/ae relation, geographical residence, racial/ethnic status, level of applicant's interest. ACT with or without writing accepted. SAT with or without Essay component accepted. High school diploma is required and GED is accepted. *Academic units required:* 4 English, 3 math, 2 science, 2 science labs, 2 foreign language, 2 history, 1 academic elective. *Academic units recommended:* 4 English, 4 math, 3 science, 3 science labs, 4 foreign language, 2 social studies, 2 history, 1 academic elective.

Financial Aid

Students should submit: FAFSA; Institution's own financial aid form; Noncustodial PROFILE. Priority filing deadline is 2/1. The Princeton Review suggests that all financial aid forms be submitted as soon as possible after October 1. *Need-based scholarships/grants offered:* College/university scholarship or grant aid from institutional funds; Federal Pell; Private scholarships; SEOG; State scholarships/grants; United Negro College Fund. *Loan aid offered:* Federal Direct Parent Loan (PLUS) and Federal Direct Student Loan (Subsidized and unsubsidized). Applicants will be notified of awards on or about 3/15. Federal Work-Study Program available. Institutional employment available.

The Inside Word

Admissions officers at Muhlenberg endeavor to get a strong sense of each candidate. After all, they are on the hunt for students who will thrive at and complement the college. Of course, that being said, academic records are of primary concern. And a strong performance in college prep courses is a must. Applicants wary of standardized tests rejoice; submission of ACT or SAT scores is optional here. Individual interviews are required for academic partnership programs (UPenn Dental and SUNY Optometry), however we highly recommend interviews for all applicants so that we may get a strong sense of each candidate.

THE SCHOOL SAYS "..."

From the Admissions Office

"Listening to our own students, we've learned that most picked Muhlenberg mainly because it has a long-standing reputation for being academically demanding on one hand but personally supportive on the other. We expect a lot from our students, but we also expect a lot from ourselves in providing the challenge and support they need to stretch, grow, and succeed. It's not unusual for professors to put their cell numbers on the course syllabus and encourage students to call them with questions. Upperclassmen are helpful to underclassmen. 'We really know about collegiality here,' says an alumna who now works at Muhlenberg. 'It's that kind of place.' The supportive atmosphere and strong work ethic produce lots of successes. The pre-med and pre-law programs are very strong, as are programs in theatre arts, English, psychology, the sciences, business, and accounting. 'When I was a student here,' recalls Dr. Walter Loy, now a professor emeritus of physics, 'we were encouraged to live life to its fullest, to do our best, to be honest, to deal openly with others, and to treat everyone as an individual. Those are important things, and they haven't changed at Muhlenberg.'"

SELECTIVITY

Admissions Rating	86
# of applicants	4,224
% of applicants accepted	66
% of acceptees attending	19
# offered a place on the wait list	497
% accepting a place on wait list	37
% admitted from wait list	22
# of early decision applicants	261
% accepted early decision	84

FRESHMAN PROFILE

Range SAT EBRW	580–680
Range SAT Math	570–660
Range SAT Composite	1170–1340
Range ACT Composite	26–31
# submitting SAT scores	353
% submitting SAT scores	66
# submitting ACT scores	146
% submitting ACT scores	27
Average HS GPA	3.4
% graduated top 10% of class	35
% graduated top 25% of class	72
% graduated top 50% of class	95

DEADLINES

Early decision	
Deadline	11/15
Notification	12/15
Other ED Deadline	2/1
Other ED Notification	2/15
Regular	
Deadline	2/1
Notification	3/15
Nonfall registration?	Yes

APPLICANTS ALSO LOOK AT AND OFTEN PREFER

Gettysburg College; Lafayette College; Brandeis University; State University of New York—Binghamton University

AND SOMETIMES PREFER

Dickinson College; Ithaca College; Skidmore College; American University; Rutgers University—New Brunswick; University of Delaware; University of Pittsburgh—Pittsburgh Campus; The College of New Jersey; Fordham University; Franklin and Marshall College

AND RARELY PREFER

Pace University

FINANCIAL FACTS

Financial Aid Rating	87
Annual tuition	$55,915
Room and board	$12,560
Required fees	$750
Books and supplies	$1400
Average frosh need-based scholarship	$38,254
Average UG need-based scholarship	$36,591
% needy frosh rec. need-based scholarship or grant aid	100
% needy UG rec. need-based scholarship or grant aid	98
% needy frosh rec. non-need-based scholarship or grant aid	15
% needy UG rec. non-need-based scholarship or grant aid	15
% needy frosh rec. need-based self-help aid	78
% needy UG rec. need-based self-help aid	75
% frosh rec. any financial aid	100
% UG rec. any financial aid	92
% UG borrow to pay for school	60
Average cumulative indebtedness	$29,609
% frosh need fully met	20
% ugrads need fully met	19
Average % of frosh need met	87
Average % of ugrad need met	84

NAZARETH COLLEGE

4245 East Avenue, Rochester, NY 14618-3790 • Admissions: 585-389-2860 • Fax: 585-389-2826

STUDENTS SAY ". . ."

Academics

Nazareth College's classic 150-acre campus in the Rochester suburbs houses a "small private school with a large amount of spirit and a grand amount of heart." Nazareth (affectionately nicknamed "Naz") boasts sixty majors, including strong programs in nursing, music, and physical therapy, and the opportunity to pursue a variety of different discourses, whether or not it's part of your official field of study. Classrooms are filled with "an array of professors that come from both theory backgrounds and real-world experience backgrounds." The class sizes are very small and intimate, so "you get to know your professor very well and feel more open to ask questions and share your ideas," and most classes are based around discussion. The school encourages interdisciplinary exploration and tries to structure courses that connect "different fields of study to benefit the students' interests and allow them to pursue fields which would typically not accept differing opinions."

The faculty is "by far one of the best strengths of Nazareth College." "Anyone who has been at Naz can attest to the caring and personable faculty and staff," says a student. These "interesting, insightful, and approachable" professors "want to see every student succeed" and "make time to see students outside of the classroom if they need extra help," fostering "a positive self-image to learn and achieve in all of their students." "They bring a passion to the classroom that makes it fun to learn the material," raves a student, and they "encourage research and encourage using outside sources for additional learning." Peckham Hall, the new science building, has "beautiful labs" for biology and chemistry, and Nazareth has "great internship and clinical experiences as we get into our later years of school." The Health Sciences Department is also well known for its top-notch facilities that allow students to run pro-bono clinics right on campus.

Life

The Nazareth College campus is "beautiful," and there are underground tunnels connecting most of the buildings, so students "hardly ever [have] to go outside in the cold or rain." Rochester is only ten minutes away and the malls and restaurants of hometown Pittsford are also popular jaunts (plus, don't forget "Wegmans!"). People here have "enormously strong community engagement" with the surrounding area, and the majority of students have jobs or participate in community service. Though most weekdays are spent at the library, "there is plenty of time for fun if you plan accordingly."

Students fill their days with "classes, on-campus jobs, clubs, intramurals, sports, [and] studying," and there are "endless activities and events that are available to students to network, learn, and grow as an individual." Campus can become inactive on the weekends, as most people leave, but during the week "Naz always has activities offered, whether that be Motivation Monday donuts and coffee, Winter Wonderland, Spring Fest, or Friday movie nights." There are also "$5 ticket deals with free transportation to major events like NHL games, Duke and Syracuse basketball games, Broadway shows, and much more," and traditional Naz events like "Grocery Bingo, Trivia Night, Family Weekend, Siblings Weekend, Movie Nights, and other random activities like glow-in-the-dark Capture the Flag, roller skating, and Late-Night-Bites."

Student Body

Since Nazareth College is a smaller school (enrollment is just over 2,100 students), "there is always a familiar face around the corner," and students are "extremely outgoing and sociable." A relatively large international contingent (as well as a conversation program that pairs international students with American ones to learn about the culture) aids in creating a student body that is "very open-minded and open to new ideas." Current students report that a high female-to-male ratio is noticeable, many of the people here are from either the Rochester or Syracuse area, and there are huge factions of musicians, dancers, and occupational/physical therapy students.

NAZARETH COLLEGE

Financial Aid: 585-389-2310 • E-Mail: admissions@naz.edu • Website: www.naz.edu

THE PRINCETON REVIEW SAYS

Admissions

Very important factors considered include: rigor of secondary school record, class rank, academic GPA, application essay, recommendation(s). *Important factors considered include:* interview, extracurricular activities, talent/ability, character/personal qualities, geographical residence, state residency, racial/ethnic status, volunteer work. *Other factors considered include:* standardized test scores, first generation, alumni/ae relation. ACT with or without writing accepted. SAT with or without Essay component accepted. High school diploma is required and GED is accepted. *Academic units required:* 3 English, 3 math, 3 science, 3 foreign language, 3 social studies. *Academic units recommended:* 4 English, 4 math, 4 science, 4 foreign language, 4 social studies.

Financial Aid

Students should submit: FAFSA; State aid form. Priority filing deadline is 2/15. The Princeton Review suggests that all financial aid forms be submitted as soon as possible after October 1. *Need-based scholarships/grants offered:* College/university scholarship or grant aid from institutional funds; Federal Pell; Private scholarships; SEOG; State scholarships/grants. *Loan aid offered:* Direct PLUS loans; Direct Subsidized Stafford Loans; Direct Unsubsidized Stafford Loans. Applicants will be notified of awards on a rolling basis beginning 2/1. Federal Work-Study Program available. Institutional employment available.

The Inside Word

Students with good test scores shouldn't sweat too much over getting accepted here. Admissions officers review each applicant's Common Application, high school transcript, recommendations, and essay. Standardized test scores are optional. Art, music, and theatre programs require additional application materials.

THE SCHOOL SAYS "..."

From the Admissions Office

"Preparing students for a changing world and careers yet to be defined is the focus at Nazareth. In addition to relevant knowledge, graduates achieve exceptional critical thinking skills and a global mindset. Working with career coaches in the Center for Life's work, real work experience is part of the curriculum that prepares students for their future.

"Nazareth offers sixty majors, including education, math and sciences, health and human services programs, business and management, visual and performing arts, humanities, and foreign languages.

"Expect high caliber, small classes, personal attention, friendliness, and nationally recognized community service programs. The uncommon core curriculum is student-focused and integrated with career goals. Global dexterity is promoted through coursework, foreign-language houses, cultural events, a diverse campus community, and numerous opportunities to travel, study, and intern overseas. Nazareth is noted for its Fulbright scholars, selected to teach around the world, and its commitment to developing student leaders.

"Nazareth is coeducational and independent, located on 150 beautiful acres in a suburb of Rochester, New York's third-largest city. New construction includes cutting-edge lab facilities in Peckham Hall Integrated Center for Math and Science, York Wellness and Rehabilitation Institute with extensive collaborative clinic spaces, and the Glazer Music Performance Center. Students attend free theatre, music, dance, and international performances at the Arts Center.

"The Golisano Athletic Training Center opened in fall 2019 to support campus fitness and develop a unique partnership with the Special Olympics. Nazareth supports 27 athletic teams and has one of the highest graduation rates in NCAA Division III."

SELECTIVITY

Admissions Rating	85
# of applicants	4,273
% of applicants accepted	64
% of acceptees attending	20
# offered a place on the wait list	486
% accepting a place on wait list	1
% admitted from wait list	20
# of early decision applicants	408
% accepted early decision	88

FRESHMAN PROFILE

Range SAT EBRW	550–630
Range SAT Math	540–640
Range ACT Composite	23–28
# submitting SAT scores	393
% submitting SAT scores	72
# submitting ACT scores	192
% submitting ACT scores	35
% graduated top 10% of class	25
% graduated top 25% of class	58
% graduated top 50% of class	88

DEADLINES

Early decision	
Deadline	11/15
Notification	12/15
Other ED Deadline	1/10
Other ED Notification	2/1
Regular	
Priority	12/1
Deadline	2/1
Notification	Rolling, 3/1
Nonfall registration?	Yes

APPLICANTS ALSO LOOK AT AND OFTEN PREFER
Ithaca College; St John Fisher College

AND SOMETIMES PREFER
Hobart and William Smith Colleges; Siena College

FINANCIAL FACTS

Financial Aid Rating	88
Annual tuition	$34,850
Room and board	$14,600
Required fees	$1,805
Books and supplies	$1,000
Average frosh need-based scholarship	$19,557
Average UG need-based scholarship	$18,131
% needy frosh rec. need-based scholarship or grant aid	100
% needy UG rec. need-based scholarship or grant aid	100
% needy frosh rec. non-need-based scholarship or grant aid	51
% needy UG rec. non-need-based scholarship or grant aid	38
% needy frosh rec. need-based self-help aid	92
% needy UG rec. need-based self-help aid	93
% frosh rec. any financial aid	98
% UG rec. any financial aid	96
% UG borrow to pay for school	86
Average cumulative indebtedness	$42,412
% frosh need fully met	42
% ugrads need fully met	34
Average % of frosh need met	85
Average % of ugrad need met	82

NEW COLLEGE OF FLORIDA

5800 Bay Shore Rd, Sarasota, FL 34243-2109 • Admissions: 941-487-5000 • Fax: 941-487-5001

STUDENTS SAY ". . ."

Academics

New College of Florida, a uniquely small and unconventional public institution, "provides challenging courses for highly self-motivated students who want a large amount of control over their academic choices." It's all about "self-directed learning" here (working closely with faculty advisers, "the student decides what he or she is going to learn and how she is going to learn it"). Those who can balance the intellectual freedom New College offers with the academic accountability it demands, wind up with "a rounded education that enables them to critically and pragmatically examine and understand the world in which we live." The academics "are undeniably awesome" at New College, while the small-school setting and the student body "encourage a love of learning, whether it be academic, political, or hobby-related." It's the sort of school where "it is very popular for groups of students to get together to talk about class readings outside of the classroom, usually at the college coffee shop, as a means of socializing." New College undergrads receive "narrative evaluations instead of grades. These evaluations give advice and help us to become better students." Many here "love having written evaluations in which our process and progress are documented, not only the final outcome. The evaluations force students to fully participate and the professors to pay close attention." All students must write a senior thesis to graduate; reports one undergrad, "recently we had a survey…on which one of the sections dealt with the possibility of making the senior thesis optional. There was an overwhelming response that this was unacceptable. I think that says a lot about how proud we are of our academic standards."

Life

Having fun "in a glorified retirement community requires ingenuity of the New College student population," but "thankfully, most grew up in suburban Florida" and so are used to a slower pace. It helps that the campus is near Lido and Siesta Beaches, "where [students] enjoy unlimited swimming, sunning, and Frisbee playing," and that "downtown Sarasota isn't that bad either," since it's home to a number of "ethnic eateries. Thai food, in particular, seems to have a cult following on campus—with constant debate as to which restaurant is the best or most authentic and student events that advertise Thai food are bound to pull in dozens of followers." On campus, students enjoy everything "from club meetings to public speakers to 'hip' bands playing shows. There's usually something to do and usually free food to be found!" There are also "school-wide parties…in a courtyard outside of the dorms. Different students get to decide the theme of each dance party and the music to be played. Most on-campus students never leave campus during the weekend because of these dance parties."

Student Body

New College students share "a few things in common: Most…are friendly, passionate about the things they believe in, very hard workers, liberal, and most of all, try to be open to new experiences." Thirty percent of the population are students of color. You'll find that students on campus are "largely…liberal." There are of course exceptions, but the school is rather small and there is "a fairly strong [LGBTQ] community here, and many transgendered people who have decided to make New College their coming-out grounds. The student body is generally aware of gender issues and respectful of {LGBTQ} people of all types."

Financial Aid: 941-487-5000 • E-Mail: admissions@ncf.edu • Website: www.ncf.edu

THE PRINCETON REVIEW SAYS

Admissions

Very important factors considered include: rigor of secondary school record, academic GPA, application essay. *Important factors considered include:* class rank, standardized test scores, recommendation(s), extracurricular activities, character/personal qualities. *Other factors considered include:* talent/ability, first generation, alumni/ae relation, geographical residence, state residency. ACT with or without writing accepted. SAT with or without Essay component accepted. High school diploma is required and GED is accepted. *Academic units required:* 4 English, 4 math, 3 science, 2 science labs, 2 foreign language, 3 social studies, 2 academic electives. *Academic units recommended:* 4 English, 4 math, 4 science, 2 science labs, 4 foreign language, 4 social studies, 4 academic electives.

Financial Aid

Students should submit: FAFSA. Priority filing deadline is 11/1. The Princeton Review suggests that all financial aid forms be submitted as soon as possible after October 1. *Need-based scholarships/grants offered:* College/university scholarship or grant aid from institutional funds; Federal Pell; Private scholarships; SEOG; State scholarships/grants. *Loan aid offered:* Direct PLUS loans; Direct Subsidized Stafford Loans; Direct Unsubsidized Stafford Loans. Applicants will be notified of awards on a rolling basis beginning 2/1. Federal Work-Study Program available. Institutional employment available.

The Inside Word

New College isn't your typical public school. The tiny student body allows admissions officers here to review each application carefully; expect a thorough going over of your essays, recommendations, and extracurricular activities. Freethinking students tend to thrive here, and the admissions staff knows that. Don't be afraid to showcase your individuality; it won't get you in here if your academics aren't top flight, but it certainly won't hurt you either.

THE SCHOOL SAYS "..."

From the Admissions Office

"Deep curiosity, inspired individualism, civic-mindedness, and a dash of quirkiness. New College students collaborate with their professors to build a program of courses, seminars, and independent and group projects to meet their individual needs and interests. The result? A remarkably rigorous and engaging education (with highly affordable tuition). New College students apply theories and methods they learn in the classroom to research and creative work of their own design. While learning to organize and execute large projects, they sharpen their critical thinking—a skillset that serves them well in grad school and the world beyond higher education. The social atmosphere is relaxed and intellectually playful; the campus celebrates creativity, service, and the value of the individual. New College welcomes admitted students to visit "in depth"—arrange to talk and tour, attend a class, perhaps lunch with a current student before making the decision to enroll. Application Materials (November 1 Early Decision Deadline): Common Application (with essay and fee/fee waiver), Self-Reported Student Academic Report (SSAR), recommendation, and SAT or ACT scores. Some Florida public college transfers can have exam scores waived—please inquire. International applicants and applicants with materials from abroad, should inquire about additional materials needed. Financial Aid (November 1 Priority FAFSA Deadline): If you seek need-based grants and/or federal student loans, please complete the Free Application for Federal Student Aid. In addition to packaging need-based aid, the College offers scholarship funding to nearly all of its entering students."

SELECTIVITY

Admissions Rating	83
# of applicants	1,226
% of applicants accepted	73
% of acceptees attending	16
# offered a place on the wait list	3
% accepting a place on wait list	67
% admitted from wait list	50

FRESHMAN PROFILE

Range SAT EBRW	620–700
Range SAT Math	560–660
Range ACT Composite	25–31
# submitting SAT scores	124
% submitting SAT scores	84
# submitting ACT scores	68
% submitting ACT scores	46
Average HS GPA	3.9
% graduated top 10% of class	22
% graduated top 25% of class	50
% graduated top 50% of class	88

DEADLINES

Early decision	
Deadline	11/1
Notification	12/15
Regular	
Priority	11/1
Deadline	4/15
Nonfall registration?	No

FINANCIAL FACTS

Financial Aid Rating	89
Annual in-state tuition	$6,916
Annual out-of-state tuition	$29,944
Room and board	$9,529
Books and supplies	$1,200
Average frosh need-based scholarship	$10,596
Average UG need-based scholarship	$10,530
% needy frosh rec. need-based scholarship or grant aid	96
% needy UG rec. need-based scholarship or grant aid	94
% needy frosh rec. non-need-based scholarship or grant aid	14
% needy UG rec. non-need-based scholarship or grant aid	16
% needy frosh rec. need-based self-help aid	80
% needy UG rec. need-based self-help aid	73
% frosh rec. any financial aid	99
% UG rec. any financial aid	96
% UG borrow to pay for school	42
Average cumulative indebtedness	$18,953
% frosh need fully met	20
% ugrads need fully met	23
Average % of frosh need met	90
Average % of ugrad need met	88

NEW JERSEY INSTITUTE OF TECHNOLOGY

Office of University Admissions, Newark, NJ 07102 • Admissions: 973-596-3300 • Fax: 973-596-3300

CAMPUS LIFE

Quality of Life Rating	**77**
Fire Safety Rating	**99**
Green Rating	**79**
Type of school	Public
Environment	Metropolis

STUDENTS

Total undergrad enrollment	8,126
% male/female	76/24
% from out of state	4
% frosh from public high school	89
% frosh live on campus	48
% ugrads live on campus	23
# of fraternities (% ugrad men join)	18 (5)
# of sororities (% ugrad women join)	6 (5)
% African American	9
% Asian	23
% Caucasian	34
% Hispanic	22
% Native American	<1
% Pacific Islander	0
% Two or more races	3
% Race and/or ethnicity unknown	3
% international	6
# of countries represented	93

SURVEY SAYS . . .

Very little drug use
Different types of students interact
Easy to get around campus

ACADEMICS

Academic Rating	**73**
% students returning for sophomore year	88
% students graduating within 4 years	37
% students graduating within 6 years	67
Calendar	Semester
Student/faculty ratio	16:1
Profs interesting rating	77
Profs accessible rating	84
Most classes have 20–29 students.	

MOST POPULAR MAJORS

Computer and Information Sciences, General; Computer Engineering, General; ENGINEERING/ ENGINEERING-RELATED TECHNOLOGIES/ TECHNICIANS

STUDENTS SAY ". . ."

Academics

New Jersey Institute of Technology provides students with the opportunity to receive a stellar education at an affordable price point. This is especially true considering the college "is incredibly generous with its scholarship money." Undergrads also benefit from "strong academic programs," with lots of individuals emphasizing that for computer science and IT, it is not only "one of the best in the country," but "unique because everyone who graduates from NJIT is technologically literate." This is, perhaps, the result of an all-in approach to certain skills: "Everyone is required to take computing classes, and apply programming skills in their math and science classes." To further prepare students, "the school stresses the importance of teamwork in the field" by introducing a lot of team projects, covering "a great portion of real-world problems," and offering "a vast amount of research opportunities" no matter your major. Some students feel that classes can be "unnecessarily difficult" and that despite being "clearly very knowledgeable," certain instructors have a "lack of compassion" wherein they "just expect students to be able to understand." Others, however, suggest that this is just a matter of motivation, and describe being greeted by professors who are "very eager to give help to students that are not afraid to go and ask."

Life

NJIT features an extremely studious student body, and accordingly, you'll find students hitting the books and working after hours in academic clubs. One student describes creating "a concrete canoe for competition against other schools" in the civil engineering club, while another notes that the solar car race team works to "build and design a car that runs on solar energy." If those pursuits don't sound relaxing to you, note that "many student organizations hold fun events like Puppy Therapy, Movie Nights, and Cookie Decorating throughout the week." Students can also be found taking advantage of the "open gym times for basketball, tennis, and volleyball," or participating in "religious groups as well as art and musical organizations." There's even a popular pub in the campus center that hosts events like karaoke night and casino night which provide "fun with awesome rewards such as tickets, T-shirts and a Nintendo Switch." And of course, students who want to take things at their own, unscheduled pace can simply enjoy the scenery ("The college has some great spaces where you can be alone") or amenities like "nice facilities for recreation after classes, and the Makerspace is a big thing here."

Student Body

NJIT undergrads pride themselves on the being "very focused" and "the most hardworking" individuals. For instance, there's a high commuter population, and on top of that, many "have part-time or even full-time jobs." Cars aside, students are "driven to succeed," a status that some attribute to the decent percentage of "first-generation college students or first-generation Americans." Be aware, though, that students note that "the school is very diverse racially, but the overwhelming majority of students are male." And while NJIT has its fair share of athletes who are "friendly to everyone," there is a bit of a divide between their sports cohorts and the students who have "nerd-like interests in video games and other technological hobbies." Some also assert that the "polytechnic" focus attracts a handful of "very introverted" students who have "little desire for any social activities." The vast majority of peers, however, are described as "very warm and welcoming no matter where you go." Moreover, they're certainly "extroverted when it comes to helping . . . the entire student body excel."

NEW JERSEY INSTITUTE OF TECHNOLOGY

Financial Aid: 973-596-3479 • E-Mail: admissions@njit.edu • Website: www.njit.edu

THE PRINCETON REVIEW SAYS

Admissions

Very important factors considered include: rigor of secondary school record, class rank, standardized test scores. *Important factors considered include:* academic GPA. *Other factors considered include:* application essay, recommendation(s), interview, extracurricular activities, talent/ability, character/personal qualities, alumni/ae relation, geographical residence, state residency, racial/ethnic status, volunteer work, work experience, level of applicant's interest. ACT with or without writing accepted. SAT with or without Essay component accepted. High school diploma is required and GED is accepted. *Academic units required:* 4 English, 4 math, 2 science, 2 science labs. *Academic units recommended:* 2 foreign language, 1 social studies, 1 history, 2 academic electives.

Financial Aid

Students should submit: FAFSA; State aid form. Priority filing deadline is 2/15. The Princeton Review suggests that all financial aid forms be submitted as soon as possible after October 1. *Need-based scholarships/grants offered:* College/university scholarship or grant aid from institutional funds; Federal Pell; Private scholarships; SEOG; State scholarships/ grants. *Loan aid offered:* Direct PLUS loans; Direct Subsidized Stafford Loans; Direct Unsubsidized Stafford Loans. Applicants will be notified of awards on a rolling basis beginning 11/15. Federal Work-Study Program available. Institutional employment available.

The Inside Word

As one of the nation's top public universities, NJIT's admissions process is rather competitive. Admitted students are generally in the top 25% of their class and have a minimum 3.0 GPA. Moreover, admissions officers look for students who like to challenge themselves. Hence applicants who have taken multiple advanced placement or IB courses are at an advantage. Given NJIT's status as a STEM school, you'll need strong grades in your math and sciences classes. Fortunately, the school does take grade trends into consideration.

THE SCHOOL SAYS "..."

From the Admissions Office

"Talented high school graduates from across the nation come to NJIT to prepare for leadership roles in architecture, business, engineering, medical, legal, science, and technological fields. Students experience a public research university conducting over $160 million in research that maintains a small-college atmosphere at a modest cost. Our attractive forty-five-acre campus is just minutes from New York City and less than an hour from the Jersey shore. Students find an outstanding faculty and a safe, diverse, and caring learning and residential community. NJIT's academic environment challenges and prepares students for rewarding careers and full-time advanced study after graduation. The campus is computing-intensive.

"Students applying for admission to NJIT may provide scores from either the SAT or the ACT. SAT Subject Test scores are not required for any major."

SELECTIVITY

Admissions Rating	85
# of applicants	8,201
% of applicants accepted	73
% of acceptees attending	23

FRESHMAN PROFILE

Range SAT EBRW	580–670
Range SAT Math	610–720
Range SAT Composite	1200–1370
Range ACT Composite	24–31
# submitting SAT scores	1,215
% submitting SAT scores	89
# submitting ACT scores	237
% submitting ACT scores	17
Average HS GPA	3.6
% graduated top 10% of class	31
% graduated top 25% of class	57
% graduated top 50% of class	85

DEADLINES

Early action	
Deadline	11/15
Notification	12/15
Regular	
Priority	12/15
Deadline	3/1
Notification	Rolling, 11/15

FINANCIAL FACTS

Financial Aid Rating	83
Annual in-state tuition	$14,448
Annual out-of-state tuition	$30,160
Room and board	$13,900
Required fees	$3,226
Books and supplies	$2,900
Average frosh need-based scholarship	$13,945
Average UG need-based scholarship	$12,341
% needy frosh rec. need-based scholarship or grant aid	95
% needy UG rec. need-based scholarship or grant aid	96
% needy frosh rec. non-need-based scholarship or grant aid	10
% needy UG rec. non-need-based scholarship or grant aid	5
% needy frosh rec. need-based self-help aid	53
% needy UG rec. need-based self-help aid	66
% frosh rec. any financial aid	82
% UG rec. any financial aid	63
% UG borrow to pay for school	58
Average cumulative indebtedness	$38,718
% frosh need fully met	15
% ugrads need fully met	13
Average % of frosh need met	58
Average % of ugrad need met	55

NEW YORK UNIVERSITY

383 Lafayette St., New York, NY 10012 • Admissions: 212-998-4500 • Fax: 212-995-4902

CAMPUS LIFE
Quality of Life Rating	86
Fire Safety Rating	98
Green Rating	96
Type of school	Private
Environment	Metropolis

STUDENTS
Total undergrad enrollment	26,612
% male/female	42/58
% from out of state	67
% frosh live on campus	89
% ugrads live on campus	49
# of fraternities	23
# of sororities	14
% African American	8
% Asian	19
% Caucasian	25
% Hispanic	16
% Native American	<1
% Pacific Islander	<1
% Two or more races	4
% Race and/or ethnicity unknown	5
% international	22
# of countries represented	110

SURVEY SAYS . . .
Internships are widely available
Students love New York, NY
Theater is popular
Active student government
Active student-run political groups

ACADEMICS
Academic Rating	83
% students graduating within 4 years	77
% students graduating within 6 years	85
Calendar	Semester
Student/faculty ratio	9:1
Profs interesting rating	85
Profs accessible rating	86

Most classes have 10–19 students.
Most lab/discussion sessions have
10–19 students.

MOST POPULAR MAJORS
Business/Commerce, General; Liberal Arts and
Sciences/Liberal Studies; Drama and Dramatics/
Theatre Arts, General

STUDENTS SAY "..."

Academics

"Location, location, location" in "the most amazing city on Earth," along with "great facilities" and "top-notch faculty," makes New York University an excellent choice for those seeking "an untraditional college experience" in "a paradise for the independent and motivated." With more than 20,000 students and ten distinct schools offering more than 230 areas of study, NYU "is about diversity. Students are from all over the world; they come from different cultures, and they have different talents and interests. Similarly, NYU offers endless opportunities for students, no matter what their interests or ambitions are." The school offers huge opportunities to participate in research, pursue an internship, or begin a career in the arts (although "you have to be active and willing to find these opportunities"). Given the school's size, many students are "actually quite surprised by the accessibility of both the faculty and administration." Although "this is not the kind of school where students really get to know all of their teachers, as it is unlikely that a student will have a professor more than once," those who make the effort report that "it is so easy to meet with [professors] outside of class, and I still get e-mails from professors about internships, jobs, and scholarship recommendations." Many here also tout the "great study abroad programs."

Life

"Living in New York City is the biggest part of going to school at New York University," NYU students agree. The school's Washington Square campus is located in the heart of Greenwich Village, one of the city's major nightlife destinations, so "there is always something to do at any hour of the day," usually within walking distance of the school. One student reports, "Every weekend there are tons of things to do, both at NYU and in New York City. NYU really takes advantage of its location, so a lot of the programming provided by residence life or the student resource center is engaging you in the city that has become your new home." Living in the Big Apple means that "on any given day you can go to a museum, concert, sporting event, or theater performance...and a lot of the times, NYU will foot the bill if you go to an event in the city with your RA or with a club." The location also provides plenty of internship opportunities, which is good because "the vast majority of students at NYU are interested in interning and finding jobs through that gateway." The school has an atypical campus; it surrounds Washington Square Park, a busy public square where students love to relax when the weather is accommodating.

Student Body

"There is no typical student at NYU," where an undergraduate student body of more than 20,000 and a broad range of academic interests ensure a broad demographic. "Each school at NYU attracts a different group," students tell us. "The Tisch School of the Arts attracts a very out-there group of actors and the like." "Hipsters are pretty pervasive throughout all schools except Stern"—although "every school has people who break those stereotypes. [Even so,] few students can find ways to not fit in because of the huge number of students" at the university. Throughout NYU, "students tend to be incredibly motivated and ambitious." Students insist that "it is also important to note that NYU students are very accepting of each other's differences," an important factor at a school that brings together "students of all different backgrounds, ethnicities, and gender identities and makes them coexist within the university."

Financial Aid: 212-998-4444 • E-Mail: admissions@nyu.edu • Website: www.nyu.edu

THE PRINCETON REVIEW SAYS

Admissions

Very important factors considered include: rigor of secondary school record, class rank, academic GPA, standardized test scores, talent/ability. *Important factors considered include:* application essay, recommendation(s), extracurricular activities, character/personal qualities. *Other factors considered include:* interview, first generation, alumni/ae relation, geographical residence, racial/ethnic status, volunteer work, work experience, level of applicant's interest. ACT with or without writing accepted. SAT with or without Essay component accepted. High school diploma is required and GED is accepted. *Academic units required:* 4 English, 3 math, 3 science, 3 science labs, 3 foreign language, 3 social studies, 3 history. *Academic units recommended:* 4 English, 4 math, 4 science, 4 science labs, 4 foreign language, 4 social studies, 4 history.

Financial Aid

Students should submit: CSS/Financial Aid PROFILE; FAFSA; Noncustodial PROFILE. The Princeton Review suggests that all financial aid forms be submitted as soon as possible after October 1. *Need-based scholarships/grants offered:* College/university scholarship or grant aid from institutional funds; Federal Nursing Scholarships; Federal Pell; Private scholarships; SEOG; State scholarships/grants. *Loan aid offered:* Direct PLUS loans; Direct Subsidized Stafford Loans; Direct Unsubsidized Stafford Loans. Applicants will be notified of awards on or about 4/1. Federal Work-Study Program available. Institutional employment available.

The Inside Word

Undergraduates can apply to more than one of NYU's degree-granting campuses. If you are interested in the New York Campus you must also apply to one of NYU's undergraduate schools and colleges: the College of Arts and Science; the Tandon School of Engineering, the Liberal Studies Program; the Stern School of Business; Meyers College of Nursing; the Gallatin School of Individualized Study; the Silver School of Social Work; the Steinhardt School of Culture, Education, and Human Development; the Tisch School of the Arts; or the School of Professional Studies. This is different from the application process at some universities and obviously requires some forethought. Remember that this is a highly competitive university; if your application doesn't reflect a serious interest in your intended area of study, your chances of gaining admission will be diminished. NYU has a flexible testing policy that includes SAT or ACT, IB, AP, and many international examinations; in some cases an audition or portfolio can be submitted in lieu of standardized testing.

THE SCHOOL SAYS "..."

From the Admissions Office

"NYU is the University without walls. We remove the boundary between your classroom and the real world to open limitless opportunities. That's why NYU has become one of the most influential universities in the world with campuses in 15 major cities across the globe including, New York, Abu Dhabi, Shanghai, London, Madrid, and Washington, D.C. Our expansive global network directly serves our students by allowing a uniquely rich academic experience led by renowned faculty with accolades ranging from the Nobel Prize and MacArthur Genius Grant to Emmy, Oscar, and Grammy Awards. But our community is more than a list of cities and fancy awards. Since our beginning in 1831, we've been champions of diversity, access, and inclusion, creating one of the most diverse student bodies on Earth with no single ethnic majority and students from over 150 countries. NYU is for risk-takers; for the bold, the curious, the innovative, for those that see a problem and find the solution simply because "we have to." For more than 180 years, we have produced some of the brightest minds, ground-breaking research, and most influential people capable of being comfortable anywhere and effective everywhere."

SELECTIVITY

Admissions Rating	97
# of applicants	79,462
% of applicants accepted	16
% of acceptees attending	45
# of early decision applicants	13,842
% accepted early decision	28

FRESHMAN PROFILE

Range SAT EBRW	660–740
Range SAT Math	690–790
Range ACT Composite	30–34
# submitting SAT scores	3,666
% submitting SAT scores	64
# submitting ACT scores	1,621
% submitting ACT scores	28
Average HS GPA	3.7

DEADLINES

Early decision	
Deadline	11/1
Notification	12/15
Other ED Deadline	1/1
Other ED Notification	2/15
Regular	
Deadline	1/1
Notification	4/1
Nonfall registration?	Yes

FINANCIAL FACTS

Financial Aid Rating	76
Annual tuition	$50,684
Room and board	$18,684
Required fees	$2,624
Books and supplies	$752
Average frosh need-based scholarship	$37,080
Average UG need-based scholarship	$32,933
% needy frosh rec. need-based scholarship or grant aid	97
% needy UG rec. need-based scholarship or grant aid	94
% needy frosh rec. non-need-based scholarship or grant aid	5
% needy UG rec. non-need-based scholarship or grant aid	6
% needy frosh rec. need-based self-help aid	78
% needy UG rec. need-based self-help aid	72
% frosh need fully met	12
% ugrads need fully met	12
Average % of frosh need met	71
Average % of ugrad need met	65

NORTH CAROLINA STATE UNIVERSITY

Box 7103, Raleigh, NC 27695 • Admissions: 919-515-2434 • Fax: 919-515-5039

STUDENTS SAY "..."

Academics

The "largest and most diverse" of North Carolina's public university system, NC State provides undergrads with a "high level education" and "great value." The campus rings with a "welcoming, down-to-earth" vibe and "Wolfpack pride" is certainly infectious. Moreover, the university maintains "opportunities to fit every single type of person no matter their interest." Academically, NC State is home to a stellar engineering school that students contend is "the best engineering program in the state of North Carolina." It offers "world-renowned faculty who conduct innovative and cutting edge research in a plethora of scientific fields." Undergrads also like to emphasize the "exceptionally rigorous" design program which is "small and personal." And we'd certainly be remiss if we didn't mention the "fantastic business school" and "great entrepreneurship program" it has developed. Inside the classroom, students find their professors to be "very enthusiastic about what they teach" and appreciate that they truly "challenge you to think." As one satisfied junior adds, "My professors are extremely knowledgeable about the course material and bring in practical demonstrations to bring the lecture to life." And just as important, "professors love to discuss future professional development plans with undergraduate students." All in all, it's highly evident that "professors and TAs here love their jobs." Simply put, "they want you to succeed."

Life

Students proffer that NC State's campus is always abuzz with activity. As one excited senior quickly shares, "There's always something to do for fun—spanking the UNC Tarheels at football, painting the Free Expression Tunnel, stalking American Idol winner Scotty McCreery, and people-watching at the State Fair are just a few examples." Athletics are extremely popular here and it often feels as though "basketball games and football games are almost required [viewing]." And, naturally, these contests are accompanied by "a large tailgate culture." Additionally, the university "sponsors many different programs, ranging from concerts to a movie at the campus cinema every weekend." And there are "quite a few service and community oriented activities that go on around campus, such as Shack-A-Thon for Habitat for Humanity and the Krispy Kreme Challenge for children's hospitals." Students also love to take advantage of the surrounding area. As one freshman tells us, "Hillsborough Street has a lot of fun restaurants to go to when we want to go out and do things. Also, there [are] lots of [places] to go to the movies and shop right outside of campus." Indeed, the "Raleigh-area is full of things to do from concerts, bars, shows, restaurants, museums, malls, etc." As another freshman sums up life at NC State, "The problem isn't finding something to do, it is finding time to do it all [while] manag[ing] to stay on task and put aside time to study."

Student Body

When you first step onto the campus of NC State, "first impressions might make it seem like everyone there is a sorority girl or a frat guy who all wear cowboy boots and come from rural NC." However, "if you look closely [you'll see a] very diverse campus with lots of opportunities." Indeed, you'll find a range from "hipster to farm boy" and everything in between. Of course, no matter the easy or convenient characterization, most undergrads agree that their peers are "welcoming" and "friendly." Students tell us that "fitting in is super easy and getting involved with any of the many programs on campus help[s] with meeting new people and making friends!" And while most students are "devoted to academics," they all still manage to "go out and have fun." Additionally, undergrads say their peers "are service oriented and always think of creative ways to give back." Finally, as one junior reveals, "NCSU is huge, so every person can find a spot—and when you do, you find a family. To me, it doesn't feel like a large school. I see someone I know walking on campus every day. I don't know anyone, particularly those that began their education living on campus, that hasn't found their niche."

NORTH CAROLINA STATE UNIVERSITY

Financial Aid: 919-515-2421 • E-Mail: undergrad-admissions@ncsu.edu • Website: http://www.ncsu.edu/

THE PRINCETON REVIEW SAYS

Admissions

Very important factors considered include: rigor of secondary school record, class rank, academic GPA, standardized test scores. *Other factors considered include:* application essay, recommendation(s), extracurricular activities, talent/ability, character/personal qualities, first generation, alumni/ae relation, geographical residence, state residency, racial/ethnic status, volunteer work, work experience, level of applicant's interest. ACT with or without writing accepted. SAT with or without Essay component accepted. High school diploma is required and GED is accepted. *Academic units required:* 4 English, 4 math, 3 science, 1 science lab, 2 foreign language, 1 social studies, 1 history. *Academic units recommended:* 4 English, 4 math, 3 science, 1 science lab, 2 foreign language, 1 social studies, 1 history.

Financial Aid

Students should submit: FAFSA. Priority filing deadline is 3/1. The Princeton Review suggests that all financial aid forms be submitted as soon as possible after October 1. *Need-based scholarships/grants offered:* College/university scholarship or grant aid from institutional funds; Federal Pell; Private scholarships; SEOG; State scholarships/grants; United Negro College Fund. *Loan aid offered:* Direct PLUS loans; Direct Subsidized Stafford Loans; Direct Unsubsidized Stafford Loans. Applicants will be notified of awards on a rolling basis beginning 4/1. Federal Work-Study Program available. Institutional employment available.

The Inside Word

As one of the nation's top research universities, NC State maintains a competitive admissions process. Successful applicants take a rigorous courseload and often have a B-plus average or better. Admissions officers also closely weigh GPA, class rank and standardized test scores. Extracurricular activities are of secondary importance.

THE SCHOOL SAYS "..."

From the Admissions Office

"Students choose NC State University for its strong and varied academic programs, national reputation for excellence and friendly atmosphere. Consistently rated best value in North Carolina, NC State is located in Raleigh, the capital of the state, and is minutes away from nationally known Research Triangle Park providing access to unlimited internships and co-op opportunities. NC State degrees earn the top return on student investment among North Carolina's public universities, and job recruiters rate our alumni among the top 20 most attractive job candidates in the country. Our students thrive with the benefits of a large school, but love the tight-knit feel of our community. NC State offers more than 100 majors and 120 minors, over 700 clubs and organizations, the opportunity to study abroad and engage in research so students have the opportunity to explore all their interests. Members of the Wolfpack aren't only successful - they're passionate. With 23 Division 1 sports and lifelong traditions, NC State students feel the power of the Pack from the roaring stadiums to the support on campus to the strong network of alumni. Once you're part of the Pack, you're a member for life."

SELECTIVITY

Admissions Rating	**92**
# of applicants	30,995
% of applicants accepted	45
% of acceptees attending	34
# offered a place on the wait list	5,093
% accepting a place on wait list	37
% admitted from wait list	0

FRESHMAN PROFILE

Range SAT EBRW	620–690
Range SAT Math	630–730
Range SAT Composite	1270–1410
Range ACT Composite	27–32
# submitting SAT scores	2,634
% submitting SAT scores	55
# submitting ACT scores	2,169
% submitting ACT scores	45
Average HS GPA	3.8
% graduated top 10% of class	50
% graduated top 25% of class	86
% graduated top 50% of class	99

DEADLINES

Early action	
Deadline	11/1
Notification	1/30
Regular	
Priority	11/1
Deadline	1/15
Notification	Rolling, 3/30
Nonfall registration?	Yes

FINANCIAL FACTS

Financial Aid Rating	**87**
Annual in-state tuition	$6,535
Annual out-of-state tuition	$26,654
Room and board	$11,601
Required fees	$2,566
Books and supplies	$1,082
Average frosh need-based scholarship	$10,812
Average UG need-based scholarship	$10,326
% needy frosh rec. need-based scholarship or grant aid	94
% needy UG rec. need-based scholarship or grant aid	92
% needy frosh rec. non-need-based scholarship or grant aid	18
% needy UG rec. non-need-based scholarship or grant aid	13
% needy frosh rec. need-based self-help aid	69
% needy UG rec. need-based self-help aid	69
% frosh rec. any financial aid	84
% UG rec. any financial aid	75
% UG borrow to pay for school	50
Average cumulative indebtedness	$15,651
% frosh need fully met	23
% ugrads need fully met	21
Average % of frosh need met	76
Average % of ugrad need met	75

NORTHEASTERN UNIVERSITY

360 Huntington Avenue, Boston, MA 02115 • Admissions: 617-373-2200 • Fax: 617-373-8780

STUDENTS SAY "..."

Academics

Founded in 1898, Northeastern University is an old Boston stalwart, but its "globally-minded and career-focused" approach to education is as current as ever. The school's focus on experiential learning is never more apparent than in the co-op programs, which have been around for more than one hundred years. Through the co-op program, students alternate rigorous classes with full-time work in career-related jobs for six months (during which they do not pay tuition and are often paid), providing "an open-minded, explorative environment where real-life work experience...combined with top-level academics to provide the best preparation possible for students post-college." Often, students receive job offers from previous co-op employers upon graduation. "My overall academic experience has been pretty grueling but completely worth it," says one satisfied student of the "strong academics in conjunction with a reasonable and healthy atmosphere."

On top of the "strong academic pipeline to university cultivated co-ops and jobs," students benefit from professors who are "passionate about the subject and about you learning the subject." While students admit that there are a handful of "not-so-great professors," they say "the ones that are great, however, are fabulous." "They always offer help or ways to give you experience, are there for you in and outside the classroom, and are extremely intelligent," a current undergrad explains. Students love how encouraging both the university and the faculty are, pushing students to study abroad, do a dialogue (a Northeastern global/international summer program that focuses on critical current issues), or complete an international co-op—"anything to experience another culture and be fully emerged in it," one student notes. Different majors benefit from unique integration of their programs with co-op learning, and the way that Northeastern "[marries] theory with practicality," no matter the course of study, is a huge benefit to students throughout their post-graduate lives.

Life

There is certainly no lack of activities in which to participate in nearby Boston (there are four T stops on campus), from movie theaters, museums, restaurants, and shopping malls to the Prudential Center and the Charles River, which "provides opportunities for running, walking, biking, [and] kayaking." "Our location means that I can get dumplings in Chinatown, see a show, or attend the Christmas tree lighting without much effort to get off campus," says a student. Weekends are traditionally for city exploring, and weekdays usually are filled with people participating in one of the many clubs the school offers. Plus, Northeastern has "a ton of amazing events and programs on campus that make the campus feel like a community." Students on co-op "tend to have a lot more free time at night and on the weekends, allowing them to get more involved and spend more time with friends." Still, life outside of school is "pretty substantial" for this "extremely social" crowd: Mission Hill is a popular spot for a Friday and Saturday night activities. Greek life is small but "becoming more popular" on campus.

Student Body

Northeastern is "both incredibly diverse as well as being a quintessential New England school." This environment is filled with many people from different backgrounds (including a sizeable international population), and "it's not unusual to hear ten languages in ten minutes walking across campus." People are "motivated and passionate about the issues or projects they care about" and "are implementing and rolling with those ideas." No one here is cookie-cutter in any way, as "everyone has their quirks and qualities that shine through." All are "very supportive and seem to genuinely care about each other," which is useful since the nature of the school requires quite a few independent student decisions and those who go here "quickly have to become an adult and take charge of [their] life."

Financial Aid: 617-373-3190 • E-Mail: admissions@northeastern.edu • Website: www.northeastern.edu

THE PRINCETON REVIEW SAYS

Admissions

Very important factors considered include: rigor of secondary school record, academic GPA, application essay, standardized test scores, recommendation(s). *Important factors considered include:* extracurricular activities, talent/ability, character/personal qualities, volunteer work. *Other factors considered include:* class rank, first generation, geographical residence, racial/ethnic status, level of applicant's interest. ACT with or without writing accepted. SAT with or without Essay component accepted. High school diploma is required and GED is accepted. *Academic units required:* 4 English, 3 math, 3 science, 2 science labs, 2 foreign language, 3 social studies, 2 history. *Academic units recommended:* 4 math, 4 science.

Financial Aid

Students should submit: Business/Farm Supplement; CSS/Financial Aid PROFILE; FAFSA; Noncustodial PROFILE. Priority filing deadline is 2/15. The Princeton Review suggests that all financial aid forms be submitted as soon as possible after October 1. *Need-based scholarships/grants offered:* College/university scholarship or grant aid from institutional funds; Federal Pell; Private scholarships; SEOG; State scholarships/grants. *Loan aid offered:* Direct PLUS loans; Direct Subsidized Stafford Loans; Direct Unsubsidized Stafford Loans. Applicants will be notified of awards on or about 4/1. Federal Work-Study Program available. Institutional employment available.

The Inside Word

Applicants to Northeastern are evaluated based on their secondary school performance, with emphasis given to the difficulty of courses you pursued, and you should go beyond minimum high school graduation requirements to show broad intellectual curiosity. The admission committee recommends having strong standardized test scores. Both the Common Application and the Coalition Application are accepted.

THE SCHOOL SAYS "..."

From the Admissions Office

"There's a certain energy about Northeastern University. It comes from our bright, ambitious students, exhibiting a strong sense of purpose in the classroom and while working or studying abroad. In the heart of Boston—the ultimate college city—and across the globe, Northeastern students challenge themselves intellectually, investigate career options, participate in community service, and graduate both personally and professionally prepared for their future careers and graduate school. A Northeastern education is like no other, integrating rigorous classroom learning with real-world experiences—through opportunities to study, work, research, and serve on seven continents. Our students learn how to apply their knowledge, to solve problems, and to make a difference in the world—before they graduate."

SELECTIVITY

Admissions Rating	97
# of applicants	62,263
% of applicants accepted	18
% of acceptees attending	27
# of early decision applicants	1,478
% accepted early decision	37

FRESHMAN PROFILE

Range SAT EBRW	680–750
Range SAT Math	710–790
Range ACT Composite	32–35
# submitting SAT scores	1,657
% submitting SAT scores	55
# submitting ACT scores	942
% submitting ACT scores	31
% graduated top 10% of class	75
% graduated top 25% of class	93
% graduated top 50% of class	99

DEADLINES

Early decision	
Deadline	11/1
Notification	12/15
Other ED Deadline	1/1
Other ED Notification	2/15
Early action	
Deadline	11/1
Notification	2/1
Regular	
Deadline	1/1
Notification	4/1
Nonfall registration?	Yes

FINANCIAL FACTS

Financial Aid Rating	90
Annual tuition	$52,420
Room and board	$16,930
Required fees	$1,086
Books and supplies	$1,000
Average frosh need-based scholarship	$35,299
Average UG need-based scholarship	$27,457
% needy frosh rec. need-based scholarship or grant aid	99
% needy UG rec. need-based scholarship or grant aid	94
% needy frosh rec. non-need-based scholarship or grant aid	47
% needy UG rec. non-need-based scholarship or grant aid	48
% needy frosh rec. need-based self-help aid	87
% needy UG rec. need-based self-help aid	84
% frosh need fully met	100
% ugrads need fully met	49
Average % of frosh need met	100
Average % of ugrad need met	87

NORTHWESTERN UNIVERSITY

1801 Hinman Ave, Evanston, IL 60204 • Admissions: 847-491-7271

CAMPUS LIFE

Quality of Life Rating	87
Fire Safety Rating	83
Green Rating	94
Type of school	Private
Environment	City

STUDENTS

Total undergrad enrollment	8,319
% male/female	49/51
% from out of state	69
% frosh from public high school	65
% frosh live on campus	100
% ugrads live on campus	60
# of fraternities	17
# of sororities	12
% African American	6
% Asian	18
% Caucasian	44
% Hispanic	12
% Native American	<1
% Pacific Islander	0
% Two or more races	6
% Race and/or ethnicity unknown	3
% international	10
# of countries represented	77

SURVEY SAYS . . .

Internships are widely available
Great financial aid
No one cheats
Recreation facilities are great
Lots of beer drinking
Frats and sororities are popular
Theater is popular
Campus newspaper is popular
Active student government

ACADEMICS

Academic Rating	87
% students returning for sophomore year	98
% students graduating within 4 years	84
% students graduating within 6 years	94
Calendar	Quarter
Student/faculty ratio	6:1
Profs interesting rating	87
Profs accessible rating	92

Most classes have 10–19 students.
Most lab/discussion sessions have
10–19 students.

MOST POPULAR MAJORS

Engineering, General; Economics, General;
Journalism

STUDENTS SAY "..."

Academics

"The strength of the school is its range." Northwestern students agree, vowing their school "has everything": "Intelligent but laid-back students, excel[lence] in academic fields," "great extracurriculars and good parties," "strong [Big Ten] sports spirit," and "so many connections and opportunities during and after graduation." Undergrads here brag of "nationally acclaimed programs for almost anything anyone could be interested in, from engineering to theater to journalism to music," and report "everything is given fairly equal weight. Northwestern students and faculty do not show a considerable bias" toward specific fields. The school accomplishes all this while maintaining a manageable scale. While its relatively small size allows for good student-professor interaction, it has "all the perks" of a big school, including "many opportunities" for research and internships. Be aware, however, "Northwestern is not an easy school. It takes hard work to be average here." If you "learn from your failures quickly and love to learn for the sake of learning rather than the grade," students say it is quite possible to stay afloat and even to excel. Helping matters are numerous resources established by administrators and professors, including tutoring programs such as Northwestern's Gateway Science Workshop. Those who take advantage of these opportunities find the going much easier than those who don't.

Life

There are two distinct sections of the Northwestern campus. The North Campus is where "you can find a party every night of the week," and "the Greek scene is strong." The South Campus, about a one-mile trek from the action to the north, is "more artsy and has minimal partying on weeknights," but is closer to town so "it is easy" to "buy dinner, see a show at the movies, and go shopping. People who live on North Campus have a harder time getting motivated to go into Evanston and tap into all that is offered." As one South Campus resident puts it, "South Campus is nice and quiet in its own way. I enjoy reading and watching movies here, and the quietude is appreciated when study time rolls around. But for more exciting fun, a trip north is a must." Regardless of where students live, extracurriculars are "incredible here. There is a group for every interest, and the groups are amazingly well-managed by students alone. This goes hand-in-hand with how passionate students at Northwestern are about what they love." Many students "are involved in plays, a cappella groups, comedy troupes, and other organizations geared toward the performing arts. Activism is also very popular, with many involved in political groups, human-rights activism, and volunteering." In addition, Northwestern's membership in the Big Ten means students "attend some of the best sporting events in the country." Chicago, of course, "is a wonderful resource. People go into the city for a wide variety of things—daily excursions, jobs, internships, nights out, parties, etc."

Student Body

The typical Northwestern student "was high school class president with a 4.0, swim team captain, and on the chess team." So it makes sense everyone here "is an excellent student who works hard" and "has a leadership position in at least two clubs, plus an on-campus job." Students also tell us "there's [a] great separation between North Campus (think: fraternities, engineering, state school mentality) and South Campus (think: closer to Chicago and its culture, arts and letters, liberal arts school mentality). Students segregate themselves depending on background and interests, and it's rare for these two groups to interact beyond a superficial level." The student body here includes sizeable Jewish, Indian, and East-Asian populations.

Financial Aid: 847-491-7400 • E-Mail: ug-admission@northwestern.edu • Website: www.northwestern.edu

THE PRINCETON REVIEW SAYS

Admissions

Very important factors considered include: rigor of secondary school record, class rank, academic GPA, standardized test scores. *Important factors considered include:* application essay, recommendation(s), extracurricular activities, talent/ability, character/personal qualities. *Other factors considered include:* interview, first generation, alumni/ae relation, racial/ethnic status, volunteer work, work experience, level of applicant's interest. ACT with or without writing accepted. SAT with or without Essay component accepted. High school diploma is required and GED is accepted. *Academic units recommended:* 4 English, 3 math, 2 science, 2 science labs, 2 foreign language, 2 social studies, 2 history, 1 academic elective.

Financial Aid

Students should submit: CSS/Financial Aid PROFILE; FAFSA; Noncustodial PROFILE. Priority filing deadline is 3/1. The Princeton Review suggests that all financial aid forms be submitted as soon as possible after October 1. *Need-based scholarships/grants offered:* College/university scholarship or grant aid from institutional funds; Federal Pell; SEOG; State scholarships/grants. *Loan aid offered:* Direct PLUS loans; Direct Subsidized Stafford Loans; Direct Unsubsidized Stafford Loans. Applicants will be notified of awards on or about 4/15. Federal Work-Study Program available. Institutional employment available.

The Inside Word

Northwestern is among the nation's most expensive undergraduate institutions, a fact that dissuades some qualified students from applying. The school is working to attract more low-income applicants by increasing the number of full scholarships available for students whose family income is less than $45,000. Low-income students who score well on the ACT may receive a letter from the school encouraging them to apply. Even if you don't receive this letter, you should consider applying if you've got the goods—you may be pleasantly surprised by the offer you receive from the financial aid office.

THE SCHOOL SAYS "..."

From the Admissions Office

"Consistent with its dedication to excellence, Northwestern provides both an educational and an extracurricular environment that enables its undergraduate students to become accomplished individuals and informed and responsible citizens. To the students in all its undergraduate schools, Northwestern offers liberal learning and professional education to help them gain the depth of knowledge that will empower them to become leaders in their professions and communities. Furthermore, Northwestern fosters in its students a broad understanding of the world in which we live as well as excellence in the competencies that transcend any particular field of study: writing and oral communication, analytical and creative thinking and expression, and quantitative and qualitative methods of thinking.

"Applicants are required to take the SAT or the ACT with the writing section."

SELECTIVITY

Admissions Rating	99
# of applicants	40,585
% of applicants accepted	9
% of acceptees attending	55
# offered a place on the wait list	3,067
% accepting a place on wait list	69
% admitted from wait list	3
# of early decision applicants	4,399
% accepted early decision	25

FRESHMAN PROFILE

Range SAT EBRW	700–760
Range SAT Math	740–790
Range SAT Composite	1450–1540
Range ACT Composite	33–35
# submitting SAT scores	1,284
% submitting SAT scores	64
# submitting ACT scores	1,070
% submitting ACT scores	53
% graduated top 10% of class	92
% graduated top 50% of class	100

DEADLINES

Early decision	
Deadline	11/1
Notification	12/15
Regular	
Deadline	1/1
Notification	4/1
Nonfall registration?	Yes

FINANCIAL FACTS

Financial Aid Rating	95
Annual tuition	$56,232
Room and board	$17,019
Required fees	$514
Books and supplies	$1,605
Average frosh need-based scholarship	$54,303
Average UG need-based scholarship	$52,629
% needy frosh rec. need-based scholarship or grant aid	98
% needy UG rec. need-based scholarship or grant aid	98
% needy frosh rec. non-need-based scholarship or grant aid	0
% needy UG rec. non-need-based scholarship or grant aid	0
% needy frosh rec. need-based self-help aid	68
% needy UG rec. need-based self-help aid	67
% UG borrow to pay for school	34
Average cumulative indebtedness	$36,350
% frosh need fully met	100
% ugrads need fully met	100
Average % of frosh need met	100
Average % of ugrad need met	100

OBERLIN COLLEGE

101 North Professor Street, Oberlin, OH 44074 • Admissions: 440-775-8411 • Fax: 440-775-6905

STUDENTS SAY "..."

Academics

Oberlin College, a school "for laid-back people who enjoy learning and expanding social norms, allows each and every student to have the undergrad experience for which he or she is looking, all the while challenging the students to change themselves and the world for the better." Oberlin is a place where students "focus on learning for learning's sake rather than making money in a career." As one student explains, "I didn't plan on becoming a scholar when I entered Oberlin.... As fate would have it, I ended up loving my college classes and professors. Now I hope to be a professor of religion." At Oberlin, "academics are very highly valued, but balanced with a strong interest in the arts and a commitment to society." Some might suggest Oberlin puts the "liberal" in "liberal arts," and the school's staunchest supporters agree, stressing the school's emphasis on open-mindedness and the belief that "one person can change the world." Among the school's offerings, "the sciences, English, politics, religion, music, environmental studies, and East-Asian studies are particularly noteworthy." The presence of a prestigious music school imbues the entire campus community. One undergrad writes, "Oberlin's greatest strength is the combination of the college and the conservatory. They are not separated, so students mix with each other all the time." Professors here—the "heart and soul of the school"—are dedicated teachers who "treat you more like collaborators and realize that even with their PhDs, they can learn and grow from you, as well as you from them." They are "excellent instructors and fantastic people" who are "focused on learning instead of deadlines." Undergrads also appreciate "a cooperative learning environment" in which "students bond over studying together for difficult exams."

Life

Life during the week at Oberlin can be "pretty bland," as "almost everyone has to crack the books and study it up." It's not always bland, though. Some here manage to find time for the many "events [going on] each weekend—operas, plays, organ pumps, etc.," or "rally to stage to help the oppressed." Thursday afternoons at Oberlin mean "Classical Thursdays," an event during which "you get free beer [or soda] from the college if you bring a professor to the on-campus pub." Another feature of campus life is "the musical scene, which has its heart in the conservatory. All of the other arts—performing, studio, whatever—are intertwined with the talent in the conservatory." On weekends, "people let loose and drink beer. Not everyone does this every weekend. Some don't do it at all," and "there is absolutely no pressure on those who don't." There are also "tons of student-produced social events like parties, fundraisers, concerts, dances, etc.," keeping students "very connected to each other and to what's going on in the community." Hometown Oberlin "is a small town, and about all there is to do there is go out for pizza or Chinese, see a movie for two or three dollars at the Apollo, or go to the Feve, the bar in town."

Student Body

"If you're a liberal, artsy, indie loner who likes to throw around the phrase 'heteronormative white privilege,'" then Oberlin might be the place for you. "We're like the Island of Misfit Toys, but together we make a great toy chest." "We're all different and unusual, which creates a common bond between students." "Musicians, jocks, science geeks, creative writing majors, straight, bi, questioning, queer, and trans [students]," all have their place here, alongside "straight-edge, international, local, and joker students." Oberlin has a reputation for a left-leaning and active student body. One undergrad observes, "They are less active politically than they would like to think, but still more active than most people elsewhere." Another adds, "Most students are very liberal, but the moderates and (few) Republicans have a fine time of it. Every student has different interests and isn't afraid to talk about them." Some here worry, "Oberlin's student body is becoming more and more mainstream each year."

Oberlin College

Financial Aid: 440-775-8142 • E-Mail: college.admissions@oberlin.edu • Website: www.oberlin.edu

THE PRINCETON REVIEW SAYS

Admissions

Very important factors considered include: rigor of secondary school record, class rank, academic GPA, standardized test scores. *Important factors considered include:* extracurricular activities, talent/ability, character/personal qualities, first generation. *Other factors considered include:* application essay, recommendation(s), interview, alumni/ae relation, racial/ethnic status, volunteer work, work experience, level of applicant's interest. ACT with or without writing accepted. SAT with or without Essay component accepted. High school diploma is required and GED is not accepted *Academic units required:* 4 English, 3 math, 3 science, 3 foreign language, 3 social studies. *Academic units recommended:* 4 science.

Financial Aid

Students should submit: Business/Farm Supplement; CSS/Financial Aid PROFILE; FAFSA; Institution's own financial aid form; Noncustodial PROFILE. Priority filing deadline is 2/1. The Princeton Review suggests that all financial aid forms be submitted as soon as possible after October 1. *Need-based scholarships/grants offered:* College/university scholarship or grant aid from institutional funds; Federal Pell; Private scholarships; SEOG; State scholarships/grants. *Loan aid offered:* Direct PLUS loans; Direct Subsidized Stafford Loans; Direct Unsubsidized Stafford Loans. Applicants will be notified of awards on or about 4/1. Federal Work-Study Program available. Institutional employment available.

The Inside Word

Oberlin's music conservatory is one of the most elite programs in the nation. Aspiring music students should expect stiff competition for one of the 600 available slots. Other applicants won't have a much easier time of it. Oberlin is a highly selective institution that attracts a highly competitive applicant pool. Your personal statement could be the make-or-break factor here.

THE SCHOOL SAYS "..."

From the Admissions Office

"Oberlin College, located in northeast Ohio, is a liberal arts college of intense energy and creativity, built on a foundation of academic, artistic, and musical excellence. The only institution in the United States where a top-ranked liberal arts college and a world-renowned conservatory of music share a seamless student culture and campus, Oberlin also boasts an art museum that is known as one of the best in the country. Noted for its sustainability initiatives and achievements, Oberlin has been recognized as one of the 'greenest' institutions in the USA and continues to challenge itself and its students to find better and more efficient ways to be environmentally responsible. Oberlin's flexible curriculum honors the individual and prepares students to tackle the complex challenges that face our planet and society. In fact, the majority of Oberlin's 2900 students continue on to prestigious fellowships and PhD programs. Oberlin has been on the front lines of changing the world for almost two centuries, often serving as the prototype for progress even in the face of strong resistance, beginning with its admission of students of color in 1835—the first in the nation to adopt this practice as policy. With its longstanding commitments to access, diversity, and inclusion, and with limitless opportunities for scholarly and cultural exploration, Oberlin is the ideal laboratory in which to debate, study, and grow."

SELECTIVITY

Admissions Rating	94
# of applicants	7,762
% of applicants accepted	34
% of acceptees attending	28
# offered a place on the wait list	1,125
% accepting a place on wait list	67
% admitted from wait list	16
# of early decision applicants	505
% accepted early decision	49

FRESHMAN PROFILE

Range SAT EBRW	650–720
Range SAT Math	630–730
Range ACT Composite	28–33
# submitting SAT scores	391
% submitting SAT scores	54
# submitting ACT scores	407
% submitting ACT scores	56
Average HS GPA	3.6
% graduated top 10% of class	58
% graduated top 25% of class	79
% graduated top 50% of class	97

DEADLINES

Early decision	
Deadline	11/15
Notification	12/15
Other ED Deadline	1/2
Other ED Notification	1/15
Regular	
Priority	1/15
Deadline	1/15
Notification	4/1
Nonfall registration?	No

FINANCIAL FACTS

Financial Aid Rating	96
Annual tuition	$55,976
Room and board	$16,826
Required fees	$842
Books and supplies	$930
Average frosh need-based scholarship	$37,998
Average UG need-based scholarship	$38,289
% needy frosh rec. need-based scholarship or grant aid	95
% needy UG rec. need-based scholarship or grant aid	85
% needy frosh rec. non-need-based scholarship or grant aid	82
% needy UG rec. non-need-based scholarship or grant aid	80
% needy frosh rec. need-based self-help aid	88
% needy UG rec. need-based self-help aid	89
% UG borrow to pay for school	42
Average cumulative indebtedness	$29,781
% frosh need fully met	100
% ugrads need fully met	100
Average % of frosh need met	100
Average % of ugrad need met	100

OCCIDENTAL COLLEGE

1600 Campus Road, Los Angeles, CA 90041-3314 • Admissions: 800-825-5262 • Fax: 323-341-4875

STUDENTS SAY "..."

Academics

An "intellectual, accepting, beautiful" liberal arts college in northeast Los Angeles, Occidental is "perfect for hard-working and involved students who not only want to be challenged academically, but also want to be pushed to learn more about the world around them." At this small school, classes are "intellectually stimulating," spearheaded by professors who "encourage critical analysis, ask interesting questions, and allow students to create informed opinions about the subject." The faculty and staff "really encourage students to take a proactive role in their education," giving them the freedom to "experiment with a wide range of courses." A current undergrad enthuses, "I love the interdisciplinary aspect of academics. I can really tailor my coursework to what I am interested in." In the classroom, Oxy professors "find ways to connect the lectures to the real world," and many are "very willing to have students help them with their research," providing valuable hands-on experience to undergraduates. Students further augment their coursework through numerous extracurricular and off-campus opportunities, including study abroad, academic conferences, and the school's popular "UN internship program." "Courses are challenging," but Oxy "professors want to see you succeed," and the favorably low student-to-faculty ratio means "there are plenty of opportunities to get extra help on the tough material." In fact, most professors "go the extra mile to make themselves available" and "are invested in cultivating real relationships with students."

Life

"People are really passionate about their extracurricular activities and internships" at Occidental, where most students are "busy from dawn to dusk, and loving it." Clubs and intramural sports, "from quidditch to women's rugby," are popular across campus, and "Greek life is getting bigger and bigger every year." On campus, "there are frequently guest speakers, dialogues, and workshops," and on the weekends, the school organizes "dances, trivia nights, movie screenings, fashion shows, concerts, food tastings, beer gardens, and many other events." When it comes to parties, the alcohol policy is "strict" (even students of legal age are "forbidden from drinking in their dorms"), so most campus get-togethers are small and subdued. Off campus, "house parties are a huge source of fun on the weekends," as are "music shows, bars, and clubs" in surrounding L.A. When they don't have anything planned, students "listen to and make music, watch movies, have impromptu dance parties, and do wacky things." You can't beat having the "intimacy of a small college with Los Angeles as your backyard," and students love the fact that Oxy is "not isolated from the surrounding community like many other college campuses." In their free time, many take advantage of the Southern California setting to "go to the beach, go shopping in L.A., go out to eat in Eagle Rock, [and] go hiking." "Having a car definitely helps" if you want to explore the surrounding city, though "the school has a 'Bengal Bus' system that provides free rides to areas close to campus."

Students

Oxy students are "well rounded," "socially and politically conscious," and "excited to be at Occidental." Though they take academics seriously, "people at Oxy are concerned with much, much more than their education. They are focused on academically succeeding, sure, but they are also concerned with social issues, identity, meeting new people, having fun, and gathering a variety of other skills to help them succeed in life outside of Oxy." Many note the "overwhelmingly left-wing atmosphere" on campus, admitting that the people and their viewpoints can feel a little "homogeneous" at times. However, "every student at Oxy treats all persons equally, regardless of sexual orientation, gender identity, or religious views," and most are readily "accepting of different opinions." With such a tiny enrollment, it's easy to find "a good niche of close friends at Oxy," and "if you're involved on campus, expect your friend group to continually grow." Despite the rigors of the academic program, "there is a communal desire to help each other succeed."

OCCIDENTAL COLLEGE

Financial Aid: 323-259-2548 • E-Mail: admission@oxy.edu • Website: www.oxy.edu

THE PRINCETON REVIEW SAYS

Admissions

Very important factors considered include: rigor of secondary school record, academic GPA, application essay. *Important factors considered include:* class rank, standardized test scores, recommendation(s), extracurricular activities, character/personal qualities, volunteer work. *Other factors considered include:* interview, talent/ability, first generation, alumni/ae relation, geographical residence, racial/ethnic status, level of applicant's interest. ACT with or without writing accepted. SAT with or without Essay component accepted. High school diploma is required and GED is accepted. *Academic units recommended:* 4 English, 4 math, 3 science, 3 foreign language, 3 social studies.

Financial Aid

Students should submit: CSS/Financial Aid PROFILE; FAFSA; Noncustodial PROFILE; State aid form. Priority filing deadline is 1/10. The Princeton Review suggests that all financial aid forms be submitted as soon as possible after October 1. *Need-based scholarships/grants offered:* College/university scholarship or grant aid from institutional funds; Federal Pell; Private scholarships; SEOG; State scholarships/grants. *Loan aid offered:* Direct PLUS loans; Direct Subsidized Stafford Loans; Direct Unsubsidized Stafford Loans. Applicants will be notified of awards on or about 3/25. Federal Work-Study Program available. Institutional employment available.

The Inside Word

The admissions team at Occidental does not use any minimums or formulas when evaluating an applicant's eligibility for the incoming class. In addition to academic achievement, they place a lot of weight on essays and recommendations in their mission to create a diverse incoming class. A demanding course load in high school is essential for competitive candidates, but successful applicants will also show what makes them unique, from volunteer experiences to artistic talent.

THE SCHOOL SAYS "..."

From the Admissions Office

"Here's what our students tell us:

'The professors have all been just amazing. They're all very willing to coordinate times to meet and discuss how you feel about a class and what you want to get out of it.'

'I realize the caliber of discussion that occurs at Oxy is not easily matched. I've developed very strong relationships with many professors, and that's something I believe is unique to Oxy.'

'The program has been awesome. Whether you want to go to med school or grad school, it's a great experience. The professors really want you to succeed.'

'I've been working with postdoctoral researchers as an undergraduate. It's very rewarding. Oxy challenges me both inside and outside the classroom.'

'Occidental opened my eyes to different beliefs, values, and ideas. Discussions in class are much more interesting, because you consider things you might not have thought about before.'

'Oxy's close-knit community and its size make me feel this is a place I can call home.'

'Oxy instills curiosity and makes students want to go out and learn a subject on their own. I've gotten a broader sense of self and have been able to fulfill my learning goals.'

"Occidental requires all applicants (including international students) to take either the SAT or ACT with the writing component. SAT Subject Tests are recommended but not required."

SELECTIVITY

Admissions Rating	93
# of applicants	7,501
% of applicants accepted	37
% of acceptees attending	20
# offered a place on the wait list	1,057
% accepting a place on wait list	53
% admitted from wait list	4
# of early decision applicants	368
% accepted early decision	49

FRESHMAN PROFILE

Range SAT EBRW	650–730
Range SAT Math	650–750
Range SAT Composite	1320–1450
Range ACT Composite	28–32
# submitting SAT scores	383
% submitting SAT scores	68
# submitting ACT scores	255
% submitting ACT scores	45
Average HS GPA	3.6
% graduated top 10% of class	53
% graduated top 25% of class	87
% graduated top 50% of class	97

DEADLINES

Early decision	
Deadline	11/15
Notification	12/15
Other ED Deadline	1/1
Other ED Notification	2/1
Regular	
Deadline	1/10
Notification	3/25
Nonfall registration?	No

APPLICANTS ALSO LOOK AT AND OFTEN PREFER

University of California, Los Angeles; University of Southern California; University of California—Berkeley; Pomona College

AND SOMETIMES PREFER

Claremont McKenna College; New York University

FINANCIAL FACTS

Financial Aid Rating	97
Annual tuition	$55,980
Room and board	$16,034
Required fees	$596
Books and supplies	$1,240
Average frosh need-based scholarship	$45,568
Average UG need-based scholarship	$43,248
% needy frosh rec. need-based scholarship or grant aid	98
% needy UG rec. need-based scholarship or grant aid	99
% needy frosh rec. non-need-based scholarship or grant aid	54
% needy UG rec. non-need-based scholarship or grant aid	45
% needy frosh rec. need-based self-help aid	82
% needy UG rec. need-based self-help aid	87
% frosh rec. any financial aid	75
% UG rec. any financial aid	74
% UG borrow to pay for school	59
Average cumulative indebtedness	$39,306
% frosh need fully met	98
% ugrads need fully met	99
Average % of frosh need met	100
Average % of ugrad need met	100

OHIO NORTHERN UNIVERSITY

525 South Main Street, Ada, OH 45810 • Admissions: 419-772-2260 • Fax: 419-772-2313

STUDENTS SAY "..."

Academics

Many students are attracted to Ohio Northern University's "prestigious" Raabe College of Pharmacy, a "six-year program" that "is focused on developing the next generation of clinical pharmacists who are well rounded leaders, clinicians, and members of society." But this comprehensive university offers its 2,900 students lots of other outstanding academic options: "The accounting program is highly ranked," "it has a great political science program that has sent many students to graduate school and politics," and "the engineering college is great." An ONU education provides practical applications for knowledge as well as theoretical ones, with a "wonderful incorporation of current events and timeless business principles." Students are also drawn to ONU's "good financial aid" and "varsity sports," with one athlete noting that ONU "was my most affordable option of Division III schools where I could play soccer and receive a quality education." Undergrads feel that their "renowned faculty" "are outstanding and all influential in the field," but also that their "professors are very friendly and down to earth" and that they "are real and treat students like people not as if they are beneath them, so it is easier to understand material." In addition to academic performance, "professors care about the student's well-being and future endeavors" and "they are always available to help." "It's great that even though there are 170-plus senior pharmacy majors, the professors still know my name." ONU's "classes are tough, no doubt about it," but "my overall academic experience has been above and beyond anything I could've expected." As a whole, students call ONU "a top-notch education with a family-like atmosphere that is very conducive for learning and excelling in many disciplines."

Life

ONU's hometown of Ada, OH, is a "small town," but one with "good places to eat and a movie theatre." There's also a "big town," Columbus, ninety minutes away "with a lot of attractions so always something to do if you have the time to drive." "Because we are in a small town, the students bond together to find fun things to do," including D3 athletics and "pick-up sports games," "fraternity house parties and local bars (The Regal Beagle and The Cask Room)," as well as "several university-sponsored events throughout the year." Socializing and academics mix freely: "People love hanging out with each other, especially when they are trying to get things done." Social life can be a "mixed bag" of "students who spend all of their time focused on school" and "a good number of students who enjoy having a good time and hanging out with friends"; still "people here are very relaxed—you do what you want and everyone is fine with you being who you are." "Students usually party on the weekends," but "hard drugs are rare." Dorm life is also popular: "It's easy to have fun in the dorms, especially during winter."

Student Body

As you might expect, "in a small town, students must get along because there are high chances they will see one another again," so at ONU, "everyone is very caring toward each other." The typical ONU student "is committed to academics, to service, and has leadership potential," and students appreciate that "everyone here finds a supportive group of friends." Many students are Midwestern and "some denomination of Christian," with a majority of ONU's population hailing from "in-state, some surrounding states and internationals." Students see themselves as involved and conscientious: ONU students often belong to "several clubs and organizations," are "always willing to help or mentor younger students, and very concerned about academic success." One undergrad offers this bit of advice: "Most students are friends with other people in the same activities that they're involved in, so join something you're interested in and don't be shy!"

OHIO NORTHERN UNIVERSITY

Financial Aid: 419-772-2272 • E-Mail: admissions-ug@onu.edu • Website: www.onu.edu

THE PRINCETON REVIEW SAYS

Admissions

Very important factors considered include: rigor of secondary school record, academic GPA, standardized test scores. *Important factors considered include:* class rank, interview, extracurricular activities. *Other factors considered include:* application essay, recommendation(s), talent/ability, character/personal qualities, first generation, alumni/ae relation, volunteer work, level of applicant's interest. ACT with or without writing accepted. SAT with or without Essay component accepted. High school diploma is required and GED is accepted. *Academic units required:* 4 English, 2 math, 2 science, 2 science labs, 2 social studies, 2 history, 4 academic electives. *Academic units recommended:* 4 English, 4 math, 3 science, 2 science labs, 2 foreign language, 3 social studies, 2 history, 4 academic electives, 1 computer science, 1 visual/performing arts.

Financial Aid

Students should submit: FAFSA. Priority filing deadline is 3/1. The Princeton Review suggests that all financial aid forms be submitted as soon as possible after October 1. *Need-based scholarships/grants offered:* College/university scholarship or grant aid from institutional funds; Federal Pell; Private scholarships; SEOG; State scholarships/grants. *Loan aid offered:* Direct PLUS loans; Direct Subsidized Stafford Loans; Direct Unsubsidized Stafford Loans. Applicants will be notified of awards on a rolling basis beginning 12/1. Federal Work-Study Program available. Institutional employment available.

The Inside Word

ONU's well-regarded pharmacy school is without question the most competitive of the university's programs, and has a Dec. 1 application deadline; Arts & Sciences, Business, and Engineering students may apply on a rolling basis. Strong high school transcripts and standardized test scores will assist any application, and particularly those seeking merit-based financial aid. Applicants are evaluated holistically, so in addition to GPAs and test scores, admissions counselors will also consider high school leadership and community service activities.

THE SCHOOL SAYS "..."

From the Admissions Office

"The purpose of Ohio Northern is to help students develop into self-reliant, mature men and women capable of clear and logical thinking and sensitive to the higher values of truth, beauty, and goodness. ONU selects its student body from among those students possessing characteristics congruent with the institution's objectives. Generally, a student must be prepared to use the resources of the institution to achieve personal and educational goals.

"Students applying for admission are urged to submit scores for the SAT or the ACT with the writing section. The student's best composite scores will be used for scholarship purposes.

"The Office of Admissions highly encourages a campus visit. To schedule a visit, please visit www.onu.edu/admissions/visit_us or call 888-408-4668."

SELECTIVITY

Admissions Rating	83
# of applicants	3,108
% of applicants accepted	69
% of acceptees attending	27

FRESHMAN PROFILE

Range SAT EBRW	480–600
Range SAT Math	530–640
Range ACT Composite	23–28
# submitting SAT scores	116
% submitting SAT scores	20
# submitting ACT scores	538
% submitting ACT scores	92
Average HS GPA	3.6
% graduated top 10% of class	32
% graduated top 25% of class	60
% graduated top 50% of class	85

DEADLINES

Regular	
Priority	12/1
Deadline	8/15
Notification	Rolling, 9/1
Nonfall registration?	Yes

FINANCIAL FACTS

Financial Aid Rating	82
Annual tuition	$32,500
Room and board	$12,040
Required fees	$940
Books and supplies	$1,800
Average frosh need-based scholarship	$25,204
Average UG need-based scholarship	$24,130
% needy frosh rec. need-based scholarship or grant aid	100
% needy UG rec. need-based scholarship or grant aid	100
% needy frosh rec. non-need-based scholarship or grant aid	0
% needy UG rec. non-need-based scholarship or grant aid	0
% needy frosh rec. need-based self-help aid	67
% needy UG rec. need-based self-help aid	72
% UG borrow to pay for school	75
Average cumulative indebtedness	$39,221
% frosh need fully met	26
% ugrads need fully met	24
Average % of frosh need met	26
Average % of ugrad need met	24

THE OHIO STATE UNIVERSITY—COLUMBUS

Student Academic Services Building, Columbus, OH 43210 • Admissions: 614-292-3980 • Fax: 614-292-3980

STUDENTS SAY " . . ."

Academics

Ohio State, one of the Midwest's premier universities, is a school with "strong name-brand recognition." Of course, it also has a massive student population, which makes the "campus feel like its own city." Nevertheless, OSU does an admirable job of "handling the large number of students that attend and creating opportunities for over 40,000 undergraduates." As one impressed student explains, "Every single student feels personally attended to and not [like] a number in the crowd of Buckeyes." Many undergrads here also appreciate that "the college is very research-based, which allows students to fully discover what exactly they want to do, and to also build connections with faculty." And while there are many great academic programs, a number of undergrads specifically highlight the "very strong business school, medical program, and engineering school." Moreover, students generally give high marks to their "friendly and approachable" professors. Though you might encounter a "couple of duds ... depend[ing] on the department," OSU's faculty are usually "very passionate about the material they teach," which even makes for "very interesting general education classes." They're also "more than willing to meet outside of their designated office hours to help a student struggling with course materials or even just to get coffee and chat." Best of all, "they truly seem to have a genuine interest in the students' academic and career success."

Life

OSU students boast that "it's impossible to be bored here" given that the university provides "thousands of opportunities" for extracurricular involvement. For starters, undergrads can participate in "countless intramural or club sport[s]," including volleyball, basketball and rock climbing. "When it's football season, game days are always the best," says a student. They go on to add, "Experiencing the atmosphere of the entire Ohio State campus in one stadium is amazing." Aside from athletics, students can join a number of clubs like "Dungeons and Dragons, ... student leadership, [and even] small [music] ensembles that don't require auditions." Buckeyes also quickly find that "going out on Thursdays, Fridays, and Saturdays is extremely popular, whether [to] the bars or frat parties." Nevertheless, one student assures that "although partying is common, there is absolutely no pressure to partake in any of it." In fact, "there are an abundance of [alternative] options [like] weekly karaoke and trivia." Finally, should you need a breather from all that campus excitement, downtown Columbus is a "great place ... [filled with] art galleries, coffee shops," and "top-notch" restaurants.

Student Body

Undergrads at Ohio State love that their peers come "from quite a range of backgrounds." Indeed, you can just as easily "find yourself meeting an individual from a very remote city in the state ... [as you can] an out of state or international student from places ... you'd think [the school] wouldn't have a reach." Thankfully, no matter where they grew up, these Buckeyes are typically "down-to-earth and have a strong desire to succeed." They also comprise "some of the most spirited fans" you'll ever meet. And while students here "take their academics quite seriously," there's still "a very friendly [and] cooperative atmosphere." As one undergrad shares, "I've never encountered anybody that didn't want to work on ... homework or [study] for an exam due to selfish competitive reasons." Students also greatly appreciate the fact that "there are so many people here that every social group is well represented." For example, "there's a party scene, a big Esports scene, a lot of gym rats, [and] a lot Christian[s] [and representatives from] other religious groups." In other words, rest assured that "there's a place for everyone" at Ohio State.

THE OHIO STATE UNIVERSITY—COLUMBUS

Financial Aid: 614-292-0300 • E-Mail: askabuckeye@osu.edu • Website: www.osu.edu

THE PRINCETON REVIEW SAYS

Admissions

Very important factors considered include: rigor of secondary school record, class rank, academic GPA, standardized test scores. *Important factors considered include:* application essay, extracurricular activities, talent/ability, first generation. *Other factors considered include:* recommendation(s), character/personal qualities, geographical residence, state residency, racial/ethnic status. ACT with or without writing accepted. SAT with or without Essay component accepted. High school diploma is required and GED is accepted. *Academic units required:* 4 English, 3 math, 3 science, 3 science labs, 2 foreign language, 2 social studies, 1 academic elective, 1 visual/performing arts. *Academic units recommended:* 4 English, 4 math, 3 science, 3 science labs, 3 foreign language, 3 social studies, 1 academic elective, 1 visual/performing arts.

Financial Aid

Students should submit: FAFSA. Priority filing deadline is 2/1. The Princeton Review suggests that all financial aid forms be submitted as soon as possible after October 1. *Need-based scholarships/grants offered:* College/university scholarship or grant aid from institutional funds; Federal Pell; Private scholarships; SEOG; State scholarships/grants. *Loan aid offered:* Direct PLUS loans; Direct Subsidized Stafford Loans; Direct Unsubsidized Stafford Loans. Federal Work-Study Program available. Institutional employment available.

The Inside Word

Despite being a huge state university, OSU truly strives to evaluate applications holistically. The school endeavors to build an incoming class filled with intellectually curious individuals who have proven leadership skills. To that end, admissions officers review all academic achievement, paying close attention to whether applicants have challenged themselves with honors, AP, or IB courses. They also consider level of extracurricular involvement, outstanding talent in a particular area, desire to engage with a diverse campus community, and whether a candidate is a first-generation college student.

THE SCHOOL SAYS "..."

From the Admissions Office

"How will you make your mark? More importantly: Where's the best environment to get started? Ohio State has the breadth and depth to take you wherever your goals lead, an environment rich in experiences and unexpected opportunities. It's a leading public institution for research with study abroad programs on every continent. You'll be in contact with world-class faculty, studying in world-class facilities, living in a smart and thriving city. Ohio State students who've made their mark say it's because they went to Ohio State. We're looking to add the best and brightest to make their mark in this year's class. Will it be you?"

SELECTIVITY
Admissions Rating	91
# of applicants	47,703
% of applicants accepted	54
% of acceptees attending	30
# offered a place on the wait list	5,801
% accepting a place on wait list	24
% admitted from wait list	8

FRESHMAN PROFILE
Range SAT EBRW	600–690
Range SAT Math	650–770
Range SAT Composite	1300–1420
Range ACT Composite	28–32
# submitting SAT scores	3,028
% submitting SAT scores	39
# submitting ACT scores	6,005
% submitting ACT scores	78
% graduated top 10% of class	60
% graduated top 25% of class	93
% graduated top 50% of class	99

DEADLINES
Early action	
Deadline	11/1
Notification	1/31
Regular	
Deadline	2/1
Notification	3/31
Nonfall registration?	Yes

APPLICANTS ALSO LOOK AT AND OFTEN PREFER
University of Michigan—Ann Arbor; University of Illinois at Urbana-Champaign

AND SOMETIMES PREFER
University of Cincinnati; Purdue University—West Lafayette; Case Western Reserve University; Penn State University Park; University of Wisconsin-Madison

AND RARELY PREFER
Miami University; Ohio University—Athens; University of Dayton

FINANCIAL FACTS
Financial Aid Rating	85
Annual in-state tuition	$11,084
Annual out-of-state tuition	$32,061
Room and board	$12,708
Books and supplies	$1,082
Average frosh need-based scholarship	$13,174
Average UG need-based scholarship	$12,037
% needy frosh rec. need-based scholarship or grant aid	92
% needy UG rec. need-based scholarship or grant aid	86
% needy frosh rec. non-need-based scholarship or grant aid	8
% needy UG rec. non-need-based scholarship or grant aid	5
% needy frosh rec. need-based self-help aid	70
% needy UG rec. need-based self-help aid	79
% frosh rec. any financial aid	87
% UG rec. any financial aid	76
% UG borrow to pay for school	50
Average cumulative indebtedness	$27,242
% frosh need fully met	29
% ugrads need fully met	23
Average % of frosh need met	74
Average % of ugrad need met	73

OHIO UNIVERSITY—ATHENS

120 Chubb Hall, Athens, OH 45701 • Admissions: 740-593-4100 • Fax: 740-593-0560

STUDENTS SAY "..."

Academics

"Academically, OHIO has something for everyone, from astro-physics to the history of rock and roll," students at this large state-run university boast. And students have an equally wide range of choices when it comes to committing themselves to academics; "You can take advantage of the vast amount of knowledge and resources directly available, or you can forget studies and party," students tell us. Those seeking a challenge will have no trouble finding it here, however; OHIO boasts "a strong engineering faculty," a noteworthy aviation program offered within the university's demanding college of engineering and technology, an "excellent and very selective early childhood education program," and "one of the best journalism schools in the country"—the E.W. Scripps School of Journalism—which offers "frequent opportunities to learn and grow outside the classroom with guest speakers and special events." The Scripps College houses "a great communications school" offering great hands-on experience; one student informs us that "Southeast Ohio depends on our college television and radio station for their news, weather, and high school sports." As at any large university, unassertive students are in danger of getting lost in the crowd, but those who make the effort to seek out faculty and administrators assure us that "the school is very supportive of the students. I have close relationships with multiple professors, and I think that they generally take a strong interest in the students."

Life

"Ohio University has a beautiful campus with lots of character, both in academia and nightlife," students here report. Though most students remain independent, Greek organizations play a role in the life of the campus, providing service to the community and serving as a social catalyst. Some undergraduates note that the school holds true to its "reputation as a party school." One says, "It is never hard to find a party on any given night, whether in the dorms or off campus." One undergrad writes, "A nationwide reputation as a party school is not something I'm proud of," but most accept things as they are, noting that "Ohio University is a school where everyone can find a group of people doing whatever they're particularly interested in," which is to say that partying is hardly the only option here. College athletics are a big draw (especially football, men's basketball, and women's volleyball), as are such annual events as Homecoming, and the school is host to literally hundreds of student clubs and organizations serving interests of every variety. Hometown Athens is a typical small college town with access to a wide variety of outdoor activities. The closest cities of note—Columbus, Ohio, and Charleston, West Virginia—are each about a ninety-minute drive from the OHIO campus.

Student Body

The OHIO student body "is pretty homogenous," with a large contingent of undergrads who are "white, middle- to upper-class, and from Ohio." "We have a small minority population, especially in the undergraduate programs," one student concedes, "but it's easy to interact with other cultures if you seek them out." Students here "try to get involved in community service, especially those involved in Greek life," and they are "generally friendly." One student observes that "students totally devoted to their schoolwork are atypical here." Yet, it should be noted that OHIO students have succeeded in claiming a number of nationally competitive academic awards in recent years, with *The Chronicle of Higher Education* having recognized Ohio University as being among the nation's top producers of U.S. Fulbright Students.

OHIO UNIVERSITY—ATHENS

Financial Aid: 740-593-4141 • E-Mail: admissions@ohio.edu • Website: www.ohio.edu

THE PRINCETON REVIEW SAYS

Admissions

Very important factors considered include: rigor of secondary school record, academic GPA, standardized test scores. *Important factors considered include:* class rank, application essay, first generation. *Other factors considered include:* recommendation(s), interview, extracurricular activities, talent/ability, character/personal qualities, alumni/ae relation, geographical residence, state residency, volunteer work, work experience. ACT with Writing recommended. SAT with Essay component recommended. High school diploma is required and GED is accepted. *Academic units required:* 4 English, 4 math, 3 science, 2 foreign language, 3 social studies, 4 academic electives, 1 unit from above areas or other academic areas. *Academic units recommended:* 1 visual/performing arts.

Financial Aid

Students should submit: FAFSA. The Princeton Review suggests that all financial aid forms be submitted as soon as possible after October 1. *Need-based scholarships/grants offered:* College/university scholarship or grant aid from institutional funds; Federal Pell; Private scholarships; SEOG; State scholarships/grants. *Loan aid offered:* Direct PLUS loans; Direct Subsidized Stafford Loans; Direct Unsubsidized Stafford Loans. Applicants will be notified of awards on or about 2/1. Federal Work-Study Program available. Institutional employment available.

The Inside Word

Admissions requirements vary from school to school at Ohio University. The Honors Tutorial College is most selective (you should be in the top 10 percent of your graduating class and earn at least a 30/1300 on your ACT/SAT for best consideration), followed by the journalism school (top 15 percent, 25/1140), the business college (top 20 percent, 24/1100), media arts and studies, engineering, and visual communication. Admissions decisions are made through holistic review; those on the cusp should get in if they've demonstrated academic improvement during their junior and senior years and show evidence of academic preparation.

THE SCHOOL SAYS "..."

From the Admissions Office

"Ohio University offers a welcoming campus and more than 240 outstanding academic programs. Our dedicated professors do more than just teach—they serve as mentors and advisors who prepare students for success. Ohio University's recently launched initiative, The OHIO Guarantee, may be of particular interest to families facing budgetary challenges: It enables undergraduate students to pay a single "fixed" rate that covers tuition, room and meal plan, and most fees for four years. In addition, Ohio University is home to an Honors Tutorial College that offers high-ability students distinctive, tutorial-based learning opportunities that mirror the instructional model used for centuries at British universities such as Cambridge and Oxford. Students can enhance their educational experiences with adventures beyond the classroom. Education abroad opportunities can range from studying the plays of Shakespeare in London to retail merchandising in China. Students also can participate in meaningful research and internships, community service, and 530 student organizations. OHIO's picturesque campus—among the most beautiful in the nation—features learning communities that create a welcoming environment for first-year students. Friendships are forged as students with diverse backgrounds study, learn, and socialize together. Many students proudly cheer on Ohio University's athletics teams. The Bobcats have garnered consistent national attention in recent years, with the football team earning multiple bowl game experiences and the men's and women's basketball teams excelling in the Mid-American Conference and playing in post-season tournaments. All told, OHIO sponsors 16 varsity sports with success both on the field and in the classroom. Many non-varsity students participate in club and intramural sports or learn to rappel, kayak, or canoe through OHIO's Outdoor Pursuits Program."

SELECTIVITY

Admissions Rating	77
# of applicants	24,179
% of applicants accepted	82
% of acceptees attending	19

FRESHMAN PROFILE

Range SAT EBRW	530–640
Range SAT Math	520–620
Range ACT Composite	21–26
# submitting SAT scores	816
% submitting SAT scores	22
# submitting ACT scores	3,292
% submitting ACT scores	90
Average HS GPA	3.6
% graduated top 10% of class	20
% graduated top 25% of class	47
% graduated top 50% of class	82

DEADLINES

Early action	
Deadline	11/15
Regular	
Priority	12/1
Deadline	2/1
Notification	Rolling, 9/15
Nonfall registration?	Yes

APPLICANTS ALSO LOOK AT AND SOMETIMES PREFER

The Ohio State University—Columbus; Miami University; University of Cincinnati

AND RARELY PREFER

Kent State University- Kent Campus; University of Dayton; University of Akron Wayne College; Bowling Green State University

FINANCIAL FACTS

Financial Aid Rating	79
Annual in-state tuition	$12,612
Annual out-of-state tuition	$22,406
Room and board	$12,172
Books and supplies	$962
Average frosh need-based scholarship	$7,410
Average UG need-based scholarship	$6,791
% needy frosh rec. need-based scholarship or grant aid	93
% needy UG rec. need-based scholarship or grant aid	80
% needy frosh rec. non-need-based scholarship or grant aid	9
% needy UG rec. non-need-based scholarship or grant aid	6
% needy frosh rec. need-based self-help aid	80
% needy UG rec. need-based self-help aid	82
% frosh rec. any financial aid	94
% UG rec. any financial aid	88
% UG borrow to pay for school	66
Average cumulative indebtedness	$28,856
% frosh need fully met	12
% ugrads need fully met	9
Average % of frosh need met	58
Average % of ugrad need met	50

OHIO WESLEYAN UNIVERSITY

61 South Sandusky Street, Delaware, OH 43015 • Admissions: 740-368-3020 • Fax: 740-368-3314

STUDENTS SAY "..."

Academics

To some, Ohio Wesleyan University offers the best of both worlds: the "smaller school" experience of a "liberal arts education" along with the "fantastic financial aid," "scholarship money," and "opportunity to play a collegiate sport" available at a "global" university. OWU offers eighteen different pre-professional majors in areas like pre-medicine and pre-engineering, along with "enriching" programs called out by students in "psychology," "economics," "Black World Studies," and others. In addition, the university facilitates special programs like "the undergraduate research program, SSRP, that allows only Ohio Wesleyan students to work with a professor over the summer," which entrusts undergrads with "a rare opportunity to get paid to do research almost always one-on-one with a PhD, where at any other school you'll be working with lab techs and graduate students." Another crown jewel of the OWU academic experience is the "Theory to Practice opportunities," which challenge students to design their own project applications "for grants through the school that allow you to do your own research [and] travel to gain new experience." Similarly, OWU's "Travel-Learning Courses" create "many opportunities to go abroad" for students with intellectual wanderlust, and with such a global focus, OWU also attracts "many international students" to its Ohio campus. The faculty participates in this global citizenship as well: "The professors are very diverse, like the students here, bringing different perspectives and knowledge to campus." They're also committed to their students, who find that professors are "good at engaging the student in classroom discussions" and "will go out of their way to help you. I have had numerous professors support me in applying for grants, applying for research experiences at other universities, as well as jobs." Students report that "a major benefit of going to a smaller school is that I am on a first-name basis with multiple professors, and even text them if I need help with something," and that they've "had professors stay until 6pm just to make sure I understood a concept." An OWU education also builds a foundation for the future: the university boasts "strong career services," and "OWU alums are very dedicated to helping provide employment to students post-graduation."

Life

OWU's "close knit community" is forged through common-interest bonds: "Most students are nerds/passionate about something. They usually fit in by finding people interested in the same things they are." The prototypical OWU student is "extremely involved in clubs/organizations," but has lots of choices of what to join: there's an "amazing club and Greek Life," "varsity sports," "jobs on campus," and "SLUs (small living units)," described as "intentional communities centered around various mission statements." All of this adds up to a robust "overall community" and "great campus culture" that "make OWU an even better school to attend. The majority of students stay on campus because of the community and friendships that they have formed." That said, a lot of students "go to class and study during the week like its [their] job," "and every night do homework followed by Netflix." "In general, everyone is in study groups during the week and watching movies with friends when free"; then "weekends are spent with friends at a frat, sorority, or sport house." "Drinking does occur, as does drug usage," but "it's not a huge party school," and "many people are devoted strongly to their academics."

Student Body

OWU is populated by enthusiastic joiners of all different stripes, and students love the "very culturally diverse" atmosphere of the school. "I've never met so many people that are religiously and culturally different in a single place. It's amazing!" Because "we only have around 1800 students" and "students and faculty alike push for acceptance of everyone," it's "very easy to make friends in this type of environment." Students extol each other as "friendly and smart," as well as "outgoing, overcommitted in student organizations, and driven," and love that "it is impossible to judge or peg people" because "everyone here is from all over with different backgrounds." At OWU, "everyone fits in somewhere."

OHIO WESLEYAN UNIVERSITY

Financial Aid: 740-368-3050 • E-Mail: owuadmit@owu.edu • Website: www.owu.edu

THE PRINCETON REVIEW SAYS

Admissions

Very important factors considered include: rigor of secondary school record, academic GPA, application essay, recommendation(s), interview, character/personal qualities. *Important factors considered include:* class rank, standardized test scores, extracurricular activities, talent/ability. *Other factors considered include:* first generation, alumni/ae relation, geographical residence, volunteer work, work experience, level of applicant's interest. ACT with or without writing accepted. SAT with or without Essay component accepted. High school diploma is required and GED is accepted. *Academic units required:* 4 English, 3 math, 3 science, 2 foreign language, 3 social studies. *Academic units recommended:* 4 English, 4 math, 4 science, 3 foreign language, 4 social studies.

Financial Aid

Students should submit: FAFSA. Priority filing deadline is 12/1. The Princeton Review suggests that all financial aid forms be submitted as soon as possible after October 1. *Need-based scholarships/grants offered:* College/university scholarship or grant aid from institutional funds; Federal Pell; Private scholarships; SEOG; State scholarships/grants. *Loan aid offered:* Direct PLUS loans; Direct Subsidized Stafford Loans; Direct Unsubsidized Stafford Loans. Federal Work-Study Program available. Institutional employment available.

The Inside Word

For students with a high school GPA of 3.0 or higher at the end of junior year, OWU no longer requires SAT or ACT scores. Students with high scores are certainly advised to submit them, and they may be required for some scholarship and honors programs. Well-roundedness is a must for any serious applicant. OWU offers both Early Decision and Early Admission options.

THE SCHOOL SAYS "..."

From the Admissions Office

"Ohio Wesleyan University is a national liberal arts university with a strong international presence. OWU is distinctive for offering the personal attention of a college with a student-to-faculty ratio of less than 10 to 1, combined with opportunities of a larger university, including more than 90 academic majors.

"Ohio Wesleyan's unique OWU Connection program guides every student to "think big, go global, and get real." The program begins with individual guidance from faculty and advisers to help students find their passion and develop a personalized four-year program that can combine mentored research, travel-learning courses, semester-abroad programs, university-funded Connection grants, interdisciplinary programs, service-learning, creative projects, work in a public-private entrepreneurship center, community and overseas service programs, and internships across the nation. Every student is guaranteed Connection experiences proven to give them real-world experience and help them prepare for the causes, careers, and graduate school opportunities they want to pursue.

"Ohio Wesleyan offers 25 varsity athletic teams, including new programs in men's wrestling and women's rowing. The university boasts a vibrant visual and performing arts program, and OWU's 100-plus clubs and activities include marching band. The residential campus features a variety of living options, from traditional residence halls to themed houses. And new in 2018, OWU students have access to 24/7 dining.

"Applicants may submit the SAT or the ACT. Best scores from either test will be considered in the application review."

SELECTIVITY

Admissions Rating	81
# of applicants	4,705
% of applicants accepted	69
% of acceptees attending	14
# of early decision applicants	77
% accepted early decision	60

FRESHMAN PROFILE

Range SAT EBRW	530–650
Range SAT Math	530–645
Range ACT Composite	22–28
# submitting SAT scores	161
% submitting SAT scores	35
# submitting ACT scores	308
% submitting ACT scores	68
Average HS GPA	3.6
% graduated top 10% of class	25
% graduated top 25% of class	53
% graduated top 50% of class	81

DEADLINES

Early decision	
Deadline	11/15
Notification	11/30
Other ED Deadline	1/15
Other ED Notification	1/30
Early action	
Deadline	12/1
Notification	12/15
Regular	
Priority	1/15
Deadline	3/1
Notification	4/1
Nonfall registration?	Yes

FINANCIAL FACTS

Financial Aid Rating	87
Annual tuition	$46,870
Room and board	$12,800
Required fees	$260
Books and supplies	$1,500
Average frosh need-based scholarship	$33,021
Average UG need-based scholarship	$32,503
% needy frosh rec. need-based scholarship or grant aid	100
% needy UG rec. need-based scholarship or grant aid	100
% needy frosh rec. non-need-based scholarship or grant aid	14
% needy UG rec. non-need-based scholarship or grant aid	15
% needy frosh rec. need-based self-help aid	87
% needy UG rec. need-based self-help aid	85
% UG borrow to pay for school	69
Average cumulative indebtedness	$33,814
% frosh need fully met	17
% ugrads need fully met	18
Average % of frosh need met	78
Average % of ugrad need met	80

OREGON STATE UNIVERSITY

104 Kerr Administration Building, Corvallis, OR 97331-2106 • Admissions: 541-737-4411 • Fax: 541-737-2482

STUDENTS SAY "..."

Academics

Located in Corvallis, Oregon, "one of the safest, smartest, and greenest college towns in the nation," Oregon State University is a "diverse school with a strong presence in the scientific community." The university "strives for equitable education along with a fair opportunity for everyone to get their hands dirty," and a "unique set of classes that can only be found in the Pacific Northwest." According to students, Oregon State "is #1 in the world for forestry and Marine Biology," and the university is one of "only a few" to "receive all the land, sun, sea, and space grants" in the country. An emphasis on sustainability is notable, and other top-notch programs include the engineering, agriculture, food science, and public health programs. The Hatfield Marine Science Center is located about an hour from the main campus and serves as a coastal campus for full-time and part-time students. "The advisors and teachers want you to succeed," says one student. "They are very accommodating and the staff tries to do everything they can to help you." The school offers "great research opportunities," "mentor programs," "access to professors and undergraduate research opportunities," "lab experiences/jobs," and "networking with professors and professionals in the field." Students also praise the administration and faculty's "transparency," led by a "humanitarian president." Academic resources include "study tables, tutoring, or even emotional support such as counselors or the health clinic." Students praise the school's "incredible infrastructure," which offers "research labs, peer education, outreach, ministries, athletics, and other interest groups." There are amazing undergraduate research opportunities that any student can get involved in. Oregon State fuels passions and provides avenues to take passions further. Professors are typically "engaged in their classrooms, and are trying to think of new ways to help their students succeed, especially in the more difficult classes."

Life

"Life is good" on Oregon State's "exceedingly beautiful campus" in "peaceful" Corvalis, a town of about 60,000. No wonder students count the school's geography as a top strength, with "so many different ecosystems within reach: the ocean, deserts, mountains, and rainforests." There's a "huge research forest right outside Corvallis" that boasts "beautiful hiking trails." Adventurers can also take weekend trips to Mary's Peak, "which is especially fun in the snow," or in warm weather, "take a float on the local river." Downtown offers "fun places to shop and eat," and the Saturday Farmer's Market is a "huge draw." A large population of students participate in Greek Life and athletics; among other university sponsored sports clubs, the Equestrian Dressage Team (along with many other equestrian teams) stands out as a unique offering. Students spend time outside of classes volunteering hours at the local Humane Society, rock climbing and slacklining" or "bouldering" at the "indoor rock gym " at Dixon," "playing volleyball," "swimming at the recreational center," or "bowling at the school's bowling alley." Fraternities and sororities "throw great socials" and "the library, MU [Memorial Union] and other public area buildings on campus are always full of students, either studying or socializing." And if the fresh air and socializing doesn't relieve all the stresses of college, OSU offers a wealth of wellness resources, which include "Counseling and Psychological Services, Student Health Services, and the Survivor Advocacy and Resource Center," all which help students to "thrive."

Student Body

Students cite international diversity as a standout aspect of the Oregon State student body. "My field of study contains mostly veteran students, immigrant and first-generation students," one student comments. "Most from places like Chili, Ecuador, or Mexico." There is a "significant number of non-binary gender students and LGBT students." Most are "eager to further sustainability and social justice issues." Another student notes that the school's "location in Northern Oregon gives us a distinct Pacific Northwest feel: the number of hydro flasks and Patagonia gear gives us away." Students are "hardworking," "accepting," and "kind-hearted," "entrepreneurial," and "motivated and passionate learners." A majority of students are "very likely to do a lot of scientific research, even in their first year." Along with a strong sense of "school spirit," students boast "a pretty great party scene."

OREGON STATE UNIVERSITY

Financial Aid: 541-737-2241 • E-Mail: osuadmit@oregonstate.edu • Website: http://oregonstate.edu/

THE PRINCETON REVIEW SAYS

Admissions

Very important factors considered include: academic GPA. *Important factors considered include:* rigor of secondary school record, application essay, talent/ability, character/personal qualities, volunteer work, work experience. *Other factors considered include:* class rank, standardized test scores, recommendation(s), extracurricular activities, level of applicant's interest. ACT with Writing required. SAT with Essay component recommended. High school diploma is required and GED is accepted. *Academic units required:* 4 English, 3 math, 3 science, 2 science labs, 2 foreign language, 3 social studies. *Academic units recommended:* 3 science labs.

Financial Aid

Students should submit: FAFSA. Priority filing deadline is 2/28. The Princeton Review suggests that all financial aid forms be submitted as soon as possible after October 1. *Need-based scholarships/grants offered:* College/university scholarship or grant aid from institutional funds; Federal Pell; Private scholarships; SEOG; State scholarships/grants. *Loan aid offered:* Direct PLUS loans; Direct Subsidized Stafford Loans; Direct Unsubsidized Stafford Loans. Applicants will be notified of awards on a rolling basis beginning 4/1. Federal Work-Study Program available. Institutional employment available.

The Inside Word

Oregon State University duly notes that academic performance and test scores are not the only criteria for admission. A broad range of characteristics and perspectives are taken into consideration during the university's admissions process to determine if prospective students are able to succeed here. OSU wants to understand you as a unique, contributing individual.

THE SCHOOL SAYS "..."

From the Admissions Office

"Since 1868, Oregon State University's mission has been to conduct world-leading research and provide a high quality, relevant and affordable education for the people of Oregon and beyond.

"We are Oregon's leading public research university with two welcoming campuses, 11 colleges, 200 academic programs, and excellent and inspiring faculty committed to the success of each student.

"Oregon State is one of only two universities in the U.S. to have land, sea, space and sun grant designations, and we take seriously our responsibility to serve the people of Oregon, the nation and the world. Our impact resounds around the globe because we are out there, addressing the most pressing challenges and providing discoveries that improve the health and prosperity of society, the economy and our planet.

"We are known for offering some of the top programs in the world, including forestry (No. 2), oceanography (No. 3) and agriculture (No. 13). Nationally, Oregon State is among the nation's academic leaders in robotics, creative writing and innovative on-line learning. In the classroom, in laboratories and in the community, we provide students the opportunities and the tools necessary to succeed, including exposure to innovations in educational technology and access to opportunities for experiential learning and discovery.

"Our students learn by doing. And what students experience at Oregon State University not only shapes their own lives, it prepares them to transform a future that is smarter, healthier, more prosperous and just."

SELECTIVITY

Admissions Rating	80
# of applicants	14,890
% of applicants accepted	81
% of acceptees attending	31

FRESHMAN PROFILE

Range SAT EBRW	540–650
Range SAT Math	540–660
Range ACT Composite	22–28
# submitting SAT scores	2,547
% submitting SAT scores	69
# submitting ACT scores	1,661
% submitting ACT scores	45
Average HS GPA	3.6
% graduated top 10% of class	28
% graduated top 25% of class	58
% graduated top 50% of class	89

DEADLINES

Early action	
Deadline	11/1
Notification	12/15
Regular	
Priority	2/1
Deadline	9/1
Notification	Rolling, 10/15
Nonfall registration?	Yes

APPLICANTS ALSO LOOK AT AND OFTEN PREFER

University of California, Davis; University of Washington

AND SOMETIMES PREFER

University of Oregon; Washington State University; Willamette University

AND RARELY PREFER

Western Oregon University; Portland State University

FINANCIAL FACTS

Financial Aid Rating	82
Annual in-state tuition	$9,390
Annual out-of-state tuition	$28,365
Room and board	$12,855
Books and supplies	$1,200
Average frosh need-based scholarship	$8,662
Average UG need-based scholarship	$7,682
% needy frosh rec. need-based scholarship or grant aid	83
% needy UG rec. need-based scholarship or grant aid	77
% needy frosh rec. non-need-based scholarship or grant aid	3
% needy UG rec. non-need-based scholarship or grant aid	2
% needy frosh rec. need-based self-help aid	96
% needy UG rec. need-based self-help aid	96
% frosh rec. any financial aid	76.3
% UG rec. any financial aid	68.7
% UG borrow to pay for school	56
Average cumulative indebtedness	$28,482
% frosh need fully met	14
% ugrads need fully met	11
Average % of frosh need met	71
Average % of ugrad need met	68

PACE UNIVERSITY

1 Pace Plaza, New York, NY 10038 • Admissions: 212-346-1323 • Fax: 212-346-1040

CAMPUS LIFE

Quality of Life Rating	**83**
Fire Safety Rating	**91**
Green Rating	**81**
Type of school	Private
Environment	Metropolis

STUDENTS

Total undergrad enrollment	8,238
% male/female	38/62
% from out of state	46
% frosh from public high school	75
% frosh live on campus	73
% ugrads live on campus	42
# of fraternities (% ugrad men join)	10 (5)
# of sororities (% ugrad women join)	11 (6)
% African American	10
% Asian	8
% Caucasian	49
% Hispanic	14
% Native American	<1
% Pacific Islander	<1
% Two or more races	4
% Race and/or ethnicity unknown	5
% international	10
# of countries represented	99

SURVEY SAYS . . .

Students love New York, NY
College radio is popular
Theater is popular
Active student government

ACADEMICS

Academic Rating	**74**
% students returning for sophomore year	78
% students graduating within 4 years	42
Calendar	Semester
Student/faculty ratio	14:1
Profs interesting rating	81
Profs accessible rating	85

Most classes have 10–19 students.
Most lab/discussion sessions have 10–19 students.

MOST POPULAR MAJORS

Registered Nursing/Registered Nurse; Accounting; Finance, General

STUDENTS SAY "..."

Academics

Starting from humble beginnings as a one-room accounting school in 1906, Pace University has since grown tremendously. The institution is now comprised of six schools and colleges spread across three campuses in New York City and Westchester County and serves more than 8,700 undergraduates. The unique Pace Path curriculum leans heavily on experiential learning, and the school has one of the largest career experience programs in the New York City metropolitan area, placing around eight thousand students in internships, co-ops, field positions, and clinicals each year. "It is the best place to really amp up your career before you even get into it," says a student. Faculty members "host meet and greets for their respective departments and events with guest speakers from different companies or speakers for relative topics," and there are plenty of "opportunities to network and expand our careers through the resources [Pace] gives us."

Instead of "just lecturing," students explain that professors "grab the students' attention" by "open[ing] the floor to students." They "use a pleasant blend of lecture with anecdotal tales that help [students] get accustomed to the conceptual side of the material," and the majority "are professionals in the field or greatly knowledgeable about it," so much so that "even in the most mundane classes, I still learn something new." There are "great options for classes that can cater one's schedule to any days and times they'd like," and innovative teaching mechanisms such as "a reverse classroom where you take notes and read for homework and then do examples in class." The university also "utilizes technology to their advantage when lecturing students," which allows for advanced learning and understanding of topics." The university itself "listens to what the students want and try their best to fulfill it in the best way possible," and is "always looking for ways to improve our experience here at Pace."

Life

Perks like "Starbucks included on the meal plan [and] flex dollars for local restaurants" are huge boons of urban life at Pace. New York City, where "you cannot get bored," obviously plays a big role in student activities, especially when Pace provides "tickets to awesome events around NYC, like the late night shows," as well as shuttles that help make it even easier to have a night out on the town. And while "most of the fun is outside of college," Pace itself doesn't skimp out on its own "campus events like therapy dogs and wellness week," "pumpkin smash in the fall and bubble soccer games in the spring," and "a multitude of clubs and campus wide activities to appeal to almost every interest." According to those in the know, "it's up to the individual on how active or inactive they want their lifestyle to be," and from the sounds of things, most "have full time jobs or internships."

Student Body

In this "very open community that is also accepting of everyone," students "are very creative and expressive" and the wide variety of schools means "there are individuals with different talents and interests, which is great for collaborations and interactions." Lest you think it's difficult to make connections because there are so many students—"I see a new face almost every day," says one undergrad—know that the First Year Interest Group is there for you. This program, which groups first-years by commonalities, leads us to believe that "It is especially easy for freshmen to make friends." There is "a large LGBTQ+ community and every single student is supportive of it," and "there is always positive energy radiating." Most of the students "are very liberal and they like to create a safe environment for everyone there."

PACE UNIVERSITY

Financial Aid: 212-346-1309 • E-Mail: undergradadmission@pace.edu • Website: www.pace.edu

THE PRINCETON REVIEW SAYS

Admissions

Very important factors considered include: rigor of secondary school record, application essay, standardized test scores. *Important factors considered include:* class rank, academic GPA, recommendation(s). *Other factors considered include:* interview, extracurricular activities, talent/ability, character/personal qualities, alumni/ae relation, volunteer work, work experience. ACT with or without writing accepted. SAT with or without Essay component accepted. High school diploma is required and GED is accepted. *Academic units required:* 4 English, 3 math, 2 science labs, 2 foreign language, 3 history, 2 academic electives.

Financial Aid

Students should submit: FAFSA. Priority filing deadline is 11/1. The Princeton Review suggests that all financial aid forms be submitted as soon as possible after October 1. *Need-based scholarships/grants offered:* College/university scholarship or grant aid from institutional funds; Federal Nursing Scholarships; Federal Pell; Private scholarships; SEOG; State scholarships/grants. *Loan aid offered:* Direct PLUS loans; Direct Subsidized Stafford Loans; Direct Unsubsidized Stafford Loans. Applicants will be notified of awards on a rolling basis beginning 12/1. Federal Work-Study Program available. Institutional employment available.

The Inside Word

Certainly, gaining admission to Pace is competitive. But you can take comfort in knowing that the university takes a holistic approach when reviewing candidates. Therefore, it's important not to slack on any facet of your application. When choosing teachers and mentors for your letters of recommendation, make sure they can really speak to your character and academic potential. Finally, we should note that auditions and/or interviews are required for any student who wants to enroll in the School of Performing Arts.

SELECTIVITY
Admissions Rating	76
# of applicants	22,411
% of applicants accepted	79
% of acceptees attending	11
# of early decision applicants	93
% accepted early decision	65

FRESHMAN PROFILE
Range SAT EBRW	530–620
Range SAT Math	520–610
Range ACT Composite	21–27
# submitting SAT scores	1,613
% submitting SAT scores	83
# submitting ACT scores	419
% submitting ACT scores	22

DEADLINES
Early decision	
Deadline	11/1
Notification	12/1
Early action	
Deadline	11/1
Notification	12/1
Regular	
Priority	2/15
Nonfall registration?	Yes

FINANCIAL FACTS
Financial Aid Rating	85
Annual tuition	$44,714
Room and board	$20,018
Required fees	$1,732
Books and supplies	$800
Average frosh need-based scholarship	$31,381
Average UG need-based scholarship	$29,960
% needy frosh rec. need-based scholarship or grant aid	100
% needy UG rec. need-based scholarship or grant aid	99
% needy frosh rec. non-need-based scholarship or grant aid	15
% needy UG rec. non-need-based scholarship or grant aid	13
% needy frosh rec. need-based self-help aid	75
% needy UG rec. need-based self-help aid	76
% frosh rec. any financial aid	98
% UG rec. any financial aid	94
% UG borrow to pay for school	64
Average cumulative indebtedness	$36,797
% frosh need fully met	17
% ugrads need fully met	17
Average % of frosh need met	74
Average % of ugrad need met	72

PENN STATE UNIVERSITY PARK

201 Shields Building, University Park, PA 16802 • Admissions: 814-865-5471 • Fax: 814-863-7590

CAMPUS LIFE
Quality of Life Rating	93
Fire Safety Rating	98
Green Rating	92
Type of school	Public
Environment	Town

STUDENTS
Total undergrad enrollment	40,385
% male/female	53/47
% from out of state	34
% ugrads live on campus	36
# of fraternities (% ugrad men join)	44 (17)
# of sororities (% ugrad women join)	47 (20)
% African American	4
% Asian	6
% Caucasian	65
% Hispanic	7
% Native American	<1
% Pacific Islander	<1
% Two or more races	3
% Race and/or ethnicity unknown	2
% international	12
# of countries represented	105

SURVEY SAYS . . .
Students are happy
Classroom facilities are great
Lab facilities are great
Great library
Career services are great
Internships are widely available
School is well run
Students are friendly
Students get along with local community
Great off-campus food
Recreation facilities are great
Lots of beer drinking
Hard liquor is popular
Everyone loves the Nittany Lions
Intramural sports are popular
Campus newspaper is popular
Alumni active on campus

ACADEMICS
Academic Rating	82
% students returning for sophomore year	94
% students graduating within 4 years	68
% students graduating within 6 years	86
Calendar	Semester
Student/faculty ratio	14:1
Profs interesting rating	87
Profs accessible rating	92

Most classes have 20–29 students.
Most lab/discussion sessions have
20–29 students.

MOST POPULAR MAJORS
Computer and Information Sciences, General;
Engineering, General

STUDENTS SAY ". . ."

Academics
Immense "pride and a sense of community" pervade every aspect of life at Penn State. Students love the remarkable "school spirit" and "strong family feel" on this vibrant campus, and they are equally proud of the "quality education" they receive. An affordable public institution, PSU offers "highly regarded programs across a wide range of academic colleges," including a "prestigious undergrad business school," top engineering and education majors, and the competitive Schreyer Honors College, which participants describe as "the finest honors program in the nation." "Classes freshman year are mostly lectures," which can be "intimidating" for new students. Fortunately, "even in lectures with hundreds of students, many professors still make an effort to get to know their class and have plenty of office hours to make themselves more accessible." Plus, the academic experience becomes more individualized as you move through the system. A current student shares, "As I have gotten into my majors, my classes are down to about fifteen to forty people and there are a lot more discussions. I know all of my professors personally now." Academics are often described as "rigorous" and "competitive," but most students are able to stay afloat; here, "professors will challenge you, but it's nothing that a hard-working student can't handle." Job-seeking seniors praise the career center, as well as the school's fantastic alumni connections, saying, "The Penn State networking web is incredible!" Not to mention, the school's enviable "location within driving distance to Philadelphia, Washington, and New York" makes it easier to score a job at graduation.

Life
If you are looking for the "full college experience," you'll find "the perfect mix of great academics, social life, and sports" at Penn State. While "the library is usually filled with students" during the week, "everyone counts down the days till the weekend, then its party, party, party." Throughout fall semester, football is a campus-wide obsession; "game days are super exciting and unifying for the student population," which turns out in large numbers to tailgate and cheer at Beaver Stadium. In addition to sports, "Greek Life dominates the social scene," though students also flock to the many bars in downtown State College. A current student jokes, "Nothing brings the Penn State community together like stumbling around downtown with 3,000 other drunken students." Those looking for a mellower night out will find "on-campus concerts, stand-up comedians, craft nights, sporting events, and other ways of having fun without drugs or alcohol." Others like to "go out to the local avenue and try new eateries, and walk around campus and enjoy the scenery." In addition to the "killer social life," there are hundreds of clubs and student groups; of particular note, many students "fit in by joining THON, the largest student-run philanthropy in the world, that raises money for children with pediatric cancer." No matter what your interests, "between football games, Late Nights at the HUB, festivities downtown, movies, shows at Eisenhower Auditorium or the Penn State Theatre, concerts at the BJC…there is something for everyone."

Student Body
With a total enrollment of more than 45,000, "Penn State is the passion and pride of a large and diverse student body." Demographically, the school draws heavily from the Northeast; in particular, there are "lots of kids from the tri-state area," and most could be described as "athletic, suburban, and friendly middle-class." While some note that "the percentage of minorities and foreign students is low," they also say, "pretty much every student will find somewhere to fit in." Especially during the first year, "there are many opportunities to meet new people," and almost "everyone is friendly," making it easy to form bonds and build relationships. The best way to make friends is to "try different clubs and find your niche"; from Greek organizations to sports, most Penn Staters have "a great enthusiasm for extracurricular and philanthropic involvement." On that note, most undergrads "take their education seriously," but achieve a "good balance of school and social life."

PENN STATE UNIVERSITY PARK

Financial Aid: 814-865-6301 • E-Mail: admissions@psu.edu • Website: www.psu.edu

THE PRINCETON REVIEW SAYS

Admissions

Very important factors considered include: academic GPA, standardized test scores. *Important factors considered include:* rigor of secondary school record. *Other factors considered include:* class rank, application essay, extracurricular activities, talent/ability, character/personal qualities, alumni/ae relation, geographical residence, state residency, racial/ethnic status, volunteer work, work experience. ACT with or without writing accepted. SAT with or without Essay component accepted. High school diploma is required and GED is accepted. *Academic units required:* 4 English, 3 math, 3 science, 2 foreign language, 3 social studies. *Academic units recommended:* 3 foreign language.

Financial Aid

Students should submit: FAFSA. Priority filing deadline is 2/15. The Princeton Review suggests that all financial aid forms be submitted as soon as possible after October 1. *Need-based scholarships/grants offered:* College/university scholarship or grant aid from institutional funds; Federal Pell; Private scholarships; SEOG; State scholarships/grants; United Negro College Fund. *Loan aid offered:* Direct PLUS loans; Direct Subsidized Stafford Loans; Direct Unsubsidized Stafford Loans. Federal Work-Study Program available. Institutional employment available.

The Inside Word

Though the school does not have any minimum requirements for an incoming student's GPA or standardized test scores, high school GPA is by far the most important factor in PSU admissions. According to the school's website, high school grades account for two-thirds of the final admissions decision. Other factors, like standardized test scores, make up the remaining third. PSU is a popular choice for Pennsylvania residents and admits on a rolling basis; prospective students should submit their applications as early as possible.

THE SCHOOL SAYS "..."

From the Admissions Office

"Founded in 1855, Penn State is a world-class public research university with a broad mission of teaching, research and public service. Ranked as one of the world's top universities, Penn State serves a total of nearly 100,000 students through its 24 campuses, which include a medical college, two law schools, an online World Campus and a school of graduate professional studies. As Pennsylvania's sole land-grant institution, Penn State educates nearly 100,000 students each year in more than 160 undergraduate and more than 160 graduate degree programs.

"Ranging in size from 600 to 4,000 students, most of Penn State's residential and commuter locations offer the first two years of baccalaureate instruction as well as a limited number of two- and four-year degree programs. These small-college settings focus on the needs of new students by offering smaller classes and close interaction with faculty. More than half of the undergraduates who complete their studies at University Park start at another Penn State campus.

"Applicants are qualified for review for any of Penn State's campuses, with preferences considered in the order requested. Choice of location and entrance difficulty are based, in part, on demand. Due to its popularity, the University Park campus is the most competitive for admission. Freshman applicants may submit the results from the SAT or the ACT with the writing component.

"Visit http://www.psu.edu for more information."

SELECTIVITY

Admissions Rating	89
# of applicants	71,903
% of applicants accepted	49
% of acceptees attending	24
# offered a place on the wait list	4,651
% accepting a place on wait list	63
% admitted from wait list	40

FRESHMAN PROFILE

Range SAT EBRW	580–670
Range SAT Math	580–700
Range ACT Composite	25–30
# submitting SAT scores	6,466
% submitting SAT scores	78
# submitting ACT scores	1,434
% submitting ACT scores	17

DEADLINES

Early action	
Deadline	11/1
Notification	12/24
Regular	
Notification	Rolling, 10/1
Nonfall registration?	Yes

FINANCIAL FACTS

Financial Aid Rating	80
Annual in-state tuition	$17,416
Annual out-of-state tuition	$34,480
Room and board	$11,884
Required fees	$1,034
Books and supplies	$1,840
Average frosh need-based scholarship	$6,517
Average UG need-based scholarship	$6,755
% needy frosh rec. need-based scholarship or grant aid	34
% needy UG rec. need-based scholarship or grant aid	45
% needy frosh rec. non-need-based scholarship or grant aid	55
% needy UG rec. non-need-based scholarship or grant aid	55
% needy frosh rec. need-based self-help aid	71
% needy UG rec. need-based self-help aid	76
% frosh rec. any financial aid	63
% UG rec. any financial aid	62
% UG borrow to pay for school	52
Average cumulative indebtedness	$40,128
% frosh need fully met	31
% ugrads need fully met	30
Average % of frosh need met	64
Average % of ugrad need met	64

PEPPERDINE UNIVERSITY

24255 Pacific Coast Highway, Malibu, CA 90263 • Admissions: 310-506-4392 • Fax: 310-506-4861

STUDENTS SAY "..."

Academics

Pepperdine University is a Christian liberal arts school situated in picturesque Malibu, California. Many students say the "professors are the greatest strength of Pepperdine," citing "mentorship [and] research collaboration" opportunities thanks to the small classes. Faculty "genuinely care about your individual success, both personally and academically." One student says that it's normal for "them to invite students to their homes for dinner or to host a Bible study group." Professors are lauded as "very passionate" and "successful in their field." Many professors take advantage of Pepperdine's location with "field trips to the beach, lagoon, waste treatment plant, museums, and organizations in Los Angeles." The great scenery doesn't just include California: Pepperdine's "absolutely fantastic" international programs are a draw for many, sending students to destinations like Argentina, Italy, Germany, Switzerland, England, and China. "The Church of Christ mission is prevalent," as all undergrads are required to take three religion courses.

Life

Students take pride in their "academically rigorous and beautiful school." They find Pepperdine's campus to be "drop dead gorgeous" with an "amazing ocean view." Its prime location in Southern California means there are plenty of options for activities outside of the classroom: students "surf, hike, [and visit] museums." Of course, church is prominent here, too. "We are ... allowed to freely incorporate our faith into our education," one student says. The school also features a Convocation Series, although some express concerns about that since it "is required [and] factors into [students'] GPA." They still find other ways to connect with religious communities, though, often "doing [community] service in an off-campus location" with a religious affiliation. Evenings bring "a lot of events on campus either sponsored by clubs, athletics, [or] the student programming board," but one thing undergrads would like to see more of is "school spirit at the athletic games." Pepperdine has a dry campus, so students looking for that kind of nightlife spend "weekends ... [taking] trips into LA [or attending] parties off campus."

Student Body

Pepperdine students rave about their "welcoming," "caring," and "tight-knit" community. "Everyone is genuinely interested in how to make the world better and people take up a real interest in each other," says a student. "Everyone always has a smile on their face" and "in times of crisis the support system is tremendously helpful." "Even though there is a large group of both the left and right," one student says this is "the most open-minded student body." Students find "diverse ... personalities and ideas" but say the school would benefit from attracting more students who don't exactly fit the "Christian, white, conservative," and affluent background. Students are "taught to live life with purpose, service, and leadership." Overall there's a "mix of driven entrepreneurs and chill surfers," and "you have your partiers and then you have the very religious" students.

Financial Aid: 310-506-4301 • E-Mail: admission-seaver@pepperdine.edu • Website: www.pepperdine.edu

THE PRINCETON REVIEW SAYS

Admissions

Very important factors considered include: rigor of secondary school record, academic GPA, application essay, extracurricular activities, talent/ability, character/personal qualities, religious affiliation/commitment. *Important factors considered include:* standardized test scores, recommendation(s), volunteer work. *Other factors considered include:* first generation, alumni/ae relation, racial/ethnic status, work experience. ACT with or without writing accepted. SAT with or without Essay component accepted. High school diploma is required and GED is accepted.

Financial Aid

Students should submit: FAFSA. Priority filing deadline is 2/15. The Princeton Review suggests that all financial aid forms be submitted as soon as possible after October 1. *Need-based scholarships/grants offered:* College/university scholarship or grant aid from institutional funds; Federal Pell; Private scholarships; SEOG; State scholarships/grants; United Negro College Fund. *Loan aid offered:* Direct PLUS loans; Direct Subsidized Stafford Loans; Direct Unsubsidized Stafford Loans. Applicants will be notified of awards on or about 4/5. Federal Work-Study Program available. Institutional employment available.

The Inside Word

Admission to Pepperdine is highly selective. Decisions are made based on a student's academic record, standardized test scores, an academic letter of recommendation, and personal statements. Applicant's demonstrated character and leadership and service experience are also factors. Students affiliated with the Church of Christ are eligible for special Church of Christ scholarships; to be considered, applicants must submit a letter of recommendation from a church leader.

THE SCHOOL SAYS "..."

From the Admissions Office

"Pepperdine's curriculum emphasizes the broad discovery of all disciplines and is at the forefront of holistically developing the next generation of global leaders through rigorous curriculum, faculty mentorship, internship experiences, and tailored research opportunities. With its renowned Malibu campus, facilities throughout California and in Washington, D.C., and international campuses in South America, Europe, and Asia, the University is a point of convergence for scholars, believers, artists, athletes, and innovators. We seek students who show promise of academic achievement at the collegiate level. We also look for students who are committed to serving others and demonstrate the potential of emerging as a leader in our community."

SELECTIVITY

Admissions Rating	93
# of applicants	12,764
% of applicants accepted	32
% of acceptees attending	18
# offered a place on the wait list	1,088
% accepting a place on wait list	58
% admitted from wait list	52

FRESHMAN PROFILE

Range SAT EBRW	610–700
Range SAT Math	620–750
Range SAT Composite	1250–1430
Range ACT Composite	27–32
# submitting SAT scores	502
% submitting SAT scores	69
# submitting ACT scores	298
% submitting ACT scores	41
Average HS GPA	3.7
% graduated top 10% of class	46
% graduated top 25% of class	77
% graduated top 50% of class	97

DEADLINES

Early action	
Deadline	11/1
Notification	1/10
Regular	
Deadline	1/15
Notification	Rolling, 4/1
Nonfall registration?	Yes

FINANCIAL FACTS

Financial Aid Rating	87
Average frosh need-based scholarship	$37,678
Average UG need-based scholarship	$38,089
% needy frosh rec. need-based scholarship or grant aid	100
% needy UG rec. need-based scholarship or grant aid	99
% needy frosh rec. non-need-based scholarship or grant aid	0
% needy UG rec. non-need-based scholarship or grant aid	0
% needy frosh rec. need-based self-help aid	73
% needy UG rec. need-based self-help aid	72
% frosh rec. any financial aid	91
% UG rec. any financial aid	88
% UG borrow to pay for school	52
Average cumulative indebtedness	$34,711
% frosh need fully met	22
% ugrads need fully met	21
Average % of frosh need met	77
Average % of ugrad need met	75

PITZER COLLEGE

1050 North Mills Avenue, Claremont, CA 91711-6101 • Admissions: 909-621-8129 • Fax: 909-621-8770

STUDENTS SAY "..."

Academics

Just outside of Los Angeles, Pitzer College is a "socially responsible and progressive" liberal arts and sciences college with "great academics" and "active students" and that "feels like a second home." Students prize Pitzer's "flexible graduation requirements," especially "the ability to create your own major," and "the options and resources offered throughout the Claremont Consortium," which includes the ability to take classes at any of the other five Claremont Colleges. Because the school is so small, with an enrollment of just under 1,100 undergrads, students feel they belong to a close and caring community: "Pitzer College is basically a year-round summer camp where people go to grow as individuals through liberal arts studies and through relationships that they build." Current students praise the school's "interdisciplinary focus and non-Western centric studies." Furthermore, students say they "love the academic support" they receive at Pitzer, especially the professors, who are "well connected but incredibly caring." "All my professors know me by name," students tell us, "even in introductory courses. [Instructors] all have PhDs from prestigious universities and demonstrate love for teaching." Experiential learning opportunities "[extend] far beyond the classroom to community service projects, the dorms, and abroad," and, because of the school's size, students often get the chance to conduct research with their professors as well. "By my second semester of my first year a professor offered me a research position," one student tells us, which "is typical for many students since class sizes are small, so we get to create intimate relationships and have direct discussions with professors."

Life

Because of the mild southern California climate, Pitzer students can be found "around the pool or in the Grove House" (a student center), as well as enjoying other idyllic locations. "I manage the school garden and care for chickens," one student tells us. "I spend a lot of afternoons just hanging out in the garden doing homework or talking to friends." Weekends are spent taking advantage of the surrounding landscapes by "hiking in the mountains by the school or [driving] into L.A. to shop or go to the beach." Students here are serious about their academics, but they do "study together and mix chatting in with homework." They also take a lot of ownership over how the campus is run: "We sit on hiring committees and our Student Senate has more power than the administration." "Multiple student-run eateries [and] strong student organizations" create a "collaborative atmosphere." On-campus there is "a very active party scene," and "on weekends, [themed] parties are usually hosted by the school." Students "love that Pitzer provides a super progressive environment."

Student Body

While Pitzer's student body contains diverse personalities and backgrounds, in one respect these Sagehens are the same: "Everyone is passionate about something. You won't find a single student who isn't somehow involved on campus outside of the classroom." At Pitzer, "most students tend to lean far left in ideology," and they are generally "outspoken about their views ... but open-minded students of any political ideology should not fear the liberal environment." "I cannot count the number of nights I have stayed up until 2:00 A.M. discussing issues ranging from Middle Eastern politics to growing up in the inner-cities," one student tells us. Students speak highly of one another and judge that their peers "are sincerely pursuing passions that they believe are reflective of themselves, as opposed to doing things for jobs/other forms of external validation." Many students are focused on "social justice" and environmental issues, though some reject the "Pitzer hippy stereotype." More than anything, they seem to agree that Pitzer students are "intellectual, and seeking to use that intellect to do good in the world."

Financial Aid: 909-621-8208 • E-Mail: admission@pitzer.edu • Website: www.pitzer.edu

THE PRINCETON REVIEW SAYS

Admissions

Very important factors considered include: rigor of secondary school record, academic GPA, application essay, character/personal qualities. *Important factors considered include:* recommendation(s), extracurricular activities, talent/ability. *Other factors considered include:* class rank, standardized test scores, interview, first generation, alumni/ae relation, geographical residence, state residency, racial/ethnic status, work experience, level of applicant's interest. ACT with or without writing accepted. SAT with or without Essay component accepted. High school diploma is required and GED is accepted. *Academic units recommended:* 4 English, 3 math, 3 science, 3 foreign language, 3 social studies.

Financial Aid

Students should submit: Business/Farm Supplement; CSS/Financial Aid PROFILE; FAFSA; Institution's own financial aid form; Noncustodial PROFILE; State aid form. Priority filing deadline is 1/1. The Princeton Review suggests that all financial aid forms be submitted as soon as possible after October 1. *Need-based scholarships/grants offered:* College/university scholarship or grant aid from institutional funds; Federal Pell; Private scholarships; SEOG; State scholarships/grants. *Loan aid offered:* Direct PLUS loans; Direct Subsidized Stafford Loans; Direct Unsubsidized Stafford Loans. Applicants will be notified of awards on or about 3/15. Federal Work-Study Program available. Institutional employment available.

The Inside Word

Prospective students will use the Common Application with the addition of a Pitzer Writing Supplement to apply for admission. Use the Writing Supplement to demonstrate not only your writing ability but your passion and creativity. It is the admission office's way to see if you would be a good fit on campus, so get to know the school's values (social responsibility, intercultural understanding, interdisciplinary learning, student engagement, and environmental sustainability), and make sure they are reflected in what you write.

THE SCHOOL SAYS "..."

From the Admissions Office

"Pitzer is about opportunities. It's about possibilities. The students who come here are looking for something different from the usual 'take two courses from column A, two courses from column B, and two courses from column C.' That kind of arbitrary selection doesn't make a satisfying education at Pitzer. So we look for students who want to have an impact on their own education, who want the chief responsibility—with help from their faculty advisors—in designing their own futures.

"Pitzer's admission policy uses a test-optional policy. Students in the top 10 percent of their class or those who have an unweighted academic GPA of 3.5 or higher are not required to submit test scores. Others are allowed to choose from a variety of choices, including standardized tests (i.e., the SAT and ACT with the writing component)."

SELECTIVITY

Admissions Rating	97
# of applicants	3,753
% of applicants accepted	16
% of acceptees attending	43
# offered a place on the wait list	675
% accepting a place on wait list	43
% admitted from wait list	8
# of early decision applicants	381
% accepted early decision	32

FRESHMAN PROFILE

Range SAT EBRW	640–740
Range SAT Math	670–750
Range ACT Composite	29–32
# submitting SAT scores	78
% submitting SAT scores	30
# submitting ACT scores	81
% submitting ACT scores	31
Average HS GPA	3.9
% graduated top 10% of class	63
% graduated top 25% of class	88
% graduated top 50% of class	100

DEADLINES

Early decision	
Deadline	11/15
Notification	12/18
Other ED Deadline	1/1
Other ED Notification	2/12
Regular	
Deadline	1/1
Notification	4/1
Nonfall registration?	No

FINANCIAL FACTS

Financial Aid Rating	97
Annual tuition	$55,734
Room and board	$17,432
Required fees	$284
Books and supplies	$1,000
Average frosh need-based scholarship	$41,042
Average UG need-based scholarship	$43,813
% needy frosh rec. need-based scholarship or grant aid	97
% needy UG rec. need-based scholarship or grant aid	98
% needy frosh rec. non-need-based scholarship or grant aid	2
% needy UG rec. non-need-based scholarship or grant aid	1
% needy frosh rec. need-based self-help aid	92
% needy UG rec. need-based self-help aid	88
% frosh rec. any financial aid	38.5
% UG rec. any financial aid	37
% UG borrow to pay for school	40
Average cumulative indebtedness	$17,848
% frosh need fully met	95
% ugrads need fully met	98
Average % of frosh need met	100
Average % of ugrad need met	100

POMONA COLLEGE

333 N. College Way, Claremont, CA 91711 • Admissions: 909-621-8134 • Fax: 909-621-8952

CAMPUS LIFE
Quality of Life Rating	94
Fire Safety Rating	97
Green Rating	95
Type of school	Private
Environment	Town

STUDENTS
Total undergrad enrollment	1,688
% male/female	47/53
% from out of state	73
% frosh from public high school	54
% frosh live on campus	100
% ugrads live on campus	98
# of fraternities	3
# of sororities	0
% African American	10
% Asian	16
% Caucasian	34
% Hispanic	17
% Native American	<1
% Pacific Islander	<1
% Two or more races	7
% Race and/or ethnicity unknown	4
% international	11
# of countries represented	60

SURVEY SAYS . . .
Lots of liberal students
Classroom facilities are great
Lab facilities are great
Great library
Internships are widely available
School is well run
Great financial aid
No one cheats
Diverse student types interact on campus
Students aren't religious
Students environmentally aware
Great food on campus
Lots of beer drinking
Active minority support groups

ACADEMICS
Academic Rating	94
% students returning for sophomore year	97
% students graduating within 4 years	89
% students graduating within 6 years	93
Calendar	Semester
Student/faculty ratio	8:1
Profs interesting rating	94
Profs accessible rating	98

Most classes have 10–19 students.
Most lab/discussion sessions have
 10–19 students.

MOST POPULAR MAJORS
Economics; Mathematics; Computer Science

STUDENTS SAY "..."
Academics
At Pomona College in Claremont, you can get "an academically rigorous education" in a "low-stress California atmosphere." At this prestigious liberal arts school, "The professors are, for the most part, fantastic—engaging, creative, and sharp," and "all classes are taught by professors, not grad students or TAs." With small class sizes in every department, "there is an emphasis on collaborative learning," and "many professors are great discussion leaders and really motivate students to get involved in class." Students have the advantage of "getting to know professors outside the classroom, in any setting, from office hours, to Thanksgiving dinner at their homes." Illustrating how personal the experience can be, a student tells us, "Today, I had a class with seven people in it, then lunch with a physics professor, and then a personal tutorial with a philosophy professor." Another student adds, "Between department barbecues, parties, and weekend retreats, by the time you're an upperclassman, you will know most of the professors in your major department quite well." In complement to the intimate academic atmosphere, Pomona "offers the resources of a large university" through The Claremont College consortium, which offers joint events and cross-registration with four adjoining colleges. Among other programs, "Pomona pays for students to take otherwise unpaid internship positions." Students praise Pomona's "efficiency in taking care of administrative tasks such as financial aid and registration," adding that the administration "is very good at responding to what students want."

Life
Pomona students are "ridiculously happy" about their lot in life, and why shouldn't they be? They're living in a "perfect world full of intelligent, engaging, and open individuals, amazing academics, brilliant opportunities to get involved in, and enough sunshine to make anyone happy to be alive." The weather is a key aspect of the experience, and "on a nice day, everyone heads outside in shorts and t-shirts to do their class work." On any given day, "you'll see people setting up telescopes outside the dorms at night to try to get a glimpse of the stars, you'll find people practicing ukulele on our quad, you'll see students filming for a project in the dining halls, [or] you'll see someone riding around campus on a bamboo bike." "Many people are involved in intramural sports," and students love "hiking, skiing, and going to the beach year round." There are many beautiful beaches in the area, and "Joshua Tree is only an hour and a half away, so there are camping trips there just about every weekend." Though the school is small, there are four other undergraduate colleges in the Claremont Consortium, and Pomona students can "take their classes, eat at their dining halls, go to their parties, swim in their pools, and generally share in a great experience." When it's time to blow off steam, "there are large 5C-sponsored parties that people go to and enjoy."

Student Body
At Pomona, only a quarter or so of students are from California, yet the California attitude reigns supreme. Here, you'll find a number of "tree-hugging, rock-climbing, Tom's shoes-wearing" undergraduates, with most students generally falling within the "liberal, upper-middle-class, hipster-athlete" continuum. Students report a "decent level of diversity and a strong international community." Studious and talented, Pomona undergraduates "excel in the classroom and usually have some sort of passion that they pursue outside of the classroom." "Underneath our sundresses and rainbow flip-flops, we're all closet nerds—everybody is really passionate about something or other." At Pomona, "you will meet the football player who got a perfect score on his SAT or the dreadlocked hippie who took multivariable calculus when he was sixteen." Dress code is uniformly casual, and "flip-flops, polo, or tank tops and shorts" are the unofficial uniform.

POMONA COLLEGE

Financial Aid: 909-621-8205 • E-Mail: admissions@pomona.edu • Website: www.pomona.edu

THE PRINCETON REVIEW SAYS

Admissions

Very important factors considered include: rigor of secondary school record, class rank, academic GPA, application essay, standardized test scores, recommendation(s), extracurricular activities, talent/ability, character/personal qualities. *Other factors considered include:* interview, first generation, geographical residence, racial/ethnic status, volunteer work, work experience. ACT with or without writing accepted. SAT with or without Essay component accepted. High school diploma or equivalent is not required. *Academic units required:* 4 English, 3 math, 2 science, 2 science labs, 3 foreign language, 2 social studies. *Academic units recommended:* 4 English, 4 math, 4 science, 3 science labs, 4 foreign language, 4 social studies.

Financial Aid

Students should submit: CSS Profile for primary and seconary households; FAFSA; State aid form. The Princeton Review suggests that all financial aid forms be submitted as soon as possible after October 1. *Need-based scholarships/grants offered:* College/university scholarship or grant aid from institutional funds; Federal Pell Grant; Private scholarships; Federal SEOG Grant; State scholarships/grants. *Loan aid offered:* Direct PLUS loans; Direct Subsidized Stafford Loans; Direct Unsubsidized Stafford Loans. Applicants will be notified of awards on or about 4/1. Federal Work-Study Program available. Institutional employment available.

The Inside Word

For first-year applicants, Pomona College offers regular decision admissions, as well as two binding early decision programs. Admissions officials evaluate a student's academic record carefully, examining the rigor of high school coursework, class rank, and grade point average. Ninety-four percent of Pomona admits rank in the top 10 percent of their class. Students are strongly encouraged to (virtually) visit campus and meet with admissions staff, though it's not required.

THE SCHOOL SAYS "..."

From the Admissions Office

"Pomona College is a place for adventurous, creative students, who have talent and passion and are prepared to dream big and work hard in order to make a difference in the world.

"Pomona students enjoy both the advantages of a small college, where professors teach every class, and the opportunities and resources of a larger university, with more than 6,000 undergraduates at The Claremont Colleges consortium.

"The founding member of The Claremont Colleges, Pomona is one of five adjacent undergraduate colleges and two graduate institutions that make up this unique, Oxford-style consortium. Students may supplement Pomona's extensive curricular offerings with classes at any of the other Claremont Colleges, each no more than a few minutes' walk away.

"Pomona's Southern California location provides its students with exciting opportunities for scientific and community-based research, engagement with a diverse artistic and creative urban community, professional internships, and a broad range of cultural and entertainment options."

SELECTIVITY

Admissions Rating	98
# of applicants	10,401
% of applicants accepted	7
% of acceptees attending	54
# offered a place on the wait list	839
% accepting a place on wait list	67
% admitted from wait list	8
# of early decision applicants	1,384
% accepted early decision	15

FRESHMAN PROFILE

Range SAT EBRW	690–750
Range SAT Math	700–790
Range SAT Composite	1410–1530
Range ACT Composite	32–35
# submitting SAT scores	267
% submitting SAT scores	64
# submitting ACT scores	210
% submitting ACT scores	50
% graduated top 10% of class	93
% graduated top 25% of class	100
% graduated top 50% of class	100

DEADLINES

Early decision	
Deadline	11/15
Notification	12/15
Other ED Deadline	1/8
Other ED Notification	2/15
Regular	
Deadline	1/8
Notification	4/1
Nonfall registration?	No

APPLICANTS ALSO LOOK AT AND OFTEN PREFER

Stanford University; Yale University; Harvard College; Brown University

AND SOMETIMES PREFER

Princeton University; Williams College; University of California—Berkeley

FINANCIAL FACTS

Financial Aid Rating	99
Annual tuition	$54,380
Room and board	$17,218
Required fees	$382
Books and supplies	$1,000
Average frosh need-based scholarship	$55,485
Average UG need-based scholarship	$55,082
% needy frosh rec. need-based scholarship or grant aid	100
% needy UG rec. need-based scholarship or grant aid	100
% needy frosh rec. non-need-based scholarship or grant aid	0
% needy UG rec. non-need-based scholarship or grant aid	0
% needy frosh rec. need-based self-help aid	100
% needy UG rec. need-based self-help aid	100
% frosh rec. any financial aid	51
% UG rec. any financial aid	55
% UG borrow to pay for school	25
Average cumulative indebtedness	$18,829
% frosh need fully met	100
% ugrads need fully met	100
Average % of frosh need met	100
Average % of ugrad need met	100

PORTLAND STATE UNIVERSITY

Office of Admissions, Portland, OR 97207-0751 • Admissions: 503-725-3511 • Fax: 503-725-5525

CAMPUS LIFE

Quality of Life Rating	**86**
Fire Safety Rating	**88**
Green Rating	**98**
Type of school	Public
Environment	Metropolis

STUDENTS

Total undergrad enrollment	17,827
% male/female	46/54
% from out of state	16
% frosh from public high school	85
% frosh live on campus	50
% ugrads live on campus	9
# of fraternities (% ugrad men join)	4 (1)
# of sororities (% ugrad women join)	6 (1)
% African American	4
% Asian	10
% Caucasian	52
% Hispanic	17
% Native American	1
% Pacific Islander	1
% Two or more races	7
% Race and/or ethnicity unknown	4
% international	5
# of countries represented	70

SURVEY SAYS . . .

Lots of liberal students
Students environmentally aware
Recreation facilities are great

ACADEMICS

Academic Rating	**74**
% students returning for sophomore year	73
% students graduating within 4 years	20
% students graduating within 6 years	47
Calendar	Quarter
Student/faculty ratio	19:1
Profs interesting rating	85
Profs accessible rating	86
Most classes have 10–19 students.	
Most lab/discussion sessions have 10–19 students.	

MOST POPULAR MAJORS

Psychology, General; Business Administration and Management, General; Biology/Biological Sciences, General

STUDENTS SAY ". . ."

Academics

Portland State University's motto is "let knowledge serve the city," and students echo this philosophy, saying their school "has a strong focus on civic engagement and sustainability." "PSU is a great learning environment in the heart of the city" and a "good value" for your tuition dollars. It's also "a green-minded urban school" that's "training students to be good community members." "There is a wealth of courses" on offer here, with degrees in social work, a range of business majors, and the hard sciences all receiving praise. "Classes are usually pretty small," and professors "promote lots of in-class discussion and are readily available to meet outside of class as well." "They really care about the student's success, and they really help broaden our scope of learning [and] thinking critically." Adjunct professors are "very connected to the community and their particular areas of expertise." Overall, students are happy with their instructors, saying, "Most professors are engaging and truly want to challenge you and help you succeed." They "are well-educated [and] well-versed in current issues and research." There's "the occasional dud thrown into the mix," though. Generally, "they are prepared and are passionate about the classes they teach. They have a wealth of experiences to bring to classroom," and they're "easily accessible for questions or further assistance, students just need to reach out."

Life

The city of Portland is a big draw for PSU students. "The campus is extraordinarily beautiful and ideally located." Outdoor activities are big here: "There's skiing, hiking, camping, [and] fishing." "The downtown area has plenty of microbrew pubs, nightlife, eateries, and theaters." "The people are friendly, and the city is gorgeous and easy to navigate. You can go to the beach or to the mountain in about two hours, and there are many things to do outdoors. There are great parks throughout the city." "The public transportation is outstanding." It's bike- and vegan-friendly. "There are lots of activist and awareness-raising events going on all the time, and lots of students are involved in volunteering (on and off campus)." Because PSU has a large nontraditional undergraduate population and the majority of students live off campus, the sense of community extends beyond the school and into the city. "There are a lot of things to do on campus, and there are different groups on campus that promote going out into the community at large and helping out." "Because the student body is so big and really diverse, PSU has tons of programs/clubs/groups that help make you feel more involved with your school. PSU is also committed to sustainability: Any new buildings are made with the latest green technology, and recycling is a big deal."

Student Body

"It is difficult to define the typical PSU student, because there are so many of us from so many different backgrounds," one student says, and diversity does indeed seem to be the name of the game at PSU. Students describe themselves as "environmentally aware, hip," and "very liberal." Overall, people at PSU are "invested in their education and are friendly." There's a large population of nontraditional undergraduates, so students are "either typical college-age…or people in their thirties and forties with kids and full-time job trying to juggle everything." Even within this large, diverse student body, "everyone finds a niche pretty quickly." "It's easy to find people you get along with, but it's also easy to find people who are completely different from you, which makes school a lot more interesting."

PORTLAND STATE UNIVERSITY

Financial Aid: 800-547-8887 • E-Mail: admissions@pdx.edu • Website: http://www.pdx.edu/

THE PRINCETON REVIEW SAYS

Admissions

Very important factors considered include: academic GPA. *Other factors considered include:* standardized test scores, recommendation(s). ACT with or without writing accepted. High school diploma is required and GED is accepted. *Academic units required:* 4 English, 3 math, 3 science, 2 foreign language, 3 social studies, 1 history. *Academic units recommended:* 1 science lab.

Financial Aid

Students should submit: FAFSA. Priority filing deadline is 2/1. The Princeton Review suggests that all financial aid forms be submitted as soon as possible after October 1. *Need-based scholarships/grants offered:* College/university scholarship or grant aid from institutional funds; Federal Pell; Private scholarships; SEOG; State scholarships/grants. *Loan aid offered:* Direct PLUS loans; Direct Subsidized Stafford Loans; Direct Unsubsidized Stafford Loans. Applicants will be notified of awards on a rolling basis beginning 2/27. Federal Work-Study Program available. Institutional employment available.

The Inside Word

PSU offers a range of admission options for new freshmen, transfers, students enrolled at local community colleges, continuing students, and those with nontraditional high school backgrounds. Regardless of an applicant's status, admissions officers look for a secondary school GPA of at least 3.0, though high test scores can make up for a lower average.

THE SCHOOL SAYS "..."

From the Admissions Office

"Portland State University is Oregon's most diverse public university located in the heart of one of America's most progressive cities. It offers more than sixty undergraduate and forty graduate programs in fine and performing arts, liberal arts and sciences, business administration, education, urban and public affairs, social work, engineering, and computer science. PSU offers more than 120 bachelor's, master's, and doctoral degrees.

"The forty-nine-acre downtown campus—whose motto is 'Let Knowledge Serve the City'—places students in a vibrant center of culture, business, and technology. Portland State's urban mission offers opportunities for every student to participate in internships and community-based projects in business, education, social services, government, technology, and the arts and sciences.

"The award-winning University Studies curriculum provides small class sizes and mentoring for undergraduates and culminates in Senior Capstone, which takes students out of the classroom and into the field, where they utilize their knowledge and skills to develop community projects.

"Portland State has taken aggressive steps to enhance the student experience and campus life, with new student housing and a comprehensive recreation complex and remodeled science and performing arts facilities. The university also has hired more academic and career advisers and created new programs to support students. Sustainability—initiatives that balance environmental, economic, and social concerns—is incorporated throughout the curriculum and across the campus."

SELECTIVITY
Admissions Rating	74
# of applicants	6,861
% of applicants accepted	96
% of acceptees attending	30

FRESHMAN PROFILE
Range SAT EBRW	500–630
Range SAT Math	500–590
Range SAT Composite	990–1220
Range ACT Composite	18–24
# submitting SAT scores	699
% submitting SAT scores	45
# submitting ACT scores	555
% submitting ACT scores	35
Average HS GPA	3.5
% graduated top 10% of class	15
% graduated top 25% of class	43
% graduated top 50% of class	83

DEADLINES
Regular	
Priority	6/1
Notification	Rolling, 1/1
Nonfall registration?	Yes

FINANCIAL FACTS
Financial Aid Rating	80
Annual in-state tuition	$8,078
Annual out-of-state tuition	$26,910
Room and board	$11,172
Required fees	$1,500
Books and supplies	$1,263
Average frosh need-based scholarship	$8,310
Average UG need-based scholarship	$6,380
% needy frosh rec. need-based scholarship or grant aid	79
% needy UG rec. need-based scholarship or grant aid	92
% needy frosh rec. non-need-based scholarship or grant aid	50
% needy UG rec. non-need-based scholarship or grant aid	61
% needy frosh rec. need-based self-help aid	65
% needy UG rec. need-based self-help aid	65
% frosh rec. any financial aid	75
% UG rec. any financial aid	70
% UG borrow to pay for school	55
Average cumulative indebtedness	$26,426
% frosh need fully met	8
% ugrads need fully met	3
Average % of frosh need met	61
Average % of ugrad need met	53

PRINCETON UNIVERSITY

PO Box 430, Princeton, NJ 08544-0430 • Admissions: 609-258-3060 • Fax: 609-258-6743

STUDENTS SAY "..."

Academics

As a member of the grand old Ivy League, Princeton University has long maintained a "sterling reputation" for quality academics; however, students say Princeton's "unique focus on the undergraduate experience" is what makes their school stand out among institutions. It attracts "really experienced and big-name professors, who actually want to teach undergraduates." Introductory lecture classes can be rather large, but "once you take upper-level courses, you'll have a lot of chances to work closely with professors and study what you are most interested in." A current undergrad enthuses, "The discussions I have in seminar are the reason I get out of bed in the morning; after a great class, I feel incredibly invigorated." Though all Princeton professors are "leading scholars in their field," students admit that some classes can be "dry." Fortunately, "the overwhelming majority of professors are wonderful, captivating lecturers" who are "dedicated to their students." While you may be taking a class from a Nobel laureate, "the humility and accessibility of world-famous researchers and public figures is always remarkable." At Princeton, "there are so many chances to meet writers, performers, and professionals you admire." A student details, "The two years I've been here, I've been in discussions with Frank Gehry, David Sedaris, Peter Hessler, John McPhee, Jeff Koons, Chang-rae Lee, Joyce Carol Oates, W.S. Merwin, and on and on." No matter what you study, Princeton is an "intellectually challenging place," and the student experience is "intense in almost every way." Hard work pays off, though "the academic caliber of the school is unparalleled," and a Princeton education is "magnificently rewarding."

Life

Princeton students "tend to participate in a lot of different activities, from varsity sports (recruits), intramural sports (high school athletes), and more academically restricted activities like autonomous vehicle design club, Engineers Without Borders, and the literary magazine." In and out of the classroom, there are a "billion opportunities to do what you know you love" on the Princeton campus, from performance to sports to research. "Princeton offers a lot of different opportunities to relax and de-stress," including "sporting events, concerts, recreational facilities," "a movie theater that frequently screens current films for free," and "arts and crafts at the student center." For some, social life is centered along Prospect Avenue, where "Princeton's eating clubs are lined up like ten booze-soaked ducklings in a row." These eating clubs—private houses that serve as social clubs and cafeterias for upperclassmen—"play a large role in the social scene at the university." On the weekends, "the eating clubs are extremely popular for partying, chatting, drinking, and dancing"—not to mention, "free beer." "The campus is gorgeous year-round"; however, when students need a break from the college atmosphere, "there's NJ Transit if you want to go to New York, Philly, or even just the local mall."

Student Body

It's not surprising that most undergraduates are "driven, competitive, and obsessed with perfection." "Academics come first," and Princeton students are typified by dedication to their studies and "a tendency to overwork." "Almost everyone at Princeton is involved with something other than school about which they are extremely passionate," and most have "at least one distinct, remarkable talent." "It's fairly easy for most people to find a good group of friends with whom they have something in common," and many students get involved in one of the "infinite number of clubs" on campus. Superficially, "the preppy Ivy League stereotype" is reflected in the student population, and many students are "well-spoken," "dress nicely," and stay in shape. A student jokes, "Going to Princeton is like being in a contest to see who can be the biggest nerd while simultaneously appearing least nerdy."

PRINCETON UNIVERSITY

Financial Aid: 609-258-3330 • E-Mail: uaoffice@princeton.edu • Website: www.princeton.edu

THE PRINCETON REVIEW SAYS

Admissions

Very important factors considered include: rigor of secondary school record, class rank, academic GPA, application essay, standardized test scores, recommendation(s), extracurricular activities, talent/ability, character/personal qualities. *Other factors considered include:* interview, first generation, alumni/ae relation, geographical residence, racial/ethnic status, volunteer work, work experience. ACT with or without writing accepted. SAT with or without Essay component accepted. High school diploma or equivalent is not required. *Academic units recommended:* 4 English, 4 math, 4 science, 2 science labs, 4 foreign language, 2 social studies, 2 history, 1 visual/performing arts.

Financial Aid

Students should submit: FAFSA; Institution's own financial aid form. Priority filing deadline is 2/1. The Princeton Review suggests that all financial aid forms be submitted as soon as possible after October 1. *Need-based scholarships/grants offered:* College/university scholarship or grant aid from institutional funds; Federal Pell; Private scholarships; SEOG; State scholarships/grants. *Loan aid offered:* Direct PLUS loans; Direct Subsidized Stafford Loans; Direct Unsubsidized Stafford Loans. Applicants will be notified of awards on or about 4/1. Federal Work-Study Program available. Institutional employment available.

The Inside Word

Not surprisingly, admission to Princeton is highly selective. Only about 7 percent of applicants are accepted, and these students usually rank at the top of their high school class. Prospective students should prepare for Princeton by excelling in honors, AP, and upper-level course work during high school. The application materials and personal essays are carefully read and evaluated, so students should also allocate time to prepare their applications. Admission to Princeton comes with a great deal of prestige, and to make the deal even sweeter, Princeton's remarkable no-loan financial aid program means that every student has 100 percent of their financial need met, without student loans.

THE SCHOOL SAYS "..."

From the Admissions Office

"Methods of instruction at Princeton vary widely, but common to all areas is a strong emphasis on individual responsibility and the free interchange of ideas. This is displayed most notably in the wide use of preceptorials and seminars, in the provision of independent study for all upperclass students and qualified underclass students, and in the availability of a series of special programs to meet a range of individual interests. The undergraduate college encourages the student to be an independent seeker of information and to assume responsibility for gaining both knowledge and judgment that will strengthen later contributions to society. Two hallmarks of the academic experience are the junior paper and senior thesis, which allow students the opportunity to pursue original research and scholarship in a field of their choosing.

"Princeton offers a distinctive financial aid program that provides grants, which do not have to be repaid, rather than loans. Princeton meets the full demonstrated financial need of all students—domestic and international—offered admission. About 60 percent of Princeton's undergraduates receive financial aid.

"All applicants must submit results for both the SAT as well as SAT Subject Tests in two different subject areas."

SELECTIVITY

Admissions Rating	99
# of applicants	35,370
% of applicants accepted	5
% of acceptees attending	69
# offered a place on the wait list	1,125
% accepting a place on wait list	75
% admitted from wait list	0

FRESHMAN PROFILE

Range SAT EBRW	710–770
Range SAT Math	730–800
Range ACT Composite	32–35
# submitting SAT scores	917
% submitting SAT scores	68
# submitting ACT scores	732
% submitting ACT scores	55
Average HS GPA	3.9

DEADLINES

Early action	
Deadline	11/1
Notification	12/15
Regular	
Deadline	1/1
Notification	4/1
Nonfall registration?	No

FINANCIAL FACTS

Financial Aid Rating	99
Annual tuition	$49,450
Room and board	$16,360
Required fees	$890
Books and supplies	$1,050
Average frosh need-based scholarship	$54,270
Average UG need-based scholarship	$53,572
% needy frosh rec. need-based scholarship or grant aid	100
% needy UG rec. need-based scholarship or grant aid	100
% needy frosh rec. non-need-based scholarship or grant aid	0
% needy UG rec. non-need-based scholarship or grant aid	0
% needy frosh rec. need-based self-help aid	100
% needy UG rec. need-based self-help aid	100
% frosh rec. any financial aid	60
% UG rec. any financial aid	60
% UG borrow to pay for school	18
Average cumulative indebtedness	$9,059
% frosh need fully met	100
% ugrads need fully met	100
Average % of frosh need met	100
Average % of ugrad need met	100

PROVIDENCE COLLEGE

Harkins Hall 103, Providence, RI 02918 • Admissions: 401-865-2535 • Fax: 401-865-2826

STUDENTS SAY ". . ."

Academics

A "small" Catholic college in Rhode Island, Providence College offers students a "strong" liberal arts curriculum and a "fun and flourishing social environment." Academically, many undergrads point to Providence's "Western Civilization program" as a highlight of their collegiate experience. This interdisciplinary series exposes students to art, literature, philosophy, and theology and shapes undergrads into "well-rounded and deep thinkers." Students are also quick to highlight Providence's "strong business school" as well. And they certainly appreciate that they are "taught to think on our feet and to apply what we have learned in the classroom to real life situations." "Small classes" are another hallmark of a Providence education. In turn, this enables students to develop "great relationships" with their professors. And speaking of professors, undergrads here happily report that their teachers are "phenomenal." Not only are they "extremely knowledgeable," they also "have a real passion for teaching." As one thankful student boasts, "My professors have met with me on the weekends, over the summer, and responded to text messages/emails/phone calls. We have gone off campus just to chat and keep up to date on how things are going." Indeed, these professors might just be Providence's "biggest asset."

Life

Life at Providence can aptly be described as a "whirlwind." This is due to the myriad of "recreational activities," "school sponsored trips," and "programmed nights" the college offers. Additionally, school spirit abounds and students are "very enthusiastic" about attending sporting events, "especially men's basketball and hockey." Students do admit that "partying is a pretty large part of the social life." And on the weekends you'll find that lots of people "go out, either to bars/clubs or senior off campus housing." One student shares, "People will sit out on the quad on nice sunny days and play catch. We have many activities such as dances and cookouts that the school holds year round." Moreover, there are "two concerts each year where [basically] the entire school attends." Many individuals are also "highly involved in intramural sports" as well as a club or two "aligning with social, political and relig[ious] interests." Of course, students here love exploring the city of Providence too, "which is a short car ride or public bus trip [away]." And undergrads "can [check out] activities around Brown University/Thayer Street, as well as DownCity where there are many shops and a large artistic influence."

Student Body

Students at Providence attest that the college is "very homogenous in regards to race and socioeconomic status," noting that most undergrads are "white" and come from "upper middle class families." Additionally, a large percentage hail from "New England, New York, [or] New Jersey." And many don "preppy" clothing; you frequently "see backwards hats, Vineyard Vines, Patagonia, and bean boots or boat shoes." Thankfully, Providence has grown "increasingly diverse" in the last few years. On top of that, undergrads gush that their peers are "genuinely nice" and quite "inclusive" regardless of background. Students are also quite impressed with how "polite" everyone seems to be. As one undergrad explains, "Doors are held, everyone thanks the professor after class, people say hello as you walk by—it's phenomenal!" Moreover, as a Catholic institution, you do find "kids who take their faith seriously." However, "you do not need to be religious to feel welcomed here." Indeed, "the college preaches about the Friar Family which the students are supposed to embody. When I first started here I thought that this motto was quite ludicrous, but it honestly seems as though it is true. The way everyone acts is just so kind towards one another. The students here really do treat everyone like family."

PROVIDENCE COLLEGE

Financial Aid: 401-865-2286 • E-Mail: pcadmiss@providence.edu • Website: www.providence.edu

THE PRINCETON REVIEW SAYS

Admissions

Very important factors considered include: rigor of secondary school record, academic GPA, application essay. *Important factors considered include:* recommendation(s), extracurricular activities, character/personal qualities. *Other factors considered include:* class rank, standardized test scores, talent/ability, first generation, alumni/ae relation, geographical residence, racial/ethnic status, volunteer work, work experience, level of applicant's interest. ACT with or without writing accepted. SAT with or without Essay component accepted. High school diploma is required and GED is not accepted. *Academic units required:* 4 English, 4 math, 3 science, 2 science labs, 3 foreign language, 2 social studies, 2 history. *Academic units recommended:* 4 English, 4 math, 4 science, 2 science labs, 4 foreign language, 2 social studies, 2 history.

Financial Aid

Students should submit: CSS/Financial Aid PROFILE; FAFSA. The Princeton Review suggests that all financial aid forms be submitted as soon as possible after October 1. *Need-based scholarships/grants offered:* College/university scholarship or grant aid from institutional funds; Federal Pell; Private scholarships; SEOG; State scholarships/grants; United Negro College Fund. *Loan aid offered:* Direct PLUS loans; Direct Subsidized Stafford Loans; Direct Unsubsidized Stafford Loans. Applicants will be notified of awards on or about 3/15. Federal Work-Study Program available. Institutional employment available.

The Inside Word

Applicants to Providence College can rest assured that the school takes a holistic approach to the admissions game. Of course, your high school transcript will still hold the most weight. And given that admission is selective, the strongest candidates have taken several honors or advanced placement classes. Beyond that, the college closely evaluates personal statements, recommendations and extracurricular involvement. Interested students should know that Providence is a test-optional school.

THE SCHOOL SAYS "..."

From the Admissions Office

"A Providence College education challenges students to find commonality among topics that seem, on the surface, to be opposites. 'Or' often becomes 'and.' There are shared academic experiences such as the Core Curriculum and the distinctive Development of Western Civilization sequence, but the college also encourages students to explore differences of opinion and unfamiliar lines of thought. PC's Catholic and Dominican identity fuels intellectual, spiritual, and emotional growth by encouraging students to view subjects through the complementary lenses of faith and reason. It also fosters a respectful, supportive community that feels like home.

"Submission of standardized test scores is optional for students applying for admission. This policy change allows each student to decide whether they wish to have their standardized test results considered as part of their application for admission. Students who choose not to submit SAT or ACT test scores will not be penalized in the review for admission. Additional details about the test-optional policy can be found on our website at https://admission.providence.edu/apply/standardized-testing/."

SELECTIVITY

Admissions Rating	88
# of applicants	11,251
% of applicants accepted	52
% of acceptees attending	18
# offered a place on the wait list	3,103
% accepting a place on wait list	32
% admitted from wait list	1
# of early decision applicants	420
% accepted early decision	76

FRESHMAN PROFILE

Range SAT EBRW	580–660
Range SAT Math	580–670
Range ACT Composite	26–30
# submitting SAT scores	487
% submitting SAT scores	46
# submitting ACT scores	255
% submitting ACT scores	24
Average HS GPA	3.4
% graduated top 10% of class	36
% graduated top 25% of class	65
% graduated top 50% of class	92

DEADLINES

Early decision	
Deadline	11/15
Notification	1/1
Other ED Deadline	1/15
Other ED Notification	2/15
Early action	
Deadline	11/1
Notification	1/1
Regular	
Deadline	1/15
Notification	4/1
Nonfall registration?	Yes

APPLICANTS ALSO LOOK AT AND OFTEN PREFER
Boston College; College of the Holy Cross

AND SOMETIMES PREFER
Villanova University

AND RARELY PREFER
Fairfield University; Loyola University Maryland

FINANCIAL FACTS

Financial Aid Rating	87
Annual tuition	$51,490
Room and board	$15,140
Books and supplies	$1,605
Average frosh need-based scholarship	$27,732
Average UG need-based scholarship	$27,621
% needy frosh rec. need-based scholarship or grant aid	94
% needy UG rec. need-based scholarship or grant aid	99
% needy frosh rec. non-need-based scholarship or grant aid	8
% needy UG rec. non-need-based scholarship or grant aid	6
% needy frosh rec. need-based self-help aid	89
% needy UG rec. need-based self-help aid	97
% frosh rec. any financial aid	79
% UG rec. any financial aid	75
% UG borrow to pay for school	68
Average cumulative indebtedness	$41,383
% frosh need fully met	27
% ugrads need fully met	23
Average % of frosh need met	86
Average % of ugrad need met	83

PURDUE UNIVERSITY—WEST LAFAYETTE

475 Stadium Mall Drive, West Lafayette, IN 47907-2050 • Admissions: 765-494-1776 • Fax: 765-494-0544

CAMPUS LIFE

Quality of Life Rating	91
Fire Safety Rating	96
Green Rating	60*
Type of school	Public
Environment	Town

STUDENTS

Total undergrad enrollment	30,831
% male/female	57/43
% from out of state	36
% frosh live on campus	94
% ugrads live on campus	41
# of fraternities (% ugrad men join)	30 (18)
# of sororities (% ugrad women join)	25 (22)
% African American	3
% Asian	8
% Caucasian	63
% Hispanic	5
% Native American	<1
% Pacific Islander	<1
% Two or more races	3
% Race and/or ethnicity unknown	2
% international	16
# of countries represented	123

SURVEY SAYS . . .

Students are happy
Lab facilities are great
Great library
Career services are great
Internships are widely available
Students are friendly
Students are very religious
Great food on campus
Recreation facilities are great
Very little drug use
Intramural sports are popular
Alumni active on campus

ACADEMICS

Academic Rating	84
% students returning for sophomore year	92
% students graduating within 4 years	51
Calendar	Semester
Student/faculty ratio	13:1
Profs interesting rating	84
Profs accessible rating	94

Most classes have 10–19 students.
Most lab/discussion sessions have
20–29 students.

MOST POPULAR MAJORS

Mechanical/Mechanical Engineering Technology/
Technician; Computer Science; Mechanical
Engineering

STUDENTS SAY "..."

Academics

Purdue is a Big Ten school that provides "a world class education" with a name "that is known all over the world and not just the state of Indiana." The university is especially "known for being a great engineering school," but has a bevy of amazing programs including "a great nursing program," "a great Pharmacy program" and a "speech pathology program [that] is one of the best." "I knew that I would receive an unparalleled education here," an Aeronautical and Astronautical Engineering major says. Purdue, "cradle of engineers and quarterbacks alike," is known for its athletics as well as its academics. There is "great school spirit exhibited in student organizations and athletic events." Yet despite the "big campus atmosphere," the school still maintains "small-school feel within its individual colleges." The "knowledgeable and helpful" professors are "very excited about their topic of teaching" and "the classes are excellent and stimulating." "Many of my professors have at least ten years under their belts with PhD's," one student boasts. Students are not going to find easy classes here. Purdue has teachers that "expect the most out of you." However, "the difficult and rigorous curriculum" is a bonding experience that "increases out of the classroom skills such as communication and collaboration." Some students did worry that "many things (such as Industrial Roundtable) are focused almost exclusively on engineers, which leaves some other majors out in the cold." "The dining services are immaculate" at Purdue, and students love how the school "promotes green technology." One Biology major explains the Purdue appeal: "It has everything a college kid could want: sports, academics, clubs, and delicious food." Purdue provides an educational experience that students will remember the rest of their lives. As one student puts it: "Once a Boilermaker, always a Boilermaker."

Life

Life at Purdue involves a lot of "time management" and "a typical student has a hard time completing all three S's (sleep, study, socialize) but has fun trying." As a Big Ten university, athletics make up a large part of campus life. "We have Ross-Ade Brigade and Paint Crew, student clubs for cheering on the athletic teams, and they're fairly large," one Biology major explains. "Partying and hard alcohol [are] common," but seem to divide the student body. Some wish the administration put "more control on partying and drinking" while others wish it was "less strict on alcohol/drug policies." "Sometimes there isn't a lot to do in West Lafayette besides drink," and "students typically spend their time partying hard on Thursday nights at the Cactus and cramming on Sunday nights." "Greek life is huge at Purdue" although "not essential." West Lafayette is "close to Chicago and Indy" for weekend trips, and "students stay on campus most of the time, so it's not a huge deal that the town around us sucks." There is "always something fun to do on campus" too, such as "a club meeting, a social event/recreational event, or just plain studying." "Most people unwind and have fun by joining a club or organization" and everyone seems to find a place to fit in. Even quiet students blossom at Purdue as "the atmosphere on campus coaxes most out of their shell sooner or later."

Student Body

Located in Indiana, Purdue has a student body that is largely "white and from the Midwest" with "conservative political views." That said, one student points out that "West Lafayette is a pretty progressive town and usually ends up going Democratic if you check election records." A fair number of students say the school needs to work to bring "better diversity." "Most students are really down to earth" and "students can all find their niche here and get along well." Students tend to bond "within their majors" which "helps create a small-school feel within a huge university," although "it is not unheard of for people involved in different things to be with different people." There is a fair amount of animosity between majors since "science and engineering majors DO look down on other majors" and tend to think that non-technical majors "are a 'joke'" to the point that people are arrogant, obnoxious, and rude." Still, most students "fit in well," and at the end of the day, "we take all kinds here and turn everyone into Boilermakers."

PURDUE UNIVERSITY—WEST LAFAYETTE

Financial Aid: 765-494-0998 • E-Mail: admissions@purdue.edu • Website: www.purdue.edu

THE PRINCETON REVIEW SAYS

Admissions

Very important factors considered include: rigor of secondary school record, academic GPA, standardized test scores. *Important factors considered include:* application essay, recommendation(s), extracurricular activities, character/personal qualities, first generation. *Other factors considered include:* class rank, talent/ability, alumni/ae relation, geographical residence, state residency, racial/ethnic status, volunteer work, work experience, level of applicant's interest. ACT with Writing required. High school diploma is required and GED is accepted. *Academic units required:* 4 English, 3 math, 3 science, 2 science labs, 3 foreign language.

Financial Aid

Students should submit: FAFSA. Priority filing deadline is 3/1. The Princeton Review suggests that all financial aid forms be submitted as soon as possible after October 1. *Need-based scholarships/grants offered:* College/university scholarship or grant aid from institutional funds; Federal Pell; Private scholarships; SEOG; State scholarships/grants. *Loan aid offered:* Direct PLUS loans; Direct Subsidized Stafford Loans; Direct Unsubsidized Stafford Loans. Applicants will be notified of awards on or about 4/15. Federal Work-Study Program available. Institutional employment available.

The Inside Word

Purdue looks at student applications holistically. Having said that, Purdue does have minimum high school course requirements, so make sure you have met or exceeded all of those requirements before applying.

THE SCHOOL SAYS "..."

From the Admissions Office

"Although it is one of America's largest universities, Purdue does not 'feel' big to its students. The campus is very compact when compared to universities with similar enrollment. Purdue is a comprehensive university with an international reputation in a wide range of academic fields. A strong work ethic prevails at Purdue. As a member of the Big Ten, Purdue has a strong and diverse athletic program. Purdue offers more than 1,000 clubs and organizations. The residence halls and Greek community offer many participatory activities for students. Numerous convocations and lectures are presented each year. Purdue is all about people, and allowing students to grow academically as well as socially, preparing them for the real world.

"Applicants seeking admission are required to have their SAT or ACT test score sent from the testing agency. Purdue accepts either test, and will use the best available score, for admission and scholarship decisions.

"To be considered for the full range of merit-based scholarships, students must complete their admission application by November 1.

"Purdue is a member of the Common Application and the Coalition Application."

SELECTIVITY

Admissions Rating	88
# of applicants	48,912
% of applicants accepted	57
% of acceptees attending	27
# offered a place on the wait list	3,664
% accepting a place on wait list	61
% admitted from wait list	4

FRESHMAN PROFILE

Range SAT EBRW	570–670
Range SAT Math	580–710
Range ACT Composite	25–31
# submitting SAT scores	5,253
% submitting SAT scores	69
# submitting ACT scores	4,529
% submitting ACT scores	60
Average HS GPA	3.8
% graduated top 10% of class	44
% graduated top 25% of class	78
% graduated top 50% of class	97

DEADLINES

Early action	
Deadline	11/1
Notification	12/12
Regular	
Priority	2/1
Notification	12/12
Nonfall registration?	Yes

APPLICANTS ALSO LOOK AT AND OFTEN PREFER
Indiana University Bloomington; University of Illinois at Urbana-Champaign

AND SOMETIMES PREFER
Georgia Institute of Technology; Penn State University Park; The Ohio State University—Columbus; University of Michigan—Ann Arbor; University of California—Berkeley; University of California, Davis; University of California—San Diego; University of Wisconsin-Madison; University of Texas at Austin

FINANCIAL FACTS

Financial Aid Rating	87
Annual in-state tuition	$9,208
Annual out-of-state tuition	$28,010
Room and board	$10,030
Required fees	$784
Books and supplies	$1,160
Average frosh need-based scholarship	$12,787
Average UG need-based scholarship	$12,621
% needy frosh rec. need-based scholarship or grant aid	77
% needy UG rec. need-based scholarship or grant aid	80
% needy frosh rec. non-need-based scholarship or grant aid	37
% needy UG rec. non-need-based scholarship or grant aid	32
% needy frosh rec. need-based self-help aid	53
% needy UG rec. need-based self-help aid	58
% frosh rec. any financial aid	74
% UG rec. any financial aid	77
% UG borrow to pay for school	40
Average cumulative indebtedness	$28,440
% frosh need fully met	38
% ugrads need fully met	35
Average % of frosh need met	77
Average % of ugrad need met	78

QUINNIPIAC UNIVERSITY

275 Mount Carmel Avenue, Hamden, CT 06518-1940 • Admissions: 203-582-8600 • Fax: 203-582-8906

STUDENTS SAY "..."

Academics

Quinnipiac University is a mid-sized Connecticut institution that uses a practice-focused, market-tested curriculum and experiential learning to prepare students for the working world. The university's job connections in Connecticut, New York, and Boston are particularly strong, and its ongoing expansion "is giving its students the opportunity to work in more and more locations throughout the world." Small classes are "tailored to the individual student," but the school "still has a big university feel. It is the best of both worlds." There are "numerous resources that are helpful to students," such as peer fellows at the Learning Commons that "put on review sessions for difficult courses like Anatomy and Organic Chemistry." All in all, faculty and staff alike "work hard to ensure the student body develops skills crucial to the workforce."

Professors at Quinnipiac are "highly educated in their fields and lecture based on personal experiences in their careers," which "truly brings the material to life when learning about it." The faculty "really want you to succeed and want to help in that process." All of the teachers here have real-world experience to bring to the classroom and "have several connections within their field." Quinnipiac is "big into projects" and "tries to limit the number of exams that students are forced to take," finding a balance between graded assignments, projects, and tests in order to cater to every student's strengths.

Life

Aside from going to and from class, the average day at Quinnipiac could be filled with "a variety of campus activities, student group meetings, or special occasions." Many students choose to work out or play sports at the Recreation Center, and many student groups offer on-campus activities and lectures, such as guest speakers or performers." Most students spend their time in the library, but venture into Hamden's surrounding towns and cities, as well as hike "the Giant," which is a mountain right in front of the main campus. In fact there are "many amazing restaurants, bars, clubs, and fun things to do" within a certain radius; QU After Dark always has events, and "there is also a good amount of night-life on the weekends in New Haven."

When students involve themselves in an activity on campus, "they are in it 100 percent." For bigger events, students set fundraising goals, and "what they raise goes beyond anyone's expectations." Everyone hangs out on the quad in the nice weather, and "all of your friend's residence halls are within a five-minute walk from each other." Quinnipiac's Division 1 athletics certainly "bring everyone together" on weekends, and hockey and basketball games draw the most students. A lot of students participate in Greek Life, but no one on campus is left out: "It is a very Panhellenic community and outsiders are encouraged to participate in events and have just as much fun as the members."

Student Body

Quinnipiac University is "the perfect size where you don't know everyone in your year, but you know a good amount of people. Most of the "not very diverse" students come from "the four big surrounding states" (New York, New Jersey, Connecticut, and Massachusetts), and tend to be from upper-middle to upper-class families. There are "more females than males," as well as a large number of health science and law students. Most of the students "love the outdoors and enjoy looking at the mountains of Sleeping Giant State Park on their walk to class." It's a "very friendly" student body. "Everyone at Quinnipiac can find a group to fit into and feel at home," says a student. "The halls are full of people who stop to say hello and ask how you are."

Financial Aid: 203-582-8750 • E-Mail: admissions@qu.edu • Website: www.qu.edu

THE PRINCETON REVIEW SAYS

Admissions

Very important factors considered include: rigor of secondary school record, academic GPA, level of applicant's interest. *Important factors considered include:* class rank, application essay, standardized test scores, recommendation(s). *Other factors considered include:* interview, extracurricular activities, talent/ability, character/personal qualities, first generation, alumni/ae relation, state residency, racial/ethnic status, work experience. ACT with or without writing accepted. SAT with or without Essay component accepted. High school diploma is required and GED is accepted. *Academic units required:* 4 English, 3 math, 3 science, 2 foreign language, 2 social studies, 3 academic electives.

Financial Aid

Students should submit: FAFSA. Priority filing deadline is 3/1. The Princeton Review suggests that all financial aid forms be submitted as soon as possible after October 1. *Need-based scholarships/grants offered:* College/university scholarship or grant aid from institutional funds; Federal Pell; Private scholarships; SEOG; State scholarships/grants. *Loan aid offered:* Direct PLUS loans; Direct Subsidized Stafford Loans; Direct Unsubsidized Stafford Loans. Applicants will be notified of awards on a rolling basis beginning 1/15. Federal Work-Study Program available. Institutional employment available.

The Inside Word

Quinnipiac University offers early decision and also admits students on a rolling basis, a process that favors those who submit their applications early. Programs for physical therapy, nursing, and occupational therapy and physician assistants are quite competitive. The school strongly recommends that those seeking spots in the physician assistant program apply no later than 10/15 and for PT, nursing, and OT no later than 11/15.

THE SCHOOL SAYS "..."

From the Admissions Office

"Quinnipiac today is 'three settings, one university,' with an undergraduate population growing to 7,100, many of whom remain at QU for the ever-expanding graduate programs, and a continuing focus on our core values: academic excellence, a student oriented environment and a strong sense of community.

"The Mount Carmel campus, the academic home to all undergraduates with traditional, suite and apartment housing for freshmen and sophomores, is 250-acres in a picturesque setting adjacent to Sleeping Giant state park. The nearby 250-acre York Hill campus is home to juniors and seniors in apartments with breathtaking views, a lodge style student center, covered parking, and the TD Bank sports center with twin arenas for hockey and basketball. The 100-acre North Haven campus, just four miles distant, is the home to graduate programs in Health Sciences, and Education, and the Frank H. Netter, MD School of Medicine.

"Academic initiatives such as the honors program, 'writing across the curriculum', QU seminar series, extensive internship experiences, study abroad opportunities and a highly-regarded emerging leaders student-life program form the foundation for excellence in business, communication, health sciences, nursing, engineering, education, liberal arts, and law."

SELECTIVITY

Admissions Rating	80
# of applicants	22,751
% of applicants accepted	72
% of acceptees attending	12
# offered a place on the wait list	3,568
% accepting a place on wait list	47
% admitted from wait list	18

FRESHMAN PROFILE

Range SAT EBRW	550–630
Range SAT Math	540–630
Range ACT Composite	23–28
# submitting SAT scores	1,357
% submitting SAT scores	71
# submitting ACT scores	414
% submitting ACT scores	22
Average HS GPA	3.4
% graduated top 10% of class	20
% graduated top 25% of class	58
% graduated top 50% of class	92

DEADLINES

Nonfall registration?	Yes

FINANCIAL FACTS

Financial Aid Rating	84
Annual tuition	$46,790
Room and board	$15,600
Required fees	$2,490
Books and supplies	$800
Average frosh need-based scholarship	$23,265
Average UG need-based scholarship	$23,028
% needy frosh rec. need-based scholarship or grant aid	98
% needy UG rec. need-based scholarship or grant aid	98
% needy frosh rec. non-need-based scholarship or grant aid	93
% needy UG rec. non-need-based scholarship or grant aid	78
% needy frosh rec. need-based self-help aid	75
% needy UG rec. need-based self-help aid	80
% frosh rec. any financial aid	98
% UG rec. any financial aid	88
% UG borrow to pay for school	70
Average cumulative indebtedness	$48,544
% frosh need fully met	19
% ugrads need fully met	16
Average % of frosh need met	67
Average % of ugrad need met	65

RANDOLPH COLLEGE

2500 Rivermont Avenue, Lynchburg, VA 24503-1555 • Admissions: 434-947-8100 • Fax: 434-947-8996

STUDENTS SAY "..."

Academics

Rest assured, at Randolph College, "You're not just a number; you matter as an individual." Indeed, this "small, tight-knit community" instantly "makes you feel welcome." Additionally, students at Randolph are grateful they attend a college that "promotes self-discovery, personal growth, and individuality." Further, "small class sizes" allow for an "emphasis on student-professor relationships," a hallmark of a Randolph education. One undergrad happily confirms, "My academic experience has been challenging, there's no doubt, but the professor support has made that challenge enjoyable and exciting." A fellow student agrees, sharing, "My professors are excellent. Everyone I have had here has been supremely knowledgeable, understanding and helpful to students. The number one goal is always to make students better thinkers." Finally, as this student gushes, "My professors are amazing! Their passion for the subject matter and course content is infectious. I look forward to each class each day and feel confident in my education. Learning is interesting and fun here, and professors are eager to answer questions and provide resources to supplement lectures and experiments. Often professors list their home phone numbers on syllabi to allow students to contact them outside of office hours. Every professor replies to e-mail quickly, and professors are all very easy to communicate with in the classroom and one-on-one."

Life

According to many undergrads, "life at Randolph is always busy and exciting." As one ecstatic student quickly asserts, "I don't think I have [been] bored [since] the day I stepped foot on this campus." And why would you be? Indeed, there are "a wide variety of clubs and organizations [in which] to become involved." Moreover, there are "many sports teams and exciting competitions to watch" as well as intramurals, which "offer a chance for non-athletes to" participate. In addition, there are a myriad of "parties and dances...sponsored by various organizations." These events are typically well-attended by students, as "they never disappoint." And for those undergrads looking for an activity a little more out of the box, there's "even a game called Humans vs Zombies where students dress up and try to 'turn people into zombies' with Nerf guns. It's a lot of fun." Randolph is also home to many proud traditions and students love to partake. An insider reveals, "The even-odd class rivalry is definitely one popular school tradition. Skeller Sings are one of the events where the even spirit society (ETAs) and odd spirit society (Gammas) will sing (read: shout) songs at each other and try to create distractions while the other group sings." Finally, when students want to look beyond the campus for fun, they can "go hiking, swimming, and boating at all the lakes, rivers, and trails. [Indeed] there is a lot of nature and history surrounding the Lynchburg area."

Student Body

Undergrads at Randolph emphatically state that there's no typical student to be found wandering around campus. As one knowing undergrad shares, "Students vary widely in background and personality, preferences, [and] habits." Additionally, a "considerable percentage of the student body is comprised of international students," which certainly adds to the diversity of the school. Of course, if pressed to throw out some adjectives, Randolph undergrads will likely say that their peers are "hardworking, artistic, and caring." They are also "intelligent," "unafraid to speak their minds," and "committed to doing excellent work." Fortunately, "being such a small campus, it is hard not [to] develop lots of friends from several different social groups," and certainly, "campus traditions help form a very strong sense of community here." Or, as one content undergrad simply states, "Everyone gets along fairly well and it's not too hard to fit in when there aren't really any labels for people."

RANDOLPH COLLEGE

Financial Aid: 434-947-8128 • E-Mail: admissions@randolphcollege.edu • Website: www.randolphcollege.com

THE PRINCETON REVIEW SAYS

Admissions

Very important factors considered include: academic GPA. *Important factors considered include:* rigor of secondary school record, standardized test scores, extracurricular activities, alumni/ae relation. *Other factors considered include:* class rank, application essay, recommendation(s), interview, talent/ability, character/personal qualities, first generation, volunteer work, work experience. ACT with or without writing accepted. SAT with or without Essay component accepted. High school diploma is required and GED is accepted. *Academic units required:* 4 English, 3 math, 3 science, 2 science labs, 2 history, 1 academic elective. *Academic units recommended:* 4 math, 4 foreign language, 3 academic electives.

Financial Aid

Priority filing deadline is 3/1. The Princeton Review suggests that all financial aid forms be submitted as soon as possible after October 1. *Need-based scholarships/grants offered:* College/university scholarship or grant aid from institutional funds; Federal Pell; Private scholarships; SEOG; State scholarships/grants; United Negro College Fund. *Loan aid offered:* Direct PLUS loans; Direct Subsidized Stafford Loans; Direct Unsubsidized Stafford Loans. Applicants will be notified of awards on a rolling basis beginning 11/15. Federal Work-Study Program available. Institutional employment available.

The Inside Word

Officers at Randolph College take a fairly traditional approach to their admissions decisions. Certainly your transcript and test scores hold the most weight. However, recommendations, personal essays, and extracurricular activities are also taken into consideration, so it's best not to slack off any facet of your application.

THE SCHOOL SAYS "..."

From the Admissions Office

"Nationally ranked for its academic programs and affordability, Randolph College offers students the best features of breadth—including a comprehensive general education curriculum and a wide range of majors—as well as specialization. Embedded within a liberal arts framework are ample opportunities for study abroad, leadership roles, research partnerships with faculty, and practical experience through internships and service learning. Throughout their college careers, students are encouraged to pursue academic goals that are personalized and meaningful to them.

"In Fall 2021, Randolph College will launch its new "TAKE2" curriculum. This unique curricular model splits the semester into two seven-week sessions. During each one, students concentrate on two courses at a time. Believed to be the only permanent one of its kind in the nation, TAKE2 was designed by faculty to enable a more successful, enjoyable, and rewarding academic experience. Students focus on two courses, rather than several, at a time, in extended class sessions that allow for more applied activities and group interaction. No classes will be held on Wednesdays, allowing for a cognitive break to study and prepare for classes, as well as extracurricular activities, community engagement, field trips, and internships.

"A graduate of Randolph College understands the intellectual foundations of the arts, sciences, and humanities while developing critical skills to learn, adapt, and succeed in a rapidly changing global environment. The college's strong emphasis on writing enables students to communicate clearly and persuasively, and the diverse student population and study abroad programs enable students to expand their horizons. The distinctive student-led honor system has long been a central part of daily life at Randolph and adds to the cohesive community feel.

"A member of the Old Dominion Athletic Conference, Randolph's holistic approach to student development enables scholar-athletes to excel in a variety of sports while focusing on academic excellence. Located in the heart of Virginia near the Blue Ridge Mountains, Randolph College's campus is part of the multi-college town of Lynchburg, with abundant cultural, entertainment, and recreational opportunities."

SELECTIVITY

Admissions Rating	74
# of applicants	1,177
% of applicants accepted	90
% of acceptees attending	14

FRESHMAN PROFILE

Range SAT EBRW	490–600
Range SAT Math	480–580
Range SAT Composite	980–1180
Range ACT Composite	19–25
# submitting SAT scores	130
% submitting SAT scores	91
# submitting ACT scores	28
% submitting ACT scores	20
Average HS GPA	3.6
% graduated top 10% of class	15
% graduated top 25% of class	49
% graduated top 50% of class	81

DEADLINES

Early action	
Deadline	11/15
Regular	
Notification	Rolling, 9/1
Nonfall registration?	Yes

APPLICANTS ALSO LOOK AT AND SOMETIMES PREFER

Virginia Commonwealth University; James Madison University; Old Dominion Radford University; George Mason University; Virginia Polytechnic Institute and State University; University of Virginia

FINANCIAL FACTS

Financial Aid Rating	82
Annual tuition	$25,000
Room and board	$11,000
Required fees	$610
Books and supplies	$1,280
Average frosh need-based scholarship	$33,484
Average UG need-based scholarship	$31,680
% needy frosh rec. need-based scholarship or grant aid	100
% needy UG rec. need-based scholarship or grant aid	100
% needy frosh rec. non-need-based scholarship or grant aid	23
% needy UG rec. non-need-based scholarship or grant aid	18
% needy frosh rec. need-based self-help aid	68
% needy UG rec. need-based self-help aid	73
% frosh rec. any financial aid	100
% UG rec. any financial aid	98
% UG borrow to pay for school	78
Average cumulative indebtedness	$27,098
% frosh need fully met	24
% ugrads need fully met	22
Average % of frosh need met	82
Average % of ugrad need met	78

RANDOLPH-MACON COLLEGE

P. O. Box 5005, Ashland, VA 23005-5505 • Admissions: 804-752-7305 • Fax: 804-752-4707

CAMPUS LIFE

Quality of Life Rating	**90**
Fire Safety Rating	**93**
Green Rating	**60***
Type of school	Private
Affiliation	Methodist
Environment	Village

STUDENTS

Total undergrad enrollment	1,530
% male/female	47/53
% from out of state	22
% frosh from public high school	77
% frosh live on campus	93
% ugrads live on campus	80
# of fraternities (% ugrad men join)	7 (29)
# of sororities (% ugrad women join)	4 (25)
% African American	10
% Asian	1
% Caucasian	77
% Hispanic	4
% Native American	<1
% Pacific Islander	<1
% Two or more races	5
% Race and/or ethnicity unknown	1
% international	2
# of countries represented	26

SURVEY SAYS . . .

Students are happy
Lab facilities are great
Career services are great
Internships are widely available
Easy to get around campus
Alumni active on campus

ACADEMICS

Academic Rating	**84**
% students returning for sophomore year	84
% students graduating within 4 years	63
% students graduating within 6 years	68
Calendar	4/1/4
Student/faculty ratio	11:1
Profs interesting rating	90
Profs accessible rating	96
Most classes have 10–19 students.	

MOST POPULAR MAJORS

Communication and Media Studies; Biology/
Biological Sciences, General; Business/Commerce,
General

STUDENTS SAY "..."

Academics

At Randolph-Macon College, "everyone from the professors, to the other students, to the staff, ... care about each student." Those lucky enough to attend have the privilege of "creating the education experience [they] want." As one student explains, "If you want to be an athlete, a triple major, and study abroad three times, you can do that!" A hallmark of a Randolph-Macon education? Small class sizes. As one undergrad notes, "The student-faculty ratio is roughly 11:1, and last year there were barely any classes over 30." That makes it rather easy to "get to know professors and ... build relationships with them." Of course, it doesn't hurt that professors at RMC "genuinely care about your success." As one student concludes, "They are willing to help me in any topic. I am not just a number in a lecture hall, and they know my name. My questions in class have never been dismissed for the sake of proceeding with new material. I am very lucky to be where I am."

Life

Academics certainly take priority at Randolph-Macon, and many students report that "Sunday through Wednesday most people can be found in the library." Nevertheless, they just as quickly assert that "Thursday through Saturday are for getting together and letting loose," and say there are "so many options" from which to choose when you want to kick back. For starters, "athletic events ... are very popular." In fact, these undergrads—whether they're part of the team or not—are so dedicated to their sports teams that "students will carpool to support their friends" in off-campus games. In case you think all these undergrads care about is athletics, know that "Greek life philanthropy events are widely supported too." Of course, students here don't just rely on school organized activities—they also make their own fun, which ranges from "random dance parties and movie nights" to days when they just "hang with ... friends, take walks together, and bake."

Student Body

Undergrads at Randolph-Macon admit that their school isn't the most diverse institution, making claims that they are a "predominantly white" student body with a mostly "middle-class status" that also tends to skew conservative. However, one undergrad insists that while many wouldn't "view Randolph-Macon as diverse, ... that is something they are working to broaden." But regardless of background, nearly everyone describes their peers as "very welcoming and kind." Another student underscores this point by sharing, "We are a tight community that works to support each other no matter if you are an athlete, a member of theater, or a part of any other organization on campus." A classmate agrees adding, "I never leave my dorm without seeing someone I know, and I can always find a friendly face in a crowd." Additionally, students report that most people are "extremely involved" and "genuinely care about the school and community." As another satisfied undergrad sums up, "I have met some of the best people here, and have definitely found lifelong friends."

Financial Aid: 804-752-7259 • E-Mail: admissions@rmc.edu • Website: www.rmc.edu

THE PRINCETON REVIEW SAYS

Admissions

Very important factors considered include: rigor of secondary school record, academic GPA. *Important factors considered include:* class rank, application essay, standardized test scores, recommendation(s). *Other factors considered include:* interview, extracurricular activities, talent/ability, character/personal qualities, first generation, alumni/ae relation, racial/ethnic status, volunteer work, work experience, level of applicant's interest. ACT with Writing recommended. SAT with Essay component recommended. High school diploma is required and GED is accepted. *Academic units required:* 4 English, 3 math, 2 science, 2 science labs, 2 foreign language, 2 social studies, 3 academic electives. *Academic units recommended:* 4 English, 4 math, 4 science, 4 science labs, 3 foreign language, 3 social studies, 4 academic electives.

Financial Aid

Students should submit: FAFSA; State aid form. Priority filing deadline is 2/15. The Princeton Review suggests that all financial aid forms be submitted as soon as possible after October 1. *Need-based scholarships/grants offered:* College/university scholarship or grant aid from institutional funds; Federal Pell; Private scholarships; SEOG; State scholarships/grants. *Loan aid offered:* Direct PLUS loans; Direct Subsidized Stafford Loans; Direct Unsubsidized Stafford Loans. Applicants will be notified of awards on or about 3/1. Federal Work-Study Program available. Institutional employment available.

The Inside Word

When it comes to their admissions process, Randolph-Macon is pretty by-the-book. Certainly, your high school transcript will be of primary importance. Admissions officers are looking for evidence that you challenged yourself, so a handful of honors, AP, or IB classes will give your application a boost. Your standardized test scores and recommendation letter also hold significant weight. Lastly, though the college offers both Early Action and Regular Decision deadlines, they insist that no special preference is given to applicants for either deadline.

THE SCHOOL SAYS "..."

From the Admissions Office

"A Randolph-Macon College education begins with your future in mind. R-MC integrates an extraordinary education and pairs it with faculty, staff, coaches and alumni that provide you with a campus-wide support system to help you make the most of your R-MC experience. Campus life offers over one hundred organizations, including eSports, an equestrian program, and 18 varsity sports, to provide a dynamic event schedule that enriches your experience. Our challenging curriculum, national and global opportunities through internships and study abroad programs, which include our unique January Term experience, make Randolph-Macon students competitive for any career or academic pursuit post-graduation. This, paired with Randolph-Macon's four-year career preparation program, The EDGE, gives students a distinct, competitive advantage after graduation in reaching their career or graduate school goals. Ideally located just outside of Richmond, Virginia and 90 miles from Washington, D.C., R-MC offers a wide range of educational and career possibilities, partnerships with prestigious medical institutions, including guaranteed admissions to qualified students to medical or nursing school. The college also offers a new Bachelor of Science in Nursing with a direct entry option for qualified students. Our Four-Year-Degree Guarantee program promises that freshmen who meet the necessary requirements will graduate within four years, which ninety-five percent of Randolph-Macon College students achieve. R-MC's loyal alumni rank twenty-second in the nation for alumni giving, a true testament to their love of, and gratitude for, their Randolph-Macon experience. Randolph-Macon helps you build an extraordinary future."

SELECTIVITY

Admissions Rating	81
# of applicants	2,460
% of applicants accepted	71
% of acceptees attending	25

FRESHMAN PROFILE

Range SAT EBRW	540–630
Range SAT Math	510–610
Range SAT Composite	1050–1230
Range ACT Composite	20–26
# submitting SAT scores	392
% submitting SAT scores	91
# submitting ACT scores	96
% submitting ACT scores	22
Average HS GPA	3.7
% graduated top 10% of class	22
% graduated top 25% of class	50
% graduated top 50% of class	79

DEADLINES

Early action	
Deadline	11/15
Notification	1/1
Regular	
Priority	2/1
Deadline	3/1
Notification	4/1
Nonfall registration?	Yes

FINANCIAL FACTS

Financial Aid Rating	89
Annual tuition	$42,490
Room and board	$12,680
Required fees	$1,450
Books and supplies	$1,200
Average frosh need-based scholarship	$30,218
Average UG need-based scholarship	$28,452
% needy frosh rec. need-based scholarship or grant aid	100
% needy UG rec. need-based scholarship or grant aid	100
% needy frosh rec. non-need-based scholarship or grant aid	30
% needy UG rec. non-need-based scholarship or grant aid	27
% needy frosh rec. need-based self-help aid	65
% needy UG rec. need-based self-help aid	68
% frosh rec. any financial aid	100
% UG rec. any financial aid	99
% UG borrow to pay for school	90
Average cumulative indebtedness	$22,206
% frosh need fully met	37
% ugrads need fully met	32
Average % of frosh need met	84
Average % of ugrad need met	82

REED COLLEGE

3203 SE Woodstock Boulevard, Portland, OR 97202-8199 • Admissions: 503-777-7511 • Fax: 503-777-7553

STUDENTS SAY "..."

Academics

Reed is a college synonymous with academic rigor and a "passion for learning" certainly permeates this campus. A political science major steadfastly agrees stating, "Reed's commitment to academic excellence blew me away. The students here work like demons and love it!" In fact, "Reedies are proud that the most popular location on campus is the library, regardless of the night of the week." Fortunately, "there is a collective humor on campus and no one takes themselves too seriously." Undergrads also closely adhere to an "Honor Principle," which ensures that "cheating, peer-pressure or antagonism of any kind [is] extremely rare." This also helps to foster a culture in which "people would rather help each other learn than be the best." Additionally, small classes are integral to the academic experience here. The 9:1 "student to faculty ratio assures that the professors have the time to devote to their students, and students have plenty of opportunities to use that time, be it in thesis meetings, regular office hours, or just to bug the professor about a question they had about that day's conference or lab." And these undergrads are eager to lap up conversation with their "brilliant" professors who "love teaching" and "will not allow you to settle for mediocrity." All in all, the college "breeds free thought, pushes students to their intellectual limits, and strengthens each student's character all in the context of the welcoming environment that is the Reed campus and the surrounding city of Portland, Oregon."

Life

Intellectual discussions and debates are most definitely woven into the fabric of life here. As a physics major reveals, "One of my favorite things about Reed is how often people will strike up engaged discussions about anything. Be it conversations about the axiom of choice, the existence of free will, or the various merits of 1990s television shows, every conversation is fascinating. Best, you'll hear these conversations everywhere you go: dining hall, dorms, academic buildings, even just people walking around campus." Of course, this isn't wholly surprising given that life at Reed "revolves around academics." But fear not; even Reedies cannot survive by books alone. And, "while work and fun are, in many cases, synonymous, the need to break free from the library manifests on the weekends by campus dances and other forms of spontaneous creativity." A psychology major quickly adds, "I'm never bored because there's always something going on and it's never the same. Glittery dance parties in the Student Union? Check. Movie night in one of the Language Houses? Check. Debate-watching in Vollum? Check. Visiting lecturers? Check. Pool hall tournament? Check. RPG gaming night? Check." Finally, undergrads may take advantage of anything downtown Portland has to offer.

Student Body

As you probably already gleaned, the typical Reedie has "an overwhelming curiosity and desire to question everything." "Socially liberal" and a tad "socially awkward," these undergrads also define their peers as "witty and talented," and "smart." A content sophomore explains, "Everyone brings their own unique spin to everything—everyone has a hidden talent or skill that they would love to teach you about, or a wealth of knowledge in some obscure subject you've probably never heard of. Everyone is passionate about something, and it creates a dynamic and wonderful atmosphere." Additionally, "fitting in isn't hard, because student interests are so diverse that there's almost always a number of other people who like the same things you like and want to do the same things you want to do." Finally, a succinct sophomore sums up, "At Reed I found the kind of student body I craved in high school."

Financial Aid: 503-777-7223 • E-Mail: admission@reed.edu • Website: www.reed.edu

THE PRINCETON REVIEW SAYS

Admissions

Very important factors considered include: rigor of secondary school record, academic GPA, application essay. *Important factors considered include:* class rank, standardized test scores, recommendation(s), interview. *Other factors considered include:* extracurricular activities, talent/ability, character/personal qualities, first generation, alumni/ae relation, geographical residence, racial/ethnic status, volunteer work, work experience. Self-reported ACT with or without writing accepted. Self-reported SAT with or without Essay component accepted. High school diploma is required and GED is accepted. *Academic units recommended:* 4 English, 4 math, 3 science, 3 foreign language, 4 social studies.

Financial Aid

Students should submit: Business/Farm Supplement; CSS/Financial Aid PROFILE; FAFSA; Noncustodial PROFILE. Completed financial aid application is due at the same time as the application for admission. The Princeton Review suggests that all financial aid forms be submitted as soon as possible after October 1. *Need-based scholarships/grants offered:* College/university scholarship or grant aid from institutional funds; Federal Pell; Private scholarships; SEOG; State scholarships/grants. *Loan aid offered:* Direct PLUS loans; Direct Subsidized Stafford Loans; Direct Unsubsidized Stafford Loans. Generally, applicants will be notified of their financial aid awards within two weeks of receiving their admission decision. Federal Work-Study Program available. Institutional employment available.

The Inside Word

While there are no fixed requirements or "cut-off" points for applicants, Reed College is definitely on the lookout for students who maintain a thirst for knowledge and take their academics seriously. A rigorous curriculum is a must, so if possible take the rigorous classes offered at your high school. Candidates who demonstrate social consciousness, a desire to join an intellectual community and who appear to be independent thinkers might have a leg up.

THE SCHOOL SAYS "..."

From the Admissions Office

"Intellectual. Intense. Inspiring. Transformative. For over 100 years, Reed has sought to provide the finest educational program in the country, offering students an extraordinary environment in which to discover their passions and pursue them with depth and determination.

"Reed provides a singular example of the liberal arts experience: a structured curriculum with an emphasis on independent inquiry; extensive feedback from professors emphasized instead of letter grades on assignments; and a deeply collaborative academic environment. You will learn how to learn—how to dedicate yourself to studying and how to work toward the production of new knowledge.

"The Reed community is self-directed and guided by the Honor Principle. This dual commitment to the independence of thought and mutual trust and respect helps to create an environment in which students feel inspired, challenged, and fulfilled.

"Students at Reed dedicate themselves to the life of the mind."

SELECTIVITY

Admissions Rating	94
# of applicants	5,815
% of applicants accepted	39
% of acceptees attending	17
# offered a place on the wait list	1,557
% accepting a place on wait list	33
% admitted from wait list	3
# of early decision applicants	225
% accepted early decision	48

FRESHMAN PROFILE

Range SAT EBRW	670–750
Range SAT Math	655–770
Range ACT Composite	30–34
# submitting SAT scores	3,634
% submitting SAT scores	62
# submitting ACT scores	2,033
% submitting ACT scores	35
% graduated top 10% of class	53
% graduated top 25% of class	83
% graduated top 50% of class	95

DEADLINES

Early decision	
Deadline	11/15
Notification	12/15
Other ED Deadline	12/20
Other ED Notification	2/1
Early action	
Deadline	11/15
Notification	2/1
Regular	
Deadline	1/15
Notification	4/1
Nonfall registration?	No

FINANCIAL FACTS

Financial Aid Rating	95
Annual tuition	$60,310
Room and board	$14,980
Required fees	$310
Books and supplies	$1,050
Average frosh need-based scholarship	$42,096
Average UG need-based scholarship	$39,742
% needy frosh rec. need-based scholarship or grant aid	99
% needy UG rec. need-based scholarship or grant aid	98
% needy frosh rec. non-need-based scholarship or grant aid	0
% needy UG rec. non-need-based scholarship or grant aid	0
% needy frosh rec. need-based self-help aid	99
% needy UG rec. need-based self-help aid	98
% frosh rec. any financial aid	55
% UG rec. any financial aid	52
% UG borrow to pay for school	48
Average cumulative indebtedness	$25,657
% frosh need fully met	100
% ugrads need fully met	100
Average % of frosh need met	100
Average % of ugrad need met	100

RENSSELAER POLYTECHNIC INSTITUTE

110 Eighth Street, Troy, NY 12180-3590 • Admissions: 518-276-6216 • Fax: 518-276-4072

CAMPUS LIFE

Quality of Life Rating	85
Fire Safety Rating	94
Green Rating	60*
Type of school	Private
Environment	City

STUDENTS

Total undergrad enrollment	6,203
% male/female	68/32
% from out of state	66
% frosh from public high school	70
% frosh live on campus	100
% ugrads live on campus	57
# of fraternities (% ugrad men join)	29 (30)
# of sororities (% ugrad women join)	5 (16)
% African American	4
% Asian	15
% Caucasian	47
% Hispanic	10
% Native American	<1
% Pacific Islander	0
% Two or more races	5
% Race and/or ethnicity unknown	3
% international	16
# of countries represented	44

SURVEY SAYS . . .

Internships are widely available
Lots of beer drinking
Very little drug use
Intramural sports are popular
Alumni active on campus

ACADEMICS

Academic Rating	85
% students returning for sophomore year	92
% students graduating within 4 years	61
% students graduating within 6 years	83
Calendar	Semester
Student/faculty ratio	13:1
Profs interesting rating	83
Profs accessible rating	93
Most classes have 10–19 students.	

MOST POPULAR MAJORS

Business/Commerce, General; Computer Engineering, General; Electrical and Electronics Engineering

STUDENTS SAY ". . ."

Academics

As the nation's oldest technological university, Rensselaer Polytechnic Institute in upstate New York has a rightfully deserved reputation in the science and engineering world, having led tens of thousands of bright minds to look at "innovation and the future." "Research opportunities" and facilities are everywhere, and students are encouraged to work in interdisciplinary programs that allow them to combine scholarly work from several departments or schools. When their four years are complete, students are encouraged to take what they learn and use it for the greater good. "Why not change the world?" asks a student.

The professors at RPI are "passionate about teaching," "very accessible, and really there for the students." Though there are certainly some "dull" professors ("I've seen the good, the bad, and the ugly!" says one student), most find that the faculty is praiseworthy and "serve as great mentors for students." "My professors in my direct major are extremely hands-on and discussion-based," says a student. Thanks to the "focus on problem-solving," professors are always looking to get students involved in projects, and one of "the greatest strengths of [the] school is the resources that they offer." On top of that, the "welcoming overall community" fosters success, as "students are not extremely competitive and everyone tends to help each other out."

The school is "rigorous," but the students "do find time to enjoy the downtime when we get it." RPI "is a place where nerds can get both an excellent education and an enjoyable four years," according to one student. The student union is entirely student-run, giving students "a lot of freedom to control our educational experience." Many of the student clubs both "suit your interests and work toward your professional career after college." All in all, "community and knowledge drive this school to push students to excel in school and after graduation."

Life

Everyone agrees that RPI is just the right size: "The kind of size where you don't know everybody but you see ten people you know as you walk across campus (and it only takes ten minutes to walk across campus)." People at RPI "don't care how weird or different you are, they let you be." "You can be anyone you want—the kid sword-fighting with his friends in quad or an avid musician who has a 4.0," says a student. Most students do have a "nerdy" side to them, and they inherently love math/science—"even the humanities at RPI are laced with the sweet smell of science," and "physics equation graffiti" can be found on some walls. Academics are definitely an important priority here, but "extracurricular activities are balanced alongside the classes, labs, homework, and studying." There are hundreds of clubs on campus (such as Engineers for a Sustainable World and the Model Railroad Society, which does model railroading of upstate New York and Vermont all circa the early- to mid-1950s), and "most people are involved in several." There are always campus events that students can attend, which range from "athletic events and cultural programs to student ensemble concerts and open mic shows." Downtown Troy has some "quaint cafes and places to explore," Albany has shopping malls, parks, and movie theaters, and a ski trip to Lake Placid is easily accomplished. "There is so much to do around here—you'll never be bored if you take the time to explore." Men's hockey games are a large part of student life here, and "Greek life accounts for about one-fourth of the undergraduate student body and is a great leadership experience and a large contributor to the social scene."

Student Body

Everyone here is pretty much without a doubt "a little bit nerdy, but friendly and helpful." This tinge of nerdiness in everyone "brings the students together and makes it a fun environment with little to no discrimination." "The typical student at my school is studious, but also social in their own way," explains a student. There is a whole spectrum of social students, which ranges "from socializing with a select few to the person that is a social butterfly," but no matter which path you choose, "people don't judge at RPI."

RENSSELAER POLYTECHNIC INSTITUTE

Financial Aid: 518-276-6813 • E-Mail: admissions@rpi.edu • Website: www.rpi.edu

THE PRINCETON REVIEW SAYS

Admissions

Very important factors considered include: rigor of secondary school record, class rank, academic GPA, standardized test scores. *Important factors considered include:* application essay, recommendation(s), extracurricular activities, character/personal qualities. *Other factors considered include:* talent/ability, first generation, alumni/ae relation, racial/ethnic status, volunteer work, work experience, level of applicant's interest. ACT with or without writing accepted. SAT with or without Essay component accepted. High school diploma is required and GED is accepted. *Academic units required:* 4 English, 4 math, 3 science, 3 social studies. *Academic units recommended:* 4 science, 3 social studies.

Financial Aid

Students should submit: CSS/Financial Aid PROFILE; FAFSA. Priority filing deadline is 2/1. The Princeton Review suggests that all financial aid forms be submitted as soon as possible after October 1. *Need-based scholarships/grants offered:* College/university scholarship or grant aid from institutional funds; Federal Pell; Private scholarships; SEOG; State scholarships/grants. *Loan aid offered:* Direct PLUS loans; Direct Subsidized Stafford Loans; Direct Unsubsidized Stafford Loans. Applicants will be notified of awards on or about 3/15. Federal Work-Study Program available. Institutional employment available.

The Inside Word

Outstanding test scores and grades are pretty much a must for any applicant hopeful of impressing the RPI admissions committee. Cohorts of underrepresented minorities and women are increasing each year. The school is unlikely to admit anyone who lacks the skills and background to survive here.

THE SCHOOL SAYS "..."

From the Admissions Office

"The oldest degree-granting technological research university in the U.S., Rensselaer was founded in 1824 to instruct students to apply 'science to the common purposes of life.' Students immerse themselves in course work that combines theory with learning by experience in unparalleled facilities, using advanced technology. Rensselaer offers more than 100 programs and 1,000 courses leading to bachelor's, master's, and doctoral degrees. Undergraduates pursue studies in architecture; engineering; humanities, arts, and social sciences; business; science; and information technology (web science). A pioneer in interactive learning, Rensselaer provides real-world, hands-on educational opportunities that cut across academic disciplines. The Rensselaer student experience, or CLASS (Clustered Learning Advocacy and Support for Students) provides programs and support for students that begins even before they arrive on campus. Students have ready access to laboratories and classes involving lively discussion, problem solving, and faculty mentoring. Students are able to take full advantage of Rensselaer's unique research platforms: the Center for Biotechnology and Interdisciplinary Studies; one of the world's most powerful academic supercomputers, the Center for Computational Innovations; and the Experimental Media and Performing Arts Center, which encourages students to explore the intersection of science, technology, and the arts. Newly renovated residence halls, wireless computing network, and studio classrooms create a fertile environment for study and learning. Rensselaer offers recreational and fitness facilities plus numerous student-run organizations and activities, including fraternities and sororities, newspaper, television and radio station, drama and musical groups, and more than 200 clubs. In addition to intramural sports, NCAA varsity sports include Division I men's and women's ice hockey teams and twenty-one Division III men's and women's teams in thirteen sports. The East Campus Athletic Village raises the bar for student athletic facilities for varsity and non-varsity athletes alike, and includes a football arena, basketball stadium, and sports medicine and training complex."

SELECTIVITY

Admissions Rating	**93**
# of applicants	18,635
% of applicants accepted	47
% of acceptees attending	19
# offered a place on the wait list	4,896
% accepting a place on wait list	64
% admitted from wait list	2
# of early decision applicants	850
% accepted early decision	65

FRESHMAN PROFILE

Range SAT EBRW	620–710
Range SAT Math	670–780
Range ACT Composite	28–34
# submitting SAT scores	1,149
% submitting SAT scores	69
# submitting ACT scores	516
% submitting ACT scores	31
Average HS GPA	3.9
% graduated top 10% of class	63
% graduated top 25% of class	92
% graduated top 50% of class	98

DEADLINES

Early decision	
Deadline	11/1
Notification	12/14
Other ED Deadline	12/15
Other ED Notification	1/18
Regular	
Notification	3/7
Nonfall registration?	Yes

FINANCIAL FACTS

Financial Aid Rating	**86**
Annual tuition	$54,000
Room and board	$15,580
Required fees	$1,375
Books and supplies	$2,858
Average frosh need-based scholarship	$40,272
Average UG need-based scholarship	$38,809
% needy frosh rec. need-based scholarship or grant aid	100
% needy UG rec. need-based scholarship or grant aid	100
% needy frosh rec. non-need-based scholarship or grant aid	21
% needy UG rec. non-need-based scholarship or grant aid	14
% needy frosh rec. need-based self-help aid	99
% needy UG rec. need-based self-help aid	97
% frosh rec. any financial aid	83
% UG rec. any financial aid	86
% UG borrow to pay for school	63
% frosh need fully met	24
% ugrads need fully met	19
Average % of frosh need met	82
Average % of ugrad need met	79

RHODES COLLEGE

2000 North Parkway, Memphis, TN 38112 • Admissions: 901-843-3700 • Fax: 901-843-3631

STUDENTS SAY "..."

Academics

Rhodes College is a small, appealing southern institution that produces "graduates that have lots of knowledge and experience." To say that the program is "academically very strong" or "unparalleled, especially in the sciences" might actually be somewhat of an understatement, considering feedback from some students who began working before even matriculating. "I was granted a position in a research lab prior to even starting my first semester as a freshman." Early opportunities like these are a common refrain from undergrads, who also talk up the school's "infinite resources," which include academic coaches, peer and professor tutors, advisors for classes and health, and many more. Rhodes also allows students to access their strong alumni network, which provides an "immense array of career opportunities," and there's also a "well-developed study abroad program."

But perhaps the highest praise is reserved for Rhodes' faculty and staff, whom many say are the school's "greatest strength." Students love that their professors "each retain their unique styles, with accessibility being the only common factor." Many "go above and beyond to help students succeed," which is apparent from the way office hours are utilized, not just for help "but for lively discussions on papers..., for finding research opportunities, or just to chat, because they're great humans." And a classmate simply sums up by saying, "Professors have challenged me, and through it all, I have learned more than I ever thought possible."

Life

Undergrads at Rhodes tend to be serious about their academics and students certainly "study very hard throughout the week." Nevertheless, there's plenty to enjoy and experience beyond classwork. For starters, undergrads can join groups as disparate as the board game club and bee-keeping club, get involved with mock trials and student government, or try out for the "really great intramural frisbee team." A number of people also like to participate in the "Rhodes Outdoor Organization, which provides totally free trips to go camping, hiking, and climbing out of Memphis, as well as trips to more local sites to rock climb indoors." Additionally, "Greek life is very big" and we're told that "frat parties are common on Saturday and Friday night." Students also make the most of the city of Memphis, whether that's heading to "Beale Street for night life" going on a taste-test of new restaurants because "the food is amazing" or "attending music and arts fests in Cooper-Young neighborhood."

Student Body

The "great community feel" at Rhodes comes down to the unifying desire to learn. "Students WANT to come to class and complete assignments, because they truly care about the work they are doing." Unsurprisingly, peers describe one another as "very motivated," "intelligent" and "extremely hardworking." Admittedly, students also state that "the campus still feels very white," but qualify this by calling out the fact that they've "met people with diverse perspectives, cultures, and interests that have allowed me to learn more about the world beyond the classroom." Regardless of background, students appraise one another as "genuine, kind, and respectful of others," and one adds that "I'm amazed by how inclusive the student body is and the opportunities they create to ensure the acceptance and safety of everyone." All in all, "finding 'your group' of people is very easy, and not difficult at all because everyone just bonds easily."

Financial Aid: 901-843-3810 • E-Mail: adminfo@rhodes.edu • Website: http://www.rhodes.edu

THE PRINCETON REVIEW SAYS

Admissions

Very important factors considered include: rigor of secondary school record, class rank, academic GPA. *Important factors considered include:* application essay, standardized test scores, recommendation(s), character/personal qualities, alumni/ae relation. *Other factors considered include:* interview, extracurricular activities, talent/ability, first generation, geographical residence, state residency, volunteer work, work experience, level of applicant's interest. ACT with or without writing accepted. SAT with or without Essay component accepted. High school diploma is required and GED is accepted. *Academic units required:* 4 English, 3 math, 2 science, 2 science labs, 2 foreign language, 2 social studies, 3 academic electives.

Financial Aid

Students should submit: CSS/Financial Aid PROFILE; FAFSA; Noncustodial PROFILE. Priority filing deadline is 11/15. The Princeton Review suggests that all financial aid forms be submitted as soon as possible after October 1. *Need-based scholarships/grants offered:* College/university scholarship or grant aid from institutional funds; Federal Pell; Private scholarships; SEOG; State scholarships/grants. *Loan aid offered:* Direct PLUS loans; Direct Subsidized Stafford Loans; Direct Unsubsidized Stafford Loans. Federal Work-Study Program available. Institutional employment available.

The Inside Word

Admissions officers at Rhodes make it their mission to find candidates who will be a great fit for the school. This means that you can expect all facets of your application to be carefully considered: from your GPA and test scores to your letters of recommendation and extracurricular involvement. And if you're confident Rhodes is your top choice, we recommend applying early decision. The school gives priority consideration to these candidates with regards to both admission and financial aid.

THE SCHOOL SAYS "..."

From the Admissions Office

"Rhodes is a residential college committed to liberal arts and sciences. Our highest priorities are intellectual engagement, service to others, and honor among ourselves. We live this life on one of the country's most beautiful campuses in the heart of Memphis, Tennessee, an economic, political, and cultural center, making Rhodes one of a handful of top-tier, liberal arts colleges in a major metropolitan area.

"Rhodes has the soul of a liberal arts college coupled with a real-world mindset. Our students put their liberal arts knowledge to work in the world starting their first year. You'll be encouraged to engage in research, leadership and service opportunities—and to take responsibility for shaping your educational experience to meet your personal interests and goals. Memphis is a thriving city right on Rhodes' doorstep, with spectacular resources for students, and the college has pioneered the establishment of programs with world-class institutions and companies, including St. Jude Children's Research Hospital, FedEx and the Memphis Zoo, which take advantage of the college's metropolitan location and provide students with real-world opportunities for academic and personal growth."

SELECTIVITY

Admissions Rating	**92**
# of applicants	5,207
% of applicants accepted	45
% of acceptees attending	22
# offered a place on the wait list	1,237
% accepting a place on wait list	27
% admitted from wait list	22
# of early decision applicants	220
% accepted early decision	66

FRESHMAN PROFILE

Range SAT EBRW	620–700
Range SAT Math	600–730
Range ACT Composite	27–32
# submitting SAT scores	184
% submitting SAT scores	36
# submitting ACT scores	373
% submitting ACT scores	72
Average HS GPA	3.7
% graduated top 10% of class	52
% graduated top 25% of class	83
% graduated top 50% of class	99

DEADLINES

Early decision	
Deadline	11/1
Notification	12/1
Other ED Deadline	1/15
Other ED Notification	2/1
Early action	
Deadline	11/15
Notification	1/15
Regular	
Notification	4/1
Nonfall registration?	Yes

APPLICANTS ALSO LOOK AT AND OFTEN PREFER

Washington University in St. Louis; Washington and Lee University

AND SOMETIMES PREFER

Vanderbilt University; The University of the South; Furman University; Davidson College

AND RARELY PREFER

Millsaps College; Elon University; University of Tennessee—Knoxville

FINANCIAL FACTS

Financial Aid Rating	**93**
Annual tuition	$48,888
Room and board	$11,631
Required fees	$310
Books and supplies	$1,125
Average frosh need-based scholarship	$35,927
Average UG need-based scholarship	$34,229
% needy frosh rec. need-based scholarship or grant aid	99
% needy UG rec. need-based scholarship or grant aid	99
% needy frosh rec. non-need-based scholarship or grant aid	43
% needy UG rec. non-need-based scholarship or grant aid	36
% needy frosh rec. need-based self-help aid	53
% needy UG rec. need-based self-help aid	59
% frosh rec. any financial aid	96
% UG rec. any financial aid	95
% UG borrow to pay for school	46
Average cumulative indebtedness	$26,155
% frosh need fully met	49
% ugrads need fully met	58
Average % of frosh need met	94
Average % of ugrad need met	91

RICE UNIVERSITY

MS-17 PO Box 1892, Houston, TX 77251-1892 • Admissions: 713-348-7423 • Fax: 713-348-5952

STUDENTS SAY "..."

Academics

A private research university in Houston, Rice University offers a top-notch "level of prestige," that, when combined with a similar "level of support provided by the university" and the "support of the residential college system," makes for "an ideal environment." In addition to being a "premier research university," Rice is an "amazing place for students because of how much professors care about teaching undergraduates." Professors, who are "easily accessible outside the classroom" and "experts in their specific fields," introduce students to "a number of perspectives" and "push [students] to think [more deeply] about [the] world." The "pre-med program offers a large number of opportunities," and "is known for its strong biochemistry and medical research," aided by its "proximity to the Texas Medical Center." Rice is also known for its "prestigious architecture program." Overall, students praise the "strong curriculum" offered with "flexibility" that makes it "easy to add/drop/change majors and minors while still graduating on time." The college is flush with resources, but if a need arises, students are empowered to take "leadership roles" and maintain "direct contact with the administration." Small class sizes foster a deep relationship with professors in every department. One grateful student says, "I have personally benefited from close working relationships with most of my professors in my major department, beginning in my freshman year." The opportunities this affords for research and collaboration cannot be understated, and the funding for students in the humanities tends to be particularly good: small numbers of students in these areas makes each department more willing to spend a greater proportion on individual students.

Life

Students are attracted to Rice's location, in the "unique and vibrant city of Houston." The innovative "residential college system is "truly special" because of its "ability to supply students with an immediate family after stepping foot onto campus." Before matriculating, each of the university's undergraduates "becomes a member of one of eleven residential colleges, which have their own dining halls, public rooms, and dorms on campus." Each student is "randomly assigned to one of the colleges, and maintains membership in the same college throughout their undergraduate years," and each college is assigned a "faculty magister," who "lives in an adjacent house." Rice students are "spoiled with opportunities [for] fun," but students "are concerned first and foremost with their academics, and prioritize that over anything else." That being said, "all welcome distractions from the daily routine." "On any given night of the week there is...some kind of event" and "crawls and parties tend to be quite frequent starting Thursday night through the weekend." Students also "support their Owls in whatever athletic contests are going on," visit the "museum district, which is close by," or "hang out in the commons of their residential colleges after class doing homework."

Student Body

Rice has been said to have "the happiest students in the United States" and "a high quality of life." Students count that as a major impressing factor on their decision to enroll: "I wanted my college years to be both happy and successful," one student says, "and I found no other schools that were as prestigious, but also dedicated to ensuring the happiness of the student body." Students describe their peers as "enthusiastic," "helpful," "politically liberal," and highly involved in "civic engagement" in the form of voter registration efforts, campaigning for local leaders, and so on. The emphasis is on collaboration: students are "incredibly supportive and encouraging" and "truly care about each other's intellectual and emotional growth," which helps Rice "foster positivity" and "inclusivity," "especially helpful" in an academically rigorous environment. There is "never any competition." "When people told me that the school was collaborative," one student says, "I never imagined that...Seniors would stay up late just to help me with things I've been struggling with, even when they have their own work to do." Rice has a "culture of care," another student reports.

Financial Aid: 713-348-4958 • E-Mail: admission@rice.edu • Website: www.rice.edu

THE PRINCETON REVIEW SAYS

Admissions

Very important factors considered include: rigor of secondary school record, class rank, academic GPA, application essay, standardized test scores, recommendation(s), extracurricular activities, talent/ability, character/personal qualities. *Other factors considered include:* interview, first generation, alumni/ae relation, geographical residence, state residency, racial/ethnic status, volunteer work, work experience, level of applicant's interest. ACT with or without writing accepted. SAT with or without Essay component accepted. High school diploma or equivalent is not required. *Academic units required:* 4 English, 3 math, 2 science, 2 science labs, 2 foreign language, 2 social studies, 3 academic electives. *Academic units recommended:* 4 English, 4 math, 4 science, 3 science labs, 4 foreign language, 3 social studies, 3 academic electives.

Financial Aid

Students should submit: CSS/Financial Aid PROFILE; FAFSA; Noncustodial PROFILE. Priority filing deadline is 2/15. The Princeton Review suggests that all financial aid forms be submitted as soon as possible after October 1. *Need-based scholarships/grants offered:* College/university scholarship or grant aid from institutional funds; Federal Pell; Private scholarships; SEOG; State scholarships/grants. *Loan aid offered:* Direct PLUS loans; Direct Subsidized Stafford Loans; Direct Unsubsidized Stafford Loans. Applicants will be notified of awards on or about 4/1. Federal Work-Study Program available. Institutional employment available.

The Inside Word

Gaining admission to Rice University isn't easy. That being said, no one metric in particular holds the most weight. The university considers everything from academic prowess and special talents to creativity, life experiences, and leadership. It should be noted that applicants must apply to one of six schools—humanities, engineering, natural sciences, architecture, music, or social sciences. The school you select is not binding but should reflect your skills and interests. For "high achieving, low-income students" Rice is a participating college in QuestBridge, which provides financial aid packages that include tuition and fees, room and board, books and supplies, and personal and travel expenses.

THE SCHOOL SAYS "..."

From the Admissions Office

"We seek students of keen intellect and diverse backgrounds who show potential to succeed at Rice and have a desire to shape the world around them.

"Rice looks for students who have demonstrated exceptional academic ability and the potential for personal and intellectual growth. Admission is competitive, and we consider not only high school grades and test scores, but also leadership, participation in extracurricular activities, and personal creativity. We practice holistic, committee-based evaluation to build a broad, diverse, and vibrant community of scholars. While students indicate an intended area of study in the application, this selection is nonbinding and acts as a lens through which we review applicants.

"Rice's signature financial aid program, The Rice Investment, is one of the best in country. It provides full-tuition scholarships and grants to degree-seeking undergraduates with family incomes between $65,000 and $130,000 who are eligible to receive need-based financial aid. In addition, students with family incomes between $130,000 and $200,000 will receive scholarships covering at least half of their tuition. Support for students from low-income families will also be significantly enhanced under the program, and students with family incomes below $65,000 will receive grant aid covering not only their full tuition, but also all of their mandatory fees and room and board."

SELECTIVITY

Admissions Rating	98
# of applicants	27,087
% of applicants accepted	9
% of acceptees attending	41
# offered a place on the wait list	2,788
% accepting a place on wait list	67
% admitted from wait list	0
# of early decision applicants	2,628
% accepted early decision	16

FRESHMAN PROFILE

Range SAT EBRW	720–770
Range SAT Math	750–800
Range SAT Composite	1470–1560
Range ACT Composite	33–35
# submitting SAT scores	646
% submitting SAT scores	67
# submitting ACT scores	318
% submitting ACT scores	33
% graduated top 10% of class	93
% graduated top 25% of class	99
% graduated top 50% of class	100

DEADLINES

Early decision	
Deadline	11/1
Notification	12/15
Regular	
Deadline	1/1
Notification	4/1
Nonfall registration?	No

FINANCIAL FACTS

Financial Aid Rating	97
Annual tuition	$48,330
Room and board	$14,140
Required fees	$782
Books and supplies	$1,200
Average frosh need-based scholarship	$46,975
Average UG need-based scholarship	$48,300
% needy frosh rec. need-based scholarship or grant aid	97
% needy UG rec. need-based scholarship or grant aid	98
% needy frosh rec. non-need-based scholarship or grant aid	11
% needy UG rec. non-need-based scholarship or grant aid	8
% needy frosh rec. need-based self-help aid	36
% needy UG rec. need-based self-help aid	40
% frosh rec. any financial aid	56
% UG borrow to pay for school	25
Average cumulative indebtedness	$24,292
% frosh need fully met	99
% ugrads need fully met	99
Average % of frosh need met	100
Average % of ugrad need met	100

RIDER UNIVERSITY

2083 Lawrenceville Road, Lawrenceville, NJ 08648-3099 • Admissions: 609-896-5042 • Fax: 609-895-6645

CAMPUS LIFE

Quality of Life Rating	83
Fire Safety Rating	85
Green Rating	97
Type of school	Private
Environment	Village

STUDENTS

Total undergrad enrollment	3,763
% male/female	44/56
% from out of state	23
% frosh live on campus	83
% ugrads live on campus	53
# of fraternities	6
# of sororities	9
% African American	14
% Asian	5
% Caucasian	55
% Hispanic	17
% Native American	<1
% Pacific Islander	<1
% Two or more races	4
% Race and/or ethnicity unknown	2
% international	3
# of countries represented	73

SURVEY SAYS . . .

Theater is popular
Students are friendly
Great off-campus food
Easy to get around campus

ACADEMICS

Academic Rating	76
% students returning for sophomore year	77
% students graduating within 4 years	54
% students graduating within 6 years	67
Calendar	Semester
Student/faculty ratio	10:1
Profs interesting rating	84
Profs accessible rating	90

Most classes have 10–19 students.
Most lab/discussion sessions have
10–19 students.

MOST POPULAR MAJORS

Business Administration; Management and
Operations; Computer Science; Information
Systems and Supply Chain Management;
Cybersecurity; Accounting; Psychology; Marketing;
Criminal Justice; Biology; Health Sciences;
Teacher Education

STUDENTS SAY "..."

Academics

New Jersey's Rider University focuses on enriching its students not only through academics, but through encouraging students to participate in a variety of engaged learning opportunities. The university's location between Philadelphia and New York City offers "fantastic internship opportunities" as well as co-ops, and this experiential learning is an integral part of the Rider curriculum. The business, education, and performing arts schools are notable highlights of the school's seventy majors, and the financial aid packages are "fantastic and extremely generous, especially for the merit-based scholarship awards." The Career Development & Success department is at the ready to help students start their careers upon graduation (for those not already hired by their internship organizations, which is common): "It's actually really incredible to see students within the business school getting very good jobs straight out of college," says a student.

One of the school's greatest strengths is "the support each student has from the faculty and staff," who are here "to support and uplift students" and encourage self-motivation. "If you need help in any way people will go to great lengths to help you in any way they can," says a student. Almost all professors hold discussion-based classes and are "extremely accessible outside of the classroom," though students admit that there are a few "that don't really have any interest in teaching," "I have had some professors who are inspirational, and so passionate about a topic that it furthers my interest," says one student. Even the adjuncts that typically teach classes at night bring their personal experience from being full-time in the field to the classroom, which allows students to see real-world experiences. "My school is all about experience, making Rider the experience you want to have in college," says a student.

Life

Rider has "a very encompassing campus life," with a "broad range" of student-run groups and events facilitated by the school: "If there is something you want to do, you can find a way to do it." The Student Entertainment Council "has made great strides" to ensure that Rider is not branded a suitcase school (as in the past), and there are events planned every weekend throughout the year, from "comedians to fashion shows and everything else under the sun." Also, there are "countless performances and workshops you can attend every week." Most people play a sport or are involved in Greek life, and the athletic community is "very supportive of each other in going to games and cheering them on." A lot of students have work study jobs on campus, and the Student Government Association "works vigorously to ensure the quality of life for students is as good as it can be." When these students have some downtime, there is a recreational center that "has video game consoles such as Xbox and PlayStation as well as pool and ping pong." New York and Philadelphia are both just train rides away, and people also "go off campus to Princeton to eat and explore."

Student Body

Rider's small enrollment allows students to create "a close-knit community within the school that promotes networking and personal relationships with peers." This "unified and impressive" group with diverse interests "are unafraid of challenging expeditions, classes, jobs, internships, and more." In fact, students know they can "rely on each other for daily interactions and fun." There is a mix of on-campus students and commuting students, and though cliques can form within areas of study, "even people with the same majors have their own unique personality."

RIDER UNIVERSITY

Financial Aid: 609-896-5188 • E-Mail: admissions@rider.edu • Website: www.rider.edu

THE PRINCETON REVIEW SAYS

Admissions

Very important factors considered include: rigor of secondary school record, academic GPA, application essay, recommendation(s). *Other factors considered include:* class rank, standardized test scores, interview, extracurricular activities, talent/ability, character/personal qualities, alumni/ae relation, geographical residence, state residency, volunteer work, work experience, level of applicant's interest. ACT with or without writing accepted. SAT with or without Essay component accepted. High school diploma is required and GED is accepted. *Academic units required:* 4 English, 3 math. *Academic units recommended:* 4 science, 4 science labs, 2 foreign language, 2 social studies, 2 history.

Financial Aid

Students should submit: FAFSA. Priority filing deadline is 2/1. The Princeton Review suggests that all financial aid forms be submitted as soon as possible after October 1. *Need-based scholarships/grants offered:* College/university scholarship or grant aid from institutional funds; Federal Pell; Private scholarships; SEOG; State scholarships/grants. *Loan aid offered:* Direct PLUS loans; Direct Subsidized Stafford Loans; Direct Unsubsidized Stafford Loans. Applicants will be notified of awards on a rolling basis beginning 2/1. Federal Work-Study Program available. Institutional employment available.

The Inside Word

To prepare for college, Rider University suggests that high school students follow a rigorous curriculum of college prep courses, including AP and honors classes. Students need at least four years of high school English and three years of math (including Algebra 2) to be considered for admission to Rider. The most recent incoming class had an average high school GPA of 3.32. Although most students major in the liberal arts and sciences, more than a quarter of undergraduates are enrolled in the business school. Rider University accepts applications on a rolling basis.

THE SCHOOL SAYS "..."

From the Admissions Office

"At Rider University, your future is wide open.

"Whether you know exactly what your future holds, or are still figuring it out, Rider provides the support to follow your drive and the freedom to explore our 100+ majors and minors.

"The majors at Rider open a world of possibility from internships, to grad school, to career opportunities and new passions you may have not discovered yet! Our Engaged Learning Program combines your academics, career goals and personal interests to guide you through eye-opening, life-changing opportunities.

"Rider is a beautiful campus, but the connections, lessons and sense of community you find here will follow you anywhere. So if you can't come to us, don't worry. Through video calls, photo galleries, texting, live chat—you name it—we'll bring the spirit of Rider to you.

"The Rider experience is an investment in your growth and potential. We're committed to making Rider affordable for all our students, and that begins with exceptional financial aid options. We encourage you to invest in yourself, and our financial aid counselors are here to answer any questions, and guide you, every step of the way.

"Whether you know exactly what you want to do or aren't yet sure where you're headed, let's figure it out together."

SELECTIVITY
Admissions Rating	79
# of applicants	9,388
% of applicants accepted	71
% of acceptees attending	13
# offered a place on the wait list	35
% accepting a place on wait list	20
% admitted from wait list	57

FRESHMAN PROFILE
Range SAT EBRW	510–600
Range SAT Math	510–600
Range SAT Composite	1040–1200
Range ACT Composite	19–26
# submitting SAT scores	484
% submitting SAT scores	56
# submitting ACT scores	77
% submitting ACT scores	9
Average HS GPA	3.3
% graduated top 10% of class	14
% graduated top 25% of class	35
% graduated top 50% of class	77

DEADLINES
Early action	
Deadline	11/15
Notification	12/15
Regular	
Priority	1/15
Notification	Rolling, 12/15
Nonfall registration?	Yes

FINANCIAL FACTS
Financial Aid Rating	86
Annual tuition	$45,120
Room and board	$15,500
Required fees	$740
Books and supplies	$1,500
Average frosh need-based scholarship	$33,611
Average UG need-based scholarship	$29,739
% needy frosh rec. need-based scholarship or grant aid	100
% needy UG rec. need-based scholarship or grant aid	99
% needy frosh rec. non-need-based scholarship or grant aid	16
% needy UG rec. non-need-based scholarship or grant aid	16
% needy frosh rec. need-based self-help aid	78
% needy UG rec. need-based self-help aid	80
% frosh rec. any financial aid	98
% UG rec. any financial aid	89
% UG borrow to pay for school	78
Average cumulative indebtedness	$35,781
% frosh need fully met	18
% ugrads need fully met	17
Average % of frosh need met	79
Average % of ugrad need met	76

RIPON COLLEGE

PO Box 248, Ripon, WI 54971 • Admissions: 920-748-8337 • Fax: 920-748-8335

CAMPUS LIFE

Quality of Life Rating	91
Fire Safety Rating	76
Green Rating	65
Type of school	Private
Environment	Village

STUDENTS

Total undergrad enrollment	787
% male/female	46/54
% from out of state	30
% frosh from public high school	75
% frosh live on campus	98
% ugrads live on campus	95
# of fraternities (% ugrad men join)	5 (38)
# of sororities (% ugrad women join)	3 (26)
% African American	4
% Asian	2
% Caucasian	78
% Hispanic	10
% Native American	<1
% Pacific Islander	<1
% Two or more races	2
% Race and/or ethnicity unknown	<1
% international	3
# of countries represented	14

SURVEY SAYS . . .

No one cheats
Lots of beer drinking
Very little drug use
Intramural sports are popular

ACADEMICS

Academic Rating	85
% students returning for sophomore year	78
% students graduating within 4 years	61
% students graduating within 6 years	68
Calendar	Semester
Student/faculty ratio	13:1
Profs interesting rating	93
Profs accessible rating	97

Most classes have 10–19 students.
Most lab/discussion sessions have
    10–19 students.

MOST POPULAR MAJORS

Business/Commerce, General; History, General;
Exercise Science; General

STUDENTS SAY ". . ."

Academics

Described as a "close-knit community," "Ripon is a place where a student's best interest matters; all other agendas are secondary." One student chose Ripon because, "I was looking for a liberal arts school that allowed me to do the things I like, namely, be involved in multiple student groups, study abroad, and take classes in different fields, all of which I have been able to do at Ripon." The "quiet beauty," "welcoming nature of the campus," along with "small class sizes and a lot of personal attention from professors" create a "friendly, home-away-from-home atmosphere." Students appreciate the education they are receiving and how it prepares them for a productive life after college. The school's motto, "more together" "is exactly what our school is all about; becoming something more with the help of those here to guide us." "Ripon College prepares students to be productive, service-minded leaders who are ready and willing to influence the direction of our nation's future." "Ripon College is not all about sitting in a classroom listening to lectures and taking notes; it's about teaching us to become more educated in the world around us and helping us to develop the skills needed to succeed." "The hands-on, experiential, service-learning projects have been particularly valuable for my own personal growth and for preparing me for life after college." Another student agrees, saying, "Ripon is a prime example of a college with a positive and supportive living and learning community." "Ripon professors provide an interesting and intellectually challenging environment for students to discuss and to learn." Students say, Ripon is an "amazing community of learners and educators who support one another" and a "unique institution that helps ordinary people uncover their extraordinary potential to do great things." Professors "are not just teachers, but mentors!" Scholarships make a Ripon College education possible for some that otherwise could not attend. One student says, "They offered me a great scholarship and were really willing to work with me to make my college education affordable."

Life

With its "tight-knit and welcoming community," Ripon conveys "a friendly environment conducive to learning, fun, and overall personal growth." It is "not uncommon to sit down to lunch with a professor, or even go over to their house for tea." Life at Ripon has proven blissful for one student who now says, "I cannot remember a time when I wanted to be anywhere else." Besides a "strong academic core," Ripon College has "many successful sports teams," and Greek life "is abundant." Greeks host events and are a big part of many students' life. Partying "is evident but not huge by any respect." "Since Ripon College is in a small town, the college sets up a lot of events on weekends for us to take part in!" "The small-town feel of Ripon forces you sometimes to create your own fun, which usually makes for the best memories." "Being close to several metropolitan areas (Chicago, Milwaukee, Madison, and the Twin Cities), there is rarely a weekend when people are not getting off campus to go explore." But if you are looking for snow days to figure into your schedule, then Ripon may not be for you "because most professors will keep classes going even in negative temperatures with two feet of snow."

Student Body

A typical Ripon student is described as "laid-back and friendly." One student cautions, "You have to plan extra time in between classes because you're guaranteed to be stopped by someone you know along the way to talk for a few minutes." Students are "outgoing, personable, and motivated," "involved in multiple clubs," and may "hold more than one internship at a time. From Student Senate to Ultimate Frisbee to volunteering in the community, there is never a lack of activities in which one can participate." Students are "always looking for something new and exciting to do, and [are] ready to volunteer their time and energy to someone in need."

RIPON COLLEGE

Financial Aid: 920-748-8301 • E-Mail: adminfo@ripon.edu • Website: www.ripon.edu

THE PRINCETON REVIEW SAYS

Admissions

Very important factors considered include: rigor of secondary school record, interview. *Important factors considered include:* class rank, academic GPA, extracurricular activities, character/personal qualities. *Other factors considered include:* application essay, standardized test scores, recommendation(s), talent/ability, volunteer work. ACT with or without writing accepted. SAT with or without Essay component accepted. High school diploma is required and GED is accepted. *Academic units required:* 4 English, 2 math, 2 science, 2 social studies. *Academic units recommended:* 4 math, 4 science, 2 foreign language, 4 social studies.

Financial Aid

Students should submit: FAFSA. Priority filing deadline is 3/1. The Princeton Review suggests that all financial aid forms be submitted as soon as possible after October 1. *Need-based scholarships/grants offered:* College/university scholarship or grant aid from institutional funds; Federal Pell; Private scholarships; SEOG; State scholarships/grants. *Loan aid offered:* Direct PLUS loans; Federal Direct Subsidized Loans; Federal Direct Unsubsidized Loans. Applicants will be notified of financial aid offers on a rolling basis beginning in early November. Federal Work-Study Program available. Institutional employment available.

The Inside Word

Ripon seeks accomplished high school students who have challenged themselves in and out of the classroom. Solid performers—those earning a B-plus average in a college-prep curriculum and exceeding 1100 SAT/22 ACT—should find a clear path awaiting them, although the school does also consider such peripherals as potential contribution to extracurricular life and the likelihood a candidate will flourish in a small-school environment.

THE SCHOOL SAYS "..."

From the Admissions Office

"Since its founding in 1851, Ripon College has adhered to the philosophy that the liberal arts offer the richest foundation for intellectual, cultural, social, and spiritual growth. Academic strength is a 150-year tradition at Ripon. We attract excellent professors who are dedicated to their disciplines; they in turn attract bright, committed students. Together with the other members of our tightly knit learning community, students at Ripon learn more deeply, live more fully, and achieve more success. Students are surprised to discover that here there are more opportunities—to be involved, to lead, to speak out, to make a difference, to explore new interests—than at a college ten times our size. Through collaborative learning, group living, teamwork, and networking, students tap into the power of a community where we all work together to ensure success—at Ripon and beyond.

"All of the best residential liberal arts colleges strive to be true learning communities like Ripon. We succeed better than most because our enrollment of about 1,000 students is perfect for fostering connections inside and outside the classroom. Our students flourish in this environment of mutual respect, where shared values are elevated and diverse ideas are valued. If you are seeking academic challenge and want to benefit from an environment of personal attention and support—then you should take a closer look at Ripon."

SELECTIVITY
Admissions Rating	79
# of applicants	2,619
% of applicants accepted	69
% of acceptees attending	15

FRESHMAN PROFILE
Range SAT EBRW	500–610
Range SAT Math	500–600
Range ACT Composite	20–27
% submitting SAT scores	19
% submitting ACT scores	63
Average HS GPA	3.4
% graduated top 10% of class	17
% graduated top 25% of class	38
% graduated top 50% of class	81

DEADLINES
Regular	
Priority	3/15
Notification	Rolling, 9/15
Nonfall registration?	Yes

FINANCIAL FACTS
Financial Aid Rating	88
Annual tuition	$46,823
Room and board	$8,653
Required fees	$300
Books and supplies	$750
Average frosh need-based scholarship	$31,709
Average UG need-based scholarship	$29,592
% needy frosh rec. need-based scholarship or grant aid	100
% needy UG rec. need-based scholarship or grant aid	100
% needy frosh rec. non-need-based scholarship or grant aid	15
% needy UG rec. non-need-based scholarship or grant aid	13
% needy frosh rec. need-based self-help aid	82
% needy UG rec. need-based self-help aid	84
% frosh rec. any financial aid	90
% UG rec. any financial aid	83
% UG borrow to pay for school	84
Average cumulative indebtedness	$37,084
% frosh need fully met	28
% ugrads need fully met	27
Average % of frosh need met	88
Average % of ugrad need met	86

THE BEST 386 COLLEGES ■ 467

ROANOKE COLLEGE

221 College Lane, Salem, VA 24153-3794 • Admissions: 540-375-2270 • Fax: 540-375-2267

STUDENTS SAY "..."

Academics

Located in the scenic Blue Ridge Mountains, Roanoke College, a small Lutheran-affiliated liberal arts institution, "values community and academic integrity over all." With its small class sizes, a key draw for students, Roanoke "aims to equip you for the real world, but also make you feel at home, like you belong." The school's "academic rigor, research opportunities, and a robust Honors Program" encourage students to push themselves. As one student puts it, "Roanoke College does not hand out A's. You really have to apply yourself, and grades really reflect your effort." Students say that "undergraduate research opportunities abound if you want it," and professors "truly do want the best for [students] and go out of their way to make sure [they] are given everything needed to succeed, but make sure [they] are challenged at the exact same time." In general, professors earn universal praise for being "approachable, knowledgeable," and "willing and able to work with every student." The required core classes earn mixed reviews, with some students saying the school's core curriculum is "very strong" while others counter that the required classes are "often treated as boring busy work instead of learning the topics." But most agree that Roanoke "[excels] in academics and learning how to relate what is learned in the classroom to real world jobs."

Life

Students are split over whether Greek life dominates campus life or simply provides ample social opportunities for those who want it. As one student puts it, "Go Greek or go home," but others say that "Greek life has a presence, but it is far from overwhelming." There are numerous other clubs on campus, as well as "many on-campus events provided by the school on the weekends." Students looking to get away from school for a bit can take the 20-minute drive to Roanoke. With its location in the scenic Blue Ridge Mountains, outdoor opportunities abound and students say "hiking and kayaking are very popular," as well as "camping trips that are organized by the Outdoor Adventure Club." A little over 75 percent of undergrads currently live on campus, but students say that it's not too hard to find off-campus accommodations.

Student Body

Roanoke students say that "it feels like one big family here," and "the small tight-knit community allows [students] to have a home away from home." Diversity is a sticking point; one student says that, "I would not say that we have a very unique student body." But others are quick to point out that Roanoke students are "people from all over the world": "Students from every corner of the globe, from Asia to Europe, from every religion, from Catholic to Islam, all congregate together in Roanoke peacefully and work together to find the common string that binds us all together as a community." Students say that overall, the atmosphere at Roanoke "is kind and inclusive, with many opportunities to meet new people in and out of your major or subject of interest."

Roanoke College

Financial Aid: 540-375-2235 • E-Mail: admissions@roanoke.edu • Website: www.roanoke.edu

THE PRINCETON REVIEW SAYS

Admissions

Very important factors considered include: rigor of secondary school record, academic GPA, character/personal qualities. *Important factors considered include:* class rank, interview, extracurricular activities. *Other factors considered include:* application essay, standardized test scores, recommendation(s), talent/ability, alumni/ae relation, racial/ethnic status, volunteer work, work experience. ACT with or without writing accepted. SAT with or without Essay component accepted. High school diploma is required and GED is accepted. *Academic units required:* 4 English, 3 math, 2 science, 2 science labs, 2 foreign language, 2 social studies, 5 academic electives. *Academic units recommended:* 2 foreign language.

Financial Aid

Students should submit: FAFSA; State aid form. Priority filing deadline is 3/1. The Princeton Review suggests that all financial aid forms be submitted as soon as possible after October 1. *Need-based scholarships/grants offered:* College/university scholarship or grant aid from institutional funds; Federal Pell; Private scholarships; SEOG; State scholarships/grants. *Loan aid offered:* Direct PLUS loans; Direct Subsidized Stafford Loans; Direct Unsubsidized Stafford Loans. Applicants will be notified of awards on a rolling basis beginning 11/15. Federal Work-Study Program available. Institutional employment available.

The Inside Word

Each part of a student's application to Roanoke is important, as the College takes a holistic approach to admission, considering the whole student, not just a string of numbers. That said, the average admitted student comes to Roanoke with a 3.6 high school GPA and nearly 40 percent of admitted applicants have a high school GPA of 3.75 or higher. The optional admissions essay should be seen as required: It gives the school a chance to get to know the real you and the reasons you think Roanoke is the best fit for you and your talents.

THE SCHOOL SAYS "..."

From the Admissions Office

"The Roanoke College experience is a full one. When enrolled students arrive, they embark on a rich personal and academic journey. They discover how to think deeply about their choices, their skills and their contributions to the world. They discover a community of people dedicated to helping them find high-value careers and lives with meaning and purpose"

"The College is nationally recognized for its innovative core curriculum and majors that allow for depth of study and research. All of Roanoke's core introductory courses are topic-based. For example, instead of Statistics 101, students might choose 'Statistics and the Weather,' and discover how statistical analysis is used in weather forecasting."

"Over 95 percent of surveyed Roanoke alumni received job offers or entered graduate school within six months of graduation. The College—where students fully participate in internships, community service and study away—has been deemed a top producer of academic scholars, including Fulbright, Goldwater and Truman awardees."

"The Cregger Center is the newest addition to campus. The 155,000-square-foot complex features an indoor track, fitness center, academic spaces and 2,500-seat arena. Ten residence halls have been constructed or renovated in the past decade, featuring a mix of traditional double rooms, singles, suites and apartment-style living."

"The College campus is known for its beautiful, lush grounds. Roanoke received 2019 Tree Campus USA recognition for promoting healthy trees, and engaging students and staff in the spirit of conservation. Not surprisingly, the College, minutes away from the Blue Ridge Mountains, has a vibrant outdoor adventures program."

SELECTIVITY
Admissions Rating	79
# of applicants	5,453
% of applicants accepted	75
% of acceptees attending	14
# offered a place on the wait list	257
% admitted from wait list	3
# of early decision applicants	100
% accepted early decision	89

FRESHMAN PROFILE
Range SAT EBRW	540–640
Range SAT Math	510–620
Range SAT Composite	1060–1250
Range ACT Composite	21–28
# submitting SAT scores	451
% submitting SAT scores	82
# submitting ACT scores	127
% submitting ACT scores	23
Average HS GPA	3.6
% graduated top 10% of class	17
% graduated top 25% of class	46
% graduated top 50% of class	82

DEADLINES
Early decision	
Deadline	11/15
Notification	12/15
Regular	
Deadline	3/15
Notification	Rolling, 10/1
Nonfall registration?	Yes

APPLICANTS ALSO LOOK AT AND OFTEN PREFER
William & Mary; James Madison University; University of Virginia

AND SOMETIMES PREFER
Christopher Newport University; University of Lynchburg; Virginia Polytechnic Institute and State University; University of Richmond

AND RARELY PREFER
Bridgewater College; Radford University; University of Mary Washington; Randolph-Macon College

FINANCIAL FACTS
Financial Aid Rating	88
Annual tuition	$45,200
Room and board	$14,580
Required fees	$1,820
Books and supplies	$1,000
Average frosh need-based scholarship	$33,684
Average UG need-based scholarship	$32,220
% needy frosh rec. need-based scholarship or grant aid	97
% needy UG rec. need-based scholarship or grant aid	98
% needy frosh rec. non-need-based scholarship or grant aid	97
% needy UG rec. non-need-based scholarship or grant aid	97
% needy frosh rec. need-based self-help aid	78
% needy UG rec. need-based self-help aid	78
% frosh rec. any financial aid	100
% UG rec. any financial aid	97
% UG borrow to pay for school	71
Average cumulative indebtedness	$37,335
% frosh need fully met	19
% ugrads need fully met	22
Average % of frosh need met	81
Average % of ugrad need met	84

ROCHESTER INSTITUTE OF TECHNOLOGY

60 Lomb Memorial Drive, Rochester, NY 14623-5604 • Admissions: 585-475-6631 • Fax: 585-475-7424

STUDENTS SAY "..."

Academics

This western New York academic stalwart boasts one of the country's oldest (and largest) co-op programs and regularly turns out job-ready students from its arts, business, and engineering programs alike. Rochester Institute of Technology is laser-focused on "creating students that are more than prepared to enter the job force," and faculty "bring the material to life" by keeping lectures work-related and placing emphasis on "how you would use what we are learning on the job site." "Professors work with the students and see them as equals," says one mechanical engineering major. "When I'm in the classroom, I feel like I'm learning and that I have a voice."

The workload is legendarily daunting and "you will have to reach out and form study groups and pull all-nighters," but professors are "more than happy to help their students" and "truly take pride in helping their students become successful." While the material may be difficult, faculty "are willing to stay after hours, meet with the student, and hold group study/review sessions to help their students understand the material." The easy A is "not very common, especially in engineering classes," but "if you work hard, you will be recognized and grades will reflect that."

The opportunity for students to dip their toes into real-world experience abounds throughout the college, and the paid co-op program (mandatory for most majors) is considered by many to be "the best thing anyone could ever choose to go through if you are a career-driven individual." Additionally, there are "plenty of materials and machines students can use for free where in other schools you still have to pay."

Life

While schoolwork takes up the majority of students' time, outside the classroom they "are constantly doing something to keep busy," whether that's joining one of the 300-plus clubs or chilling at the lab. "RIT has a culture for everybody," so if you are interested in a broad topic like computing, "there are a dozen different clubs/societies that you can join to learn more about whatever niche topic interests you."

Students cop to their being "a large gamer population" at RIT, and both electronic and tabletop gaming clubs and tournaments are wildly popular, as is anime. Hockey is a huge part of RIT and "it is very common to see a large number of students at the games." People also "go to the free on-campus movies, see guest speakers, listen to comedians, and attend events hosted by the College Activities Board."

The atmosphere and layout of the campus are beautifully balanced in that "it is not very spread out but not very small at the same time." More than half of the growing population of students live in on-campus, meaning housing "is not always available for everyone who applies" and dorms can be crowded. As one student notes: "The existing infrastructure is okay at best."

Student Body

RIT is a place "where diversity is highlighted [and] academics are prominent," and the population is "as unique and diverse as they come." This environment "allows for a good [facsimile] of the real world." The school's internationally recognized National Technical Institute for the Deaf means there are "amazing accommodations for deaf and hard of hearing students that attend the university," including "notetaking, interpreters, [and C Print® technology]," and a vibrant LGBT+ community also exists on campus. "Video games are a way of life" and students tend to have a nerdy streak ("We are geeky and we love it"). Large groups and clubs for "anime, World of Warcraft, [and] chain mail" happily thrive among students that are all "very accepting of each other's interests." "This is where students are able to create what their minds generate. It's like teenager's dream," says one.

ROCHESTER INSTITUTE OF TECHNOLOGY

Financial Aid: 585-475-2186 • E-Mail: admissions@rit.edu • Website: www.rit.edu

THE PRINCETON REVIEW SAYS

Admissions

Very important factors considered include: rigor of secondary school record, academic GPA. *Important factors considered include:* class rank, standardized test scores. *Other factors considered include:* application essay, recommendation(s), interview, extracurricular activities, talent/ability, character/personal qualities, first generation, alumni/ae relation, geographical residence, racial/ethnic status, volunteer work, work experience, level of applicant's interest. ACT with or without writing accepted. SAT with or without Essay component accepted. High school diploma is required and GED is accepted. *Academic units required:* 4 English, 2 math, 2 science, 1 science lab, 4 social studies, 10 academic electives. *Academic units recommended:* 4 English, 3 math, 3 science, 2 science labs, 3 foreign language, 4 social studies, 5 academic electives.

Financial Aid

Students should submit: FAFSA; State aid form. Priority filing deadline is 2/15. The Princeton Review suggests that all financial aid forms be submitted as soon as possible after October 1. *Need-based scholarships/grants offered:* College/university scholarship or grant aid from institutional funds; Federal Pell; Private scholarships; SEOG; State scholarships/grants. *Loan aid offered:* Direct PLUS loans; Direct Subsidized Stafford Loans; Direct Unsubsidized Stafford Loans. Applicants will be notified of awards on a rolling basis beginning 3/1. Federal Work-Study Program available. Institutional employment available.

The Inside Word

Competition to gain admission into Rochester Institute of Technology is tough. The admissions committee is on the lookout for bright, highly motivated students who will make the most out of the university's experiential learning opportunities, and the majority of students must choose their intended course of study during the admissions process. In addition to a sense of direction, you'll need a transcript that reflects a rigorous high school curriculum (including APs and honors classes) to have a shot at admission here.

THE SCHOOL SAYS "..."

From the Admissions Office

"RIT is a kaleidoscope of curious minds working together through creativity and innovation to find new ways to move the world forward. Through an intentional blending of technology, the arts and design, we provide engaged, socially conscious, and intellectually curious individuals with a wide range of academic opportunities, including expansive experiential learning opportunities, a leading research program and an internationally recognized education for deaf and hard-of-hearing students. As one of the world's leading technological universities, RIT offers undergraduate and graduate programs in areas such as engineering, computing, engineering technology, business, hospitality, science, visual arts, biomedical sciences, game design and development, psychology, advertising, public relations, and public policy. Students may choose from more than eighty different minors to develop personal and professional interests. RIT attracts students from every state and nearly 2,500 international students from more than 100 countries. Embodying our commitment to diversity, more than 3,400 students of color have elected to study at RIT. Adding a social and educational dynamic not found at any other university are nearly 1,000 deaf and hard-of-hearing students supported by RIT's National Technical Institute for the Deaf. Experiential learning has been a hallmark of an RIT education since 1912. Every academic program offers some form of experiential education opportunity, which may include cooperative education, internships, study abroad, and undergraduate research. Students work hard, but learning is complemented with plenty of organized and spontaneous events and activities. RIT is a unique blend of rigor and fun, creativity and specialization, intellect and practice. It is a launching pad for a brilliant career, and a highly unique state of mind. It is a perfect environment in which to pursue your passion."

SELECTIVITY

Admissions Rating	**86**
# of applicants	19,744
% of applicants accepted	71
% of acceptees attending	19
# offered a place on the wait list	376
% accepting a place on wait list	98
% admitted from wait list	22
# of early decision applicants	1,373
% accepted early decision	84

FRESHMAN PROFILE

Range SAT EBRW	600–690
Range SAT Math	620–720
Range SAT Composite	1230–1400
Range ACT Composite	27–32
# submitting SAT scores	2,012
% submitting SAT scores	75
# submitting ACT scores	724
% submitting ACT scores	27
Average HS GPA	3.6
% graduated top 10% of class	40
% graduated top 25% of class	74
% graduated top 50% of class	95

DEADLINES

Early decision	
Deadline	11/1
Notification	12/15
Other ED Deadline	1/1
Other ED Notification	1/15
Regular	
Priority	1/15
Notification	Rolling, 2/15
Nonfall registration?	Yes

APPLICANTS ALSO LOOK AT AND OFTEN PREFER
Carnegie Mellon University; Cornell University

AND SOMETIMES PREFER
Penn State University Park; State University of New York at Binghamton (Binghamton University); Worcester Polytechnic Institute; State University of New York—Buffalo State ; Rensselaer Polytechnic Institute; Syracuse University

AND RARELY PREFER
Clarkson University; Drexel University

FINANCIAL FACTS

Financial Aid Rating	**93**
Annual tuition	$50,564
Room and board	$13,976
Required fees	$676
Books and supplies	$1,082
Average frosh need-based scholarship	$29,745
Average UG need-based scholarship	$28,045
% needy frosh rec. need-based scholarship or grant aid	83
% needy UG rec. need-based scholarship or grant aid	94
% needy frosh rec. non-need-based scholarship or grant aid	20
% needy UG rec. non-need-based scholarship or grant aid	33
% needy frosh rec. need-based self-help aid	78
% needy UG rec. need-based self-help aid	88
% frosh rec. any financial aid	77
% UG rec. any financial aid	77
% UG borrow to pay for school	75
Average cumulative indebtedness	$41,202
% frosh need fully met	67
% ugrads need fully met	80
Average % of frosh need met	87
Average % of ugrad need met	85

ROLLINS COLLEGE

1000 Holt Avenue, Winter Park, FL 32789-4499 • Admissions: 407-646-2161 • Fax: 407-646-1502

CAMPUS LIFE

Quality of Life Rating	89
Fire Safety Rating	97
Green Rating	87
Type of school	Private
Environment	Town

STUDENTS

Total undergrad enrollment	1,984
% male/female	39/61
% from out of state	42
% frosh from public high school	51
% frosh live on campus	82
% ugrads live on campus	59
# of fraternities (% ugrad men join)	6 (33)
# of sororities (% ugrad women join)	7 (33)
% African American	4
% Asian	3
% Caucasian	60
% Hispanic	16
% Native American	<1
% Pacific Islander	0
% Two or more races	4
% Race and/or ethnicity unknown	3
% international	10
# of countries represented	57

SURVEY SAYS . . .

Internships are widely available
Class discussions encouraged
Lots of beer drinking

ACADEMICS

Academic Rating	86
% students returning for sophomore year	83
% students graduating within 4 years	67
% students graduating within 6 years	73
Calendar	Semester
Student/faculty ratio	10:1
Profs interesting rating	89
Profs accessible rating	93
Most classes have 10–19 students.	

MOST POPULAR MAJORS

Economics, General; International Business/Trade/
Commerce; Communication and Media Studies,
Other

STUDENTS SAY "..."

Academics

Located in sunny central Florida, Rollins College is "small enough to help the individual but is fortunate enough to have a large endowment capable of providing each student with necessary academic means." The generous academic merit scholarships bring in a smart crowd, and the small class sizes, dedicated faculty, and numerous "student leadership opportunities, internships, academic presentations, [and] conference opportunities" sweeten the pot.

Rollins is "all about individual growth personally and educationally," but it also stresses "responsible community leadership both on and off campus." Students have a great deal of freedom to study what they choose, and many large projects are individualized toward the student, meaning a student "can tailor my topic to my interests." In addition to the autonomy this approach grants students, it "reinforces the idea of a holistic education," which helps to "make [students] competitive in an ever-changing job market." Working at this speed, students are able to "discover purpose and identify goals." Many services are also available to students, such as free tutoring and counseling.

Professors "perform very well" and create an "open and invigorating classroom environment" that is "open to diverse ideas and perspectives." Teachers "know every student's name, and they will remember you throughout your college experience." "My first year, one called my cell phone when I missed class," says a student. "The interactions that I have with the professors are second to none," says another. The small class sizes (even introductory courses are tiny) make it "very easy to learn and share your opinion," and since professors are "very engaging and willing to hear all points of view," "no one is left feeling like they don't matter."

Life

The "very beautiful and relaxing" campus can often feel sort of like a "country club" in both appearance and attitude. With "so many attractions in the Orlando area, the accessibility of the lake and the beach it is hard not to bring your books outside." Some people like "to go out to nearby downtown Orlando" (which is fifteen minutes away from school), some "live for Disney World," and some just stay in and hang out. A favorite activity among students is "walking up Park Avenue and exploring the delicious culinary endeavors there," and Lake Virginia is a great spot for perching, wakeboarding, or sailing. Students here tend "to travel a lot and explore other towns in Florida during the school year."

There are "always events on campus that are fun," like "a student who is a DJ [who] had a concert on the lawn one night," and almost one-third of the school is involved in Greek life. Community service is also "a pretty big part of the campus," and there is "always something service-related going on either from student groups or from the community engagement office."

Student Body

Rollins is such a small school that "everyone knows everyone." It's a true split at Rollins between in-staters and out-of-staters (and the international contingent) and among socioeconomic classes. "There are extremely wealthy spoiled kids driving Mercedes and smoking, [and] then there are true nerds who busted their butts to get in," says a student. Since the two groups mix constantly, "it is often hard to differentiate between the students who are set to inherit their parent's company after they graduate and those here on scholarship." Luckily, the "family environment and the closeness of all of the campus bring all the students together as scholars." Everyone may have small groups to which they belong, but "there is intermingling going on all the time."

Financial Aid: 407-646-2395 • E-Mail: admission@rollins.edu • Website: http://www.rollins.edu

THE PRINCETON REVIEW SAYS

Admissions

Very important factors considered include: rigor of secondary school record, academic GPA. *Important factors considered include:* application essay, standardized test scores, recommendation(s), extracurricular activities, talent/ability. *Other factors considered include:* class rank, character/personal qualities, first generation, alumni/ae relation, volunteer work, work experience, level of applicant's interest. ACT with Writing recommended. SAT with or without Essay component accepted. High school diploma is required and GED is accepted. *Academic units required:* 4 English, 3 math, 2 science, 2 foreign language, 2 social studies, 2 history, 2 academic electives. *Academic units recommended:* 4 English, 4 math, 4 science, 3 foreign language, 3 social studies, 3 history, 3 academic electives.

Financial Aid

Students should submit: FAFSA. Priority filing deadline is 3/1. The Princeton Review suggests that all financial aid forms be submitted as soon as possible after October 1. *Need-based scholarships/grants offered:* College/university scholarship or grant aid from institutional funds; Federal Pell; Private scholarships; SEOG; State scholarships/grants. *Loan aid offered:* Direct PLUS loans; Direct Subsidized Stafford Loans; Direct Unsubsidized Stafford Loans. Applicants will be notified of awards on a rolling basis beginning 3/1. Federal Work-Study Program available. Institutional employment available.

The Inside Word

Rollins is a test optional school, and both academic and need-based scholarships are available to students who choose to not submit standardized test scores. It's the school's way of creating another opportunity for students whose test results do not match their overall academic performance, and it's characteristic of the individualized approach taken here (about 10 percent of applicants opt for this method). Each applicant is assigned an admissions officer who acts as his or her liaison, ensuring a personalized admissions experience. Early decision applicants are given priority in admissions as well as in considerations for merit-based scholarships and need-based financial aid.

THE SCHOOL SAYS "..."

From the Admissions Office

"Rollins' mission is to nurture global citizenship and responsible leadership within its students so they are prepared to lead meaningful lives and productive careers. As you begin the college selection process, remember that you are in control of your destiny. Your academic record—course load, grades earned, test scores—is the most important part of your application credentials. But Rollins also pays close attention to your personal dimension—interests, strengths, values, and potential to contribute to college life. Don't sell yourself short in the application process. Be proud of what you've accomplished and who you are, and be honest when you describe yourself. Finally, the admission committee always likes to see candidates who express interest in the college. If we're your first choice, apply early decision. Each year we admit approximately one-third of the entering class through the early decision process. Are you unsure about your choice? If you can, schedule some visits, meet with an admission counselor, tour campus, and spend time in a class so you can see for yourself what Rollins and other colleges are all about. Take control of your destiny, and enjoy the process along the way."

SELECTIVITY

Admissions Rating	86
# of applicants	5,297
% of applicants accepted	64
% of acceptees attending	16
# offered a place on the wait list	206
% accepting a place on wait list	41
% admitted from wait list	6

FRESHMAN PROFILE

Range SAT EBRW	605–680
Range SAT Math	590–670
Range ACT Composite	25–30
# submitting SAT scores	231
% submitting SAT scores	42
# submitting ACT scores	220
% submitting ACT scores	42
Average HS GPA	3.3
% graduated top 10% of class	36
% graduated top 25% of class	67
% graduated top 50% of class	88

DEADLINES

Early decision	
Deadline	11/15
Notification	12/15
Other ED Deadline	12/15
Other ED Notification	1/15
Regular	
Deadline	2/1
Notification	4/1
Nonfall registration?	Yes

FINANCIAL FACTS

Financial Aid Rating	87
Annual tuition	$51,700
Room and board	$15,034
Books and supplies	$716
Average frosh need-based scholarship	$36,026
Average UG need-based scholarship	$35,036
% needy frosh rec. need-based scholarship or grant aid	94
% needy UG rec. need-based scholarship or grant aid	93
% needy frosh rec. non-need-based scholarship or grant aid	23
% needy UG rec. non-need-based scholarship or grant aid	17
% needy frosh rec. need-based self-help aid	61
% needy UG rec. need-based self-help aid	68
% frosh rec. any financial aid	92.5
% UG rec. any financial aid	89.1
% UG borrow to pay for school	45
Average cumulative indebtedness	$31,459
% frosh need fully met	23
% ugrads need fully met	17
Average % of frosh need met	84
Average % of ugrad need met	84

ROSE-HULMAN INSTITUTE OF TECHNOLOGY

5500 Wabash Avenue, Terre Haute, IN 47803-3999 • Admissions: 812-877-8213 • Fax: 812-877-8941

CAMPUS LIFE

Quality of Life Rating	93
Fire Safety Rating	96
Green Rating	78
Type of school	Private
Environment	Town

STUDENTS

Total undergrad enrollment	2,146
% male/female	75/25
% from out of state	64
% frosh from public high school	63
% frosh live on campus	99
% ugrads live on campus	58
# of fraternities (% ugrad men join)	8 (36)
# of sororities (% ugrad women join)	3 (34)
% African American	3
% Asian	5
% Caucasian	68
% Hispanic	5
% Native American	<1
% Pacific Islander	<1
% Two or more races	5
% Race and/or ethnicity unknown	1
% international	15
# of countries represented	11

SURVEY SAYS . . .

Students always studying
Students are happy
Classroom facilities are great
Lab facilities are great
Career services are great
Internships are widely available
School is well run
Students are friendly
Diverse student types interact on campus
Students involved in community service
Dorms are like palaces
Easy to get around campus
Recreation facilities are great
Very little drug use
Intramural sports are popular
Frats and sororities are popular

ACADEMICS

Academic Rating	92
% students returning for sophomore year	91
% students graduating within 4 years	67
Calendar	Quarter
Student/faculty ratio	11:1
Profs interesting rating	95
Profs accessible rating	99

Most classes have 20–29 students.
Most lab/discussion sessions have 20–29 students.

MOST POPULAR MAJORS

Chemical Engineering; Mechanical Engineering; Computer Science

STUDENTS SAY "..."

Academics

Rose-Hulman Institute of Technology, in Terre Haute, Indiana, earns its "reputation as an excellent undergraduate engineering school" with a combination of strong academics and "personal attention, small class sizes, and a family atmosphere," a rarity among tech schools. More succinctly, "Rose-Hulman is where nerds go to finally feel like they belong." Sure, "the workload is fairly heavy, especially sophomore year with the engineering curriculum." One mechanical engineering student describes the course work: "The material is difficult...but the culture is supportive, so you make it work." Rose-Hulman features an unusually robust support system, and that mitigates the strain. "The transition is made as smooth as possible from high school to college for freshmen" with "on-campus tutoring in the learning center (an excellent resource for students to get homework help)" and "professors who are always available outside of class." One student elaborates, "If you are walking down the hall, [professors] will say hello and usually ask how you are doing." Not only are those professors "happy to be teaching," but they have "real-world industry experience" to back it up. One student sums up the teaching philosophy as "theory is important, but application is everything." All of this hard work pays dividends in the form "a great alumni base" and a near 99 percent job placement rate six months after graduation.

Life

"Life at Rose is academically demanding," but "the community here is so supportive and safe that you get through it," and while "students do a lot of homework and study a lot," they do occasionally find time to close the books and relax. "It's all work and little play Sunday through Thursday," but come Friday "we play hard.'" Students inform us "there's always something to do on campus, whether it's going to a fraternity party or attending a concert or going to a dance or just watching a movie with friends." Greek life is big, "but it's not your typical Animal House," and both intramural and Division III intercollegiate athletics have their supporters. There are also "tons of different groups to get involved in" on campus. Hometown Terre Haute, on the other hand, isn't so lively. "There isn't much to do" in town other than "go to the shadiest bars and check out the locals." As one student points out, "We are located in the middle of nowhere...not much they can do about it, but it is not so great."

Student Body

"The kids who attend Rose-Hulman are smart, dedicated, and consequently, nerds," but "this is not a negative thing. Within the students here, there are no outcasts, and even our athletes are most likely also mathletes." "Everyone definitely marches to the beat of his own drum," students assure us. Personality types run the gamut from "geniuses, average students, student-athletes, outspoken, quiet, etc." Demographically, undergrads are "mostly white male engineers from the Midwest" (partly a function of Rose-Hulman's location), but "we are slowly expanding the Rose-Hulman name and getting people from all over the United States and globe." The population "is mostly boys, although the females are catching up." About half of the incoming freshman class played varsity sports in high school, which is about as many as had been involved in the performing arts.

ROSE-HULMAN INSTITUTE OF TECHNOLOGY

Financial Aid: 812-877-8259 • E-Mail: admissions@rose-hulman.edu • Website: www.rose-hulman.edu

THE PRINCETON REVIEW SAYS

Admissions

Very important factors considered include: rigor of secondary school record, class rank, academic GPA. *Important factors considered include:* standardized test scores, recommendation(s), extracurricular activities, character/personal qualities, volunteer work. *Other factors considered include:* application essay, talent/ability, alumni/ae relation, geographical residence, racial/ethnic status. ACT with or without writing accepted. SAT with or without Essay component accepted. High school diploma is required and GED is not accepted *Academic units required:* 4 English, 4 math, 3 science, 3 science labs, 2 social studies, 4 academic electives. *Academic units recommended:* 5 math, 4 science.

Financial Aid

Students should submit: FAFSA. Priority filing deadline is 3/10. The Princeton Review suggests that all financial aid forms be submitted as soon as possible after October 1. *Need-based scholarships/grants offered:* College/university scholarship or grant aid from institutional funds; Federal Pell; SEOG; State scholarships/grants. *Loan aid offered:* Direct PLUS loans; Direct Subsidized Stafford Loans; Direct Unsubsidized Stafford Loans. Applicants will be notified of awards on or about 3/10. Federal Work-Study Program available. Institutional employment available.

The Inside Word

Admission to Rose-Hulman is selective, and the admissions committee isn't shy about the fact that they are looking for the best and the brightest. They expect students to be in the top 25 percent of their graduating class (but will look at other factors like the rigor of your classes if your high school doesn't rank). It's a fantastic idea to apply sooner rather than later: Rose-Hulman's Early Action is non-binding, so you can find out if you were admitted sooner in the process without having to commit to attending.

THE SCHOOL SAYS "..."

From the Admissions Office

"Imagine a college where your classes are taught by professors who know you by name, and who also happen to be among the best in the world; a place with a rigorous curriculum that prepares you for today's jobs and for careers that don't yet exist; a place where you have access to state-of-the-art labs, equipment, and research opportunities that are off-limits to undergrads at most schools; a friendly, safe, and collaborative place where you're surrounded by people who love science, engineering, and math as much as you do; and a place where everyone on campus, from your residence hall housekeeper to your academic adviser, will take the time to help you when needed.

"That place is Rose-Hulman, and our culture is the secret to our success.

"Here, your STEM education isn't just about getting a degree, or even a job. It's about taking what you learn and applying it to match your passions. You'll be the center of your experience; not stuck with a one-size-fits-all college career.

"Rose-Hulman has been recognized for the past two decades as the best undergraduate engineering school in the U.S., and we have a track record of excelling at career placement rate—averaging 98 percent—with some of the best-known companies in the world seeking out our students for paid internships and full-time employment.

"There are many more accomplishments we're proud of, but we're prouder of *why* we're so highly regarded. To fully appreciate that, schedule a visit and come see for yourself."

SELECTIVITY

Admissions Rating	91
# of applicants	4,473
% of applicants accepted	61
% of acceptees attending	20
# offered a place on the wait list	379
% accepting a place on wait list	40
% admitted from wait list	25

FRESHMAN PROFILE

Range SAT EBRW	610–690
Range SAT Math	650–760
Range ACT Composite	27–32
# submitting SAT scores	288
% submitting SAT scores	52
# submitting ACT scores	395
% submitting ACT scores	71
Average HS GPA	4.0
% graduated top 10% of class	64
% graduated top 25% of class	91
% graduated top 50% of class	100

DEADLINES

Early action	
Deadline	11/1
Notification	12/15
Regular	
Priority	11/1
Deadline	2/1
Notification	12/15
Nonfall registration?	No

FINANCIAL FACTS

Financial Aid Rating	88
Annual tuition	$46,641
Room and board	$14,766
Required fees	$930
Books and supplies	$1,500
Average frosh need-based scholarship	$30,676
Average UG need-based scholarship	$28,385
% needy frosh rec. need-based scholarship or grant aid	99
% needy UG rec. need-based scholarship or grant aid	99
% needy frosh rec. non-need-based scholarship or grant aid	45
% needy UG rec. non-need-based scholarship or grant aid	90
% needy frosh rec. need-based self-help aid	69
% needy UG rec. need-based self-help aid	73
% frosh rec. any financial aid	99
% UG rec. any financial aid	98
% UG borrow to pay for school	58
Average cumulative indebtedness	$43,459
% frosh need fully met	19
% ugrads need fully met	16
Average % of frosh need met	65
Average % of ugrad need met	62

RUTGERS UNIVERSITY—NEW BRUNSWICK

Admissions Office, Piscataway, NJ 08854-8097 • Admissions: 732-932-4636 • Fax: 732-445-8088

CAMPUS LIFE

Quality of Life Rating	83
Fire Safety Rating	77
Green Rating	60*
Type of school	Public
Environment	Town

STUDENTS

Total undergrad enrollment	35,760
% male/female	50/50
% from out of state	6
% frosh live on campus	81
% ugrads live on campus	43
# of fraternities	50
# of sororities	29
% African American	6
% Asian	29
% Caucasian	36
% Hispanic	13
% Native American	<1
% Pacific Islander	<1
% Two or more races	4
% Race and/or ethnicity unknown	2
% international	10
# of countries represented	87

SURVEY SAYS . . .

Lots of beer drinking
Hard liquor is popular
Campus newspaper is popular

ACADEMICS

Academic Rating	77
% students returning for sophomore year	93
% students graduating within 4 years	65
% students graduating within 6 years	84
Calendar	Semester
Profs interesting rating	81
Profs accessible rating	90

MOST POPULAR MAJORS

Computer and Information Sciences, General; Registered Nursing/Registered Nurse; Business Administration and Management, General

STUDENTS SAY "..."

Academics

Rutgers is "a big school with many different types of people," a "diverse university in all aspects of the word—academically, culturally, politically, ethnically, linguistically, and socially," which offers "opportunities around every corner." No matter what students seek from their educations, they're likely to find it here, from engineering to business to pharmacy programs and more. That kind of all-encompassing diversity means the school "offers everyone the opportunity to pursue anything they're interested in." It also means, however, that your instructors will run the gamut "from vivacious to narcoleptic"; students will have their "fair share of great professors, average professors, and bad professors." However, for every professor who is "rude when dealing with students," there are ten who are "intelligent people who have a lot of information to share and a lot of experience that allows them to elaborate on many topics." The best of these professors are "experienced, intelligent, and helpful," as well as "diverse, accessible, proactive, involved in research, and interested in students who take initiative." These educators know how to make learning "enjoyable and informative." Most classes employ a traditional lecture format, but many elective classes "are much smaller and thus much more open to discussion and student presentation." Even more attractive for many, Rutgers' status as a research university means there are ample opportunities for undergraduates "to conduct research and work with professors in any number of fields."

Life

A big campus, "awesome" public transportation, and activities of every type mean staying active at Rutgers is easy. There is certainly no lack of things to do. "There is always something going on," students boast, with sports, "movie screenings, arcade games at the RutgersZone, performing arts, local theaters, university-sponsored concerts, free food events, community service days, Greek life," and more filling whatever down time students might have. Local restaurants abound. School clubs and organizations exist by the hundreds, including those dedicated to theater, music, dance, and community service. "The party scene is definitely present, more so in the warmer months," and there are plenty of bars popular with students. The on-campus party scene tends to be safe, since the school "sends out (campus) police to patrol around the campus twenty-four hours to ensure student safety." Maybe most popular of all is rooting for the scarlet. "During football season…everyone can be found cheering in the student section at the games." For those who need to get off campus, New York City and Philadelphia are both a modest train or bus drive away. With so many opportunities, "Rutgers allows students to do well in school, be a part of an organization, have relationships with friends, and even have a job." Here, "there's rarely a dull moment."

Student Body

Typical student? Not here. The universal refrain from Rutgers students is there is no such thing. "The one common thread most students have is that they are from New Jersey, since it is a state school." Other than that, "Rutgers is truly a melting pot of people from all over the world of all different backgrounds with different interests." Rather than making it more difficult to fit in, students say this melting pot makes it easier because "no matter what you're interested in, there is a group of students here who share the same exact interests. It's really easy to find your own niche." Most students are "dedicated to academics and community service and also to having fun," students who, no matter which group they fall in with, are "very friendly, funny, and nice." Notice the combination of strong academics and a dedication to fun? That, too, is a frequently cited trait common at Rutgers. Even though "there is not one typical student," at the very least most are "serious about their work and studying but know how to party and have fun." With a large, diverse campus having more than 50,000 students, it doesn't matter the kind of person you are. "It is not uncommon to meet someone new weekly.... With so many students here, everyone is able to find someone to befriend and interact with."

RUTGERS UNIVERSITY—NEW BRUNSWICK

Financial Aid: 848-932-7057 • E-Mail: admissions@ugadm.rutgers.edu • Website: www.newbrunswick.rutgers.edu

THE PRINCETON REVIEW SAYS

Admissions

Very important factors considered include: rigor of secondary school record, academic GPA, standardized test scores. *Important factors considered include:* extracurricular activities. *Other factors considered include:* class rank, application essay, interview, talent/ability, character/ personal qualities, first generation, geographical residence, state residency, racial/ethnic status, volunteer work, work experience. ACT with or without writing accepted. SAT with or without Essay component accepted. High school diploma is required and GED is accepted. *Academic units required:* 4 English, 3 math, 2 science, 2 foreign language, 5 academic electives.

Financial Aid

Students should submit: FAFSA. Priority filing deadline is 12/1. The Princeton Review suggests that all financial aid forms be submitted as soon as possible after October 1. *Need-based scholarships/grants offered:* College/university scholarship or grant aid from institutional funds; Federal Nursing Scholarships; Federal Pell; SEOG; State scholarships/grants. *Loan aid offered:* Direct PLUS loans; Direct Subsidized Stafford Loans; Direct Unsubsidized Stafford Loans. Applicants will be notified of awards on a rolling basis beginning 2/15. Federal Work-Study Program available. Institutional employment available.

The Inside Word

One does not need to jump through hoops to get into Rutgers. Because of the vast number of applications the university gets each year, applicants will be reviewed based on the standard criteria—grades, the quality of your high school curriculum, standardized test scores, and your student essay—without much beyond that. Solid students should find acceptance into Rutgers a relatively painless process.

THE SCHOOL SAYS "..."

From the Admissions Office

"The Rutgers story runs deeper than top-notch research, high-caliber academics, a diverse student body, and Big Ten athletics. We encourage you to look closer and discover what Rutgers can offer you.

- You will study with some of the best and brightest minds around; from award-winning faculty who are leaders in their fields to students who are smart, diverse, ambitious, and engaged with the world around them.

- With more than 100 undergraduate majors, study abroad programs in 60+ countries, and a student-to-faculty ratio of 16:1, your education will be all about you.

- At the doorsteps of New York City and Philadelphia, Rutgers hosts 650+ employers each year for career and internship fairs allowing you access to companies like Bloomberg, Johnson & Johnson, Capital One, Amazon, and Google.

- Whether you're cheering on your beloved Scarlet Knights at a Big Ten football game, joining one of over 500 student organizations, or raising $1 million for children with cancer through Rutgers Dance Marathon, there are hundreds of ways to join in, find your niche, and make lifelong memories.

- Rutgers is among the most diverse universities in the nation, with students from all 50 states and 87+ countries.

"With the prestigious honor of being a member of the Association of American Universities (a highly selective organization comprising the 62 top research institutions in North America), the flagship university of the State University of New Jersey is the ultimate beginning to your remarkable future."

SELECTIVITY

Admissions Rating	88
# of applicants	41,286
% of applicants accepted	61
% of acceptees attending	29

FRESHMAN PROFILE

Range SAT EBRW	590–680
Range SAT Math	620–750
Range ACT Composite	25–32
# submitting SAT scores	6,585
% submitting SAT scores	90
# submitting ACT scores	1,303
% submitting ACT scores	18
% graduated top 10% of class	38
% graduated top 25% of class	73
% graduated top 50% of class	94

DEADLINES

Early action	
Deadline	11/1
Notification	1/31
Regular	
Priority	12/1
Nonfall registration?	Yes

APPLICANTS ALSO LOOK AT AND OFTEN PREFER
University of Pennsylvania; Cornell University; Princeton University

AND SOMETIMES PREFER
Penn State University Park; New York University; Boston University; University of Maryland, College Park; The College of New Jersey

FINANCIAL FACTS

Financial Aid Rating	70
Annual in-state tuition	$12,230
Annual out-of-state tuition	$29,012
Room and board	$13,075
Required fees	$3,177
Books and supplies	$1,350
% needy frosh rec. need-based scholarship or grant aid	0
% needy UG rec. need-based scholarship or grant aid	0
% needy frosh rec. non-need-based scholarship or grant aid	0
% needy UG rec. non-need-based scholarship or grant aid	0
% needy frosh rec. need-based self-help aid	0
% needy UG rec. need-based self-help aid	0
% frosh need fully met	0
% ugrads need fully met	0

SACRED HEART UNIVERSITY

5151 Park Avenue, Fairfield, CT 06825 • Admissions: 203-371-7880 • Fax: 203-365-7607

STUDENTS SAY ". . ."

Academics
Sacred Heart is a university that's imbued with a tremendous amount of "school spirit" and "an amazing sense of community." The university offers a wide range of majors and many students are quick to laud the "strong nursing and business programs." A number also cheer for the performing arts department's "professional, conservatory-style Dance program, and Theater Arts Program." Moreover, students love that the campus is "very modern," with whiteboard-stacked classrooms that feature "many unique features other schools lack" and "VR for classroom exercises, which enhanced the learning experience." At Sacred Heart, you're getting brand-new facilities and "state-of-the-art technology designed to give every student the best experience possible."

These aren't bells and whistles; Sacred Heart prioritizes "real work experience" and provides "a lot of networking opportunities that are very valuable." Undergrads also suggest that small classes help "make the learning experience very personal." Students also seem to hold their professors in high regard as well. Adjectives like "lively" and "passionate" abound, as do anecdotes about a particular religion teacher who "would literally get up on the desk with so much enthusiasm" so as to "engage us with his humor." Sacred Heart professors are also defined by their accessibility. As this undergrad shares, "They are always available for extra help and genuinely want their students to succeed."

Life
Out of all the things you'll learn at Sacred Heart University, the one thing you might forget is what boredom is. Undergrads assert that "there are countless clubs and organizations to get involved in, activities at all hours of the day, and there is so much spirit here!" One student's typically packed (and far from complete) list of experiences goes as follows: "I go to Greek life talent shows, tie-dye shirts, make mugs, play with therapy dogs, [and] participate in dodgeball [and] cornhole games." A number of students also enjoy giving back and you'll often find undergrads working with "the school's Habitat for Humanity Chapter" or even embarking on "service trips to places like Mexico, Puerto Rico, and South Dakota." Having a bunch of D1 athletes also means that there are plenty of games to watch, as well as various high-quality performing arts. And if you're intrigued by fraternities or sororities, you'll be glad to hear that "a large population of students here participate in Greek life." Of course, these undergrads are also happy to indulge in simple pleasures too. For example, once it snows, it's not uncommon for students to "go sledding [or start] snowball fights." Finally, undergrads like to visit "downtown Fairfield, which is only 15 minutes away from campus [and has] tons of restaurants and shops."

Student Body
When they first arrive on campus, Sacred Heart students are generally pleased to discover just how "selfless" and "supportive" their classmates truly are. "Every day when I go to class, a fellow student is always holding open the door for me." Another undergrad explains, "There is an enthusiasm that you can't fake that comes from the President all the way down to the students. People here genuinely care for others." It's an active concern too, or as one student puts it, "We push each other to do the best we can in school and in sports." As a result of such "happy, positive, and hardworking" peers, it's not hard to find common ground, though students still marvel at how easy it is to meet people. "Whenever I walk down the hall there is always someone I know... so you have to be ready to say hello or give a smile." Those looking for diversity should know that "even though most students are from the Northeast, I still believe that we are all very different and bring unique ideas to the table, which makes for an overall great campus environment. "

SACRED HEART UNIVERSITY

Financial Aid: 203-371-7980 • E-Mail: enroll@sacredheart.edu • Website: www.sacredheart.edu

THE PRINCETON REVIEW SAYS

Admissions

Very important factors considered include: rigor of secondary school record, academic GPA, volunteer work, work experience, level of applicant's interest. *Important factors considered include:* class rank, application essay, recommendation(s), interview, extracurricular activities, talent/ability, character/personal qualities. *Other factors considered include:* standardized test scores, alumni/ae relation. ACT with or without writing accepted. SAT with or without Essay component accepted. High school diploma is required and GED is accepted. *Academic units required:* 4 English, 3 math, 3 science, 1 science lab, 2 foreign language, 3 social studies, 3 history, 3 academic electives. *Academic units recommended:* 4 English, 4 math, 4 science, 2 science labs, 4 foreign language, 4 social studies, 4 history, 4 academic electives.

Financial Aid

Students should submit: CSS/Financial Aid PROFILE; FAFSA; Noncustodial PROFILE. The Princeton Review suggests that all financial aid forms be submitted as soon as possible after October 1. *Need-based scholarships/grants offered:* College/university scholarship or grant aid from institutional funds; Federal Pell; Private scholarships; SEOG; State scholarships/grants. *Loan aid offered:* Direct PLUS loans; Direct Subsidized Stafford Loans; Direct Unsubsidized Stafford Loans. Applicants will be notified of awards on a rolling basis beginning 2/1. Federal Work-Study Program available. Institutional employment available.

The Inside Word

Sacred Heart takes a holistic approach to the admissions process and the school aims to get a sense of every candidate beyond their quantitative metrics. Nevertheless, while recommendation letters and extracurricular participation are important, academic achievement still carries the most weight. To be seen as a competitive candidate, you should take at least several honors or advanced placement courses during high school. It's also important to note that Sacred Heart is a test-optional school (with the exception of homeschooled students).

THE SCHOOL SAYS "..."

From the Admissions Office

"Sacred Heart University is recognized for cutting-edge technology, academic programs with excellent career outcomes, championship Division I athletic programs, and its beautiful suburban campus, with many new facilities and features. Along with exceptional growth in enrollment, academic programs continue to expand and include new majors in engineering, technology, business fields, communications and the sciences. The physical campus was recently expanded to include the 66-acre former world headquarters of General Electric, now SHU's West Campus, which houses the IDEA Lab; NeXReality AR/VR/XR labs; the iHub powered by Verizon co-working and incubator space; the Finance Lab; and a Center for Career & Professional Development satellite office. New campus buildings also include the Center for Healthcare Education, a new health and recreation center and four new residence halls. With an ideal New England location 55 miles from New York City in Fairfield County, Connecticut, plentiful undergraduate research and internship experiences are in place for all majors, the Career Center works with students as soon as they arrive as freshmen. Students also gain real-world experience taking a wide variety of courses at SHU's two international campuses in Europe and study abroad locations around the globe. On campus, an exciting student life program for both residential and commuter students offers more than 100 student organizations including strong performing arts programs in dance, theater arts, band, orchestra, and choral; Greek life; media clubs; an array of community service organizations; 32 Division I varsity sports; and 36 club sports teams."

SELECTIVITY

Admissions Rating	85
# of applicants	11,748
% of applicants accepted	64
% of acceptees attending	21
# of early decision applicants	252
% accepted early decision	85

FRESHMAN PROFILE

Range SAT EBRW	570–630
Range SAT Math	550–630
Range ACT Composite	23–28
# submitting SAT scores	838
% submitting SAT scores	52
# submitting ACT scores	173
% submitting ACT scores	11
Average HS GPA	3.6
% graduated top 10% of class	10
% graduated top 25% of class	35
% graduated top 50% of class	69

DEADLINES

Early decision	
Deadline	12/1
Notification	12/15
Early action	
Deadline	12/15
Notification	1/31
Regular	
Priority	2/15
Notification	4/1
Nonfall registration?	Yes

APPLICANTS ALSO LOOK AT AND SOMETIMES PREFER

Marist College; Quinnipiac University; University of Connecticut; University of Rhode Island; Fairfield University

FINANCIAL FACTS

Financial Aid Rating	84
Annual tuition	$42,800
Room and board	$15,960
Required fees	$270
Books and supplies	$1,200
Average frosh need-based scholarship	$18,503
Average UG need-based scholarship	$18,140
% needy frosh rec. need-based scholarship or grant aid	100
% needy UG rec. need-based scholarship or grant aid	99
% needy frosh rec. non-need-based scholarship or grant aid	18
% needy UG rec. non-need-based scholarship or grant aid	15
% needy frosh rec. need-based self-help aid	77
% needy UG rec. need-based self-help aid	80
% frosh rec. any financial aid	99.9
% UG rec. any financial aid	96.6
% UG borrow to pay for school	72
Average cumulative indebtedness	$45,630
% frosh need fully met	19
% ugrads need fully met	18
Average % of frosh need met	59
Average % of ugrad need met	58

SAINT ANSELM COLLEGE

100 Saint Anselm Drive, Manchester, NH 03102-1310 • Admissions: 603-641-7500 • Fax: 603-641-7550

CAMPUS LIFE

Quality of Life Rating	**93**
Fire Safety Rating	**85**
Green Rating	**63**
Type of school	Private
Affiliation	Roman Catholic
Environment	City

STUDENTS

Total undergrad enrollment	2,043
% male/female	39/61
% from out of state	86
% frosh from public high school	65
% frosh live on campus	91
% ugrads live on campus	94
% African American	2
% Asian	1
% Caucasian	87
% Hispanic	4
% Native American	<1
% Pacific Islander	0
% Two or more races	2
% Race and/or ethnicity unknown	4
% international	1
# of countries represented	9

SURVEY SAYS . . .

Students are happy
Lab facilities are great
Great library
Internships are widely available
Students are friendly
Students are very religious
Students get along with local community
Great food on campus
Very little drug use
Intramural sports are popular
Alumni active on campus
Active student-run political groups

ACADEMICS

Academic Rating	**86**
% students returning for sophomore year	89
% students graduating within 4 years	74
% students graduating within 6 years	78
Calendar	Semester
Student/faculty ratio	11:1
Profs interesting rating	90
Profs accessible rating	95

Most classes have 10–19 students.

MOST POPULAR MAJORS

Business Administration and Management, General; Nursing; Political Science and Government, General

STUDENTS SAY " . . ."

Academics

Nestled in New Hampshire, an hour north of Boston, Saint Anselm College is a small, Catholic Benedictine liberal arts college founded in 1889. Its prime location provides not only a beautiful environment in which to learn, but also makes it "the Benedictine college with a box seat on America's most riveting political theater" according to *The Washington Post*, and adds indelible "real-world experience" for those pursuing an education in politics. The small size of the college—in 2019 there were 2,041 students—allows Saint Anselm College to provide "a welcoming community" and a "personalized experience" for all students. It encourages "Catholic ideals" of "service and community" and offers "a challenging, quality education" with "in depth learning both inside and outside of the classroom." Students call Saint Anselm a "close knit yet academically motivating environment, with countless opportunities to gain internship and other leadership experiences." "Each individual can thrive in some way," notes an English major, and "be involved, serve others, and have a life-long second home." "The education here is incredible," says a Forensic Science major, and "the teachers are more than happy to help you succeed." Students feel "challenged and enthused" by their professors and note that "discussions inside and outside of class are fantastic," "the lectures and labs prepare" them well for exams, "homework is almost always extremely relevant and beneficial," and professors "rarely lecture [or] read off power points." Professors "seem to love their job" and "come to class ready to stimulate your creative thinking." Students say that there is an "accessible, friendly, and inviting atmosphere in the classroom" and that "the teachers are always accessible." Community service is encouraged, making Saint Anselm a good fit for students who want to "become a better person as a whole and create an intelligent and kind community of students." As one student notes: "Saint Anselm College prepared me for life, and a wonderful, happy, and successful one at that."

Life

Saint Anselm College "is a school with rigorous academics on the weekdays," notes a Communication major, "and tons of different things to be involved in on the weekends." On campus, students hang out and "watch movies," play "pool in their dorms," and attend "sports events." The Campus Activities Board "brings magicians, comedians, and musicians" to campus that students can "see for free." Students can also enjoy the "Abbey Players or various theater performances at the Dana Center," and "many students grab a bite to eat at the Coffee Shop" afterward. "There are plenty of options to keep busy!" says an International Relations major. Including community service work, which is a "big part of Saint Anselm's mission."

Student Body

Saint Anselm students describe their classmates as "smart," "kind," "hardworking" and "friendly." They can be "very preppy" and are "committed to the community and family." A typical student at Saint Anselm College is "very well rounded," communicates well, and "can multi-task." Most students engage in a variety of on-campus opportunities, and "have a lot of experience in their field of study," by engaging in "research studies, literature reviews, and advanced studying." They are inspired by "the generosity of the monks that serve the campus," and are community service oriented. "Never in my life can I recall seeing such a diverse community of people so well integrated and committed to its success as a whole," notes one student. "Students fit in by being Anselmian."

Financial Aid: 603-641-7110 • E-Mail: admission@anselm.edu • Website: www.anselm.edu

THE PRINCETON REVIEW SAYS

Admissions

Very important factors considered include: rigor of secondary school record, academic GPA. *Important factors considered include:* recommendation(s), extracurricular activities, character/ personal qualities, volunteer work. *Other factors considered include:* class rank, application essay, standardized test scores, talent/ability, first generation, alumni/ae relation, geographical residence, racial/ethnic status, level of applicant's interest. ACT with or without writing accepted. SAT with or without Essay component accepted. High school diploma is required and GED is accepted. *Academic units required:* 4 English, 3 math, 3 science, 2 science labs, 2 foreign language, 2 social studies. *Academic units recommended:* 4 English, 4 math, 4 science, 2 science labs, 4 foreign language, 4 social studies.

Financial Aid

Students should submit: CSS/Financial Aid PROFILE; FAFSA; Noncustodial PROFILE. Priority filing deadline is 2/15. The Princeton Review suggests that all financial aid forms be submitted as soon as possible after October 1. *Need-based scholarships/grants offered:* College/university scholarship or grant aid from institutional funds; Federal Pell; Private scholarships; SEOG; State scholarships/grants. *Loan aid offered:* Direct PLUS loans; Direct Subsidized Stafford Loans; Direct Unsubsidized Stafford Loans. Federal Work-Study Program available. Institutional employment available.

The Inside Word

Saint Anselm College uses the Common Application and ACT and SAT scores (although test scores are optional), but places an added focus on personal character and community service extracurriculars in their admissions process. Applicants who feel their grades and test scores are not as high as they'd like should make sure to emphasize their out-of-class skills and experiences in their application. Note that nursing applicants must apply early action or early decision.

THE SCHOOL SAYS "..."

From the Admissions Office

"Saint Anselm is New England's only Benedictine College, a place where a 1,500 year tradition that values a love of learning and a balanced life is coupled with a contemporary liberal arts education. The college offers over eighty academic programs and is particularly well-known for nursing, politics, business, criminal justice, and psychology. Located in the first in the nation primary state, Saint Anselm is the home of the New Hampshire Institute of Politics, which hosts national debates and provides opportunities for students of any major to engage with candidates, journalists, and elected officials. A student who wants to meet the next President of the United States has a good chance of doing so here. Saint Anselm has been ranked 18th nationally for student engagement in community service by the Princeton Review, hailed by the Carnegie Foundation with Classification in both Curricular Engagement and Outreach and Partnerships, and recognized as a first tier best national liberal arts college by U.S. News & World Report. Faculty from many departments teach in the seminar-based program where students contemplate questions of value and moral choice. The college's Dana Center for the Humanities, used by students and the public, hosts a broad range of theater programming including contemporary dance and music. The Alva De Mars Megan Chapel Art Center provides an extraordinary array of art exhibitions from classic to contemporary. Eighty-five percent of the college's students participates in athletics, intramurals, and club sports. The college also offers fifty student organizations, study abroad, and community service."

SELECTIVITY

Admissions Rating	81
# of applicants	3,742
% of applicants accepted	75
% of acceptees attending	18
# offered a place on the wait list	471
% accepting a place on wait list	24
% admitted from wait list	24
# of early decision applicants	33
% accepted early decision	82

FRESHMAN PROFILE

Range SAT EBRW	570–660
Range SAT Math	550–650
Range ACT Composite	24–29
# submitting SAT scores	286
% submitting SAT scores	56
# submitting ACT scores	40
% submitting ACT scores	8
Average HS GPA	3.4
% graduated top 10% of class	28
% graduated top 25% of class	61
% graduated top 50% of class	91

DEADLINES

Early decision	
Deadline	12/1
Notification	1/1
Early action	
Deadline	11/15
Notification	1/15
Regular	
Deadline	2/1
Notification	3/15
Nonfall registration?	Yes

APPLICANTS ALSO LOOK AT AND OFTEN PREFER

Boston College; Colby College; College of the Holy Cross; Villanova University

AND SOMETIMES PREFER

Fairfield University; Fordham University; Providence College; Wheaton College (MA); Quinnipiac University; Sacred Heart University; Saint Michael's College; Salve Regina University; Stonehill College

FINANCIAL FACTS

Financial Aid Rating	88
Annual tuition	$41,510
Room and board	$15,120
Required fees	$1,330
Books and supplies	$1,000
Average frosh need-based scholarship	$28,533
Average UG need-based scholarship	$27,299
% needy frosh rec. need-based scholarship or grant aid	100
% needy UG rec. need-based scholarship or grant aid	100
% needy frosh rec. non-need-based scholarship or grant aid	26
% needy UG rec. non-need-based scholarship or grant aid	19
% needy frosh rec. need-based self-help aid	77
% needy UG rec. need-based self-help aid	81
% frosh rec. any financial aid	99
% UG rec. any financial aid	98
% UG borrow to pay for school	80
Average cumulative indebtedness	$32,769
% frosh need fully met	34
% ugrads need fully met	26
Average % of frosh need met	85
Average % of ugrad need met	80

ST. BONAVENTURE UNIVERSITY

3261 West State Road, St. Bonaventure, NY 14778 • Admissions: 716-375-2434 • Fax: 716-375-4005

STUDENTS SAY "..."

Academics

St. Bonaventure University is a small Franciscan school of around 1,800 undergraduates. It provides "a well-rounded college experience that allows [students] to feel confident after graduation," great academic programs, and "an enormously huge heart." St. Bonaventure University is "very responsive to the need of having small class sizes to improve education outcomes" and the 12:1 student-faculty ratio guarantees personal relationships with the professors and thoughtful discussions with peers. Students "know just about everyone. You go through the same classes with the same students throughout [your] career and it makes it easier to work in groups and get help," says a student. This is a group of eager learners who have a drive to learn and succeed not only in the classroom but "beyond, in meaningful applications to current and future employment endeavors."

The faculty comes equipped with real-world experience and sparks students' interests in a variety of academic disciplines, and "every single teacher goes out of their way to help students in any way they can." If students need help and show that they really want to learn the material, "[the faculty] will devote so much time to you." Professors "really work hard to make their classes better" and "really take our teacher evaluations to heart." Bonaventure's small size provides each student with "the opportunity to tutor, teach, do research and lead during their undergrad," and the school shows excellent career placement rates.

Life

Between the great people and gorgeous scenery, "it's not that hard to go to school in the middle of nowhere." During the week, the most popular place to be between classes is "either the dining hall or the library." The small campus means students "can roll out of bed 10 minutes before class and still make it on time," and it features "a beautiful trail to walk." Division I athletics at SBU receive a lot of accolades, and students say there's nothing better than cheering for Bona basketball in the Reilly Center. "You can always tell when game day is for the men's basketball team just by walking through campus, it gets pretty crazy." Extracurricular clubs are extremely popular, as is spending time in the Rathskeller, "an on campus bar that features two pool tables, ping-pong, multiple TVs, a dance floor with a DJ usually, [and] other games." Off campus parties are "very common" on weekends. Everyone pretty much sticks to campus or hometown Olean, but for those that do want to venture further (and have access to a car), they can always "spend the day exploring the nearby national forest, or take a trip to Buffalo or Erie."

Student Body

Here in the Bona Bubble, students "look out for each other both during and after our collegiate careers." The campus culture encourages students "to be respectful with each other." "All of my peers know that the bubble we have on campus is unquestionably unique," says one. Besides holding the doors for each other all around campus ("If door holding was an Olympic sport we would win gold"), these "unfailingly kind" students "bond and form a group passionate for their small-town school." "Once a Bonnie, always a Bonnie," says a student. The familial atmosphere that students revel in here often keeps people so tightly knit "that going home for break can be difficult because you miss them so much."

St. Bonaventure University

Financial Aid: 716-375-7888 • E-Mail: admissions@sbu.edu • Website: www.sbu.edu

THE PRINCETON REVIEW SAYS

Admissions

Very important factors considered include: rigor of secondary school record, academic GPA, recommendation(s), character/personal qualities. *Important factors considered include:* application essay, standardized test scores, extracurricular activities, talent/ability. *Other factors considered include:* class rank, interview, first generation, alumni/ae relation, geographical residence, state residency, work experience, level of applicant's interest. ACT with or without writing accepted. SAT with or without Essay component accepted. High school diploma is required and GED is accepted. *Academic units recommended:* 4 English, 3 math, 3 science, 3 science labs, 2 foreign language, 4 social studies.

Financial Aid

Students should submit: FAFSA; State aid form. Priority filing deadline is 2/1. The Princeton Review suggests that all financial aid forms be submitted as soon as possible after October 1. *Need-based scholarships/grants offered:* College/university scholarship or grant aid from institutional funds; Federal Pell; Private scholarships; SEOG; State scholarships/grants. *Loan aid offered:* Direct PLUS loans; Direct Subsidized Stafford Loans; Direct Unsubsidized Stafford Loans. Applicants will be notified of awards on a rolling basis beginning 1/1. Federal Work-Study Program available. Institutional employment available.

The Inside Word

Prospective students at Bonaventure are evaluated individually and accepted based on their capacity for success in college. St. Bonaventure recommends that applicants submit academic transcripts, standardized test scores, recommendations, and a personal essay, and the admissions committee will consider any other supporting materials that prove a student's overall eligibility for admission. St. Bonaventure has a rolling admissions program, so applications are reviewed as soon as they arrive at the admissions office, and encouraged to apply early in the admission cycle.

THE SCHOOL SAYS "..."

From the Admissions Office

"For more than 160 years, St. Bonaventure University has been dedicated to education excellence as informed by our Franciscan and liberal arts traditions. We seek to transform the lives of our students, inspiring in them a lifelong commitment to service and citizenship.

"The charm of our campus and the inspirational beauty of the surrounding hills provide a special place where growth in learning and living is abundantly realized. St. Bonaventure establishes pathways to internships, graduate schools and careers through its innovate Career and Professional Readiness Center, which engages students from the time they step onto campus. The Richter Recreation Center provides all students with state-of-the-art facilities for athletics and wellness. As a student at one of the smallest Division I schools in the country, you get the benefits of big-time sports along with those of a small, student-centered university. St. Bonaventure is a member of the Atlantic 10.

"Academics at St. Bonaventure are challenging. Small classes and personalized attention encourage individual growth and development. St. Bonaventure's schools of Arts and Sciences, Business, (Jandoli School of) Communications, Education and Health Professions offer fifty majors. The School of Graduate Studies also offers several programs —on-ground, on-line and hybrid formats—leading to the master's degree.

"While St. Bonaventure has adopted a test-optional policy for standardized tests (ACT and SAT), such scores will still be required for some specific majors, and to be eligible for the university's top three scholarship levels. The biology Subject Test is required only for students applying to one of our many dual-degree medical programs."

SELECTIVITY

Admissions Rating	79
# of applicants	3,058
% of applicants accepted	75
% of acceptees attending	21

FRESHMAN PROFILE

Range SAT EBRW	510–620
Range SAT Math	520–620
Range SAT Composite	1030–1220
Range ACT Composite	19–26
# submitting SAT scores	440
% submitting SAT scores	89
# submitting ACT scores	147
% submitting ACT scores	30
Average HS GPA	3.3
% graduated top 10% of class	16
% graduated top 25% of class	39
% graduated top 50% of class	73

DEADLINES

Regular	
Priority	2/15
Deadline	7/30
Notification	Rolling, 10/15
Nonfall registration?	Yes

FINANCIAL FACTS

Financial aid Rating	87
Annual tuition	$35,450
Room and board	$13,620
Required fees	$1,065
Books and supplies	$800
Average frosh need-based scholarship	$25,442
Average UG need-based scholarship	$24,215
% needy frosh rec. need-based scholarship or grant aid	100
% needy UG rec. need-based scholarship or grant aid	99
% needy frosh rec. non-need-based scholarship or grant aid	94
% needy UG rec. non-need-based scholarship or grant aid	91
% needy frosh rec. need-based self-help aid	82
% needy UG rec. need-based self-help aid	83
% frosh rec. any financial aid	98
% UG rec. any financial aid	94
Average cumulative indebtedness	$34,877
% frosh need fully met	24
% ugrads need fully met	24
Average % of frosh need met	73
Average % of ugrad need met	70

ST. JOHN'S COLLEGE (MD)

60 College Avenue, Annapolis, MD 21401 • Admissions: 410-626-2522 • Fax: 410-269-7916

STUDENTS SAY "..."

Academics

At St. John's College in Maryland, the "great books," or texts commonly viewed as the foundation of Western culture, form the backbone of the unique curriculum. St. John's is a liberal arts college with two campuses that encourages exploration and dissection of original, foundational texts so that students may develop critical analysis skills within a "safe and prosperous learning environment." "The teaching of St. John's College is all about allowing individuals to collectively discover the essence of being a human being," sums up one student. Classes are pretty straightforward: "We read, and we talk about what we read." The curriculum includes obscure texts as well as the major classic players, and one of the greatest things about studying here is "engaging with difficult and renowned texts without worrying about impressing others or having to show off."

The "largely brilliant and caring" faculty members at St. John's are "some of the most wonderful and interesting people," and are "willing to meet for coffee or lunch to discuss essays, questions from class, concerns, and even non-program texts." They are "engaged and enthralled by the learning process at St. John's, just as the students are." The college has a unique evaluation system in place, so students at St. John's "are faced with reports not just on their academic success, but also on the way that they treat and interact with their peers, via classroom dynamic." The college has made academic rigor an "overwhelmingly social issue," and the "'too cool for school' attitude is not socially rewarded" here. Not only do students discuss the same works and questions, "they do so in a respectful, tactful manner." In any classroom "you get the sense of togetherness" where everyone listens and "no one's points are any more or less important to the discussion than any other's."

Life

There are "no two Johnnies that are alike" and students at St. John's display a wide range of interests. Most participate in "a study group of some sort, at least one artistic extracurricular, and an intramural sport." St. John's "robust intramural program" is a major component of campus social life, and creates a "fantastic" community in which students are alphabetically sorted onto teams "where anyone can participate in various seasonal sports." "Although I have never been athletic, this is a very welcoming group regardless of ability, and playing intramural sports here has given me a lot of confidence," says one student. A large amount of extracurricular time is spent studying and reading, but there are also "very many popular club options," including "swing dance lessons, fencing, the croquet team, student play productions, orchestra, various choral groups, community service, [and the] environmental club." St. John's also offers students spots in classes run by non-faculty members of the Annapolis community, including "writing classes, poetry, watercolor, and sculpture." Off campus, people often go out to eat at many of the great restaurants in Annapolis, or head to the museums and monuments in Washington, D.C., which is "just a short train ride away." Students can also transfer between the Annapolis or the Santa Fe campuses, and many in Maryland spend a year studying in New Mexico.

Student Body

The student body at St. John's is "intellectual, but far from pretentious," and given that all students go through the same academic program "there is a strong and warm sense of camaraderie." Upperclassmen "couldn't care less that you're a freshmen," and people "who would have never become friends anywhere else are able to come together here and form bonds that start in the classroom but continue into life outside the academics." The curiosity students develop here extends to outside the program as well, so while the program at St. John's is classically oriented, students at the college "are aware of pop culture, current events, and politics." The bubble at St. John's is "real, but in no way impenetrable."

Financial Aid: 410-626-2502 • E-Mail: Annapolis.Admissions@sjc.edu • Website: www.sjc.edu

THE PRINCETON REVIEW SAYS

Admissions

Very important factors considered include: application essay. *Important factors considered include:* rigor of secondary school record, recommendation(s), character/personal qualities. *Other factors considered include:* class rank, academic GPA, standardized test scores, interview, extracurricular activities, talent/ability, first generation, alumni/ae relation, geographical residence, volunteer work, work experience. ACT with or without writing accepted. SAT with or without Essay component accepted. High school diploma is required and GED is accepted. *Academic units required:* 3 math, 2 foreign language. *Academic units recommended:* 4 English, 4 math, 3 science, 3 science labs, 4 foreign language, 2 history.

Financial Aid

Students should submit: FAFSA; State aid form. Priority filing deadline is 2/1. The Princeton Review suggests that all financial aid forms be submitted as soon as possible after October 1. *Need-based scholarships/grants offered:* College/university scholarship or grant aid from institutional funds; Federal Pell; Private scholarships; SEOG; State scholarships/grants. *Loan aid offered:* Direct PLUS loans; Direct Subsidized Stafford Loans; Direct Unsubsidized Stafford Loans. Applicants will be notified of awards on a rolling basis beginning 12/15. Federal Work-Study Program available. Institutional employment available.

The Inside Word

St. John's is a unique environment, best suited to students of a quirky yet serious intellectual predilection. To test the waters before you jump in, consider taking a campus tour or even sitting in on an active tutorial session with students. You can also send your questions about academics and life on campus to a current student through the St. John website. Each applicant is evaluated individually for potential success in the program, and submitting standardized test scores is optional. St. John's also features rolling admission beginning 2/15 with notification within three weeks of completing the application.

THE SCHOOL SAYS "..."

From the Admissions Office

"St. John's College is centered on reading and discussing the greatest books in history. With teachers such as Plato, Shakespeare, Euclid, Nietzsche, Einstein, Austen, and Du Bois, students at St. John's are original and unconventional, love big questions and discussion, and are excited to join an intellectual community of thinkers and seekers.

"All students at St. John's explore our great books curriculum in interdisciplinary classes focused on philosophy, classics, literature, politics, religion, biology, chemistry, physics, mathematics, music, history, language, and more. With a 7:1 student to faculty ratio, every class is a discussion led by one or two faculty members. Instead of choosing a major, all students graduate with a BA in the Liberal Arts. The college regularly ranks among the best for undergraduate teaching and student-faculty relationships.

"Over 70% of Johnnies attend graduate school, particularly in law, business, and journalism, and the college is among the best for students receiving PhDs in the humanities and sciences. Students are free to transfer between the campuses in Annapolis, MD, and Santa Fe, NM.

"On the Annapolis campus, 500 students experience an idyllic college town along the Chesapeake Bay. Annapolis is close to Washington, DC, with dozens of nearby museums and cultural offerings. The college was founded here in 1696, and students embrace long-held traditions such as waltz parties, intramural sports, and the annual croquet match against the Naval Academy. Popular student groups include musical ensembles, community service organizations, and the college's theatrical troupe, King Williams Players."

SELECTIVITY

Admissions Rating	89
# of applicants	753
% of applicants accepted	55
% of acceptees attending	30
# offered a place on the wait list	32
% accepting a place on wait list	100
% admitted from wait list	25

FRESHMAN PROFILE

Range SAT EBRW	630–710
Range SAT Math	650–740
Range ACT Composite	26–32
# submitting SAT scores	61
% submitting SAT scores	50
# submitting ACT scores	23
% submitting ACT scores	19
Average HS GPA	3.5
% graduated top 10% of class	36
% graduated top 25% of class	59
% graduated top 50% of class	87

DEADLINES

Early action	
Deadline	11/15
Notification	12/15
Regular	
Priority	11/15
Notification	Rolling, 12/15
Nonfall registration?	Yes

APPLICANTS ALSO LOOK AT AND OFTEN PREFER
Brown University; The University of Chicago; Harvard College

AND SOMETIMES PREFER
Bard College; Reed College; William & Mary

AND RARELY PREFER
University of Maryland, College Park

FINANCIAL FACTS

Financial Aid Rating	89
Annual tuition	$35,000
Room and board	$13,635
Required fees	$635
Books and supplies	$630
Average frosh need-based scholarship	$38,747
Average UG need-based scholarship	$36,575
% needy frosh rec. need-based scholarship or grant aid	98
% needy UG rec. need-based scholarship or grant aid	99
% needy frosh rec. non-need-based scholarship or grant aid	16
% needy UG rec. non-need-based scholarship or grant aid	19
% needy frosh rec. need-based self-help aid	89
% needy UG rec. need-based self-help aid	87
% frosh rec. any financial aid	99
% UG rec. any financial aid	99
% UG borrow to pay for school	74
Average cumulative indebtedness	$16,705
% frosh need fully met	23
% ugrads need fully met	25
Average % of frosh need met	88
Average % of ugrad need met	87

ST. JOHN'S COLLEGE (NM)

1160 Camino Cruz Blanca, Santa Fe, NM 87505 • Admissions: 505-984-6060

CAMPUS LIFE

Quality of Life Rating	92
Fire Safety Rating	73
Green Rating	71
Type of school	Private
Environment	Town

STUDENTS

Total undergrad enrollment	322
% male/female	56/44
% from out of state	89
% frosh from public high school	50
% frosh live on campus	96
% ugrads live on campus	83
# of fraternities	0
# of sororities	0
% African American	1
% Asian	2
% Caucasian	55
% Hispanic	9
% Native American	<1
% Pacific Islander	0
% Two or more races	6
% Race and/or ethnicity unknown	1
% international	26
# of countries represented	28

SURVEY SAYS . . .

Students always studying
Students are happy
Great library
Class discussions encouraged
No one cheats
Diverse student types interact on campus
Students aren't religious
Easy to get around campus
Lots of beer drinking
Intramural sports are popular

ACADEMICS

Academic Rating	96
% students returning for sophomore year	68
% students graduating within 4 years	42
% students graduating within 6 years	48
Calendar	Semester
Student/faculty ratio	8:1
Profs interesting rating	99
Profs accessible rating	98
Most classes have 10–19 students.	

STUDENTS SAY "..."

Academics

At St. John's College in Santa Fe, students read and explore a common body of "great books"—including many of the most important books in history—in close partnership with their classmates and teachers. Every professor "must teach (learn) Euclid, Plato, and Darwin, whether he or she has a PhD in mathematics, classics, or biology." This common curriculum and dedication to the liberal arts means that "students are respected for what they can bring, and need never feel self-conscious about whether they're 'smart enough.'" Everywhere you look, there is a "commitment, sincerity, and passion for learning of the community and the faculty." This truly is an academic community that sincerely loves "the journey in its pursuit of knowledge, not simply the destination." The "liberation of the mind" at SJC comes primarily by means of the Socratic Method. SJC does not have professors, but tutors, who are there not to lecture, but to "help lead the class through the curriculum." The tutors are "very different in personality," but also "very knowledgeable and excitable about what we do." As experienced academics, they are "skillful when it comes to managing the classroom discussions and helping students articulate their thoughts" and are "truly open-minded and give everyone a chance to participate." "They really care about their students and treat us as peers in the classroom since they consider themselves also to be constantly learning." "Everyone shares fundamental values of how to treat others in the classroom," says a student. The greatest asset of SJC is the community; with everyone on board this nontraditional learning train, it's hard not to be at your best. "You're thinking nonstop at SJC," says a student. Though the self-selecting student body pretty much ensures success, students can choose how connected they wish to be to the rest of the school. "You can go four years without having an interaction with the president of the college, or you can see him every Tuesday at the Foreign Relations study group," says a student.

Life

At St. John's, "you have to work intensely and relax intensely. Life is more distilled, here." "Is it hard work?" asks a student. "Yes and no. Does staying up until 1:00 A.M. reading Shakespeare or Darwin sound like work?" Santa Fe is "stunning," and the proximity of the mountains (for hiking and skiing) is more than welcome. Though each week is "epic" in its schoolwork, there are dozens of clubs and activities to take part in, from "dance (beginners always welcome) to search and rescue to astronomy to rock-climbing." If you're artsy, there are many galleries in Santa Fe, or "you can stay on campus, join a study group or sports team, or go to the gym." The student government is also responsible for dispersing several thousand dollars to support student clubs annually, so "if you can get signatures to show support, you can probably get funding for snacks or supplies." Many say that food services could have better hours and prices. There are "frequent" field trips to some of the extraordinary places in New Mexico.

Student Body

Most of the 350 undergrads at St. John's are "friendly," "big readers," and "interested in discussions." It's easy to find commonalities, since "you're always able to discuss the program as long as they're the same year or lower." All are here "because we have a genuine interest in the larger questions that are posed in life through academia," and "that's enough for most of us to feel like we're 'fitting in,' however that may be defined." Johnnies are "fascinated with learning in a way different from most schools" and "thrive on epiphanies through the 'great books,' especially ones shared with others."

ST. JOHN'S COLLEGE (NM)

Financial Aid: 505-984-6058 • E-Mail: SantaFe.Admissions@sjc.edu • Website: www.sjc.edu

THE PRINCETON REVIEW SAYS

Admissions

Very important factors considered include: application essay. *Important factors considered include:* rigor of secondary school record, recommendation(s), character/personal qualities. *Other factors considered include:* class rank, academic GPA, standardized test scores, interview, extracurricular activities, talent/ability, first generation, alumni/ae relation, geographical residence, volunteer work, work experience. ACT with or without writing accepted. SAT with or without Essay component accepted. High school diploma is required and GED is accepted. *Academic units required:* 3 math, 2 foreign language. *Academic units recommended:* 4 English, 4 math, 3 science, 3 science labs, 4 foreign language, 2 history.

Financial Aid

Students should submit: FAFSA. The Princeton Review suggests that all financial aid forms be submitted as soon as possible after October 1. *Need-based scholarships/grants offered:* College/university scholarship or grant aid from institutional funds; Federal Pell; Private scholarships; SEOG; State scholarships/grants. *Loan aid offered:* Direct PLUS loans; Direct Subsidized Stafford Loans; Direct Unsubsidized Stafford Loans. Applicants will be notified of awards on a rolling basis beginning 12/15. Federal Work-Study Program available. Institutional employment available.

The Inside Word

Self-selection drives this admissions process—more than one-half of the entire applicant pool each year indicates that St. John's is their first choice, and half of those admitted send in tuition deposits. Even so, no one in admissions takes things for granted, and neither should any student considering an application. The admissions process is highly personal on both sides of the coin. Only the intellectually curious and highly motivated need apply. St. John's also features rolling admission beginning 2/15 with notification within three weeks of completing the application.

THE SCHOOL SAYS "..."

From the Admissions Office

"St. John's College is centered on reading and discussing the greatest books in history. With teachers such as Plato, Shakespeare, Euclid, Nietzsche, Einstein, Austen, and Du Bois, students at St. John's are original and unconventional, love big questions and discussion, and are excited to join an intellectual community of thinkers and seekers.

"All students at St. John's explore our great books curriculum in interdisciplinary classes focused on philosophy, classics, literature, politics, religion, biology, chemistry, physics, mathematics, music, history, language, and more. With a 7:1 student to faculty ratio, every class is a discussion led by one or two faculty members. Instead of choosing a major, all students graduate with a BA in the Liberal Arts. The college regularly ranks among the best for undergraduate teaching and student-faculty relationships.

"Over 70% of Johnnies attend graduate school, particularly in law, business, and journalism, and the college is among the best for students receiving PhDs in the humanities and sciences. Students are free to transfer between the campuses in Annapolis, MD, and Santa Fe, NM.

"The Santa Fe campus, in the foothills of the Rocky Mountains, is a one-minute walk to the best hiking, biking, and skiing in the southwest. Santa Fe is also home to more than 250 art galleries, great food, and live music. Nearly 400 Johnnies embrace the stunning natural environment and rich cultural heritage of New Mexico while reading great books on the placita, hiking 12,000-foot mountains, sculpting in the pottery studio, or socializing in the student-run coffee shop."

SELECTIVITY

Admissions Rating	87
# of applicants	342
% of applicants accepted	63
% of acceptees attending	32
# offered a place on the wait list	14
% accepting a place on wait list	100
% admitted from wait list	100

FRESHMAN PROFILE

Range SAT EBRW	630–670
Range SAT Math	560–680
Range ACT Composite	23–32
# submitting SAT scores	29
% submitting SAT scores	41
# submitting ACT scores	17
% submitting ACT scores	24
Average HS GPA	3.5
% graduated top 10% of class	37
% graduated top 25% of class	48
% graduated top 50% of class	74

DEADLINES

Early action	
Deadline	11/15
Notification	12/15
Regular	
Priority	11/15
Notification	Rolling, 12/15
Nonfall registration?	Yes

APPLICANTS ALSO LOOK AT AND OFTEN PREFER
Colorado College; Reed College; University of California—Berkeley

AND SOMETIMES PREFER
Kenyon College; Thomas Aquinas College; University of Puget Sound

AND RARELY PREFER
University of New Mexico

FINANCIAL FACTS

Financial Aid Rating	87
Annual tuition	$35,000
Room and board	$12,860
Required fees	$1,410
Books and supplies	$400
Average frosh need-based scholarship	$42,153
Average UG need-based scholarship	$39,930
% needy frosh rec. need-based scholarship or grant aid	100
% needy UG rec. need-based scholarship or grant aid	100
% needy frosh rec. non-need-based scholarship or grant aid	28
% needy UG rec. non-need-based scholarship or grant aid	17
% needy frosh rec. need-based self-help aid	31
% needy UG rec. need-based self-help aid	89
% frosh rec. any financial aid	97
% UG rec. any financial aid	84
% UG borrow to pay for school	71
Average cumulative indebtedness	$18,434
% frosh need fully met	41
% ugrads need fully met	21
Average % of frosh need met	86
Average % of ugrad need met	88

ST. JOHN'S UNIVERSITY (NY)

8000 Utopia Parkway, Queens, NY 11439 • Admissions: 718-990-2000 • Fax: 718-990-2096

STUDENTS SAY "..."

Academics

St. John's University upholds the Catholic and Vincentian traditions set forth at its founding in 1870. At the residential Queens, New York, campus, located in a suburban area (as well as at the two additional New York City campuses found in Staten Island and Manhattan), students receive "a well-nurtured education that can help one turn into a specialist in whatever field they desire." A wide range of support systems, such as career services, campus ministry, the writing center, and a focus on mentoring ensure that "every student has a safe, healthy, and challenging academic career" while at St. John's.

Most professors are generous "when it comes to providing help and any aids for you to succeed" and "are here to help you and prepare you for the rest of your life." "Almost all my experiences with professors have been positive. If you are willing to put in the work they are willing to work with you," says one actuarial science major. They are very helpful "in making sure you actually understand the information rather than memorize it and not use it outside the classroom," and "provide guidance with classwork, finding jobs and internships, and more." On top of faculty help, the career services office is "amazing." "They help you with your résumé, cover letter, [telling] you when there are career fairs, picking graduate schools, [and] finding internships."

Classes are "easy to follow and there are never any surprises from the professors," and most are discussion-based. Students in all majors find that "the workload is not overwhelming and the assignments are helpful and relevant to the subjects." For commuter and non-commuter students alike, the Monday and Thursday afternoon common hour provides a universal time for most social and academic clubs to meet.

Life

From athletics to coffeehouse shows and cultural events, there are "multiple things to do on campus every day." Many people take advantage of the gym and the classes it offers, or "hang out on the Great Lawn and play frisbee and other similar games." Students "sometimes have to wait a long time for their next class" so the school provides "too many extracurricular activities to count" to help time pass. There are clubs to represent "almost every racial, religious and interest group" and "there's never a day where there isn't anything to do." Basketball season is a huge rally booster (the men's team plays some games at Madison Square Garden), and St. John's also hosts "many great events on off days such as family day, picnics, barbecues, and more." There are a fair number of commuters, and those who live on campus often venture into the city to "enjoy the fast pace and vibrant life of New York City." Between "the spring carnival, the free commuter breakfasts, and reduced prices on movie tickets, [and] Broadway shows, St. John's wants their students' experience to be unforgettable."

Student Body

This "very diverse" group has students from all over the country and world (it "falls perfectly into place with the diversity of the New York City area as a whole"), which "exposes everyone to new ideas and helps us better define where we stand on our own views." "There's an atmosphere of the core staples of the University: Catholic, Vincentian, and metropolitan," says a student. People speak of the sense of unity that comes from everyone being "more than happy to be here, excited to learn, and [willing to] participate in campus activities." There is a lot of collaboration when it comes to student organizations, and students also "have great initiative when it comes to getting their voice heard."

St. John's University (NY)

Financial Aid: 718-990-2000 • E-Mail: admhelp@stjohns.edu • Website: www.stjohns.edu

THE PRINCETON REVIEW SAYS

Admissions

Very important factors considered include: rigor of secondary school record, academic GPA. *Important factors considered include:* standardized test scores. *Other factors considered include:* class rank, application essay, recommendation(s), extracurricular activities, talent/ability, character/personal qualities, alumni/ae relation, volunteer work, work experience, level of applicant's interest. ACT with or without writing accepted. SAT with or without Essay component accepted. High school diploma is required and GED is accepted. *Academic units required:* 4 English, 2 math, 2 science, 2 foreign language. *Academic units recommended:* 4 English, 3 math, 3 science, 2 foreign language, 2 social studies, 2 history.

Financial Aid

Students should submit: FAFSA; State aid form. Priority filing deadline is 12/15. The Princeton Review suggests that all financial aid forms be submitted as soon as possible after October 1. *Need-based scholarships/grants offered:* College/university scholarship or grant aid from institutional funds; Federal Pell; Private scholarships; SEOG; State scholarships/grants. *Loan aid offered:* Direct PLUS loans; Direct Subsidized Stafford Loans; Direct Unsubsidized Stafford Loans. Applicants will be notified of awards on a rolling basis beginning 2/15. Federal Work-Study Program available. Institutional employment available.

The Inside Word

The admissions process at St. John's doesn't include many surprises. High school grades and standardized test scores are undoubtedly the most important factors, though volunteer work and extracurricular activities are also highly regarded. The university doesn't consider religious affiliation at all when making admissions decisions; there are students of every religious stripe here.

THE SCHOOL SAYS "..."

From the Admissions Office

"Founded in 1870, St. John's is a Catholic and Vincentian University that prepares students for personal and professional success—and emphasizes academic excellence without bounds—by providing talented students with an outstanding education that builds upon their abilities and aspirations. On the playing courts and athletic fields, St. John's is New York City's team, with 17 NCAA Division I men's and women's athletic teams.

"St. John's offers more than 100 associate, bachelor's, master's, and doctoral degrees in areas including the arts, business, communication arts, education, law, pharmacy, and the natural and applied sciences. More than 94 percent of our full-time professors hold a Ph.D. or comparable terminal degree in their field. Our 16:1 student/faculty ratio ensures personal attention.

"Faith, service, and student success are central to a St. John's education. Each year, students perform more than 100,000 service hours. With world-class academics, renowned professors, outstanding resources, and a storied tradition of academic excellence and service, St. John's prepares you to change the world for the better.

"Our students enjoy both a metropolitan and global experience that starts at our three New York City campuses—in Queens, on Staten Island, and in Manhattan—and a graduate center in Hauppauge, NY; an international campus in Rome, Italy; and study abroad locations in Paris, France, and Limerick, Ireland, and around the world. Enhancing the University's cosmopolitan character, students come from nearly 50 states and 119 foreign countries—all of them benefiting from the University's network of more than 190,000 alumni."

SELECTIVITY

Admissions Rating	81
# of applicants	29,059
% of applicants accepted	72
% of acceptees attending	15
# offered a place on the wait list	1,075
# of early decision applicants	180
% accepted early decision	28

FRESHMAN PROFILE

Range SAT EBRW	540–640
Range SAT Math	540–660
Range SAT Composite	1100–1300
Range ACT Composite	23–29
# submitting SAT scores	2,425
% submitting SAT scores	77
# submitting ACT scores	333
% submitting ACT scores	11
Average HS GPA	3.5
% graduated top 10% of class	21
% graduated top 25% of class	48
% graduated top 50% of class	79

DEADLINES

Early decision	
Deadline	11/15
Notification	12/15
Early action	
Deadline	12/1
Notification	1/1
Regular	
Priority	2/1
Notification	Rolling, 12/15
Nonfall registration?	Yes

FINANCIAL FACTS

Financial Aid Rating	82
Annual tuition	$43,160
Room and board	$18,312
Required fees	$1,600
Books and supplies	$656
Average frosh need-based scholarship	$8,495
Average UG need-based scholarship	$8,790
% needy frosh rec. need-based scholarship or grant aid	72
% needy UG rec. need-based scholarship or grant aid	73
% needy frosh rec. non-need-based scholarship or grant aid	100
% needy UG rec. non-need-based scholarship or grant aid	99
% needy frosh rec. need-based self-help aid	60
% needy UG rec. need-based self-help aid	64
% frosh rec. any financial aid	99
% UG rec. any financial aid	98
% UG borrow to pay for school	68
Average cumulative indebtedness	$31,237
% frosh need fully met	15
% ugrads need fully met	12
Average % of frosh need met	72
Average % of ugrad need met	68

SAINT JOSEPH'S UNIVERSITY (PA)

5600 City Avenue, Philadelphia, PA 19131 • Admissions: 888-BE-A-HAWK • Fax: 610-660-1314

STUDENTS SAY ". . ."

Academics

A Roman Catholic Jesuit university, Saint Joseph's, situated in the suburbs of Philadelphia, strives to incorporate "Jesuit values like solidarity, service, living greater, and reflection" into the fabric of the school. Fortunately, the administration does this thoughtfully and "without shoving religion down your throat." Saint Joseph's also does a phenomenal job of making "everyone who attends feel valued and welcome." Many students flock here because it has "one of the best business schools in the country" as well as the wonderful College of Arts and Sciences. It also offers a robust "online option for [non-traditional students as well as individuals] not living close to campus." Undergrads experience "small classes" and a "well-rounded curriculum." And they speak quite highly of their "extraordinarily caring and dedicated" professors. Most students here feel that SJU instructors work diligently "to present the material in an engaging way and genuinely care that we are learning something important and relevant." They also "really like to make you think and challenge you to strengthen your mind and reasoning skills." Best of all, professors here are quite "accessible and you can definitely tell they want you to succeed." As one appreciative student reveals, "They also get to know you on a personal level and remember you."

Life

Life at Saint Joseph's is definitely hectic. However, that's exactly how these Hawks like it! Certainly, it's "pretty common to meet up with your friends in the library and work on some homework while casually catching up with them." Of course, SJU undergrads also manage to step away from the books once in awhile. Many individuals are involved with "service [clubs]" like SJU Dance Marathon, Hand in Hand (a special needs carnival held every year), [and] the Make a Wish club." The university is also "a big basketball school, so students like to attend basketball and other sporting events." Moreover, SJU has a very active Student Union Board (SUB) "that plans events on and off campus [like concerts and comedians] for free or discount prices." Once the weekend rolls around, "upperclassmen [often head to the] bars…[while first-years] go to fraternity parties." When undergrads are getting a little antsy, they "like to travel to neighboring towns such as Manayunk, Ardmore, and Lower Merion." And if they're looking for a little more excitement, they can easily head into Philadelphia. Indeed, Saint Joseph's is only "a ten minute ride away from Center City." Students often take the trip to enjoy the restaurants, arts, and culture that Philadelphia offers.

Student Body

Undergrads at SJU are quick to pronounce their peers "considerate, passionate and intelligent." They're also "selfless…and dedicate[d] to others." As one impressed Saint Joseph's student explains, "Most of the people I know here participate in some kind of service, social justice, or faith-based activities like Weekly Service, APEX (a service immersion trip during Spring Break), or other similar programs that encourage us to learn more about the world around us." Students also note that their fellow Hawks are "super friendly" and "very welcoming." Moreover, it's incredibly evident that they "want the best for one another." Another thrilled student shares, "I am always greeted with smiling faces whether or not I know them." Undergrads do acknowledge that the majority of the student body is a somewhat "homogenous group from the New Jersey, Pennsylvania, and Maryland area" and that many students "come from wealthy families." But they also note that "the school has taken great strides to become more diverse and to celebrate the existing diversity." Thankfully, no matter an individual's background, "the sense of community and school spirit on campus flows through each student." As one grateful undergrad concludes, "We all hold SJU close to our hearts and are proud to be Hawks."

SAINT JOSEPH'S UNIVERSITY (PA)

Financial Aid: 610-660-1556 • E-Mail: admit@sju.edu • Website: www.sju.edu

THE PRINCETON REVIEW SAYS

Admissions

Very important factors considered include: rigor of secondary school record, class rank, academic GPA. *Important factors considered include:* application essay, standardized test scores, recommendation(s). *Other factors considered include:* interview, extracurricular activities, talent/ability, character/personal qualities, first generation, alumni/ae relation, geographical residence, racial/ethnic status, volunteer work, work experience, level of applicant's interest. ACT with or without writing accepted. SAT with or without Essay component accepted. High school diploma is required and GED is accepted. *Academic units required:* 4 English, 3 math, 3 science, 2 foreign language, 3 social studies, 5 academic electives.

Financial Aid

Students should submit: FAFSA. Priority filing deadline is 12/1. The Princeton Review suggests that all financial aid forms be submitted as soon as possible after October 1. *Need-based scholarships/grants offered:* College/university scholarship or grant aid from institutional funds; Federal Pell; Private scholarships; SEOG; State scholarships/grants. *Loan aid offered:* Direct PLUS loans; Direct Subsidized Stafford Loans; Direct Unsubsidized Stafford Loans. Applicants will be notified of awards on a rolling basis beginning 3/31. Federal Work-Study Program available. Institutional employment available.

The Inside Word

Saint Joseph's University is on the lookout for applicants that are serious about their education and excited for learning. And they certainly want students who have found success in the classroom. After all, GPAs for admitted students ed range from 3.27–3.92 (on a 4.0 scale). Fortunately, individuals who dread standardized tests can rejoice; both the ACT and SAT are optional at Saint Joseph's. Beyond academics, admissions officers also look for community involvement and service.

THE SCHOOL SAYS "..."

From the Admissions Office

"Rooted in the Jesuit, Catholic tradition, Saint Joseph's University provides a rigorous, intense education that both disciplines and expands the mind. At the core of this education is a General Education Program (G.E.P.), which exposes students to primary fields of inquiry and the cultural values that shape our world. An emphasis on engaged teaching and mentoring permeates the university.

"Saint Joseph's students engage enthusiastically in all facets of campus life—academic, social, athletic, ethical and spiritual. Their active participation creates a vibrant, dynamic campus community and produces a supportive, humane and tolerant environment for individual success and service to others.

"Alumni of Saint Joseph's rise to the highest levels of leadership, and use this influence to transform their organizations into exemplary models of success and integrity. Bound by a lasting pride in their alma mater, the Saint Joseph's alumni network of over 66,000 is strong and eager to help students find meaningful employment after graduation.

"As a Jesuit institution, Saint Joseph's University educates for a higher purpose: students are expected to improve the common good by utilizing their skills and knowledge to promote tolerance, compassion and social justice. Curricular and co-curricular programs engage students with important social concerns—both domestic and international—and prepare them to lead as informed citizens, socially responsive professionals and active community members.

"Located on the edge of metropolitan Philadelphia, Saint Joseph's provides ready access to the vast career opportunities and cultural resources of America's fifth-largest city, while affording students a cohesive and intimate campus experience."

SELECTIVITY

Admissions Rating	80
# of applicants	8,692
% of applicants accepted	75
% of acceptees attending	17
# of early decision applicants	139
% accepted early decision	58

FRESHMAN PROFILE

Range SAT EBRW	570–650
Range SAT Math	550–650
Range ACT Composite	23–29
# submitting SAT scores	799
% submitting SAT scores	72
# submitting ACT scores	174
% submitting ACT scores	18
Average HS GPA	3.7
% graduated top 10% of class	22
% graduated top 25% of class	52
% graduated top 50% of class	82

DEADLINES

Early decision	
Deadline	11/1
Notification	12/20
Other ED Deadline	1/15
Other ED Notification	2/1
Early action	
Deadline	11/1
Notification	12/20
Regular	
Deadline	2/1
Notification	Rolling, 3/15
Nonfall registration?	Yes

FINANCIAL FACTS

Financial Aid Rating	87
Annual tuition	$46,350
Room and board	$14,840
Required fees	$200
Books and supplies	$893
Average frosh need-based scholarship	$27,663
Average UG need-based scholarship	$25,171
% needy frosh rec. need-based scholarship or grant aid	99
% needy UG rec. need-based scholarship or grant aid	98
% needy frosh rec. non-need-based scholarship or grant aid	16
% needy UG rec. non-need-based scholarship or grant aid	17
% needy frosh rec. need-based self-help aid	75
% needy UG rec. need-based self-help aid	74
% frosh rec. any financial aid	98
% UG rec. any financial aid	93
% frosh need fully met	24
% ugrads need fully met	27
Average % of frosh need met	82
Average % of ugrad need met	79

ST. LAWRENCE UNIVERSITY

23 Romoda Drive, Canton, NY 13617 • Admissions: 315-229-5261 • Fax: 315-229-5818

STUDENTS SAY "..."

Academics

Nestled in the uppermost reaches of New York State on a scenic one thousand-acre campus, St. Lawrence University is a vibrant liberal arts institution of around 2,400 undergraduates and a very long reach. The "alumni network is super active," students have "lots of opportunities for hands-on research" and nearly two-thirds of SLU undergrads study abroad. With almost seventy majors to choose between, and the option to design one's own course of study in the multi-field major program, there are "a plethora of options for one's academic path." Small class sizes—an average of sixteen students in each—further focus those options, as enrollees note that they "feel more comfortable asking questions and having conversation," which "fosters learning." Adding to that comfort is a First-Year Program that helps with the transition to college and which is described as "a great way to bond" through living-learning communities in the dorms. The school also offers Community-Based Learning (CBL) courses that immerse students in the real world: "I am currently taking a CBL course at the local correctional facility that allows me to take a philosophy course in a classroom at the jail with ten SLU students and ten inmates as my classmates."

As for the staff, "I've never felt so supported and believed in." Students specifically note that the "compassion professors have for individual success is incredible," particularly in the way that they "know people have different styles of learning" and so "are responsive to questions and always try to make the class [as] interactive as possible." Their classes work "to deliver a well-rounded education and develop our interpersonal skills," and "a lot of the intro classes are very reasonable and give you the right amount of work." And for those interested, you can dive into research from your very first year: "I was offered an opportunity to study and train wildlife detection dogs with a focus on locating amphibians, all thanks to my professors." Overall, students suggest that "St. Lawrence is a place for students to explore past thinkers and ideas while also conversing with their peers to help them establish their own thoughts and views."

Life

Ninety-eight percent of students live on this "walking campus" and "have the opportunity to live in theme houses or Greek houses, which support high-quality residential communities." There are nearly one hundred and forty clubs and organizations, and "skiing, hiking, rock climbing and other outdoor activities are popular" among this nature-loving group. "The incredible outdoors that SLU has around us is insane," says a student. And while remote Canton "is a small and rural town" where "there is not a hopping night scene," students actually appreciate knowing "where everyone is going to be on a Saturday night." This means that "sports events are popular," as is "spend[ing] time in the student center to talk and grab coffee, go outside and sit in hammocks if the weather is permitting, and do homework in the library."

Student Body

St. Lawrence students "wear many different hats and are involved in almost all aspects of the school community and culture," including the "large student-athlete population." Undergrads describe this society as "tight knit," such that "even if you don't know someone, you treat them as if you do," and they speak warmly of the "extremely positive and loving" atmosphere this creates. Peers are seen as "a welcoming family in which everybody can find friends," something that's only enhanced by "very low-key people who work very hard in the classroom as well as [at] athletics, but [who] treat it like it is no big deal." One student posits that it might be the cold of being so close to Canada, which "brings a level of closeness and different atmosphere," but based on responses, we think SLU just chooses warm students.

St. Lawrence University

Financial Aid: 315-229-5265 • E-Mail: admissions@stlawu.edu • Website: www.stlawu.edu

THE PRINCETON REVIEW SAYS

Admissions

Very important factors considered include: rigor of secondary school record, academic GPA, application essay, recommendation(s), character/personal qualities. *Important factors considered include:* class rank, interview, extracurricular activities. *Other factors considered include:* standardized test scores, talent/ability, first generation, alumni/ae relation, geographical residence, volunteer work, work experience, level of applicant's interest. ACT with or without writing accepted. SAT with or without Essay component accepted. High school diploma is required and GED is accepted. *Academic units recommended:* 4 English, 3 math, 3 science, 3 foreign language, 3 social studies.

Financial Aid

Students should submit: FAFSA. Priority filing deadline is 2/1. The Princeton Review suggests that all financial aid forms be submitted as soon as possible after October 1. *Need-based scholarships/grants offered:* College/university scholarship or grant aid from institutional funds; Federal Pell; Private scholarships; SEOG; State scholarships/grants. *Loan aid offered:* Direct PLUS loans; Direct Subsidized Stafford Loans; Direct Unsubsidized Stafford Loans. Federal Work-Study Program available. Institutional employment available.

The Inside Word

At St. Lawrence, you're not required to submit scores from the SAT or the ACT (unless you're an international student), but that means your high school transcript and teacher recommendations had better be stellar. Merit scholarships selection is based on your overall academic profile.

THE SCHOOL SAYS "..."

From the Admissions Office

"Situated in an ideal location, St. Lawrence University is a diverse liberal arts learning community of talented students and inspiring faculty, guided by tradition and focused on the future. We are a vibrant, collaborative community of learners who value thought and action. Students tap into their full potential, as they embrace the natural environment, engage with global challenges, and experience the relevance and adventure of a liberal arts education in a complex and changing world.

"Our faculty has chosen St. Lawrence intentionally because they know there is institutional commitment to support great teaching. They are dedicated to making each student's experience challenging and rewarding. Our graduates make up one of the strongest networks of support among any alumni body and are ready, willing, and able to connect with students and help them succeed.

"Every student has diverse opportunities to connect classroom theory to hands-on, real-world experience through internships, international study, and community projects. Faculty know their students and act as their mentors, guides, and colleagues on their journeys. Creative degree paths allow students to discover new dimensions of themselves and prepare for lives of personal fulfillment and career success.

"Our location on the edge of the Adirondack Mountains gives us easy access to enviable outdoor spaces to learn and to practice environmental sustainability and to participate year-round in all things outdoors. You must visit and meet our students to get a sense of the energy on campus to begin to understand just what makes St. Lawrence University a place our students, faculty, staff, and alumni call home."

SELECTIVITY
Admissions Rating	89
# of applicants	6,998
% of applicants accepted	42
% of acceptees attending	20
# offered a place on the wait list	166
% accepting a place on wait list	27
% admitted from wait list	36
# of early decision applicants	297
% accepted early decision	74

FRESHMAN PROFILE
Range SAT EBRW	580–670
Range SAT Math	580–680
Range SAT Composite	1170–1340
Range ACT Composite	24–30
# submitting SAT scores	335
% submitting SAT scores	55
# submitting ACT scores	121
% submitting ACT scores	20
Average HS GPA	3.6
% graduated top 10% of class	42
% graduated top 25% of class	77
% graduated top 50% of class	97

DEADLINES
Early decision	
Deadline	11/1
Other ED Deadline	2/1
Regular	
Deadline	3/12
Notification	3/31
Nonfall registration?	Yes

FINANCIAL FACTS
Financial Aid Rating	89
Annual tuition	$58,330
Room and board	$15,150
Required fees	$420
Books and supplies	$750
Average frosh need-based scholarship	$43,621
Average UG need-based scholarship	$40,913
% needy frosh rec. need-based scholarship or grant aid	99
% needy UG rec. need-based scholarship or grant aid	99
% needy frosh rec. non-need-based scholarship or grant aid	31
% needy UG rec. non-need-based scholarship or grant aid	23
% needy frosh rec. need-based self-help aid	76
% needy UG rec. need-based self-help aid	80
% frosh rec. any financial aid	97
% UG rec. any financial aid	98
% UG borrow to pay for school	60
Average cumulative indebtedness	$32,390
% frosh need fully met	31
% ugrads need fully met	34
Average % of frosh need met	89
Average % of ugrad need met	87

SAINT LOUIS UNIVERSITY

Office of Admissions, DuBourg Hall, Saint Louis, MO 63103 • Admissions: 314-977-2500 • Fax: 314-977-7136

CAMPUS LIFE

Quality of Life Rating	92
Fire Safety Rating	89
Green Rating	81
Type of school	Private
Affiliation	Roman Catholic-Jesuit
Environment	Metropolis

STUDENTS

Total undergrad enrollment	7,127
% male/female	40/60
% from out of state	61
% frosh live on campus	92
% ugrads live on campus	55
% of ugrad men in fraternities	15
% of ugrad women in sororities	25
% African American	6
% Asian	11
% Caucasian	67
% Hispanic	7
% Native American	<1
% Pacific Islander	<1
% Two or more races	4
% Race and/or ethnicity unknown	1
% international	5
# of countries represented	82

SURVEY SAYS . . .

Students are happy
Great library
Students are very religious
Students involved in community service
Active student government
Active minority support groups

ACADEMICS

Academic Rating	85
% students returning for sophomore year	91
% students graduating within 4 years	73
% students graduating within 6 years	80
Calendar	Semester
Student/faculty ratio	9:1
Profs interesting rating	90
Profs accessible rating	93

Most classes have 20–29 students.
Most lab/discussion sessions have 20–29 students.

MOST POPULAR MAJORS

Exercise Science and Kinesiology; Registered Nursing/Registered Nurse; Biology/Biological Sciences, General

STUDENTS SAY "..."

Academics

At Saint Louis University, a Jesuit institution in Missouri, the focus is squarely on "educating the whole person and serving others to make the world a better place." In the Jesuit tradition, the school is about "shaping the whole person: mind, body, and spirit." The "generally open-minded, non-judgmental, and welcoming" campus, located in the heart of Saint Louis, is a "big-city school with a small-town feel," with approximately 7,200 undergraduates. The "small class size" is a big draw in academically rigorous courses, and students say, "SLU is all about having unique experiences that challenge preconceived notions and promote learning and growth." Professors on the whole "really engage the students and you can tell they are passionate about what they do," though some, as at any school, just "go through the motions and lack enthusiasm." Some students make it clear that SLU professors go above and beyond. One student notes, "Every single professor I've had, whether it is a [large, 200-] person lecture or a 30-student lecture, genuinely cares about you. They are accommodating and understanding of everyone's circumstances and are always willing to try to help you." According to some students, the school's academic strengths are not equally divided, as SLU "has great science/medical programs (e.g., nursing, pre-med track, engineering, etc.), but not as strong liberal arts or music."

Life

The school's location in Saint Louis provides much of the off-campus entertainment for students. In fact, students "all receive Metro Passes to get around the city as much as [they] please." Popular spots include The Arch and Forest Park, "which is a massive beautiful park in the middle of Saint Louis." On campus, students note, "Intramurals are popular as is Greek life, but at SLU Greek life does not define your college experience." Even so, other students declare, "Greek life is very popular on SLU's campus." Despite SLU's city location, students emphasize that, "Although we are urban, our campus is very traditional in that there is a lot of green space, a traditional quad, and hammocks everywhere for studying/relaxing." Service opportunities abound, as per SLU's Jesuit principles, and students praise the "emphasis on community service" on and off campus. Some students say that safety can be a concern, being in an urban environment like Saint Louis, cautioning that "during the day it is perfectly fine, but at night it is smart to have someone to walk with for safety." Overall, students say, "Clubs and extracurriculars are very popular, but people seem to put a greater emphasis on making friendships, seeking a faith or spiritual life, and definitely on working hard in school to achieve one's intended career path."

Student Body

While there's less emphasis on the Ugg boot-wearing, North Face jacket-toting girls and American Eagle jean-clad boys than in previous years, SLU still struggles with being a fairly homogenous campus. As some students bluntly put it, "We are too white," and "SLU could admit more students of color." Others counter that "The student body at SLU is extremely diverse, and no one is exactly the same. SLU encourages diversity and uniqueness." In keeping with the school's religious ideals, students say, "We are encouraged by the Jesuit Mission, being men and women for others to work on behalf of people whose voices are not ordinarily heard." Describing their peers as "insightful, intelligent, warm, and [caring] about the well-being of the world," SLU students emphasize that, "SLU is unique in that the community is exceptionally strong. There really is a palpable feeling of acceptance and support when you join the community in any capacity."

SAINT LOUIS UNIVERSITY

Financial Aid: 314-977-2350 • E-Mail: admission@slu.edu • Website: www.slu.edu

THE PRINCETON REVIEW SAYS

Admissions

Very important factors considered include: academic GPA, standardized test scores. *Important factors considered include:* rigor of secondary school record, application essay, extracurricular activities, talent/ability, character/personal qualities, volunteer work. *Other factors considered include:* recommendation(s), interview, work experience. ACT with or without writing accepted. SAT with or without Essay component accepted. High school diploma is required and GED is accepted. *Academic units required:* 4 English, 4 math, 3 science, 3 foreign language, 3 social studies, 3 academic electives. *Academic units recommended:* 4 English, 4 math, 3 science, 3 foreign language, 3 social studies, 3 academic electives.

Financial Aid

Students should submit: FAFSA. Priority filing deadline is 2/1. The Princeton Review suggests that all financial aid forms be submitted as soon as possible after October 1. *Need-based scholarships/grants offered:* College/university scholarship or grant aid from institutional funds; Federal Nursing Scholarships; Federal Pell; Private scholarships; SEOG; State scholarships/grants. *Loan aid offered:* Direct PLUS loans; Direct Subsidized Stafford Loans; Direct Unsubsidized Stafford Loans; Federal Nursing Loans. Applicants will be notified of awards on a rolling basis beginning 11/26. Federal Work-Study Program available. Institutional employment available.

The Inside Word

Despite being known for mostly drawing its students from the immediate region, SLU continues to expand its range and now 61 percent of students are from out of state. The average high school GPA for admitted first-year is 3.91, with 70 percent of accepted students coming to SLU with a GPA of 3.75 or higher. In addition to grades and standardized test scores, the university also weighs each applicant's' commitment to the Jesuit ideals of service to the community, so volunteering for Habitat for Humanity can be just as important as scoring off the charts on your SAT.

THE SCHOOL SAYS "..."

From the Admissions Office

"Saint Louis University gives students the knowledge, skills, and values to build a successful career and make a difference in the lives of those around them. Students live and learn in a safe and attractive campus environment. The beautiful urban, residential campus offers many internship, outreach, and recreational opportunities. Ranked as one of the best educational values in the country, the university welcomes students—from all 50 states and 82 foreign countries—who pursue rigorous majors that invite individualization. Accessible faculty, study abroad opportunities, and many small, interactive classes make SLU a great place to learn.

"Founded in 1818, Saint Louis University is one of the nation's oldest and most prestigious Catholic institutions. Rooted in Jesuit values and its pioneering history as the first university west of the Mississippi River, SLU offers nearly 12,000 students a rigorous, transformative education of the whole person. At the core of the University's diverse community of scholars is SLU's service-focused mission, which challenges and prepares students to make the world a better, more just place. Saint Louis University's admission process is standardized-test-optional for all undergraduate programs, beginning with students applying for admission to the 2021-2022 academic year. Applicants may submit ACT or SAT test scores, but those who choose not to will not be disadvantaged in the admission process."

SELECTIVITY

Admissions Rating	88
# of applicants	15,573
% of applicants accepted	58
% of acceptees attending	21

FRESHMAN PROFILE

Range SAT EBRW	590–680
Range SAT Math	580–700
Range SAT Composite	1180–1370
Range ACT Composite	25–30
# submitting SAT scores	682
% submitting SAT scores	36
# submitting ACT scores	1,452
% submitting ACT scores	77
Average HS GPA	3.9
% graduated top 10% of class	38
% graduated top 25% of class	72
% graduated top 50% of class	92

DEADLINES

Regular	
Notification	Rolling, 10/15
Nonfall registration?	Yes

FINANCIAL FACTS

Financial Aid Rating	84
Annual tuition	$46,400
Room and board	$12,920
Required fees	$724
Books and supplies	$1,200
Average frosh need-based scholarship	$29,200
Average UG need-based scholarship	$26,797
% needy frosh rec. need-based scholarship or grant aid	96
% needy UG rec. need-based scholarship or grant aid	96
% needy frosh rec. non-need-based scholarship or grant aid	19
% needy UG rec. non-need-based scholarship or grant aid	19
% needy frosh rec. need-based self-help aid	63
% needy UG rec. need-based self-help aid	68
% UG borrow to pay for school	55
Average cumulative indebtedness	$34,188
% frosh need fully met	26
% ugrads need fully met	23
Average % of frosh need met	83
Average % of ugrad need met	77

SAINT MARY'S COLLEGE OF CALIFORNIA

1928 St. Mary's Road, PMB 4800, Moraga, CA 94575-4800 • Admissions: 925-631-4224 • Fax: 925-376-7193

STUDENTS SAY "..."

Academics

Intimacy rules the day at Saint Mary's, a Catholic college where "small class sizes" and professors who you "get to know personally" are the rule rather than the exception. "They make time for me outside of class," one student boasts, "I even have some of their phone numbers." This intimacy offers "unlimited opportunities for students and very direct interaction with staff and faculty," and makes it feel as if "the professors are learning at the same time from the students." These teachers are "are very optimistic and love what they teach, so it's great to be taught by them because they're so passionate about their subject. It helps make learning about the subject fun and interesting." Indeed, as one student points out, "It's usually very difficult for a math or physics professor to inject their personality into their classes, but the faculty that Saint Mary's employs somehow manage to do it." Some do complain that "when they teach they go really fast and it makes it hard to keep up with them," but that may be a result of the attitude that "lectures are overrated." Instead, "professors help students learn by engaging one another in meaningful dialogue and debate." The idea is to help you to "learn how to talk more in public settings and [give] you life skills that you can rely on and use the rest of your life." The bottom line is, "Saint Mary's offers students an unparalleled education with small class sizes, seminars, high accessibility to professors, and a strong alumni and network association."

Life

Don't expect non-stop parties at Saint Mary's. This is a "distinguished, calm campus" with students focused on their studies. When it comes time to wind down, sports, clubs, and mellow socializing are far more prevalent than rowdy keggers. Saint Mary's "is what you make it, it takes time to adjust," but "there are vast opportunities provided by the school to get involved with others inside and outside of the community." There is "a grove that is a secluded area where everyone goes to just leave the urban world for a bit and just relax," while others "go on great hiking and outdoor adventure trips the rec sports provides the students with." The school is six miles off the freeway, so access to other communities isn't as easy as at other schools, but nearby Orinda has beautiful theaters and restaurants, and all that San Francisco has to offer is accessible to students willing to make the journey. The biggest draw is sports and athletic recreation. Students here are "very active. Everyone wears some sort of active clothes because everyone is basically a regularly active individual. Sports are a big focus at my school, whether it be intercollegiate or just for fun."

Student Body

The "smart, humble, dedicated, and compassionate" students of Saint Mary's make up a group with a "wide range of students from a large spectrum of life and socioeconomic status. Students mix easily and the college climate promotes equality and understanding." At this "very welcoming" school you'll find "few cliques among students," only "normal people who are looking to go on and succeed at life." The "hard-working" students of Saint Mary's have a reputation for being friendly. "You walk through the halls and say hi to almost everyone even if you have never seen them before." Indeed, "students always smile and say have a good day. Students fit in by taking the time to meet others. A simple smile can make a day for a lot of people." Typical students are "involved in sports or some type of club on campus. They are a big part of the community, and are avid NCAA college basketball fans." That, or they are engaged in their studies. Saint Mary's is filled with people serious about their educations—but not at the expense of social interaction. "Students can engage in complex discussion and easily switch to witty banter at any given moment."

SAINT MARY'S COLLEGE OF CALIFORNIA

Financial Aid: 925-631-4370 • E-Mail: smcadmit@stmarys-ca.edu • Website: www.stmarys-ca.edu

THE PRINCETON REVIEW SAYS

Admissions

Very important factors considered include: rigor of secondary school record, academic GPA. *Important factors considered include:* standardized test scores, first generation. *Other factors considered include:* class rank, application essay, recommendation(s), interview, extracurricular activities, talent/ability, character/personal qualities, alumni/ae relation, geographical residence, volunteer work, work experience, level of applicant's interest. ACT with or without writing accepted. SAT with or without Essay component accepted. High school diploma is required and GED is accepted. *Academic units required:* 4 English, 3 math, 3 science, 1 science lab, 2 foreign language, 2 social studies, 1 history. *Academic units recommended:* 4 English, 4 math, 2 science, 1 science lab, 3 foreign language, 2 social studies, 1 history.

Financial Aid

Students should submit: FAFSA. Priority filing deadline is 2/15. The Princeton Review suggests that all financial aid forms be submitted as soon as possible after October 1. *Need-based scholarships/grants offered:* College/university scholarship or grant aid from institutional funds; Federal Pell; Private scholarships; SEOG; State scholarships/grants. *Loan aid offered:* Direct PLUS loans; Direct Subsidized Stafford Loans; Direct Unsubsidized Stafford Loans. Applicants will be notified of awards on a rolling basis beginning 12/16. Federal Work-Study Program available. Institutional employment available.

The Inside Word

Saint Mary's has a deep commitment to serving underprivileged students and offering opportunities for low-income students with strong academic potential, which is why the school sets aside 25 percent of its undergraduate population for low economic status students. That core philosophy of the school won't be changing anytime soon, so students with economic difficulties should not hesitate to apply if their academics are strong.

THE SCHOOL SAYS "..."

From the Admissions Office

"The first day of the rest of your life begins at Saint Mary's College of California. Charting a path toward transformative growth that embraces a culture of inclusivity, academic distinction, a vibrant and affirming community, and human understanding through faith-centered values is the hallmark of a highly sought-after Saint Mary's education. A top-ranked liberal arts college founded in 1863, Saint Mary's lives out its Catholic Lasallian values that embody compassion, dignity, and social justice. Our faculty are world-class academicians, and our students are passionate learners who take risks, seek adventure, and are eager to explore all that Saint Mary's and the world have to offer. We are a community of scholars committed to cultivating a community of future leaders who are eager and excited to be agents of change in business, politics, the arts, science, and more. The future of a Saint Mary's student knows no bounds. You will become smarter, wiser, and more generous with your heart, and you'll discover your life's calling. At Saint Mary's, our students break the mold by expanding their intellect, fostering innovation, growing their spirit, and embracing the 'Gael Force' attributes of enthusiasm, diversity, belonging, passion, and pride."

SELECTIVITY

Admissions Rating	76
# of applicants	6,069
% of applicants accepted	81
% of acceptees attending	10
# offered a place on the wait list	124
% accepting a place on wait list	45
% admitted from wait list	91

FRESHMAN PROFILE

Range SAT EBRW	540–630
Range SAT Math	520–620
Range ACT Composite	22–28
# submitting SAT scores	369
% submitting SAT scores	72
# submitting ACT scores	162
% submitting ACT scores	31
Average HS GPA	3.5

DEADLINES

Early action	
Deadline	11/15
Notification	1/1
Regular	
Priority	11/15
Deadline	1/15
Notification	Rolling, 12/1
Nonfall registration?	Yes

APPLICANTS ALSO LOOK AT AND SOMETIMES PREFER

San Jose State University; University of San Francisco

FINANCIAL FACTS

Financial Aid Rating	81
Annual tuition	$50,460
Room and board	$15,706
Required fees	$200
Books and supplies	$1,080
Average frosh need-based scholarship	$17,916
Average UG need-based scholarship	$16,751
% needy frosh rec. need-based scholarship or grant aid	61
% needy UG rec. need-based scholarship or grant aid	70
% needy frosh rec. non-need-based scholarship or grant aid	100
% needy UG rec. non-need-based scholarship or grant aid	86
% needy frosh rec. need-based self-help aid	70
% needy UG rec. need-based self-help aid	78
% frosh rec. any financial aid	99
% UG rec. any financial aid	92
% UG borrow to pay for school	85
Average cumulative indebtedness	$30,693
Average % of frosh need met	74
Average % of ugrad need met	67

ST. MARY'S COLLEGE OF MARYLAND

47645 College Drive, St. Mary's City, MD 20686-3001 • Admissions: 240-895-5000 • Fax: 240-895-5001

CAMPUS LIFE
Quality of Life Rating	82
Fire Safety Rating	88
Green Rating	99
Type of school	Public
Environment	Rural

STUDENTS
Total undergrad enrollment	1,466
% male/female	41/59
% from out of state	5
% frosh from public high school	81
% frosh live on campus	91
% ugrads live on campus	80
# of fraternities	0
# of sororities	0
% African American	10
% Asian	4
% Caucasian	71
% Hispanic	7
% Native American	<1
% Pacific Islander	<1
% Two or more races	6
% Race and/or ethnicity unknown	2
% international	<1
# of countries represented	4

SURVEY SAYS . . .
Lots of liberal students
Students are happy
Students are friendly
Students environmentally aware
Theater is popular

ACADEMICS
Academic Rating	83
% students returning for sophomore year	85
% students graduating within 4 years	68
% students graduating within 6 years	77
Calendar	Semester
Student/faculty ratio	9:1
Profs interesting rating	91
Profs accessible rating	94

Most classes have 10–19 students.
Most lab/discussion sessions have
10–19 students.

MOST POPULAR MAJORS
English Language and Literature, General; Biology/
Biological Sciences, General; Psychology, General

STUDENTS SAY "..."

Academics

Students fortunate enough to attend St. Mary's College of Maryland receive a "top tier education" wherein they have ample "opportunity to try new things and explore their interests." That extends beyond the applauded "research-based curriculum" to the environment—"the campus is absolutely gorgeous"—and even the food in the "great dining hall." Where St. Mary's shines most, however, is in its academic offerings, which "reflect the challenges that [students] will face in the workplace," particularly for those in the STEM field who "can really get a leg up by doing publishable work even prior to grad school." In this, the faculty are routinely praised for "always [being] super helpful," noting that they "care about your experience and want you to understand the material" and "genuinely try to engage students during lectures." Enrollees feel they're able to properly assess their teachers because of the "small class sizes," which truly allow "you get to know your professors really well, and build relationships and networks with them." This sort of backing makes the rigor tolerable, at least according to those who say "I've . . . definitely had to work hard but also had the support of professors when I needed it" and note that "They are willing to work with you, to enable and encourage you to have the best academic experience possible!"

Life

There's never a dull moment at St. Mary's thanks to an "extremely active" campus life (and the potential for getaways to nearby DC). Undergrads have the opportunity to participate in "a wide range of clubs from windsurfing to student government to theater and sword fighting." Moreover, "there are multiple events on campus each week including guest magicians, comedians, and musicians," as well as "a murder mystery." The quality of those events has recently improved, as well, with the addition of "a brand-new stadium" which has led to an increasing number of students attending sporting events. And those looking to see a sillier side of their faculty appreciate the various "social events where you can play a game of Cornhole with your professors and get to know them more." St. Mary's gorgeous waterfront location also gets a lot of love: "During the warmer months the river center has free kayak and boat and paddleboard rentals for students and many students go swimming in the river or just sit on the docks." As for weekend-specific activities, it's not only common to find "parties [happening] all over campus," but "most of the time you can just walk [in]...and join...without an invitation."

Student Body

Though the St. Mary's community isn't the most diverse campus around, students emphasize that they are very proud of the diversity they do have, describing their "very creative" and "unique" peers as "extremely accepting." Undergrads are quick to note that "minority communities [are] visible and present" and that the school is "super inclusive [with regards to] LGBT+ students." This applies to personal opinions as well; while many individuals identify as "fairly liberal," classmates are described as "very open to different cultural viewpoints." In fact, some even refer to the friendliness as "quite bold" in that "I've never been at a place where more people will randomly walk up to you and just start a conversation." Indeed, "You can't walk for five minutes in any direction without getting a friendly greeting from someone." Of course, you'll definitely find a range of personality types, "from the athletes to dancers to light-saber fighters" as well as "hippie/hipsters, and nerdy academic students." Ultimately, when it comes down to it, there "seems to be a place for everyone to fit into at St. Mary's."

ST. MARY'S COLLEGE OF MARYLAND

Financial Aid: 240-895-3000 • E-Mail: admissions@smcm.edu • Website: www.smcm.edu

THE PRINCETON REVIEW SAYS

Admissions

Very important factors considered include: rigor of secondary school record, academic GPA, application essay, recommendation(s). *Important factors considered include:* class rank, extracurricular activities, talent/ability, character/personal qualities. *Other factors considered include:* standardized test scores, interview, first generation, alumni/ae relation, geographical residence, state residency, racial/ethnic status, work experience, level of applicant's interest. ACT with or without writing accepted. SAT with or without Essay component accepted. High school diploma is required and GED is accepted. *Academic units required:* 4 English, 3 math, 3 science, 2 science labs, 2 social studies, 1 history. *Academic units recommended:* 4 math, 4 foreign language, 3 social studies.

Financial Aid

Students should submit: FAFSA. Priority filing deadline is 2/28. The Princeton Review suggests that all financial aid forms be submitted as soon as possible after October 1. *Need-based scholarships/grants offered:* College/university scholarship or grant aid from institutional funds; Federal Pell; Private scholarships; SEOG; State scholarships/grants. *Loan aid offered:* Direct PLUS loans; Direct Subsidized Stafford Loans; Direct Unsubsidized Stafford Loans. Applicants will be notified of awards on a rolling basis beginning 12/1. Federal Work-Study Program available. Institutional employment available.

The Inside Word

St. Mary's is a public honors college, which means earning admission is no easy feat. The school is looking for intellectually curious students who will be thoroughly engaged in the classroom as well as campus life. Top candidates tend to have taken a rigorous course-load in high school, so you'll want to load up on honors and AP classes. And if you're test-averse, you'll be delighted to hear that St. Mary's just became a test-optional school (with the exception of home-school applicants and students who must demonstrate proficiency with English).

THE SCHOOL SAYS "..."

From the Admissions Office

"St. Mary's College of Maryland, The National Public Honors College, believes that a rigorous, relevant and experiential education should be accessible for those with the talent, ambition and potential to do the work. Our students enjoy the prestige of attending a nationally highly-ranked public honors college with the enriched experience of a diverse student body. Our Learning through Experiential and Applied Discovery (LEAD) curriculum blends a liberal arts and sciences academic experience with professional skill development in which students learn how disciplines connect, the power of collaboration, critical thinking skills, multiple ways to approach problems, and so much more. Through the Honors College Promise, every student is guaranteed an internship, research, or international experience. It is this mix of academic excellence, experiential learning and affordability that makes St. Mary's College an education that is uncommonly worth it."

SELECTIVITY

Admissions Rating	77
# of applicants	1,621
% of applicants accepted	84
% of acceptees attending	23
# of early decision applicants	38
% accepted early decision	89

FRESHMAN PROFILE

Range SAT EBRW	540–650
Range SAT Math	520–640
Range SAT Composite	1070–1290
Range ACT Composite	21–29
# submitting SAT scores	279
% submitting SAT scores	87
# submitting ACT scores	70
% submitting ACT scores	22
Average HS GPA	3.4
% graduated top 10% of class	26
% graduated top 25% of class	55
% graduated top 50% of class	83

DEADLINES

Early decision	
Deadline	11/1
Notification	12/1
Early action	
Deadline	11/1
Notification	1/1
Regular	
Priority	11/1
Deadline	1/15
Notification	4/1
Nonfall registration?	Yes

FINANCIAL FACTS

Financial Aid Rating	82
Annual in-state tuition	$12,116
Annual out-of-state tuition	$28,192
Room and board	$13,595
Required fees	$3,008
Books and supplies	$800
Average frosh need-based scholarship	$8,827
Average UG need-based scholarship	$9,406
% needy frosh rec. need-based scholarship or grant aid	87
% needy UG rec. need-based scholarship or grant aid	86
% needy frosh rec. non-need-based scholarship or grant aid	78
% needy UG rec. non-need-based scholarship or grant aid	65
% needy frosh rec. need-based self-help aid	60
% needy UG rec. need-based self-help aid	70
% frosh rec. any financial aid	92
% UG rec. any financial aid	83
% UG borrow to pay for school	52
Average cumulative indebtedness	$25,579
% frosh need fully met	7
% ugrads need fully met	4
Average % of frosh need met	75
Average % of ugrad need met	69

SAINT MICHAEL'S COLLEGE

One Winooski Park, Box 7, Colchester, VT 05439 • Admissions: 802-654-3000 • Fax: 802-654-2906

STUDENTS SAY "..."

Academics

"Small classes" help to ensure that "you are not just another number in a lecture hall." Indeed, the college "really wants to help its students realize their full potential." Many tout the "strong academics" and highlight the education, biology, and religion departments in particular. Classes are often "discussion-based" and "require a conscientious student who will actively participate in discussion." Moreover, undergrads here speak effusively about their professors. As one Biology major shares, "Regardless of which class you're in, you can tell that each professor's #1 priority is that the students succeed." A history major succinctly adds, "Whether you like it or not, your professor will know your name," while a Media Studies major notes that their "professors aren't just professors. They're lifelong teachers," with a Business Administration major stating, "I've had professors set up weekend study sessions before exams, bring in donuts for 8:00 A.M. classes, and invite students over for dinner or out for coffee. My professors have also really helped me in beginning my career—setting up research studies in my field of interest, writing incredible letters of recommendation for grad school, or networking to get me internships." It's been said that St. Mike's "could improve the Media Studies, Journalism, and Digital Arts Facility," and that "there are not enough seats in popular or required classes for the amount of students that need to take them."

Life

Burlington Vermont (less than ten minutes from campus minutes by bus) is "one of the greatest places to be in this part of the country. There is so much to do in such a small, convenient area." Of Burlington, students say that "Church Street is crowded with unique shops, fantastic restaurants, and interesting people." Many also love to take advantage of Vermont's outdoor recreational options and the school counts many avid skiers, snowboarders, and hikers among it ranks. In fact, "Saint Michael's provides amazing ski pass deals and transportation to amazing ski resorts in the area." St. Mike's campus is "tiny, but in the cold months of winter, five minute walks to class are a godsend." Life at St. Mike's is "pretty chill." "If a student is one that likes to party, they are able to find it on campus. If a person is more reserved, there are thousands of other things that that person can do." "St. Mike's students have their heads on straight when it comes to making decisions." Students feel that the food "lacks flavor," although it should be noted that this is the way of most undergraduate dining experiences.

Student Body

In their own words: "the typical student is upper-middle class, environmentally and politically aware, and always says 'Hi,'" and who quickly dons "North Faces and UGGs during the cold Vermont winters," and, although St. Mike's is a Catholic school, students "are all different in regards to religions, races, sexual orientations and genders." The most frequent comment made by first-years "is that they were shocked when a student held the door open for them." Giving back to the community is a main theme in terms of the typical student here at St. Mike's, as exemplified by the statement that "nearly all students participate in at least one service project during their four years here. Most students are concerned about the environment and social justice." Students are "very relaxed for the most part" and enjoy "the outdoors that this great state provides for us." "If you're genuine and true to who you are, you're bound to do well at St. Mike's."

SAINT MICHAEL'S COLLEGE

Financial Aid: 802-654-3243 • E-Mail: admission@smcvt.edu • Website: www.smcvt.edu

THE PRINCETON REVIEW SAYS

Admissions

Very important factors considered include: rigor of secondary school record, class rank, academic GPA. *Important factors considered include:* application essay, standardized test scores, recommendation(s), talent/ability, character/personal qualities. *Other factors considered include:* interview, extracurricular activities, first generation, alumni/ae relation, geographical residence, state residency, racial/ethnic status, volunteer work, work experience, level of applicant's interest. ACT with Writing recommended. SAT with Essay component recommended. High school diploma is required and GED is accepted. *Academic units required:* 4 English, 4 math, 3 science, 2 science labs, 2 foreign language, 3 social studies, 3 history. *Academic units recommended:* 4 English, 4 math, 4 science, 3 science labs, 4 foreign language, 4 social studies, 4 history.

Financial Aid

Students should submit: FAFSA. Priority filing deadline is 2/1. The Princeton Review suggests that all financial aid forms be submitted as soon as possible after October 1. *Need-based scholarships/grants offered:* Federal Pell; Private scholarships; SEOG; State scholarships/grants. *Loan aid offered:* Direct PLUS loans; Direct Subsidized Stafford Loans; Direct Unsubsidized Stafford Loans. Applicants will be notified of awards on a rolling basis beginning 2/1. Federal Work-Study Program available. Institutional employment available.

The Inside Word

Applicants to St. Mike's are more than just a number, and admissions officers do their utmost to consider candidates in their entirety. Officers consider everything from essays to extracurricular activities, though most weight is given to academic record. The College has been standardized test optional for nearly a decade, and applicants are not penalized in the admission or scholarship process if they choose not to submit their scores.

THE SCHOOL SAYS "..."

From the Admissions Office

"A residential Catholic college welcoming to all, Saint Michael's is steeped in the spirit of our founders, the Society of Saint Edmund. Their example inspires our community to embrace the values of intellectual inquiry, peace, justice, and service to others. Students at St. Mike's are challenged to do well and driven to do good.

"Choosing a major is not always easy. At St. Mike's, students can take advantage of the flexible structure of their majors and our liberal arts core to explore then pursue more than one academic interest. In fact, over 80 percent of our students complete more than just their major, with nearly 40 percent completing at least a double major or double minor. We help students find and follow their passions and excel at them.

"Outside the classroom, students grow into impressive leaders through their experiences with the Adventure Sports Center, Fire & Rescue, our MOVE service work program, varsity and club athletics, a uniquely active student government, our student run radio station WWPV, the student paper, the College farm, the Center for the Environment, and numerous other opportunities.

"Named among the 'best college towns' in the country, nearby Burlington is a vibrant city with a wealth of professional experiences, arts, and culture. Campus is also located just ninety minutes from the multicultural center of Montreal, Quebec. Students enjoy a deeply discounted season's pass to Sugarbush, access to our campus 440-acre Natural Area for research and recreation, and meaningful internships at top companies.

"St. Mike's will take you wherever you want to go."

SELECTIVITY

Admissions Rating	77
# of applicants	3,967
% of applicants accepted	83
% of acceptees attending	12
# offered a place on the wait list	112
% accepting a place on wait list	24
% admitted from wait list	33

FRESHMAN PROFILE

Range SAT EBRW	585–660
Range SAT Math	570–650
Range ACT Composite	25–29
# submitting SAT scores	187
% submitting SAT scores	47
# submitting ACT scores	42
% submitting ACT scores	11
Average HS GPA	3.4
% graduated top 10% of class	21
% graduated top 25% of class	49
% graduated top 50% of class	79

DEADLINES

Early action	
Deadline	11/1
Notification	12/21
Regular	
Priority	11/1
Deadline	2/1
Notification	4/1
Nonfall registration?	Yes

APPLICANTS ALSO LOOK AT AND OFTEN PREFER
Providence College; College of the Holy Cross; Boston College

AND SOMETIMES PREFER
University of Vermont; University of New Hampshire; University of Massachusetts Amherst; Stonehill College; St. Lawrence University

AND RARELY PREFER
Saint Anselm College; Assumption University

FINANCIAL FACTS

Financial Aid Rating	88
Annual tuition	$46,175
Room and board	$13,600
Required fees	$2,000
Books and supplies	$1,250
Average frosh need-based scholarship	$29,809
Average UG need-based scholarship	$27,022
% needy frosh rec. need-based scholarship or grant aid	99
% needy UG rec. need-based scholarship or grant aid	99
% needy frosh rec. non-need-based scholarship or grant aid	19
% needy UG rec. non-need-based scholarship or grant aid	17
% needy frosh rec. need-based self-help aid	80
% needy UG rec. need-based self-help aid	81
% frosh rec. any financial aid	100
% UG rec. any financial aid	98
% UG borrow to pay for school	72
Average cumulative indebtedness	$38,040
% frosh need fully met	23
% ugrads need fully met	24
Average % of frosh need met	80
Average % of ugrad need met	76

ST. OLAF COLLEGE

1520 St. Olaf Avenue, Northfield, MN 55057 • Admissions: 507-786-3025 • Fax: 507-786-3832

STUDENTS SAY "..."

Academics

With roots in a "Norwegian heritage," St. Olaf College in Northfield, Minnesota, provides students "a wonderful liberal arts education" with a strong focus on "classical music appreciation," while still offering "academic opportunities for everyone." St. Olaf emphasizes the need for "globally conscious citizens." To help them "[build] a global perspective," St. Olaf encourages students "to ask questions and explore their beliefs." Students agree that "the professors here are simply phenomenal in every respect, and their approachability is absolutely a hallmark of this campus." Nearly everyone we heard from praised their professors as "readily available to help," offering "late night review sessions," encouraging "academic conversations outside of the classroom," and "[extending] office hours to all five days a week the week before" major projects are due. St. Olaf students feel their professors "care about their students as whole people." But "this does not mean that they are lax and let students walk all over them." St. Olaf faculty maintain "high expectations" for their students, "but [they] want to see students succeed" as well. "Being a professor isn't just a 9-to-5 job for them," one student explains, "but a life they truly enjoy." While the school is affiliated with the Lutheran church, students assure us that "even if you aren't religious, you won't feel out of place at St. Olaf," explaining how "the religious aspect of the school" is rooted in its history "and allows those that are religious to find a community of people who are religious as well."

Life

Oles enjoy an active and engaging campus life where "most students are busy on school days and nights either studying or attending school functions." Olaf students take their community and club involvement seriously. With "250 student clubs and organizations" that "[provide] opportunities for students to explore and nourish their passions," students find that "it is really easy to get involved in multiple activities." While this can make it so their "days are pretty full, sometimes hectic," "being an Ole means you are fully devoted to your school or your community." Even so, Oles say they have "a pretty good work/life balance since there are so many opportunities to de-stress and spend time with friends (even if you are just working in the same room)." Among the "million extra activities" that Oles love, "choir and music are hugely popular—[about 25 percent] of students are in a music ensemble and [many] students participate in the nationally renowned St. Olaf Christmas Festival." During the Christmas Festival, "alumni from all over [flock] back to the Hill to relive their Ole days. The campus is decorated everywhere, and the cafeteria even serves Norwegian food for the big weekend." And for Oles this "close knit, inquisitive student body" is "literally home." "I leave for break, excited to see my family" one environmental science major explains, "But to be honest? I find myself longing for the day when I come back to campus. Back to my home."

Student Body

Students express concern about the "lack of diversity on campus," but they hold one another in high esteem. "It's an accepting and trusting community" where students are comfortable "leaving laptops and backpacks around" without worry, and "if you lose your ID or wallet, you can expect it to appear in your PO box within a few hours." Students tend to be "a little preppy, type A personalities" who are "trustworthy" and considerate: "a local florist sells 'Friday flowers'—which people buy for their friends and leave in their POs with notes." These "sincere" students "wear Norwegian sweaters non-ironically" and exude a "very mid-western ... niceness." Olaf is an alcohol-free school, and "although it definitely has a presence on campus," students "agree that there is no pressure to drink" from fellow Oles. "I would say if you're not into socializing at parties and are into good clean fun," one student explains, "then there are options for you." With such strong music programs, it is no wonder that "music is very important to the average St. Olaf student, especially choir."

Financial Aid: 507-786-3019 • E-Mail: admissions@stolaf.edu • Website: http://wp.stolaf.edu

THE PRINCETON REVIEW SAYS

Admissions

Very important factors considered include: rigor of secondary school record, academic GPA, application essay. *Important factors considered include:* class rank, standardized test scores, recommendation(s), interview, extracurricular activities, talent/ability, character/personal qualities. *Other factors considered include:* first generation, alumni/ae relation, geographical residence, state residency, religious affiliation/commitment, racial/ethnic status, volunteer work, work experience, level of applicant's interest. ACT with or without writing accepted. SAT with or without Essay component accepted. High school diploma is required and GED is accepted. *Academic units recommended:* 4 English, 4 math, 4 science, 2 science labs, 4 foreign language, 4 social studies.

Financial Aid

Students should submit: CSS/Financial Aid PROFILE; FAFSA; Noncustodial PROFILE. Priority filing deadline is 1/15. The Princeton Review suggests that all financial aid forms be submitted as soon as possible after October 1. *Need-based scholarships/grants offered:* College/university scholarship or grant aid from institutional funds; Federal Pell; Private scholarships; SEOG; State scholarships/grants. *Loan aid offered:* Direct Subsidized Stafford Loans; Direct Unsubsidized Stafford Loans. Applicants will be notified of awards on or about 4/1. Federal Work-Study Program available. Institutional employment available.

The Inside Word

As St. Olaf's academic reputation steadily rises, so too does competition to gain admission. First and foremost, admissions officers here assess the rigor of each applicant's course load (and subsequent success in the classroom). Of course, as a tight-knit community, the college also looks to admit students who will complement St. Olaf's ethos. To that end, admissions officers also closely analyze personal essays, recommendations and participation in extracurricular activities.

THE SCHOOL SAYS "…"

From the Admissions Office

"With so many great liberal arts colleges, how do you choose? What makes St. Olaf stand apart? We think it's this: St. Olaf doesn't produce ordinary college grads. It turns out Oles (Oh-Lees). Oles are the people that companies want, because they know how to get stuff done. They think harder, approach problems differently, persevere with enthusiasm. Oles are born of St. Olaf's intense academic program—an academic program that hones minds, while its emphasis on global engagement helps broaden perspectives. Oles aren't necessarily religious, but our religious tradition encourages deep self-reflection. Most important, perhaps, is the Ole community—a vibrant community that accepts, supports and encourages, generating lifelong friendships and invaluable business connections. Today more than ever, the world needs idealistic, tireless problem solvers. In other words, Oles.

"Facts about Oles: St. Olaf's 3,000 students come from 80 countries, every state, and a variety of religious and non-religious backgrounds. Oles choose from more than 85 majors, concentrations, and pre-professional tracks. 95 percent of Oles live on campus or in college-owned houses nearby. Two thirds of Oles study abroad. Oles participate on 27 varsity teams, numerous club sports and intramurals. They belong to 200 student organizations and have countless opportunities to get involved."

SELECTIVITY

Admissions Rating	89
# of applicants	5,964
% of applicants accepted	48
% of acceptees attending	30
# offered a place on the wait list	942
% accepting a place on wait list	50
% admitted from wait list	7
# of early decision applicants	402
% accepted early decision	76

FRESHMAN PROFILE

Range SAT EBRW	590–710
Range SAT Math	600–720
Range ACT Composite	26–32
# submitting SAT scores	243
% submitting SAT scores	30
# submitting ACT scores	596
% submitting ACT scores	74
Average HS GPA	3.6
% graduated top 10% of class	46
% graduated top 25% of class	74
% graduated top 50% of class	96

DEADLINES

Early decision	
Deadline	11/15
Notification	12/15
Other ED Deadline	1/8
Other ED Notification	2/1
Regular	
Deadline	1/15
Notification	3/20
Nonfall registration?	No

APPLICANTS ALSO LOOK AT AND SOMETIMES PREFER

Carleton College; Macalester College; University of Minnesota—Twin Cities Campus; University of Wisconsin-Madison

AND RARELY PREFER

Luther College; Gustavus Adolphus College

FINANCIAL FACTS

Financial Aid Rating	95
Annual tuition	$51,450
Room and board	$11,660
Books and supplies	$1,000
Average frosh need-based scholarship	$39,727
Average UG need-based scholarship	$37,646
% needy frosh rec. need-based scholarship or grant aid	100
% needy UG rec. need-based scholarship or grant aid	100
% needy frosh rec. non-need-based scholarship or grant aid	36
% needy UG rec. non-need-based scholarship or grant aid	26
% needy frosh rec. need-based self-help aid	91
% needy UG rec. need-based self-help aid	100
% frosh rec. any financial aid	100
% UG rec. any financial aid	100
% UG borrow to pay for school	60
Average cumulative indebtedness	$28,950
% frosh need fully met	100
% ugrads need fully met	80
Average % of frosh need met	100
Average % of ugrad need met	96

SALISBURY UNIVERSITY

1101 Camden Avenue, Salisbury, MD 21801 • Admissions: 410-543-6161 • Fax: 410-546-6016

CAMPUS LIFE

Quality of Life Rating	**86**
Fire Safety Rating	**96**
Green Rating	**98**
Type of school	Public
Environment	Town

STUDENTS

Total undergrad enrollment	7,459
% male/female	44/56
% from out of state	13
% frosh from public high school	85
% frosh live on campus	88
% ugrads live on campus	31
# of fraternities (% ugrad men join)	11 (10)
# of sororities (% ugrad women join)	7 (7)
% African American	14
% Asian	4
% Caucasian	70
% Hispanic	5
% Native American	<1
% Pacific Islander	<1
% Two or more races	2
% Race and/or ethnicity unknown	3
% international	1
# of countries represented	30

SURVEY SAYS . . .

Great library
Frats and sororities are popular
Intramural sports are popular

ACADEMICS

Academic Rating	**79**
% students returning for sophomore year	81
% students graduating within 4 years	52
% students graduating within 6 years	70
Calendar	4/1/4
Student/faculty ratio	15:1
Profs interesting rating	87
Profs accessible rating	91

Most classes have 20–29 students.
Most lab/discussion sessions have
20–29 students.

MOST POPULAR MAJORS

Speech Communication and Rhetoric; Exercise
Science and Kinesiology; Registered Nursing/
Registered Nurse

STUDENTS SAY "..."

Academics

Located on Maryland's Eastern Shore, Salisbury University is a public school with a "stellar reputation [of] various programs and challenging courses." Of those options, undergrads make particular note of an "amazing nursing program," an "impressive business school," and "health science programs [that] are pretty great." Some also boast about an education program with a great track record. Students are also pleased with the small class sizes this mid-size school features, finding that "most professors take the time to really get to know their students over the semesters." One student concurs: "The faculty is amazing. I haven't had a professor that doesn't truly care about [my] education." Praise for the staff doesn't stop there: "The faculty and staff take time to understand the demands put on the students," adds another. To further help with those demands, SU also provides "everything a student needs to succeed, be that academic help, support systems, clubs, sports, anything; the university provides them all."

Life

Students at Salisbury are "very studious during the week," and a lot of time is spent at the "*huge* brand new library and study area ... where there are coffee shops [and] food." A particular strength of that new library that many note are the "student aid resources provided, such as the Center for Student Achievement, the Writing Center, and [Supplemental Instruction] meetings." One undergrad elaborates, "The campus community works really hard to make ... different opportunities available to us free of extra fees. So it gives us students a variety of options of how to study and learn." That variety also extends to extracurriculars: "Students are encouraged to join clubs and participate in some of the abundant activities offered on campus in order to create a more active student body." So while studies tend to come first at SU, undergrads are also "focused on fun" and "try to enjoy their college life while they are here." Popular activities on and off campus include "playing music in the Red Square, attending school events, ... enjoying food at the Commons or at the Chick-Fil-A, [and] playing ping pong or pool." On the weekends, "since Salisbury is right next to Ocean City, many will take trips to the beach."

Student Body

Salisbury undergrads are thankful to have a community of "friendly and inclusive peers." "Nobody ever really feels alone," one student states; they're enveloped in a group that is "academically driven and focused," which cultivates a cooperative environment. "I feel as though I am surrounded by others who push me to better myself, instead of focusing only on bettering themselves," says another student. While many note that diversity might be lacking, most agree that "the school provides *many* multicultural related resources, clubs, [and] presentations, so [minorities] still feel very comfortable and involved." One Salisbury Sea Gull sums it up: "There's a place for everyone."

SALISBURY UNIVERSITY

Financial Aid: 410-543-6165 • E-Mail: https://www.salisbury.edu/admissions/ • Website: https://www.salisbury.edu/

THE PRINCETON REVIEW SAYS

Admissions

Very important factors considered include: rigor of secondary school record, academic GPA. *Important factors considered include:* class rank, standardized test scores. *Other factors considered include:* application essay, recommendation(s), extracurricular activities, talent/ability, character/personal qualities, first generation, alumni/ae relation, geographical residence, state residency, racial/ethnic status, volunteer work, work experience, level of applicant's interest. ACT with or without writing accepted. SAT with or without Essay component accepted. High school diploma is required and GED is accepted. *Academic units required:* 4 English, 4 math, 3 science, 2 science labs, 2 foreign language, 3 social studies. *Academic units recommended:* 4 English, 4 math, 4 science, 3 science labs, 3 foreign language, 3 social studies, 3 academic electives.

Financial Aid

Students should submit: FAFSA. Priority filing deadline is 3/1. The Princeton Review suggests that all financial aid forms be submitted as soon as possible after October 1. *Need-based scholarships/grants offered:* College/university scholarship or grant aid from institutional funds; Federal Pell; Private scholarships; SEOG; State scholarships/grants. *Loan aid offered:* Direct PLUS loans; Direct Subsidized Stafford Loans; Direct Unsubsidized Stafford Loans. Applicants will be notified of awards on or about 2/15. Federal Work-Study Program available. Institutional employment available.

The Inside Word

The SU Admissions Office takes a comprehensive view of a student's application and puts top priority on the academic record, including curriculum and performance. Preference is for a college preparatory curriculum and a strong history of leadership experience and community service. The university has an SAT/ACT optional admissions policy for students with a GPA of 3.5 or above. Test scores are required for scholarship consideration. Other requirements include recommendations and a personal essay. Portfolio required for Bachelor of Fine Arts applicants.

THE SCHOOL SAYS "..."

From the Admissions Office

"Salisbury University is a must-see, with flowering trees, green spaces, and traditional red brick echoing the natural beauty of coastal Maryland. Comfortably situated in the Salisbury community between restaurants, retail shops, and a historic downtown district, the campus is ideally located to meet student needs while maintaining the friendly ambience of nearby beach communities. An academic leader and top producer of student and faculty Fulbright awards, SU affords students access to research as early as their first semester. Faculty mentors coach them toward opportunities for study abroad, experiential learning, and national fellowships. Expansive facilities, including the $117 million Guerrieri Academic Commons (GAC)—the hub of academic life—serve faculty and students. This state-of-the-art "library of the future" also is home to academic events, instruction, digital scholarship, outreach programs, research, and scholastic enrichment. The GAC complements SU's five primary academic divisions, including its new College of Health and Human Services, which provide the perfect environment for students to develop a liberal arts foundation, hone their skills in communication and entrepreneurship, conduct scientific and scholarly research, and engage in public service. The explosive growth of the Honors College and SU's strong job placement rankings are testaments to its commitment to students. Academic success is matched by the spirit of community involvement in over 100 student clubs and multiple service projects. Students cheer on SU's Division III athletic programs (with 20 national championships) in new facilities. The campus also is known nationally for sustainability. The University seeks students who want to make a difference in their work and in the world."

SELECTIVITY

Admissions Rating	82
# of applicants	8,421
% of applicants accepted	74
% of acceptees attending	24
# of early decision applicants	348
% accepted early decision	71

FRESHMAN PROFILE

Range SAT EBRW	570–640
Range SAT Math	550–640
Range SAT Composite	1150–1260
Range ACT Composite	19–23
# submitting SAT scores	729
% submitting SAT scores	50
# submitting ACT scores	202
% submitting ACT scores	14
Average HS GPA	3.7
% graduated top 10% of class	15
% graduated top 25% of class	45
% graduated top 50% of class	81

DEADLINES

Early decision	
Deadline	11/15
Notification	12/15
Early action	
Deadline	12/1
Notification	1/15
Regular	
Deadline	1/15
Notification	3/15
Nonfall registration?	Yes

FINANCIAL FACTS

Financial Aid Rating	81
Annual in-state tuition	$7,264
Annual out-of-state tuition	$17,330
Room and board	$12,360
Required fees	$2,780
Books and supplies	$1,300
Average frosh need-based scholarship	$8,029
Average UG need-based scholarship	$7,098
% needy frosh rec. need-based scholarship or grant aid	85
% needy UG rec. need-based scholarship or grant aid	78
% needy frosh rec. non-need-based scholarship or grant aid	0
% needy UG rec. non-need-based scholarship or grant aid	0
% needy frosh rec. need-based self-help aid	64
% needy UG rec. need-based self-help aid	71
% frosh rec. any financial aid	87
% UG rec. any financial aid	78
% UG borrow to pay for school	63
Average cumulative indebtedness	$27,355
% frosh need fully met	12
% ugrads need fully met	9
Average % of frosh need met	56
Average % of ugrad need met	53

SAN DIEGO STATE UNIVERSITY

5500 Campanile Drive, San Diego, CA 92182-7455 • Admissions: 619-594-6336

STUDENTS SAY "..."

Academics

Students lucky enough to attend San Diego State University receive a "quality, affordable education," all while they soak up that brilliant "San Diego sun!" And with a "wide array [of] majors and minors" along with a good deal of "flexibility in course choices," it's understandable why individuals are drawn to this institution. Speaking of majors (and minors), undergrads at SDSU rush to underscore a handful of really stellar academic departments. For starters, the "science programs have vigorous requirements that [truly] prepare you for grad school or medical school." Additionally, the "music program strives to create the best educators and performers." The nursing school is also "amazing" and really works to "accommodate...each individual." And the international business program is considered "one of the top...in the nation."

When it comes to professors, while there's the occasional bad or "boring" apple, the vast majority at SDSU are "dedicated and eager to teach." Moreover, they typically approach their time in the classroom with "enthusiasm" and manage to "bring life to every lecture." Indeed, they "make learning the material easy and fun." It's also quite apparent that they "care about their students," taking the time to "check in with them" and making themselves "accessible outside of the classroom." And, as a grateful religious studies major explains, they often "inspire [you] to become a more intellectual person and involved student."

Life

Simply put, life at San Diego State is "wonderful." And, no matter whether you opt to participate in "Greek life, a student organization or a sport, everyone [finds] something to do." Additionally, SDSU's Associated Students is great about sponsoring a number of "fun" events such as Aztec Nights, which in past years have included "Distress Fest, Haunted Montezuma and the Polar Plunge." A thrilled speech pathology major rushes to brag, "Every Thursday, there is a farmer's market on campus where students can enjoy a wide array of international cuisines prepared by local restaurants. SDSU also has "amazing athletics" and undergrads love "attending football [games], basketball [games] and other sporting events." Of course, given that San Diego has "[beautiful] weather year round," you won't catch SDSU students...spend[ing] much time indoors." It's quite common to see students riding "bikes or skateboards across campus." And a business administration major pipes in, "The beach is a huge draw for people whether you like surfing, paddle boarding, or just swimming." Additionally, the "campus is located 10 minutes from Fashion Valley or Balboa Park, and there are tons of good restaurants around. It is also very close to the Mexican border for easy day trips."

Student Body

San Diego State is comprised of a "diverse community of students who are as laid-back as they are hard-working." Indeed, the university does a great job of attracting undergrads "from all over the world and all walks of life." Students happily report that their peers are both "social" and "academically driven." Even better, "they are supportive and seem to always be open to help others who are struggling." Undergrads also appreciate that there are "endless opportunities to meet new people because the campus is swarming with students." And, for the most part, San Diego undergrads are "very accepting of one another and open minded." Of course, all of this goodwill can partially be attributed to the lovely surroundings. As one business students sums up, "It's hard not to be happy when living in beautiful San Diego."

SAN DIEGO STATE UNIVERSITY

Financial Aid: 619-594-6323 • Website: www.sdsu.edu

THE PRINCETON REVIEW SAYS

Admissions

Very important factors considered include: rigor of secondary school record, academic GPA, standardized test scores. *Important factors considered include:* geographical residence, state residency. ACT with or without writing accepted. SAT with or without Essay component accepted. High school diploma is required and GED is accepted. *Academic units required:* 4 English, 3 math, 2 science, 2 science labs, 2 foreign language, 1 social studies, 1 history, 1 academic elective, 1 visual/performing arts. *Academic units recommended:* 4 math.

Financial Aid

Students should submit: FAFSA; State aid form. Priority filing deadline is 4/1. The Princeton Review suggests that all financial aid forms be submitted as soon as possible after October 1. *Need-based scholarships/grants offered:* College/university scholarship or grant aid from institutional funds; Federal Pell; Private scholarships; SEOG; State scholarships/grants. *Loan aid offered:* Direct PLUS loans; Direct Subsidized Stafford Loans; Direct Unsubsidized Stafford Loans. Applicants will be notified of awards on a rolling basis beginning 3/15. Federal Work-Study Program available. Institutional employment available.

The Inside Word

The admissions process at San Diego State is very by the book. Similar to other universities within the California State system San Diego relies on the eligibility index as the crux of their decision making. Hence, your GPA and standardized test scores will be critical. Moreover, the application is major specific; candidates will be ranked against all other individuals applying to that particular major. You will not be able to change your major during this process (though, aside from nursing, you will once you arrive on campus). Finally, all music, dance, and/or theater candidates will have to audition as well.

THE SCHOOL SAYS "..."

From the Admissions Office

"Founded in 1897, San Diego State University is a major public research institution that provides transformative experiences for its more than 36,000 students. SDSU ranks as the number 1 California State University in federal research support, is a long-standing Hispanic-Serving Institution (HSI) and resides on Kumeyaay land.

"The university is known for offering transformational research, international experiences, sustainability and entrepreneurship initiatives, internships and mentoring, and a broad range of student life and leadership opportunities. SDSU is committed to excellence and known for its efforts advancing diversity and inclusion.

"SDSU is nationally recognized for its study abroad initiatives, veterans' programs and support of LGBTQA+ students, as well as its powerhouse Division I Athletics Program. Recognized as a national leader in higher education, students have access to more than 400 student clubs and organizations and an inclusive environment with a diverse range of programs and offerings.

"About 54% of SDSU's undergraduates and graduates are students of color. The university's rich campus life and ideal location offers opportunities for students to lead and engage with the creative and performing arts, career and internship opportunities with SDSU's more than 400,000 living alumni, and the vibrant cultural life of the greater San Diego and U.S.- Mexico region."

SELECTIVITY

Admissions Rating	91
# of applicants	69,842
% of applicants accepted	34
% of acceptees attending	22
# offered a place on the wait list	3,529
% accepting a place on wait list	46
% admitted from wait list	32

FRESHMAN PROFILE

Range SAT EBRW	560–650
Range SAT Math	550–670
Range ACT Composite	22–29
# submitting SAT scores	4,527
% submitting SAT scores	86
# submitting ACT scores	1,985
% submitting ACT scores	38
Average HS GPA	3.8
% graduated top 10% of class	33
% graduated top 25% of class	70
% graduated top 50% of class	94

DEADLINES

Regular	
Deadline	11/30
Notification	3/1
Nonfall registration?	No

FINANCIAL FACTS

Financial Aid Rating	82
Annual in-state tuition	$5,742
Annual out-of-state tuition	$17,622
Room and board	$17,752
Required fees	$1,768
Books and supplies	$1,969
Average frosh need-based scholarship	$10,300
Average UG need-based scholarship	$10,100
% needy frosh rec. need-based scholarship or grant aid	63
% needy UG rec. need-based scholarship or grant aid	71
% needy frosh rec. non-need-based scholarship or grant aid	48
% needy UG rec. non-need-based scholarship or grant aid	41
% needy frosh rec. need-based self-help aid	100
% needy UG rec. need-based self-help aid	94
% frosh rec. any financial aid	57
% UG rec. any financial aid	59
% UG borrow to pay for school	44
Average cumulative indebtedness	$21,172
% frosh need fully met	11
% ugrads need fully met	20
Average % of frosh need met	67
Average % of ugrad need met	66

SANTA CLARA UNIVERSITY

500 El Camino Real, Santa Clara, CA 95053 • Admissions: 408-554-4700 • Fax: 408-554-5255

STUDENTS SAY "..."

Academics

Located "in the heart of Silicon Valley," Santa Clara University is a mid-size Jesuit school that blends "the Jesuit philosophy of social justice" with access to the "the tech capital of the world." That proximity means "job opportunities are never-ending," and that students have easy access to a "great alumni network." Overall, undergrads note that "academics are challenging but not unbearable," mentioning popular majors in business, art, and engineering. Taking advantage of its prime location, the school offers opportunities outside the classroom as well—"Students ... get involved on all levels, whether it be on campus, domestically, or internationally." This is achieved through "clubs, immersion trips, fellowship programs, ... and study abroad" programs. These initiatives serve to offer a "holistic curriculum [that] encompasses all aspects of knowledge," one undergrad says. Faculty members take the same approach, and one student notes that professors "are caring about not just the students' learning, but their lives outside of the classroom." A few students comment that some professors are "only teaching because they have to in order to do research," but the general impression is one of "qualified and knowledgeable" industry professionals who are "leaders in their fields." One student offers a summation of praise: "Good academics, great professors, beautiful campus."

Life

The Santa Clara campus is always buzzing with activity because "students are highly involved in at least one aspect of university life, whether it be academic commitment, extracurricular activities, career development, or social networking." Fitness is a popular focus of choice: Most days you'll "see people packing the gym" because Broncos "*love* to work out." Of course, this is if they find the extra time—students are often "engaged in internships" or "studying in the library, socializing in the student center, or hanging out in their ... residence halls." And because "the weather here is absolutely amazing," people "are usually outside ... for studying, reading, [or] relaxing." They also manage to squeeze in Although Greek life is not sanctioned by the university, students note that "Sorority and fraternity culture is prevalent (but not dominating), and that involves a lot of partying," one student says. Others add, "there are a lot of parties going on throughout the week," but say it is balanced with "non-drinking on-campus alternatives." Beyond campus, "SCU is a stone's throw away from [the mountains and beach in] Santa Cruz, San Francisco, [and] Lake Tahoe." It's a "great local area [with] so much to do," declares one happy student.

Student Body

Santa Clara Broncos say their peers are "collaborative," "caring," and "helpful." Many comment on the "strong sense of community" created by students who are "willing to work and help each other accomplish success in their areas of study." And while "the academic scene is very competitive," the majority of people "here are interested in helping others and working together to create positive change in the world." Many "students come from the Bay Area" and are "mostly upper-class people from private schools," and while the consensus is that SCU's student body is "not diverse, ... [it is] generally very positive and welcoming." It is "a warm and inclusive atmosphere," one undergrad says. Politically, "the school is fairly liberal but also has a big conservative base to it."

Financial Aid: 408-551-1000 • E-Mail: Admission@scu.edu • Website: www.scu.edu

THE PRINCETON REVIEW SAYS

Admissions

Very important factors considered include: rigor of secondary school record, academic GPA, application essay. *Important factors considered include:* class rank, standardized test scores, recommendation(s), extracurricular activities, talent/ability, character/personal qualities, first generation, alumni/ae relation, racial/ethnic status, volunteer work. *Other factors considered include:* geographical residence, state residency, religious affiliation/commitment, work experience, level of applicant's interest. ACT with or without writing accepted. SAT with or without Essay component accepted. High school diploma is required and GED is accepted. *Academic units required:* 4 English, 3 math, 2 science, 2 foreign language, 3 social studies. *Academic units recommended:* 4 English, 4 math, 3 science, 3 foreign language, 3 social studies, 1 visual/performing arts.

Financial Aid

Students should submit: CSS/Financial Aid PROFILE; FAFSA. Priority filing deadline is 2/1. The Princeton Review suggests that all financial aid forms be submitted as soon as possible after October 1. *Need-based scholarships/grants offered:* College/university scholarship or grant aid from institutional funds; Federal Pell; Private scholarships; SEOG; State scholarships/grants. *Loan aid offered:* Direct PLUS loans; Direct Subsidized Stafford Loans; Direct Unsubsidized Stafford Loans, college/university loans from institutional funds; private credit based loans. Applicants will be notified of awards on or about 4/1. Federal Work-Study Program available. Institutional employment available.

The Inside Word

Applications for Santa Clara University come mostly from within California, and although an acceptance rate of nearly 50 percent might not seem overly competitive, admissions criteria is stringent and growing tougher. The number of applications has been increasing over the last few years, and the university's Silicon Valley address ensures even more attention is coming the school's way. Admissions officers consider high school transcripts, standardized test scores, as well as community service and involvement. Applicants apply to one of SCU's three schools: Arts and Sciences, School of Business, and School of Engineering. School visits are available. There are no admissions interviews offered.

THE SCHOOL SAYS "..."

From the Admissions Office

"Santa Clara University is a comprehensive Jesuit, Catholic university located forty miles south of San Francisco in Silicon Valley. We'll challenge you to think critically, take risks, and take charge within a dynamic and caring community, with more than fifty majors, numerous interdisciplinary programs, and some 3,669 courses from which to choose. There's something special about living and learning in one of the most innovative places on Earth, where more than 80 percent of our students have at least one internship before graduating and undergraduates conduct important research alongside professors in a way that is usually reserved for graduate students. The University blends a sense of tradition and history—as the oldest college in California—with a vision that values innovation and a deep commitment to social justice. We offer an experience so great that 94 percent of first-year students return for their sophomore year. People of all backgrounds flourish here. One thing they have in common? They want to make a difference. Santa Clara students are driven to build a better, kinder, more humane, and more sustainable planet. Distinguished nationally by one of the highest graduation rates, SCU provides rigorous undergraduate curricula in the arts and sciences, business, and engineering. Find out why SCU is the right fit for you at scu.edu."

SELECTIVITY

Admissions Rating	91
# of applicants	16,300
% of applicants accepted	49
% of acceptees attending	17
# offered a place on the wait list	2,162
% accepting a place on wait list	52
% admitted from wait list	20
# of early decision applicants	453
% accepted early decision	68

FRESHMAN PROFILE

Range SAT EBRW	630–700
Range SAT Math	650–740
Range SAT Composite	1300–1420
Range ACT Composite	28–32
# submitting SAT scores	942
% submitting SAT scores	68
# submitting ACT scores	600
% submitting ACT scores	43
Average HS GPA	3.7
% graduated top 10% of class	52
% graduated top 25% of class	88
% graduated top 50% of class	99

DEADLINES

Early decision	
Deadline	11/1
Notification	12/31
Other ED Deadline	1/7
Other ED Notification	2/15
Early action	
Deadline	11/1
Notification	12/31
Regular	
Deadline	1/7
Notification	Late March
Nonfall registration?	No

APPLICANTS ALSO LOOK AT AND OFTEN PREFER

Stanford University; University of Southern California; University of California—Berkeley; University of Washington

AND SOMETIMES PREFER

California Polytechnic State University; University of California, Los Angeles; Boston College

FINANCIAL FACTS

Financial Aid Rating	84
Annual tuition	$54,987
Room and board	$15,972
Required fees	$642
Books and supplies	$1,080
Average frosh need-based scholarship	$33,925
Average UG need-based scholarship	$32,076
% needy frosh rec. need-based scholarship or grant aid	83
% needy UG rec. need-based scholarship or grant aid	71
% needy frosh rec. non-need-based scholarship or grant aid	41
% needy UG rec. non-need-based scholarship or grant aid	34
% needy frosh rec. need-based self-help aid	47
% needy UG rec. need-based self-help aid	40
% frosh rec. any financial aid	70
% UG rec. any financial aid	72
% UG borrow to pay for school	35
Average cumulative indebtedness	$26,603
% frosh need fully met	32
% ugrads need fully met	26
Average % of frosh need met	77
Average % of ugrad need met	74

SARAH LAWRENCE COLLEGE

1 Mead Way, Bronxville, NY 10708-5999 • Admissions: 914-395-2510 • Fax: 914-395-2515

STUDENTS SAY "..."

Academics

Sarah Lawrence College is a stalwart liberal arts jewel located just north of New York City, offering students an interdisciplinary education in which they are able to select their "own course of study" and design their own personalized projects (which can take any form, including creative works of art and fiction, but are most often academic papers about a topic that the student is interested in). The school's didactical approach gives students "the benefit of seminar settings combined with independent research in one-on-one coordination with faculty," and the campus' location means they have "a ton of fieldwork and internship opportunities." The five credit system (three classes per semester, along with independent study) prioritizes in-depth study of topics over broader surveys, and every class is "a combination of different topics and attracts connection-drawing, instead of trying to categorize everything." Sarah Lawrence also has an "excellent writing program," where the workshop is constructive and the conference "helps a student to build a story as high as it can go."

Professors here are beloved, and aside from being "extremely accessible and intelligent," they "talk to us almost like colleagues" and "respect what we have to say and use what we say to steer us in a direction for further enrichment." They are "nothing short of brilliant, caring, and absolute joys" who are "so invested in your life it hurts." Various accolades and awards aside, the professors at this school demonstrate "such intelligence, fluency in their work, and a unique compassion and drive to TEACH students." The administration is incredibly receptive to ideas, and "students have a say in who teaches here" in that student input is considered during faculty searches. At Sarah Lawrence, students are not asked to test themselves "but rather to prove our abilities and intelligence through graduate level work." Sarah Lawrence "essentially offers a build-your-own education, and for those who are dedicated and passionate, it's perfect."

Life

With Grand Central Station just a thirty-minute train ride away, a lot of students escape to the city when the chance arises, because "there is not much to do in Bronxville." Very few classes meet on Fridays, so that's often when students "catch up on homework, work out at the gym, or maybe go into the city for an internship." Guest lectures are terrifically popular among students because "they are genuinely interesting, even if it's on a topic that seems wicked niche (octopi, for example)." Students continue intellectual discussions outside of the classroom because "they care about what they are learning in the real world." This isn't a party scene—"a Sarah Lawrence party is usually just a group of friends hanging out at someone's dorm"—and in their down time, people choose instead to "attend theater performances, take the free Met van into the city on Saturdays, hang their hammocks to the trees on the side of the road, sit and chat on large rocks, sun bathe on the green lawn, and go get coffee or bagels in Bronxville."

Student Body

Students are "creative, talented and hardworking," but above all else they are "passionate," and their passions are "fully interwoven in their art and coursework." Sarah Lawrence is "known for its individuality;" the LGBTQA+ population is "present and vocal," and pronouns are "part of introductions in many classes." Most students here are activists who "devote themselves to matters of social justice." It's not uncommon for students to "organize a bus to a rally, volunteer in underprivileged communities, or run phone banks in our milkshake café." They are often "fiercely passionate about niche topics" and "generally very liberal," and though school spirit is "not driven by pride in sports," students here at this "kind of academic utopia" take pride in "the friends they make and the classes they take."

SARAH LAWRENCE COLLEGE

Financial Aid: 914-395 2570 • E-Mail: slcadmit@sarahlawrence.edu • Website: www.sarahlawrence.edu

THE PRINCETON REVIEW SAYS

Admissions

Very important factors considered include: rigor of secondary school record, application essay, recommendation(s). *Important factors considered include:* academic GPA, extracurricular activities, talent/ability, character/personal qualities. *Other factors considered include:* class rank, standardized test scores, interview, first generation, alumni/ae relation, geographical residence, racial/ethnic status, volunteer work, work experience, level of applicant's interest. ACT with or without writing accepted. SAT with or without Essay component accepted. High school diploma is required and GED is accepted. *Academic units required:* 4 English, 2 math, 2 science, 2 foreign language, 2 history. *Academic units recommended:* 4 math, 4 science, 4 foreign language, 4 social studies, 4 history.

Financial Aid

Students should submit: FAFSA; State aid form. Priority filing deadline is 1/15. The Princeton Review suggests that all financial aid forms be submitted as soon as possible after October 1. *Need-based scholarships/grants offered:* College/university scholarship or grant aid from institutional funds; Federal Pell; Private scholarships; SEOG; State scholarships/grants. *Loan aid offered:* Direct PLUS loans; Direct Subsidized Stafford Loans; Direct Unsubsidized Stafford Loans. Applicants will be notified of awards on or about 4/1. Federal Work-Study Program available. Institutional employment available.

The Inside Word

Gaining admission to Sarah Lawrence is certainly competitive. Thankfully, admissions officers take a well-rounded approach. Of course, a strong college prep curriculum and solid GPA are of utmost importance, though submitting standardized test scores is optional. Candidates are encouraged to submit scores only if it will enhance their application. Additionally, interviews are optional, but may offer an opportunity to demonstrate what you can bring to this unique community.

THE SCHOOL SAYS "..."

From the Admissions Office

"Students who come to Sarah Lawrence are curious about the world, and they have an ardent desire to satisfy that curiosity. Sarah Lawrence offers such students two innovative academic structures: the seminar/conference system and the arts components. Courses in the humanities, social sciences, natural sciences, and mathematics are taught in the seminar/conference style. The seminars enroll an average of eleven students and consist of lecture, discussion, readings, and assigned papers. For each seminar, students also meet one-on-one in biweekly conferences, for which they conceive of individualized projects and shape them under the direction of professors. Arts components let students combine history and theory with practice. Painters, printmakers, photographers, sculptors, filmmakers, composers, musicians, choreographers, dancers, actors, and directors work in readily available studios, editing facilities, and darkrooms, guided by accomplished professionals. The suburban, wooded campus is thirty minutes from midtown Manhattan, and the diversity of people and ideas at Sarah Lawrence make it an extraordinary educational environment.

"Sarah Lawrence College is 'test optional,' accepting and reviewing standardized test scores if they are submitted; however, they are not required as part of the admission application."

SELECTIVITY

Admissions Rating	89
# of applicants	4,053
% of applicants accepted	53
% of acceptees attending	18
# offered a place on the wait list	1,088
% accepting a place on wait list	46
% admitted from wait list	6
# of early decision applicants	129
% accepted early decision	66

FRESHMAN PROFILE

Range SAT EBRW	640–720
Range SAT Math	600–702
Range ACT Composite	28–31
# submitting SAT scores	180
% submitting SAT scores	45
# submitting ACT scores	105
% submitting ACT scores	26
Average HS GPA	3.7
% graduated top 10% of class	36
% graduated top 25% of class	67
% graduated top 50% of class	93

DEADLINES

Early decision	
Deadline	11/1
Other ED Deadline	1/2
Early action	
Deadline	11/1
Regular	
Deadline	1/15
Nonfall registration?	No

FINANCIAL FACTS

Financial Aid Rating	86
Annual tuition	$56,020
Room and board	$15,820
Required fees	$1,500
Books and supplies	$600
Average frosh need-based scholarship	$37,854
Average UG need-based scholarship	$35,692
% needy frosh rec. need-based scholarship or grant aid	90
% needy UG rec. need-based scholarship or grant aid	97
% needy frosh rec. non-need-based scholarship or grant aid	15
% needy UG rec. non-need-based scholarship or grant aid	13
% needy frosh rec. need-based self-help aid	74
% needy UG rec. need-based self-help aid	81
% frosh rec. any financial aid	83
% UG rec. any financial aid	78
% UG borrow to pay for school	55
Average cumulative indebtedness	$26,808
% frosh need fully met	16
% ugrads need fully met	16
Average % of frosh need met	81
Average % of ugrad need met	75

SCRIPPS COLLEGE

1030 Columbia Avenue, Claremont, CA 91711-3948 • Admissions: 909-621-8149

STUDENTS SAY ". . ."

Academics

Scripps College has an "absolutely gorgeous" campus and terrific Southern California vibes, but the reason applicants clamor to attend is because of its "dedication to empowering female voices and education." The focus may be on its "supportive, small community of women who want to fight to make the world a better place," but students won't have to worry about missing out on the resources often attributed to larger institutions, as Scripps is part of the Claremont Colleges, a consortium that grants undergraduates access "to all of the benefits and resources within [four] other colleges."

Access is key across the "challenging and engaging" academic offerings at Scripps, whether that's one-on-one time with professors or simply having opportunity for undergraduate research. This extends to "discussion-based [classes], which allows students to raise questions ..., [gain] a better understanding of the course, and connect to the subject more intimately." It helps, too, that professors "are very good at creating interesting courses," and are "generally accepting of a wide range of student opinions, " though students should be aware that these freedoms come with "high expectations." Ultimately, what undergrads appreciate the most is that it's "very easy to form close connections with professors both in class and out of class."

Life

Scripps students are fairly studious and during the week you'll often find them congregating in one of the "many outdoor study spaces, such as courtyards, lawns, or the lounge chairs by the pool." Of course, there's lots of fun to be had beyond academics. For example, undergrads can take advantage of "a ton of free fitness courses on campus like CrossFit, yoga, and Zumba" as well as unique "intramural sports like inner-tube water polo." Additionally, "there are hundreds of clubs to join that are both specific to Scripps and also across all the Claremont Colleges." Don't like the dance team and have no interest in roller derby? Consider getting your inner baker on, as "Scripps Challah for Hunger bakes and sells challah every week." And if you've got opinions, "political clubs. . . are also popular," as are school-sponsored "speakers, screenings, presentations, workshops, [and] de-stress activities." Should you need a respite from that overflowing campus life, the surrounding area provides many options. "The train to downtown Los Angeles is about a ten-minute walk away, Mt. Baldy is about a 20-minute drive, and the village in Claremont is filled with shops and eateries."

Student Body

When asked to describe their peers, Scripps undergrads are prone to using effusive adjectives such as "passionate, driven, [and] creative." Many students also "identify as liberal, feminist, [and] social-justice oriented." As one individual explains, "From reproductive rights, prison abolition, racial justice, everyone you talk to has the desire to change the world." Indeed, they are certainly "not afraid to let their voices be heard." A number of undergrads appreciate that the college attracts "many transgender and non-binary students, which creates a very open and safe environment." However, a few do caution that there is a little "tension between white feminism and intersectionality" on campus. Fortunately, most everyone enjoys the fact their classmates are often "intelligent and ready to have in depth conversations about topics from politics to *The Bachelor* to data on climate change." Undergrads here also tend to be "very supportive of one another" and "very accepting" as well. In fact, when strolling through campus, it's even common to "receive smiles from students [you] don't know." All in all, the Scripps student body offers the "type of community that will cheer with and for you when you succeed and be a shoulder to cry on when needed."

Financial Aid: 909-621-8275 • E-Mail: admission@scrippscollege.edu • Website: www.scrippscollege.edu

THE PRINCETON REVIEW SAYS

Admissions

Very important factors considered include: rigor of secondary school record, class rank, academic GPA, application essay, recommendation(s), extracurricular activities, talent/ability, character/personal qualities. *Other factors considered include:* interview, first generation, alumni/ae relation, geographical residence, racial/ethnic status, volunteer work, work experience. ACT with or without writing accepted. SAT with or without Essay component accepted. High school diploma is required and GED is accepted. *Academic units required:* 4 English, 3 math, 3 science, 3 foreign language, 3 social studies.

Financial Aid

Students should submit: Business/Farm Supplement; CSS/Financial Aid PROFILE; FAFSA; Noncustodial PROFILE; State aid form. Priority filing deadline is 2/1. The Princeton Review suggests that all financial aid forms be submitted as soon as possible after October 1. *Need-based scholarships/grants offered:* College/university scholarship or grant aid from institutional funds; Federal Pell; Private scholarships; SEOG; State scholarships/grants. *Loan aid offered:* Direct PLUS loans; Direct Subsidized Stafford Loans; Direct Unsubsidized Stafford Loans. Applicants will be notified with admission decision. Federal Work-Study Program available.

The Inside Word

Admissions officers at Scripps truly strive to get to know each applicant. After all, they are looking for the students who will best complement the college and take advantage of the opportunities offered. Therefore, expect every part of your application to be carefully vetted. Your academic achievements will still hold the most weight, but your recommendations, personal statement and extracurriculars are of great importance. Your scores, thanks to Scripps being test-optional, should not affect your chances of gaining admission.

THE SCHOOL SAYS "..."

From the Admissions Office

"Scripps College, a top liberal arts college in the country, offers students a life-changing experience that combines demanding academic rigor with the powerful support of a collaborative women's college community. At Scripps, students thrive in an intellectually challenging yet collaborative community where undergraduate research and critical-thinking skills are top priorities. Scripps' faculty are distinguished teachers and leaders who are experts in their field, and classes are purposefully small (an average of sixteen students or fewer) to promote discussion and debate. More than sixty-five majors are available to Scripps students, which include a number of joint and intercollegiate programs. The College's Core Curriculum in Interdisciplinary Studies is a three-semester interdisciplinary program that provides a common academic experience for all students. As they explore provocative and relevant topics, students gain a foundation for the critical thinking, writing, and dialogue that distinguish the Scripps curriculum and graduate with new perspectives on the most complex issues facing the world today. Sixty percent of students study abroad, more than 80 percent hold at least one internship, and students can participate in eleven NCAA Division III sports. Scripps is a member of The Claremont Colleges, a consortium of five prestigious undergraduate institutions all located within walking distance, and two distinguished graduate institutions. Scripps College meets 100 percent of demonstrated financial need for admitted students, and all first-year applicants to the College are automatically considered for merit-based scholarships."

SELECTIVITY

Admissions Rating	97
# of applicants	3,022
% of applicants accepted	32
% of acceptees attending	29
# offered a place on the wait list	711
% accepting a place on wait list	50
% admitted from wait list	7
# of early decision applicants	247
% accepted early decision	47

FRESHMAN PROFILE

Range SAT EBRW	673–740
Range SAT Math	660–750
Range SAT Composite	1330–1470
Range ACT Composite	30–33
# submitting SAT scores	176
% submitting SAT scores	62
# submitting ACT scores	144
% submitting ACT scores	51
Average HS GPA	4.2
% graduated top 10% of class	78
% graduated top 25% of class	98
% graduated top 50% of class	100

DEADLINES

Early decision	
Deadline	11/15
Notification	12/15
Other ED Deadline	1/3
Other ED Notification	2/15
Regular	
Deadline	1/3
Notification	4/1
Nonfall registration?	No

FINANCIAL FACTS

Financial Aid Rating	96
Annual tuition	$59,192
Room and board	$18,286
Required fees	$218
Books and supplies	$800
Average frosh need-based scholarship	$39,084
Average UG need-based scholarship	$39,007
% needy frosh rec. need-based scholarship or grant aid	98
% needy UG rec. need-based scholarship or grant aid	99
% needy frosh rec. non-need-based scholarship or grant aid	0
% needy UG rec. non-need-based scholarship or grant aid	0
% needy frosh rec. need-based self-help aid	69
% needy UG rec. need-based self-help aid	80
% UG borrow to pay for school	32
Average cumulative indebtedness	$30,150
% frosh need fully met	100
% ugrads need fully met	100
Average % of frosh need met	100
Average % of ugrad need met	100

SEATTLE UNIVERSITY

Admissions Office, WA 98122-1090 • Admissions: 206-296-2000 • Fax: 206-296-5656

CAMPUS LIFE

Quality of Life Rating	90
Fire Safety Rating	97
Green Rating	99
Type of school	Private
Affiliation	Roman Catholic-Jesuit
Environment	Metropolis

STUDENTS

Total undergrad enrollment	4,751
% male/female	39/61
% from out of state	59
% frosh from public high school	62
% frosh live on campus	92
% ugrads live on campus	50
# of fraternities	0
# of sororities	0
% African American	3
% Asian	16
% Caucasian	42
% Hispanic	12
% Native American	<1
% Pacific Islander	1
% Two or more races	8
% Race and/or ethnicity unknown	6
% international	11
# of countries represented	80

SURVEY SAYS . . .

Students love Seattle, WA
Great food on campus
Students are happy

ACADEMICS

Academic Rating	83
% students returning for sophomore year	85
% students graduating within 4 years	61
% students graduating within 6 years	73
Calendar	Differs By Program
Student/faculty ratio	11:1
Profs interesting rating	88
Profs accessible rating	92

Most classes have 10–19 students.
Most lab/discussion sessions have 10–19 students.

MOST POPULAR MAJORS

Liberal Arts and Sciences, General Studies and Humanities, Other; Business/Commerce, General; Registered Nursing/Registered Nurse

STUDENTS SAY "..."

Academics

Though Seattle University is renowned for its excellent academics and programs, particularly its nursing program, it is the Jesuit philosophy of holistic education that underscores the mission of the university. The university requires its 4,800 undergraduates to take a collection of Core classes that are more than "just a random collection of math, writing, and social science classes. There's a lot more philosophy, theology, psychology, ethics, and actual service learning" involved, and students say that "often times the Core classes that [they are] required to take ended up being the most memorable classes." The dynamic professors "ensure the students have a chance not only to digest and memorize the information but also a chance to critically think about it and discuss different viewpoints." The university's commitment to social justice is "more than just rhetoric—there are classes structured around specific kinds of service learning." There is a growing sentiment "that SU is increasingly known for the Albers School of Business [and Economics]." Overall, students feel that Seattle U "is about finding community in a large city, and being able to discuss and have deep meaningful conversations about the issues we encounter in our everyday lives."

Life

It's "very much a city lifestyle" at Seattle U; "however, the mountains are not too far away." Here "you have the best of both worlds. You can go to happy hours, brunch, clubs, bars and restaurants, hiking, skiing, canoeing, and swimming in the summer. There is a lot to do in the area." In fact, "as soon as you step off campus, you are in the hustle and bustle of Capitol Hill, a booming, youthful neighborhood that is LGBT friendly. There are coffee shops... concert venues, and parks within a two-block radius." It's "a quick bus ride to downtown and Pike Place Market or a nice half-hour walk. [The International District] is nearby, too." And it's fine if you don't feel like walking because "the university loans out bus passes free of charge." Living in the heart of Seattle means that you can never run out of fun things to do on weekends. You could "see plays, go to the Seattle Art Museum, eat all sorts of different types of food, hang out in the International District, [or] attend film festivals. You name it, Seattle has it!" The campus is "super green," providing students with "composting and recycling options in every location possible." The food is not only "delicious," but is largely "locally grown, organic, and well-prepared."

Student Body

As "one of the most liberal Catholic schools," Seattle University is a place where "all faiths are not only accepted, but they are welcomed and encouraged." The "majority of students are liberal," and "everyone is aware of social issues." There is a "very large LGBTQ community" on campus, as well as "lots of international students." At Seattle U, students "frequently discuss gender norms, privilege, and how race influences identity. Identity is a popular topic of discussion—how we all use who we are to impact how we interact in the world." Here, "students are creative, insightful, and dedicated to making their educational experience unique and personal. Community is strongly felt [among] students and staff."

SEATTLE UNIVERSITY

Financial Aid: 206-296-8020 • E-Mail: admissions@seattleu.edu • Website: www.seattleu.edu

THE PRINCETON REVIEW SAYS

Admissions

Very important factors considered include: rigor of secondary school record, academic GPA, standardized test scores, character/personal qualities. *Important factors considered include:* application essay, recommendation(s), extracurricular activities. *Other factors considered include:* class rank, interview, talent/ability, first generation, alumni/ae relation, geographical residence, state residency, religious affiliation/commitment, racial/ethnic status, volunteer work, work experience. ACT with or without writing accepted. High school diploma is required and GED is accepted. *Academic units required:* 4 English, 3 math, 2 science, 2 science labs, 2 foreign language, 3 social studies, 1 history, 2 academic electives. *Academic units recommended:* 4 English, 3 math, 2 science, 2 science labs, 2 foreign language, 3 social studies, 1 history, 2 academic electives.

Financial Aid

Students should submit: FAFSA. Priority filing deadline is 2/1. The Princeton Review suggests that all financial aid forms be submitted as soon as possible after October 1. *Need-based scholarships/grants offered:* College/university scholarship or grant aid from institutional funds; Federal Nursing Scholarships; Federal Pell; Private scholarships; SEOG; State scholarships/grants. *Loan aid offered:* Direct PLUS loans; Direct Subsidized Stafford Loans; Direct Unsubsidized Stafford Loans. Applicants will be notified of awards on a rolling basis beginning 3/1. Federal Work-Study Program available. Institutional employment available.

The Inside Word

At this Jesuit Catholic school, admissions officers tend to value community service as well as overall "life experience." Those who demonstrate a significant commitment to volunteerism will find themselves at an advantage, as will those who convey a clear sense of their academic and career goals. Applicants should keep in mind that Seattle University has more stringent test score and course work requirements for certain majors.

THE SCHOOL SAYS "..."

From the Admissions Office

"Students who are adventurous, forward-thinking, creative and have an interest in social justice are drawn to Seattle University, located in the heart of a city with unparalleled access to innovation, technology, the arts and culture. Personalized learning—with an 11:1 student-faculty ratio—provides opportunities for research alongside accomplished faculty. Internships and community engagement give students relevant experience for their resumes and the chance to be noticed by some of the world's most influential nonprofits and companies that call the Seattle area home, such as Microsoft, the Gates Foundation, Starbucks, Amazon, Boeing and Costco. Seattle U is a school of action with an ever-growing impact on the city, the region and throughout the world. In Washington state, where dozens of different languages are spoken and every race, religion and perspective is represented, Seattle U's nearly 4,800 undergraduate students from 53 states and territories and 89 nations fit right in. Service is a cornerstone of the Seattle U experience with four out of five students participating in some form of service learning—that's nearly 3× the national average. That spirit is especially visible in the Seattle University Youth Initiative, recognized by the White House in 2012 with its highest recognition for community service. As the university's largest-ever community engagement project, the Youth Initiative is transforming lives of Seattle's underserved children while becoming a model of service.

"Discover Seattle University's sustainable campus, which is pesticide-free and wins top awards for its environmental leadership and energy conservation. The urban campus is woven into Seattle's thriving Capitol Hill neighborhood, which abounds with culture and entertainment options."

SELECTIVITY

Admissions Rating	82
# of applicants	8,640
% of applicants accepted	76
% of acceptees attending	17

FRESHMAN PROFILE

Range SAT EBRW	570–660
Range SAT Math	560–660
Range ACT Composite	24–30
# submitting SAT scores	800
% submitting SAT scores	74
# submitting ACT scores	419
% submitting ACT scores	39
Average HS GPA	3.6
% graduated top 10% of class	27
% graduated top 25% of class	64
% graduated top 50% of class	94

DEADLINES

Early action	
Deadline	11/15
Notification	12/23
Regular	
Priority	1/15
Notification	Rolling, 3/1
Nonfall registration?	Yes

FINANCIAL FACTS

Financial Aid Rating	85
Annual tuition	$45,765
Room and board	$12,531
Required fees	$825
Books and supplies	$1,200
Average frosh need-based scholarship	$26,998
Average UG need-based scholarship	$26,825
% needy frosh rec. need-based scholarship or grant aid	81
% needy UG rec. need-based scholarship or grant aid	89
% needy frosh rec. non-need-based scholarship or grant aid	82
% needy UG rec. non-need-based scholarship or grant aid	61
% needy frosh rec. need-based self-help aid	69
% needy UG rec. need-based self-help aid	72
% frosh rec. any financial aid	98
% UG rec. any financial aid	86
% UG borrow to pay for school	66
Average cumulative indebtedness	$36,140
% frosh need fully met	18
% ugrads need fully met	14
Average % of frosh need met	82
Average % of ugrad need met	80

SETON HALL UNIVERSITY

Office of Admission, Seton Hall, South Orange, NJ 07079 • Admissions: (800) THE HALL • Fax: 973-275-2339

CAMPUS LIFE

Quality of Life Rating	83
Fire Safety Rating	92
Green Rating	60*
Type of school	Private
Affiliation	Roman Catholic
Environment	Village

STUDENTS

Total undergrad enrollment	5,295
% male/female	41/59
% from out of state	22
% frosh from public high school	70
% frosh live on campus	74
% ugrads live on campus	41
# of fraternities	11
# of sororities	11
% African American	13
% Asian	8
% Caucasian	51
% Hispanic	16
% Native American	<1
% Pacific Islander	<1
% Two or more races	2
% Race and/or ethnicity unknown	7
% international	2
# of countries represented	71

SURVEY SAYS . . .

Easy to get around campus
College radio is popular
Everyone loves the Pirates

ACADEMICS

Academic Rating	72
% students returning for sophomore year	85
Calendar	Semester
Student/faculty ratio	14:1
Profs interesting rating	87
Profs accessible rating	91

MOST POPULAR MAJORS

Criminal Justice/Safety Studies; Communication, Journalism, and Related Programs, Other; Speech Communication and Rhetoric

STUDENTS SAY ". . ."

Academics

Founded in 1856, New Jersey's Seton Hall University is a Catholic school offering students "a chance at an affordable, quality college education" composed of challenging coursework and a "diversity of programming." The school "has a very high employment rate," and "the financial aid is wonderful." Seton Hall also features an "excellent career center," making for a good return on investment. Building on that, the proximity to New York City (about fifteen miles away) helps in the "abundance of available internships" and "the opportunity to network with Seton Hall alumni [who] are now business professionals." The Honors Program "is very thorough and well put together," the business and nursing schools are notably strong, and the school has done its share of innovating by adding features such as "one-day classes for credit, tech courses online, and money management courses," as well as group-oriented sessions where students "are allowed to stand up and freely discuss the topic at hand" rather than "being bound to a desk."

Professors are "usually experts [in] their fields" who "bring their experience into the classroom," although some students note there are a handful of "weaker professors." Accessibility is important to the faculty, and "if their office hours don't work for you, they'll come up with an alternate time or even give out their cell or suggest a Skype session." There are also "plenty of opportunities to connect with peers and find the academic help that you need" via the Academic Resource Center (ARC) and the Writing Center.

Life

This is an academically serious group that also makes time for "lots of outings to NYC and events on campus." The "environment and energy" at athletic games "draws people together," and the school "has extensive programming that allows opportunities for cultural, social, and service oriented events" while "always [providing] fun things to do on the green when the weather is nice." After class ends, many students "meet up together for lunch on or off campus" or work out; "the Rec Center is always bustling with yoga classes or intramural sports." People generally "fill their days by hanging out in various spots on campus like lounges in the dorms, the dining hall, The Cove, the Living Room, or the library." Some mention the areas around campus "can make students feel unsafe travelling off campus," but note that it's "not unsafe as long as [you are] using common sense." Weekends can involve "various social activities exclusive to Greek Life, trips hosted by the Student Activities Board into New York City, as well as club events hosted on campus." In addition, "there are so many different clubs or organizations that allow each student to find their place on campus."

Student Body

This is a "big name and small community atmosphere" in which the "empowered and ambitious students" are "fairly diverse in regards to race" and "eager to jump start their careers." "Christianity is the dominant faith" and Seton Hall's "Catholic values bring in a large range of religious students." One student adds, "It is very easy to build relationships and make connections with people outside your particular field of study." Another goes on to describe the overall feel of campus: "There's never a time I'm on campus where I don't see a friendly face," says a student, and others note that "there's a general familial air around campus." Since the campus draws many students, "there is a heavy commuter population," but those living on campus "are often members of Greek life or have a leadership position in clubs."

SETON HALL UNIVERSITY

Financial Aid: 973-761-9332 • E-Mail: thehall@shu.edu • Website: http://admissions.shu.edu/

THE PRINCETON REVIEW SAYS

Admissions

ACT with or without writing accepted. High school diploma is required and GED is accepted. *Academic units required:* 4 English, 3 math, 1 science, 1 science lab, 2 foreign language, 2 social studies, 4 academic electives.

Financial Aid

Students should submit: FAFSA. The Princeton Review suggests that all financial aid forms be submitted as soon as possible after October 1. Federal Work-Study Program available. Institutional employment available.

The Inside Word

Seton Hall accepts both its own online application and the Common Application. Students' average test scores are 1230 for the SAT and 26 for the ACT. Students with reasonably solid high school transcripts, strong recommendations, and test scores within the median range won't have trouble getting in, and Seton Hall makes an effort to sweeten the deal financially for standout students: generally, the higher a student's academic standing, the higher the scholarship award.

THE SCHOOL SAYS "..."

From the Admissions Office

"A leading Catholic university since 1856, Seton Hall educates great minds like in a challenging, supportive and rigorous environment. With approximately 6,000 undergraduate students and a 14:1 student to faculty ratio, students develop a mentoring relationship with faculty. At Seton Hall, students have unprecedented access to research, conferences, clinicals, corporate mentors, internships, study abroad and many other hands-on learning opportunities as early as freshman year. Located just 14 miles from New York City in suburban South Orange, New Jersey, Seton Hall benefits from all the opportunities the Big Apple has to offer. Seton Hall is ranked No. 4 in the nation for providing internships by *The International Business Times*. Graduates also have 50 percent higher mid-career earnings than the national average. Seton Hall offers over 17,000 internships. Students have found internships or employment upon graduation at Goldman Sachs, CNN, Pfizer, Google, the United Nations, ABC, NBC, CBS, Lockheed Martin, Morgan Stanley, *The Wall Street Journal*, HBO, Amazon, Prudential, Lincoln Center, Standard and Poor's, The State Department and *The New York Times*, as well as acclaimed hospitals, schools and nonprofit organizations. Seton Hall has been rated as one of the best schools for a return on investment and for having the highest paid graduates for the investment. Seton Hall also provides more than $96 million dollars a year in scholarships and grants to students; 98 percent of students receive some form of financial assistance from the University."

SELECTIVITY

Admissions Rating	77
# of applicants	10,180
% of applicants accepted	84
% of acceptees attending	17

FRESHMAN PROFILE

Range SAT EBRW	490–590
Range SAT Math	510–610
Range ACT Composite	22–27
# submitting SAT scores	1355
% submitting SAT scores	93
# submitting ACT scores	324
% submitting ACT scores	22
Average HS GPA	3.5
% graduated top 10% of class	37
% graduated top 25% of class	61
% graduated top 50% of class	86

DEADLINES

Early action	
Deadline	12/15
Notification	1/1
Regular	
Priority	3/1
Notification	Rolling, 11/15
Nonfall registration?	Yes

FINANCIAL FACTS

Financial Aid Rating	68
Annual tuition	$35,940
Room and board	$11,522
Required fees	$1,782
% frosh rec. any financial aid	97
% UG rec. any financial aid	97

SIENA COLLEGE

515 Loudon Road, Loudonville, NY 12211-1462 • Admissions: 518-783-2423 • Fax: 518-783-2436

STUDENTS SAY ". . ."

Academics

Siena College and its "beautiful campus [are] just the perfect distance from the city of Albany." The "small Franciscan Catholic school" is home to just over 3,000 Siena Saints who cite "many research opportunities" and "the reputation [Siena has] among peers and companies" as a few of the reasons they chose the school. Others comment on "awesome opportunities for jobs and internships in the Capital Region." One student attributes this to the school's "strong internship office and strong alumni connection." Science and Business are popular programs, but Siena offers a broad mix. "I am a physics major, and I have friends in marketing, environmental science, social work, comp sci, biochemistry, and business," shares another student. Regardless of program, students generally have high praise for the faculty, who are "not only here to teach material and lessons … they are here to mentor and help shape the path you wish to take in your future." And students appreciate that professors "are always offering office hours and one-on-one attention." On the other hand, some note that opportunities are more plentiful for those who seek them out on their own, stating, "You definitely have to work to succeed at Siena." But succeed, they do.

Life

"The best part of Siena is the sense of community both inside and outside the classroom," one student shares. "We hold the door for one another," which "is representative of Franciscan values" and contributes to an atmosphere that "feels like a big family." In daily life, academics comes first. "A typical day is usually going to class and then the library to do homework." But there's more to Siena than just work. "The student government organizations and over 100 clubs are always hosting events on campus," and activities include "international food events or free ice skating," "bingo, dances, [and] movie showings." Clubs and intramural sports are also popular, as is spending time at the "recently renovated athletic center." No matter your interests, there are opportunities to get involved. The school suggests that "Saints don't sit on the sideline," and gives students—regardless of their interests—the opportunity to get involved. In fact, the campus sidelines themselves hold chances for outlets beyond the classroom here: Nearby "Troy and Albany are fun places to go on the weekends, because there are lots of good restaurants, cafés, and bars." Overall, students agree that the "close knit community, and strong sense of tradition" at Siena help make "college feel even more like home."

Student Body

"School spirit … is amazing" at Siena, which bolsters "a strong sense of community." And Siena Saints are "passionate about service and committed to living selfless lives" outside of the classroom. The plurality of students are in the liberal arts, with the rest "divided among [the] School of Business and School of Science," but as a business major says, "Weekend activities … afford the opportunity to mix with kids from other schools (liberal arts and science)." Many students are "upper middle class [and] mostly from across New York state," which leads some to note that the school is "lacking diversity." However, "there is a big initiative toward inclusion and diversity acceptance." And the students are ready to achieve that broader acceptance, overall being "very friendly [on a] campus [where] everyone is there to help others succeed."

SIENA COLLEGE

Financial Aid: 518-783-2427 • E-Mail: admissions@siena.edu • Website: https://www.siena.edu

THE PRINCETON REVIEW SAYS

Admissions

Very important factors considered include: rigor of secondary school record, academic GPA. *Important factors considered include:* recommendation(s), interview. *Other factors considered include:* class rank, application essay, standardized test scores, extracurricular activities, talent/ability, character/personal qualities, first generation, alumni/ae relation, geographical residence, racial/ethnic status, volunteer work, work experience, level of applicant's interest. ACT with or without writing accepted. SAT with or without Essay component accepted. High school diploma is required and GED is accepted. *Academic units required:* 4 English, 3 math, 3 science, 3 science labs, 2 foreign language, 2 social studies, 2 history. *Academic units recommended:* 4 English, 4 math, 4 science, 4 science labs, 3 foreign language, 2 social studies, 2 history.

Financial Aid

Students should submit: FAFSA; State aid form. Priority filing deadline is 2/15. The Princeton Review suggests that all financial aid forms be submitted as soon as possible after October 1. *Need-based scholarships/grants offered:* College/university scholarship or grant aid from institutional funds; Federal Pell; Private scholarships; SEOG; State scholarships/grants. *Loan aid offered:* Direct Subsidized Stafford Loans; Direct Unsubsidized Stafford Loans. Applicants will be notified of awards on or about 2/15. Federal Work-Study Program available. Institutional employment available.

The Inside Word

The admissions process at Siena is fairly stringent. With a 78 percent acceptance rate and an average SAT score of 1160 for incoming freshman, admissions officers look for a strong academic record. Academic interests and extracurricular activities also play a role. Prior to applying, a campus tour or participation in an admissions program is strongly encouraged.

THE SCHOOL SAYS "..."

From the Admissions Office

"At Siena College, education isn't something you get, it's something you get to do. Located just 10 minutes from New York's state capital of Albany, the Siena experience is built for a new generation of leaders eager to create a more just, peaceful, and humane world. It empowers them through a transformative journey of intellectual, spiritual, and personal discovery. Saints have more than 1,200 unique ways to customize their degree to reach their personal and professional goals. But that's just the beginning. From internships to research to service, they get real world experience now, not later. Hundreds of student life options join with Siena's 21-sport Division I athletics program providing students the opportunity to get in the game, whatever their interests may be. Extensive study abroad programs and immersive service-learning allow for discovery and reflection. Saints are challenged ethically and morally and work closely with top scholars (100% faculty taught classes, 12:1 student-faculty ratio), taking advantage of state-of-the-art resources, and exclusive research opportunities in all fields. Siena's Franciscan, liberal arts tradition is our soul. Saints lead by putting others first, thinking creatively, and developing innovative solutions that make the world a better place. Saints succeed. A Siena education provides access to a powerful and connected alumni network. The average salary after attending is $57,100. Nearly 90 percent of alumni say their job allows them to make a positive contribution to society. Are you ready to get off the sidelines?"

SELECTIVITY

Admissions Rating	76
# of applicants	7,728
% of applicants accepted	81
% of acceptees attending	13

FRESHMAN PROFILE

Range SAT EBRW	530–630
Range SAT Math	540–650
Range SAT Composite	1080–1260
Range ACT Composite	22–28
# submitting SAT scores	546
% submitting SAT scores	65
# submitting ACT scores	113
% submitting ACT scores	14
Average HS GPA	3.5
% graduated top 10% of class	19
% graduated top 25% of class	51
% graduated top 50% of class	88

DEADLINES

Early decision	
Deadline	12/1
Notification	1/1
Early action	
Deadline	12/1
Notification	1/7
Regular	
Deadline	3/1
Notification	3/15
Nonfall registration?	Yes

APPLICANTS ALSO LOOK AT AND OFTEN PREFER

Marist College; St. John's University (NY); State University of New York—Binghamton University; State University of New York College at Oneonta; State University of New York—University at Albany; State University of New York—University at Buffalo

AND SOMETIMES PREFER

Le Moyne College; Sacred Heart University; State University of New York at Geneseo; State University of New York—New Paltz

AND RARELY PREFER

Fairfield University; Quinnipiac University; State University of New York—Plattsburgh; State University of New York—Stony Brook University

FINANCIAL FACTS

Financial Aid Rating	89
Annual tuition	$39,200
Room and board	$15,915
Required fees	$975
Books and supplies	$1,293
Average frosh need-based scholarship	$26,609
Average UG need-based scholarship	$24,358
% needy frosh rec. need-based scholarship or grant aid	100
% needy UG rec. need-based scholarship or grant aid	100
% needy frosh rec. non-need-based scholarship or grant aid	97
% needy UG rec. non-need-based scholarship or grant aid	96
% needy frosh rec. need-based self-help aid	73
% needy UG rec. need-based self-help aid	77
% frosh rec. any financial aid	98
% UG rec. any financial aid	93
% frosh need fully met	34
% ugrads need fully met	31
Average % of frosh need met	80
Average % of ugrad need met	80

SIMMONS UNIVERSITY

300 The Fenway, Boston, MA 02115 • Admissions: 617-521-2051

STUDENTS SAY "..."

Academics

Located in the middle of Boston, the all-women Simmons University is a liberal arts center, offering its 1,800 undergraduates more than sixty majors and programs, including a well-known nursing school, as well as some that are "pretty uncommon, like library science and children's literature." Some courses require field trips and city exploration or internships relevant to the course, while others involve projects that "place students in volunteering jobs to work with the surrounding communities." "Classes involve significant amounts of discussions and presentations," and with small class sizes, students generally get to know all of their peers. Similarly, students enjoy "the ability to create strong personal relationships with professors and advisors" and say that teachers "truly are there for you as human beings, not just professors."

The workload is "heavy, but always doable" at Simmons, and clinicals tend to let students in earlier than many other schools would. "Labs go above and beyond" here, and the school incorporates video lectures into its courses "so that class periods can be more discussion-based." One student says, "Even as a first-year I have already been given multiple research opportunities that amaze and excite me." There are many accelerated programs to which undergraduate students can apply in order to achieve a graduate degree at a faster rate (many at Simmons go on to graduate school), and employers are well-aware of the school's curriculum, which requires every student to partake in "at least one internship, clinical, research [project], or other type of real-world learning." "When I say I attend Simmons, people know I have received a quality education," says a student.

Life

There are two campuses at Simmons: academic and residential. The academic campus has "lots of places to study," such as the library, multicultural center, and cafés, but most students stay on the residential campus when classes aren't going on, and more than half live there. Most in this "nomadic bunch" like to use their free time to explore Boston and surrounding neighborhoods, including nearby Fenway Park. "I spend my days living my best city life," says a student. There are no parties on this "very academics-oriented" campus, especially given the "strict drug and alcohol policy." This is a campus of "all-around intellectuals who are serious about their careers after university [who] will more likely be found studying than partying." A lot of students work "either on campus or in hospitals or restaurants." Boston sporting events are popular pastimes, as is going to the gym, and "there is always something to do off campus." Almost all students go out into the city only on weekends, as "there usually isn't anything going on on-campus," and they get discounts or free admission to many events or institutions, like the Museum of Fine Arts and the Isabella Stewart Gardener Museum, "both of which are right down the street from campus."

Student Body

The women here are "generally highly liberal and outspoken," and "you have to find your niche." Students at Simmons are typically "advocates for a number of causes" and are extremely political. A huge number are healthcare majors, and everyone is "incredibly passionate and intelligent [and] invested in the community." This group is "very centered around acceptance of various identities as well as female empowerment," and "there is a theme of personal growth reflected in the gender identity."

Financial Aid: 617-521-2001 • E-Mail: sfs@simmons.edu • Website: www.simmons.edu

THE PRINCETON REVIEW SAYS

Admissions

Very important factors considered include: rigor of secondary school record, academic GPA, application essay, standardized test scores, recommendation(s). *Important factors considered include:* extracurricular activities. *Other factors considered include:* class rank, interview, volunteer work, work experience. ACT with or without writing accepted. SAT with or without Essay component accepted. High school diploma is required and GED is accepted. *Academic units required:* 4 English, 4 math, 3 science, 3 foreign language, 3 social studies, 3 history.

Financial Aid

Students should submit: FAFSA. Priority filing deadline is 11/1. The Princeton Review suggests that all financial aid forms be submitted as soon as possible after October 1. *Need-based scholarships/grants offered:* College/university scholarship or grant aid from institutional funds; Federal Pell; Private scholarships; SEOG; State scholarships/grants. *Loan aid offered:* Direct PLUS loans; Direct Subsidized Stafford Loans; Direct Unsubsidized Stafford Loans. Applicants will be notified of awards on a rolling basis beginning 12/19. Federal Work-Study Program available.

The Inside Word

Simmons evaluates prospective students on both academic strength and personal qualities, including community involvement or leadership. Applicants to Simmons should use their personal essays, letters of recommendation, and applications to show the admissions committee who they are as a person. Although a personal interview isn't required, it can be a great way to augment your application, as well as a chance to experience the unique environment at Simmons. Please note, Simmons will be test-optional for those applying for spring or fall 2021, due to limits in standardized test taking.

THE SCHOOL SAYS "..."

From the Admissions Office

"Simmons University helps students find their passion and build successful careers through an education that combines liberal arts and sciences with professional preparation. We empower women who are intellectually curious, ambitious, and socially conscious to become leaders in their careers, communities, and beyond.

"Located in the heart of Boston, Simmons is best known for its small classes, access to faculty, and internship and research opportunities. Students say that Simmons's location offers the best of both worlds—an intimate college experience in the heart of a vibrant city. Simmons's nearly 2,000 undergraduates love the fact that they can easily access the city's rich social and cultural resources but also come home to a safe, friendly campus.

"Simmons offers a learning experience that is highly collaborative and much more personal than that of large universities. Simmons professors include distinguished researchers, published authors, Fulbright scholars, health professionals, and community leaders. Seventy percent of faculty are women, and nearly 100 percent hold a terminal degree. They advise numerous government, nonprofit, and corporate organizations in the United States and in the world.

"To help students succeed, career support starts as soon as students step on campus and continues as an ongoing, lifelong service. Ninety-one percent of Simmons graduates are employed or in graduate school within six months of graduation. As the only women's university in Boston, employers see Simmons as a beacon of leadership with a reputation for professionalism and well-prepared graduates."

SELECTIVITY

Admissions Rating	82
# of applicants	2,933
% of applicants accepted	73
% of acceptees attending	20

FRESHMAN PROFILE

Range SAT EBRW	570–660
Range SAT Math	540–630
Range ACT Composite	23–29
# submitting SAT scores	393
% submitting SAT scores	88
# submitting ACT scores	50
% submitting ACT scores	12
Average HS GPA	3.9
% graduated top 10% of class	28
% graduated top 25% of class	69
% graduated top 50% of class	72

DEADLINES

Early action	
Deadline	11/1
Notification	12/15
Early action II	
Deadline	12/1
Notification	1/15
Regular	
Deadline	2/1
Notification	Rolling, 2/15
Nonfall registration?	Yes

FINANCIAL FACTS

Financial Aid Rating	87
Annual tuition	$42,080
Room and board	$15,660
Required fees	$1,250
Books and supplies	$1,280
Average frosh need-based scholarship	$32,347
Average UG need-based scholarship	$30,651
% needy frosh rec. need-based scholarship or grant aid	99
% needy UG rec. need-based scholarship or grant aid	100
% needy frosh rec. non-need-based scholarship or grant aid	29
% needy UG rec. non-need-based scholarship or grant aid	15
% needy frosh rec. need-based self-help aid	68
% needy UG rec. need-based self-help aid	81
% frosh rec. any financial aid	82
% UG rec. any financial aid	75
% UG borrow to pay for school	77
Average cumulative indebtedness	$37,935
% frosh need fully met	35
% ugrads need fully met	20
Average % of frosh need met	86
Average % of ugrad need met	79

SKIDMORE COLLEGE

815 North Broadway, Saratoga Springs, NY 12866-1632 • Admissions: 518-580-5570 • Fax: 518-580-5584

CAMPUS LIFE

Quality of Life Rating	93
Fire Safety Rating	98
Green Rating	94
Type of school	Private
Environment	Town

STUDENTS

Total undergrad enrollment	2,649
% male/female	40/60
% from out of state	66
% frosh from public high school	58
% frosh live on campus	100
% ugrads live on campus	89
# of fraternities	0
# of sororities	0
% African American	5
% Asian	6
% Caucasian	62
% Hispanic	9
% Native American	<1
% Pacific Islander	0
% Two or more races	5
% Race and/or ethnicity unknown	2
% international	11
# of countries represented	65

SURVEY SAYS ...

Lots of liberal students
Students are happy
Great library
Internships are widely available
Great financial aid
Students aren't religious
Students environmentally aware
Students love Saratoga Springs, NY
Great food on campus
Great off-campus food
Dorms are like palaces
Easy to get around campus
Theater is popular

ACADEMICS

Academic Rating	91
% students returning for sophomore year	91
% students graduating within 4 years	85
% students graduating within 6 years	89
Calendar	Semester
Student/faculty ratio	8:1
Profs interesting rating	92
Profs accessible rating	95

Most classes have 10–19 students.
Most lab/discussion sessions have 10–19 students.

MOST POPULAR MAJORS

English Language and Literature, General; Psychology, General; Business/Commerce, General

STUDENTS SAY "..."

Academics

Just thirty miles north of Albany lies Skidmore College, a small liberal arts school that is home to around 2,500 students. Skidmore thrives on combining academics with creative expression, and the school works to cultivate students who want to explore ideas across traditional disciplinary boundaries. "The pursuit of knowledge is valued here," says a student, so "you won't be barred from an academic department just because you aren't enrolled in it." Another student states that the school is "excellent when it comes to every path or field of study," and "you can pursue everything you are interested in." This all happens in classrooms run by "very helpful, understanding, motivating," and "understanding faculty who know that we are human beings before we are students." Students also enjoy "small class sizes [that] allow for the formation of impactful and lasting relationships." Furthermore, "all teachers are accessible outside the classroom," which helps teaching extend beyond the traditional four walls. Other examples of this include "environmental studies [classes that] take place in the North Woods" and an artist interview class "in which each student chooses an artist they admire and [interview] that artist." One student sums up the Skidmore academic experience by saying, "Learning feels important and productive towards society."

Life

People "are constantly on the go at Skidmore," but this "doesn't mean that students ... don't take care of themselves." A typical day involves "going to classes, eating meals with friends, ... meeting for a group project, studying in the library, maybe [taking] a nap, and getting outdoors." The outdoorsy crowd find great joy with the Adirondack Mountains and Lake George being just about an hour away. Those looking to stay a little closer to campus also have options: Saratoga Springs, which some call "an amazing town" to be near, is just a ten-minute walk from campus. And Boston, New York City, and Montreal are just a few hours away as well. Regardless of whether they're spent on campus or off, days are "always full of activity and connection," and there are more than one hundred student clubs and organizations, making it "easy to integrate and be part of the community." Those clubs "host tons of lectures and events for students," and "the arts are a huge strength at Skidmore." Anywhere you look, "students are constantly collaborating and playing shows," and there is "a good culture of attending events on campus and supporting the student body."

Student Body

This is an "active and involved" student body, with the average Skidmore student having "at least a major and a minor [and getting] involved in multiple clubs, [while] probably working more than one job as well." One member of this "well-rounded and over accomplished" group says, "Skidmore is the school for students who want to do it all." Plus, it's a place where everyone is "super welcoming and friendly" with a student body that "puts the 'liberal' in liberal arts." That's all representative of the "drive for creativity" on campus and the fact that students "support creativity in one another." As one student jokes, "there are more shades of hair here (mostly unnatural) than there are people." But despite any differences, everyone at Skidmore "has 'their people' and is welcome in many other circles and friend groups as well."

SKIDMORE COLLEGE

Financial Aid: 518-580-5750 • E-Mail: admissions@skidmore.edu • Website: www.skidmore.edu

THE PRINCETON REVIEW SAYS

Admissions

Very important factors considered include: rigor of secondary school record. *Important factors considered include:* class rank, academic GPA, application essay, recommendation(s), extracurricular activities, talent/ability, character/personal qualities, volunteer work. *Other factors considered include:* standardized test scores, interview, first generation, alumni/ae relation, geographical residence, racial/ethnic status. ACT with or without writing accepted. SAT with or without Essay component accepted. High school diploma is required and GED is accepted. *Academic units recommended:* 4 English, 4 math, 4 science, 3 science labs, 4 foreign language, 4 social studies.

Financial Aid

Students should submit: CSS/Financial Aid PROFILE; Noncustodial PROFILE. The Princeton Review suggests that all financial aid forms be submitted as soon as possible after October 1. *Need-based scholarships/grants offered:* College/university scholarship or grant aid from institutional funds; Federal Pell; Private scholarships; SEOG; State scholarships/grants. *Loan aid offered:* Direct PLUS loans; Direct Subsidized Stafford Loans; Direct Unsubsidized Stafford Loans. Applicants will be notified of awards on or about 4/1. Federal Work-Study Program available. Institutional employment available.

The Inside Word

Admission to Skidmore is highly competitive, and the admissions staff carefully considers each applicant's academic background. Consistent with their motto ("Creative Thought Matters"), Skidmore carefully reviews a student's extracurricular talents, achievements, and passions when making decisions. Standardized tests are optional in most cases, and students should check with the school for exceptions. While admissions interviews aren't a requirement for Skidmore applicants, students may request a personal interview on campus or with an alumnus in their area.

THE SCHOOL SAYS "..."

From the Admissions Office

"At Skidmore, we believe a great education is about putting academic theory and creative expression into practice; hence, our belief that creative thought matters. It's a place where faculty and students work together, then figure out how to use what they've learned to make a difference. This often leads to multidisciplinary approaches, where students carry more than one major, student-faculty research is common, most students study abroad, and service learning courses, internships and community service are standard. Skidmore students develop into independent, creative problem-solvers who aren't restricted to looking at things in traditional ways. This personal journey starts with the First-Year Experience—fifty seminars from which to choose, faculty and peer mentors and planned gatherings beyond the classroom. It's meant to ensure that first-year students hit the ground running on day one, connected and involved. When it comes to your major, you can choose from 44 offerings in the sciences, social sciences, arts and humanities, as well as pre-professional fields like management and business. Since we have no fraternities or sororities, student life centers on the 120 student clubs and organizations, which range from the Environmental Action Club to a capella groups to snowboarding. Add to this the prominence of the arts, which has long set Skidmore apart. Science classes collaborate on exhibits at the Tang Museum. Hundreds of students perform, often in the Zankel Music Center. Enroll in dance courses. Do theater performances. Most are not even arts majors. At Skidmore, the arts don't dominate, they permeate. As for location, who wouldn't want to go to college in Saratoga Springs? A downtown brimming with shops, galleries, coffeehouses, and great restaurants. Boston, New York City, and Montreal are a three-hour car ride from campus. The Adirondacks, Berkshires, and Green Mountains provide opportunities for skiing, mountain biking, hiking, rock-climbing, and kayaking."

SELECTIVITY	
Admissions Rating	94
# of applicants	11,102
% of applicants accepted	30
% of acceptees attending	22
# offered a place on the wait list	2,184
% accepting a place on wait list	47
# of early decision applicants	631
% accepted early decision	58

FRESHMAN PROFILE	
Range SAT EBRW	610–700
Range SAT Math	610–700
Range SAT Composite	1230–1390
Range ACT Composite	28–32
# submitting SAT scores	390
% submitting SAT scores	53
# submitting ACT scores	159
% submitting ACT scores	22
% graduated top 10% of class	32
% graduated top 25% of class	62
% graduated top 50% of class	90

DEADLINES	
Early decision	
Deadline	11/15
Notification	12/15
Other ED Deadline	1/15
Other ED Notification	2/15
Regular	
Deadline	1/15
Notification	4/1
Nonfall registration?	No

APPLICANTS ALSO LOOK AT AND OFTEN PREFER
Wesleyan University

AND SOMETIMES PREFER
Connecticut College; New York University

AND RARELY PREFER
University of Vermont

FINANCIAL FACTS	
Financial Aid Rating	97
Annual tuition	$55,136
Room and board	$15,000
Required fees	$1,186
Books and supplies	$1,300
Average frosh need-based scholarship	$46,850
Average UG need-based scholarship	$47,800
% needy frosh rec. need-based scholarship or grant aid	100
% needy UG rec. need-based scholarship or grant aid	100
% needy frosh rec. non-need-based scholarship or grant aid	4
% needy UG rec. non-need-based scholarship or grant aid	4
% needy frosh rec. need-based self-help aid	94
% needy UG rec. need-based self-help aid	92
% frosh rec. any financial aid	63
% UG rec. any financial aid	53
% UG borrow to pay for school	34
Average cumulative indebtedness	$31,381
% frosh need fully met	100
% ugrads need fully met	97
Average % of frosh need met	100
Average % of ugrad need met	99

SMITH COLLEGE

7 College Lane, Northampton, MA 01063 • Admissions: 413-585-2500 • Fax: 413-585-2527

CAMPUS LIFE
Quality of Life Rating	89
Fire Safety Rating	84
Green Rating	91
Type of school	Private
Environment	Town

STUDENTS
Total undergrad enrollment	2,484
% male/female	0/100
% from out of state	81
% frosh from public high school	62
% frosh live on campus	100
% ugrads live on campus	95
# of sororities	0
% African American	7
% Asian	9
% Caucasian	48
% Hispanic	12
% Native American	<1
% Pacific Islander	<1
% Two or more races	5
% Race and/or ethnicity unknown	6
% international	14
# of countries represented	59

SURVEY SAYS . . .
Lots of liberal students
Classroom facilities are great
Lab facilities are great
Career services are great
Internships are widely available
Class discussions encouraged
Great financial aid
No one cheats
Students environmentally aware
Recreation facilities are great
Alumni active on campus
Active minority support groups
Active student-run political groups

ACADEMICS
Academic Rating	94
% students returning for sophomore year	93
% students graduating within 4 years	82
% students graduating within 6 years	88
Calendar	Semester
Student/faculty ratio	8:1
Profs interesting rating	93
Profs accessible rating	96
Most classes have 10–19 students.	

MOST POPULAR MAJORS
Economics, General; Political Science and Government, General; Psychology, General

STUDENTS SAY "..."

Academics

Smith College is "an incredibly prestigious, diverse, academically rigorous, socially liberal, and well-respected institution," located in the consummate college town of Northampton, Massachusetts. A Smith education is all about "finding and pursuing your passions." Offering "academic freedom," "Smith doesn't have course requirements" beyond the major, other than a writing-intensive course for first-years, and "self-scheduled finals" allow students to take exam week at their own pace. "One of the most prominent women's colleges in the country," Smith "builds the self-confidence of smart women," and "most classes, even in math and sciences, are very interdisciplinary and often have a feminist bias." Classes are "engaging and promote critical thought," and professors are "inspiring, dynamic, accessible, and brilliant." Smith professors "care deeply about students" and "take the time to get to know you on a first-name basis." Smith also offers fabulous academic facilities and "countless resources" to augment your education, including a "wonderful study abroad department" and ample opportunities for research. There's "a large number of undergrads doing serious scientific research" in addition to course work. If they can't find what they need amid Smith's ample course selection, students "can take classes at the other four schools nearby (UMass Amherst, Amherst College, Hampshire College, and Mount Holyoke College)" through the Five College Consortium. When graduation approaches, Smith students benefit from the school's "excellent alumnae network." "The Career Development Office will do everything in its power to help you get a job."

Life

Smith attracts hardworking and idealistic students, who are "striving to succeed in our classes, as well as make a difference in the Smith College community and the outside community." There's a decided "focus on academics" at Smith, and most students "study, write papers, rehearse, or practice the majority of the time." Students augment course work with "lectures and symposium on campus," as well as "involvement in community service and activism for global issues, women's rights, LGBTQ rights, the environment, and pretty much anything that fights oppression." When they want to relax, Smithies can attend "free movies and concerts, plays, speakers, sports events, and dances," as well as "school-sponsored house parties almost every weekend." When they want to branch out or rub elbows with the opposite sex, students "go to other college parties at surrounding campuses," or head out in Northampton, which is "always bustling" with "concerts, restaurants, and cute shops." The "quality of life is outstanding" on campus, where "the dorms are not dorms but beautiful houses," and cafeteria food is a cut above the average.

Student Body

"Smithies are passionate about everything they do," especially academics. Throughout the semester, undergraduates are known to "study hard" and get "ridiculously stressed" about course work. "It's the nature of Smithies to be driven, but we all want to see our friends and housemates succeed as well." Smith's unique environment attracts "a great mix of nerdy, edgy, [and] traditional" students, including "hipsters, WASPs, crazy partiers, international students, and the average New Englander." Fortunately, there's a "strong sense of community," and "students fit in easily, even if they have different interests." Despite diversity, "one thing all students have in common here is the will for women's empowerment and acceptance of any gender or sexual preference." On that note, many students "love the queer life on campus," where some students are either gay or have "a fluid perception of sexuality." Though there's some political diversity on campus, most Smithies hold "very liberal views," and many are "very conscious and aware, not only of their community but the world in general."

Financial Aid: 413-585-2530 • E-Mail: admission@smith.edu • Website: www.smith.edu

THE PRINCETON REVIEW SAYS

Admissions

Very important factors considered include: rigor of secondary school record, academic GPA, application essay, recommendation(s), character/personal qualities. *Important factors considered include:* class rank, interview, extracurricular activities, talent/ability. *Other factors considered include:* standardized test scores, first generation, alumni/ae relation, racial/ethnic status, volunteer work, work experience. ACT with or without writing accepted. SAT with or without Essay component accepted. High school diploma or equivalent is not required *Academic units recommended:* 4 English, 3 math, 3 science, 3 science labs, 3 foreign language, 2 history, 1 academic elective.

Financial Aid

Students should submit: CSS/Financial Aid PROFILE; FAFSA; Institution's own financial aid form; Noncustodial PROFILE. The Princeton Review suggests that all financial aid forms be submitted as soon as possible after October 1. *Need-based scholarships/grants offered:* College/university scholarship or grant aid from institutional funds; Federal Pell; Private scholarships; SEOG; State scholarships/grants. *Loan aid offered:* Direct PLUS loans; Direct Subsidized Stafford Loans; Direct Unsubsidized Stafford Loans. Applicants will be notified of awards on or about 4/1. Federal Work-Study Program available. Institutional employment available.

The Inside Word

Every prospective Smithie is carefully evaluated by at least two members of the admissions staff. No hard numbers guarantee admission: Smith is looking for students who will succeed academically and socially in college, evaluating each applicant for both personal and intellectual qualities. To best prepare for admission, Smith recommends that students follow a rigorous college prep curriculum in high school. If you're feeling particularly enthused about your future at Smith, you can become a fan of the admissions department on Facebook, take the online tour, or read student blogs on the admission page.

THE SCHOOL SAYS "..."

From the Admissions Office

"Smith students choose from 1,000 courses in more than fifty areas of study. There are no specific course requirements outside the major; students meet individually with faculty advisers to plan a balanced curriculum. Smith programs offer unique opportunities, including interdisciplinary concentrations, the chance to study abroad, or at another college in the United States, and a semester in Washington, D.C. The Ada Comstock Scholars Program encourages women beyond the traditional age to return to college and complete their undergraduate studies. Smith is located in the scenic Connecticut River valley of western Massachusetts near a number of other outstanding educational institutions. Through the Five College Consortium, Smith, Amherst, Hampshire, and Mount Holyoke colleges, and the University of Massachusetts enrich their academic, social, and cultural offerings by means of joint faculty appointments, joint courses, student and faculty exchanges, shared facilities, and other cooperative arrangements. Smith has the largest and oldest women-only ABET-accredited engineering program in the country; it's also the only college in the country that offers a guaranteed paid internship program ('Praxis')."

SELECTIVITY

Admissions Rating	96
# of applicants	5,780
% of applicants accepted	31
% of acceptees attending	36
# offered a place on the wait list	923
% accepting a place on wait list	50
% admitted from wait list	15
# of early decision applicants	578
% accepted early decision	49

FRESHMAN PROFILE

Range SAT EBRW	670–750
Range SAT Math	670–770
Range ACT Composite	31–34
# submitting SAT scores	262
% submitting SAT scores	43
# submitting ACT scores	185
% submitting ACT scores	30
Average HS GPA	4.0
% graduated top 10% of class	72
% graduated top 25% of class	96
% graduated top 50% of class	100

DEADLINES

Early decision	
Deadline	11/15
Notification	12/15
Other ED Deadline	1/1
Other ED Notification	1/31
Regular	
Deadline	1/15
Notification	3/31
Nonfall registration?	No

FINANCIAL FACTS

Financial Aid Rating	97
Annual tuition	$53,940
Room and board	$18,130
Required fees	$284
Books and supplies	$800
Average frosh need-based scholarship	$50,491
Average UG need-based scholarship	$52,924
% needy frosh rec. need-based scholarship or grant aid	96
% needy UG rec. need-based scholarship or grant aid	97
% needy frosh rec. non-need-based scholarship or grant aid	3
% needy UG rec. non-need-based scholarship or grant aid	2
% needy frosh rec. need-based self-help aid	90
% needy UG rec. need-based self-help aid	93
% frosh rec. any financial aid	70
% UG rec. any financial aid	71
% UG borrow to pay for school	58
Average cumulative indebtedness	$22,083
% frosh need fully met	100
% ugrads need fully met	100
Average % of frosh need met	100
Average % of ugrad need met	100

SONOMA STATE UNIVERSITY

1801 East Cotati Avenue, Rohnert Park, CA 94928 • Admissions: 707-664-2778 • Fax: 707-664-2060

STUDENTS SAY ". . ."

Academics

A member of the reputable California state university system, Sonoma State University distinguishes itself from similar institutions through its low-key atmosphere and strong "focus on undergraduates." Employing "teachers who are willing to take the time to make a difference in students' lives," SSU limits most classes to fewer than fifty, giving students the opportunity to "develop close and meaningful relationships with professors and classmates that will continue even after graduation." During class time, professors often "allow open discussions and emphasize a comfortable, safe environment to express oneself." After class, they "are always available through e-mail or in person during their office hours." Most SSU instructors are excellent in the classroom, but the school is big enough that you'll find "a wide variety of professors, ranging from spectacular to pretty poor." Fortunately, professors are generally "experts in their field" and "stay up to date on current events that affect our field of study." While students benefit from a very low in-state tuition, SSU has been affected by California budget cuts, and the resulting unit cap "makes it almost impossible to graduate in four years." The school could also improve some of its bureaucratic processes; for example, the class "registration process is notoriously buggy." For those hoping to stay in California after graduation, "Sonoma County and the city of San Francisco are two places very rich in career opportunities for Sonoma State students."

Life

SSU boasts a "gorgeous campus" and "impressive" facilities, including "incredible" dormitories and "a new rec center with [a] climbing wall and indoor courts, as well as outside fields." A current student enthuses, "Just come look at the housing and you realize that Sonoma is trying to make everyone as comfortable as possible." With its "beautiful setting in the heart of wine country," "the pace here seems to be a slower one, which creates a peaceful and calm environment to take classes and study in; the stress level here is relatively low." After class, students might "hang out by the pools" or study in the "many little redwood groves" around campus. "There are hundreds of clubs" on campus, including many popular Greek organizations, and, for those with a little initiative, "the leadership opportunities are endless." Off campus, surrounding Rohnert Park is a "more suburban" environment, so "it is difficult to go anywhere unless you have a car." With a set of wheels, students love to take day trips to San Francisco, or go miniature golfing, hiking, and bowling nearby. "Outdoor activities are abundant year-round" and, for those of legal drinking age, "there are also a lot of wineries and vineyards to go wine tasting!" Come the weekend, "a lot of students like to party," while others "enjoy on-campus activities like midnight improv and free movies."

Students

"Many students pick Sonoma because it is close to home," whether they live on campus or commute. Southern Californians and other in-staters round out the largely "Bay Area" crowd, and there are a number of older students mixed in with traditional undergrads. In broad strokes, "most students here come from middle- to upper-class backgrounds, and they are all fairly down-to-earth and really very nice and socially aware." More superficially, you'll notice "a lot of white girls wearing yoga pants, Nike shocks, and drinking Starbucks coffee." That said, "everyone has their own thing" at SSU. Though the school is "not really racially diverse" there is an "eclectic group of students," making it easy to fit in. A wise junior advises, "The important thing is to find your passions, your niche, and pursue it. In the process, you'll come upon like-minded students who share the same interests." "Most of the students here are part of the Greek life," telling us that fraternities and sororities are the best way to make friends and have fun (though others complain that "Greeks feel like they run the school," to the detriment of non-affiliated students). Even if you don't pledge, "the residential community helps build great friendships" for those who live on campus, and "because everyone is friendly most people find it easy to make friends."

SONOMA STATE UNIVERSITY

Financial Aid: 707-664-2389 • E-Mail: student.outreach@sonoma.edu • Website: www.sonoma.edu

THE PRINCETON REVIEW SAYS

Admissions

Very important factors considered include: academic GPA, standardized test scores. *Other factors considered include:* geographical residence. ACT with or without writing accepted. High school diploma is required and GED is accepted. *Academic units required:* 4 English, 3 math, 2 science, 1 science lab, 2 foreign language, 2 history, 1 academic elective, 1 visual/performing arts, 1 unit from above areas or other academic areas.

Financial Aid

Students should submit: FAFSA. Priority filing deadline is 3/2. The Princeton Review suggests that all financial aid forms be submitted as soon as possible after October 1. *Need-based scholarships/grants offered:* College/university scholarship or grant aid from institutional funds; Federal Pell; Private scholarships; SEOG; State scholarships/grants; United Negro College Fund. *Loan aid offered:* Direct PLUS loans; Direct Subsidized Stafford Loans; Direct Unsubsidized Stafford Loans. Applicants will be notified of awards on a rolling basis beginning 3/25. Federal Work-Study Program available. Institutional employment available.

The Inside Word

SSU makes admissions decisions based on an "eligibility index" number, which is calculated using a student's standardized test scores and GPA; note that honors and advanced placement course work is weighted more heavily than regular courses in calculating a grade point average. Because of the school's budget problems, students applying for admission to impacted majors must meet a higher index number. Currently, impacted majors include communication studies, biology, kinesiology, liberal studies, pre-nursing, and psychology.

THE SCHOOL SAYS "..."

From the Admissions Office

"Sonoma State University occupies 269 acres in the beautiful wine country of Sonoma county, in northern California. Located at the foot of the Sonoma hills, the campus is an hour's drive north of San Francisco and centrally located between the Pacific Ocean to the west and the wine country to the north and east. SSU is deeply committed to the teaching of the liberal arts and sciences with selected professional programs. Within its thirty-four academic departments, SSU awards bachelor's degrees in forty-six areas of specialization and master's degrees in fifteen areas. In addition, the university offers a joint master's degree in mathematics with San Francisco State University and a joint Ed.D. with UC Davis.

"All freshmen applicants are required to provide SAT or ACT scores."

SELECTIVITY

Admissions Rating	74
# of applicants	14,129
% of applicants accepted	92
% of acceptees attending	14

FRESHMAN PROFILE

Range SAT EBRW	490–590
Range SAT Math	490–580
Range ACT Composite	18–23
# submitting SAT scores	1,596
% submitting SAT scores	89
# submitting ACT scores	653
% submitting ACT scores	36
Average HS GPA	3.2

DEADLINES

Regular	
Priority	3/1
Deadline	11/30
Notification	3/1
Nonfall registration?	Yes

FINANCIAL FACTS

Financial Aid Rating	80
Annual in-state tuition	$5,742
Annual out-of-state tuition	$17,622
Room and board	$13,960
Required fees	$2,056
Books and supplies	$1,916
Average frosh need-based scholarship	$10,887
Average UG need-based scholarship	$10,192
% needy frosh rec. need-based scholarship or grant aid	71
% needy UG rec. need-based scholarship or grant aid	73
% needy frosh rec. non-need-based scholarship or grant aid	36
% needy UG rec. non-need-based scholarship or grant aid	36
% needy frosh rec. need-based self-help aid	54
% needy UG rec. need-based self-help aid	55
% frosh rec. any financial aid	59
% UG rec. any financial aid	51
% frosh need fully met	6
% ugrads need fully met	5
Average % of frosh need met	57
Average % of ugrad need met	55

SOUTHERN METHODIST UNIVERSITY

P.O. Box 750181, Dallas, TX 75275-0181 • Admissions: 214-768-2058 • Fax: 214-768-0103

STUDENTS SAY "..."

Academics

Located on a tree-lined, "beautiful campus" in the heart of Dallas, Southern Methodist University is a mid-size private university with a lot going on. The school has a "unique culture" that relies on "top academics" and a "long-standing history of strong traditions" to build "incredible alumni support," which in turn brings students excellent internship and job opportunities. SMU offers everything "from a great social life and extracurricular activities to fun and interesting classes," including a "phenomenal business school" and "amazing" facilities. The school prides itself on being "a close-knit community of the intellectually elite," and this translates into "a wealth of academic resources [with which] to be successful, a flood of opportunities for those who want them, and thus a community of intellectuals who happen to genuinely care about each other." Professors are "incredibly gifted in their fields and exceptional communicators." They "love interacting with students" and "are willing to put in extra time to convey the material accurately to students." "If their office hours don't match yours, they will change their schedule to accommodate people," says a student. Most have worked in the industry that they teach in, and therefore they "can offer real-life connections to the material we learn." The syllabus is also modeled "to what you'll face in the real world." The legion of SMU alumni provides excellent connections into the business world (among others), and a "dedicated career services center" only sweetens the employment pot. Since many attend SMU for the Cox School of Business, it helps that the school is in the ideal location "to secure great jobs with Fortune 500 companies right here in Dallas." The school's administration also "understands that studying abroad, internships, extracurriculars, etc., also play a crucial role in developing students into the adults and professionals they want to become." "SMU puts the 'classy' back in classical education," says a student.

Life

Despite the fact it is located in the heart of Dallas, "the atmosphere is very calm and relaxing." SMU students frequently head to uptown Dallas "for fine dining and dancing" and often see movies, shop, and attend concerts and sports games. Everyone is always on campus for the football games for "boulevarding" ("basically tailgating but on steroids"), and "we love to have alums come visit us for the tailgate," says a student. Students generally fit in with this "vibrant social life" best once they have found an extracurricular organization that is right for them, and oftentimes "sororities and fraternities tend to be this venue." However, some wish there was "less emphasis on Greek Life," since "if you're not Greek, you can sometimes feel left out or looked down on." Students devote a large portion of their time to their studies, but "there is always a social event every weekend night to blow off steam." This heavy concentration on future careers means that most here are "definitely wanting to become leaders in their field or profession," so "fraternity parties and formals are popular, but at the same time, so are speeches from prominent members of the community and theatrical performances."

Student Body

This student body is "happy and leads a balanced life" at a school that it loves. Most students at SMU "tend to be a bit preppy," "polite," and tend to come from "influential backgrounds." Many "work a lot for pay or do internships," take a lot of class hours, "are involved...and have fun a lot." "They are very busy people, and they prefer it that way," says one student. All of these "motivated, outgoing," people "thrive on leadership" and are "dedicated to academics and involvement, both at SMU and in the greater community." Fashion "is a big part of SMU culture." This group is "very social" and frequently interacts with the Dallas community and "amazing arts and restaurant scene around campus."

SOUTHERN METHODIST UNIVERSITY

Financial Aid: 214-768-3417 • E-Mail: ugadmission@smu.edu • Website: www.smu.edu

THE PRINCETON REVIEW SAYS

Admissions

Very important factors considered include: rigor of secondary school record, academic GPA, application essay, standardized test scores, recommendation(s). *Important factors considered include:* class rank, extracurricular activities, talent/ability, character/personal qualities. *Other factors considered include:* first generation, alumni/ae relation, racial/ethnic status, volunteer work, work experience, level of applicant's interest. ACT with or without writing accepted. SAT with or without Essay component accepted. High school diploma is required and GED is not accepted. *Academic units required:* 4 English, 3 math, 3 science, 2 science labs, 2 foreign language, 3 social studies. *Academic units recommended:* 4 English, 4 math, 3 science, 2 science labs, 3 foreign language, 3 history, 3 academic electives.

Financial Aid

Students should submit: CSS PROFILE; FAFSA; Noncustodial CSS PROFILE. Priority filing deadline is 11/1. The Princeton Review suggests that all financial aid forms be submitted as soon as possible after October 1. *Need-based scholarships/grants offered:* College/university scholarship or grant aid from institutional funds; Federal Pell; Private scholarships; SEOG; State scholarships/grants. *Loan aid offered:* Direct PLUS loans; Direct Subsidized Stafford Loans; Direct Unsubsidized Stafford Loans; Alternative and Private Loans. Applicants will be notified of awards soon after an offer of admission. Federal Work-Study Program available. Institutional employment available.

The Inside Word

SMU boasts a potent combination: high-caliber academics, a desirable location, and a beautiful campus. No surprise then that gaining admission is challenging, and growing more so all the time. Solid high school grades and a compelling list of extracurricular activities will usually do the trick. "Special talent" students—artists and athletes in particular—can make up for academic deficiencies; those in the arts must undergo an audition/portfolio review, while promising athletes are scouted. Except for those in the performing arts, all admitted students enter as "pre-majors" in the Dedman College of Humanities and Sciences.

THE SCHOOL SAYS "..."

From the Admissions Office

"At SMU, we seek bright, hardworking students. We match our rigorous academics, powerful opportunities and incredible classroom-to-career experiences with access to outstanding financial resources. We want students to achieve their goals regardless of financial need. When students apply to SMU, they are automatically considered for generous academic awards, many of which can be combined. Nearly 80% of first-years are awarded grants and/or scholarships. We respond to what employers want. The flexibility of our curriculum and our vibrant community in the global gateway of Dallas offer students robust preparation for the demands of a rapidly changing world. All students have the chance to pursue career-boosting internships. Many SMU students choose to double or triple major, demonstrating expertise in different disciplines. Employers tell us that SMU graduates are creative, ethical and critical thinkers who hit the ground running faster because they know how to lead, solve problems and communicate with emotional and cultural intelligence. Students often partner with our professors as co-creators of knowledge, thriving on personal attention in small classes. They can participate in undergraduate research as early as their first year. Our enterprising spirit has long been part of our DNA. Through our Big iDeas program, students work in cross-disciplinary teams to win funding to start a company. The SMU Incubator is a dedicated campus space where entrepreneurial students and faculty work on generating business-friendly solutions. The George W. Bush Presidential Center and renowned Tate Lecture Series offer students access to dignitaries ranging from former presidents to Nobel Laureates."

SELECTIVITY

Admissions Rating	91
# of applicants	13,959
% of applicants accepted	47
% of acceptees attending	23
# offered a place on the wait list	2,407
% accepting a place on wait list	45
% admitted from wait list	4
# of early decision applicants	485
% accepted early decision	65

FRESHMAN PROFILE

Range SAT EBRW	640–720
Range SAT Math	660–760
Range ACT Composite	29–33
# submitting SAT scores	605
% submitting SAT scores	39
# submitting ACT scores	854
% submitting ACT scores	55
Average HS GPA	3.6
% graduated top 10% of class	49
% graduated top 25% of class	79
% graduated top 50% of class	97

DEADLINES

Early decision	
Deadline	11/1
Notification	12/31
Other ED Deadline	1/15
Other ED Notification	4/1
Early action	
Deadline	11/1
Notification	12/31
Regular	
Priority	1/15
Deadline	7/31
Notification	4/1
Nonfall registration?	Yes

APPLICANTS ALSO LOOK AT AND OFTEN PREFER
University of Southern California; New York University; Duke University

AND SOMETIMES PREFER
Vanderbilt University; Boston University

AND RARELY PREFER
Texas Christian University; Tulane University

FINANCIAL FACTS

Financial Aid Rating	87
Annual tuition	$51,958
Room and board	$17,110
Required fees	$6,582
Books and supplies	$800
Average frosh need-based scholarship	$21,993
Average UG need-based scholarship	$22,114
% needy frosh rec. need-based scholarship or grant aid	63
% needy UG rec. need-based scholarship or grant aid	71
% needy frosh rec. non-need-based scholarship or grant aid	77
% needy UG rec. non-need-based scholarship or grant aid	69
% needy frosh rec. need-based self-help aid	71
% needy UG rec. need-based self-help aid	76
% frosh rec. any financial aid	77.7
% UG rec. any financial aid	73.7
% UG borrow to pay for school	28
Average cumulative indebtedness	$30,697
% frosh need fully met	44
% ugrads need fully met	36
Average % of frosh need met	85
Average % of ugrad need met	85

SOUTHWESTERN UNIVERSITY

Admission Office, Georgetown, TX 78627-0770 • Admissions: 512-863-1200 • Fax: 512-863-9601

STUDENTS SAY ". . ."

Academics

Known as "Texas' first university," Southwestern University is a small liberal arts school of around 1,600 or so for students who develop a passion for lifelong learning and a desire to contribute to society. The school focuses on building connections between different disciplines, which is at the heart of the unique "Paideia experience." Paideia is actually a common occurrence in all classes, and professors "actively seek to make connections across disciplines and encourage students to do the same," with social justice and environmentalism both common themes. The University also "has excellent institutions built in," and the "stellar" career services program, helmed by a small staff that "is very invested in student's well being and success," sets the school apart. To that end, more than half of all students complete an internship during their time at Southwestern, with similar numbers for study abroad participation.

"Discussion is the primary mode of delivery, and critical thinking is encouraged," and since the classes are small, professors "all know you by name (even if you don't have their class!)." They teach the course material "with passion and interesting perspectives/mediums that allow for better retention and integrative understanding." Most are available at any time "to assist in understanding, clarification, and extrapolation of the ideas discussed in class," which also leads to many research opportunities with faculty. They "not only push us to be better but know we are capable of it, even if we as students aren't sure that we are." The course load here is "very demanding but worth it," and communication via classroom technology and email between the teachers and the students is excellent. "Southwestern is all about making a connection with the people around you while making connections between the subjects you study," says a student.

Life

Southwestern is a draw for "thinkers and learners, for people who like to be challenged and have fun at the same time." The students here are definitely academically focused, and "even those involved in other organizations (which most of us are) are still excellent students." In fact, Southwestern is all about balance, and "the academics and the athletics really work together to make sure that everybody maintains a high GPA." Students are assigned "a substantial amount of homework," but "you can study anywhere...from the hammocks to the chairs around campus," which is easily traversed via the campus bikes. Greek life is very prevalent and "is sort of the social heart of the campus," but the school also offers lots of other activities for students who are not involved with the Greek system, such as events held every Friday and Saturday night. Georgetown, Texas is not a typical college town, but there are shops and restaurants for when students want to get off campus. There is plenty to do outdoors—luckily, it's warm a large part of the year, so "people go to the hiking trails, go swimming, or hang out on the academic mall."

Student Body

Students are, across the board, "highly involved and motivated." "Almost everyone has a major, minor, and one or two organizations in which they are heavily involved," says a student. The culture here is largely one of "acceptance and stimulating engagement." Everyone here "celebrates a range of personalities and points of view," and is "unashamedly passionate about our goals." A uniting force is "involvement in social justice and activism," and the University "offers a unique scholarly bubble that makes you feel like a scholar yourself." It's a small school, so "you don't feel lost in the crowd," and the atmosphere is "very similar" to nearby Austin and the "Keep Austin Weird" stereotype.

SOUTHWESTERN UNIVERSITY

Financial Aid: 512-863-1259 • E-Mail: admission@southwestern.edu • Website: www.southwestern.edu

THE PRINCETON REVIEW SAYS

Admissions

Very important factors considered include: rigor of secondary school record, class rank, academic GPA, application essay, standardized test scores, recommendation(s). *Important factors considered include:* interview, extracurricular activities, talent/ability, character/personal qualities, first generation, alumni/ae relation, geographical residence, state residency, racial/ethnic status, volunteer work. *Other factors considered include:* religious affiliation/commitment, work experience, level of applicant's interest. ACT with or without writing accepted. SAT with or without Essay component accepted. High school diploma is required and GED is accepted. *Academic units required:* 4 English, 4 math, 3 science, 2 science labs, 2 foreign language, 2 social studies, 1 history, 1 academic elective. *Academic units recommended:* 4 English, 4 math, 4 science, 3 science labs, 3 foreign language, 3 social studies, 1 history, 1 academic elective.

Financial Aid

Students should submit: FAFSA. Priority filing deadline is 3/1. The Princeton Review suggests that all financial aid forms be submitted as soon as possible after October 1. *Need-based scholarships/grants offered:* College/university scholarship or grant aid from institutional funds; Federal Pell; Private scholarships; SEOG; State scholarships/grants. *Loan aid offered:* Direct PLUS loans; Direct Subsidized Stafford Loans; Direct Unsubsidized Stafford Loans. Applicants will be notified of awards on a rolling basis beginning 11/15. Federal Work-Study Program available. Institutional employment available.

The Inside Word

Successful applicants to Southwestern University demonstrate intellectual curiosity and a strong desire to participate in an active collegiate community. Students need to be well-rounded and highly motivated. The vast majority of those who receive the coveted thick envelope are in the top quarter of their class and have above-average standardized test scores.

THE SCHOOL SAYS "..."

From the Admissions Office

"Southwestern is the leading liberal arts institution in Texas. As Texas' first institution of higher learning, Southwestern has been providing students with a distinctive, values-centered education since 1840. Our tree-lined residential campus is everything you imagine when you dream about going to college, and then some. Grand, century-old limestone buildings accent the heart of campus, offering spacious sports and recreational facilities, multiple research laboratories, two live-performance theaters, roomy residence halls, and so much more. Our community Pirate Bike program is unlike anything in Texas. These bright yellow bikes scattered across campus are ready to ride anytime, day or night. The Paideia experience introduces students to intentional connections. Through collaboration, participation in civic engagement activities, intercultural learning experiences and undergraduate research, students think across the disciplines to form new solutions, ultimately integrating their knowledge, high-level problem solving skills and deep learning as they apply their scholarship to essential questions of the world around them. The results are impressive, Post Graduate Survey data for 2016 reports that 91 percent of students are either employed, attending medical, law and other professional schools or pursuing advanced studies. Georgetown has much to offer, but if at the end of the day you are in the mood for a quick drive, grab your friends and help 'Keep Austin Weird!' Experience SXSW Music, Film and Interactive, ACL Music Festival, or face your fears at Bat Fest. What's more, with the year-round sunshine and a wealth of recreational activities within your reach, the outdoors becomes a popular playground."

SELECTIVITY

Admissions Rating	89
# of applicants	4,766
% of applicants accepted	49
% of acceptees attending	19
# offered a place on the wait list	294
% accepting a place on wait list	12
% admitted from wait list	24
# of early decision applicants	92
% accepted early decision	26

FRESHMAN PROFILE

Range SAT EBRW	580–670
Range SAT Math	560–650
Range SAT Composite	1150–1310
Range ACT Composite	23–29
# submitting SAT scores	342
% submitting SAT scores	77
# submitting ACT scores	225
% submitting ACT scores	51
Average HS GPA	3.5
% graduated top 10% of class	35
% graduated top 25% of class	67
% graduated top 50% of class	94

DEADLINES

Early decision	
Deadline	11/1
Notification	12/1
Early action	
Deadline	12/1
Notification	3/1
Regular	
Priority	2/1
Deadline	2/1
Notification	4/1
Nonfall registration?	No

APPLICANTS ALSO LOOK AT AND OFTEN PREFER

University of Texas at Austin; Trinity University; St. Edward's University; Texas A&M University

AND SOMETIMES PREFER

Baylor University; Austin College; The University of Texas at Dallas

AND RARELY PREFER

Rhodes College; Rice University; University of Dallas

FINANCIAL FACTS

Financial Aid Rating	89
Annual tuition	$45,120
Room and board	$12,450
Books and supplies	$1,300
Average frosh need-based scholarship	$32,843
Average UG need-based scholarship	$31,693
% needy frosh rec. need-based cholarship or grant aid	100
% needy UG rec. need-based scholarship or grant aid	99
% needy frosh rec. non-need-based scholarship or grant aid	98
% needy UG rec. non-need-based scholarship or grant aid	98
% needy frosh rec. need-based self-help aid	78
% needy UG rec. need-based self-help aid	81
% frosh rec. any financial aid	100
% UG rec. any financial aid	98
% UG borrow to pay for school	61
Average cumulative indebtedness	$34,551
% frosh need fully met	26
% ugrads need fully met	27
Average % of frosh need met	89
Average % of ugrad need met	86

SPELMAN COLLEGE

350 Spelman Lane, Atlanta, GA 30314-4399 • Admissions: 404-270-5193 • Fax: 404-270-5201

CAMPUS LIFE
Quality of Life Rating	87
Fire Safety Rating	87
Green Rating	60*
Type of school	Private
Environment	Metropolis

STUDENTS
Total undergrad enrollment	2,166
% male/female	0/100
% from out of state	74
% frosh live on campus	99
% ugrads live on campus	65
# of sororities (% ugrad women join)	4 (3)
% African American	97
% Asian	0
% Caucasian	<1
% Hispanic	<1
% Native American	<1
% Pacific Islander	0
% Two or more races	0
% Race and/or ethnicity unknown	0
% international	1
# of countries represented	7

SURVEY SAYS . . .
Lots of liberal students
Lab facilities are great
Internships are widely available
Students are very religious
Very little drug use

ACADEMICS
Academic Rating	85
% students returning for sophomore year	91
% students graduating within 4 years	69
% students graduating within 6 years	75
Calendar	Semester
Student/faculty ratio	11:1
Profs interesting rating	87
Profs accessible rating	91

Most classes have 10–19 students.
Most lab/discussion sessions have
10–19 students.

MOST POPULAR MAJORS
Psychology, General; Political Science and
Government, General

STUDENTS SAY ". . ."

Academics

A historically black women's institution, Spelman College has built a strong reputation for "molding intelligent, goal-oriented young ladies into determined, successful, free-thinking women." Many prospective students are attracted to the school's "powerful history," including the "long list of successful, educated, strong, black women who have attended Spelman College" during the century since its founding. Once on campus, students are happy to report that Spelman's "professors are committed to the mission of the school," and they really "bring out the best" in their students. In the classroom, students are "encouraged to state our opinions," and professors "allow room for us to challenge and discuss what they present." You'll definitely work hard to stay afloat in this "challenging academic environment," because professors "do not allow for even a minute amount of slacking when it comes to completing assignments and being on time for class." Fortunately, there are "many academic resources available to help us, such as tutoring services and a writing center." Plus, the majority of Spelman professors "take additional time outside of instructional time to assist their students" with course work. Of particular note, Spelman is "very focused on the sciences and improving the number of African American women in this field, and they offer many facilities, faculty, and opportunities" for advanced study. As graduation approaches, the "Career Counseling Center is extremely strong and has helped numerous students find employment and graduate school placements." While the future looks bright for Spelman grads, many say this private institution could better serve its students by providing "more money for scholarships and financial aid."

Life

There's a "strong sense of tradition and loyalty" on the Spelman campus, and most students are deeply involved in the community. From service groups to sororities, "there are so many organizations and clubs that you're bound to find one that fits you." There are tons of "opportunities to obtain leadership positions" outside the classroom, and many students are "very involved in campus life." A first-year student details, "In my freshman year already, I've walked in a fashion show, I was crowned Miss Glee Club, I write for the campus newspaper." There's a constant buzz of activity on campus, and "informational forums, career fairs, college fairs, performances, and sporting events are at the forefront of everyone's campus life." Socially, "Greek Life is quite important at Spelman College, but isn't a must." Even if you don't join a sorority, "there are a lot of social events on campus," and two other historically black colleges, Clark Atlanta and Morehouse, "are only inches away." Spelman undergrads say, "The camaraderie between the schools is great," and "joint homecoming with Morehouse is the highlight of the entire year." Off campus, students "go skating, bowling, and to Six Flags Over Georgia, as well as to Atlanta Falcons, Hawks, and Braves [games]." Nearby, Atlantic Station is home to "a major movie theater, shopping, [and] restaurants."

Student Body

Spelman College is "full of warm, welcoming, sisterly, and highly educated African American women." A unique environment, "Spelman College offers a chance for African American women to be the majority," and students appreciate being "surrounded and empowered by other young, intelligent, and goal-oriented women like myself." At the same time, "the institution promotes diversity within the student body," and Spelman women "come in all shapes and sizes and from all walks of life, though linked by our African descent. Anyone can find their place here." Confidence and individuality are prized at Spelman, and the typical undergraduate "speaks her mind, wears what she wants, [and] is comfortable in her own skin, yet she has empathy and a strong sense of social justice." Many students "love to do service for the community" and are involved in philanthropic projects around Atlanta. Spelman women are "hardworking and focused on academics." However, most are "excellent at balancing a full course load and an active social life."

Financial Aid: 404-270-5212 • E-Mail: admiss@spelman.edu • Website: www.spelman.edu

THE PRINCETON REVIEW SAYS

Admissions

Very important factors considered include: rigor of secondary school record, academic GPA, application essay, standardized test scores, recommendation(s), character/personal qualities. *Important factors considered include:* class rank, extracurricular activities, volunteer work. *Other factors considered include:* talent/ability, alumni/ae relation, geographical residence, work experience, level of applicant's interest. ACT with or without writing accepted. SAT with or without Essay component accepted. High school diploma is required and GED is accepted. *Academic units required:* 4 English, 2 math, 2 science, 1 science lab, 2 foreign language, 2 social studies, 2 history, 1 academic elective. *Academic units recommended:* 4 English, 4 math, 4 science, 2 science labs, 2 foreign language, 3 social studies.

Financial Aid

Students should submit: FAFSA. Priority filing deadline is 2/1. The Princeton Review suggests that all financial aid forms be submitted as soon as possible after October 1. *Need-based scholarships/grants offered:* College/university scholarship or grant aid from institutional funds; Federal Pell; Private scholarships; SEOG; State scholarships/grants; United Negro College Fund. *Loan aid offered:* Direct PLUS loans; Direct Subsidized Stafford Loans; Direct Unsubsidized Stafford Loans. Applicants will be notified of awards on a rolling basis beginning 12/15. Federal Work-Study Program available. Institutional employment available.

The Inside Word

The best way to prepare for admission to Spelman is to pursue a strong, precollege academic curriculum during high school. In 2018, admitted students had an average GPA of 3.80. Students who are particularly interested in Spelman have two early application options: early decision, which is binding, and early action, which is nonbinding, but allows students to receive a response more quickly.

THE SCHOOL SAYS " . . ."

From the Admissions Office

"As an outstanding Historically Black College for women, Spelman strives for academic excellence in liberal arts education. This predominantly residential private college provides students with an academic climate conducive to the full development of their intellectual and leadership potential. The college is a member of the Atlanta University Center Consortium, and Spelman students enjoy the benefits of a small college while having access to the resources of the other three participating institutions. The purpose extends beyond intellectual development and professional career preparation of students. It seeks to develop the total person. The college provides an academic and social environment that strengthens those qualities that enable women to be self-confident as well as culturally and spiritually enriched. This environment attempts to instill in students both an appreciation for the multicultural communities of the world and a sense of responsibility for bringing about positive change in those communities.

"Applicants are required to submit standardized test scores from an appropriate venue (i.e., ACT, TOEFL, SAT). The highest composite score will be used in admissions decisions. Writing scores from either the SAT or ACT will not be taken into consideration in the admission process."

SELECTIVITY

Admissions Rating	89
# of applicants	9,451
% of applicants accepted	39
% of acceptees attending	15
# offered a place on the wait list	529
% accepting a place on wait list	20
% admitted from wait list	14
# of early decision applicants	233
% accepted early decision	36

FRESHMAN PROFILE

Range SAT EBRW	560–630
Range SAT Math	520–590
Range ACT Composite	22–26
# submitting SAT scores	402
% submitting SAT scores	70
# submitting ACT scores	317
% submitting ACT scores	55
Average HS GPA	3.7
% graduated top 10% of class	10
% graduated top 25% of class	25
% graduated top 50% of class	50

DEADLINES

Early decision	
Deadline	11/1
Notification	12/15
Early action	
Deadline	11/15
Notification	12/31
Regular	
Deadline	2/1
Notification	4/1
Nonfall registration?	Yes

FINANCIAL FACTS

Financial Aid Rating	83
Annual tuition	$25,942
Room and board	$14,338
Required fees	$4,280
Books and supplies	$3,000
Average frosh need-based scholarship	$11,706
Average UG need-based scholarship	$14,611
% needy frosh rec. need-based scholarship or grant aid	99
% needy UG rec. need-based scholarship or grant aid	89
% needy frosh rec. non-need-based scholarship or grant aid	10
% needy UG rec. non-need-based scholarship or grant aid	13
% needy frosh rec. need-based self-help aid	85
% needy UG rec. need-based self-help aid	85
% frosh rec. any financial aid	26
% UG rec. any financial aid	90
% UG borrow to pay for school	82
Average cumulative indebtedness	$35,582
% frosh need fully met	50
% ugrads need fully met	48
Average % of frosh need met	32
Average % of ugrad need met	34

STANFORD UNIVERSITY

Undergraduate Admission, Stanford, CA 94305-6106 • Admissions: 650-723-2091 • Fax: 650-723-6050

CAMPUS LIFE

Quality of Life Rating	94
Fire Safety Rating	89
Green Rating	99
Type of school	Private
Environment	City

STUDENTS

Total undergrad enrollment	6,994
% male/female	50/50
% from out of state	61
% frosh from public high school	59
% frosh live on campus	100
% ugrads live on campus	97
# of fraternities (% ugrad men join)	16 (18)
# of sororities (% ugrad women join)	14 (24)
% African American	7
% Asian	23
% Caucasian	32
% Hispanic	17
% Native American	1
% Pacific Islander	<1
% Two or more races	9
% Race and/or ethnicity unknown	<1
% international	11
# of countries represented	90

SURVEY SAYS . . .

Students are happy
Classroom facilities are great
Lab facilities are great
Great library
Career services are great
Internships are widely available
School is well run
Great financial aid
No one cheats
Students are friendly
Diverse student types interact on campus
Great food on campus
Recreation facilities are great
Lots of beer drinking
Everyone loves the Cardinal
Alumni active on campus
Active minority support groups

ACADEMICS

Academic Rating	93
% students returning for sophomore year	99
% students graduating within 4 years	73
% students graduating within 6 years	94
Calendar	Quarter
Student/faculty ratio	5:1
Profs interesting rating	89
Profs accessible rating	94

Most classes have 10–19 students.
Most lab/discussion sessions have
fewer than 10 students.

MOST POPULAR MAJORS
Computer Science; Human Biology; Economics

STUDENTS SAY "..."

Academics

There are few universities that can match the prestige and caliber of Stanford University. At "the forefront of [nearly] every field of study," it's easy to understand why so many students are attracted to the school. Of course, far more than simply offering access to highly rated departments, Stanford strives to "expand your creativity, challenge and deepen your world view, and make you a passionate and informed citizen of the world." Moreover, the opportunities for research "are incredible" and "the support for students (residential, emotional, academic) is unrivaled." And while the university is certainly "academically rigorous," it is "without the competitive edge that many top-tier institutions are known for." Inside the classroom, undergrads are privy to "dynamic" professors who easily "draw [students] into the material because they are so excited to share their passion for the subject." Though instructors are "at the top of their respective fields," most are also "engaging and approachable." A mechanical engineering major supports this sentiment sharing, "I play basketball on Friday mornings with my major adviser and will often bring my homework with me in order to talk to him about problems I'm stuck on afterward." Ultimately, as this senior boasts, "At Stanford, anything is possible; I've lived on a schooner with faculty studying sharks, snorkeled on the Great Barrier Reef, hiked in the Australian rainforest, studied Antarctic phytoplankton with world-class scientists, and spent countless nights discussing philosophy, politics, film, and art until sunrise."

Life

Undergrads agree that "it's pretty much impossible to be bored" at Stanford. Though students "work insanely hard during the week," they "also make it a priority to have a great time." And with so much to take advantage of, having fun is pretty easy. For example, the university sponsors "Cardinal Nights," a non-alcoholic program that hosts a number of events including "trips to Great America, a local amusement park, *The Great Gatsby* movie pre-screening, and Stanford's Got Talent. All of the events are either free or extremely cheap for students." Undergrads also look forward to "special dinners...a common event in upper class housing." These are "nice on-campus dinners that are catered by house chefs. The meals usually have themes, such as Saturday Night Live or Moulin Rouge." Moreover, while there is certainly a drinking scene, it's pretty laid back. A sophomore explains, "you can find as much or as little of a party culture here as you're looking for. There's always a frat party to attend on the weekends, and there's always people to just hang out with at the dorm." Finally, students love the fact that hometown Palo Alto leaves them in close proximity to San Francisco. "A trip to the city is a short train-ride or car-ride away, so going to concerts and events in the city is always a fun option. Same goes for the nearby beaches." However, "there's always so much going on on-campus that sometimes it's hard to leave!"

Student Body

Stanford undergrads speak glowingly of their peers: "Everyone here is smart and has some story that will blow you out of the water if you ask, but are very humble and really just looking to have a good time." They also steadfastly assert, "There really is no typical Stanford student." And, thankfully, that "makes it easy to be an integrated and diverse student body." That being said, most Stanford undergrads are "very driven, independently motivated and willing to seek out opportunities." One senior elaborates by sharing, "Everyone fits in because we're united by a fire that drives us all to be excited about what we do. The trends you'll see will be along the lines of leadership and crazy intellect." Ultimately, students at Stanford are "ridiculously friendly and you can meet new people all over campus at almost every type of event."

STANFORD UNIVERSITY

Financial Aid: 650-723-3058 • E-Mail: admission@stanford.edu • Website: www.stanford.edu

THE PRINCETON REVIEW SAYS

Admissions

Very important factors considered include: rigor of secondary school record, class rank, academic GPA, application essay, standardized test scores, recommendation(s), extracurricular activities, talent/ability, character/personal qualities. *Other factors considered include:* interview, first generation, alumni/ae relation, geographical residence, racial/ethnic status, volunteer work, work experience. ACT with or without writing accepted. SAT with or without Essay component accepted. High school diploma is required and GED is accepted. *Academic units recommended:* 4 English, 4 math, 4 science, 4 science labs, 4 foreign language, 4 social studies.

Financial Aid

Students should submit: CSS/Financial Aid PROFILE; FAFSA; Noncustodial PROFILE. Priority filing deadline is 2/16. The Princeton Review suggests that all financial aid forms be submitted as soon as possible after October 1. *Need-based scholarships/grants offered:* College/university scholarship or grant aid from institutional funds; Federal Pell; Private scholarships; SEOG; State scholarships/grants. *Loan aid offered:* Direct PLUS loans; Direct Subsidized Stafford Loans; Direct Unsubsidized Stafford Loans. Applicants will be notified of awards on a rolling basis beginning 4/1. Federal Work-Study Program available. Institutional employment available.

The Inside Word

Receiving a highly coveted acceptance letter from Stanford is no easy feat! Indeed, competition to gain admission is fierce. And, unfortunately, there is no magic formula. Clearly, a stellar academic record is a must. Beyond strong transcripts and test scores, successful applicants readily display intellectual curiosity and vigor, commitment to the topics and activities they are passionate about and initiative in seeking out opportunity.

THE SCHOOL SAYS "..."

From the Admissions Office

"Stanford looks for distinctive students who exhibit energy, personality, a sense of intellectual vitality and extraordinary impact outside the classroom. While there is no minimum grade point average, class rank, or test score one needs to be admitted to Stanford, the vast majority of successful applicants will be among the strongest students (academically) in their secondary schools. We want to understand the impact you have had at your job, in your family, in a club, in your school, or in the larger community, and we want to learn of the impact that experience has had on you. By focusing on your achievements in context, we evaluate how you have excelled in your school environment and how you have taken advantage of what is available to you in your school and community.

"The Common Application or The Coalition for College application *and* Stanford Writing Supplement are both required and must be submitted online. In the Stanford Writing Supplement, accessed at www.commonapp.org and/or www.coalitionforcollegeaccess.org, candidates write about an idea or experience important to their intellectual development, as well as a note to their future roommate. In the final essay, candidates are asked to write about something meaningful to them and why.

"While the SAT or ACT is required for admission, SAT subject tests are not required (and only recommended). AP scores are also not required but can be used for placement/credit purposes if an admitted student decides to enroll.

"Tuition charges are covered for undergrads with family incomes below $150,000. Zero parent contribution for undergrads with family incomes below $65,000."

SELECTIVITY

Admissions Rating	99
# of applicants	47,498
% of applicants accepted	4
% of acceptees attending	82
# offered a place on the wait list	750
% accepting a place on wait list	77
% admitted from wait list	1

FRESHMAN PROFILE

Range SAT EBRW	700–770
Range SAT Math	740–800
Range SAT Composite	1440–1550
Range ACT Composite	32–35
# submitting SAT scores	1,140
% submitting SAT scores	67
# submitting ACT scores	846
% submitting ACT scores	50
Average HS GPA	4.0
% graduated top 10% of class	98
% graduated top 25% of class	100
% graduated top 50% of class	100

DEADLINES

Early action	
Deadline	11/1
Notification	12/15
Regular	
Deadline	1/2
Notification	4/1
Nonfall registration?	No

FINANCIAL FACTS

Financial Aid Rating	98
Annual tuition	$55,473
Room and board	$17,255
Required fees	$696
Books and supplies	$1,290
Average frosh need-based scholarship	$55,394
Average UG need-based scholarship	$52,823
% needy frosh rec. need-based scholarship or grant aid	98
% needy UG rec. need-based scholarship or grant aid	98
% needy frosh rec. non-need-based scholarship or grant aid	3
% needy UG rec. non-need-based scholarship or grant aid	4
% needy frosh rec. need-based self-help aid	67
% needy UG rec. need-based self-help aid	74
% frosh rec. any financial aid	86
% UG rec. any financial aid	85
% UG borrow to pay for school	17
Average cumulative indebtedness	$22,897
% frosh need fully met	93
% ugrads need fully met	89
Average % of frosh need met	100
Average % of ugrad need met	100

STATE UNIVERSITY OF NEW YORK—BINGHAMTON UNIVERSITY

PO Box 6001, Binghamton, NY 13902-6001 • Admissions: 607-777-2171 • Fax: 607-777-4445

STUDENTS SAY "..."

Academics

As one of the central institutions in one of the country's strongest public university systems, Binghamton University upholds rigorous academic, cultural, and engagement standards. The research university's six schools are spread across 930 acres of the beautiful upstate Susquehanna Valley. The nursing, business, and engineering schools are three standouts, but no matter what course a student chooses to study, you're sure to get the "best bang for your buck." Binghamton's multi-disciplinary education "prepares you not only for your career, but for the rest of your life," by instilling students with leadership, academic and social skills, and "employers rave about the school, especially if you are applying to jobs in New York City or on Long Island." "Binghamton is all about giving students many options to do what they want," and the career services office is an excellent complement to that; fellow students and alums are also "very willing to give out information that will benefit others, such as an internship or winter program."

Faculty members here are "dedicated and willing to invest in the university," and hold regular office hours, though students "have so many places to go if they are not available." As students get into their major-specific courses, "there is more discussion and less lecturing." Professors are "supportive, reasonable, accessible, clear and fair," and "as long as you are genuinely interested in the subject and willing to put in the work, you will succeed." High-quality research endeavors are available to all (especially those in the sciences), through programs like First-year Research Immersion, which provides first-year students with a three semester-long research experience in sciences, engineering, and public health. The Source Project provides similar research experiences for students in the humanities and social sciences.

Life

The "excellent student board" organizes tons of events throughout the week and is "keen on getting the students...involved and [making] a difference." The university's 450+ organizations carry various roles "from community service to professionalism," and it has "almost any kind of club out there," from club sports to the hula hoop club to L.O.C.K.S. (Ladies Owning their Curls Kinks and Straights). The school's residential college system is modeled after the one at Oxford University, with students living in six different communities, each with its own personality. The living communities "really help break it up and make it feel smaller," and "there are a lot of study spaces and a lot of places to spend time." Though academics take priority, when students do leave their books, "Binghamton offers so many activities to do on campus that it is hard to ever be bored."

The town of Vestal is small and quiet, and there is a 190-acre nature preserve on campus that is frequently hiked by students. The nearby city and communities of Binghamton are constantly improving: "Change happens all of the time and the students are getting ready for it." People here do like to party on the weekends, and "going out into downtown Binghamton on Friday and Saturday nights to hit up the bars is popular." For those who prefer to keep it more low-key, the University Union always has "games, arts and crafts, free bowling (with free shoe rentals), ping pong (you do have to rent the paddles if you don't bring your own), billiards, and movie rentals," and there are often performances or movies shown on campus.

Student Body

A high proportion of students are from Long Island or Westchester, but they do report "a surprising amount of diversity" on campus, and students are "happy to step outside of their comfort zones and learn about different cultures." The majority of students "worked hard to afford school and to get into a school as intense as Binghamton" and there is "a very friendly and homey atmosphere at the school." This "extremely loving and generous" group is "multi-disciplined" and "involved in many organizations, leadership roles, jobs, internships, or research.'

STATE UNIVERSITY OF NEW YORK—BINGHAMTON UNIVERSITY

Financial Aid: 607-777-2428 • E-Mail: admit@binghamton.edu • Website: www.binghamton.edu

THE PRINCETON REVIEW SAYS

Admissions

Very important factors considered include: rigor of secondary school record, academic GPA, standardized test scores. *Important factors considered include:* class rank, application essay, recommendation(s), extracurricular activities. *Other factors considered include:* talent/ability, character/personal qualities, first generation, alumni/ae relation, geographical residence, state residency, racial/ethnic status, volunteer work, work experience, level of applicant's interest. ACT with Writing required. SAT with Essay component recommended. High school diploma is required and GED is accepted. *Academic units required:* 4 English, 3 math, 2 science, 3 foreign language, 2 social studies. *Academic units recommended:* 4 math, 4 science, 4 social studies, 4 history.

Financial Aid

Students should submit: FAFSA; New York state aid forms, including Excelsior and STEM applications. Priority filing deadline is January 1. The Princeton Review suggests that all financial aid forms be submitted as soon as possible after October 1. *Need-based and merit-based scholarships/grants offered:* College/university scholarship or grant aid from institutional funds; Federal Pell; Federal SEOG; state scholarships/grants. *Loan aid offered:* Federal Direct PLUS loans; Federal Direct Subsidized Loans; Federal Direct Unsubsidized Loans; Federal Nursing Loans; Private Education loans. Applicants will be notified of awards on a rolling basis beginning 1/31. Federal Work Study Program as well as Institutional employment available.

The Inside Word

Like the vast majority of New York state schools, Binghamton accepts the single-apply SUNY application. Binghamton also accepts the Common Application, making it easy to apply to Binghamton University and other schools at the same time. Binghamton is one of the top public universities in the country—it's often referred to as a "public Ivy"—so expect competition to be stiff.

THE SCHOOL SAYS "..."

From the Admissions Office

"Binghamton has established itself as the premier public university in the Northeast, because of our outstanding undergraduate programs, vibrant campus culture, and committed faculty. Students are academically motivated, but there is a great deal of mutual help as they compete against the standard of a class rather than each other. Faculty and students work side by side in research labs or on artistic pursuits. Achievement, exploration, and leadership are hallmarks of a Binghamton education. Add to that a campus-wide commitment to internationalization that includes a robust education abroad program, cultural offerings, languages and international studies, and you have a place where graduates leave prepared for success. Binghamton University graduates lead the nation in top starting salaries among public universities, demonstrating that our students are recognized by employers and recruiters for having strong abilities to be leaders, critical thinkers, decision makers, analysts, and researchers in many fields and industries."

SELECTIVITY

Admissions Rating	92
# of applicants	37,516
% of applicants accepted	41
% of acceptees attending	19
# offered a place on the wait list	5,331
% accepting a place on wait list	37
% admitted from wait list	17

FRESHMAN PROFILE

Range SAT EBRW	630–700
Range SAT Math	650–740
Range SAT Composite	1295–1430
Range ACT Composite	29–32
Average HS GPA	4.0

DEADLINES

Early action	
Deadline	11/1
Notification	1/15
Regular	
Deadline	1/15
Notification	4/1
Nonfall registration?	Yes

APPLICANTS ALSO LOOK AT AND OFTEN PREFER
Cornell University

AND SOMETIMES PREFER
Boston University; New York University

AND RARELY PREFER
Rutgers University–Newark; State University of New York—Stony Brook University

FINANCIAL FACTS

Financial Aid Rating	84
Annual in-state tuition	$6,870
Annual out-of-state tuition	$23,710
Room and board	$15,058
Required fees	$2,934
Books and supplies	$1,000
Average frosh need-based scholarship	$9,908
Average UG need-based scholarship	$9,655
% needy frosh rec. need-based scholarship or grant aid	83
% needy UG rec. need-based scholarship or grant aid	83
% needy frosh rec. non-need-based scholarship or grant aid	14
% needy UG rec. non-need-based scholarship or grant aid	8
% needy frosh rec. need-based self-help aid	98
% needy UG rec. need-based self-help aid	98
% frosh rec. any financial aid	87
% UG rec. any financial aid	73
% UG borrow to pay for school	50
Average cumulative indebtedness	$27,470
% frosh need fully met	15
% ugrads need fully met	19
Average % of frosh need met	70
Average % of ugrad need met	70

STATE UNIVERSITY OF NEW YORK—COLLEGE OF ENVIRONMENTAL SCIENCE AND FORESTRY

Office of Undergraduate Admissions, Syracuse, NY 13210-2779 • Admissions: 315-470-6600 • Fax: 315-470-6933

CAMPUS LIFE

Quality of Life Rating	86
Fire Safety Rating	98
Green Rating	98
Type of school	Public
Environment	City

STUDENTS

Total undergrad enrollment	1,854
% male/female	53/47
% from out of state	19
% frosh from public high school	90
% frosh live on campus	96
% ugrads live on campus	35
# of fraternities (% ugrad men join)	26 (2)
# of sororities (% ugrad women join)	21 (2)
% African American	1
% Asian	4
% Caucasian	78
% Hispanic	6
% Native American	<1
% Pacific Islander	0
% Two or more races	3
% Race and/or ethnicity unknown	4
% international	3
# of countries represented	7

SURVEY SAYS . . .

Students environmentally aware
Dorms are like palaces
Active student government

ACADEMICS

Academic Rating	79
% students returning for sophomore year	83
% students graduating within 6 years	74
Calendar	Semester
Student/faculty ratio	15:1
Profs interesting rating	88
Profs accessible rating	89

Most classes have 10–19 students.
Most lab/discussion sessions have 20–29 students.

MOST POPULAR MAJORS

Environmental Biology; Landscape Architecture; Environmental Science

STUDENTS SAY "..."

Academics

The State University of New York—College of Environmental Science and Forestry is the country's oldest college dedicated entirely to environmental discovery, learning, and sustainability. Campus occupies 12 acres in Syracuse and the institution uses 25,000 acres located across central New York and the Adirondacks as a "living laboratory" for hands-on projects and research. ESF's 1,600 undergrads choose from twenty-six majors (as well as plenty of specialized courses) and are able to take classes and use facilities and resources at neighboring Syracuse University. The school reports an excellent job placement rate, and students tell us "the student body and faculty care about each other and help everyone get the most out of the experience."

The professors here are "so down to earth and passionate." They "seem to love what they do, and they are all conducting their own research," and this research "is sprinkled into the undergraduate experience." Every class "is applied directly to your major and field of interest." Be it paper engineering and renewable materials science, forest resources, or environmental interpretation, "ESF will cater to your specific needs." The small campus size allows plentiful opportunities for students to gain close relationships with professors, often eventually leading to projects or teaching assistant positions." When it comes to jobs in the environmental field, ESF is well recognized, and "the name alone will likely set you ahead in your career." The school "truly does provide you with the necessary experience for your field with challenging courses and endless volunteer, research, and internship opportunities throughout your time at ESF."

Life

ESF is home to is an extremely active student body, with "students participating in several clubs at a time and holding several leadership positions at a time." There are a lot of wonderful organizations on campus to get involved in, but when students are tired of those things, "the school shares a border with a 160 acre forested cemetery and it is a very popular place for students to explore and hang out." Central New York is also filled with things to do for students with cars, mostly parks and waterfalls. "Here at 'tree school,' we spend most of our time studying, chilling with pals, or appreciating nature," says one student, adding that students looking for a more active social life enjoy "using Syracuse University facilities and attending their parties." ESF students have the option of pledging Greek organizations at Syracuse, as well. ESF is a smaller school so "everyone really does know everyone." The off-campus housing situation illustrates this pretty well; "most of the students from our school live along this one street."

Student Body

Students describe ESF as "fostering a community that uses the knowledge it gains through schooling to make real changes to our world." Though "everyone takes a different path towards the end goal of helping our planet prosper, it's a main concern for all of us," according to one student. With this common goal, students feel "an almost instantaneous camaraderie." This is "one of the most accepting groups of students" out there, and students here "are free to rock their own styles." "Of course we have hippies and rednecks and everyone in between, but no one is afraid to be themselves and it is a very open…environment," says a student. While some are more focused on wildlife and others on timber resources, "everyone enjoys being outdoors," and students are "often caught discussing class or lab topics in their free time."

STATE UNIVERSITY OF NEW YORK—COLLEGE OF ENVIRONMENTAL SCIENCE AND FORESTRY

Financial Aid: 315-470-6706 • E-Mail: esfinfo@esf.edu • Website: www.esf.edu

THE PRINCETON REVIEW SAYS

Admissions

Very important factors considered include: rigor of secondary school record, academic GPA, application essay, standardized test scores, level of applicant's interest. *Important factors considered include:* class rank, recommendation(s), extracurricular activities, talent/ability. *Other factors considered include:* interview, character/personal qualities, first generation, alumni/ae relation, geographical residence, state residency, racial/ethnic status, volunteer work, work experience. ACT with or without writing accepted. SAT with or without Essay component accepted. High school diploma is required and GED is accepted. *Academic units required:* 4 English, 3 math, 3 science, 3 social studies, 1 history. *Academic units recommended:* 4 math, 4 science, 3 science labs, 3 foreign language.

Financial Aid

Students should submit: FAFSA; State aid form. Priority filing deadline is 2/1. The Princeton Review suggests that all financial aid forms be submitted as soon as possible after October 1. *Need-based scholarships/grants offered:* College/university scholarship or grant aid from institutional funds; Federal Pell; Private scholarships; SEOG; State scholarships/grants. *Loan aid offered:* Direct PLUS loans; Direct Subsidized Stafford Loans; Direct Unsubsidized Stafford Loans. Applicants will be notified of awards on a rolling basis beginning 2/1. Federal Work-Study Program available. Institutional employment available.

The Inside Word

ESF is an excellent value even for students hailing from outside the Empire State. While there are many specialized bachelor of science degrees, there are also coordinated programs between the college and the Upstate Medical University, as well as a host of pre-professional programs. Statistics—test scores and GPA—are an important factor in ESF's admission calculus, but level of demonstrated interest carries as much weight as SAT scores. Aspiring Mighty Oaks should make their interest known early and often.

SELECTIVITY

Admissions Rating	87
# of applicants	2,018
% of applicants accepted	61
% of acceptees attending	31
# of early decision applicants	163
% accepted early decision	80

FRESHMAN PROFILE

Range SAT EBRW	560–660
Range SAT Math	560–650
Range ACT Composite	23–29
# submitting SAT scores	337
% submitting SAT scores	87
# submitting ACT scores	167
% submitting ACT scores	43
Average HS GPA	3.7
% graduated top 10% of class	25
% graduated top 25% of class	63
% graduated top 50% of class	95

DEADLINES

Early decision	
Deadline	12/1
Notification	1/15
Regular	
Priority	2/1
Notification	Rolling, 2/1
Nonfall registration?	Yes

FINANCIAL FACTS

Financial Aid Rating	87
Annual in-state tuition	$7,070
Annual out-of-state tuition	$16,980
Room and board	$16,270
Required fees	$2,045
Books and supplies	$1,200
Average frosh need-based scholarship	$7,510
Average UG need-based scholarship	$6,648
% needy frosh rec. need-based scholarship or grant aid	98
% needy UG rec. need-based scholarship or grant aid	92
% needy frosh rec. non-need-based scholarship or grant aid	72
% needy UG rec. non-need-based scholarship or grant aid	65
% needy frosh rec. need-based self-help aid	69
% needy UG rec. need-based self-help aid	66
% frosh rec. any financial aid	91
% UG rec. any financial aid	93
% UG borrow to pay for school	68
Average cumulative indebtedness	$26,679
% frosh need fully met	35
% ugrads need fully met	48
Average % of frosh need met	70
Average % of ugrad need met	66

STATE UNIVERSITY OF NEW YORK—GENESEO

1 College Circle, Geneseo, NY 14454 • Admissions: 585-245-5571 • Fax: 585-245-5550

CAMPUS LIFE

Quality of Life Rating	85
Fire Safety Rating	98
Green Rating	77
Type of school	Public
Environment	Village

STUDENTS

Total undergrad enrollment	5,222
% male/female	38/62
% from out of state	1
% frosh live on campus	98
% ugrads live on campus	55
# of fraternities (% ugrad men join)	13 (20)
# of sororities (% ugrad women join)	13 (21)
% African American	3
% Asian	5
% Caucasian	77
% Hispanic	8
% Native American	<1
% Pacific Islander	<1
% Two or more races	2
% Race and/or ethnicity unknown	3
% international	1
# of countries represented	18

SURVEY SAYS . . .

Frats and sororities are popular
Students love Geneseo, NY
Lab facilities are great

ACADEMICS

Academic Rating	76
% students returning for sophomore year	85
% students graduating within 4 years	72
% students graduating within 6 years	80
Calendar	Semester
Student/faculty ratio	17:1
Profs interesting rating	81
Profs accessible rating	88

Most classes have 20–29 students.
Most lab/discussion sessions have
10–19 students.

MOST POPULAR MAJORS

Biology, General; Psychology, General;
Communication and Business

STUDENTS SAY "..."

Academics

As a public liberal arts college, State University of New York at Geneseo attracts students searching for a "quality education at an affordable price." Undergrads say this academics-focused college provides "challenging but rewarding" courses taught by faculty who are "here to teach and prepare students for the real world." Students find professors to be "fair in terms of tests and expectations," and note that they "really push the students." While most professors use traditional teaching methods, "giving very interesting lectures or leading good group discussions," other notable forms of learning include "live experiments in class," labs that "develop skills necessary for future studies . . . as well as for general team work," and "counseling services for local businesses." Some classes seem needlessly difficult to students, with the sole purpose of "weeding people out" of competitive majors, but thankfully there are "great resources available to anyone who needs help regardless of the subject matter." Professors provide generous office hours and are mostly "accommodating as long as you reach out to them" and students can "seek help and work with peers through challenging material and problems" at the tutoring centers. Students seeking a challenging liberal arts college environment with a state school price are pleased with the choice to attend Geneseo.

Life

At Geneseo, which sits on a "gorgeous campus [with] beautiful sunsets," students "focus on their academics," but they also make time for clubs or athletics—hockey games in particular bring out school spirit. In addition to team sports, undergrads stay active by "going to the gym or various classes offered by [the] school such as spin, yoga, or Zumba." On warm days, students love to "hang out and do work on the quad, put up a hammock between two trees, or throw a frisbee around ... with friends." Greek life is a big part of the Geneseo experience for some students, as are college sponsored events by the organization Geneseo Late Knight, which "puts on events every single weekend that are free for students." The weekends are also when "students definitely like to party," and they spend time at nearby bars. For those looking to get outside, the "scenery of the Geneseo area" has much more to offer: Students mention it's also great for hiking. Despite this, they note that "the town around us is small so there's not a lot to do," which makes trips to Rochester popular: "it's a short drive away" and reachable via a bus shuttle on the weekends.

Student Body

With its small campus, Geneseo is a "tightly knit community" of "intelligent and kind individuals" where "all members support each other." Students value the "strong sense of community" and say all types of people can be found at Geneseo, although some do claim that their peers are "mostly white," however, students come from "very different upbringings and are from different social classes." One student describes her friends as a mix of "some quiet, some outgoing, some party-animals, and some bookworms." Regardless of this broad range, almost everyone is there to "receive a higher education and be successful." Campus culture is generally liberal, featuring "inclusivity involving ethnicity, religion, and sexuality," but some describe social life as cliquey, noting "it is much harder to make friends if you are not in Greek life." On a final note, one student reassures us, "once you find your people you will feel right at home."

STATE UNIVERSITY OF NEW YORK—GENESEO

Financial Aid: 585-245-5731 • E-Mail: admissions@geneseo.edu • Website: www.geneseo.edu

THE PRINCETON REVIEW SAYS

Admissions

Very important factors considered include: rigor of secondary school record, standardized test scores. *Important factors considered include:* class rank, academic GPA, application essay, recommendation(s), extracurricular activities, talent/ability. *Other factors considered include:* character/personal qualities, first generation, alumni/ae relation, state residency, volunteer work, work experience, level of applicant's interest. ACT with or without writing accepted. SAT with or without Essay component accepted. High school diploma is required and GED is accepted. *Academic units recommended:* 4 English, 4 math, 4 science, 4 foreign language, 4 social studies.

Financial Aid

Students should submit: FAFSA. The Princeton Review suggests that all financial aid forms be submitted as soon as possible after October 1. *Need-based scholarships/grants offered:* Federal Pell; SEOG; State scholarships/grants. *Loan aid offered:* Direct PLUS loans; Direct Subsidized Stafford Loans; Direct Unsubsidized Stafford Loans. Applicants will be notified of awards on a rolling basis beginning 3/15. Federal Work-Study Program available. Institutional employment available.

The Inside Word

While the current acceptance rate is high, the applicant pool for SUNY Geneseo grows increasingly competitive each year. Grades and test scores carry the most weight with the admissions committee here, followed by the rigor of an applicant's high school classes. The personal essay, résumé of co-curricular activities, and recommendations round out the holistic application review.

THE SCHOOL SAYS "..."

From the Admissions Office

"Geneseo occupies a distinctive niche among the nation's premier public liberal arts colleges, allowing it to attract highly motivated and talented students from across the state, around the nation, and from all corners of the world. Its highly-regarded professional programs as well as its cultural, social, recreational, and volunteer service opportunities, lead Geneseo students to attest that "there is no place like here." Geneseo's status as the only SUNY undergraduate college with a chapter of Phi Beta Kappa, the world's most prestigious academic honor society, further solidifies the college's reputation for being a community of outstanding scholars. Inspired by a transformative core curriculum and extraordinary active learning opportunities, Geneseo students are able to pursue independent study, take advantage of global experiences and get involved in research activities with faculty who value close working relationships with exceptional students. And for savvy students who recognize Geneseo's value and the financial advantage it affords, the College is a first-choice and a smart investment. Founded in 1871, the College occupies a beautiful 220-acre campus in the historic Village of Geneseo, which contributes to its inclusive sense of community. It's this intellectual and supportive environment—a hallmark of the Geneseo experience—that inspires students to successfully pursue life and career goals. Over 40% of students pursue graduate study immediately upon graduation, making Geneseo among the country's top ten master's-awarding colleges for the number of doctorates earned, and in the top five for those who earn doctorates in STEM fields."

SELECTIVITY

Admissions Rating	85
# of applicants	10,433
% of applicants accepted	65
% of acceptees attending	18
# offered a place on the wait list	1,756
% accepting a place on wait list	46
% admitted from wait list	25
# of early decision applicants	279
% accepted early decision	84

FRESHMAN PROFILE

Range SAT EBRW	560–650
Range SAT Math	560–660
Range SAT Composite	1140–1300
Range ACT Composite	23–28
# submitting SAT scores	1,088
% submitting SAT scores	88
# submitting ACT scores	145
% submitting ACT scores	12
Average HS GPA	3.6
% graduated top 10% of class	28
% graduated top 25% of class	63
% graduated top 50% of class	93

DEADLINES

Early decision	
Deadline	11/15
Notification	12/15
Regular	
Deadline	1/1
Notification	3/1
Nonfall registration?	Yes

APPLICANTS ALSO LOOK AT AND OFTEN PREFER

State University of New York at Binghamton (Binghamton University); State University of New York—University at Buffalo; University at Albany—SUNY; SUNY College at Oneonta; SUNY Oswego; CUNY Hunter College

AND SOMETIMES PREFER

Fordham University; Skidmore College; Hamilton College; University of Delaware; Ithaca College; Rochester Institute of Technology; Syracuse University; State University of New York at New Paltz

FINANCIAL FACTS

Financial Aid Rating	79
Annual in-state tuition	$7,070
Annual out-of-state tuition	$16,320
Room and board	$12,906
Required fees	$1,807
Books and supplies	$1,000
Average frosh need-based scholarship	$6,837
Average UG need-based scholarship	$6,513
% needy frosh rec. need-based scholarship or grant aid	76
% needy UG rec. need-based scholarship or grant aid	77
% needy frosh rec. non-need-based scholarship or grant aid	20
% needy UG rec. non-need-based scholarship or grant aid	20
% needy frosh rec. need-based self-help aid	75
% needy UG rec. need-based self-help aid	70
% frosh rec. any financial aid	53
% UG rec. any financial aid	49
% UG borrow to pay for school	58
Average cumulative indebtedness	$23,666
% frosh need fully met	15
% ugrads need fully met	15
Average % of frosh need met	41
Average % of ugrad need met	44

STATE UNIVERSITY OF NEW YORK—PURCHASE COLLEGE

735 Anderson Hill Road, Purchase, NY 10577 • Admissions: 914-251-6300 • Fax: 914-251-6314

CAMPUS LIFE
Quality of Life Rating	82
Fire Safety Rating	60*
Green Rating	92
Type of school	Public
Environment	Town

STUDENTS
Total undergrad enrollment	3,978
% male/female	42/58
% from out of state	13
% frosh live on campus	86
% ugrads live on campus	68
% African American	12
% Asian	4
% Caucasian	51
% Hispanic	25
% Native American	<1
% Pacific Islander	<1
% Two or more races	5
% Race and/or ethnicity unknown	1
% international	2
# of countries represented	39

SURVEY SAYS . . .
Lots of liberal students
Students aren't religious
Theater is popular
Active student government

ACADEMICS
Academic Rating	80
% students returning for sophomore year	81
% students graduating within 4 years	53
% students graduating within 6 years	61
Calendar	Semester
Student/faculty ratio	14:1
Profs interesting rating	89
Profs accessible rating	88

Most classes have 10–19 students.
Most lab/discussion sessions have
 10–19 students.

MOST POPULAR MAJORS
Arts, Entertainment, and Media Management;
Liberal Arts and Sciences/Liberal Studies;
Psychology

STUDENTS SAY "..."

Academics

Its motto "Think Wide Open" perfectly sums up SUNY Purchase, long the artsy lodestone in the SUNY system: the conservatory here "deserves and receives the highest respect." Beyond the School of the Arts, the School of Liberal Arts & Sciences offers twenty-three major options, as well as the chance to design an individualized, interdisciplinary major through the Liberal Arts program. Nearly all bachelor's students must complete a senior project in which they devote two semesters to in-depth, original, and creative study, and students welcome the chance to explore. "We're all about finding new ways to think about things, from science to art to management," says one.

Classes tend to be about "learning through discussion" rather than lecture, and professors "go out of their way to make sure that everyone is on the same page, and don't leave anyone behind." They often actively work in the field in which they teach, and therefore "bring the material life and take learning outside the classroom." Classes in both the creative arts and general education are "rich and exciting," such as the professor who "teaches classes about Jack Kerouac on a train and walks the path of *On the Road*." Students benefit from the school's proximity to New York City (less than an hour away), where auditions, showcases, and a fertile alumni network thrive, and "some of the best artists in the NY area become adjunct faculty at this school at some point."

Life

For fun, there's "a TON of things going on": weekly dance parties and concerts, student clubs, lectures, an on-campus museum, free yoga classes, zumba, and tons of festivals. People "pay a lot of money to see bands and they support music and musicians here," and theatre is also "very, very big and popular." Though there are 17 Division III athletics teams, students feel that they get less emphasis, and Greek life is non-existent. Students receive email digests of all the events on campus, and for those who want to get off campus, it's easy to take a bus into White Plains or take the train into Manhattan. "The question isn't 'What to do for fun?' but rather 'Where do you even start?'" Professors usually "know a lot about what's going on" and will often get free tickets to performances for students. While the Student Center (Stood) and library facilities are admittedly great ("there are different levels, so students never have to be isolated in one spot"), many say that Purchase could improve the dorms, as "a lot of the on-campus living needs to be updated badly." Luckily, a new residence hall housing upper class students opened in August 2019.

Student Body

Overwhelmingly accepting of "the weird and strange," the school is known as a beacon for those that didn't fit in in high school. This "artsy, unique, passionate, intelligent" group of students has "a definite sense of unity and acceptance," meaning that everyone is free to be themselves. "People walk around confident in who they are and they aren't afraid to show their unique styles and personalities," says one student. There are a lot of "free spirits" and the atmosphere is "filled with liberal ideologies," and the high concentration of visual/multi-media artists, musicians, and dancers means that "creativity and the arts flourish." The decent number of commuters don't have any real problem integrating with the resident population, and "you can always incorporate your craft into whatever you create at Purchase."

STATE UNIVERSITY OF NEW YORK—PURCHASE COLLEGE

E-Mail: admissions@purchase.edu • Website: www.purchase.edu

THE PRINCETON REVIEW SAYS

Admissions

Very important factors considered include: academic GPA, application essay, talent/ability. *Important factors considered include:* rigor of secondary school record. *Other factors considered include:* class rank, standardized test scores (optional), recommendation(s), interview, extracurricular activities, character/personal qualities. ACT with or without writing accepted. SAT with or without Essay component accepted. High school diploma is required and GED is accepted. *Academic units recommended:* 4 English, 4 math, 3 science, 3 foreign language, 4 social studies, 2 academic electives.

Financial Aid

Students should submit: FAFSA; State aid form. Priority filing deadline is 2/1. The Princeton Review suggests that all financial aid forms be submitted as soon as possible after October 1. *Need-based scholarships/grants offered:* College/university scholarship or grant aid from institutional funds; Federal Pell; Private scholarships; SEOG; State scholarships/grants. *Loan aid offered:* Direct PLUS loans; Direct Subsidized Stafford Loans; Direct Unsubsidized Stafford Loans. Applicants will be notified of awards on a rolling basis beginning 3/1. Federal Work-Study Program available. Institutional employment available.

The Inside Word

Almost 40 percent of Purchase students are enrolled in the highly selective School of the Arts. Arts applicants should know that to apply to the programs in dance, theatre arts, music, School of Art+Design, or School of Film and Media Studies—the audition, portfolio, or other applicable work samples in addition to academic performance are of paramount importance. Purchase College is test optional, and standardized test scores will only be reviewed if a student chooses to submit them.

THE SCHOOL SAYS "..."

From the Admissions Office

"Whether for our top-ranked and innovative liberal arts majors or our world-class arts programs, Purchase attracts students from around the globe seeking to cultivate their intellectual identity, develop their talents, expand their minds and transform their passions into action. By choosing Purchase, students make a conscious decision to join an intense community with a deep respect for individuality and diversity and an unparalleled environment of creativity and innovation.

"Our dynamic faculty are not only among the most accomplished in their fields but also partner with students on research projects and work tirelessly to ensure students succeed in their chosen fields of study or career. The intimate classroom setting and engaged faculty inspire lively classroom discussion and debate, critical thinking, originality, and discovery and invention.

"Purchase students represent a broad spectrum of familial, social, ethnic, economic, and geographical backgrounds. The student body is also diverse in terms of gender identity and sexual orientation. Highly talented, motivated, and entrepreneurial, Purchase students strive to impact our society through civic and cultural engagement.

"Still a relatively young college, Purchase offers students an opportunity to build upon established campus traditions as well as create new ones. Our proximity to New York City provides students access to outstanding cultural and career-related opportunities. On campus, students can see world-class performances at the PAC and notable exhibitions at the Neuberger Museum.

"We seek to enroll highly motivated, hard-working and academically strong students with a consistent record of achievement in a challenging high school curriculum. Admission criteria vary amongst programs."

SELECTIVITY

Admissions Rating	87
# of applicants	6,486
% of applicants accepted	52
% of acceptees attending	24

FRESHMAN PROFILE

Range SAT EBRW	540–640
Range SAT Math	520–620
Range ACT Composite	23–30
# submitting SAT scores	313
% submitting SAT scores	39
# submitting ACT scores	73
% submitting ACT scores	9
Average HS GPA	3.3

DEADLINES

Early action	
Deadline	11/15
Notification	1/1
Regular	
Deadline	7/1
Notification	Rolling, 10/1
Nonfall registration?	Yes

FINANCIAL FACTS

Financial Aid Rating	80
Annual in-state tuition	$7,070
Annual out-of-state tuition	$16,980
Room and board	$14,548
Required fees	$2,093
Books and supplies	$1,240
Average frosh need-based scholarship	$10,465
Average UG need-based scholarship	$10,870
% needy frosh rec. need-based scholarship or grant aid	95
% needy UG rec. need-based scholarship or grant aid	98
% needy frosh rec. non-need-based scholarship or grant aid	14
% needy UG rec. non-need-based scholarship or grant aid	18
% needy frosh rec. need-based self-help aid	82
% needy UG rec. need-based self-help aid	88
% UG borrow to pay for school	68
Average cumulative indebtedness	$23,987
% frosh need fully met	5
% ugrads need fully met	2
Average % of frosh need met	49
Average % of ugrad need met	50

STATE UNIVERSITY OF NEW YORK—STONY BROOK UNIVERSITY

Office of Undergraduate Admissions, Stony Brook, NY 11794-1901 • Admissions: 631-632-6868 • Fax: 631-632-9898

STUDENTS SAY ". . ."

Academics

Stony Brook University offers a world class research university experience with excellent value. There are more than 200 academic programs that attract "a diverse array of students with interests and passions in everything under the sun," with STEM programs receiving particularly high praise. The large campus population means students need to be motived self-advocates, and the university does a good job of making students aware of opportunities and structuring their curriculum. "Advising [is] very organized and helpful," and "larger lectures are broken down into smaller groups to help facilitate better learning." After the first year, "class sizes reduce drastically." "Research is a key part of the academic process" and those who choose to attend Stony Brook "are often interested in making discoveries in this world." Undergraduate Research and Creative Activities (URECA) is a program that gives students the ability to get involved with research or other on-campus experiences with faculty.

Professors are "always willing to give educational and professional advice" and "are all very enthusiastic about the courses they teach." They are great at "offering creative problems that show the real-world applications of our studies." Many teachers at Stony Brook "combine the theory of the textbook with what they experienced," which "is extremely dynamic." Students agree that there are some professors that focus too heavily on their research, but once you get to more advanced courses, "actually interacting with and getting help from professors and TAs is far easier and more worthwhile."

Life

During the week, students "spend a lot time in class, studying, or doing homework" in the dorms and the library. On the weekend, students typically "go out with friends either to restaurants, parties, the movie theaters, [or the] mall," and a large portion of students head home. Still, there are plenty of school-sponsored activities, and the university sends out twice-weekly emails to the student body publicizing events on campus, "which is a wonderful gesture." There is "a surplus of clubs" that mostly meet on Wednesdays from 1–2 P.M. (there are no classes scheduled at this time), and it "is hard to get bored. If you aren't involved, you aren't trying." Stony Brook has a "spectacular" recreational center where students can play sports, work out, or take fitness classes (such as kick boxing, self-defense, and yoga), and the campus is "surrounded with historic sites, beaches" and not too far away from New York City, with a train near campus. School spirit infuses annual Stony Brook traditions "such as Roth Regatta (a boat race of boats made from only cardboard and duct tape), Earthstock, and semesterly concerts."

Student Body

Students describe the campus population as very diverse, "with people from different places, of different ethnicities, and of different ages," which makes for "a very inclusive and inviting environment." With a large international student population, it "is so easy to become socially aware of other cultures simply by talking to people." This "cheerful and helpful" crew is "incredibly knowledgeable," and the work ethic most students display motivates others to work harder. "A Seawolf doesn't hesitate when another needs anything," says one student.

STATE UNIVERSITY OF NEW YORK—STONY BROOK UNIVERSITY

Financial Aid: 631-632-6840 • E-Mail: enroll@stonybrook.edu • Website: www.stonybrook.edu/

THE PRINCETON REVIEW SAYS

Admissions

Very important factors considered include: rigor of secondary school record, academic GPA, standardized test scores. *Important factors considered include:* application essay, recommendation(s). *Other factors considered include:* class rank, interview, extracurricular activities, talent/ability, character/personal qualities, first generation, alumni/ae relation, geographical residence, state residency, volunteer work, work experience, level of applicant's interest. ACT with Writing recommended. SAT with Essay component recommended. High school diploma is required and GED is accepted. *Academic units required:* 4 English, 4 math, 4 science, 4 social studies. *Academic units recommended:* 4 English, 4 math, 4 science, 3 foreign language, 4 social studies.

Financial Aid

Students should submit: FAFSA; State aid form. Priority filing deadline is 3/1. The Princeton Review suggests that all financial aid forms be submitted as soon as possible after October 1. *Need-based scholarships/grants offered:* College/university scholarship or grant aid from institutional funds; Federal Pell; Private scholarships; SEOG; State scholarships/grants. *Loan aid offered:* Direct PLUS loans; Direct Subsidized Stafford Loans; Direct Unsubsidized Stafford Loans. Applicants will be notified of awards on a rolling basis beginning 4/1. Federal Work-Study Program available. Institutional employment available.

The Inside Word

Admission to Stony Brook University is competitive. Successful applicants for the freshman class will have typically followed a rigorous college prep curriculum in high school and have strong standardized test scores, and the university will also give special consideration to leadership experience or talents demonstrated through extracurricular activities or volunteer work. Students with a particularly strong academic record may be considered for the university's special programs, including the Honors College, the University Scholars program, and Women in Science and Engineering.

THE SCHOOL SAYS "..."

From the Admissions Office

"Stony Brook University is going beyond the expectations of what today's public universities can accomplish, offering students an elite education with an outstanding return on investment. Stony Brook offers more than 200 majors, minors and combined-degree programs. Among our innovative programs are a fast-track MBA program and the award-winning Undergraduate Research and Creative Activities (URECA) program, which involves undergraduates in research in nearly every discipline and has produced Goldwater, Marshall and Truman scholars. Unique research opportunities abound at our medical center, in our marine sciences program and at nearby Brookhaven National Laboratory, which Stony Brook has a role in running. We offer a variety of honors programs—such as University Scholars, Honors College, and Women in Science and Engineering, as well as honors tracks in Computer Science and Business—to challenge and inspire our most gifted students. Faculty include Nobel laureates, Guggenheim fellows, MacArthur grant recipients, Fields medalists and Pulitzer-Prize winners. Students enjoy a dynamic first-year experience in one of six small undergraduate communities, reside in comfortable campus housing, and have access to outstanding recreational facilities, including an 12,300-seat stadium, a modern student activities center, a sports complex housing a 4,000-seat arena, and a state-of-the-art campus recreation center devoted entirely to the health and well-being of the campus community. The Staller Center for the Arts features spectacular theatrical and musical performances throughout the year. Beyond the campus, Stony Brook offers unique study abroad programs on six continents in nearly 30 different countries."

SELECTIVITY

Admissions Rating	91
# of applicants	37,079
% of applicants accepted	44
% of acceptees attending	21
# offered a place on the wait list	3,500
% accepting a place on wait list	43
% admitted from wait list	10

FRESHMAN PROFILE

Range SAT EBRW	590–690
Range SAT Math	640–750
Range ACT Composite	26–32
# submitting SAT scores	2,906
% submitting SAT scores	86
# submitting ACT scores	686
% submitting ACT scores	20
Average HS GPA	3.8
% graduated top 10% of class	51
% graduated top 25% of class	80
% graduated top 50% of class	96

DEADLINES

Regular	
Priority	1/15
Deadline	1/15
Notification	4/1
Nonfall registration?	Yes

APPLICANTS ALSO LOOK AT AND OFTEN PREFER

Cornell University; Rensselaer Polytechnic Institute; State University of New York at Binghamton (Binghamton University); New York University

AND SOMETIMES PREFER

Penn State University Park; Rutgers University–New Brunswick; University of Connecticut; State University of New York—University at Buffalo; State University of New York at Geneseo

AND RARELY PREFER

Adelphi University; Hofstra University; Pace University

FINANCIAL FACTS

Financial Aid Rating	84
Annual in-state tuition	$7,070
Annual out-of-state tuition	$24,740
Room and board	$14,278
Required fees	$3,105
Books and supplies	$900
Average frosh need-based scholarship	$10,477
Average UG need-based scholarship	$9,443
% needy frosh rec. need-based scholarship or grant aid	91
% needy UG rec. need-based scholarship or grant aid	87
% needy frosh rec. non-need-based scholarship or grant aid	10
% needy UG rec. non-need-based scholarship or grant aid	7
% needy frosh rec. need-based self-help aid	89
% needy UG rec. need-based self-help aid	88
% frosh rec. any financial aid	79
% UG rec. any financial aid	70
% UG borrow to pay for school	49
Average cumulative indebtedness	$25,678
% frosh need fully met	13
% ugrads need fully met	16
Average % of frosh need met	65
Average % of ugrad need met	65

STEPHENS COLLEGE

1200 East Broadway, Columbia, MO 65215 • Admissions: 573-876-7207 • Fax: 573-876-7237

CAMPUS LIFE

Quality of Life Rating	94
Fire Safety Rating	84
Green Rating	66
Type of school	Private
Environment	City

STUDENTS

Total undergrad enrollment	724
% male/female	1/99
% from out of state	37
% frosh from public high school	80
% frosh live on campus	99
% ugrads live on campus	76
# of fraternities	0
# of sororities	2
% African American	13
% Asian	2
% Caucasian	69
% Hispanic	4
% Native American	<1
% Pacific Islander	<1
% Two or more races	6
% Race and/or ethnicity unknown	4
% international	<1
# of countries represented	1

SURVEY SAYS . . .

Students are happy
Great library
Career services are great
Internships are widely available
Great financial aid
No one cheats
Students are friendly
Diverse student types interact on campus
Students get along with local community
Students love Columbia, MO
Great off-campus food
Easy to get around campus
Very little drug use
Theater is popular
Alumni active on campus
Active student government
Active minority support groups

ACADEMICS

Academic Rating	84
% students returning for sophomore year	69
Calendar	Semester
Student/faculty ratio	9:1
Profs interesting rating	93
Profs accessible rating	93

Most classes have fewer than 10 students.

MOST POPULAR MAJORS

Biology/Biological Sciences, General; Fashion/Apparel Design; Health Professions And Related Programs

STUDENTS SAY "..."

Academics

Stephens College is one of the oldest all women's educational institutions in the country, having spent more than 180 years "empowering women to be independent and show that we can change the world." Class sizes are very small, so it makes for "a very intensive learning experience," but luckily the programs here are "so awesome and creative, no Stephens woman is ever bored." The fashion program is wildly popular and an annual fashion show is one of the school's most anticipated events, and a strong theatre program "consistently produces great performers." "Although we are small, we are mighty," says a student. "It feels like a warm hug every day on campus."

Stephens is "blessed" to have an incredible teaching staff. "By creating an amazing and comfortable environment to learn in and ask questions we are set up to succeed in our futures," says a student. "They also make class time meaningful and always worth going." "You hit up your favorite professors...during their office hours and catch up with them the same way you caught up with your friends in the morning over coffee," says a student. All professors "make time to work with you on a personal level" both inside and outside of the classroom and "include lesson plans for every type of learner," taking time for the experts and the newbies no matter their skill level. Each student gets an adviser in their department who is "attentive to their needs and goals," and the student body and staff "have amazing communication amongst each other" as well.

Life

Stephens 'Susies' "enjoy having a great time, but realize when it is time to study." School-sponsored events can be as frequent as two to four in a day with big events (such as "Half the Sky Day, Citizen Jane, and Diversity Week") happening once or twice a week. When students "aren't throwing little parties or fighting the good fight, we just chill." People enjoy "making meals together in the community kitchens" or at an on-campus apartment, and the lobbies have TVs so "self-organized movie nights are popular," as well. Some dorm halls "could use a bit of an update," but all speak lovingly of the "cozy" hallway parties and ensuing friendships. Also of note: the school allows pets on campus.

Most girls are committed to multiple clubs or sports, as "you'd have to go out of your way to not participate in something." Columbia itself is a great three-college town filled with everything from "awesome food joints like Gumby's Pizza and Strange Donuts to art galleries, clubs/bars, Saturday college football games, arcades, geek/novelty stores, and much more." Students like to go out and shop, hit the bars (if they're of age), or just go hiking or exploring the local caves and trails surrounding the city.

Student Body

This community of "inspiring, supportive and motivating women" is "a melting pot of women" where everyone "appreciates the outcasts and black sheep." There are no cookie-cutter college groups here, and a quick survey of the campus will reveal a group of "genuine" women who embody what they love, and whether that means "wearing riding boots, stage makeup, or toting a way too heavy light kit, students are always working on something and looking to achieve their dreams." "We come from literally all over the world. It's such a welcoming, diverse atmosphere," says one girl. Unsurprisingly, feminism "runs strong" here and Stephens is also a "very liberal LGBT+ friendly" place. "Imagine if Katniss from *The Hunger Games*, Rey from *Star Wars*, Anna and Elsa from *Frozen*, Hermione from *Harry Potter*, and Tris from *The Hunger Games* all went to school together," says a student. "Yeah, it's that."

STEPHENS COLLEGE

Financial Aid: 573-876-7106 • E-Mail: apply@stephens.edu • Website: http://www.stephens.edu/

THE PRINCETON REVIEW SAYS

Admissions

Very important factors considered include: rigor of secondary school record, academic GPA, standardized test scores. *Important factors considered include:* recommendation(s), extracurricular activities, talent/ability, character/personal qualities. *Other factors considered include:* class rank, application essay, interview, volunteer work, work experience, level of applicant's interest. ACT with or without writing accepted. SAT with or without Essay component accepted. High school diploma is required and GED is accepted. *Academic units recommended:* 4 English, 3 math, 2 science, 2 foreign language, 1 social studies.

Financial Aid

Students should submit: FAFSA. Priority filing deadline is 2/1. The Princeton Review suggests that all financial aid forms be submitted as soon as possible after October 1. *Need-based scholarships/grants offered:* College/university scholarship or grant aid from institutional funds; Federal Pell; Private scholarships; SEOG; State scholarships/grants. *Loan aid offered:* Direct PLUS loans; Direct Subsidized Stafford Loans; Direct Unsubsidized Stafford Loans. Applicants will be notified of awards on a rolling basis beginning 10/1. Federal Work-Study Program available. Institutional employment available.

The Inside Word

Even with only half the population eligible for admission, the applicant pool at Stephens is still quite small, so anyone bearing less than a solid B average had better have the test scores and activities to make up space. A little over half of all applicants get in, and early decision is recommended for students who know this distinctive college is where they want to be.

THE SCHOOL SAYS "..."

From the Admissions Office

"Stephens College prepares students to become leaders and innovators in a rapidly changing world, and engages lifelong learners in an educational experience characterized by intellectual rigor, creative expression and professional practice. Since its founding in 1833, the College has been offering innovative, career-focused programs sound in the liberal arts with a focus on creative arts and sciences. Stephens takes a hands-on, experiential approach to education, making sure students get both quality classroom instruction and external work experiences.

"The second-oldest women's college in the U.S., Stephens is committed to educating and empowering women at all stages in life. At Stephens, women learn to think critically, communicate powerfully, lead responsibly and engage for change. The curriculum is thoughtful and respects those values.

"Stephens is a pet-friendly campus proudly located in Columbia, Missouri, home to more than 36,000 college students, and the campus is located just minutes from Columbia's thriving downtown district."

SELECTIVITY

Admissions Rating	83
# of applicants	1,168
% of applicants accepted	61
% of acceptees attending	22

FRESHMAN PROFILE

Range SAT EBRW	450–620
Range SAT Math	440–570
Range ACT Composite	20–25
# submitting SAT scores	16
% submitting SAT scores	10
# submitting ACT scores	149
% submitting ACT scores	93
Average HS GPA	3.3
% graduated top 10% of class	14
% graduated top 25% of class	44
% graduated top 50% of class	79

DEADLINES

Early decision	
Deadline	12/31
Notification	11/1
Early action	
Deadline	12/31
Notification	12/31
Regular	
Priority	1/18
Notification	Rolling, 1/1
Nonfall registration?	Yes

FINANCIAL FACTS

Financial Aid Rating	85
Annual tuition	$30,144
Room and board	$10,424
Books and supplies	$1,000
Average frosh need-based scholarship	$16,000
Average UG need-based scholarship	$14,000
% needy frosh rec. need-based scholarship or grant aid	100
% needy UG rec. need-based scholarship or grant aid	100
% needy frosh rec. non-need-based scholarship or grant aid	84
% needy UG rec. non-need-based scholarship or grant aid	93
% needy frosh rec. need-based self-help aid	100
% needy UG rec. need-based self-help aid	100
% frosh rec. any financial aid	100
% UG rec. any financial aid	98
% UG borrow to pay for school	93
Average cumulative indebtedness	$9,238
Average % of frosh need met	80
Average % of ugrad need met	70

STETSON UNIVERSITY

421 N. Woodland Blvd, DeLand, FL 32723 • Admissions: 386-822-7100 • Fax: 386-822-7112

CAMPUS LIFE
Quality of Life Rating	86
Fire Safety Rating	81
Green Rating	76
Type of school	Private
Environment	Town

STUDENTS
Total undergrad enrollment	3,135
% male/female	43/57
% from out of state	25
% frosh from public high school	75
% frosh live on campus	83
% ugrads live on campus	65
# of fraternities (% ugrad men join)	9 (24)
# of sororities (% ugrad women join)	6 (23)
% African American	8
% Asian	2
% Caucasian	58
% Hispanic	18
% Native American	<1
% Pacific Islander	<1
% Two or more races	5
% Race and/or ethnicity unknown	1
% international	6
# of countries represented	58

SURVEY SAYS . . .
Frats and sororities are popular
Intramural sports are popular
Easy to get around campus

ACADEMICS
Academic Rating	80
% students returning for sophomore year	77
% students graduating within 4 years	60
% students graduating within 6 years	65
Calendar	Semester
Student/faculty ratio	13:1
Profs interesting rating	89
Profs accessible rating	93

Most classes have 10–19 students.
Most lab/discussion sessions have
   10–19 students.

MOST POPULAR MAJORS
Health Sciences; Psychology; Business
Administration

STUDENTS SAY ". . ."

Academics

Stetson University in Central Florida may offer more than fifty-five majors to 3,000 undergraduate students, but students say the focus remains on the individual. Between "small class sizes," "readily available" technology (like a 3-D printer), numerous "opportunities for involvement and learning," and a "multitude of hands-on activities," the institution not only works to cater to each enrollee, but seeks to engage them in the world with "classes where we spend time in the classroom working on community and global problems and then address them ... through volunteering." Stetson never limits itself or its students, which is why those in the Honors Program can design a class of their choice, "which gives students the opportunity to explore something not otherwise offered at Stetson," and offers "countless opportunities to study abroad."

Professors "inherently care about our paths and experiences and always want to enhance them in the best way possible," which often means that they "encourage outdoor activity rather than remaining in one environment to learn." As one student puts it, "They truly care about making sure that students understand the material, and are willing to go out of their way to make that happen." This extra layer of focus on student well-being isn't just because of the low student-to-faculty ratio, though respondents note that this feature is "allowing me to work closely with my professors and developing a unique relationship with some of the best professionals in my field of study." Rather, this level of individualized aid is built into university life, with the school offering "so much support to [its] students. Between one-on-one tutoring, career counseling, the Writing Center, and professors who want to know their students, Stetson does an amazing job making sure we are never alone."

Life

Stetson highly encourages involvement out of the classroom as well, and students suggest that many are "very engaged in campus activities." Some programs, such as mixers and social networking events, are even "specifically catered towards commuters that make you engage with campus and other students." That vibe extends beyond school-sanctioned meetings as well, with undergrads noting that "there are always on-campus events going on, which are generally very well-attended." Even weekdays are busy—"the outside of the student union is filled with tabling events," notes one student, and others add that "there are clubs and organizations to support all religions, faiths, races, and orientations." There's a lot of emphasis on the outdoors as well, whether that comes from the Hollis Center (the on-campus gym), which "has a program called SOAR where they organize outdoor activities" or just from students in general: "If it's a nice day out, I and other students typically grab lunch and eat under the trees." As for the weekend, nearby Main Street is known for having a "surprisingly ... nice nightlife that's fun, even if low-key," and of course, there's always room to "take trips to the beach together."

Student Body

The general consensus is that "Stetson is a place where genuine, lifelong friendships develop." Students feel that the school's relatively smaller size makes it "easier to make connections and friends, especially in classes," but also note that the general culture "is inviting, accessible, and open." All of the opportunities to engage and get involved result in an "incredibly driven group of people" and what some positively describe as "a dynamic vibe on campus." As one puts it, "everyone is a leader in some form on campus." And most importantly about the school to some is not only that there is "a wide range of diversity in its students' background and experience," but that this so often tends to lead to a place where "people are supportive of one another, like a family."

STETSON UNIVERSITY

Financial Aid: 800-688-7120 • E-Mail: admissions@stetson.edu • Website: stetson.edu

THE PRINCETON REVIEW SAYS

Admissions

Very important factors considered include: rigor of secondary school record, academic GPA. *Important factors considered include:* class rank, application essay, standardized test scores, recommendation(s), interview, extracurricular activities, talent/ability, character/personal qualities. *Other factors considered include:* alumni/ae relation, geographical residence, state residency, racial/ethnic status. ACT with or without writing accepted. SAT with or without Essay component accepted. High school diploma is required and GED is accepted. *Academic units required:* 4 English, 3 math, 3 science, 2 foreign language, 2 social studies.

Financial Aid

Students should submit: FAFSA. Priority filing deadline is 11/1. The Princeton Review suggests that all financial aid forms be submitted as soon as possible after October 1. *Need-based scholarships/grants offered:* College/university scholarship or grant aid from institutional funds; Federal Pell; Private scholarships; SEOG; State scholarships/grants. *Loan aid offered:* Direct PLUS loans; Direct Subsidized Stafford Loans; Direct Unsubsidized Stafford Loans. Applicants will be notified of awards on a rolling basis beginning 12/1. Federal Work-Study Program available. Institutional employment available.

The Inside Word

Stetson University operates with early action deadlines on November 1 (Early Action I), January 15 (Early Action II), and March 1 (Regular Decision). Applicants are required to submit an official transcript, at least one letter of recommendation, and a writing sample, with standardized test scores being optional but recommended. Stetson's acceptance rate is deceptively high: this school attracts go-getters, and each year's freshman class profile is more impressive than the last.

THE SCHOOL SAYS "..."

From the Admissions Office

"Creative problem solving and innovation are traditional hallmarks of a Stetson education. In fact, Stetson University is home to many Florida firsts: the first private university in the state, the first collegiate newspaper, the first schools of business, music, and law, and in 1962, one of the first private universities in the state to integrate.

"Stetson University students are daring, hardworking, open-minded, and caring. Our mission is providing a challenging education in a creative community where learning, leadership and values meet. We mentor students, cultivating in them the qualities of mind and heart, and preparing them to gain confidence as informed citizens of local communities and the world. Undergraduate leadership, research, internships, and community-engaged learning flourish here.

"Stetson University is home to 17 NCAA Division I athletics teams, over 100 clubs, and 73 academic programs with both undergraduate and graduate studies in many areas. Accredited by numerous accrediting agencies, including the Southern Association of College and Schools Commission on Colleges, Stetson is among only a handful of schools worldwide where both Business and Accounting programs are accredited by AACSB International at the undergraduate and graduate levels. Stetson is also a proud member of Phi Beta Kappa, joining less than 10% of colleges and universities in the country within this prestigious academic institution.

"Academic and campus life programs are centered on a rigorous examination of values with leadership potential, records of personal growth, and community service. Here, graduation isn't just the end goal. It's one stop along the way, as students pursue something greater for themselves and the world around them.

"At Stetson University, we encourage students to go beyond expectations."

SELECTIVITY

Admissions Rating	80
# of applicants	13,005
% of applicants accepted	72
% of acceptees attending	10
# offered place on wait list	760
% accepting place on wait list	95
% admitted from wait list	48

FRESHMAN PROFILE

Range SAT EBRW	570–660
Range SAT Math	540–640
Range SAT Composite	1130–1290
Range ACT Composite	22–29
# submitting SAT scores	505
% submitting SAT scores	54
# submitting ACT scores	278
% submitting ACT scores	30
Average HS GPA	3.9
% graduated top 10% of class	23
% graduated top 25% of class	56
% graduated top 50% of class	87

DEADLINES

Early action	
Deadline	11/1
Regular	
Priority	11/1
Notification	Rolling, 9/1
Nonfall registration?	Yes

APPLICANTS ALSO LOOK AT AND OFTEN PREFER
University of Central Florida; University of Florida; Florida State University

AND SOMETIMES PREFER
Rollins College; University of Tampa

AND RARELY PREFER
Elon University; Florida Southern College; University of Miami

FINANCIAL FACTS

Financial Aid Rating	87
Annual tuition	$49,140
Room and board	$14,540
Required fees	$360
Books and supplies	$1,200
Average frosh need-based scholarship	$35,451
Average UG need-based scholarship	$33,564
% needy frosh rec. need-based scholarship or grant aid	100
% needy UG rec. need-based scholarship or grant aid	99
% needy frosh rec. non-need-based scholarship or grant aid	25
% needy UG rec. non-need-based scholarship or grant aid	20
% needy frosh rec. need-based self-help aid	75
% needy UG rec. need-based self-help aid	75
% frosh rec. any financial aid	100
% UG rec. any financial aid	98
% UG borrow to pay for school	65
Average cumulative indebtedness	$32,601
% frosh need fully met	27
% ugrads need fully met	23
Average % of frosh need met	82
Average % of ugrad need met	78

THE BEST 386 COLLEGES ■ 549

STEVENS INSTITUTE OF TECHNOLOGY

One Castle Point Terrace, Hoboken, NJ 07030 • Admissions: 201-216-5194 • Fax: 201-216-8348

CAMPUS LIFE

Quality of Life Rating	84
Fire Safety Rating	99
Green Rating	95
Type of school	Private
Environment	Town

STUDENTS

Total undergrad enrollment	3,420
% male/female	71/29
% from out of state	38
% frosh live on campus	91
% ugrads live on campus	60
# of fraternities (% ugrad men join)	13 (29)
# of sororities (% ugrad women join)	7 (42)
% African American	2
% Asian	15
% Caucasian	64
% Hispanic	11
% Native American	<1
% Pacific Islander	0
% Two or more races	0
% Race and/or ethnicity unknown	4
% international	4
# of countries represented	48

SURVEY SAYS . . .

Students love Hoboken, NJ
Great off-campus food
Frats and sororities are popular

ACADEMICS

Academic Rating	76
% students returning for sophomore year	95
% students graduating within 4 years	42
% students graduating within 6 years	83
Calendar	Semester
Student/faculty ratio	10:1
Profs interesting rating	79
Profs accessible rating	87

Most classes have 20–29 students.
Most lab/discussion sessions have 20–29 students.

MOST POPULAR MAJORS

Computer Science; Computer Engineering, General; Mechanical Engineering

STUDENTS SAY ". . ."

Academics

It's no surprise that students at Stevens Institute of Technology feel as if they're receiving an "Ivy League caliber education at a more affordable" price. Indeed, there's much talk of the "high job placement rate" and overall "return on investment," particularly within the "rigorous but fair" physics classes and the "strong engineering department." But undergrads also find the school itself to be "very collaborative and supportive," with plenty of attention given to teaching about the "work ethic and moving past perceived failures." That means that there's room to foster relationships with professors, which can "lead to hands-on, paid research positions and connections to the professional world." As for that faculty, students describe a decent percentage as being "very enthusiastic about their material" and who "look to pass on their knowledge as best they can." If anything, "many professors are so qualified that they begin teaching the material at a level slightly above a beginner's understanding," which can sometimes be demanding, but the overall impression is that there are some great opportunities to learn from experienced mentors.

Life

Life at Stevens can be hectic in the best way, which is to say that there's so much to take advantage of. Students are often "running around to different events, club meetings, eboard meetings, study groups, classes, etc," and you'll likely find every sort of topic covered, whether it's the poker or anime club, the society of women engineers, or intramural sports like floor hockey. According to some proud undergrads, "We are definitely a nerdy school with some of our most popular events being Lan Parties and the Epic Lans where people can play video games and board games and compete in friendly Melee and Ultimate tournaments." Greek life provides a nice counter-balance for some students and many find themselves busy with "service trips [and] rush events" along with the occasional party. Additionally, there's "a movie theater within walking distance" and "a ton of great restaurants on the main street right next to campus." There's also the affordable PATH train just "a 10 minute walk away from campus," which means that "New York City is so close," and a frequent weekend getaway for students looking for even more to do.

Student Body

Some students may throw around terms for their peers like "very ambitious and driven" in a negative light, but not so at Stevens. Here, "nearly everyone is very smart and intelligent without being snobby or arrogant." More importantly, they're also quite supportive of one another. "If you have a huge assignment due and are stressing over it, your friends motivate you by cheering you on and checking up on your progress." A few do complain that "there is a large chunk of students that are very quiet and won't do anything besides schoolwork and video games," but that doesn't lead a negative impact. "Everyone finds a friend group no matter what." It does, however, leave the school "almost split between the Greek community and the non-Greek community." Some also note that "diversity is lacking." Indeed, "almost everyone that attends Stevens is either white, or an international student (predominantly Asian)." Moreover, "the student body is 70% male" and many hail "from New Jersey." Nevertheless, Stevens undergrads do have varied interests and you're bound to encounter "artistic students, gamers, athletes, and pretty much every other kind." Best of all, you'll discover that "a great sense of community" permeates the campus.

STEVENS INSTITUTE OF TECHNOLOGY

Financial Aid: 201-216-8142 • E-Mail: admissions@stevens.edu • Website: http://www.stevens.edu/princetonreview

THE PRINCETON REVIEW SAYS

Admissions

Very important factors considered include: rigor of secondary school record, academic GPA, standardized test scores. *Important factors considered include:* talent/ability, character/personal qualities. *Other factors considered include:* class rank, application essay, recommendation(s), interview, extracurricular activities, first generation, alumni/ae relation, geographical residence, state residency, racial/ethnic status, volunteer work, work experience, level of applicant's interest. ACT with or without writing accepted. SAT with or without Essay component accepted. High school diploma is required and GED is accepted. *Academic units required:* 4 English, 4 math, 3 science, 3 science labs, 2 foreign language, 2 history. *Academic units recommended:* 4 science, 4 science labs, 4 foreign language, 4 history.

Financial Aid

Students should submit: CSS/Financial Aid PROFILE; FAFSA. Priority filing deadline is 2/15. The Princeton Review suggests that all financial aid forms be submitted as soon as possible after October 1. *Need-based scholarships/grants offered:* College/university scholarship or grant aid from institutional funds; Federal Pell; Private scholarships; SEOG; State scholarships/grants; United Negro College Fund. *Loan aid offered:* Direct PLUS loans; Direct Subsidized Stafford Loans; Direct Unsubsidized Stafford Loans; State Loans. Federal Work-Study Program available. Institutional employment available.

The Inside Word

The admissions process at Stevens Institute of Technology is definitely competitive. To be a serious contender, you will need a strong GPA and solid standardized test scores. Most highly qualified applicants also have plenty of honors, advanced placement or IB classes on their transcript. And given that Stevens is a tech school, your science and math courses will be closely evaluated. Finally, if you think the college is your top choice, it's a good idea to take advantage of applying early decision.

THE SCHOOL SAYS "..."

From the Admissions Office

"Technological innovation has been the driving force behind a Stevens education since the university's founding in 1870 by America's 'first family of inventors.' Whether they're designing an award-winning solar-powered home for the future, launching the next great technology startup or performing cutting-edge research, Stevens students and faculty collaborate in an interdisciplinary, student-centric, entrepreneurial environment to confront global challenges. Leading-edge programs in more than thirty undergraduate majors in business, computer science, arts, humanities, engineering and sciences teach students how to create and leverage technology in ways that matter to today's society. Tying education to a career path is a long-standing tradition at Stevens, which is why the university is consistently ranked among the nation's elite for student ROI, career services and mid-career salaries of alumni. A host of experiential learning opportunities provide real-world work and research experiences so that when students graduate from the university, they are ready to hit the ground running. Our location in Hoboken, NJ, minutes from New York City and the surrounding metro area, cultivates unmatched internship, cooperative education, and other project-based learning opportunities for Stevens students. Entrepreneurship programs encourage students to think creatively and to pursue big ideas. The annual Innovation Expo is a celebration of senior capstone projects, which are often undertaken in collaboration with students from other disciplines, mentored by faculty, and sponsored by industry partners. A robust student life, an exciting college town, and more than 125 student organizations and 25 NCAA Division III athletics teams add to an enriching student experience."

SELECTIVITY

Admissions Rating	94
# of applicants	9,265
% of applicants accepted	41
% of acceptees attending	26
# offered a place on the wait list	1,503
% accepting a place on wait list	42
# of early decision applicants	655
% accepted early decision	59

FRESHMAN PROFILE

Range SAT EBRW	640–710
Range SAT Math	690–770
Range SAT Composite	1330–1480
Range ACT Composite	30–33
# submitting SAT scores	693
% submitting SAT scores	69
# submitting ACT scores	296
% submitting ACT scores	29
Average HS GPA	3.9
% graduated top 10% of class	72
% graduated top 25% of class	96
% graduated top 50% of class	100

DEADLINES

Early decision	
Deadline	11/15
Notification	12/15
Other ED Deadline	1/15
Other ED Notification	2/15
Regular	
Deadline	1/15
Notification	4/1
Nonfall registration?	No

FINANCIAL FACTS

Financial Aid Rating	82
Annual tuition	$52,134
Room and board	$15,770
Required fees	$1,880
Books and supplies	$1,200
Average frosh need-based scholarship	$15,291
Average UG need-based scholarship	$13,203
% needy frosh rec. need-based scholarship or grant aid	71
% needy UG rec. need-based scholarship or grant aid	65
% needy frosh rec. non-need-based scholarship or grant aid	99
% needy UG rec. non-need-based scholarship or grant aid	96
% needy frosh rec. need-based self-help aid	78
% needy UG rec. need-based self-help aid	78
% frosh rec. any financial aid	99
% UG rec. any financial aid	94
% UG borrow to pay for school	64
Average cumulative indebtedness	$40,588
% frosh need fully met	13
% ugrads need fully met	16
Average % of frosh need met	70
Average % of ugrad need met	69

STONEHILL COLLEGE

320 Washington Street, Easton, MA 02357-5610 • Admissions: 508-565-1373 • Fax: 508-565-1545

CAMPUS LIFE

Quality of Life Rating	**91**
Fire Safety Rating	**98**
Green Rating	**84**
Type of school	Private
Affiliation	Roman Catholic
Environment	Village

STUDENTS

Total undergrad enrollment	2,486
% male/female	41/59
% from out of state	35
% frosh from public high school	67
% frosh live on campus	92
% ugrads live on campus	86
# of fraternities	0
# of sororities	0
% African American	4
% Asian	2
% Caucasian	83
% Hispanic	5
% Native American	<1
% Pacific Islander	0
% Two or more races	2
% Race and/or ethnicity unknown	3
% international	1
# of countries represented	15

SURVEY SAYS . . .

Students are happy
Lab facilities are great
Great library
Career services are great
Internships are widely available
Students are friendly
Students involved in community service
Easy to get around campus
Recreation facilities are great
Very little drug use
Active student government

ACADEMICS

Academic Rating	**86**
% students returning for sophomore year	83
% students graduating within 4 years	77
% students graduating within 6 years	82
Calendar	Semester
Student/faculty ratio	12:1
Profs interesting rating	91
Profs accessible rating	93
Most classes have 20–29 students.	
Most lab/discussion sessions have 10–19 students.	

MOST POPULAR MAJORS

Psychology, General; Finance, General; Criminology

STUDENTS SAY "..."

Academics

Stonehill College, resting between Boston and Providence, is a place where students say "I can be myself," and "I am supported in all my endeavors" by a community of people who "want [me] to succeed." At this Roman Catholic liberal arts college, students feel like the academics place a productive emphasis on developing all the "necessary training, knowledge and skills that will allow us to succeed post-graduation." "My résumé is unique, and I feel secure that I will have a successful job after I leave," one student reports, listing "a full-time internship in L.A." and the chance to travel "abroad to do service in South Africa next semester" among the career-building opportunities to be found at Stonehill. Students also praise "the invaluable Career Development Center, providing ample career opportunities and professional training." This "strong liberal arts program geared toward traditional students" provides students with "fully-integrated classrooms and laboratories" and professors who are "friendly, with intimate class sizes of ten to twenty-five students." The "knowledgeable and passionate" professors are "accessible to students" outside of class and "challenge students to work hard and think critically." They are genuinely interested in their students and want to help them succeed. They "really do care about you and make an effort to get to know you (academically as well as outside the classroom, i.e., hobbies, etc.). One student describes a professor they had their first semester who "still says hi to me when he sees me in the hallways (and I haven't had him as a professor in three years)," and many other students tell us about how professors are "willing to meet with you to go over a test or paper" to make sure "you succeed."

Life

Stonehill College is "aesthetically beautiful, idealistically comfortable with a suburban yet grandiose green appeal." Life during the week is structured around academics, and you will find students "[making] use of one of the countless awesome study spots on campus to do some homework alone or with friends" or else "scattered about doing various different clubs and sports, and eating in the dining hall." Study-weary students can always find a chance to relax and enjoy themselves at "fun events around campus both during the week and on weekends, between sporting events, intense BINGO, a musical or dancing performance, or other fun activities." Students try to "make an effort to volunteer both on and off campus to give back to the community," either "on campus volunteering at the farm... to help provide fresh produce to the surrounding area" or at a local organization, like the "Big Sister Big Brother program." Stonehill students are an active bunch; "When it's nice out, you can expect to see people playing frisbee or spikeball on the quad," and "intramural sports is a big [past] time." It isn't a "huge party school," but "many upperclassmen students party...on-campus and off-campus on Thursday and there are parties on-campus on Friday and Saturday nights."

Student Body

Stonehill students are quick to tell you just how nice everyone is. People "always say hello even if they don't know you," and "if you run out of money at the dining hall, someone will almost always help you out." It is rare to "see people eating alone in the cafeteria," and students say they "strive towards creating an accepting, welcoming community and [that they] are committed to making our world just for all." Demographically, "Stonehill is primarily white, Catholic students from New England," though some students say that the administration has "been working on [increasing diversity] in the past couple years." Stonehill is a place where you will find people who are "kind and thoughtful," "friendly to everyone and passionate about their areas of study, service and [extracurricular activities]."

STONEHILL COLLEGE

Financial Aid: 508-565-1088 • E-Mail: admission@stonehill.edu • Website: www.stonehill.edu

THE PRINCETON REVIEW SAYS

Admissions

Very important factors considered include: rigor of secondary school record, class rank, academic GPA, talent/ability. *Important factors considered include:* application essay, recommendation(s), extracurricular activities. *Other factors considered include:* standardized test scores, interview, character/personal qualities, first generation, alumni/ae relation, geographical residence, religious affiliation/commitment, racial/ethnic status, volunteer work, work experience, level of applicant's interest. ACT with or without writing accepted. SAT with or without Essay component accepted. High school diploma is required and GED is accepted. *Academic units required:* 4 English, 3 math, 3 science, 3 science labs, 3 foreign language, 3 history. *Academic units recommended:* 4 English, 4 math, 4 science, 3 science labs, 4 foreign language, 4 history.

Financial Aid

Students should submit: CSS/Financial Aid PROFILE; FAFSA; Noncustodial PROFILE. Priority filing deadline is 12/1. The Princeton Review suggests that all financial aid forms be submitted as soon as possible after October 1. *Need-based scholarships/grants offered:* College/university scholarship or grant aid from institutional funds; Federal Pell; Private scholarships; SEOG; State scholarships/grants. *Loan aid offered:* Direct PLUS loans; Direct Subsidized Stafford Loans; Direct Unsubsidized Stafford Loans. Applicants will be notified of awards on or about 4/1. Federal Work-Study Program available. Institutional employment available.

The Inside Word

Maybe not as selective as some of the other schools in the Boston area, Stonehill still has high expectations for students they admit. In the class of 2021, 71 percent of students took at least one AP course and 65 percent took part in some kind of community service. Standardized tests scores are optional.

THE SCHOOL SAYS "..."

From the Admissions Office

"Founded by the Congregation of Holy Cross, Stonehill is a Catholic college that values integrity, tradition, diversity and the rewards that come when you pair rigorous academics with world-class faculty committed to empowering future leaders. Our approach to liberal arts education is distinctive because it melds challenging courses, nationally recognized experiential learning and life-changing service opportunities to shape compassionate leaders and global thinkers.

"Stonehill is on a beautiful 384-acre campus with architecture ranging from traditional brick-and-ivy academic buildings to our new May School of Arts & Sciences and Meehan School of Business. With its ideal location between Boston and Providence, Stonehill is perfectly situated for internships, professional networking, cultural experiences, pro sports and countless entertainment options.

"More than 90 percent of our students study abroad, complete an internship or perform field research before graduation. Such experiences along with 49 majors and 54 minors in the liberal arts, sciences and business prepare them for productive careers or lives of leadership and service. Our students are also active outside of class. Whether its Ultimate Disc, dance or one of our Division II varsity teams, most participate in some form of athletics. With a student/faculty ratio of 12:1 and an average class size of nineteen, individual attention is a Stonehill hallmark. Whether collaborating on research or mentoring students on careers and graduate school, our faculty puts students first. The result shows in their successes: 94 percent of alumni respondents report being in careers, top graduate programs, or volunteer positions within six months of graduation."

SELECTIVITY

Admissions Rating	84
# of applicants	6,961
% of applicants accepted	68
% of acceptees attending	14
# offered a place on the wait list	1,133
% accepting a place on wait list	23
% admitted from wait list	19
# of early decision applicants	128
% accepted early decision	88

FRESHMAN PROFILE

Range SAT EBRW	570–650
Range SAT Math	550–640
Range SAT Composite	1130–1280
Range ACT Composite	24–29
# submitting SAT scores	364
% submitting SAT scores	56
# submitting ACT scores	48
% submitting ACT scores	7
Average HS GPA	3.3
% graduated top 10% of class	19
% graduated top 25% of class	51
% graduated top 50% of class	88

DEADLINES

Early decision	
Deadline	12/1
Notification	12/31
Other ED Deadline	2/1
Other ED Notification	2/15
Early action	
Deadline	11/1
Notification	12/31
Regular	
Deadline	1/15
Notification	3/15
Nonfall registration?	Yes

APPLICANTS ALSO LOOK AT AND OFTEN PREFER

Boston College; College of the Holy Cross; Villanova University

AND SOMETIMES PREFER

Assumption University; Bentley University; Fairfield University; Northeastern University; Providence College; Quinnipiac University; Saint Michael's College

FINANCIAL FACTS

Financial Aid Rating	91
Annual tuition	$44,420
Room and board	$16,620
Books and supplies	$893
Average frosh need-based scholarship	$28,288
Average UG need-based scholarship	$26,331
% needy frosh rec. need-based scholarship or grant aid	99
% needy UG rec. need-based scholarship or grant aid	99
% needy frosh rec. non-need-based scholarship or grant aid	33
% needy UG rec. non-need-based scholarship or grant aid	35
% needy frosh rec. need-based self-help aid	64
% needy UG rec. need-based self-help aid	64
% frosh rec. any financial aid	100
% UG rec. any financial aid	98
% UG borrow to pay for school	71
Average cumulative indebtedness	$38,359
% frosh need fully met	48
% ugrads need fully met	52
Average % of frosh need met	90
Average % of ugrad need met	90

SUFFOLK UNIVERSITY

8 Ashburton Place, Boston, MA 02108 • Admissions: 617-573-8460 • Fax: 617-557-1574

STUDENTS SAY "..."

Academics

Suffolk University's focus on experiential learning is abetted by its longstanding relationships with Boston area businesses, government, and arts organizations, and public service is a key component of a Suffolk education. This institution is "about gathering all of the information that we learn in the classroom and translating it to the real world in order to prepare for our careers." The curriculum is built into a "great class structure," with general education requirements in one tier, major/minor requirements in another, and then a tier of electives, which "allows students to easily transfer into the university and study abroad." There are many tutoring options for help if a student needs it, and the school has systems in place to "actually make [sure] we know what we are doing when we do get the degree." Suffolk truly prepares the students to take on professional careers "by exposing us to numerous internship/job opportunities all around the city."

Suffolk professors are "experienced professionals with a lot of feedback on the subject they teach," "very clear and easy to understand," and "have a great amount of really valuable knowledge" that students will be able to utilize later in the real world. Many faculty members work in the field they are teaching in, "so you know that what they are teaching you is life experience, not just the bold words in a book." The school's small size means they "can really interact and help students and create strong relationships" and most classes are discussion-based. Teachers "make an immense amount of effort to actually get to know you as an individual." "I jokingly call my professors 'Mom' and 'Dad' because of how supportive they are in every aspect of my college career," says a student. Whether students need help with a class or a personal problem, they are always "there to listen and help however they [can]."

Life

Going to a city school means "you sign up for a certain way of life," and it is up to the student "to either sit in their room or go out and embrace all the school and city have to offer." Suffolk doesn't have a typical campus so "when you leave the dorms or classroom buildings you are in the heart of downtown Boston," and the majority of free fun time is "spent exploring Boston and what it has to offer." Suffolk is just a minute from a train station, within "walking distance from places like Newbury Street, Copley [Square], and Chinatown," and situated near many other major colleges where students can visit and expand their social horizons. "Suffolk is all about making all of Boston your campus," says a student. It's easy "to find a place to eat, get a cup of coffee, go shopping, or go to the gym with one's free time," and "you can go from class to shopping or relaxing in the Boston Common or in the winter, skating."

Student Body

Being in the heart of the city "can be a little overwhelming as the hustle and bustle of Boston never ends," but this is a welcoming and friendly "collective group of individuals" and Boston is a huge college town so "it is easy to make friends from other schools to hang out with." Many students are commuters and most work while in school, and there can be a partition felt between these two groups. "It's really hard for commuters to integrate," but "when a student immerses themselves in the school, there is no divide." The student body at Suffolk is "very protective of its very large LGBTQ+ community," and there is also a large international population here, and this "vast mixture of international and American students makes it a university plagued with opportunity."

SUFFOLK UNIVERSITY

Financial Aid: 617-573-8470 • E-Mail: admission@suffolk.edu • Website: www.suffolk.edu

THE PRINCETON REVIEW SAYS

Admissions

Very important factors considered include: rigor of secondary school record, academic GPA. *Important factors considered include:* application essay, recommendation(s), character/personal qualities. *Other factors considered include:* class rank, standardized test scores, interview, extracurricular activities, talent/ability, first generation, alumni/ae relation, volunteer work, work experience, level of applicant's interest. ACT with or without writing accepted. SAT with or without Essay component accepted. High school diploma is required and GED is accepted. *Academic units required:* 4 English, 3 math, 2 science, 1 science lab, 2 foreign language, 1 social studies, 1 history, 4 academic electives. *Academic units recommended:* 4 English, 4 math, 4 science, 3 science labs, 4 foreign language, 2 social studies, 3 history, 4 academic electives.

Financial Aid

Students should submit: FAFSA. Priority filing deadline is 3/1. The Princeton Review suggests that all financial aid forms be submitted as soon as possible after October 1. *Need-based scholarships/grants offered:* College/university scholarship or grant aid from institutional funds; Federal Pell; Private scholarships; SEOG; State scholarships/grants. *Loan aid offered:* Direct PLUS loans; Direct Subsidized Stafford Loans; Direct Unsubsidized Stafford Loans. Applicants will be notified of awards on a rolling basis beginning 2/1. Federal Work-Study Program available. Institutional employment available.

The Inside Word

Suffolk emphasizes its mission to provide access and opportunity to college-bound students. A personal statement, a transcript or GED results, and one letter of recommendation are required. Suffolk is test-optional. Standardized test scores are required for some students. Students are automatically considered for merit scholarships upon applying, and high achievers may be invited to join the Honors Program if accepted.

THE SCHOOL SAYS "..."

From the Admissions Office

"Located in the heart of downtown Boston, Suffolk University gives students unparalleled access to this dynamic city and transforms their lives. Suffolk offers more than 60 undergraduate programs and over 50 graduate degree programs, along with our doctoral program in clinical psychology and numerous certificate options. Students in our College of Arts & Sciences, Sawyer Business School, and Law School come to Suffolk to gain the knowledge and hands-on experiential learning they need to become leaders in their chosen fields. We take pride in being a personal, student-centered university, where faculty members lead small classes and nurture their students' success. Suffolk offers a 15:1 student-faculty ratio and the average class size is 20 students. Undergraduates may study at both our flagship Boston campus and our campus in Madrid, Spain. We are steps—or a short T ride—away from Boston's top employers, and we prepare students for professional success from day one. Our partnerships with myriad institutions in Boston, across Massachusetts, and around the world grant Suffolk students a wealth of choices when it comes to internships and co-op experiences. Indeed, 96 percent of the Class of 2018 were employed or enrolled in graduate school within a year of graduation."

SELECTIVITY

Admissions Rating	76
# of applicants	8,362
% of applicants accepted	84
% of acceptees attending	16

FRESHMAN PROFILE

Range SAT EBRW	510–610
Range SAT Math	510–600
Range SAT Composite	1030–1210
Range ACT Composite	21–26
# submitting SAT scores	935
% submitting SAT scores	83
# submitting ACT scores	143
% submitting ACT scores	13
Average HS GPA	3.3
% graduated top 10% of class	15
% graduated top 25% of class	43
% graduated top 50% of class	81

DEADLINES

Early action	
Deadline	11/15
Notification	12/15
Regular	
Priority	2/15
Notification	Rolling, 2/15
Nonfall registration?	Yes

FINANCIAL FACTS

Financial Aid Rating	83
Annual tuition	$41,242
Room and board	$18,134
Required fees	$666
Books and supplies	$1,200
Average frosh need-based scholarship	$13,164
Average UG need-based scholarship	$10,563
% needy frosh rec. need-based scholarship or grant aid	91
% needy UG rec. need-based scholarship or grant aid	88
% needy frosh rec. non-need-based scholarship or grant aid	93
% needy UG rec. non-need-based scholarship or grant aid	93
% needy frosh rec. need-based self-help aid	87
% needy UG rec. need-based self-help aid	85
% frosh rec. any financial aid	95
% UG rec. any financial aid	87
% UG borrow to pay for school	73
Average cumulative indebtedness	$28,582
% frosh need fully met	9
% ugrads need fully met	11
Average % of frosh need met	71
Average % of ugrad need met	68

SUSQUEHANNA UNIVERSITY

514 University Avenue, Selinsgrove, PA 17870 • Admissions: 570-372-4260 • Fax: 570-372-2722

STUDENTS SAY "..."

Academics

Susquehanna University is an institution that "thrives on building strong leaders and independent thinkers." The school's "small" size means undergrads are joining a "close-knit community" replete with a "strong alumni network." Perhaps more importantly, it's evident that the school "is invested...in the success of their students." While Susquehanna offers a variety of great majors, students are prone to highlight the "top-notch creative writing program," "outstanding music education program," and "strong" science departments. Undergrads also praise a more unique aspect of a Susquehanna education—mandatory study off campus in a culture different from one's own (95 percent of students choose to go abroad). One senior elated about this requirement shares, "I believe that every young adult should have access to a cross-cultural experience and I value Susquehanna for making such an experience a priority for its students." Thankfully, for the most part, undergrads enjoy their on-campus education as well. By and large, this can be attributed to "fantastic" professors who "take a personal interest in their students." Indeed, the "friendly" teachers here really strive to make themselves "accessible." And, as one impressed creative writing major adds, a handful "often invite [students] up to their houses for dinner and discussion." However, one neuroscience major does caution that "you usually have to fight to get into a class with a 'good' professor and the registration process is always a hassle."

Life

There is always something exciting to seek out at Susquehanna! To begin with, "there are over [150] clubs and organizations (academic, cultural, religious, arts, service, special interest, etc.)" in which students can participate. Additionally, "the Student Activities Committee [sponsors] a lot of free events—including the occasional trapeze and gyroscope!" Many undergrads also enjoy the "on-campus nightclub [which] hosts free dances on the weekends." Moreover, Susquehanna is a fairly athletic school. Indeed, "varsity sports are huge on campus; we have a large number of athletic teams for such a small school. Students love "tailgating [at] sporting events" as well. Undergrads also flock to "Charlie's Coffeehouse to watch movies or hang out with friends during the week." And, for students looking to unwind, "every Wednesday, Friday and Saturday night there is usually off campus partying happening." If students are itching to escape for a bit, they can take advantage of several "recreational places off campus (Bounce Plex, bowling alley, racetrack, rock climbing, hiking, etc.)" And though Selinsgrove "is a small town, it's got everything you need." A senior confidently proclaims that "there are plenty of places to eat and shop!"

Student Body

It can easily feel as though most Susquehanna students hail from "upper-middle class" homes located in either the "Mid-Atlantic [region or] New England." Fortunately, to the delight of many students, the "campus has been steadily diversifying over the years." And besides, these "outgoing" undergrads are able to forge bonds that go well beyond geography. After all, this is the type of student body that "will hold the door for you, even if you are 100 feet away." However, there are a handful of students who feel that, to fully fit in, you have to be "part of either Greek life or a sport." Naturally, other undergrads vehemently disagree, emphatically stating that "students find their niche quickly and make friends easily." A history major helps clarify by relaying that "roughly 25 percent of students are athletes and 17 percent are involved in Greek life. However, for the most part students from every range of the spectrum interact and support each other." And one immensely proud and satisfied speech communication major triumphantly sums up, "We are all awesome. There's no other way to describe it besides awesomeness."

SUSQUEHANNA UNIVERSITY

Financial Aid: 570-372-4450 • E-Mail: suadmiss@susqu.edu • Website: www.susqu.edu

THE PRINCETON REVIEW SAYS

Admissions

Very important factors considered include: rigor of secondary school record, academic GPA. *Important factors considered include:* class rank, application essay, standardized test scores, recommendation(s), interview, extracurricular activities, talent/ability, character/personal qualities, alumni/ae relation. *Other factors considered include:* first generation, geographical residence, state residency. ACT with or without writing accepted. SAT with or without Essay component accepted. High school diploma is required and GED is accepted. *Academic units required:* 4 English, 3 math, 2 science, 2 science labs, 2 foreign language, 2 social studies, 2 history, 2 academic electives. *Academic units recommended:* 4 English, 4 math, 3 science, 3 science labs, 4 foreign language, 4 social studies, 2 history, 3 academic electives.

Financial Aid

Students should submit: FAFSA; State aid form. Priority filing deadline is 12/1. The Princeton Review suggests that all financial aid forms be submitted as soon as possible after October 1. *Need-based scholarships/grants offered:* College/university scholarship or grant aid from institutional funds; Federal Pell; Private scholarships; SEOG; State scholarships/grants. *Loan aid offered:* Direct PLUS loans; Direct Subsidized Stafford Loans; Direct Unsubsidized Stafford Loans. Applicants will be notified of awards on a rolling basis beginning 11/15. Federal Work-Study Program available. Institutional employment available.

The Inside Word

Admissions officers at Susquehanna aim to understand the candidate behind the numbers. They want students who demonstrate intellect, creativity and leadership. The university also realizes that standardized test scores aren't always representative of a student's abilities. Therefore, applicants who believe their test scores do not reflect their abilities may apply Test Score Optional. Finally, Susquehanna operates on a rolling admissions policy.

THE SCHOOL SAYS "..."

From the Admissions Office

"No matter your major or career plans, you will graduate from Susquehanna with the broad-based academic foundation, intercultural competence and transferable career skills—critical thinking, writing, teamwork and communication skills—that employers and graduate schools seek. Our challenging and innovative academic preparation—plus internships, practica and research completed by 90 percent of students—result in 94 percent of new graduates employed or in graduate school within six months.

"Choose from more than 100 majors and minors in liberal arts and science or preprofessional programs. Our business school guarantees international internships and is AACSB-accredited, placing it among the top 5 percent of business schools worldwide.

"Susquehanna faculty members are exceptional teachers and scholars, and many involve students in their research. Esteemed mentors, they advise students about career choices or strategies for getting into graduate school, and support you with letters of recommendation. Many professors stay connected and follow their students' careers after graduation.

"You and 100% of your classmates will study off campus through our nationally-recognized Global Opportunities (GO) program. By completing a cross-cultural experience for at least two weeks in the U.S. or abroad, you'll broaden your perspective and professional options through your ability to connect with people from other backgrounds, be they coworkers or clients.

"You will enjoy first-rate learning and living facilities on our beautiful 325-acre residential campus. Make friends through 150+ student-run clubs and organizations, 23 NCAA Division III intercollegiate sports, fraternities, sororities and service groups. With easy access to major East Coast cities, you'll network with alumni, pursue internships, explore professional opportunities and have fun!"

SELECTIVITY

Admissions Rating	78
# of applicants	4,863
% of applicants accepted	85
% of acceptees attending	15
# of early decision applicants	63
% accepted early decision	56

FRESHMAN PROFILE

Range SAT EBRW	560–650
Range SAT Math	540–640
Range SAT Composite	1110–1240
Range ACT Composite	22–28
# submitting SAT scores	457
% submitting SAT scores	74
# submitting ACT scores	90
% submitting ACT scores	15
Average HS GPA	3.7
% graduated top 10% of class	25
% graduated top 25% of class	63
% graduated top 50% of class	88

DEADLINES

Early decision	
Deadline	11/15
Notification	12/1
Early action	
Deadline	11/1
Notification	12/1
Regular	
Notification	Rolling, 10/1
Nonfall registration?	Yes

APPLICANTS ALSO LOOK AT AND OFTEN PREFER

Dickinson College; Bucknell University; Gettysburg College

AND SOMETIMES PREFER

Penn State University Park; Muhlenberg College; Juniata College; Ithaca College

AND RARELY PREFER

Elizabethtown College

FINANCIAL FACTS

Financial Aid Rating	88
Annual tuition	$50,500
Room and board	$13,680
Required fees	$640
Books and supplies	$1,200
Average frosh need-based scholarship	$37,380
Average UG need-based scholarship	$35,382
% needy frosh rec. need-based scholarship or grant aid	100
% needy UG rec. need-based scholarship or grant aid	100
% needy frosh rec. non-need-based scholarship or grant aid	23
% needy UG rec. non-need-based scholarship or grant aid	18
% needy frosh rec. need-based self-help aid	74
% needy UG rec. need-based self-help aid	80
% frosh rec. any financial aid	98.5
% UG rec. any financial aid	100
% UG borrow to pay for school	84
Average cumulative indebtedness	$40,455
% frosh need fully met	27
% ugrads need fully met	22
Average % of frosh need met	86
Average % of ugrad need met	82

SWARTHMORE COLLEGE

500 College Avenue, Swarthmore, PA 19081 • Admissions: 610-328-8300 • Fax: 610-328-8580

STUDENTS SAY "..."

Academics

Swarthmore College "has a lovely campus, the people are almost unbelievably friendly, it's a safe environment, and it's really, really challenging academically," and "although it's not one of the most well-known schools, those who do know of it also know of its wonderful reputation. It's where to go for a real education—for learning for the sake of truly learning, rather than just for grades." Students warn that "academics here are definitely stressful, especially when you sign up for extracurricular activities that take up some more time—and almost everyone here is involved in something outside of classes, because you don't want to just go to class, study, and sleep every day." As a result, "Swarthmore is truly challenging. It teaches its students tough lessons not only about classes but about life, and though it may be extremely, almost unbearably difficult sometimes, it's totally worth it." Undergrads also note that "there are tons of resources to help you—professors, academic mentors, writing associates (who are really helpful to talk to when you have major papers), residential assistants, psychological counseling, multicultural support groups, queer/trans support groups—basically, whenever you need help with something, there's someone you can talk to." Swatties also love how "Swarthmore is amazingly flexible. The requirements are very limited, allowing you to explore whatever you are interested in and change your mind millions of times about your major and career path. If they don't offer a major you want, you can design your own with ease."

Life

The Swarthmore community is "a family of students who are engaged in academics, learning, politics, activism, and civic responsibility, with a work hard, play hard, intense mentality, who don't get enough sleep because they're too busy doing all they want to do in their time here, and who (this is kind of cheesy, but true) when you really think about it are really just smart students who care about the world and want to make it better." There "is a misconception that Swarthmore students do nothing but study, [but] while we certainly do a lot of it, we still find many ways to have fun." Not so much in hometown Swarthmore—"there isn't a lot to do right in the area"—but "with a train station on campus, Philly is very accessible." Additionally, "there are so many organizations and clubs on campus that you'd be pressed to find none of the activities interesting. Even then, you can start your own club, so that takes care of it." The small size of the school means that "opportunities to participate in many different programs" are usually available. On-campus activities "are varied, and there is almost always something to do on the weekend. There are student musical performances, drama performances, movies, speakers, and comedy shows," as well as "several parties every weekend, with and without alcohol, and a lot of pre-partying with friends." One student sums up, "While it is tough to generalize on the life of a Swarthmore student, one word definitely applies to us all: busy. All of us are either working on extracurriculars, studying, or fighting sleep to do more work."

Student Body

Students are "not sure if there is a typical Swattie" but suspect that "the defining feature among us is that each person is brilliant at something: maybe dance, maybe quantum physics, maybe philosophy. Each person here has at least one thing that [he or she does] extraordinarily well." A Swattie "is [typically] liberal, involved in some kind of activism group or multicultural group, talks about classes all the time, was labeled a nerd by people in high school, and is really smart—one of those people where you just have to wonder, how do they get all their homework done and manage their extracurriculars and still have time for parties?" The campus "is very diverse racially but not in terms of thought—in other words, pretty much everyone's liberal, you don't get many different points of view. Multicultural and queer issues are big here, but you don't have to be involved in that to enjoy Swarthmore. You just have to accept it."

SWARTHMORE COLLEGE

Financial Aid: 610-328-8358 • E-Mail: admissions@swarthmore.edu • Website: www.swarthmore.edu

THE PRINCETON REVIEW SAYS

Admissions

Very important factors considered include: rigor of secondary school record, class rank, academic GPA, application essay, recommendation(s), character/personal qualities. *Important factors considered include:* standardized test scores, extracurricular activities. *Other factors considered include:* interview, talent/ability, first generation, alumni/ae relation, geographical residence, state residency, religious affiliation/commitment, racial/ethnic status, volunteer work, work experience, level of applicant's interest. ACT with or without writing accepted. SAT with or without Essay component accepted. High school diploma or equivalent is not required. *Academic units recommended:* 4 English, 3 math, 3 science, 3 foreign language, 3 social studies, 3 history.

Financial Aid

Students should submit: CSS/Financial Aid PROFILE; FAFSA; Noncustodial PROFILE; State aid form. Priority filing deadline is 1/1. The Princeton Review suggests that all financial aid forms be submitted as soon as possible after October 1. *Need-based scholarships/grants offered:* College/university scholarship or grant aid from institutional funds; Federal Pell; Private scholarships; SEOG; State scholarships/grants. *Loan aid offered:* Direct PLUS loans; Direct Subsidized Stafford Loans; Direct Unsubsidized Stafford Loans. Applicants will be notified of awards on or about 4/1. Federal Work-Study Program available. Institutional employment available.

The Inside Word

Competition for admission to Swarthmore remains fierce, as the school consistently receives applications from top students across the country. Applicants should understand that Swarthmore receives more than enough applications from well-qualified students to fill its classrooms. The optional Writing components are not required for either the SAT or ACT. Admissions officers comb applications carefully for evidence of intellectually curious, highly motivated, and creative-minded candidates.

THE SCHOOL SAYS "..."

From the Admissions Office

"Swarthmore College is a highly selective college of liberal arts and engineering located half an hour outside of Philadelphia. The college empowers students to intertwine academic curiosity with social responsibility and a sense of purpose. Swarthmore's staff are fully behind this mission, from world-class professors who engage directly with students in meaningful ways, to staff in the dining hall and libraries, who can come to feel like friends. Close relationships fuel life at Swarthmore. Many students collaborate with professors on joint research projects, and the exchange of intellectual ideas is facilitated by small class sizes. The Honors Program extends the depth of free and critical discussion of ideas via small-group seminars. One trademark of a "Swattie" is the desire to learn for the sake of knowledge. Swatties can be astrophysicists who write poetry, economists who love to code, and athletes with a passion for choreography. Almost half of students enjoy playing sports, at the Division III level or in club and intramural teams. The College's Quaker roots emphasize the concept of access regardless of income; the annual activity fee covers digital printing, sporting events, campus movie screenings, and dance performances. Swarthmore's financial aid program ensures affordability—without loans. Fifty-three percent of the Class of 2022 received aid in 2017–2018, with an average aid award of $54,967. Swarthmore makes admissions decisions for U.S. citizens, permanent residents, and undocumented or DACA-eligible students graduating from U.S. high schools without considering a family's ability to pay. International applicants are admitted on a need-aware basis and are eligible for financial aid."

SELECTIVITY

Admissions Rating	98
# of applicants	11,442
% of applicants accepted	9
% of acceptees attending	41
# of early decision applicants	992
% accepted early decision	24

FRESHMAN PROFILE

Range SAT EBRW	680–750
Range SAT Math	700–790
Range ACT Composite	31–35
# submitting SAT scores	284
% submitting SAT scores	68
# submitting ACT scores	156
% submitting ACT scores	37
% graduated top 10% of class	87
% graduated top 25% of class	100
% graduated top 50% of class	100

DEADLINES

Early decision	
Deadline	11/15
Notification	12/15
Other ED Deadline	1/1
Other ED Notification	2/15
Regular	
Deadline	1/1
Notification	4/1
Nonfall registration?	No

FINANCIAL FACTS

Financial Aid Rating	97
Annual tuition	$54,256
Room and board	$16,088
Required fees	$400
Books and supplies	$1,400
Average frosh need-based scholarship	$55,233
Average UG need-based scholarship	$54,217
% needy frosh rec. need-based scholarship or grant aid	99
% needy UG rec. need-based scholarship or grant aid	100
% needy frosh rec. non-need-based scholarship or grant aid	0
% needy UG rec. non-need-based scholarship or grant aid	0
% needy frosh rec. need-based self-help aid	97
% needy UG rec. need-based self-help aid	97
% frosh rec. any financial aid	58
% UG rec. any financial aid	52
% UG borrow to pay for school	26
Average cumulative indebtedness	$24,099
% frosh need fully met	100
% ugrads need fully met	100
Average % of frosh need met	100
Average % of ugrad need met	100

SYRACUSE UNIVERSITY

100 Crouse-Hinds Hall, Syracuse, NY 13244-2130 • Admissions: 315-443-3611 • Fax: 315-443-4226

STUDENTS SAY "..."

Academics

The Orange of Syracuse University love their school and want the world to know it. Those who brave the northern winters are rewarded with a choice of around 200 majors and 100 minors, and one of Syracuse's greatest strengths is "the distinct tracks students can take within each of the professional schools." There is so much to do with your education and it can be as specific or broad as you would like," says one student. "If you put in the work…it can make a world of a difference to your college experience." The school does a good job of being cohesive for its size, and "there is a sense of connection between all years of study." Alumni form an "everlasting network between Syracuse students" and the school has a "big reach" for a relatively tucked away school: "There is somebody from Syracuse everywhere you look." On top of the alumni, the school provides "ample amounts of resources in regard to finding jobs or applying to graduate programs," which "makes looking for that next step easy and not so intimidating."

Professors are "very intelligent and qualified individuals who have a strong base in what they teach," and are here "as a tool to enhance your knowledge and to help in any way possible." In general education classes, professors are "attentive and aware that students of varying interests and backgrounds are enrolled in the 101-level class and adjust teaching strategies accordingly." They are "quick to respond to emails," and "always open to meeting with you if you need help with anything, academic or personal." Professors typically "do justice to both sides of various arguments" and classroom discussions don't feel biased.

Life

The atmosphere of Syracuse is "always electric, with something going on at all times." Student life can revolve around athletics, and campus is "the most fun place on the planet when the basketball team is doing well, but could be very dreary if they're not and the weather is bad." Students are especially eager to don their orange apparel and "tailgate until the wee hours," but they "always get studying done first." Greek life is popular for many students and "once the sun goes down, you will find a lot of the students all gathering at the fraternities and the bars on Marshall street," though 'Cuse still offers alternative activities, including the Orange After Dark program, "bowling, shopping, whitewater rafting, day trips to NYC, [and] movie nights" for students who have no interest in parties. The gym is always thumping: "it's a social thing here."

As this is Central NY, life takes a little hit when winter comes, and indoor socializing is more prominent. "Floors become close" and "movies and video games" are popular distractions. Dining hall food can be less than pleasant and a lot of people go off-campus when they get sick of it, also travelling to Destiny USA (one of the country's largest malls) or Armory Square, where there are restaurants and shops.

Student Body

School spirit "runs rampant" here, and this "energized" group can be found "seeking the fun out of every opportunity thrown at them." Syracuse is "not as diverse as a city school but still pretty diverse nonetheless," with most students hailing from the northeast. No matter their background, students "very quickly find a home" whether it's with a sports team, club, organization, or Greek life, and everyone is active in the community. There is "very little competition" among this "practical student body…that doesn't take flack or do unnecessary work," and if there is any divide, it is between the driven students and those just here for a degree. Students "love to party, especially on game days, but also understand that they are here for academics."

Financial Aid: 315-443-1513 • E-Mail: orange@syr.edu • Website: https://www.syracuse.edu

THE PRINCETON REVIEW SAYS

Admissions

Very important factors considered include: rigor of secondary school record, class rank, academic GPA, application essay, standardized test scores, recommendation(s), interview, extracurricular activities, talent/ability, character/personal qualities, volunteer work, level of applicant's interest. *Other factors considered include:* first generation, alumni/ae relation, geographical residence, state residency, racial/ethnic status, work experience. ACT with or without writing accepted. SAT with or without Essay component accepted. High school diploma is required and GED is accepted. *Academic units recommended:* 4 English, 4 math, 4 science, 4 science labs, 3 foreign language, 4 social studies, 4 history.

Financial Aid

Students should submit: CSS/Financial Aid PROFILE; FAFSA; Noncustodial PROFILE. The Princeton Review suggests that all financial aid forms be submitted as soon as possible after October 1. *Need-based scholarships/grants offered:* College/university scholarship or grant aid from institutional funds; Federal Pell; Private scholarships; SEOG; State scholarships/grants. *Loan aid offered:* Direct PLUS loans; Direct Subsidized Stafford Loans; Direct Unsubsidized Stafford Loans. Applicants will be notified of awards on or about 3/15. Federal Work-Study Program available. Institutional employment available.

The Inside Word

Syracuse's admissions process is competitive. Successful candidates will have strong GPAs and solid test scores. It's also important to note that students interested in applying to any fine or performing arts or architecture programs will need to audition and/or submit a portfolio. Finally, applicants who strongly feel that Syracuse is their first choice are highly encouraged to apply early decision.

THE SCHOOL SAYS "..."

From the Admissions Office

"Syracuse University is a private, global research university with distinctive, outstanding academics, diverse opportunities for student research, and unique experiences beyond the classroom. Established nearly 150 years ago in the geographic heart of New York State, Syracuse University offers a quintessential college campus experience, along with innovative online learning programs and opportunities for international travel and study.

"The depth and breadth of the university's program offerings are a testament to its enduring strength, with more than 200 majors and 100 minors offered through 13 schools and colleges and 18 online degree programs. More than 15,000 undergraduates and 7,500 graduate students, who come from all 50 states and 123 countries, join a global network of more than 240,000 alumni spanning 160 countries.

"Dedicated to preparing students for a rapidly changing world, Syracuse University consistently ranks among the nation's highest quality international study programs. With 7 overseas centers and more than 100 programs within 60 countries, nearly half of Syracuse University students study abroad at some point during their academic careers. As a Carnegie classification Research 1 institution, Syracuse offers students hands-on opportunities and support to conduct research in their fields.

"Syracuse University has earned a reputation as the best university for veterans and military-connected students, who make up more than 5 percent of the student body. Opening in 2020, the National Veterans Resource Center (NVRC) will be dedicated to advancing the social and economic well-being of the nation's veterans and their families on the campus of Syracuse University and beyond."

SELECTIVITY

Admissions Rating	90
# of applicants	35,299
% of applicants accepted	44
% of acceptees attending	23
# offered a place on the wait list	8,859
% accepting a place on wait list	36
% admitted from wait list	19
# of early decision applicants	2,090
% accepted early decision	60

FRESHMAN PROFILE

Range SAT EBRW	580–670
Range SAT Math	600–710
Range SAT Composite	1210–1368
Range ACT Composite	26–30
# submitting SAT scores	2,542
% submitting SAT scores	70
# submitting ACT scores	1,171
% submitting ACT scores	32
Average HS GPA	3.6
% graduated top 10% of class	33
% graduated top 25% of class	66
% graduated top 50% of class	91

DEADLINES

Early decision	
Deadline	11/15
Notification	12/15
Regular	
Priority	11/15
Deadline	1/1
Nonfall registration?	Yes

FINANCIAL FACTS

Financial Aid Rating	91
Annual tuition	$54,270
Room and board	$16,356
Required fees	$1,656
Books and supplies	$1,564
Average frosh need-based scholarship	$38,431
Average UG need-based scholarship	$34,854
% needy frosh rec. need-based scholarship or grant aid	97
% needy UG rec. need-based scholarship or grant aid	97
% needy frosh rec. non-need-based scholarship or grant aid	18
% needy UG rec. non-need-based scholarship or grant aid	12
% needy frosh rec. need-based self-help aid	87
% needy UG rec. need-based self-help aid	91
% frosh rec. any financial aid	87
% UG rec. any financial aid	80
% UG borrow to pay for school	54
Average cumulative indebtedness	$37,563
% frosh need fully met	71
% ugrads need fully met	54
Average % of frosh need met	98
Average % of ugrad need met	94

TEMPLE UNIVERSITY

1801 North Broad Street (041-09), Philadelphia, PA 19122 • Admissions: 215-204-7200 • Fax: 215-204-5694

STUDENTS SAY " . . ."

Academics
Temple University, Philadelphia's largest university, is constantly growing, and not just in size. Currently, the nearly 30,000 undergraduates have more than 150 majors to choose from. But the school is also "constantly improving and upgrading its resources," which means that students always have access to something new, most recently a library that features "one of the world's first robot book fetchers." It also means that "career opportunities are plentiful and are available for all students" or as another respondent puts it, "Attending such a large school allows limitless internship, scholarship, academic, and social opportunities." There's even a nod to how the "Gen Ed courses are a great help to discover your interests." The university as a whole "is very well-rounded, and you are going to receive a really good education no matter what major you choose."

Such achievements wouldn't be nearly as effective if not for the faculty, and accordingly, professors are praised as being "extremely accessible," "highly skilled at relaying information and teaching," and providing "many opportunities outside of the classroom for students." It's not just about relaying information as it is about facilitating interactions and collaborations. Professors "genuinely care about how well you learn the material and try as hard as they can to get you as excited to learn as they are to teach," which is why classes involve "lots of discussion-based lectures and ways of challenging students to think outside the box." You're never alone at Temple either: "For example, for Calculus help I could go to the tutoring center, the student success center, MCC (Mathematics Counseling Center), or I could attend PASS (Peer Assisted Study Sessions) sessions offered for group tutoring before the exam."

Life
The Temple campus is described as "a major highlight," one that "sits right in Philadelphia but maintains a distinct campus-like feel." Students rejoice in the freedom this offers: "Living in a city allows people largely to exist as they wish," which means students don't have to choose between "just their academic life or their partying life" and "are not confined to campus and can venture out into the major city." That said, those who choose to remain local will find "plenty of clubs and organizations to join as well as Greek life organizations," and "people enjoy going to sports games either for Temple teams or Philadelphia teams." Physical activities in particular are referenced by undergrads, with attention called to the campus's three gyms, and a "recreation center open on Wednesday and Friday nights for net sports."

Student Body
This is "a very likable campus" where everyone "respects everyone and who they choose to be and they celebrate it." Many at Temple are "engaged in public service" and the school "has amazing diversity, which is what Temple strives to have and support." A lot of students here "are commuters and spend their days in class or at the library/tech center," while many others "either live on campus or off campus close by in an apartment and work when not in class." There are also "lots of international students from many different countries." Students here "have their lives together…but also know how to have a good time."

TEMPLE UNIVERSITY

Financial Aid: 215-204-2244 • E-Mail: askanowl@temple.edu • Website: www.temple.edu

THE PRINCETON REVIEW SAYS

Admissions

Very important factors considered include: rigor of secondary school record, academic GPA. *Other factors considered include:* class rank, application essay, standardized test scores, recommendation(s), extracurricular activities, talent/ability, character/personal qualities, alumni/ae relation, geographical residence, state residency, volunteer work, work experience. ACT with or without writing accepted. SAT with or without Essay component accepted. High school diploma is required and GED is accepted. *Academic units required:* 4 English, 3 math, 2 science, 1 science lab, 2 foreign language, 2 social studies, 1 history, 1 academic elective, 1 visual/performing arts. *Academic units recommended:* 4 English, 4 math, 3 science, 2 science labs, 2 foreign language, 2 social studies, 1 history, 3 academic electives, 1 visual/performing arts.

Financial Aid

Students should submit: FAFSA; State aid form. Priority filing deadline is 3/1. The Princeton Review suggests that all financial aid forms be submitted as soon as possible after October 1. *Need-based scholarships/grants offered:* College/university scholarship or grant aid from institutional funds; Federal Nursing Scholarships; Federal Pell; Private scholarships; SEOG; State scholarships/grants; United Negro College Fund. *Loan aid offered:* Direct PLUS loans; Direct Subsidized Stafford Loans; Direct Unsubsidized Stafford Loans; Federal Nursing Loans; State Loans; College/university loans from institutional funds. Applicants will be notified of awards on a rolling basis beginning 2/14. Federal Work-Study Program available. Institutional employment available.

The Inside Word

Gaining admission to Temple is competitive and a solid academic record is a must. Students need to have earned at least a minimum of a B-minus average or a 3.0 GPA in college prep courses to be considered serious contenders, and should demonstrate a well-rounded academic background and course distribution. Submitting SAT or ACT scores is optional.

THE SCHOOL SAYS "..."

From the Admissions Office

"Temple University attracts some of the most diverse, driven and motivated minds from across the nation and around the world. These students and faculty bring the university to life and move Temple forward and upward in academics, athletics, research and the arts. Powering Temple's ascent are innovative approaches to admissions and affordability; a campus transformation; plentiful creative and research opportunities; rigorous academic programs; an indelible bond with the city of Philadelphia; and groundbreaking work in science, research and technology. Temple is home to over 39,000 students, is among the 35 largest public, four-year institutions in the U.S. and offers more than 600 academic programs in 17 schools and colleges, on eight campuses, including locations in Japan and Italy. More than 3,900 distinguished faculty members; five professional schools; and dozens of renowned programs make Temple an academic powerhouse. Students enjoy the advantages of a large urban, public research university with the individualized attention of a 13:1 student-to-faculty ratio. The majority of first-year students live on campus, steps away from classes; the state-of-the-art Charles Library; the TECH Center; fitness and recreation facilities; dining options such as cafés, dining halls and food trucks; and the many arts, cultural, sports and scholarly events that happen daily at Temple and throughout the city. By living and learning in an urban environment, Temple students are well prepared for the world. Employers laud Owls for their tenacity, teamwork and talent. Students also have access to an immense alumni network 340,000 strong for guidance, job opportunities and mentoring."

SELECTIVITY

Admissions Rating	87
# of applicants	35,599
% of applicants accepted	60
% of acceptees attending	23
# offered a place on the wait list	2,190
% accepting a place on wait list	48
% admitted from wait list	99

FRESHMAN PROFILE

Range SAT EBRW	570–660
Range SAT Math	550–660
Range SAT Composite	1140–1310
Range ACT Composite	24–30
# submitting SAT scores	3,777
% submitting SAT scores	76
# submitting ACT scores	826
% submitting ACT scores	17
Average HS GPA	3.5
% graduated top 10% of class	36
% graduated top 25% of class	76
% graduated top 50% of class	92

DEADLINES

Early action	
Deadline	11/1
Notification	1/10
Regular	
Priority	11/1
Deadline	2/1
Nonfall registration?	Yes

APPLICANTS ALSO LOOK AT AND OFTEN PREFER

Drexel University; Penn State University Park; Rutgers University–New Brunswick

AND SOMETIMES PREFER

West Chester University of Pennsylvania; University of Delaware; University of Maryland, College Park; University of Pittsburgh—Pittsburgh Campus; University of Connecticut; University of Pennsylvania; Montclair State University; Virginia Commonwealth University; Ithaca College

AND RARELY PREFER

Saint Joseph's University (PA); Syracuse University; Rowan University

FINANCIAL FACTS

Financial Aid Rating	82
Annual in-state tuition	$18,858
Annual out-of-state tuition	$33,236
Room and board	$12,188
Required fees	$890
Books and supplies	$1,478
Average frosh need-based scholarship	$10,829
Average UG need-based scholarship	$9,596
% needy frosh rec. need-based scholarship or grant aid	96
% needy UG rec. need-based scholarship or grant aid	91
% needy frosh rec. non-need-based scholarship or grant aid	65
% needy UG rec. non-need-based scholarship or grant aid	52
% needy frosh rec. need-based self-help aid	80
% needy UG rec. need-based self-help aid	83
% frosh rec. any financial aid	90
% UG rec. any financial aid	82
% UG borrow to pay for school	71
Average cumulative indebtedness	$38,634
% frosh need fully met	5
% ugrads need fully met	3
Average % of frosh need met	63
Average % of ugrad need met	61

TEXAS A&M UNIVERSITY—COLLEGE STATION

P.O. Box 30014, College Station, TX 77843-3014 • Admissions: 979-845-1060 • Fax: 979-458-1808

STUDENTS SAY "..."

Academics

The "untold spirit at Texas A&M" lies in its tradition, which is "the underlying pulse of Aggieland." This large research school has "deep-rooted values" and "runs as a tight-knit family despite the numerous population." This strong family dynamic makes the school an "open, friendly place to learn and grow," and the incredibly strong engineering and life science programs certainly don't hurt. The academics can be "difficult," but "the goal is to set [students] apart from the rest, so [they] can excel." The "wonderful" professors "do their best to bring the topics from pages to the real world." They "all have life experiences working with the topics that they teach making them the perfect resource for information." These "top-notch" professors (well, aside from a very few who are "extremely dry") come back to A&M after working in powerful industry positions "because they love the atmosphere and the students." "I have never skipped a class because I thoroughly enjoy going," says one student. Particularly with the sciences, professors offer students the opportunity to participate in "world-changing research," and all such experiences "have had something useful to add to the material," which helps students when they go out into the real world. The "Aggie network" is something to behold; it reaches far across the nation ("Aggie alumni are loyal to their school forever") and "is good for getting jobs after graduation." The sense of pride here motivates students to do well "because they're part of something bigger than themselves." There is "great support" from both the faculty and staff together. "The mindset they have is to effectively prepare students for world-class challenges," says one student. "At Texas A&M, you learn to be a well-rounded, moral, and ethical person."

Life

Student organizations positively abound at Texas A&M (there are more than 1,000), and they are a huge social outlet for students looking to find those with similar interests. "Get involved in something you're passionate about; there is a club for just about *everything*," says a student. Off-campus, there are "four-dollar movies, many dancehalls, endless restaurants to eat at, and a large mall," as well as "an ice-skating rink, bowling alley, and miniature golf place." Students at Texas A&M are "loyal to one another and are always willing to support their fellow Aggies." "Tradition and chivalry run the school," and students all "work hard during the week so we can party hard on the weekends," usually at Northgate, the "bar street." "Texas A&M is kind of like a cult—a really happy cult," explains a student. The "immense school spirit" is derived from the many "time-honored traditions," including the Big Event, which is the largest one-day, student-run service project in the nation. That's not even to mention the football: "Saturdays in the fall are owned by football." "Although the school is very large, whenever the…Aggies at Kyle Field are belting the war hymn and linking arms, I feel like I am part of a huge family." As one student cryptically sums up his school's mythology, "From the outside looking in, you can't understand it. From the inside looking out, you can't explain it."

Student Body

A typical student is "white," "conservative," "involved in at least one club, spends a fair amount of time studying, and learns to two-step for Thursday nights." This being Texas, "some wear cowboy boots, a flannel shirt, a cowboy hat/baseball cap, and jeans." There is also a strong faction of members of the Corps of Cadets, as well as religious folk (the school has "the largest Bible study in the world"). Though lacking cultural diversity, interests and hobbies run the gamut, and "students from other races and classes fit in just fine and are able to make friends just like anybody else." While it's a big school, "a lot of classes are pretty small, so it's easy to make friends in class." There are "no pretenses" among Aggies, and "everyone shows who they are." "Most of the people I have met here are truly genuine individuals," says a student.

Financial Aid: 979-845-3236 • E-Mail: admissions@tamu.edu • Website: www.tamu.edu

THE PRINCETON REVIEW SAYS

Admissions

Very important factors considered include: rigor of secondary school record, class rank, academic GPA, standardized test scores, extracurricular activities, talent/ability. *Important factors considered include:* application essay, first generation, geographical residence, state residency, volunteer work. *Other factors considered include:* recommendation(s), character/personal qualities, level of applicant's interest. ACT with Writing required. SAT with Essay component required. High school diploma is required and GED is accepted. *Academic units required:* 4 English, 3 math, 3 science, 1 science lab, 2 foreign language, 3 social studies, 5 academic electives, 1 visual/performing arts, 1 unit from above areas or other academic areas. *Academic units recommended:* 4 English, 4 math, 4 science, 2 science labs, 2 foreign language, 4 social studies, 7 academic electives, 1 visual/performing arts.

Financial Aid

Students should submit: FAFSA. Priority filing deadline is 12/15. The Princeton Review suggests that all financial aid forms be submitted as soon as possible after October 1. *Need-based scholarships/grants offered:* College/university scholarship or grant aid from institutional funds; Federal Pell; Private scholarships; SEOG; State scholarships/grants. *Loan aid offered:* Direct PLUS loans; Direct Subsidized Stafford Loans; Direct Unsubsidized Stafford Loans. Applicants will be notified of awards on a rolling basis beginning 2/25. Federal Work-Study Program available. Institutional employment available.

The Inside Word

Texas A&M uses some cut-and-dried admissions criteria: Students graduating in the top 10 percent of a recognized public or private high school in the state of Texas are automatically in; all they have to do is get their applications in on time. Applicants in the top quarter of their graduating class who have a combined SAT math/critical reading score of 1300 (minimum score of 600 in each component) are also automatically in, as are such students who earn a composite ACT score of 30 (minimum 27 on the math and English sections). Students must also take the writing component of the SAT and/or ACT for the test score to be considered. All other applications are deemed "Review Admits" to be sorted through by the admissions committee.

THE SCHOOL SAYS "..."

From the Admissions Office

"Established in 1876 as the first public college in the state, Texas A&M University has become a world leader in teaching, research, and public service. Located in College Station in the heart of Texas, it is centrally situated among three of the country's ten largest cities: Dallas, Houston, and San Antonio. Texas A&M is ranked nationally in these four areas: enrollment, enrollment of top students, value of research, and endowment.

"Freshman applicants are required to take the SAT or the ACT. We will use the applicant's best single testing date score in decision making."

SELECTIVITY

Admissions Rating	90
# of applicants	42,899
% of applicants accepted	58
% of acceptees attending	43

FRESHMAN PROFILE

Range SAT EBRW	580–680
Range SAT Math	580–710
Range SAT Composite	1180–1390
Range ACT Composite	26–31
# submitting SAT scores	6,631
% submitting SAT scores	62
# submitting ACT scores	3,986
% submitting ACT scores	38
% graduated top 10% of class	70
% graduated top 25% of class	93
% graduated top 50% of class	99

DEADLINES

Regular	
Deadline	12/1
Notification	Rolling, 12/15
Nonfall registration?	Yes

FINANCIAL FACTS

Financial Aid Rating	83
Annual in-state tuition	$7,579
Annual out-of-state tuition	$34,073
Room and board	$10,400
Required fees	$3,652
Books and supplies	$1,222
Average frosh need-based scholarship	$12,388
Average UG need-based scholarship	$10,740
% needy frosh rec. need-based scholarship or grant aid	90
% needy UG rec. need-based scholarship or grant aid	86
% needy frosh rec. non-need-based scholarship or grant aid	10
% needy UG rec. non-need-based scholarship or grant aid	7
% needy frosh rec. need-based self-help aid	46
% needy UG rec. need-based self-help aid	56
% frosh rec. any financial aid	76
% UG rec. any financial aid	70
% UG borrow to pay for school	43
Average cumulative indebtedness	$24,590
% frosh need fully met	21
% ugrads need fully met	18
Average % of frosh need met	72
Average % of ugrad need met	69

TEXAS CHRISTIAN UNIVERSITY

TCU, Fort Worth, TX 76129 • Admissions: 817-257-7490 • Fax: 817-257-7268

STUDENTS SAY "..."

Academics

Undergrads at Texas Christian University certainly feel that their college offers it all—"strong academics, driven student body, great opportunities, [and] valuable connections." It also combines a small school atmosphere with the resources of a large university. Many students are attracted to TCU thanks to its "very nice facilities," "great honors [college]," and the fact that the university "provides large amounts of merit-based financial aid." "Small class sizes" mean that students here are "not just a number." While the university has many fabulous departments and programs, students tout the Neeley School of Business and Harris College of Nursing & Health Sciences as standouts. Texas Christian professors are typically "experts in [their] field of study." Although classes are frequently "challenging," it's obvious that instructors are wholly committed to "serving and helping students." Indeed, "they demand much, but also provide plenty of resources in order for students to meet and exceed expectations." They're also "extremely open and respectful to all students" and truly want them to "become more interested in the subject as well." Faculty members make themselves "readily available through office hours and emails."

Life

Students at TCU, as at many universities, subscribe to a work hard, play hard lifestyle. "Libraries are usually semi-full or packed with students studying for classes and exams." When undergrads are itching for a study break, there is "a plethora of on-campus organizations [in which] to participate." One club in particular, "the Crew, comes up with some new activity or program for students every day." Their activities can "range from petting zoos to bouncy houses to circus performers." The university also brings speakers to campus "pretty often to talk about current issues/academic [topics] of interest." And of course, "Saturdays in the fall are strictly dedicated to football." "Thursdays, Fridays, and Saturdays are the big nights for people to go out. This usually includes fraternity parties and the bar," The Bottom. Finally, heading into downtown Fort Worth is pretty popular. Students love to take advantage of the "shopping, bars, and movie theaters." And outdoorsy types will be excited to learn that "there are some trails that wind with the Trinity River which many people run and bike along."

Student Body

The vibe on Texas Christian University's campus can be summed up with the phrase "southern hospitality." Undergrads find their peers to be "friendly [and] welcoming." Many are also "football fanatics who...happen to be pretty smart." The majority of TCU students are "engaged, generally extroverted individuals who are optimistic about their potential to change the world." TCU is "big on Greek life, it can seem like everyone is a stereotypical sorority sister or fraternity brother." However, we've been assured that "there are many pockets within the student body where individuals can find their group of like-minded people," and that "everyone gets along very well in general." TCU undergrads typically "have a lot of school spirit and love to support the university" and are "friendly and personable." One student shares, "People tend to remember you just from a few interactions and never shy [away] from saying 'hi' whenever they see you on campus." Lastly, undergrads admit that TCU is not the most ethnically diverse institution. Even though there is an "abundance" of "international students," the "campus remains to be predominately white." Nevertheless, you can find "a wide array of...ideological" beliefs.

TEXAS CHRISTIAN UNIVERSITY

Financial Aid: 817-257-7858 • E-Mail: frogmail@tcu.edu • Website: www.tcu.edu

THE PRINCETON REVIEW SAYS

Admissions

Very important factors considered include: rigor of secondary school record, academic GPA. *Important factors considered include:* application essay, standardized test scores, recommendation(s), extracurricular activities, character/personal qualities, first generation, alumni/ae relation. *Other factors considered include:* class rank, interview, talent/ability, geographical residence, state residency, religious affiliation/commitment, level of applicant's interest. ACT with or without writing accepted. SAT with or without Essay component accepted. High school diploma is required and GED is not accepted. *Academic units required:* 4 English, 3 math, 3 science, 1 science lab, 2 foreign language, 3 social studies, 2 academic electives. *Academic units recommended:* 4 English, 4 math, 4 science, 1 science lab, 4 foreign language, 4 social studies.

Financial Aid

Students should submit: CSS/Financial Aid PROFILE; FAFSA; Noncustodial PROFILE. Priority filing deadline is 2/1. The Princeton Review suggests that all financial aid forms be submitted as soon as possible after October 1. *Need-based scholarships/grants offered:* College/university scholarship or grant aid from institutional funds; Federal Pell; Private scholarships; SEOG; State scholarships/grants. *Loan aid offered:* Direct PLUS loans; Direct Subsidized Stafford Loans; Direct Unsubsidized Stafford Loans. Applicants will be notified of awards on a rolling basis beginning 12/15. Federal Work-Study Program available. Institutional employment available.

The Inside Word

Admissions officers at Texas Christian University make it a priority to find applicants who will enrich the TCU community. The school does not maintain strict minimums for GPA or test scores. Admitted applicants are typically in the top 13 percent of their graduating class, with a roster of challenging courses behind them. Evaluations, essays, and activities will all be closely evaluated. Interviews are optional and standardized tests are required.

THE SCHOOL SAYS "..."

From the Admissions Office

"TCU is a major teaching and research university with the feel of a small college. The TCU academic experience includes small classes with top faculty; cutting-edge technology; a liberal arts and sciences core curriculum; and real-life application through faculty-directed research, group projects, and internships. While TCU faculty members are recognized for research, their main focus is on teaching and mentoring students. The friendly campus community welcomes new students at Frog Camp before classes begin, where students find three days of fun meeting new friends, learning campus traditions, and serving the community. Campus life includes 200 clubs and organizations, a spirited NCAA Division I athletics program in the Big 12 Conference, and numerous professional-scale productions from the TCU College of Fine Arts. More than half of the students participate in a wide array of intramural sports, and about 40 percent are involved in Greek organizations, including ones emphasizing ethnic diversity as well as the Christian faith. The historic relationship to the Christian Church (Disciples of Christ) means that instead of teaching a particular viewpoint, TCU encourages students to consider and follow their own beliefs. The university's mission—to educate individuals to think and act as ethical leaders and responsible citizens in a global community—influences everything from course work to study abroad to the way Horned Frogs act and interact. From National Merit Scholars to those just now realizing their academic potential, TCU attracts and serves students who are learning to change the world.

"TCU will accept either the SAT or the ACT (with or without the writing component) in admission and scholarship processes."

SELECTIVITY

Admissions Rating	89
# of applicants	19,028
% of applicants accepted	47
% of acceptees attending	24
# offered a place on the wait list	1,690
% accepting a place on wait list	46
% admitted from wait list	44
# of early decision applicants	855
% accepted early decision	51

FRESHMAN PROFILE

Range SAT EBRW	580–670
Range SAT Math	570–680
Range SAT Composite	1150–1340
Range ACT Composite	25–31
# submitting SAT scores	877
% submitting SAT scores	41
# submitting ACT scores	1,259
% submitting ACT scores	58
% graduated top 10% of class	47
% graduated top 25% of class	75
% graduated top 50% of class	95

DEADLINES

Early decision	
Deadline	11/1
Notification	12/1
Early action	
Deadline	11/1
Notification	12/15
Regular	
Deadline	2/1
Notification	4/1
Nonfall registration?	Yes

APPLICANTS ALSO LOOK AT AND OFTEN PREFER
Vanderbilt University; University of Southern California

AND SOMETIMES PREFER
Baylor University; Southern Methodist University; Texas A&M University; University of Texas at Austin; Trinity University; University of Miami; The University of Alabama—Tuscaloosa; Santa Clara University; Gonzaga University; Clemson University; Miami University

FINANCIAL FACTS

Financial Aid Rating	86
Annual tuition	$51,570
Room and board	$14,040
Required fees	$90
Books and supplies	$900
Average frosh need-based scholarship	$30,724
Average UG need-based scholarship	$31,070
% needy frosh rec. need-based scholarship or grant aid	94
% needy UG rec. need-based scholarship or grant aid	94
% needy frosh rec. non-need-based scholarship or grant aid	74
% needy UG rec. non-need-based scholarship or grant aid	68
% needy frosh rec. need-based self-help aid	72
% needy UG rec. need-based self-help aid	73
% frosh rec. any financial aid	82
% UG rec. any financial aid	78
% UG borrow to pay for school	34
Average cumulative indebtedness	$47,931
% frosh need fully met	36
% ugrads need fully met	25
Average % of frosh need met	71
Average % of ugrad need met	64

TEXAS STATE UNIVERSITY

429 North Guadalupe St., San Marcos, TX 78666 • Admissions: 512-245-2364 • Fax: 512-245-8044

CAMPUS LIFE

Quality of Life Rating	86
Fire Safety Rating	95
Green Rating	79
Type of school	Public
Environment	Town

STUDENTS

Total undergrad enrollment	33,917
% male/female	42/58
% from out of state	2
% frosh from public high school	98
% frosh live on campus	91
% ugrads live on campus	20
# of fraternities (% ugrad men join)	19 (5)
# of sororities (% ugrad women join)	13 (5)
% African American	9
% Asian	3
% Caucasian	43
% Hispanic	40
% Native American	<1
% Pacific Islander	<1
% Two or more races	4
% Race and/or ethnicity unknown	<1
% international	0
# of countries represented	50

SURVEY SAYS . . .

Students love San Marcos, TX
Students are happy
Great library
Great off-campus food
Recreation facilities are great
Active student government
Active minority support groups

ACADEMICS

Academic Rating	74
% students returning for sophomore year	76
% students graduating within 4 years	29
% students graduating within 6 years	54
Calendar	Semester
Student/faculty ratio	20:1
Profs interesting rating	84
Profs accessible rating	89

Most classes have 20–29 students.
Most lab/discussion sessions have 10–19 students.

MOST POPULAR MAJORS

Multi-/Interdisciplinary Studies, Other; Exercise Science and Kinesiology; Psychology, General

STUDENTS SAY "..."

Academic

Texas State University is a large research university that offers students the "diversity, quality of instruction, [and] resources of a large university with the feel of a smaller school." This is "a friendly institution that is growing in population and academics," and its size lends to "well-funded programs, activities, learning opportunities," and "merit-based financial aid." Additionally, "there are countless programs to help students succeed" and "lots of student outreach programs," and the school puts on events, exhibitions, and performances throughout the year built around a central theme (most recently "Innovation").

The "very student-focused" professors at Texas State "are fantastic and try to help you reach your full potential." To do this, they "attempt to make everyone feel as if they are important [in addition to] their opinions and ideas" being important as well. They "come from actual job experience that they share with students" and "make an effort to keep you up to date on new findings in their field," all while being "very aware of current events [which they] easily relate ... to our topic of class." The "small school feel helps people to find what's right for them," and the faculty and staff at Texas State "give the students as many opportunities as possible." As one student sums it up: "It's big enough that there are tons of opportunities to get involved in internships or organizations," but it's "very helpful to have academic advisors that you can visit at any time."

Life

With great natural features at the "big-but-not-too big" school, including the San Marcos River running right through the main campus, activities like "floating the river, swimming, hiking, [and] biking" are popular pastimes, so people "spend the majority of time outside or doing something active." One student says, "Nature brings everyone together. The river is a symbol of our school." At Texas State, "there is an organization for everyone in one way or another," and "many people go out during the week, whether it's to go drink at bars, ... go bowling, [or] watch a movie." Nearby San Marcos also holds plenty of opportunities for fun because it features "great food and recreational places in the city," and during downtime, people will "go to the town square [which] is lined with bars and restaurants," and where "coffee shops and study spots are abundant.

Student Body

This is "an inclusive campus"—more than half of all Texas State students are minorities and students come "from all ... races [and] sexual orientations," making the school feel "unique and very diverse." This range means there are "a lot of opposing ideas on everything from politics to social issues," but "students engage each other in a productive manner" in this "open-minded and engaging campus climate." (One student notes the variety even more specifically, mentioning "a healthy mix of people invested in studies, in parties, in their specific interests, or in nothing at all.") Since students are mainly Texans, people "are friendly and easy to talk to," and though it's a big school, "it's easy to make friends within your classes." One student brags, "There's a sense of community among the students and it's really heartwarming."

TEXAS STATE UNIVERSITY

Financial Aid: 512-245-2315 • E-Mail: admissions@txstate.edu • Website: www.txstate.edu

THE PRINCETON REVIEW SAYS

Admissions

Very important factors considered include: class rank, standardized test scores. *Other factors considered include:* rigor of secondary school record, application essay, extracurricular activities, talent/ability, first generation. ACT with Writing recommended. SAT with Essay component recommended. High school diploma is required and GED is accepted. *Academic units required:* 4 English, 4 math, 4 science, 2 science labs, 2 foreign language, 2 social studies, 2 history, 6 academic electives, 1 visual/performing arts, 1 unit from above areas or other academic areas. *Academic units recommended:* 4 English, 4 math, 4 science, 2 science labs, 2 foreign language, 2 social studies, 2 history, 6 academic electives, 1 visual/performing arts.

Financial Aid

Students should submit: FAFSA. Priority filing deadline is 1/15. The Princeton Review suggests that all financial aid forms be submitted as soon as possible after October 1. *Need-based scholarships/grants offered:* College/university scholarship or grant aid from institutional funds; Federal Pell; Private scholarships; SEOG; State scholarships/grants. *Loan aid offered:* Direct PLUS loans; Direct Subsidized Stafford Loans; Direct Unsubsidized Stafford Loans. Applicants will be notified of awards on a rolling basis beginning 5/1. Federal Work-Study Program available. Institutional employment available.

The Inside Word

Competition to become a Bobcat is fierce; first-year applicants should have four years of math, science, and English; three years of social studies; and two years of a foreign language, among other requirements. The state of Texas requires that all students meet specific college readiness standards, and assured admission is granted to all students with certain diploma types who meet specific test score and class ranking standards—students should visit the school's website in order to see if they qualify. Even if a student does not meet assured admission requirements, their application will be holistically reviewed by the school.

SELECTIVITY

Admissions Rating	82
# of applicants	23,583
% of applicants accepted	81
% of acceptees attending	33

FRESHMAN PROFILE

Range SAT EBRW	510–600
Range SAT Math	500–580
Range ACT Composite	19–25
# submitting SAT scores	4,685
% submitting SAT scores	74
# submitting ACT scores	1,672
% submitting ACT scores	26
% graduated top 10% of class	12
% graduated top 25% of class	46
% graduated top 50% of class	90

DEADLINES

Regular	
Priority	3/1
Deadline	5/1
Notification	Rolling, 9/1
Nonfall registration?	Yes

APPLICANTS ALSO LOOK AT AND OFTEN PREFER
University of Texas at Austin

AND SOMETIMES PREFER
Texas A&M University

AND RARELY PREFER
The University of Texas at San Antonio; Texas Tech University; University of Houston

FINANCIAL FACTS

Financial Aid Rating	83
Annual in-state tuition	$8,627
Annual out-of-state tuition	$21,287
Room and board	$11,102
Required fees	$2,630
Books and supplies	$800
Average frosh need-based scholarship	$9,713
Average UG need-based scholarship	$8,081
% needy frosh rec. need-based scholarship or grant aid	82
% needy UG rec. need-based scholarship or grant aid	80
% needy frosh rec. non-need-based scholarship or grant aid	18
% needy UG rec. non-need-based scholarship or grant aid	9
% needy frosh rec. need-based self-help aid	76
% needy UG rec. need-based self-help aid	77
% frosh rec. any financial aid	77
% UG rec. any financial aid	70
% UG borrow to pay for school	65
Average cumulative indebtedness	$24,950
% frosh need fully met	23
% ugrads need fully met	19
Average % of frosh need met	71
Average % of ugrad need met	63

THOMAS AQUINAS COLLEGE

10,000 Ojai Road, Santa Paula, CA 93060 • Admissions: 805-525-4417 • Fax: 805-421-5905

STUDENTS SAY " . . ."

Academics

Thomas Aquinas College is a small, private Roman Catholic-affiliated liberal arts school located in Southern California. Students have a wide spectrum of terms with which to describe their unique education: "difficult, mind blowing, extremely enjoyable, and intensely interesting." Instead of taking the standard mix of general education requirements, electives, and coursework for majors and minors, TAC has a set curriculum for all first-years, sophomores, juniors, and seniors that is comprised entirely of reading and discussing the great books of Western civilization with the goal of "grappling with the greatest thinkers directly instead of … through a secondary text." Students say professors are excellent at facilitating discussions, "always accessible outside of their class hours," and "strong role models and mentors." With class sizes of "just over a dozen students," they typically rely on the Socratic Method with little to no lecturing. Students say the combination of curriculum and pedagogy allows them to "find the truth themselves," hone their critical thinking skills, and, by senior year, grasp essential "core ideas of the highest nature such as relativity, time, space and being." Some do note that courses could focus more on developing writing skills by assigning "more essays and papers" in addition to the heavy reading. By contrast, some students feel that while a classical education "may not prepare one for a specific job, it prepares one to be a good man [or woman]." One student sums the academic experience up by saying, "You have to work very hard, but … you see [it] pay off instantly in class."

Life

During the week, Thomas Aquinas College students focus on preparing for class and on their work-study jobs, if they've taken one on. When they're looking for a break, they often find it in the college's intramural sports, which are "open to all students regardless of skill." Sports like basketball, ultimate frisbee, tennis, soccer, baseball, or volleyball "bring the community together without taking over" campus life. Outside of athletics, students would like more variety in school sponsored extracurricular activities, but this outdoorsy student body has a plethora of options in their backyard. The campus is "a mile walk from the Los Padres National Forest, which is a beautiful location for hiking and mountain biking," and the local beach in Ventura is a popular swimming and surfing destination.

Campus rules "strongly reflect [TAC's] Catholic identity" and include a dress code and curfew. For some, this conservative culture "does not feel like college life but high school life," while others say it creates a peaceful environment where it's easy to prioritize coursework. Instead of traditional campus nightlife there are frequent "small, informal waltz or swing nights." (Drinking isn't tolerated on campus, so those looking for such activities must head off campus.) Classes take turns hosting monthly themed dances, which are "often highlights of everyone's year." When they're not busy with this wide array of options, students simply "sit around and talk in the commons," play board games, read poetry, make music and movies, sing in the choir, knit, and hang out in the coffee shop.

Student Body

With a student body of about 400 undergrads, "each individual is a relevant member of the community." TAC students take pride in the "culture of casual kindnesses," where everyone "is friendly and comfortable with each other" and is "always willing to have a good conversation." Additionally, students describe their peers as "kind," "quirky," "genuine," and united by "a desire for [pursuing] knowledge for its own sake." This sense of community is bolstered by a "wide range of backgrounds and cultures," primarily from a traditional Catholic or Christian background—"most students attend mass daily." One student sums it up: "There are the athletic students, the studious students, the party-goers, and the introverted students," although "we joke that . . . everyone falls under the common category of nerd."

THOMAS AQUINAS COLLEGE

Financial Aid: 800-634-9797 • E-Mail: admissions@thomasaquinas.edu • Website: www.thomasaquinas.edu

THE PRINCETON REVIEW SAYS

Admissions

Very important factors considered include: rigor of secondary school record, application essay, standardized test scores, recommendation(s), character/personal qualities, level of applicant's interest. *Important factors considered include:* academic GPA. *Other factors considered include:* class rank, interview, extracurricular activities, talent/ability, religious affiliation/commitment, volunteer work, work experience. ACT with or without writing accepted. SAT with or without Essay component accepted. High school diploma is required and GED is accepted. *Academic units required:* 4 English, 3 math, 2 science, 2 foreign language, 2 history. *Academic units recommended:* 4 English, 4 math, 3 science, 2 science labs, 2 history, 3 academic electives.

Financial Aid

Students should submit: CSS/Financial Aid PROFILE; FAFSA; Noncustodial PROFILE; State aid form. The Princeton Review suggests that all financial aid forms be submitted as soon as possible after October 1. *Need-based scholarships/grants offered:* College/university scholarship or grant aid from institutional funds; Federal Pell; Private scholarships; State scholarships/grants. *Loan aid offered:* Direct PLUS loans; Direct Subsidized Stafford Loans; Direct Unsubsidized Stafford Loans. Applicants will be notified of awards on a rolling basis beginning 2/1. Institutional employment available.

The Inside Word

A unique academic institution, Thomas Aquinas College thoroughly analyzes applicants to ensure accepted students will be a good fit on campus. Therefore, academic prowess is a must, and candidates should also demonstrate intellectual curiosity. Because of their holistic approach, admissions officers pay close attention to the application essays. The college operates on a rolling admissions schedule and, if interested, you should apply as early as possible. Note that a second campus location has been opened in western Massachusetts. Prospective students can only apply for admission at one location—each campus has separate applications.

THE SCHOOL SAYS "..."

From the Admissions Office

"Thomas Aquinas College holds with confidence that the human mind is capable of knowing the truth about reality, that living according to the truth is necessary for human happiness, and that truth is best comprehended through the harmonious work of faith and reason. The intellectual virtues are understood to be essential, and the college considers the cultivation of those virtues the primary work of Catholic liberal education.

"The academic program is comprehensive and unified, and it includes no textbooks or lecture classes. Students read the greatest written works in every subject—from philosophy, theology, mathematics, and science to language, music, literature, and history. From the ancients to the moderns, authors in the curriculum include Plato, Einstein, Shakespeare, Aristotle, Galileo, St. Augustine, Freud, Austen, Locke, and St. Thomas Aquinas, to name a few. Instead of attending lecture classes, students gather in small seminars for Socratic-style discussions and in laboratories for biology, chemistry, and physics investigation and experimentation.

"One mark of the program's success is the variety of professions and careers that graduates enter. Many alumni attend graduate and professional schools in a wide array of disciplines; among them, philosophy, theology, law, literature, and the sciences are most often chosen. Interested students may consider attending one of the College's summer programs, held annually on both campuses."

SELECTIVITY
Admissions Rating	88
# of applicants	170
% of applicants accepted	76
% of acceptees attending	73
# offered a place on the wait list	24
% accepting a place on wait list	100
% admitted from wait list	63

FRESHMAN PROFILE
Range SAT EBRW	590–710
Range SAT Math	570–680
Range ACT Composite	27–31
# submitting SAT scores	75
% submitting SAT scores	81
# submitting ACT scores	20
% submitting ACT scores	22
Average HS GPA	3.8
% graduated top 10% of class	25
% graduated top 25% of class	67
% graduated top 50% of class	83

DEADLINES
Regular	
Notification	Rolling, 10/1
Nonfall registration?	No

FINANCIAL FACTS
Financial Aid Rating	97
Annual tuition	$26,000
Room and board	$9,400
Average frosh need-based scholarship	$14,359
Average UG need-based scholarship	$14,019
% needy frosh rec. need-based scholarship or grant aid	91
% needy UG rec. need-based scholarship or grant aid	83
% needy frosh rec. non-need-based scholarship or grant aid	0
% needy UG rec. non-need-based scholarship or grant aid	0
% needy frosh rec. need-based self-help aid	97
% needy UG rec. need-based self-help aid	99
% frosh rec. any financial aid	79
% UG rec. any financial aid	77
% UG borrow to pay for school	82
Average cumulative indebtedness	$18,967
% frosh need fully met	100
% ugrads need fully met	100
Average % of frosh need met	100
Average % of ugrad need met	100

TRANSYLVANIA UNIVERSITY

300 North Broadway, Lexington, KY 40508-1797 • Admissions: 859-233-8242 • Fax: 859-281-3649

CAMPUS LIFE

Quality of Life Rating	88
Fire Safety Rating	90
Green Rating	60*
Type of school	Private
Affiliation	Disciples of Christ
Environment	Metropolis

STUDENTS

Total undergrad enrollment	989
% male/female	40/60
% from out of state	21
% frosh from public high school	78
% frosh live on campus	90
% ugrads live on campus	70
# of fraternities (% ugrad men join)	4 (44)
# of sororities (% ugrad women join)	4 (42)
% African American	5
% Asian	2
% Caucasian	80
% Hispanic	4
% Native American	<1
% Pacific Islander	0
% Two or more races	5
% Race and/or ethnicity unknown	5
% international	0
# of countries represented	8

SURVEY SAYS . . .

Internships are widely available
Class discussions encouraged
Students love Lexington, KY
Easy to get around campus
Recreation facilities are great
Frats and sororities are popular
Theater is popular

ACADEMICS

Academic Rating	85
% students returning for sophomore year	82
% students graduating within 4 years	69
% students graduating within 6 years	75
Calendar	Other
Student/faculty ratio	11:1
Profs interesting rating	93
Profs accessible rating	95

Most classes have 10–19 students.
Most lab/discussion sessions have
  10–19 students.

MOST POPULAR MAJORS

Business/Commerce, General; Accounting;
Psychology, General

STUDENTS SAY "..."

Academics

For many thrilled students, Transylvania University in Lexington, Kentucky feels "like home" from the minute they set foot on campus. This is due in large part to its "small size," which allows "Transy" to maintain a very "supportive" environment. When it comes to academics, undergrads at Transylvania savor the breadth of courses that are available. And they rush to highlight the "inclusive fine arts program," which lets non-majors still actively participate in "music or theatre." Many also note student success with graduate school, boasting of a "96%" acceptance rate to medical school and a whopping "100%" acceptance rate to law school. Much of this can be attributed to "rigorous" classes that "require you to think deeply and critically." Transy's "brilliant faculty" is owed some credit as well. They are "highly dedicated" instructors who continually demonstrate "interest...in [their] students' lives and ambitions." Even better, "they all have open office hours multiple days a week and often will meet with students other times as well." And one incredulous student interjects, "I am close enough with my professors to join them for department dinners or drinks with guest lecturers. It is a one-of-a-kind situation that I wouldn't trade for the world."

Life

It is pretty easy to lead a fun and robust life at Transylvania. While academics take top priority, there are also "many opportunities to get involved on campus." For example, "there are frequently guest speakers and movie nights that students can attend for fun and for class credit." The university hosts "a lot of theater productions and music concerts" as well. Most "people are involved with school-affiliated organizations, like the school's "environmental conservation group" and the "Student Activities Board." Athletics are a big draw too and you can often find undergrads playing "volleyball, basketball, soccer," and "intramurals." Those looking for instant community will be happy to hear that "Greek life is extremely popular." When students are itching to get a break from campus life, downtown Lexington offers a plethora of great options including "a ton of neat places within walking distance, such as the malls at the Square and at the Central Bank Center, Triangle Park, the Mary Todd Lincoln House, and the Lexington Opera House." All in all, there's "so much to do, and there's always something new to discover."

Student Body

Transylvania manages to foster a "very safe and accepting" atmosphere. Much of that can be attributed to the "incredibly welcoming and friendly" student body. And though the university is set in Kentucky, we're told you find a nice "mix of classic south[ern] and northern attitudes." You're also likely to discover both "liberal" and "conservative" students. Unfortunately, some undergrads do caution that Transylvania is "not very diverse." But many people insist that their peers "seem willing and curious to learn about different cultures and perspectives." As one undergrad shares, "The majority of students on campus are open-minded, creative people, and incredibly accepting of others no matter their gender, race, sexual/gender orientation, or socioeconomic status. They do not hesitate to band together to aid another student in need." Students also love that their peers are "goal oriented" and "take their education seriously." They "push to excel academically, socially, and athletically." And they all enjoy being "extremely involved on campus." Of course, the best aspect of Transy's student body is the fact that "anywhere you go you can always find a friend or at least some people that are easy to talk to."

TRANSYLVANIA UNIVERSITY

Financial Aid: 859-233-8239 • E-Mail: admissions@transy.edu • Website: www.transy.edu

THE PRINCETON REVIEW SAYS

Admissions

Very important factors considered include: rigor of secondary school record, academic GPA, application essay, standardized test scores. *Important factors considered include:* recommendation(s), extracurricular activities, talent/ability, character/personal qualities. *Other factors considered include:* class rank, interview, first generation, alumni/ae relation, geographical residence, racial/ethnic status, volunteer work, work experience. ACT with or without writing accepted. SAT with or without Essay component accepted. High school diploma is required and GED is accepted. *Academic units required:* 4 English, 3 math, 3 science, 2 science labs, 2 foreign language, 2 social studies, 2 academic electives. *Academic units recommended:* 4 English, 4 math, 4 science, 3 science labs, 2 foreign language, 2 social studies, 1 history, 2 academic electives.

Financial Aid

Students should submit: FAFSA. Priority filing deadline is 10/15. The Princeton Review suggests that all financial aid forms be submitted as soon as possible after October 1. *Need-based scholarships/grants offered:* College/university scholarship or grant aid from institutional funds; Federal Pell; Private scholarships; SEOG; State scholarships/grants. *Loan aid offered:* Direct PLUS loans; Direct Subsidized Stafford Loans; Direct Unsubsidized Stafford Loans. Students who wish to compete for the highest scholarships should apply by 12/1. Federal Work-Study Program available. Institutional employment available.

The Inside Word

Admissions officers at Transylvania realize that students are more than the mere sum of their GPA and test scores. And they strive to get a clear picture of the entire applicant. Therefore, while high school transcripts hold the most weight, the committee also closely considers your personal statement, extracurricular activities, and recommendations. And applicants wary of the SATs and ACTs can breathe a sigh of relief; Transylvania is a test optional school. You will not be at a disadvantage if you choose not to submit your scores.

THE SCHOOL SAYS "..."

From the Admissions Office

"Bright, highly motivated students choose Transylvania for our personal approach to learning and our record of success in preparing them for rewarding careers and fulfilling lives. They attend small classes with highly qualified professors (no teaching assistants) and tackle faculty-directed student research projects in intriguing subjects like neurotransmitters and receptors, computer animation, and local Hispanic culture. Transylvania graduates have won prestigious scholarships and distinguished themselves at highly selective graduate and professional schools. Transylvania students consider the world their classroom. They enjoy May term travel courses studying the ancient polis in Greece, language and culture in France, and tropical ecology in Hawaii. Study abroad takes them to Germany, England, Japan, Mexico, and other destinations for a summer, a semester, or a year. You'll find Transylvania, a small college, nestled in a big city. Transylvania students soak up the advantages of Lexington, Kentucky, with its population of 300,000, numerous internships and job opportunities, and lots of entertainment. On campus, we have more than fifty co-curricular activities, and twenty-seven varsity athletic teams with twenty-three competing in NCAA Division III. While Transylvania is the nation's sixteenth oldest college and proud of its rich history, its commitments to the exploration of a variety of disciplines, to intellectual inquiry, and to critical thinking have never been more relevant than in today's rapidly changing twenty-first-century world.

"Transylvania University is a Test Optional school and does not require that students submit standardized test scores as part of the admission process. Read more at www.transy.edu/optional."

SELECTIVITY

Admissions Rating	77
# of applicants	1,662
% of applicants accepted	89
% of acceptees attending	20

FRESHMAN PROFILE

Range SAT EBRW	560–640
Range SAT Math	540–670
Range ACT Composite	24–30
# submitting SAT scores	33
% submitting SAT scores	11
# submitting ACT scores	244
% submitting ACT scores	82
Average HS GPA	3.7
% graduated top 10% of class	30
% graduated top 25% of class	67
% graduated top 50% of class	90

DEADLINES

Regular	
Priority	11/1
Notification	Rolling, 11/1
Nonfall registration?	Yes

APPLICANTS ALSO LOOK AT AND OFTEN PREFER
University of Kentucky; Centre College

AND SOMETIMES PREFER
Bellarmine University; Eastern Kentucky University; Georgetown College; Hanover College; University of Louisville; Western Kentucky University

AND RARELY PREFER
Northern Kentucky University; University of Cincinnati; Morehead State University; University of Tennessee, Knoxville; Butler University; DePauw University

FINANCIAL FACTS

Financial Aid Rating	87
Annual tuition	$38,570
Room and board	$10,770
Required fees	$1,640
Books and supplies	$1,000
Average frosh need-based scholarship	$27,254
Average UG need-based scholarship	$25,644
% needy frosh rec. need-based scholarship or grant aid	100
% needy UG rec. need-based scholarship or grant aid	100
% needy frosh rec. non-need-based scholarship or grant aid	17
% needy UG rec. non-need-based scholarship or grant aid	16
% needy frosh rec. need-based self-help aid	76
% needy UG rec. need-based self-help aid	76
% frosh rec. any financial aid	99
% UG rec. any financial aid	98
% UG borrow to pay for school	55
Average cumulative indebtedness	$33,037
% frosh need fully met	24
% ugrads need fully met	23
Average % of frosh need met	81
Average % of ugrad need met	78

TRINITY COLLEGE (CT)

300 Summit Street, Hartford, CT 06106 • Admissions: 860-297-2180 • Fax: 860-297-2287

STUDENTS SAY "..."

Academics

"[It's all] about getting a top-notch education in small classes with professors who know you and being able to also have a good time outside of class" at Trinity College, a small and prestigious liberal arts school located in Connecticut's state capital. A "great political science department" exploits TC's location "about two blocks away from the state capital, which is great for internships." Other social sciences, including economics and history, earn students' praises, as do offerings in engineering and education. Strength across the liberal arts bolsters the school's Humanities Gateway Program, in which students undertake a fixed curriculum of interdisciplinary study to survey the entirety of European cultures from the classical age to the present. In all disciplines, "small classes, very involved professors, and a very conscious student body" combine to provide "an excellent liberal arts education that will provide [students] with the skills to be thoughtful, independent adults." Professors "are always available to talk and offer help to students. They often invite students out to lunch." Likewise, administrators are easy to access. Students also appreciate that "the career services office is amazing" here.

Life

"The fraternity scene is the draw for the majority of campus" at Trinity College, where "on a typical weekend night, people go out to dinner, go back to their room and nap, get ready for the evening, and go meet up with a friend or two where they chill out and then go to someone's room for pregaming.... Then when it's about 1:00 A.M., they go out and do some frat hopping. It's great for people who like their life to be predictable." The frats are hardly the only option, though; in fact, "there are a ton of underappreciated options on or near campus. Hartford has amazing restaurants, there are movie theaters and bowling alleys nearby, the Cinestudio is a ninety-second walk from the main dining hall." There is also a Health and Wellness Residence Hall. "Plus, plenty of student groups hold events" in such places as "the arts and cultural houses." Trinity's theater and dance department offer regular performances. Hometown Hartford "may be [an economically] depressed city, but it is still a city, and it affords benefits that tiny college towns just can't match."

Student Body

The stereotype about Trinity undergrads is that "most...are from the tristate area and appear to have just stepped off a yacht or out of a country club," and students confirm that while "there are a lot of students who are not" in this crowd, the preppy contingent is "the main group" and "socially dominant" here. "There are definitely some very preppy girls and boys—blond hair, sunglasses, Chanel flats, a polo," one student concedes before adding that "sometimes people identify these students as typical Trinity students; however, there are many students who are not like that at all." All students tend to be "well-rounded" and "very passionate," "intelligent but also social," with "good verbal skills." They "care deeply about their work and really like to have fun when they can," and while many gravitate to the Greek community for their fun, "there are [also] communities here for those who do not enjoy the frat scene, for people who are passionate about music and acting, and [for] those who want to spend their weekends giving back to the community."

TRINITY COLLEGE (CT)

Financial Aid: 860-297-2047 • E-Mail: admissions.office@trincoll.edu • Website: www.trincoll.edu

THE PRINCETON REVIEW SAYS

Admissions

Very important factors considered include: rigor of secondary school record, character/personal qualities. *Important factors considered include:* academic GPA, application essay, recommendation(s), extracurricular activities, talent/ability. *Other factors considered include:* class rank, standardized test scores, interview, first generation, alumni/ae relation, racial/ethnic status, volunteer work, work experience. ACT with or without writing accepted. SAT with or without Essay component accepted. High school diploma is required and GED is accepted. *Academic units required:* 4 English, 3 math, 2 science, 2 science labs, 3 foreign language, 2 history.

Financial Aid

Students should submit: CSS/Financial Aid PROFILE; FAFSA; Noncustodial PROFILE. Priority filing deadline is 2/1. The Princeton Review suggests that all financial aid forms be submitted as soon as possible after October 1. *Need-based scholarships/grants offered:* College/university scholarship or grant aid from institutional funds; Federal Pell; Private scholarships; SEOG; State scholarships/grants. *Loan aid offered:* Direct PLUS loans; Direct Subsidized Stafford Loans; Direct Unsubsidized Stafford Loans. Applicants will be notified of awards on or about 4/1. Federal Work-Study Program available. Institutional employment available.

The Inside Word

Students describe Trinity as "the home of Yale rejects," an appraisal that accurately, if somewhat hyperbolically, characterizes the school's reputation as an Ivy safety. The hefty tuition and fees here ensure that a large percentage of the student body is made up of wealthy, preppy types, but the school does offer generous financial aid packages to top candidates who can't afford the considerable price of attending. The school would love to broaden its demographic, so competitive minority students should receive a very welcome reception here.

THE SCHOOL SAYS "..."

From the Admissions Office

"An array of distinctive curricular options—including an interdisciplinary neuroscience major and a professionally accredited engineering degree program, a unique Human Rights Program, a Health Fellows Program, and interdisciplinary programs such as the Cities Program, Interdisciplinary Science Program, and InterArts—is one reason record numbers of students are applying to Trinity. In fact, applications are up 80 percent over the past five years. In addition, the college has been recognized for its commitment to diversity; students of color have represented approximately 20 percent of the freshman class for the past four years, setting Trinity apart from many of its peers. Trinity's capital city location offers students unparalleled 'real-world' learning experiences to complement classroom learning. Students take advantage of extensive opportunities for internships for academic credit and community service, and these opportunities extend to Trinity's global learning sites in cities around the world. Trinity's faculty is a devoted and accomplished group of exceptional teacher-scholars; our 100-acre campus is beautiful; Hartford is an educational asset that differentiates Trinity from other liberal arts colleges; our global connections and foreign study opportunities prepare students to be good citizens of the world; and our graduates go on to excel in virtually every field. We invite you to learn more about why Trinity might be the best choice for you.

"Students applying for admission may submit the following testing options: SAT or ACT with writing."

SELECTIVITY

Admissions Rating	92
# of applicants	6,073
% of applicants accepted	34
% of acceptees attending	28
# of early decision applicants	508
% accepted early decision	56

FRESHMAN PROFILE

Range SAT EBRW	600–680
Range SAT Math	610–690
Range ACT Composite	28–32
# submitting SAT scores	192
% submitting SAT scores	34
# submitting ACT scores	141
% submitting ACT scores	25
% graduated top 10% of class	50
% graduated top 25% of class	78
% graduated top 50% of class	96

DEADLINES

Early decision	
Deadline	11/15
Notification	12/15
Other ED Deadline	1/1
Other ED Notification	2/15
Regular	
Deadline	1/1
Notification	4/1
Nonfall registration?	Yes

FINANCIAL FACTS

Financial Aid Rating	96
Annual tuition	$52,280
Room and board	$14,200
Required fees	$2,490
Books and supplies	$1,000
Average frosh need-based scholarship	$44,394
Average UG need-based scholarship	$44,812
% needy frosh rec. need-based scholarship or grant aid	97
% needy UG rec. need-based scholarship or grant aid	97
% needy frosh rec. non-need-based scholarship or grant aid	4
% needy UG rec. non-need-based scholarship or grant aid	6
% needy frosh rec. need-based self-help aid	59
% needy UG rec. need-based self-help aid	68
% frosh rec. any financial aid	49
% UG rec. any financial aid	45
% UG borrow to pay for school	43
Average cumulative indebtedness	$29,506
% frosh need fully met	100
% ugrads need fully met	100
Average % of frosh need met	100
Average % of ugrad need met	100

TRINITY UNIVERSITY

Northrup Hall Room 140, San Antonio, TX 78212-7200 • Admissions: 210-999-7207 • Fax: 210-999-8164

STUDENTS SAY "..."

Academics

Located in San Antonio, Trinity University is a small liberal arts college that offers substantial financial aid and encourages the exploration of academic interests and personal goals. Strong science programs and research opportunities abound, and students are interested in many different branches of academia and extracurricular life: "It's rare to find a student with one major and no minor." The Dean and President "have steady communication with the student body," and "they're open to criticism and willing to change the school's policy in order to advocate for the students' needs." The "highly intelligent" faculty "know their stuff and love what they do"; they are "very self-aware and are constantly trying to improve themselves and their students." The most distinguishable trait about Trinity professors is "the deeply-ingrained willingness to connect with and help their students," which is possible due to Trinity's small class sizes. Academics here are rigorous, and professors "expect their students to treat the class ... as if it was the only class students have." Luckily, they will "bend over backwards to help you understand and complete material," and some professors even hold extra study sessions on Sundays (one-on-one attention from professors is common, as the university does not have TAs).

Above all else, Trinity University encourages students to take a wide range of classes and pursue a wide variety of interests, and a fair number of students choose to study abroad their junior year. The school "focuses on building a community based on the individual" and "fosters a space for the easy transfer of knowledge between faculty and students as well as the creation of new knowledge in research."

Life

Most students at Trinity live on campus (and it's "hard to get off campus and do things if you don't have a car"), so there are always campus-wide events happening. Most people here are "happily overcommitted" and the "lovely campus" is big enough for all sorts of people to find their niche, but small enough "that you can connect with others who share similar interests as you within and without your major." Intramural sports and Greek life are popular, and "there's no tension between Greeks and non-Greeks." A healthy mix of activities complements the healthy mix of academic areas, and some people go out to parties on weekends, other people get ahead on studies, other people sleep." For those looking for some city culture, downtown San Antonio is ten minutes away, Austin is just a 90-minute drive, and "there are tons of restaurants and historical monuments and museums" nearby. Cowboys, the local country dance club ("only in Texas") gets a lot of Trinity students visiting on weekends, and many people here "enjoy outdoor pursuits." Laid back, casual fun is the name of the game at Trinity, and students are perfectly happy to "catch a movie at the nearby theater, go to the local farmers' market, go to Spurs' games ... or just hang out on campus."

Student Body

There is an "open-minded open-to-all mindset" that is readily seen on campus: "At Trinity, you're cool if you competitively roller skate, are an amateur baker, play a competitive sport, are freaky good at laser tag (ninja status), or anything else you can do well and makes you happy," says a student. Though most are "pretty middle- to upper middle-class," the school "encourages interactions with others from all walks of life." For the most part, everyone is "smart, committed, and involved," and an "overarching friendliness" pervades the entire student population.

Financial Aid: 210-999-8898 • E-Mail: admissions@trinity.edu • Website: www.trinity.edu

THE PRINCETON REVIEW SAYS
Admissions
Very important factors considered include: rigor of secondary school record, class rank, academic GPA, standardized test scores. *Important factors considered include:* application essay, recommendation(s), interview, extracurricular activities, talent/ability, character/personal qualities. *Other factors considered include:* first generation, alumni/ae relation, geographical residence, volunteer work, work experience, level of applicant's interest. ACT with or without writing accepted. SAT with or without Essay component accepted. High school diploma is required and GED is accepted. *Academic units required:* 4 English, 3 math, 3 science, 2 science labs, 2 foreign language, 3 social studies. *Academic units recommended:* 4 English, 3 math, 3 science, 2 science labs, 2 foreign language, 3 social studies.

Financial Aid
Students should submit: CSS/Financial Aid PROFILE; FAFSA. Priority filing deadline is 2/15. The Princeton Review suggests that all financial aid forms be submitted as soon as possible after October 1. *Need-based scholarships/grants offered:* College/university scholarship or grant aid from institutional funds; Federal Pell; Private scholarships; SEOG; State scholarships/grants. *Loan aid offered:* Direct PLUS loans; Direct Subsidized Stafford Loans; Direct Unsubsidized Stafford Loans. Applicants will be notified of awards on or about 3/15. Federal Work-Study Program available. Institutional employment available.

The Inside Word
As Trinity embraces a small, close-knit community of students, admissions officers are looking for the complete package: bright, capable, motivated students who are ready to take advantage of all the school has to offer. While academic performance is the factor considered most heavily on each application, recommendations, extracurricular activities, and standardized test scores should all be very strong as well.

THE SCHOOL SAYS "..."
From the Admissions Office
"Three qualities separate Trinity University from other selective, academically challenging institutions around the country. First, Trinity is unusual in the quality and quantity of resources devoted almost exclusively to its undergraduate students. Those resources give rise to a second distinctive aspect of Trinity—its emphasis on undergraduate research. Our students prefer being involved over observing. With superior laboratory facilities and strong, dedicated faculty, our undergraduates fill many of the roles formerly reserved for graduate students, and our professors often go to their undergraduates for help with their research. Other experiential learning opportunities including internships, study abroad, and service projects are also available to students. Finally, Trinity stands apart for the attitude of its students. In an atmosphere of academic camaraderie, our students work together to stretch their minds and broaden their horizons across academic disciplines. For quality of resources, for dedication to undergraduate research, and for the disposition of its student body, Trinity University holds a unique position in American higher education.

"Students applying for admission must submit either the SAT or the ACT. The highest composite test scores from one or multiple dates are evaluated. The SAT writing section and ACT writing component are not required."

SELECTIVITY
Admissions Rating	93
# of applicants	9,864
% of applicants accepted	28
% of acceptees attending	23
# offered a place on the wait list	1,236
% accepting a place on wait list	42
% admitted from wait list	6
# of early decision applicants	159
% accepted early decision	63

FRESHMAN PROFILE
Range SAT EBRW	650–720
Range SAT Math	640–730
Range SAT Composite	1290–1420
Range ACT Composite	29–32
# submitting SAT scores	353
% submitting SAT scores	55
# submitting ACT scores	289
% submitting ACT scores	49
Average HS GPA	3.6
% graduated top 10% of class	50
% graduated top 25% of class	82
% graduated top 50% of class	98

DEADLINES
Early decision	
Deadline	11/1
Notification	12/1
Other ED Deadline	1/15
Other ED Notification	2/1
Early action	
Deadline	11/1
Notification	12/15
Regular	
Deadline	2/1
Notification	4/1
Nonfall registration?	Yes

FINANCIAL FACTS
Financial Aid Rating	91
Annual tuition	$44,064
Room and board	$13,584
Required fees	$616
Books and supplies	$1,000
Average frosh need-based scholarship	$34,754
Average UG need-based scholarship	$33,705
% needy frosh rec. need-based scholarship or grant aid	100
% needy UG rec. need-based scholarship or grant aid	99
% needy frosh rec. non-need-based scholarship or grant aid	42
% needy UG rec. non-need-based scholarship or grant aid	21
% needy frosh rec. need-based self-help aid	57
% needy UG rec. need-based self-help aid	62
% frosh rec. any financial aid	99
% UG rec. any financial aid	97
% UG borrow to pay for school	47
Average cumulative indebtedness	$43,005
% frosh need fully met	62
% ugrads need fully met	44
Average % of frosh need met	98
Average % of ugrad need met	92

TRUMAN STATE UNIVERSITY

100 E. Normal Ave., Kirksville, MO 63501 • Admissions: 660-785-4114 • Fax: 660-785-7456

STUDENTS SAY "..."

Academics
Simply put, Truman State University in Kirksville, Missouri offers undergraduates a "great education" at a "great price." Students fortunate enough to attend join a "strong community" that quickly becomes a "home away from home." Academically, undergrads here applaud the school's wide "variety of classes, majors and minors." This virtually guarantees, "There is a way for everyone to study what they enjoy." Of course, some undergrads do note that Truman is especially known for its "education program and nursing program." Many individuals also site the "very low" student-professor ratio as being a huge advantage. Indeed, these "small" classes translate into a "more personal" learning experience. As one thankful student expounds, "The professors want to get to know you and know your name and do everything they can to help you succeed in life." While classes "are demanding," the workload is certainly "not unreasonable." Nevertheless, some students do caution, "you have to be prepared to really engage with the material in order to do well at Truman." Though they just as readily acknowledge that this emphasis on critical thinking translates into "very good ... job placement/graduate school entrance rates." All in all, undergrads concur that a Truman education is "really worth the hard work."

Life
Truman has plenty to offer when it comes to extracurricular opportunities and entertainment. For starters, there are "several hundred clubs" in which students can participate. Additionally, "the school does a good job of hosting different events, such as performers, comedians, or informational speakers." The Student Union is fairly active as well, sponsoring everything "from movie marathons to dances." On the weekends, it's relatively easy to stumble upon "parties ... in fraternities or people's off-campus houses." And while they are often well attended, a handful of students assure us that they "don't usually get too crazy." Additionally, when the weather's nice, undergrads can often be found sneaking off to "hang out at Thousand Hills State Park" and squeezing in a little hiking. Further, while some might describe hometown Kirksville as "boring," others insist there are plenty of low-key options. Students "grab coffee on the Square, go to $1 bowling," and "check out the Farmer's market." Finally, when students want a little more action, they often take a "day trip to Columbia," which tends to offer "better food and shopping."

Student Body
Not surprisingly, a large percentage of Truman undergrads hail from the Midwest and "most are Missouri residents." Therefore, it often feels as though the majority of students here hold "similar small town/suburban midwestern conservative values." Beyond these shared morals, Truman undergrads are also united in their "eager[ness] to learn" and the library is continually "packed ... with students trying to better themselves." Many also describe their peers as "very open" and "friendly." More importantly, Truman undergrads "are always willing to help each other." And while they do recognize that "there is not much ethnic diversity," students rush to assert that "the school overall shows a considerable warm and accepting atmosphere." Rest assured, "racial nor gender discrimination is tolerated on campus." Many also love that the university is "big enough that you can always meet new people, but small enough that you always see someone you know no matter where you go." And they greatly appreciate that their classmates "are always prepared for conversation." As one supremely satisfied student sums up, "Truman has led me to my very best friends." And what more could you hope for in your collegiate experience?

TRUMAN STATE UNIVERSITY

Financial Aid: 660-785-4130 • E-Mail: admissions@truman.edu • Website: http://www.truman.edu

THE PRINCETON REVIEW SAYS

Admissions

Very important factors considered include: rigor of secondary school record, class rank, academic GPA, standardized test scores. *Important factors considered include:* application essay, *Other factors considered include:* recommendation(s), extracurricular activities, talent/ability, character/personal qualities, first generation, alumni/ae relation, geographical residence, state residency, racial/ethnic status, volunteer work, work experience, level of applicant's interest. ACT with or without writing accepted. SAT with or without Essay component accepted. High school diploma is required and GED is accepted. *Academic units required:* 4 English, 3 math, 3 science, 2 science labs, 2 foreign language, 2 social studies, 1 history, 5 academic electives, 1 visual/performing arts, 3 units from above areas or other academic areas. *Academic units recommended:* 4 English, 4 math, 3 science, 2 science labs, 2 foreign language, 2 social studies, 1 history, 5 academic electives, 1 visual/performing arts, 3 units from above areas or other academic areas.

Financial Aid

Students should submit: FAFSA. Priority filing deadline is 2/1. The Princeton Review suggests that all financial aid forms be submitted as soon as possible after October 1. *Need-based scholarships/grants offered:* College/university scholarship or grant aid from institutional funds; Federal Pell; Private scholarships; SEOG; State scholarships/grants. *Loan aid offered:* Direct PLUS loans; Direct Subsidized Stafford Loans; Direct Unsubsidized Stafford Loans. Applicants will be notified of awards on a rolling basis beginning 1/1. Federal Work-Study Program available. Institutional employment available.

The Inside Word

Truman State prides itself on taking a well-rounded approach to the admissions process. The university truly believes that students are more than just the sum of their grades and test scores. Therefore, expect that all application facets, from transcripts to extracurricular participation, will be heavily scrutinized. We do want to note that intended music majors will have to sit for an audition in addition to the regular application. And nursing candidates will need to be admitted to both the university overall as well as the specific nursing program.

THE SCHOOL SAYS "..."

From the Admissions Office

"Truman's talented student body enjoys small classes where undergraduate research and personal interaction with professors are the norm. Our outstanding internship and study abroad opportunities allow students to attend top graduate schools and have great job prospects. Truman is recognized consistently as one of the nation's 'Best Values' in higher education. The university offers a variety of competitive scholarships, and there is no separate scholarship application. Students wishing to be considered for all scholarship programs are strongly encouraged to apply for admission by December 1st.

"Students applying to Truman State University can submit scores from both the ACT and the SAT. The best composite score from either test will be considered in admission and scholarship selection. The writing section is not required. Admission requirements are selective and there is no application fee.

"At Truman, we believe a quality college experience does not stop at the classroom door. It should permeate the entire campus, offering opportunities that entertain, pique students' interest, and invite them to fully embrace this extraordinary journey. It is about making great friends, getting involved in one of over 200 student organizations, exploring the amazing world that surrounds them and creating memories that will last a lifetime. This is a university that transforms lives. Truman's success as one of the nation's premier public liberal arts and sciences institutions can be traced to one guiding principle: an unwavering devotion to the pursuit of knowledge, wherever your journey leads you."

SELECTIVITY

Admissions Rating	89
# of applicants	4,595
% of applicants accepted	63
% of acceptees attending	31

FRESHMAN PROFILE

Range SAT EBRW	580–680
Range SAT Math	570–670
Range ACT Composite	24–31
# submitting SAT scores	92
% submitting SAT scores	10
# submitting ACT scores	823
% submitting ACT scores	92
Average HS GPA	3.8
% graduated top 10% of class	57
% graduated top 25% of class	82
% graduated top 50% of class	97

DEADLINES

Regular	
Priority	12/1
Notification	Rolling, 9/1
Nonfall registration?	Yes

APPLICANTS ALSO LOOK AT AND OFTEN PREFER

Missouri State University; Saint Louis University; University of Missouri

AND SOMETIMES PREFER

Washington University in St. Louis

FINANCIAL FACTS

Financial Aid Rating	89
Annual in-state tuition	$7,796
Annual out-of-state tuition	$14,990
Room and board	$9,012
Required fees	$674
Books and supplies	$1,000
Average frosh need-based scholarship	$8,696
Average UG need-based scholarship	$8,083
% needy frosh rec. need-based scholarship or grant aid	99
% needy UG rec. need-based scholarship or grant aid	95
% needy frosh rec. non-need-based scholarship or grant aid	98
% needy UG rec. non-need-based scholarship or grant aid	82
% needy frosh rec. need-based self-help aid	67
% needy UG rec. need-based self-help aid	76
% frosh rec. any financial aid	99.36
% UG rec. any financial aid	84.71
% UG borrow to pay for school	52
Average cumulative indebtedness	$25,660
% frosh need fully met	43
% ugrads need fully met	35
Average % of frosh need met	86
Average % of ugrad need met	83

TUFTS UNIVERSITY

Bendetson Hall, Medford, MA 02155 • Admissions: 617-627-3170 • Fax: 617-627-3860

STUDENTS SAY "..."

Academics

The campus culture at Tufts University in Massachusetts is "thriving and alive," and as such it really encourages students to merge their academic and social interests and "pursue both in a passionate way." This is a place where, through active discussion and a student body with a zest for life, "passion meets reality." The academic experience here is marked by "small classes with knowledgeable and interesting professors." "I have had the opportunity to explore a huge amount of academic subjects and really challenge myself," says a student. If students actively seek out their "highly accessible and prompt" professors, they will be rewarded with "a better learning experience and with incomparable relationships with brilliant (yet down to earth) professors." "Whenever I ask them a question that they might not know the answer to, they do research on it immediately and return quickly with a detailed response." The academic curriculum is a "perfect mix of liberal arts and university," and the professors are actively concerned with making sure that students leave with a true understanding of the course material, "not just a book list under their arms." These "global minded, ambitious" students rise to the challenge and beyond, as "most every student focuses on life beyond their education" and seeks out a well-rounded life. "It is far easier to succeed here than to fail, as long as you are committed to getting as strong an education as possible," advises a student. "I've literally been offered a research position by asking questions multiple times," says another. The international relations program at this globally-aware school is particularly strong (as are study abroad options), but activism spills over into the entirety of the student body. "Change is easily made here," and "if you have a problem with something, you can easily address it." A lot of effort is put into ensuring that every student transitions well into college and success. A strong alumni network and excellent internship opportunities also "open up a world of opportunities after graduation."

Life

Though the campus itself is gorgeous, "the true beauty of the school is in the unique and quirky nature of its student body." Generally, there are "always a lot of events going on around campus that attract students every weekend" and the variety of clubs and activities available is "amazing." "Almost everything here is run by clubs and student organizations," and the Tufts Dance Collective and Quidditch clubs are some of the most popular and fun options, as is a capella. Public transportation "makes everything accessible," and on the weekends, students often go into Boston or Davis Square and spend the day shopping and "eating non-dining hall food," and at night "there are usually good parties to go to." "There is more to do in this city than anyone can possibly do in four years," says a student.

People here are "always thinking about politics" and all have a lot of spirit for Tufts, and "it's really nice to walk around campus knowing that you're in a place where almost everyone is excited to be there." "This is a great place to share knowledge you have, because everyone wants to hear it and share their own experiences and thoughts," says a student.

Student Body

This is a group of go-getters, so here "everyone has the same passion for excellence" and "is engaged in so many activities on campus." Tufts is "a quirky (yet normal) compilation of a bunch of young adults with not only big dreams for the world, but with dedication and motivation to complete them." "It's like a competition to be the "most interesting man/woman in the world," says a senior. Even better, "being nerdy is cool!" "We here embrace weirdness. If talking to new people in daily life is awkward, we know it and we revel in it," says a sophomore. There is "no discrimination whatsoever," though "it can actually get frustrating how politically correct everyone is." From "dancing and singing to teaching and tutoring to international community service," students here are "stunningly busy and happy to be so."

Financial Aid: 617-627-2000 • E-Mail: undergraduate.admissions@tufts.edu • Website: www.tufts.edu

THE PRINCETON REVIEW SAYS

Admissions

Very important factors considered include: rigor of secondary school record, class rank, academic GPA, application essay, standardized test scores (optional), recommendation(s), character/personal qualities. *Important factors considered include:* extracurricular activities, talent/ability. *Other factors considered include:* interview, first generation, alumni/ae relation, geographical residence, racial/ethnic status, volunteer work, work experience, level of applicant's interest. ACT with or without writing accepted. SAT with or without Essay component accepted. High school diploma is required and GED is accepted. *Academic units required:* 4 English, 4 math, 4 science, 3 foreign language, 4 social studies. *Academic units recommended:* 4 foreign language.

Financial Aid

Students should submit: CSS/Financial Aid PROFILE; FAFSA; Noncustodial PROFILE. The Princeton Review suggests that all financial aid forms be submitted as soon as possible after October 1. *Need-based scholarships/grants offered:* College/university scholarship or grant aid from institutional funds; Federal Pell; Private scholarships; SEOG; State scholarships/grants. *Loan aid offered:* Direct PLUS loans; Direct Subsidized Stafford Loans; Direct Unsubsidized Stafford Loans. Applicants will be notified of awards on or about 4/1. Federal Work-Study Program available. Institutional employment available.

The Inside Word

Admission at Tufts is competitive. You'll need a stellar transcript to get accepted here, rounded out with strong recommendations and extracurriculars that reflect substantive engagement with your school or community. The Common App with Tufts' own writing supplement is required. Note that starting with the Class of 2025, Tufts is instituting a test-optional admissions policy. More information can be found online.

THE SCHOOL SAYS ". . ."

From the Admissions Office

"Tufts is a medium-sized liberal arts university with a focus on faculty relationships, research, and celebrating diverse experiences. Our 5,800 undergraduate students pursue majors in one of three schools: the School of Arts and Sciences, the School of Engineering, or the School of the Museum of Fine Arts (SMFA). As part of a tier one research university, our students delve into world-class research easily and early, exploring fields from soft-bodied robotics to the rebirth of urban democracy, microbial communities to musical theater. Tufts offers the chance to join a close-knit community that supports intellectual risk-taking and a global outlook, all in a beautiful campus setting just five miles from downtown Boston.

"You can't fit Tufts students into a box. They are intellectually powerful, down-to-earth, driven, and civic-minded. At Tufts, they learn how to make a measurable difference and then start making it—even as undergraduates. On campus, the Tisch College of Civic Life leads the way, allowing students to take curricular courses in social change or even enroll in the 1+4 Bridge-Year Service Learning Program or Civic Semester. Whether they are engineers, studio artists, environment advocates, or poets, our students graduate from Tufts ready to enact positive change in the communities they join."

SELECTIVITY

Admissions Rating	98
# of applicants	22,766
% of applicants accepted	15
% of acceptees attending	47
# offered a place on the wait list	1,441
% accepting a place on wait list	36
% admitted from wait list	16

FRESHMAN PROFILE

Range SAT EBRW	680–750
Range SAT Math	710–790
Range ACT Composite	32–34
# submitting SAT scores	906
% submitting SAT scores	56
# submitting ACT scores	706
% submitting ACT scores	44
% graduated top 10% of class	80
% graduated top 25% of class	95
% graduated top 50% of class	99

DEADLINES

Early decision	
Deadline	11/1
Notification	12/15
Other ED Deadline	1/1
Other ED Notification	2/15
Regular	
Deadline	1/1
Notification	4/1
Nonfall registration?	No

APPLICANTS ALSO LOOK AT AND OFTEN PREFER

Brown University; Georgetown University; Harvard College; University of Pennsylvania

AND SOMETIMES PREFER

Dartmouth College; Johns Hopkins University; Northwestern University; The University of Chicago; Washington University in St. Louis; Cornell University

AND RARELY PREFER

Boston College; Boston University; Carnegie Mellon University; New York University

FINANCIAL FACTS

Financial Aid Rating	96
Annual tuition	$57,324
Room and board	$15,086
Required fees	$1,254
Books and supplies	$1,000
Average frosh need-based scholarship	$48,886
Average UG need-based scholarship	$45,887
% needy frosh rec. need-based scholarship or grant aid	92
% needy UG rec. need-based scholarship or grant aid	92
% needy frosh rec. non-need-based scholarship or grant aid	3
% needy UG rec. non-need-based scholarship or grant aid	4
% needy frosh rec. need-based self-help aid	84
% needy UG rec. need-based self-help aid	88
% frosh rec. any financial aid	38
% UG rec. any financial aid	36
% UG borrow to pay for school	33
Average cumulative indebtedness	$28,014
% frosh need fully met	100
% ugrads need fully met	97
Average % of frosh need met	100
Average % of ugrad need met	98

TULANE UNIVERSITY

6823 St. Charles Avenue, New Orleans, LA 70118 • Admissions: 504-865-5731 • Fax: 504-862-8715

STUDENTS SAY " . . ."

Academics

Tulane University, located in the heart of New Orleans, is an institution where "academics are rigorous" and which "encourages exploration, trying new things … and learn[ing] from people who are different from you." Attending students benefit from a myriad of research opportunities—"it's very easy to get into a lab or other research through relationships with professors," says a student—as well as an "extensive alumni network." They're also quick to taut the academic flexibility which lets undergrads "explore [all] possible majors and minors." This is largely due to the fact that all students "are admitted into every school at Tulane" so everyone has access to the business, science and engineering, liberal arts, public health, and architecture programs in equal measure. When it comes to specific disciplines, a few individuals note that "the Public Health Program is incredible." And some students make a point of highlighting the Business School's "high rate of job placement." Overall, undergrads find their professors "extremely knowledgeable," "really passionate," and "incredibly accomplished." Additionally, "most of them have had … careers outside the classroom [that] bring the lessons to life." But perhaps their "greatest strength is their commitment to working with students." As this undergrad illustrates, "Office hours are easy, and all of my professors are willing and even eager to meet when I reach out for help."

Life

Due to the intensity of their coursework, most students spend the majority of their week hitting the books at one of the "great study spots" around campus. But when these dedicated scholars need a break, there are plenty of events and activities to enjoy. For example, students can take advantage of everything from "community service projects [to] art shows." And they have the opportunity of "attending guest lectures with friends" as well as "student theatrical [and] dance performances or … cultural demonstrations" presented by various departments. Many undergrads here are also rather active and health conscious. Therefore, a large number of "students exercise at the athletic center, run around campus or Audubon Park, or play sports in their free time." Nevertheless, "once Thursday rolls around, students are ready to go out." As one undergrad explains, "Bars around campus are [frequented] throughout the late week and into the weekend. [Additionally,] frat parties are typically thrown on the weekends and attendance is high." Not surprisingly, the city of New Orleans itself is also a big draw. A good number of students spend their free time exploring "all of the different music and food festivals that are constantly happening." And they are quick to note that "there are [an] infinite number of restaurants to try, jazz concerts to attend, [and] neighborhoods to explore."

Student Body

Tulane undergrads admit that the majority of their "peers are … white, upper-class individuals" who primarily hail "from the Northeast, Chicago, and the West Coast." Fortunately, these same classmates have proven themselves to be "extremely open minded and some of the most accepting and kind people [you'll] ever [meet]." Of course, it probably doesn't hurt that many are also rather quick to adopt that "Southern hospitality mentality." Moreover, a vast number are "excited to learn" and "eager to get involved on campus." And they tend to be "enthusiastic, spontaneous, intellectual, curious, [and] exciting." But perhaps what really unites these undergrads is their desire to "pick each other up and work together to make the world a better place." Indeed, Tulane students "would [prefer to] pull someone up with them to get ahead rather than stepping on the shoulders of others." As one undergrad adds, "We are not a competitive student body; we collaborate because we want to see each other succeed." That attitude makes it easy to understand the "positive vibe" permeating the campus and the fact that, ultimately, students find that those "at Tulane are overall really happy."

Financial Aid: 504-865-5723 • E-Mail: https://admission.tulane.edu/ • Website: www.tulane.edu

THE PRINCETON REVIEW SAYS
Admissions

Very important factors considered include: rigor of secondary school record, class rank, academic GPA, standardized test scores. *Important factors considered include:* application essay, recommendation(s), character/personal qualities. *Other factors considered include:* interview, extracurricular activities, talent/ability, first generation, alumni/ae relation, volunteer work, work experience, level of applicant's interest. ACT with or without writing accepted. SAT with or without Essay component accepted. High school diploma is required and GED is accepted. *Academic units recommended:* 4 English, 3 math, 3 science, 3 science labs, 3 foreign language, 3 social studies.

Financial Aid

Students should submit: Business/Farm Supplement; CSS/Financial Aid PROFILE; FAFSA; Noncustodial PROFILE. Priority filing deadline is 2/15. The Princeton Review suggests that all financial aid forms be submitted as soon as possible after October 1. *Need-based scholarships/grants offered:* College/university scholarship or grant aid from institutional funds; Federal Pell; Private scholarships; SEOG; State scholarships/grants. *Loan aid offered:* Direct PLUS loans; Direct Subsidized Stafford Loans; Direct Unsubsidized Stafford Loans. Applicants will be notified of awards on a rolling basis beginning 12/15. Federal Work-Study Program available. Institutional employment available.

The Inside Word

When it comes to evaluating applicants, Tulane takes a fairly straight-forward approach. Expect admissions officers to closely consider your high school transcript and standardized test scores. Moreover, be aware that the most successful candidates will have taken a rigorous course-load; load up on those honors and AP classes if possible! You should also know that extracurricular activities will be of secondary importance. Additionally, alumni interviews are optional. It will not affect your candidacy if you decide against it. Finally, if you're a budding architecture student, it's highly recommended that you submit a portfolio.

THE SCHOOL SAYS "..."
From the Admissions Office

"With more than 6,600 full-time undergraduate students in five schools, Tulane University offers the personal attention and teaching excellence traditionally associated with small colleges together with the facilities and interdisciplinary resources found only at major research universities. As the only major research university in America with a public service requirement for graduation, Tulane students are wholly committed to giving back to their communities. The opportunities for students to be involved in the rebirth of New Orleans offer an experience unavailable at any other place, at any other time.

"Tulane is committed to undergraduate education. Senior faculty members teach most introductory and lower-level courses, and most classes have twenty-five or fewer students. The close student-teacher relationship pays off. Tulane graduates are among the most likely to be selected for several prestigious fellowships that support graduate study abroad. Founded in 1834 and reorganized as Tulane University in 1884, Tulane is one of the major private research universities in the South.

"As previously mentioned, Tulane students highly value balance, and most of all they're happy with their choice and love the school."

SELECTIVITY

Admissions Rating	97
# of applicants	42,185
% of applicants accepted	13
% of acceptees attending	34
# offered a place on the wait list	5,412
% accepting a place on wait list	25
# of early decision applicants	2,163
% accepted early decision	33

FRESHMAN PROFILE

Range SAT EBRW	660–750
Range SAT Math	700–770
Range SAT Composite	1370–1480
Range ACT Composite	31–33
# submitting SAT scores	480
% submitting SAT scores	26
# submitting ACT scores	1,320
% submitting ACT scores	72
Average HS GPA	3.6
% graduated top 10% of class	64
% graduated top 25% of class	88
% graduated top 50% of class	97

DEADLINES

Early decision	
Deadline	11/1
Notification	12/15
Other ED Deadline	1/6
Other ED Notification	1/31
Early action	
Deadline	11/15
Notification	1/15
Regular	
Priority	11/1
Deadline	11/15
Notification	4/1
Nonfall registration?	Yes

APPLICANTS ALSO LOOK AT AND SOMETIMES PREFER

Boston University; Northeastern University; University of Miami; University of Michigan--Ann Arbor; University of Southern California; Vanderbilt University; Emory University; Washington University in St. Louis; University of Virginia

FINANCIAL FACTS

Financial Aid Rating	92
Annual tuition	$52,760
Room and board	$16,464
Required fees	$4,040
Books and supplies	$1,200
Average frosh need-based scholarship	$37,284
Average UG need-based scholarship	$37,297
% needy frosh rec. need-based scholarship or grant aid	98
% needy UG rec. need-based scholarship or grant aid	97
% needy frosh rec. non-need-based scholarship or grant aid	32
% needy UG rec. non-need-based scholarship or grant aid	26
% needy frosh rec. need-based self-help aid	71
% needy UG rec. need-based self-help aid	72
% frosh rec. any financial aid	94
% UG rec. any financial aid	93
% UG borrow to pay for school	34
Average cumulative indebtedness	$31,306
% frosh need fully met	51
% ugrads need fully met	48
Average % of frosh need met	94
Average % of ugrad need met	93

TUSKEGEE UNIVERSITY

Margaret Murray Washington Hall, Tuskegee, AL 36088 • Admissions: 334-727-8500 • Fax: 334-727-5750

CAMPUS LIFE
Quality of Life Rating	78
Fire Safety Rating	97
Green Rating	60*
Type of school	Private
Environment	Rural

STUDENTS
Total undergrad enrollment	2,480
% male/female	39/61
% from out of state	70
% frosh from public high school	88
% frosh live on campus	98
% ugrads live on campus	55
# of fraternities (% ugrad men join)	5 (6)
# of sororities (% ugrad women join)	6 (5)
% African American	78
% Asian	<1
% Caucasian	<1
% Hispanic	<1
% Native American	<1
% Pacific Islander	0
% Two or more races	0
% Race and/or ethnicity unknown	21
% international	<1
# of countries represented	19

SURVEY SAYS . . .
Lots of liberal students
Students are very religious
Very little drug use
Frats and sororities are popular

ACADEMICS
Academic Rating	75
% students returning for sophomore year	73
Calendar	Semester
Student/faculty ratio	14:1
Profs interesting rating	81
Profs accessible rating	88
Most classes have 10–19 students.	

MOST POPULAR MAJORS
Electrical and Electronics Engineering

STUDENTS SAY ". . ."

Academics

For the past 132 years, Tuskegee University has strived to continue the legacy of higher learning created by Booker T. Washington and upheld by its other notable presidents and benefactors. The "rich history" of the school has always been about "achieving the…highest level of performance" in all areas of service, leadership, and academics, and everyone in the community works to ensure that "the Tuskegee Experience is like none other." The veterinary and engineering schools are standouts here, but the school can transform any individual into a leader. "Tuskegee, figuratively speaking, is often given coal, and it *always* produces diamonds," says one student. Academics are "a top priority" for Tuskegee, and the classes and structure are designed to "effectively nurture students' academic, social, and professional potentials and produce great leaders in society." "School is about gaining independence and responsibility so that you will be able to grow and compete in the real world." Small classes and personal interaction with professors help further this process along, and the school aims for "excellence within every aspect of education offered at the institution." "My professors don't teach because it's their job, they do it because they care and want you to learn and succeed. It's very obvious," says one student. Though the alumni network is positively rock solid, and fundraising isn't a problem, some students question the allocation of funds. Many agree that "the development of new facilities/buildings around the campus" is a sore spot, and though the administration is in the process of updating some, "there is a lot of work to be done," particularly in the student housing arena.

Life

The heritage of Tuskegee is felt in every step; "We literally walk on historic grounds," says a student of going to school on the only college or university campus in the nation to be designated a National Historic Site by Congress. The traditional festivities the school usually hosts are "quite enjoyable," and the school is in a "very quaint" town, which "allows for constant interaction among students on campus to occur." When there is nothing to do in Tuskegee, students usually go to Auburn, Montgomery, or even Atlanta. TU is for "academically inclined individuals," but when the books do shut, most people "go to the local clubs (The Soul Inn or Club Extreme)," or hang out at houses off campus. "Home football and basketball games are usually really fun" as well. "Even though people are serious about their work and classes, we all know how to have fun," says one student. "We're a school of weekend warriors." "It can be raining cats and dogs…and you will still see people going to class, or if it's the weekend you will see students going to a party."

Student Body

At this go-getter university, the typical student here is "someone who is driven to becoming successful in the future through studious methods." Though this HBCU is naturally predominantly black, there is much diversity in that "people from all across the country come to school in this small city in Alabama." Most students here are "very outspoken and easy to work with" and "open to meeting and interacting with new people"; with students from all over the world, "the diverse environment helps keep the campus from getting too dull."

TUSKEGEE UNIVERSITY

Financial Aid: 334-727-8088 • E-Mail: admissions@mytu.tuskegee.edu • Website: www.tuskegee.edu

THE PRINCETON REVIEW SAYS

Admissions

Very important factors considered include: rigor of secondary school record, class rank, academic GPA, standardized test scores, recommendation(s), talent/ability. *Important factors considered include:* character/personal qualities, alumni/ae relation. *Other factors considered include:* application essay, interview, extracurricular activities, first generation, geographical residence, state residency, volunteer work, work experience. ACT with or without writing accepted. High school diploma is required and GED is accepted. *Academic units required:* 4 English, 3 math, 2 science, 3 social studies, 4 academic electives.

Financial Aid

Students should submit: CSS/Financial Aid PROFILE; FAFSA; Institution's own financial aid form. Priority filing deadline is 3/31. The Princeton Review suggests that all financial aid forms be submitted as soon as possible after October 1. *Need-based scholarships/grants offered:* College/university scholarship or grant aid from institutional funds; Federal Nursing Scholarships; Federal Pell; Private scholarships; SEOG; State scholarships/grants; United Negro College Fund. *Loan aid offered:* Direct PLUS loans; Direct Subsidized Stafford Loans; Direct Unsubsidized Stafford Loans. Federal Work-Study Program available. Institutional employment available.

The Inside Word

Tuskegee presents its students with a myriad of opportunities for discovery and research. Therefore, Tuskegee seeks applicants who have proven themselves successful in the classroom. Admissions counselors consider each application holistically and individually. What they really like to see, though, is a GPA of at least 3.0 and a composite ACT score of 21 or better. Note also that requirements for the nursing and engineering programs are more stringent. For example, you'll probably need four years of high school math if you want to major in engineering here. Prospective students interested in either field should investigate the specific criteria.

THE SCHOOL SAYS "..."

From the Admissions Office

"Tuskegee University, located in south central Alabama, was founded in 1881 under the dynamic and creative leadership of Booker T. Washington. As a state-related, independent institution, Tuskegee offers undergraduate and graduate degrees through five colleges and two schools: the College of Agriculture, Environment and Nutrition Sciences; the Brimmer College of Business and Information Sciences; the College of Engineering; the College of Veterinary Medicine, Nursing and Allied Health; the Taylor School of Architecture and Construction Science; and the School of Education. Substantial research and service programs make Tuskegee University an effective comprehensive institution geared toward preparing tomorrow's leaders today.

"First-year applicants must take the SAT or ACT; the SAT is preferred. International applicants must complete the TOEFL. Nursing applicants must complete the National Nursing exam."

SELECTIVITY

Admissions Rating	84
# of applicants	9,582
% of applicants accepted	36
% of acceptees attending	17

FRESHMAN PROFILE

Range SAT EBRW	440–510
Range SAT Math	420–520
Range ACT Composite	18–23
# submitting SAT scores	262
% submitting SAT scores	44
# submitting ACT scores	434
% submitting ACT scores	73
Average HS GPA	3.2
% graduated top 10% of class	20
% graduated top 25% of class	60
% graduated top 50% of class	100

DEADLINES

Early action	
Deadline	8/31
Notification	10/1
Regular	
Priority	3/31
Deadline	7/15
Notification	3/15
Nonfall registration?	Yes

FINANCIAL FACTS

Financial Aid Rating	81
Annual tuition	$18,100
Room and board	$8,510
Required fees	$3,525
Books and supplies	$1,282
Average frosh need-based scholarship	$1,500
Average UG need-based scholarship	$1,500
% needy frosh rec. need-based scholarship or grant aid	100
% needy UG rec. need-based scholarship or grant aid	100
% needy frosh rec. non-need-based scholarship or grant aid	17
% needy UG rec. non-need-based scholarship or grant aid	22
% needy frosh rec. need-based self-help aid	100
% needy UG rec. need-based self-help aid	68
% frosh rec. any financial aid	90
% UG rec. any financial aid	92
% UG borrow to pay for school	49
Average cumulative indebtedness	$18,100
% frosh need fully met	0
% ugrads need fully met	0
Average % of frosh need met	70
Average % of ugrad need met	70

UNION COLLEGE (NY)

Grant Hall, Schenectady, NY 12308 • Admissions: 518-388-6112 • Fax: 518-388-6986

STUDENTS SAY "..."

Academics

Founded in 1795, Union College in upstate New York is a small, independent liberal arts college that provides a wide "breadth of education" that allows students to learn across the curriculum and graduate with a respected degree and a true liberal arts education. The "great historical roots" are apparent all around the "beautiful campus full of school-spirited students," but the school keeps a firm eye on the future as well, and "encourages students to develop and be prepared for graduation."

The professors are "interested in the lives of their students" and "work to make sure the student gets the academic support needed to succeed," and best of all, "you will never EVER have a teaching assistant instead of a professor at Union." Professors have an open door policy to always allow students right on in—"students are their main priority." Research opportunities are plentiful—"any professor with a lab is always looking for new recruits"—and a strong engineering department ensures that the sciences get a fair shake at a traditionally liberal arts school. The school also strives "to create interesting interdisciplinary classes that combine science and humanities in innovative ways."

Union is small, so "the sense of community is very important to the overall experience." The administration "wants you to enjoy your four years of college not just by studying but get to know other people and do things you never did before." A senior neuroscience major agrees: "Union is all about finding the best mix of the challenging courses and millions of activities happening each night." The trimester schedule is "fantastic," and the school "melds academic, social, and cultural life together seamlessly." "Union is also a prestigious institution that is small enough to allow every student a presence on campus," says one.

Life

The unique Minerva House system blends academic, social, and residential interests. All students and faculty are assigned to one of the seven houses, which host hundreds of events each year (some professors even teach preceptorials there). There are also "Theme Houses," which are on-campus housing where people who have similar interests can live, such as the Ozone House for environmentally-oriented people.

Between Greek and Minerva life, there is "a vibrant social life" for all students, though quite a few admit that the emphasis on the "huge" Greek life "could certainly be reduced." "Most of the campus attends parties on weekends," which is "a great way to relieve the stress caused by being at such an academically rigorous school and also meet new people." In class, however, "we're all nerds at heart, and we can talk books and numbers all day long." Everyone also goes to free campus movies and other events like "concerts, magicians, comedians, roller skating, and others."

The Capital Region is "all around us, so if you're bored you're just not trying hard enough," says a student. There is a bounty of events and organizations, so "one has to try to NOT be involved." "I never feel like the campus runs out of things for me to do," says a senior. Dating is "thin" at Union: "it is not a couples' school;" however, it IS a hockey school.

Student Body

Most come to Union from "some part of the northeast," are "from middle/upper-middle class families," and are "very active, career-oriented, [and] serious about academics." One student tells us, "I'm not going to lie, it's a pretty white campus." "Everyone fits in because everyone seems to love Union." These "intellectuals" tend to dress "very preppy" ("wearing Patagonia jackets, Lilly Pulitzer handbags, and Ugg boots is basically the uniform") and are "a great group of people"; "there don't seem to be any barriers between them."

UNION COLLEGE (NY)

Financial Aid: 518-388-6123 • E-Mail: admissions@union.edu • Website: www.union.edu

THE PRINCETON REVIEW SAYS

Admissions

Very important factors considered include: rigor of secondary school record, class rank, academic GPA. *Important factors considered include:* application essay, standardized test scores, recommendation(s), extracurricular activities, talent/ability, character/personal qualities. *Other factors considered include:* interview, first generation, alumni/ae relation, geographical residence, state residency, racial/ethnic status, level of applicant's interest. ACT with or without writing accepted. SAT with or without Essay component accepted. High school diploma is required and GED is not accepted. *Academic units required:* 4 English, 3 math, 2 science, 2 science labs, 2 foreign language, 1 social studies, 1 history. *Academic units recommended:* 4 English, 4 math, 4 science, 4 science labs, 4 foreign language, 2 social studies, 2 history.

Financial Aid

Students should submit: CSS/Financial Aid PROFILE; FAFSA; Noncustodial PROFILE; State aid form. Priority filing deadline is 1/15. The Princeton Review suggests that all financial aid forms be submitted as soon as possible after October 1. *Need-based scholarships/grants offered:* College/university scholarship or grant aid from institutional funds; Federal Pell; Private scholarships; SEOG; State scholarships/grants. *Loan aid offered:* Direct PLUS loans; Direct Subsidized Stafford Loans; Direct Unsubsidized Stafford Loans. Applicants will be notified of awards on or about 3/25. Federal Work-Study Program available. Institutional employment available.

The Inside Word

Union College is an SAT-optional college. Students may simply indicate on their application if they would like the admissions committee to consider their test scores or not. However, applicants to the Leadership in Medicine Program (an eight-year MD/MBA program with Albany Medical College and Clarkson University Capital Region Campus) and to the Law and Public Policy program (a combined BA and JD with Albany Law School) must submit test scores for consideration. For students who know that Union is their first choice, the school offers two early decision deadlines.

THE SCHOOL SAYS "..."

From the Admissions Office

"The Union academic program is characterized by breadth and flexibility across a range of disciplines and interdisciplinary programs in the liberal arts, sciences, and engineering. With nearly 1,000 courses to choose from, Union students may major in a single field, combine work in two or more departments or create their own organizing-theme major. Opportunities for undergraduate research are robust and give students a chance to work closely with professors year-round, take part in professional-level conferences and use sophisticated scientific equipment. More than half of Union's students take advantage of the college's extensive international study program, and the College places students in internships with more than 500 companies and organizations. A rich array of service learning programs and strong athletic, cultural, and social activities also enhance the overall Union experience. Union's seven student-run Minerva Houses are lively hubs for intellectual and social activities. They bring together students, faculty and staff for hundreds of events, from dinners with invited speakers, lectures, and live bands, to trips to local attractions.

"The Union community welcomes talented and diverse students, and we work closely with each one to help identify and cultivate their passions. Admission to the college is based on excellent academic credentials as reflected in the high school transcript, quality of courses selected, teacher and counselor recommendations, and personal essays. Personal interviews are strongly recommended. All candidates who apply to Union receive a thorough and thoughtful review of their application. Submission of SAT and ACT scores is optional except for the law and medicine programs."

SELECTIVITY

Admissions Rating	93
# of applicants	6,086
% of applicants accepted	43
% of acceptees attending	21
# offered a place on the wait list	753
% accepting a place on wait list	44
% admitted from wait list	32
# of early decision applicants	357
% accepted early decision	61%

FRESHMAN PROFILE

Range SAT EBRW	600–680
Range SAT Math	620–740
Range ACT Composite	27–32
# submitting SAT scores	322
% submitting SAT scores	59
# submitting ACT scores	126
% submitting ACT scores	23
Average HS GPA	3.5
% graduated top 10% of class	63
% graduated top 25% of class	86
% graduated top 50% of class	98

DEADLINES

Early decision	
Deadline	11/15
Notification	12/15
Other ED Deadline	1/15
Other ED Notification	2/8
Early action	
Deadline	11/1
Notification	12/31
Regular	
Deadline	1/15
Notification	4/1
Nonfall registration?	Yes

APPLICANTS ALSO LOOK AT AND OFTEN PREFER

Colgate University; Cornell University; Tufts University

AND SOMETIMES PREFER

Hamilton College; Lafayette College; University of Rochester

AND RARELY PREFER

University of Vermont; Boston University

FINANCIAL FACTS

Financial Aid Rating	97
Annual tuition	$59,031
Room and board	$14,583
Required fees	$471
Books and supplies	$1,500
Average frosh need-based scholarship	$40,535
Average UG need-based scholarship	$39,940
% needy frosh rec. need-based scholarship or grant aid	100
% needy UG rec. need-based scholarship or grant aid	100
% needy frosh rec. non-need-based scholarship or grant aid	4
% needy UG rec. non-need-based scholarship or grant aid	6
% needy frosh rec. need-based self-help aid	97
% needy UG rec. need-based self-help aid	97
% frosh rec. any financial aid	82
% UG rec. any financial aid	80
% UG borrow to pay for school	53
Average cumulative indebtedness	$36,921
% frosh need fully met	100
% ugrads need fully met	100
Average % of frosh need met	100
Average % of ugrad need met	100

UNITED STATES AIR FORCE ACADEMY

HQ USAFA/RRS, USAF Academy, CO 80840-5025 • Admissions: 719-333-2520 • Fax: 719-333-3012

STUDENTS SAY ". . ."

Academics

Students who seek out a United States Air Force Academy education note their satisfaction in how "values of integrity, service, and excellence . . . are actually the norm." This esteemed institution not only promotes a "culture of excellence" that molds students into "leaders of character," but also offers "prestige in both the military and private sector." It does so, incidentally, while offering free tuition and a "guaranteed job" following graduation. Of course, if you decide to attend, be prepared to "be challenged physically and mentally" and held "to a higher standard" than at your average college. In return, however, students suggest you'll also get "incredible opportunities" not found elsewhere. These opportunities can range from taking "trips around the world" or "operating a real DoD satellite" to "jumping out of planes [and] getting a secret clearance." Additionally, undergrads benefit from "extremely small" class sizes. As one cadet shares, "the biggest class I've had in four years was 24 students." The faculty itself is a nice "mix of military and civilian" instructors who "tend to make class interesting" and often excel at "bring[ing] their life experiences into the classroom." The majority also do their utmost to ensure that they are "accessible for extra instruction, exam review, etc." Many students also feel that their professors "really seem to care about your performance and work with you on a one-on-one basis." As one cadet frames it, "Their only focus is supporting us."

Life

As you might have suspected, life at the Air Force Academy is rather regimented and cadets "don't have much free time." Students "go to class from 0730 to 1530 [and] freshmen have physical training multiple times a week after[wards]." Additionally, everyone "participate[s] in an athletic activity [whether] it be NCAA athletics, club sports, or intramurals." And on the weekends it's quite common to "have the Cadet Wing marching" or to have to perform "other military duties." Students also make a point of mentioning that "once every semester we have mandatory fitness tests, and throughout the semester [there are] random mandatory military briefs in the evenings." Even with a schedule packed with academic obligations and military training, one individual notes that there are "various clubs and activities for different interests, as well as religious services, all [of] which take [place] intermittently throughout the week." And if they do have a moment to relax, cadets will typically kick back with "Netflix or video games." Of course, when students really want to have fun, they generally leave "USAFA and [go] out into CO Springs or Denver" or they will "take advantage of outdoor areas for hiking, fishing, etc."

Student Body

Air Force Academy cadets seem to agree that the school attracts a number of "type A personalities" and "hard working" individuals who are "much more motivated than many other normal college students." They are also united in their deep desire "to serve [the] country" and are often "team oriented" as well. Further, cadets pride themselves on being "more fit than the general population," though cadets at USAFA "come from all over the nation, territories included, and from allied partner nations." While there may be a "healthy diversity of thought" at the academy, students do acknowledge a disparity in gender. A few individuals also grumble that some of their peers can be "very cynical." Thankfully, students view themselves as "one brotherhood and sisterhood looking out for each other." One cadet delves deeper adding, "We hold each other to an honor code the best we can and feel very close as a student body because we all live on campus and spend a majority of our time together." All in all, "there is a definite culture of helping out fellow cadets and of striving to bring peers up that helps people to perform at their best."

UNITED STATES AIR FORCE ACADEMY

E-Mail: rr_admissions@usafa.edu • Website: www.academyadmissions.com/about-the-academy

THE PRINCETON REVIEW SAYS

Admissions

Very important factors considered include: rigor of secondary school record, class rank, academic GPA, application essay, standardized test scores, recommendation(s), interview, extracurricular activities, character/personal qualities, level of applicant's interest. *Important factors considered include:* talent/ability, geographical residence, volunteer work. *Other factors considered include:* first generation, alumni/ae relation, racial/ethnic status. ACT with Writing recommended. SAT with Essay component recommended. High school diploma is required and GED is accepted. *Academic units required:* 4 English, 4 math, 4 science, 3 social studies, 1 history. *Academic units recommended:* 4 English, 4 math, 4 science, 2 science labs, 2 foreign language, 4 social studies, 3 history, 1 computer science.

Financial Aid

The Princeton Review suggests that all financial aid forms be submitted as soon as possible after October 1.

The Inside Word

Earning admission to the United States Air Force Academy is no easy feat. The process is extraordinarily competitive, and you'll need a very high GPA and class rank to be in contention. Beyond strong academics, your teacher evaluations and letters of recommendation will be extremely important. The school uses them to assess your moral character and leadership capabilities. Additionally, cadet life is physically demanding, and you'll have to meet specific fitness requirements. Finally, you must be a U.S. citizen in order to apply.

THE SCHOOL SAYS "..."

From the Admissions Office

"The United States Air Force Academy offers one of the most prestigious and respected undergraduate programs available. With twenty-seven majors and four minors offered at the Academy, there are programs of study for every interest. The academic challenges and expectations are high—but so are the rewards. You will emerge from the Academy with a well-rounded knowledge in many fields, an intimate knowledge in your major area of study, and the ability to serve our nation as a Second Lieutenant in the world's greatest air, space, and cyberspace force.

"At the United States Air Force Academy, every cadet is an athlete. Our extensive athletic program includes twenty-nine men's and women's NCAA Division I intercollegiate teams, intramural sports, physical education courses, and physical fitness tests tailored to prepare you for Air Force leadership by building confidence, physical courage, and the ability to perform under pressure.

"The Academy experience requires cadets to become active participants in leadership roles and opportunities that give a sense of honor and duty. The Air Force Academy's mission is to educate, train, and inspire men and women to become officers of character motivated to lead the United States Air Force in service to our nation. If you choose to accept the challenges, you will be rewarded with unique experiences and opportunities incomparable to any other college experience and the honor of serving your country in the United States Air Force."

SELECTIVITY

Admissions Rating	99
# of applicants	10,354
% of applicants accepted	11
% of acceptees attending	98

FRESHMAN PROFILE

Range SAT EBRW	610–700
Range SAT Math	620–740
Range ACT Composite	28–33
# submitting SAT scores	562
% submitting SAT scores	50
# submitting ACT scores	571
% submitting ACT scores	50
Average HS GPA	3.8
% graduated top 10% of class	54
% graduated top 25% of class	82
% graduated top 50% of class	97

DEADLINES

Early action	
Deadline	11/1
Notification	1/15
Regular	
Deadline	12/31
Notification	Rolling, 10/15
Nonfall registration?	No

FINANCIAL FACTS

Financial Aid Rating	60*
Annual tuition	$0

UNITED STATES COAST GUARD ACADEMY

31 Mohegan Avenue, New London, CT 06320-8103 • Admissions: 860-444-8500 • Fax: 860-701-6700

CAMPUS LIFE
Quality of Life Rating	85
Fire Safety Rating	91
Green Rating	61
Type of school	Public
Environment	City

STUDENTS
Total undergrad enrollment	898
% male/female	65/35
% from out of state	95
% frosh from public high school	76
% frosh live on campus	100
% ugrads live on campus	100
# of fraternities	0
# of sororities	0
% African American	4
% Asian	7
% Caucasian	67
% Hispanic	10
% Native American	<1
% Pacific Islander	<1
% Two or more races	8
% Race and/or ethnicity unknown	2
% international	2
# of countries represented	12

SURVEY SAYS . . .
Students always studying
School is well run
Great financial aid
No one cheats
Diverse student types interact on campus
Very little drug use
Everyone loves the Bears
Intramural sports are popular
Alumni active on campus

ACADEMICS
Academic Rating	87
% students returning for sophomore year	90
Calendar	Semester
Student/faculty ratio	8:1
Profs interesting rating	87
Profs accessible rating	98

Most classes have 10–19 students.
Most lab/discussion sessions have
10–19 students.

MOST POPULAR MAJORS
Business Administration and Management,
General; Oceanography, Chemical and Physical;
Political Science and Government, General

STUDENTS SAY ". . ."

Academics

Students at the United States Coast Guard Academy recommend their school as "highly demanding, immensely rewarding, professionally oriented, and the best choice to make the best friends you are ever going to have." Many appreciate the "regimented environment," which, according to one management major, "Gives me a standard to live up to and hold myself to, even when I am away from here." Cadets are "pushed to [the] limits" "academically, emotionally, and physically," and they wouldn't have it any other way. Importantly, "the academy fosters camaraderie amongst the Corps of Cadets that can't be found anywhere else. With a student body numbering a little less than 1,000, the Coast Guard Academy is truly unique in its ability to provide an environment where classmates become shipmates, friends, and eventually family." Though there are a number of excellent programs, cadets call the most attention to the strong engineering department. The academics are "challenging but rewarding." Professors challenge cadets "to reach farther, expand their horizons, and to develop outside the classroom as much as inside of it." An electrical engineering major expounds, "The most surprising and excellent trait that all teachers have is that they are always willing to help outside of the class rooms. Always." Some students contend "the best part about my school is the summer training programs." Students have traveled "across the Atlantic Ocean" stopping "in London, Iceland, and Nova Scotia." Others have been to "Bermuda, St. Pierre France, Guantanamo Bay, and St. Petersburg Florida since coming to the Academy, which is absolutely amazing."

Life

"Life at USCGA is unique. Only way to put it," says one junior. Day-to-day life at the Coast Guard Academy is "orderly and predictable." During the week, it's difficult for people to do anything "outside of their military, athletic, and academic obligations." As one honest marine and environmental science major reveals, "Every moment of every day is planned out." Required sports credits "keep people active and involved either intercollegiate or intramurals." Of course, life at the Academy isn't 100 percent work and stress. Free time is at a premium on weekdays but "weekends are the time to explore New England, New York City, and the downtown New London area." A senior shares, cadets "go to the beach, head up to Vermont for some hiking or skiing ... there is a lot to do if you look for it." While "students aren't allowed off campus during the week," unless participating in an academy sanctioned activity, "most try and get away for the weekend." Another senior elaborates, "Underage students tend to go to the movies or the local mall. Of-age students usually spend their time off drinking at the bars downtown." Life at USCGA can be "very challenging and demanding at times, but the goal of becoming an officer makes it worth it." A "guaranteed job upon graduation" is pretty persuasive as well.

Student Body

While in past, USGCA has been described as homogeneous; "the academy has been stressing diversity in its admissions and has had a good deal of success." Luckily, a civil engineering major assures us, "Those students of different backgrounds easily fit in with everyone else." In fact, one cadet goes so far to say "sometimes, I don't think that cadets recognize diversity because we all wear the same uniforms, take the same classes, and are going through the same experiences." Not surprisingly, the academy seems to attract "highly motivated [people] with a strong desire to serve in the Coast Guard." Certainly, another hallmark of Coast Guard cadets is that they're "hard working, smart, motivated, and in great shape." A naval architecture and marine engineering major adds, "Type-A personalities are most common among the Corps." A senior describes student as "very close with each other and for the most part, everyone has a group of friends that they fit in quite well with." This sophomore cheekily sums up his peers, "A typical student here is just like a typical student anywhere else but works harder, follows stricter rules, is in better shape, and is owned by the federal government."

UNITED STATES COAST GUARD ACADEMY

E-Mail: USCGA.Admissions@uscga.edu • Website: www.uscga.edu

THE PRINCETON REVIEW SAYS

Admissions

Very important factors considered include: rigor of secondary school record, class rank, academic GPA, standardized test scores, extracurricular activities, character/personal qualities. *Important factors considered include:* application essay, recommendation(s), talent/ability. *Other factors considered include:* interview, first generation, alumni/ae relation, geographical residence, state residency, religious affiliation/commitment, racial/ethnic status, volunteer work, work experience, level of applicant's interest. ACT with Writing required. High school diploma is required and GED is accepted. *Academic units required:* 4 English, 4 math, 3 science, 3 science labs. *Academic units recommended:* 4 English, 4 math, 4 science, 3 science labs.

Financial Aid

The Princeton Review suggests that all financial aid forms be submitted as soon as possible after October 1.

The Inside Word

Gaining acceptance into the Coast Guard Academy is a highly competitive process. The admissions committee is looking not only for outstanding academic achievement but also for applicants who demonstrate leadership ability and strong moral character. In addition, unlike other colleges, you'll also need a physical fitness examination and evaluation.

THE SCHOOL SAYS "..."

From the Admissions Office

"Established in 1876, the Coast Guard Academy educates, trains, and inspires Cadets to serve their country and humanity. Leadership and character development are emphasized in academic life, athletic pursuits, and military training. Commitment to helping those in need is a personal quality shared by every student selected to attend the Coast Guard Academy. High levels of personal accountability are expected of Cadets and graduates.

"Fourth Class (freshmen) arrive in June to begin a strenuous seven week training program (Swab Summer) that prepares them to join the Corps of Cadets in August. Swab Summer culminates with a week at sea aboard America's only active tall ship, the EAGLE.

"The Corps of Cadets is comprised of talented Cadets from all fifty states and about twenty other nations. The Academy is diverse: Women and students of color, as groups, each comprise over 30 percent of the student body. Most Cadets are athletes—over 60 percent play on at least one NCAA Division III team. The opportunity to play is nearly unmatched in college athletics.

"The Academy's value proposition is also tough to beat. This is the only small, highly selective four year college in the U.S. that is free of charge to attend. This is possible because Academy grads go straight to a position of responsibility as a commissioned officer in the Coast Guard. All are obligated to serve for five years, and most make it a career. Aside from the satisfaction of saving lives and protecting others, the opportunity to fly is exceptional. And, about 85 percent of officers also earn a graduate degree at Coast Guard expense.

"If you are smart, adventuresome, physically fit, and want to achieve a higher purpose in your life, the U.S. Coast Guard Academy may be for you!"

SELECTIVITY

Admissions Rating	97
# of applicants	2,214
% of applicants accepted	18
% of acceptees attending	75
# offered a place on the wait list	148
% accepting a place on wait list	100
% admitted from wait list	24
# of early decision applicants	648
% accepted early decision	24%

FRESHMAN PROFILE

Range SAT EBRW	570–660
Range SAT Math	610–690
Range ACT Composite	26–31
# submitting SAT scores	220
% submitting SAT scores	76
# submitting ACT scores	183
% submitting ACT scores	63
Average HS GPA	3.8
% graduated top 10% of class	45
% graduated top 25% of class	79
% graduated top 50% of class	96

DEADLINES

Early action	
Deadline	11/15
Notification	2/1
Regular	
Priority	11/15
Deadline	2/1
Notification	4/15
Nonfall registration?	No

FINANCIAL FACTS

Financial Aid Rating	60*
Annual tuition	$0

UNITED STATES MERCHANT MARINE ACADEMY

Office of Admissions, Kings Point, NY 11024-1699 • Admissions: 516-726-5643 • Fax: 516-773-5390

CAMPUS LIFE

Quality of Life Rating	68
Fire Safety Rating	98
Green Rating	63
Type of school	Public
Environment	Town

STUDENTS

Total undergrad enrollment	952
% male/female	83/17
% from out of state	87
% frosh from public high school	75
% frosh live on campus	100
% ugrads live on campus	100
# of fraternities	0
# of sororities	0
% African American	3
% Asian	8
% Caucasian	75
% Hispanic	10
% Native American	<1
% Pacific Islander	<1
% Two or more races	0
% Race and/or ethnicity unknown	3
% international	1
# of countries represented	4

SURVEY SAYS . . .

Lots of conservative students
Great financial aid
Very little drug use
Alumni active on campus

ACADEMICS

Academic Rating	65
% students returning for sophomore year	89
% students graduating within 4 years	81
Calendar	Trimester
Student/faculty ratio	8:1
Profs interesting rating	63
Profs accessible rating	77

Most classes have 20–29 students.

MOST POPULAR MAJORS

Naval Architecture and Marine Engineering;
Engineering, General; Transportation and Materials
Moving, Other

STUDENTS SAY ". . ."

Academics

Tucked away on Long Island, the United States Merchant Marine Academy offers students the chance to pursue a prestigious though rigorous and regimented education. Further, it allows undergrads to join "a group of elite students who work hard and [are] honest and patriotic." Students here caution that the academics are "extremely difficult," especially given the "fast-paced classroom environment." Additionally, when asked about their professors, students dole out mixed reviews. Though most assert that their teachers are "very intelligent," some bemoan a "lack of enthusiasm." While some professors are described as "fair, approachable, and extremely helpful," other professors come across as "heartless and condescending." Regardless of which classes you enroll in, the Merchant Marine Academy is "a school that requires plenty of effort on behalf of the student." As one midshipman proudly sums up, "The opportunities afforded by this Academy are unparalleled by any other college I have come across. Despite the immense sacrifices and hardships of this school, it is completely worth it for the right person."

Life

Undergrads at the Merchant Marine Academy don't mince words about life at their school. Indeed, the majority seem to be in agreement that because "it is a military academy, fun is generally limited." As one straightforward student explains, "We are restricted to the campus grounds during the week until senior year. Life is pretty drab, dull, and boring [with] most time spent either in class, studying, or working out." Moreover, undergrads are "restricted by the regiment and disciplinary system." Of course, even these hardworking midshipmen get to kick back every now and again. Another undergrad cheerfully shares, "When the spring comes, everyone gets out to play rec sports (Ultimate Frisbee, tag football, soccer, swim, or bike ride) and goes to the park to BBQ." A fellow student chimes in, "We have a good time, and usually, it is the little things that make us happy. We enjoy hanging out on weekends and doing things that normal college students would do. Recently a few friends and I had a Nerf gun battle, which was pretty fun." When they are allowed, midshipmen rush to get off campus. Indeed, students here love to take advantage of the fact that they are "only twenty minutes from downtown NYC." As this wise midshipman concludes, "New York City in uniform boils down to cheap food, movies, plays, concerts, easy way to meet girls, you name it ... we work hard all week, but when it comes time, we get to play hard as well."

Student Body

At first glance, the average Merchant Marine Academy midshipman could be described as "a white, conservative male." Of course, there's definitely more to these students than race, gender, and political views. Certainly, undergrads can also be depicted as "respectful," "athletic," and "outgoing." They can also be categorized as "those that want to work in the maritime industry and those that want to join the military." Moreover, many are "hardworking and serious." As one undergrad explains, "If you aren't willing to work, you won't be here long." Another student continues, "The typical student has tons on his plate, whether it's regimental duties or academic ones. [However], no matter what, if you need help with something, somebody will be there for you." A fellow midshipman concurs, summing up, "The students here are all a family. Each one of us here at the Merchant Marine Academy [has] experienced the same rigorous training and tough treatment plebe year. We all work together in everything we do, and without one another it is almost impossible to succeed at the Academy." Actually, the U.S. Merchant Marine Academy is increasing the diversity of its student body every year.

UNITED STATES MERCHANT MARINE ACADEMY

Financial Aid: 516-773-5295 • E-Mail: admissions@usmma.edu • Website: www.usmma.edu

THE PRINCETON REVIEW SAYS

Admissions

Very important factors considered include: rigor of secondary school record, class rank, standardized test scores, extracurricular activities, character/personal qualities. *Important factors considered include:* academic GPA, application essay, recommendation(s), talent/ability. *Other factors considered include:* interview, first generation, geographical residence, state residency, racial/ethnic status, volunteer work, work experience. ACT with or without writing accepted. SAT with or without Essay component accepted. High school diploma is required and GED is accepted. *Academic units required:* 3 English, 3 math, 1 science, 1 science lab, 8 academic electives. *Academic units recommended:* 4 English, 4 math, 3 science, 2 science labs, 2 foreign language.

Financial Aid

Students should submit: FAFSA. The Princeton Review suggests that all financial aid forms be submitted as soon as possible after October 1. *Need-based scholarships/grants offered:* Federal Pell; Private scholarships; State scholarships/grants. *Loan aid offered:* Direct PLUS loans; Direct Subsidized Stafford Loans; Direct Unsubsidized Stafford Loans. Applicants will be notified of awards on a rolling basis beginning 5/1.

The Inside Word

Securing admittance to the Merchant Marine Academy is no easy feat. The admissions committee is looking for stellar candidates who have the intelligence, fortitude, and leadership capabilities to survive (and thrive) at this institution. In addition to your transcripts and test scores, the admissions crew will closely assess your letters of recommendation. Moreover, unlike traditional colleges, you'll also have to pass a fitness requirement and secure a nomination from a U.S. representative or senator.

THE SCHOOL SAYS "..."

From the Admissions Office

"The U. S. Merchant Marine Academy (USMMA) at Kings Point, New York, is a federal service academy with the mission to educate and graduate licensed Merchant Marine Officers of exemplary character who serve America's marine transportation and defense needs in peace and war. The Academy's four-year program is a demanding academic schedule that includes hands on experience. In addition, each cadet participates in Sea Year, during which cadets acquire more hands-on experience working aboard commercial and military vessels sailing around the world. Due to the Academy's unique mission, its graduates have civilian and military career choices that are unmatched by any other federal or maritime academy.

"Kings Point graduates earn (1) a Bachelor of Science degree, (2) an unlimited U.S. Coast Guard license (Deck or Engine), as well as (3) an officer's commission in one of the U.S. Armed Forces. Graduates are obligated to serve as a licensed officer in the U.S. Merchant Marine for five years, and as a commissioned officer in one of the U.S. Armed Forces reserves for eight years following graduation. Alternatively, graduating midshipmen can apply for an active duty commission in any branch of the U.S Armed Forces or the National Oceanic and Atmospheric Administration (NOAA) Corps.

"USMMA graduates are highly sought after as officers in the military and the U.S. Merchant Marine. Further, according to recent reports from the Department of Education and others, Kings Point graduates earn some of the highest salaries of college graduates in the United States."

SELECTIVITY

Admissions Rating	96
# of applicants	1,855
% of applicants accepted	22
% of acceptees attending	68
# offered a place on the wait list	204
% accepting a place on wait list	100
% admitted from wait list	65

FRESHMAN PROFILE

Range SAT EBRW	570–660
Range SAT Math	630–660
% submitting SAT scores	66
% submitting ACT scores	75
% graduated top 10% of class	22
% graduated top 25% of class	64
% graduated top 50% of class	96

DEADLINES

Regular	
Deadline	3/1
Notification	Rolling, 4/1
Nonfall registration?	No

FINANCIAL FACTS

Financial Aid Rating	60*
Annual tuition	$0
Required fees	$1,050
Books and supplies	$2,880

UNITED STATES MILITARY ACADEMY

646 Swift Road, West Point, NY 10996-1905 • Admissions: 845-938-4041 • Fax: 845-938-3021

CAMPUS LIFE

Quality of Life Rating	88
Fire Safety Rating	91
Green Rating	60*
Type of school	Public
Environment	Village

STUDENTS

Total undergrad enrollment	4,491
% male/female	78/22
% from out of state	94
% frosh from public high school	80
% frosh live on campus	100
% ugrads live on campus	100
# of fraternities	0
# of sororities	0
% African American	12
% Asian	8
% Caucasian	62
% Hispanic	10
% Native American	<1
% Pacific Islander	<1
% Two or more races	3
% Race and/or ethnicity unknown	1
% international	1
# of countries represented	29

SURVEY SAYS . . .

Lots of conservative students
Students always studying
Students are happy
Classroom facilities are great
Lab facilities are great
Great library
Career services are great
Internships are widely available
Class discussions encouraged
Great financial aid
No one cheats
Diverse student types interact on campus
Students get along with local community
Students involved in community service
Recreation facilities are great
Very little drug use
Everyone loves the Black Knights
Intramural sports are popular
Alumni active on campus

ACADEMICS

Academic Rating	99
% students returning for sophomore year	98
% students graduating within 4 years	83
% students graduating within 6 years	85
Calendar	Semester
Student/faculty ratio	7:1
Profs interesting rating	97
Profs accessible rating	99

Most classes have 10–19 students.
Most lab/discussion sessions have 10–19 students.

MOST POPULAR MAJORS
Engineering/Industrial Management; Economics, General; Business Administration and Management, General

STUDENTS SAY ". . ."

Academics
Throughout its more than 200 year history, the United States Military Academy in West Point, New York has produced United States presidents, NASA astronauts, notable generals, business leaders and many medal of honor recipients. So it is no wonder that cadets say the academy's "leadership training is second to none." Cadets praise the school for "helping the students succeed not only in the classroom, but also outside in our daily lives as people and as leaders" by pairing "academic vigor" with "[experiences] which enrich your character and ultimately make you a better person." The academy extends its holistic education "with countless academic enrichment activities," like "trips all over the world during spring break with the history department," "scuba diving with NASA" or parachuting lessons. The United States Military Academy also "sends cadets all over the world for study abroad" and gives students practical experience to apply what they learn in the classroom through programs like Advanced Individual Academic Development where students say they can work at "government research facilities during the summer doing relevant and cutting edge research." Professors are universally admired as "amazing," "very accessible and devoted" to their students. Students say this contributes an environment where "everyone goes to all classes and cares about academics." "Academics are hard," but because professors "[teach] only a few sections," "aren't sidetracked by research while they are teaching" and are willing to "bend over backwards to accommodate" the busy schedules of West Point cadets, any student can "succeed if you're willing to ask" for help.

Life
To put it mildly, "life is extremely busy" at West Point. "Time management is one the biggest things that you [will] learn" one cadet advises. Most days start with "formation in the morning before 7:30 A.M. classes" and cadets "are either working, in class, or exercising for most of the day. After classes are over at 4:00 P.M.," time is divided between activities and studies. "Every cadet is required to play a sport," but that doesn't necessarily mean that everyone is an athlete. While most admit that they "live a regimented lifestyle," cadets still nonetheless find ways to relax and socialize: "upper class [cadets] often go to one of the bars on post and drink till TAPS, when everyone must be in their rooms. We play video games, go to clubs, play instruments, and go to NYC on the weekends for fun." The academic schedules of first and second year students are pre-selected "but junior and senior classes are chosen on your own depending on your major." Students praise the system because "you don't have to worry about a class filling up," and cadets "can study ANY major they want because we are all guaranteed a great job after graduation." And like any old institution there are "a lot of silly traditions that we hold on to long after we're gone."

Student Body
The academy's unique application process requires students be nominated by their congressional representative, so cadets assure us that they "never cease to be impressed with [their] peers," who are some "of the smartest sons and daughters of America." Cadets provide a litany of praise for their peers: "People are courteous, respectful, honest, honorable, and simply amazing at West Point USMA." Cadets say that their "shared hardships foster an environment of camaraderie unparalleled anywhere else in the world." Many stress the importance of teamwork, cooperation, and leadership, explaining that "by the time you become a senior, you may be responsible for 120 other people." Cadets say the student body is geographically diverse with "students from every state in the US" represented as well as "some students from other countries like, Nigeria, Qatar, and France."

594 ■ FOR MORE FREE CONTENT, VISIT PRINCETONREVIEW.COM

E-Mail: admissions@usma.edu • Website: www.westpoint.edu

THE PRINCETON REVIEW SAYS

Admissions

Very important factors considered include: rigor of secondary school record, class rank, academic GPA, standardized test scores, extracurricular activities, character/personal qualities. *Important factors considered include:* application essay, recommendation(s), talent/ability, level of applicant's interest. *Other factors considered include:* interview, first generation, racial/ethnic status, volunteer work, work experience. ACT with Writing required. SAT with Essay component required. High school diploma is required and GED is accepted. *Academic units recommended:* 4 English, 4 math, 4 science, 2 science labs, 2 foreign language, 3 social studies, 1 history, 3 academic electives.

Financial Aid

The Princeton Review suggests that all financial aid forms be submitted as soon as possible after October 1.

The Inside Word

The fact that you must be nominated by your Congressional representative in order to apply to West Point tells you all you need to know about the school's selectivity. Contact your district's Congressional representative to learn the deadline for nomination requests; typically these are made in the spring of your junior year. Successful candidates must demonstrate excellence in academics, physical conditioning, extracurricular involvement, and leadership. They must also be willing to commit to five years of active duty and three years of reserve duty upon graduation. The rigorous requirements and demanding commitments of a West Point education hardly dissuade applicants. More than 15,000 applied for the 1,150 available slots.

THE SCHOOL SAYS "..."

From the Admissions Office

"West Point is searching for applicants who possess the leadership skills, cultural sensibilities, and the moral fiber to handle the volatile, uncertain, complex, and ambiguous contemporary operating environment of today's world as a future U.S. Army Officer. As a crucible for leadership, we are looking for critical thinkers that have who have the judgment and experience to become a leader of character upon graduation.

"To assess your ability and preparation, admissions looks at more than your GPA or standardized test scores. The applications of almost 15,000 students are evaluated based on academic, physical, and leadership potential to find approximately 1,150 candidates who are ready to be offered the challenge of admission into the Corps of Cadets. With an amazingly high offer-acceptance rate, only the most dedicated, enthusiastic applicants make it to the finish line for the report date each June.

"If you accept the challenge, you will be immersed in a military training program that ranges from marksmanship to orienteering, an academic program that offers over forty majors ranging from electrical engineering to philosophy, and a physical program that finds every cadet participating in an intercollegiate, club, or intramural-level sport. The fully funded, four-year college education includes tuition, room, board, and full medical and dental care. In return, you will graduate with a Bachelor of Science degree and be commissioned as a U.S. Army Officer with an active duty service obligation of five years active and three years reserve. Complete admissions guidance found online."

SELECTIVITY

Admissions Rating	99
# of applicants	12,973
% of applicants accepted	10
% of acceptees attending	98

FRESHMAN PROFILE

Range SAT EBRW	585–690
Range SAT Math	600–710
Range ACT Composite	23–28
# submitting SAT scores	1,076
% submitting SAT scores	86
# submitting ACT scores	1,029
% submitting ACT scores	82
% graduated top 10% of class	46
% graduated top 25% of class	74
% graduated top 50% of class	94

DEADLINES

Regular	
Deadline	2/28
Notification	Rolling, 2/28
Nonfall registration?	No

APPLICANTS ALSO LOOK AT AND SOMETIMES PREFER

United States Air Force Academy; United States Coast Guard Academy; United States Naval Academy

FINANCIAL FACTS

Financial Aid Rating	60*
Annual tuition	$0

UNITED STATES NAVAL ACADEMY

52 King George Street, Annapolis, MD 21402 • Admissions: 410-293-1858 • Fax: 410-293-4348

CAMPUS LIFE

Quality of Life Rating	91
Fire Safety Rating	77
Green Rating	60*
Type of school	Public
Environment	Town

STUDENTS

Total undergrad enrollment	4,512
% male/female	72/28
% from out of state	94
% frosh from public high school	60
% frosh live on campus	100
% ugrads live on campus	100
# of fraternities	0
# of sororities	0
% African American	7
% Asian	7
% Caucasian	63
% Hispanic	12
% Native American	<1
% Pacific Islander	1
% Two or more races	9
% Race and/or ethnicity unknown	1
% international	1
# of countries represented	29

SURVEY SAYS . . .

Classroom facilities are great
Lab facilities are great
Great library
Career services are great
Internships are widely available
Great financial aid
No one cheats
Diverse student types interact on campus
Students are very religious
Students get along with local community
Students involved in community service
Students love Annapolis, MD
Very little drug use
Everyone loves the Navy
Intramural sports are popular
Alumni active on campus

ACADEMICS

Academic Rating	88
% students returning for sophomore year	97
% students graduating within 4 years	90
% students graduating within 6 years	91
Calendar	Semester
Student/faculty ratio	8:1
Profs interesting rating	86
Profs accessible rating	96
Most classes have 10–19 students.	

MOST POPULAR MAJORS

Econometrics and Quantitative Economics;
Political Science and Government, General;
Mechatronics, Robotics, and Automation
Engineering

STUDENTS SAY ". . ."

Academics

It's a matter of moral, mental, and physical development for the proud 4,500 midshipmen of the United States Naval Academy, who serve at least five years in the Navy or Marine Corps. Make no mistake: this is a "regimented, disciplined, controlled environment," but that's to get all midshipmen to graduation in a forty-seven month program. Students are "fully immersed in a military environment and have to keep up many different standards" to attend, but midshipmen are granted "endless ... unique travel opportunities" not found at traditional colleges, such as "attending political functions in D.C. [and] foreign travel to Morocco to learn French." "From [subjects covering] CEOs to war heroes, we learn and learn and learn," says a student. The Naval Academy gives students "the resources to truly become great leaders in whatever naval warfare field [they] go into on top of a well-balanced and challenging college education."

All incoming freshman take part in a rigorous seven-week mental and physical training program known as "Plebe Summer," and students find the "greatest strengths [on campus] are endurance and multitasking." Class sizes are small and the "vast majority of professors are extremely passionate and competent." "They take feedback well and are always trying to improve their teaching and classes," says a student. Many classes focus entirely around class discussions rather than lectures, pushing students "to [lead] outside the classroom and then discuss our actions and others' reactions," and classes about Seamanship and Navigation take midshipmen on actual ships to practice; in the summer, students also go on different training courses to experience the military first-hand.

Life

Attending USNA is undoubtedly "a busy lifestyle that allows for little free time." Students undergo "lots of work, sports, [and] military training" on any given day, so "free time is [spent] either trying to get more than four to five hours of sleep or playing video games [and] watching movies." Students spend almost every day in class or at mandatory events, followed by meetings and homework, and the schedule is very regimented: "Morning quarters formation, classes, noon meal formation, more classes, sports period, evening meal, then study." A lot of people work out "almost obsessively" as well. There is no drinking allowed and everyone lives in the same dorm (no members of the opposite sex are allowed in rooms), so "a lot of socializing" takes place elsewhere. Everything here is "mission-oriented" and has a purpose: to foster a "camaraderie, understanding of others, and a no-person-left-behind mentality." Students love Annapolis, where USNA is located, because they are a "very active" crowd and "there are a lot of places to go for outdoor activities."

Student Body

Unsurprisingly, this "bright, hard-working" group has a lot of "type-A personalities who are very outgoing, ambitious, and driven," so those one student calls "the average Joe who just gets by flying under the radar" are rare. This is "an extremely challenging environment that forces you to grow into both a person of character and caliber," says another student. Fortunately, the student body is "capable of helping each other through any conflict," and students find that their "friendships are true relationships." Due to the constraints placed on the midshipmen, there can be a great deal of "happy cynicism," which results in a bit of "sarcasm and [a] make-our-own fun attitude." USNA students are "quite competitive in all aspects," but there are "so many people and resources available ... committed to your success."

UNITED STATES NAVAL ACADEMY

E-Mail: inquire@usna.edu • Website: www.usna.edu

THE PRINCETON REVIEW SAYS

Admissions

Very important factors considered include: rigor of secondary school record, class rank, academic GPA, application essay, recommendation(s), interview, extracurricular activities, character/personal qualities, level of applicant's interest. *Important factors considered include:* standardized test scores, talent/ability. *Other factors considered include:* first generation, alumni/ae relation, geographical residence, state residency, racial/ethnic status, volunteer work, work experience. ACT with or without writing accepted. SAT with or without Essay component accepted. High school diploma or equivalent is not required. *Academic units recommended:* 4 English, 4 math, 2 science, 1 science lab, 2 foreign language, 2 history, 1 unit from above areas or other academic areas.

Financial Aid

The Princeton Review suggests that all financial aid forms be submitted as soon as possible after October 1.

The Inside Word

Securing admission to the Naval Academy is no easy feat. To begin with, a top-notch academic record is a must. In addition to strong GPA and test scores, applicants also have to secure an official nomination (typically granted by a U.S. representative, U.S. senator, or the Vice President). Further, candidates need to prove physical fitness, be an unmarried U.S. citizen between the ages of seventeen and twenty-three with no dependents. And, perhaps most importantly, applicants should also demonstrate strong moral character. Finally, the earlier you apply the better.

THE SCHOOL SAYS "..."

From the Admissions Office

"The finest young men and women in the country come to the Naval Academy to develop into leaders to serve the nation; USNA is the school of admirals, presidents, Nobel Prize winners, astronauts, jet pilots and CEOs. At USNA, you will have the opportunity to pursue a four-year degree program that develops you mentally, morally, and physically as no civilian college can. As you might expect, this program is demanding, but the opportunities are limitless and more than worth the effort.

"Upon throwing the iconic Midshipmen hat into the air at graduation, you will serve your country in one of dozens of professional fields—primarily aviation, submarines, ships, or the Marine Corps, but with additional limited options for the SEALs, medical, and other communities."

SELECTIVITY

Admissions Rating	98
# of applicants	16,086
% of applicants accepted	9
% of acceptees attending	87
# offered a place on the wait list	216
% accepting a place on wait list	77
% admitted from wait list	8

FRESHMAN PROFILE

Range SAT EBRW	560–680
Range SAT Math	590–690
Range ACT Composite	26–32
# submitting SAT scores	859
% submitting SAT scores	71
# submitting ACT scores	818
% submitting ACT scores	68
Average HS GPA	4.1
% graduated top 10% of class	57
% graduated top 25% of class	81
% graduated top 50% of class	96

DEADLINES

Regular	
Deadline	1/31
Notification	4/15
Nonfall registration?	No

FINANCIAL FACTS

Financial Aid Rating	60*
Annual tuition	$0

THE UNIVERSITY OF ALABAMA—BIRMINGHAM

Office of Undergraduate Admissions, Birmingham, AL 35294-4412 • Admissions: 205-934-8221 • Fax: 205-975-7114

CAMPUS LIFE

Quality of Life Rating	92
Fire Safety Rating	95
Green Rating	84
Type of school	Public
Environment	Metropolis

STUDENTS

Total undergrad enrollment	13,328
% male/female	39/61
% from out of state	13
% frosh live on campus	72
% ugrads live on campus	23
# of fraternities (% ugrad men join)	13 (7)
# of sororities (% ugrad women join)	13 (9)
% African American	24
% Asian	7
% Caucasian	56
% Hispanic	6
% Native American	<1
% Pacific Islander	0
% Two or more races	4
% Race and/or ethnicity unknown	1
% international	2
# of countries represented	53

SURVEY SAYS . . .

Lab facilities are great
Great library
Internships are widely available
Diverse student types interact on campus
Students are very religious
Recreation facilities are great
Alumni active on campus

ACADEMICS

Academic Rating	80
% students returning for sophomore year	83
% students graduating within 4 years	40
% students graduating within 6 years	63
Calendar	Semester
Student/faculty ratio	19:1
Profs interesting rating	88
Profs accessible rating	93

Most classes have 10–19 students.
Most lab/discussion sessions have 20–29 students.

MOST POPULAR MAJORS

Biology/Biological Sciences, General; Psychology, General; Accounting

STUDENTS SAY "..."

Academics

At the University of Alabama at Birmingham, professors and administrators "care about you." "For many of the professors, it's not just about a grade in a class that you are taking. Rather it's an experience and preparation for any of our further endeavors." The professors here are "experts in their fields," they're "accessible and exciting," and "they're down-to-earth enough to give students a real view of what it's like to enter the world of academia." Despite the fact that this is a large university, there are "small class sizes in even the 100-level classes," and "many professors are available for help outside the classroom and care about teaching their subjects to the students." Of particular note, students say professors in the science departments "are great. They do a great job with interactive learning, and they really put forth every effort to make sure that those who want help get it." Academically, students feel that the workload is rigorous, but "certainly worth the challenge." As one student notes, a graduate tends to feel like "a better person for having experienced the challenge of UAB as well as the diversity." With a biannual student forum, "the faculty and administration are very close with students and actively look to pursuing perfection and improving the collegiate experience."

Life

"Campus life is vibrant and exciting," boasts the student body. With UAB being "in the city of Birmingham, right outside of the school is something for everyone. There are malls, many restaurants, museums, and live music." UAB "strongly encourages their students to get involved on campus in some shape or form," presenting the student body with such opportunities as "the widely used Campus Recreation Center where students can take free U-Fit Classes (kickboxing, krunk/hip-hop class, yoga, spin, etc.), swim in the wave pool, climb the rock wall, or play intramurals (flag football, dodgeball, soccer, volleyball, slow pitch softball, etc.)." In addition, the surrounding city of Birmingham offers many venues for arts and entertainment; "students can dine or shop at the many malls located throughout the city. There are also many museums, art shows, concerts, dance clubs, [and] movie theaters to choose from." Students say that the list of attractions in Birmingham "goes on and on." "Students have the problem of having to narrow down their opportunities, rather than having to find something to do." Students "love the size of the school," finding it "like a small town in a big city." The impression is that "the campus is large enough that [you] meet and see new faces daily, but small enough to where [you] have personal relationships with teachers and the administration." Additionally, "there is a genuine interest among students in learning about the other cultures and religions represented on campus and in other cultures around the world."

Student Body

"Everyone is so diverse that there is...something for everyone to get involved in." With more than 250 campus organizations, students say you'd "have to choose to not become involved." Many students love "how no one looks down on anyone," and how "everyone is so down-to-earth!" Most feel that they all come "from modest households." Regarding potential changes that could be made, "the meal plan situation could use some serious help." At UAB students feel, "it is easy to find a place where you fit in," although the student body will insist that "there is no typical student!" In general, students are "hardworking and serious," while doing their best to always "enjoy weekend fun with friends."

THE UNIVERSITY OF ALABAMA—BIRMINGHAM

Financial Aid: 205-934-8223 • E-Mail: chooseuab@uab.edu • Website: www.uab.edu

THE PRINCETON REVIEW SAYS

Admissions

Very important factors considered include: rigor of secondary school record, academic GPA, standardized test scores. ACT with or without writing accepted. SAT with or without Essay component accepted. High school diploma is required and GED is accepted. *Academic units required:* 4 English, 3 math, 3 science, 2 science labs, 1 foreign language, 3 social studies, 3 academic electives.

Financial Aid

Students should submit: FAFSA. Priority filing deadline is 3/1. The Princeton Review suggests that all financial aid forms be submitted as soon as possible after October 1. *Need-based scholarships/grants offered:* College/university scholarship or grant aid from institutional funds; Federal Pell; Private scholarships; SEOG; State scholarships/grants; United Negro College Fund. *Loan aid offered:* Direct PLUS loans; Direct Subsidized Stafford Loans; Direct Unsubsidized Stafford Loans. Applicants will be notified of awards on a rolling basis beginning 3/15. Federal Work-Study Program available. Institutional employment available.

The Inside Word

UAB's incoming class tends to have an average GPA of 3.5. The most important factors for admission are GPA and test scores. At the minimum, students need a GPA of 2.25 and a 950 SAT score. Administrators here are looking to admit a student body that's friendly, diverse, and intelligent with students who strive to be active in the community.

THE SCHOOL SAYS "..."

From the Admissions Office

"The University of Alabama at Birmingham (UAB) is a young, dynamic teaching and research university that has—in just four decades—won international renown for our collaborative and interdisciplinary culture. Our academic programs afford students unrivaled, hands-on experience in research and scholarship as UAB is first in the nation among public universities of federal research dollars per freshman. With over 120 areas of study, UAB attracts the best and brightest students from Alabama, the nation, and 109 countries around the globe.

"UAB students learn from—and work alongside—some of the world's top researchers, scholars, performers, and experts. Programs from the sciences and engineering to the arts and humanities give students the benefit of globally recognized faculty, exciting academic challenges, and experiences that will prepare them for a future in the job market.

"At UAB, we understand that having a fulfilling student life experience is as important as having a fulfilling academic experience. UAB has a rich mix of academic organizations, honor clubs, social fraternities and sororities, volunteer groups, and activities ranging from intramural sports and SGA to program-related clubs and supporting Blazer athletics. With 250 campus organizations to keep students involved, UAB offers the chance to make lifelong friendships while assisting in the development of skills essential to leadership and teamwork."

SELECTIVITY

Admissions Rating	78
# of applicants	8,298
% of applicants accepted	74
% of acceptees attending	38

FRESHMAN PROFILE

Range SAT EBRW	560–680
Range SAT Math	530–685
Range SAT Composite	1100–1360
Range ACT Composite	22–29
# submitting SAT scores	312
% submitting SAT scores	13
# submitting ACT scores	2,162
% submitting ACT scores	92
Average HS GPA	3.8
% graduated top 10% of class	29
% graduated top 25% of class	57
% graduated top 50% of class	87

DEADLINES

Regular	
Priority	6/1
Notification	Rolling, 8/1
Nonfall registration?	Yes

FINANCIAL FACTS

Financial Aid Rating	81
Annual in-state tuition	$10,710
Annual out-of-state tuition	$25,500
Room and board	$10,910
Books and supplies	$1,200
Average frosh need-based scholarship	$4,862
Average UG need-based scholarship	$4,950
% needy frosh rec. need-based scholarship or grant aid	56
% needy UG rec. need-based scholarship or grant aid	63
% needy frosh rec. non-need-based scholarship or grant aid	78
% needy UG rec. non-need-based scholarship or grant aid	50
% needy frosh rec. need-based self-help aid	24
% needy UG rec. need-based self-help aid	14
% UG borrow to pay for school	60
Average cumulative indebtedness	$29,914
% frosh need fully met	21
% ugrads need fully met	15
Average % of frosh need met	66
Average % of ugrad need met	55

THE UNIVERSITY OF ALABAMA—TUSCALOOSA

Box 870132, Tuscaloosa, AL 35487-0132 • Admissions: 205-348-5666 • Fax: 205-348-9046

CAMPUS LIFE
Quality of Life Rating	91
Fire Safety Rating	83
Green Rating	60*
Type of school	Public
Environment	City

STUDENTS
Total undergrad enrollment	31,900
% male/female	45/55
% from out of state	61
% frosh live on campus	95
% ugrads live on campus	25
# of fraternities (% ugrad men join)	43 (28)
# of sororities (% ugrad women join)	24 (42)
% African American	10
% Asian	1
% Caucasian	77
% Hispanic	5
% Native American	<1
% Pacific Islander	<1
% Two or more races	4
% Race and/or ethnicity unknown	0
% international	2
# of countries represented	57

SURVEY SAYS . . .
Students are happy
Classroom facilities are great
Lab facilities are great
Great library
School is well run
Recreation facilities are great
Lots of beer drinking
Frats and sororities are popular
Alumni active on campus
Active student government

ACADEMICS
Academic Rating	76
% students returning for sophomore year	87
% students graduating within 4 years	50
% students graduating within 6 years	71
Calendar	Semester
Student/faculty ratio	20:1
Profs interesting rating	87
Profs accessible rating	91

Most classes have 20–29 students.
Most lab/discussion sessions have 20–29 students.

MOST POPULAR MAJORS
Business Administration and Management, General; Marketing/Marketing Management, General; Finance, General

STUDENTS SAY "..."

Academics

University of Alabama—Tuscaloosa is an institution where "students reach their full potential and accomplish their dreams." Undergrads here are drawn to the school's rich history, beautiful campus and wide range of challenging academic programs. A major benefit is the fact that "there's a lot of funding for scholarships...[as well as] research and facilities." As with any large university, students are likely to encounter a range of professors, but for the most part, Alabama undergrads enjoy their time in the classroom. They report that the majority of their teachers are "caring," "engaging," and "highly intelligent." Professors hail "from a myriad of backgrounds, and a lot are here to carry on research that they are interested in." Fortunately, "their passion drives classes and makes learning very interesting and fun." Even better, "they are willing to help you if you need it and sincerely want you to succeed." Standout programs include business, communication studies, engineering, and nursing. The honors college offers "smaller class sizes and more theory-based assignments."

Life

Life at UA is active: "there are over 400 clubs and organizations to fill your time here." Crimson Tide football is dominant; "Tailgating before games and then going out to party after games is common." Beyond football, "intramural sports are popular [as is] going to the rec centers to exercise." Greek life is popular and a big part of the social scene. "Fraternities and sororities have swaps on Thursday nights. Friday nights the fraternities have band parties or DJ's come in." The university sponsors plenty of alternative options as well. Undergrads can attend "concerts and fairs," "movie nights," "book clubs," and cultural events like the "Japanese festival." And when students want to take a breather from campus life, they can easily head to "Riverwalk, a walking trail close to campus that goes along the Black Warrior River." Moreover, hometown Tuscaloosa "has more restaurants than you could try in four years so we go out to eat a lot." Finally, if undergrads want to further explore the surrounding area, "Birmingham [is only] 50 minutes away."

Student Body

Over the past few years, University of Alabama has done a great job of attracting large numbers of out-of-state students. As such, undergrads here report "the culture is definitely shifting from ultra-conservative to more progressive." "School spirit permeates every aspect of campus and student life" and we're assured that "all students bond over the love of the Tide no matter what differences they may have in passions, interests, or politics." And just as important, regardless of a student's hometown, we're told that "Southern hospitality" shines through. Hence it's not surprising that many students describe their peers as "friendly," "polite," "warm, and inclusive." The vast majority promise that there's "something here for everyone, and there are people on campus that fill every academic and social niche imaginable." As one content student conveniently sums up, "There are the students who are here just for football and partying; there are students here strictly for academics; and there are students...that will be with you at 2:00 A.M. in the library or at 2:00 A.M. in a frat house."

THE UNIVERSITY OF ALABAMA—TUSCALOOSA

Financial Aid: 205-348-7949 • E-Mail: admissions@ua.edu • Website: www.ua.edu

THE PRINCETON REVIEW SAYS

Admissions

Very important factors considered include: rigor of secondary school record, academic GPA, standardized test scores. *Important factors considered include:* class rank. *Other factors considered include:* application essay, recommendation(s), interview, extracurricular activities, talent/ability, character/personal qualities, first generation, alumni/ae relation, volunteer work, work experience. ACT with or without writing accepted. SAT with or without Essay component accepted. High school diploma is required and GED is accepted. *Academic units required:* 4 English, 3 math, 3 science, 2 science labs, 1 foreign language, 4 social studies, 5 academic electives. *Academic units recommended:* 4 English, 3 math, 3 science, 2 science labs, 2 foreign language, 4 social studies, 5 academic electives.

Financial Aid

Students should submit: FAFSA and Application for Academic Scholarship. Priority filing deadline is 3/1. The Princeton Review suggests that all financial aid forms be submitted as soon as possible after October 1. *Need-based scholarships/grants offered:* College/university scholarship or grant aid from institutional funds; Federal Nursing Scholarships; Federal Pell; Private scholarships; SEOG; State scholarships/grants. *Loan aid offered:* Direct PLUS loans; Direct Subsidized Stafford Loans; Direct Unsubsidized Stafford Loans. Applicants will be notified of awards on a rolling basis beginning 4/1. Institutional employment available.

The Inside Word

The admissions process at Alabama is pretty straightforward. The university is looking for students who are strongly committed to their studies and demonstrate the ability to successfully tackle the school's academic rigor. To that end, admissions officers closely review each applicant's GPA, standardized test scores, and high school course schedule. Students who have earned a minimum GPA of 3.0 as well as a 21 on the ACT or 1080 on the new/current SAT will be competitive candidates.

THE SCHOOL SAYS "..."

From the Admissions Office

"Since its founding in 1831 as the first public university in the state, the University of Alabama has been committed to providing the best, most complete education possible for its students. Our commitment to that goal means that as times change, we sharpen our focus and methods to keep our graduates competitive in their fields. By offering outstanding teaching in a solid core curriculum enhanced by multimedia classrooms and campuswide computer labs, the University of Alabama keeps its focus on the future while maintaining a traditional college atmosphere. Extensive international study opportunities, internship programs, and cooperative education placements help our students prepare for successful futures. Consisting of eleven colleges and schools offering 193 degrees in more than 100 fields of study, the university gives its students a wide range of choices and offers courses of study at the bachelor's, master's, specialist, and doctoral levels. The university emphasizes quality and breadth of academic opportunities and challenging programs for well-prepared students through its Honors College, including the University Honors Program, International Honors Program, and Computer-Based Honors Programs and Blount Undergraduate Initiative (liberal arts program). Thirty-one percent of undergraduates are from out of state, providing an enriching social and cultural environment.

"Applicants may submit either the SAT or the ACT. The writing component is accepted but not required for admission."

SELECTIVITY
Admissions Rating	84
# of applicants	38,505
% of applicants accepted	83
% of acceptees attending	21

FRESHMAN PROFILE
Range SAT EBRW	550–660
Range SAT Math	530–680
Range SAT Composite	1080–1340
Range ACT Composite	23–31
# submitting SAT scores	1,808
% submitting SAT scores	27
# submitting ACT scores	4,892
% submitting ACT scores	72
Average HS GPA	3.8
% graduated top 10% of class	40
% graduated top 25% of class	61
% graduated top 50% of class	84

DEADLINES
Regular	
Priority	2/1
Notification	Rolling, 7/15
Nonfall registration?	Yes

APPLICANTS ALSO LOOK AT AND OFTEN PREFER
Florida State University; University of Georgia; University of Tennessee, Knoxville

AND SOMETIMES PREFER
Auburn University; The University of Alabama at Birmingham; University of Florida

FINANCIAL FACTS
Financial Aid Rating	83
Annual in-state tuition	$10,780
Annual out-of-state tuition	$30,250
Room and board	$10,836
Books and supplies	$1,000
Average frosh need-based scholarship	$14,016
Average UG need-based scholarship	$13,730
% needy frosh rec. need-based scholarship or grant aid	77
% needy UG rec. need-based scholarship or grant aid	75
% needy frosh rec. non-need-based scholarship or grant aid	63
% needy UG rec. non-need-based scholarship or grant aid	54
% needy frosh rec. need-based self-help aid	63
% needy UG rec. need-based self-help aid	73
% frosh rec. any financial aid	81
% UG rec. any financial aid	74
% UG borrow to pay for school	47
Average cumulative indebtedness	$34,975
% frosh need fully met	23
% ugrads need fully met	20
Average % of frosh need met	56
Average % of ugrad need met	54

UNIVERSITY OF ARIZONA

PO Box 210073, Tucson, AZ 85721-0073 • Admissions: 520-621-3237 • Fax: 520-621-9799

CAMPUS LIFE
Quality of Life Rating	**87**
Fire Safety Rating	**91**
Green Rating	**95**
Type of school	Public
Environment	Metropolis

STUDENTS
Total undergrad enrollment	35,801
% male/female	46/54
% from out of state	39
% frosh from public high school	99
% frosh live on campus	76
% ugrads live on campus	20
# of fraternities	25
# of sororities	24
% African American	4
% Asian	5
% Caucasian	49
% Hispanic	27
% Native American	<1
% Pacific Islander	<1
% Two or more races	5
% Race and/or ethnicity unknown	2
% international	6
# of countries represented	120

SURVEY SAYS . . .
Students are happy
Recreation facilities are great
Everyone loves the Wildcats
Frats and sororities are popular
Active student government

ACADEMICS
Academic Rating	**78**
% students returning for sophomore year	83
% students graduating within 4 years	47
% students graduating within 6 years	65
Calendar	Semester
Student/faculty ratio	15:1
Profs interesting rating	84
Profs accessible rating	89

Most classes have 10–19 students.
Most lab/discussion sessions have
20–29 students.

MOST POPULAR MAJORS
Psychology, General; Public Health, General;
Registered Nursing/Registered Nurse

STUDENTS SAY "..."

Academics

When it was first established in 1885, the University of Arizona had a graduating class of just three students. Today, this public research institution has over 35,000 undergrads, and more than 280 majors; as those enrolled put it, "there are so many resources and opportunities available." Moreover, while the "great programs" themselves are lauded, their availability gets even more praise, with creative class schedules available for those who may need to attend after work.

"Some seminar courses require students to attend poetry readings as the lectures, while others require students to attend talks typically at night and in a non-traditional setting." Presentation matters, too, which is why many classes incorporate "active learning or engagement rooms that set up in small groups to allow for discussion or answering questions," as well as "collaborative spaces, in which microphones, mobile device answering, and white boards are incorporated into learning." And, because it's important to offer "better opportunities to [help] get your foot in the door," Arizona's classes are "based on intensive research so every day is filled with great knowledge." Rest assured, struggling students have access to an on-campus resource called Think Tank, which "can be used by anyone to get help with any subject." The university also offers hands-on opportunities for students to participate in "experiential learning through volunteering [and] internships," as well as through "excellent scientific research."

Attending Arizona is a "large school experience but with professors and staff who share the heart and care of a much smaller school." Instructors "work hard to make these classes meaningful, regardless of the medium," and "a lot of guest lecturers are brought into class to demonstrate their expertise and innovative [and] exciting projects." Professors here are "wonderful, knowledgeable, accessible, and devoted" to student success. Most of them are "always open for further conversations either during class, right after, or during office hours," and make every effort to be "open-minded and love to hear the experiences of their students as well."

Life

Spread across a full square mile of red-bricked campus, the University of Arizona is "small [and] centralized," meaning "everything is easy to find." Students with packed academic and social calendars are particularly grateful for the layout "because it can take them less than fifteen minutes to walk to any given class" or on-campus activity. And when classes end, those looking for more will find that the day's really only just begun. With over 600 clubs and organizations, "there is always something to do" and plenty of ways "for everyone to become involved in campus." Some flock to "outdoors activities [which] are very common since the weather is perfect." Others point to how "student centers host different events every other night." And then there are the seventeen Division I sports teams, which feature "great athletics and fan support," with students displaying "a high interest in sports from the professional to the intramural level. So far as the weekend goes, Saturday is when "people usually party and hang out with friends" or "love exploring the immediate area of Tucson." That's not to say Sundays are dull, but students do note that it tends to be "study day and there are usually a lot of people in the library." Ultimately, whether it's Tuesdays after class or midnight on a Saturday, students find that "most people socialize all the time."

Student Body

This group is "very diverse and is made up of many different people from different backgrounds and places." The student population feels eclectic, with "artists, athletes, gym rats, mathematicians, researchers, performers, performance goers, and dedicated students young and old." On the sunny Arizona campus, many note that fellow undergrads are also "very active and health conscious individuals." Overall, the "community is very supportive of one another," and "students on campus are always smiling and ready to engage with one another." Many enrollees agree that students here try to find a balance of all of the things that make the University of Arizona what it is. "There are people who study very hard here and there are people who party very hard," but the school "is unique because while the University of Arizona is a fun and athletic school, academics are also important."

Financial Aid: 520-621-1858 • E-Mail: admissions@arizona.edu • Website: http://www.arizona.edu

THE PRINCETON REVIEW SAYS

Admissions

Very important factors considered include: rigor of secondary school record, academic GPA. *Important factors considered include:* extracurricular activities, talent/ability, character/personal qualities, level of applicant's interest. *Other factors considered include:* standardized test scores, class rank, application essay, recommendation(s), volunteer work, work experience. ACT with or without writing accepted. SAT with or without Essay component accepted. High school diploma is required and GED is accepted. *Academic units required:* 4 English, 4 math, 3 science, 3 science labs, 2 foreign language, 2 social studies, 1 visual/performing arts. *Academic units recommended:* 4 English, 4 math, 3 lab science, 2 foreign language, 2 social studies, 1 visual/performing arts.

Financial Aid

Students should submit: FAFSA; Institution's own financial aid form. Priority filing deadline is 3/1. The Princeton Review suggests that all financial aid forms be submitted as soon as possible after October 1. *Need-based scholarships/grants offered:* College/university scholarship or grant aid from institutional funds; Federal Pell; Private scholarships; SEOG; State scholarships/grants. *Loan aid offered:* Direct PLUS loans; Direct Subsidized Stafford Loans; Direct Unsubsidized Stafford Loans. Applicants will be notified of awards on a rolling basis beginning 2/1. Federal Work-Study Program available. Institutional employment available.

The Inside Word

Admission to the University of Arizona is competitive, and you'll need to demonstrate achievement in college prep courses. Prospective students should take note that those who graduate in the top 25 percent of their class with a GPA of 3.0 or higher in core competencies and meet all course requirements gain automatic acceptance through the assured admission program. Applicants should also recognize that some programs, such as the College of Engineering, College of Nursing, and College of Fine Arts, mandate additional materials and requirements.

THE SCHOOL SAYS "..."

From the Admissions Office

"From day one, University of Arizona students step into an unrivaled mix of academics, student life, and experiential learning enhanced with opportunities that only a top research institution can offer. A sunny campus, welcoming atmosphere, and diverse student body offer a place for everyone to pursue their passions. Students spend their days learning from a world-class faculty of Pulitzer and Nobel Prize winners, participating in countless recreation activities, and being valued members of a close-knit, active community. Through services like Student Engagement and Career Development, the university connects students with education-enhancing experiences like internships, research, or volunteering. Slated for completion in 2022, a new Student Success District in the heart of campus will elevate student support in areas like academics, career, and health and wellness. Thanks to the knowledge and experience they gain here, Wildcats are often sought after by top employers because they graduate with a diverse set of knowledge and skills that can apply to the workplace. As the network of 275,000 global alumni can attest to, an Arizona education pays you back for a lifetime—one of the many reasons why Arizona is repeatedly recognized for its outstanding academics and exceptional value. From ground-breaking research to a bustling student life with 600+ student clubs, cultural centers, and unrivaled school spirit with winning athletics programs, the University of Arizona offers an ideal college experience."

SELECTIVITY

Admissions Rating	82
# of applicants	40,854
% of applicants accepted	85
% of acceptees attending	22

FRESHMAN PROFILE

Range SAT EBRW	560–670
Range SAT Math	550–690
Range SAT Composite	1120–1350
Range ACT Composite	21–29
# submitting SAT scores	3,932
% submitting SAT scores	51
# submitting ACT scores	3,821
% submitting ACT scores	50
Average HS GPA	3.4
% graduated top 10% of class	36
% graduated top 25% of class	65
% graduated top 50% of class	88

DEADLINES

Regular	
Priority	5/1
Deadline	5/1
Notification	Rolling, 9/1
Nonfall registration?	Yes

FINANCIAL FACTS

Financial Aid Rating	83
Annual in-state tuition	$11,299
Annual out-of-state tuition	$35,326
Room and board	$13,050
Required fees	$1,412
Books and supplies	$800
Average frosh need-based scholarship	$13,720
Average UG need-based scholarship	$11,716
% needy frosh rec. need-based scholarship or grant aid	96
% needy UG rec. need-based scholarship or grant aid	91
% needy frosh rec. non-need-based scholarship or grant aid	17
% needy UG rec. non-need-based scholarship or grant aid	11
% needy frosh rec. need-based self-help aid	46
% needy UG rec. need-based self-help aid	58
% frosh rec. any financial aid	92
% UG rec. any financial aid	80
% UG borrow to pay for school	45
Average cumulative indebtedness	$26,414
% frosh need fully met	19
% ugrads need fully met	13
Average % of frosh need met	67
Average % of ugrad need met	61

UNIVERSITY OF ARKANSAS—FAYETTEVILLE

232 Silas H. Hunt Hall, Fayetteville, AR 72701 • Admissions: 479-575-5346 • Fax: 479-575-7515

STUDENTS SAY "..."

Academics

The University of Arkansas—Fayetteville "is a large university with a community feel. It's big enough to have a lot of great opportunities, but small enough you see people you know on campus." With Fayetteville's outdoorsy culture, some students "would describe [the school] as a weird cross between Southern and hippie." Research opportunities abound, and prospective students are drawn to both the Honors College and the Sam Walton School of Business. Students also single out U of A's "strong engineering program, with the depth and diversity in every discipline from mechanical to computer science [and] biomedical." Even with the relaxed atmosphere—one student coins it as "Fayettechill"—students say that there are "tough programs that really make you work for your grade so you can be sure you are worth your degree." Professors are hit or miss; while some students say, "Most of my professors are extremely helpful," others lament that while "I enjoy most of my professors, but I do sometimes get the impression that they don't care about my individual success." Students in the larger majors say they often lack individualized attention. As one student points out: "My major is located in a smaller department so I know my professors very well. However, in larger classes and departments it is easy to 'get lost' or go unnoticed."

Life

Football (this is Razorback country) and Greek activities are prevalent on campus, though some students say, "The school is very centered around Greek life, so for some students it is harder for them to find their place outside of Greek life." The school's location in the Ozark Mountains gives students ample opportunities for "hiking, kayaking, [and] rock climbing" on the weekends. Popular destinations "nearby to take daytrips with your friends [include] Devil's Den or Crystal Bridges." Students say, "The pace of life is comfortably slow, but still full of fun opportunities," and Fayetteville "is an incredibly vibrant city because it is a refreshing combination of elements of the old South and collegiate culture." One popular destination is Dickson Street, "home to a plethora of bars and restaurants." On campus, when the Razorbacks are playing, "The whole state turns up to 'Call the Hogs' on to victory." For those who aren't as interested in athletics, luckily, a "school this big has enough people of diverse interests to create a club or event almost incredibly tailored to you."

Student Body

Students describe their peers as "friendly" and living "relaxed lifestyles" but are quick to point out that this doesn't mean "they are not high-achieving students." In general, students say they're an "adventurous, fun loving, welcoming, genuine, [and] creative" bunch. While some say the school is "very diverse for a Southern university," others lament the lack of diversity and say that the campus is "very much white, upper-middle class" students from Arkansas and the surrounding states, noting that more could be done in "advocating for marginalized groups." But despite the lack of diversity, students say that their peers are "accepting" and "kind," and that "the campus has a very warm feeling to it."

UNIVERSITY OF ARKANSAS—FAYETTEVILLE

Financial Aid: 479-575-3806 • E-Mail: uofa@uark.edu • Website: http://www.uark.edu

THE PRINCETON REVIEW SAYS

Admissions

Very important factors considered include: academic GPA, standardized test scores. *Important factors considered include:* Other factors considered include: rigor of secondary school record, class rank, application essay, recommendation(s), extracurricular activities, talent/ability, character/personal qualities, first generation, alumni/ae relation, geographical residence, state residency, volunteer work, work experience. Require ACT with or without writing accepted SAT with or without Essay component accepted High school diploma is required and GED is accepted. *Academic units required:* 4 English, 4 math, 3 science, 1 science lab, 1 social studies, 2 history, 2 academic electives. *Academic units recommended:* 4 English, 4 math, 3 science, 1 science lab, 2 foreign language, 1 social studies, 2 history, 2 academic electives.

Financial Aid

Students should submit: FAFSA. The Princeton Review suggests that all financial aid forms be submitted as soon as possible after October 1. *Need-based scholarships/grants offered:* College/university scholarship or grant aid from institutional funds; Federal Pell; Private scholarships; SEOG; State scholarships/grants. *Loan aid offered:* Direct PLUS loans; Direct Subsidized Stafford Loans; Direct Unsubsidized Stafford Loans. Applicants will be notified of awards on or about 4/1. Federal Work-Study Program available. Institutional employment available.

The Inside Word

Admissions requirements differ for in-state and out-of-state applicants but are still very simple: Arkansas residents need a 3.0 high school GPA and a minimum score of 20 on the ACT. Generally, out-of-state applicants have the same minimum requirements as Arkansas residents, however, a holistic review process may occur in years where demand increases (or when class size is limited). If you are taking the SAT, it's best to check the school's website for comparable minimum SAT scores needed for admission. University of Arkansas has a rolling admissions policy, with the process beginning on September 1 for admission next fall. It's always in a prospective student's best interest to apply as early as possible. The school encourages students who do not meet the minimum admissions requirements to apply anyway, as records indicating academic improvement are considered on a case-by-case basis.

THE SCHOOL SAYS "..."

From the Admissions Office

"The University of Arkansas is located in Fayetteville, consistently named among the top five places to live in the country. Nestled in the beautiful Ozark Mountains, the university is both a land-grant university for Arkansas and the state's flagship university, encompassing more than 130 buildings on 718 acres and providing more than 230 graduate and undergraduate academic programs—more than any other university in the state. At the same time, the University of Arkansas maintains a low student-to-faculty ratio—currently 18:1—that makes personal attention possible. The university aggressively promotes undergraduate research in virtually every discipline and makes higher education affordable with competitively priced tuition and generous financial aid. University undergraduates have earned many honors; 57 received Goldwater Scholarships. There have been 142 National Science Foundation Graduate Research Fellows; 96 Fulbright Students; eight British Marshall Scholars; and 24 Truman Scholars. Nine undergraduates have received Udall scholarships; seven earned Madison scholarships; and 10 received Rhodes scholarships. Quality programs in 10 colleges and schools, affordable tuition, and the level of student achievement all contribute to the University of Arkansas consistently being ranked in the top tier of national universities. The Carnegie Foundation categorizes the university among institutions with the highest level of research activity. Northwest Arkansas is the headquarters to several major international corporations that have close ties to the university: Tyson Foods, the world's largest protein producer; J.B. Hunt Transport Services Inc., a major transportation and logistics company; and Wal-Mart Stores Inc., the world's largest corporation."

SELECTIVITY

Admissions Rating	83
# of applicants	17,913
% of applicants accepted	77
% of acceptees attending	33
# offered a place on the wait list	187
% accepting a place on wait list	98
% admitted from wait list	90

FRESHMAN PROFILE

Range SAT EBRW	570–650
Range SAT Math	550–650
Range SAT Composite	1130–1280
Range ACT Composite	23–30
# submitting SAT scores	1,178
% submitting SAT scores	26
# submitting ACT scores	4,105
% submitting ACT scores	89
Average HS GPA	3.7
% graduated top 10% of class	25
% graduated top 25% of class	52
% graduated top 50% of class	83

DEADLINES

Early action	
Deadline	11/1
Notification	12/15
Regular	
Priority	11/1
Deadline	8/1
Notification	Rolling, 9/1
Nonfall registration?	Yes

FINANCIAL FACTS

Financial Aid Rating	82
Annual in-state tuition	$7,568
Annual out-of-state tuition	$24,056
Room and board	$11,330
Required fees	$1,816
Books and supplies	$1,100
Average frosh need-based scholarship	$7,324
Average UG need-based scholarship	$7,799
% needy frosh rec. need-based scholarship or grant aid	79
% needy UG rec. need-based scholarship or grant aid	75
% needy frosh rec. non-need-based scholarship or grant aid	11
% needy UG rec. non-need-based scholarship or grant aid	9
% needy frosh rec. need-based self-help aid	66
% needy UG rec. need-based self-help aid	68
% frosh rec. any financial aid	77
% UG rec. any financial aid	70
% UG borrow to pay for school	47
Average cumulative indebtedness	$25,778
% frosh need fully met	14
% ugrads need fully met	13
Average % of frosh need met	55
Average % of ugrad need met	56

UNIVERSITY OF CALIFORNIA—BERKELEY

110 Sproul Hall, Berkeley, CA 94720-5800 • Admissions: 510-642-6000

CAMPUS LIFE
Quality of Life Rating	82
Fire Safety Rating	96
Green Rating	99
Type of school	Public
Environment	City

STUDENTS
Total undergrad enrollment	31,780
% male/female	46/53
% from out of state	16
% frosh live on campus	94
% ugrads live on campus	27
# of fraternities (% ugrad men join)	38 (3)
# of sororities (% ugrad women join)	19 (9)
% African American	2
% Asian	36
% Caucasian	24
% Hispanic	16
% Native American	<1
% Pacific Islander	<1
% Two or more races	6
% Race and/or ethnicity unknown	4
% international	13

SURVEY SAYS . . .
Lots of liberal students
Great library
Great off-campus food
Everyone loves the Golden Bears
Students politically aware
Campus newspaper is popular

ACADEMICS
Academic Rating	83
% students returning for sophomore year	97
% students graduating within 4 years	75
Calendar	Semester
Student/faculty ratio	19:1
Profs interesting rating	85
Profs accessible rating	87

Most classes have 10–19 students.
Most lab/discussion sessions have
20–29 students.

MOST POPULAR MAJORS
Computer Engineering, General; Political Science;
Economics; Business Administration

STUDENTS SAY "..."

Academics

The flagship campus of the University of California school system with a "highly respectable name," UC Berkeley "has great faculty, great research, great classes, and everyone knows it." The school "really encourages us to go out and learn, both inside and outside the classroom," and there is a real commitment to "a well- rounded, diverse education" that permeates the curriculum. "Berkeley is defined by its open, liberal education and culture for independent and collaborative thinking across all fields," sums up a senior molecular toxicology major.

Professors here are "fantastic," "the best in their fields," and each "offers a diverse perspective" toward the academic experience. There are some complaints that larger freshman courses can be "somewhat terrible" and "experience from professors can range widely" (though graduate student instructors "are very accessible and helpful"), but it is universally agreed that "after getting through lower division prerequisite classes, [the] academic experience has significantly improved." All faculty "have full command of their subjects and are determined to find an answer to anything they don't know, within their discipline."

UC Berkeley is known for having "some of the best engineering programs across the board among colleges," and it doesn't hurt that the school's Silicon Valley home is the "best location in the country for entrepreneurship and innovation." "Top-notch" research abounds, and there are "plenty of opportunities for undergrads to engage in it." "Berkeley will offer you all the opportunity you can handle, it's up to you to take hold of it," says a student.

Life

There's "a constant buzz of student activity that drives everyday life" at Cal, where "academics are a priority" and "every single person has something that they are very passionate about and talking to them for five minutes about it makes you wonder if you should change your major." Students also really appreciate all of the tradition present at Cal. "It's a great choice for students who want the feeling of a big state school but want to also be pushed to their limits," says one. Berkeley is "very hard so free time isn't like it is at other places," but an "amazing community" of student-run organizations and "clubs, sports, student-run classes, seminars, [and] research opportunities" are among the "many different venues for people to find their passion." There's a lot to do off-campus in the downtown Berkeley area, and using the BART is "really convenient and time-saving to go to San Francisco." On campus, there is everything "from frat houses to coffee shop discussions, hiking the fire trails to studying for finals." In those moments that studying abates (a particular rarity for engineers), a lot of students enjoy going to football games, restaurant hopping, or (especially during welcome week) party hopping. Many people here do like to party and drink, but "if that's not your style there are plenty of others to spend time with."

Student Body

Berkeley is a large school, so clusters naturally form along lines such as major or dorm, but all "mix among each other easily." "From clubs to DeCal courses, there is no way a student will not make a group of friends while here at Cal," says a junior. Most Berkeley students are generally "politically liberal, nonreligious, and pretty independent," and there is a large Asian student contingent here. One of the defining characteristics of a Cal student is "the ability to hold high-level conversation about basically anything." Everyone is accepted in here, "regardless of their sexual orientation, religion, or political beliefs."

UNIVERSITY OF CALIFORNIA—BERKELEY

Website: www.berkeley.edu

THE PRINCETON REVIEW SAYS

Admissions

Very important factors considered include: rigor of secondary school record, academic GPA, application essay, standardized test scores. *Important factors considered include:* extracurricular activities, character/personal qualities. *Other factors considered include:* recommendation(s), first generation, state residency. ACT with Writing required. SAT with Essay component required. High school diploma is required and GED is accepted. *Academic units required:* 4 English, 3 math, 2 science, 2 science labs, 2 foreign language, 2 history, 1 academic elective, 1 visual/performing arts. *Academic units recommended:* 4 English, 4 math, 3 science, 3 science labs, 3 foreign language, 2 history, 1 academic elective, 1 visual/performing arts.

Financial Aid

Students should submit: FAFSA; State aid form. Priority filing deadline is 3/2. The Princeton Review suggests that all financial aid forms be submitted as soon as possible after October 1. *Need-based scholarships/grants offered:* College/university scholarship or grant aid from institutional funds; Federal Pell; Private scholarships; SEOG; State scholarships/grants. *Loan aid offered:* Direct PLUS loans; Direct Subsidized Stafford Loans; Direct Unsubsidized Stafford Loans. Applicants will be notified of awards on or about 3/31. Federal Work-Study Program available. Institutional employment available.

The Inside Word

UC Berkeley is a top-notch public university with a well-regarded English and Literature department. Importance is placed on the totality of a student's application with a joint focus on the personal statement and academic excellence as noted by a student's GPA. Class rank isn't considered. The school is home to an incredible amount of students with as wide a range of interests. Successful applicants here are generally stellar both academically and personally. Applications, especially the personal statement, should create a picture of a unique candidate with a diversity of skills to offer this active community.

THE SCHOOL SAYS "..."

From the Admissions Office

"One of the top public universities in the nation and the world, the University of California—Berkeley offers a vast range of courses and a full menu of extracurricular activities. Berkeley's academic programs are internationally recognized for their excellence. Undergraduates can choose one of 100 majors. Thirty-five departments are top ranked, more than any other college or university in the country. Access to one of the foremost university libraries enriches studies. There are twenty-three specialized libraries on campus and distinguished museums of anthropology, paleontology, and science.

"All applicants must take the ACT plus writing or the SAT Reasoning Test. UC admissions requirements are found at http://www.universityofcalifornia.edu/admissions/freshman/requirements/index.html."

SELECTIVITY

Admissions Rating	97
# of applicants	87,398
% of applicants accepted	17
% of acceptees attending	44
# offered a place on the wait list	7,531
% accepting a place on wait list	53
% admitted from wait list	28

FRESHMAN PROFILE

Range SAT EBRW	640–740
Range SAT Math	660–790
Range SAT Composite	1330–1520
Range ACT Composite	28–34
# submitting SAT scores	5,265
% submitting SAT scores	81
# submitting ACT scores	2,681
% submitting ACT scores	41
Average HS GPA	3.9
% graduated top 10% of class	98
% graduated top 25% of class	100
% graduated top 50% of class	100

DEADLINES

Regular	
Deadline	11/30
Notification	3/31
Nonfall registration?	Yes

FINANCIAL FACTS

Financial Aid Rating	87
Annual in-state tuition	$11,442
Annual out-of-state tuition	$41,196
Room and board	$19,556
Required fees	$2,784
Books and supplies	$1,091
Average frosh need-based scholarship	$23,767
Average UG need-based scholarship	$22,420
% needy frosh rec. need-based scholarship or grant aid	92
% needy UG rec. need-based scholarship or grant aid	94
% needy frosh rec. non-need-based scholarship or grant aid	3
% needy UG rec. non-need-based scholarship or grant aid	2
% needy frosh rec. need-based self-help aid	64
% needy UG rec. need-based self-help aid	62
% frosh rec. any financial aid	41
% UG rec. any financial aid	44
% UG borrow to pay for school	32
Average cumulative indebtedness	$19,733
% frosh need fully met	29
% ugrads need fully met	29
Average % of frosh need met	83
Average % of ugrad need met	83

UNIVERSITY OF CALIFORNIA—DAVIS

178 Mrak Hall, One Shields Ave, Davis, CA 95616 • Admissions: 530-752-2971 • Fax: 530-752-1280

STUDENTS SAY ". . ."

Academics
Situated on a "large campus [with] lots of land" in northern California, the University of California, Davis is "a prestigious research university with great professors and brilliant students." With a longtime "focus on the agriculture and biological science," Davis has cultivated a "strong science-based education." Students also praise its "other great programs such as engineering and political science," as well as the "large variety of majors and [programs] offered" by the university. "Davis does have a fast-paced quarter system," but the "resources available to assist students" help them "feel at ease with their quarters." Beyond the "abundant research, internship, and job opportunities," Davis students rave about the support they receive from "tutoring and advising resources, opportunities to have a focus within each major, study abroad opportunities," and "all the counselors who can answer every question." "Professors here are true experts," and they have generated "a great research legacy in the animal, ag, environmental, health, and food sciences." "Top researchers are clearly going to get a place at UC Davis," which means that "classes are full of challenging, hands-on experiences." Students benefit from "passionate and devoted" scholars who "have their own research projects going on, and apply what they are teaching to their work." Students point out that "research skills do not translate into teaching skills," so some professors who "are pioneers," "superb at research," "and enthusiastic about their field of study" "might not be too good at teaching." But even when professors "seem to be more focused on research," "teaching assistants who want to help students" and "are also really great and amazing people" provide support. These stellar "TAs have a HUGE impact on classes" and contribute to the "very supportive campus community." Overall, UC Davis students agree that "the majority of my professors [care] very deeply about teaching" and provide a "challenging, but rewarding and successful academic experience."

Life
UC Davis students boast about belonging to a "green school" that "promotes sustainability." Many students gravitate towards "outdoor activities to fill their time," like "pick-up soccer, slack lining," visiting the local farmers market or "reading at the arboretum." Students tell us that "even if you don't have a car," the "bike paths make it really easy to get around the city and campus" and the "free convenient bus systems" ensure there are "plenty of transportation options" available to students. Many say that Davis owes its "relaxed vibe" to the "close-knit" campus community where "everyone is very supportive of each other" and to the surrounding town that "supports the school." But many students point out that "despite the friendly community, we can still be educationally competitive." The "fast paced quarter system" keeps students busy, but students still say they maintain a good "balance between school life and their social life because of all the opportunities and activities to do on campus." With "700+ clubs on campus including seventy-one Greek organizations," many students spend their weeknights at club events. The downtown Davis nightlife is "mostly low-key," but students can enjoy "good food, open mic night, trivia night," " local shows, line dancing, and just about everything in between." And because it is near "Tahoe, San Francisco, [and] Napa," Davis is "a great location for day trips or weekend trips."

Student Body
Davis is a "pretty diverse community" where most students are "very friendly and thoughtful" and "few are quick to judge." "Most students spend their days biking furiously from class to class," but "everyone is very nice and welcoming." "Anyone can ask any student for directions and the student will gladly stop biking to help out." While Davis "is a top university, you don't feel like everyone is competing against you" and "help from your peers" is easy to find. And while Davis students "are academically rigorous," they are "quirky and [creative]" too, creating "the perfect mixture of serious about studying and down to earth and fun." They like to take advantage of the "beautiful campus," and "on sunny days, the quad is always filled with students lying down or sleeping in the hammocks." "Most people get involved in one of the clubs or athletics" groups, and "most are also very open to making new friends or trying something new."

UNIVERSITY OF CALIFORNIA—DAVIS

Financial Aid: 530-752-2396 • E-Mail: undergraduateadmissions@ucdavis.edu • Website: www.ucdavis.edu

THE PRINCETON REVIEW SAYS

Admissions

Very important factors considered include: rigor of secondary school record, academic GPA, application essay, standardized test scores. *Important factors considered include:* extracurricular activities, talent/ability, character/personal qualities. *Other factors considered include:* first generation, state residency, work experience. ACT with Writing required. SAT with Essay component required. High school diploma is required and GED is accepted. *Academic units required:* 4 English, 3 math, 2 science, 2 science labs, 2 foreign language, 2 history, 1 academic elective, 1 visual/performing arts. *Academic units recommended:* 4 English, 4 math, 3 science, 3 science labs, 3 foreign language, 2 history, 1 academic elective, 1 visual/performing arts.

Financial Aid

Students should submit: FAFSA; State aid form. Priority filing deadline is 3/2. The Princeton Review suggests that all financial aid forms be submitted as soon as possible after October 1. *Need-based scholarships/grants offered:* College/university scholarship or grant aid from institutional funds; Federal Pell; Private scholarships; SEOG; State scholarships/grants. *Loan aid offered:* Direct PLUS loans; Direct Subsidized Stafford Loans; Direct Unsubsidized Stafford Loans. Applicants will be notified of awards on a rolling basis beginning 3/10. Federal Work-Study Program available. Institutional employment available.

The Inside Word

Admission to UC Davis is not as competitive as, say, admission to Berkeley. Nevertheless, every school in the UC system is world-class, and the UC system in general is geared toward the best and brightest of not only California's high school students but the nation and the globe.

THE SCHOOL SAYS "..."

From the Admissions Office

"One of the world's top-tier public research universities, UC Davis offers undergraduates a challenging education and unmatched research opportunities in more than 100 majors. Our community encourages students to ask questions and work alongside faculty members, who are engaged in research and solving today's critical issues. UC Davis supports student involvement in leadership and honors programs, career exploration through internships, learning by studying abroad and volunteering through programs like our student-run community clinics.

"UC Davis students are part of an active, diverse student community on a beautiful campus immersed in the arts and sciences. Aggies enjoy world-class cultural programs at the Robert and Margrit Mondavi Center for the Performing Arts, cheer on our NCAA Division I sports teams, learn how to ride at the Equestrian Center and stay fit at the Activities and Recreation Center. The friendly, supportive nature of our campus and surrounding community welcomes exploration of all kinds: learning about new cultures at a cultural celebration or in a themed residence hall, meeting new friends through our more than 750 student-run organizations, or building a career network before graduation.

"Apply and discover why the value of a UC Davis education and the income potential of our graduates placed UC Davis on The Princeton Review's elite list of *Colleges That Pay You Back*. The UC application is available in August. Freshman applicants are required to take the ACT Assessment plus Writing or the SAT Reasoning Test no later than December. SAT subject tests are not required."

SELECTIVITY

Admissions Rating	90
# of applicants	76,647
% of applicants accepted	41
% of acceptees attending	20
# offered a place on the wait list	9,213
% accepting a place on wait list	35
% admitted from wait list	1

FRESHMAN PROFILE

Range SAT EBRW	570–670
Range SAT Math	580–740
Range ACT Composite	25–31
# submitting SAT scores	4,544
% submitting SAT scores	71
# submitting ACT scores	1,829
% submitting ACT scores	29
Average HS GPA	4.0

DEADLINES

Regular	
Deadline	11/30
Notification	3/31
Nonfall registration?	No

FINANCIAL FACTS

Financial Aid Rating	85
Annual in-state tuition	$11,442
Annual out-of-state tuition	$40,434
Room and board	$15,863
Required fees	$3,050
Books and supplies	$1,159
Average frosh need-based scholarship	$21,402
Average UG need-based scholarship	$19,236
% needy frosh rec. need-based scholarship or grant aid	96
% needy UG rec. need-based scholarship or grant aid	97
% needy frosh rec. non-need-based scholarship or grant aid	2
% needy UG rec. non-need-based scholarship or grant aid	2
% needy frosh rec. need-based self-help aid	53
% needy UG rec. need-based self-help aid	51
% frosh rec. any financial aid	67
% UG rec. any financial aid	71
% UG borrow to pay for school	48
Average cumulative indebtedness	$18,575
% frosh need fully met	24
% ugrads need fully met	22
Average % of frosh need met	83
Average % of ugrad need met	81

UNIVERSITY OF CALIFORNIA—LOS ANGELES

1147 Murphy Hall, Los Angeles, CA 90095-1436 • Admissions: 310-825-3101 • Fax: 310-206-1206

CAMPUS LIFE

Quality of Life Rating	88
Fire Safety Rating	92
Green Rating	93
Type of school	Public
Environment	Metropolis

STUDENTS

Total undergrad enrollment	31,441
% male/female	42/58
% from out of state	13
% frosh from public high school	74
% frosh live on campus	98
% ugrads live on campus	48
# of fraternities (% ugrad men join)	35 (11)
# of sororities (% ugrad women join)	35 (13)
% African American	3
% Asian	28
% Caucasian	26
% Hispanic	22
% Native American	<1
% Pacific Islander	<1
% Two or more races	6
% Race and/or ethnicity unknown	3
% international	11
# of countries represented	116

SURVEY SAYS . . .

Great library
Recreation facilities are great
Campus newspaper is popular

ACADEMICS

Academic Rating	82
% students returning for sophomore year	96
% students graduating within 4 years	79
% students graduating within 6 years	91
Calendar	Quarter
Student/faculty ratio	18:1
Profs interesting rating	82
Profs accessible rating	86

Most classes have 10–19 students.
Most lab/discussion sessions have
20–29 students.

MOST POPULAR MAJORS

Biology/Biological Sciences, General; Psychology,
General; Business/Managerial Economics

STUDENTS SAY "..."

Academics

Undergrads at this esteemed university don't mince words when boasting about all that UCLA has to offer. As a geography and environmental science double-major proudly declares, "There's nothing that can't be accomplished at UCLA. The possibilities are endless, and the resources are unparalleled." Moreover, students appreciate the "ideal" location as well as the "pride of going to a Division I school with more NCAA championships than any other college/university." Perhaps more notable, "UCLA is the kind of school that pushes you to work hard academically but reminds you that interaction with people outside of the classroom is just as important." Students are continually impressed by their professors who are "leaders in their field." Indeed, most consider it "a privilege to study under them." While some undergrads caution that you might encounter some teachers simply "in it for the research," others insist, "Most professors care about their students." A political science major interjects, saying that professors "are willing to work extra hours with students and help us with anything we need." An English major concurs, sharing, "I have never had a professor that I did not feel comfortable approaching, which has made my academic experience incredibly more beneficial." As this grateful junior succinctly explains, "UCLA is the campus. The people, the weather, the academics, the sports; it has absolutely everything I could ever want."

Life

There's so much "hustle and bustle" at UCLA that it would be virtually "impossible to [be] bored." While nearly everyone's "main focus is on school," most students also know how to "play hard." Indeed, "whether it be in Greek life, a club or organization, everybody has somewhere they can go to relax and have some fun. The apartments are close to campus, so nearly everybody lives in a small area with close proximity." Sports "are extremely popular here, and conversations about the Bruins are common." There are also "tons of movie showings on campus, recreation centers, pools, activities, [and] events." Additionally, students love being located in Los Angeles. A happy senior reveals, "You can take a five-minute drive and you'll be soaking in the Pacific Ocean, or take an hour drive where you can be hitting the slopes in Big Bear. You can walk down to the theater and run into Jennifer Lopez. The possibilities are endless here, with or without money."

Student Body

UCLA "is the mold that fits you." More than 30,000 undergraduates and more than 1,000 student groups virtually assure that "there is no 'typical' student" to be found at UCLA. This wide range of individuals and activities guarantees that "everyone has their niche." Certainly, the Bruin community is a "vibrant" one, and "the unmatched diversity broadens students' horizons culturally and socially." Of course, undergrads here do tread some common ground. Many define their peers as "very hardworking and ambitious," and they typically "strive for success and to do their absolute best." They "know how to have a good time, but they also know when it is time to study." Further, it's an active student body, and it often "seems like everyone is in at least one club or organization." Friendliness is another trademark of UCLA undergrads as a physiology major assures us, "It is very easy to talk to and meet new people and make new friends." Fortunately, most people are "laid-back," and while "academically invested,...[they're] not outright competitive with other students." This bio major sums up his peers easily by saying, "Everyone comes from different backgrounds with varied interests. The only common denominator is truly an appetite for excellence."

UNIVERSITY OF CALIFORNIA—LOS ANGELES

Financial Aid: 310-206-0400 • Website: www.ucla.edu

THE PRINCETON REVIEW SAYS

Admissions

Very important factors considered include: rigor of secondary school record, academic GPA, application essay, standardized test scores. *Important factors considered include:* extracurricular activities, talent/ability, character/personal qualities. *Other factors considered include:* first generation, geographical residence, state residency. ACT with Writing required. SAT with Essay component required. High school diploma is required and GED is accepted. *Academic units required:* 4 English, 3 math, 2 science, 2 science labs, 2 foreign language, 2 history, 1 academic elective, 1 visual/performing arts. *Academic units recommended:* 4 English, 4 math, 3 science, 3 science labs, 3 foreign language, 2 history, 1 academic elective, 1 visual/performing arts.

Financial Aid

Students should submit: FAFSA. Priority filing deadline is 3/2. The Princeton Review suggests that all financial aid forms be submitted as soon as possible after October 1. *Need-based scholarships/grants offered:* College/university scholarship or grant aid from institutional funds; Federal Pell; Private scholarships; SEOG; State scholarships/grants. *Loan aid offered:* Direct PLUS loans; Direct Subsidized Stafford Loans; Direct Unsubsidized Stafford Loans. Applicants will be notified of awards on a rolling basis beginning 3/15. Federal Work-Study Program available. Institutional employment available.

The Inside Word

Competition is fierce to secure admittance to one of the nation's top public universities. Academic success is paramount, and your GPA and standardized test scores factor heavily into admissions decisions. You'll want to load up on challenging courses in high school. Indeed, taking advanced placement, IB, or honors classes is a must. Of course, UCLA also wants students who will actively contribute to their community, and it's also important to demonstrate commitment to extracurricular activities.

THE SCHOOL SAYS "..."

From the Admissions Office

"Undergraduates arrive at UCLA from throughout California and around the world with exceptional levels of academic preparation. They are attracted by our acclaimed degree programs, distinguished faculty, and the beauty of a park-like campus set amid the dynamism of the nation's second-largest city. UCLA's highly ranked undergraduate programs incorporate cutting-edge technology and teaching techniques that hone the critical-thinking skills and the global perspectives necessary for success in our rapidly changing world. The diversity of these programs draws strength from a student body that mirrors the cultural and ethnic vibrancy of Los Angeles. Generally ranked among the nation's top half-dozen universities, UCLA is at once distinguished and dynamic, academically rigorous, and responsive.

"All applicants must take the ACT plus writing or the SAT Reasoning Test. Be sure to complete these tests by December. Engineering applicants are strongly urged to take the SAT Subject Test in math level 2, to demonstrate the proficiency in mathematics needed for success in Engineering courses."

SELECTIVITY

Admissions Rating	98
# of applicants	111,322
% of applicants accepted	12
% of acceptees attending	43

FRESHMAN PROFILE

Range SAT EBRW	640–740
Range SAT Math	640–790
Range SAT Composite	1290–1510
Range ACT Composite	27–34
# submitting SAT scores	4,735
% submitting SAT scores	80
# submitting ACT scores	2,586
% submitting ACT scores	44
Average HS GPA	3.9
% graduated top 10% of class	97
% graduated top 25% of class	100
% graduated top 50% of class	100

DEADLINES

Regular	
Deadline	11/30
Notification	3/31
Nonfall registration?	No

FINANCIAL FACTS

Financial Aid Rating	87
Annual in-state tuition	$11,442
Annual out-of-state tuition	$40,434
Room and board	$15,902
Required fees	$1,784
Books and supplies	$1,464
Average frosh need-based scholarship	$20,926
Average UG need-based scholarship	$20,775
% needy frosh rec. need-based scholarship or grant aid	96
% needy UG rec. need-based scholarship or grant aid	96
% needy frosh rec. non-need-based scholarship or grant aid	4
% needy UG rec. non-need-based scholarship or grant aid	2
% needy frosh rec. need-based self-help aid	54
% needy UG rec. need-based self-help aid	55
% frosh rec. any financial aid	53
% UG rec. any financial aid	54
% UG borrow to pay for school	42
Average cumulative indebtedness	$22,390
% frosh need fully met	27
% ugrads need fully met	24
Average % of frosh need met	81
Average % of ugrad need met	82

University of California—Merced

5200 Lake Road, Merced, CA 95343 • Admissions: 209-228-7178 • Fax: 209-228-4244

STUDENTS SAY "..."

Academic

University of California—Merced is quickly building a name for itself as a cutting-edge research university with a focus on sustainability, and it has acted as a boon to the San Joaquin Valley since it opened. Undergraduates can avail themselves of twenty-four "new, groundbreaking majors" and twenty-five minors. The campus has several specialized research institutes and centers and plenty of further opportunities "for growth and creation since it's such a new school." Students find that "the school is great at supporting you on every single level." In fact, "there are multiple programs to help support students mentally and educationally." That educational support is nowhere more apparent than in the fact that "no faculty or staff will ever turn down a question, comment or concern." As such, professors "are always there for students," and it is "extremely easy to make an appointment when necessary." One student comments, "They all go out of their way to make sure every question is answered." Therefore, students find it's easy to "connect with your professor on a personal level and get advice from them for your career path and educational goals." Plus, "they bring their love for the community and the material into the class." Overall, "class sizes are kept reasonably small" and "even in a lecture class, it's a discussion." More generally, the school "is always ahead of modern technology," which "gives the students a feeling of importance and relevance to the growing research" at the school. UC Merced "always displays and announces any new project they are launching"; it "has all the benefits of a research school as well as the benefits of a small college."

Life

Students note that, because of the school's rural location, there's "not much to do on campus except study." Because students are required to live on campus for their first two years, this leads "students [to] get creative." It also means "there's no need to force school spirit because everyone has it." At UC Merced, "it's extremely easy to get involved in things you believe in." After getting back to the dorms from classes, "friends hang out on their [dorms'] lounge or activities room," and "a lot of people head to the gym to work out." Students who enjoy outdoor physical exercise note that "there are tons of bike trails and beautiful landscapes to see." For those with cars (or friend with cars), long weekends offer even more outdoors opportunities, like a "drive to Yosemite for a nice hike" or a visit to Fresno and the Bay Area: "Merced [is] the perfect distance ... from all major cities in California."

Student Body

There is a common "craving for knowledge" among this group of "people from many backgrounds that have come together to learn." More than half of the student body is Hispanic, with almost three-quarters being first-generation college students. But regardless of background, students categorize their peers as "kind," "curious," and "motivated." One says, "If you're struggling you can ask for help and actually receive it." This "incredibly unified and inclusive" bunch makes UC Merced feel "almost as if it [is] a party for intellectuals." As evidence of this, "friends are easily made in and out of classes," and they "are always willing to lend a hand, whether [it] be personally, academically, or financially."

UNIVERSITY OF CALIFORNIA—MERCED

Financial Aid: 209-228-7178 • E-Mail: admissions@ucmerced.edu • Website: http://www.ucmerced.edu

THE PRINCETON REVIEW SAYS

Admissions

Very important factors considered include: rigor of secondary school record, academic GPA, application essay, standardized test scores. *Important factors considered include:* extracurricular activities, talent/ability. *Other factors considered include:* recommendation(s), character/personal qualities, first generation, geographical residence, state residency, volunteer work, work experience. ACT with Writing required. SAT with Essay component required. High school diploma is required and GED is accepted. *Academic units required:* 4 English, 3 math, 2 science, 2 science labs, 2 foreign language, 2 history, 1 academic elective, 1 visual/performing arts. *Academic units recommended:* 4 math, 3 science, 3 science labs, 3 foreign language.

Financial Aid

The Princeton Review suggests that all financial aid forms be submitted as soon as possible after October 1. Federal Work-Study Program available. Institutional employment available.

The Inside Word

For a student to be considered for admission at UC Merced, they must have taken at least fifteen college-prep courses and have a minimum 3.0 GPA if they are a California resident, or a minimum 3.4 GPA if they are out-of-state. Test scores from either the ACT or SAT (with Writing/Essay sections) are also required. University of California campuses share scores, so if your scores are sent to one UC campus, they will also be available to sister campuses where you've applied. All academics are viewed through the context of the student's background, extracurriculars, and personal achievements. Note that the middle 50 percent of admitted students have a GPA ranging from 3.46–3.96, so B students need to have impressive non-academic aspects to get in.

THE SCHOOL SAYS "..."

From the Admissions Office

"The fastest-growing public university in the country, UC Merced is in the midst of an innovative expansion project that will double the physical size of the campus by 2020, while remaining environmentally sustainable. From new housing and labs to recreational areas and classrooms, UC Merced offers undergraduates an opportunity to take control of their education in 24 different majors. As a high-level research institution, undergraduate research opportunities with cutting-edge researchers and pioneers of change in the Central Valley and state of California are available as soon as students arrive on campus.

"Undergraduates can explore Yosemite National Park as a member of the Yosemite Leadership Program or create the newest start-up as a member of an Engineering Service Learning team. With an undergraduate curriculum that reflects the university's mission of interdisciplinarity, students can earn intellectual experience badges in areas like sustainability, leadership, ethics, and media and visual analysis through coursework and co-curricular activities. Living Learning Communities supplement undergraduate curriculum by connecting students with a faculty advisor and graduate student who share a passion in science, leadership, social justice and other areas.

"Students are prepared for a career after college through a strategic approach to talent development. Students are introduced to internship programs and partnerships with organizations that will help them build the skills necessary for the jobs of the future, not the past. With small class sizes and lab opportunities, students can build connections with faculty that facilitate continuation into graduate degrees."

SELECTIVITY
Admissions Rating	77
# of applicants	25,368
% of applicants accepted	72
% of acceptees attending	12

FRESHMAN PROFILE
Range SAT EBRW	490–590
Range SAT Math	490–590
Range ACT Composite	17–22
# submitting SAT scores	1,931
% submitting SAT scores	92
# submitting ACT scores	891
% submitting ACT scores	42
Average HS GPA	3.6

DEADLINES
Regular	
Deadline	11/30
Notification	Rolling, 3/1
Nonfall registration?	Yes

FINANCIAL FACTS
Financial Aid Rating	88
Annual in-state tuition	$11,502
Annual out-of-state tuition	$39,516
Room and board	$16,454
Required fees	$2,125
Books and supplies	$1,106
Average frosh need-based scholarship	$24,018
Average UG need-based scholarship	$21,453
% needy frosh rec. need-based scholarship or grant aid	99
% needy UG rec. need-based scholarship or grant aid	98
% needy frosh rec. non-need-based scholarship or grant aid	1
% needy UG rec. non-need-based scholarship or grant aid	1
% needy frosh rec. need-based self-help aid	69
% needy UG rec. need-based self-help aid	62
% frosh rec. any financial aid	94
% UG rec. any financial aid	90
% UG borrow to pay for school	71
Average cumulative indebtedness	$18,187
% frosh need fully met	26
% ugrads need fully met	24
Average % of frosh need met	86
Average % of ugrad need met	83

UNIVERSITY OF CALIFORNIA—RIVERSIDE

3106 Student Services Building, Riverside, CA 92521 • Admissions: 951-827-3411 • Fax: 951-827-6344

STUDENTS SAY ". . ."

Academics

Undergraduates at the University of California—Riverside have the opportunity to get "a great education while also having fun." The university goes to great lengths to ensure that "everyone feels welcome and wanted on campus" and that's palpable to the students. Undergrads here also greatly benefit from all the research being conducted at Riverside. As one giddy student explains, "There are so many different projects happening in [a variety of] fields" and the opportunities to participate are quite "generous." Additionally, UCR undergrads appreciate that "there are so many programs to help student[s] stay on track academically and even more to help student[s] in academic recovery." Students have an abundance of courses and majors from which to choose; highlights include the "very prestigious entomology and agriculture departments." In general, students report that professors are "very helpful and friendly." They tend to be "passionate and engaged" as well as "knowledgeable." And they make it abundantly clear that "they love their field, their job, and their students." As one amazed student reveals, "I have not yet met a professor that wasn't happy to rearrange their plans, so they could help a student in need."

Life

Boredom is virtually non-existent at UC Riverside. After all, "there is always something to do on campus throughout the day." For example, "Every week there is a mini-concert in the middle of campus to showcase a local group (small band or DJ)." There are also a number of "career workshops, movie screenings [and] cultural events" of which to take advantage. Additionally, students have the opportunity to participate in "over 400 clubs on campus, many of which organize their own activities and will often go on excursions or trips." A number of undergrads also report that the "party scene is decent," though it's often relegated to the weekend. Outdoor enthusiasts love that UCR is adjacent to the Box Spring Mountains. Hence, there are "a plethora of trails for hiking." Plenty of students can also be found hanging at the Hub which has "a game room where you can play pool, board games or watch TV." Even more enticing, "the recreation center has a hot tub and a recreational pool with vortex current as well as lap pool. It's also possible to play volleyball, basketball, badminton, racquetball, and other games [as well as use] the rock climbing wall." But the best aspect of the rec center? It "provides free massages twice a week."

Student Body

Individuals greatly interested in UC Riverside will be delighted to learn that the school maintains a "very diverse" student body. In turn, this allows all undergrads to truly "feel welcome." Of course, the fact that most students here are "extremely friendly and supportive" also helps. One proud undergrad agrees sharing, "It is easy to approach most people and start a conversation." Beyond their general openness, Riverside students also describe their classmates as "liberal and politically-engaged." Additionally, the vast majority seem to have "an appetite to learn and discover." Perhaps more importantly, undergrads readily assert that their fellow students "are committed to the success of the [Riverside] community as a whole." Indeed, they empathize "with those who are struggling and they seek to be involved both on and off campus." And while they are certainly "passionate about what they believe in," they're also "respectful of...[the] opinions [of others]." Overall, as this grateful undergrad explains, "My peers at the University of California, Riverside make my college experience a great one. They make college feel safe, fun, and exciting." And this fellow student wholeheartedly agrees exclaiming, "College life is stressful but it is easier with the right people surrounding you. And that's what I have here at UCR."

UNIVERSITY OF CALIFORNIA—RIVERSIDE

Financial Aid: 951-827-3878 • E-Mail: admissions@ucr.edu • Website: www.ucr.edu

THE PRINCETON REVIEW SAYS

Admissions

Very important factors considered include: academic GPA, application essay. *Important factors considered include:* rigor of secondary school record. *Other factors considered include:* first generation, standardized test scores, talent/ability, state residency. High school diploma is required and GED is accepted. *Academic units required:* 4 English, 3 math, 2 science, 2 science labs, 2 foreign language, 2 history, 1 academic elective, 1 visual/performing arts. *Academic units recommended:* 4 English, 4 math, 3 science, 3 science labs, 3 foreign language, 2 history, 1 academic elective, 1 visual/performing arts.

Financial Aid

Students should submit: FAFSA; State aid form. Priority filing deadline is 3/2. The Princeton Review suggests that all financial aid forms be submitted as soon as possible after October 1. *Need-based scholarships/grants offered:* College/university scholarship or grant aid from institutional funds; Federal Pell; Private scholarships; SEOG; State scholarships/grants. *Loan aid offered:* Direct PLUS loans; Direct Subsidized Stafford Loans; Direct Unsubsidized Stafford Loans. Applicants will be notified of awards on a rolling basis beginning 3/1. Federal Work-Study Program available. Institutional employment available.

The Inside Word

As one of the top ranking universities within the California system, the admissions process at UC Riverside is certainly competitive. To determine who earns a coveted acceptance letter, the school closely evaluates each student's GPA and standardized test scores. Successful applicants typically have a minimum 3.0 GPA. Admissions officers are also on the lookout for students who have earned a C or higher in AP/IB courses. Lastly, extra consideration is given to both first generation and low income applicants.

THE SCHOOL SAYS "..."

From the Admissions Office

"The University of California, Riverside offers the quality, rigor, and facilities of a world-class research institution, while assuring its undergraduates personal attention and a welcoming campus community. Academic programs, teaching, advising and student services all reflect the supportive attitudes that characterize the campus. Exceptional opportunities include undergraduate research, University Honors, and the Thomas Haider Program (up to 24 spots to the UCR School of Medicine are guaranteed to UCR undergraduates each year). UCR's largest undergraduate program is biology, and it offers the only Bachelor of Arts in Creative Writing in the UC system. Students are actively involved in campus life—thanks to a variety of athletic and cultural events, ethnic and gender programs, community service opportunities and more than 450 student organizations.

All applicants may submit ACT or SAT scores; however, they are not required for admission. Additionally, SAT Subject Tests are not required for admission, but students who are interested in admission to any major in the College of Natural and Agricultural Sciences or the Marlan and Rosemary Bourns College of Engineering are strongly encouraged to take the SAT Subject Test math level 2 and the SAT Subject Test in chemistry or physics."

SELECTIVITY

Admissions Rating	92
# of applicants	49,518
% of applicants accepted	57
% of acceptees attending	17
# offered a place on the wait list	7,776
% accepting a place on wait list	52
% admitted from wait list	34

FRESHMAN PROFILE

Range SAT EBRW	560–650
Range SAT Math	550–690
Range SAT Composite	1130–1330
Range ACT Composite	24–30
# submitting SAT scores	4,470
% submitting SAT scores	94
# submitting ACT scores	1,648
% submitting ACT scores	34
Average HS GPA	3.8
% graduated top 10% of class	94
% graduated top 25% of class	100
% graduated top 50% of class	100

DEADLINES

Regular	
Deadline	11/30
Notification	3/31
Nonfall registration?	No

FINANCIAL FACTS

Financial Aid Rating	86
Annual in-state tuition	$11,442
Annual out-of-state tuition	$41,196
Room and board	$17,350
Required fees	$2,411
Average frosh need-based scholarship	$20,381
Average UG need-based scholarship	$17,670
% needy frosh rec. need-based scholarship or grant aid	96
% needy UG rec. need-based scholarship or grant aid	96
% needy frosh rec. non-need-based scholarship or grant aid	2
% needy UG rec. non-need-based scholarship or grant aid	2
% needy frosh rec. need-based self-help aid	81
% needy UG rec. need-based self-help aid	68
% frosh rec. any financial aid	89
% UG rec. any financial aid	87
% UG borrow to pay for school	62
Average cumulative indebtedness	$20,779
% frosh need fully met	17
% ugrads need fully met	15
Average % of frosh need met	85
Average % of ugrad need met	81

UNIVERSITY OF CALIFORNIA—SAN DIEGO

9500 Gilman Drive, La Jolla, CA 92093-0021 • Admissions: 858-534-4831 • Fax: 858-534-5723

CAMPUS LIFE

Quality of Life Rating	84
Fire Safety Rating	85
Green Rating	97
Type of school	Public
Environment	Metropolis

STUDENTS

Total undergrad enrollment	30,645
% male/female	50/50
% from out of state	7
# of fraternities (% ugrad men join)	16 (14)
# of sororities (% ugrad women join)	12 (14)
% African American	3
% Asian	36
% Caucasian	19
% Hispanic	21
% Native American	<1
% Pacific Islander	<1
% Two or more races	0
% Race and/or ethnicity unknown	2
% international	18
# of countries represented	120

SURVEY SAYS . . .

Students are happy
Great library
Very little drug use

ACADEMICS

Academic Rating	79
% students returning for sophomore year	93
% students graduating within 4 years	55
% students graduating within 6 years	85
Calendar	Quarter
Student/faculty ratio	19:1
Profs interesting rating	81
Profs accessible rating	86

Most classes have 10–19 students.
Most lab/discussion sessions have 10–19 students.

STUDENTS SAY "..."

Academics

UC San Diego is widely regarded by students as "one of the top science universities in the United States." As a result, the school attracts bright students who benefit from "access to cutting edge technology and theories" and "great opportunities for undergraduates to do research." Professors "are incredibly knowledgeable about their material, and many of them are actively doing research in their field." Research opportunities are widely available to undergraduate science majors. However, sciences are not the only attraction here. The university is home to six colleges, a system that students say is "a great way to not feel like a small fish in a huge ocean." Whereas it might seem like some science professors "are more interested in research than teaching," students say, "Humanities professors tend to be more accessible and more interested in their students as well as what they are teaching." Overall, however, "professors are very helpful and willing to take extra time to help students understand material." Given the fact that this is a large public university, students say, "Professors are extremely willing to help and mentor students if you seek them out." Another major benefit to attending a large university is that "there are a lot of resources, and there is always a faculty member or organization that will help you achieve what you want." Students say, "This university will undoubtedly set the new standard of what it means to be an elite public university in the years to come."

Life

Students love to take advantage of UC San Diego's "unbeatable location," ten minutes from the beach and a quick ride away from downtown San Diego. It is easy to enjoy "all the nature around the campus by hiking, biking, [and] camping," or taking surf lessons, which "are offered on campus for a modest fee." It is also "super easy to get to San Diego proper for a fun night out." There is a perception that social life is somewhat lacking on the campus itself, which may be the result of UC San Diego being such a large, academically intensive school. While some students have trouble fitting a social life into their busy study schedules, others say that, in fact, there are "tons of resources and ways to get involved" on campus; students "just have to actively seek them." Plenty of people "play sports or participate in clubs." "Lots of people enjoy ... small parties but the party scene isn't too big here." In the spring, the Sun God Festival is "always a popular event" that brings the entire campus together. There "is not really a huge emphasis on the athletics department," much to the annoyance of some students. However, students who make the most of their experience here maintain, "There is always an event going on and so many clubs to be involved in. From the Greek life, to the intramural sports, to the variety of clubs, there is literally a place for everyone."

Student Body

The typical student at UC San Diego "is a little nerdy and studies a lot." "Doing well academically at UC San Diego is an extreme priority, even to students who are not good students. Most of the students are geared toward extended education or professional school." However, "there are plenty of students who balance academics with other things, like sports or clubs." The student body "has such a diverse range of personalities" that almost anyone "can fit in here because it's such a big school, and there are so many different organizations and places where you can find people that enjoy the same things as you." Students say that the population of students in the humanities has been growing "rapidly" in recent years, but some still see room for improvement among the diversity of the student body. There are those who would love "to see more students become socially conscious" to enhance the overall student body experience on campus.

UNIVERSITY OF CALIFORNIA—SAN DIEGO

Financial Aid: 858-534-4480 • E-Mail: admissionsinfo@ucsd.edu • Website: www.ucsd.edu

THE PRINCETON REVIEW SAYS

Admissions

Very important factors considered include: rigor of secondary school record, academic GPA, application essay, standardized test scores. *Important factors considered include:* extracurricular activities, talent/ability, character/personal qualities, state residency, volunteer work. *Other factors considered include:* first generation, geographical residence, work experience. ACT with Writing required. SAT with Essay component required. High school diploma is required and GED is accepted. *Academic units required:* 4 English, 3 math, 2 science, 2 science labs, 2 foreign language, 2 history, 1 academic elective, 1 visual/performing arts. *Academic units recommended:* 4 English, 4 math, 3 science, 3 science labs, 3 foreign language, 2 history, 1 academic elective, 1 visual/performing arts.

Financial Aid

Students should submit: FAFSA; State aid form. Priority filing deadline is 3/2. The Princeton Review suggests that all financial aid forms be submitted as soon as possible after October 1. *Need-based scholarships/grants offered:* College/university scholarship or grant aid from institutional funds; Federal Pell; Private scholarships; SEOG; State scholarships/grants. *Loan aid offered:* Direct PLUS loans; Direct Subsidized Stafford Loans; Direct Unsubsidized Stafford Loans. Applicants will be notified of awards on a rolling basis beginning 3/15. Federal Work-Study Program available. Institutional employment available.

The Inside Word

UC San Diego is rapidly earning its place as one of the gems of the UC system, and admission is competitive. Applications are reviewed thoroughly by at least two readers. Applicants will need excellent grades and test scores, and to demonstrate personal qualities like leadership, tenacity, compassion, and independence.

THE SCHOOL SAYS "..."

From the Admissions Office

"UC San Diego is recognized for the exceptional quality of its academic programs. UC San Diego ranks fifth in the nation and first in the University of California system for the amount of federal research dollars spent on research and development; and the university ranks tenth in the nation in the excellence of its graduate programs and the quality of its faculty, according to the most recent National Research Council college rankings.

"About 40 percent of UC San Diego's undergraduates participate in research, developing critical thinking and effective communication skills as well as greater cultural understanding. Their faculty mentors are in the divisions and schools of arts and humanities, biology, engineering, medicine, pharmacy, physical sciences, social sciences, and UC San Diego's Scripps Institution of Oceanography, California Institute for Telecommunications and Information Technology and the San Diego Supercomputer Center. Undergraduates also participate in research at the Salk Institute for Biological Studies and other nearby research institutes and biotechnology companies."

SELECTIVITY

Admissions Rating	97
# of applicants	99,133
% of applicants accepted	32
% of acceptees attending	19

FRESHMAN PROFILE

Range SAT EBRW	610–710
Range SAT Math	620–780
Range ACT Composite	24–33
# submitting SAT scores	5,311
% submitting SAT scores	88
# submitting ACT scores	2,232
% submitting ACT scores	37
Average HS GPA	4.1
% graduated top 10% of class	100
% graduated top 25% of class	100
% graduated top 50% of class	100

DEADLINES

Regular	
Deadline	11/30
Notification	3/31
Nonfall registration?	No

APPLICANTS ALSO LOOK AT AND OFTEN PREFER

University of California, Los Angeles; University of California—Berkeley; Stanford University

AND SOMETIMES PREFER

University of Southern California; University of California, Davis; University of California, Irvine

FINANCIAL FACTS

Financial Aid Rating	87
Annual in-state tuition	$12,570
Annual out-of-state tuition	$42,324
Room and board	$14,295
Required fees	$2,046
Books and supplies	$1,128
Average frosh need-based scholarship	$19,366
Average UG need-based scholarship	$19,496
% needy frosh rec. need-based scholarship or grant aid	94
% needy UG rec. need-based scholarship or grant aid	95
% needy frosh rec. non-need-based scholarship or grant aid	3
% needy UG rec. non-need-based scholarship or grant aid	2
% needy frosh rec. need-based self-help aid	69
% needy UG rec. need-based self-help aid	70
% frosh rec. any financial aid	77
% UG rec. any financial aid	63
% UG borrow to pay for school	45
Average cumulative indebtedness	$21,061
% frosh need fully met	23
% ugrads need fully met	25
Average % of frosh need met	85
Average % of ugrad need met	83

UNIVERSITY OF CALIFORNIA—SANTA BARBARA

Office of Admissions, Santa Barbara, CA 93106-2014 • Admissions: 805-893-2881 • Fax: 805-893-2676

CAMPUS LIFE

Quality of Life Rating	92
Fire Safety Rating	95
Green Rating	98
Type of school	Public
Environment	City

STUDENTS

Total undergrad enrollment	22,186
% male/female	46/54
% from out of state	4
% frosh from public high school	80
% frosh live on campus	95
% ugrads live on campus	38
# of fraternities (% ugrad men join)	12 (4)
# of sororities (% ugrad women join)	20 (8)
% African American	2
% Asian	21
% Caucasian	34
% Hispanic	26
% Native American	<1
% Pacific Islander	<1
% Two or more races	6
% Race and/or ethnicity unknown	1
% international	8
# of countries represented	82

SURVEY SAYS . . .

Students are happy
Lab facilities are great
Students are friendly
Easy to get around campus
Recreation facilities are great
Lots of beer drinking
Hard liquor is popular

ACADEMICS

Academic Rating	83
% students returning for sophomore year	92
% students graduating within 4 years	72
% students graduating within 6 years	88
Calendar	Quarter
Student/faculty ratio	17:1
Profs interesting rating	89
Profs accessible rating	93
Most classes have 20–29 students.	
Most lab/discussion sessions have 20–29 students.	

MOST POPULAR MAJORS

Economics, General; Biology/Biological Sciences, General; Psychology, General

STUDENTS SAY ". . ."

Academics

It's easy to be dazzled by this University of California's "incredible location" in stunning Santa Barbara, but UCSB is much more than a "safe and beautiful campus." "It has one of the top chemical engineering departments in the country," a "highly ranked" mechanical engineering program, and is generally "strong in the sciences." Outstanding students can enroll in the College of Creative Studies, which acts as the university's Honors program and requires a supplemental application: CCS students report that it "allows me to pursue my academic interests with maximum freedom." While they love the "laid-back" atmosphere, students regard their course work in any school as both "academically challenging" and "down to earth": "Every other college on my list seemed locked in an ivory tower. UCSB was the exception with both the warm, sun-kissed charm of a beach town and excellent academics." "I would challenge any Ivy school to match" the quality of professors at UCSB, asserts one student, and another says the "outstanding professors" "are definitely an important source of inspiration for me." Some students comment on the "wide range of professors," and point out that "many of [the] professors are Nobel Prize winners or well-known in their field; however, these individuals are not necessarily the best teachers." Overall, though, UBSB undergrads name the "accessibility and knowledge of the professors" as one of the university's strengths. If you're seeking a dynamic college experience with choices within and outside the classroom, UCSB could be for you: "UCSB is the perfect blend of academics and social life. I get to study at a renowned research university and work closely with professors, while living on the beach and making lifelong friendships."

Life

No matter the activity, UCSB students love to be involved: "85 percent of our student body is in at least one extracurricular activity—and I've met the smartest people of my life here." Outdoor pastimes like "rock climbing, beach volleyball," "surfing, hiking," "bik[ing], and skateboard[ing]," figure prominently in students' favorite ways to spend free time wholesomely. After the sun goes down, "a lot of people party at UCSB. What do you expect, we live on a beach? But don't be fooled. I've met some of the smartest, most hardworking people at UCSB." Social life at UCSB is as "varied" as you want it to be: "People think of UCSB exclusively as a party school but it's what you make of it." The party scene "is totally avoidable if you want," but "UCSB is famous for its party life" for a reason. Students looking to avoid drinking and drug culture entirely might be best advised to look elsewhere, and insiders say that "substance abuse is somewhat common off campus and not as much on campus; campus alcohol and drug policies are typically enforced strictly." At the end of the day, "everything is give and take here. You spend your week busting your butt in your internship and churning out research papers, and finish everything up in time to go indulge in some of the debauchery that is DP on a Friday night."

Student Body

To find your place at a big school, get ready to get out and do something: "The typical student is active and involved. Whether it be with sports, or in a community service or environmental club, rock climbing, politics, the list goes on. Students fit in by finding a good group of friends in the dorms and by getting involved in extracurricular activities." Because the university is accessible to so many different types of students, "there is a great sense of community among the students, and those with all sorts of socio-economic backgrounds feel at home here." UCSB undergrads care about more than partying, and are "intelligent, sociable, engaging" as well as "very motivated and driven to succeed academically." People are "laid-back but hard-working," at least partially because "the sunny weather keeps people happy." UCSB is "extremely diverse personality wise": "We've got the hippies, the sorority girls, the surfer dudes, the Jesus-lovers, the anarchists, the school-oriented folk and everything in between. Everyone finds their niche here."

UNIVERSITY OF CALIFORNIA—SANTA BARBARA

Financial Aid: 805-893-2432 • E-Mail: admissions@sa.ucsb.edu • Website: www.ucsb.edu

THE PRINCETON REVIEW SAYS

Admissions

Very important factors considered include: academic GPA, application essay, standardized test scores. *Important factors considered include:* rigor of secondary school record. *Other factors considered include:* extracurricular activities, talent/ability, character/personal qualities, first generation, geographical residence, state residency, volunteer work, work experience. ACT with Writing required. SAT with Essay component required. High school diploma is required and GED is accepted. *Academic units required:* 4 English, 3 math, 2 science, 2 science labs, 2 foreign language, 2 history, 1 academic elective, 1 visual/performing arts. *Academic units recommended:* 4 English, 4 math, 3 science, 3 science labs, 3 foreign language, 2 history, 1 academic elective, 1 visual/performing arts.

Financial Aid

Students should submit: FAFSA. Priority filing deadline is 3/2. The Princeton Review suggests that all financial aid forms be submitted as soon as possible after October 1. *Need-based scholarships/grants offered:* College/university scholarship or grant aid from institutional funds; Federal Pell; SEOG; State scholarships/grants. *Loan aid offered:* Direct PLUS loans; Direct Subsidized Stafford Loans; Direct Unsubsidized Stafford Loans. Federal Work-Study Program available. Institutional employment available.

The Inside Word

UCSB uses a "minimum eligibility" index as a formula to calculate a student's viability for admission; other standards in high school courseload and standardized tests are synthesized with a 3.0 minimum GPA for California students and a 3.4 for out-of-state applicants. Weakness in one area may be balanced out by strength in another, but don't be fooled by the fact that it's a state school: UCSB is competitive.

THE SCHOOL SAYS "..."

From the Admissions Office

"The University of California—Santa Barbara is a major research institution offering undergraduate and graduate education in the arts, humanities, sciences and technology, and social sciences. Large enough to have excellent facilities for study, research, and other creative activities, the campus is also small enough to foster close relationships among faculty and students. The faculty numbers more than 1,000. A member of the most distinguished system of public higher education in the nation, UC—Santa Barbara is committed equally to excellence in scholarship and instruction. Through the general education program, students acquire good grounding in the skills, perceptions, and methods of a variety of disciplines. In addition, because they study with a research faculty, they not only acquire basic skills and broad knowledge but also are exposed to the imagination, inventiveness, and intense concentration that scholars bring to their work. UCSB is one of sixty-two members of the prestigious Association of American Universities.

"All applicants must take the ACT plus writing or the SAT Reasoning Test. SAT Subject Tests are no longer required by the University of California. Students applying to engineering majors are encouraged to take SAT Subject Tests in math (level 2) and a science exam of their choice."

SELECTIVITY

Admissions Rating	95
# of applicants	80,319
% of applicants accepted	33
% of acceptees attending	17
# offered a place on the wait list	6,650
% accepting a place on wait list	60
% admitted from wait list	24

FRESHMAN PROFILE

Range SAT EBRW	620–710
Range SAT Math	620–760
Range ACT Composite	26–32
# submitting SAT scores	3,373
% submitting SAT scores	74
# submitting ACT scores	2,565
% submitting ACT scores	57
Average HS GPA	4.1
% graduated top 10% of class	100
% graduated top 25% of class	100
% graduated top 50% of class	100

DEADLINES

Regular	
Deadline	11/30
Notification	3/1
Nonfall registration?	No

APPLICANTS ALSO LOOK AT AND OFTEN PREFER
University of California, Los Angeles; University of California—Berkeley

AND SOMETIMES PREFER
University of California, Davis; University of California, Irvine

AND RARELY PREFER
California Polytechnic State University; University of California—Santa Cruz

FINANCIAL FACTS

Financial Aid Rating	86
Annual in-state tuition	$12,570
Annual out-of-state tuition	$42,324
Room and board	$15,111
Required fees	$1,875
Books and supplies	$1,143
Average frosh need-based scholarship	$21,635
Average UG need-based scholarship	$20,707
% needy frosh rec. need-based scholarship or grant aid	94
% needy UG rec. need-based scholarship or grant aid	95
% needy frosh rec. non-need-based scholarship or grant aid	0
% needy UG rec. non-need-based scholarship or grant aid	0
% needy frosh rec. need-based self-help aid	0
% needy UG rec. need-based self-help aid	0
% frosh rec. any financial aid	61
% UG rec. any financial aid	59
% UG borrow to pay for school	50
Average cumulative indebtedness	$20,004
% frosh need fully met	18
% ugrads need fully met	17
Average % of frosh need met	81
Average % of ugrad need met	80

UNIVERSITY OF CALIFORNIA—SANTA CRUZ

Office of Admissions, Cook House, Santa Cruz, CA 95064 • Admissions: 831-459-4008 • Fax: 831-459-4452

CAMPUS LIFE

Quality of Life Rating	78
Fire Safety Rating	80
Green Rating	97
Type of school	Public
Environment	City

STUDENTS

Total undergrad enrollment	17,517
% male/female	52/48
% from out of state	4
% frosh from public high school	81
% frosh live on campus	97
% ugrads live on campus	50
# of fraternities (% ugrad men join)	7 (7)
# of sororities (% ugrad women join)	13 (8)
% African American	2
% Asian	22
% Caucasian	31
% Hispanic	26
% Native American	<1
% Pacific Islander	<1
% Two or more races	8
% Race and/or ethnicity unknown	2
% international	9
# of countries represented	55

SURVEY SAYS . . .

Students environmentally aware
Students politically aware
Students are happy
Students are friendly

ACADEMICS

Academic Rating	74
% students graduating within 4 years	52
% students graduating within 6 years	75
Calendar	Quarter
Student/faculty ratio	25:1
Profs interesting rating	77
Profs accessible rating	81

MOST POPULAR MAJORS

Computer Science; Psychology, General; Business/
Managerial Economics

STUDENTS SAY "..."

Academics

The University of California—Santa Cruz offers one of the nation's best combinations of "focus on scholastic endeavors in a beautiful forest setting" and is, by all accounts "a great place to live and study!" Students attribute their enthusiasm to "intelligent, eloquent, and easily accessible professors," academics that are "impressive and challenging," and fellow students who are "happy, open-minded, and a little bit crazy." This school is best suited to those who can motivate themselves in a "chill" environment and the sort of student whose motto might be, "There's no point in learning if you're too stressed to enjoy it." The sciences are "world-class" at UCSC, and the school also boasts "one of the finest engineering programs in the UCs" as well as "a great marine biology program." While the "professors all do research," what sets them apart from those at the typical research-driven university is that "they are very passionate about their subject even when teaching undergrads," and they "also tend to be quite approachable despite having large class sizes and allow students to attend their office hours for extra help." The school also offers undergrads "a lot of opportunities in terms of internships, research opportunities, job opportunities, and networking." "There's a focus on undergraduate study" here, one student contentedly reports.

Life

Undergrads rave about the "take-your-breath-away beauty" of the heavily wooded UCSC campus; one says it's like "taking paths through the forest that resemble Endor only to find a lecture hall at the end." Another adds, "Almost every time my friends and I walk around outside, someone comments on how lucky we are to be surrounded by such beauty. Whether the silvery ocean, the fog in the trees, the wind in the fields of green, the wildlife such as deer, raccoons, squirrels, newts, etc., it all comes together like a painting." The school's setting means "there is much to do recreationally, such as hiking, biking, swimming, trail running, tree climbing, or rock-climbing. You can walk in any direction and find some hiking trail that leads to some other part of the forest." Students note that, "It is also nice to get off campus from time to time and enjoy the city of Santa Cruz. Downtown is lively and usually has something fun going on such as local farmer's markets and cultural festivals." Ambitious students "may head to San Jose or San Francisco on the weekend for a more rowdy bar or club scene." Both cities are "readily accessible via public transportation." The party scene on and off campus consists of "mostly decentralized, smaller parties, due to the near-absence of fraternities and sororities."

Student Body

"The 'stereotypical' Santa Cruz student is a hippie," and the school certainly has its fair share of those, but "there are many different types who attend UCSC." "The typical student is very hardworking," and "it seems that almost every student here has a personal passion, whether it be an activism or cause of some sort, etc.," one student writes. "Everyone is so... alive." "Most are liberal," and there's a definite propensity for earnestness; it's the sort of place where students declare without irony that they "not only possess a great respect for one another but the world and life in general. The world to an average UCSC student is a sacred and beautiful place to be shared and enjoyed by all its inhabitants."

UNIVERSITY OF CALIFORNIA—SANTA CRUZ

Financial Aid: 831-459-2963 • E-Mail: admissions@ucsc.edu • Website: www.ucsc.edu

THE PRINCETON REVIEW SAYS

Admissions

Very important factors considered include: rigor of secondary school record, academic GPA, application essay, standardized test scores, state residency. *Important factors considered include:* extracurricular activities, talent/ability, character/personal qualities, first generation, geographical residence. *Other factors considered include:* volunteer work, work experience. ACT with Writing required. SAT with Essay component required. High school diploma is required and GED is accepted. *Academic units required:* 4 English, 3 math, 2 science, 2 science labs, 2 foreign language, 1 social studies, 1 history, 1 academic elective, 1 visual/performing arts. *Academic units recommended:* 4 English, 4 math, 3 science, 3 science labs, 3 foreign language, 1 social studies, 1 history, 1 academic elective, 1 visual/performing arts.

Financial Aid

Students should submit: FAFSA; State aid form. The Princeton Review suggests that all financial aid forms be submitted as soon as possible after October 1. *Need-based scholarships/grants offered:* College/university scholarship or grant aid from institutional funds; Federal Pell; Private scholarships; SEOG; State scholarships/grants. *Loan aid offered:* Direct PLUS loans; Direct Subsidized Stafford Loans; Direct Unsubsidized Stafford Loans. Applicants will be notified of awards on a rolling basis beginning 4/1. Federal Work-Study Program available. Institutional employment available.

The Inside Word

Professionally-trained Admissions readers conduct an in-depth review of your academic and personal achievements in light of the opportunities available to you and your demonstrated capacity to contribute to the intellectual and cultural life at UCSC. UCSC's acceptance rate belies the high caliber of applicants it regularly receives.

THE SCHOOL SAYS "..."

From the Admissions Office

"UC—Santa Cruz students, faculty, and researchers are working together to make a world of difference. Within our extraordinary educational community, students participate in the creation of new knowledge, new technologies, and new forms of expressing and understanding cultures. From helping teachers improve their skills to building more efficient solar cells and working to save endangered sea turtles, our focus is on improving our planet and the lives of all its inhabitants. The academic programs at UCSC are challenging and rigorous, and many of them are in newer fields that focus on interdisciplinary thinking. At UCSC, undergraduates conduct and publish research, working closely with faculty on leading-edge projects. Taking advantage of the campus' proximity to centers of industry and innovation such as the Monterey Bay National Marine Sanctuary and Silicon Valley, many students at UC—Santa Cruz take part in fieldwork and internships that complement their studies and provide practical experience in their fields.

"All frosh applicants must take the ACT assessment plus the ACT writing test or the SAT test."

SELECTIVITY

Admissions Rating	94
# of applicants	55,866
% of applicants accepted	52
% of acceptees attending	13
# offered a place on the wait list	12,859
% accepting a place on wait list	59
% admitted from wait list	62

FRESHMAN PROFILE

Range SAT EBRW	590–680
Range SAT Math	600–710
Range SAT Composite	1200–1360
Range ACT Composite	24–30
# submitting SAT scores	3,189
% submitting SAT scores	86
# submitting ACT scores	1,223
% submitting ACT scores	33
Average HS GPA	3.6
% graduated top 10% of class	96
% graduated top 25% of class	100
% graduated top 50% of class	100

DEADLINES

Regular	
Deadline	11/30
Notification	3/31
Nonfall registration?	No

FINANCIAL FACTS

Financial Aid Rating	83
Annual in-state tuition	$11,442
Annual out-of-state tuition	$40,434
Room and board	$16,916
Required fees	$2,612
Books and supplies	$1,085
Average frosh need-based scholarship	$20,343
Average UG need-based scholarship	$21,020
% needy frosh rec. need-based scholarship or grant aid	92
% needy UG rec. need-based scholarship or grant aid	93
% needy frosh rec. non-need-based scholarship or grant aid	2
% needy UG rec. non-need-based scholarship or grant aid	1
% needy frosh rec. need-based self-help aid	73
% needy UG rec. need-based self-help aid	71
% frosh rec. any financial aid	51
% UG rec. any financial aid	57
% UG borrow to pay for school	58
Average cumulative indebtedness	$22,092
% frosh need fully met	23
% ugrads need fully met	24
Average % of frosh need met	83
Average % of ugrad need met	84

UNIVERSITY OF CENTRAL FLORIDA

P.O. Box 160111, Orlando, FL 32816-0111 • Admissions: 407-823-3000 • Fax: 407-823-5625

CAMPUS LIFE

Quality of Life Rating	88
Fire Safety Rating	94
Green Rating	90
Type of school	Public
Environment	City

STUDENTS

Total undergrad enrollment	58,998
% male/female	45/55
% from out of state	7
% frosh live on campus	71
% ugrads live on campus	18
# of fraternities (% ugrad men join)	21 (5)
# of sororities (% ugrad women join)	20 (6)
% African American	11
% Asian	6
% Caucasian	47
% Hispanic	28
% Native American	<1
% Pacific Islander	<1
% Two or more races	4
% Race and/or ethnicity unknown	1
% international	3
# of countries represented	140

SURVEY SAYS . . .

Everyone loves the Knights
Active student government
Students love Orlando, FL
Recreation facilities are great

ACADEMICS

Academic Rating	75
% students returning for sophomore year	92
% students graduating within 4 years	44
% students graduating within 6 years	72
Calendar	Semester
Student/faculty ratio	30:1
Profs interesting rating	82
Profs accessible rating	86

Most classes have 20–29 students.
Most lab/discussion sessions have 30–39 students.

MOST POPULAR MAJORS

Psychology, General; Health Professions And Related Programs; Business Administration and Management, General

STUDENTS SAY "..."

Academics

The University of Central Florida is a massive institution that yields over 68,000 students. Yet, despite its overwhelming population, UCF "strives to make everyone feel welcome." And undergrads stress that you'll "never [feel] completely anonymous." Moreover, the university's size means that it's able to provide students with "a ton of resources to help students succeed academically." Indeed, the sheer variety of academic disciplines astounds, and "there are countless opportunities to get involved in internships, co-ops, [and] work experience programs." Undergrads here greatly appreciate all of these "opportunities for professional development" and a number highlight the fact that there are "lots of resources to help students with résumés and cover letters."

When it comes to the classroom, undergrads admit that their "general education" professors can be "hit or miss." Thankfully, many students are eager to sing the praises of the "outstanding," "welcoming," and "very knowledgeable" faculty in their respective majors (regardless of the department). "They care about the material, they know how to present it, and they are willing to work with [us] to facilitate the learning process," says a student. Best of all, they are "very friendly and will go out of their way to help you succeed."

Life

Undergrads at UCF can't help but have a good time. After all, one student says "there are so many extracurricular activities and clubs that you can always find something to your liking." Another points out, "on a typical walk across campus you will see ROTC training, people playing guitar and singing on Memory Mall, people hammocking in the palm trees, free items being handed out, people dancing by the Union, [and] students studying out front of the fountain." For the sporty types, there's the "climbing course and the Rec fields [along with] swim[ming] in the leisure pool [and] play[ing] racquetball." You can even borrow kayaks and go boating on the lake on campus. Of course, "football games are also very popular" and students report that "tailgating is a fun activity" as well. Additionally, "fraternity and sorority life are present for those who want to participate." Finally, students love to take advantage of their prime Orlando location. You better believe that "Disney [and] Universal Studios ... are [both] popular destination spots." As one student claims, "there is no excuse for feeling lonely or bored at this school!"

Student Body

UCF Knights value the fact that "the student body is very diverse." One student explains, "We've got every kind of student you can imagine, ... and we come together to make one great community that people find hard to resist." Indeed, you can find "ambitious high achievers and classic frat [guys] and sorority girls" and everything in between. Students have "strength in passion ... and achievement," and they "love what they are studying (even if they don't love the course load)." Additionally, undergrads describe their classmates as "enthusiastic," "inspiring," and "very school spirited." As one happy student shares, "I would never have expected for everyone ... I have met to be so helpful and kind, but they truly are." A fellow Knight adds, "The students here are amicable and always happy to lend a hand to their peers." All in all, rest assured that "you'll find a niche in which you'll fit" and that UCF has "something for everyone."

UNIVERSITY OF CENTRAL FLORIDA

Financial Aid: 407-823-2827 • E-Mail: admission@ucf.edu • Website: www.ucf.edu

THE PRINCETON REVIEW SAYS

Admissions

Very important factors considered include: rigor of secondary school record, academic GPA, standardized test scores. *Important factors considered include:* application essay, *Other factors considered include:* class rank, extracurricular activities, talent/ability, character/personal qualities, first generation, alumni/ae relation, geographical residence, state residency, volunteer work, work experience, level of applicant's interest. ACT with or without writing accepted. SAT with or without Essay component accepted. High school diploma is required and GED is accepted. *Academic units required:* 4 English, 4 math, 3 science, 2 science labs, 2 foreign language, 3 social studies, 2 academic electives.

Financial Aid

Students should submit: FAFSA. Priority filing deadline is 12/1. The Princeton Review suggests that all financial aid forms be submitted as soon as possible after October 1. *Need-based scholarships/grants offered:* College/university scholarship or grant aid from institutional funds; Federal Pell; Private scholarships; SEOG; State scholarships/grants. *Loan aid offered:* Direct PLUS loans; Direct Subsidized Stafford Loans; Direct Unsubsidized Stafford Loans. Applicants will be notified of awards on a rolling basis beginning 3/1. Federal Work-Study Program available. Institutional employment available.

The Inside Word

Like many state schools, earning admission to UCF is primarily a numbers game, meaning that the college largely considers your GPA and standardized test scores. We should also mention that grades earned in honors, IB, advanced placement, AICE and/or dual enrollment classes will be given greater weight. UCF does not require applicants to submit a personal statement, however, you are likely to give your candidacy a modest boost if you include one. Finally, we should note that students graduating from a Florida high school in the top 10 percent of their class (or with a recalculated academic core 3.9 GPA if their high school does not rank) and minimum test scores (1090 SAT or 21 ACT) will be guaranteed admission to the fall, summer, or spring semester.

THE SCHOOL SAYS "..."

From the Admissions Office

"The University of Central Florida offers competitive advantages to its student body. We're committed to teaching, providing advisement, and academic support services for all students. Our undergraduates have access to state-of-the-art wireless buildings, high-tech classrooms, research labs, web-based classes, and an undergraduate research and mentoring program.

"Our Career Services professionals help students gain practical experiences at NASA, schools, hospitals, high-tech companies, local municipalities, and the entertainment industry. With an international focus to our curricula and research programs, we enroll international students from 140 nations. Our study abroad programs and other study and research opportunities include agreements with ninety-eight institutions and thirty-six countries.

"UCF's 1,415-acre campus provides a safe and serene setting for learning, with natural lakes and woodlands. The bustle of Orlando lies a short distance away: the pro sport teams, the Kennedy Space Center, film studios, Walt Disney World, Universal Orlando, Sea World, and sandy beaches are all nearby.

"UCF recently set new records for diversity: 46 percent of students are minorities, including 26 percent Hispanic. Over the past 25 years, UCF's minority enrollment has increased 191 percent."

SELECTIVITY

Admissions Rating	91
# of applicants	45,118
% of applicants accepted	44
% of acceptees attending	37
# offered a place on the wait list	6,742
% accepting a place on wait list	45
% admitted from wait list	17

FRESHMAN PROFILE

Range SAT EBRW	590–670
Range SAT Math	580–670
Range ACT Composite	25–30
# submitting SAT scores	5,788
% submitting SAT scores	79
# submitting ACT scores	1,535
% submitting ACT scores	21
Average HS GPA	4.1
% graduated top 10% of class	36
% graduated top 25% of class	74
% graduated top 50% of class	97

DEADLINES

Regular	
Priority	1/1
Deadline	5/1
Notification	Rolling, 9/1
Nonfall registration?	Yes

FINANCIAL FACTS

Financial Aid Rating	82
Annual in-state tuition	$6,368
Annual out-of-state tuition	$22,467
Room and board	$9,580
Books and supplies	$1,200
Average frosh need-based scholarship	$7,339
Average UG need-based scholarship	$7,160
% needy frosh rec. need-based scholarship or grant aid	68
% needy UG rec. need-based scholarship or grant aid	74
% needy frosh rec. non-need-based scholarship or grant aid	80
% needy UG rec. non-need-based scholarship or grant aid	41
% needy frosh rec. need-based self-help aid	36
% needy UG rec. need-based self-help aid	49
% frosh rec. any financial aid	85.4
% UG rec. any financial aid	74.29
% UG borrow to pay for school	49
Average cumulative indebtedness	$22,561
% frosh need fully met	27
% ugrads need fully met	15
Average % of frosh need met	75
Average % of ugrad need met	64

THE UNIVERSITY OF CHICAGO

1101 E. 58th Street, Chicago, IL 60637 • Admissions: 773-702-8650 • Fax: 773-702-4199

CAMPUS LIFE

Quality of Life Rating	91
Fire Safety Rating	97
Green Rating	87
Type of school	Private
Environment	Metropolis

STUDENTS

Total undergrad enrollment	6,734
% male/female	51/49
% from out of state	82
% frosh live on campus	99
% ugrads live on campus	52
% African American	6
% Asian	19
% Caucasian	37
% Hispanic	14
% Native American	<1
% Pacific Islander	0
% Two or more races	7
% Race and/or ethnicity unknown	2
% international	15
# of countries represented	125

SURVEY SAYS . . .

Students always studying
Students are happy
Classroom facilities are great
Lab facilities are great
Great library
Career services are great
Internships are widely available
Great financial aid
Students love Chicago, IL
Dorms are like palaces
Easy to get around campus
Theater is popular

ACADEMICS

Academic Rating	96
% students returning for sophomore year	99
% students graduating within 4 years	90
% students graduating within 6 years	95
Calendar	Quarter
Student/faculty ratio	5:1
Profs interesting rating	90
Profs accessible rating	93

Most classes have fewer than 10 students.
Most lab/discussion sessions have
  10–19 students.

MOST POPULAR MAJORS

Biology/Biological Sciences, General; Mathematics, General; Econometrics and Quantitative Economics

STUDENTS SAY ". . ."

Academics

Described as "an academic paradise near an awesome city," the University of Chicago is a research institution dedicated to "cultivating a rigorous mentality that enables students to think through and solve any problem they might confront." Students say, UChicago "is a rigorous institution," but they celebrate the fact that "you can't just stick up your hand and not expect to be challenged by your professors and your peers," and note that the professors "are really good at asking students 'Why?' instead of the usual 'What?'" Classrooms are small and foster a "collaborative learning environment." It's a place that "pushes smart people to make new discoveries, challenge their limits, and find new ways of understanding the world." Students say of the faculty that "there's really nothing that compares to working with people on the cutting edge of research and discussing books with their authors," and that they are "very focused on inspiring conversation between students." The "wide array of strong academic programs" offered at UChicago are set on the quarter system, which can be "a bit intensive." "The sheer amount of material one covers in any given quarter is simply massive." If you are up for it, you can "learn a ton" in this fast-paced system.

Life

The College Houses are a very important aspect of student life and gets rave reviews for being a "supportive, fun, community environment" with a "family atmosphere." "Your house becomes your family and the center of your social life on campus. You go to parties with your House, your best friends come from the House, and you will likely move off campus with members of your House. The House system is truly one of the great aspects of the University of Chicago." Although the "harsh Chicago winter" may not appeal to everyone, the city of Chicago clearly does. Students report that "there are a lot of really cool lectures and events for undergrads on campus that enable us to take advantage of the whole university." Students feel that "the nice thing is that everyone here is so unique; you can go from talking about a TV show to religion to career plans—really anything is fair game. And the Common Core gives every student some grounds of connection." In terms of social life, one student reports that "I like to have the option of going downtown for fun, or just staying in with friends, or going out. You really do get the best of all of these worlds and have choices, but never are you pressured into doing anything. There is always a group of people willing to do any of those things, so you never have to go through it alone!"

Student Body

Students find it difficult to describe a typical student except as someone "you wouldn't expect. Football players are computer programmers, sorority girls are poets, nerds are hip-hop dance prodigies," and "the lead role in the play is going into investment banking." "It runs the gamut from complete nerd to complete jock. It even includes people who are both!" What students do "have in common is a genuine interest in ideas and a profound investment in the life of the mind." While "students almost always looked stressed...they also look like they are loving their stress." Students "fit in by finding other like-minded individuals—either through the House system (the easiest method), by joining clubs, or through classes." Continuing the theme of having dedicated and intelligent students, one notes that "everyone here is so intelligent that sometimes people think they're unintelligent for being surrounded by so many smart people. Everyone is dedicated to something and most everyone has been through significant struggles of some kind." "A typical student loves to learn, does a lot of homework, enjoys their time here, but also loves to complain about it, is probably not religious, has probably considered majoring in econ at one point," driving home the point that economics is, in fact, popular.

THE UNIVERSITY OF CHICAGO

Financial Aid: 773-702-8666 • E-Mail: collegeadmissions@uchicago.edu • Website: uchicago.edu

THE PRINCETON REVIEW SAYS

Admissions

Very important factors considered include: rigor of secondary school record, application essay, recommendation(s), extracurricular activities, talent/ability, character/personal qualities. *Other factors considered include:* class rank, academic GPA, standardized test scores, first generation, alumni/ae relation, geographical residence, state residency, religious affiliation/commitment, racial/ethnic status, volunteer work, work experience, level of applicant's interest. ACT with or without writing accepted. SAT with or without Essay component accepted. High school diploma is required and GED is accepted. *Academic units recommended:* 4 English, 4 math, 4 science, 3 foreign language, 2 social studies, 2 history.

Financial Aid

Students should submit: CSS/Financial Aid PROFILE; FAFSA; Institution's own financial aid form. Priority filing deadline is 2/15. The Princeton Review suggests that all financial aid forms be submitted as soon as possible after October 1. *Need-based scholarships/grants offered:* College/university scholarship or grant aid from institutional funds; Federal Pell; Private scholarships; SEOG; State scholarships/grants. *Loan aid offered:* Direct PLUS loans; Direct Subsidized Stafford Loans; Direct Unsubsidized Stafford Loans. Applicants will be notified of awards on or about 3/15. Federal Work-Study Program available. Institutional employment available.

The Inside Word

Students at the University of Chicago dwell on deep thoughts and big ideas. In your application, you'll need to demonstrate outstanding grades in tough courses and that you will fit in with a bunch of big thinkers. Although the University of Chicago uses the Common Application, essay topics remain "uncommon" and thought-provoking.

THE SCHOOL SAYS "..."

From the Admissions Office

"The University of Chicago is universally recognized for its devotion to open and rigorous inquiry. The strength of our intellectual traditions—intense critical analysis, lively debate, and creative solutions to complex problems—rests on the scholars who continue to engage them. Graduates of the college have made discoveries in every field of academic study; they are ambitious thinkers who are unafraid to take on the most pressing questions of our time. Their accomplishments have helped establish the University's legacy as one of the world's finest academic institutions. The University of Chicago has been home to 91 Nobel Prize winners, 32 MacArthur "Genius" Fellows, and 21 Pulitzer Prize winners. With over 150 research centers and institutes, numerous cultural opportunities, and three of the nation's top professional schools in law, business, and medicine—all within blocks of one another on our campus—UChicago is known for the unparalleled resources it provides its undergraduate students.

"UChicago maintains a student-faculty ratio of five to one, ensuring that every classroom experience exemplifies our commitment to a student's ability to interact closely with our faculty. Our Core curriculum provides students with a common vocabulary and a well-balanced academic experience, while allowing the flexibility to explore their own particular interests in small discussion-style seminars. Students also enjoy a successful Division III sports program, small but active Greek life, over 30 student theatrical productions a year, a rich music scene, celebrations of culture and community—and the extraordinary opportunities in politics, music, theater, commerce, architecture, and neighborhood life in the city of Chicago."

SELECTIVITY

Admissions Rating	99
# of applicants	34,641
% of applicants accepted	6
% of acceptees attending	81

FRESHMAN PROFILE

Range SAT EBRW	730–770
Range SAT Math	770–800
Range ACT Composite	33–35
# submitting SAT scores	925
% submitting SAT scores	54
# submitting ACT scores	884
% submitting ACT scores	51
Average HS GPA	4.2
% graduated top 10% of class	99
% graduated top 25% of class	100
% graduated top 50% of class	100

DEADLINES

Early decision	
Deadline	11/1
Notification	12/18
Other ED Deadline	1/4
Other ED Notification	2/12
Early action	
Deadline	11/1
Notification	12/18
Regular	
Deadline	1/4
Notification	4/1
Nonfall registration?	No

FINANCIAL FACTS

Financial Aid Rating	97
Annual tuition	$55,425
Room and board	$16,350
Required fees	$2,805
Books and supplies	$1,800
Average frosh need-based scholarship	$55,458
Average UG need-based scholarship	$52,471
% needy frosh rec. need-based scholarship or grant aid	99
% needy UG rec. need-based scholarship or grant aid	99
% needy frosh rec. non-need-based scholarship or grant aid	22
% needy UG rec. non-need-based scholarship or grant aid	16
% needy frosh rec. need-based self-help aid	72
% needy UG rec. need-based self-help aid	74
% frosh rec. any financial aid	56
% UG rec. any financial aid	57
% UG borrow to pay for school	17
Average cumulative indebtedness	$26,619
% frosh need fully met	99
% ugrads need fully met	99
Average % of frosh need met	100
Average % of ugrad need met	100

UNIVERSITY OF CINCINNATI

P.O. Box 210091, Cincinnati, OH 45221-0091 • Admissions: 513-556-1100 • Fax: 513-556-1105

STUDENTS SAY "...

Academics

At the University of Cincinnati, professors emphasize "the importance of gaining professional experience while [still] in school" and students are often encouraged "out of [their] comfort zones to go to networking events." Students mention "experiential learning the university provides through internships and co-ops," and many call it a "catalyst in [personal] growth." Students point to cross-disciplinary and pre-professional training in the university's co-op program, which while generally considered to be "a great program," has been said by some to "need a little bit of tweaking." With the Design, Architecture, Art, and Planning School (DAAP), a highly-ranked program with "studios [that] allow cross-collaboration with peers," "students are always tackling projects from different perspectives … and [appreciating] different learning styles." Many DAAP students love that they "are on a first-name basis" with their professors, who are "very passionate about what they are teaching." But other DAAP students mention that the demands are "too stress-inducing … and [that] the curriculum does not regard the well-being of the students." In contrast, students in other UC programs emphasize that their professors encourage them to "seek help at every turn, to lead healthy lives, and study in more effective ways." There is "plenty of opportunity for study outside of class including Supplemental Instruction (SI) sessions, office hours, and tutoring."

Life

"We're so lucky to be right in the center of Cincinnati," says one student. And indeed, UC students "take full advantage of the restaurants, bars, museums, concerts, and local festivals in the city." This includes student tickets to Bengals and Reds games, free concerts, and farmers markets. Plus, "Oktoberfest is always popular," adds another Bearcat. Downtown Cincinnati also holds "many other interesting places to eat, drink, and socialize." Students de-stress on campus at the recreational facilities, which include an indoor track, a lazy river, and a hot tub, which one student stresses is "*super* nice." On the weekends, students go out to bars and restaurants near campus. They also "hang out in the student center, outdoors, or in the library between and after classes," and they often "attend the free sporting events or club meetings after." UC is "highly involved in the [professional soccer] FC Cincinnati games, which take place in the football stadium on campus." If you're hungry, head over to the Tangeman Center where you will find "many restaurants to choose from" or you can grab food at On the Green, the newest "super nice and … healthy" food court. Some find UC to be "fairly landlocked," with a "large number of students in a fairly small radius." They comment that this makes it "feel like a college city."

Student Body

The student body at the University of Cincinnati is "a fairly diverse community, with cultures from all across Ohio, the United States, and … the entire globe." "First-generation and minority students are well-represented and encouraged through programs such as Emerging Ethnic Engineers," says a student. Students describe themselves and each other as "motivated," "experienced," and "real-world-ready." "In addition to their academic prowess," students take on "numerous activities like intramural athletics, student government, [and] mental health initiatives." One Bearcat attributes the school's strengths to school spirit, saying, "[It] binds us." Another student says that everyone has "a different story and reason for being here, but all [share] a same liking of the institution."

UNIVERSITY OF CINCINNATI

Financial Aid: 513-556-1000 • E-Mail: admissions@uc.edu • Website: www.uc.edu

THE PRINCETON REVIEW SAYS

Admissions

Very important factors considered include: rigor of secondary school record, academic GPA, standardized test scores. *Important factors considered include:* application essay, recommendation(s), talent/ability. *Other factors considered include:* class rank, extracurricular activities, character/personal qualities, first generation, geographical residence, state residency, racial/ethnic status, volunteer work, work experience. ACT with or without writing accepted. SAT with or without Essay component accepted. High school diploma is required and GED is not accepted *Academic units required:* 4 English, 4 math, 3 science, 3 social studies, 5 units from above areas or other academic areas. *Academic units recommended:* 2 foreign language.

Financial Aid

Students should submit: FAFSA. Priority filing deadline is 12/1. The Princeton Review suggests that all financial aid forms be submitted as soon as possible after October 1. *Need-based scholarships/grants offered:* College/university scholarship or grant aid from institutional funds; Federal Pell; Private scholarships; SEOG; State scholarships/grants; United Negro College Fund. *Loan aid offered:* Direct PLUS loans; Direct Subsidized Stafford Loans; Direct Unsubsidized Stafford Loans. Applicants will be notified of awards on a rolling basis beginning 3/1. Federal Work-Study Program available. Institutional employment available.

The Inside Word

The University of Cincinnati admissions officers advise students that they are looking for those who have been academically successful in past coursework, who show drive and a willingness to challenge themselves, and who are passionate about leaving a positive mark on the world. Essay prompts should be chosen with the goal of showing your authentic self in order to reveal something that wouldn't otherwise be apparent from other application material. All aspects of each student's application—from GPA to personal statements—are considered when making an admission decision. A letter of recommendation is optional for first-year applicants, although one is highly encouraged.

THE SCHOOL SAYS "..."

From the Admissions Office

"The University of Cincinnati provides a unique learning experience to students from around the globe. All students hone their skills outside the classroom through co-cop, internships, clinicals, undergraduate research, study abroad, service-learning, performances, or other approved activities. This focus on experience-based learning not only builds a student's resume, but allows students to network and build confidence within their chosen field. When combined with top academic programs, location, diversity, scope of majors and programs, and campus setting, the University of Cincinnati stands out among the top research universities in the country. Students and counselors agree:

"'I fell in love with the University of Cincinnati during an afternoon visit a few years ago. Cincinnati is one of the few out-of-state institutions I STRONGLY recommend for our students to consider.'

–Heidi Clark-Smitley; Director of Guidance and College Counseling, Catholic Central High School (Grand Rapids, MI)

"'I knew the co-op program would allow me to have numerous professional experiences working in the design field and the university setting appealed to me more than a small art school. I am involved in several organizations and attend sporting events—which are both possible because DAAP is part of a larger university.'

–Hannah, Architecture major

"Come visit and find out how Cincinnati can benefit you both inside and outside the classroom: admissions.uc.edu/visit."

SELECTIVITY

Admissions Rating	83
# of applicants	23,609
% of applicants accepted	77
% of acceptees attending	30

FRESHMAN PROFILE

Range SAT EBRW	560–660
Range SAT Math	560–690
Range SAT Composite	1140–1330
Range ACT Composite	23–29
# submitting SAT scores	1,192
% submitting SAT scores	22
# submitting ACT scores	4,883
% submitting ACT scores	89
Average HS GPA	3.7
% graduated top 10% of class	24
% graduated top 25% of class	51
% graduated top 50% of class	83

DEADLINES

Regular	
Priority	12/1
Deadline	3/1
Notification	1/1
Nonfall registration?	Yes

FINANCIAL FACTS

Financial Aid Rating	74
Annual in-state tuition	$9,982
Annual out-of-state tuition	$25,316
Room and board	$11,530
Required fees	$1,678
Books and supplies	$1,200
Average frosh need-based scholarship	$6,790
Average UG need-based scholarship	$6,506
% needy frosh rec. need-based scholarship or grant aid	39
% needy UG rec. need-based scholarship or grant aid	42
% needy frosh rec. non-need-based scholarship or grant aid	58
% needy UG rec. non-need-based scholarship or grant aid	41
% needy frosh rec. need-based self-help aid	70
% needy UG rec. need-based self-help aid	73
% UG borrow to pay for school	58
Average cumulative indebtedness	$30,350
% frosh need fully met	14
% ugrads need fully met	9
Average % of frosh need met	43
Average % of ugrad need met	36

UNIVERSITY OF COLORADO—BOULDER

552 UCB, Boulder, CO 80309-0552 • Admissions: 303-492-6301 • Fax: 303-735-2501

CAMPUS LIFE

Quality of Life Rating	92
Fire Safety Rating	95
Green Rating	88
Type of school	Public
Environment	City

STUDENTS

Total undergrad enrollment	30,673
% male/female	55/45
% from out of state	42
% frosh from public high school	86
% frosh live on campus	94
% ugrads live on campus	28
# of fraternities (% ugrad men join)	32 (12)
# of sororities (% ugrad women join)	18 (22)
% African American	2
% Asian	6
% Caucasian	67
% Hispanic	13
% Native American	<1
% Pacific Islander	<1
% Two or more races	6
% Race and/or ethnicity unknown	1
% international	6
# of countries represented	76

SURVEY SAYS . . .

Students are happy
Great library
Students environmentally aware
Students love Boulder, CO
Great off-campus food
Easy to get around campus
Recreation facilities are great
Lots of beer drinking
Hard liquor is popular
Intramural sports are popular

ACADEMICS

Academic Rating	82
% students returning for sophomore year	87
% students graduating within 4 years	46
% students graduating within 6 years	69
Calendar	Semester
Student/faculty ratio	18:1
Profs interesting rating	88
Profs accessible rating	92

Most classes have 10–19 students.
Most lab/discussion sessions have
20–29 students.

MOST POPULAR MAJORS

Psychology, General; Finance, General; Public
Relations, Advertising, and Strategic
Communication

STUDENTS SAY "..."

Academics

Located in the Rocky Mountain region, the University of Colorado Boulder is a "comprehensive public research university" boasting "five Nobel laureates and more than fifty members of prestigious academic academies." It "provides a modern, research-based education that focuses on creating aware citizens to go on to change the world (while having fun)." Students call it a "strong school academically with all the perks of a big state university" including "excellent diversity in subjects and courses, school spirit, packed sports games, and a fun, beautiful college town." Students get to enjoy a "beautiful campus with outdoor-oriented people" in addition to "a great research university," notes an international affairs major. Boulder offers a wide variety of degree programs, but students praise the "top-notch leadership program," "great business program," and "strong physics reputation" in particular. CU Boulder also offers a "strong environmental program" with opportunities for "both on- and off-campus" study. Students say the professors are "amazing," "approachable," "interested in students personally," and "will treat you as an adult." Professors are "consistently excellent across the wide variety of subjects I have taken courses in, from geography to astronomy and economics to literature," notes one student. "In my four years as an undergrad," says an environmental studies major, "I have traveled places and learned things that I never imagined I would or could experience." In addition, "the price for an education of this caliber is phenomenal," a creative writing major notes. "I was going to a private college for two years and can safely say that this education is significantly better, while the cost is relatively minimal." CU Boulder is a perfect fit for students who want to be in a "college town surrounded by other young intellectuals."

Life

"Boulder is the best college town in the U.S.," raves one student. With the foothills of the Rockies as their home, "being active and outdoors is a staple for students." "Regardless of the time of day, students can be seen outside relaxing, exercising, or just hanging out with friends," according to one marketing major. Students "go hiking when the weather is nice" and many "go skiing in the mountains on days that [they] don't have classes." Snowboarding is also "extremely popular." And there is also a "prominent night life at the bars," including a music scene that is "diverse and active." Students "go shopping and eat out on Pearl Street" in "downtown Boulder" and "Farrand Field is always busy on nice days with students playing Frisbee, football, soccer, and tanning." It's a "fun college town," and many students "[like] to go out and party on the weekends."

Student Body

CU Boulder students consider themselves a diverse bunch from "diverse backgrounds" with "diverse passions." "There isn't really a typical student, which is awesome," notes a marketing major. But an international affairs major says, "Students are mostly upper-middle class white kids from Colorado, California, Texas, or Illinois." Typical CU Boulder students are "kind," "genuine," "smart," and "athletic." They are "outdoorsy, outgoing, and always up for anything." They "love to be outside and often will spend their weekends in the mountains." And though "partying is big," "most take school very seriously and are irritated by [its] depiction as a 'party school'" in the "media." "The school is so large that everyone fits into a group, no matter what your interests are," says an environmental studies major. In addition to those attracted to Greek life, there are "hippy concert going types and everything in between." An architecture major says, those "who make an effort to meet new people and try new things, will be very happy, and have a great time at CU Boulder." As one student notes: "When I stepped foot on CU's campus, I immediately felt at home." She adds: "Everyone is so friendly and welcoming. It's such a community atmosphere. Everyone watches out for each other and has each other's backs, even strangers."

UNIVERSITY OF COLORADO—BOULDER

Financial Aid: 303-492-5091 • Website: www.colorado.edu/

THE PRINCETON REVIEW SAYS

Admissions

Very important factors considered include: rigor of secondary school record, academic GPA, standardized test scores. *Important factors considered include:* application essay, recommendation(s), extracurricular activities, talent/ability, character/personal qualities, first generation. *Other factors considered include:* class rank, alumni/ae relation, geographical residence, state residency, racial/ethnic status, volunteer work, work experience. ACT with or without writing accepted. SAT with or without Essay component accepted. High school diploma is required and GED is accepted. *Academic units required:* 4 English, 4 math, 3 science, 2 science labs, 3 foreign language, 3 social studies, 1 history, 1 unit from above areas or other academic areas.

Financial Aid

Students should submit: FAFSA. Priority filing deadline is 2/15. The Princeton Review suggests that all financial aid forms be submitted as soon as possible after October 1. *Need-based scholarships/grants offered:* College/university scholarship or grant aid from institutional funds; Federal Pell; Private scholarships; SEOG; State scholarships/grants. *Loan aid offered:* Direct PLUS loans; Direct Subsidized Stafford Loans; Direct Unsubsidized Stafford Loans. Applicants will be notified of awards on a rolling basis beginning 3/15. Federal Work-Study Program available. Institutional employment available.

The Inside Word

Applicants must apply to a specific school within CU Boulder. Some programs are more competitive than others. Engineering and Applied Science and the Leeds School of Business are the most competitive. Those who apply to a competitive school within CU Boulder and are not selected will be automatically entered into consideration for admission to the College of Arts and Sciences.

THE SCHOOL SAYS "..."

From the Admissions Office

"Located at the foot of the Rocky Mountains, the University of Colorado Boulder has a breathtaking view from campus. But don't just come for the view. CU Boulder and its nationally and internationally ranked faculty have built a global reputation for outstanding teaching, research and creative work across more than 150 academic fields. Our innovative academic programs, hands-on opportunities, and rigorous coursework will prepare you for a complex global society. While working with faculty, you'll develop a broad understanding of the world, strong leadership skills and an enhanced ability to think critically.

"Within CU Boulder's inclusive community, you'll find many ways to get involved and make lifelong friends. We have one of the most active college campuses in the nation, where recreation, sports and student groups play a key role in the unique CU Boulder experience. We don't claim that we can change the world. Instead, we teach, inspire and encourage our students, faculty and researchers. So they can change the world. Live in spectacular surroundings and learn in a campus environment of extraordinary opportunities.

"Come to CU Boulder and discover what you can be.

"To find out if CU Boulder is the place for you, we encourage you to learn more. Check out our website, visit campus or take a virtual tour online.

"Be inspired. Be unique. Be driven.

"Be Boulder."

SELECTIVITY

Admissions Rating	81
# of applicants	40,740
% of applicants accepted	78
% of acceptees attending	22
# offered a place on the wait list	4,380
% accepting a place on wait list	32
% admitted from wait list	40

FRESHMAN PROFILE

Range SAT EBRW	580–670
Range SAT Math	560–690
Range SAT Composite	1150–1350
Range ACT Composite	25–31
# submitting SAT scores	5,518
% submitting SAT scores	72
# submitting ACT scores	3,371
% submitting ACT scores	47
Average HS GPA	3.7
% graduated top 10% of class	26
% graduated top 25% of class	56
% graduated top 50% of class	86

DEADLINES

Early action	
Deadline	11/15
Notification	2/1
Regular	
Priority	11/15
Deadline	1/15
Nonfall registration?	Yes

FINANCIAL FACTS

Financial Aid Rating	87
Annual in-state tuition	$10,728
Annual out-of-state tuition	$36,546
Room and board	$14,778
Required fees	$1,772
Books and supplies	$1,200
Average frosh need-based scholarship	$12,225
Average UG need-based scholarship	$11,882
% needy frosh rec. need-based scholarship or grant aid	77
% needy UG rec. need-based scholarship or grant aid	74
% needy frosh rec. non-need-based scholarship or grant aid	6
% needy UG rec. non-need-based scholarship or grant aid	4
% needy frosh rec. need-based self-help aid	84
% needy UG rec. need-based self-help aid	83
% frosh rec. any financial aid	77
% UG rec. any financial aid	60
% UG borrow to pay for school	40
Average cumulative indebtedness	$27,568
% frosh need fully met	42
% ugrads need fully met	39
Average % of frosh need met	80
Average % of ugrad need met	80

UNIVERSITY OF CONNECTICUT

2131 Hillside Road, Storrs, CT 06268-3088 • Admissions: 860-486-3137 • Fax: 860-486-1476

CAMPUS LIFE

Quality of Life Rating	87
Fire Safety Rating	96
Green Rating	99
Type of school	Public
Environment	Town

STUDENTS

Total undergrad enrollment	19,030
% male/female	50/50
% from out of state	22
% frosh from public high school	88
% frosh live on campus	97
% ugrads live on campus	67
# of fraternities (% ugrad men join)	23 (12)
# of sororities (% ugrad women join)	13 (17)
% African American	6
% Asian	11
% Caucasian	60
% Hispanic	10
% Native American	<1
% Pacific Islander	<1
% Two or more races	3
% Race and/or ethnicity unknown	5
% international	6
# of countries represented	71

SURVEY SAYS . . .

Lots of beer drinking
Everyone loves the Huskies
Students are happy

ACADEMICS

Academic Rating	78
% students returning for sophomore year	92
% students graduating within 4 years	70
% students graduating within 6 years	82
Calendar	Semester
Student/faculty ratio	16:1
Profs interesting rating	83
Profs accessible rating	88

Most classes have 10–19 students.
Most lab/discussion sessions have 10–19 students.

MOST POPULAR MAJORS

Economics, General; Communication and Media Studies; Psychology, General

STUDENTS SAY ". . ."

Academics

The University of Connecticut may be "known for our amazing athletics," but it's also "one of the top research universities and state schools," a "university [that] truly cares about their students." As one political science major puts it, UConn is "unique because it is comprised of all different types of students both in backgrounds and ethnicities. What makes us different than other universities is our cohesiveness despite these differences. We all go to one school, we all cheer on the same team, and we all bleed blue." While "basketball games are like religion," students say that, "UConn is focused on academic achievement." For one student, the school's main appeal is that it is a "large, public university [with] a variety of programs and diversity on campus." As the "flagship state school," UConn provides "research opportunities for undergrads" and "every student is supported in order to be the most successful student possible; UConn cares." When it comes to professors, the "performance level [varies], more so during the first couple years when the students are required to take general education requirements." Students say that in more advanced, major-specific courses, "the professors tend to be more interested in the topics of the course and thus more engaging." Those professors are "truly amazing, inspiring, and add so much to my academics," but the general consensus is that "UConn is a really big university, so professors can be hit or miss."

Life

"Since it's a big school, there is always something going on on-campus, whether it's free movies, lectures, concerts, food, or more." For students who want to experience nature, "There's always the opportunity to go outdoors and walk to Horsebarn Hill, go on runs around campus or go on hikes in the UConn forest." Even though the campus a little off the beaten path—one transfer student laments "the nickname for Storrs is Snores"—students say "the downtown area has developed into its own mini city" with restaurants and cafés. As one student puts it, "I am never bored on the weekend between the many shows and concerts, movies and other activities offered by the university." Greek life plays a significant role on campus—some say that "Greek life dominates many aspects of social scene," while others say only that there are "frat parties if you're into that kind of scene." The school's reputation for top notch athletics is legendary; as one student puts it, "the celebrations after victories are unlike anything I've ever experienced elsewhere." Some students are frustrated that "athletics sometimes overshadows academic achievements in funding," but others underscore the rigorousness of UConn's academics, saying "UConn is a research school so classes are difficult and professors will not go out of their way to ensure you get a good grade." When it comes to kicking back after a long week, one student succinctly sums up the alcohol culture at the school: "UConn doesn't seem to be a party school, it is a drinking school—there is a difference."

Student Body

UConn students are typically "very diverse due to the large student body"—you can find "students who love to go out every weekend at the bar [and] you can find students whose hobby is knitting or [to] go to ComiCONN…there really is a peer group for everyone." The students, "the majority of which are from Connecticut," are "uniquely passionate and spirited." As one student puts it, the school is composed of "many small communities based on academics, sports, clubs, and interests, that come together to form a large community connected by a mutual love of UConn." Some pinpoint the average student as "white, upper middle class and wears L.L. Bean boots, North Face coats," but others stress that "it's a big school, so there is no one word to describe my peers." With "more happening on campus than you expect," there are "athletic teams and Greek life" but also "human rights organizations, activists, and volunteers."

UNIVERSITY OF CONNECTICUT

Financial Aid: 860-486-2819 • E-Mail: beahusky@uconn.edu • Website: www.uconn.edu

THE PRINCETON REVIEW SAYS

Admissions

Very important factors considered include: rigor of secondary school record, class rank, academic GPA, standardized test scores. *Important factors considered include:* application essay, recommendation(s), extracurricular activities, talent/ability, character/personal qualities, first generation. *Other factors considered include:* alumni/ae relation, geographical residence, state residency, racial/ethnic status, work experience, level of applicant's interest. ACT with or without writing accepted. SAT with or without Essay component accepted. High school diploma is required and GED is accepted. *Academic units required:* 4 English, 3 math, 2 science, 2 science labs, 2 foreign language, 2 social studies, 3 academic electives. *Academic units recommended:* 3 foreign language.

Financial Aid

Students should submit: FAFSA. Priority filing deadline is 3/1. The Princeton Review suggests that all financial aid forms be submitted as soon as possible after October 1. *Need-based scholarships/grants offered:* College/university scholarship or grant aid from institutional funds; Federal Pell; Private scholarships; SEOG; State scholarships/grants. *Loan aid offered:* Direct PLUS loans; Direct Subsidized Stafford Loans; Direct Unsubsidized Stafford Loans. Applicants will be notified of awards on a rolling basis beginning 3/1. Federal Work-Study Program available. Institutional employment available.

The Inside Word

The UConn admissions committee looks at every aspect of a prospective first year's application, taking everything from GPA, class rank, extracurricular activities, standardized test scores, a required essay, and two letters of recommendation into consideration. The university is a very selective school—college preparatory coursework in high school is required, with additional requirements for School of Engineering and School of Nursing applicants—and students should be sure that all aspects of their application pass muster.

THE SCHOOL SAYS "..."

From the Admissions Office

"Founded in 1881, the University of Connecticut is ranked as one of the best public universities in the United States. With a combination of dynamic faculty, strong athletic pride and an extraordinary sense of community, UConn is a university like no other. Offering over 110 majors and the ability to create a major of your own, a broad range of academic choices is provided. Faculty members are top experts in their fields, and serve as mentors and advisors to students. Distinctive research opportunities pair undergraduate students with faculty in every academic discipline offered. The main campus in Storrs is located in a safe New England town midway between New York City and Boston. With one of the highest percentages of students living on campus of any public university in the United States, UConn is its own community within a thriving rural town. With on-campus museums and performances, and newly released movies right inside the Student Union's theater, UConn students work hard and play hard. Over 650 student clubs and organizations allow students to pursue their passions outside the classroom. School spirit permeates the campus. Students can cheer on one of our twenty-four Division I teams, or join one of our intramural or club sports teams. No matter how students are involved, they exemplify the Husky Spirit.

"Interested in learning more about what UConn can offer you? For details on the admissions process or to schedule a campus tour, visit admissions.uconn.edu."

SELECTIVITY

Admissions Rating	89
# of applicants	35,980
% of applicants accepted	49
% of acceptees attending	22
# offered a place on the wait list	3,386
% accepting a place on wait list	53
% admitted from wait list	8

FRESHMAN PROFILE

Range SAT EBRW	600–680
Range SAT Math	610–710
Range ACT Composite	26–31
# submitting SAT scores	3,011
% submitting SAT scores	82
# submitting ACT scores	1,233
% submitting ACT scores	33
% graduated top 10% of class	51
% graduated top 25% of class	84
% graduated top 50% of class	98

DEADLINES

Regular	
Deadline	1/15
Notification	Rolling, 3/1
Nonfall registration?	Yes

FINANCIAL FACTS

Financial Aid Rating	81
Annual in-state tuition	$13,798
Annual out-of-state tuition	$36,466
Room and board	$13,258
Required fees	$3,428
Books and supplies	$950
Average frosh need-based scholarship	$14,041
Average UG need-based scholarship	$13,049
% needy frosh rec. need-based scholarship or grant aid	67
% needy UG rec. need-based scholarship or grant aid	71
% needy frosh rec. non-need-based scholarship or grant aid	40
% needy UG rec. non-need-based scholarship or grant aid	33
% needy frosh rec. need-based self-help aid	62
% needy UG rec. need-based self-help aid	72
% frosh rec. any financial aid	49
% UG rec. any financial aid	48
% UG borrow to pay for school	59
Average cumulative indebtedness	$28,028
% frosh need fully met	15
% ugrads need fully met	12
Average % of frosh need met	58
Average % of ugrad need met	57

UNIVERSITY OF DALLAS

1845 East Northgate Drive, Irving, TX 75062 • Admissions: 972-721-5266 • Fax: 972-721-5017

STUDENTS SAY "..."

Academics

The University of Dallas is a small Catholic university that aims to unite its "community of learners" by having them "[investigate] the same essential questions of human life." This is accomplished through the school's Great Books curriculum, which puts all 1,500 undergrads through a sequence of nineteen core English, philosophy, and history courses. While this focus on primary texts leads to a "heavy homework load," students embrace this "rigorous, but reasonably so" coursework, saying that it creates "thoughtful and provoking discussions" that encourage them to develop "independent and opposing viewpoints to aid in a well-rounded education." Further setting UD apart from other institutions is the way it uses its "extremely well-established" Rome Program to encourage students to visit notable cities from their studies: "it's one thing to read and discuss the Great Books in a Texas classroom, and another to do so while immersed in the places where those books were written."

University of Dallas professors are the cornerstone of enrollee support. Instructors "care about their students and the UD community at large," as illustrated in the ways that "combine academic expertise and experience, classroom rapport, and interest in their students." And given the ten-to-one student-to-faculty ratio, it is no surprise that students and faculty form close relationships. Undergrads appreciate how professors treat them as intelligent individuals, saying they "are not trying to push their own agenda onto the students" and "lead us to reach our own conclusions and develop our own ideas rather than having us regurgitate lecture material." Many attest that the faculty at UD "want [them] to succeed," and their teachers' unending support has "made this university [their] home."

Life

At this "very academic focused" university "most students study together" across campus "in lounges, [the] library, the cafeteria, empty classrooms, [and other] main areas", as the "majority of the week is spent doing homework." But when undergrads are ready for a break, the school "has really unique traditions that offer plenty of occasions for fun activities." For instance, the Campus Activities Board hosts weekly TGIT (Thank. Goodness. It's. Thursday!) events at the bar and grill on campus, which include live music, drinks, and themes, as well as Quiz Bowl on Wednesdays, where students "can win gift cards and prizes." For those looking for relief in the form of a spiritual community, "daily Mass is also a popular weekday activity." On the weekends, you're never too far from your friends since all students under the age of twenty-one are required to live on campus in one of seven residence halls. In the dorms, undergrads enjoy participating in "programs put on by the resident assistants." Many also make plans to "attend sporting events [together] or hang out in each other's dorm rooms for fun." And when they're looking to get off campus for a bit, students "love to have bonfires, go on road trips, hang out in coffee shops, and have get-togethers."

Student Body

Community is strong at University of Dallas. Everyone at UD is "very close and welcoming [which] makes it easy to find a group of people with which you can learn and grow together," and the core "really does bond students together in the first years of college before getting more specific major-only classes." As one undergrad notes, "Every student, no matter what major, can relate to any other student because they all have the same academic background to some extent." With more than seventy-five percent of this "fun and respectful student body" identifying as Catholic, "the authenticity of the Catholic tradition is prevalent on campus and stays true to its nature." Enrollees find that with so much in common between their academics and their commitment to Catholic values, students will "talk all the time and for hours about everything, and it's awesome." Above all, undergrads at UD agree that they choose to "[gild] their days spending genuine and meaningful time with one another when they aren't studying."

UNIVERSITY OF DALLAS

Financial Aid: 972-721-5266 • E-Mail: crusader@udallas.edu • Website: www.udallas.edu

THE PRINCETON REVIEW SAYS

Admissions

Very important factors considered include: rigor of secondary school record, academic GPA, application essay, recommendation(s), character/personal qualities. *Important factors considered include:* standardized test scores (optional), class rank, talent/ability. *Other factors considered include:* interview, extracurricular activities, first generation, alumni/ae relation, volunteer work, work experience, level of applicant's interest. ACT with or without writing accepted. SAT with or without Essay component accepted. High school diploma is required and GED is accepted. *Academic units required:* 4 English, 3 math, 3 science, 2 foreign language, 3 social studies, 3 history, 3 academic electives, 1 visual/performing arts. *Academic units recommended:* 4 English, 4 math, 4 science, 3 science labs, 3 foreign language, 4 social studies, 4 history, 4 academic electives, 2 visual/performing arts.

Financial Aid

Students should submit: FAFSA. Priority filing deadline is 1/15. The Princeton Review suggests that all financial aid forms be submitted as soon as possible after October 1. *Need-based scholarships/grants offered:* College/university scholarship or grant aid from institutional funds; Federal Pell; Private scholarships; SEOG; State scholarships/grants. *Loan aid offered:* Direct PLUS loans; Direct Subsidized Stafford Loans; Direct Unsubsidized Stafford Loans. Applicants will be notified of awards on a rolling basis beginning 12/1. Federal Work-Study Program available. Institutional employment available.

The Inside Word

Because of University of Dallas's distinction as a Catholic liberal arts school, its applicant pool is frequently small but self-selective. As such, don't be fooled by its relatively high acceptance rate—strong academic performance and test scores are closely considered, as are students who demonstrate moral and ethical commitment in addition to intellectual curiosity.

THE SCHOOL SAYS "..."

From the Admissions Office

"Undergraduates at UD, whether they choose to major in art history, business, pastoral ministry, or one of 30 other programs, all share the formative experience of the Core Curriculum. 'The Core', which consists of courses in humanities, sciences, and fine arts, provides a common cross-disciplinary foundation that students carry forth into their various majors. This curriculum roots all further studies in the great deeds and works of Western civilization and inspires an ongoing dialogue with the past that helps in understanding the present. The common Core fuels robust discussion both inside and outside of the classroom, even more so when students travel to Rome for a semester as part of our renowned Rome Program, where all classes are part of the Core. While there, students can experience firsthand much of what they have learned about in class. We believe that education is more than just a means to an end, so our curriculum is designed to provide students with wisdom, knowledge, and skills that can be applied to all areas of life – intellectual, professional, spiritual and personal. As students develop life skills, such as independent and critical thinking, UD also offers them the support and encouragement of a dedicated faith community that enables them to engage the world beyond graduation as people of faith. All in all, the undergraduate UD experience is an inquiry into the fundamental aspects of being and our relationship with God, nature, and our fellow human beings, all while pursuing wisdom, truth, and virtue as the proper and primary ends of education."

SELECTIVITY
Admissions Rating	89
# of applicants	4,676
% of applicants accepted	45
% of acceptees attending	18

FRESHMAN PROFILE
Range SAT EBRW	590–700
Range SAT Math	540–660
Range SAT Composite	1150–1340
Range ACT Composite	24–30
# submitting SAT scores	257
% submitting SAT scores	67
# submitting ACT scores	193
% submitting ACT scores	51
Average HS GPA	3.8
% graduated top 10% of class	32
% graduated top 25% of class	66
% graduated top 50% of class	91

DEADLINES
Early action	
Deadline	12/1
Notification	1/15
Regular	
Priority	12/1
Deadline	8/1
Notification	Rolling, 9/15
Nonfall registration?	Yes

FINANCIAL FACTS
Financial Aid Rating	88
Annual tuition	$41,660
Room and board	$13,080
Required fees	$3,150
Books and supplies	$1,040
Average frosh need-based scholarship	$31,943
Average UG need-based scholarship	$29,804
% needy frosh rec. need-based scholarship or grant aid	97
% needy UG rec. need-based scholarship or grant aid	99
% needy frosh rec. non-need-based scholarship or grant aid	17
% needy UG rec. non-need-based scholarship or grant aid	15
% needy frosh rec. need-based self-help aid	63
% needy UG rec. need-based self-help aid	68
% frosh rec. any financial aid	99
% UG rec. any financial aid	98
% UG borrow to pay for school	60
Average cumulative indebtedness	$34,205
% frosh need fully met	20
% ugrads need fully met	20
Average % of frosh need met	82
Average % of ugrad need met	79

THE BEST 386 COLLEGES ■ 633

UNIVERSITY OF DAYTON

300 College Park, Dayton, OH 45469-1669 • Admissions: 937-229-4411 • Fax: 937-229-4729

STUDENTS SAY "..."

Academics

University of Dayton, a Catholic school in the Marianist tradition, has done a tremendous job fostering a sense of community throughout the campus. Dayton is an institution that places an emphasis on service, and undergrads feel that the school is the "perfect size." Academically, undergrads are quick to mention that "UD has a very strong engineering program...that encourages creativity and innovation." And overall, there are also lots of "good opportunities [to participate] in research." Students also benefit from "small" class sizes as well as professors who are "so passionate about their field[s]." They are usually quite "receptive to questions" and "never treat [students] like [they're] below them." UD professors are also great at making "their material very interesting [by fostering] discussions and [demonstrating real world] applications." Time and again they prove that they "are genuinely interested in student success...[and] always more than willing to talk and meet outside of the classroom." As this grateful student concludes, "I know all of my professors well at the end of the semester as we are able to develop a personal relationship."

Life

Undergrads at the University of Dayton are diligent about their studies, but they also understand the importance of stepping away from their books. You can find many UD students working out on a "daily [basis] at the "Rec Plex," and "intramural sports are also very popular." There are "over 250 clubs" in which students can (and do!) participate. For example, as one busy undergrad reveals, "I enjoy playing Quidditch two to three days per week. I am also in the Flyer Pep Band which is a fantastic way to get involved in the student section at basketball games." Further, "the school's activity board usually puts on a movie or different events [throughout the semester]." Dayton students also report that "the weekends are really fun, and everyone lets loose by going to the student neighborhood." There you'll find kids "hanging out on porches and filling their houses...with music and laughter." While drinking certainly occurs there, students assure us that "for the most part people practice safe behaviors." Lastly, when UD undergrads want a respite from collegiate life, they can head into downtown Dayton to enjoy the city's numerous restaurants and "vibrant arts scene."

Student Body

University of Dayton works hard to attract (and admit) students who are "very friendly and welcoming to others." As one undergrad gushes, "I have never been surrounded by a more positive group of people; everyone that attends is absolutely in love with the school and their passion for UD shows in everything they do." Many are also keen "to spend their time volunteering to improve Dayton and the wider Ohio community." Moreover, a laid back and "comfortable" lot, we're told that "leggings and sweatshirts are standard attire"—at least when it comes to attending class. Of course, some students do lament the fact that UD "is not very diverse." After all, students say the "majority [of undergrads] are white, upper-class [and] Catholic." Still, there's "always a place for someone new at the table." And no matter their background or ethnicity, Dayton students are united in their desire to both "work hard and have fun." As this incredibly content undergrad gently concludes, "there is no every man for himself mindset. Every person on campus is invested in helping one another to make UD feel like home. The day you choose to be a Flyer, you become a member of our family."

UNIVERSITY OF DAYTON

Financial Aid: 800-427-5029 • E-Mail: admission@udayton.edu • Website: www.udayton.edu

THE PRINCETON REVIEW SAYS

Admissions

Very important factors considered include: rigor of secondary school record, class rank, academic GPA, application essay, UD is moving to test optional for Fall 2021 admission. *Important factors considered include:* recommendation(s), extracurricular activities, character/personal qualities, alumni/ae relation. *Other factors considered include:* talent/ability, first generation, racial/ethnic status, volunteer work, work experience. ACT with or without writing accepted. SAT with or without Essay component accepted. High school diploma is required and GED is accepted. *Academic units recommended:* 4 English, 4 math, 4 science, 1 science lab, 2 foreign language, 4 social studies, 4 history, 4 computer science, 4 visual/performing arts.

Financial Aid

Students should submit: FAFSA. Priority filing deadline is 2/1. The Princeton Review suggests that all financial aid forms be submitted as soon as possible after October 1. *Need-based scholarships/grants offered:* College/university scholarship or grant aid from institutional funds; Federal Pell; Private scholarships; SEOG; State scholarships/grants. Federal Work-Study Program available. Institutional employment available.

The Inside Word

When it comes to the admissions process at the University of Dayton, academics take top priority. Indeed, the committee pays close attention to both your GPA and grade pattern throughout your high school tenure. Course selection, class rank, and UD is moving to test optional for Fall 2021. To a lesser extent, the university considers factors such as letters of recommendation. Finally, it will be a boon to your application if you can demonstrate strong interest in the university (in earnest of course).

THE SCHOOL SAYS "..."

From the Admissions Office

"The University of Dayton is a top-tier national, Catholic research university. Founded in 1850 by the Society of Mary (Marianists), UD is distinguished by our academics, research and commitment to the common good. Through experiential opportunities, our students go beyond learning by doing—they learn by doing good in the world. We offer more than 80 undergraduate and 50 graduate and doctoral programs, plus bachelor plus – master programs, and we provide credit for college-level courses and exams, as well as personalized, preliminary credit evaluations to help determine the credit students could receive at UD. Our students can work alongside GE Aviation and Emerson professionals in on-campus research facilities or study abroad at locations around the world. Academic programs are offered in the College of Arts and Sciences and the Schools of Business Administration, Education and Health Sciences, Engineering, and Law. Classes are small, which is just one reason 97 percent of our students find success within six months of graduation. We're also a strong research institution; UD performed $170.5 million in sponsored research last year, and our faculty are committed to teaching undergraduate students and involving them in their research projects. Dedicated to transparent affordability, we provide locked-in net tuition all four years, with no fees. We also offer scholarships for textbooks and studying abroad. Since we launched this innovative tuition plan, our students have reduced borrowing by more than 28 percent, and our graduation rate is now 81.5 percent. Because we are a Marianist university, a strong sense of community is core to the UD experience; eighty-five percent of our students live on campus all four years, either in our residence halls or our unique, porch-clad student neighborhood."

SELECTIVITY

Admissions Rating	81
# of applicants	17,462
% of applicants accepted	72
% of acceptees attending	16

FRESHMAN PROFILE

Range SAT EBRW	560–650
Range SAT Math	560–670
Range ACT Composite	23–29
# submitting SAT scores	687
% submitting SAT scores	34
# submitting ACT scores	1,709
% submitting ACT scores	84
Average HS GPA	3.7
% graduated top 10% of class	27
% graduated top 25% of class	59
% graduated top 50% of class	89

DEADLINES

Early action	
Deadline	11/1
Notification	12/15
Regular	
Priority	11/1
Deadline	3/1
Nonfall registration?	Yes

FINANCIAL FACTS

Financial Aid Rating	95
Annual tuition	$44,890
Room and board	$14,580
Books and supplies	$1,000
Average frosh need-based scholarship	$27,521
Average UG need-based scholarship	$25,093
% needy frosh rec. need-based scholarship or grant aid	99
% needy UG rec. need-based scholarship or grant aid	99
% needy frosh rec. non-need-based scholarship or grant aid	7
% needy UG rec. non-need-based scholarship or grant aid	9
% needy frosh rec. need-based self-help aid	75
% needy UG rec. need-based self-help aid	82
% frosh rec. any financial aid	97
% UG rec. any financial aid	94
% UG borrow to pay for school	63
Average cumulative indebtedness	$19,344
% frosh need fully met	98
% ugrads need fully met	94
Average % of frosh need met	82
Average % of ugrad need met	82

THE BEST 386 COLLEGES ■ 635

UNIVERSITY OF DELAWARE

210 South College Ave., Newark, DE 19716 • Admissions: 302-831-8123 • Fax: 302-831-6905

STUDENTS SAY ". . ."

Academics

As the largest university in the state, the University of Delaware is a medium-sized interdisciplinary school with "a wide range of opportunities [and] full of students with pride, ambition and eagerness to make an impact during the college years and beyond." This research university offers over 150 majors and plenty of chances to get into the lab, classroom, or a real-world setting for your major (particularly for the school's notable STEM and health-related programs). One strong aspect of UD is their range of 4+1 programs, which allow a student to receive a master's degree in the year immediately following the completion of their bachelor's, and "the unusual schedule (Winter Session)" allows for students to take advantage of the "variety of study abroad programs" through a short-term study abroad program.

Professors here are "helpful and available outside of the classroom," "invested in their classes," and "truly want students to succeed." The school's "many support systems and safety nets" ensure that students never get lost in the crowd. "Those who are falling behind have many resources they can refer to," says an early childhood education major. Students admit that teaching here can be "hit or miss" in terms of the quality of lectures, so "it is usually good to get in touch with other students and find out what professors are good or bad." Many professors conduct research or are involved with organizations around campus, and "they're always willing to let students join them or get more involved," as well.

Life

The beautiful campus is "so pleasing" that students immediately fall in love with the campus and offers "many places to study or just hang out and enjoy the company of fellow Blue Hens." Hanging out on Main Street is also "a big thing here," and its proximity means that "you don't feel confined to a campus because you can enjoy different restaurants and shopping." Schoolwork is "a large part of the day," however, "everyone gets their work done to be able to be social during the night." Small mixers and socials are held during the week, while weekends find a large chunk of students going to bars or house parties. Greek life is "definitely prominent" and tends to be popular on campus, and some say "you can't go a single day without seeing a fraternity or sorority event or fundraiser." For students who aren't on the hunt for a party, "there are more and more alternatives to parties for the students who are not big into partying," such as the weekly events at the student center on Friday and Saturday nights.

Student Body

Students have "a plethora of opportunities to get involved with any number of clubs and activities all over campus" and the majority are involved with "Greek life, club sports, interest clubs, or working for the university." The Delaware student body "has a lot of school spirit" and is a welcoming bunch: "Everyone is so friendly and nice it seems impossible to think you would ever meet someone otherwise." Though UD is "not very diverse in a sense of...ethnicity," it is "very diverse...regarding personality," so "everyone should be able to find the right group for them." There is a strong interest in the many registered student organizations on campus grounds to help students find communities, but no matter what your interests are at UD, "whenever you go anywhere you see many smiling faces."

Financial Aid: 302-831-0520 • E-Mail: admissions@udel.edu • Website: http://www.udel.edu

THE PRINCETON REVIEW SAYS

Admissions

Very important factors considered include: rigor of secondary school record, academic GPA, state residency. *Important factors considered include:* application essay, standardized test scores, recommendation(s), extracurricular activities, talent/ability, character/personal qualities, volunteer work, work experience. *Other factors considered include:* class rank, remote interview, first generation, alumni/ae relation, geographical residence, racial/ethnic status, level of applicant's interest. SAT or ACT. High school diploma is required and GED is accepted. *Academic units required:* 4 English, 3 math, 3 science, 2 science labs, 2 foreign language, 4 history/social studies, 2 academic electives. *Academic units recommended:* 4 English, 4 math, 4 science, 3 science labs, 4 foreign language, 4 history/social studies, 2 academic electives.

Financial Aid

Students should submit: FAFSA. Priority filing deadline is 1/15. The Princeton Review suggests that all financial aid forms be submitted as soon as possible after October 1. *Need-based scholarships/grants offered:* College/university scholarship or grant aid from institutional funds; Federal Pell; Private scholarships; SEOG; State scholarships/grants. *Loan aid offered:* Direct PLUS loans; Direct Subsidized Stafford Loans; Direct Unsubsidized Stafford Loans. Applicants will be notified of awards on a rolling basis after the offer of admission. Federal Work-Study Program available. Institutional employment available.

The Inside Word

UD is state assisted but privately governed. Out-of-state students also benefit from the school's academic and social offerings at a reasonable tuition. Even so, the school is expressly committed to supporting Delawarean students, who compose about 34 percent of each incoming class. More details and samples of qualifying high school curricula are available on the admissions department website. In all admissions decisions, UD considers the entirety of a student's application; there are no minimum test scores or GPAs.

THE SCHOOL SAYS "..."

From the Admissions Office

"The University of Delaware, was chartered in 1743 and is located in Newark, DE, a vibrant college town midway between New York City and Washington, D.C. At UD, you can go from a concert in our music halls to a lecture on bioengineering to tours of the ancient world while taking advantage of our many study abroad programs. For each of our 17,000 undergraduate students, we foster connections: connections to ideas, to professors and to alumni, connections that can be cultivated into assets for the future. In each of our 150+ majors, our broad academic selections and our priority for hands-on research is designed to stimulate a passion for learning, curiosity and a connection with the larger world.

"Our distinguished faculty includes internationally known authors, scientists, business professionals and artists. State-of-the-art facilities support UD's academic, research and service activities. You'll find campus life is welcoming, enriched by distinguished speakers from various fields, NCAA Division I intercollegiate athletics, 350-plus student organizations, and a host of cultural activities."

SELECTIVITY

Admissions Rating	87
# of applicants	26,866
% of applicants accepted	68
% of acceptees attending	23
# offered a place on the wait list	3,194
% accepting a place on wait list	7
% admitted from wait list	31

FRESHMAN PROFILE

Range SAT EBRW	590–670
Range SAT Math	580–690
Range ACT Composite	24–30
# submitting SAT scores	3,189
% submitting SAT scores	77
# submitting ACT scores	900
% submitting ACT scores	22
Average HS GPA	3.8
% graduated top 10% of class	34
% graduated top 25% of class	69
% graduated top 50% of class	94

DEADLINES

Regular	
Deadline	1/15
Notification	Rolling, 11/1
Nonfall registration?	Yes

APPLICANTS ALSO LOOK AT AND OFTEN PREFER
University of Maryland, College Park; Penn State University Park

AND SOMETIMES PREFER
University of Connecticut; University of Pittsburgh

FINANCIAL FACTS

Financial Aid Rating	82
Annual in-state tuition	$12,730
Annual out-of-state tuition	$34,160
Room and board	$13,208
Required fees	$1,550
Books and supplies	$1,000
Average frosh need-based scholarship	$12,694
Average UG need-based scholarship	$10,805
% needy frosh rec. need-based scholarship or grant aid	96
% needy UG rec. need-based scholarship or grant aid	87
% needy frosh rec. non-need-based scholarship or grant aid	9
% needy UG rec. non-need-based scholarship or grant aid	7
% needy frosh rec. need-based self-help aid	74
% needy UG rec. need-based self-help aid	80
% frosh rec. any financial aid	58
% UG rec. any financial aid	50
% UG borrow to pay for school	59
Average cumulative indebtedness	$37,447
% frosh need fully met	12
% ugrads need fully met	10
Average % of frosh need met	61
Average % of ugrad need met	55

UNIVERSITY OF DENVER

Office of Admission, Denver, CO 80208 • Admissions: 303-871-2036 • Fax: 303-871-3301

STUDENTS SAY "..."

Academics

At the University of Denver—the oldest private university in the Rocky Mountain region—the faculty and staff are "extremely dedicated to ensuring that the students receive a high-quality, worthwhile education." The business and accountancy programs are the standouts of the "plethora of classes to choose from," but the school is all about "a global view and interdisciplinary courses" and so has one of the best study abroad programs in the nation, giving students the option to do so without straying from their majors or incurring additional expense, and offering international travel interterm courses to students.

The "lively, passionate" professors teach with hands-on, real-life examples that "prompt students to critically think and apply what is learned in the classroom to our future careers and life." Teachers usually allow students to dictate speed and amount of discussion on a topic as the class allows, and take a vested interest in each student's success: They "care more about how you do in the long run than how you may perform in individual classes." "If you try hard, they will engage with you and truly become your friends." "The face-to-face time you get with them is a big reason why I feel so connected to my school," says another student.

Networking here "happens almost without effort; it is ingrained in every aspect of most classes and activities" and there is a "good connection with [the] Denver business community." DU has "basically every resource on campus for advising, counseling, health, and assistance with school work," an "awesome" library, and "there are a lot of 'green' initiatives…it feels quite progressive." Though the common curriculum isn't universally beloved, students appreciate that DU runs on a quarterly system, so people "can take more credits than other semester schools…if you don't like a particular class ... you are done within ten weeks and you can move on with classes you enjoy."

Life

DU is close enough to the city of Denver that it is possible for students to head downtown whenever they feel like it (the light rail stops on campus and is free for students), but "far enough away that I still get the 'campus' feel." "The nightlife is great around the DU area (for students of age) and downtown has amazing bars and restaurants." The residential living communities and programs get high marks, and "there is never a dull moment on campus." "Everyone is so active and there is so much going on that you almost feel bad if you're not doing anything," says a student. "Microbrews! Pub Quizzes! Poetry Slams! Sleep! Reading! Concerts!" sums up another.

If there's one trait that DU students share, it's "outdoorsy." Many students spend their weekends being active, active, active and enjoy meeting people through the Alpine Club, which "sponsors trips to nearby mountains, deserts, and parks for outdoor activities like skiing, hiking, biking, and backpacking." "Find a friend who comes from one of the ski towns, and see if you can bum a ride from them for a weekend on the slopes," suggests a student. About a quarter of the student population goes Greek, and intramurals and hockey are huge. Denver also has an amazing music scene; "Red Rocks Amphitheatre is—no exaggeration—the best music venue on the globe."

Student Body

DU has a wide variety of people (the majority being "white and middle to upper class") who are "pretty driven," while still "[knowing] how to make time to do something outdoorsy on the weekends." Everybody "respects themselves and the people around them, especially in the learning environment." Obviously, everyone here "loves to ski" and social lives are a huge part of the DU campus culture, so "many join club sports, student orgs, or student alliances" through which they "are able to easily find people to relate to."

University of Denver

Financial Aid: 303-871-4020 • E-Mail: admission@du.edu • Website: http://www.du.edu

THE PRINCETON REVIEW SAYS

Admissions

Very important factors considered include: rigor of secondary school record, academic GPA, standardized test scores. *Important factors considered include:* application essay, recommendation(s), extracurricular activities, talent/ability, character/personal qualities. *Other factors considered include:* first generation, alumni/ae relation, geographical residence, racial/ethnic status, volunteer work, work experience, level of applicant's interest. ACT with or without writing accepted. SAT with or without Essay component accepted. High school diploma is required and GED is accepted. *Academic units recommended:* 4 English, 4 math, 4 science, 2 science labs, 4 foreign language, 4 social studies.

Financial Aid

Students should submit: CSS/Financial Aid PROFILE; FAFSA; Noncustodial PROFILE. Priority filing deadline is 2/15. The Princeton Review suggests that all financial aid forms be submitted as soon as possible after October 1. *Need-based scholarships/grants offered:* College/university scholarship or grant aid from institutional funds; Federal Pell; Private scholarships; SEOG; State scholarships/grants. *Loan aid offered:* Direct PLUS loans; Direct Subsidized Stafford Loans; Direct Unsubsidized Stafford Loans. Applicants will be notified of awards on or about 3/1. Federal Work-Study Program available. Institutional employment available.

The Inside Word

Admission officers at University of Denver take a holistic approach to the application process. Therefore, they strive to look beyond quantitative factors and will also review your essay, recommendations, and extracurricular activities. The average high school GPA for fall 2017 accepted students was 3.7.

THE SCHOOL SAYS "..."

From the Admissions Office

"At the University of Denver—in our setting of great natural beauty, cultural richness, and intellectual energy—you'll experience meaningful interaction with professors who set you on paths toward personal discovery, paths that can change the course of your future. Our diverse student body, engaged faculty, and prime location provide a culture of opportunity that is unique and unrivaled. DU is continually developing educational initiatives that help students prepare for an ever-changing world. Our Living and Learning Communities and Pioneer Leadership Program provide extracurricular and co-curricular programming in specialized areas; the Partners in Scholarship (PinS) program funds undergraduate research for students wishing to pursue a topic of personal interest in greater depth; and nearly 80 percent of our students are taking advantage of invaluable internship opportunities in laboratories, corporate offices, government agencies, and cultural settings. One of the university's signature offerings is the Cherrington Global Scholars program, which allows students to study abroad at the same cost of a quarter spent on campus at DU. Over 70 percent of our students study abroad, which ranks DU fourth in the nation among doctoral and research institutions for percentage of students participating. Outside the classroom, DU students put ideas and ideals into action. They are active members of our community and they take advantage of the numerous recreational opportunities available to them, including club, intramural, and 17 Division I sports. Whatever their majors and interests, DU students are inspired by Denver's Rocky Mountain spirit of exploration and openness, and are encouraged to engage in and personalize their educational journey."

SELECTIVITY

Admissions Rating	82
# of applicants	21,028
% of applicants accepted	59
% of acceptees attending	11
# offered a place on the wait list	472
% accepting a place on wait list	43
% admitted from wait list	28
# of early decision applicants	363
% accepted early decision	46%

FRESHMAN PROFILE

# submitting SAT scores	739
% submitting SAT scores	55
# submitting ACT scores	743
% submitting ACT scores	56

DEADLINES

Early decision	
Deadline	11/1
Notification	12/15
Other ED Deadline	1/15
Other ED Notification	2/20
Early action	
Deadline	11/1
Notification	1/15
Regular	
Deadline	1/15
Notification	3/15
Nonfall registration?	Yes

APPLICANTS ALSO LOOK AT AND OFTEN PREFER

Colorado College; Colorado State University; University of Colorado Boulder

AND SOMETIMES PREFER

Boston University; University of Puget Sound; University of Vermont; Santa Clara University; Southern Methodist University; The George Washington University; University of Southern California

FINANCIAL FACTS

Financial Aid Rating	89
Annual tuition	$52,596
Room and board	$14,178
Books and supplies	$1,000
Average frosh need-based scholarship	$36,795
Average UG need-based scholarship	$36,561
% needy frosh rec. need-based scholarship or grant aid	99
% needy UG rec. need-based scholarship or grant aid	99
% needy frosh rec. non-need-based scholarship or grant aid	25
% needy UG rec. non-need-based scholarship or grant aid	23
% needy frosh rec. need-based self-help aid	68
% needy UG rec. need-based self-help aid	68
% frosh rec. any financial aid	85
% UG rec. any financial aid	85
% UG borrow to pay for school	44
Average cumulative indebtedness	$27,938
% frosh need fully met	29
% ugrads need fully met	31
Average % of frosh need met	84
Average % of ugrad need met	84

UNIVERSITY OF FLORIDA

201 Criser Hall, Gainesville, FL 32611-4000 • Admissions: 352-392-1365 • Fax: 352-392-2115

CAMPUS LIFE

Quality of Life Rating	86
Fire Safety Rating	88
Green Rating	93
Type of school	Public
Environment	City

STUDENTS

Total undergrad enrollment	35,405
% male/female	44/56
% from out of state	8
% frosh from public high school	84
% frosh live on campus	83
% ugrads live on campus	24
# of fraternities (% ugrad men join)	36 (17)
# of sororities (% ugrad women join)	28 (23)
% African American	6
% Asian	9
% Caucasian	52
% Hispanic	23
% Native American	<1
% Pacific Islander	<1
% Two or more races	4
% Race and/or ethnicity unknown	3
% international	2
# of countries represented	114

SURVEY SAYS . . .

Great library
Career services are great
Recreation facilities are great
Lots of beer drinking
Everyone loves the Gators
Intramural sports are popular
Campus newspaper is popular
Alumni active on campus

ACADEMICS

Academic Rating	79
% students returning for sophomore year	97
% students graduating within 4 years	67
% students graduating within 6 years	88
Calendar	Semester
Student/faculty ratio	17:1
Profs interesting rating	83
Profs accessible rating	90

MOST POPULAR MAJORS

Biology/Biological Sciences, General; Psychology, General; Finance, General

STUDENTS SAY "..."

Academics

Located in the heart of the "Gator Nation," Gainesville, Florida, the University of Florida offers "a hell of a deal" on "one of the best educations in the nation." Students are proud that UF is "the best state school in Florida" and "one of the top public universities in the nation"; they also love that it's "a great school with a large alumni network," that there's plenty of "intellectual stimulation" to be found there, and that UF's "research opportunities are abundant." Though the school has "strong academic standards" across the board, programs in Business and Journalism are particularly "highly ranked." "Access to alumni" pays off when students seek "opportunities for networking and research," and they find that "as a large school, [UF] has a lot of funding and a large number of opportunities for student involvement." Students say that the university's size doesn't sacrifice individuals' ability to focus on their course of study: "Classes for your major are hard, but they prepare you for more than easier classes would. They better prepare you for your career." Moreover, "as a research university with nearly every graduate program imaginable, the opportunities are endless." Students praise the "truly incredible faculty and staff" and appreciate that "one of the greatest strengths of UF is the fact there is always someone to turn to for help." Class structure is still impacted by the school's size in that "lectures are 80–90 percent of class activities," but conversely, students love "having experts in my field teaching all of my classes for my major." If "breadth of opportunities" for a value price is a priority for you, "The Gator Nation is one where anyone can build a future for themselves."

Life

In terms of town-gown relations, "Gainesville revolves around UF, most everything is catered to the students and student life." "Bars are the big scene," and students "love going out with friends on the weekends to Midtown. It is a UF staple to party at Grog, Balls, and Salty Dog once you turn twenty-one." "Tons of school spirit" ranks high on the list of things students love about UF, as "A lot of UF culture is based around sports." "Greek life...is a big deal in both the social and extracurricular scene," and "when you are in the Greek community, there are many things to do." For other students, "I find myself working or studying in a computer lab most of the time," and "there is a really intense nightlife, but when it comes to exams, papers and finals week, it is pretty quiet everywhere." Extracurricular life can also be as forward-looking as you want it to be: "In addition to classes, I research in a lab with the College of Medicine and volunteer at the hospital located on campus." Students "play sports," and "For fun, there are several places to go such as Paynes Prairie, Devil's Millhopper, or other outdoor activities." If you want to get involved, join one of the many clubs: "There is literally a club for everyone at UF," and "you make it what you want. You can party every day or you can study every day. I keep it pretty balanced."

Student Body

While "everyone is different," "fraternity and sorority participation...dominates the student culture." Students are "hard working and interested in getting ahead," and "even though UF is considered a party school, it is full of people who put their future careers first." "Students fit in by taking part in and participating in the various things our campus offers" and are often "busy and focused usually on one subject matter or area of interest to be involved in through extracurricular activities." Even though it's a large campus, one student remarks on the sense of community: "We're students? I thought we were all part of one big family!" They find each other "mostly accepting and friendly," but as a whole "hard to define. Gators are religious and non-religious, Greek and non-Greek, obsessed with athletics and some couldn't care less." Overall, the typical UF student "knows how to balance their school work and still have a good time."

UNIVERSITY OF FLORIDA

Financial Aid: 352-294-3226 • E-Mail: https://admissions.ufl.edu/staff • Website: www.ufl.edu

THE PRINCETON REVIEW SAYS

Admissions

Very important factors considered include: rigor of secondary school record, academic GPA, application essay, extracurricular activities, talent/ability, character/personal qualities, volunteer work. *Important factors considered include:* standardized test scores, first generation. *Other factors considered include:* class rank, geographical residence, state residency, level of applicant's interest. ACT with or without writing accepted. SAT with or without Essay component accepted. High school diploma is required and GED is accepted. *Academic units required:* 4 English, 4 math, 3 science, 2 science labs, 2 foreign language, 3 social studies.

Financial Aid

Students should submit: FAFSA. Priority filing deadline is 12/15. The Princeton Review suggests that all financial aid forms be submitted as soon as possible after October 1. *Need-based scholarships/grants offered:* College/university scholarship or grant aid from institutional funds; Federal Pell; Private scholarships; SEOG; State scholarships/grants; United Negro College Fund. *Loan aid offered:* Direct PLUS loans; Direct Subsidized Stafford Loans; Direct Unsubsidized Stafford Loans. Applicants will be notified of awards on a rolling basis beginning 2/22. Federal Work-Study Program available. Institutional employment available.

The Inside Word

Unlike many state universities, UF doesn't publish an admissions formula, saying rather that they use a "holistic review" process to determine candidates' eligibility. Their application's short-answer and essay questions are emphasized in factors considered, and first-generation college students from low-income backgrounds should take note of the Florida Opportunity Scholars program, which covers four years of tuition in full.

THE SCHOOL SAYS "..."

From the Admissions Office

"University of Florida students come from more than 147 countries, all fifty states, and every one of the sixty-seven counties in Florida. Thirty-two percent of the student body is composed of graduate students. Within the undergraduate population, approximately 2,061 African-American students, 7,999 Hispanic students, and 3,237 Asian American students attend UF. Ninety percent of the entering freshmen rank above the national mean of scores on standard entrance exams. UF consistently ranks near the top among public universities in the number of new National Merit and Achievement scholars in attendance.

"Students must submit the SAT with or without the Essay or the ACT with or without the writing section. UF considers your highest section scores across all SAT test dates."

SELECTIVITY

Admissions Rating	96
# of applicants	38,069
% of applicants accepted	37
% of acceptees attending	47

FRESHMAN PROFILE

Range SAT EBRW	650–720
Range SAT Math	660–750
Range SAT Composite	1320–1450
Range ACT Composite	28–33
# submitting SAT scores	5,540
% submitting SAT scores	85
# submitting ACT scores	3,281
% submitting ACT scores	50
Average HS GPA	4.5
% graduated top 10% of class	81
% graduated top 25% of class	98
% graduated top 50% of class	100

DEADLINES

Regular	
Priority	11/1
Deadline	3/1

FINANCIAL FACTS

Financial Aid Rating	85
Annual in-state tuition	$6,381
Annual out-of-state tuition	$28,658
Room and board	$10,590
Books and supplies	$890
Average frosh need-based scholarship	$9,083
Average UG need-based scholarship	$8,476
% needy frosh rec. need-based scholarship or grant aid	53
% needy UG rec. need-based scholarship or grant aid	62
% needy frosh rec. non-need-based scholarship or grant aid	88
% needy UG rec. non-need-based scholarship or grant aid	68
% needy frosh rec. need-based self-help aid	28
% needy UG rec. need-based self-help aid	41
% frosh rec. any financial aid	90
% UG rec. any financial aid	85
% UG borrow to pay for school	38
Average cumulative indebtedness	$21,800
% frosh need fully met	29
% ugrads need fully met	24
Average % of frosh need met	99
Average % of ugrad need met	98

UNIVERSITY OF GEORGIA

Terrell Hall, 210 South Jackson Street, Athens, GA 30602-1633 • Admissions: 706-542-8776

CAMPUS LIFE

Quality of Life Rating	92
Fire Safety Rating	88
Green Rating	95
Type of school	Public
Environment	City

STUDENTS

Total undergrad enrollment	22,919
% male/female	44/56
% from out of state	11
% frosh from public high school	65
% frosh live on campus	98
% ugrads live on campus	33
# of fraternities (% ugrad men join)	37 (20)
# of sororities (% ugrad women join)	29 (31)
% African American	8
% Asian	10
% Caucasian	69
% Hispanic	6
% Native American	<1
% Pacific Islander	<1
% Two or more races	4
% Race and/or ethnicity unknown	1
% international	2
# of countries represented	90

SURVEY SAYS . . .

Great library
Great food on campus
Recreation facilities are great
Lots of beer drinking
Hard liquor is popular
Everyone loves the Bulldogs
Intramural sports are popular
Frats and sororities are popular
Alumni active on campus

ACADEMICS

Academic Rating	80
% students returning for sophomore year	96
% students graduating within 4 years	63
Calendar	Semester
Student/faculty ratio	17:1
Profs interesting rating	87
Profs accessible rating	90
Most classes have 10–19 students.	

MOST POPULAR MAJORS

Biology/Biological Sciences, General; Finance, General; Psychology, General

STUDENTS SAY "..."

Academics

As at many large universities, UGA has a "mixed bag of professors," but there are "more good teachers" than bad. Though students don't love the core curriculum classes due to their large size and the prevalence of TAs, "once [you're] in your particular program, the teachers are outstanding and easy to reach." "The professors really do want to see you at office hours if you have questions," and they "want to share their love of learning with you." "My major-related classes are very small, and each student receives individual attention." The honors program also receives raves: "Many of my best classes and favorite teachers have come from the honors program, but non-honors classes are generally good as well." "The study spaces are well-equipped and quiet," but "the school of social work is still housed in an old dorm." "Administration is a pain (not the people, only the requirements), but I think that describes academia in general." In general, students "feel that the administration can be very accommodating at times, but at other times it can seem like it is full of red tape." Registration technology "needs to be brought out of the 1980s and into the twenty-first century." "The administration [can] seem like a bunch of penny-pinchers, but they must be to run a major research facility."

Life

Life at UGA seems to be a good mix of the two different worlds of sports and arts: football, frats, and tailgating on campus come together nicely with the coffee shops and music scene in downtown Athens. "On Saturday afternoons in the fall, nearly everyone on campus is at the football game. It's a way of life here." "Everybody really gets behind the team, and Saturdays in Athens feel like mini vacations." Fraternities and sororities dominate the party scene, but "there is definitely plenty to do, even if you don't go Greek." Students love to brag about the high number of bars per capita in Athens, but there's plenty more to boast about. "The Athens music and art scene is very inspiring, and there are tons of opportunities for creativity here." "Downtown Athens is fabulous! Whether you drink or don't drink, all are welcome and all congregate there." Campus life offers plenty of activity too. "Fun is a part of daily life...with a dozen intramural sports each semester...and many community activities (multiple movie theaters, bowling allies, golf course)." "Ultimate Frisbee, walks around the multiple parks, days lounging on North Campus, and spending *lots* of time downtown are a couple ways I like to have fun at school." "There are so many organizations that everyone can find a place that will feel like home or find a place to meet new people." "It's no secret that UGA knows how to party. However, most of the students know how to manage social and academic time."

Student Body

"Students are generally white, upper-middle-class, smart, [and] involved, and [they] have a good time," "seem to be predominantly conservative," and "are usually involved in at least one organization whether it be Greek, a club, or sports." "The typical student at UGA is one who knows how and when to study but allows himself or herself to have a very active social life." The majority are Southerners, with many students from within Georgia. "The stereotype is Southern, Republican, football-loving, and beer-drinking. While many, many of UGA's students do not fit this description, there is no lack of the above," and "there is a social scene for everyone in Athens." "There are a great number of atypical students in the liberal arts," which "creates a unique and exciting student body with greatly contrasting opinions."

Financial Aid: 706-542-6147 • E-Mail: adm-info@uga.edu • Website: www.uga.edu

THE PRINCETON REVIEW SAYS

Admissions

Very important factors considered include: rigor of secondary school record, academic GPA. *Important factors considered include:* standardized test scores. *Other factors considered include:* application essay, recommendation(s), extracurricular activities, talent/ability, character/personal qualities, first generation, volunteer work, work experience. ACT with or without writing accepted. SAT with or without Essay component accepted. High school diploma is required and GED is accepted. *Academic units required:* 4 English, 4 math, 4 science, 2 science labs, 2 foreign language, 3 social studies. *Academic units recommended:* 4 English, 4 math, 4 science, 2 science labs, 3 foreign language, 3 social studies, 1 academic elective.

Financial Aid

Students should submit: FAFSA. Priority filing deadline is 12/15. The Princeton Review suggests that all financial aid forms be submitted as soon as possible after October 1. *Need-based scholarships/grants offered:* College/university scholarship or grant aid from institutional funds; Federal Pell; Private scholarships; SEOG; State scholarships/grants. *Loan aid offered:* Direct PLUS loans; Direct Subsidized Stafford Loans; Direct Unsubsidized Stafford Loans. Applicants will be notified of awards on a rolling basis beginning 5/1. Federal Work-Study Program available. Institutional employment available.

The Inside Word

A school as large as UGA must start winnowing applicants by the numbers. If you fail to meet certain baseline curricular, GPA, and standardized-test-score floors, only exceptional talent elsewhere (a gift for the arts or, better still, throwing a football) will get you past the first cut. Some students here are Georgia residents reaping the benefits of the state's HOPE/Zell Miller scholarship programs, which pay tuition and most school-related fees for state residents who earn at least a 3.7 GPA in high school, a 1200 SAT or 26 ACT score, and maintain a 3.3 in college. Georgia state residents who earn at least a 3.0 in high school will also have a large portion of their tuition paid.

THE SCHOOL SAYS "..."

From the Admissions Office

"The University of Georgia offers students the advantages and resources of a top public research university, including a wide range of majors and exceptional academic facilities such as the 260,000 square-foot Miller Learning Center. At the same time, UGA provides opportunities more common to smaller, private schools, such as first-year seminars led by distinguished faculty and learning communities that connect students with similar academic interests. The university is committed to challenging its academically superior students in the classroom and beyond, with increased emphasis on undergraduate research, service-learning, and study abroad. UGA students taking advantage of such offerings find themselves well positioned to compete with the best undergraduates in the country, as evidenced by their recent string of successes in winning Rhodes, Marshall, Truman, and other major scholarships. The UGA campus, considered one of the most beautiful in the nation, adjoins vibrant downtown Athens. While Athens is renowned for its local music scene, UGA also houses the Performing Arts Center, the Hugh Hodgson School of Music, the Lamar Dodd School of Art, and the Georgia Museum of Art. Sports—from football to gymnastics—are also a major attraction, with UGA teams perennially ranked among the best in the country. To experience the excitement of UGA, most prospective students visit campus, a ninety-minute drive northeast of the Atlanta airport. See the admissions website to sign up for a tour with the Visitors Center, view the weekday schedule of admissions information sessions, and find application details. Applicants for first-year admission will be required to submit either the SAT or ACT. Students submitting only the ACT must also submit the optional ACT writing test."

SELECTIVITY

Admissions Rating	90
# of applicants	24,165
% of applicants accepted	54
% of acceptees attending	45
# offered a place on the wait list	889
% accepting a place on wait list	60
% admitted from wait list	6

FRESHMAN PROFILE

Range SAT EBRW	610–690
Range SAT Math	590–680
Range ACT Composite	26–31
# submitting SAT scores	3,946
% submitting SAT scores	68
# submitting ACT scores	4,319
% submitting ACT scores	74
Average HS GPA	4.0
% graduated top 10% of class	54
% graduated top 25% of class	90
% graduated top 50% of class	99

DEADLINES

Early action	
Deadline	10/15
Notification	12/1
Regular	
Priority	10/15
Deadline	1/1
Nonfall registration?	Yes

FINANCIAL FACTS

Financial Aid Rating	86
Annual in-state tuition	$12,080
Annual out-of-state tuition	$31,120
Room and board	$10,314
Books and supplies	$986
Average frosh need-based scholarship	$11,114
Average UG need-based scholarship	$9,776
% needy frosh rec. need-based scholarship or grant aid	97
% needy UG rec. need-based scholarship or grant aid	92
% needy frosh rec. non-need-based scholarship or grant aid	25
% needy UG rec. non-need-based scholarship or grant aid	18
% needy frosh rec. need-based self-help aid	43
% needy UG rec. need-based self-help aid	50
% frosh rec. any financial aid	45.6
% UG rec. any financial aid	44.9
% UG borrow to pay for school	43
Average cumulative indebtedness	$22,872
% frosh need fully met	31
% ugrads need fully met	26
Average % of frosh need met	79
Average % of ugrad need met	74

UNIVERSITY OF HAWAI'I—MĀNOA

2500 Campus Road, Honolulu, HI 96822-2301 • Admissions: 808-956-8975 • Fax: 808-956-4148

CAMPUS LIFE
Quality of Life Rating	86
Fire Safety Rating	89
Green Rating	60*
Type of school	Public
Environment	Metropolis

STUDENTS
Total undergrad enrollment	12,609
% male/female	43/57
% from out of state	28
% frosh live on campus	52
% ugrads live on campus	23
# of fraternities (% ugrad men join)	2 (1)
# of sororities (% ugrad women join)	3 (1)
% African American	2
% Asian	40
% Caucasian	20
% Hispanic	2
% Native American	<1
% Pacific Islander	17
% Two or more races	16
% Race and/or ethnicity unknown	<1
% international	3
# of countries represented	67

SURVEY SAYS . . .
Students love Honolulu, HI
Recreation facilities are great
Students are happy
Students are friendly
Diverse student types interact on campus
Students get along with local community

ACADEMICS
Academic Rating	75
% students returning for sophomore year	79
% students graduating within 4 years	32
Calendar	Semester
Student/faculty ratio	10:1
Profs interesting rating	81
Profs accessible rating	87

Most classes have 10–19 students.
Most lab/discussion sessions have
10–19 students.

MOST POPULAR MAJORS
Registered Nursing/Registered Nurse; Biology/
Biological Sciences, General; Psychology, General

STUDENTS SAY "..."

Academics

This flagship school of the University of Hawai'i system offers nearly one hundred bachelor's programs to the 13,000 or so students who call the O'ahu campus home during the school year. A lot of the school's vibe is "very laid back, just like the Hawaiian lifestyle," and students often show up to class with bikinis and swim trunks under their clothes from that morning's beach trip. Nearly 250 degree programs across seventeen schools are available to students but no matter the course of study, Hawai'i plays TA. "When someone goes to UH Mānoa, they aren't expecting to receive a Hawaiian education but that is exactly what they get. Whether they are learning the Hawaiian language, Hawaiian culture, or about the Hawaiian ecosystem, there is a lot for everyone that goes along with their major," says a student. "UH really incorporates how important Hawai'i really is."

Sciences are particularly strong here, and the language offerings are incredibly diverse (think Ilocano and Tagalog). Teachers are "always willing to go the extra mile to help students by offering office hours" and many professors challenge students while simultaneously "letting us know what content will be useful in our future careers and/or graduate level exams." However, the real gold here is in the added resources for extra help in classes. There is "free one-on-one tutoring" and review sessions through the learning center, a writing center, a learning emporium for certain subjects, and "[you] can even walk into the library where librarians will help to find sources for papers and guide students in a great direction."

Life

UH Mānoa is on an island that offers a bit of everything. Here you can find "the city, the country, the surf, the mountains, the malls, and so on and so on. Oahu has something to fit my every mood and need," says a student. There are always cultural festivals and activities, and Hawai'i is made for active people who "like to get lost in nature's beauty." Whether you're "running up Koko Head, swimming with dolphins on the west side, catching some rays between classes on the Waikiki strip, or jumping off rocks on the north shore, there's no way to escape the beauty that is Hawai'i." On the weekend, many local students travel home so the campus can get very quiet, but students do use their IDs for free bus transportation to explore the relatively small island and student services and student affairs are "excellent." As is common with college students, "many of us do not have enough money to enjoy the nightlife, therefore we enjoy our free time at the beach." Still, students "have work that we can't just blow off for a swim or something." People like to use the grill that the school has set up, and there are "always people walking from place to place until late at night, hanging out with friends in the courtyards, skateboarding, or cooking out."

Student Body

This group—mainly from the Asia-Pacific region and mainland USA, with the occasional European or South American throw in—is a "huge melting pot" that is just "filled with Aloha." An "incredible amount of culture is exhibited here," most of all the Hawaiian cool: "I have never been on another college campus where it is completely normal to ride your skateboard barefoot or walk around with your surfboard." This is good news for the plenty of exchange students from Asia are here "trying to have an American campus experience"; ROTC also has a "very large" presence. On the whole, this is a "very relaxed and cool" bunch of students with whom "you can strike up friendly conversations with strangers in the cafeteria, or while waiting to cross the street, or while ordering food."

Financial Aid: 808-956-7251 • E-Mail: manoa.admissions@hawaii.edu • Website: http://manoa.hawaii.edu

THE PRINCETON REVIEW SAYS

Admissions

Very important factors considered include: rigor of secondary school record, academic GPA, standardized test scores. *Important factors considered include:* class rank, state residency. *Other factors considered include:* application essay, recommendation(s), interview, extracurricular activities, talent/ability, geographical residence. ACT with Writing required. SAT with or without Essay component accepted. High school diploma is required and GED is accepted. *Academic units required:* 4 English, 3 math, 3 science, 3 social studies, 5 academic electives.

Financial Aid

Students should submit: FAFSA. Priority filing deadline is 2/1. The Princeton Review suggests that all financial aid forms be submitted as soon as possible after October 1. *Need-based scholarships/grants offered:* College/university scholarship or grant aid from institutional funds; Federal Pell; Private scholarships; SEOG; State scholarships/grants. *Loan aid offered:* Direct PLUS loans; Direct Subsidized Stafford Loans; Direct Unsubsidized Stafford Loans. Applicants will be notified of awards on a rolling basis beginning 4/1. Federal Work-Study Program available. Institutional employment available.

The Inside Word

All students must have a minimum GPA of 2.8, be in the top 40 percent of their high school class, and must take either the SAT or the ACT. All applicants are encouraged to apply by the priority consideration deadline of January 5, as this deadline increases your chance of receiving financial aid and student housing. Certain programs (nursing, social work, education, and others) may have earlier admission deadlines.

THE SCHOOL SAYS "..."

From the Admissions Office

"Aloha and welcome to UH Mānoa, the largest campus in the University of Hawai'i System. We are located on the island of O'ahu, in Honolulu's lush Mānoa valley. With almost 100 undergraduate majors, over 200 student organizations, and a variety of Division I and intramural sports to choose from, you will agree that UH Mānoa is a great place for you to realize your academic, professional, and personal dreams.

"UH Mānoa is one of only a handful of institutions to hold the distinction of being a land-, sea-, and space-grant research institution. Classified by the Carnegie Foundation as having 'very high research activity,' UH Mānoa is known for its pioneering research in such fields as oceanography, astronomy, Pacific Islands and Asian area studies, linguistics, cancer research, and genetics.

"Applicants to UH Mānoa are expected to have a minimum score of 510 on all three sections of the SAT (or a 22 on all four sections of the ACT), and have completed a college preparatory high school curriculum. All applicants are encouraged to apply for priority consideration. Applying by this deadline (January 5 for fall admission, September 1 for spring) increases your chance of receiving financial aid and student housing.

"Experience the University of Hawai'i at Mānoa first hand. We welcome you to tour our Mānoa campus guided by our very own Rainbow Warrior students. Experience a campus tour by calling (808) 956-7137 or email visituhm@hawaii.edu.

SELECTIVITY

Admissions Rating	77
# of applicants	9,350
% of applicants accepted	83
% of acceptees attending	28

FRESHMAN PROFILE

Range SAT EBRW	530–620
Range SAT Math	525–620
Range ACT Composite	20–25
# submitting SAT scores	1,601
% submitting SAT scores	73
# submitting ACT scores	1,014
% submitting ACT scores	46
Average HS GPA	3.6
% graduated top 10% of class	25
% graduated top 25% of class	54
% graduated top 50% of class	86

DEADLINES

Regular	
Priority	1/5
Deadline	3/1
Notification	Rolling, 9/1
Nonfall registration?	Yes

FINANCIAL FACTS

Financial Aid Rating	86
Annual in-state tuition	$11,088
Annual out-of-state tuition	$33,120
Room and board	$12,686
Required fees	$882
Books and supplies	$1,040
Average frosh need-based scholarship	$10,706
Average UG need-based scholarship	$10,428
% needy frosh rec. need-based scholarship or grant aid	99
% needy UG rec. need-based scholarship or grant aid	95
% needy frosh rec. non-need-based scholarship or grant aid	27
% needy UG rec. non-need-based scholarship or grant aid	22
% needy frosh rec. need-based self-help aid	52
% needy UG rec. need-based self-help aid	57
% frosh rec. any financial aid	56
% UG rec. any financial aid	59
% UG borrow to pay for school	45
Average cumulative indebtedness	$24,233
% frosh need fully met	34
% ugrads need fully met	29
Average % of frosh need met	75
Average % of ugrad need met	70

UNIVERSITY OF HOUSTON

Office of Admissions, Houston, TX 77204-2023 • Admissions: 713-743-1010 • Fax: 713-743-7542

CAMPUS LIFE

Quality of Life Rating	82
Fire Safety Rating	96
Green Rating	88
Type of school	Public
Environment	Metropolis

STUDENTS

Total undergrad enrollment	37,689
% male/female	50/50
% from out of state	2
% frosh from public high school	94
% frosh live on campus	45
% ugrads live on campus	17
# of fraternities (% ugrad men join)	22 (3)
# of sororities (% ugrad women join)	18 (4)
% African American	10
% Asian	23
% Caucasian	22
% Hispanic	36
% Native American	<1
% Pacific Islander	<1
% Two or more races	3
% Race and/or ethnicity unknown	2
% international	4
# of countries represented	106

SURVEY SAYS . . .

Students love Houston, TX
Intramural sports are popular
Recreation facilities are great
Students are happy
Students are friendly
Diverse student types interact on campus
Students get along with local community

ACADEMICS

Academic Rating	74
% students returning for sophomore year	85
% students graduating within 4 years	32
% students graduating within 6 years	61
Calendar	Semester
Student/faculty ratio	23:1
Profs interesting rating	82
Profs accessible rating	87

Most classes have 20–29 students.
Most lab/discussion sessions have 20–29 students.

MOST POPULAR MAJORS

Biology/Biological Sciences, General; Psychology, General; Business Administration and Management, General

STUDENTS SAY ". . ."

Academics

Those who attend the University of Houston tap into a wealth of resources: a long list of majors, plentiful student organizations, and an extensive alumni network. The "diversity of programs" brings with it "a lot of super hands-on programs," and in that, "the university provides many different ways to get ahead." This is evidenced by the "high job placement" students cite. To that benefit, there are "plenty of opportunities to volunteer within the college" and to get your foot in the door—the school is near the epicenter of a number of different fields, including healthcare, oil and gas, and many Fortune 500 companies. With all of that, one student says, "It really seems my future is cared for and cultivated here."

That cultivation wouldn't be possible without the instructors at UH. However, students admit that professors can be "a mixed bag" in terms of their teaching efficacy. Don't let that worry you too much, though—there are "some real hidden gems at this school" and most of the faculty "put effort into teaching the student on the fundamentals of the course." That's often done with "fun and engaging class projects, such as a Shark Tank simulation," "discussion-based exams," or TED Talks. They're also fairly accessible outside of class: "Making appointments with advisors is not very difficult," says one student. And given that it's a Tier One research university, there are opportunities for "nearly one-on-one researching" with faculty.

Life

This is a "very organized and ... active student body," the sort of place where you'll find that students "go to the rec [center] to work out before or after classes." Everyone is "very social"—between classes, "there are always clusters of people, and the school does a good job of providing a lot of group space" for collaboration. However, if you need some time to yourself, the campus also has plenty of "individual spaces when you need" them. Those attending campus events will find they "always have games [and] free food," which is great for the students who also "enjoy walking around campus and trying out the different food trucks" when there aren't events going on. Student organizations are also "very involved on campus ... and try to help students do better or to provide opportunities for [growth]." Even with all of the options presented to them, for the most part "people are very focused on their studies." And since so many people here commute, "most students try to pack all their classes into two days," tending to "fill their day on campus with classes and studying/socializing in public places," such as the "really beautiful fountains and park-like areas around campus that are great for relaxing when it's warm out."

Student Body

The University is "extremely diverse both racially and culturally." As one student explains: "No two students sitting next to each other are the same." This diversity "makes for an environment that is collectively considerate about the circumstances of others." Even better, students are "approachable and just overall easy to talk to on campus" and "amazing with school spirit," particularly during athletic events. And while "many commute from home" and don't necessarily stick around to show that school spirit, "if you choose to get involved, you will meet some interesting and exciting people."

UNIVERSITY OF HOUSTON

Financial Aid: 713-743-1010 • E-Mail: admissions@uh.edu • Website: www.uh.edu

THE PRINCETON REVIEW SAYS

Admissions
Very important factors considered include: rigor of secondary school record, class rank, academic GPA, standardized test scores. *Other factors considered include:* application essay, recommendation(s), extracurricular activities, talent/ability, first generation, volunteer work, work experience. ACT with or without writing accepted. SAT with or without Essay component accepted. High school diploma is required and GED is accepted. *Academic units required:* 4 English, 3 math, 3 science, 2 science labs, 3 social studies. *Academic units recommended:* 4 math, 4 science, 2 foreign language, 1 history, 1 visual/performing arts.

Financial Aid
Students should submit: FAFSA. Priority filing deadline is 1/15. The Princeton Review suggests that all financial aid forms be submitted as soon as possible after October 1. *Need-based scholarships/grants offered:* College/university scholarship or grant aid from institutional funds; Federal Pell; Private scholarships; SEOG; State scholarships/grants. *Loan aid offered:* Direct PLUS loans; Direct Subsidized Stafford Loans; Direct Unsubsidized Stafford Loans. Applicants will be notified of awards on a rolling basis beginning 2/1. Federal Work-Study Program available. Institutional employment available.

The Inside Word
The school's large size means that acceptance is easier to achieve than at some smaller schools. Students who meet the State of Texas Uniform Admissions Policy and satisfy a certain scale of requirements for class ranking and/or SAT or ACT scores are assured admission. But even if your grades aren't seemingly up to par, the admissions committee will consider students individually based on a holistic review of certain aspects, such as first-generation, socioeconomic background, rigor of high school curriculum, family responsibilities, special talents, public service, and strong letters of recommendation or a persuasive statement explaining your special circumstances.

THE SCHOOL SAYS "..."

From the Admissions Office
"The University of Houston is a public research university recognized throughout the world as a leader in energy and health research, law, business, and environmental education. Located in America's fourth-largest city, the University of Houston is one of the most ethnically diverse metropolitan research universities in the United States. Its 46,100 students hail from 106 countries.

"In addition to preparing its students to succeed in today's global economy, the University of Houston also is a catalyst within its own community—changing lives through health, education, and outreach projects that help build a future for children in Houston, in Texas, and in the world.

"Other distinctive merits of the University of Houston include the establishment of a Phi Beta Kappa chapter, which indicates a strong foundation for undergraduate education and academic achievement, a historic Division I athletic program, with premier facilities, top-level arts programs, and an internationally recognized faculty including a Nobel Laureate; winners of the National Medal of Science, Pulitzer, and Tony awards; and members of prestigious National Academies. The Princeton Review has chosen the University of Houston for inclusion in its guidebook of the nation's best colleges.

"Discover the greatness of the University of Houston's dynamic campus of more than 857 acres—nestled just minutes from Houston's bustling theater and museum districts—where innovative teaching, revolutionary research, and nationally recognized and motivated students work together to create a globally competitive educational environment."

SELECTIVITY
Admissions Rating	86
# of applicants	25,393
% of applicants accepted	65
% of acceptees attending	34

FRESHMAN PROFILE
Range SAT EBRW	570–650
Range SAT Math	570–660
Range SAT Composite	1150–1300
Range ACT Composite	22–27
# submitting SAT scores	5,008
% submitting SAT scores	88
# submitting ACT scores	2,030
% submitting ACT scores	36
Average HS GPA	3.7
% graduated top 10% of class	32
% graduated top 25% of class	64
% graduated top 50% of class	88

DEADLINES
Regular	
Priority	11/15
Deadline	6/1
Nonfall registration?	Yes

FINANCIAL FACTS
Financial Aid Rating	82
Annual in-state tuition	$10,274
Annual out-of-state tuition	$25,934
Room and board	$9,368
Required fees	$1,002
Books and supplies	$1,338
Average frosh need-based scholarship	$10,738
Average UG need-based scholarship	$9,099
% needy frosh rec. need-based scholarship or grant aid	88
% needy UG rec. need-based scholarship or grant aid	84
% needy frosh rec. non-need-based scholarship or grant aid	4
% needy UG rec. non-need-based scholarship or grant aid	3
% needy frosh rec. need-based self-help aid	49
% needy UG rec. need-based self-help aid	53
% frosh rec. any financial aid	83
% UG rec. any financial aid	77
% UG borrow to pay for school	44
Average cumulative indebtedness	$22,858
% frosh need fully met	13
% ugrads need fully met	12
Average % of frosh need met	61
Average % of ugrad need met	59

UNIVERSITY OF IDAHO

UI Admissions Office, Moscow, ID 83844-4264 • Admissions: 208-885-6326 • Fax: 208-885-9119

CAMPUS LIFE

Quality of Life Rating	89
Fire Safety Rating	89
Green Rating	97
Type of school	Public
Environment	Town

STUDENTS

Total undergrad enrollment	7,227
% male/female	51/49
% from out of state	23
% frosh live on campus	90
% ugrads live on campus	39
# of fraternities (% ugrad men join)	18 (21)
# of sororities (% ugrad women join)	10 (22)
% African American	1
% Asian	2
% Caucasian	75
% Hispanic	11
% Native American	<1
% Pacific Islander	<1
% Two or more races	4
% Race and/or ethnicity unknown	2
% international	4
# of countries represented	45

SURVEY SAYS . . .

Students are happy
Great library
Students love Moscow, ID

ACADEMICS

Academic Rating	78
% students returning for sophomore year	77
% students graduating within 4 years	35
% students graduating within 6 years	56
Calendar	Semester
Student/faculty ratio	16:1
Profs interesting rating	85
Profs accessible rating	90

Most classes have 10–19 students.
Most lab/discussion sessions have
10–19 students.

MOST POPULAR MAJORS

Mechanical Engineering; Psychology, General;
Marketing/Marketing Management, General

STUDENTS SAY "..."

Academics

University of Idaho is truly a school that invests in its students. Despite its large size, the university manages to create a "personalized learning experience" for all undergrads. Idaho also provides numerous "networking opportunities" for their students. One lucky beneficiary explains, "Being here at UI, I've had the chance to meet many people in industry, which helped me land an internship at NASA JPL this past summer." Academically, Idaho offers students a wide range of stellar departments. However, undergrads especially like to tout the fantastic "engineering, agriculture, business, and law programs." Fortunately, no matter what you choose to study, the university is "incredible at creating an environment [in which] to build great relationships between professors and students." Though it's certainly helped by the fact that "the faculty here really cares about the students and genuinely wants to see them succeed." Undergrads also value that their professors "don't want students who [simply] suck up information and then vomit it back on a test." Instead, they're hoping to form "well-educated students with the ability to think." They're also happy to "host study sessions [in preparation] for exams and quizzes, and they are willing to answer all of your questions." And, best of all, Idaho professors "are very interesting and really bring their lectures to life."

Life

Undergrads at Idaho happily report that "there are always a lot of activities going on around campus." For starters, the student recreation center is often a big draw where students can "work out, play a variety of indoor sports, take classes, climb the rock wall, or just hang out." Students also love to explore the "two arboretums on campus." Idaho also has "a very involved Greek system that is always holding a philanthropic event somewhere on campus or in the community." The university sponsors a number of great cultural affairs including "an amazing Jazz Festival, Native American celebrations, African American celebrations, and many many more throughout the year." In fact, "on the weekends there is almost always [an] event to attend that is hosted by an organization at the university, whether it is just for fun or to raise money for a cause." Finally, students also love taking advantage of everything hometown Moscow has to offer. As one pleased Vandal elaborates, "There is usually something going on every night, be it trivia nights at local restaurants, local musicians playing at a coffee shop, or a book signing at Book People."

Student Body

On the surface, the student body at University of Idaho might appear a bit homogenous. After all, "most people are white," and it often feels like the vast majority hail from "Idaho, Washington, or Oregon." Nevertheless, the "population is slowly becoming more and more diverse." This is partially thanks to a "surprising number of international students." In turn, "this creates a unique opportunity to learn from people of different cultures." Undergrads also take great solace in the fact that their peers are "all very, very friendly" and united in their "kindness." Simply stroll across campus and you'll notice that "everyone smiles and says hi." An ecstatic student rushes to add, "My peers are the most supportive and uplifting people I've ever been surrounded by.... It's not uncommon to see students giving directions to lost tours or inviting perfect strangers to something like the farmers market or a film downtown." A lot of these Idaho Vandals also find common ground in their love of the outdoors, with many students looking to "take advantage of Moscow Mountain nearby for hiking, mountain biking, or snowshoeing." Finally, when it comes to political leanings, we're told that Idaho has an "unusually large number of libertarian-minded students here." Thankfully, most undergrads "are very respectful, even when they strongly disagree." As one contemplative student states, "We rarely talk about tolerance here, but we act on it daily."

Financial Aid: 208-885-6312 • E-Mail: admappl@uidaho.edu • Website: http://www.uidaho.edu/

THE PRINCETON REVIEW SAYS

Admissions

Very important factors considered include: academic GPA, standardized test scores. ACT with or without writing accepted. SAT with or without Essay component accepted. High school diploma is required and GED is accepted. *Academic units required:* 4 English, 3 math, 3 science, 1 science lab, 2.5 social studies, 1.5 academic electives, 1 unit from above areas or other academic areas.

Financial Aid

Students should submit: FAFSA. Priority filing deadline is 12/1. The Princeton Review suggests that all financial aid forms be submitted as soon as possible after October 1. *Need-based scholarships/grants offered:* College/university scholarship or grant aid from institutional funds; Federal Pell; Private scholarships; SEOG; State scholarships/grants. *Loan aid offered:* Direct PLUS loans; Direct Subsidized Stafford Loans; Direct Unsubsidized Stafford Loans. Applicants will be notified of awards on a rolling basis beginning 12/20. Federal Work-Study Program available. Institutional employment available.

The Inside Word

The admissions process at University of Idaho is fairly by the book. Indeed, officers closely consider each applicant's GPA and standardized test scores. They also check to make sure that every candidate has completed their core requirements. Both home-schooled and GED students will have to submit three letters of recommendation attesting to their academic abilities. They'll also be expected to draft a written statement that discusses their educational goals and professional objectives.

THE SCHOOL SAYS "..."

From the Admissions Office

"A leading public research university in the West, the University of Idaho offers a traditional residential campus experience in a spectacular natural setting. It provides more than 130 undergraduate degree options and graduate degrees in forty-seven discipline areas, which helps provide unprecedented undergraduate research opportunities. Idaho has become known for its academic excellence, student-centered, experiential learning, and an exceptional student living environment that coupled with dedicated faculty, world-class facilities, and renowned research has produced a proven track record of high-achieving graduates. The student population of 12,000 includes first-generation college students and ethnically diverse scholars, who select from hands-on learning experiences in the colleges of Agricultural and Life Sciences; Art and Architecture; Business and Economics; Education; Engineering; Law; Letters, Arts, and Social Sciences; Natural Resources; and Science. The university also provides medical education for the state through the WWAMI program. Increasingly its interdisciplinary teams involved in environmental, sustainability, engagement, and resource management have gained national recognition. Idaho combines the strength of a large, land grant university with the intimacy of a small learning community to help students succeed and become leaders. It is home to the Vandals and competes in the Western Athletic Conference.

"Students applying for admission are required to take either the SAT or the ACT. The writing component is not required from the ACT. SAT Subject Test scores are not used for admission purposes."

SELECTIVITY

Admissions Rating	78
# of applicants	8,071
% of applicants accepted	78
% of acceptees attending	24

FRESHMAN PROFILE

Range SAT EBRW	510–630
Range SAT Math	500–610
Range SAT Composite	1010–1220
Range ACT Composite	20–27
# submitting SAT scores	1,448
% submitting SAT scores	98
# submitting ACT scores	504
% submitting ACT scores	34
Average HS GPA	3.5
% graduated top 10% of class	18
% graduated top 25% of class	44
% graduated top 50% of class	75

DEADLINES

Regular	
Priority	2/15
Deadline	8/1
Nonfall registration?	Yes

FINANCIAL FACTS

Financial Aid Rating	84
Annual in-state tuition	$6,182
Annual out-of-state tuition	$25,418
Room and board	$9,080
Required fees	$2,122
Books and supplies	$1,130
Average frosh need-based scholarship	$4,839
Average UG need-based scholarship	$5,069
% needy frosh rec. need-based scholarship or grant aid	57
% needy UG rec. need-based scholarship or grant aid	65
% needy frosh rec. non-need-based scholarship or grant aid	81
% needy UG rec. non-need-based scholarship or grant aid	67
% needy frosh rec. need-based self-help aid	68
% needy UG rec. need-based self-help aid	70
% frosh rec. any financial aid	93
% UG rec. any financial aid	81
% UG borrow to pay for school	61
Average cumulative indebtedness	$23,105
% frosh need fully met	37
% ugrads need fully met	33
Average % of frosh need met	77
Average % of ugrad need met	76

UNIVERSITY OF ILLINOIS—URBANA-CHAMPAIGN

901 West Illinois Street, Champaign, IL 61801-3028 • Admissions: 217-333-0302 • Fax: 217-244-4614

CAMPUS LIFE
Quality of Life Rating	**86**
Fire Safety Rating	**60***
Green Rating	**98**
Type of school	Public
Environment	City

STUDENTS
Total undergrad enrollment	32,884
% male/female	54/46
% from out of state	14
% frosh live on campus	99
% ugrads live on campus	50
# of fraternities (% ugrad men join)	NR (21)
# of sororities (% ugrad women join)	NR (27)
% African American	6
% Asian	18
% Caucasian	45
% Hispanic	11
% Native American	<1
% Pacific Islander	<1
% Two or more races	3
% Race and/or ethnicity unknown	<1
% international	16
# of countries represented	90

SURVEY SAYS . . .
Great library
Recreation facilities are great
Lots of beer drinking
Hard liquor is popular
Frats and sororities are popular

ACADEMICS
Academic Rating	**81**
% students returning for sophomore year	92
% students graduating within 4 years	70
% students graduating within 6 years	85
Calendar	Semester
Student/faculty ratio	20:1
Profs interesting rating	84
Profs accessible rating	90

Most classes have 10–19 students.
Most lab/discussion sessions have 20–29 students.

STUDENTS SAY "..."

Academics

The University of Illinois' massive size means "opportunities, lots of classes, lots of student groups," and "an incredibly lively campus." "The research support is phenomenal on campus" and "there are a lot of resources to supplement your studies." Students find the university's "fantastic library system" and "phenomenal advisors" to be "such a benefit for research projects," and "countless on-campus resources such as the Career Center, Writers Workshop, Office of Minority Student Affairs, free tutoring services, and the Study Abroad Office" also support students' academic experiences. They praise their professors as "wonderful," "not just good at research but also instructing and mentoring," and "very approachable," and students thrive on the emphasis on experiences outside the classroom: "The field work (tons of field work) that they make us do really helped in getting used to the field." "Most professors here are devoted to teaching, not researching." Classes can be big—"As an underclassman, many classes I've taken have been with very large classes"— but "the professors are engaging and know how to keep a class of 700-plus entertained." U of I's programs in business and engineering have long been recognized as among the best, and one student says, "I liked the breadth of the engineering program and the opportunities associated with it." Even if you're not sure what you want to study yet, its undergrads feel that the university has "an amazing reputation and strong programs in many different majors, and that if I needed to change majors (which I ended up doing) I would still be getting a great degree."

Life

In terms of location, "campus is located perfectly between Chicago, Indianapolis, and St. Louis, providing a unique atmosphere in town but close access to other urban areas for a change of pace." Students call social life "very exciting," and say, "The bars in downtown Champaign are great and super relaxed, plus there is an awesome music scene that most people don't expect from a college town." "People here like to party, but there are a lot of other fun things to do," whether it's "going to the Krannert Center to see plays or concerts" or the "movie theater and mall...on Saturday afternoons. Champaign-Urbana seems small to city kids, but to me it's the land of opportunity." Students relish the "nineteen-year-old bar age," and U of I also has "one of the largest Greek communities in the country." The combination of these facts does mean that "drinking culture is huge here" but "there's also tons to do beyond the bars." The range of social opportunities is nearly limitless: "There are 40,000 students, thousands of clubs, two gyms and several sport facilities, and array of establishments to explore on Green Street." As a whole, students report happily that "life is busy, but rewarding."

Student Body

"The diversity of the students here is astounding. Race, religion, major, you've got it all." Because in-state tuition is a major draw, "a majority of the students that you meet here will be from the Chicago suburbs," but the school also attracts "a wide variety of students from all across the world." "University of Illinois houses so many different types of students that the only way we are alike is our dedication to getting an education and our loyalty to UIUC." Undergrads feel that their peers "really know how to be academically successful," and shed state-school stereotypes like so many dirty socks: "It obviously takes a lot to get into this school so students aren't ready to throw it all away to sleep in every day." Social life changes as you find your "niche": "The typical student starts out going to a school of 40,000 students and is lucky if they know a handful of people. Within one week, life as that freshman student grows. There are so many opportunities to get involved on the floor of your residence hall, in organizations, in your classes, that it's hard not to make friends and close relationships."

■ FOR MORE FREE CONTENT, VISIT <u>PrincetonReview.com</u>

University of Illinois—Urbana-Champaign

Financial Aid: 217-333-0100 • E-Mail: http://admissions.illinois.edu/contact_u • Website: illinois.edu

THE PRINCETON REVIEW SAYS

Admissions

Very important factors considered include: rigor of secondary school record, academic GPA. *Important factors considered include:* application essay, standardized test scores, extracurricular activities, talent/ability. *Other factors considered include:* class rank, character/personal qualities, first generation, geographical residence, state residency, racial/ethnic status, volunteer work, work experience. ACT with or without writing accepted. SAT with or without Essay component accepted. High school diploma is required and GED is accepted. *Academic units required:* 4 English, 3 math, 2 science, 2 science labs, 2 foreign language, 2 social studies, 2 academic electives. *Academic units recommended:* 4 English, 4 math, 4 science, 4 science labs, 4 foreign language, 4 social studies, 4 academic electives.

Financial Aid

Students should submit: FAFSA. Priority filing deadline is 3/15. The Princeton Review suggests that all financial aid forms be submitted as soon as possible after October 1. *Need-based scholarships/grants offered:* College/university scholarship or grant aid from institutional funds; Federal Pell; Private scholarships; SEOG; State scholarships/grants; United Negro College Fund. *Loan aid offered:* Direct PLUS loans; Direct Subsidized Stafford Loans; Direct Unsubsidized Stafford Loans. Applicants will be notified of awards on a rolling basis beginning 3/10. Federal Work-Study Program available. Institutional employment available.

The Inside Word

The University of Illinois' application review process distinguishes itself from that of many state schools in that every application is considered individually—no small feat for a campus of about 30,000 students. Don't be fooled by the university's high acceptance rate: U of I's applicant pool tends to be self-selective, and those without sufficient qualifications won't make the cut.

THE SCHOOL SAYS "..."

From the Admissions Office

"The campus has been aptly described as a collection of neighborhoods constituting a diverse and vibrant city. The neighborhoods are of many types: students and faculty within a department; people sharing a room or house; the members of a professional organization, a service club, or an intramural team; or simply people who, starting out as strangers sharing a class or a study lounge or a fondness for a weekly film series, have become friends. The city of this description is the university itself—a rich cosmopolitan environment constructed by students and faculty to meet their educational and personal goals. The quality of intellectual life parallels that of other great universities, and many faculty and students who have their choice of top institutions select Illinois over its peers. While such choices are based often on the quality of individual programs of study, another crucial factor is the 'tone' of the campus life that is linked with the virtues of Midwestern culture. There is an informality and a near-absence of pretension, which, coupled with a tradition of commitment to excellence, creates an atmosphere that is unique among the finest institutions.

"Applicants are required to take the SAT or the ACT with the writing section."

SELECTIVITY

Admissions Rating	89
# of applicants	38,093
% of applicants accepted	60
% of acceptees attending	33
# offered a place on the wait list	2,846
% accepting a place on wait list	74
% admitted from wait list	17

FRESHMAN PROFILE

Range SAT EBRW	580–690
Range SAT Math	700–790
Range ACT Composite	26–32
# submitting SAT scores	1564
% submitting SAT scores	21
# submitting ACT scores	6422
% submitting ACT scores	85
% graduated top 10% of class	49
% graduated top 25% of class	82
% graduated top 50% of class	99

DEADLINES

Early action	
Deadline	11/1
Notification	12/16
Regular	
Priority	11/1
Deadline	12/1
Nonfall registration?	No

FINANCIAL FACTS

Financial Aid Rating	80
Annual in-state tuition	$12,036
Annual out-of-state tuition	$28,156
Room and board	$11,308
Required fees	$3,832
Books and supplies	$1,200
Average frosh need-based scholarship	$14,652
Average UG need-based scholarship	$14,244
% needy frosh rec. need-based scholarship or grant aid	81
% needy UG rec. need-based scholarship or grant aid	64
% needy frosh rec. non-need-based scholarship or grant aid	17
% needy UG rec. non-need-based scholarship or grant aid	8
% needy frosh rec. need-based self-help aid	74
% needy UG rec. need-based self-help aid	60
% UG borrow to pay for school	47
Average cumulative indebtedness	$25,222
% frosh need fully met	13
% ugrads need fully met	9
Average % of frosh need met	67
Average % of ugrad need met	65

UNIVERSITY OF IOWA

107 Calvin Hall, Iowa City, IA 52242-1396 • Admissions: 319-335-3847 • Fax: 319-333-1535

STUDENTS SAY "..."

Academics

The University of Iowa manages to pull off an amazing feat: It's a "Big Ten university full of exciting opportunities," yet it's still able to maintain "a small-college feel." Moreover, as the state's flagship school, Iowa provides a "great education" at a "reasonable price." Additionally, students here welcome the fact that "requirements are minimal." In turn, this truly encourages undergrads to "make [their] education [their] own." While there are certainly a "[wide] range of degree programs" from which to choose, students here are especially impressed with Iowa's journalism, premed, writing, nursing, and engineering departments. Though professors certainly run the gamut from "amazing" to "boring," the majority of them are "very engaged with students and are always helpful to any student looking to push their learning beyond the classroom." A fellow student concurs adding that her professors are "passionate, encouraging, and invested in the success of their students both inside and outside of academia." Undergrads at Iowa also appreciate that their teachers really "do a nice job of balancing lectures with real-world applications of the material." Finally, as this pleased undergrad summarizes her school, "The University of Iowa is a platform to launch yourself to the top of your field at an affordable price."

Life

If there's one thing that undergrads tend to agree on, it's that "life is pretty fun at The University of Iowa." To begin with, sports culture is definitely big here. As one student relays, "During football season, Saturdays get crazy. There is just a sea of black and gold swarming toward the stadium. Nothing can really compare to 70,000 Hawkeye fans in one place." Additionally, students love the new rec center, which frequently runs trips "to go rock-climbing, camping, hiking, or kayaking." Of course, the university also sponsors a number of other events outside of athletics. For example, "there are always concerts and comedians on campus, [and] many [of these shows] are even free to students. There are also free movies shown at the Iowa Memorial Union." Students also stress that the university has a lively drinking scene. Indeed, "there is always a party going on here at Iowa." Lastly, undergrads also love hometown Iowa City, which offers a "vibrant downtown" that's "literally across the street from campus." Students happily take advantage of the city's "unique places to eat, shop, or go out." As this undergrad poetically concludes, "When a man is tired of Iowa City, he is tired of life."

Student Body

With such a large student body, undergrads here all posit that there is no "typical" student. One pleased undergrad elaborates, "Everyone is unique and has a different story, but that's one thing that makes life here so great. You have the ability to meet people from around the country and around the world, and we all get to share the experience of college together." Indeed, students feel very fortunate to be surrounded by such diversity. "We have a strong LGBTQA presence on campus, [along with] different religious places near campus. [In addition,] there are many different organizations for minorities, religions, and everything else here on campus. I couldn't imagine someone coming here and not being able to find a student organization that is for them." Of course, if pressed to generalize, students will describe their fellow Hawkeyes as "friendly, hardworking, and studious" but also "laid-back" and "very social." However, what ultimately unites this student body is the fact that most undergrads have "their season football tickets by June."

Financial Aid: 319-335-1450 • E-Mail: admissions@uiowa.edu • Website: www.uiowa.edu

THE PRINCETON REVIEW SAYS

Admissions

Very important factors considered include: rigor of secondary school record, class rank, academic GPA, standardized test scores. *Other factors considered include:* recommendation(s), talent/ability, character/personal qualities, state residency. ACT with Writing recommended. SAT with or without Essay component accepted. High school diploma is required and GED is accepted. *Academic units required:* 4 English, 3 math, 3 science, 2 foreign language, 3 social studies. *Academic units recommended:* 4 math.

Financial Aid

Students should submit: FAFSA. Priority filing deadline is 12/1. The Princeton Review suggests that all financial aid forms be submitted as soon as possible after October 1. *Need-based scholarships/grants offered:* College/university scholarship or grant aid from institutional funds; Federal Pell; Private scholarships; SEOG; State scholarships/grants. *Loan aid offered:* Direct PLUS loans; Direct Subsidized Stafford Loans; Direct Unsubsidized Stafford Loans. Applicants will be notified of awards on a rolling basis beginning 11/15. Federal Work-Study Program available. Institutional employment available.

The Inside Word

Like many large public universities, admissions officers at the University of Iowa rely heavily on quantitative factors when determining an applicant's status. Therefore, GPA and standardized test scores will likely hold the most weight. It should also be noted that the majority of applicants are admitted to the College of Liberal Arts & Sciences or the College of Engineering. Students interested in other programs (say within the College of Business or Nursing) often apply after they have enrolled in the university.

THE SCHOOL SAYS "..."

From the Admissions Office

"The University of Iowa offers all of the opportunities and resources of a large, research university, while putting a strong emphasis on the undergraduate student experience. As the first public university to enroll men and women on an equal basis, Iowa is proud of its history in providing a world-class education to students from all backgrounds. Today, the University of Iowa offers nationally ranked academic programs, strong pre-professional programs in the health sciences and law, and access to world-renowned faculty. With an emphasis on small class sizes, students interact with faculty both inside and outside the classroom. Located in one of the top college towns in America, Iowa's campus is undergoing a historic physical makeover to compliment a newly constructed residence hall, school of music, school of art and art history, and Hancher Auditorium, the UI's world-renowned performing arts venue."

SELECTIVITY

Admissions Rating	82
# of applicants	25,928
% of applicants accepted	83
% of acceptees attending	23
# offered a place on the wait list	12
% accepting a place on wait list	83
% admitted from wait list	40

FRESHMAN PROFILE

Range SAT EBRW	560–660
Range SAT Math	570–680
Range ACT Composite	22–29
# submitting SAT scores	1,440
% submitting SAT scores	29
# submitting ACT scores	4,320
% submitting ACT scores	·87
Average HS GPA	3.8
% graduated top 10% of class	32
% graduated top 25% of class	63
% graduated top 50% of class	93

DEADLINES

Regular	
Deadline	5/1
Notification	Rolling, 8/1
Nonfall registration?	Yes

FINANCIAL FACTS

Financial Aid Rating	82
Annual in-state tuition	$8,073
Annual out-of-state tuition	$30,036
Room and board	$11,400
Required fees	$1,533
Books and supplies	$950
Average frosh need-based scholarship	$9,744
Average UG need-based scholarship	$9,095
% needy frosh rec. need-based scholarship or grant aid	83
% needy UG rec. need-based scholarship or grant aid	82
% needy frosh rec. non-need-based scholarship or grant aid	47
% needy UG rec. non-need-based scholarship or grant aid	10
% needy frosh rec. need-based self-help aid	78
% needy UG rec. need-based self-help aid	78
% frosh rec. any financial aid	91
% UG rec. any financial aid	78
% UG borrow to pay for school	48
Average cumulative indebtedness	$28,328
% frosh need fully met	14
% ugrads need fully met	13
Average % of frosh need met	51
Average % of ugrad need met	52

UNIVERSITY OF KANSAS

1502 Iowa St., Lawrence, KS 66045-7576 • Admissions: 785-864-3911 • Fax: 785-864-5017

STUDENTS SAY "..."

Academics

Located in the heartland's quintessential college town, University of Kansas's flagship campus is a "place of tradition" as well as opportunity, combining "stimulating academics with a community that is passionate about the school." Most of KU's 2,800 faculty members are "actively engaged in research in their particular field," but there is nonetheless a real emphasis on undergraduate teaching. Here, "the faculty is obviously willing to do what it takes to help," and "teachers are always urging students to contact them with questions or visit their office hours." An undergrad details, "The personalities and teaching styles of KU's professors vary widely, but all of the instructors I have had are fully engaged in teaching and truly enjoy helping students learn." That said, "there are a lot of giant lecture halls your freshmen and sophomore year," which some students find "overwhelming." On the flip side, the big-school setting proffers "abundant resources," including "research opportunities" for undergraduates and "one of the best study abroad programs in the nation." In fact, many say, "The experience outside of the classroom is what sets you up for success after college." Speaking of life after graduation, KU's "career center is committed to getting students hired," and "there are many job opportunities" in nearby Topeka and Kansas City. To make the deal sweeter, KU graduates aren't strapped with insurmountable debt: "In-state tuition is very affordable."

Life

In the pursuit of an "incredible college experience," KU undergrads definitely keep busy: "The typical student probably volunteers in the community, has a part time job, [and] has some special hobby (from rock climbing to tightrope walking)." Incoming freshman will find more than 500 student groups in which to participate, ranging from "Quidditch to chess club to the arts," and "there is never a dull night" on campus, where "Student Union Activities brings in comedians, authors, and movies on a regular basis." During the winter months, "KU basketball is our religion, and Allen Fieldhouse is our church." An undergrad admits, "I schedule everything in my life around the KU men's basketball schedule, as does much of the student population." Described as "the perfect college town," "Lawrence has a great live music scene, cool coffee shops, and eclectic stores," as well as bars and nightclubs popular with students. "People in Lawrence are also very outdoorsy," and, when the weather is nice, "you can rent camping equipment from the rec for a weekend out at the lake" or "go rock climbing" nearby. For a more cosmopolitan outing, "being close to Kansas City provides a lot of entertainment from museums and art shows to music and dining."

Students

Students say you'd be surprised by the diversity on this friendly Midwestern campus, lauding the KU's "ability to unite 30,000 people of different values and backgrounds." There are "students from every county in Kansas, every state, and over 100 countries," with noticeable representations from out-of-state cities like St. Louis and Denver mixing into the large in-state crowd. "KU students find a great balance in work and play," with some undergrads tipping the scales in one direction or the other: "You have your 'here for a good time' types, absolutely rock-star scholars, and dedicated students who balance their GPA and their social calendar." In terms of making friends and fitting in, getting involved is the best way to mitigate the campus's size: "There are so many opportunities at KU that it can seem a bit overwhelming, but students really find their niche and run with it." Of particular note, "there is definitely a big Greek life presence" on campus, which some say causes a "schism" in the undergraduate community. In counterpoint, a student reassures us, "The Greek community does intermingle frequently with non-Greeks. I'm not Greek, but I see it a lot and have a lot of Greek friends."

UNIVERSITY OF KANSAS

Financial Aid: 785-864-4700 • E-Mail: adm@ku.edu • Website: https://www.ku.edu/

THE PRINCETON REVIEW SAYS

Admissions

Very important factors considered include: academic GPA, standardized test scores. *Other factors considered include:* rigor of secondary school record, class rank, application essay, extracurricular activities, talent/ability, character/personal qualities, first generation, alumni/ae relation, geographical residence, state residency, racial/ethnic status, volunteer work, work experience, level of applicant's interest. ACT with or without writing accepted. SAT with or without Essay component accepted. High school diploma is required and GED is accepted. *Academic units required:* 4 English, 3 math, 3 science, 1 science lab, 3 social studies, 3 academic electives. *Academic units recommended:* 4 English, 4 math, 3 science, 3 social studies, 3 academic electives.

Financial Aid

Students should submit: FAFSA. Priority filing deadline is 11/1. The Princeton Review suggests that all financial aid forms be submitted as soon as possible after October 1. *Need-based scholarships/grants offered:* College/university scholarship or grant aid from institutional funds; Federal Pell; Private scholarships; SEOG; State scholarships/grants. *Loan aid offered:* Direct PLUS loans; Direct Subsidized Stafford Loans; Direct Unsubsidized Stafford Loans. Federal Work-Study Program available. Institutional employment available.

The Inside Word

KU has a great program for assured admission! The standards for 2018 are: 2.0 GPA (resident) or 2.5 GPA (nonresident) in the Kansas Qualified high school core curriculum and 21 ACT/1060 SAT and 3.25 cumulative GPA or 24 ACT/1160 SAT and 3.0 cumulative GPA. Professional schools have different standards. SAT only includes math and critical reading.

THE SCHOOL SAYS "..."

From the Admissions Office

"The University of Kansas has a tradition of academic excellence. The mission of KU is to lift students and society by educating leaders, building healthy communities, and making discoveries that will change the world. Outstanding students from around the world attend KU for its outstanding academics, challenging opportunities, the Jayhawk community, and incredible value including four-year renewable scholarships. KU provides students exceptional opportunities in the University Honors Program, experiential learning, undergraduate research, internships, study abroad, and more than 600 clubs and organizations. The university is located in Lawrence (forty minutes from Kansas City), a vibrant community of 93,000 consistently recognized as one of the nation's top ten college towns.

"All students are encouraged to apply. KU does an individual review of each application. We consider many factors that are provided on the application such as cumulative high school GPA, ACT or SAT scores, GPA in the core curriculum, and strength of courses. We may also ask you to respond to short essay questions that will provide additional information to support your application."

SELECTIVITY

Admissions Rating	76
# of applicants	15,093
% of applicants accepted	93
% of acceptees attending	29

FRESHMAN PROFILE

Range ACT Composite	22–29
# submitting ACT scores	4,021
% submitting ACT scores	98
Average HS GPA	3.6
% graduated top 10% of class	29
% graduated top 25% of class	55
% graduated top 50% of class	83

DEADLINES

Regular	
Priority	2/1
Deadline	8/19
Notification	Rolling, 7/1
Nonfall registration?	Yes

FINANCIAL FACTS

Financial Aid Rating	87
Annual in-state tuition	$10,092
Annual out-of-state tuition	$26,960
Room and board	$10,350
Required fees	$1,074
Books and supplies	$1,212
Average frosh need-based scholarship	$9,739
Average UG need-based scholarship	$8,305
% needy frosh rec. need-based scholarship or grant aid	90
% needy UG rec. need-based scholarship or grant aid	80
% needy frosh rec. non-need-based scholarship or grant aid	15
% needy UG rec. non-need-based scholarship or grant aid	9
% needy frosh rec. need-based self-help aid	65
% needy UG rec. need-based self-help aid	70
% frosh rec. any financial aid	80
% UG rec. any financial aid	67
% UG borrow to pay for school	53
Average cumulative indebtedness	$28,176
% frosh need fully met	46
% ugrads need fully met	40
Average % of frosh need met	81
Average % of ugrad need met	77

UNIVERSITY OF KENTUCKY

100 W.D. Funkhouser Building, Lexington, KY 40506 • Admissions: 859-257-2000 • Fax: 859-257-3823

STUDENTS SAY " . . ."

Academics

Founded in 1865, the University of Kentucky in Lexington offers more than two hundred academic programs to its 22,000 undergraduate students. It is one of only eight institutions in the country with the full set of liberal arts, engineering, professional, agricultural and medical colleges. With a "great variety in majors and classes" available, many undergraduates find UK has "available opportunities for students in all fields of study." Enrollees find support outside their standard classroom work with "so many study abroad options" and the chance to "become involved in undergraduate research." Many courses also incorporate "active technology learning classrooms," and some degree programs have hybrid classes. From classroom to campus, Kentucky makes sure that "everything is there to help the students—all of the resources you could need."

Undergrads say the faculty is "passionate about giving us more than just degrees" and most have "a great base of knowledge, enthusiasm, and accessibility." Students enthusiastically recommend registering for courses with seasoned teachers who have industry experience because they "are the best at their job," and "are able to answer questions from personal experience more so than just textbook knowledge." But regardless of if you're learning from a TA or a tenured faculty member, undergrads appreciate the fact that their instructors "do their best to make the material interesting and engaging." Many enrollees also value "the availability of professors and their willingness to help" after class and during offices hours. "They are more than professors, they are mentors for me and networking connections for the field," says a student.

Life

The University of Kentucky has made great efforts at "transforming itself into a more modern and thriving university city." "There is so much to do" at UK, and the "campus is close to downtown, so people will go out to eat or attend events happening there." The university is also located in "horse country and in a wonderful proximity to good hiking, so a lot of time is spent outdoors." During the week, you'll find students "[sitting] in common areas around campus to hang out and relax before the next class." After class, they will "usually study at the library or go to work" (UK has "a lot of opportunities for student employment"), but weekends are a time to let loose. "Sporting events are always popular," and students are "filled to the brim with pride." Home to a multitude of active Greek chapters, "Sorority/fraternity life is huge," as "Greek life is really important on campus." Beyond the Greek scene, "there are a lot of clubs that are very diverse and a lot of intramural sports," as well as opportunities to volunteer in Lexington and on campus.

Student Body

Many students express "a love for [their] school" and the "very friendly" community that comes with it. As one undergrad notes, "Big Blue Nation makes everyone feel a part of the school pride here at the University of Kentucky." The culture of being a Kentucky Wildcat unifies enrollees in many aspects of their college career. "Students of every major and discipline find commonality in a variety of things," including "great pride about the state of Kentucky and its values." And while the student body is diverse with "a healthy number of in-state and out-of-state students," as well as "many international students and nontraditional students," walking around campus, "there is a comfortable atmosphere," which "helps each student to learn how to communicate with people from many different backgrounds." "There isn't a sense of elitism here," but "students still value academia." In the end, "all of UK's students contribute to a very diverse atmosphere that creates its unique environment." As one student explains, "It's one big community, and people are so happy to engage in it."

Financial Aid: 859-257-3172 • E-Mail: admissions@uky.edu • Website: www.uky.edu

THE PRINCETON REVIEW SAYS

Admissions

Very important factors considered include: rigor of secondary school record, academic GPA, standardized test scores. *Important factors considered include:* application essay, recommendation(s). *Other factors considered include:* class rank, interview, extracurricular activities, talent/ability, character/personal qualities, alumni/ae relation, geographical residence, state residency, volunteer work. ACT with or without writing accepted. SAT with or without Essay component accepted. High school diploma is required and GED is accepted. *Academic units required:* 4 English, 3 math, 3 science, 1 science lab, 3 foreign language, 3 social studies, 7 academic electives, 1 visual/performing arts, 1 unit from above areas or other academic areas.

Financial Aid

Students should submit: FAFSA. Priority filing deadline is 2/15. The Princeton Review suggests that all financial aid forms be submitted as soon as possible after October 1. *Need-based scholarships/grants offered:* College/university scholarship or grant aid from institutional funds; Federal Pell; Private scholarships; SEOG; State scholarships/grants. *Loan aid offered:* Direct PLUS loans; Direct Subsidized Stafford Loans; Direct Unsubsidized Stafford Loans. Applicants will be notified of awards on a rolling basis beginning 3/15. Federal Work-Study Program available.

The Inside Word

The University of Kentucky's admissions team is about as objective as they come. If you have the GPA, class rank, and test scores, you'll in all likelihood be welcomed into the Wildcat community. The university is continually looking to improve its selectivity, so hitting the books is a must if you want to be a serious contender. Freshman applicants who have completed the pre-college curriculum, but do not have the requisite GPA, test scores or both, may be placed on a wait list.

THE SCHOOL SAYS "..."

From the Admissions Office

"The University of Kentucky has sixteen academic colleges, including the Lewis Honors College and the Graduate School. Only 2 percent of all colleges and universities in the country are comprehensive research-intensive institutions like UK. We are one of only eight institutions in the country which host a university medical center and colleges of pharmacy, medicine, and agriculture on one campus.

"UK has invested over $2.27 billion since July 2011 to transform the University of Kentucky campus. In addition to housing and dining revitalization accomplished through public private partnerships, UK has prioritized other student quality-of-life projects, including the new Gatton Student Center, campus recreation, and athletics facilities. Over $600 million in new and renovated spaces include the Jacobs Science Building and the Gatton College of Business and Economics among others.

"The University has a close connection with the city of Lexington, a vibrant, growing community with a culture students describe as close-knit, opportunity-rich and supportive of all things local. Students get the best of both worlds—urban bustle adjacent to campus and beautiful rolling hills, immaculate horse farms, and wilderness adventures just a short drive out of town."

SELECTIVITY

Admissions Rating	76
# of applicants	18,925
% of applicants accepted	96
% of acceptees attending	27
# offered a place on the wait list	637
% accepting a place on wait list	100
% admitted from wait list	73

FRESHMAN PROFILE

Range SAT EBRW	550–660
Range SAT Math	530–660
Range ACT Composite	22–28
# submitting SAT scores	821
% submitting SAT scores	17
# submitting ACT scores	4,468
% submitting ACT scores	92
Average HS GPA	3.7
% graduated top 10% of class	29
% graduated top 25% of class	58
% graduated top 50% of class	86

DEADLINES

Early action	
Deadline	12/1
Regular	
Priority	2/15
Deadline	2/15
Notification	8/1
Nonfall registration?	Yes

FINANCIAL FACTS

Financial Aid Rating	79
Annual in-state tuition	$10,896
Annual out-of-state tuition	$27,750
Room and board	$12,982
Required fees	$1,349
Books and supplies	$1,000
Average frosh need-based scholarship	$5,557
Average UG need-based scholarship	$5,664
% needy frosh rec. need-based scholarship or grant aid	42
% needy UG rec. need-based scholarship or grant aid	47
% needy frosh rec. non-need-based scholarship or grant aid	62
% needy UG rec. non-need-based scholarship or grant aid	76
% needy frosh rec. need-based self-help aid	58
% needy UG rec. need-based self-help aid	53
% frosh rec. any financial aid	40
% UG rec. any financial aid	38
% UG borrow to pay for school	54
Average cumulative indebtedness	$42,090
% frosh need fully met	19
% ugrads need fully met	18
Average % of frosh need met	53
Average % of ugrad need met	54

UNIVERSITY OF LOUISIANA AT LAFAYETTE

P.O. Drawer 41210, Lafayette, LA 70504-1008 • Admissions: 337-482-6553 • Fax: 337-482-1112

CAMPUS LIFE

Quality of Life Rating	91
Fire Safety Rating	94
Green Rating	60*
Type of school	Public
Environment	City

STUDENTS

Total undergrad enrollment	13,639
% male/female	43/57
% from out of state	6
% frosh live on campus	57
% ugrads live on campus	24
# of fraternities (% ugrad men join)	11 (9)
# of sororities (% ugrad women join)	9 (12)
% African American	21
% Asian	3
% Caucasian	64
% Hispanic	6
% Native American	<1
% Pacific Islander	<1
% Two or more races	3
% Race and/or ethnicity unknown	3
% international	1
# of countries represented	101

SURVEY SAYS . . .

Students are happy
Great library
Students are very religious
Students get along with local community
Students love Lafayette, LA
Great off-campus food
Recreation facilities are great
Everyone loves the Ragin' Cajuns
Intramural sports are popular
Frats and sororities are popular

ACADEMICS

Academic Rating	77
% students returning for sophomore year	76
% students graduating within 4 years	23
% students graduating within 6 years	51
Calendar	Semester
Student/faculty ratio	20:1
Profs interesting rating	84
Profs accessible rating	90
Most classes have 20–29 students.	

MOST POPULAR MAJORS

Biology/Biological Sciences, General; Business
Administration and Management, General;
Nursing/Registered Nurse (Rn, Asn, Bsn, Msn)

STUDENTS SAY ". . ."

Academics

With a "beautiful campus" and "friendly atmosphere," it's quite easy to understand how students could be drawn to University of Louisiana at Lafayette. This public research university strives to provide undergrads with an affordable education and offers an "abundance [of] scholarship opportunities." Undergrads also appreciate the breadth of fantastic academic departments, from the "wonderful" nursing program and the "exceptional biology program" to the "good architecture program" and "phenomenal art [department]." And, since it's "smaller than most state schools," undergrads here are really able to interact with their professors and receive "quality in-class instruction." Indeed, students seem to thoroughly enjoy their courses. This can definitely be attributed to "amazing faculty." As an English major explains, "Most of the professors I've had have been very passionate about their subjects, which in turn makes the student interested in the class. They're all very open to questions and discussions." A fellow English student agrees, "My professors have been helpful and knowledgeable, and they are always willing to help their students succeed." Perhaps this pre-med student best sums up the experience here: "UL is all about melding creativity, spicy Cajun culture, and academia into a gumbo-pot of successful scholars!"

Life

Students who attend University of Louisiana at Lafayette will likely never be bored. There's always something of which to take advantage. To begin with, we're told that "a lot of the buzz around campus [surrounds] sports." An English major confirms, "Football is a major thing in South Louisiana. I think we're the second biggest 'sports fan base' behind LSU, of course." Come game day, many people "tailgate and there is a big community of RV's and tents from [both] out-of-towners and [those who reside] on campus." Students also report that "the Ragin Cajun Catholics and Christian community is awesome and dynamic!" Many undergrads can also be found "working out in the gym." And a large number participate in Greek life as well. Lastly, students love the area surrounding UL. A biology major happily shares, "Throughout the year, there are tons of festivals unique to Lafayette, all of which are free to attend, such as Festivale Acadiens, which celebrates Cajun culture, as well as Festivale Internationale, which is the largest free world-music festival in the world."

Student Body

Undergrads at UL steadfastly insist that "there is no typical...student." Those who enroll here will discover all types, "from quiet students [and] outgoing students [to] sporty students [and] artsy students." A biology major explains, "We have students of all ethnicities, races, religions, and styles. There are very few social boundaries and mostly everyone is accepting of our diverse student body." Of course, when pressed, one journalism major admits that there is a typical UL Lafayette undergrad, one that "reflects Lafayette's culture: creative, friendly, and food-loving." Many are also "involved in Greek life, and therefore [frequently participate] in community service and [embody] school spirit." By and large, undergrads also report that their peers are "dedicated and determined to succeed." Finally, an art education major encapsulates her fellow students by simply stating, "Everyone accepts one another for who they are. There are friends for everyone." And "as long as you make it a point to get out of your dorm once in a while, you will have close knit circle of friends in no time."

UNIVERSITY OF LOUISIANA AT LAFAYETTE

Financial Aid: 337-482-6506 • E-Mail: enroll@louisiana.edu • Website: www.louisiana.edu

THE PRINCETON REVIEW SAYS

Admissions

Very important factors considered include: rigor of secondary school record, class rank, academic GPA, standardized test scores. *Other factors considered include:* state residency. ACT with or without writing accepted. High school diploma is required and GED is accepted. *Academic units required:* 4 English, 4 math, 3 science, 2 foreign language, 1 social studies, 2 history, 1 visual/performing arts, 1 unit from above areas or other academic areas.

Financial Aid

Students should submit: FAFSA. Priority filing deadline is 5/1. The Princeton Review suggests that all financial aid forms be submitted as soon as possible after October 1. *Need-based scholarships/grants offered:* College/university scholarship or grant aid from institutional funds; Federal Nursing Scholarships; Federal Pell; Private scholarships; SEOG; State scholarships/grants. Applicants will be notified of awards on a rolling basis beginning 4/1. Federal Work-Study Program available. Institutional employment available.

The Inside Word

Students hoping to attend the University of Louisiana at Lafayette must make sure they take a solid college prep curriculum in high school. Applicants need to complete 4 units of English, 4 units of math, 4 units of social studies, 4 units of science, 2 units of foreign language and 1 unit within the arts in order to qualify. Students must have a minimum overall GPA of 2.0 (on a 4 point scale), a composite ACT score of 23 and/or SAT score of 1050 (critical reading & math) to gain admission. Finally, any candidate requiring remedial classes should complete that coursework prior to enrolling at UL.

THE SCHOOL SAYS "..."

From the Admissions Office

"The University of Louisiana at Lafayette offers students from throughout the United States and more than ninety countries strong academic training and personal enrichment opportunities in a friendly, comfortable, student-centered environment. UL Lafayette students are taught, mentored, and advised by some of the brightest and most accomplished faculty members in the United States. Although UL Lafayette offers more than 100 programs of study and the research opportunities, internship possibilities, and facilities of a major research-intensive university, average class size is approximately the same as that at many high schools and smaller higher education institutions. UL students receive a good deal of individual attention and support—both personal and academic—from faculty and staff.

"A wide range of cultural, recreational, and social activities are available on and off campus, including more than 150 campus organizations and clubs, NCAA Division I and intramural athletics, a state-of-the-art recreation and aquatic center, a thriving arts scene, a wide range of live music venues, shopping, a great variety of excellent restaurants, theaters, the second largest Mardi Gras in the nation, and an international music festival. In fact, *Utne Reader* magazine selected the city of Lafayette as Louisiana's 'Most Enlightened Town.' Recently, Lafayette was also listed as one of America's most optimistic cities.

"Our generous financial aid and scholarship programs, including an out-of-state tuition waiver for qualified students, make UL Lafayette one of the most affordable universities in the nation. Students who have completed the required college preparatory core curriculum in high school may qualify for admission on the basis of a combination of their high school cumulative grade point average and ACT or SAT scores."

SELECTIVITY

Admissions Rating	85
# of applicants	9,138
% of applicants accepted	68
% of acceptees attending	41

FRESHMAN PROFILE

Range SAT EBRW	510–618
Range SAT Math	510–650
Range ACT Composite	21–26
# submitting SAT scores	114
% submitting SAT scores	4
# submitting ACT scores	2,498
% submitting ACT scores	99
Average HS GPA	3.4
% graduated top 10% of class	17
% graduated top 25% of class	38
% graduated top 50% of class	65

DEADLINES

Regular	
Priority	7/20
Nonfall registration?	Yes

FINANCIAL FACTS

Financial Aid Rating	82
Annual in-state tuition	$5,407
Annual out-of-state tuition	$19,135
Room and board	$10,708
Required fees	$4,975
Books and supplies	$1,220
Average frosh need-based scholarship	$7,180
Average UG need-based scholarship	$6,558
% needy frosh rec. need-based scholarship or grant aid	96
% needy UG rec. need-based scholarship or grant aid	88
% needy frosh rec. non-need-based scholarship or grant aid	15
% needy UG rec. non-need-based scholarship or grant aid	9
% needy frosh rec. need-based self-help aid	48
% needy UG rec. need-based self-help aid	59
% frosh rec. any financial aid	87
% UG rec. any financial aid	72
% frosh need fully met	15
% ugrads need fully met	9
Average % of frosh need met	61
Average % of ugrad need met	52

UNIVERSITY OF LOUISVILLE

Admissions Office, Louisville, KY 40292-0001 • Admissions: 502-852-6531 • Fax: 502-852-4776

CAMPUS LIFE

Quality of Life Rating	85
Fire Safety Rating	98
Green Rating	97
Type of school	Public
Environment	Metropolis

STUDENTS

Total undergrad enrollment	14,303
% male/female	47/53
% from out of state	18
% frosh from public high school	88
% frosh live on campus	68
% ugrads live on campus	23
# of fraternities (% ugrad men join)	20 (16)
# of sororities (% ugrad women join)	13 (14)
% African American	12
% Asian	4
% Caucasian	70
% Hispanic	6
% Native American	<1
% Pacific Islander	0
% Two or more races	6
% Race and/or ethnicity unknown	0
% international	1
# of countries represented	60

SURVEY SAYS . . .

Recreation facilities are great
Everyone loves the Cardinals
Students love Louisville, KY

ACADEMICS

Academic Rating	75
% students returning for sophomore year	80
% students graduating within 4 years	37
% students graduating within 6 years	59
Calendar	Semester
Student/faculty ratio	14:1
Profs interesting rating	82
Profs accessible rating	88

Most classes have 20–29 students.

MOST POPULAR MAJORS

Biology/Biological Sciences, General; Registered
Nursing/Registered Nurse; Psychology, General

STUDENTS SAY "..."

Academics

University of Louisville is an institution that affords undergraduates "endless opportunities." Certainly, as one of Kentucky's premiere public universities, a Louisville education means students are getting a "great value" and an affordable price tag. And when you combine those attributes with a "beautiful" campus that's "easy to navigate," well it's understandable why students eagerly exclaim that Louisville "feels...like home." With regards to academics, undergrads truly appreciate the university's "[emphasis on] critical thinking" as well as the "personalized" attention they receive. Therefore, it's no surprise to hear that Louisville professors "generally [seem to] care about student success [both] in[side] and outside the classroom." As one satisfied biology student further explains, "They are willing to go above and beyond to help you gain a better understanding of course material and obtain supplementary experience outside of the classroom using their own collaborations and affiliations in the field." However, some students do find cause to mention that professors in "higher up courses...are better than professors who teach gen-ed courses." Fortunately, students are pleased to discover that, for the most part, "U of L is about immersing yourself in a diverse community where you have the chance to grow academically, socially, spiritually, and in whatever other ways you choose."

Life

As one excited junior quickly exclaims, life at University of Louisville is "always lively." Indeed, "there is always something going on both on and off campus and numerous ways to get involved and have a great time." To begin with, Greek life is "fairly prominent." And, naturally, there's a small party scene to go with it. Fortunately, we're assured that "things never get out of hand; it's just students trying to wind down and have a good time." Sporting events are extremely popular as well and these undergrads generate a lot of Cardinal pride. As one music education major boasts, "We have several conference championships already this year and our basketball team looks to repeat as national champions." Additionally, Louisville students like to give back and community service is a common activity here. An impressed junior reveals, "People are pretty conscientious. They volunteer a lot and there are a million and one volunteer groups throughout the city. Same goes for environmental groups." Of course Louisville itself is a vibrant city and one which undergrads love to take advantage. For example, students flock to "4th Street Live!, a popular hangout." And they also "enjoy Churchill Downs and going to horse races as well as the eclectic Highlands area of Bardstown Road."

Student Body

Undergrads at University of Louisville really value the amount of diversity found among their student body. As a highly content nursing student immediately chimes in, "We have so many people with different backgrounds, religions, and interests that no matter where you come from or what you are interested in you will fit in." This sentiment is bolstered by a peer who states, "We have a little bit of everyone, from sorority girls to hippies to those who study all the time. You will not have trouble finding friends here." Certainly, there are also plenty of similarities to be found across the student body as well. After all, many undergrads hail from "the Louisville area" and hold "moderate political views." Students also say that "the majority of [individuals] are extremely nice and easy to get along with." And they are more than "willing to help" their peers whenever they're in need. Then again that's not terribly surprising given that, as this music education major eloquently states, "We are all Cardinals."

Financial Aid: 502-852-5511 • E-Mail: admitme@louisville.edu • Website: www.louisville.edu

THE PRINCETON REVIEW SAYS

Admissions

Very important factors considered include: rigor of secondary school record, academic GPA, standardized test scores. *Other factors considered include:* class rank, recommendation(s), extracurricular activities, talent/ability, state residency, racial/ethnic status, volunteer work, work experience. High school diploma is required and GED is accepted. *Academic units required:* 4 English, 3 math, 3 science, 1 science lab, 2 foreign language, 3 social studies, 5 academic electives, 1 visual/performing arts, 5 units from above areas or other academic areas. *Academic units recommended:* 4 math, 4 science, 3 foreign language.

Financial Aid

Students should submit: FAFSA. Priority filing deadline is 2/15. The Princeton Review suggests that all financial aid forms be submitted as soon as possible after October 1. *Need-based scholarships/grants offered:* College/university scholarship or grant aid from institutional funds; Federal Nursing Scholarships; Federal Pell; Private scholarships; SEOG; State scholarships/grants. *Loan aid offered:* Direct PLUS loans; Direct Subsidized Stafford Loans; Direct Unsubsidized Stafford Loans. Federal Work-Study Program available. Institutional employment available.

The Inside Word

By and large, admissions decisions at University of Louisville are highly dependent on quantitative data. This means that each applicant's class rank, GPA and standardized test scores will be of utmost importance. Attention will also be paid to course selection; a strong college prep curriculum should be a given. Requirements will vary depending on the specific school to which a candidate is applying. For example, applicants interested in the School of Music must also pass an audition. And nursing students face a two-part process; applying for the lower-level division in freshman year and then applying for the upper-level division in junior year.

THE SCHOOL SAYS "..."

From the Admissions Office

"The University of Louisville (UofL) has transformed into a premier metropolitan university—and it keeps getting better. It is a tight knit community with the feel of a small college where you can walk anywhere on campus in only ten minutes. Over the past ten years it has dramatically improved its on-campus environment with the addition of new residence halls, new apartments near campus, a new state-of-the-art student recreation center and restaurants and shopping near campus with the right mix of local flavor. Located in a vibrant city that is known worldwide for the Kentucky Derby, students quickly learn to navigate its great parks, discover local restaurants and explore a revitalized downtown and neighborhoods with an eclectic environment.

"With over 50 percent of our entering freshmen beginning their studies with college credit, U of L is a strong academic environment with opportunities inside and outside the classroom to prepare you for professional school or your first job. The city and UofL are closely linked, providing opportunities for internships, coops, part-time jobs and service learning experiences. Our commitment to diversity has created a culture with support for LGBT students and students of all socioeconomic and ethnic backgrounds.

"Although widely known for our engineering, business and medical programs, we offer over 200 academic programs and in recent years have added undergraduate programs in Public Health, Social Work, Asian Studies and Latin American and Latino Studies, demonstrating a desire to prepare students for the 21st Century needs of our city, region and beyond."

SELECTIVITY
Admissions Rating	83
# of applicants	14,447
% of applicants accepted	70
% of acceptees attending	28

FRESHMAN PROFILE
Range ACT Composite	22–29
# submitting SAT scores	0
% submitting SAT scores	0
# submitting ACT scores	2,528
% submitting ACT scores	100
Average HS GPA	3.6

DEADLINES
Regular	
Priority	2/15
Deadline	8/1
Notification	Rolling, 8/1
Nonfall registration?	Yes

FINANCIAL FACTS
Financial Aid Rating	84
Annual in-state tuition	$11,732
Annual out-of-state tuition	$27,758
Room and board	$9,452
Required fees	$196
Books and supplies	$1,200
Average frosh need-based scholarship	$11,724
Average UG need-based scholarship	$10,623
% needy frosh rec. need-based scholarship or grant aid	98
% needy UG rec. need-based scholarship or grant aid	92
% needy frosh rec. non-need-based scholarship or grant aid	16
% needy UG rec. non-need-based scholarship or grant aid	11
% needy frosh rec. need-based self-help aid	55
% needy UG rec. need-based self-help aid	60
% frosh rec. any financial aid	67
% UG rec. any financial aid	61
% UG borrow to pay for school	51
Average cumulative indebtedness	$24,840
% frosh need fully met	21
% ugrads need fully met	17
Average % of frosh need met	62
Average % of ugrad need met	59

UNIVERSITY OF LYNCHBURG

1501 Lakeside Drive, Lynchburg, VA 24501 • Admissions: 434-544-8300 • Fax: 434-544-8653

STUDENTS SAY ". . ."

Academics
Beneath the Blue Ridge mountains in Lynchburg, Virginia, the University of Lynchburg students experience an "academic environment [that] is the perfect level of challenge and excitement." Lynchburg is "huge on community service" and opportunities on and around campus make it easy for students to "get out there and get involved in the local community." Students enjoy a "friendly environment" among peers who are "willing to help you out when needed." Students say that the academic environment is convivial, classes are "very discussion based and allow for conversation." Students appreciate that "class sizes are so small" and explain that this means "participation is necessary" from everyone. A low student-to-faculty ratio also means that it is "very easy to ask questions during class and meet with your professors" outside of class hours. One student in Lynchburg's well-regarded nursing program tells us "we have incredible faculty members who are caring, compassionate, and experienced. They go above and beyond for us each day to make us the best nurses possible." Lynchburg boasts "other amazing programs such as Exercise Physiology, Biology, Teaching, [and] Business," all of which "are backed by the liberal arts education that allows us to expand our thinking and look at the world in a broader view." "I have been given nothing but support and encouragement throughout my time in the program," one student tells us. This nurturing atmosphere helps students become "the best version of ourselves." It isn't uncommon to hear students say, "I wasn't very successful academically in high school but I have done extremely well in college. I would attribute that to the professors" who offer plenty of office hours to get in contact with them, as well as most classes having a class tutor with weekly study sessions to help you along with the class."

Life
There is plenty going on around the University of Lynchburg campus to keep students busy. "Our inboxes are bombarded with everything going on throughout our campus," one students explains. During the week "most people go to class and then have meetings for clubs," which are well attended at Lynchburg. "Very often, students are involved in at least two campus organizations," and it is a great way for them to get involved in the community: "Students spend a great deal of their out-of-class time working on planning events, service, and projects for these organizations." Athletics are popular on campus and "nearly 1 in 5 students is involved in Greek Life." Students say they can "always fill any free time...exploring the city of Lynchburg," where they can check out "a movie, trampoline parks, skating rinks" or catch a bite downtown where "the restaurants and bars ... are absolutely amazing." Outside the city, students can explore the foothills of the Blue Ridge Mountains where there are "lots of opportunities for hiking, cave diving, and rafting."

Student Body
Many identify their peers as "primarily Caucasian, wealthy, athletes" who are "friendly and willing to work together and help each other out." Students agree that "a good portion" of Lynchburg students hail "from Northern states (e.g., Delaware, Maryland) while the majority are from Virginia or neighboring states." But they are quick to point out that diversity on campus is on the rise. Lynchburg is "beginning to have more cultural diversity," one student tells us. "Most of my friends are from other states or sometimes other countries," another points out. Lynchburg students are "open to ideas and accepting to others" while extending their welcoming Southern hospitality. Students will "hold the door for you and give you a sincere smile as you walk by them on the way to class." "I never walk to class without saying hey to at least three people," another student boasts. "Everyone is very helping," one student explains. "If someone is not able to help you with a homework question or a project then they will find you someone that can. It does feel like one giant family here."

UNIVERSITY OF LYNCHBURG

Financial Aid: 434-544-8230 • E-mail: admissions@lynchburg.edu • Website: www.lynchburg.edu

THE PRINCETON REVIEW SAYS

Admissions

Very important factors considered include: rigor of secondary school record, academic GPA, standardized test scores. *Important factors considered include:* interview. *Other factors considered include:* application essay, recommendation(s), extracurricular activities, talent/ability, character/personal qualities, volunteer work, work experience, level of applicant's interest. ACT with or without writing accepted. SAT with or without Essay component accepted. High school diploma is required and GED is accepted. *Academic units required:* 4 English, 3 math, 3 science, 2 science labs, 2 foreign language, 2 social studies, 2 history. *Academic units recommended:* 4 English, 4 math, 4 science, 2 science labs, 3 foreign language, 2 social studies, 2 history, 1 academic elective.

Financial Aid

Students should submit: FAFSA; State aid form. Priority filing deadline is 11/1. The Princeton Review suggests that all financial aid forms be submitted as soon as possible after October 1. *Need-based scholarships/grants offered:* College/university scholarship or grant aid from institutional funds; Federal Pell; SEOG. *Loan aid offered:* Direct PLUS loans; Direct Subsidized Stafford Loans; Direct Unsubsidized Stafford Loans. Applicants will be notified of awards on a rolling basis beginning 12/1. Federal Work-Study Program available. Institutional employment available.

The Inside Word

Lynchburg uses rolling admission, so students can apply any time after their junior year of high school, and they recommend that students apply by the fall of their senior year. You only need to submit transcripts and standardized test scores, but they highly recommend including a letter of recommendation from a teacher or counselor and a writing sample. The writing sample can be an essay on a topic of your choice or a graded essay from a class. Accepted students are automatically considered for academic scholarship based on their application materials.

THE SCHOOL SAYS "..."

From the Admissions Office

"The University of Lynchburg offers over 100 academic programs and offers degrees at the undergraduate, masters, and doctoral levels. Throughout their years at Lynchburg, students discover new things about themselves and their interests. Lynchburg provides an engaging and challenging curriculum of liberal arts, sciences, and professional programs that develops broad-based understanding and specialized knowledge, leading to fulfilling careers.

"Lynchburg students make many new connections starting with their first days on campus. They benefit from personal interaction with expert faculty. A vibrant campus life helps students forge meaningful connections with each other and with alumni who have exceled in countless career paths.

"Lynchburg students and alumni achieve excellence in the classroom, where they consistently earn places in competitive graduate programs; athletics, including multiple national and conference championships; and in the global workforce. Lynchburg students express high satisfaction with their school, giving it high marks in all five benchmarks of the National Survey of Student Engagement, which measures how colleges engage their students in activities related to learning and personal development. These areas include student-faculty interaction, supportive campus environment, level of academic challenge, active and collaborative learning, and enriching education experiences.

"From the moment prospective students step onto this beautiful campus, they begin to appreciate the Lynchburg experience. Students and families are invited to attend one of the many visit events throughout the year."

SELECTIVITY

Admissions Rating	73
# of applicants	4,205
% of applicants accepted	97
% of acceptees attending	12

FRESHMAN PROFILE

Range SAT EBRW	500–600
Range SAT Math	470–570
Range ACT Composite	18–26
# submitting SAT scores	430
% submitting SAT scores	90
# submitting ACT scores	115
% submitting ACT scores	24
Average HS GPA	3.4
% graduated top 10% of class	13
% graduated top 25% of class	22
% graduated top 50% of class	67

DEADLINES

Early decision	
Deadline	11/15
Notification	12/15
Regular	
Notification	Rolling, 9/1
Nonfall registration?	Yes

FINANCIAL FACTS

Financial Aid Rating	88
Annual tuition	$39,720
Room and board	$11,450
Required fees	$970
Books and supplies	$1,200
Average frosh need-based scholarship	$29,511
Average UG need-based scholarship	$27,544
% needy frosh rec. need-based scholarship or grant aid	100
% needy UG rec. need-based scholarship or grant aid	100
% needy frosh rec. non-need-based scholarship or grant aid	24
% needy UG rec. non-need-based scholarship or grant aid	17
% needy frosh rec. need-based self-help aid	70
% needy UG rec. need-based self-help aid	78
% frosh rec. any financial aid	80
% UG rec. any financial aid	75
% UG borrow to pay for school	81
Average cumulative indebtedness	$36,036
% frosh need fully met	27
% ugrads need fully met	21
Average % of frosh need met	80
Average % of ugrad need met	75

UNIVERSITY OF MAINE

5713 Chadbourne Hall, Orono, ME 04469-5713 • Admissions: 207-581-1561 • Fax: 207-581-1213

CAMPUS LIFE

Quality of Life Rating	83
Fire Safety Rating	99
Green Rating	91
Type of school	Public
Environment	Village

STUDENTS

Total undergrad enrollment	8,832
% male/female	54/46
% from out of state	33
% frosh live on campus	89
% ugrads live on campus	38
# of fraternities	17
# of sororities	9
% African American	2
% Asian	2
% Caucasian	84
% Hispanic	4
% Native American	<1
% Pacific Islander	0
% Two or more races	4
% Race and/or ethnicity unknown	2
% international	2
# of countries represented	51

SURVEY SAYS . . .

Hard liquor is popular
Intramural sports are popular
Recreation facilities are great

ACADEMICS

Academic Rating	74
% students returning for sophomore year	74
% students graduating within 4 years	38
% students graduating within 6 years	57
Calendar	Semester
Student/faculty ratio	15:1
Profs interesting rating	83
Profs accessible rating	88

Most classes have 10–19 students.
Most lab/discussion sessions have
  10–19 students.

MOST POPULAR MAJORS

Psychology, General; Registered Nursing/
Registered Nurse; Business Administration and
Management, General

STUDENTS SAY "..."

Academics

Up in the Northeast corner of the United States, the University of Maine is a public research university with "all the opportunities of a large state school, while having the atmosphere of a small school." Students majoring in Business, Engineering, Marine Sciences, Forestry, Animal Science, Music, and Education majors all rave about their departments, but they also say that with nearly 100 majors, minors and degree programs, "the class choices are amazing." The great value is another draw: "UMaine provides one of the most affordable university educations in the area" with "great scholarships if you have decent high school grades [and] SAT scores." As for the classes themselves, undergrads caution that "the courses are rather challenging," but there's a sense of "camaraderie and willingness to ... help—not just in professors but in your peers as well." Professors are generally "passionate, helpful, and actually want to see you at their office hours," and also bring "real-world experience into their classrooms." Juniors and seniors advise that "building a relationship with faculty is key" to success both at UMaine and beyond as they "are eager to recruit students to help with their [own] research" and provide connections to outside jobs and research positions in their fields. Other hands-on learning opportunities abound at UMaine, with some examples including "drilling through the ice to collect sediment samples" on a frozen lake and caring for "horses and dairy cows" on the university farm. Students also find "well-established connections outside of college" in the form of hospital internships to placements at local primary schools. Because of this, students seeking "opportunity and a sense of community" find this campus to "feel like home."

Life

UMaine Black Bears are a very active bunch, and "sports, especially hockey, [are] a huge part of the ... culture." At games, "the student section goes crazy (in the best way)" and "the school spirit is . . . incredible." Additionally, the school is situated in "such a unique place" that is "super green in the summer and pure white in the winter," providing this outdoorsy student body with miles of "trails for running and biking and a river [where] people often go paddling, kayaking, swimming and fishing." (Yes, there's an on-campus canoe rental.) Both coastal Arcadia National Park and remote Baxter State Park, where "the Appalachian Trail ends . . . [atop] pristine Mount Katahdin," are just an hour's drive away. The winter season is popular for cross-country and alpine skiing, snowboarding and other sports. Other forms of physical activity are available in UMaine's recreation center, which students boast is the "best in New England" and features "tons of equipment and ... classes for people of all experience levels." For those who would rather stay inside during the winter, the campus puts on free movies, "drag shows, trivia nights, [and] amazing Collins Center performances." As for nightlife, while there are plenty of parties and drinking at downtown bars on weekends, there is little pressure to partake—students say their peers are "chill and accepting of whatever you do and do not do." While the school may be in a rural environment, that doesn't mean the students are bored or lonely. As one undergrad puts it: "When everyone's in the middle of nowhere, no one is."

Student Body

UMaine's "campus is filled with very welcoming people" who are "down to earth," "helpful," "hardworking," and, as one undergrad phrases it, "wicked friendly." The student body hails "mostly from the state of Maine or the surrounding New England area" and is predominantly white. Yet students emphasize that the campus is diverse, maintaining a "significant LGBT+ presence on campus" and a mix of social classes, religions, and political affiliations. Whatever the background, most students "share the love and passion of the outdoors." Additionally, one student tells us, "Everyone has their own different quirks and no one is judged for that." That acceptance also goes for nontraditional students. For example, the "veteran community is fantastic" and there are "many people with military partners [or] family members." Another student sums it up: "There is a unique sense of Maine here, and we are quite united under the Black Bear banner."

Financial Aid: 207-581-1324 • E-Mail: umaineadmissions@maine.edu • Website: www.umaine.edu

THE PRINCETON REVIEW SAYS

Admissions

Very important factors considered include: rigor of secondary school record, class rank, academic GPA. *Important factors considered include:* application essay, recommendation(s). *Other factors considered include:* interview, extracurricular activities, talent/ability, character/personal qualities, volunteer work, work experience. ACT with or without writing accepted. SAT with or without Essay component accepted. High school diploma is required and GED is accepted. *Academic units required:* 4 English, 3 math, 2 science, 2 science labs, 2 social studies, 4 academic electives. *Academic units recommended:* 4 English, 4 math, 4 science, 3 science labs, 2 foreign language, 2 social studies, 1 history, 4 academic electives.

Financial Aid

Students should submit: FAFSA. Priority filing deadline is 3/1. The Princeton Review suggests that all financial aid forms be submitted as soon as possible after October 1. *Need-based scholarships/grants offered:* College/university scholarship or grant aid from institutional funds; Federal Pell; Private scholarships; SEOG; State scholarships/grants. *Loan aid offered:* Direct PLUS loans; Direct Subsidized Stafford Loans; Direct Unsubsidized Stafford Loans. Applicants will be notified of awards on a rolling basis beginning 1/1. Federal Work-Study Program available. Institutional employment available.

The Inside Word

Though they are not required, interviews, campus visits, and tours (run through the Heritage House) are highly recommended as a means of standing out among the many local UMaine applicants. Regular admissions are rolling with a recommended deadline of March 1 in order to optimize financial aid and housing prospects. Applicants for Mechanical Engineering should apply by February 28. Early Action applications maximize merit-based scholarships and have a December 1 deadline.

THE SCHOOL SAYS "..."

From the Admissions Office

"Maine's Flagship and Public Research University is at the forefront of national and international research, student engagement, innovation and collaboration. With experiential learning at its core, UMaine offers celebrated academics, student research opportunities and a close-knit community that strives for diversity, inclusion and excellence. UMaine offers more than one hundred undergraduate academic programs, eighty-seven master's programs and thirty-five doctoral programs. Top students are invited to join UMaine's Honors College, one of the country's oldest and most accomplished. The National Science Foundation ranks UMaine among the top third of public institutions engaged in research. Classified as a 'High Research Activity Institution' by the Carnegie Foundation for the Advancement of Teaching, its sixteen major research centers include The Laboratory for Surface Science and Technology, a hub for cutting-edge sensor and nanotechnology research, and the Advanced Structures and Composites Center, a global leader in deep water offshore wind energy development.

"Maine boasts a 16:1 student-to-faculty ratio, where faculty and administration members are known for having an open-door policy. Our students work alongside some of the most renowned scholars and scientists in their fields, whether they're talking civil engineering over lunch or traversing an Antarctic ice sheet with climate researchers.

"UMaine students gain real-world experience to prepare them for their professional careers after college. SPIFFY, our student investment club, manages a $3.2 million real-money portfolio. Wildlife ecology majors learn about bear behavior by going out and tagging cubs. Engineering majors take advantage of internships that often lead to employment after graduation. Marine science undergrads spend a semester by the sea at our internationally renowned Darling Marine Center."

SELECTIVITY

Admissions Rating	75
# of applicants	13,118
% of applicants accepted	90
% of acceptees attending	18

FRESHMAN PROFILE

Range SAT EBRW	530–630
Range SAT Math	520–630
Range ACT Composite	21–27
# submitting SAT scores	2,002
% submitting SAT scores	94
# submitting ACT scores	213
% submitting ACT scores	11
Average HS GPA	3.3
% graduated top 10% of class	20
% graduated top 25% of class	46
% graduated top 50% of class	79

DEADLINES

Early action	
Deadline	12/1
Notification	1/15
Regular	
Priority	2/1
Deadline	2/1
Notification	Rolling, 12/2
Nonfall registration?	Yes

APPLICANTS ALSO LOOK AT AND OFTEN PREFER
University of New Hampshire

AND SOMETIMES PREFER
Husson University; University of Connecticut; University of Massachusetts Amherst; University of New England; University of Rhode Island; University of Southern Maine; University of Vermont; University of Massachusetts Lowell; Merrimack College

FINANCIAL FACTS

Financial Aid Rating	84
Annual in-state tuition	$9,000
Annual out-of-state tuition	$29,310
Room and board	$10,966
Required fees	$2,438
Books and supplies	$1,000
Average frosh need-based scholarship	$11,243
Average UG need-based scholarship	$9,614
% needy frosh rec. need-based scholarship or grant aid	99
% needy UG rec. need-based scholarship or grant aid	94
% needy frosh rec. non-need-based scholarship or grant aid	14
% needy UG rec. non-need-based scholarship or grant aid	10
% needy frosh rec. need-based self-help aid	76
% needy UG rec. need-based self-help aid	79
% frosh rec. any financial aid	99
% UG rec. any financial aid	93
% UG borrow to pay for school	75
Average cumulative indebtedness	$34,703
% frosh need fully met	22
% ugrads need fully met	18
Average % of frosh need met	73
Average % of ugrad need met	68

UNIVERSITY OF MARY WASHINGTON

1301 College Avenue, Fredericksburg, VA 22401 • Admissions: 540-654-2000 • Fax: 540-654-1857

CAMPUS LIFE

Quality of Life Rating	89
Fire Safety Rating	93
Green Rating	91
Type of school	Public
Environment	City

STUDENTS

Total undergrad enrollment	4,371
% male/female	36/64
% from out of state	9
% frosh from public high school	79
% frosh live on campus	86
% ugrads live on campus	56
# of fraternities	0
# of sororities	0
% African American	8
% Asian	4
% Caucasian	68
% Hispanic	10
% Native American	<1
% Pacific Islander	<1
% Two or more races	6
% Race and/or ethnicity unknown	3
% international	1
# of countries represented	50

SURVEY SAYS . . .

Students are happy
Students love Fredericksburg, VA
Frats and sororities are popular

ACADEMICS

Academic Rating	80
% students returning for sophomore year	82
% students graduating within 4 years	60
% students graduating within 6 years	71
Calendar	Differs By Program
Student/faculty ratio	14:1
Profs interesting rating	90
Profs accessible rating	93

Most classes have 20–29 students.
Most lab/discussion sessions have 20–29 students.

MOST POPULAR MAJORS

Biology/Biological Sciences, General; Business Administration and Management, General; Psychology, General

STUDENTS SAY ". . ."

Academics

University of Mary of Washington offers a "sense of community" and tons of "school spirit." Students describe it as a "great liberal arts school with small class sizes." And the university itself truly excels at providing students with the "strategies and tools necessary to think critically and succeed in the workforce." It's also important to mention that "undergraduate research opportunities" abound. Perhaps what students here value most is the level of communication they have with their professors. As one impressed undergrad explains, "UMW professors go the extra mile to help students and ensure that they succeed and students never hesitate to take time out of their day to go see their professors during their office hours for extra help." Another amazed undergrad rushes to add, "Every professor I have had has made attempts to learn every student's name and what they are interested in." And in general, undergrads at UMW seem to find their professors "wonderful" and "very engaging." It's quite evident that "they love what they teach and want you to love it as well." What more could you want from your classroom experience?

Life

University of Mary Washington's campus is frequently abuzz with activity. To begin with, when the weather is nice you can find "students chilling on lawn chairs or reading on the grass or playing Frisbee." Additionally, "almost all students participate in clubs." And many UMW undergrads are "involved in community service both on and around campus." Moreover, "every weekend there are $1 movie nights for students, and one of the biggest weekly events is bingo on Tuesday nights." Although "there is no Greek Life officially on campus…there are nationally recognized fraternities and sororities operating off campus." And we've been informed that "parties are most often hosted by either these groups or by athletic teams." Students also declare "Fredericksburg is a great place to live." After all, "there are a plethora of historic sites to visit and an abundance of eateries to enjoy" along with "shops, movie theatres, and a bowling alley." And should these undergrads desire to get a little further away, they can easily capitalize on the fact that the university is "smack-dab in the middle of Richmond and Washington, D.C."

Student Body

Undergrads at University of Mary Washington tend to be "very relaxed and easy-going." And while they don't necessarily "party too hard," rest assured that they "definitely know how to have fun." Students also report that "Mary Washington is unique because everyone is so friendly." Indeed, "you cannot make it between buildings without someone saying hi or smiling at you. Everyone is so kind and welcoming." This grateful undergrad agrees sharing, "I'm never afraid to speak to someone new because at Mary Washington my peers are always accepting and willing to speak and form new friendships." Of course, it's important to mention that while "there is some diversity in demographics," the "student body is predominantly white." However, undergrads also rush to point out that the school has a nice combination of "on-campus and commuter students as well as a mix of traditional and non-traditional students. [In turn,] working with such a mix gives students a very unique education because you can learn so much from your [peers'] various viewpoints and…experiences." All in all, University of Mary Washington undergrads "care about each other, help each other and respect each other." Or, as this student succinctly states, "[This] community feels like a second family."

Financial Aid: 540-654-1682 • E-Mail: admit@umw.edu • Website: www.umw.edu

THE PRINCETON REVIEW SAYS

Admissions

Very important factors considered include: rigor of secondary school record, academic GPA, standardized test scores. *Important factors considered include:* class rank, application essay, recommendation(s). *Other factors considered include:* interview, extracurricular activities, talent/ability, character/personal qualities, first generation, alumni/ae relation, geographical residence, state residency, racial/ethnic status, volunteer work, work experience, level of applicant's interest. ACT with or without writing accepted. SAT with or without Essay component accepted. High school diploma is required and GED is accepted. *Academic units required:* 4 English, 3 math, 3 science, 3 science labs, 3 foreign language, 3 social studies. *Academic units recommended:* 4 English, 4 math, 4 science, 4 science labs, 4 foreign language, 2 social studies, 2 history.

Financial Aid

Students should submit: FAFSA. Priority filing deadline is 2/1. The Princeton Review suggests that all financial aid forms be submitted as soon as possible after October 1. *Need-based scholarships/grants offered:* College/university scholarship or grant aid from institutional funds; Federal Pell; Private scholarships; SEOG; State scholarships/grants. *Loan aid offered:* Direct PLUS loans; Direct Subsidized Stafford Loans; Direct Unsubsidized Stafford Loans. Applicants will be notified of awards on a rolling basis beginning 12/1. Federal Work-Study Program available. Institutional employment available.

The Inside Word

When considering candidates for admissions, University of Mary Washington does not subscribe to any particular formula. Indeed, the committee simply strives to create a diverse and well-rounded incoming class. Therefore, all aspects of your application will hold some weight. Of course, strong emphasis is placed on the quality and rigor of your high school curriculum. And successful students tend to have taken a handful of honors, advanced placement and/or IB classes.

THE SCHOOL SAYS "..."

From the Admissions Office

"The University of Mary Washington is one of the nation's premier public, liberal arts and sciences institutions. Highly respected for its commitment to academic excellence, the University boasts three colleges—business, education and arts and sciences and three campuses, conveniently located between Richmond, VA, and Washington, D.C. These two capitals provide a rich resource for undergraduate student internships, as well as a promising job market for graduates. Mary Washington's talented and intellectually curious students work collaboratively in small, interactive classes with innovative and accessible master teachers, including Fulbright scholars, who motivate them to think critically, engage meaningfully and communicate effectively.

"In addition to rigorous academics, the UMW experience is based on a culture of honor as well as community and global service, exemplified in the 2019 Peace Corps ranking of Mary Washington as one of the nation's top volunteer producers among small colleges. With multiple opportunities for student research and service learning, UMW graduates thrive in our fast-changing society.

"Distinctive to UMW is one of the nation's leading historic preservation programs, as well as strong creative writing and debate programs. Other top majors include political science and international affairs, English, biology, psychology, earth and environmental science, history, visual and performing arts, economics and business. With its classic Jeffersonian architecture, and beautifully manicured grounds, UMW offers an unparalleled American college experience. Nearly 150 student organizations and clubs provide opportunities for leadership. UMW Eagles varsity teams compete at the championship level in NCAA Division III."

SELECTIVITY

Admissions Rating	82
# of applicants	5,909
% of applicants accepted	72
% of acceptees attending	22
# offered a place on the wait list	773
% accepting a place on wait list	16
% admitted from wait list	29
# of early decision applicants	127
% accepted early decision	85

FRESHMAN PROFILE

Range SAT EBRW	540–649
Range SAT Math	510–620
Range ACT Composite	22–29
# submitting SAT scores	812
% submitting SAT scores	87
# submitting ACT scores	197
% submitting ACT scores	21
Average HS GPA	3.6
% graduated top 10% of class	16
% graduated top 25% of class	46
% graduated top 50% of class	81

DEADLINES

Early decision	
Deadline	11/1
Notification	12/15
Early action	
Deadline	11/15
Notification	1/31
Regular	
Priority	2/1
Deadline	2/1
Notification	4/1
Nonfall registration?	Yes

APPLICANTS ALSO LOOK AT AND OFTEN PREFER
William & Mary; University of Virginia

AND SOMETIMES PREFER
James Madison University; Virginia Polytechnic Institute and State University; Christopher Newport University

AND RARELY PREFER
George Mason University; Virginia Commonwealth University

FINANCIAL FACTS

Financial Aid Rating	79
Annual in-state tuition	$6,522
Annual out-of-state tuition	$23,014
Room and board	$11,612
Required fees	$6,576
Books and supplies	$1,200
Average frosh need-based scholarship	$3,505
Average UG need-based scholarship	$3,368
% needy frosh rec. need-based scholarship or grant aid	68
% needy UG rec. need-based scholarship or grant aid	67
% needy frosh rec. non-need-based scholarship or grant aid	82
% needy UG rec. non-need-based scholarship or grant aid	57
% needy frosh rec. need-based self-help aid	69
% needy UG rec. need-based self-help aid	75
% frosh rec. any financial aid	93
% UG rec. any financial aid	81
% UG borrow to pay for school	56
Average cumulative indebtedness	$32,820
% frosh need fully met	12
% ugrads need fully met	10
Average % of frosh need met	43
Average % of ugrad need met	43

UNIVERSITY OF MARYLAND, BALTIMORE COUNTY

1000 Hilltop Circle, Baltimore, MD 21250 • Admissions: 410-455-2292 • Fax: 410-455-1094

CAMPUS LIFE

Quality of Life Rating	87
Fire Safety Rating	65
Green Rating	92
Type of school	Public
Environment	Metropolis

STUDENTS

Total undergrad enrollment	10,955
% male/female	55/45
% from out of state	5
% frosh from public high school	91
% frosh live on campus	71
% ugrads live on campus	36
# of fraternities (% ugrad men join)	11 (3)
# of sororities (% ugrad women join)	6 (5)
% African American	19
% Asian	22
% Caucasian	39
% Hispanic	8
% Native American	<1
% Pacific Islander	<1
% Two or more races	5
% Race and/or ethnicity unknown	2
% international	4
# of countries represented	82

SURVEY SAYS . . .

School is well run
Students are happy
Career services are great

ACADEMICS

Academic Rating	82
% students returning for sophomore year	87
% students graduating within 4 years	42
% students graduating within 6 years	71
Calendar	4/1/4
Student/faculty ratio	17:1
Profs interesting rating	87
Profs accessible rating	90

Most classes have 10–19 students.
Most lab/discussion sessions have 20–29 students.

MOST POPULAR MAJORS

Biology/Biological Sciences, General; Management Information Systems and Services; Psychology

STUDENTS SAY "..."

Academics

The University of Maryland, Baltimore County has a "great...reputation" as a "quiet academic school" where "students take education seriously." Undergraduates are enthusiastic about the "academic opportunities and scholarship programs available," and say, "UMBC wants to see every student succeed—they provide you with the tools, people, and resources to make sure you get where you want to go in life." The university is particularly known for its "strong" science and mathematics programs and a commitment to the performing arts. Some students grumble, "The school needs to serve those with different majors apart from the sciences," but others are quick to point out that "UMBC is changing a bit to offer more to the fine arts students," including a new technologically advanced Performing Arts & Humanities Building. Most agree the university has "extremely intelligent professors that have a knack for inspiring the students," and say, "UMBC is a place where professors aren't just talking heads." Although some complain about dull lectures, a common consensus is that "this is a university where teaching comes first, followed by research, and it shows," and that "most of the professors are so helpful, you can find most of them sitting in their office, and they don't mind if you come and ask them questions."

Life

With 70 percent of first-year students living on campus, UMBC no longer deserves its commuter school reputation, though one ancient studies major says, "There are a lot of activities held by student organizations on campus during the week and on the weekends, but many students live close to campus and choose to go home for the weekend." While some may see this as a downside, others say, "The location of UMBC is true brilliance—so close to Baltimore. We hop over there on the weekdays even to go shopping or go out to eat." Most lament the absence of a football team, and there are complaints about the parking facilities, as well as a desire for "better buildings and food options." Despite these criticisms, a sociology major says, "Everyone on campus is nice and helpful to other students. People will always hold a door for you, help you pick up a dropped folder, or offer to share their notes with a student who missed class."

Student Body

More than one student says, "UMBC is a place where it is cool to be smart, and everything about the campus, including the students, exudes 'nerd-chic.'" In fact, an English major says that even "our president likes to say that it's cool to be smart at UMBC." This mentality is captured by a student who remarks, "Life at UMBC, aside from special events, revolves around classes and learning," and most undergrads agree: "The typical student at UMBC is interested in doing well academically and not just here to party until graduation." However, despite their dedication to hard work, UMBC students call themselves "enthusiastic and bright" and say "that almost every student at UMBC is involved with at least a couple of extracurricular activities, which connect them to the campus." The school has a strong reputation for diversity and students feel "it enriches our school and everyone gets to know everyone despite culture or ethnicity." A mechanical engineering student says, "This is even reflected in the high number of interracial couples I see on campus." Overall, it seems, "People fit in by being intellectually creative and finding a community with which to discuss important issues."

UNIVERSITY OF MARYLAND, BALTIMORE COUNTY

Financial Aid: 410-455-2387 • E-Mail: admissions@umbc.edu • Website: www.umbc.edu

THE PRINCETON REVIEW SAYS

Admissions

Very important factors considered include: rigor of secondary school record, academic GPA, application essay, standardized test scores, recommendation(s). *Important factors considered include:* class rank, talent/ability. *Other factors considered include:* extracurricular activities, character/personal qualities, first generation, volunteer work, work experience. ACT with or without writing accepted. SAT with or without Essay component accepted. High school diploma is required and GED is accepted. *Academic units required:* 4 English, 4 math, 3 science, 2 foreign language, 3 social studies, 3 history, 3 units from above areas or other academic areas. *Academic units recommended:* 4 English, 4 math, 3 science, 2 foreign language.

Financial Aid

Students should submit: FAFSA. Priority filing deadline is 2/14. The Princeton Review suggests that all financial aid forms be submitted as soon as possible after October 1. *Need-based scholarships/grants offered:* College/university scholarship or grant aid from institutional funds; Federal Pell; Private scholarships; SEOG; State scholarships/grants; United Negro College Fund. *Loan aid offered:* Direct PLUS loans; Direct Subsidized Stafford Loans; Direct Unsubsidized Stafford Loans. Applicants will be notified of awards on a rolling basis beginning 3/25. Federal Work-Study Program available. Institutional employment available.

The Inside Word

UMBC offers a large number of admissions events, online chats, a virtual tour, and other opportunities for prospective students to connect with the admissions team. The admissions committee considers the strength of your secondary school curriculum and class rank in combination with traditional factors, such as GPA, test scores, and essay when making an acceptance decision. Additionally, it's suggested that at least one letter of recommendation be written by a teacher.

THE SCHOOL SAYS "..."

From the Admissions Office

"At just over 50 years old, UMBC is established as a university where highly motivated students are taught and mentored by faculty who have been consistently recognized for their commitment to undergraduate teaching. Innovative approaches to learning take place in world-class facilities—such as the Howard Hughes Medical Institute at UMBC and the world-class Performing Arts and Humanities building. UMBC celebrates undergraduate research and creative achievement, which means even freshman are involved in research with their classmates and professors. The location of UMBC is just right—nestled just outside of Baltimore, in a quiet, green setting. UMBC is also a short commute to D.C., an advantage for jobs, internships, and networking opportunities. Perhaps that's why 87 percent of the UMBC class of 2018 are in prestigious graduate programs and careers within six months of graduation. Student life is abundant at UMBC. With more students living on campus each year (over 70 percent of freshman), Division 1 sports, a brand new 85 million dollar UMBC Event Center and 250 student organizations, students are creating experiences and friendships that will last a lifetime."

SELECTIVITY

Admissions Rating	87
# of applicants	11,842
% of applicants accepted	61
% of acceptees attending	24
# offered a place on the wait list	444
% accepting a place on wait list	100
% admitted from wait list	93

FRESHMAN PROFILE

Range SAT EBRW	590–670
Range SAT Math	590–690
Range ACT Composite	24–29
# submitting SAT scores	1,570
% submitting SAT scores	92
# submitting ACT scores	341
% submitting ACT scores	20
Average HS GPA	3.9
% graduated top 10% of class	21
% graduated top 25% of class	51
% graduated top 50% of class	83

DEADLINES

Early action	
Deadline	11/1
Notification	12/15
Regular	
Priority	11/1
Deadline	2/1
Notification	Rolling, 12/15
Nonfall registration?	Yes

APPLICANTS ALSO LOOK AT AND OFTEN PREFER
American University; Johns Hopkins University; Virginia Polytechnic Institute and State University; University of Maryland, College Park

AND SOMETIMES PREFER
Boston University; Penn State University Park

FINANCIAL FACTS

Financial Aid Rating	82
Annual in-state tuition	$8,704
Annual out-of-state tuition	$24,338
Room and board	$12,000
Required fees	$3,324
Books and supplies	$1,200
Average frosh need-based scholarship	$11,119
Average UG need-based scholarship	$10,079
% needy frosh rec. need-based scholarship or grant aid	88
% needy UG rec. need-based scholarship or grant aid	78
% needy frosh rec. non-need-based scholarship or grant aid	35
% needy UG rec. non-need-based scholarship or grant aid	13
% needy frosh rec. need-based self-help aid	42
% needy UG rec. need-based self-help aid	56
% frosh rec. any financial aid	89
% UG rec. any financial aid	62
% UG borrow to pay for school	49
Average cumulative indebtedness	$26,315
% frosh need fully met	19
% ugrads need fully met	11
Average % of frosh need met	63
Average % of ugrad need met	56

UNIVERSITY OF MARYLAND, COLLEGE PARK

Mitchell Building, College Park, MD 20742-5235 • Admissions: 301-314-8385 • Fax: 301-314-9693

STUDENTS SAY "..."

Academics

The University of Maryland—College Park is a grand mix of "twenty-minute walks to class across one of the country's most beautiful campuses, [an introduction] to high-level courses taught by the nation's top researchers, [and] a motivated 'green' campus" as well as "crowded, smelly frat parties, [and] living-learning communities that can make the gigantic campus much smaller." Students are quick to boast about sports, too, especially the men's and women's basketball teams. In short, it's a quintessential large university, offering "a great experience with a variety of opportunities that are what you make of them." Students crow about Maryland's "nationally recognized business program," a "top-ranked criminology program," a solid engineering school, a great political science department that capitalizes on the school's proximity to Washington, D.C., and the "top-notch honors program." Most of all, they love the "great price. This school gives you a great education for a really cheap price." Low cost doesn't translate to budget accommodations. On the contrary, "the administration shows a desire to always upgrade facilities, as can be witnessed by the tremendous business school and the brand new engineering building." In conclusion, students applaud "the widely diverse opportunities available at UMD. You can never get bored because there is always something to do."

Life

"Life at UMD is awesome," with "a good mix of fun activities" including "school-sponsored parties, games," a "campus recreation center that has virtually everything you could wish for, including pools, an extensive gym, a rock wall, squash courts, an indoor track," and a student union "loaded with fun places like the arcade area, bowling alley," and "tons of places to eat as well." In addition, "there are always open games of soccer, football, or ultimate Frisbee being played on the mall and elsewhere." There are bars close to campus, and "students are always having parties," especially along College Park's raucous Frat Row. Terrapin sports are a passion for many. If all that isn't enough, "the proximity to D.C. makes clubbing, nights out on the town, and general visits to D.C. frequent." With all this going on, no wonder students say that "the social life at UMD is unsurpassed." Some warn the surrounding area is dicey; "It's pretty annoying and scary to get crime alerts from the police informing us of incidents close to campus," one student explains. Undergrads also warn that parking regulations are brutal. "Bus transportation around campus provided by the university is great, but for students and visitors with cars, it's a huge hassle. Permits are expensive, and free parking for visitors is impossible to find. School officials are strict with violations, and tickets are seventy-five dollars. They are hard to refute and very costly."

Student Body

"The University of Maryland is a very large school," so "there is no 'typical' student here. Everyone will find that they can fit in somewhere." Better still, "different groups are very accepting of other groups. Students in Greek life are just as accepting of students in non-Greek life. Athletes blend in with non-athletes. UMD provides a great environment for students to meet people they would normally not know and helps to provide great connections with these people." UMD is "an especially diverse school," and this makes people "more tolerant and accepting of people from different backgrounds and cultures." A student from New Jersey explains it this way: "Coming from a very diverse area, I thought it was going to be hard to find a school that had that same representation of minority and atypical students until I found Maryland. I don't think I have ever learned so much about different religions, cultures, orientations, or lifestyles. All of them are accepted and even celebrated" at UMD.

UNIVERSITY OF MARYLAND, COLLEGE PARK

Financial Aid: 301-314-9000 • E-Mail: ApplyMaryland@umd.edu • Website: http://www.umd.edu

THE PRINCETON REVIEW SAYS

Admissions

Very important factors considered include: rigor of secondary school record, academic GPA, standardized test scores. *Important factors considered include:* class rank, application essay, recommendation(s), talent/ability, first generation, state residency. *Other factors considered include:* extracurricular activities, character/personal qualities, alumni/ae relation, geographical residence, racial/ethnic status, volunteer work, work experience. ACT with Writing required. SAT with or without Essay component accepted. High school diploma is required and GED is accepted. *Academic units required:* 4 English, 4 math, 3 science, 2 science labs, 2 foreign language, 3 social studies. *Academic units recommended:* 4 English, 4 math, 3 science, 2 science labs, 2 foreign language, 3 social studies.

Financial Aid

Students should submit: FAFSA. Priority filing deadline is 1/1. The Princeton Review suggests that all financial aid forms be submitted as soon as possible after October 1. *Need-based scholarships/grants offered:* College/university scholarship or grant aid from institutional funds; Federal Pell; Private scholarships; SEOG; State scholarships/grants. *Loan aid offered:* Direct PLUS loans; Direct Subsidized Stafford Loans; Direct Unsubsidized Stafford Loans. Applicants will be notified of awards on a rolling basis beginning 4/1. Federal Work-Study Program available. Institutional employment available.

The Inside Word

Maryland admissions officers don't simply crunch numbers and apply a formula. The school considers no fewer than twenty-five factors when determining who's in and who's out. Essays, recommendations, extracurricular activities, talents and skills, and demographic factors all figure into the mix along with high school transcript and standardized test scores. Give all aspects of your application your utmost attention; admissions is very competitive.

THE SCHOOL SAYS "..."

From the Admissions Office

"The University of Maryland (UMD) is a top-ranked flagship public research university, located within minutes from Washington, D.C. Students have opportunities to learn, explore and succeed through interaction with outstanding faculty that include Nobel Prize, Pulitzer Prize, Emmy and Tony winners. The beautifully landscaped 1,335-acre campus's proximity to major East Coast cities allows students to extend their education beyond the classroom through education abroad programs, and internships at U.S. federal agencies, research labs, global think tanks, major media outlets, world-class museums, and thriving companies. The university strongly encourages innovation, entrepreneurship and creativity by assisting students to launch startups, and serves as a model of cultural excellence through its arts programming. The University of Maryland also thrives on diversity, inclusion and engagement to prepare graduates to become excellent leaders in their communities and careers."

SELECTIVITY

Admissions Rating	94
# of applicants	32,987
% of applicants accepted	44
% of acceptees attending	29
# offered a place on the wait list	207

FRESHMAN PROFILE

Range SAT EBRW	630–720
Range SAT Math	650–760
Range SAT Composite	1290–1460
Range ACT Composite	29–33
# submitting SAT scores	3,520
% submitting SAT scores	82
# submitting ACT scores	1,342
% submitting ACT scores	31
Average HS GPA	4.3
% graduated top 10% of class	69
% graduated top 25% of class	89
% graduated top 50% of class	99

DEADLINES

Early action	
Deadline	11/1
Notification	1/31
Regular	
Priority	11/1
Deadline	1/20
Notification	Rolling, 4/1
Nonfall registration?	Yes

FINANCIAL FACTS

Financial Aid Rating	80
Annual in-state tuition	$8,824
Annual out-of-state tuition	$34,936
Room and board	$12,935
Required fees	$1,955
Books and supplies	$1,250
Average frosh need-based scholarship	$10,398
Average UG need-based scholarship	$10,577
% needy frosh rec. need-based scholarship or grant aid	78
% needy UG rec. need-based scholarship or grant aid	75
% needy frosh rec. non-need-based scholarship or grant aid	10
% needy UG rec. non-need-based scholarship or grant aid	5
% needy frosh rec. need-based self-help aid	84
% needy UG rec. need-based self-help aid	91
% frosh rec. any financial aid	86.4
% UG rec. any financial aid	71.7
% UG borrow to pay for school	39
Average cumulative indebtedness	$29,133
% frosh need fully met	21
% ugrads need fully met	15
Average % of frosh need met	63
Average % of ugrad need met	60

UNIVERSITY OF MASSACHUSETTS AMHERST

University Admissions Center, Amherst, MA 01003 • Admissions: 413-545-0222 • Fax: 413-545-4312

STUDENTS SAY " . . ."

Academics

As a large research institution and the state's flagship campus, the University of Massachusetts Amherst offers "immense resources and opportunities" for enrollees. Students at this university can choose from over 110 majors. Many are eager to sign up for exciting courses such as a botany class where undergrads visit a "new garden where food is made for [the] dining halls" or a "bookbinding class," and even a "science course called the science of craft where [students] get to learn how to blacksmith, make pottery, brew, and blow glass." There are also "many niche seminars for first year students that allow them to explore their identities and eccentric interests." In addition to "unique and interesting courses," undergrads say "the ongoing research and new ideas coming from here are amazing." With access to "new facilities and very high tech labs" and "great research opportunities" from professors who "eagerly accept undergraduate assistants," many agree that "school keeps [them] busy, but it's worth it." And if there's somehow not enough for students to do at Amherst itself, there's a free inter-campus bus for those who want to take advantage of cross-registering at one of the five other Massachusetts colleges that the school is in a consortium with.

Behind these "very engaging" courses and research opportunities are "kind and knowledgeable" professors. Students note that faculty are "super personable" and make it "easy to ask questions in big lectures with TAs and office hours." While every instructor's course is different, the "group-based [and] interactive learning" complements the "big lectures" offered by the school. Students feel that professors are constantly "bringing the class to life with new teaching styles" in order to "make sure that each individual is grasping the material." Many undergrads indicate that their instructors "obviously care about the subjects [they teach]" and "care about their students' well-being." Above all, it feels like professors "want their students to succeed."

Life

On campus at UMass Amherst and in the nearby cities, "there's always something to do if you keep your eyes peeled and are willing." You can find students hanging out in the dining halls (where "the food is off the charts good"), tinkering in the craft center, or exercising at the rec center's fitness classes. The university has "an array of fun activities" for "people with many interests like sports, music, theater, and other clubs." On the weekends, people tend to "hang out a lot and sometimes go to parties." Amherst also has twenty-one Division I sports, so attending games—particularly cheering on the "great hockey team" and showing your spirit at "fun tailgates"—is a frequent pastime. The school "has so many interesting opportunities to get involved that it's nearly impossible to be surrounded by completely identical people."

The school's location in the Northeast "gives [students] many opportunities to explore" the surrounding area. Consequently, students love to "travel to nearby cities like NYC or Boston." The neighboring city of Northampton has several "fun shops" and students can be found in downtown Amherst "sitting in a local tea shop" and trying out "cool little restaurants." On the whole, "there's always something to do."

Student Body

While finding your place among 24,000 undergrads might sound intimidating, students note that it's "a large school that you can make smaller so easily by building your own community." There are so many potential new friends to choose from amongst this "diverse, tolerant, inclusive" group, most of whom are described as "very kind and respectful" and who "love to have a good time and learn." The size is actually an advantage, in that it's easier to "find people you identify with . . . which helps a lot when moving in the first year." Ultimately, students suggest that "there's a place for everyone," whether you're from Massachusetts, like much of the campus's population, or from "different parts of the country or the world."

UNIVERSITY OF MASSACHUSETTS AMHERST

Financial Aid: 413-545-0801 • E-Mail: mail@admissions.umass.edu • Website: www.umass.edu

THE PRINCETON REVIEW SAYS

Admissions

Very important factors considered include: rigor of secondary school record, academic GPA. *Important factors considered include:* standardized test scores, application essay, recommendation(s), extracurricular activities, talent/ability, character/personal qualities, first generation. *Other factors considered include:* alumni/ae relation, geographical residence, state residency, racial/ethnic status, volunteer work. ACT with Writing recommended. SAT with Essay component recommended. High school diploma is required and GED is accepted. *Academic units required:* 4 English, 4 math, 3 science, 3 science labs, 2 foreign language, 2 social studies, 2 academic electives.

Financial Aid

Students should submit: FAFSA. Priority filing deadline is 3/1. The Princeton Review suggests that all financial aid forms be submitted as soon as possible after October 1. *Need-based scholarships/grants offered:* College/university scholarship or grant aid from institutional funds; Federal Pell; Private scholarships; SEOG; State scholarships/grants. *Loan aid offered:* Direct PLUS loans; Direct Subsidized Stafford Loans; Direct Unsubsidized Stafford Loans. Applicants will be notified of awards on a rolling basis beginning 12/15. Federal Work-Study Program available. Institutional employment available.

The Inside Word

UMass Amherst takes a fairly straightforward approach to the admissions game. High school transcripts and standardized test scores will be of primary importance. When assessing an applicant's transcript, UMass Amherst takes into consideration course grades but also grade trends, course selection, and grades related to a desired major. Applicants to the Architecture, Art, Dance, and Music majors are encouraged to contact the appropriate department and apply as early as possible to allow enough time for an audition or portfolio review. For all applicants, a strong senior year schedule is also admired. The university is forward-thinking and socially conscious and therefore invites applications from and encourages the enrollment of undocumented students and students granted Deferred Action for Childhood Arrivals (DACA).

THE SCHOOL SAYS "..."

From the Admissions Office

"The University of Massachusetts Amherst is the flagship campus of the Commonwealth and the largest public university in New England, offering its students an almost limitless variety of academic programs and activities. The Commonwealth Honors College Residential Complex is a national model and welcomes students who seek additional academic challenge and meet the requirements for acceptance. The school takes a holistic view of the student's application package and considers test scores (SAT or ACT) as only part of the evaluation criteria. Greater weight in the selection process is placed on the student's performance in a rigorous curriculum. Increased applications in recent years have made admission more selective. Over one hundred majors are offered, including a unique program called Bachelor's Degree with Individual Concentration (BDIC) in which students create their own program of study. First-year students participate in the Residential First-Year Experience with opportunities to explore every possible interest through residential life. The extensive library system is the largest at any public institution in the Northeast. The campus completes in NCAA Division I sports for men and women, with teams winning national recognition. About 6,500 students a year participate in the intramural sports program. The town of Amherst is consistently ranked one of the top college towns in the country. Through the Five College Interchange, students enroll in classes at nearby Amherst, Hampshire, Mount Holyoke, and Smith Colleges at no extra charge. A free bus system connects these five campuses, allowing students to participate in a wide array of social and cultural events."

SELECTIVITY

Admissions Rating	86
# of applicants	42,157
% of applicants accepted	64
% of acceptees attending	21
# offered a place on the wait list	2,188
% accepting a place on wait list	46
% admitted from wait list	0

FRESHMAN PROFILE

Range SAT EBRW	590–680
Range SAT Math	600–710
Range SAT Composite	1210–1370
Range ACT Composite	26–32
# submitting SAT scores	5,141
% submitting SAT scores	89
# submitting ACT scores	1,052
% submitting ACT scores	18
Average HS GPA	3.9
% graduated top 10% of class	31
% graduated top 25% of class	70
% graduated top 50% of class	96

DEADLINES

Early action	
Deadline	11/5
Regular	
Deadline	1/15
Nonfall registration?	Yes

APPLICANTS ALSO LOOK AT AND OFTEN PREFER

Boston College; Boston University; Northeastern University

AND SOMETIMES PREFER

Syracuse University; University of Connecticut; Worcester Polytechnic Institute

AND RARELY PREFER

University of Massachusetts Lowell; University of New Hampshire; University of Rhode Island; University of Vermont; Fordham University; Penn State University Park

FINANCIAL FACTS

Financial Aid Rating	85
Annual in-state tuition	$16,784
Annual out-of-state tuition	$36,763
Room and board	$14,006
Books and supplies $1,000	
Average frosh need-based scholarship	$11,467
Average UG need-based scholarship	$11,180
% needy frosh rec. need-based scholarship or grant aid	92
% needy UG rec. need-based scholarship or grant aid	90
% needy frosh rec. non-need-based scholarship or grant aid	8
% needy UG rec. non-need-based scholarship or grant aid	6
% needy frosh rec. need-based self-help aid	86
% needy UG rec. need-based self-help aid	90
% frosh rec. any financial aid	90.4
% UG rec. any financial aid	90.8
% UG borrow to pay for school	62
Average cumulative indebtedness	$31,755
% frosh need fully met	13
% ugrads need fully met	13
Average % of frosh need met	80
Average % of ugrad need met	82

UNIVERSITY OF MIAMI

P.O. Box 248025, Coral Gables, FL 33124-4616 • Admissions: 305-284-4323 • Fax: 305-284-2507

STUDENTS SAY ". . ."

Academics

"Gorgeous" University of Miami offers an "incredible range" of courses of study, chief among them "great programs in the sciences, engineering [and] music." Class sizes are small and internship opportunities are plentiful. Students here feel that they're getting a "well-rounded education," and "making connections" that they can capitalize on in the future. Though many undergrads report that their "courses are difficult," they also find them incredibly "rewarding." Inside the classroom, Miami students are delighted to find the majority of their professors are "easily approachable" and "incredibly knowledgeable." They clearly want "their students to learn and succeed." Indeed, "they are always there for you and open to helping in any way they can." Moreover, professors here are "well informed on the topic and are [typically] accessible after class." As one grateful student sums up, "I have had great academic success at UM largely because of my supportive and helpful professors. They deserve a lot more credit than they receive."

Life

"There is always something going on" at the University of Miami. The campus is frequently abuzz with a multitude of fun events like the "farmers market, patio jams...and random activities [such as] laser tag, corn hole, food trucks [and] Frisbee game[s]." "The majority of students are involved in more than one campus club or activity" and a number of undergrads seek out volunteer opportunities. As one student explains, "We also have special service days that get good turnouts including Gandhi Day, Orientation Outreach, and MLK Day of Service." And plenty of undergrads spend their time "poolside, beachside, tailgating, anything they can find to have a good time." University of Miami also has a "very active/sporty population" with many students participating in both "club sports [and] intramural sports." Additionally, "Greek life is relatively popular, though the community is very welcoming and non-exclusive." And students also love "Canes After Dark [which often sponsors] cool activities like movies by the pool or snowball fights." Finally, nearby Miami "provides a lot of opportunity for adventure." Indeed, it has a "vibrant night life," a "wide array of cuisine," world-class museums, and beautiful beaches. You couldn't ask for anything more!

Student Body

Many undergrads at University of Miami proudly report that their peers are "very diverse." Indeed, you'll find that "there are people here from all over the world with different cultures, different experiences, and different likes and dislikes." As one amazed student shares, "You can hear so many different languages being spoken on campus." Nevertheless, while you might encounter people from around the country and the globe, a handful of undergrads insist that a number of their fellow students are "frat bros and girls that [simply] want to have fun." Additionally, a lot of students appear to come from "very affluent" families and "luxury cars and going out to clubs on South Beach aren't out of the ordinary." However, others are quick to describe the culture as "very inclusive and understanding." And many assert that University of Miami students are "always willing to help out and assist you in finding your way." Another undergrad bolsters this claim by sharing, "I was lost on the first day of my first semester and an upperclassman pointed me in the direction of my class without being asked! It really made my day." Perhaps most importantly, we've been assured that "everyone can find their own social group here."

Financial Aid: 305-284-2270 • E-Mail: admission@miami.edu • Website: www.miami.edu

THE PRINCETON REVIEW SAYS

Admissions

Very important factors considered include: rigor of secondary school record, class rank, academic GPA, application essay, standardized test scores, recommendation(s), extracurricular activities, character/personal qualities. *Important factors considered include:* talent/ability. *Other factors considered include:* first generation, alumni/ae relation, geographical residence, state residency, racial/ethnic status, level of applicant's interest. ACT with or without writing accepted. SAT with or without Essay component accepted. High school diploma is required and GED is accepted. *Academic units recommended:* 4 English, 4 math, 3 science, 2 science labs, 2 foreign language, 2 social studies.

Financial Aid

Students should submit: Business/Farm Supplement; CSS/Financial Aid PROFILE; FAFSA; Noncustodial PROFILE. Priority filing deadline is 1/1. The Princeton Review suggests that all financial aid forms be submitted as soon as possible after October 1. *Need-based scholarships/grants offered:* College/university scholarship or grant aid from institutional funds; Federal Pell; Private scholarships; SEOG; State scholarships/grants. *Loan aid offered:* Direct PLUS loans; Direct Subsidized Stafford Loans; Direct Unsubsidized Stafford Loans. Applicants will be notified of awards on a rolling basis beginning 1/20. Federal Work-Study Program available. Institutional employment available.

The Inside Word

Interested candidates should be aware that the admissions process at University of Miami is competitive. Fortunately, the committee does its utmost to consider the whole candidate. Therefore, everything from the strength of your high school curriculum and standardized test scores to extracurricular activities and awards earned will be reviewed thoroughly. Ultimately, the university is looking for intellectually curious students who will be leaders both inside and outside the classroom.

THE SCHOOL SAYS "..."

From the Admissions Office

"At the University of Miami, we educate leaders, problem solvers, and change makers. With the flexibility to choose from more than 180 majors and programs across 11 schools and colleges, students design their education based on the topics that excite them most. Here, coursework integrates academic rigor and theory with hands-on experience so students are able to convert knowledge into fulfilling achievements. As early as freshman year, students collaborate with award-winning faculty on projects that make meaningful contributions beyond the classroom. Projects range from volunteer experiences to cutting-edge research in topics such as climate change, public health, and privacy in the age of social media.

"With 10,000 undergraduate students, our close-knit campus combines the personal attention of a small college with the academic opportunity of a large research university. Our international location, just seven miles from downtown Miami, provides students with meaningful opportunities for experiential learning locally and in countries around the world. On campus, we are united in our diversity and working to cultivate a culture of belonging.

"Our students are passionate about learning, driven to contribute to their community, and encouraged to innovate. Whether you seek to make your mark in science, service, or the arts, the University of Miami will help you develop the skills needed to carve your own path to success."

SELECTIVITY

Admissions Rating	93
# of applicants	34,279
% of applicants accepted	32
% of acceptees attending	21
# offered a place on the wait list	10,405
% accepting a place on wait list	39
% admitted from wait list	1
# of early decision applicants	1,232
% accepted early decision	56

FRESHMAN PROFILE

Range SAT EBRW	620–690
Range SAT Math	630–740
Range ACT Composite	29–32
# submitting SAT scores	1,204
% submitting SAT scores	51
# submitting ACT scores	1,013
% submitting ACT scores	43
Average HS GPA	3.6
% graduated top 10% of class	55
% graduated top 25% of class	83
% graduated top 50% of class	95

DEADLINES

Early decision	
Deadline	11/1
Notification	12/15
Other ED Deadline	1/1
Other ED Notification	2/15
Early action	
Deadline	11/1
Notification	1/31
Regular	
Deadline	1/1
Notification	4/15
Nonfall registration?	Yes

FINANCIAL FACTS

Financial Aid Rating	93
Annual tuition	$48,720
Room and board	$14,108
Required fees	$1,506
Books and supplies	$1,000
Average frosh need-based scholarship	$34,643
Average UG need-based scholarship	$33,923
% needy frosh rec. need-based scholarship or grant aid	76
% needy UG rec. need-based scholarship or grant aid	75
% needy frosh rec. non-need-based scholarship or grant aid	48
% needy UG rec. non-need-based scholarship or grant aid	40
% needy frosh rec. need-based self-help aid	57
% needy UG rec. need-based self-help aid	61
% frosh rec. any financial aid	70
% UG rec. any financial aid	72
% UG borrow to pay for school	36
Average cumulative indebtedness	$22,000
% frosh need fully met	98
% ugrads need fully met	89
Average % of frosh need met	95
Average % of ugrad need met	93

UNIVERSITY OF MICHIGAN—ANN ARBOR

515 E. Jefferson St, Ann Arbor, MI 48109-1316 • Admissions: 734-764-7433 • Fax: 734-936-0740

STUDENTS SAY "..."

Academics

Among the many allures of the University of Michigan—Ann Arbor is that the school offers "a great environment both academically and socially." One student explains, "It has the social, fun atmosphere of any Big Ten university, but most people are still incredibly focused on their studies. It's great to be at a place where there is always something to do, but your friends completely understand when you have to stay in and get work done." With "an amazing honors program," a "wide range of travel-abroad opportunities," and "research strength" all available "at a low cost," it's no wonder students tell us that UM "provides every kind of opportunity at all times to all people." Academically, Michigan "is very competitive, and the professors have high academic standards for all the students." In fact, some here insist that "Michigan is as good as Ivy League schools in many disciplines." Standout offerings include business ("We have access to some of the brightest leaders" in the business world, students report), a "great engineering program," and "a good undergraduate program for medical school preparation." Those seeking add-on academic experiences here will find "a vast amount of resources. Internships, career opportunities, tutoring, community service projects, a plethora of student organizations, and a wealth of other resources" are all available, but "you need to make the first move" because no one "will seek you out."

Life

Michigan is a huge university, meaning that students have endless extracurricular options here. One explains: "If you seek it out, you can find organizations for *any* interest. There are always people out there who share your interests. That's part of the benefit of 40,000-plus students!" There is a robust party scene. Students tell us that "most students go to house parties [or] hit the bars." There's also a vigorous social scene for the non-drinking crowd, with "great programs like UMix…phenomenal cultural opportunities in Ann Arbor especially music and movies," and "the hugely popular football Saturdays. The sense of school spirit here is impressive." Michigan students tend to be both academically serious and socially outgoing, which "is great because you can have a stimulating conversation with someone one day, and, the next day, be watching a silly movie or playing video games with this person."

Student Body

The Michigan student body "is hugely diverse," which "is one of the things Michigan prides itself on." "If you participate in extracurricular activities and make an effort to get to know other students in class and elsewhere, you'll definitely end up with a pretty diverse group of friends," undergrads assure us. Although varied, students tend to be similar in that they "are social but very academically driven." A number of students "are on the cutting edge of both research and progressive thinking," and there is a decided liberal tilt to campus politics. Even so, there's a place for everyone here, because "there are hundreds of mini-communities within the campus, made of everything from service fraternities to political organizations to dance groups. If you have an interest, you can find a group of people who enjoy the same thing."

Financial Aid: 734-763-6600 • E-Mail: financial.aid@umich.edu • Website: umich.edu

THE PRINCETON REVIEW SAYS

Admissions

Very important factors considered include: rigor of secondary school record, academic GPA. *Important factors considered include:* application essay, standardized test scores, recommendation(s), character/personal qualities, first generation. *Other factors considered include:* extracurricular activities, talent/ability, alumni/ae relation, geographical residence, state residency, volunteer work, work experience, level of applicant's interest. ACT with or without writing accepted. SAT with or without Essay component accepted. High school diploma is required and GED is accepted. *Academic units required:* 4 English, 3 math, 3 science, 1 science lab, 2 foreign language, 1 social studies, 3 history. *Academic units recommended:* 4 English, 4 math, 4 science, 1 science lab, 4 foreign language, 1 social studies, 3 history, 1 computer science, 2 visual/performing arts.

Financial Aid

Students should submit: CSS/Financial Aid PROFILE; FAFSA. Priority filing deadline is 3/31. The Princeton Review suggests that all financial aid forms be submitted as soon as possible after October 1. *Need-based scholarships/grants offered:* College/university scholarship or grant aid from institutional funds; Federal Pell; Private scholarships; SEOG; State scholarships/grants. *Loan aid offered:* Direct PLUS loans; Direct Subsidized Stafford Loans; Direct Unsubsidized Stafford Loans. Applicants will be notified of awards on a rolling basis beginning 3/15. Federal Work-Study Program available. Institutional employment available.

The Inside Word

Michigan admissions are extremely competitive, so you will need high test scores, exemplary grades in challenging courses, and strong teacher recommendations to make the cut here. Though Michigan receives over 60,000 applications, each one is read three times. Use your extracurricular activities to demonstrate leadership and originality to stand out from the crowd.

THE SCHOOL SAYS "..."

From the Admissions Office

"The University of Michigan is one of the great public research universities in the U.S. and the world, located in vibrant Ann Arbor. Since 1817, U-M has been a global model of a diverse, comprehensive academic institution committed to the public good. Nineteen schools and colleges offer over 275 degree programs, featuring tremendous academic breadth and opportunity for discovery. Our thriving innovation ecosystem cultivates the ingenuity and entrepreneurial spirit of students across campus. Students study the liberal arts and the sciences in an immersive, cross-disciplinary environment that encourages inquiry in the classroom and in undergraduate research, with a 15:1 student/faculty ratio and 1,300 students participating in undergraduate research partnerships with faculty. Numerous service learning programs link academics with volunteerism, such as Semester in Detroit. U-M is the fourth-largest all-time producer of Peace Corps volunteers. Starting freshman year, students can join Living-Learning Programs to explore and experience college life with other students who share similar interests, making a large campus small. With access to top-ranked programs and distinguished faculty, students have the resources and support they need to reach their full potential, to find their true voice, and to make a positive impact on the world. And with more than 580,000 living alumni around the world, new graduates can easily make personal and professional connections to other Michigan grads."

SELECTIVITY

Admissions Rating	97
# of applicants	64,972
% of applicants accepted	23
% of acceptees attending	46
# offered a place on the wait list	12,527
% accepting a place on wait list	39
% admitted from wait list	2

FRESHMAN PROFILE

Range SAT EBRW	660–740
Range SAT Math	680–790
Range SAT Composite	1340–1530
Range ACT Composite	31–34
# submitting SAT scores	4,315
% submitting SAT scores	63
# submitting ACT scores	3,288
% submitting ACT scores	48
Average HS GPA	3.9

DEADLINES

Early action	
Deadline	11/1
Notification	12/24
Regular	
Priority	11/1
Deadline	2/1
Nonfall registration?	Yes

APPLICANTS ALSO LOOK AT AND OFTEN PREFER

Cornell University; University of California—Berkeley

AND SOMETIMES PREFER

University of California, Los Angeles

AND RARELY PREFER

Grand Valley State University; Michigan State University; Oakland University; Wayne State University; Purdue University—West Lafayette; Western Michigan University

FINANCIAL FACTS

Financial Aid Rating	90
Annual in-state tuition	$16,212
Annual out-of-state tuition	$52,669
Room and board	$11,996
Required fees	$328
Books and supplies	$1,048
Average frosh need-based scholarship	$21,330
Average UG need-based scholarship	$21,665
% needy frosh rec. need-based scholarship or grant aid	76
% needy UG rec. need-based scholarship or grant aid	81
% needy frosh rec. non-need-based scholarship or grant aid	70
% needy UG rec. non-need-based scholarship or grant aid	66
% needy frosh rec. need-based self-help aid	68
% needy UG rec. need-based self-help aid	73
% frosh rec. any financial aid	70
% UG rec. any financial aid	59
% UG borrow to pay for school	38
Average cumulative indebtedness	$25,777
% frosh need fully met	66
% ugrads need fully met	74
Average % of frosh need met	90
Average % of ugrad need met	92

UNIVERSITY OF MINNESOTA—TWIN CITIES

240 Williamsom Hall, Minneapolis, MN 55455-0213 • Admissions: 612-625-2008 • Fax: 612-626-1693

CAMPUS LIFE

Quality of Life Rating	**89**
Fire Safety Rating	**88**
Green Rating	**96**
Type of school	Public
Environment	Metropolis

STUDENTS

Total undergrad enrollment	31,367
% male/female	47/53
% from out of state	27
% frosh live on campus	86
% ugrads live on campus	23
# of fraternities	31
# of sororities	12
% African American	5
% Asian	10
% Caucasian	65
% Hispanic	5
% Native American	<1
% Pacific Islander	<1
% Two or more races	4
% Race and/or ethnicity unknown	2
% international	8
# of countries represented	147

SURVEY SAYS . . .

Students are happy
Great library
Students love Minneapolis, MN
Recreation facilities are great
Everyone loves the Golden Gophers
Intramural sports are popular

ACADEMICS

Academic Rating	**81**
% students returning for sophomore year	93
% students graduating within 4 years	69
% students graduating within 6 years	83
Calendar	Semester
Student/faculty ratio	17:1
Profs interesting rating	85
Profs accessible rating	89
Most classes have 20–29 students.	
Most lab/discussion sessions have 10–19 students.	

MOST POPULAR MAJORS

Journalism; Psychology, General; Computer Science

STUDENTS SAY "..."

Academics

"Great research opportunities," and "phenomenal engineering programs" among other fantastic departments, attract students to the University of Minnesota, Twin Cities. "A top-ranked university in a beautiful city that has a lot of great job opportunities"—how could you resist? And, given its "large" size, it's a virtual guarantee that "anyone can find what they want to do." Even better, the university really makes an effort to "help students discover themselves." An impressed psych major explains, "Our school pushes us to expand our horizons, to go outside of our comfort zones, and to try things that we never would have considered trying before." And Minnesota deftly maintains "a small school feeing" amidst "an urban setting," something many undergrads here value. By and large, Minnesota professors tend to be "approachable and are more than willing to take time out of their day to ensure you understand the material." They are also "very knowledgeable" and "strive to make [the subject matter] exciting." In short, "the University of Minnesota is a place with endless opportunity for those willing to discover their passions."

Life

Attending the University of Minnesota means that your life is likely to be "full of variety." Indeed, from "biking [and] outdoor games [to] reading in the park, going to the farmers market, attending events at Coffman or TCF Bank Stadium, or taking the green line down town to explore," undergrads here "can get involved in almost anything." UMN also "hosts a lot of lectures and discussions with prominent figures" like Sandra Day O'Connor and the Dalai Lama. Further, as a member of the Big 10 conference, it's no surprise that "sporting events are widely popular, even if we aren't doing very well." As if that wasn't enough, "the Coffman building always has something going on—movies, book signings—and there are a ton of student groups to join, no experience necessary." There is also a "thriving" Greek population on campus, and a social scene that also involves a handful of "house parties," which typically feature "alcohol and lots of dancing." And, of course, the Twin Cities themselves have "a lot going on!" As a political science student succinctly puts it, "If you're bored on a weekend, then you're not looking hard enough."

Student Body

Given the university's large undergraduate population, it's rather difficult to put "[students] into one category." Indeed, Minnesota truly manages to net "a wide variety of people." A dental hygiene student confirms this stating, "We have so much diversity here, that it is hard to pinpoint a general student type." And a mechanical engineering major quickly follows up, "Due to its size, everyone can find their niche and be free to express who they are." That being said, undergrads report that most of their peers are "generally quite friendly and outgoing." And everyone is "pretty willing to go out of their way for others, we are Minnesota nice after all." Further, many "students are driven to succeed and to make the most of the vast opportunities offered by the UMN." And a political science major matter-of-factly asserts that a large number of students are "white, middle to upper middle-class Midwesterner[s], most likely hailing from Minnesota, Wisconsin, or the Dakotas." Of course, at the very least, nearly all Minnesota undergrads can "fit in by bonding over how much [they] hate winter."

UNIVERSITY OF MINNESOTA—TWIN CITIES

Financial Aid: 612-624-1111 or 1-800-400-8636 • Website: https://twin-cities.umn.edu/

THE PRINCETON REVIEW SAYS

Admissions

Very important factors considered include: rigor of secondary school record, class rank, academic GPA, standardized test scores. *Other factors considered include:* extracurricular activities, talent/ability, character/personal qualities, first generation, alumni/ae relation, geographical residence, racial/ethnic status, volunteer work, work experience. ACT with Writing recommended. SAT with Essay component recommended. High school diploma is required and GED is accepted. *Academic units required:* 4 English, 4 math, 3 science, 1 science lab, 2 foreign language, 3 social studies, 1 visual/performing arts. *Academic units recommended:* 4 English, 4 math, 4 science, 1 science lab, 2 foreign language, 3 social studies, 1 visual/performing arts.

Financial Aid

Students should submit: FAFSA; Institution's own financial aid form. Priority filing deadline is 3/1. The Princeton Review suggests that all financial aid forms be submitted as soon as possible after October 1. *Need-based scholarships/grants offered:* College/university scholarship or grant aid from institutional funds; Federal Nursing Scholarships; Federal Pell; Private scholarships; SEOG; State scholarships/grants. *Loan aid offered:* Direct PLUS loans; Direct Subsidized Stafford Loans; Direct Unsubsidized Stafford Loans. Applicants will be notified of awards on a rolling basis beginning 2/15. Federal Work-Study Program available. Institutional employment available.

The Inside Word

University of Minnesota, Twin Cities is a well-regarded institution and gaining admission is no easy feat. Academic preparation and performance are of primary concern. Therefore, course selection, GPA, class rank, and standardized test scores will hold the most weight. However, plenty of consideration is also given to secondary factors such as outstanding talent and achievement in a particular area, military service, strong leadership experience, and extenuating circumstances.

THE SCHOOL SAYS "..."

From the Admissions Office

"The University of Minnesota is one of the nation's top public research universities. That means your college experience will be enhanced by world-renowned faculty, state-of-the-art learning facilities, and an unprecedented variety of options (such as 150 majors). Eighty-one percent of our classes have fewer than fifty students, and our caring advisers will help you find opportunities that are right for you. Hands-on courses, volunteer opportunities, internships, study abroad, and undergraduate research are part of the U of M experience. Students benefit from programs and traditions designed to support their success, like Welcome Week, where freshmen explore campus, meet their classmates, and connect with faculty and staff before the school year begins. Our classic Big Ten campus is located in the heart of the vibrant Twin Cities. Just minutes away, intern at a Fortune 500 company, volunteer at a major hospital, or relax at the beautiful Chain of Lakes. With a wealth of cultural, career, and recreational opportunities, there's no better place to earn your degree. Last year, we awarded over $12 million in four-year scholarship packages. Residents of Minnesota benefit from in-state tuition. Minnesota residents may also qualify for the University of Minnesota Promise Scholarship, which guarantees tuition aid to eligible students with a family income up to $120,000. Residents of North Dakota, South Dakota, Wisconsin, or Manitoba qualify for special reciprocity tuition rates.

"The University of Minnesota has been named a 'Best Value in Public Colleges' by multiple ranking organizations. As a U of M student, you will experience this value first-hand: you will step into a thriving academic community with some of the world's most renowned researchers. In fact, you'll often find that your professors are leading discoveries in their fields and developing curricula used across the country. With direct access to these incredible resources, you will get a great education and a prestigious degree that helps you achieve your dreams."

SELECTIVITY

Admissions Rating	89
# of applicants	40,673
% of applicants accepted	57
% of acceptees attending	27

FRESHMAN PROFILE

Range SAT EBRW	600–710
Range SAT Math	660–770
Range ACT Composite	26–31
# submitting SAT scores	1,127
% submitting SAT scores	18
# submitting ACT scores	5,560
% submitting ACT scores	89
% graduated top 10% of class	50
% graduated top 25% of class	83
% graduated top 50% of class	98

DEADLINES

Regular	
Notification	3/31
Nonfall registration?	Yes

FINANCIAL FACTS

Financial Aid Rating	84
Annual in-state tuition	$13,318
Annual out-of-state tuition	$31,616
Room and board	$10,768
Required fees	$1,709
Books and supplies	$1,000
Average frosh need-based scholarship	$12,676
Average UG need-based scholarship	$11,235
% needy frosh rec. need-based scholarship or grant aid	88
% needy UG rec. need-based scholarship or grant aid	86
% needy frosh rec. non-need-based scholarship or grant aid	10
% needy UG rec. non-need-based scholarship or grant aid	7
% needy frosh rec. need-based self-help aid	78
% needy UG rec. need-based self-help aid	80
% UG borrow to pay for school	55
Average cumulative indebtedness	$27,077
% frosh need fully met	27
% ugrads need fully met	25
Average % of frosh need met	77
Average % of ugrad need met	74

UNIVERSITY OF MISSISSIPPI

145 Martindale, University, MS 38677 • Admissions: 662-915-7226 • Fax: 662-915-5869

CAMPUS LIFE

Quality of Life Rating	94
Fire Safety Rating	90
Green Rating	69
Type of school	Public
Environment	Village

STUDENTS

Total undergrad enrollment	16,932
% male/female	43/57
% from out of state	44
% frosh live on campus	98
% ugrads live on campus	25
# of fraternities (% ugrad men join)	20 (32)
# of sororities (% ugrad women join)	15 (43)
% African American	12
% Asian	2
% Caucasian	78
% Hispanic	4
% Native American	<1
% Pacific Islander	<1
% Two or more races	2
% Race and/or ethnicity unknown	0
% international	1

SURVEY SAYS . . .

Students are very religious
Lots of beer drinking
Hard liquor is popular
Everyone loves the Ole Miss Rebels
Frats and sororities are popular
Alumni active on campus

ACADEMICS

Academic Rating	78
% students returning for sophomore year	85
% students graduating within 4 years	37
% students graduating within 6 years	60
Calendar	Semester
Student/faculty ratio	18:1
Profs interesting rating	88
Profs accessible rating	94

Most classes have 10–19 students.
Most lab/discussion sessions have
20–29 students.

MOST POPULAR MAJORS

Accounting; Marketing/Marketing Management,
General

STUDENTS SAY "..."

Academics

Ole Miss is a prime example of Southern hospitality combined with the opportunity for greatness. Founded in 1848, the legendary university offers "'big-time' SEC athletics in the safe, quaint, and picturesque town of Oxford." Many of the school's services "are cheap if not free," and the school "puts on many programs that bring together lots of different people of different backgrounds." "It has a togetherness about it…there is something for a person with any interest here," says a student. There is also "a highly academic side to Ole Miss that many outsiders do not see." Business and international studies are programs of note, and the Honors College is a particular standout here, as it provides "unparalleled academic opportunities, such as beginning research as a freshman."

Most of the professors "hit the ball out of the park" when it comes to teaching, being available, and helping students acquire internships. Professors constantly organize discussion groups, dinner events, and other gatherings in order to "develop our ability to speak academically in a non-academic setting." Going to class is "critical"; professors "add much more than the textbook has to offer." Classes are designed to be "informative but also engaging and dynamic," and there is a deep understanding that individuals have an effect on the whole. "The teachers care, the university cares, [and] the students all care about the school and what it stands for."

It can be said again and again, but even beyond the "world-class programs and faculty," the thing that students at Ole Miss value the most is the traditions and legacy of this school. People "are proud to have graduated from Ole Miss," and the tremendous amount of alumni support "gives Ole Miss a lot of confidence."

Life

An Ole Miss existence is "always super busy." There is "a lot of work to be done" as "school and grades are a very important aspect of life," but there are also "a lot of opportunities for fun." "During football season, the Grove consumes our weekends. It's an amazing experience!" says a student. As a school that most admit is "known for its Greek life, beautiful women, and great parties," it's a common misconception that "most people's minds revolve around drinking, college football, and church on Sunday." If you take a closer look, you'll find that there is a huge literary scene "with Thacker Mountain Radio on Thursdays and poetry readings monthly at Proud Larry's," and students here also "really want to be active in making changes in the world."

The closeness of the community makes it easy to feel part of the University. "You'll hear the term the 'Ole Miss family,' and it won't seem forced or strange," explains a student. Oxford is also very appealing due to its "small, hometown feel," and the rich history you see everywhere you go (the Square is the center of town life, and most students can be found there at some point in a week). Basically, "there is never a dull moment, especially on the weekends."

Student Body

Ole Miss is a fairly diverse campus, with most students possessing "decent grades and an extravagant social life." One-third of the student body "belongs to either a fraternity or sorority, fancying the appropriate attire of a Polo shirt and loafers or baggy t-shirts and Nike shorts." The divide between Greek and non-Greek is stark here, though the two groups are not necessarily always adverse toward each other; this is a group of "open minds" in "a small-town" setting, with "a blend of Southern charm and laid-back manners" thrown in, after all. "Studying for your next exam over a glass of sweet tea is a common practice." As there are a lot of different groups on campus, "you can find a group of friends without much effort."

Financial Aid: 800-891-4596 • E-Mail: admissions@olemiss.edu • Website: www.olemiss.edu

THE PRINCETON REVIEW SAYS

Admissions

Important factors considered include: academic GPA, standardized test scores. *Other factors considered include:* rigor of secondary school record, class rank. ACT with or without writing accepted. High school diploma is required and GED is accepted. *Academic units required:* 4 English, 3 math, 3 science, 2 science labs, 2 foreign language, 3 social studies, 0.5 computer science, 1 visual/performing arts. *Academic units recommended:* 4 English, 4 math, 4 science, 2 science labs, 2 foreign language, 4 social studies, 0.5 computer science, 1 visual/performing arts, 2 units from above areas or other academic areas.

Financial Aid

Students should submit: FAFSA. Priority filing deadline is 3/1. The Princeton Review suggests that all financial aid forms be submitted as soon as possible after October 1. *Need-based scholarships/grants offered:* College/university scholarship or grant aid from institutional funds; Federal Pell; Private scholarships; SEOG; State scholarships/grants. *Loan aid offered:* Direct PLUS loans; Direct Subsidized Stafford Loans; Direct Unsubsidized Stafford Loans. Applicants will be notified of awards on a rolling basis beginning 4/1. Federal Work-Study Program available. Institutional employment available.

The Inside Word

Ole Miss offers students tremendous educational opportunities and its admissions policies are designed to help in-state students attain a college degree. In-state applicants must have a 3.2 GPA or greater, or a 2.5 GPA and a 16 on the ACT or 760 on the SAT). Non-residents will need a 2.75 GPA and score 22 on the ACT or 980 on the SAT.

THE SCHOOL SAYS "..."

From the Admissions Office

"The state's flagship university, affectionately known as Ole Miss, offers extraordinary opportunities through more than 120 areas of study from medicine and law to creative writing and accountancy. Its acclaimed offerings include the Sally McDonnell Barksdale Honors College, the Croft Institute for International Studies and the Center for Manufacturing Excellence, which incorporates coursework from schools of engineering, accountancy and business into its curriculum. Its Patterson School of Accountancy is nationally ranked for undergraduate and graduate education, the School of Law is a national leader in the fields of air and space law and sports law, and nearly 100 percent of School of Pharmacy graduates pass the national licensure exam on their first try. It was the state's first public university to shelter a chapter of the nation's oldest and most prestigious honor society, Phi Beta Kappa. Strong academic programs and a rich and varied campus life have helped Ole Miss produce twenty-six Rhodes Scholars and fifteen Truman Scholars. Since 1998 alone, UM has produced ten Goldwater Scholars, nineteen Fulbright Scholars, and twenty-one Boren Scholars.

"The campuses are diverse; 45 percent come from out of state, with all fifty states and ninety foreign countries represented, and 13 percent are black Americans. Recent significant campus improvements include several new residence halls and a totally renovated and expanded dining facility. Ole Miss is home to twenty research and education centers, including the National Center for Justice and the Rule of Law, which provides training on investigating and prosecuting cybercrime; the National Center for Physical Acoustics, which is helping to quiet jet engines and use infrasound to detect tornadoes; and the National Center for Natural Products Research, where scientists are working to find new drugs to treat cancer, AIDS, fungal infections, and more. Students applying must take the SAT or the ACT but are not required to take the ACT writing section. The university will not consider the writing section of either exam when evaluating students for admission, but certain specialty programs may request these scores."

SELECTIVITY

Admissions Rating	76
# of applicants	16,253
% of applicants accepted	88
% of acceptees attending	23

FRESHMAN PROFILE

Range SAT EBRW	520–630
Range SAT Math	500–620
Range ACT Composite	21–29
# submitting SAT scores	853
% submitting SAT scores	26
# submitting ACT scores	2,753
% submitting ACT scores	85
Average HS GPA	3.6
% graduated top 10% of class	25
% graduated top 25% of class	49
% graduated top 50% of class	76

DEADLINES

Regular	
Priority	4/1
Notification	Rolling, 9/15
Nonfall registration?	Yes

FINANCIAL FACTS

Financial Aid Rating	86
Annual in-state tuition	$8,550
Annual out-of-state tuition	$24,504
Room and board	$10,696
Required fees	$100
Books and supplies	$1,200
Average frosh need-based scholarship	$10,013
Average UG need-based scholarship	$8,954
% needy frosh rec. need-based scholarship or grant aid	91
% needy UG rec. need-based scholarship or grant aid	85
% needy frosh rec. non-need-based scholarship or grant aid	15
% needy UG rec. non-need-based scholarship or grant aid	10
% needy frosh rec. need-based self-help aid	63
% needy UG rec. need-based self-help aid	71
% frosh rec. any financial aid	86
% UG rec. any financial aid	80
% UG borrow to pay for school	50
Average cumulative indebtedness	$30,731
% frosh need fully met	19
% ugrads need fully met	14
Average % of frosh need met	78
Average % of ugrad need met	75

UNIVERSITY OF MISSOURI

230 Jesse Hall, Columbia, MO 65211 • Admissions: 573-882-7786 • Fax: 573-882-7887

STUDENTS SAY ". . ."

Academics

The "gorgeous campus" at the University of Missouri is filled with "a diverse group of students who are eager to learn and a staff that is eager to teach them." The school is all about "learning while networking," and the administration always has an ear to the students. "When we say there is a problem, it gets fixed," one student says. Mizzou takes pride in tradition, which is to be found "in all aspects that involve the University name," which makes for "a campus full of pride and spirit." There is a "constant focus on beautification, which makes for a great campus," and "top-of-the-line facilities" are available to all. One of the university's greatest strengths is its dependability: "From mass e-mails to mass texts, if there is an issue anywhere on campus you will know about it."

Professors teach "comprehensive courses" and "are always available to answer a question"; "even with large classes they are very attentive to individuals." "I've always had professors who have had a million ways to explain any given theory, problem, or question," says a student. The school boasts one of the country's best and most "intense" journalism schools (nursing is also a strong suit), and there are tons of "participation opportunities" for whatever area you choose to study. Classes may be hard, but "good grades are attainable." In addition to the "quality" academics, the advising system is "great," and Mizzou sets itself as a real model for its students: "It is always striving to achieve better, and not in just one specific category or area, but all around." "I came into college undecided and wanted to have plenty of options and opportunities to decide on a major," says a student of her reasoning for choosing Mizzou.

Life

"There is never a dull moment to be had" at the University of Missouri. All athletic events are "heavily attended," especially football and basketball. Everyone walks or bikes everywhere in Columbia "because it's such a pedestrian friendly place," and "there are plenty of opportunities to chill out downtown." It is "the perfect mixture of small town and big city," and local attractions include a mall, small shops, micro-breweries, and tons of parks and hiking trails. If you're used to bigger cities, then it also happens to be located between Kansas City and St. Louis. "Best of both worlds!" says a student. The school has "a huge Greek Life," and "it's a pretty close community." "Students enjoy going to off-campus parties or the bars downtown." "A lot of students spend their time in class, but every night of the week there is a party to go to," explains a student. Many agree that both the residential life system and the dorms "could use some work," and "having a car is the key to living off campus."

Student Body

The school has a giant spectrum of diversity, meaning "everyone is different. Anyone could fit in and find a group here." If a typical student has to be defined, most here are "friendly, outgoing, social, [and] very involved." Most of all, they are "proud to be Tiger[s]." "We all fit in because we have this in common," says a student. "It's pretty great company." "Classes have always felt like big families," and the majority of students find friends "by joining one of our million organizations," which is a common pastime among this "on-the-go" group. As everyone is "pretty easygoing and easy to get along with," "fitting in is easy; you just act like yourself!"

Financial Aid: 573-882-7506 • E-Mail: MU4U@missouri.edu • Website: www.missouri.edu

THE PRINCETON REVIEW SAYS

Admissions

Very important factors considered include: class rank, academic GPA, standardized test scores. *Other factors considered include:* rigor of secondary school record, application essay, recommendation(s), talent/ability. ACT with or without writing accepted. SAT with or without Essay component accepted. High school diploma is required and GED is accepted. *Academic units required:* 4 English, 4 math, 3 science, 1 science lab, 2 foreign language, 3 social studies, 1 unit from above areas or other academic areas.

Financial Aid

Students should submit: FAFSA. Priority filing deadline is 2/1. The Princeton Review suggests that all financial aid forms be submitted as soon as possible after October 1. *Need-based scholarships/grants offered:* College/university scholarship or grant aid from institutional funds; Federal Nursing Scholarships; Federal Pell; Private scholarships; SEOG; State scholarships/grants. *Loan aid offered:* Direct PLUS loans; Direct Subsidized Stafford Loans; Direct Unsubsidized Stafford Loans. Applicants will be notified of awards on a rolling basis beginning 3/15. Federal Work-Study Program available. Institutional employment available.

The Inside Word

If your application suggests that you can handle the workload here, the school will find a place for you. Average test scores in conjunction with a college-prep high school curriculum should be all it takes. Even those who don't meet these criteria have a chance; admissions officers consider essays, recommendations, and special talents in the cases of borderline candidates.

THE SCHOOL SAYS "..."

From the Admissions Office

"Founded in 1839 as the first public university west of the Mississippi River, MU is a member of the nation's most prestigious group of sixty-three public and private teaching/research institutions: the Association of American Universities. The National Science Foundation has recognized MU as one of the top ten universities in the country for integrating research into undergraduate education; Mizzou offers twelve major undergraduate research programs, some with freshmen participants.

"Mizzou is nestled in the heart of Columbia, Missouri, a bright and lively college town where something is always happening. Galleries, concert halls, theaters, shops, festivals and restaurants are just steps from campus. It's hard to tell where campus ends and downtown begins.

"Hands-on learning is central to the Mizzou academic experience. Called the Missouri Method, Students get right into the mix, from reporting news on the local NBC TV station, making ice cream, healing animals, trading stocks or teaching kindergarteners.

"Mizzou's Freshman Interest Groups (FIGs) program places freshmen in halls alongside students with similar interests. Freshmen take courses and participate in activities with others in the same FIG, creating a sense of community and leading to academic success.

"Mizzou has more than 300 degree programs to choose from. And if one of those doesn't quite meet a student's needs, they can create their own major.

"Students can find admissions requirements at missouri.edu. As students apply online, it is clear whether they are admissible or not. That may partially explain Missouri's high acceptance rate."

SELECTIVITY

Admissions Rating	82
# of applicants	20,015
% of applicants accepted	81
% of acceptees attending	34

FRESHMAN PROFILE

Range SAT EBRW	560–660
Range SAT Math	560–680
Range ACT Composite	23–29
# submitting SAT scores	542
% submitting SAT scores	10
# submitting ACT scores	4,869
% submitting ACT scores	90
% graduated top 10% of class	33
% graduated top 25% of class	63
% graduated top 50% of class	91

DEADLINES

Regular	
Deadline	Rolling
Notification	Rolling
Nonfall registration?	Yes

FINANCIAL FACTS

Financial Aid Rating	73
Annual in-state tuition	$9,120
Annual out-of-state tuition	$26,991
Room and board	$11,618
Required fees	$1,357
Books and supplies	$1,232
% needy frosh rec. need-based scholarship or grant aid	91
% needy UG rec. need-based scholarship or grant aid	84
% needy frosh rec. non-need-based scholarship or grant aid	11
% needy UG rec. non-need-based scholarship or grant aid	7
% needy frosh rec. need-based self-help aid	56
% needy UG rec. need-based self-help aid	62
% frosh rec. any financial aid	85
% UG rec. any financial aid	77
% frosh need fully met	22
% ugrads need fully met	17
Average % of frosh need met	65
Average % of ugrad need met	62

THE UNIVERSITY OF MONTANA—MISSOULA

Lommasson Center 101, Missoula, MT 59812 • Admissions: 406-243-6266 • Fax: 406-243-5711

CAMPUS LIFE
Quality of Life Rating	88
Fire Safety Rating	90
Green Rating	82
Type of school	Public
Environment	City

STUDENTS
Total undergrad enrollment	7,515
% male/female	44/56
% from out of state	30
% frosh live on campus	76
% ugrads live on campus	37
# of fraternities (% ugrad men join)	6 (6)
# of sororities (% ugrad women join)	4 (6)
% African American	1
% Asian	1
% Caucasian	78
% Hispanic	5
% Native American	<1
% Pacific Islander	<1
% Two or more races	5
% Race and/or ethnicity unknown	5
% international	1
# of countries represented	43

SURVEY SAYS . . .
Recreation facilities are great
Everyone loves the Grizzlies
Students are happy
Students love Missoula, MT

ACADEMICS
Academic Rating	75
% students returning for sophomore year	71
% students graduating within 4 years	30
% students graduating within 6 years	49
Calendar	Semester
Student/faculty ratio	16:1
Profs interesting rating	87
Profs accessible rating	89

Most classes have 10–19 students.
Most lab/discussion sessions have 10–19 students.

MOST POPULAR MAJORS
Business Administration and Management, General; Forest Management/Forest Resources Management; Psychology, General

STUDENTS SAY ". . ."

Academics

Nestled in beautiful Missoula, The University of Montana is "a great place to live, work, and study." Indeed, Montana's awesome location and solid reputation coupled with low in-state tuition make it "hard to beat." Moreover, while it has a substantial number of students, we're assured that you're never "just a number" here. Undergrads also appreciate the university's focus on "environmental sustainability…and social justice" along with the fact that the University of Montana strives to develop "creative thinkers and engaged citizens." While the university maintains a fantastic liberal arts program, students especially laud the wildlife biology, forestry, physical therapy, and forensic anthropology departments. Moreover, undergrads at Montana are highly complementary of their teachers who are generally "helpful, engaging, and accessible." One thrilled student claims that the professors are "amazing! Math and science has never come easy for me, and my professors have taught in a way I completely understand the material." Another enthusiastic student summarizes her experience by stating, "The professors here are very knowledgeable and passionate about what they are teaching, because of this, the learning experience is always interesting and inviting. I truly appreciate all the effort that is put forward to help students succeed and prepare for the next steps in their life."

Life

Undergrads seem to truly enjoy life at U of M. Indeed, the campus is often buzzing with activity. As one student happily shares, "When it's not snowing in the fall or spring you can find people playing Frisbee, walking their dogs, catching footballs, and even playing with lightsabers." Additionally, there are "many music concerts and dance parties" one can attend. "Football is [also] really big here," and games are often packed with students. Beyond the campus, Montana offers a myriad of options for the outdoor enthusiast. As one ecstatic undergrad tells us, "Western Montana is a divine place for hiking, hunting, fishing, camping, snowshoeing, swimming, huckleberry picking, going to hot springs, mushroom picking, antler collecting, and just being immersed in nature. Near where I live there is access to the Rattlesnake Wilderness, mountains surround the valley, and the Clark Fork River runs right through town." Those with a more adventurous spirit can delight in "skiing and skydiving, hand gliding and parasailing, mountain climbing and repelling, caving and biking." As this pleased undergrad summarizes, "There is always something to do no matter what your interests are and great people to do them with."

Student Body

The University of Montana attracts a student body that's "pretty laid-back and easygoing." Many are "outdoorsy" and self-described as "hippies." Indeed, there are "quite a few granola kids" and "Carhartt-sporting, plaid-proud, future biologists" types. Though many students hail from within the state, one undergrad assures us that "increasing diversity efforts have begun to show in the past three years." Fortunately, for the most part, everyone is "accepting, friendly, and very involved in college and community life." Another student expands on this idea, stating, "People here do not seem to judge others or hold stereotypes against each other. If you're lost or need to ask a question you can ask anyone, and they're willing to give you the best answer they know in order to help you out even if they don't know you." A fellow undergrad agrees softly, sharing, "I feel like I've stepped into a melting pot of all beliefs and ideals. You can be yourself, and never be looked down on for that at this school."

THE UNIVERSITY OF MONTANA—MISSOULA

Financial Aid: 406-243-5373 • E-Mail: admiss@umontana.edu • Website: www.umt.edu

THE PRINCETON REVIEW SAYS

Admissions

Very important factors considered include: rigor of secondary school record, class rank, academic GPA, standardized test scores. *Important factors considered include:* extracurricular activities, talent/ability. ACT with Writing recommended. SAT with Essay component recommended. High school diploma is required and GED is accepted. *Academic units required:* 4 English, 3 math, 2 science, 2 science labs, 3 social studies, 2 history. *Academic units recommended:* 2 foreign language, 2 computer science, 2 visual/performing arts.

Financial Aid

Students should submit: FAFSA. Priority filing deadline is 12/1. The Princeton Review suggests that all financial aid forms be submitted as soon as possible after October 1. *Need-based scholarships/grants offered:* College/university scholarship or grant aid from institutional funds; Federal Pell; Private scholarships; SEOG; State scholarships/grants. *Loan aid offered:* Direct PLUS loans; Direct Subsidized Stafford Loans; Direct Unsubsidized Stafford Loans. Applicants will be notified of awards on a rolling basis beginning 3/16. Federal Work-Study Program available. Institutional employment available.

The Inside Word

The admissions game at the University of Montana is fairly straightforward. Officers here rely heavily on quantitative data. Applicants who meet standardized test and GPA minimums and are in the top half of their graduating class generally receive an acceptance letter. Those who did not meet the minimum requirements can often enroll on a conditional basis.

THE SCHOOL SAYS "..."

From the Admissions Office

"There's something special about this place. It's something different for each person. For some, it's the blend of academic quality and outdoor recreation. The University of Montana ranks fifth in the nation among public institutions for producing Rhodes scholars, and *Outside* Magazine lists Missoula in its 'Top Ten Amazing Places for Outdoor Recreation.' For others, it's size—not too big, not too small. The University of Montana is a midsized university in the heart of the Rocky Mountains—accessible in both admission and tuition bills—that produces graduates considered among the best and brightest in the world. It is located in a community that could pass for a cozy college town or a bustling big city, depending on your point of view. There's a lot happening, but you won't get lost. People are friendly and diverse. They come from all over the world to study and learn and to live a good life. They come to a place to be inspired, a place where they feel comfortable yet challenged. Some never leave. Most never want to."

SELECTIVITY

Admissions Rating	75
# of applicants	4,910
% of applicants accepted	94
% of acceptees attending	32

FRESHMAN PROFILE

Range SAT EBRW	535–635
Range SAT Math	520–610
Range ACT Composite	20–26
# submitting SAT scores	454
% submitting SAT scores	39
# submitting ACT scores	820
% submitting ACT scores	71
Average HS GPA	3.4
% graduated top 10% of class	16
% graduated top 25% of class	40
% graduated top 50% of class	73

DEADLINES

Regular	
Priority	3/1
Notification	Rolling, 6/15
Nonfall registration?	Yes

FINANCIAL FACTS

Financial Aid Rating	80
Annual in-state tuition	$5,352
Annual out-of-state tuition	$24,144
Room and board	$9,966
Required fees	$2,002
Books and supplies	$1,100
Average frosh need-based scholarship	$5,168
Average UG need-based scholarship	$4,991
% needy frosh rec. need-based scholarship or grant aid	56
% needy UG rec. need-based scholarship or grant aid	61
% needy frosh rec. non-need-based scholarship or grant aid	80
% needy UG rec. non-need-based scholarship or grant aid	52
% needy frosh rec. need-based self-help aid	95
% needy UG rec. need-based self-help aid	91
% frosh rec. any financial aid	74
% UG rec. any financial aid	63
% UG borrow to pay for school	58
Average cumulative indebtedness	$27,132
% frosh need fully met	12
% ugrads need fully met	11
Average % of frosh need met	69
Average % of ugrad need met	61

UNIVERSITY OF NEBRASKA—LINCOLN

1410 Q Street, Lincoln, NE 68588-0417 • Admissions: 402-472-2023 • Fax: 402-472-0670

CAMPUS LIFE

Quality of Life Rating	91
Fire Safety Rating	86
Green Rating	81
Type of school	Public
Environment	City

STUDENTS

Total undergrad enrollment	20,253
% male/female	52/48
% from out of state	25
% frosh live on campus	86
% ugrads live on campus	41
# of fraternities (% ugrad men join)	33 (19)
# of sororities (% ugrad women join)	23 (27)
% African American	3
% Asian	3
% Caucasian	75
% Hispanic	7
% Native American	<1
% Pacific Islander	0
% Two or more races	3
% Race and/or ethnicity unknown	1
% international	8
# of countries represented	100

SURVEY SAYS . . .

Students are happy
Students love Lincoln, NE
Recreation facilities are great
Everyone loves the Cornhuskers
Intramural sports are popular
Frats and sororities are popular

ACADEMICS

Academic Rating	78
% students returning for sophomore year	84
% students graduating within 4 years	41
% students graduating within 6 years	65
Calendar	Semester
Student/faculty ratio	17:1
Profs interesting rating	84
Profs accessible rating	90

Most classes have 20–29 students.
Most lab/discussion sessions have 20–29 students.

MOST POPULAR MAJORS

Public Relations, Advertising, and Applied Communication; Psychology, General; Business Administration and Management, General

STUDENTS SAY ". . ."

Academics

The University of Nebraska–Lincoln, is situated in a great spot—Nebraska's capital city—to make "connections with companies in Lincoln, Omaha, and surrounding areas," and provides "tons of undergraduate research opportunities," "amazing internships," and "leadership opportunities." Students find the university to pair this practical focus on "job placement," which is aided by "career coaches and employer-in residences, and partnerships with "local businesses," with the recognition and prestige of a Big 10, "rigorous" research institution. Students also praise "phenomenal advisors," especially for pre-health students, "great study abroad programs," and other specific schools and programs such as the business school, the honors academy, and Raikes School of Computer Science and Management. Professors are "passionate," and Nebraska being a research institution, can teach from "real world examples." After their first year, students typically begin "moving toward…project based courses where you…are paired with a company or using a real world example" instead of textbooks to do homework. Faculty is known to be accessible and generous with students, offering "personal advice," orienting students and "introducing campus resources," and sometimes even "welcoming [students] to their home." Nebraska is also known to have a "fantastic financial aid and scholarship program that makes it very affordable to attend," offering "great scholarships, especially to out-of-state students" who would have a higher tuition bill.

Life

Nebraska is the "smallest Big 10 public school," so students say their "beautiful campus" is "great if you're looking for a prestigious school, but a bit smaller." Students overwhelmingly name the Division 1 football team ("Go Big Red!") as being a generator of school spirit that spreads into the "incredible college town." "Since this is the only football team here in Nebraska, many people are very excited for game days here in Lincoln," one student reports. Intramural sports are also popular: "there are always pick-up games of soccer, ultimate Frisbee, football" and so on "on the outdoor Astroturf fields, as well as the indoor practice facilities, which includes an "indoor football field for students … [donated] by the Athletic Department and the Husker Football Team."

About "20 percent of students are in Greek Life," and "the whole campus is always attending their philanthropy events." And with over 600 clubs, students need not leave campus to pack their schedules with activities outside of studying. However, campus is right next to downtown, so the campus isn't isolated; students are "part of the Lincoln community," which offers a "small town feel with big town amenities." In the city, students "catch a movie at the downtown movie theater," "take swing dancing classes at the Pla Mor ballroom," go "ice skating," and "jogging" or "shop in the Haymarket area."

Student Body

University of Nebraska–Lincoln's student body is made up of an "array of students from small town Nebraska, the big cities of Lincoln and Omaha" as well as a number of "out-of-state and international students." "Kindness permeates interactions across campus," and the "passion that the students have for their institution is palpable." Students are by and large "friendly but conservative," a "mixture of rural and city kids." "The mix of cultures works really well" reflecting "Midwestern manners of kind, friendly people." Students are studious but interconnected, especially through their identification with "Husker power." "Sports aren't my main concern," says another, "but it is super awesome attending a Big 10 university" because of the "pride" and "positive and outgoing" Lincoln community.

Financial Aid: 402-472-2030 • E-Mail: admissions@unl.edu • Website: http://www.unl.edu

THE PRINCETON REVIEW SAYS

Admissions

Very important factors considered include: class rank, academic GPA, standardized test scores. *Important factors considered include:* rigor of secondary school record. ACT with or without writing accepted. SAT with or without Essay component accepted. High school diploma is required and GED is accepted. *Academic units required:* 4 English, 4 math, 3 science, 1 science lab, 2 foreign language, 1 social studies, 2 history.

Financial Aid

Students should submit: FAFSA. Priority filing deadline is 4/1. The Princeton Review suggests that all financial aid forms be submitted as soon as possible after October 1. *Need-based scholarships/grants offered:* College/university scholarship or grant aid from institutional funds; Federal Pell; Private scholarships; SEOG; State scholarships/grants. *Loan aid offered:* Direct PLUS loans; Direct Subsidized Stafford Loans; Direct Unsubsidized Stafford Loans. Applicants will be notified of awards on a rolling basis beginning 12/15. Federal Work-Study Program available. Institutional employment available.

The Inside Word

Nebraska offers more than 150 majors. All applications will be weighed on the combined strength of course work, GPAs, and test scores. Applicants interested in applying to a specific school within the university should take into account those school's specialized requirements as they may include additional high school course work than what is required by the university's general studies program. To be considered for leadership and diversity scholarships, you must write a 500-word essay that focuses on leadership, career goals, and community service.

THE SCHOOL SAYS "..."

From the Admissions Office

"We are Nebraska. We believe in the power of every person. We don't rest on our strengths—we stretch them. Sweat them. Combine them. Growing flexible, nimble, and strong minds. That's how we do big things. Our faculty and researchers work hard to help students succeed and to solve real-world issues. Students can quickly access the programs they desire, get involved in the university community and build their skills—all elements that will help them create the future they want. Nebraska has a low student-to-faculty ratio, a substantial out-of-state scholarship program and one of the nation's leading undergraduate research programs.

"The university is the heart of Lincoln, a growing, thriving contemporary city. Tech start-ups are flocking to Lincoln to recruit talent from the university and get involved with our cutting-edge Innovation Campus. The city's downtown is steps away from campus and home to a rich arts and music scene. Campus upgrades to the student union and rec centers, plus several building projects, contribute to a vibrant and dynamic culture. More than 200,000 alumni from the University of Nebraska–Lincoln's nearly 150-year history have made a difference in the world and opened doors for those who've followed."

SELECTIVITY

Admissions Rating	83
# of applicants	16,829
% of applicants accepted	78
% of acceptees attending	36

FRESHMAN PROFILE

Range SAT EBRW	560–670
Range SAT Math	560–690
Range ACT Composite	22–28
# submitting SAT scores	591
% submitting SAT scores	12
# submitting ACT scores	4,393
% submitting ACT scores	92
Average HS GPA	3.6
% graduated top 10% of class	28
% graduated top 25% of class	56
% graduated top 50% of class	87

DEADLINES

Regular	
Priority	3/1
Deadline	5/1
Notification	Rolling, 8/1
Nonfall registration?	Yes

APPLICANTS ALSO LOOK AT AND OFTEN PREFER
University of Nebraska at Omaha; University of Nebraska at Kearney; Creighton University; Nebraska Wesleyan University; Wayne State College

AND SOMETIMES PREFER
Iowa State University; University of Kansas; Kansas State University; Doane University; University of Iowa

AND RARELY PREFER
University of Minnesota—Twin Cities Campus; Hastings College; Northwest Missouri State University; Colorado State University; South Dakota State University

FINANCIAL FACTS

Financial Aid Rating	84
Annual in-state tuition	$7,560
Annual out-of-state tuition	$24,000
Room and board	$11,330
Required fees	$1,806
Books and supplies	$1,044
Average frosh need-based scholarship	$8,781
Average UG need-based scholarship	$8,304
% needy frosh rec. need-based scholarship or grant aid	91
% needy UG rec. need-based scholarship or grant aid	85
% needy frosh rec. non-need-based scholarship or grant aid	12
% needy UG rec. non-need-based scholarship or grant aid	8
% needy frosh rec. need-based self-help aid	64
% needy UG rec. need-based self-help aid	64
% frosh rec. any financial aid	93
% UG rec. any financial aid	77
% UG borrow to pay for school	55
Average cumulative indebtedness	$22,290
% frosh need fully met	21
% ugrads need fully met	16
Average % of frosh need met	77
Average % of ugrad need met	71

UNIVERSITY OF NEW ENGLAND

11 Hills Beach Road, Biddeford, ME 04005-9599 • Admissions: 207-602-2847 • Fax: 207-602-5900

CAMPUS LIFE
Quality of Life Rating	86
Fire Safety Rating	99
Green Rating	93
Type of school	Private
Environment	Town

STUDENTS
Total undergrad enrollment	2,449
% male/female	31/69
% from out of state	73
% frosh live on campus	95
% ugrads live on campus	62
# of fraternities	0
# of sororities	0
% African American	2
% Asian	3
% Caucasian	88
% Hispanic	<1
% Native American	<1
% Pacific Islander	<1
% Two or more races	2
% Race and/or ethnicity unknown	4
% international	<1
# of countries represented	7

SURVEY SAYS . . .
Intramural sports are popular
Everyone loves the Nor'Easters
Students are happy

ACADEMICS
Academic Rating	78
% students returning for sophomore year	82
% students graduating within 4 years	59
% students graduating within 6 years	68
Calendar	Semester
Student/faculty ratio	13:1
Profs interesting rating	86
Profs accessible rating	90

Most classes have 10–19 students.
Most lab/discussion sessions have
 10–19 students.

MOST POPULAR MAJORS
Biomedical Sciences, General; Exercise Science
and Kinesiology; Registered Nursing/Registered
Nurse

STUDENTS SAY ". . ."
Academics
With its prime location on the southern coast of Maine, the University of New England is known for preparing students for careers in healthcare and the sciences and for "creating socially, environmentally, and intellectually aware students to effectively change the world around them through liberal arts education." A small school with less than 5,000 undergraduates (roughly 75 percent of the student body is female), students say that around UNE, things are mostly "studious, not too many party animals around here." Despite the university's continued growth in recent years, students still appreciate small class sizes when they can get them, with one student saying that "the class sizes are small enough to have one-on-one interaction with your professor, but they are not too small." With "high-intensity courses to prepare you for the future" and "internships, research, and job [opportunities]," students praise the connections they develop at UNE. The school's location is a boon for marine biology and other similar science majors, with one student noting that the "location of campus with all ecosystems available" was a key reason for choosing UNE. Professors at UNE "truly care about their students and their dreams to succeed"; they are "enthusiastic about teaching and excited to teach." Some students do note that "the higher-level classes are more meaningful," and some "professors are rarely available out of the classroom."

Life
While there are school-sponsored events on campus, such as the popular Bingo Night, many students gripe that UNE "is not a very lively campus" and that there's "not much to do here in terms of fun" unless there's an athletic event going on. "Most people focus mainly on their studies," students agree, and the vibe is "definitely focused on academics as opposed to partying, though there are definite social offerings as well." Those students with cars often make the twenty-minute drive to nearby Portland "for shopping and restaurants" and in general "spending time in Portland and at the beach is common." Sports are a big draw, both playing and watching, and "a lot of people participate in Division III sports." Even so, some students feel as though their peers "seem primarily focused on school and then leave on the weekends." As the school continues to expand, parking needs grow, too, as do the need for more dorm space.

Student Body
As one student puts it, "UNE is definitely a melting pot. People of all races, ethnicities, genders, [and] personalities" come together in a single school. Not all students agree with this assessment, though, seeing their peers as "mostly white [and] mostly upper-middle class." UNE students generally are "super friendly and supportive," while still being "very driven students who put academics before anything else." The school "foster[s] a student body that tends to be passionate about the environment," which makes sense for a university that, as one student describes it, is "mostly science majors." One student sums up the atmosphere on campus by explaining, "Every university has students that come to college for athletics or the social atmosphere, although at UNE many of the students are academics first and student involvement second." Even so, the prevailing opinion of UNE students is that "everyone is extremely friendly and always willing to help you out no matter what."

Financial Aid: 207-602-2342 • E-Mail: admissions@une.edu • Website: www.une.edu

THE PRINCETON REVIEW SAYS

Admissions

Very important factors considered include: rigor of secondary school record, academic GPA. *Important factors considered include:* class rank. *Other factors considered include:* application essay, standardized test scores, recommendation(s), extracurricular activities, talent/ability, character/ personal qualities, alumni/ae relation, geographical residence, volunteer work, work experience. ACT with or without writing accepted. SAT with or without Essay component accepted. High school diploma is required and GED is accepted. *Academic units required:* 4 English, 3 math, 3 science, 2 science labs, 2 social studies, 2 history. *Academic units recommended:* 4 math, 4 science, 3 science labs, 2 foreign language, 4 social studies, 4 history, 4 academic electives.

Financial Aid

Students should submit: FAFSA. Priority filing deadline is 5/1. The Princeton Review suggests that all financial aid forms be submitted as soon as possible after October 1. *Need-based scholarships/grants offered:* College/university scholarship or grant aid from institutional funds; Federal Pell; Private scholarships; SEOG; State scholarships/grants. *Loan aid offered:* Direct PLUS loans; Direct Subsidized Stafford Loans; Direct Unsubsidized Stafford Loans. Applicants will be notified of awards on a rolling basis beginning 12/1. Federal Work-Study Program available. Institutional employment available.

The Inside Word

A strong high school transcript is the best way to get the attention of the admissions department at University of New England. The average high school GPA for admitted students is 3.33. Since the school is so heavily focused in the sciences, students with a rigorous math and science course load in high school will likely do well. For those students who apply with set career aspirations, the Early Assurance Program is intended to allow talented undergraduate applicants the opportunity to combine their UNE admission with admission to one of the school's graduate programs. Any student who wants an admissions answer sooner rather than later should consider applying Early Action—it's non-binding.

THE SCHOOL SAYS "..."

From the Admissions Office

"New for students entering in 2021, University of New England (UNE) is piloting a test-blind policy. UNE is a private top-ranked university offering flagship programs in the health and life sciences as well as degrees in business, education, the social sciences and the liberal arts. UNE's three beautiful campuses in Biddeford and Portland, Maine, and Tangier, Morocco, are home to an active and close-knit student community engaged in rigorous academic experiences. With over 40 undergraduate degree programs, UNE students have plenty of opportunities for extensive fieldwork, clinical experiences, research, internships, and global experiences. Qualified UNE students can pursue UNE graduate or professional degrees through Early Assurance in applied nutrition, dental medicine, education, health informatics, occupational therapy, osteopathic medicine, ocean food systems, pharmacy, physical therapy, physician assistant, public health, and social work.

"UNE's Student Academic Success Center provides academic support services to help students attain their personal education goals. The Career Services Office provides academic and career exploration assistance, guidance in applying to graduate schools, self-assessment, résumé help, and information and access to job listings and job fairs.

"UNE's campuses offer a variety of cultural and social events and students are encouraged to become involved in activities, clubs, and sports. Popular interests include scuba diving, skiing, hiking, biking, surfing, music, theater, community service, and student leadership programs. UNE's Department of Athletics operates an NCAA Division III varsity athletics program. Varsity sports for men are basketball, cross country, football, golf, ice-hockey, lacrosse, and soccer. Varsity sports for women are basketball, cross country, field hockey, ice hockey, lacrosse, rugby, soccer, softball, swimming, and volleyball."

SELECTIVITY

Admissions Rating	76
# of applicants	5,175
% of applicants accepted	84
% of acceptees attending	16

FRESHMAN PROFILE

Range SAT EBRW	520–620
Range SAT Math	520–610
Range SAT Composite	1050–1230
Range ACT Composite	21–27
# submitting SAT scores	597
% submitting SAT scores	84
# submitting ACT scores	84
% submitting ACT scores	12
Average HS GPA	3.4

DEADLINES

Early action	
Deadline	12/1
Notification	12/31
Regular	
Priority	12/1
Deadline	2/15
Notification	Rolling, 12/15
Nonfall registration?	Yes

FINANCIAL FACTS

Financial Aid Rating	74
Annual tuition	$37,390
Room and board	$14,410
Required fees	$1,360
Books and supplies	$1,400
Average frosh need-based scholarship	$7,988
Average UG need-based scholarship	$7,290
% needy frosh rec. need-based scholarship or grant aid	78
% needy UG rec. need-based scholarship or grant aid	72
% needy frosh rec. non-need-based scholarship or grant aid	100
% needy UG rec. non-need-based scholarship or grant aid	100
% needy frosh rec. need-based self-help aid	93
% needy UG rec. need-based self-help aid	91
% UG rec. any financial aid	98
% UG borrow to pay for school	94
Average cumulative indebtedness	$40,683

UNIVERSITY OF NEW HAMPSHIRE

UNH Office of Admissions, Durham, NH 03824 • Admissions: 603-862-1360 • Fax: 603-862-0077

STUDENTS SAY ". . ."

Academics

The benefits of going to a large, well-established state school, such as the University of New Hampshire, are exactly what one expects—its low in-state tuition, firmly established reputation, and place in the system allow it to offer "many resources to help students out in life." Located in tiny, beautiful Durham, the school "emphasizes research in every field, including non-science fields," and a lot of importance is placed "on the outdoors and the environment." The small town really fosters "lots of school spirit," and the laid-back denizens of UNH make it known that "having a good time" is a priority in their lives: "Weekends are for the Warriors." Most professors "truly care" about the students' learning so that "you never feel like a number at the school but rather a respected student," and professors "will get down and dirty when it comes to experiencing what they're teaching firsthand." Though there are definitely complaints that some can be "sub-par," a student "just needs to possess the initiative to go to their office hours" and they will get all the help they need. Some of the general education classes "are *huge*," and TAs can be difficult to understand, but for the most part, students report that they've had a "good experience" and that their academic career has been "very successful." The Honors program is particularly challenging (in a very positive way) and offers "great seminar/inquiry classes that have about fifteen students." Students universally pan the administration, claiming it "is a massive bureaucracy that gets little done," partially due to poor communication, or one student puts it that "the left hand has no idea what the right hand is doing." "The school is way more challenging than I thought it would be because the administration makes things harder than they need to be," says a sophomore.

Life

The school is just "fifteen minutes to the beach, one hour to the mountains, and one hour to Boston," making the world a Wildcat's oyster. Partying is big here, and the weekends are crazy; "Everyone goes out pretty much every Thursday, Friday, and Saturday night." The small number of bars in town "makes the age limit pretty well enforced." After a hard night out, "there are many late night convenience stores and food places to go to." In fact, it can be "difficult to find activities to do on the weekend that don't involve drinking," though UNH does a good job of bringing in "popular comedians, musicians, bands, political figures, etc.," and the school has tons of "amazing" a capella groups, so there is "almost always something to go see." Sports are also big here: "We love our hockey and football," says a student. Though there's a pretty big housing crunch, the oft-used athletic and recreational facilities here are both convenient and excellent, and since everything on this "beautiful" campus is only about ten minutes away, "you walk pretty much everywhere," though public transportation and school-provided buses run often. Students do a lot of socializing over meals at the "eight cafés or in any of the three dining halls."

Student Body

This being New Hampshire, people are "very politically and socially aware." Students here are mostly middle-class and hail from New England (especially from New Hampshire, naturally), and a main point of contention among students is that there "is not a lot of ethnic/racial diversity," though the school is working on it. The size of UNH means that "even the most unique individual will find a group of friends," and even the most atypical students "fit in perfectly well." Most of these "laid-back" and "easy-to-get-along-with" Wildcats party, and it can be "hard to find one that doesn't." "*Everyone* skis or snowboards," and in the cold weather "Uggs and North Face fleece jackets abound."

UNIVERSITY OF NEW HAMPSHIRE

Financial Aid: 603-862-3600 • E-Mail: admissions@unh.edu • Website: www.unh.edu

THE PRINCETON REVIEW SAYS

Admissions

Very important factors considered include: rigor of secondary school record, academic GPA. *Important factors considered include:* recommendation(s). *Other factors considered include:* class rank, application essay, standardized test scores, extracurricular activities, talent/ability, character/personal qualities, first generation, alumni/ae relation, geographical residence, state residency, racial/ethnic status, volunteer work, work experience. ACT with or without writing accepted. SAT with or without Essay component accepted. High school diploma is required and GED is accepted. *Academic units required:* 4 English, 3 math, 3 science, 2 science labs, 2 foreign language, 3 social studies. *Academic units recommended:* 4 English, 4 math, 4 science, 3 science labs, 3 foreign language, 3 social studies, 1 visual/performing arts.

Financial Aid

Students should submit: FAFSA. Priority filing deadline is 3/1. The Princeton Review suggests that all financial aid forms be submitted as soon as possible after October 1. *Need-based scholarships/grants offered:* College/university scholarship or grant aid from institutional funds; Federal Pell; Private scholarships; SEOG; State scholarships/grants. *Loan aid offered:* Direct PLUS loans; Direct Subsidized Stafford Loans; Direct Unsubsidized Stafford Loans. Applicants will be notified of awards on a rolling basis beginning 12/1. Federal Work-Study Program available. Institutional employment available.

The Inside Word

New Hampshire's emphasis on academic accomplishment in the admissions process makes it clear that the admissions committee is looking for students who have taken high school seriously. Standardized tests take as much of a backseat here as is possible at a large, public university.

THE SCHOOL SAYS "..."

From the Admissions Office

"At UNH, you are always on the edge of a new vista; a new possibility. That's because we are spectacularly located near the Atlantic coast, the White Mountains and Boston. It's because we are a research university where relationships matter. The big opportunities and the small ones, what you learn, the friends you make, the adventures you have and the passions you discover will be relevant and rewarding for the rest of your life.

"The University of New Hampshire is an institution best defined by the students who take advantage of its opportunities. Enrolled students who are willing to engage in a high-quality academic community in some meaningful way, who have genuine interest in discovering or developing new ideas, and who believe in each person's obligation to improve the community they live in typify the most successful students at UNH. Undergraduate students practice these three basic values in a variety of ways: by undertaking their own, independent research projects; by collaborating in faculty research; and by participating in study abroad, residential communities, community service, and other cultural programs."

SELECTIVITY

Admissions Rating	76
# of applicants	18,040
% of applicants accepted	84
% of acceptees attending	18

FRESHMAN PROFILE

Range SAT EBRW	540–640
Range SAT Math	530–630
Range ACT Composite	22–28
# submitting SAT scores	2,541
% submitting SAT scores	93
# submitting ACT scores	368
% submitting ACT scores	13
Average HS GPA	3.5
% graduated top 10% of class	22
% graduated top 25% of class	49
% graduated top 50% of class	85

DEADLINES

Early action	
Deadline	11/15
Notification	1/15
Regular	
Deadline	2/1
Notification	Rolling, 12/1
Nonfall registration?	Yes

FINANCIAL FACTS

Financial Aid Rating	80
Annual in-state tuition	$15,520
Annual out-of-state tuition	$32,050
Room and board	$11,942
Required fees	$3,359
Books and supplies	$1,000
Average frosh need-based scholarship	$7,116
Average UG need-based scholarship	$6,230
% needy frosh rec. need-based scholarship or grant aid	9
% needy UG rec. need-based scholarship or grant aid	82
% needy frosh rec. non-need-based scholarship or grant aid	12
% needy UG rec. non-need-based scholarship or grant aid	8
% needy frosh rec. need-based self-help aid	93
% needy UG rec. need-based self-help aid	94
% frosh rec. any financial aid	91
% UG rec. any financial aid	81
% UG borrow to pay for school	80
Average cumulative indebtedness	$42,246
% frosh need fully met	17
% ugrads need fully met	16
Average % of frosh need met	76
Average % of ugrad need met	75

UNIVERSITY OF NEW HAVEN

300 Boston Post Road, West Haven, CT 06516 • Admissions: 203-932-7319 • Fax: 203-931-6093

STUDENTS SAY "..."

Academics

The University of New Haven is a comprehensive school that offers its 5,000 undergraduates access to an experiential education achieved via over 60 majors, generous financial aid, numerous satellite campuses, and more than 500 study abroad programs worldwide. The resources available to students are comprehensive, keeping the school "full of academic, social, and professional opportunity," and the relatively small population "allows the professors to get to know you and gives multiple opportunities for research and other advancements." The forensics and criminal justice programs are among the top of their kind in the nation, and the specificity of all of the programs "fully prepares students for the practicalities of their professions." "So much extra help" is provided by the professors and tutoring center, and the faculty and staff are "fair and [will] work with you in whatever way possible." It is also "quite easy to form study groups," and peers tend to be "very open-minded in online discussions."

The "down to earth" professors "are amazing and want to help in any way they can," and "most of them are accessible outside of the classroom either by their office hours or by appointment." They are "open to feedback from students" and work to create a suitable learning environment tailored to each student, truly believing that "their main purpose is to help us be ready for our future and to prepare us to become leaders." Teachers here are both very knowledgeable in the textbook material as well as the real world applications, and "take material from the classroom and show how to use it after college." As hands-on learning is a requirement, students must either have an internship, study abroad, or complete an independent study or service-based learning course in order to graduate.

Life

There are "so many" clubs on campus, and students participate in a range of activities, from "Music with a Mission to Greek life to ROTC, and everyone gets involved with competitive sports through the rec center. There "is always at least one or two activities happening on any given day," and "every student is involved in some way on the campus" and loves being there. At the West Haven campus, there's a shuttle bus "that goes everywhere, such as Walmart, Target, Starbucks, the mall, city of New Haven," and "everything a student could need is on Boston Post Road." Students avail themselves of the numerous study rooms to work or hang out, and during the spring and fall the grounds are "much more alive with people hanging out in the quads." The "very convenient" campus is small and everything is in walking distance. The marching band is "a very large part of campus life"; UNH is also a decently close distance from Boston and NYC so that "if you did want to spend a weekend in the city, you could."

Student Body

The "huge melting pot" of UNH has "a refreshingly diverse campus" in all senses of the term; there is "a nice blend of ethnicities, majors, places of origin, sexualities, gender identities, [and] extracurricular interests." Due to the location there are "a lot of military veterans," and everyone is "friendly and has a positive and welcoming attitude" toward everyone else, making the school "such a welcoming environment." Students here "know what it is they want and they are going for it," and overall most "care about the quality of their education and want to participate in extracurriculars."

Financial Aid: 203-932-7220 • E-Mail: admissions@newhaven.edu • Website: www.newhaven.edu

THE PRINCETON REVIEW SAYS

Admissions

Very important factors considered include: academic GPA. *Important factors considered include:* application essay, recommendation(s). *Other factors considered include:* rigor of secondary school record, standardized test scores, interview, extracurricular activities, character/personal qualities, volunteer work, work experience, level of applicant's interest. ACT with or without writing accepted. SAT with or without Essay component accepted. High school diploma is required and GED is accepted. *Academic units recommended:* 4 English, 3 math, 3 science, 2 science labs, 2 foreign language, 3 social studies.

Financial Aid

Students should submit: FAFSA. Priority filing deadline is 3/1. The Princeton Review suggests that all financial aid forms be submitted as soon as possible after October 1. *Need-based scholarships/grants offered:* College/university scholarship or grant aid from institutional funds; Federal Pell; Private scholarships; SEOG; State scholarships/grants. *Loan aid offered:* Direct PLUS loans; Direct Subsidized Stafford Loans; Direct Unsubsidized Stafford Loans. Applicants will be notified of awards on a rolling basis beginning 1/15. Federal Work-Study Program available. Institutional employment available.

The Inside Word

The University of New Haven isn't a terribly difficult school to get into. There are four options for (rolling) admission: early decision, two early action deadlines, and regular decision. The school asks that applicants use the Common Application, which also covers the personal essay application requirement. Please note that those applying Early Decision must also complete a personal interview with an admissions counselor.

THE SCHOOL SAYS "..."

From the Admissions Office

"The University of New Haven is a national leader in experiential education, offering several unique and innovative majors housed in five distinct colleges and schools: the College of Arts & Sciences, AACSB-accredited College of Business, Tagliatela College of Engineering (ABET-accredited), Henry C. Lee College of Criminal Justice and Forensic Sciences, and the School of Health Sciences.

"We offer our students a number of exciting facilities on campus, such as our National Crime Scene Training & Technology Center, Cyber Forensics Research and Education Lab, Digital & Analog Recording Studios, Dental Center, Finance & Technology Center, Healthcare Simulation Lab, and new state-of-the-art Bergami Center for Science, Technology & Innovation.

"We pride ourselves on providing students with great experiences and opportunities through Faculty-Mentored Student Research, Internships and Co-Ops, Academic Service Learning & Community Service, and Study Abroad. Our satellite campus in Prato, Italy is popular as well as our two-week intensive study abroad programs where students can earn six credits at a number of different places around the world.

"Some of our newest academic offerings include undergraduate degrees in Genetics & Biotechnology, Cybersecurity, Paramedicine, International Affairs, Homeland Security & Emergency Management, and Esports & Gaming in addition to graduate programs in Data Science, Forensic Technology, Biomedical Engineering, and Public Health.

"NCAA Division II athletics, a 275-member marching band, student-run 88.7 FM radio station (WNHU), an amazing theater production company, Model United Nations team, and full-service sixty-seat restaurant managed entirely by our students are just a few more of the great things you can get involved with at the University of New Haven."

SELECTIVITY

Admissions Rating	76
# of applicants	10,997
% of applicants accepted	83
% of acceptees attending	14
# offered a place on the wait list	594
% accepting a place on wait list	98
% admitted from wait list	11
# of early decision applicants	81
% accepted early decision	99

FRESHMAN PROFILE

Range SAT EBRW	520–620
Range SAT Math	510–600
Range SAT Composite	1050–1210
Range ACT Composite	21–27
# submitting SAT scores	1,193
% submitting SAT scores	93
# submitting ACT scores	202
% submitting ACT scores	16
Average HS GPA	3.5
% graduated top 10% of class	17
% graduated top 25% of class	42
% graduated top 50% of class	75

DEADLINES

Early decision	
Deadline	12/1
Notification	12/15
Early action	
Deadline	12/15
Notification	1/15
Regular	
Priority	3/1
Notification	Rolling, 9/1
Nonfall registration?	Yes

APPLICANTS ALSO LOOK AT AND OFTEN PREFER

University of Connecticut; Southern Connecticut State University; University of Hartford; Quinnipiac University

AND SOMETIMES PREFER

University of Rhode Island; University of Bridgeport; City University of New York—John Jay College of Criminal Justice; Roger Williams University

FINANCIAL FACTS

Financial Aid Rating	84
Annual tuition	$40,440
Room and board	$16,852
Books and supplies	$1,000
Average frosh need-based scholarship	$22,933
Average UG need-based scholarship	$21,357
% needy frosh rec. need-based scholarship or grant aid	100
% needy UG rec. need-based scholarship or grant aid	99
% needy frosh rec. non-need-based scholarship or grant aid	12
% needy UG rec. non-need-based scholarship or grant aid	12
% needy frosh rec. need-based self-help aid	80
% needy UG rec. need-based self-help aid	81
% frosh rec. any financial aid	
% UG rec. any financial aid	
% UG borrow to pay for school	78
Average cumulative indebtedness	$47,457
% frosh need fully met	14
% ugrads need fully met	15
Average % of frosh need met	60
Average % of ugrad need met	59

UNIVERSITY OF NEW MEXICO

Office of Admissions, Albuquerque, NM 86131 • Admissions: 505-277-2446 • Fax: 505-277-6686

CAMPUS LIFE

Quality of Life Rating	**76**
Fire Safety Rating	**80**
Green Rating	**60***
Type of school	Public
Environment	Metropolis

STUDENTS

Total undergrad enrollment	18,913
% male/female	44/56
% from out of state	13
% frosh live on campus	25
% ugrads live on campus	6
# of fraternities (% ugrad men join)	10 (5)
# of sororities (% ugrad women join)	10 (6)
% African American	2
% Asian	4
% Caucasian	32
% Hispanic	49
% Native American	<1
% Pacific Islander	<1
% Two or more races	4
% Race and/or ethnicity unknown	1
% international	2
# of countries represented	92

SURVEY SAYS . . .

Diverse student types interact on campus
Students get along with local community
Great off-campus food
Students are happy

ACADEMICS

Academic Rating	**71**
% students graduating within 4 years	16
% students graduating within 6 years	44
Calendar	Semester
Student/faculty ratio	16:1
Profs interesting rating	76
Profs accessible rating	78

Most classes have 10–19 students.
Most lab/discussion sessions have 20–29 students.

MOST POPULAR MAJORS
Biology/Biological Sciences, General; Business Administration and Management, General; Psychology, General

STUDENTS SAY ". . ."

Academics

Offering a "solid education" in a beautiful setting, the University of New Mexico offers "academic excellence...through some of the best teachers and tough classes." Students also cited affordability and excellent scholarships awarded to both in-state and out-of-state applicants as a decisive factor in attending UNM. The affordability also extends to "amazing opportunities to travel abroad." At UNM, "there is something here for everyone." The education program and variety of science programs—including Earth and planetary sciences, biology, and the premed and nursing programs—also attract students. Some students express frustration with it at times being "difficult to work your way around the student services system," but the "very knowledgeable" teaching faculty are roundly praised as "teachers who care." UNM students also agree that "professors are helpful [and] genuinely interested in your personal success." Professors are approachable both in class and out and "talk to and with you and not just at you." "It's very easy to come to instructors outside of class with questions," and "most professors are willing to meet with you at your convenience." As for UNM's greatest strengths, students cite both the "research-oriented staff" and "the research opportunities available. Oftentimes the research can be done with top-of-the-line equipment" nearby at Sandia National Labs, Los Alamos National Labs, and other well-known research institutes. In UNM's collaborative environment, students also often work together and "are eager to form study groups." Also, students who need additional help can rely on academic support with "tutoring, study groups, and supplemental instruction for most courses."

Life

With "ways for everyone to get involved," UNM offers "hundreds of great student organizations" providing "opportunities for fun events." There is a student group "that will fit everyone," and at UNM, "everyone seems to find their niche." Offering another opportunity to become more involved on campus, the Greek community "makes up a lot of the senate and other extracurricular activities" and "with them, any activity has fun attached." UNM students are divided in their support of the school's athletics program. With some thinking "this school should concentrate less on sports and more on academics," other students feel "attending games is a must." Students enjoy spending time at the Student Union Building (SUB), because "there is always something going on." Even with a dry campus, "a lot of people drink, just like at any college." Students often leave campus for Albuquerque and its "excellent nightlife." UNM students also mention attending concerts and art shows for fun. Students also go to the weekly free movies at The Cellar, and to stay active, students frequent the Johnson Gym. Students say that "hanging out at the duck pond is a great way to pass time between classes in warmer months," and "during the winter season, there are numerous ski resorts and places to go snowboarding that are not far away."

Student Body

Time and time again, students select UNM's "diversity" as its greatest strength, and one student even stated "no one will ever feel ethnically alone since there are so many different kinds of people." This also means at UNM, "people never get boring," and "you meet someone different every day." In addition to the diversity, the prevailing atmosphere is a friendly one where "people get along regardless of origin," but "like any school there are cliques...but that does not mean they do not interact with each other." One student reserved special praise for the university, "UNM is sensitive and very engaged with its diverse population of students...concerned with facilitating in-depth inquiry and learning," and more than one student observed that at UNM, "everyone brings something to the table."

Financial Aid: 505-277-8900 • E-Mail: apply@unm.edu • Website: www.unm.edu

THE PRINCETON REVIEW SAYS

Admissions

Very important factors considered include: rigor of secondary school record, academic GPA. *Important factors considered include:* standardized test scores. *Other factors considered include:* application essay, interview, extracurricular activities, talent/ability, volunteer work, work experience. ACT with or without writing accepted. SAT with or without Essay component accepted. High school diploma is required and GED is accepted. *Academic units required:* 4 English, 4 math, 3 science, 2 science labs, 2 foreign language, 2 social studies, 1 history.

Financial Aid

Students should submit: FAFSA. Priority filing deadline is 3/1. The Princeton Review suggests that all financial aid forms be submitted as soon as possible after October 1. *Need-based scholarships/grants offered:* College/university scholarship or grant aid from institutional funds; Federal Nursing Scholarships; Federal Pell; Private scholarships; SEOG; State scholarships/grants; United Negro College Fund. *Loan aid offered:* Direct PLUS loans; Direct Subsidized Stafford Loans; Direct Unsubsidized Stafford Loans. Applicants will be notified of awards on a rolling basis beginning 4/15. Federal Work-Study Program available.

The Inside Word

UNM offers online applications through its website, and you will also find specific scholastic standards for traditional and nontraditional students interested in applying to UNM. Traditional applicants should have completed core coursework, taken the ACT or SAT exam and have an average or above-average GPA if they would like to be considered for admission at UNM.

THE SCHOOL SAYS "..."

From the Admissions Office

"The University of New Mexico is a major research institution nestled in the heart of multicultural Albuquerque on one of the nation's most beautiful and unique campuses. Students learn in an environment graced by distinctive Southwestern architecture, beautiful plazas and fountains, spectacular art and a national arboretum...all within view of the 10,000-foot Sandia Mountains. At UNM, diversity is a way of learning with education enriched by a lively mix of students being taught by a world-class research faculty that includes a Nobel laureate, a MacArthur Fellow, and members of several national academies. UNM offers more than 200 degree programs and majors and has earned national recognition in dozens of disciplines, ranging from primary care medicine and clinical law to engineering, photography, Latin American history, and intercultural communications. Research and the quest for new knowledge fuels the university's commitment to an undergraduate education where students work side-by-side with many of the finest scholars in their fields.

"The university will continue to accept SAT or ACT scores, but the University of New Mexico does not require the writing component at this time. The SAT critical reading portion will be used with the SAT math to be considered in any admission decision based on formula. The use of ACT composite remains unchanged. These requirements are subject to change."

SELECTIVITY

Admissions Rating	89
# of applicants	11,347
% of applicants accepted	49
% of acceptees attending	57

FRESHMAN PROFILE

Range SAT EBRW	460–590
Range SAT Math	470–580
Range ACT Composite	19–25
# submitting SAT scores	101
% submitting SAT scores	3
# submitting ACT scores	2,801
% submitting ACT scores	87
Average HS GPA	3.4

DEADLINES

Regular	
Priority	5/1
Nonfall registration?	Yes

FINANCIAL FACTS

Financial Aid Rating	66
Annual in-state tuition	$8,863
Annual out-of-state tuition	$24,500
Room and board	$10,262
Books and supplies	$1,266
Average frosh need-based scholarship	$5,560
Average UG need-based scholarship	$6,069
% needy frosh rec. need-based scholarship or grant aid	94
% needy UG rec. need-based scholarship or grant aid	89
% needy frosh rec. non-need-based scholarship or grant aid	1
% needy UG rec. non-need-based scholarship or grant aid	3
% needy frosh rec. need-based self-help aid	44
% needy UG rec. need-based self-help aid	53
% UG borrow to pay for school	43
Average cumulative indebtedness	$20,532
% frosh need fully met	13
% ugrads need fully met	12

UNIVERSITY OF NEW ORLEANS

University of New Orleans Privateer Enrollment Center, New Orleans, LA 70148 • Admissions: 504-280-6595 • Fax: 504-280-3973

STUDENTS SAY "..."

Academics

The University of New Orleans is a public research university in one of the world's most fascinating and unique cities. This "not too big, not too small" school is a "diverse environment that makes it a welcoming area to be" and provides "lots of opportunities to develop our personality, leadership skills, and career skills." The diversity is a huge draw to students from all over the world (international students can even receive financial aid), and UNO "opens doors to students who come from different social and economic backgrounds," giving them "the opportunity to get an education that helps students to get a better future."

Professors at this "inclusive" school "push students to do excellence." You "can always find them in their office during office hours," and they "really connect with students." The engineering, film, and accounting programs are all popular programs at UNO (accounting is one of the few accredited by AACSB International), and classes stress real-world applicability. "There has never been a moment at UNO that I wasn't able to leave the classroom and go apply what I learned to my job immediately," says one part-time student. "My professors are generous with their time and knowledge," says another. Class sizes are small, and many classes focus on discussion, which "allows for increased learning and understanding." The school is "blessed" with having a large traditional student body matched with an equal percentage of nontraditional students (adult education), which "allows great mentorship between students and also pushed both sides to be aware of how they can positively affect the other generation's education."

Life

Obviously, the fact that the school is located in New Orleans "is a big plus," and "there is never a dull moment." "Eating and nightlife in New Orleans is a big part of our lives," says a student. "There is so much to do on campus and around the city, students often have to make efforts to keep their social calendars in check so that they have time to study," says a student. The campus is large enough to offer "many diverse academic, extracurricular, and social activities," yet small enough to easily access all classes. However, "upgrading facilities" (and cleaning them) is on the wish list of pretty much everyone here.

UNO offers "plenty of on campus activities" for students "to meet and work with other students of all backgrounds," including sports, movies, and "a lot of free entertainment." There are also "always political discussions happening on campus, as well as debates." "You can feel at home here but not get bored," says a student. The older students feel similarly comfortable in their environment. "I am unusual in that I am a much older student living on campus. Yet, the younger students have accepted me warmly and I have many friends," says one.

Student Body

More so than most schools, there really is no typical at this "very eclectic university," other than "determined, hardworking, and considerate." The school's large number of international students, adult learners, commuters, and locals "tend to get along rather well," with "those who live right on or near campus probably being more close-knit." Many students live off campus and work full time, which "creates in an environment where the people in your classes are there for a purpose." People here are "very colorful and outgoing" and "have no problem expressing themselves whether it's through clothing, lifestyles, or speech." "It is very easy to make friends here," says a student.

UNIVERSITY OF NEW ORLEANS

Financial Aid: 504-280-6603 • E-Mail: admissions@uno.edu • Website: www.uno.edu

THE PRINCETON REVIEW SAYS

Admissions

Very important factors considered include: academic GPA, standardized test scores. ACT with or without writing accepted. High school diploma is required and GED is accepted. *Academic units required:* 4 English, 4 math, 4 science, 2 foreign language, 4 social studies, 1 visual/performing arts.

Financial Aid

Students should submit: FAFSA; Institution's own financial aid form. Priority filing deadline is 5/1. The Princeton Review suggests that all financial aid forms be submitted as soon as possible after October 1. *Need-based scholarships/grants offered:* College/university scholarship or grant aid from institutional funds; Federal Pell; Private scholarships; SEOG; State scholarships/grants; United Negro College Fund. *Loan aid offered:* Direct PLUS loans; Direct Subsidized Stafford Loans; Direct Unsubsidized Stafford Loans. Applicants will be notified of awards on or about 1/15. Federal Work-Study Program available. Institutional employment available.

The Inside Word

Admission is straightforward here. Complete a basic college-bound high school curriculum with a GPA of at least 2.5 (with no remedial course work) and get at least a 23 on your ACT (SAT 1060), including a minimum score at or above 19 Math (460 SAT), 18 English (450 SAT). Nontraditional students who don't want to pay the exorbitant prices of the more well-known private universities in New Orleans can find their niche at UNO; if you're twenty-five or older, the only requirement for admission is a legitimate high school diploma or a GED.

THE SCHOOL SAYS "..."

From the Admissions Office

"The University of New Orleans has a wide array of academic programs. Quality student life programs include a campus bar, first-run movies, and a host of exciting student activities.

"UNO embraces its mission by providing the best educational opportunities for undergraduate and graduate students, conducting world-class research, and serving a diverse and cultured community in critical areas. UNO's most outstanding offerings include planning and urban studies; hotel, restaurant and tourism administration; computer science; educational leadership; earth and environmental studies; one of the nation's few programs in naval architecture and marine engineering; a leading jazz studies program; one of the top film programs in the region; and the only graduate arts administration program in the Gulf South.

"UNO will use the total score from the critical reading/verbal and math sub sections of the SAT or the composite score for the ACT. The writing components of the ACT and SAT will be used for placement purposes, but not for admission purposes, at the time."

SELECTIVITY

Admissions Rating	87
# of applicants	3,736
% of applicants accepted	57
% of acceptees attending	45

FRESHMAN PROFILE

Range SAT EBRW	520–640
Range SAT Math	510–610
Range ACT Composite	20–25
# submitting SAT scores	61
% submitting SAT scores	6
# submitting ACT scores	917
% submitting ACT scores	96
Average HS GPA	3.2
% graduated top 10% of class	15
% graduated top 25% of class	34
% graduated top 50% of class	64

DEADLINES

Regular	
Priority	12/15
Deadline	7/15
Notification	Rolling, 9/1
Nonfall registration?	Yes

FINANCIAL FACTS

Financial Aid Rating	81
Annual in-state tuition	$6,090
Annual out-of-state tuition	$10,926
Room and board	$10,575
Required fees	$2,394
Books and supplies	$1,300
Average frosh need-based scholarship	$5,550
Average UG need-based scholarship	$5,126
% needy frosh rec. need-based scholarship or grant aid	80
% needy UG rec. need-based scholarship or grant aid	78
% needy frosh rec. non-need-based scholarship or grant aid	65
% needy UG rec. non-need-based scholarship or grant aid	51
% needy frosh rec. need-based self-help aid	55
% needy UG rec. need-based self-help aid	56
% UG borrow to pay for school	48
Average cumulative indebtedness	$20,723
% frosh need fully met	16
% ugrads need fully met	12
Average % of frosh need met	67
Average % of ugrad need met	64

UNIVERSITY OF NORTH CAROLINA ASHEVILLE

One University Heights, Asheville, NC 28804-8502 • Admissions: 828-251-6481 • Fax: 828-251-6482

CAMPUS LIFE
Quality of Life Rating	93
Fire Safety Rating	97
Green Rating	91
Type of school	Public
Environment	Town

STUDENTS
Total undergrad enrollment	3,286
% male/female	43/57
% from out of state	11
% frosh from public high school	87
% frosh live on campus	96
% ugrads live on campus	46
# of fraternities (% ugrad men join)	2 (1)
# of sororities (% ugrad women join)	2 (2)
% African American	5
% Asian	2
% Caucasian	74
% Hispanic	9
% Native American	<1
% Pacific Islander	<1
% Two or more races	4
% Race and/or ethnicity unknown	4
% international	1
# of countries represented	15

SURVEY SAYS . . .
Lots of liberal students
Students are happy
Students aren't religious
Students get along with local community
Students environmentally aware
Students love Asheville, NC
Great off-campus food
Active student government
Active minority support groups

ACADEMICS
Academic Rating	82
% students returning for sophomore year	73
% students graduating within 4 years	39
% students graduating within 6 years	59
Calendar	Semester
Student/faculty ratio	13:1
Profs interesting rating	92
Profs accessible rating	94

Most classes have 10–19 students.
Most lab/discussion sessions have
10–19 students.

MOST POPULAR MAJORS
Environmental Studies; Psychology, General;
Business Administration and Management,
General

STUDENTS SAY "..."

Academics

Offering "small class sizes," "local art culture," and "environmental sustainability," UNC Asheville is "the only [designated] public liberal arts school" in North Carolina. Professors are "some of the best in their respective fields" and "have time to invest interest in your individual advancement—not only in the course, but in your life...may come to you with job, internship or volunteer opportunities." Students praise the fruitful relationships with faculty and opportunities for hands-on research. Says one first-year student, "I...am able to be a research assistant to a teacher who is working on a cloud computing model for ALS research, an amazing opportunity that I only would get at UNC Asheville." Students also have opportunities to learn through experiences like the campus "bee garden," field trips (e.g., "climbing up Roan Mountain for Earth History"; "visiting a Cherokee Indian reservation and the Katua mound, a sacred Native American site, with an indigenous studies class"; and "hiking through Asheville for a history honors course.") There is actually a space designated the "Outdoor Classroom," "where any class can go—not just environmental classes." UNC Asheville offers an emphasis on service-learning courses, as well, which does "a lot of work in schools and through afterschool programs," or helping "prepare actual tax returns for low-income families in the area." One student says "because western North Carolina has such rich history, biodiversity, and social issues, it attracts wonderful and passionate intellectuals, and as a result, UNC Asheville has an exceptional team of professors." Others describe faculty as "incredibly passionate about their subjects," and invested in student learning in "holistic, intersectional ways."

Life

UNC Asheville students feel that they are truly cared for from the day they step on campus: "The university's intense focus on physical and mental health," says one student, "make[s] it harder to burn out during one's [otherwise] stressful first year." The school's proximity to the city of Asheville "makes it easy for students to get off-campus jobs and explore the downtown scene safely," especially as "the bus system goes through campus." The "town and the mountains make living here an exceptional experience," says another student. Another praises the "vibrancy of Asheville" as a music student, where it "was crucial" to be "in a rich music and art scene." Downtown Asheville offers plenty of dining options as well as "farmers markets and food co-ops," "thrift stores," and other shops. With only 3,286 students, the campus is "small" but there is a big "range of activities and clubs." Most are "required to do service projects, which help students engage with and help out the community." The botanical gardens are also on campus, which provide both job and research opportunities for budding botanists and environmental studies majors, and rest and relaxation for casual strollers. Nice days bring students out to the Quad to study or catch some sun, and the "Free Store," run by the Student Environmental Center "offers an alternative to our throw-away culture." UNC Asheville's "student-led, student-run, and student-funded programming board," Asheville Campus Entertainment (ACE), plans events ranging from open mic nights to DIY activities.

Student Body

"My peers are inquisitive, mindful, compassionate, and hungry for justice," says one student. "They go to extremes to live sustainably and waste-free, on and off campus." Parties usually mean "student bands performing in a basement" with many "intellectual conversations" going on upstairs and "vegetarian potluck dishes spread around the house." Students at UNC Asheville also truly "care about the environment," and are generally "compassionate," "open-minded," and "accepting." There is a large LGBTQ population within a culture that has all students regularly asking for others' preferred pronouns. Communicating one's political beliefs is "basically chill" in that "everyone can voice their opinions...and people don't try to...force an argument." The campus gardens "grow healthy organic food and also offer a place for students to experiment with metal art and design."

UNIVERSITY OF NORTH CAROLINA ASHEVILLE

Financial Aid: 828-251-6535 • E-Mail: admissions@unca.edu • Website: www.unca.edu

THE PRINCETON REVIEW SAYS

Admissions

Very important factors considered include: rigor of secondary school record, class rank, academic GPA, application essay, standardized test scores, recommendation(s). *Important factors considered include:* extracurricular activities, talent/ability, character/personal qualities. *Other factors considered include:* first generation, alumni/ae relation, geographical residence, state residency, racial/ethnic status, volunteer work, work experience, level of applicant's interest. ACT with or without writing accepted. SAT with or without Essay component accepted. High school diploma is required and GED is not accepted. *Academic units required:* 4 English, 4 math, 3 science, 1 science lab, 2 foreign language, 2 social studies.

Financial Aid

Students should submit: FAFSA. Priority filing deadline is 3/1. The Princeton Review suggests that all financial aid forms be submitted as soon as possible after October 1. *Need-based scholarships/grants offered:* College/university scholarship or grant aid from institutional funds; Federal Pell; Private scholarships; SEOG; State scholarships/grants; McRae and Provost Scholarships awarded from $1,000 to $10,000 per year. *Loan aid offered:* Direct PLUS loans; Direct Subsidized Stafford Loans; Direct Unsubsidized Stafford Loans. Applicants will be notified of awards on a rolling basis beginning 2/15. Federal Work-Study Program available. Institutional employment available.

The Inside Word

UNC Asheville looks for candidates who are "independent thinkers, curious learners and service volunteers." Applicants to UNC Asheville can apply via either the Common Application or The College Foundation of NC online application. In addition to your standardized test scores and high school GPA (the average accepted student's unweighted GPA is 3.40), most students graduated in the top 50 percent of their high school class with 25th to 75th percentile SAT scores ranging from 1100–1250. Students who view UNC Asheville as a first-choice destination should apply Early Decision. Those granted admission through Early Decision are guaranteed an enrollment opportunity. All students, whether choosing Early or Regular Decision—are encouraged to apply early. Enrollment and scholarship opportunities are considered on a space and funds availability basis. The priority application date for transfers is April 15.

THE SCHOOL SAYS "..."

From the Admissions Office

"With a focus on collaborative, interdisciplinary education, UNC Asheville prepares students to be innovative critical thinkers, giving them the tools they need to thrive as experts in their area of study and beyond. Over thirty majors prepare students to understand and define their place in our ever-changing world. UNC Asheville students ask important questions and pursue answers across disciplines with a commitment to making an impact and building community. The result is a competitive advantage, not only for graduates but also for the organizations they work for, where the convergence of art and science leads the way in today's dynamic economy.

"Admission at UNC Asheville is competitive, so interested students should be sure to apply early for maximum consideration for both admission and merit scholarships."

SELECTIVITY
Admissions Rating	76
# of applicants	3,750
% of applicants accepted	84
% of acceptees attending	21

FRESHMAN PROFILE
Range SAT EBRW	560–650
Range SAT Math	530–620
Range SAT Composite	1100–1250
Range ACT Composite	22–27
# submitting SAT scores	409
% submitting SAT scores	63
# submitting ACT scores	393
% submitting ACT scores	60
Average HS GPA	3.4
% graduated top 10% of class	14
% graduated top 25% of class	39
% graduated top 50% of class	78

DEADLINES
Early decision	
Deadline	11/1
Notification	12/15
Other ED Deadline	1/15
Other ED Notification	2/1
Regular	
Deadline	2/1
Notification	Begins 2/15
Nonfall registration?	Yes

FINANCIAL FACTS
Financial Aid Rating	86
Annual in-state tuition	$4,246
Annual out-of-state tuition	$21,594
Room and board	$9,950
Required fees	$3,220
Books and supplies	$1,200
Average frosh need-based scholarship	$8,006
Average UG need-based scholarship	$7,762
% needy frosh rec. need-based scholarship or grant aid	95
% needy UG rec. need-based scholarship or grant aid	88
% needy frosh rec. non-need-based scholarship or grant aid	41
% needy UG rec. non-need-based scholarship or grant aid	23
% needy frosh rec. need-based self-help aid	68
% needy UG rec. need-based self-help aid	69
% frosh rec. any financial aid	83
% UG rec. any financial aid	73
% UG borrow to pay for school	59
Average cumulative indebtedness	$24,476
% frosh need fully met	22
% ugrads need fully met	25
Average % of frosh need met	76
Average % of ugrad need met	75

UNIVERSITY OF NORTH CAROLINA—CHAPEL HILL

Jackson Hall, Chapel Hill, NC 27599-2200 • Admissions: 919-962-2211 • Fax: 919-962-3045

STUDENTS SAY "..."

Academics

Citing "academic prestige" and "affordability," the "beautiful," "historic" setting, and "world-renowned" faculty, students take pride in "being a Tar Heel" at the University of North Carolina at Chapel Hill. The professors at UNC-Chapel Hill are "top-notch, many of them being academic celebrities," but "like the students, are never flashy" and remain "humble." Students find that their professors frequently stress that they are here to "learn from you all as much as you are here to learn from me." UNC offers undergrads "bountiful resources" as "one of the top public research universities in the nation," and students have the opportunity to participate in this research by applying for "generous academic grants." Academics are "rigorous," but the "quality of teaching makes the material intellectually stimulating." The college is fairly large, so students will likely attend "large lecture-hall style classes," yet students stress that as they advance, "class sizes are smaller," and this leads to "the opportunity to build more personal relationships with professors." UNC's "reputation and ranking in STEM programs," along with its well-regarded business school, are among its greatest strengths. Said one transfer student, "I visited countless top universities," but UNC was the only one that had a "population...both economically and ethnically diverse."

Life

UNC offers its "more than 19,000 undergrads" a host of opportunities to socialize, relax, and pack themselves all together at the Dean E. Smith Center to cheer on the men's basketball team. Carolina has strong athletics, including opportunities for "potential student-athletes." For non-athletes, it's a great school to be a fan, "as basketball games especially create a special campus atmosphere that nothing can recreate." Despite the university's size, life on campus generally moves at a "slow pace"—in a good way. The campus is full of "gorgeous old buildings, towering oak trees, and ubiquitous birds, squirrels, and chipmunks," and students "love walking through the upper quad," a "beautiful green area with lots of old trees." Raleigh is "only 30 minutes away" and "Durham only 15," so students will head out there on weekends, and if they need to unwind during the week, they go "out to bars on Franklin Street." There's "always a party going on at UNC," but there are also "plenty of ways to have fun if you're not into the party scene." There are several "day hikes somewhat close to campus," and Carrboro is "within walking distance," providing a "hip space for social life including a farmers market, concert venue[s], and many bars and restaurants."

Student Body

The student body is "as helpful as it is inquisitive, and as creative as it is caring." For every "get-to-know-you question someone asks you," there is a "student happy to direct you to your classes." Everyone at Carolina is "fun, energetic, and passionate about something." UNC is "unified unlike any other school I have encountered," says one student, "whether it's in the common support of a sports team, music group, or simply the pride in saying you are a Tar Heel." Another student agrees, "Donning Carolina blue almost constantly, we all just really love our school!" The students "are smart, but they aren't haughty and ostentatious about it." Students are "generally liberal, but there is a vocal religious/conservative presence on campus as well." Although there is a "large Greek population, Greek life isn't quite as conservative as it is at many other southern schools."

UNIVERSITY OF NORTH CAROLINA—CHAPEL HILL

Financial Aid: 919-962-8396 • E-Mail: unchelp@admissions.unc.edu • Website: www.unc.edu

THE PRINCETON REVIEW SAYS

Admissions

Very important factors considered include: rigor of secondary school record, application essay, standardized test scores, recommendation(s), extracurricular activities, talent/ability, character/personal qualities, state residency. *Important factors considered include:* class rank, academic GPA, volunteer work, work experience. *Other factors considered include:* first generation, alumni/ae relation, racial/ethnic status. ACT with or without writing accepted. SAT with or without Essay component accepted. High school diploma is required and GED is not accepted *Academic units required:* 4 English, 4 math, 3 science, 1 science lab, 2 foreign language, 1 social studies, 1 history, 1 academic elective.

Financial Aid

Students should submit: CSS/Financial Aid PROFILE; FAFSA. Priority filing deadline is 3/1. The Princeton Review suggests that all financial aid forms be submitted as soon as possible after October 1. *Need-based scholarships/grants offered:* College/university scholarship or grant aid from institutional funds; Federal Pell; Private scholarships; SEOG; State scholarships/grants. *Loan aid offered:* Institutional Loans; Direct PLUS Loans; Direct Subsidized Stafford Loans; Direct Unsubsidized Stafford Loans. Applicants will be notified of awards on a rolling basis beginning 1/31. Federal and Institutional Work-Study Programs available. Institutional employment available.

The Inside Word

UNC's admissions process is highly selective. North Carolina students compete against other students from across the state for 82 percent of all spaces available in the freshman class; out-of-state students compete for the remaining 18 percent of the spaces. State residents will find the admissions standards high, and out-of-state applicants will find that it's one of the hardest offers of admission to come by in the country. While there's no formula, a fact UNC is proud of, students should expect to offer a compelling portrait to the admissions committee of their talents and achievements.

THE SCHOOL SAYS "..."

From the Admissions Office

"Carolina is proudly public and has earned a reputation as one of the best universities in the world, preparing its students for a lifetime of leadership and service. Carolina is best known for having one of the strongest and most diverse student bodies in the nation. Carolina's most recently admitted class includes students who will be the first in their families to graduate from college (21 percent of the class), are high school valedictorians or salutatorians (15 percent of the class), and are committed to serving their communities (87 percent volunteered during high school). Carolina offers academic opportunities that prepare students to empower themselves and their communities; 93 percent of graduates earn jobs or enter graduate school within six months of graduating.

"Admission to Carolina is competitive, but we are dedicated to making it fair and considerate. We don't use formulas or cutoffs; instead, we know that students travel many roads to Carolina, and we celebrate the variety of interests, backgrounds, and aspirations they bring. We actively seek excellence in academics, arts, athletics, leadership, service, citizenship, and character. This list isn't exhaustive or prescriptive. When we read an application, we're interested in what a student has done, what they care about, and the difference they will make as a member of Carolina's community. We're committed to ensuring that every student who earns a place at Carolina can afford to attend, and our financial aid program meets full need and enables qualified low-income students to graduate debt-free through the Carolina Covenant."

SELECTIVITY

Admissions Rating	97
# of applicants	42,466
% of applicants accepted	23
% of acceptees attending	44
# offered a place on the wait list	5,572
% accepting a place on wait list	67
% admitted from wait list	4

FRESHMAN PROFILE

Range SAT EBRW	650–730
Range SAT Math	650–760
Range SAT Composite	1300–1470
Range ACT Composite	27–33
# submitting SAT scores	2,180
% submitting SAT scores	52
# submitting ACT scores	2,902
% submitting ACT scores	69
Average HS GPA	4.4
% graduated top 10% of class	78
% graduated top 25% of class	95
% graduated top 50% of class	99

DEADLINES

Early action	
Deadline	10/15
Notification	1/31
Regular	
Priority	10/15
Deadline	1/15
Notification	3/31
Nonfall registration?	No

APPLICANTS ALSO LOOK AT AND SOMETIMES PREFER

Duke University; University of Virginia; Vanderbilt University; Harvard College; Yale University; University of Pennsylvania

AND RARELY PREFER

North Carolina State University; Appalachian State University

FINANCIAL FACTS

Financial Aid Rating	94
Annual in-state tuition	$7,019
Annual out-of-state tuition	$34,198
Room and board	$11,740
Required fees	$2,027
Books and supplies	$990
Average frosh need-based scholarship	$15,532
Average UG need-based scholarship	$17,217
% needy frosh rec. need-based scholarship or grant aid	93
% needy UG rec. need-based scholarship or grant aid	91
% needy frosh rec. non-need-based scholarship or grant aid	11
% needy UG rec. non-need-based scholarship or grant aid	6
% needy frosh rec. need-based self-help aid	54
% needy UG rec. need-based self-help aid	64
% frosh rec. any financial aid	64.5
% UG rec. any financial aid	62.8
% UG borrow to pay for school	37
Average cumulative indebtedness	$21,203
% frosh need fully met	81
% ugrads need fully met	76
Average % of frosh need met	100
Average % of ugrad need met	100

UNIVERSITY OF NORTH CAROLINA—GREENSBORO

PO Box 26170, Greensboro, NC 27402-6170 • Admissions: 336-334-5243 • Fax: 336-334-4180

STUDENTS SAY "..."

Academics

The University of North Carolina at Greensboro is a big school yet students "[don't] feel like a number." They find their professors are often "incredibly personable" and that they give advice "about finding internships and other opportunities to network." They're a great resource for getting "all the information and guidance [students] need to succeed." The Lloyd International Honors College "has an emphasis on … experiential learning," including visits to nearby Guilford forest where students "[learn] about the important points of the Underground Railroad." As standout offerings, students comment on the "superb online programs" offered by the school as well as the "great art, [music], and science programs." "Many programs are oriented toward student help and health" to make sure students don't fall behind. "I think the greatest strength of UNCG is that they are very good at [pointing] students in the right direction," says a student. They continue: "For example, [if] you approach your advisors … with a problem, they will show up with a big list of possible solutions."

Life

"There is always something to do on this beautiful campus," boasts a student of UNCG. During their study time, plenty sit in the "Salad Bowl, [which is] a huge garden space with really huge trees canopying over top." Some get "geeky, fun, and athletic" with the Quidditch Club, which a student calls "the highlight of UNCG." With "a pool, lazy river, and sauna along with all of the athletic equipment … and group fitness classes," students call the recreation center "insane"—but they mean that in the best possible way. "People eat on Tate Street, [which has] very popular off-campus eateries," and take "day trips to Piney Lake for paddle boarding." Located in the center of North Carolina, "just a few hours east or west [of the school] will take you to the coast or the mountains if you need a change of scenery." On weekends, "many people go to clubs like Limelight or Arizona Pete's," and "there is a jazz night at Tate Street Coffee House…, which is a really fun thing."

Student Body

The student body at UNC Greensboro is "racially, economically, [and] ideologically diverse." "The political viewpoint … is [majorly] liberal," says a student. "What makes UNCG unique is our strong acceptance of the others of society," the student continues. Students note that the school's integrated programs "get all levels of students working together." The student body here is one with a "huge music/theater concentration but also a mix of athletes and fraternity/sorority members." As a "minority-serving institution, … the culture is rich and eclectic," and students say that it's "one of the most LGBTQ+ friendly campuses." One student puts it this way: "It is rare that I walk into a class of students [who] look like myself." They don't see this as a drawback, though, and say that it makes the campus feel "lively" and "diverse in many ways."

UNIVERSITY OF NORTH CAROLINA—GREENSBORO

Financial Aid: 336-334-5702 • E-Mail: admissions@uncg.edu • Website: www.uncg.edu

THE PRINCETON REVIEW SAYS

Admissions

Very important factors considered include: rigor of secondary school record, academic GPA. *Important factors considered include:* standardized test scores. *Other factors considered include:* class rank, application essay, recommendation(s), extracurricular activities, volunteer work. ACT with or without writing accepted. SAT with or without Essay component accepted. High school diploma is required and GED is accepted. *Academic units required:* 4 English, 4 math, 3 science, 1 science lab 2 foreign language, 2 social studies.

Financial Aid

Students should submit: FAFSA. Priority filing deadline is 12/1. The Princeton Review suggests that all financial aid forms be submitted as soon as possible after October 1. *Need-based scholarships/grants offered:* College/university scholarship or grant aid from institutional funds; Federal Pell; Private scholarships; SEOG; State scholarships/grants. *Loan aid offered:* Direct PLUS loans; Direct Subsidized Stafford Loans; Direct Unsubsidized Stafford Loans. Applicants will be notified of awards on a rolling basis beginning 3/15. Federal Work-Study Program available. Institutional employment available.

The Inside Word

UNCG emphasizes GPA and test scores above all else in the admissions process. However, they also consider high school course selection and progression, Senior class schedule, all test scores, and community standards concerns. Students who aren't accepted in the school of their choice can make use of the college redirection program, which will match students with an NC university that has admission slots available for qualified students. Fall applicants need to apply on or before December 1 to be eligible for merit scholarships and to receive an admission decision by January 31. Applications are reviewed on a rolling basis from December 1 through March 1. Applications received after March 1 are only reviewed on a space-available basis.

THE SCHOOL SAYS "..."

From the Admissions Office

"With a history spanning more than 125 years, UNC Greensboro is one of the original three institutions in the UNC System. Now, UNCG is a growing higher-research university, with noted strengths in health and wellness, visual and performing arts, nursing, and education. With more than 20,000 students and 2,700 faculty and staff members representing more than 90 nationalities, UNCG is among the most diverse universities in the state.

"UNCG is committed to transforming its students through challenging academics and enriching extracurricular opportunities. Undergraduates can choose from more than 125 degree programs including familiar degrees like business, education, and nursing, and unique majors like fashion and retail, interior architecture, sign language interpreting, and information science.

"One common factor that drives UNCG students is a passion for making an impact. UNCG alumni have built careers that make an everyday difference. (UNCG graduates 400+ educators and 300+ nurses every year.) Student success is supported by our faculty and staff who are committed to giving students unique opportunities—like supervised research and service learning—that help them stand out in the job market.

"UNCG is consistently recognized for the value of its education and is regularly listed among the "Best Colleges" in the U.S. Known for being one of the most diverse campuses in North Carolina, UNCG students bring a dynamic energy to class discussions and campus events. All of these factors contribute to a truly meaningful college experience for students at UNCG. Find your way here."

SELECTIVITY

Admissions Rating	77
# of applicants	9,972
% of applicants accepted	82
% of acceptees attending	33

FRESHMAN PROFILE

Range SAT EBRW	500–590
Range SAT Math	500–570
Range ACT Composite	19–24
# submitting SAT scores	1,795
% submitting SAT scores	65
# submitting ACT scores	1,694
% submitting ACT scores	62
Average HS GPA	3.7
% graduated top 10% of class	13
% graduated top 25% of class	39
% graduated top 50% of class	77

DEADLINES

Regular	
Priority	12/1
Deadline	3/1
Notification	Rolling, 12/1
Nonfall registration?	Yes

FINANCIAL FACTS

Financial Aid Rating	82
Annual in-state tuition	$7,403
Annual out-of-state tuition	$22,562
Room and board	$9,264
Average frosh need-based scholarship	$9,080
Average UG need-based scholarship	$8,340
% needy frosh rec. need-based scholarship or grant aid	85
% needy UG rec. need-based scholarship or grant aid	80
% needy frosh rec. non-need-based scholarship or grant aid	13
% needy UG rec. non-need-based scholarship or grant aid	16
% needy frosh rec. need-based self-help aid	74
% needy UG rec. need-based self-help aid	76
% frosh rec. any financial aid	74
% UG rec. any financial aid	68
% UG borrow to pay for school	71
Average cumulative indebtedness	$23,317
% frosh need fully met	13
% ugrads need fully met	10
Average % of frosh need met	63
Average % of ugrad need met	59

UNIVERSITY OF NORTH DAKOTA

3501 University Avenue Stop 8357, Grand Forks, ND 58202 • Admissions: 701-777-3000 • Fax: 701-777-2721

CAMPUS LIFE

Quality of Life Rating	85
Fire Safety Rating	87
Green Rating	83
Type of school	Public
Environment	Town

STUDENTS

Total undergrad enrollment	9,519
% male/female	56/44
% from out of state	62
% frosh from public high school	92
% frosh live on campus	92
% ugrads live on campus	25
# of fraternities (% ugrad men join)	13 (11)
# of sororities (% ugrad women join)	7 (13)
% African American	2
% Asian	2
% Caucasian	80
% Hispanic	4
% Native American	1
% Pacific Islander	1
% Two or more races	5
% Race and/or ethnicity unknown	1
% international	5
# of countries represented	78

SURVEY SAYS . . .

Lots of conservative students
Recreation facilities are great
Everyone loves the Fighting Hawks
Intramural sports are popular
Frats and sororities are popular

ACADEMICS

Academic Rating	74
% students returning for sophomore year	78
% students graduating within 4 years	32
% students graduating within 6 years	61
Calendar	Semester
Student/faculty ratio	17:1
Profs interesting rating	84
Profs accessible rating	88

Most classes have 20–29 students.
Most lab/discussion sessions have 10–19 students.

MOST POPULAR MAJORS

Aviation; Engineering; Health Professions and Related Programs; Business; Education

STUDENTS SAY "..."

Academics

If you love hockey, want to study at the nation's foremost aerospace and aviation school, and you're not afraid of the cold temperatures, the University of North Dakota in Grand Forks, wants you on their team. The largest university in the state, UND is internationally recognized in the aviation industry for its aerospace program, which offers "the highest level of flight training," "incredible professors" who "know the industry." Other schools including the college of business and public administration, the college of engineering and mines, and the school of medicine and health sciences are praised for their "innovation and intelligence." UND also benefits from its "strong and active alumni network." Students have mixed experiences with the quality of advisement and experiences with faculty seeming to vary depending on the students' interests. "General education teachers are very hit or miss," one student says. But another offers, "Every single professor that I've had has been engaging, interested in my learning… are dedicated….and have also given me opportunities for success by introducing me to internships or jobs that I should apply for, as well as being willing to write recommendation letters or talk during their office hours whenever possible." UND offers "great on-campus resources for its students, including "counseling, student health, LGBTQ+ office, International Center, Student Government, and *The Dakota Student,* the student newspaper." Small class sizes "make for a more personalized learning experience," and "tuition costs are still reasonable compared to other schools and states," proving "bang for your buck." And there are "numerous resources and organizations available for students on campus to help them succeed…academically, socially, and mentally—including a "strategic plan recently implemented that focuses more on the student experience and being a leader in action."

Life

Students love the "tight knit community support," and say "everyone in Grand Forks wants the students at UND to succeed." School spirit "is very strong…which makes it extremely fun to attend basketball, football, volleyball, or hockey games." Emphasis on the hockey games: "There is nothing that brings us together more than hockey." The Ralph Engelstad Arena "nearly sells out at any home game" and "many people begin lining up in the cold as early as 8:00 A.M. on some game days." The city has a lot of outdoor skating rinks. The "greenway is great in the warmer months." The "beautiful campus" is "relatively compact in size," so traveling to and from classes is easy and "convenient." There is "support for Greek organizations and other organizations that support leadership opportunities," and the "attitude of all people, staff, and workers is always uplifting." Most students' days are "filled with studying and homework," but in between classes students visit the "local coffee shop, Archives," or visit the Wellness Center, which "is always busy, either with individual workouts, group exercise classes, intramural or pick-up games, or cooking classes." Sometimes students take "weekend trips to Winnipeg, Canada." "Greek life is popular," and "drinking is huge here."

Student Body

The "conservative" student body "is mostly comprised of Midwestern students," a "large majority from Minnesota and North Dakota," with the aviation program bringing in "a decent amount of diversity from around the U.S. and the world." "It takes a special kind of person to be able to suffer through the long, dark, and extremely cold winters," one student says proudly. "Despite these treacherous temperatures, many still show up in negative twenty degree wind chills to wait in line for two hours to cheer on the hockey team." Everyone that comes through campus is "willing to lend a helping hand," "not only for the campus but for the community as well." "The school isn't exactly diverse," one student says, "but that is mostly due to location I'd say. There are many contract students within aviation so there is diversity in that major."

UNIVERSITY OF NORTH DAKOTA

Financial Aid: 701-777-3121 • E-Mail: admissions@UND.edu • Website: http://und.edu

THE PRINCETON REVIEW SAYS

Admissions

Very important factors considered include: academic GPA. *Important factors considered include:* standardized test scores, rigor of secondary school record. *Other factors considered include:* recommendation(s). ACT with or without writing accepted. SAT with or without Essay component accepted. High school diploma is required and GED is accepted. *Academic units required:* 4 English, 3 math, 3 science, 3 science labs, 3 social studies, 1 additional unit from any category listed or a world language.

Financial Aid

Students should submit: FAFSA. Priority filing deadline is 2/1. The Princeton Review suggests that all financial aid forms be submitted as soon as possible after October 1. *Need-based scholarships/grants offered:* College/university scholarship or grant aid from institutional funds; Federal Pell; Private scholarships; SEOG; State scholarships/grants. *Loan aid offered:* Direct PLUS loans; Direct Subsidized Stafford Loans; Direct Unsubsidized Stafford Loans. Applicants will be notified of awards on a rolling basis beginning 12/1. Federal Work-Study Program available. Institutional employment available.

The Inside Word

As a potential incoming student, you will find that the University of North Dakota is ready and willing to help you apply. The website has applications broken down by student type, and you'll also find admissions guidelines to help you see if you would be accepted for admission. The higher your GPA, the lower your SAT and ACT scores can be, and vice-versa. However, the school says that everyone should apply for admission, even if you don't meet these standards, since your application will be reviewed by a committee that may make the decision based on other factors. If you're twenty-five plus years old on the first day of class OR you've completed twenty-four (including in progress) transferable college credits after graduating high school, you're not required to submit ACT or SAT test scores. However, if you've taken the ACT or SAT, it's highly recommended that you submit your official scores to UND for proper placement into English and math courses.

THE SCHOOL SAYS "..."

From the Admissions Office

"Founded in 1883, UND offers more than 225 fields of study, including aerospace, nursing, education, engineering, business, medicine, law, the arts and more. With so many options, you can explore all of your interests to discover your passion. You'll get the experience you need to succeed through internships, hands-on learning and real world projects, such as building a hydrogen-powered car, writing and producing a magazine, running a capitalist venture fund, or simulating a mission to Mars. And you'll graduate with the skills that will get you hired by today's employers.

"Nestled in a classic college town of 65,000, UND offers the atmosphere of a small college campus while giving you opportunities found only at large universities. You can do what you love by joining one of 250+ student organizations—ranging from Swing Dance Club to Robotics Club to the Photography Society. And, if you're up for an adventure, you can study abroad in more than 40 countries around the world.

"Like to work out? You'll be at home in one of the best campus Wellness Centers in the nation. Love sports? Whether you're an athlete or a fan, you can get in the game with our Fighting Hawks NCAA Division I athletic teams and 20+ intramural and club sports. And did we mention that our 8-time national men's hockey champions play in the finest collegiate hockey venue in the world? After all, there's a reason Grand Forks was named as America's Best Hockey Town—five years in a row!"

SELECTIVITY

Admissions Rating	77
# of applicants	4,964
% of applicants accepted	81
% of acceptees attending	42

FRESHMAN PROFILE

Range SAT EBRW	500–620
Range SAT Math	510–630
Range SAT Composite	1010–1210
Range ACT Composite	20–26
# submitting SAT scores	215
% submitting SAT scores	13
# submitting ACT scores	1,479
% submitting ACT scores	88
Average HS GPA	3.5
% graduated top 10% of class	19
% graduated top 25% of class	44
% graduated top 50% of class	78

DEADLINES

Regular	
Priority	5/1
Nonfall registration?	Yes

APPLICANTS ALSO LOOK AT AND OFTEN PREFER
Saint Cloud State University; University of Minnesota Duluth

AND SOMETIMES PREFER
Concordia College (Moorhead, MN) ; University of Minnesota, Crookston; North Dakota State University

FINANCIAL FACTS

Financial Aid Rating	83
Annual in-state tuition	$8,212
Annual out-of-state tuition	$12,318
Room and board	$9,544
Required fees	$1,524
Books and supplies	$1,000
Average frosh need-based scholarship	$5,996
Average UG need-based scholarship	$5,823
% needy frosh rec. need-based scholarship or grant aid	89
% needy UG rec. need-based scholarship or grant aid	78
% needy frosh rec. non-need-based scholarship or grant aid	10
% needy UG rec. non-need-based scholarship or grant aid	7
% needy frosh rec. need-based self-help aid	80
% needy UG rec. need-based self-help aid	82
% frosh rec. any financial aid	92
% UG rec. any financial aid	77
% UG borrow to pay for school	69
% frosh need fully met	45
% ugrads need fully met	39
Average % of frosh need met	61
Average % of ugrad need met	55

UNIVERSITY OF NOTRE DAME

220 Main Building, Notre Dame, IN 46556 • Admissions: 574-631-7505 • Fax: 574-631-8865

STUDENTS SAY "..."

Academics

Notre Dame has many traditions, including a "devotion to undergraduate education" you might not expect from a school with such an athletic reputation. Professors here are, by all accounts, "wonderful": "Not only are they invested in their students," they're "genuinely passionate about their fields of study," "enthusiastic and animated in lectures," and "always willing to meet outside of class to give extra help." Wary that distance might breed academic disengagement, professors ensure "large lectures are broken down into smaller discussion groups once a week to help with class material and...give the class a personal touch." For its part, "the administration tries its best to stay on top of the students' wants and needs." They make it "extremely easy to get in touch with anyone." Like the professors, administrators try to make personal connections with students. For example, "our president (a priest), as well as both of our presidents emeritus, make it a point to interact with the students in a variety of ways—teaching a class, saying mass in the dorms, etc." Overall, "while classes are difficult," "students are competitive against one another," and "it's necessary to study hard and often, [but] there's also time to do other things."

Life

Life at Notre Dame is centered around two things—"residential life" and "sports." The "dorms on campus provide the social structure" and supply undergrads with tons of opportunities to get involved and have fun. "During the school week" students "study a lot, but on the weekends everyone seems to make up for the lack of partying during the week." The school "does not have any fraternities or sororities, but campus is not dry, and drinking/partying is permitted within the residence halls." The administration reportedly tries "to keep the parties on campus due to the fact that campus is such a safe place and they truly do care about our safety." In addition to parties the dorms are really competitive in the Interhall Sport System, and "virtually every student plays some kind of sport [in] his/her residence hall." Intercollegiate sports, to put it mildly, "are huge." "If someone is not interested in sports upon arrival, he or she will be by the time he or she leaves." "Everybody goes to the football games, and it's common to see 1,000 students at a home soccer game." Beyond residential life and sports, "religious activities," volunteering, "campus publications, student government, and academic clubs round out the rest of ND life."

Student Body

Undergrads at Notre Dame report "the vast majority" of their peers are "very smart" "white kids from upper- to middle-class backgrounds from all over the country, especially the Midwest and Northeast." The typical student "is a type-A personality that studies a lot, yet is athletic and involved in the community. They are usually the outstanding seniors in their high schools," the "sort of people who can talk about the BCS rankings and Derrida in the same breath." Additionally, something like "85 percent of Notre Dame students earned a varsity letter in high school." "Not all are Catholic" here, though most are, and it seems that most undergrads "have some sort of spirituality present in their daily lives." "ND is slowly improving in diversity concerning economic backgrounds, with the university's policy to meet all demonstrated financial need." As things stand now, those who "don't tend to fit in with everyone else hang out in their own groups made up by others like them (based on ethnicity, sexual orientation, etc.)."

UNIVERSITY OF NOTRE DAME

Financial Aid: 574-631-6436 • E-Mail: admissions@nd.edu • Website: www.nd.edu

THE PRINCETON REVIEW SAYS

Admissions

Very important factors considered include: rigor of secondary school record. *Important factors considered include:* class rank, academic GPA, application essay, standardized test scores, recommendation(s), extracurricular activities, talent/ability, character/personal qualities, alumni/ae relation, volunteer work. *Other factors considered include:* first generation, religious affiliation/commitment, racial/ethnic status, work experience, level of applicant's interest. ACT with or without writing accepted. SAT with or without Essay component accepted. High school diploma is required and GED is accepted. *Academic units required:* 4 English, 3 math, 2 science, 2 science labs, 2 foreign language, 2 history, 3 academic electives. *Academic units recommended:* 4 English, 4 math, 4 science, 2 science labs, 4 foreign language, 4 history.

Financial Aid

Students should submit: CSS/Financial Aid PROFILE; FAFSA; Noncustodial PROFILE. Priority filing deadline is 11/15. The Princeton Review suggests that all financial aid forms be submitted as soon as possible after October 1. *Need-based scholarships/grants offered:* College/university scholarship or grant aid from institutional funds; Federal Pell; Private scholarships; SEOG; State scholarships/grants. *Loan aid offered:* Direct PLUS loans; Direct Subsidized Stafford Loans; Direct Unsubsidized Stafford Loans. Applicants will be notified of awards on a rolling basis beginning 2/15. Federal Work-Study Program available. Institutional employment available.

The Inside Word

Notre Dame is one of the most selective colleges in the country. Almost everyone who enrolls is in the top 10 percent of their graduating class and possesses test scores in the highest percentiles. But, as the student respondents suggest, strong academic ability isn't enough to get you in here. The school looks for students with other talents, and seems to have a predilection for athletic achievement. Legacy students get a leg up but are by no means assured of admission.

THE SCHOOL SAYS "..."

From the Admissions Office

"Notre Dame is a Catholic university, which means it offers unique opportunities for academic, ethical, spiritual, and social service development. The First Year of Studies program provides special assistance to our students as they make the adjustment from high school to college. The first-year curriculum includes many core requirements, while allowing students to explore several areas of possible future study. Each residence hall is home to students from all classes; most will live in the same hall for all their years on campus. An average of 93 percent of entering students will graduate within five years.

"The highest critical reading score and the highest math score from either test will be accepted; the writing component score is not required. The ACT is also accepted (with or without writing component) in lieu of the SAT."

SELECTIVITY
Admissions Rating	98
# of applicants	22,200
% of applicants accepted	16
% of acceptees attending	58
# offered a place on the wait list	1,600
% accepting a place on wait list	64
% admitted from wait list	10.5

FRESHMAN PROFILE
Range SAT EBRW	680–760
Range SAT Math	720–790
Range ACT Composite	32–35
# submitting SAT scores	1,188
% submitting SAT scores	47
# submitting ACT scores	1,326
% submitting ACT scores	53
% graduated top 10% of class	90
% graduated top 25% of class	99
% graduated top 50% of class	100

DEADLINES
Early action	
Deadline	11/1
Notification	12/15
Regular	
Deadline	1/1
Notification	4/1
Nonfall registration?	Yes

FINANCIAL FACTS
Financial Aid Rating	96
Annual tuition	$57,192
Room and board	$15,984
Required fees	$507
Books and supplies	$1,050
Average frosh need-based scholarship	$44,087
Average UG need-based scholarship	$42,382
% needy frosh rec. need-based scholarship or grant aid	97
% needy UG rec. need-based scholarship or grant aid	97
% needy frosh rec. non-need-based scholarship or grant aid	30
% needy UG rec. non-need-based scholarship or grant aid	27
% needy frosh rec. need-based self-help aid	85
% needy UG rec. need-based self-help aid	86
% frosh rec. any financial aid	63
% UG rec. any financial aid	75
% UG borrow to pay for school	39.5
Average cumulative indebtedness	$27,460
% frosh need fully met	100
% ugrads need fully met	100
Average % of frosh need met	100
Average % of ugrad need met	100

UNIVERSITY OF OKLAHOMA

1000 Asp Avenue, Norman, OK 73019 • Admissions: 405-325-2251 • Fax: 405-325-7124

STUDENTS SAY "..."

Academics

The University of Oklahoma (OU), located in Norman, OK, outranks all other public and private universities in National Merit Scholars, and boasts 134 undergraduate degree programs. It is an "intellectually fertile, opportunity-laden public research institution" with a "rich tradition of community" that offers "an Ivy League quality education within a public university." OU has over 30,000 students, but still manages to have a "small town feel" that is "very comfortable and welcoming." Students call OU "not just a school," but "a place to meet others in the OU family, be a part of long-standing traditions," and "receive a quality education from challenging courses." Home of the Sooners football team, which won seven national championships, it's no wonder OU's school spirit is strong. The University also boasts 38 overall NCAA National Championships, and a host of other athletic championships and accolades. Though OU "might be known for its athletic program," students say "academics don't suffer from it." OU has "fantastic," "engaging," "encouraging" "professors that truly care for the well-being of the students." "The professors here don't feel like your average teachers," notes a Psychology and Economics major, "but exceptional instructors who relate on a personal basis and actually help you comprehend the material." OU gives "tons of opportunities to its students," including "jobs, networking, study abroad" programs and more. The university combines "tradition with advancement to encourage you to become the best version of yourself possible" says an Elementary Education major. Student after student noted the sense of "family" everyone has at OU, as well as the importance of "tradition, unity, and togetherness."

Life

OU is home to a host of strong athletic teams and students frequent "football games and other athletic events for fun." During the fall, "most students attend at least one football game." "Greek life" is also "very important." Some complain that "if you're not in a fraternity or sorority, there's not a lot to do on campus on the weekends." Others, though, say "there are many opportunities to be involved on campus," including "free movie nights and pool." There is always "something going on, and whether it be a sports event or a fine arts event, the quality is always excellent." Students can visit the world-renowned art in the Fred Jones Jr. Museum of Art or the twenty-six-foot tall dinosaur (an Apatosaurus!) at OU's Sam Noble Museum of Natural History. There is also "Campus Corner," which has "restaurants, bars and boutiques." And it's also "an easy drive to the movies, a nice restaurant, or night life." Students note that the "social atmosphere is very alive most of the time." But it's not all about football and parties. "People are very considerate of one another and make efforts to support each other during rough times," notes a Psychology and Mathematics major. That extends beyond campus as well, and students take advantage of "all kinds of volunteering opportunities." In fact, "every year everyone on campus drops what they're doing for one weekend to spend all day volunteering in the local Norman and Oklahoma City communities." Students value their commitment to community service. "We genuinely care for one another and are very passionate about the university," says one student. "I cannot imagine there being a happier campus than OU anywhere in the country." Or, as another says: "Life is great."

Student Body

A typical OU student is "friendly," "down to earth," "aware," and "motivated." They have a "nice balance" between their "academic and social lives" and are committed to "volunteering," "sports" and "Greek life." Many students join a fraternity or sorority. Incoming students are most likely to "fit in" by "being involved on campus" and joining "lots of organizations." Students describe their classmates as primarily "white, upper-middle class, and Christian," but "with a broad mix of international and minority students."

UNIVERSITY OF OKLAHOMA

Financial Aid: 405-325-5505 • E-Mail: admissions@ou.edu • Website: www.ou.edu

THE PRINCETON REVIEW SAYS

Admissions

Very important factors considered include: rigor of secondary school record, class rank, academic GPA, standardized test scores. *Important factors considered include:* application essay, recommendation(s). *Other factors considered include:* interview, extracurricular activities, talent/ability, character/personal qualities, alumni/ae relation, volunteer work, work experience, level of applicant's interest. ACT with or without writing accepted. SAT with or without Essay component accepted. High school diploma is required and GED is accepted. *Academic units required:* 4 English, 3 math, 3 science, 3 science labs, 1 social studies, 2 history, 2 academic electives. *Academic units recommended:* 4 math, 4 science, 2 foreign language, 1 computer science.

Financial Aid

Students should submit: FAFSA. Priority filing deadline is 3/1. The Princeton Review suggests that all financial aid forms be submitted as soon as possible after October 1. *Need-based scholarships/grants offered:* College/university scholarship or grant aid from institutional funds; Federal Pell; Private scholarships; SEOG; State scholarships/grants; United Negro College Fund. *Loan aid offered:* Direct PLUS loans; Direct Subsidized Stafford Loans; Direct Unsubsidized Stafford Loans. Applicants will be notified of awards on a rolling basis beginning 3/15. Federal Work-Study Program available. Institutional employment available.

The Inside Word

Accepted students at OU graduated from high school with an average GPA of 3.6. But while academic grades and standardized test scores (ACT/SAT) are very important to the admissions process at OU, they also place importance on community service, leadership, and extracurricular activities. In fact, the applicant's "engagement" accounts for a quarter of their decision.

THE SCHOOL SAYS "..."

From the Admissions Office

"Ask yourself some significant questions. What are your ambitions, goals, and dreams? Do you desire opportunity, and are you ready to accept challenge? What do you hope to gain from your educational experience? Are you looking for a university that will provide you with the tools, resources, and motivation to convert ambitions, opportunities, and challenges into meaningful achievement? To effectively answer these questions you must carefully seek out your options, look for direction, and make the right choice. The University of Oklahoma combines a unique mixture of academic excellence, varied social cultures, and a variety of campus activities to make your educational experience complete. At OU, comprehensive learning is our goal for your life. Not only do you receive a valuable classroom learning experience, but OU is also one of the finest research institutions in the United States. This allows OU students the opportunity to be a part of technology in progress. It's not just learning, it's discovery, invention, and dynamic creativity, a hands-on experience that allows you to be on the cutting edge of knowledge. Make the right choice and consider the University of Oklahoma!

"The SAT (or ACT) will be used when considering freshman applicants for admission. The writing component of either test is not required of students and is not used in determining admission to the university. The student's best composite score from any one test will be used."

SELECTIVITY

Admissions Rating	81
# of applicants	15,673
% of applicants accepted	80
% of acceptees attending	36
# offered a place on the wait list	2,261
% accepting a place on wait list	100
% admitted from wait list	14

FRESHMAN PROFILE

Range SAT EBRW	560–650
Range SAT Math	550–660
Range SAT Composite	1130–1310
Range ACT Composite	23–29
# submitting SAT scores	1,898
% submitting SAT scores	42
# submitting ACT scores	3,717
% submitting ACT scores	82
Average HS GPA	3.6
% graduated top 10% of class	33
% graduated top 25% of class	61
% graduated top 50% of class	89

DEADLINES

Regular	
Priority	12/15
Deadline	2/1
Notification	Rolling, 9/1
Nonfall registration?	Yes

FINANCIAL FACTS

Financial Aid Rating	89
Annual in-state tuition	$4,788
Annual out-of-state tuition	$20,169
Room and board	$10,994
Required fees	$6,975
Books and supplies	$667
Average frosh need-based scholarship	$6,689
Average UG need-based scholarship	$6,412
% needy frosh rec. need-based scholarship or grant aid	50
% needy UG rec. need-based scholarship or grant aid	57
% needy frosh rec. non-need-based scholarship or grant aid	58
% needy UG rec. non-need-based scholarship or grant aid	51
% needy frosh rec. need-based self-help aid	64
% needy UG rec. need-based self-help aid	67
% frosh rec. any financial aid	88
% UG rec. any financial aid	81
% UG borrow to pay for school	43
Average cumulative indebtedness	$30,258
% frosh need fully met	82
% ugrads need fully met	79
Average % of frosh need met	84
Average % of ugrad need met	82

UNIVERSITY OF OREGON

1217 University of Oregon, Eugene, OR 97403-1217 • Admissions: 541-346-3201 • Fax: 541-346-5815

CAMPUS LIFE

Quality of Life Rating	86
Fire Safety Rating	93
Green Rating	96
Type of school	Public
Environment	City

STUDENTS

Total undergrad enrollment	18,743
% male/female	46/54
% from out of state	43
# of fraternities (% ugrad men join)	19 (16)
# of sororities (% ugrad women join)	18 (18)
% African American	2
% Asian	6
% Caucasian	59
% Hispanic	14
% Native American	<1
% Pacific Islander	0
% Two or more races	8
% Race and/or ethnicity unknown	2
% international	7
# of countries represented	74

SURVEY SAYS . . .

Students environmentally aware
Recreation facilities are great
Lots of beer drinking
Everyone loves the Ducks

ACADEMICS

Academic Rating	79
% students returning for sophomore year	86
% students graduating within 4 years	56
% students graduating within 6 years	74
Calendar	Quarter
Student/faculty ratio	16:1
Profs interesting rating	86
Profs accessible rating	90

Most classes have 10–19 students.
Most lab/discussion sessions have
20–29 students.

MOST POPULAR MAJORS

Business/Commerce, General; Social Sciences,
General; Economics, General

STUDENTS SAY "..."

Academics

If the University of Oregon excels at anything, it is in providing students with a wealth of academic opportunities. Indeed, students feel it is "a perfect place for someone seeking a well-rounded liberal arts secondary education," a school that has "all of the creative perks of a small learning environment with all of the excitement of a big school." Sports are a big deal here, "but there is also an emphasis on rigorous academics." Business, architecture, ecology, journalism, international studies, and political science all win accolades. If there is a chink in UO's armor, it is the "inability for some students to get the classes they need." With such a wide array of fields of study available, some students find that essential classes are only available at difficult hours. Students also give mixed grades to the professors, who range from "remarkable" and "really passionate" educators who "are invested in their students" to a few "quite terrible" teachers who "are not dedicated to the students." Those attending UO should be self-motivating, since "the weight falls on the students to create relationships with professors." It is worth the effort, though, as "doing so can open many doors." When it all clicks—and many students report that once they were focused on their major things began to fall into place—students have enjoyed an education that "deeply altered the way I see things."

Life

Eugene, Oregon, is not going to give the nation's big cities a run for their money, but students here like it that way. When the weather is nice, students can be found outside "playing Frisbee, football, soccer, or just lounging in the grass," and when the rainy weather of the Pacific Northwest forces people indoors, "you find students in coffee shops on campus and off, studying, visiting, or relaxing." Music, hiking, and other outdoor activities are also popular pastimes. Indeed, the scenery proves a draw for many. "The coast is an hour away, hiking trails and mountains are everywhere, and you can even drive or take a bus up to Portland to get some city life." Greek life is growing on campus but does not dominate the school, and despite prohibitions on drinking in the dorms, students manage it anyway. With the gorgeous scenery and wealth of things to do, it's no wonder students think that "life at school is pretty great."

Student Body

What kind of student attends the University of Oregon? The typical answer is that there is no typical answer. "You have your hipsters, hippies, jocks, athletes, drunks, nerds, and every other cliché you can think of"—students from "dreadlocked hippies to straight-laced conservatives, and everything else in between." That diversity in the student body means, "if you're willing to put forth any sort of effort into meeting people, you'll find a group" who will click with you. "No matter who you are," another student agrees, "there are programs and clubs on campus to take part in." Greek or non-Greek does make a difference. Students say there is a "huge divide between Greek-life and the rest of the student body." But overall, University of Oregon students are "friendly, open-minded, and generally environmentally/socially conscious." In other words, "there are all sorts of students at Oregon, and it is pretty diverse."

Financial Aid: 541-346-3221 • E-Mail: uoadmit@uoregon.edu • Website: www.uoregon.edu

THE PRINCETON REVIEW SAYS

Admissions

Very important factors considered include: rigor of secondary school record, academic GPA. *Important factors considered include:* application essay, standardized test scores. *Other factors considered include:* class rank, recommendation(s), extracurricular activities, talent/ability, character/personal qualities, first generation, geographical residence, state residency, racial/ethnic status, volunteer work, work experience. ACT with or without writing accepted. SAT with or without Essay component accepted. High school diploma is required and GED is accepted. *Academic units required:* 4 English, 3 math, 3 science, 2 foreign language, 3 social studies. *Academic units recommended:* 1 science lab 1 visual/performing arts.

Financial Aid

Students should submit: FAFSA. Priority filing deadline is 3/1. The Princeton Review suggests that all financial aid forms be submitted as soon as possible after October 1. *Need-based scholarships/grants offered:* College/university scholarship or grant aid from institutional funds; Federal Pell; Private scholarships; SEOG; State scholarships/grants. *Loan aid offered:* Direct PLUS loans; Direct Subsidized Stafford Loans; Direct Unsubsidized Stafford Loans. Applicants will be notified of awards on a rolling basis beginning 4/15. Federal Work-Study Program available. Institutional employment available.

The Inside Word

Your ticket to UO is a strong GPA in challenging college prep courses, even if your standardized test scores are less than stellar. If your high school grades dropped due to personal circumstances, or indicate an upward trajectory due to personal growth, consider addressing that in your personal statement.

THE SCHOOL SAYS "..."

From the Admissions Office

"At the UO, you'll be part of a community dedicated to making a difference in the world and you'll find the inspiration and resources you'll need to succeed. You'll attend classes alongside students from all fifty states and more than 100 countries, and learn from people whose cultural, ethnic, political, and religious perspectives differ from your own. You'll have opportunities to participate in cutting-edge research and study with renowned faculty. You'll graduate with the critical thinking skills and professional preparation necessary to succeed in an increasingly global job market. Set in a 295-acre arboretum, the UO is literally green. Academic and outdoor programs will bring you into forests, mountains, rivers, and lakes. The state-of-the-art Lewis Integrative Science Building earned a 'platinum' certification from the U.S. Green Building Council's Leadership in Energy and Environmental Design program; the new student union and recreation center are both on track for the same distinction. You'll have access to nationally recognized programs in sustainable architecture, psychology, geography, economics, education, and business. With a student/teacher ratio of sixteen to one and median class size of 20 students, you'll find a campus that meets your individual needs. You'll also have the benefits of a premier research university: more than 300 academic programs, excellent academic facilities, and more than 250 student organizations. To be eligible for freshman admission, submit your official high school transcript and SAT or ACT scores, graduate from an accredited high school, and write an essay."

SELECTIVITY

Admissions Rating	80
# of applicants	27,358
% of applicants accepted	82
% of acceptees attending	20

FRESHMAN PROFILE

Range SAT EBRW	560–660
Range SAT Math	540–650
Range SAT Composite	1140–1340
Range ACT Composite	22–28
# submitting SAT scores	3,160
% submitting SAT scores	70
# submitting ACT scores	1,502
% submitting ACT scores	33
Average HS GPA	3.7
% graduated top 10% of class	26
% graduated top 25% of class	57
% graduated top 50% of class	86

DEADLINES

Early action	
Deadline	11/1
Notification	12/15
Regular	
Deadline	1/15
Notification	4/1
Nonfall registration?	Yes

FINANCIAL FACTS

Financial Aid Rating	80
Annual in-state tuition	$10,440
Annual out-of-state tuition	$34,335
Room and board	$13,482
Required fees	$2,280
Books and supplies	$1,178
Average frosh need-based scholarship	$10,512
Average UG need-based scholarship	$10,061
% needy frosh rec. need-based scholarship or grant aid	75
% needy UG rec. need-based scholarship or grant aid	72
% needy frosh rec. non-need-based scholarship or grant aid	4
% needy UG rec. non-need-based scholarship or grant aid	4
% needy frosh rec. need-based self-help aid	62
% needy UG rec. need-based self-help aid	66
% frosh rec. any financial aid	69
% UG rec. any financial aid	65
% UG borrow to pay for school	44
Average cumulative indebtedness	$26,548
% frosh need fully met	7
% ugrads need fully met	6
Average % of frosh need met	55
Average % of ugrad need met	55

UNIVERSITY OF PENNSYLVANIA

1 College Hall, Philadelphia, PA 19104-6228 • Admissions: 215-898-7507 • Fax: 215-898-7507

STUDENTS SAY "..."

Academics

At the University of Pennsylvania, students share an intellectual curiosity and top-notch resources but don't "buy into the stigma of being an Ivy League school." Students here are "very passionate about what they do outside the classroom" and the "flexible core requirements." The university is composed of four undergraduate schools (and "a library for pretty much any topic"). "You can take courses in any of the schools, including graduate-level courses." Luckily, there's a vast variety of disciplines available to students: "I can take a course in old Icelandic and even another one about the politics of food," says a student. Wharton, Penn's highly regarded, "highly competitive undergraduate business school" attracts "career-oriented" students who don't mind a "strenuous course load." There are "more than enough" resources, funding, and opportunity here for any student to take advantage of, and "Penn encourages students to truly take advantage of it all!" Professors can "sometimes seem to be caught up more in their research than their classes," but all "are incredibly well-versed in their subject (as well as their audience)." If you're willing to put in the time and effort, your professors "will be happy to reciprocate." In general, the instructors here are "very challenging academically" and are "always willing to offer their more than relevant life experience in class discussion."

Life

Penn students don't mind getting into intellectual conversations during dinner—"Politics and religion come up often, but so does baseball, types of wine, and restaurants"—but some "partying is a much higher priority here than it is at other Ivy League schools." "Campus is split between the downtown club scene and the frat/bar scene, depending on your preference." However, when it comes down to midterms and finals, "people get really serious and…buckle down and study." There's easy access to downtown Philadelphia, yet "still the comfortable feeling of having our own campus," giving students plenty of access to restaurants (BYO restaurants in Philly are "a huge hit"), shopping, concerts, and sports games, as well as plain old "hanging out with hallmates playing Mario Kart." "It's the perfect mix between an urban setting a traditional college campus." The school provides plenty of guest speakers, cultural events, clubs, and organizations for students to channel their energies (all of which "makes the campus feel smaller"), and seniors can even attend "Feb Club" in the month of February, which is essentially an event every night. The weekend buses to/from New York and D.C. "are always packed." It's a busy life at Penn, and "people are constantly trying to think about how they can balance getting good grades academically and their weekend plans."

Student Body

This "determined" bunch "is either focused on one specific interest, or very well-rounded." Pretty much everyone "was an overachiever ('that kid') in high school," and some students "are off-the-charts brilliant," making everyone here "sort of fascinated by everyone else." Everyone has "a strong sense of personal style and his or her own credo," but no group deviates too far from the more mainstream stereotypes. There's a definite lack of "emos" and hippies. There's "the career-driven Wharton kid who will stab you in the back to get your interview slot" and "the nursing kid who's practically nonexistent," but on the whole, there's tremendous school diversity, with "people from all over the world of all kinds of experiences of all perspectives."

UNIVERSITY OF PENNSYLVANIA

Financial Aid: 215-898-1988 • E-Mail: info@admissions.upenn.edu • Website: www.upenn.edu

THE PRINCETON REVIEW SAYS

Admissions

Very important factors considered include: rigor of secondary school record, academic GPA, application essay, standardized test scores, recommendation(s), character/personal qualities. *Important factors considered include:* class rank, interview, extracurricular activities, talent/ability. *Other factors considered include:* first generation, alumni/ae relation, geographical residence, state residency, racial/ethnic status, volunteer work, work experience, level of applicant's interest. ACT with or without writing accepted. SAT with or without Essay component accepted. High school diploma or equivalent is not required. *Academic units recommended:* 4 English, 4 math, 3 science, 3 science labs, 4 foreign language, 2 social studies, 3 history.

Financial Aid

Students should submit: Business/Farm Supplement; CSS/Financial Aid PROFILE; FAFSA; Institution's own financial aid form; Noncustodial PROFILE. Priority filing deadline is 2/15. The Princeton Review suggests that all financial aid forms be submitted as soon as possible after October 1. *Need-based scholarships/grants offered:* College/university scholarship or grant aid from institutional funds; Federal Pell; Private scholarships; SEOG; State scholarships/grants. *Loan aid offered:* Direct PLUS loans; Direct Subsidized Stafford Loans; Direct Unsubsidized Stafford Loans. Applicants will be notified of awards on or about 4/1. Federal Work-Study Program available. Institutional employment available.

The Inside Word

After a small decline four cycles ago, applications are once again climbing at Penn—the fifth increase in six years. The competition in the applicant pool is formidable. Applicants can safely assume that they need to be one of the strongest students in their graduating class in order to be successful.

THE SCHOOL SAYS "..."

From the Admissions Office

"Founded by Benjamin Franklin in 1740 to push the frontiers of knowledge and to benefit society, Penn continues to nurture a sense of public mindedness in its students, inspiring them to make vital contributions as they become engaged citizens in an evolving world. Penn's students and faculty work toward the shared goal of enacting change by questioning, thinking, and doing—often across traditional academic disciplines. The integration of knowledge and learning spans four undergraduate schools: the College of Arts & Sciences, the School of Engineering & Applied Science, the Wharton School of Business, and the School of Nursing. Penn offers more than ninety majors, eighty minors, and the ability to earn more than one degree in four years.

"The Penn community thrives on the open exchange of ideas and shared learning experiences, made possible by the faculty and students of all four undergraduate and twelve graduate schools who coexist and collaborate on one beautiful 300 acre campus in Philadelphia. Students regularly conduct research with faculty and actively participate in over 500 clubs and organizations. Education through engagement is made possible by Penn's extensive partnerships around the world and close to our Philadelphia campus, ranging from over 150 Academically-Based Community Service courses to internships in twenty-two foreign countries.

"Penn understands that the best minds should have access to the finest education, regardless of their families' ability to pay. To achieve this, Penn practices need-blind admissions for applicants who are citizens and permanent residents of the United States, Canada, and Mexico, meets 100 percent of demonstrated financial need, and provides an all-grant aid package for all undergraduates receiving financial aid. Our goal is to allow students to pursue their aspirations without assuming a burden of debt."

SELECTIVITY

Admissions Rating	99
# of applicants	44,961
% of applicants accepted	8
% of acceptees attending	70
# offered a place on the wait list	2,932
% accepting a place on wait list	70
% admitted from wait list	5
# of early decision applicants	7,109
% accepted early decision	18%

FRESHMAN PROFILE

Range SAT EBRW	700–760
Range SAT Math	750–800
Range ACT Composite	33–35
# submitting SAT scores	1,499
% submitting SAT scores	62
# submitting ACT scores	901
% submitting ACT scores	38
Average HS GPA	3.9
% graduated top 10% of class	94
% graduated top 25% of class	98
% graduated top 50% of class	100

DEADLINES

Early decision	
Deadline	11/1
Notification	12/15
Regular	
Deadline	1/5
Notification	Rolling, 4/1
Nonfall registration?	No

FINANCIAL FACTS

Financial Aid Rating	96
Annual tuition	$53,166
Room and board	$16,784
Required fees	$6,876
Books and supplies	$1,358
Average frosh need-based scholarship	$53,107
Average UG need-based scholarship	$51,403
% needy frosh rec. need-based scholarship or grant aid	99
% needy UG rec. need-based scholarship or grant aid	99
% needy frosh rec. non-need-based scholarship or grant aid	0
% needy UG rec. non-need-based scholarship or grant aid	0
% needy frosh rec. need-based self-help aid	100
% needy UG rec. need-based self-help aid	100
% frosh rec. any financial aid	46
% UG rec. any financial aid	46
% UG borrow to pay for school	22
Average cumulative indebtedness	$23,009
% frosh need fully met	100
% ugrads need fully met	100
Average % of frosh need met	100
Average % of ugrad need met	100

UNIVERSITY OF PITTSBURGH—PITTSBURGH CAMPUS

4227 Fifth Avenue, Pittsburgh, PA 15260 • Admissions: 412-624-7488 • Fax: 412-648-8815

CAMPUS LIFE

Quality of Life Rating	91
Fire Safety Rating	91
Green Rating	93
Type of school	Public
Environment	City

STUDENTS

Total undergrad enrollment	19,017
% male/female	47/53
% from out of state	34
% frosh live on campus	96
% ugrads live on campus	42
# of fraternities (% ugrad men join)	24 (10)
# of sororities (% ugrad women join)	15 (12)
% African American	5
% Asian	11
% Caucasian	68
% Hispanic	5
% Native American	<1
% Pacific Islander	<1
% Two or more races	4
% Race and/or ethnicity unknown	1
% international	5
# of countries represented	58

SURVEY SAYS . . .

Students are happy
Lab facilities are great
Students love Pittsburgh, PA
Everyone loves the Panthers

ACADEMICS

Academic Rating	81
% students returning for sophomore year	93
% students graduating within 4 years	65
% students graduating within 6 years	83
Calendar	Semester
Student/faculty ratio	14:1
Profs interesting rating	86
Profs accessible rating	90

Most classes have 10–19 students.
Most lab/discussion sessions have
20–29 students.

MOST POPULAR MAJORS

Biology/Biological Sciences, General; Psychology,
General; Registered Nursing/Registered Nurse

STUDENTS SAY "..."

Academics

Approximately 19,000 undergraduates attend the University of Pittsburgh (or "Pitt"), a "research powerhouse," that offers a "great value" for students. Pitt "attracts highly-skilled faculty," who are "incredibly accomplished," "engaging," and "bring real life experience to the classroom." One student notes, "Even in classes of over 100 people, my professors frequently pause to answer questions and check to make sure students are following their lectures." Outside of class, professors are "concerned with students' personal career development" and will often "reach out for internship and job opportunities if you build a relationship with them." One student recounts being able to "obtain a paid research position and present at a conference" as a first-year. Pitt has an "outstanding relationship with employers both local and throughout the country," a fact that is "reflected in the size of our school's co-op program" and "the Internship Guarantee policy." Pitt's Medical Center (UPMC) offers pre-med students opportunities for research and internships as well. In terms of work-life balance, students note that course loads are often "rigorous, but not so much as to prevent engaging in extracurricular activities or research and having an active social life." Students note that the University Chancellor and Dean of Students "are loved" for being "very visible on campus." "Their presence reinforces how much they care" and "the quality of the education" Pitt students can count on."

Campus Life

With a home base in Pittsburgh's Oakland neighborhood, students love that Pitt is "centrally located in one of the most growing cities in the country." Pittsburgh offers a "strong economy, diversity, arts, and opportunity that is becoming unrivaled across the nation." Students also find "plenty of entertainment in Oakland and on campus," with tons of programs put on by "student groups, the Pitt Program Council, and the Residential Student Association." Pitt has a "unique atmosphere"—it's a "fairly large school, but nevertheless, has a tight-knit community." The student body has "an abundance of pride" in its "twelve Division I varsity sports," NFL-grade stadium, and a "host of other club sports." Students can also get in some exercise at Tree Halls or the Baierl Fitness Center, "world class fitness facilities," or play "Ultimate Frisbee on the Peterson Events Center or Cathedral of Learning lawn." With the "free public transportation given to Pitt students," traveling to races and festivals or "visiting local museums and landmarks" across the city is no problem.

Student Body

"Diverse" and "hardworking" are the words University of Pittsburgh students consistently use to describe their peers. Pitt's student body is made up from a "variety of cultural, socioeconomic, and educational backgrounds." "Diversity initiatives" are first rate at Pitt, especially the BRIDGES program designed to provide resources for diversity scholarship students." Described as "motivated, accepting, empowering, and brilliant," the "vast majority of students work hard," but the atmosphere around campus is "definitely not cutthroat: everyone wants to see their peers succeed." The diversity of the university is reflected in its more than 600 student organizations; each student has "unique interests and passions," and students report that Pitt does a "great job accommodating them." One student notes their pride in "efforts Pitt students take to volunteer in various neighborhoods of the city on a regular basis" and says: "Pittsburgh students truly make Pittsburgh a better place." There is also a large contingent of international students. "There is no typical description of a Pitt student," says one student. "Our common denominator is that we all love this university."

UNIVERSITY OF PITTSBURGH—PITTSBURGH CAMPUS

Financial Aid: 412-624-7488 • E-Mail: oafa@pitt.edu • Website: www.pitt.edu

THE PRINCETON REVIEW SAYS

Admissions

Very important factors considered include: rigor of secondary school record, academic GPA, standardized test scores. *Important factors considered include:* application essay, *Other factors considered include:* class rank, recommendation(s), interview, extracurricular activities, talent/ability, character/personal qualities, first generation, alumni/ae relation, geographical residence, state residency, racial/ethnic status, volunteer work, work experience, level of applicant's interest. ACT with or without writing accepted. SAT with or without Essay component accepted. High school diploma is required and GED is not accepted. *Academic units required:* 4 English, 3 math, 3 science, 3 science labs, 2 foreign language, 2 social studies, 3 academic electives. *Academic units recommended:* 4 English, 4 math, 4 science, 4 science labs, 3 foreign language, 3 social studies, 5 academic electives.

Financial Aid

Students should submit: FAFSA; State aid form. Priority filing deadline is 3/1. The Princeton Review suggests that all financial aid forms be submitted as soon as possible after October 1. *Need-based scholarships/grants offered:* College/university scholarship or grant aid from institutional funds; Federal Nursing Scholarships; Federal Pell; Private scholarships; SEOG; State scholarships/grants. *Loan aid offered:* Direct PLUS loans; Direct Subsidized Stafford Loans; Direct Unsubsidized Stafford Loans. Applicants will be notified of awards on a rolling basis beginning 2/1. Federal Work-Study Program available. Institutional employment available.

The Inside Word

University of Pittsburgh operates on a rolling admission policy and although there is no specific deadline to apply for admission, your chances are better if you apply on the earlier side. Pitt reviews applications for the School of Medicine Guaranteed Admissions Application through November 15, and the Academic Scholarships Priority Review Application through December 15. Pitt offers extensive need- and merit-based financial aid, including the prestigious Chancellor's Scholarship. Students should count on submitting SAT/ACT scores, and while the Short Answer Questions section of the Pitt application is optional, it is highly recommended.

THE SCHOOL SAYS "..."

From the Admissions Office

"The University of Pittsburgh, a public research university, is a member of the Association of American Universities. Home to sixteen undergraduate, graduate, and professional schools, including an internationally renowned health sciences educational and research complex, Pitt is also affiliated with the University of Pittsburgh Medical Center. Its five-campus system offers more than 480 degree programs, and awards academic merit scholarships and guaranteed admission to graduate and professional programs. Pitt faculty have pioneered major medical advances including the Salk polio vaccine, multiple-organ transplantation, and CPR. Pitt alumni have won the Nobel Peace prize, the Nobel Prize in Medicine, the Pulitzer Prize, the National Medal of Science, Olympic gold medals, Academy Awards, and Super Bowl championships. University Honors College students have a proven track record of earning prestigious honors including Rhodes, Marshall, Goldwater, Truman, Udall Scholarships, Humanity in Action Scholarship, as well as a Gates Cambridge Scholarship; Pitt educates the whole student through a unique Outside the Classroom Curriculum program that helps students develop holistically; University Center for International Studies certificate programs; and Engineering Co-Op program; study abroad just about anywhere in the world; and more. There are 630 student organizations and student-athletes participate in Division I college athletics, supported by one of the most recognizable student-led fan bases in the nation. Encouraging students to take advantage of the city as their campus, Pitt grants fare-free access to city buses and discounted tickets to cultural events, opening them to the full experiences of a city that has been cited as the most livable in the U.S."

SELECTIVITY

Admissions Rating	89
# of applicants	32,091
% of applicants accepted	57
% of acceptees attending	22
# offered a place on the wait list	3,518
% accepting a place on wait list	36
% admitted from wait list	46

FRESHMAN PROFILE

Range SAT EBRW	630–700
Range SAT Math	630–740
Range ACT Composite	28–33
# submitting SAT scores	3,335
% submitting SAT scores	83
# submitting ACT scores	1,376
% submitting ACT scores	34
Average HS GPA	4.1
% graduated top 10% of class	53
% graduated top 25% of class	86
% graduated top 50% of class	98

DEADLINES

Regular	
Notification	Rolling, 9/1
Nonfall registration?	Yes

APPLICANTS ALSO LOOK AT AND OFTEN PREFER

Boston University; Case Western Reserve University; New York University; Carnegie Mellon University; University of Michigan—Ann Arbor; University of Pennsylvania; University of Virginia

AND SOMETIMES PREFER

Rochester Institute of Technology; Temple University; University of Delaware; Penn State University Park; The Ohio State University—Columbus; University of Maryland, College Park

AND RARELY PREFER

Drexel University

FINANCIAL FACTS

Financial Aid Rating	80
Annual in-state tuition	$18,628
Annual out-of-state tuition	$32,656
Room and board	$11,250
Required fees	$1,090
Books and supplies	$755
Average frosh need-based scholarship	$11,636
Average UG need-based scholarship	$10,519
% needy frosh rec. need-based scholarship or grant aid	79
% needy UG rec. need-based scholarship or grant aid	73
% needy frosh rec. non-need-based scholarship or grant aid	11
% needy UG rec. non-need-based scholarship or grant aid	8
% needy frosh rec. need-based self-help aid	72
% needy UG rec. need-based self-help aid	78
% frosh rec. any financial aid	61.6
% UG rec. any financial aid	54.2
% UG borrow to pay for school	61
Average cumulative indebtedness	$39,417
% frosh need fully met	20
% ugrads need fully met	9
Average % of frosh need met	59
Average % of ugrad need met	53

UNIVERSITY OF PUGET SOUND

1500 North Warner Street CMB 1062, Tacoma, WA 98416-1062 • Admissions: 253-879-3211 • Fax: 253-879-3993

CAMPUS LIFE

Quality of Life Rating	91
Fire Safety Rating	91
Green Rating	78
Type of school	Private
Environment	City

STUDENTS

Total undergrad enrollment	2,298
% male/female	41/59
% from out of state	75
% frosh from public high school	72
% frosh live on campus	99
% ugrads live on campus	67
# of fraternities (% ugrad men join)	4 (25)
# of sororities (% ugrad women join)	5 (25)
% African American	2
% Asian	7
% Caucasian	67
% Hispanic	10
% Native American	<1
% Pacific Islander	0
% Two or more races	10
% Race and/or ethnicity unknown	3
% international	<1
# of countries represented	9

SURVEY SAYS . . .

Lots of liberal students
Lab facilities are great
Great library
Students aren't religious
Students environmentally aware
Easy to get around campus
Recreation facilities are great
College radio is popular
Active minority support groups

ACADEMICS

Academic Rating	87
% students returning for sophomore year	81
% students graduating within 4 years	65
% students graduating within 6 years	76
Calendar	Semester
Student/faculty ratio	11:1
Profs interesting rating	92
Profs accessible rating	95

Most classes have 10–19 students.
Most lab/discussion sessions have
10–19 students.

MOST POPULAR MAJORS

Biology/Biological Sciences, General; Psychology,
General; Business Administration and
Management, General

STUDENTS SAY "..."

Academics

Armed with a "beautiful campus" and "excellent academics," the University of Puget Sound is a great option for anyone hoping to study in the Pacific Northwest. The school provides students with "an amazing support system" and truly strives to "help them [meet] their goal[s] in whatever capacity necessary." Academically, undergrads here are especially quick to highlight Puget Sound's "great arts programs, whether [in] English, music, or theater." They also applaud the fact that there are ample "project-based learning opportunities such as relevant work study [and] summer research for all majors and interests." Additionally, students benefit from small class sizes, which lead to plenty of "open discussion and interactive engagement with the course material." This also allows undergrads to develop "close student-professor relationships." And speaking of professors, they work hard to ensure their classes are "challenging" yet "accessible." Importantly, "they have open office hours that all students are encouraged to attend, and there is no shame in [doing so]." As one grateful student sums up, "Professors are genuinely excited to make time for students in their schedule for advice, homework help, or even just sharing a coffee. The level of concern of the professors for undergraduate education is almost unmatched."

Life

It's no secret that undergrads at Puget Sound are "very dedicated to their studies." In fact, "most students have a fun time studying in [the] two different cafés on campus." Of course, even these dedicated scholars need to kick back, so they frequently take advantage of the various "performances, talks, or events going on almost every week." Additionally, many students flock to "the athletic center to get in a workout, attend a dance class, or rock climb." A good number also participate in "at least one club or are [involved] in Greek life." Puget Sound undergrads report that "on any given Friday night you can find a party" to attend. No need to worry if that's not your scene. Students here are an "outdoorsy" lot, and when the weekend rolls around, many of them can be found "hiking, skiing, kayaking" or "[taking] camping trips to the Olympic Peninsula or out to Eastern Washington." People are also just as happy to stay local and explore all that the surrounding area has to offer including "the Bridge of Glass, Point Defiance park, and the Puget Sound waterfront."

Student Body

At first glance, the University of Puget Sound's student body appears "fairly homogenous." After all, most undergrads come from "white middle-class families along the West Coast." However, the school is making strides to become "more diverse," especially "in terms of gender expression and sexuality." What's more, Puget Sound students are "not afraid to voice their [opinions or] their views [on] everything from political to social issues." In turn, students also caution that "more conservative views can [either] fall on deaf ears [or] can be met with a strong argument." However, others quickly assert that no matter your background or leanings, Puget Sound students are "open and welcoming to all." As one undergrad shares, "[Students are] not just nice in passing, but they have depth and consideration; when you run into someone in a café and [make] small talk, it doesn't feel surface level." This makes for a "general vibe ... [that is] laid back." Students also tend to describe their classmates as "unique," "adventurous," and "passionate" people who maintain a strong "desire for new experiences." Of course, if you're looking to easily pinpoint these undergrads, you'd simply say that the "typical [Puget Sound] student loves the outdoors, is a critical thinker, and knows what makes a good raincoat."

Financial Aid: 253-879-3214 • E-Mail: admission@pugetsound.edu • Website: www.pugetsound.edu

THE PRINCETON REVIEW SAYS

Admissions

Very important factors considered include: rigor of secondary school record, academic GPA, application essay, character/personal qualities. *Important factors considered include:* recommendation(s), extracurricular activities, talent/ability. *Other factors considered include:* class rank, standardized test scores (optional), interview, first generation, alumni/ae relation, racial/ethnic status, volunteer work, work experience, level of applicant's interest. ACT with or without writing accepted. SAT with or without Essay component accepted. High school diploma is required and GED is accepted. *Academic units recommended:* 4 English, 4 math, 4 science, 4 science labs, 3 foreign language, 3 social studies, 3 history, 1 visual/performing arts.

Financial Aid

Students should submit: FAFSA. Priority filing deadline is 1/15. The Princeton Review suggests that all financial aid forms be submitted as soon as possible after October 1. *Need-based scholarships/grants offered:* College/university scholarship or grant aid from institutional funds; Federal Pell; Private scholarships; SEOG; State scholarships/grants. *Loan aid offered:* Direct PLUS loans; Direct Subsidized Stafford Loans; Direct Unsubsidized Stafford Loans. Applicants will be notified of awards on or about 3/15. Federal Work-Study Program available. Institutional employment available.

The Inside Word

University of Puget Sound is a selective school, so gaining admission is certainly competitive. The college is eager to build a diverse student body that actively contributes to campus life. Thus, you can expect the admissions committee to take a holistic approach; everything from GPA to personal statements to extracurricular involvement will be closely considered. Nevertheless, the rigor of your high school curriculum will be of the utmost importance. It is also highly recommended that you sit for an interview, although it is not required. Finally, Puget Sound is a test optional school for most students (those who are home-schooled or attend secondary schools that don't assign grades must submit test scores). However, applicants who opt out will have to answer a few short, supplemental questions.

THE SCHOOL SAYS "..."

From the Admissions Office

"We're a classic, forward-thinking and entrepreneurial liberal arts college with a renowned School of Music and an innovative business and leadership program. Our 2,300 undergraduate students are proudly unclassifiable and universally kind. Our professors win a metric ton of teaching awards and do research with students that pushes the figurative envelope. We're ambitious and modest. We're collaborative and independent minded. We're rooted in the innovative Pacific Northwest and in love with the world. None of these things are contradictions. All of them make sense. They add up to an education that is perfectly suited to this vast, brave, unclassifiable world."

SELECTIVITY

Admissions Rating	83
# of applicants	5,182
% of applicants accepted	84
% of acceptees attending	14
# offered a place on the wait list	46
% accepting a place on wait list	30
% admitted from wait list	14
# of early decision applicants	80
% accepted early decision	81

FRESHMAN PROFILE

Range SAT EBRW	590–690
Range SAT Math	560–680
Range ACT Composite	25–30
# submitting SAT scores	362
% submitting SAT scores	59
# submitting ACT scores	230
% submitting ACT scores	37
Average HS GPA	3.6
% graduated top 10% of class	30
% graduated top 25% of class	64
% graduated top 50% of class	91

DEADLINES

Early decision	
Deadline	11/15
Notification	12/15
Early action	
Deadline	11/15
Notification	1/15
Regular	
Priority	1/15
Deadline	1/15
Notification	3/15
Nonfall registration?	Yes

FINANCIAL FACTS

Financial Aid Rating	87
Annual tuition	$53,520
Room and board	$13,480
Required fees	$280
Books and supplies	$1,000
Average frosh need-based scholarship	$35,896
Average UG need-based scholarship	$33,262
% needy frosh rec. need-based scholarship or grant aid	99
% needy UG rec. need-based scholarship or grant aid	99
% needy frosh rec. non-need-based scholarship or grant aid	16
% needy UG rec. non-need-based scholarship or grant aid	12
% needy frosh rec. need-based self-help aid	78
% needy UG rec. need-based self-help aid	78
% frosh rec. any financial aid	100
% UG rec. any financial aid	99
% UG borrow to pay for school	48
Average cumulative indebtedness	$36,290
% frosh need fully met	16
% ugrads need fully met	15
Average % of frosh need met	84
Average % of ugrad need met	80

UNIVERSITY OF REDLANDS

1200 E. Colton Avenue, Redlands, CA 92373-0999 • Admissions: 909-748-8074 • Fax: 909-335-4089

STUDENTS SAY "..."

Academics

A small institution in Redlands, California, offering both liberal arts and professional studies, the University of Redlands is passionate about "helping students find what they are interested in," and about "allowing them to pursue avenues that will make them successful throughout life." Boasting a small student-to-faculty ratio (12:1), and more than forty programs of study, this stunning West Coast university provides a "warm, friendly, and inspirational environment inside and outside classes." Most seniors complete a research capstone, and because Redlands is a liberal arts college, students "get a well-rounded education and can easily befriend students in other disciplines." Students love that Redlands is "not a super competitive nor a high-stress environment," and "the size of our classrooms (25 max students per class) ensures that we reach our full potential." The administration and professors "really care about the success students acquire," and the system is structured in a way that "caters to students off all mindsets." No matter how you learn, the University of Redlands "will cultivate and inspire you to be the better version of yourself."

Professors are "thoughtful, engaging, enthusiastic," "very personable," and "love [us] to use their first name and get to know each student individually." Instructors are "extremely knowledgeable in their field of study" and make an effort "to engage their students in discussions during class time rather than lecture." Almost all the professors are easily accessible either after class or during their office hours. This "intimate learning environment" caters to each person differently, and faculty remain "very attentive to [students'] needs." Although certain courses aren't offered every semester, they happen "often enough for students to take them," and some classes are split into two, allowing for "more variety."

Life

The University of Redlands "absolutely gorgeous" campus has "the classic feel of a small liberal arts university with the California vibe," with outdoor programs that give students "the opportunity to experience California." Academics fill Sundays through Thursdays, but many people also find time to "work out, go sit outside on the quad, go hiking, study in the library, or grab food with friends." Students also find it fun to go downtown, "especially on Thursdays for Market Night," and on weekends they can often be found nearby at the "beach, the mountains, Disneyland, or Los Angeles." ("Everything is about an hour away" from campus). Though there is a shuttle downtown, "one needs a car here to go do fun things," but "thankfully, parking is free." There are also "on-campus parties, outdoor program trips, and activities" provided through the school. Greek life and sports are big here, and "attendance at sports events is pretty impressive": Even during the week, "the student body tends to fill a majority of the student section at basketball games."

Student Body

This is a "truly inclusive," "ecologically-minded," student body, with the majority being "open-minded with liberal inclinations." Since this is a small campus, everyone is "really close," and "there is a niche for all types of people." "You can't go anywhere on campus without running into someone you know," says a student. It is easy to get involved on campus, and "there is a good dynamic between students and professors." There tends to be a bit of a divide between the 200 or so students living and studying in the Johnston Center for Integrative Studies (who are more on the "creative" side) and the College of Arts and Sciences: "a weird dynamic, not a bad or troubling one."

UNIVERSITY OF REDLANDS

Financial Aid: 909-748-8047 • E-Mail: admissions@redlands.edu • Website: www.redlands.edu

THE PRINCETON REVIEW SAYS

Admissions

Very important factors considered include: academic GPA. *Important factors considered include:* rigor of secondary school record, application essay, standardized test scores, recommendation(s). *Other factors considered include:* class rank, interview, extracurricular activities, talent/ability, character/personal qualities, first generation, alumni/ae relation, geographical residence, racial/ethnic status, volunteer work, work experience. ACT with or without writing accepted. SAT with or without Essay component accepted. High school diploma is required and GED is accepted. *Academic units required:* 4 English, 3 math, 2 science, 2 science labs, 2 foreign language, 2 social studies. *Academic units recommended:* 3 science, 3 foreign language, 3 social studies.

Financial Aid

Students should submit: FAFSA. Priority filing deadline is 11/15. The Princeton Review suggests that all financial aid forms be submitted as soon as possible after October 1. *Need-based scholarships/grants offered:* College/university scholarship or grant aid from institutional funds; Federal Pell; Private scholarships; SEOG; State scholarships/grants. *Loan aid offered:* Direct PLUS loans; Direct Subsidized Stafford Loans; Direct Unsubsidized Stafford Loans. Applicants will be notified of awards on a rolling basis beginning 2/17. Federal Work-Study Program available.

The Inside Word

The admit rate at the University of Redlands is 68 percent, and students with above-average high school records and respectable standardized test scores should consider the school a target. Candidates who are interested in pursuing the self-designed programs available through the Johnston Center will find the admissions process to be distinctly more personal. Note, though, that you have to be admitted as a regular student in the College of Arts and Sciences first.

THE SCHOOL SAYS "..."

From the Admissions Office

"We've created an unusually blended curriculum of the liberal arts and pre-professional study because we think education is about learning how to think and learning how to do. For example, our environmental studies students have synthesized their study of sociology, biology, and economics to develop an actual resource management plan for the local mountain communities. Our creative writing program encourages internships with publishing or television production companies. We educate managers, poets, environmental scientists, teachers, musicians, and speech therapists to be reflective about culture and society so that they can better understand and improve the world they'll enter upon graduation.

"First-year students applying for admission are required to submit the results of either the SAT or the ACT. We do not require the essay sections for either the SAT or ACT.

"International students for whom English is not their first language, may meet our English proficiency requirement through the SAT, ACT, TOEFL, or IELTS. Please check our website for score requirements."

SELECTIVITY
Admissions Rating	77
# of applicants	4,562
% of applicants accepted	75
% of acceptees attending	17
# offered a place on the wait list	40
% accepting a place on wait list	40
% admitted from wait list	100

FRESHMAN PROFILE
Range SAT EBRW	490–590
Range SAT Math	490–600
Range ACT Composite	22–27
# submitting SAT scores	428
% submitting SAT scores	72
# submitting ACT scores	290
% submitting ACT scores	49
Average HS GPA	3.5
% graduated top 10% of class	22
% graduated top 25% of class	55
% graduated top 50% of class	88

DEADLINES
Early action	
Deadline	11/15
Notification	1/15
Regular	
Priority	11/15
Deadline	1/15
Notification	Rolling, 1/10
Nonfall registration?	Yes

FINANCIAL FACTS
Financial Aid Rating	88
Annual tuition	$47,722
Room and board	$13,862
Required fees	$350
Books and supplies	$1,850
Average frosh need-based scholarship	$29,047
Average UG need-based scholarship	$28,598
% needy frosh rec. need-based scholarship or grant aid	100
% needy UG rec. need-based scholarship or grant aid	99
% needy frosh rec. non-need-based scholarship or grant aid	23
% needy UG rec. non-need-based scholarship or grant aid	21
% needy frosh rec. need-based self-help aid	81
% needy UG rec. need-based self-help aid	82
% frosh rec. any financial aid	94
% UG rec. any financial aid	94
% UG borrow to pay for school	68
Average cumulative indebtedness	$32,662
% frosh need fully met	27
% ugrads need fully met	25
Average % of frosh need met	84
Average % of ugrad need met	84

UNIVERSITY OF RHODE ISLAND

Newman Hall, Kingston, RI 02881 • Admissions: 401-874-7100 • Fax: 401-874-5523

STUDENTS SAY "..."

Academics

Located in the village of Kingston in the southern part of the state, The University of Rhode Island is a public research institution known for having "excellent science programs," including a "marine biology program [that] is one of the best in the Northeast." URI is a school that challenges me to think big and outside the box," says one student. Other stand-out majors include "nursing, pharmacy," which students feel is "excellent—one of the top in the country," and engineering." Students feel that "all professors have a unique style of teaching. Most are very willing to adapt their style to fit students' needs though" and many "are able to share stories from their experiences that make the material more accessible and interesting." Another student observes that the staff is also "great at helping freshmen transferring from home to college, and there are lots of different programs offered to help students excel academically." Overall, URI is known to have a solid liberal ideology with "openness to creative and critical exploration." This engineering major finds the environment to be rather "forward-thinking [with an] emphasis on today's global workforce."

Life

The school's proximity to the beach and to other major cities like Providence and Boston make it appealing to students from all over the Northeast. One student reports that "driving to one of the nearby beaches to just clear your mind and relax is one of the many benefits of URI's location." Students are said to have a "two brain track" in terms of serious attention to study followed by equal attention to "relaxing and having a good time." If fine dining is meaningful to your quality of life, it's worth noting that URI's dining hall has "won a national award the past two years in a row." And, while there are complaints about the dry campus, one senior notes that this is a surmountable obstacle, in that "people usually live in the surrounding neighborhoods, so you can travel to your friends' houses and party." Others say that students who live nearby still choose to stay on campus during weekends, since this is where their social life is centered. Life isn't all about "getting wasted," chides one sophomore. "Sometimes we get together [to] make dinner and just have a movie night inside our apartment."

Student Body

URI, as an affordable state school, naturally attracts a large percentage of Rhode Islanders. Rumor has it that this group "sticks to their friends from high school," yet one undergrad observes, "Rhody-borns are so afraid of college turning into another four years of high school that we go searching for new people to meet." The typical URI student "is involved in at least one student organization, but many are involved in more than one. They usually go out about once a week on average and study about an hour a day." There are "many students...involved in at least one type of extracurricular activity," "then there are students who are not involved at all." Campus diversity is strong, and most groups intermingle without issue.

UNIVERSITY OF RHODE ISLAND

Financial Aid: 401-874-7530 • E-Mail: admission@uri.edu • Website: www.uri.edu

THE PRINCETON REVIEW SAYS

Admissions

Very important factors considered include: rigor of secondary school record, academic GPA. *Important factors considered include:* standardized test scores. *Other factors considered include:* class rank, application essay, recommendation(s), extracurricular activities, talent/ability, character/personal qualities, first generation, alumni/ae relation, geographical residence, state residency, racial/ethnic status, volunteer work, work experience, level of applicant's interest. ACT with or without writing accepted. SAT with or without Essay component accepted. High school diploma is required and GED is accepted. *Academic units required:* 4 English, 3 math, 2 science, 1 science lab, 2 foreign language, 2 social studies, 5 academic electives.

Financial Aid

Students should submit: FAFSA. Priority filing deadline is 3/1. The Princeton Review suggests that all financial aid forms be submitted as soon as possible after October 1. *Need-based scholarships/grants offered:* College/university scholarship or grant aid from institutional funds; Federal Pell; Private scholarships; SEOG; State scholarships/grants; United Negro College Fund. *Loan aid offered:* Direct PLUS loans; Direct Subsidized Stafford Loans; Direct Unsubsidized Stafford Loans. Applicants will be notified of awards on a rolling basis beginning 3/15. Federal Work-Study Program available. Institutional employment available.

The Inside Word

Applications here are evaluated on the basis of course selection, academic performance, standardized test scores, and unique talents. Don't forget to apply to URI's merit-based scholarships, which are open to international students as well. Remember if you're a resident of another New England state (besides Rhode Island) you may be eligible, depending on your major, for discounted tuition.

THE SCHOOL SAYS "..."

From the Admissions Office

"One only needs to visit this beautiful school to know that it is a university on the move. In the past twelve years, URI has invested over $900 million in new facilities and improvements. The most recent two are the new $150 million engineering complex and a new 500-bed residence hall. Couple these enhancements with the hiring of 346 new faculty members in the last eight years, one can see the transformation of this university.

"The University of Rhode Island is competitively priced, especially for out-of-state students. The University offers a range of merit scholarships to students who have demonstrated academic success in a challenging college preparatory curriculum. You may be eligible for these awards if you have earned a recalculated GPA of 3.2 on a 4.0 scale at the end of your junior year, as well as a minimum required SAT score of 1130 or ACT score of 23, and have demonstrated leadership and involvement in your school and/or community. All applicants are considered for these scholarships by submitting a complete application by February 1. There is no separate scholarship application. Please note that merit scholarships for first-year students are awarded only to students enrolling in the fall semester. To be considered for our highest scholarships, we recommend that you apply by our December 1 Early Action deadline. We also strongly recommend that students interested in engineering, nursing, and the doctorate in pharmacy apply by December 1 as spaces are limited in these programs."

SELECTIVITY

Admissions Rating	82
# of applicants	21,259
% of applicants accepted	72
% of acceptees attending	21
# offered a place on the wait list	1,340
% accepting a place on wait list	35
% admitted from wait list	19

FRESHMAN PROFILE

Range SAT EBRW	511–668
Range SAT Math	501–677
Range SAT Composite	1029–1324
Range ACT Composite	20–29
# submitting SAT scores	2,751
% submitting SAT scores	92
# submitting ACT scores	454
% submitting ACT scores	15
Average HS GPA	3.5
% graduated top 10% of class	18
% graduated top 25% of class	49
% graduated top 50% of class	85

DEADLINES

Early action	
Deadline	12/1
Notification	1/31
Regular	
Deadline	2/1
Notification	3/31
Nonfall registration?	Yes

FINANCIAL FACTS

Financial Aid Rating	85
Annual in-state tuition	$12,590
Annual out-of-state tuition	$29,710
Room and board	$12,510
Required fees	$1,976
Books and supplies	$1,250
Average frosh need-based scholarship	$10,885
Average UG need-based scholarship	$10,736
% needy frosh rec. need-based scholarship or grant aid	94
% needy UG rec. need-based scholarship or grant aid	87
% needy frosh rec. non-need-based scholarship or grant aid	21
% needy UG rec. non-need-based scholarship or grant aid	12
% needy frosh rec. need-based self-help aid	82
% needy UG rec. need-based self-help aid	69
% frosh rec. any financial aid	91
% UG rec. any financial aid	90
% UG borrow to pay for school	63
Average cumulative indebtedness	$35,883
% frosh need fully met	63
% ugrads need fully met	45
Average % of frosh need met	68
Average % of ugrad need met	57

UNIVERSITY OF RICHMOND

Queally Center: 142 UR Drive, University of Richmond, VA 23173 • Admissions: 804-289-8640 • Fax: 804-287-6003

CAMPUS LIFE

Quality of Life Rating	95
Fire Safety Rating	94
Green Rating	95
Type of school	Private
Environment	City

STUDENTS

Total undergrad enrollment	3,069
% male/female	48/52
% from out of state	76
% frosh from public high school	59
% frosh live on campus	99
% ugrads live on campus	91
# of fraternities (% ugrad men join)	8 (18)
# of sororities (% ugrad women join)	8 (27)
% African American	7
% Asian	7
% Caucasian	58
% Hispanic	9
% Native American	<1
% Pacific Islander	0
% Two or more races	5
% Race and/or ethnicity unknown	4
% international	9
# of countries represented	63

SURVEY SAYS . . .

Students always studying
Students are happy
Classroom facilities are great
Lab facilities are great
Great library
Career services are great
Internships are widely available
Class discussions encouraged
School is well run
Students love Richmond, VA
Great food on campus
Great off-campus food
Easy to get around campus
Recreation facilities are great
Lots of beer drinking
Frats and sororities are popular
Active student government

ACADEMICS

Academic Rating	95
% students returning for sophomore year	94
% students graduating within 4 years	84
% students graduating within 6 years	89
Calendar	Semester
Student/faculty ratio	8:1
Profs interesting rating	94
Profs accessible rating	98

Most classes have 10–19 students.
Most lab/discussion sessions have
10–19 students.

MOST POPULAR MAJORS

Biology/Biological Sciences, General; Business
Administration and Management, General;
Organizational Behavior Studies

STUDENTS SAY "..."

Academics

At the University of Richmond, students "like to enjoy themselves but most have their priorities straight," and they know that "school comes first." As one student puts it, "There is a good balance of work and play here, and students are competitive, but to a healthy extent. The expectations for students here really push you to be involved, get at least two internships or research opportunities, and secure a good job by graduation." Students praise the University of Richmond's "unparalleled resources," particularly the "high number of research, internship, and study abroad opportunities available." As one business administration major gushes, at the University of Richmond "we combine the resources of a major research institution, the breadth of development of a liberal arts education, and amplifying effect of out of classroom opportunities (speakers, programs, student activities) to deliver an undergraduate experience that is both unique to every student and universally top notch." One key resource available to all students that "the university is willing to pay $4,000 for all students to participate in an [otherwise unpaid] internship, research opportunity, or project." This allows all students "an opportunity to have meaningful, career-oriented experiences." Professors at the University of Richmond earn generally high marks, with one student admitting, "My professors showed me how to love to learn again." Another echoes that "the entire University of Richmond staff treats everyone like an individual and not just another student circling through the system." "The schoolwork is difficult, but manageable," and "Richmond is incredibly generous with not only need-based but merit-based aid, which is unusual for liberal arts colleges of a similar caliber."

Life

"The student body is academic but also enjoys having a social life," and which tends to be centered on the Greek system. Though there are no dedicated fraternity or sorority houses on campus (lodges are "our equivalent of Greek houses" where Greek events are thrown), "the social scene is generally dominated by events thrown by Greek life; however, these events are open to all students no matter your affiliation." Most students are involved in more than one extracurricular activity: "There's also plenty to get involved with, so you would have a hard time finding a student who is not involved with some sport, artistic group, club, or organization." As one student puts it, "Everyone is doing some sort of juggling act," but "students are also academically driven, and because classes are difficult and demanding, people will find themselves doing a lot of academic work throughout the week." Weekends are a time to kick back and enjoy what Richmond has to offer in the way of "clubs downtown," "the Virginia Museum of Fine Arts, over 900 restaurants, Carytown (a hipster area with boutiques and unique restaurants), various festivals and events and athletic competitions."

Student Body

"In general, the typical Richmond student cares not only about performing extremely well in class and extracurriculars, but knows it is important to look the part, as well." Some students say that the University of Richmond is getting more diverse, branching out from "New England prepsters and Old South heirs/heiresses" to a more inclusive view that sees the university's students as "diverse, from their backgrounds, races, religions, and ethnicity to their interests, beliefs, goals, and hobbies." One student estimates that "fraternity brothers [and] sorority girls are a large group." But there "is no cut throat competition to do better than your peers when it comes to grades—students are laid back in the sense that they are happy to see their peers do well." Students stress the friendliness of their fellow Spiders, saying, "Everyone that I have met has been super helpful and kind—even as a first year."

Financial Aid: 804-289-8438 • E-Mail: admission@richmond.edu • Website: www.richmond.edu

THE PRINCETON REVIEW SAYS

Admissions

Very important factors considered include: rigor of secondary school record, academic GPA. *Important factors considered include:* class rank, application essay, standardized test scores, recommendation(s), extracurricular activities, talent/ability, character/personal qualities. *Other factors considered include:* first generation, alumni/ae relation, geographical residence, state residency, racial/ethnic status, volunteer work, work experience, level of applicant's interest. ACT with or without writing accepted. SAT with or without Essay component accepted. High school diploma is required and GED is accepted. *Academic units required:* 4 English, 3 math, 2 science, 2 science labs, 2 foreign language, 2 history. *Academic units recommended:* 4 English, 4 math, 4 science, 4 science labs, 4 foreign language, 4 history.

Financial Aid

Students should submit: CSS/Financial Aid PROFILE; FAFSA; Noncustodial PROFILE. The Princeton Review suggests that all financial aid forms be submitted as soon as possible after October 1. *Need-based scholarships/grants offered:* College/university scholarship or grant aid from institutional funds; Federal Pell; Private scholarships; SEOG; State scholarships/grants. *Loan aid offered:* Direct PLUS loans; Direct Subsidized Stafford Loans; Direct Unsubsidized Stafford Loans. Applicants will be notified of awards on or about 4/1. Federal Work-Study Program available. Institutional employment available.

The Inside Word

University of Richmond office of admission takes a holistic view towards applications, and demonstration of character, leadership, and independence is evaluated alongside academic record. That said, applicants will need strong transcripts and high test scores to compete in this applicant pool. The school offers generous merit-based scholarships to those who demonstrate exemplary academic achievement.

THE SCHOOL SAYS "..."

From the Admissions Office

"University of Richmond is one of less than one percent of colleges that is need blind and meets 100 percent of demonstrated financial need for U.S. citizens and permanent residents. University of Richmond combines the characteristics of a small college with the dynamics and resources of a large university. Our unique size, beautiful suburban campus and outstanding facilities offer students an extraordinary range of opportunities for intellectual achievement and personal growth. While faculty-student interaction and dialogue are at the forefront of the academic experience, research, internships and international experiences are important components of students' lives. Richmond is committed to providing students with rigorous academics and experiential learning. The university offers funding for undergraduate research, summer fellowships and internships. Our global approach to education shines through our many study-abroad and language immersion programs. We are committed to diversity and believe in leveraging its benefits in all aspects of college life. The student body is composed of scholars from a variety of backgrounds. Nearly one in four undergraduates is a domestic student of color; one in seven is the first in his or her family to attend college; one in eleven is an international student; and 76 percent hail from outside of Virginia. The University of Richmond is planning a temporary change in its admission practice by providing a test-optional policy for first-year students entering in 2021. Students who wish to do so may still choose to submit standardized test results or other materials to support their applications for admission."

SELECTIVITY

Admissions Rating	95
# of applicants	12,356
% of applicants accepted	28
% of acceptees attending	23
# offered a place on the wait list	4,027
% accepting a place on wait list	31
% admitted from wait list	6
# of early decision applicants	725
% accepted early decision	48

FRESHMAN PROFILE

Range SAT EBRW	640–710
Range SAT Math	650–750
Range SAT Composite	1300–1450
Range ACT Composite	30–33
# submitting SAT scores	536
% submitting SAT scores	64
# submitting ACT scores	296
% submitting ACT scores	36
% graduated top 10% of class	59
% graduated top 25% of class	86
% graduated top 50% of class	96

DEADLINES

Early decision	
Deadline	11/1
Notification	12/15
Other ED Deadline	1/15
Other ED Notification	2/15
Early action	
Deadline	11/1
Notification	1/20
Regular	
Deadline	1/15
Notification	4/1
Nonfall registration?	No

APPLICANTS ALSO LOOK AT AND OFTEN PREFER
Georgetown University; University of Virginia; Boston College; William & Mary; University of Pennsylvania

AND SOMETIMES PREFER
The University of North Carolina at Chapel Hill; Emory University; Wake Forest University; Washington University in St. Louis; University of Southern California

FINANCIAL FACTS

Financial Aid Rating	91
Annual tuition	$56,860
Room and board	$13,430
Books and supplies	$1,100
Average frosh need-based scholarship	$46,186
Average UG need-based scholarship	$45,919
% needy frosh rec. need-based scholarship or grant aid	99
% needy UG rec. need-based scholarship or grant aid	98
% needy frosh rec. non-need-based scholarship or grant aid	24
% needy UG rec. non-need-based scholarship or grant aid	19
% needy frosh rec. need-based self-help aid	72
% needy UG rec. need-based self-help aid	78
% frosh rec. any financial aid	61
% UG rec. any financial aid	68
% UG borrow to pay for school	41
Average cumulative indebtedness	$28,341
% frosh need fully met	89
% ugrads need fully met	83
Average % of frosh need met	100
Average % of ugrad need met	100

UNIVERSITY OF ROCHESTER

300 Wilson Blvd., Rochester, NY 14627 • Admissions: 585-275-3221 • Fax: 585-461-4595

STUDENTS SAY "..."

Academics

The University of Rochester is a private research university in western New York. The school's programs are rigorous, but students appreciate the freedom to create their own paths. Rochester "does not require general education classes, but instead encourages students to pursue their passions through the cluster system," which groups classes together in divisions of Humanities, Social Sciences, and Natural Sciences and Engineering. While the programs offer flexibility, the academic requirements are demanding, but regardless of field of study, "tutoring services, [the] University Counseling Center, and staff [who] focus on creating a supportive environment" are always available. "Most people ... spend all of their time studying," says one student. But the intellectual efforts come with benefits: the combination of motivated peers and academics "makes ... a better student and learner." Faculty also play an important role here with professors who are "really knowledgeable and passionate" about what they're teaching. One student comments that professors "keep material interesting, [are] approachable, and [are] very fair." And class structures are varied so as to "incorporate design thinking" or to feature "more interactive problems." Added benefits to that structure include "small class sizes and individual attention," and "so many opportunities ... [are] offered to students both inside and outside of class."

Life

University of Rochester is "very much an academically driven institution," and course work is the top priority. But as one student says, "The weekend [is] when most people fill their days with different activities." One such activity that many students rave about is movie night: "School movie nights are [the] best school-provided weekend activity." Athletics are, of course, present, but as one student notes, "Rochester varsity sports are not very competitive, [however] ... a lot of people ... do club sports." Other students mention weekend hikes, dance groups, plays and recitals. One thing to contend with at Rochester is the long winter; as some students put it, it's "winter 90 percent of the time." Both the school and students have adapted, and one student offers assurances that Rochester has "established a tunnel system which provides convenience." Dining halls on campus also provide comfort, and anyone looking for a tasty bite to eat can rest easy: "There are a bunch of places to eat on campus." Another way to socialize on campus is through Greek life, but even that is "not as fratty" as you'd expect. As for parties? "There is not a huge party scene on campus, but it's there if you want it," claims one Yellowjacket. Off-campus activities are plentiful, "if you have a car." Otherwise, students rely on the shuttle system. Overall, "there is always something to do on the weekend for entertainment" if students need a study break.

Student Body

Diversity is key at UR, "both [in] background and academic interests." As one student states, "In my class alone, 46 percent of us are international students." Those different backgrounds branch into an even wider range of activities. "Some [students] are filmmakers, some are dancers, some love sailing, some love art. Everyone has their own passions," another student describes. The variety is a benefit, with students claiming "the best thing about the UR community is that nobody can be put into a box." Undergrads describe their peers as "charmingly nerdy" or "chill nerds" who are "very down to have interesting and academic conversations." While most students are "academically focused" and "really care about what they do here," they are for the most part "more collaborative than competitive." "People range from passionate to apathetic, party animals to total nerds." However, amidst all the diversity is a strong sense of camaraderie, and "everyone holds each other accountable in terms of pursuing their absolute best."

Financial Aid: 585-275-3226 • E-Mail: admit@admissions.rochester.edu • Website: www.rochester.edu

THE PRINCETON REVIEW SAYS

Admissions

Very important factors considered include: rigor of secondary school record, recommendation(s), character/personal qualities. *Important factors considered include:* academic GPA, application essay, standardized test scores, interview, extracurricular activities, talent/ability. *Other factors considered include:* class rank, first generation, alumni/ae relation, geographical residence, racial/ethnic status, volunteer work, work experience, level of applicant's interest. ACT with or without writing accepted. SAT with or without Essay component accepted. High school diploma is required and GED is accepted.

Financial Aid

Students should submit: CSS/Financial Aid PROFILE; FAFSA; Noncustodial PROFILE; State aid form. Priority filing deadline is 2/15. The Princeton Review suggests that all financial aid forms be submitted as soon as possible after October 1. *Need-based scholarships/grants offered:* College/university scholarship or grant aid from institutional funds; Federal Pell; Private scholarships; SEOG; State scholarships/grants. *Loan aid offered:* Direct PLUS loans; Direct Subsidized Stafford Loans; Direct Unsubsidized Stafford Loans. Applicants will be notified of awards on or about 4/1. Federal Work-Study Program available. Institutional employment available.

The Inside Word

The University of Rochester's academic reputation is supported by its competitive 29 percent acceptance rate. The test-flexible policy considers a variety of academic records, including SAT, ACT, AP, IB, A-Level, SAT Subject exams, and many international exams. In addition to test scores, admissions officers take a holistic approach, seeking applicants from around the world who have demonstrated intellectual curiosity, extracurricular engagement, and ethical character. In-person interviews, held from July to January, offer prospective students an opportunity to stand out and are strongly recommended if you're seeking a merit-based scholarship.

THE SCHOOL SAYS "..."

From the Admissions Office

"Rochester believes that excellence requires freedom. In the Rochester Curriculum, students are free to select the courses that appeal to them most. There are no required subjects; students' interests drive their education. Students major in either sciences and engineering, humanities, or social sciences and complete a 'cluster' of at least three related courses in each of the other two areas. Because Rochester is among America's smallest research universities, its students can pursue advanced studies and research in graduate courses, in arts and science or in any one of Rochester's nationally ranked schools of engineering, medicine, nursing, music, education, and business.

"Learning here takes place on a personal scale. Rochester remains one of the most collegiate among top research universities, with smaller classes and a ten to one student-faculty ratio—all within a university setting that attracts more than $400 million in research funding each year. Rochester faculty publish articles across the globe, win awards for their work, and collaborate with undergraduate students on a level that is rare in higher education.

"The expectation is that each student will live up to Rochester's motto, 'Meliora' (ever better), recognizing that they are future leaders in industry, education, and culture. Navigating through world-renowned facilities and resources, a day in the life of two Rochester students or any two days in the life of a single student are never the same."

SELECTIVITY

Admissions Rating	94
# of applicants	20,474
% of applicants accepted	30
% of acceptees attending	23
# offered a place on the wait list	3,605
% accepting a place on wait list	65
% admitted from wait list	3
# of early decision applicants	1,567
% accepted early decision	33

FRESHMAN PROFILE

Range SAT EBRW	640–720
Range SAT Math	670–780
Range SAT Composite	1320–1460
Range ACT Composite	30–34
% submitting SAT scores	72
% submitting ACT scores	31
Average HS GPA	3.7
% graduated top 10% of class	69
% graduated top 25% of class	95
% graduated top 50% of class	100

DEADLINES

Early decision	
Deadline	11/1
Notification	12/15
Other ED Deadline	1/5
Other ED Notification	2/7
Regular	
Priority	12/1
Deadline	1/5
Notification	3/15
Nonfall registration?	Yes

FINANCIAL FACTS

Financial Aid Rating	96
Annual tuition	$55,040
Room and board	$16,548
Required fees	$990
Books and supplies	$1,310
Average frosh need-based scholarship	$48,013
Average UG need-based scholarship	$46,633
% needy frosh rec. need-based scholarship or grant aid	99
% needy UG rec. need-based scholarship or grant aid	99
% needy frosh rec. non-need-based scholarship or grant aid	16
% needy UG rec. non-need-based scholarship or grant aid	12
% needy frosh rec. need-based self-help aid	79
% needy UG rec. need-based self-help aid	82
% frosh rec. any financial aid	85
% UG borrow to pay for school	55
Average cumulative indebtedness	$28,503
% frosh need fully met	93
% ugrads need fully met	91
Average % of frosh need met	98
Average % of ugrad need met	96

UNIVERSITY OF SAN DIEGO

5998 Alcala Park, San Diego, CA 92110-2492 • Admissions: 619-260-4506 • Fax: 619-260-6836

STUDENTS SAY "..."

Academics

The University of San Diego is a private Catholic institution that prides itself on its status as a "Changemaker," which represents its dedication to creating sustainable solutions locally and afar. In fact, 50 percent of students take advantage of the school's vast study abroad network, which includes programs and internships in forty-four countries. "USD encourages its students to apply what they learn in the world to make positive, impactful, sustainable change," says one. Strong curricula and academic advising help students construct four-year plans and create enjoyable schedules, and "projects, seminars, field trips, study abroad programs, and team-taught courses are some of the ways the university gets students engaged." "My class took a trip to the U.S.-Mexico border and talked to border patrol agents, and then we went to an immigrant safe house facility to talk to people who help immigrants with their visa/citizenship status," says one student.

Professors "are eager to share" their passion for their subject with students and offer "personalized one-on-one learning through office hours." They "communicate directly with the students on what material they find to be important." Most "adapt to the new research that has come out on how students learn best" and "bring in speakers to show how [students] can implement Changemaking into ... future classrooms." That also extends into "many informative meetings about research opportunities and internships." Speaking of which, the "Career Center [is] very helpful with landing students jobs."

Life

The "weather is so perfect and the campus so beautiful [that] most students spend time outside" at USD, which is "ten minutes away from both the beach and city." Here it's easy for students to take their pick of a litany of activities—they can "lay out on the lawn, take in the sun, skateboard, surf, [or] go out in the town or beach." "San Diego [is] such a large city that there is so much to do and see," and weekends tend to be devoted to exploring; however, there are plenty of social activities and clubs to join on campus. The "Torero Program Board makes sure there is always something for the students to do." One student comments on the "very accepting Greek Life system," citing their motto: "These hands don't haze." Of all first-year students, 95 percent live on campus, and all first years (and transfers) participate in a Living Learning Community, which "puts people from the same general living area in a class together focused on a general theme" such as innovation or advocacy. USD is a place where students "can thrive because [their] physical and mental wellness is cared for alongside [their] education."

Student Body

This is "truly ... a campus of Changemakers" and "people passionate about causes [where] everyone is hard working yet still socially engaged." USD "does a great job of making sure that students feel like they have a home," and the school just recently "created a commons area where there are ... LGBTQ+, Black Students, Multicultural Students, and Women's commons." Because of the "sunny, more relaxed environment" students enjoy on this California campus, they lean "towards casual" in their attire—"balanced and stylish," as one student describes. Many here come from a "strong religious background and greatly utilize the ministry services on campus," and everyone is "welcoming and enjoyable to be around."

UNIVERSITY OF SAN DIEGO

Financial Aid: 619-260-4514 • E-Mail: admissions@sandiego.edu • Website: www.sandiego.edu

THE PRINCETON REVIEW SAYS

Admissions

Very important factors considered include: rigor of secondary school record, academic GPA, standardized test scores. *Important factors considered include:* class rank, application essay, recommendation(s), extracurricular activities, talent/ability, character/personal qualities, alumni/ae relation, religious affiliation/commitment, volunteer work. *Other factors considered include:* interview, first generation, geographical residence, racial/ethnic status, work experience, level of applicant's interest. ACT with or without writing accepted. SAT with or without Essay component accepted. High school diploma is required and GED is accepted. *Academic units required:* 4 English, 3 math, 3 science, 2 science labs, 3 foreign language, 2 social studies. *Academic units recommended:* 4 English, 4 math, 4 science, 3 science labs, 4 foreign language, 3 social studies.

Financial Aid

Students should submit: FAFSA. The Princeton Review suggests that all financial aid forms be submitted as soon as possible after October 1. *Need-based scholarships/grants offered:* College/university scholarship or grant aid from institutional funds; Federal Nursing Scholarships; Federal Pell; Private scholarships; SEOG; State scholarships/grants. *Loan aid offered:* Direct PLUS loans; Direct Subsidized Stafford Loans; Direct Unsubsidized Stafford Loans. Applicants will be notified of awards on a rolling basis beginning 3/1. Federal Work-Study Program available. Institutional employment available.

The Inside Word

Admissions officers at University of San Diego really aim to take a well-rounded approach to the application process. Hence, they thoroughly evaluate all aspects of a candidate's application, from test scores to personal statements and recommendations. Of course, since gaining admission to the university is competitive (each year USD admits around half of those who apply), a strong academic showing is a must, and the school calculates a weighted GPA that awards credit for any honors, AP, or IB classes that have been completed. Admissions officers really keep an eye out for students who demonstrate talent and leadership or who show genuine interest in participating in community service.

THE SCHOOL SAYS " . . ."

From the Admissions Office

"The University of San Diego has received many local, regional, and national honors in its short, sixty eight year history. We are known around the world for our beautiful campus, our outstanding faculty, our sustainability efforts, study abroad programs and the community service work done by our students. Perhaps most significantly, USD has been selected as a "changemaker" campus, one of only 36 in the world so designated by the Ashoka Foundation. It is this honor that captures the spirit of USD and ties together all the others.

"We believe that the world's problems can be solved. We believe that the solution to these problems will not be found through a single discipline or focus. Instead, we know that the world's problems will be solved through innovation, collaboration, and compassion. USD was founded six decades ago with the principles of Catholic social teaching, a living tradition to work for socially just and peaceful societies and a mission to prepare generations of people changing the world for the better.

"We seek students who also believe in social innovation and change. Students at USD are bright, as our rapidly-growing student profile attests. But they also bring a passion for learning and making a difference. Through our strong liberal arts curriculum, international experiences, faculty and programs, we take that passion and turn it into a lifetime of making the world a better place."

SELECTIVITY

Admissions Rating	88
# of applicants	13,755
% of applicants accepted	49
% of acceptees attending	17
# offered a place on the wait list	2,529
% accepting a place on wait list	37
% admitted from wait list	34

FRESHMAN PROFILE

Range SAT EBRW	600–680
Range SAT Math	590–690
Range ACT Composite	26–31
# submitting SAT scores	788
% submitting SAT scores	69
# submitting ACT scores	489
% submitting ACT scores	43
Average HS GPA	3.9
% graduated top 10% of class	33
% graduated top 25% of class	74
% graduated top 50% of class	97

DEADLINES

Regular	
Deadline	12/15
Notification	Rolling, 2/20
Nonfall registration?	Yes

APPLICANTS ALSO LOOK AT AND OFTEN PREFER

University of California, Los Angeles; University of California—San Diego; University of Southern California; Loyola Marymount University

AND SOMETIMES PREFER

University of California, Irvine; Chapman University; San Diego State University; California Polytechnic State University; Santa Clara University; University of California—Santa Barbara

AND RARELY PREFER

Pepperdine University; University of San Francisco

FINANCIAL FACTS

Financial Aid Rating	86
Annual tuition	$50,450
Room and board	$14,126
Required fees	$736
Books and supplies	$1,970
Average frosh need-based scholarship	$33,573
Average UG need-based scholarship	$31,967
% needy frosh rec. need-based scholarship or grant aid	98
% needy UG rec. need-based scholarship or grant aid	97
% needy frosh rec. non-need-based scholarship or grant aid	54
% needy UG rec. non-need-based scholarship or grant aid	51
% needy frosh rec. need-based self-help aid	70
% needy UG rec. need-based self-help aid	74
% frosh rec. any financial aid	82
% UG rec. any financial aid	76
% UG borrow to pay for school	45
Average cumulative indebtedness	$30,497
% frosh need fully met	14
% ugrads need fully met	13
Average % of frosh need met	80
Average % of ugrad need met	74

UNIVERSITY OF SAN FRANCISCO

2130 Fulton Street, San Francisco, CA 94117 • Admissions: 415-422-6563 • Fax: 415-422-2217

STUDENTS SAY "..."

Academics

Students find the quality of University of San Francisco's location to be inseparable from the school's "small-ish private liberal arts college" appeal: "San Francisco is a global city with a wealth of opportunity." However, USF is more than a "diverse education in an even more diverse setting" in its "dedication to social justice." "USF is known for its Jesuit pursuit of social justice, and does so through philanthropy and a relatively left and liberal style of teaching." Undergrads love USF's "small class sizes, good work opportunities in the city," and "comprehensive core curriculum." "USF is interested in developing the individual into a strong leader with a particular emphasis on the forces of self-reflection and self-awareness," and the school's "Jesuit education…is outstanding for students who care about their community and the world beyond themselves." Holding true to its mission to students to "change the world from here," a USF education empowers students to make "an impact in the world in an area that you are passionate about." The "extremely talented, well-educated, hard-working, and passionate professors" are "well qualified and deeply care for my education," facilitating "fun and learning combined" in "interesting, engaging classes that are small." In class, students find "the opportunity to discuss, to ask questions, and to give feedback. It was not the professor's classroom, where the professor was controlling the classroom, it was our classroom, all of us together." Students are encouraged to think for themselves in an intellectual atmosphere that "emphasizes acceptance, diversity, and critical thinking." That said, the university offers plenty of support: "We have academic success advisers who help make sure we are on track with graduation, help with major changes, and choosing class schedules." USF's "very prestigious nursing program" and a "five-year program for obtaining a Master's in Education" stand out as major attractions, as do its "financial aid" resources.

Life

To many students, USF is all about "getting to know each other academically, socially and morally while allowing ourselves to get distracted by the city of San Francisco." One can't help but note that the campus is "in a beautiful location" that's "the ultimate city to be in as a young person," and "USF is located near the Haight, which means that there's always something to do even near the campus." "The Muni bus pass that USF gives you" makes it easy to get around the city (and also means that "public transportation becomes your best friend"), and "students very often go off-campus on weekends to visit tourist attractions, go hiking, explore new food places, go shopping," "hit the nightclubs and bars around the city," and enjoy "concerts and trips to various museums, shows, and performances." "The city is full of activities and free, fun things to do," and "whether you enjoy hiking and nature (Golden Gate Park) or enjoy small coffee shops for a nice read, you'll always be able to find something." USF tends not to "care for Greek life/sports," and on "weekends campus is barren because everyone is out exploring," but campus is still a "welcoming, second home for all of its students."

Student Body

At USF, students combine in "in one of the best cities in the world" to form what they perceive as "a culturally diverse community that teaches respect, dignity, and honor for all individuals." They describe themselves and their peers as "artistic, smart, morally sound," "quirky and interesting." True to San Francisco's long history as a home for immigrants and trailblazers, at USF, students will find a "very LGBT friendly environment" where it may even be "more normal to be diverse and weird or queer." Students "care about the community and believe in taking action to demonstrate their beliefs," and "the average student may be working for an NGO or volunteering regularly at one of the many non-profits in San Francisco." They "come from all over the world," as well as from many "different cultural backgrounds and hobbies and interests," but hold a common interest of being "committed to their education" and, for the most part, "everyone gets along very well."

UNIVERSITY OF SAN FRANCISCO

Financial Aid: 415-422-3387 • E-Mail: admission@usfca.edu • Website: www.usfca.edu

THE PRINCETON REVIEW SAYS

Admissions

Very important factors considered include: rigor of secondary school record, academic GPA. *Important factors considered include:* application essay, character/personal qualities, volunteer work. *Other factors considered include:* class rank, standardized test scores (optional), recommendation(s), interview, extracurricular activities, talent/ability, first generation, alumni/ae relation, racial/ethnic status, work experience, level of applicant's interest. ACT with or without writing accepted. SAT with or without Essay component accepted. High school diploma is required and GED is accepted. *Academic units required:* 4 English, 3 math, 2 science, 2 science labs, 2 foreign language, 3 social studies, 6 academic electives.

Financial Aid

Students should submit: FAFSA; State aid form. The Princeton Review suggests that all financial aid forms be submitted as soon as possible after October 1. *Need-based scholarships/grants offered:* College/university scholarship or grant aid from institutional funds; Federal Pell; Private scholarships; SEOG; State scholarships/grants. *Loan aid offered:* Direct PLUS loans; Direct Subsidized Stafford Loans; Direct Unsubsidized Stafford Loans. Applicants will be notified of awards on or around 4/1. Federal Work-Study Program available. Institutional employment available.

The Inside Word

USF offers attractive financial aid packages in a gorgeous city, but getting in isn't purely a competitive numbers game: successful applications show genuine intellectual and moral curiosity. Make sure there's real heart in your essay and recommendations. Also, interested students are encouraged to check out USF's early action and decision options and their multicultural recruitment.

THE SCHOOL SAYS "..."

From the Admissions Office

"The University of San Francisco has experienced a significant increase in applications for admission over the past five years. We select applicants with strong academic credentials who will make the most of the university's academic opportunities, location in San Francisco, and its mission to change the world from here. Community outreach and service to others, along with academic excellence, are characteristics that help distinguish those offered admission.

"SAT and ACT tests are optional for admission, but once admitted, students will be asked to provide their standardized test scores to be used in advising and course placement."

SELECTIVITY

Admissions Rating	85
# of applicants	21,867
% of applicants accepted	64
% of acceptees attending	9
# offered a place on the wait list	1,704
% accepting a place on wait list	51
% admitted from wait list	87
# of early decision applicants	203
% accepted early decision	33

FRESHMAN PROFILE

Range SAT EBRW	570–660
Range SAT Math	560–670
Range SAT Composite	1130–1310
Range ACT Composite	23–29
# submitting SAT scores	1,013
% submitting SAT scores	78
# submitting ACT scores	446
% submitting ACT scores	35
Average HS GPA	3.5
% graduated top 10% of class	32
% graduated top 25% of class	66
% graduated top 50% of class	95

DEADLINES

Early decision	
Deadline	11/1
Notification	12/1
Early action	
Deadline	11/1
Notification	12/14
Regular	
Priority	1/15
Deadline	1/15
Notification	Rolling, 3/15
Nonfall registration?	Yes

FINANCIAL FACTS

Financial Aid Rating	84
Annual tuition	$51,930
Room and board	$15,990
Required fees	$552
Books and supplies	$1,600
Average frosh need-based scholarship	$30,296
Average UG need-based scholarship	$29,709
% needy frosh rec. need-based scholarship or grant aid	99
% needy UG rec. need-based scholarship or grant aid	98
% needy frosh rec. non-need-based scholarship or grant aid	8
% needy UG rec. non-need-based scholarship or grant aid	6
% needy frosh rec. need-based self-help aid	76
% needy UG rec. need-based self-help aid	75
% frosh rec. any financial aid	87
% UG rec. any financial aid	81
% UG borrow to pay for school	49
Average cumulative indebtedness	$33,752
% frosh need fully met	9
% ugrads need fully met	7
Average % of frosh need met	68
Average % of ugrad need met	67

THE UNIVERSITY OF SCRANTON

800 Linden Street, Scranton, PA 18510 • Admissions: 570-941-7540 • Fax: 570-941-5928

STUDENTS SAY "..."

Academics

Pennsylvania's The University of Scranton does a tremendous job of creating a "home away from home" for its students. A Catholic and Jesuit institution with an undergraduate enrollment of around 3,800 students, The University of Scranton places an emphasis on "doing service for others," which is something that the students here appreciate. They also like the fact that they are required to take courses in the "humanities, philosophy, and theology irrespective of [their] major." In turn, this ensures that students receive a well-rounded education. While there are many fantastic departments, a lot of undergrads highlight Scranton's strong science programs, which result in a "high rate of students getting acceptance to medical schools." Inside the classroom, undergrads are generally greeted by "awesome," "caring" and "really supportive" professors. It's evident that they really "want their students to excel" and "care about their...success." As one grateful student recounts, "They are always open to meeting with you outside of class and love to talk about their topic of expertise." Even better, "they're just so engaging and really know how to present the material in such a way that it's interesting for us as students." Lastly, students applaud the "new improvements constantly being made to update campus including residence halls and academic buildings."

Life

Undergrads at The University of Scranton are an active lot. For starters, many students "utilize the gym either for lifting or to get [in] their cardio." They can also frequently be found "play[ing] pickup basketball games in the gymnasium." Moreover, when "the [weather] is nice out, people play football, baseball, frisbee, or other sports around campus." Of course, there are also plenty of activities beyond athletics. After all, Scranton offers over "eighty clubs and organizations, retreats...and service opportunities." One undergrad further elaborates, "There's always something fun to do on campus whether it be a comedy show or a paint night." And lots of students enjoy attending "Late-Night-Scranton," which often sponsors "movies, games, and free food." For those interested, you can typically find "parties every Thursday, Friday, and Saturday." However, there isn't too much peer pressure to attend. When students want a break from campus life, they can easily head into town. Indeed, "it's...fun to walk downtown by the courthouse square and grab coffee at the local cafes." Individuals that are hoping to get a little further away can easily "sign up for weekend trips to NYC to see a Broadway show or just to tour the city."

Student Body

On the surface The University of Scranton might not appear to be the most diverse school. After all, "the student body...is mostly white, upper middle class individuals from New Jersey, New York, Connecticut, and the greater Philadelphia area." Moreover, everyone seems to have "some sort of religious background." Fortunately, you'll still find an array of personality types. As one undergrad explains, "My peers are a diverse group of individuals that range from athletes and musicians [to] the academics and partiers." Regardless of background and interests, we're told that Scranton is filled with "lots of genuinely good people" who tend to be "laid back" and display a "casual vibe in clothing and demeanor." They're also quite "welcoming and friendly." As another impressed undergrad shares, "New people are constantly saying hi to you whenever you pass by." A fellow student immediately concurs adding, "Everyone is always holding doors or helping someone in need." But perhaps that's to be expected when you find yourself surrounded by individuals who are "exceptionally kind and upbeat." Ultimately Scranton students agree that, "We're all a family here. We look out for each other and help each other." And you can't really ask more of your classmates than that.

Financial Aid: 570-941-7701 • E-Mail: admissions@scranton.edu • Website: www.scranton.edu

THE PRINCETON REVIEW SAYS

Admissions

Very important factors considered include: rigor of secondary school record, class rank, academic GPA, standardized test scores. *Important factors considered include:* extracurricular activities. *Other factors considered include:* application essay, recommendation(s), interview, talent/ability, character/personal qualities, alumni/ae relation, volunteer work, work experience, level of applicant's interest. ACT with or without writing accepted. SAT with or without Essay component accepted. High school diploma is required and GED is accepted. *Academic units required:* 4 English, 3 math, 1 science, 2 foreign language, 2 history, 4 units from above areas or other academic areas. *Academic units recommended:* 4 English, 4 math, 2 science, 2 foreign language, 3 history.

Financial Aid

Students should submit: FAFSA; State aid form. Priority filing deadline is 2/15. The Princeton Review suggests that all financial aid forms be submitted as soon as possible after October 1. *Need-based scholarships/grants offered:* College/university scholarship or grant aid from institutional funds; Federal Pell; Private scholarships; SEOG; State scholarships/grants. *Loan aid offered:* Direct PLUS loans; Direct Subsidized Stafford Loans; Direct Unsubsidized Stafford Loans. Applicants will be notified of awards on a rolling basis beginning 1/15. Federal Work-Study Program available. Institutional employment available.

The Inside Word

When it comes to reviewing applicants, The University of Scranton takes a holistic approach. Everything from coursework and standardized test scores to leadership potential and community involvement will be considered. Science and health science majors are the most competitive programs, especially nursing and occupational therapy, and exceptional high school applicants can apply for a guaranteed seat in the Doctor of Physical Therapy program. All candidates hoping to gain entrance to those departments are highly encouraged to apply Early Action, which is non-binding.

THE SCHOOL SAYS "..."

From the Admissions Office

"The University of Scranton is a premier Catholic and Jesuit university that provides rigorous academics grounded in the liberal arts. Our fifty-eight-acre campus offers the best of both worlds—the city and the mountains. We are in the heart of the city of Scranton, in Pennsylvania's Pocono Northeast, just two hours from New York City and Philadelphia. In recent years, we have invested more than $245 million in campus improvements, including new residence halls, an athletics campus, a science center and the state-of-the-art Leahy Hall, which houses our physical therapy, occupational therapy and exercise science departments.

"This university is more than a respected institution; we are also a caring, nurturing community whose graduates are known for their devotion to the welfare of others and by their special commitment to social justice.

"We offer 68 majors, more than 80 clubs and organizations, and 23 Division III athletic teams to the 3,800 undergraduate students in attendance.

"Scranton develops leaders in every sense through rigorous preparation in students' chosen fields coupled with a commitment to educating the whole person. Students extend their academic experience through participation in honors programs, internships, faculty-student research and study abroad, and the university provides excellent preparation for medical and other health professions doctoral programs, law school, graduate school, and post-graduate fellowships and scholarships. Our AACSB-accredited Kania School of Management has received national recognition for our business programs.

"Students can apply online for free at scranton.edu/apply, or schedule a visit online at scranton.edu/visit or by calling us at 1-888-SCRANTON."

SELECTIVITY

Admissions Rating	83
# of applicants	9,545
% of applicants accepted	76
% of acceptees attending	14
# offered a place on the wait list	893
% accepting a place on wait list	18
% admitted from wait list	25

FRESHMAN PROFILE

Range SAT EBRW	570–650
Range SAT Math	550–660
Range ACT Composite	24–29
# submitting SAT scores	835
% submitting SAT scores	83
# submitting ACT scores	208
% submitting ACT scores	21
Average HS GPA	3.6
% graduated top 10% of class	34
% graduated top 25% of class	68
% graduated top 50% of class	92

DEADLINES

Early action	
Deadline	11/15
Notification	12/15
Regular	
Priority	11/15
Deadline	3/1
Notification	Rolling, 12/15
Nonfall registration?	Yes

FINANCIAL FACTS

Financial Aid Rating	84
Annual tuition	$44,132
Room and board	$15,182
Required fees	$400
Books and supplies	$1,300
Average frosh need-based scholarship	$15,786
Average UG need-based scholarship	$16,402
% needy frosh rec. need-based scholarship or grant aid	81
% needy UG rec. need-based scholarship or grant aid	82
% needy frosh rec. non-need-based scholarship or grant aid	83
% needy UG rec. non-need-based scholarship or grant aid	74
% needy frosh rec. need-based self-help aid	75
% needy UG rec. need-based self-help aid	78
% frosh rec. any financial aid	99
% UG rec. any financial aid	94
% UG borrow to pay for school	75
Average cumulative indebtedness	$41,570
% frosh need fully met	18
% ugrads need fully met	19
Average % of frosh need met	71
Average % of ugrad need met	69

THE UNIVERSITY OF THE SOUTH

735 University Avenue, Sewanee, TN 37383-1000 • Admissions: 931-598-1238 • Fax: 931-538-3248

STUDENTS SAY ". . ."

Academics

Courses are "demanding and strenuous" at The University of the South, "but not impossible." This private institution features small classes with a "strong emphasis on critical thinking and writing," and professors "know your name and care if you do well" because of that. Beyond that, teachers are "ridiculously accessible," host dinners, classes, or even "'Congratulations, you finished the final!' cookies" at their homes. (Students do note that lately the administration is not maintaining quite as low of a student-to-faculty ratio for intro-level courses.)

Overall, the campus community "loves and venerates our liberal-arts tradition," which emphasizes "learning and personal growth" and a "well-rounded education to use in careers and in life" over competition or job-specific training. Yet according to one student, the school "shows that you can get a good job with any degree here. Even the lampooned Art History major has a high job rate." Undergrads think confidently of their post-graduation prospects, giving credit once again to faculty who are "always willing to share their professional contacts" in addition to an "extensive alumni network [that] will support you after college" and the school's "great reputation around the South."

Life

The University of the South "facilitates the idea of [being] a Spartan: fit in both mind and body," a student shares. This is appropriate given the boundless outdoor activities the school's forested campus provides. The student body loves to rock climb, sunbathe, hike, swim, and mountain bike. Making the most of campus is a necessity as the school "is pretty isolated—Nashville is [an] hour away." When they're not outdoors, the library is the go-to spot for students "studying or catching up with friends." And although students "revolve their schedules around school work," weekends are generally occupied with "sporting events and parties." Greek life "serves as the central social network" of the school, although "it isn't the stereotypical Greek life where everyone must fit a cookie-cutter mold." Members proudly note that frats and sororities are welcoming and diverse: "parties are open to all students, making the environment very friendly." That said, students are divided on the issue of drinking and pledging, with some feeling that it is difficult to build a social life without joining Greek life, and others suggesting that there is "a large group of students who do not drink" to help provide alternatives. The popular Sewanee Outing Program leads trips on afternoons and weekends, and "for spring break, they're kayaking the Amazon river," says one excited student. For those more culturally inclined, options include "open mic nights, cinema guild, theatre, stand-up comedy, … academic lectures, poetry readings, [and] creative writing workshops."

Student Body

The University of the South students describe themselves as a mix of "preppy, work-hard-party-hard" types and "hemp-wearing hippies," although the "overlap between . . . groups is substantial." One student boasts: "It is a delicate balance that wouldn't work anywhere but here." That said, the school is concerned with traditions of courtesy, respect, and academic commitment," and has a reputation for conservative Southern values. The University of the South attracts "mostly white, wealthy, Southern students" who are "unique, fun, well-rounded, down-to-earth" and friendly. So, racially, "the campus isn't diverse, but it is growing." And the school itself has a mostly liberal student body and faculty, and "encourages diversity of faiths, backgrounds, sexual identities, etc." One thing students have in common is a "shared desire to excel in classes," and the "school spirit … bonds people" into a "tight-knit community" on campus. Students here are grateful that their peers are "unique in their passions and supportive of each other's endeavors" and that they "treat one another with a lot of respect."

THE UNIVERSITY OF THE SOUTH

Financial Aid: 931-598-1312 • E-Mail: admiss@sewanee.edu • Website: www.sewanee.edu

THE PRINCETON REVIEW SAYS

Admissions

Very important factors considered include: rigor of secondary school record, academic GPA, recommendation(s). *Important factors considered include:* application essay, extracurricular activities, character/personal qualities, volunteer work. *Other factors considered include:* class rank, standardized test scores, interview, talent/ability, first generation, alumni/ae relation, geographical residence, level of applicant's interest. ACT with or without writing accepted. SAT with or without Essay component accepted. High school diploma is required and GED is not accepted *Academic units required:* 4 English, 3 math, 2 science, 2 science labs, 2 foreign language, 1 social studies, 1 history. *Academic units recommended:* 4 English, 4 math, 4 science, 3 science labs, 4 foreign language, 2 social studies, 2 history.

Financial Aid

Students should submit: CSS/Financial Aid PROFILE; FAFSA. Priority filing deadline is 12/1. The Princeton Review suggests that all financial aid forms be submitted as soon as possible after October 1. *Need-based scholarships/grants offered:* College/university scholarship or grant aid from institutional funds; Federal Pell; Private scholarships; SEOG; State scholarships/grants. *Loan aid offered:* Direct PLUS loans; Direct Subsidized Stafford Loans; Direct Unsubsidized Stafford Loans. Applicants will be notified of awards on a rolling basis beginning 2/1. Federal Work-Study Program available. Institutional employment available.

The Inside Word

The admissions office at The University of the South is very personable and accessible to students. Its staff includes some of the most well-respected admissions professionals in the South, and that shows in the way they work with students. Despite a fairly high acceptance rate, candidates who take the admissions process here lightly may find themselves disappointed. Applicant evaluation is too personal for a lackadaisical approach to yield success. A demonstrated interest in attending, evidenced by campus visits or reaching out to the admissions office, is advised.

THE SCHOOL SAYS "..."

From the Admissions Office

"Sewanee is consistently ranked among the top tier of national liberal arts universities. Sewanee is committed to a rigorous academic curriculum that focuses on the liberal arts as the most enlightening and valuable form of undergraduate education. It offers 36 majors, 43 minors, and pre-professional programs including business, medicine, and education. Founded by leaders of the Episcopal Church in 1857, Sewanee continues to be owned by twenty-eight Episcopal dioceses in twelve states. The university is located on a 13,000-acre campus atop Tennessee's Cumberland Plateau between Chattanooga and Nashville. Largely forested, rich in biodiversity, this land is a distinctive asset offering an unparalleled outdoor laboratory and boundless recreational opportunities.

"The university has an impressive record of academic achievement—26 Rhodes Scholars and 34 NCAA postgraduate scholarship recipients have graduated from Sewanee. Four Tennessee Professors of the Year have been members of Sewanee's faculty. Professors are leading scholars and researchers with a commitment to teaching, and in Sewanee's close community they develop rich and enduring relationships with their students.

"As of 2009, prospective students may choose not to submit standardized test scores. Other critical factors long considered in the Sewanee admission process remain, including strength of the high school curriculum, high school academic performance, extracurricular activities, and evidence of character and talent."

SELECTIVITY

Admissions Rating	85
# of applicants	3,545
% of applicants accepted	67
% of acceptees attending	19
# offered a place on the wait list	466
% accepting a place on wait list	19
% admitted from wait list	14
# of early decision applicants	166
% accepted early decision	84

FRESHMAN PROFILE

Range SAT EBRW	580–680
Range SAT Math	570–660
Range SAT Composite	1160–1330
Range ACT Composite	25–30
# submitting SAT scores	176
% submitting SAT scores	40
# submitting ACT scores	268
% submitting ACT scores	61
% graduated top 10% of class	32
% graduated top 25% of class	60
% graduated top 50% of class	86

DEADLINES

Early decision	
Deadline	11/15
Notification	12/15
Other ED Deadline	1/15
Other ED Notification	2/15
Early action	
Deadline	12/1
Notification	2/15
Regular	
Deadline	2/1
Notification	3/31
Nonfall registration?	Yes

FINANCIAL FACTS

Financial Aid Rating	89
Annual tuition	$47,708
Room and board	$13,700
Required fees	$272
Books and supplies	$1,200
Average frosh need-based scholarship	$28,542
Average UG need-based scholarship	$30,501
% needy frosh rec. need-based scholarship or grant aid	98
% needy UG rec. need-based scholarship or grant aid	98
% needy frosh rec. non-need-based scholarship or grant aid	22
% needy UG rec. non-need-based scholarship or grant aid	20
% needy frosh rec. need-based self-help aid	76
% needy UG rec. need-based self-help aid	72
% frosh rec. any financial aid	95.9
% UG rec. any financial aid	93.4
% UG borrow to pay for school	44
Average cumulative indebtedness	$31,737
% frosh need fully met	31
% ugrads need fully met	33
Average % of frosh need met	77
Average % of ugrad need met	83

University of South Carolina—Columbia

Office of Undergraduate Admissions, Columbia, SC 29208 • Admissions: 803-777-7700 • Fax: 803-777-0101

CAMPUS LIFE

Quality of Life Rating	89
Fire Safety Rating	96
Green Rating	60*
Type of school	Public
Environment	City

STUDENTS

Total undergrad enrollment	27,066
% male/female	46/54
% from out of state	39
% frosh live on campus	94
% ugrads live on campus	27
# of fraternities (% ugrad men join)	22 (22)
# of sororities (% ugrad women join)	16 (33)
% African American	8
% Asian	3
% Caucasian	76
% Hispanic	5
% Native American	<1
% Pacific Islander	<1
% Two or more races	4
% Race and/or ethnicity unknown	1
% international	3
# of countries represented	115

SURVEY SAYS . . .

Lots of conservative students
Students are happy
Great library
Recreation facilities are great
Everyone loves the Fighting Gamecocks
Frats and sororities are popular
Campus newspaper is popular

ACADEMICS

Academic Rating	78
% students returning for sophomore year	89
% students graduating within 4 years	64
% students graduating within 6 years	77
Calendar	Semester
Student/faculty ratio	17:1
Profs interesting rating	86
Profs accessible rating	90

Most classes have 10–19 students.
Most lab/discussion sessions have
20–29 students.

MOST POPULAR MAJORS

Criminal Justice/Law Enforcement Administration;
Experimental Psychology; Registered Nursing,
Nursing Administration, Nursing Research and
Clinical Nursing

STUDENTS SAY "..."

Academics

More than 200 years of southern traditions and academic leadership provide the foundation for the University of South Carolina—Columbia, a historic institution that is "constantly working on being the absolute best university it can be for its students" and "open to any suggestions." The school provides "a wealth of opportunities for undergraduate research, study abroad, service learning, and unique organizations," and advisors and the Student Success Center are "always looking to help" students find post-graduation plans. "The University of South Carolina is about what you make it, as the university provides opportunities for everyone to make the absolute most of their time here," says one student.

Those who teach here are "intent on getting their students involved outside of the classroom," and "able to relate their in-class lectures to the real world." "I've had a ton of professors present me with opportunities for research, internship, or part-time employment on campus which has all developed me into being a very employable prospect upon graduation," says one student. While classes "can sometimes be very difficult," there are tutors and supplemental instructors through the university ("for free!") who "will always fill in the gaps that you are missing." UofSC's size "lends itself to interdisciplinary degree programs and individual projects," and faculty fosters academic exploration in asking for student opinions and "[encouraging] us to argue and consider other students' opinions."

Life

The students at the University of South Carolina are "extraordinarily social:" "From tailgates to intramural sports to Greek life, there is always something to do." Saturday football games are such a tradition that "traffic patterns are altered because it is such a huge deal." Traditions are "highly important" to the school, and events such as Tiger Burn and Homecoming are dotted throughout the year. Greene Street (the main street on campus) is closed off to traffic 24/7, which allows students to walk freely between classes and also allows organizations and activities such as Hip Hop Wednesdays and a farmer's market to take place. The weather is usually beautiful, and many students can be found "sitting on the horseshoe between classes or grabbing a bite to eat" or availing themselves of the "ton of outdoor recreation activities run through the university."

On the weekends, many upperclassmen spend time in Five Points, a "very student-friendly bar district beside campus," and Columbia's central location "grants shorter distances to the beach as well as the mountains"; the town itself is very easy to get around on foot and "very artsy." There is "literally a club for everything," from "skydiving to latin dance to language," and service opportunities are also very popular. Additionally, the amenities that UofSC provides are "phenomenal," and include everything from "free athletic tickets to twelve free counseling sessions a year." UofSC really cares about the well-being and safety of its students, and "offers so many things to help the students here to succeed."

Student Body

This medium-sized, genteel Southern institution is "all about being a family and feeling like the University of South Carolina is your home away from home." There is a "good mix" of people of different ethnicity, genders, and personalities, and a lot of the student body is "relatively laid-back in dress and attitude." There is "certainly that southern charm, especially because of the large Greek population" on campus, and this is "a unified student body in relation to each other and between students and faculty and staff." "The university welcomes everyone with open arms to make everyone feel included in the Gamecock experience," says a student.

UNIVERSITY OF SOUTH CAROLINA—COLUMBIA

Financial Aid: 803-777-8134 • E-Mail: admissions-ugrad@sc.edu • Website: www.sc.edu

THE PRINCETON REVIEW SAYS

Admissions

Very important factors considered include: rigor of secondary school record, academic GPA, standardized test scores. *Other factors considered include:* class rank, application essay, recommendation(s), extracurricular activities, talent/ability, character/personal qualities, first generation, state residency, racial/ethnic status, volunteer work, work experience. ACT with or without writing accepted. SAT with or without Essay component accepted. High school diploma is required and GED is accepted. *Academic units required:* 4 English, 4 math, 3 science, 3 science labs, 2 foreign language, 2 social studies, 1 history, 2 academic electives, 1 visual/performing arts, 1 unit from above areas or other academic areas.

Financial Aid

Students should submit: FAFSA. Priority filing deadline is 4/1. The Princeton Review suggests that all financial aid forms be submitted as soon as possible after October 1. *Need-based scholarships/grants offered:* College/university scholarship or grant aid from institutional funds; Federal Nursing Scholarships; Federal Pell; Private scholarships; SEOG; State scholarships/grants; United Negro College Fund. *Loan aid offered:* Direct PLUS loans; Direct Subsidized Stafford Loans; Direct Unsubsidized Stafford Loans. Applicants will be notified of awards on a rolling basis beginning 4/1. Federal Work-Study Program available. Institutional employment available.

The Inside Word

At University of South Carolina, as at most large schools, admissions decisions are based almost entirely on a prospective student's grades, test scores, and high school curriculum. A personal statement is required. Applicants with an A-minus average and SAT scores (Critical Reading plus Math) in the 1150–1280 range (or an ACT composite of 25–30) often get in. Higher standardized scores can offset a lower GPA, and vice versa.

THE SCHOOL SAYS "..."

From the Admissions Office

"The University of South Carolina is a destination of choice for students from all fifty states and more than 100 countries. UofSC is one of only forty public research institutions to earn both the top-tier research classification and the community service classification from the Carnegie Foundation. As early as their freshman year, undergraduates are encouraged to compete for research grants. As South Carolina's flagship institution, UofSC offers more than 300 degree programs. More than 35,000 students seek baccalaureate, masters, or doctoral degrees. UofSC is known for its top-ranked academic programs, including its international business and exercise science programs—both rated number one nationally. Other notable programs include chemical and nuclear engineering; health education; hotel, restaurant, and tourism; marine science; law; medicine; nursing; and psychology, among others. UofSC is recognized for its pioneering efforts in freshman outreach, and the South Carolina Honors College is ranked number one in the country compared to all other honors colleges in public university settings. UofSC offers student support in such areas as career development, leadership training, research grants, pre-professional planning, and study abroad. On campus, students enjoy a state-of-the-art fitness center, an 18,000-seat arena, an 80,000-seat stadium, and more than 400 student organizations. Off campus, South Carolina's world-famous beaches and the Blue Ridge Mountains are each less than a three-hour drive away. The University of South Carolina is located in the state's capital city, making it a great place for internships and job opportunities."

SELECTIVITY

Admissions Rating	86
# of applicants	31,268
% of applicants accepted	69
% of acceptees attending	29
# offered a place on the wait list	2,588
% accepting a place on wait list	0
% admitted from wait list	73

FRESHMAN PROFILE

Range SAT EBRW	600–680
Range SAT Math	580–690
Range ACT Composite	25–31
# submitting SAT scores	4,062
% submitting SAT scores	65
# submitting ACT scores	2,182
% submitting ACT scores	35
Average HS GPA	4.0
% graduated top 10% of class	28
% graduated top 25% of class	59
% graduated top 50% of class	90

DEADLINES

Early action	
Deadline	10/15
Notification	12/15
Regular	
Priority	12/1
Deadline	12/1
Notification	3/15
Nonfall registration?	Yes

FINANCIAL FACTS

Financial Aid Rating	81
Annual in-state tuition	$12,688
Annual out-of-state tuition	$33,928
Room and board	$12,184
Books and supplies	$1,085
Average frosh need-based scholarship	$6,767
Average UG need-based scholarship	$5,958
% needy frosh rec. need-based scholarship or grant aid	35
% needy UG rec. need-based scholarship or grant aid	43
% needy frosh rec. non-need-based scholarship or grant aid	93
% needy UG rec. non-need-based scholarship or grant aid	70
% needy frosh rec. need-based self-help aid	72
% needy UG rec. need-based self-help aid	78
% frosh rec. any financial aid	96
% UG rec. any financial aid	87
% UG borrow to pay for school	52
Average cumulative indebtedness	$30,449
% frosh need fully met	30
% ugrads need fully met	25
Average % of frosh need met	77
Average % of ugrad need met	72

THE UNIVERSITY OF SOUTH DAKOTA

414 East Clark, Vermillion, SD 57069 • Admissions: 605-677-5434 • Fax: 605-677-6323

STUDENTS SAY "..."

Academics

With an honors program that is "the best-kept secret in the country" and professors who are "nearly always willing to go the extra mile for students," the University of South Dakota offers a "great student to faculty communicative experience at a reasonable price." Numerous departments garner praise from students, and the University boasts winners "almost every year for big scholarships like the Goldwater and Truman, competing with big, Ivy League, private colleges that charge quadruple the amount for the same education." While the nursing school is the most frequently praised, the "business, biology, premed, law, and psychology classes are very solid," and the "dental hygiene, music, and journalism schools" also stand out, with the most copious laurels heaped on the music department's professors who are "some of the best." All told, the wide selection of quality academics "gives students many options as far as majors go," and for students willing to throw themselves into their studies, "the odds of getting into a professional or graduate program are good."

Life

"We work hard, so we can play hard," sums up the undergraduate philosophy at USD. "Although there is a lot of partying that happens, the students keep themselves occupied with school work, intramural sports, and hanging out with their friends." Vermillion's small size seems to be a double-edged sword; some insist that "the size of the town means no one is more than a 10-minute walk/bike ride away!" and that "since it is a smaller campus students have more opportunities to be involved in internships and various other activities." But the fact remains that "many of the upperclassmen live in the larger cities to the north and south." In general, "students have to make their own fun, which often involves partying or taking small road trips to other cities in the area." For those planning to roam further afield, "Vermillion is located very close to Yankton, Sioux City (IA), and Sioux Falls (all within an hour). They are bigger cities and offer everything a person would want to do (shopping, movies, entertainment)."

Student Body

A typical USD student "would be a conservative Midwesterner. He or she would be Caucasian" and would most likely have originated in "small towns in South Dakota, Iowa, and Nebraska." "Many people join a Greek system or are athletes or musicians. Those who do not fit into these three main groups seem to focus on their academics" and "[fit] in fine with the majority because of the open mindedness of most students." For example, "gay students are able to get along with the rest of student population." There's no denying that "partying is a definite part of the culture, though many of the 'smart' kids both party and work hard." Student organizations call out to many, and "it seems like every person on campus is part of at least one of them. It is a great way to meet new people and [to participate in] activities."

THE UNIVERSITY OF SOUTH DAKOTA

Financial Aid: 605-677-5446 • E-Mail: admissions@usd.edu • Website: www.usd.edu

THE PRINCETON REVIEW SAYS

Admissions

Very important factors considered include: rigor of secondary school record, class rank, academic GPA, standardized test scores. *Other factors considered include:* application essay, recommendation(s). ACT with or without writing accepted. SAT with or without Essay component accepted. High school diploma is required and GED is accepted. *Academic units required:* 4 English, 3 math, 3 science labs, 3 social studies. *Academic units recommended:* 4 math, 4 science, 2 foreign language.

Financial Aid

Students should submit: FAFSA. Priority filing deadline is 4/1. The Princeton Review suggests that all financial aid forms be submitted as soon as possible after October 1. *Need-based scholarships/grants offered:* College/university scholarship or grant aid from institutional funds; Federal Pell; Private scholarships; SEOG; State scholarships/grants; United Negro College Fund. *Loan aid offered:* Direct PLUS loans; Direct Subsidized Stafford Loans; Direct Unsubsidized Stafford Loans. Federal Work-Study Program available. Institutional employment available.

The Inside Word

To be a candidate for general admission to USD, you must meet one of three general requirements: rank in the top 50 percent of your graduating class or obtain an ACT/SAT composite score of 21/990 or higher or have a minimum grade point average of at least 2.6 on a 4.0 scale in all high school courses. An applicant's high school curricula must also meet certain minimum requirements.

THE SCHOOL SAYS "..."

From the Admissions Office

"The University of South Dakota is the perfect fit for students looking for a smart educational investment. USD is South Dakota's only designated liberal arts university and is consistently rated among the top doctoral institutions in the country. Annually, USD awards $7.2 million in scholarships. More than 80 percent of USD students receive financial aid through grants, loans and work-study jobs.

"USD students earn the nation's most prestigious scholarships. Our quality of teaching and research prepares students to pursue their passions all over the world, at institutions such as Columbia, Princeton, John Hopkins, Harvard Medical School, Massachusetts Institute of Technology, The University of Chicago and beyond. One hundred and three students have been awarded prestigious Fulbright, Rhodes, National Science Foundation, Boren, Truman, Udall, Gilman and Goldwater scholarships and grants for graduate study. Personal attention from our award-winning faculty and our welcoming environment makes students feel right at home.

"As the flagship liberal arts institution in South Dakota, USD—founded in 1862—has long been regarded as a leader in the state and the region. Notable undergraduate and postgraduate alumni include author and former news anchor Tom Brokaw, U.S. Senator Tim Johnson, U.S. Representative Kevin Brady, *USA Today* founder Al Neuharth and U.S. Senator John Thune.

"Applicants are not required to take the writing test for either SAT or ACT. USD recommends taking the ACT over the SAT. Students who wish to send their SAT scores will have their scores converted to ACT scores for placement and scholarship consideration."

SELECTIVITY

Admissions Rating	77
# of applicants	4,119
% of applicants accepted	86
% of acceptees attending	41

FRESHMAN PROFILE

Range SAT EBRW	520–620
Range SAT Math	510–640
Range ACT Composite	20–25
# submitting SAT scores	67
% submitting SAT scores	5
# submitting ACT scores	1,320
% submitting ACT scores	93
Average HS GPA	3.4
% graduated top 10% of class	13
% graduated top 25% of class	37
% graduated top 50% of class	68

DEADLINES

Regular	
Notification	Rolling, 8/1
Nonfall registration?	Yes

FINANCIAL FACTS

Financial Aid Rating	80
Annual in-state tuition	$7,697
Annual out-of-state tuition	$11,172
Room and board	$8,409
Required fees	$1,635
Books and supplies	$1,200
Average frosh need-based scholarship	$4,655
Average UG need-based scholarship	$4,720
% needy frosh rec. need-based scholarship or grant aid	45
% needy UG rec. need-based scholarship or grant aid	46
% needy frosh rec. non-need-based scholarship or grant aid	73
% needy UG rec. non-need-based scholarship or grant aid	57
% needy frosh rec. need-based self-help aid	80
% needy UG rec. need-based self-help aid	84
% frosh rec. any financial aid	94
% UG rec. any financial aid	81
% UG borrow to pay for school	73
Average cumulative indebtedness	$29,548
% frosh need fully met	19
% ugrads need fully met	16
Average % of frosh need met	57
Average % of ugrad need met	57

UNIVERSITY OF SOUTH FLORIDA

4202 East Fowler Avenue, Tampa, FL 33620-9951 • Admissions: 813-974-3350 • Fax: 813-974-9689

STUDENTS SAY "..."

Academics

The University of South Florida provides undergraduates with a "beautiful campus," a strong "sense of community," and "great financial aid," so it's easy to understand why students clamor to attend. From the moment you step onto the grounds, it's clear that the university is "committed to [your] success and [that] there are countless opportunities and support programs" available. This is showcased everywhere from the "many unique study abroad programs" to "tutoring [resources] for a variety of subjects." Academically, students are quick to highlight USF's "strong STEM programs" and note the abundance of "nursing/medical opportunities," which are courtesy of the university partnering with the "incredible [number] of hospitals in the vicinity." However, undergrads here have decidedly mixed reviews for their teachers. Indeed, they generally witness "less enthusiasm from [general education] professors." Fortunately, when it comes to their core major classes, students happily report that instructors are truly "passionate about what they teach." As one eager undergrad shares, "[Professors] go above and beyond to make their class lectures interesting and understandable." Students also enjoy the "blend of lecture and discussion" in courses. Another thrilled undergrad simply concludes, "My professors are the best [because they] encourage me not only with my work ... but also ... in my overall life."

Life

Admittedly, the University of South Florida has "a lot of commuters," but that doesn't mean the campus transforms into a ghost town once classes are finished! In fact, there are numerous activities and events of which to take advantage. For example, you can always find students enjoying "movies on the lawn, international fairs, [and] artistic presentations." Every Wednesday is "Bull Market, [which consists of] a collection of various student orgs and off-campus vendors ... giving away freebies ... or selling baked goods or raffle tickets to raise money." Need something a little more active? Well then you will be delighted to learn that "USF recreation ... has its own park where you can rent kayaks and go down the Hillsborough river." Of course, many undergrads simply love "lounging in a campus hammock" or kicking back in "the student commons [with some] foosball, video games, or pool." And when you need a respite from collegiate life, downtown Tampa also offers a good deal of excitement. There's a wide array of bars and restaurants as well as Busch Gardens, which is only "five minutes from campus ... [and] a popular hangout." The pristine beaches of St. Pete's and Walt Disney World are within driving distance as well.

Student Body

Undergrads at USF proudly proclaim that their school is "very diverse" and "like a mini-city." Indeed, you'll find "many cultures and ... tons of international students." "I have met such a variety of people from different ethnic backgrounds, religions, abilities, talents, ideologies, sexual orientations, gender expressions, interests, and life experiences," says a student. The age of students also varies widely on-campus, with one undergrad sharing, "I've seen students with grey hair, students who look fresh out of high school, and everything in between." Importantly, it's not hard for these Bulls to find common ground. That's because USF students are all typically "helpful, accommodating, and kind." Another student further explains, "My peers are very personable, smart, and caring. Everyone I met has helped me in some way and has been very pleasant to be around." And a fellow undergrad concurs by stating, "Everyone has an aura about them that makes you feel comfortable and welcomed."

UNIVERSITY OF SOUTH FLORIDA

Financial Aid: 813-974-3039 • E-Mail: admissions@usf.edu • Website: www.usf.edu

THE PRINCETON REVIEW SAYS

Admissions

Very important factors considered include: academic GPA, standardized test scores. *Important factors considered include:* rigor of secondary school record. *Other factors considered include:* class rank, talent/ability, first generation, geographical residence. ACT with or without writing accepted. SAT with or without Essay component accepted. High school diploma is required and GED is accepted. *Academic units required:* 4 English, 4 math, 3 science, 2 science labs, 2 foreign language, 3 social studies, 2 academic electives.

Financial Aid

Students should submit: FAFSA. Priority filing deadline is 1/1. The Princeton Review suggests that all financial aid forms be submitted as soon as possible after October 1. *Need-based scholarships/grants offered:* College/university scholarship or grant aid from institutional funds; Federal Pell; Private scholarships; SEOG; State scholarships/grants. *Loan aid offered:* Direct PLUS loans; Direct Subsidized Stafford Loans; Direct Unsubsidized Stafford Loans. Applicants will be notified of awards on a rolling basis beginning 3/1. Federal Work-Study Program available. Institutional employment available.

The Inside Word

USF keeps the admissions process streamlined and simplified. In other words, the university takes a fairly quantitative and objective approach, so expect that your GPA and standardized test scores will hold the most weight. The admissions committee will also consider the rigor of your coursework, which means applicants who have taken multiple AP, IB, honors, or AICE courses are at a definite advantage. Finally, grade trends also matter; don't panic if your high school career began inauspiciously as long as your grades steadily improved. If they declined over time, you may have to make up for that elsewhere in your application.

THE SCHOOL SAYS "..."

From the Admissions Office

"Located in the Tampa Bay metropolitan area, USF is recognized as a top-fifty public research university. USF takes great pride in its global faculty. Professors in all academic areas are responsible for discovering new solutions to existing and emerging problems. As an undergraduate at USF, you can participate actively in the creation of the knowledge that will be taught on other college campuses for decades to come. The faculty at USF is diverse as well.

"As students begin the application process, they should become familiar with USF's admission requirements. USF used extensive institutional research to validate that the high school GPA coupled with grade trends and the rigor of student's curriculum in high school are the most critical factors in student academic success at USF. Preference in admission, therefore, is given to students who complete at least three AP or IB courses, at least two college-level courses through dual enrollment, and additional coursework in math, science or foreign language beyond minimum requirements. SAT and ACT scores, while important, are less critical in USF's admission decisions when the high school GPA and rigor of curriculum are both strong. USF does use the SAT writing and the ACT English/writing components to make decisions, as scores of 550 and 24 respectively are additional indicators of potential for academic success. USF also takes into account special talents in and outside of the classroom as well as whether a student would be in the first generation of the family to attend college. With some of the best weather in the country, it's always a great time to visit USF. Campus tours, information sessions and tours of the residence halls are offered on weekdays throughout the year and on most Saturday mornings from September through April. Reservations are strongly encouraged."

SELECTIVITY

Admissions Rating	89
# of applicants	36,986
% of applicants accepted	48
% of acceptees attending	29

FRESHMAN PROFILE

Range SAT EBRW	590–660
Range SAT Math	580–670
Range SAT Composite	1180–1310
Range ACT Composite	25–29
# submitting SAT scores	3,799
% submitting SAT scores	74
# submitting ACT scores	1,339
% submitting ACT scores	26
Average HS GPA	4.0
% graduated top 10% of class	34
% graduated top 25% of class	68
% graduated top 50% of class	92

DEADLINES

Regular	
Priority	12/1
Deadline	4/1
Notification	Rolling, 11/15
Nonfall registration?	Yes

FINANCIAL FACTS

Financial Aid Rating	83
Annual in-state tuition	$4,559
Annual out-of-state tuition	$15,473
Room and board	$11,836
Required fees	$1,851
Books and supplies	$1,100
Average frosh need-based scholarship	$12,167
Average UG need-based scholarship	$9,911
% needy frosh rec. need-based scholarship or grant aid	93
% needy UG rec. need-based scholarship or grant aid	84
% needy frosh rec. non-need-based scholarship or grant aid	14
% needy UG rec. non-need-based scholarship or grant aid	6
% needy frosh rec. need-based self-help aid	40
% needy UG rec. need-based self-help aid	53
% frosh rec. any financial aid	97
% UG rec. any financial aid	78
% UG borrow to pay for school	50
Average cumulative indebtedness	$21,463
% frosh need fully met	21
% ugrads need fully met	13
Average % of frosh need met	73
Average % of ugrad need met	64

UNIVERSITY OF SOUTHERN CALIFORNIA

Office of Admission (University Park Campus), Los Angeles, CA 90089-0911 • Admissions: 213-740-1111 • Fax: 213-821-0200

CAMPUS LIFE
Quality of Life Rating	83
Fire Safety Rating	97
Green Rating	86
Type of school	Private
Environment	Metropolis

STUDENTS
Total undergrad enrollment	19,908
% male/female	48/52
% from out of state	35
% frosh from public high school	54
% frosh live on campus	98
% ugrads live on campus	30
# of fraternities (% ugrad men join)	32 (26)
# of sororities (% ugrad women join)	26 (27)
% African American	5
% Asian	21
% Caucasian	37
% Hispanic	16
% Native American	<1
% Pacific Islander	<1
% Two or more races	6
% Race and/or ethnicity unknown	2
% international	13
# of countries represented	114

SURVEY SAYS . . .
Everyone loves the Trojans
Theater is popular
Alumni active on campus

ACADEMICS
Academic Rating	81
% students returning for sophomore year	96
% students graduating within 4 years	77
% students graduating within 6 years	92
Calendar	Semester
Student/faculty ratio	8:1
Profs interesting rating	83
Profs accessible rating	88

Most classes have 10–19 students.
Most lab/discussion sessions have 20–29 students.

MOST POPULAR MAJORS
Visual and Performing Arts, General; Business Administration and Management, General; Social Sciences, General

STUDENTS SAY " . . ."

Academics

The University of Southern California boasts "a dynamic and culturally diverse campus located in a world-class city which is equally dynamic and culturally diverse." Everything related to cinema is "top notch." Among the other 150 or so majors here, programs in journalism, business, engineering, and architecture are particularly notable. The honors programs are "very good" too. One of the best perks about USC is its "large and enthusiastic alumni network." Becoming "part of the Trojan Family" is a great way to jumpstart your career because USC graduates love to hire other USC graduates. "Almost everyone talks about getting job offers based solely on going to USC." "The school seems to run very smoothly, with few administrative issues ever being problematic enough to reach the awareness of the USC student community," says an international relations major. The top brass "is a bit mysterious and heavy handed," though. Also, "they milk every dime they can get from you." Academically, some students call the general education courses "a complete waste of time." There are a few "real narcissists" on the faculty as well as some professors "who seem to just be there because they want to do research." Overall, though, students report professors "make the subject matter come alive" and make themselves "very available" outside the classroom. "My academic experience at USC is fabulous," gushes an aerospace engineering major. "I would not choose any other school."

Life

On campus, life is "vibrant." There are more than 850 student organizations. Theatrical and musical productions are "excellent." School spirit is "extreme" and "infectious." "Football games are huge." "There is absolutely nothing that can top watching our unbelievable football team throttle the competition," says a merciless sophomore. "Drinking is a big part of the social scene" as well. "We definitely have some of the sickest parties ever," claims an impressed freshman. "Greek life is very big" and, on the weekends, a strong contingent of students "religiously" visits "The Row, the street lined with all the fraternity and sorority houses." Students also have "the sprawling city of Los Angeles as their playground." It's an "eclectic place with both high and low culture and some of the best shopping in the world." "Hollywood clubs and downtown bars" are popular destinations. Art exhibits, concerts, and "hip restaurants" are everywhere. However, "you need a car." Los Angeles traffic may be "a buzz kill," but students report that it's considerably preferable to the "absolutely terrible" public transportation system.

Student Body

The one thing that unites everyone here is "tons of Trojan pride." USC students are also "intensely ambitious" and, while there are some "complete slackers," many students hit the books "harder than they let on." Otherwise, students insist that, "contrary to popular belief, USC has immense diversity." "The stereotypical USC student is a surfer fraternity bro or a tan, trendy sorority girl from the O.C." You'll find plenty of those. Many students are also "extremely good looking." "No one cares what your orientation is," says a first-year student. There are "prissy Los Angeles types" and "spoiled" kids. In some circles, "family income and the brands of clothes you wear definitely matter." However, "though there are quite a few who come from mega wealth, there are also many who are here on a great deal of financial aid." There are "lots of nerds," too, and a smattering of "band geeks and film freaks."

UNIVERSITY OF SOUTHERN CALIFORNIA

Financial Aid: 213-740-4444 • E-Mail: admitusc@usc.edu • Website: www.usc.edu

THE PRINCETON REVIEW SAYS

Admissions

Very important factors considered include: rigor of secondary school record, academic GPA, application essay, standardized test scores, recommendation(s). *Important factors considered include:* extracurricular activities, talent/ability, character/personal qualities. *Other factors considered include:* first generation, alumni/ae relation, racial/ethnic status, volunteer work, work experience. ACT with or without writing accepted. SAT with or without Essay component accepted. High school diploma is required and GED is not accepted. *Academic units required:* 4 English, 3 math, 2 science, 2 science labs, 2 foreign language, 2 social studies, 3 academic electives. *Academic units recommended:* 4 English, 4 math, 3 science, 3 science labs, 3 foreign language, 3 social studies, 3 academic electives.

Financial Aid

Students should submit: Business/Farm Supplement; CSS/Financial Aid PROFILE; FAFSA; Noncustodial PROFILE. Priority filing deadline is 2/17. The Princeton Review suggests that all financial aid forms be submitted as soon as possible after October 1. *Need-based scholarships/grants offered:* College/university scholarship or grant aid from institutional funds; Federal Pell; Private scholarships; SEOG; State scholarships/grants. *Loan aid offered:* Direct PLUS loans; Direct Subsidized Stafford Loans; Direct Unsubsidized Stafford Loans. Applicants will be notified of awards on or about 4/1. Federal Work-Study Program available. Institutional employment available.

The Inside Word

USC doesn't have the toughest admissions standards in California but it's up there. Your grades and test scores need to be outstanding to compete. Even if you are a borderline candidate, though, USC is certainly worth a shot. Few schools on the planet have a better alumni network and the "Trojan Family" really does create all kinds of opportunities for its members upon graduation.

THE SCHOOL SAYS " . . ."

From the Admissions Office

"One of the best ways to discover if USC is right for you is to walk around campus, talk to students, and get a feel for the area both as a place to study and a place to live. If you can't visit, we hold admission information programs around the country. Watch your mailbox for an invitation, or send us an e-mail if you're interested.

"Freshman applicants are required to submit a standardized writing exam. We will accept either the SAT or the ACT with its optional writing section."

SELECTIVITY

Admissions Rating	98
# of applicants	66,198
% of applicants accepted	11
% of acceptees attending	42

FRESHMAN PROFILE

Range SAT EBRW	670–740
Range SAT Math	690–790
Range ACT Composite	31–34
# submitting SAT scores	2,138
% submitting SAT scores	68
# submitting ACT scores	1,337
% submitting ACT scores	42
Average HS GPA	3.8
% graduated top 10% of class	0
% graduated top 25% of class	0
% graduated top 50% of class	0

DEADLINES

Regular	
Priority	12/1
Deadline	1/15
Notification	4/1
Nonfall registration?	Yes

FINANCIAL FACTS

Financial Aid Rating	94
Annual tuition	$58,133
Room and board	$15,916
Required fees	$1,389
Books and supplies	$1,200
Average frosh need-based scholarship	$39,568
Average UG need-based scholarship	$38,603
% needy frosh rec. need-based scholarship or grant aid	85
% needy UG rec. need-based scholarship or grant aid	89
% needy frosh rec. non-need-based scholarship or grant aid	74
% needy UG rec. non-need-based scholarship or grant aid	55
% needy frosh rec. need-based self-help aid	89
% needy UG rec. need-based self-help aid	93
% frosh rec. any financial aid	68
% UG rec. any financial aid	65
% UG borrow to pay for school	35
Average cumulative indebtedness	$28,228
% frosh need fully met	92
% ugrads need fully met	85
Average % of frosh need met	100
Average % of ugrad need met	100

THE UNIVERSITY OF TAMPA

401 West Kennedy Boulevard, Tampa, FL 33606-1490 • Admissions: 813-253-6211 • Fax: 813-258-7398

CAMPUS LIFE
Quality of Life Rating	88
Fire Safety Rating	98
Green Rating	62
Type of school	Private
Environment	Metropolis

STUDENTS
Total undergrad enrollment	8,685
% male/female	42/58
% from out of state	69
% frosh from public high school	75
% frosh live on campus	95
% ugrads live on campus	49
# of fraternities (% ugrad men join)	15 (2)
# of sororities (% ugrad women join)	12 (5)
% African American	4
% Asian	2
% Caucasian	61
% Hispanic	12
% Native American	<1
% Pacific Islander	<1
% Two or more races	3
% Race and/or ethnicity unknown	9
% international	8
# of countries represented	132

SURVEY SAYS . . .
Students love Tampa, FL
Easy to get around campus
Recreation facilities are great

ACADEMICS
Academic Rating	78
% students returning for sophomore year	78
% students graduating within 4 years	49
% students graduating within 6 years	58
Calendar	Semester
Student/faculty ratio	17:1
Profs interesting rating	86
Profs accessible rating	90

Most classes have 20–29 students.
Most lab/discussion sessions have
10–19 students.

MOST POPULAR MAJORS
Marketing/Marketing Management, General;
Criminology; Finance, General

STUDENTS SAY " . . ."

Academics

The sunny University of Tampa is a growing, global university that affords its undergraduates the choice of more than two hundred areas of study, as well as "so many resources and opportunities ... [that provide] hands-on and experiential learning." Students rarely feel overwhelmed, and they find they "have a lot of support from staff and peers." Everyone is "eager to help and provide opportunities to make up any missed work or [to] obtain extra credit." The business and the science programs here are "amazing and what UT's forefront is about," and the campus location near downtown means "job opportunities are everywhere." The school hosts "seminars going on all the time about ... jobs, social skills, law school, [and] medical school."

"Professors are very personal with students" and "are very much available for extra help or extra explanations both during and outside of class." Faculty members are often also researchers, which gives students "the opportunity to create and carry out experiments," and additionally, there are "many internship and career opportunities that are available while you are still in college." Classes often take on a non-traditional format, featuring guest lectures from professionals or graduate professors. The experiential learning offered at UT means that "undergraduate time is not wasted and is truly going to prepare students for post-graduate [life]."

Life

A typical day for students "is always planned around knowing it's going to be a sunny day." The university's campus "feels like summer every day," and it's within walking distance of downtown as well as "within a five minute drive from Hyde Park, Ybor, and Soho, which all offer a wide variety of activities." The nearby theme parks are also a fun getaway. "A lot of students come [to UT] for the warm weather, the nice campus, and the city life," says one. Many students study by the river or walk around campus with others; "hammocks are super popular" (there's even a Hammock Club), and "renting bikes and biking the Riverwalk is also a fun way to pass time." Although students typically start partying on Thursday nights, some point out that "nothing is crazy" in that regard. "Many people are involved in Greek Life," and others enjoy extracurricular clubs. Of course, students are always happy to head to the beach. "There is just so much to do so that every day is not exactly the same," one student says.

Student Body

The University of Tampa is "very diverse in that people from all different cultures make up the community." There is a large international student population and plenty of people from out of state (only half of all undergraduates are from Florida), and "many are very outgoing and will go out of their way to be there for other students." "I've met people from Sweden, Bermuda, Nigeria, and many other nations.... The diversity among the ... cultures [at] UT is something," says a student. There is much promotion of diversity among students, so they are introduced to "a large variety of beliefs, backgrounds, ethnicities, and ideologies." Many who go here "are in athletics or just use the gym regularly," but they are "motivated to do well in their field of study" at the same time.

THE UNIVERSITY OF TAMPA

Financial Aid: 813-253-6219 • E-Mail: admissions@ut.edu • Website: www.ut.edu

THE PRINCETON REVIEW SAYS

Admissions

Very important factors considered include: rigor of secondary school record, academic GPA, standardized test scores. *Important factors considered include:* application essay, recommendation(s), talent/ability. *Other factors considered include:* class rank, interview, extracurricular activities, character/personal qualities, first generation, alumni/ae relation, volunteer work, work experience, level of applicant's interest. ACT with Writing recommended. SAT with Essay component recommended. High school diploma is required and GED is accepted. *Academic units required:* 4 English, 3 math, 3 science, 2 science labs, 2 foreign language, 3 social studies, 3 academic electives.

Financial Aid

Students should submit: FAFSA. Priority filing deadline is 10/1. The Princeton Review suggests that all financial aid forms be submitted as soon as possible after October 1. *Need-based scholarships/grants offered:* College/university scholarship or grant aid from institutional funds; Federal Nursing Scholarships; Federal Pell; Private scholarships; SEOG; State scholarships/grants. *Loan aid offered:* Direct PLUS loans; Direct Subsidized Stafford Loans; Direct Unsubsidized Stafford Loans. Applicants will be notified of awards on a rolling basis beginning 3/1. Federal Work-Study Program available. Institutional employment available.

The Inside Word

The University of Tampa accepts either the Common Application, Coalition Application, or its own application, and admissions officers look for applicants with high standardized test scores and an average high school GPA of 3.4. A rigorous high school course load is encouraged, as are extracurricular activities such as participation in sports, internship experience, and volunteer work. Early Action applications are due by November 15.

THE SCHOOL SAYS "..."

From the Admissions Office

"High school students may apply for admission after their junior year. Applicants are evaluated holistically using many criteria; guidance counselor or teacher recommendations and an essay are not required if you have graduated high school and completed seventeen or more college credit hours.

"A college preparatory curriculum is required, including a minimum of eighteen academic units: four English courses, three sciences (two must be laboratory sciences), three mathematics, three social studies, two foreign languages and three academic electives. The 2018–2019 class had an average (unweighted) GPA of 3.4 on the 4.0 scale, 1190 SAT or a score of 25 on the ACT. Certain majors require separate departmental applications and/ or requirements.

"The interdisciplinary Honors Program allows students to go beyond the classroom and regular coursework to study one-on-one with faculty through enrichment tutorials, Honors Abroad, internships, research and classroom-to-community outreach. One of the program's salient benefits is the Oxford Semester Abroad, awarded to UT's most qualified undergraduates each semester. Students are automatically considered for the Honors Program when they apply and are admitted to the University.

"While the University's facilities are state-of-the-art, our greatest features and benefits include our diverse student body (students from fifty states and 132 countries) and internships within walking distance of campus. UT's historic campus, coupled with our downtown, riverfront location, provides the perfect environment for academic enrichment and career preparation."

SELECTIVITY

Admissions Rating	88
# of applicants	23,341
% of applicants accepted	44
% of acceptees attending	20
# offered a place on the wait list	3,591
% accepting a place on wait list	8
% admitted from wait list	0

FRESHMAN PROFILE

Range SAT EBRW	550–630
Range SAT Math	550–620
Range SAT Composite	1120–1250
Range ACT Composite	23–28
# submitting SAT scores	1,678
% submitting SAT scores	77
# submitting ACT scores	782
% submitting ACT scores	36
Average HS GPA	3.4
% graduated top 10% of class	19
% graduated top 25% of class	47
% graduated top 50% of class	81

DEADLINES

Early action	
Deadline	11/15
Notification	11/15
Regular	
Priority	11/15
Notification	Rolling, 10/1
Nonfall registration?	Yes

FINANCIAL FACTS

Financial Aid Rating	83
Annual tuition	$27,790
Room and board	$11,136
Required fees	$2,002
Average frosh need-based scholarship	$15,330
Average UG need-based scholarship	$14,141
% needy frosh rec. need-based scholarship or grant aid	98
% needy UG rec. need-based scholarship or grant aid	97
% needy frosh rec. non-need-based scholarship or grant aid	96
% needy UG rec. non-need-based scholarship or grant aid	95
% needy frosh rec. need-based self-help aid	82
% needy UG rec. need-based self-help aid	84
% frosh rec. any financial aid	96
% UG rec. any financial aid	93
% UG borrow to pay for school	58
Average cumulative indebtedness	$35,046
% frosh need fully met	11
% ugrads need fully met	9
Average % of frosh need met	61
Average % of ugrad need met	58

UNIVERSITY OF TENNESSEE—KNOXVILLE

320 Student Service Building, Knoxville, TN 37996-0230 • Admissions: 865-974-1111

STUDENTS SAY "..."

Academics

A popular saying at the University of Tennessee, Knoxville is "I Will Give My All For Tennessee Today," a rallying cry that rings true for UT students. After all, the student body, comprised of over 23,000 undergraduates, is imbued with tremendous "school spirit." And, given the "palpable" "community feel and family atmosphere that permeates [the] campus," it's easy to understand why. Academically and professionally, Knoxville undergrads benefit from the fact that the university has cultivated great relationships with "international businesses and governmental institutions such as Oak Ridge National Lab and the TVA (Tennessee Valley Authority)." Of course, prospective students should not expect their undergraduate years to be a proverbial cake walk. Students caution that classes can be "a challenge" and that UT professors certainly "make sure you earn your degree." Despite that fact (or perhaps because of it), Knoxville undergrads speak quite highly of their professors. They describe the vast majority of instructors as "extremely knowledgeable" individuals who routinely conduct "interesting research." Students also appreciate how their professors are "open to discussion on topics indirectly related to the lecture material." Best of all, they seem to "actually care about their students." Indeed, UT professors "are willing to get to know you outside of the classroom, and they want to help you succeed."

Life

Without a doubt, there's fun to be had at the University of Tennessee, Knoxville. For starters, "when the weather is nice, there are always people doing things outside. People will set up hammocks, slacklines, and play Frisbee." You'll also frequently see "people playing sports in campus facilities and people running on the sidewalks." And we're told that "there are a lot of shows and productions...that are fun to watch." As one might expect, there are numerous clubs to join as well. Undergrads can participate in everything from "Habitat for Humanity" and "marching band" to the "Society of Physics Students (SPS)" and even "Humans versus Zombies." Moreover, "Greek life is big and tends to keep people busy." And, of course, "during the fall, every Saturday is dedicated to Tennessee football." Lastly, there's plenty to do off-campus as well. For example, "there is a popular farmer's market...that is within walking distance from campus so many people go to that." Additionally, "there are several music venues so [students often attend] concerts." And since UT is "located close to the Smoky Mountains" you'll discover that "a lot of people will go hiking on pretty days." Truly, there is something for everyone.

Student Body

Fortunately, University of Tennessee, Knoxville is a school that's "big enough [to guarantee you'll find] all kinds of people." And though the "student body is made up of many Tennesseans," it still manages to "attract a large population [of] out-of-state and international students." Nevertheless, some undergrads do note that the "campus tends to be conservative leaning, with small liberal and leftist groups existing." Political beliefs aside, many report that their peers are generally "kind, compassionate, and caring people that demonstrate Southern class and values." As one grateful undergrad elaborates, "If you ever need anything, you could go up to a random person and they would gladly take the time to talk to you. I have never experienced any sort of exclusiveness here, as everyone is truly a part of the Big Orange Family." A fellow classmate agrees, "We can all come together to celebrate the traditions of our school and community. We embrace the differences and work together to continuously improve the university for future students." However, a handful of undergrads did note that the campus can sometimes feel "uncomfortable...for anyone who is not cis-gender, white, and/or heterosexual."

UNIVERSITY OF TENNESSEE—KNOXVILLE

Financial Aid: 865-974-1111 • E-Mail: admissions@utk.edu • Website: http://www.utk.edu

THE PRINCETON REVIEW SAYS

Admissions

Very important factors considered include: academic GPA, standardized test scores. *Important factors considered include:* rigor of secondary school record, application essay, *Other factors considered include:* class rank, recommendation(s), extracurricular activities, talent/ability, character/personal qualities, first generation, alumni/ae relation, geographical residence, state residency, racial/ethnic status, volunteer work, work experience, level of applicant's interest. ACT with or without writing accepted. SAT with or without Essay component accepted. High school diploma is required and GED is accepted. *Academic units recommended:* 4 English, 4 math, 3 science, 3 science labs, 2 foreign language, 1 social studies, 1 history, 1 visual/performing arts.

Financial Aid

Students should submit: FAFSA. Priority filing deadline is 2/15. The Princeton Review suggests that all financial aid forms be submitted as soon as possible after October 1. *Need-based scholarships/grants offered:* College/university scholarship or grant aid from institutional funds; Federal Pell; Private scholarships; SEOG; State scholarships/grants. *Loan aid offered:* Direct PLUS loans; Direct Subsidized Stafford Loans; Direct Unsubsidized Stafford Loans. Applicants will be notified of awards on a rolling basis beginning 2/15. Federal Work-Study Program available.

The Inside Word

The University of Tennessee, Knoxville is looking for bright, competitive students to join the school's ranks. And, to find them, the school takes a holistic approach to the admissions process. UT considers everything from rigor of high school curriculum and overall GPA to personal statements and special skills. Finally, certain colleges within the university have specific requirements. For example, applicants must audition for the UT School of Music, and applicants to the Tickle College of Engineering must meet minimum standardized test scores.

THE SCHOOL SAYS "..."

From the Admissions Office

"The University of Tennessee, Knoxville, offers students the great program diversity of a major university, opportunities for research or original creative work in every degree program, and a welcoming campus environment. Nine colleges offer more than 360 undergraduate programs of study to students from all fifty states and 100 foreign countries, Honors and Scholars Programs serve the needs of the most ambitious students. Students from all majors enjoy an intimate college experience that integrates academic achievement and student life within a culture of intellectual and civic engagement. More than 500 clubs and organizations on campus allow students to further individualize their college experience in service, recreation, academics, and professional development. UT blends more than 200 years of history, tradition, and 'Volunteer Spirit' with the latest technology and innovation."

SELECTIVITY

Admissions Rating	84
# of applicants	21,764
% of applicants accepted	79
% of acceptees attending	31

FRESHMAN PROFILE

Range SAT EBRW	580–660
Range SAT Math	570–670
Range SAT Composite	1140–1310
Range ACT Composite	24–30
# submitting SAT scores	1,189
% submitting SAT scores	23
# submitting ACT scores	4,605
% submitting ACT scores	88
Average HS GPA	4.0
% graduated top 10% of class	35
% graduated top 25% of class	63
% graduated top 50% of class	88

DEADLINES

Early action	
Deadline	11/1
Notification	12/15
Regular	
Deadline	8/20
Notification	Rolling, 9/15
Nonfall registration?	Yes

FINANCIAL FACTS

Financial Aid Rating	82
Annual in-state tuition	$11,332
Annual out-of-state tuition	$29,522
Room and board	$11,482
Required fees	$1,932
Books and supplies	$1,598
Average frosh need-based scholarship	$12,794
Average UG need-based scholarship	$11,138
% needy frosh rec. need-based scholarship or grant aid	92
% needy UG rec. need-based scholarship or grant aid	87
% needy frosh rec. need-based self-help aid	99
% needy UG rec. need-based self-help aid	98
% frosh rec. any financial aid	93.43
% UG rec. any financial aid	87.63
% UG borrow to pay for school	50
Average cumulative indebtedness	$27,060
% frosh need fully met	16
% ugrads need fully met	14
Average % of frosh need met	62
Average % of ugrad need met	57

THE UNIVERSITY OF TEXAS AT AUSTIN

P.O. Box 8058, Austin, TX 78713-8058 • Admissions: 512-475-7399 • Fax: 512-475-7478

CAMPUS LIFE

Quality of Life Rating	90
Fire Safety Rating	84
Green Rating	83
Type of school	Public
Environment	Metropolis

STUDENTS

Total undergrad enrollment	39,783
% male/female	45/55
% from out of state	5
% frosh live on campus	67
% ugrads live on campus	18
# of fraternities (% ugrad men join)	NR (13)
# of sororities (% ugrad women join)	NR (17)
% African American	4
% Asian	23
% Caucasian	39
% Hispanic	24
% Native American	<1
% Pacific Islander	<1
% Two or more races	4
% Race and/or ethnicity unknown	1
% international	5
# of countries represented	101

SURVEY SAYS . . .

Great library
Internships are widely available
Students environmentally aware
Students love Austin, TX
Recreation facilities are great
Lots of beer drinking
Hard liquor is popular
Everyone loves the Longhorns
Intramural sports are popular
Alumni active on campus

ACADEMICS

Academic Rating	81
% students returning for sophomore year	96
% students graduating within 4 years	66
% students graduating within 6 years	86
Calendar	Semester
Student/faculty ratio	18:1
Profs interesting rating	86
Profs accessible rating	88

Most classes have 10–19 students.
Most lab/discussion sessions have
  10–19 students.

MOST POPULAR MAJORS

Engineering; Social Sciences; Business Marketing;
Biological/Life Sciences

STUDENTS SAY "..."

Academics

Students insist that the University of Texas at Austin has "everything you want in a college: academics, athletics, social life, location," and it's hard to argue with them. UT is "a huge school and has a lot to offer," meaning students have "an infinite number of possibilities open to them and can use them in their own way to figure out what they want for their lives." As one student tells us about arriving on campus, "I did not realize how much was available to me just as an enrolled student. There is free tutoring, gym membership, professional counseling, doctor visits, legal help, career advising, and many distinguished outside speakers. The campus is crawling with experts in every field you can imagine." Standout academic departments are numerous: from the sciences to the humanities to creative arts, UT makes a strong bid for the much-sought-after mantle of "Harvard of the south." Also, the school does a surprisingly good job of avoiding the factory-like feel of many large schools. One student observes: "coming to a large university, there was a prejudgment that the huge classes will make it impossible to know your professor, and vice versa. The university has dispelled that myth with professors who want to know you and [who] provide opportunities to get to know them." While professors "can vary greatly across a spectrum from 'I'm smarter than him' to 'I want to follow in his footsteps,'" "the class offerings at UT are generally vast and diverse, and students can often avoid taking the less-qualified professors with a little research."

Life

Life at UT Austin is "very relaxed.... Students usually wear shorts and a t-shirt to class. When the weather gets cold, you might find students wearing the same shorts and t-shirt with a sweatshirt. Students and faculty frequently picnic all over campus. There are plenty of outdoor tables and grassy areas to sit." Undergrads "are often found throwing a Frisbee outside the tower or taking a nap under a tree. It's truly what you see in one of those cheesy brochures with everyone studying and smiling. Of course, the smiles aren't so bright during finals. We switch to an over-caffeinated, glazed-eye look instead." Hometown Austin "provides a social education that a college student newly out on his own would not find anywhere else," with "festivals or fairs of some kind going on downtown all the time" and "the infamous 6th Street with nightlife that dies down only after the bars close." Campus and the surrounding area offer "many hike-and-bike trails and fitness organizations. It's possible for students to train for marathons, half marathons, and triathlons while in school. Barton Springs pool is a natural spring that is very popular year-round. On any given Saturday you will find students throwing a football, going for a run, biking through the hills, kayaking in the river, having a late lunch at one of Austin's great restaurants, or just sleeping in."

Student Body

"Because of the huge Greek life at UT, a 'typical student' would be a sorority girl or fraternity boy," but—and it's a big but—such students "are hardly the majority, since UT is actually made of more 'atypical' people than most other schools. Everyone here has his own niche, and I could not think of any type of individual who would not be able to find one of his own." Indeed, "everyone at Texas is different! When you walk across campus, you see every type of ethnicity. There are a lot of minorities at Texas. Also, I see many disabled people, whom the school accommodates well. Everyone seems to get along. The different types of students just blend in together." Especially by Texas standards, "Austin is known for being 'weird.' If you see someone dressed in a way you've never seen before, you just shrug it off and say 'That's Austin!'"

Financial Aid: 512-475-6282 • E-Mail: admissions@austin.utexas.edu • Website: http://www.utexas.edu

THE PRINCETON REVIEW SAYS

Admissions

Very important factors considered include: rigor of secondary school record, class rank, academic GPA, application essay, standardized test scores, recommendation(s), extracurricular activities, talent/ability, character/personal qualities, first generation, geographical residence, state residency, religious affiliation/commitment, racial/ethnic status, volunteer work, work experience. ACT with or without writing accepted. SAT with or without Essay component accepted. High school diploma is required and GED is accepted. *Academic units required:* 4 English, 4 math, 4 science, 2 foreign language, 4 social studies, 6 academic electives.

Financial Aid

Students should submit: FAFSA; Institution's own financial aid form. Priority filing deadline is 1/15. The Princeton Review suggests that all financial aid forms be submitted as soon as possible after October 1. *Need-based scholarships/grants offered:* College/university scholarship or grant aid from institutional funds; Federal Pell; Private scholarships; SEOG; State scholarships/grants. *Loan aid offered:* Direct PLUS loans; Direct Subsidized Stafford Loans; Direct Unsubsidized Stafford Loans. Applicants will be notified of awards on a rolling basis beginning 1/15. Federal Work-Study Program available. Institutional employment available.

The Inside Word

The university is required to automatically admit enough Texas applicants to fill 75 percent of available spaces set aside for students from Texas. The university will admit applicants from Texas who are in the top 6 percent of their high school class for the summer/fall 2018 and the spring 2019 entering freshman class. All students, including those eligible for automatic admission, should submit the strongest possible application to increase the likelihood of admission to the university and to their requested major. Admissions are quite competitive. Space for out-of-state students is limited, meaning they'll have even higher hurdles to clear.

THE SCHOOL SAYS "..."

From the Admissions Office

"Like the state it calls home, The University of Texas at Austin is a bold, ambitious leader committed to innovative learning and research, and encourages creativity, analysis, and critical thinking. Ranked among the top research universities in the country, UT Austin is home to more than 51,000 students and 3,000 teaching faculty. Through more than 170 undergraduate fields of study across 13 colleges and schools (and hundreds of study abroad programs, comprehensive student services, exceptional cultural centers, and more than 1,100 student organizations), you will find an engaging, diverse, multi-dimensional experience that will unlock your future potential and prepare you to make an impact on the world. Our students enjoy a vibrant college experience on our urban campus in the heart of the city of Austin—consistently recognized as the nation's best place to live—and an HQ for creatives and entrepreneurs. Longhorns are part of a strong community, and inherit a storied history and rich tradition of success that's as evident in our Big 12 athletics as it is in the classroom or laboratory. Almost half a million alumni lead worldwide industries from technology to politics to entertainment, and provide a robust network of UT connections around the world and in every field. Together, we're working to make the world a better place, united by the belief that creating and sharing knowledge can transform society. It's why we say 'What starts here changes the world.'"

SELECTIVITY

Admissions Rating	95
# of applicants	53,525
% of applicants accepted	32
% of acceptees attending	48

FRESHMAN PROFILE

Range SAT EBRW	620–720
Range SAT Math	610–760
Range SAT Composite	1240–1470
Range ACT Composite	27–33
# submitting SAT scores	6,416
% submitting SAT scores	79
# submitting ACT scores	4,397
% submitting ACT scores	54
% graduated top 10% of class	87
% graduated top 25% of class	96
% graduated top 50% of class	99

DEADLINES

Regular	
Priority	11/1
Deadline	12/1
Nonfall registration?	Yes

FINANCIAL FACTS

Financial Aid Rating	82
Annual in-state tuition	$10,824
Annual out-of-state tuition	$38,326
Room and board	$11,812
Books and supplies	$700
Average frosh need-based scholarship	$9,958
Average UG need-based scholarship	$9,659
% needy frosh rec. need-based scholarship or grant aid	76
% needy UG rec. need-based scholarship or grant aid	77
% needy frosh rec. non-need-based scholarship or grant aid	73
% needy UG rec. non-need-based scholarship or grant aid	50
% needy frosh rec. need-based self-help aid	57
% needy UG rec. need-based self-help aid	62
% frosh rec. any financial aid	41
% UG borrow to pay for school	40
Average cumulative indebtedness	$24,263
% frosh need fully met	27
% ugrads need fully met	18
Average % of frosh need met	74
Average % of ugrad need met	68

THE UNIVERSITY OF TEXAS AT DALLAS

Admission & Enrollment, Richardson, TX 75080-3021 • Admissions: 972-883-2270 • Fax: 972-883-2599

CAMPUS LIFE

Quality of Life Rating	87
Fire Safety Rating	95
Green Rating	94
Type of school	Public
Environment	Metropolis

STUDENTS

Total undergrad enrollment	20,994
% male/female	57/43
% from out of state	5
% frosh from public high school	95
% frosh live on campus	52
% ugrads live on campus	24
# of fraternities (% ugrad men join)	12 (5)
# of sororities (% ugrad women join)	11 (7)
% African American	6
% Asian	33
% Caucasian	31
% Hispanic	19
% Native American	<1
% Pacific Islander	<1
% Two or more races	4
% Race and/or ethnicity unknown	2
% international	5
# of countries represented	68

SURVEY SAYS . . .

Classroom facilities are great
Lab facilities are great
Career services are great
Very little drug use

ACADEMICS

Academic Rating	75
% students returning for sophomore year	88
% students graduating within 4 years	53
% students graduating within 6 years	71
Calendar	Semester
Student/faculty ratio	24:1
Profs interesting rating	84
Profs accessible rating	90

Most classes have 40–49 students.
Most lab/discussion sessions have 20–29 students.

MOST POPULAR MAJORS

Computer and Information Sciences, General; Mechanical Engineering; Biology/Biological Sciences, General

STUDENTS SAY "..."

Academics

The University of Texas at Dallas provides its more than 20,000 undergraduates with a wealth of resources, financial aid, and opportunities, striving for "a future of talented and smart individuals." UTD has "one of the best tech schools around" and draws a good deal of students to its STEM programs (one student lovingly calls it "the nerd capital of the UT system"), causing a senior computer engineer to remark: "Engineering and the sciences for the win." The school is without large sports programs (notably football), but instead "emphasizes academics, which is what we are all here for."

Administration is responsive and invested in UTD's growing reputation, and the school "grows and changes year by year, continually getting better and better," with students acting as "a big part of that process." Someone is "always willing to help you with any problem you encounter," and the tutoring available also "really helps in understanding the material." They are dedicated to their students, this being apparent in "their open office hours and timely replies to e-mails."

Most of the professors "are very enthused about what they are teaching and genuinely want us to learn," and bring new topics to light through "very informative" discussion. "Their passion for their subject makes it easy to love your classes!" says a student. "I get pushed academically, but I love it," says another. One of the shining benefits of UTD is the chance to get "actively involved with the faculty in research," which provides "several opportunities for honors, and ultimately allows you to prepare for a continued education after undergrad."

Life

The "well-kept campus" is "not too large," though "parking is a bit of an issue sometimes." There is a lot of studying going on, so "you can always find a group or just a lot of people hanging around in a specific area studying." "Some people practically build shrines to their GPA's and worship them on weekends," says one sophomore.

A lot of students commute (which makes life "pretty quiet"), and there is no football team to rally around, so "it's hard to have a lot of school spirit"; however, "the social scene is definitely growing," and the Student Union acts as the "hub" for the entire school where "students can mingle and find friends." Computer labs also give many the chance to game and have fun (the video game culture is "strong"), and "there are usually always at least five to ten gamers in the room at once." The school provides "many things to do," with campus events like movies happening every week, and people often leave campus to seek more options, such as "movies, bowling, shopping, skating, concert, etc."

Student Body

There is "no clear majority of one race, creed, or background" at UT Dallas. Since most of the "exceptionally nice" and "very diverse" people are here for the science, technology, and business, there are "lots of smart people everywhere" and "everyone here is so open about the geeky side in everyone." Most agree that there could stand to be a bit more of a creative voice on campus and the school would do well to attract "more students to fine arts." Most students are "serious about their academics, but not too serious" and remember to take the time to relax; "video games/card games and…anime" are popular here, as are clubs and organizations.

Financial Aid: 972-883-2941 • E-Mail: admission@utdallas.edu • Website: www.utdallas.edu

THE PRINCETON REVIEW SAYS

Admissions

Very important factors considered include: rigor of secondary school record, class rank, academic GPA, standardized test scores. *Important factors considered include:* application essay, *Other factors considered include:* recommendation(s), extracurricular activities, talent/ability, character/personal qualities, geographical residence, state residency, volunteer work, work experience, level of applicant's interest. ACT with Writing required. SAT with Essay component required. High school diploma is required and GED is accepted. *Academic units required:* 4 English, 4 math, 3 science, 3 science labs, 2 foreign language, 3 social studies, 1.5 academic electives, 0.5 visual/performing arts. *Academic units recommended:* 4 English, 4 math, 3 science, 3 science labs, 3 foreign language, 4 social studies, 2.5 academic electives, 1 computer science, 1 visual/performing arts.

Financial Aid

Students should submit: FAFSA. Priority filing deadline is 3/15. The Princeton Review suggests that all financial aid forms be submitted as soon as possible after October 1. *Need-based scholarships/grants offered:* College/university scholarship or grant aid from institutional funds; Federal Pell; Private scholarships; SEOG; State scholarships/grants. *Loan aid offered:* Direct PLUS loans; Direct Subsidized Stafford Loans; Direct Unsubsidized Stafford Loans. Applicants will be notified of awards on a rolling basis beginning 3/1. Federal Work-Study Program available. Institutional employment available.

The Inside Word

UT Dallas is one of those by-the-numbers schools for the majority of its admitted students. Texas law requires that prospective students are automatically admitted to the university as first-time freshmen if they graduated from an accredited Texas high school among the top 10 percent of their class. Students outside of the top 10 percent are subject to a more holistic review based on individual strengths.

THE SCHOOL SAYS "..."

From the Admissions Office

"Founded in 1969, The University of Texas at Dallas has evolved into one of the top research institutions in Texas. UT Dallas provides some of the state's most-lauded business, engineering, and science programs, and also has developed a breadth of highly diverse educational paths with 142 academic programs across eight schools, including innovative and traditional programs in the liberal arts.

"The University's faculty consists of more than 570 tenured and tenure-track members hailing from the world's best colleges and includes members of the National Academy of Sciences and the National Academy of Engineering. In addition, UT Dallas is home to members of the National Academies of Arts and Sciences, Engineering, Inventors, and Sciences.

"UT Dallas students graduate with less debt than most college students in the country and are highly marketable upon graduation."

SELECTIVITY

Admissions Rating	86
# of applicants	14,327
% of applicants accepted	79
% of acceptees attending	36

FRESHMAN PROFILE

Range SAT EBRW	610–710
Range SAT Math	630–750
Range ACT Composite	26–33
# submitting SAT scores	3,478
% submitting SAT scores	85
# submitting ACT scores	1,704
% submitting ACT scores	42
% graduated top 10% of class	39
% graduated top 25% of class	71
% graduated top 50% of class	95

DEADLINES

Regular	
Priority	12/1
Deadline	5/1
Nonfall registration?	Yes

APPLICANTS ALSO LOOK AT AND OFTEN PREFER

University of Texas at Austin; Texas A&M University

AND SOMETIMES PREFER

University of Oklahoma; University of North Texas; The University of Texas at Arlington; Texas Woman's University; Texas Tech University

AND RARELY PREFER

Baylor University; Austin College; University of Arkansas

FINANCIAL FACTS

Financial Aid Rating	85
Annual in-state tuition	$13,442
Annual out-of-state tuition	$38,168
Room and board	$12,076
Books and supplies	$1,200
Average frosh need-based scholarship	$11,957
Average UG need-based scholarship	$9,706
% needy frosh rec. need-based scholarship or grant aid	87
% needy UG rec. need-based scholarship or grant aid	88
% needy frosh rec. non-need-based scholarship or grant aid	13
% needy UG rec. non-need-based scholarship or grant aid	6
% needy frosh rec. need-based self-help aid	82
% needy UG rec. need-based self-help aid	88
% frosh rec. any financial aid	72
% UG rec. any financial aid	65
% UG borrow to pay for school	32
Average cumulative indebtedness	$23,176
% frosh need fully met	22
% ugrads need fully met	14
Average % of frosh need met	72
Average % of ugrad need met	65

THE UNIVERSITY OF TULSA

800 South Tucker Drive, Tulsa, OK 74104 • Admissions: 918-631-2307 • Fax: 918-631-5003

CAMPUS LIFE

Quality of Life Rating	90
Fire Safety Rating	97
Green Rating	83
Type of school	Private
Affiliation	Presbyterian
Environment	Metropolis

STUDENTS

Total undergrad enrollment	3,276
% male/female	54/46
% from out of state	42
% frosh from public high school	72
% frosh live on campus	81
% ugrads live on campus	72
# of fraternities (% ugrad men join)	392 (23)
# of sororities (% ugrad women join)	339 (23)
% African American	7
% Asian	6
% Caucasian	54
% Hispanic	9
% Native American	3
% Pacific Islander	<1
% Two or more races	8
% Race and/or ethnicity unknown	1
% international	13
# of countries represented	55

SURVEY SAYS . . .

Students are happy
Intramural sports are popular

ACADEMICS

Academic Rating	83
% students returning for sophomore year	87
% students graduating within 4 years	49
% students graduating within 6 years	72
Calendar	Semester
Student/faculty ratio	11:1
Profs interesting rating	87
Profs accessible rating	92

Most classes have 10–19 students.
Most lab/discussion sessions have 10–19 students.

MOST POPULAR MAJORS

Computer Science; Psychology, General; Business Statistics; Petroleum Engineer; Mechanical Engineer; Management

STUDENTS SAY "..."

Academics

The many students at The University of Tulsa, a small private research university, find it to be the total package. After all, it combines "the friendly environment of a smaller university and the academic, employment, extracurricular, and service opportunities of a larger university." It also does a tremendous job of fostering an atmosphere that's "conducive to collaboration and growth." In general, students describe the academics as "challenging." And a number of undergrads emphasize TU's "strong engineering school," which thoroughly prepares students for "work[ing] in the industry, especially [within the] energy [sector]." All undergraduates, no matter their major, benefit from "small class sizes." In turn, this affords students the opportunity to build "close relationships...with [the] faculty," full of professors who "are great resources for [both] internships and real-world advice." Aside from being great contacts, Tulsa professors are "very knowledgeable and passionate about their subjects." They also "make their students a priority" and they're "very accessible outside of class." As one student expounds, "Many of my professors frequently invite students to their office hours and remind us of their availability....[It's clear they] care about my academic experience, career readiness, and about me as a person."

Life

While University of Tulsa undergrads say that "a good portion of [their] time is...spent studying," there's still plenty of fun to be had outside the confines of the library and/or classroom. For example, "there are a ton of active student organizations" and you can always find "an event to attend or free food to eat." Popular options include "homecoming...dog petting days, bowling, [and] carnivals." One excited student adds, "TU is good about providing events bi-weekly, like S'mores at the Student Union, an outdoor movie, or a play." If the Greek scene interests you, you'll be happy to learn that "the fraternities on campus...usually [host] events Thursday through Saturday." A number of undergrads also love to take advantage of the "many [beautiful] lawns" on the TU campus. And you're sure to find a handful of students playing any number of games, from "baseball [and] football [to] Capture the Flag." If you prefer your athletics to be a little more structured, there's also a "very popular... intramural sports [program]." As for hometown Tulsa, "there's a great food, music, and art culture in downtown Tulsa so you can always find something to do." And we're told that "the restaurants here are awesome, small and large concert venues attract all types of artists, and there all festivals of all types throughout the year."

Student Body

The student body at The University of Tulsa is comprised of "friendly" and "inclusive" individuals. Of course, it probably helps that the school is home to "a diverse group of students from various economic, academic, religious, political, and ethnic backgrounds." Indeed, "Division I athletes, international students, military veterans, sorority sisters, petroleum engineering majors, and piano performance majors represent a few of the many groups woven together on TU's campus." Undergrads are "committed to doing well in school": As one student explains, "We are all here to do well, but we are here to do well together." Undergrads also describe their classmates as "smart," "engaging," and "extremely focused on their studies." And most "are incredibly involved at TU, whether it be in Greek life, athletics, music, [or] research." Additionally, a lot of "TU students look for opportunities to challenge themselves and impact their community." One thrilled undergrad sums up the campus experience: "TU honestly feels like a small town community. Everyone is so friendly and kind, and it's like having one giant family."

Financial Aid: 918-631-2526 • E-Mail: admission@utulsa.edu • Website: utulsa.edu

THE PRINCETON REVIEW SAYS

Admissions

Very important factors considered include: rigor of secondary school record, academic GPA, standardized test scores. *Important factors considered include:* class rank, application essay, recommendation(s), interview. *Other factors considered include:* extracurricular activities, talent/ability, character/personal qualities, first generation, alumni/ae relation, racial/ethnic status, volunteer work, work experience. ACT with or without writing accepted. SAT with or without Essay component accepted. High school diploma is required and GED is accepted. *Academic units recommended:* 4 English, 4 math, 3 science, 3 science labs, 2 foreign language, 3 social studies, 1 computer science, 1 visual/performing arts.

Financial Aid

Students should submit: FAFSA. The Princeton Review suggests that all financial aid forms be submitted as soon as possible after October 1. *Need-based scholarships/grants offered:* College/university scholarship or grant aid from institutional funds; Federal Pell; Private scholarships; SEOG; State scholarships/grants. *Loan aid offered:* Direct PLUS loans; Direct Subsidized Stafford Loans; Direct Unsubsidized Stafford Loans. Applicants will be notified of awards on a rolling basis beginning 2/15. Federal Work-Study Program available. Institutional employment available.

The Inside Word

The admissions process at TU is fairly straightforward. For starters, the school closely evaluates high school transcripts and standardized test scores. Candidates are strongly encouraged to sit for an admissions interview, as well. It's also important to note that The University of Tulsa evaluates applications on a rolling basis. The earlier you apply, the more slots will be available. In fact, it's recommended that students submit their applications by January 15 for full consideration for scholarships.

THE SCHOOL SAYS "..."

From the Admissions Office

"The University of Tulsa is a private university with a comprehensive scope. Students choose from more than sixty majors offered through four undergraduate colleges—Kendall College of Arts and Sciences, Collins College of Business, Oxley College of Health Sciences, and the College of Engineering and Natural Sciences. Curricula can be customized with collaborative and interdisciplinary research, joint undergraduate and graduate programs, the Global Scholars Program and an honors program. Professors are equally committed to teaching undergraduates and to scholarly research. This results in extraordinary individual achievement, resulting in the nationally competitive scholarships students have won since 1995: sixty-five Goldwaters, seventy National Science Foundation scholars, twelve Trumans, nine Department of Defense scholars, twenty-two Fulbrights, eleven Phi Kappa Phi, nine Udalls, five British Marshalls, and three Rhodes Scholars, including one in 2017. In the past decade, over 1,000,000 square feet of facilities have been added. These include athletic venues, additional apartments, fitness center, Legal Information Center, library expansion and renovation, two new engineering buildings and a new performing arts center. Over 200 registered clubs, and interest groups, including intramural and recreational sports teams exist along with seven fraternities and nine sororities. The 8,300 seat Reynolds Center is home to the men's and women's basketball teams, campus events, and concerts. A forty-acre sports complex includes the fitness center and indoor tennis center. An outdoor freshman orientation program launches an entire first-year experience dedicated to developing students' full potential.

"Due to lack of available testing during the COVID-19 global pandemic, freshman applicants for the spring 2021 and fall 2021 entry terms are not required to submit an official ACT or SAT test score for admission. Submission of an official score is optional."

SELECTIVITY

Admissions Rating	93
# of applicants	9,793
% of applicants accepted	36
% of acceptees attending	24

FRESHMAN PROFILE

Range SAT EBRW	550–670
Range SAT Math	540–690
Range SAT Composite	1110–1350
Range ACT Composite	24–31
# submitting SAT scores	327
% submitting SAT scores	39
# submitting ACT scores	682
% submitting ACT scores	82
Average HS GPA	3.97
% graduated top 10% of class	65
% graduated top 25% of class	80
% graduated top 50% of class	93

DEADLINES

Regular	
Priority	1/15
Notification	Rolling, 11/1
Nonfall registration?	Yes

APPLICANTS ALSO LOOK AT AND OFTEN PREFER

Texas Christian University; University of Texas at Austin; University of Oklahoma; St. Louis University

AND SOMETIMES PREFER

Southern Methodist University; Baylor University; Colorado School of Mines; Oklahoma State University; Trinity University; University of Arkansas

AND RARELY PREFER

Creighton University; Texas Tech; University of Missouri

FINANCIAL FACTS

Financial Aid Rating	88
Annual tuition	$42,950
Room and board	$12,062
Required fees	$1,025
Books and supplies	$1,200
Average frosh need-based scholarship	$32,334
Average UG need-based scholarship	$29,696
% needy frosh rec. need-based scholarship or grant aid	98
% needy UG rec. need-based scholarship or grant aid	97
% needy frosh rec. non-need-based scholarship or grant aid	84
% needy UG rec. non-need-based scholarship or grant aid	62
% needy frosh rec. need-based self-help aid	64
% needy UG rec. need-based self-help aid	62
% frosh rec. any financial aid	96
% UG rec. any financial aid	88
% UG borrow to pay for school	50
Average cumulative indebtedness	$34,869
% frosh need fully met	38
% ugrads need fully met	35
Average % of frosh need met	88
Average % of ugrad need met	82

UNIVERSITY OF UTAH

201 South 1460 East, Salt Lake City, UT 84112 • Admissions: 801-581-8761 • Fax: 801-585-7864

STUDENTS SAY ". . ."

Academics

Nestled amid Salt Lake City's snowcapped mountains, the University of Utah is a large public school that offers extensive academic programs, ample research opportunities, and a surprisingly student-friendly atmosphere. No matter what your interests, you'll find like minds at The U. "I have studied everything from Tai Chi/Yoga movement and stage combat to differential equations and linear algebra," says a junior. "The one thing that has remained consistent throughout is the appreciation and dedication the people have for the topic they are involved in." The U is a research university that actually takes teaching seriously, and "every teacher ... shows incredible knowledge in their area, as well as personality and wit." "Classes are informative, challenging, and genuinely enjoyable." As is the case in many larger universities, students note that many "general education courses are taught by grad students," whose teaching abilities can range from great to below average. "Ninety percent of my professors are fantastic; the ones that aren't are usually grad students," explains a junior. On this large campus, students have little contact with the school's administration and "there's definitely no hand-holding at The U. If you're unsure of your major or career plans, it's easy to slip through the cracks." However, students assure us, "The administration puts student interests first whenever possible with a focus on keeping tuition low, creating a diverse environment, and providing opportunities and experience in order to prepare students to be productive citizens."

Life

While a large percentage of the undergraduate community at the University of Utah commutes to campus, there are still plenty of activities for the school's 4,000 resident students. There are many people "active in politics, environmental issues, and international issues," and, after hours, "the school holds different events throughout the year, such as Crimson Nights that feature activities such as bowling, crafts, games, food, and music." Socially, "Greek life is not as large as at other schools but is definitely a lot of fun and the best way to get to know more people your age." In addition, "during football season there are great tailgate parties with friends, drinks, and food." Right off campus, there are a range of great restaurants, and "the nightlife is hard to keep up with." There's always something good going on—whether it's at the bars and clubs downtown, or at small music venues." For outdoorsy types, The U is a paradise. "We have all four seasons and some of the best outdoors in the nation," explains one student. "Killer snow, amazing hills, mountains, lakes, and streams." In this natural wonderland, "hiking, biking, boating, snow-skiing, and snowboarding are just a few of the hundreds of activities available to students."

Student Body

Located in Salt Lake City, The U has "plenty of social niches to fall into, and none of them are rigidly exclusive." One student notes that part of the student body is "the typical Utah Mormon, and [the rest] is a mix of everything. The two [groups] usually stay separate but they get along." University of Utah students agree that "there is more diversity here than in any other part of the state." However, out-of-state students are not as common, and "those of us not from Utah are definitely in the minority." While there are a number of residential students, a very large percentage of students also choose to commute to school while living with their parents or family. In addition, "there are a lot of older students and a lot of married students." Academically, however, U undergraduates are "independent, smart, and come to class ready to discuss ideas."

UNIVERSITY OF UTAH

Financial Aid: 801-581-6211 • E-Mail: admissions@utah.edu • Website: www.utah.edu

THE PRINCETON REVIEW SAYS

Admissions

Very important factors considered include: rigor of secondary school record, academic GPA. *Important factors considered include:* standardized test scores. *Other factors considered include:* class rank, interview, extracurricular activities, talent/ability, character/personal qualities, first generation, alumni/ae relation, geographical residence, state residency, racial/ethnic status, volunteer work, work experience. ACT with or without writing accepted. SAT with or without Essay component accepted. High school diploma is required and GED is accepted. *Academic units required:* 4 English, 2 math, 3 science, 1 science lab, 2 foreign language, 1 history, 4 academic electives.

Financial Aid

Students should submit: FAFSA. Priority filing deadline is 2/1. The Princeton Review suggests that all financial aid forms be submitted as soon as possible after October 1. *Need-based scholarships/grants offered:* College/university scholarship or grant aid from institutional funds; Federal Nursing Scholarships; Federal Pell; Private scholarships; SEOG; State scholarships/grants. *Loan aid offered:* Direct PLUS loans; Direct Subsidized Stafford Loans; Direct Unsubsidized Stafford Loans. Applicants will be notified of awards on a rolling basis beginning 3/1. Federal Work-Study Program available. Institutional employment available.

The Inside Word

Admission is based primarily on the big three: Course selection, grades, and test scores. If you have a 3.0 GPA or better and average test scores, you're close to a sure bet for admission.

THE SCHOOL SAYS "..."

From the Admissions Office

"Salt Lake is the U's 'college city,' pairing outdoor adventure—including world-class skiing and five national parks (plus low-cost campus equipment rentals and outings to help students explore)—with sophisticated urban offerings from Utah Jazz NBA games to Broadway shows.

"However, students don't have to leave campus to experience outstanding music, theater, and dance performances. Talented students and faculty create and perform hundreds of shows each year, and the student government has hosted concerts featuring such artists as B.o.B and Icona Pop. Recent speakers have included former U.S. Vice President Joe Biden and the creator of Humans of New York.

"Salt Lake City is top in the nation for diversity of jobs, according to LinkUp, which means there is an abundance of companies providing internship and employment opportunities. And, when students land that job downtown, their transportation is covered. U students have access to public transportation to, from, and around campus and the Salt Lake Valley for no additional cost.

"The U offers an affordable investment in a high-quality and high-value degree by having one of the lowest out-of-state cost of attendances in the Pac-12, along with the opportunity to meet requirements for in-state tuition after just one year.

"As a leader in global research and innovation, the U provides students with exciting ways to discover and nurture their interests. From Lassonde Studios (an on-campus entrepreneurial center) to its international campus in Incheon, South Korea, to its hundreds of undergrad research opportunities, the possibilities are only limited by the imagination."

SELECTIVITY

Admissions Rating	87
# of applicants	24,404
% of applicants accepted	62
% of acceptees attending	28

FRESHMAN PROFILE

Range SAT EBRW	573–680
Range SAT Math	570–700
Range SAT Composite	1150–1370
Range ACT Composite	22–29
# submitting SAT scores	1,114
% submitting SAT scores	26
# submitting ACT scores	3,342
% submitting ACT scores	79
Average HS GPA	3.7

DEADLINES

Regular	
Priority	11/1
Deadline	4/1
Nonfall registration?	Yes

FINANCIAL FACTS

Financial Aid Rating	83
Annual in-state tuition	$9,286
Annual out-of-state tuition	$29,996
Room and board	$11,844
Books and supplies	$1,322
Average frosh need-based scholarship	$9,754
Average UG need-based scholarship	$8,361
% needy frosh rec. need-based scholarship or grant aid	91
% needy UG rec. need-based scholarship or grant aid	85
% needy frosh rec. non-need-based scholarship or grant aid	20
% needy UG rec. non-need-based scholarship or grant aid	10
% needy frosh rec. need-based self-help aid	75
% needy UG rec. need-based self-help aid	84
% frosh rec. any financial aid	46
% UG rec. any financial aid	44
% UG borrow to pay for school	46
Average cumulative indebtedness	$19,656
% frosh need fully met	15
% ugrads need fully met	13
Average % of frosh need met	71
Average % of ugrad need met	65

UNIVERSITY OF VERMONT

University of Vermont Admissions, Burlington, VT 05401-3596 • Admissions: 802-656-3370 • Fax: 802-656-8611

STUDENTS SAY "..."

Academics

A public research university in Burlington, the University of Vermont offers the complete package: "great academics ... in a great area [with] lots to do while getting a great education." This is bolstered by professors who are "engaging and clearly very passionate about what they teach." One student says, "[Professors] have opened my eyes to new interests, new ways of thinking, new skills, and new innovations." While some students voice concerns of "too many general education requirements" and the need for "access to quality counseling, advising, and therapists," they overall appreciate the variety of "rigorous yet interesting" programs. The pre-med programs benefit from the school's proximity to the UVM Medical Center, and students also note strong environmental, social justice, and STEM programs. Plus, the opportunity to study across departments and colleges "allows and encourages students to take a variety of classes outside of their major requirements." As one student says, "I was able to pick which college I wanted to be in and had a wide array of classes to choose from."

Life

While being considered "absolutely ... academically rigorous," there's also a strong focus on extracurriculars, and there are plentiful opportunities to get involved: "UVM offers lots of clubs to participate in, and if you don't see something you want, you can start your own club." In addition to clubs, the school is "always putting on different events," and on top of those options, many are drawn to the recreation the nearby terrain offers as well. One student says, "It is simply an outdoorsy school. Hiking, fishing, boating, skiing, snowboarding, [and] running ... are all extremely popular." Off campus, "Students go downtown to cafés, restaurants, galleries, and shops." Many students are drawn to the "chill, small town atmosphere" of Burlington and its "amenities of urban life," and the "small community feel" of the school itself complements that. One student remarks, "I cannot walk across campus ... without seeing at least eight to ten friends." An enthusiastic peer states that it's one of "the best places to live as a college student on the East Coast."

Student Body

UVM undergrads think highly of each other, saying things like: "All of my peers are intelligent, hardworking, cooperative, and all around good people." They also note a range of personalities on campus—"there is no one stereotype that UVM students conform to"— claiming that "there is truly a place for everyone, whether you're a sorority girl or a member of our woodsmen team." However, there is still a common thread that holds them all together: "exceptional passion for what they do, whether in the classroom or out." Some would like to see the school improve its "racial/ethnic/religious diversity, which the school is aware of but needs to make great strides to achieve." Overall, UVM students are "friendly, passionate, and involved" and they "care about cultural, societal, and political situations both locally and globally."

Financial Aid: 802-656-5700 • E-Mail: admissions@uvm.edu • Website: www.uvm.edu

THE PRINCETON REVIEW SAYS

Admissions

Very important factors considered include: rigor of secondary school record. *Important factors considered include:* class rank, academic GPA, application essay, standardized test scores, character/personal qualities, state residency. *Other factors considered include:* recommendation(s), extracurricular activities, talent/ability, first generation, alumni/ae relation, geographical residence, racial/ethnic status, volunteer work, work experience, level of applicant's interest. ACT with or without writing accepted. SAT with or without Essay component accepted. High school diploma is required and GED is accepted. *Academic units required:* 4 English, 3 math, 2 science, 1 science lab, 2 foreign language, 3 social studies.

Financial Aid

Students should submit: FAFSA. Priority filing deadline is 2/1. The Princeton Review suggests that all financial aid forms be submitted as soon as possible after October 1. *Need-based scholarships/grants offered:* College/university scholarship or grant aid from institutional funds; Federal Pell; Private scholarships; SEOG; State scholarships/grants. *Loan aid offered:* Direct PLUS loans; Direct Subsidized Stafford Loans; Direct Unsubsidized Stafford Loans. Applicants will be notified of awards on a rolling basis beginning 3/15. Federal Work-Study Program available. Institutional employment available.

The Inside Word

Admissions officers take a broad view of an applicant's academic program, class standing, grades, standardized test results, and trends in performance. Students that get in have an average GPA of 3.7 (out of 4.0), SAT scores between 1180–1350, or an ACT score of 27–32. Applicants must select one of seven undergraduate schools based on their desired major. Early action is an option. Be aware of deadline variations for first-year, transfer, and international applicants.

THE SCHOOL SAYS " . . ."

From the Admissions Office

"Since 1791, the University of Vermont has worked to advance humankind through education and discovery focused on the health of our societies and on the health of our environment. Campus looks out across one of America's most vibrant small cities to Lake Champlain and the Adirondack Mountains beyond. Students' lives are enriched by UVM's location in Burlington, a Northeast hub acclaimed for business innovation as well as world-class recreation, and by the dual values of "Freedom and Unity" emanating from Vermont's landscape and resonating in its motto.

"As a land grant university, UVM offers a breadth of opportunities and resources—these include a major academic medical center right on campus and newly constructed STEM facilities housing one of the fastest supercomputers in the country—yet our community is small compared to many national universities and fosters close faculty-student connections. UVM professors are acclaimed researchers, scholars, and artists who bring new discoveries into their classrooms and engage students in their labs and field research activities around the globe. Here, you'll find students testing new vaccines at our medical center; studying the effects of climate change aboard the Melosira, our research vessel; furthering the application of nanotechnology; performing alongside Grammy-winning artists; and launching socially responsible start-ups.

"Undergraduates, regardless of major, take courses across disciplines and have internships and other experiences that expand skills and perspective. The value of a UVM education shows in students' success after graduation: 92 percent of recent graduates have jobs or are continuing their education within six months (2016-18 average); many are selected for Fulbright, Truman, Udall and other top national awards.

"The fifth oldest university in New England, UVM boasts a legacy of important firsts, including first to admit women and African-Americans to Phi Beta Kappa. Today, the university continues to provide students endless ways to challenge ideas, explore the world, and develop skills and networks needed to address the most pressing issues of our time. UVM graduates are making discoveries, leading social change, and improving environmental and human health—everywhere."

SELECTIVITY

Admissions Rating	87
# of applicants	19,233
% of applicants accepted	67
% of acceptees attending	20
# offered a place on the wait list	3,802
% accepting a place on wait list	44
% admitted from wait list	0

FRESHMAN PROFILE

Range SAT EBRW	600–680
Range SAT Math	580–680
Range SAT Composite	1200–1360
Range ACT Composite	26–31
# submitting SAT scores	2,084
% submitting SAT scores	79
# submitting ACT scores	821
% submitting ACT scores	31
Average HS GPA	3.7
% graduated top 10% of class	34
% graduated top 25% of class	75
% graduated top 50% of class	98

DEADLINES

Early action	
Deadline	11/1
Notification	12/15
Regular	
Deadline	1/15
Notification	3/31
Nonfall registration?	Yes

FINANCIAL FACTS

Financial Aid Rating	84
Annual in-state tuition	$16,392
Annual out-of-state tuition	$41,280
Room and board	$13,354
Required fees	$2,670
Books and supplies	$1,200
Average frosh need-based scholarship	$19,338
Average UG need-based scholarship	$17,313
% needy frosh rec. need-based scholarship or grant aid	98
% needy UG rec. need-based scholarship or grant aid	96
% needy frosh rec. non-need-based scholarship or grant aid	13
% needy UG rec. non-need-based scholarship or grant aid	11
% needy frosh rec. need-based self-help aid	64
% needy UG rec. need-based self-help aid	68
% frosh rec. any financial aid	96
% UG rec. any financial aid	87
% UG borrow to pay for school	57
Average cumulative indebtedness	$31,684
% frosh need fully met	18
% ugrads need fully met	16
Average % of frosh need met	71
Average % of ugrad need met	66

UNIVERSITY OF VIRGINIA

Office of Admission, Charlottesville, VA 22903 • Admissions: 434-982-3200 • Fax: 434-924-3587

STUDENTS SAY " . . ."

Academics

Along with the low in-state tuition, academic rigor is the reason many students choose UVA. "All our schools are pretty strong and we have beautiful facilities, numerous options to choose from in regards to liberal arts education, and most professors are so excited to be here and be teaching," a sophomore reports. The school's greatest strengths, according to one senior, "include its location in Charlottesville, the wide variety of courses and their high level of academic rigor, and the many ways to work or volunteer outside the classroom." "Each class caters to the smartest kids and elevates everyone." On the whole, students are very happy with their professors, who are "extremely knowledgeable, passionate, excellent teachers, with a few exceptions. The teachers are generally very accessible and responsive to emails, and are genuinely interested in helping students succeed and encouraging exploration of interesting topic material outside of class." While students note that in large lecture classes it can be a challenge to engage, "professors are very accessible if you seek them out," and "are genuinely interested in helping students succeed and encouraging exploration of interesting topic material outside of class." Academics here are almost universally described as rigorous and challenging, with a particularly tough grading curve in the sciences, but students praise the available resources and academic advising. "Having a personal relationship with faculty members outside of the classroom helps with the academic experience."

Life

Between the gorgeous campus (called "Grounds" within the community) and "the bucolic college town of Charlottesville," students are very happy with life outside the classroom here. Studying occupies much of the week, in the many libraries and study spaces available. There's a lot of school spirit and varsity sporting events are well-attended. On weekends, "there is a significant party culture here…but not necessarily more than at other public universities." "Frat parties dominate the social scene" for first- and second-year students, with juniors and seniors migrating off-campus to bars and apartment parties. Roughly a quarter of the student body goes Greek. That said, "if students don't like the party scene, Charlottesville's adorable downtown mall is easily accessible by bus and has lots of fun activities!" "There's an ice skating rink downtown, as well as various restaurants and shopping. "There is always a lot going on on Grounds," as well. "Head to the lawn and you'll never be bored!" "During the warmer months you can always find people outside tossing a Frisbee, or maybe setting up an impromptu volleyball game. There are plenty of great hiking trails in the area and the athletics facilities are great." Students report "lots of student involvement and wide-range of opportunities of activities offered outside the classroom from research to internships to clubs," and "community service is very popular." Some students are eager to see the school make changes in policies pertaining to student safety and sexual misconduct; the administration is responding and has shared a lengthy, proposed new policy with the UVA community for review and comment.

Student Body

"The typical UVA student is reasonably wealthy, white, and very preppy. Other groups can be found within the student body, but you have to actively seek them out." This sums up how students describe themselves, though they're quick to acknowledge that there are other types beyond the typical. Roughly two-thirds of the student body is from Virginia. Some praise the diversity of the school while others would like to see even more. "Preppy" and "involved" are also common adjectives. "The typical student is very involved outside of academics and usually has a million things to do," including socialize. "Students are highly involved in academics, extracurriculars, and socially. Your average UVA student is very well-rounded and extremely busy, but enjoys that lifestyle." This involvement makes it easy for students to find niches within the larger community that suit their interests, and there's no question that everyone here is very driven in the direction of their choosing.

Financial Aid: 434-982-4757 • E-Mail: undergradadmission@virginia.edu • Website: www.virginia.edu

THE PRINCETON REVIEW SAYS

Admissions

Very important factors considered include: rigor of secondary school record, class rank, academic GPA, recommendation(s), character/personal qualities, state residency. *Important factors considered include:* application essay, standardized test scores, extracurricular activities, talent/ability. *Other factors considered include:* first generation, alumni/ae relation, geographical residence, racial/ethnic status, volunteer work, work experience. ACT with or without writing accepted. SAT with or without Essay component accepted. High school diploma is required and GED is accepted. *Academic units required:* 4 English, 4 math, 2 science, 2 foreign language, 1 social studies. *Academic units recommended:* 5 math, 5 science, 5 foreign language, 5 social studies.

Financial Aid

Students should submit: CSS/Financial Aid PROFILE; FAFSA. Priority filing deadline is 3/1. The Princeton Review suggests that all financial aid forms be submitted as soon as possible after October 1. *Need-based scholarships/grants offered:* College/university scholarship or grant aid from institutional funds; Federal Nursing Scholarships; Federal Pell; Private scholarships; SEOG; State scholarships/grants. *Loan aid offered:* Direct PLUS loans; Direct Subsidized Stafford Loans; Direct Unsubsidized Stafford Loans. Applicants will be notified of awards on or about 4/5. Federal Work-Study Program available. Institutional employment available.

The Inside Word

Unlike many public universities, UVA does not use a formula or minimum scores in its admission process, but applicants must have stellar academic records and demonstrate willingness to rise to the school's academic challenges. The most important parts of the application are GPA, rigor of high school curriculum, test scores (the SAT or ACT is required), and recommendations. Admission here is competitive, particularly for students from out of state.

THE SCHOOL SAYS "..."

From the Admissions Office

"Admission to the University of Virginia is competitive. Students who stretch themselves and take rigorous courses in high school (honors-level, AP, A-level, IB, and DE courses, when offered) are more qualified for admission than those who do not. Many students applying to the University present solid academic credentials, but we are also looking beyond the numbers and are interested in a student's life and contributions outside of the classroom. Non-cognitive factors play a significant role in our review, and we are especially interested in students who exhibit strong leadership and personal qualities. Love of learning, the ability to think critically, analytically, and globally, strong writing skills, and the desire to make a difference in the world are also attributes of UVA students.

"SAT or ACT is required but neither is preferred. The writing section on either test is not required, and SAT Subject Tests are optional."

SELECTIVITY

Admissions Rating	98
# of applicants	40,839
% of applicants accepted	24
% of acceptees attending	40
# offered a place on the wait list	5,486
% accepting a place on wait list	54
% admitted from wait list	0

FRESHMAN PROFILE

Range SAT EBRW	670–740
Range SAT Math	670–780
Range SAT Composite	1340–1500
Range ACT Composite	30–34
# submitting SAT scores	3,105
% submitting SAT scores	79
# submitting ACT scores	1,350
% submitting ACT scores	34
Average HS GPA	4.3
% graduated top 10% of class	90
% graduated top 25% of class	98
% graduated top 50% of class	99

DEADLINES

Early decision	
Deadline	10/15
Notification	12/15
Early action	
Deadline	11/1
Notification	1/31
Regular	
Deadline	1/1
Notification	4/1
Nonfall registration?	No

FINANCIAL FACTS

Financial Aid Rating	95
Annual in-state tuition	$15,848
Annual out-of-state tuition	$50,516
Room and board	$12,350
Required fees	$3,120
Books and supplies	$1,356
Average frosh need-based scholarship	$24,625
Average UG need-based scholarship	$24,776
% needy frosh rec. need-based scholarship or grant aid	88
% needy UG rec. need-based scholarship or grant aid	87
% needy frosh rec. non-need-based scholarship or grant aid	9
% needy UG rec. non-need-based scholarship or grant aid	7
% needy frosh rec. need-based self-help aid	57
% needy UG rec. need-based self-help aid	61
% frosh rec. any financial aid	57.6
% UG rec. any financial aid	52.2
% UG borrow to pay for school	33
Average cumulative indebtedness	$26,023
% frosh need fully met	100
% ugrads need fully met	100
Average % of frosh need met	100
Average % of ugrad need met	100

UNIVERSITY OF WASHINGTON

1410 NE Campus Parkway, Seattle, WA 98195-5852 • Admissions: 206-543-9686 • Fax: 206-685-3655

CAMPUS LIFE

Quality of Life Rating	**89**
Fire Safety Rating	**95**
Green Rating	**98**
Type of school	Public
Environment	Metropolis

STUDENTS

Total undergrad enrollment	31,042
% male/female	46/54
% from out of state	19
% frosh live on campus	72
% ugrads live on campus	29
# of fraternities (% ugrad men join)	32 (14)
# of sororities (% ugrad women join)	16 (15)
% African American	3
% Asian	26
% Caucasian	37
% Hispanic	9
% Native American	<1
% Pacific Islander	<1
% Two or more races	8
% Race and/or ethnicity unknown	1
% international	16
# of countries represented	76

SURVEY SAYS ...

Great library
Internships are widely available
No one cheats
Students environmentally aware
Students love Seattle, WA
Recreation facilities are great
Very little drug use
Everyone loves the Huskies

ACADEMICS

Academic Rating	**81**
% students returning for sophomore year	95
% % students graduating within 4 years	66
% students graduating within 6 years	84
Calendar	Quarter
Student/faculty ratio	21:1
Profs interesting rating	85
Profs accessible rating	90
Most classes have 20–29 students.	
Most lab/discussion sessions have 20–29 students.	

MOST POPULAR MAJORS

Engineering, General; Business Administration and Management, General; Computer Science

STUDENTS SAY "..."

Academics

Students find "a great combination of high-powered academics, an excellent social life, and a wide variety of courses, all in the midst of the exciting Seattle life" at the University of Washington, the state's flagship institution of higher learning. UW offers "a lot of really stellar programs and the best bang for the buck, especially for in-state students or those in the sciences." Indeed, science programs "are incredible. The research going on here is cutting-edge and the leaders of biomedical sciences, stem cell research, etc. are accessible to students." Undergrads warn, however, that science programs are extremely competitive, "high pressure," and "challenging," with "core classes taught in lectures that seat more than 500 people," creating the sense that "professors don't seem to care too much whether you succeed." Pre-professional programs in business, law, nursing, medicine, and engineering all earn high marks, although again with the caveat that the workload is tough and the hand-holding nominal. As one student puts it, "The University of Washington provides every resource and opportunity for its students to succeed. You just have to take advantage of them. No one will do it for you." For those fortunate enough to get in, the Honors Program "creates a smaller community of highly motivated students...It puts this school on top."

Life

UW students typically "have a good balance in their lives of education and fun." They "generally study hard and work in the libraries, but once the nighttime hits, they look forward to enjoying the night with their friends." Between the large university community and the surrounding city of Seattle, undergrads have a near-limitless selection of extracurricular choices. As one student explains, "There are tons of options for fun in Seattle. Going down to Pike's Market on a Saturday and eating your way through is always popular. There are tons of places to eat on 'The Ave,'" the shopping district that abuts campus, "and the UVillage shopping mall is a five minute walk from campus with chain-store comfort available. Intramural sports are big for activities, and going to undergraduate theater productions is never a disappointing experience. During autumn or spring renting a canoe and paddling around lake Washington down by the stadium is fun." Husky football games "are amazing," and the Greek community "is very big" without dominating campus social life. In short, "the UW has anything you could want to do in your free time."

Student Body

"At such a large university, there is no 'typical' student," undergrads tell us, observing "one can find just about any demographic here and there is a huge variety in personalities." There "are quite a lot of yuppies, but then again, it's Seattle," and by and large "the campus is ultraliberal. Most students care about the environment, are not religious, and are generally accepting of other diverse individuals." Otherwise, "you've got your stereotypes: the Greeks, the street fashion pioneers, the various ethnic communities, the Oxford-looking grad students, etc." In terms of demographics, "the typical student at UW is white, middle-class, and is from the Seattle area," but "there are a lot of African American students and a very large number of Asian students." All groups "seem to socialize with each other."

UNIVERSITY OF WASHINGTON

Financial Aid: 206-543-6101 • Website: admit.uw.edu

THE PRINCETON REVIEW SAYS

Admissions

Very important factors considered include: rigor of secondary school record, grade trends, GPA, application essay. *Important factors considered include:* extracurricular activities, talent/ability, first generation. *Other factors considered include:* character/personal qualities, state residency. High school diploma or equivalent is not required. *Academic units required:* 4 English, 3 math, 3 science, 2 science labs, 2 foreign language, 3 social studies, 0.5 academic electives, 1 visual/performing arts. *Academic units recommended:* 4 English, 4 math, 4 science, 3 science labs, 3 foreign language, 4 social studies, 1 history, 1 computer science, 1 visual/performing arts.

Financial Aid

Students should submit: FAFSA. Priority filing deadline is 1/15. The Princeton Review suggests that all financial aid forms be submitted as soon as possible after October 1. *Need-based scholarships/grants offered:* College/university scholarship or grant aid from institutional funds; Federal Pell; Private scholarships; SEOG; State scholarships/grants. *Loan aid offered:* Direct PLUS loans; Direct Subsidized Stafford Loans; Direct Unsubsidized Stafford Loans. Applicants will be notified of awards on or about 4/1. Federal Work-Study Program available. Institutional employment available.

The Inside Word

UW performs a thorough review of all freshman applications. Its holistic approach allows admissions officers to take into account a student's background, the degree to which he or she has overcome personal adversity, and such intangibles as leadership quality and special skills. The result has been an increased racial and socioeconomic diversity on campus.

THE SCHOOL SAYS "..."

From the Admissions Office

"Are you curious about everything, from comet dust to computer game design, salmon to Salman Rushdie, ancient Rome to the atmospherics of Mars? Do you seek the freedom to chart your own course—and work on breakthrough research? Are you ready to cheer on the Division I Huskies and spend your weekends sea kayaking? Would you like to walk to class on a 700-acre stunning, ivy-covered campus, yet be only eight minutes from downtown Seattle? If the answers are yes, then the University of Washington may be the place for you. Offering more than 180 majors and 900 student organizations, the UW is looking for students who are both excited about the vast academic and social possibilities available to them and eager to contribute to the campus' cultural and intellectual life.

"We encourage you to take advantage of every opportunity in the application, especially the personal statement and activities summary, to tell us why the University of Washington would be good fit for you and how you will contribute to our community."

SELECTIVITY

Admissions Rating	89
# of applicants	45,579
% of applicants accepted	52
% of acceptees attending	30
# offered a place on the wait list	7,775
% accepting a place on wait list	39
% admitted from wait list	79

FRESHMAN PROFILE

Range SAT EBRW	600–700
Range SAT Math	620–770
Range SAT Composite	1240–1440
Range ACT Composite	27–33
# submitting SAT scores	5,638
% submitting SAT scores	81
# submitting ACT scores	2,099
% submitting ACT scores	30
Average HS GPA	3.8

DEADLINES

Regular	
Deadline	11/15
Notification	Rolling, 3/15
Nonfall registration?	No

FINANCIAL FACTS

Financial Aid Rating	83
Annual in-state tuition	$10,370
Annual out-of-state tuition	$37,071
Room and board	$13,296
Required fees	$1,095
Books and supplies	$900
Average frosh need-based scholarship	$16,842
Average UG need-based scholarship	$16,746
% needy frosh rec. need-based scholarship or grant aid	85
% needy UG rec. need-based scholarship or grant aid	87
% needy frosh rec. non-need-based scholarship or grant aid	4
% needy UG rec. non-need-based scholarship or grant aid	3
% needy frosh rec. need-based self-help aid	40
% needy UG rec. need-based self-help aid	47
% frosh rec. any financial aid	38
% UG rec. any financial aid	39
% UG borrow to pay for school	33
Average cumulative indebtedness	$19,198
% frosh need fully met	22
% ugrads need fully met	19
Average % of frosh need met	78
Average % of ugrad need met	77

UNIVERSITY OF WISCONSIN—MADISON

702 West Johnson Street, Suite 101, Madison, WI 53715-1007 • Admissions: 608-262-3961 • Fax: 608-262-7706

STUDENTS SAY "   "

Academics

The University of Wisconsin—Madison is a large research campus sitting on an isthmus between two lakes that lets almost 30,000 undergraduates avail themselves of 4,700 courses, 129 majors, and "an abundance of research opportunities in all fields." Resources abound here: students have "access to state-of-the-art technology" and "lots of programs and opportunities to go abroad." First-years "can easily work in a lab, and … there is potential for publication" if they spend enough time there. The school "provides amazing opportunities to its students and is extremely accommodating." As one student describes, "Academic tutoring happens around campus for almost every single class and mental health resources are available 24/7."

Professors "know that the university culture involves lots of interaction and mentoring of students" and therefore "are truly about teaching and learning." "Tests are generally fair and … outlined well," says a student. Another notes that some courses are styled as "active learning classes," in which "students watch short lecture videos" and work out homework with the assistance of the professor and TAs during class time. There are "multiple avenues to gain research experience on campus" thanks to the "insane number of labs." Since "there is very little downtime here," the academic curriculum "does not occupy your time with busy work." Though students admit that there are a few faculty members with areas for improvement, they say "Wisconsin does a pretty good job of keeping professors who don't like to teach" out of the classroom, which is done by including teaching expectations in all faculty contracts.

Life

Even during cold weather "people spend a lot of time outside" and students can often be found "by the beautiful lakes [and hanging] out in the city, student unions, or parks." The "bus system is excellent" and "makes getting around campus very easy," which is useful as the campus sits on 936 acres. It "is part of a city environment," so students can go "to State Street to grab food or coffee," and "there are several concert venues around that attract pretty intriguing acts." Additionally, the school itself hosts "lots of free activities like concerts and art events and food events and speakers" that are "always well-attended." Several of the dorms "are top-notch" and the "dorm food is usually very good."

"It's never hard to find a party" here, but even though "students may go out and be social at night, the library is full by 9 A.M. the next morning." "The average student … parties a lot, and studies even more," says one. But regardless of what you like to do, students are confident that even "if you do not drink, you will find other people" to hang out with.

Student Body

Most students here "are from around the Midwest, especially Wisconsin," and "midwestern kindness prevails" among this "fun and intellectually diverse student body," which is "not too big or too small." Students are "extremely active in extracurriculars," and they take full advantage of the more than one thousand student organizations on offer. "Everyone gets so excited about sports," particularly during football and basketball season ("athletic games are sacred places for [the] Badger teams"). "Everyone is genuinely thrilled to be at this school, whether it be on a football Saturday or just another day of class," says a student. Most here "care about preparing for their future, but don't get too competitive about grades," and "it's easy to pick up new study partners in any class by introducing yourself on the first day."

UNIVERSITY OF WISCONSIN—MADISON

Financial Aid: 608-262-3060 • E-Mail: onwisconsin@admissions.wisc.edu • Website: www.wisc.edu

THE PRINCETON REVIEW SAYS

Admissions

Very important factors considered include: rigor of secondary school record, application essay. *Important factors considered include:* academic GPA, standardized test scores, state residency. *Other factors considered include:* class rank, recommendation(s), extracurricular activities, talent/ability, character/personal qualities, first generation, racial/ethnic status, volunteer work, work experience, level of applicant's interest. ACT with or without writing accepted. SAT with or without Essay component accepted. High school diploma is required and GED is accepted. *Academic units required:* 4 English, 4 math, 3 science, 3 foreign language, 3 social studies, 2 units from above areas or other academic areas. *Academic units recommended:* 4 English, 4 math, 4 science, 2 science labs, 4 foreign language, 4 social studies, 2 units from above areas or other academic areas.

Financial Aid

Students should submit: FAFSA. Priority filing deadline is 12/1. The Princeton Review suggests that all financial aid forms be submitted as soon as possible after October 1. *Need-based scholarships/grants offered:* College/university scholarship or grant aid from institutional funds; Federal Pell; Private scholarships; SEOG; State scholarships/grants. *Loan aid offered:* Direct PLUS loans; Direct Subsidized Stafford Loans; Direct Unsubsidized Stafford Loans. Applicants will be notified of awards on a rolling basis beginning 3/1. Federal Work-Study Program available. Institutional employment available.

The Inside Word

Though UW—Madison is a large state school, it still manages to take a holistic approach to the admissions game. Indeed, there are no minimum GPAs, class ranks, or test scores required. That said, a strong academic record is paramount. Looking beyond your transcript, Wisconsin wants candidates who will actively contribute to campus life. And it also seeks diversity in both background and personal experience. Finally, students who intend to major in either dance or music must schedule an audition as well as submit a regular application.

THE SCHOOL SAYS "..."

From the Admissions Office

"UW-Madison is the university of choice for some of the best students from around the world. The middle 50 percent of our Fall 2019 freshman class had an ACT score range of 27–32, an SAT score range of 630–710 (ERBW) and 680–780 (Math), a GPA range of 3.8–4.0, and ranked in the 85–97 percentile of their class.

"These factors combine to make admission to UW-Madison both competitive and selective. We consider academic record, strength of curriculum (honors, AP, IB, etc.), grade trend, class rank, results of the ACT/SAT, and non-academic factors. There is no prescribed minimum test score, GPA, or class rank criteria. Rather, we admit the best and most well-prepared students—students who have challenged themselves and who will contribute to Wisconsin's strength and diversity—for the limited space available. "Each application is personally reviewed by our admission counselors. All freshman applications completed by February 1 receive full and equal consideration. We offer two decision plans for freshman applicants. To receive a decision during the Early Action period, you must complete the application by November 1 and submit all required materials (application fee, official transcript(s), official test scores, personal essays, and one required academic letter of recommendation) by our materials deadline. Early Action period applicants will receive a decision by the end of January. All students who complete their application during the Regular Decision period (after November 1 but before the February 1 deadline) will receive a decision by the end of March. UW-Madison has a commitment to a holistic, competitive, and selective admission process for all applicants."

SELECTIVITY

Admissions Rating	93
# of applicants	43,921
% of applicants accepted	53
% of acceptees attending	32

FRESHMAN PROFILE

Range SAT EBRW	630–710
Range SAT Math	680–780
Range SAT Composite	1330–1450
Range ACT Composite	27–32
# submitting SAT scores	2,079
% submitting SAT scores	28
# submitting ACT scores	5,964
% submitting ACT scores	79
Average HS GPA	3.9
% graduated top 10% of class	57
% graduated top 25% of class	90
% graduated top 50% of class	100

DEADLINES

Early action	
Deadline	11/1
Notification	12/31
Regular	
Deadline	2/1
Notification	3/31
Nonfall registration?	Yes

FINANCIAL FACTS

Financial Aid Rating	87
Annual in-state tuition	$9,273
Annual out-of-state tuition	$36,333
Room and board	$11,114
Books and supplies	$1,200
Average frosh need-based scholarship	$17,084
Average UG need-based scholarship	$15,143
% needy frosh rec. need-based scholarship or grant aid	75
% needy UG rec. need-based scholarship or grant aid	76
% needy frosh rec. non-need-based scholarship or grant aid	10
% needy UG rec. non-need-based scholarship or grant aid	9
% needy frosh rec. need-based self-help aid	71
% needy UG rec. need-based self-help aid	72
% UG borrow to pay for school	44
Average cumulative indebtedness	$27,973
% frosh need fully met	47
% ugrads need fully met	41
Average % of frosh need met	83
Average % of ugrad need met	80

UNIVERSITY OF WYOMING

Dept 3435, Laramie, WY 82071 • Admissions: 307-766-5160 • Fax: 307-766-4042

CAMPUS LIFE

Quality of Life Rating	87
Fire Safety Rating	91
Green Rating	74
Type of school	Public
Environment	Town

STUDENTS

Total undergrad enrollment	9,646
% male/female	49/51
% from out of state	35
% frosh live on campus	87
% ugrads live on campus	25
# of fraternities (% ugrad men join)	10 (6)
# of sororities (% ugrad women join)	6 (7)
% African American	1
% Asian	1
% Caucasian	74
% Hispanic	7
% Native American	1
% Pacific Islander	<1
% Two or more races	4
% Race and/or ethnicity unknown	10
% international	3
# of countries represented	60

SURVEY SAYS . . .

Lots of conservative students
Recreation facilities are great

ACADEMICS

Academic Rating	75
% students returning for sophomore year	76
% students graduating within 4 years	27
% students graduating within 6 years	57
Calendar	Semester
Student/faculty ratio	15:1
Profs interesting rating	84
Profs accessible rating	89

Most classes have 20–29 students.
Most lab/discussion sessions have
20–29 students.

MOST POPULAR MAJORS

Psychology; Elementary Education;
Kinesiology & Health Promotion

STUDENTS SAY ". . ."

Academics

The only four-year university in the state, University of Wyoming has a lot to offer students with its large campus and small class sizes that give students the best of both worlds, and teachers "work hard for the students," "care about the material they are teaching and make it interesting," and are "knowledgeable and supportive." Doors are always open, and professors are "always happy to talk to you about experiences with work or research or school." Student Support resources are similarly very helpful; though there have been complaints of recent budget cuts, "there are a lot of options for academic help as well as personal help if you are going through a rough time." In that vein, school advisors "really get to know you and try to find the best options for you." Professors actually teach the classes instead of relying on TAs, and "eager to clarify any topics both in the classroom as well as in office hours." These dedicated instructors often assist with club programs, and are happy to help students in those clubs make connections with working professionals to improve their chances of finding future employment. The variety of courses available to students is a huge draw (there are more than 80 undergraduate majors to choose from), with a lot of niche classes and "some engineering programs that aren't found in many other universities." Students support one another and "although some programs are competitive, it is not very cutthroat." On top of the quality education available right on campus, the school also has "great study abroad programs." The university also offers research to undergraduate students as early as their first semester, for those that want to begin padding their academic résumé.

Life

Wyoming is "known for how untouched by civilization it is," and the small town of Laramie is almost entirely college-oriented. Lots of people go swing dancing, hike, fish, and ski, and "hunting is common." The outdoors is very important to the majority of the student body, and "Yes, it gets cold and snowy, but that just means the snow sculptures students make last longer!" University of Wyoming athletics are "always enjoyable to watch" and the newest addition to the campus is "a huge gym." Despite the great wide open that characterizes the state of Wyoming, the campus itself is condensed into "a smallish area" so students can walk to class from any building and be there in under ten minutes.

Outside of Laramie, it's easy enough to travel to Cheyenne or Fort Collins for shopping or other activities. The university sponsors plenty of events to keep students occupied, such as "movie nights, musical productions, [and other] de-stressors," and on Thursdays there is always live music in the student union, as well as some event usually scheduled for Friday evening.

Student Body

The University of Wyoming student body "is not full of the stereotypical cowboys" that many would expect; this is a young (mostly white) university composed of "a strong mix of western blue collar cowboy culture mixed with the more liberal ideas of bordering Colorado," all of which "combines to create a very libertarian atmosphere." There are quite a few veterans and international students here, and a simple stroll through campus lets one "see the wide range of personal expression that makes our campus a fun place." School pride is the best at UW and "there is always a sea of gold on Saturdays. We bleed brown and gold and aren't afraid to show it." To wit, "everyone here is in support of the WHOLE state, not just our region."

Financial Aid: 307-766-2116 • E-Mail: admissions@uwyo.edu • Website: www.uwyo.edu

THE PRINCETON REVIEW SAYS

Admissions

Very important factors considered include: rigor of secondary school record, academic GPA, standardized test scores. *Other factors considered include:* application essay. ACT with or without writing accepted. SAT with or without Essay component accepted. High school diploma is required and GED is accepted. *Academic units required:* 4 English, 4 math, 4 science, 3 science labs, 2 foreign language, 3 social studies, 2 academic electives, 2 units from above areas or other academic areas. *Academic units recommended:* 4 English, 4 math, 4 science, 3 science labs, 2 foreign language, 3 social studies, 2 academic electives.

Financial Aid

Students should submit: FAFSA. Priority filing deadline is 3/1. The Princeton Review suggests that all financial aid forms be submitted as soon as possible after October 1. *Need-based scholarships/grants offered:* College/university scholarship or grant aid from institutional funds; Federal Pell; Private scholarships; SEOG; State scholarships/grants. *Loan aid offered:* Direct PLUS loans; Direct Subsidized Stafford Loans; Direct Unsubsidized Stafford Loans. Applicants will be notified of awards on a rolling basis beginning 12/20. Federal Work-Study Program available. Institutional employment available.

The Inside Word

The admissions process at University of Wyoming is formula-driven. An unweighted high school GPA of 3.0 in a traditional college prep curriculum combined with some solid test scores will open the door to this university.

THE SCHOOL SAYS "..."

From the Admissions Office

"The University of Wyoming offers a personalized education for a fraction of the cost of other public universities. Located in Laramie, UW is regularly recognized as one of the nation's best college values. This comes as no surprise, as UW is a national research university offering countless academic opportunities.

"Explore 200+ programs of study through seven colleges and three specialized schools. From Engineering to Business, Performing Arts to Geology and Agricultural Economics to Nursing, we are sure you will find your program at UW.

"Over the past seven years, the UW campus has experienced incredible growth. 750 million dollars have been invested in new facilities including a new Business building, Creative Arts facility, UW Library and most recently the introduction of the NCAR supercomputer. The NCAR computer is a joint partnership between UW and the National Center for Atmospheric Research. Undergraduate students have access to all these facilities for instruction, internships and research.

"Set at 7,200 feet above sea level, UW and Laramie are in a pristine location to attend school and enjoy the outdoors. UW was recently recognized by *Outside* magazine as the fifteenth best college campus in the country for outdoor adventure. Just thirty miles from campus is over two million acres of national forest with peaks climbing over 12,000 feet. Campus life is exciting with 200+ student clubs and organizations as well as NCAA Division 1-A sports in the Mountain West conference."

SELECTIVITY

Admissions Rating	75
# of applicants	5,348
% of applicants accepted	96
% of acceptees attending	33

FRESHMAN PROFILE

Range SAT EBRW	540–640
Range SAT Math	520–640
Range SAT Composite	1080–1270
Range ACT Composite	22–28
# submitting SAT scores	654
% submitting SAT scores	37
# submitting ACT scores	1,306
% submitting ACT scores	74
Average HS GPA	3.5
% graduated top 10% of class	24
% graduated top 25% of class	51
% graduated top 50% of class	83

DEADLINES

Regular	
Deadline	8/10
Nonfall registration?	Yes

FINANCIAL FACTS

Financial Aid Rating	82
Annual in-state tuition	$4,350
Annual out-of-state tuition	$18,090
Room and board	$10,615
Required fees	$1,441
Books and supplies	$1,200
Average frosh need-based scholarship	$4,945
Average UG need-based scholarship	$5,185
% needy frosh rec. need-based scholarship or grant aid	58
% needy UG rec. need-based scholarship or grant aid	66
% needy frosh rec. non-need-based scholarship or grant aid	87
% needy UG rec. non-need-based scholarship or grant aid	74
% needy frosh rec. need-based self-help aid	46
% needy UG rec. need-based self-help aid	54
% frosh rec. any financial aid	92.2
% UG rec. any financial aid	87
% UG borrow to pay for school	46
Average cumulative indebtedness	$23,444
% frosh need fully met	26
% ugrads need fully met	16
Average % of frosh need met	64
Average % of ugrad need met	59

Ursinus College

601 East Main Street, Collegeville, PA 19426 • Admissions: 610-409-3200 • Fax: 610-409-3197

STUDENTS SAY "..."

Academics

Located just outside of Philadelphia, Ursinus College has done a remarkable job of building a "close-knit community" dedicated to helping students succeed with strong academics and "plenty of opportunities for leadership involvement through clubs, student jobs, and internships." The "liberal arts curricula [encourages undergrads] to explore different fields" and potentially uncover new academic areas of interest. Even better, there's a tremendous "focus on research." Students also rush to highlight the "science and pre-health prep program[s]," duly noting Ursinus's "high medical school acceptance rate." Some of that success can likely be attributed to "small" classes, which are a staple here. As one first-year student brags, "My smallest class size is seven and my largest is twenty-one." She continues, "I receive...[so much] attention that [it] makes it feel as though I have a seal team of PhDs looking out for me, and that is truly amazing." Indeed, professors here are "very supportive, intelligent, and passionate about the subjects they are teaching." And they work hard to make sure they're accessible. As one student shares, "Their office hours are incredibly flexible (at certain times and by appointment as well). I've gone into some professors' office hours three times a week for the entirety of the semester, I've had professors come in on Sundays to help, and I've been to their houses for dinner ... I've grown substantially ... with their help."

Life

We've been assured that "there's never a dull moment" at Ursinus. After all, the college "offer[s] so many activities [with which] to get involved." Extracurricular clubs range from a "pre-medicine help group...to a nerf club where [members] battle on the weekends in academic buildings." Community service is also pretty popular here, too. For example, "on Saturdays, groups of people will generally wake up and volunteer at the soup kitchen or go to the local nursing home and either visit or sing songs to them." Once the weekend rolls around, you can certainly find "a lot of parties." Then again, that's probably a given considering that "many students are [involved] in Greek life." However, if you aren't down for drinking it's not a problem. There "are always people who will just hang out and watch movies or play silly board games." Students who love to laugh will be delighted to learn that Ursinus sponsors a number of "comedy events," either "hosted by the UC improv club or...a guest comedian [brought in by the school.]" Finally, the "Campus Activities Board also puts on events multiple times a month that can be anything from trivia to Pinterest nights." It's virtually impossible not to have fun here!

Student Body

Students at Ursinus speak enthusiastically about their classmates. Of course, it's difficult to say something negative about people who "are always smiling" and "very welcoming." Undergrads do admit that the majority of their peers are "white [and] middle class": "While the college is homogeneous...in ethnic terms, it is ideologically very heterogeneous." As one undergrad explains, "I have encountered many ideas and beliefs that have challenged my own...[which] I very much appreciate." Students also stress that their classmates are "hardworking" and "down to earth." Moreover, as you might expect with college students, these undergrads also "tend to be curious." Indeed, "Everyone has something they really want to know more about." Interests and passions seem to run the gamut at Ursinus; you'll find everyone from "athletes [and] bio nerds [to] theatre kids" along with "prep[s and] hipsters." You "truly get a bit of everything here." Another happy student concludes, "Ursinus is a school where everyone fits in and you are encouraged to be yourself no matter how weird you may be. [It's a place that] appreciates people with different backgrounds, interests, and abilities."

Financial Aid: 610-409-3600 • E-Mail: admission@ursinus.edu • Website: www.ursinus.edu

THE PRINCETON REVIEW SAYS

Admissions

Very important factors considered include: rigor of secondary school record, academic GPA, character/personal qualities. *Important factors considered include:* class rank, application essay, recommendation(s), interview, extracurricular activities, talent/ability. *Other factors considered include:* standardized test scores, first generation, alumni/ae relation, geographical residence, state residency, racial/ethnic status, volunteer work, work experience, level of applicant's interest. ACT with or without writing accepted. SAT with or without Essay component accepted. High school diploma is required and GED is accepted. *Academic units required:* 4 English, 3 math, 1 science, 1 science lab, 2 foreign language, 1 social studies, 5 academic electives. *Academic units recommended:* 4 English, 4 math, 4 science, 3 science labs, 3 foreign language, 4 social studies.

Financial Aid

Students should submit: FAFSA; State aid form. Priority filing deadline is 2/1. The Princeton Review suggests that all financial aid forms be submitted as soon as possible after October 1. *Need-based scholarships/grants offered:* College/university scholarship or grant aid from institutional funds; Federal Pell; Private scholarships; SEOG; State scholarships/grants. *Loan aid offered:* Direct PLUS loans; Direct Subsidized Stafford Loans; Direct Unsubsidized Stafford Loans. Applicants will be notified of awards on or about 3/15. Federal Work-Study Program available. Institutional employment available.

The Inside Word

Admissions officers at Ursinus are looking for motivated students who demonstrate intellectual curiosity. They want applicants who have pushed themselves academically in high school, beyond basic college prep courses. Students who have filled their schedules with some advanced placement or IB classes might find they have a leg up. Ursinus is test optional. Those students who choose to submit can use either the new SAT or ACT. Finally, to be considered for all possible scholarships, it's best to apply either Early Action or Early Decision.

THE SCHOOL SAYS "..."

From the Admissions Office

"Located in suburban Philadelphia, the college boasts a beautiful 170-acre campus that features a highly individualized academic experience; the nationally recognized Common Intellectual Experience first-year seminar, which is a component of the Quest: Open Questions Open Minds core curriculum; residential village housing for students; the Floy Lewis Bakes Athletic Center with an indoor track and fieldhouse; the Berman Museum of Art; The Kaleidoscope performing arts center; and the new Innovation and Discovery Center. Ursinus is a member of the Centennial Conference along with Dickinson, Franklin & Marshall, Gettysburg, Muhlenberg, and Swarthmore. The academic environment is enhanced by a chapter of Phi Beta Kappa; a direct admission partnership with Saint Joseph's University (MBA program); dual-degree engineering agreements with Columbia University and Case Western Reserve; an affiliation agreement with the Villanova University M. Louise Fitzpatrick College of Nursing (accelerated BSN); the Peace Corps Preparatory program; international study abroad; the Philadelphia Experience; and three centers: the Center for Science and the Common Good, the U-Imagine Center for Integrative and Entrepreneurial Studies, and the Melrose Center for Global Civic Engagement. The college offers student research carried out with one-on-one faculty attention and extensive internship opportunities. Financial aid and scholarships are generous with special awards for outstanding academics; distinguished creative writing; music, dance and theater auditions; and Bonner leadership in service. Intercollegiate and intramural sports are very popular on campus. The Ursinus admission application requires strong and consistent performance in a college preparatory curriculum. Submission of standardized test scores is optional."

SELECTIVITY

Admissions Rating	80
# of applicants	3,530
% of applicants accepted	79
% of acceptees attending	15
# offered a place on the wait list	42
% accepting a place on wait list	26
% admitted from wait list	55
# of early decision applicants	75
% accepted early decision	93%

FRESHMAN PROFILE

Range SAT EBRW	580–670
Range SAT Math	570–680
Range SAT Composite	1160–1330
Range ACT Composite	24–30
# submitting SAT scores	310
% submitting SAT scores	72
# submitting ACT scores	74
% submitting ACT scores	17
Average HS GPA	3.4
% graduated top 10% of class	21
% graduated top 25% of class	50
% graduated top 50% of class	83

DEADLINES

Early decision	
Deadline	12/1
Notification	12/15
Other ED Deadline	2/1
Early action	
Deadline	11/1
Notification	12/15
Regular	
Deadline	2/1
Notification	3/15
Nonfall registration?	Yes

FINANCIAL FACTS

Financial Aid Rating	88
Annual tuition	$55,210
Room and board	$13,530
Books and supplies	$1,000
Average frosh need-based scholarship	$36,593
Average UG need-based scholarship	$36,659
% needy frosh rec. need-based scholarship or grant aid	98
% needy UG rec. need-based scholarship or grant aid	99
% needy frosh rec. non-need-based scholarship or grant aid	21
% needy UG rec. non-need-based scholarship or grant aid	17
% needy frosh rec. need-based self-help aid	75
% needy UG rec. need-based self-help aid	77
% frosh rec. any financial aid	99
% UG rec. any financial aid	99
% UG borrow to pay for school	70
Average cumulative indebtedness	$41,654
% frosh need fully met	27
% ugrads need fully met	24
Average % of frosh need met	80
Average % of ugrad need met	81

VANDERBILT UNIVERSITY

2305 West End Ave., Nashville, TN 37203 • Admissions: 615-322-2561 • Fax: 615-343-7765

CAMPUS LIFE

Quality of Life Rating	**99**
Fire Safety Rating	**91**
Green Rating	**99**
Type of school	Private
Environment	Metropolis

STUDENTS

Total undergrad enrollment	6,871
% male/female	48/52
% from out of state	89
% frosh from public high school	64
% frosh live on campus	100
% ugrads live on campus	85
# of fraternities (% ugrad men join)	17 (27)
# of sororities (% ugrad women join)	15 (43)
% African American	11
% Asian	14
% Caucasian	44
% Hispanic	10
% Native American	<1
% Pacific Islander	<1
% Two or more races	6
% Race and/or ethnicity unknown	5
% international	10
# of countries represented	51

SURVEY SAYS . . .

Students are happy
Classroom facilities are great
Lab facilities are great
Great library
Career services are great
Internships are widely available
School is well run
Great financial aid
Students are friendly
Students get along with local community
Students involved in community service
Students love Nashville, TN
Great food on campus
Great off-campus food
Dorms are like palaces
Easy to get around campus
Recreation facilities are great
Frats and sororities are popular
Theater is popular
Campus newspaper is popular
Active student government
Active minority support groups

ACADEMICS

Academic Rating	**93**
% students returning for sophomore year	97
% students graduating within 4 years	90
% students graduating within 6 years	93
Calendar	Semester
Student/faculty ratio	7:1
Profs interesting rating	95
Profs accessible rating	97

Most classes have 10–19 students.
Most lab/discussion sessions have
10–19 students.

MOST POPULAR MAJORS

Engineering Science; Multi-/Interdisciplinary
Studies, Other; Social Sciences, General

STUDENTS SAY "..."

Academics

The word "balance" is much used by students in describing Vanderbilt University, with its "top academics, vibrant social life, student organizations, community service, SEC football, and the city of Nashville" or the "unique balance [that] exists between social life and schoolwork." Students say this "balance" is why at Vanderbilt you'll get "an amazing education while having a good time and exploring all your interests along the way." As one student explains, "Vanderbilt is a place for students who are intelligent, but are more than just book-smart"—"it combines rigorous academics with a great social life." Another student says, "At Vanderbilt, I could [pursue] my interest in music while majoring in engineering, which was not the case in most other schools." The school is heavily influenced by the "diverse," "vibrant" city of Nashville. The "beautiful campus" is "only minutes away from being in the heart of the city," where there's a "crazy fun social scene, all with a Southern twist" and people "like being involved." This correlates well with Vanderbilt students who participate in an "array of extracurriculars" and take advantage of the school's "amazing community service opportunities" on campus and around Nashville. Within the 430 student organizations on campus, a student is hard-pressed not to find a few organizations that they can relate to. "The professors are engaging and the academics [are] challenging but rewarding." Professors are "approachable and helpful" and "are really invested in their students and will go out of their way to help them succeed." Besides the "rigorous but rewarding" academic environment, there are many "opportunities that challenge me beyond the books," says a student.

Life

"Everyone here knows how to be a student when it's time to be a student, and a college kid when outside of the classroom." Students say there's an "academic environment" but Vandy students "take the work hard/play hard mentality to heart when it comes to weekend activities." As one student puts it, "Everyone is outgoing and friendly, that's why we came to the South!" There is "a vibrant Greek [life] community" on campus and students say the social scene is inclusive and interwoven: "It is not unusual for a student to be a tour guide, RA, Fraternity officer, and still kill it in the classroom." The "beautiful" campus provides the "perfect balance between your classic college campus and big city school" and the students are "passionate, caring, [and] genuine." Even though "academics are usually at the top of everyone's lists," there's "always so much to do on campus or downtown in Nashville," with one student adding that it's also fun to "visit one of the many state parks that are close by, or go to one of the thousands of concerts Nashville has annually." On the whole, the atmosphere is "friendly and welcoming" and students say their peers are "clearly of high intellect, they are not competitive with each other academically and enjoy other things besides school."

Student Body

Vanderbilt has "a very interesting student body that blends traditional Southern students and culture with very distinct Northern influence," and students say that "you can find such a diverse group of people here...not just racially or ethnically or economically, but also in personality." The typical Vandy student is "well-rounded, engaged" and "committed to both learning and to extracurriculars." There's an atmosphere of collaboration rather than competition, students say: "People here don't worry about scoring higher than the person next to them. We're all in this together." While some say that "many fit the stereotype of rich, white, and upper class," most counter that Vanderbilt has "a diverse student body" and "students come from all over, and the freshman experience does a good job making us a united class."

VANDERBILT UNIVERSITY

Financial Aid: 800-288-0204 • E-Mail: admissions@vanderbilt.edu • Website: www.vanderbilt.edu

THE PRINCETON REVIEW SAYS

Admissions

Very important factors considered include: rigor of secondary school record, class rank, academic GPA, application essay, standardized test scores, extracurricular activities, character/personal qualities. *Important factors considered include:* recommendation(s), talent/ability. *Other factors considered include:* interview, first generation, alumni/ae relation, geographical residence, state residency, racial/ethnic status, volunteer work, work experience. ACT with or without writing accepted. SAT with or without Essay component accepted. *Academic units required:* 4 English, 3 math, 3 science, 2 science labs, 2 foreign language, 2 social studies, 1 history, 3 academic electives. *Academic units recommended:* 4 English, 4 math, 4 science, 3 science labs, 2 foreign language, 3 social studies, 1 history, 3 academic electives.

Financial Aid

Students should submit: CSS/Financial Aid PROFILE; FAFSA. Priority filing deadline is 2/1. The Princeton Review suggests that all financial aid forms be submitted as soon as possible after October 1. *Need-based scholarships/grants offered:* College/university scholarship or grant aid from institutional funds; Federal Pell; Private scholarships; SEOG; State scholarships/grants; United Negro College Fund. *Loan aid offered:* Direct PLUS loans; Direct Subsidized Stafford Loans; Direct Unsubsidized Stafford Loans. Applicants will be notified of awards on or about 4/1. Federal Work-Study Program available. Institutional employment available.

The Inside Word

Vanderbilt deliberately keeps its incoming first-year class small at roughly 1,600 students and with over 34,000 applicants a year, competition is tough for this very selective Nashville institution. With the admission committee's holistic approach to reviewing candidates, interested students should take stock of more than just their GPAs and standardized test scores. Many students take the early decision route—Vanderbilt has two early decision deadlines. A final note: Most successful candidates present the equivalent of 5 academic subjects each year for 4 years of high school.

THE SCHOOL SAYS "..."

From the Admissions Office

"The Vanderbilt undergraduate experience is often described as uniquely balanced. Within the context of an outstanding academic landscape, students are encouraged to participate in a broad spectrum of campus organizations among a highly diverse population. Many students take classes in all four undergraduate schools, stretching their intellectual experience far beyond that of their declared major. Students typically live on campus all four years, beginning with a year at The Martha Rivers Ingram Commons, a living and learning residential community for first-year students. E. Bronson Ingram College, the newest residential college, expanded living-learning opportunities for upperclass students. Students take full advantage of Nashville, often participating in government-, business-, or education-related internships, and enjoying cultural offerings of the city, honored by Forbes, 2019 as one of the '#3 Best Big Cities for Jobs.'

"Through Opportunity Vanderbilt, the university makes three commitments regarding financial aid:

1. Vanderbilt's admissions process is need-blind for all U.S. citizens and eligible noncitizens.
2. Vanderbilt meets 100 percent of a family's demonstrated financial need for all admitted students.
3. Financial aid awards do not include loans, and instead include grant assistance and a reasonable work-study component. This does not involve income bands or 'cut-offs' that impact or limit eligibility.

"The admissions process is holistic—Vanderbilt does not employ cutoffs for standardized testing or grade point averages. Students admitted to Vanderbilt typically show exceptional academic accomplishment and are highly engaged in their communities, often serving in leadership roles. The prescreening video and audition are of primary importance for students applying to the Blair School of Music."

SELECTIVITY
Admissions Rating	99
# of applicants	37,310
% of applicants accepted	9
% of acceptees attending	47
# of early decision applicants	4,321
% accepted early decision	20%

FRESHMAN PROFILE
Range SAT EBRW	710–760
Range SAT Math	750–800
Range SAT Composite	1460–1560
Range ACT Composite	33–35
# submitting SAT scores	789
% submitting SAT scores	49
# submitting ACT scores	837
% submitting ACT scores	52
Average HS GPA	3.8
% graduated top 10% of class	90
% graduated top 25% of class	7
% graduated top 50% of class	2

DEADLINES
Early decision	
Deadline	11/1
Notification	12/15
Other ED Deadline	1/1
Other ED Notification	2/15
Regular	
Priority	1/1
Deadline	1/1
Notification	4/1
Nonfall registration?	No

FINANCIAL FACTS
Financial Aid Rating	99
Annual tuition	$50,800
Room and board	$16,910
Required fees	$2,106
Books and supplies	$1,294
Average frosh need-based scholarship	$54,417
Average UG need-based scholarship	$52,242
% needy frosh rec. need-based scholarship or grant aid	98
% needy UG rec. need-based scholarship or grant aid	99
% needy frosh rec. non-need-based scholarship or grant aid	10
% needy UG rec. non-need-based scholarship or grant aid	5
% needy frosh rec. need-based self-help aid	49
% needy UG rec. need-based self-help aid	54
% frosh rec. any financial aid	54
% UG borrow to pay for school	22
Average cumulative indebtedness	$22,727
% frosh need fully met	100
% ugrads need fully met	100
Average % of frosh need met	100
Average % of ugrad need met	100

VASSAR COLLEGE

Box 10, 124 Raymond Avenue, Poughkeepsie, NY 12604 • Admissions: 845-437-7300

STUDENTS SAY "..."

Academics

Vassar College is a small "academically challenging" school that offers a "perfect liberal arts feel" and seeks to broaden students' perspectives. The "strong sense of community" is apparent both in and out of the classroom, where the school drums home the idea that "it's all about being unique and letting your quirky characteristics shine." "We're asked to critically think about the world we live in and how our privilege plays into these systems," says a student. This freedom of character is a main reason why everyone here is "excited to be with each other, which creates this school spirit that isn't necessarily based on sports."

The lack of core requirements is "a great opportunity for students to explore anything they want before settling into a major." "Amazing" professors are "super accessible" and "fully engaged in the total Vassar community." "They are willing to meet you outside their office hours if they don't work for you," says a student. "My professors are...spectacular at illuminating difficult material," says a junior psychology major. Classes are all small and "most are very discussion-based"; students are "not competitive with each other, but with themselves," which creates a more relaxed environment despite the very high academics. Many do admit that there could stand to be "more sections of the most popular classes so that the most amount of people can be happy with their course selections."

Opportunities are there for students' voices to be heard, and "the administration is very willing to work with the student organization to accomplish goals," such as a ban on bottled water from dining services as a result of an initiative by the environmental group on campus. "Vassar students will do things in any way but the traditional way," says a sophomore. "No problem goes undiscussed." "Incredible" study abroad opportunities and a "beautiful campus" don't hurt, either.

Life

"When you get here it starts to feel like home very quickly," says a student of the "stunning" campus. "The vibe of the whole school is so chill," but does not hamper a "vibrant extracurricular scene." Vassar is "bursting at the seams with orgs": there are "a ton of intramural sports teams," nine a cappella groups, plenty of political organizations, a large performing arts contingent, and "basically anything else you can think of." "Close-knit dormitory communities" and an emphasis on being "hyper-socially aware" lead students to be "very politically conscious and deeply involved in volunteerism and activism."

New York City isn't far, so some people take advantage of that, and "there are always parties you can go to if you want to," but "there is nothing wrong with staying in and watching a movie or chatting with friends." There is no Greek life; intellectual conversations abound at all hours, and students spend "significant time thinking about the state of the world and what's going on within the campus community." There are always a decent amount of weekend activities such as "concerts, comedy shows, plays, dances, etc." Be warned: "transportation is limited to get off campus unless you own a car."

Student Body

The "left wing, artsy, intelligent," and "open-minded" individuals that make up the "eclectic" student body "thrive" in the "welcoming" environs of Vassar. The "very generous" amount of need-based financial aid that is awarded "allows for wide socioeconomic diversity," and "Freshman Orientation is a great way for people to make friends here." Many here are philosophically minded and "strive to be as politically correct as possible," and there is "a good amount of hipsters." "You can definitely find at least one other student for every obscure interest you have," assures a student.

VASSAR COLLEGE

Financial Aid: 845-437-5320 • E-Mail: admissions@vassar.edu • Website: www.vassar.edu

THE PRINCETON REVIEW SAYS

Admissions

Very important factors considered include: rigor of secondary school record, academic GPA. *Important factors considered include:* class rank, application essay, standardized test scores, recommendation(s), extracurricular activities, talent/ability, character/personal qualities. *Other factors considered include:* interview, first generation, alumni/ae relation, geographical residence, racial/ethnic status, volunteer work, work experience. ACT with or without writing accepted. SAT with or without Essay component accepted. High school diploma is required and GED is accepted. *Academic units recommended:* 4 English, 4 math, 4 science, 3 science labs, 4 foreign language, 2 social studies, 2 history.

Financial Aid

Students should submit: CSS/Financial Aid PROFILE; FAFSA; Noncustodial PROFILE. Priority filing deadline is 3/30. The Princeton Review suggests that all financial aid forms be submitted as soon as possible after October 1. *Need-based scholarships/grants offered:* College/university scholarship or grant aid from institutional funds; Federal Pell; Private scholarships; SEOG; State scholarships/grants. *Loan aid offered:* Direct PLUS loans; Direct Subsidized Stafford Loans; Direct Unsubsidized Stafford Loans. Federal Work-Study Program available. Institutional employment available.

The Inside Word

With acceptance rates hitting record lows, stellar academic credentials are a must for any serious Vassar candidate. Standardized test scores are required, but come second to high school transcripts. Once admissions officers see you meet their rigorous scholastic standards, they'll closely assess your personal essay, recommendations, and extracurricular activities. The college prides itself on selecting students who will add to the vitality of the campus. Demonstrating an intellectual curiosity that extends outside the classroom is as important as success within it.

THE SCHOOL SAYS "..."

From the Admissions Office

"Vassar presents a rich variety of social and cultural activities, clubs, living arrangements, and regional attractions. Vassar also fields 23 Varsity sports plus 4 intercollegiate club teams, and more than 23 percent of students participate. Vassar is a vital, residential college community recognized for its respect for the rights and individuality of others.

"Candidates must submit standardized test results from either the SAT or the ACT. Vassar superscores the results of either test."

SELECTIVITY

Admissions Rating	96
# of applicants	8,312
% of applicants accepted	25
% of acceptees attending	34
# offered a place on the wait list	1,138
% accepting a place on wait list	50
% admitted from wait list	8
# of early decision applicants	679
% accepted early decision	44%

FRESHMAN PROFILE

Range SAT EBRW	680–740
Range SAT Math	690–770
Range ACT Composite	31–33
# submitting SAT scores	418
% submitting SAT scores	61
# submitting ACT scores	332
% submitting ACT scores	48
% graduated top 10% of class	61
% graduated top 25% of class	91
% graduated top 50% of class	98

DEADLINES

Early decision	
Deadline	11/15
Notification	12/15
Other ED Deadline	1/1
Other ED Notification	2/1
Regular	
Deadline	1/1
Notification	4/1
Nonfall registration?	No

APPLICANTS ALSO LOOK AT AND SOMETIMES PREFER

Brown University; Wesleyan University; Tufts University; Yale University

FINANCIAL FACTS

Financial Aid Rating	99
Annual tuition	$54,410
Room and board	$12,900
Required fees	$800
Books and supplies	$900
Average frosh need-based scholarship	$51,903
Average UG need-based scholarship	$49,190
% needy frosh rec. need-based scholarship or grant aid	99
% needy UG rec. need-based scholarship or grant aid	99
% needy frosh rec. non-need-based scholarship or grant aid	0
% needy UG rec. non-need-based scholarship or grant aid	0
% needy frosh rec. need-based self-help aid	95
% needy UG rec. need-based self-help aid	97
% frosh rec. any financial aid	64
% UG rec. any financial aid	66
% UG borrow to pay for school	49
Average cumulative indebtedness	$21,473
% frosh need fully met	100
% ugrads need fully met	100
Average % of frosh need met	100
Average % of ugrad need met	100

VILLANOVA UNIVERSITY

Austin Hall, 800 Lancaster Avenue, Villanova, PA 19085 • Admissions: 610-519-4000 • Fax: 610-519-6450

CAMPUS LIFE

Quality of Life Rating	86
Fire Safety Rating	97
Green Rating	93
Type of school	Private
Affiliation	Roman Catholic
Environment	Village

STUDENTS

Total undergrad enrollment	6,857
% male/female	47/53
% from out of state	79
% frosh from public high school	53
% frosh live on campus	98
% ugrads live on campus	66
# of fraternities (% ugrad men join)	14 (17)
# of sororities (% ugrad women join)	14 (32)
% African American	5
% Asian	6
% Caucasian	74
% Hispanic	8
% Native American	<1
% Pacific Islander	0
% Two or more races	3
% Race and/or ethnicity unknown	2
% international	2
# of countries represented	49

SURVEY SAYS . . .

Career services are great
Internships are widely available
School is well run
Students are very religious
Recreation facilities are great
Very little drug use
Intramural sports are popular

ACADEMICS

Academic Rating	84
% students returning for sophomore year	95
% students graduating within 4 years	87
% students graduating within 6 years	90
Calendar	Semester
Student/faculty ratio	12:1
Profs interesting rating	92
Profs accessible rating	98

MOST POPULAR MAJORS

Registered Nursing/Registered Nurse; Finance, General; Mass Communication/Media Studies

STUDENTS SAY "..."

Academics

Known for being a basketball powerhouse, Villanova University (located in Pennsylvania) has developed an equally impressive reputation for academics. The school's admissions standards have continued to rise, and there is a "great support system" in place to help students achieve, between professors, advisors, tutors, research librarians, as well as a writing, math, and language learning center. Nova's career center and internship offices focus on getting students into jobs after college, and "the opportunities outside of the classroom really complement your education." "Villanova is full of resources for my success now, as a student, and will continue to be after I graduate as an alum," says a student. There is a real sense of community here, "stemming from service, school spirit around the basketball team, and everyone actively pursuing their own area of academic interest." The "passionate" professors are "true teachers and scholars," and they "go above and beyond their office hours." They are "easily accessible," and though some will seek you out, "it is mostly up to you to take advantage of them as a resource." "If you want to succeed, the community will do everything in its power to make sure you can do so," says a student. In addition to superior classroom quality (the faculty gets "fired up about what they teach"), there are "a lot of projects across majors that have real-world applications and are designed to help students in the long run." Classes are often a mixture of "lecture, discussion, individual/group projects, [and] fieldtrips." Villanova's "emphasis on service" is a point of praise for the student body, and everyone here embraces a sense of duty to make the world a better place. "We are the Nova Nation, built upon an unbreakable foundation of community," says a student.

Life

Many buildings are new or have been recently renovated, and "most residence halls are really impressive and kept up very well." Most of campus "has a focused atmosphere during the week," but come Thursday afternoon, "you can feel campus relax and people are more likely to go out," mainly off campus. During basketball season, "people get their work done early to flock to the [Pavilion] for games." Almost everyone is involved in at least one (but probably more) extracurricular activities and clubs, and "a ton of students get involved with intramurals or club sports teams, as well." The Campus Activity Team puts on different events over the weekend, including "a cinema that is always showing a movie," and the school also offers great service experiences, whether "week-long service break experiences all over the world, cheering on the athletes at Special Olympics Fall Festival, or driving into Philly to play with kids and help them with their studies." Formals are also "a big deal" on campus. For those who want to take a break from college life, the massive King of Prussia Mall is found nearby (with a free weekend shuttle), and it is "an easy short train ride to go to Philadelphia."

Student Body

This "outstanding community" is built on "a lot of mutual respect." People are "well-rounded," "very friendly," and "proud of Villanova," and almost everyone here "dresses well" and is "extremely affable, professional, and an achiever." "Sometimes I think of Villanova as a school full of all the high school superstars," says one student. Balance is a skill that all Villanovans possess, and most are involved in some sort of volunteer activity; many also "party on the weekends, and show up ready to all of their classes." One can find a "very attractive student body" here as well.

VILLANOVA UNIVERSITY

Financial Aid: 610-519-4010 • E-Mail: gotovu@villanova.edu • Website: www.villanova.edu

THE PRINCETON REVIEW SAYS

Admissions

Very important factors considered include: rigor of secondary school record, class rank, academic GPA, standardized test scores. *Important factors considered include:* application essay, recommendation(s), extracurricular activities, talent/ability, character/personal qualities. *Other factors considered include:* first generation, alumni/ae relation, geographical residence, state residency, racial/ethnic status, level of applicant's interest. ACT with Writing required. SAT with Essay component required. High school diploma is required and GED is accepted. *Academic units required:* 4 English, 4 math, 4 science, 2 science labs, 2 foreign language, 2 academic electives, 4 units from above areas or other academic areas. *Academic units recommended:* 4 English, 4 math, 4 science, 3 science labs, 4 foreign language, 2 academic electives.

Financial Aid

Students should submit: CSS/Financial Aid PROFILE; FAFSA; Noncustodial PROFILE. Priority filing deadline is 1/15. The Princeton Review suggests that all financial aid forms be submitted as soon as possible after October 1. *Need-based scholarships/grants offered:* College/university scholarship or grant aid from institutional funds; Federal Pell; Private scholarships; SEOG; State scholarships/grants. *Loan aid offered:* Direct PLUS loans; Direct Subsidized Stafford Loans; Direct Unsubsidized Stafford Loans. Applicants will be notified of awards on or about 4/1. Federal Work-Study Program available. Institutional employment available.

The Inside Word

Villanova's growing academic reputation means its application process is growing more competitive as well: 93 percent of the most recent admitted freshman class ranked in the top 20 percent of their high school graduating class. Although academic achievement is important, the university looks at the whole package when considering applicants and expects candidates to be well rounded. As a private university, Villanova is not exactly cheap, but the school offers a wide variety of scholarships and aid to qualifying students.

THE SCHOOL SAYS "..."

From the Admissions Office

"Villanova is the oldest and largest Catholic university in Pennsylvania, founded in 1842 by the Order of Saint Augustine. Students of all faiths are welcome. The university tends to attract students who are interested in volunteerism. Villanovans provide more than 249,000 hours of service annually and host the largest student-run Special Olympics in the nation. Villanova's scenic campus is located twelve miles west of Philadelphia. The university offers programs through four undergraduate colleges: the College of Liberal Arts and Sciences, the College of Engineering, the M. Louise Fitzpatrick College of Nursing, and the Villanova School of Business. There are 265 student organizations and thirty-six National Honor Societies at Villanova. Incoming freshmen can opt to be part of a Learning Community, through which student groups live together in specially-designated residence halls and learn together in courses and co-curricular programs. The university offers Naval and Marine Reserve Officers Training Corps (ROTC) programs and hundreds of options for studying abroad. Nova's alumni body is comprised of more than 123,000 people. Some prominent grads include: Bert Jacobs, co-founder, Life Is Good Co.; Dr. Jill Biden, Second Lady of the United States of America; and James C. Davis, chairman, Allegis Group.

"If you're looking to join Nova Nation, be prepared: The competition for admission is getting tougher every year."

SELECTIVITY

Admissions Rating	95
# of applicants	21,112
% of applicants accepted	36
% of acceptees attending	23
# offered a place on the wait list	6,276
% accepting a place on wait list	41
% admitted from wait list	8

FRESHMAN PROFILE

Range SAT EBRW	620–710
Range SAT Math	630–730
Range ACT Composite	30–33
# submitting SAT scores	710
% submitting SAT scores	39
# submitting ACT scores	730
% submitting ACT scores	61
Average HS GPA	4.1
% graduated top 10% of class	65
% graduated top 25% of class	95
% graduated top 50% of class	98

DEADLINES

Early action	
Deadline	11/1
Notification	12/20
Regular	
Priority	12/15
Deadline	1/15
Notification	4/1

APPLICANTS ALSO LOOK AT AND OFTEN PREFER
Boston College; University of Notre Dame

AND SOMETIMES PREFER
Lehigh University; Penn State University Park; University of Maryland, College Park; University of Pittsburgh—Pittsburgh Campus

AND RARELY PREFER
Boston University; Fordham University; Northeastern University; University of Delaware

FINANCIAL FACTS

Financial Aid Rating	84
Annual tuition	$52,578
Room and board	$14,020
Required fees	$820
Books and supplies	$1,100
Average frosh need-based scholarship	$37,141
Average UG need-based scholarship	$35,229
% needy frosh rec. need-based scholarship or grant aid	92
% needy UG rec. need-based scholarship or grant aid	90
% needy frosh rec. non-need-based scholarship or grant aid	7
% needy UG rec. non-need-based scholarship or grant aid	4
% needy frosh rec. need-based self-help aid	92
% needy UG rec. need-based self-help aid	92
% frosh rec. any financial aid	65
% UG rec. any financial aid	68
% UG borrow to pay for school	53
Average cumulative indebtedness	$35,552
% frosh need fully met	9
% ugrads need fully met	7
Average % of frosh need met	82
Average % of ugrad need met	79

VIRGINIA TECH

925 Prices Fork Road, Blacksburg, VA 24061 • Admissions: 540-231-6267 • Fax: 540-231-3242

CAMPUS LIFE

Quality of Life Rating	91
Fire Safety Rating	94
Green Rating	97
Type of school	Public
Environment	Town

STUDENTS

Total undergrad enrollment	27,730
% male/female	57/43
% from out of state	24
% frosh live on campus	98
% ugrads live on campus	33
# of fraternities (% ugrad men join)	30 (13)
# of sororities (% ugrad women join)	21 (19)
% African American	4
% Asian	10
% Caucasian	65
% Hispanic	6
% Native American	<1
% Pacific Islander	<1
% Two or more races	5
% Race and/or ethnicity unknown	3
% international	7
# of countries represented	116

SURVEY SAYS . . .

Lab facilities are great
Career services are great
School is well run
Diverse student types interact on campus
Students get along with local community
Great food on campus
Recreation facilities are great
Lots of beer drinking
Very little drug use
Everyone loves the Hokies
Intramural sports are popular
Alumni active on campus

ACADEMICS

Academic Rating	82
% students graduating within 4 years	63
% students graduating within 6 years	84
Calendar	Semester
Student/faculty ratio	14:1
Profs interesting rating	87
Profs accessible rating	94

Most classes have 20–29 students.
Most lab/discussion sessions have 20–29 students.

MOST POPULAR MAJORS

Mechanical Engineering; Biology/Biological Sciences, General; Management Science

STUDENTS SAY ". . ."

Academics

Virginia Tech is a school with a reputation as big as its campus. Known for its "beautiful campus, amazing community feel, top-notch engineering field," and as a "good value"—not to mention its renowned athletics—Virginia Tech offers "a perfect blend of challenging and fun, encompassed in an unparalleled community feel." That community feel is a big part of the attraction to this top-ranked school, with students saying they feel "more comfortable here than anywhere in the world." Students are here, of course, for an education at a well-respected research university. At Virginia Tech, that education is provided by "passionate professors who bring real-life examples and cases into their teachings." The school's size and correspondingly large teaching staff mean that at times "professors are hit-or-miss," with "a few who just see it as another job." Most, however, "are really there to help you know as much as you can," a group who are "are extremely helpful and devoted to their students." The best of this school's professors "really makes students eager to learn." One student enthuses, "My professors here have changed the way I look at the world and have become some of my biggest heroes." But maybe another student sums it up best: "I would definitely say that my academic experience has been outstanding and that it has opened my eyes to even more possibilities."

Life

Living "in the middle of nowhere" may seem like a recipe for boredom, but members of VT's Hokie Nation make the most of this "perfect college town." After all, when "there are 30,000 people around you that are the same age as you, you find stuff to do." When not consumed with Virginia Tech football—you'll see more maroon and orange in a single day here than most people will see in a lifetime—students here do, well, a little bit of everything. "School-related and Greek-life functions are the main sources of weekend activities," students say, but deceptively quiet Blacksburg and the surrounding area offer plenty of other options. On weekends, students "go out to parties or downtown with friends, we go out to eat, we play tennis, lay out on the 'drillfield,' play in the snow when we have some, go on hikes, and go to the river." That's just a start. Students find "there is always something fun going on to do with your friends," including "bowling, movies, club sports, video games," and more. If you can't find it in Blacksburg, it's ten minutes away in Christiansburg. Students enjoy relaxing, getting into discussions, or having outdoor adventures in a pastoral setting. When autumn arrives, "football games dominate the social scene."

Student Body

Better be ready to be part of the Hokie Nation, because the "typical student is someone who has a love for all things Virginia Tech." Those who attend VT "are proud of our school," and "A typical student here wears Virginia Tech clothes practically every day." Indeed, "you will find them at every VT football game." But the student body is about more than cheering for the maroon and orange. These "middle-class, decent-looking" students study hard "but play harder." Education matters here, but maybe not as much as living life. "The typical student is serious about schoolwork," students say, "but also knows how to have a good time." Most of the student body are "white and from Virginia or North Carolina," a group who are "smart, approachable, and kind." "While we may be lacking in racial diversity," one student notes, "we have every personality type and quirk you could ever imagine." If you are "well-rounded, involved, and [have] lots of school spirit," you are likely to fit in at VT.

Financial Aid: 540-231-5179 • E-Mail: admissions@vt.edu • Website: www.vt.edu

THE PRINCETON REVIEW SAYS

Admissions

Very important factors considered include: rigor of secondary school record, academic GPA, application essay, standardized test scores. *Other factors considered include:* extracurricular activities, talent/ability, character/personal qualities, first generation, alumni/ae relation, geographical residence, state residency, racial/ethnic status, volunteer work, work experience, level of applicant's interest. ACT with or without writing accepted. SAT with or without Essay component accepted. High school diploma is required and GED is accepted. *Academic units required:* 4 English, 3 math, 2 science, 2 science labs, 1 social studies, 1 history, 4 academic electives. *Academic units recommended:* 4 math, 3 science, 3 foreign language.

Financial Aid

Students should submit: FAFSA. Priority filing deadline is 1/15. The Princeton Review suggests that all financial aid forms be submitted as soon as possible after October 1. *Need-based scholarships/grants offered:* College/university scholarship or grant aid from institutional funds; Federal Pell; Private scholarships; SEOG; State scholarships/grants; United Negro College Fund. *Loan aid offered:* Direct PLUS loans; Direct Subsidized Stafford Loans; Direct Unsubsidized Stafford Loans. Applicants will be notified of awards on or about 4/1. Federal Work-Study Program available. Institutional employment available.

The Inside Word

With some 20,000 applications pouring into the admissions office each year, it's no wonder that the game here is all about numbers, numbers, numbers. Your high school grades will be top priority, so maintain strong grades. Standardized tests also play a big role. Most solid performers will find that acceptance comes with few problems, though the school's competitive disciplines—engineering and architecture, for example—will demand a higher caliber of student.

THE SCHOOL SAYS "..."

From the Admissions Office

"Virginia Tech offers the opportunities of a large research university in a small-town setting. Undergraduates choose from more than seventy majors in seven colleges, including nationally ranked architecture, business, forestry, and engineering schools, as well as excellent computer science, biology, and communication studies, and architecture programs. Technology is a key focus, both in classes and in general. All first-year students are required to own a personal computer, each residence hall room has Ethernet connections, and every student is provided e-mail and Internet access. Faculty incorporate a wide variety of technology into class, utilizing chat rooms, online lecture notes, and multimedia presentations. The university offers cutting-edge facilities for classes and research, abundant opportunities for advanced study in the honors program, undergraduate research opportunities, study abroad, internships, and cooperative education. Students enjoy nearly 700 organizations which offer something for everyone. Tech offers the best of both worlds—everything a large university can provide and a small-town atmosphere.

"Freshman applicants must take the SAT or ACT with or without the writing section. We will use the highest scores from any SAT or ACT test scores submitted."

SELECTIVITY

Admissions Rating	87
# of applicants	31,936
% of applicants accepted	65
% of acceptees attending	30
# of early decision applicants	2,952
% accepted early decision	45

FRESHMAN PROFILE

Range SAT EBRW	590–680
Range SAT Math	590–710
Range ACT Composite	25–31
# submitting SAT scores	5,486
% submitting SAT scores	87
# submitting ACT scores	1,946
% submitting ACT scores	31
Average HS GPA	4.0
% graduated top 10% of class	38
% graduated top 25% of class	77
% graduated top 50% of class	97

DEADLINES

Early decision	
Deadline	11/1
Notification	12/15
Early action	
Deadline	12/1
Notification	2/22
Regular	
Deadline	1/15
Notification	4/1
Nonfall registration?	Yes

FINANCIAL FACTS

Financial Aid Rating	81
Annual in-state tuition	$11,420
Annual out-of-state tuition	$29,960
Room and board	$9,342
Required fees	$2,271
Books and supplies	$1,100
Average frosh need-based scholarship	$7,785
Average UG need-based scholarship	$7,432
% needy frosh rec. need-based scholarship or grant aid	60
% needy UG rec. need-based scholarship or grant aid	69
% needy frosh rec. non-need-based scholarship or grant aid	49
% needy UG rec. non-need-based scholarship or grant aid	34
% needy frosh rec. need-based self-help aid	68
% needy UG rec. need-based self-help aid	71
% frosh rec. any financial aid	65
% UG rec. any financial aid	75
% UG borrow to pay for school	48
Average cumulative indebtedness	$31,494
% frosh need fully met	16
% ugrads need fully met	15
Average % of frosh need met	55
Average % of ugrad need met	56

VIRGINIA WESLEYAN UNIVERSITY

5817 Wesleyan Drive, Virginia Beach, VA 23455 • Admissions: 757-455-3208 • Fax: 757-461-5238

STUDENTS SAY "..."

Academics

Virginia Wesleyan is the quintessential small liberal arts university, providing undergraduates with "a close-knit community" where one "can easily build strong relationship[s]." Indeed, you're guaranteed to be "more than a number" on this Virginia Beach campus of 1,500 undergrads. "Small classes" are a hallmark of a Virginia Wesleyan education with many being "discussion or interaction based." And students love the fact that they are "always taught by...professors"—no teaching assistants here! Speaking of professors, VWU undergrads are full of praise for theirs. They seem to "genuinely care about their students and are approachable outside the classroom." A current student agrees, "I have never met a faculty so invested in my own personal success." And an earth and environmental studies student excitedly interjects, "I have never experienced [a] learning environment like this one. Professors not only care about their students, but they go above and beyond to ensure that every student understands the material. Professors make lifelong connections with students." All in all, Virginia Wesleyan offers individuals a college experience that's "all about making every single student feel as though this is their second home and that every person they come into contact with is looking out for the student's best interest."

Life

Despite students reporting that "the food could be better," by and large undergrads seem to enjoy life at Virginia Wesleyan. To begin with, there are plenty of activities with which to get involved, be it "Greek life, music, arts, religion, sciences, business, etc." Indeed, there's truly something for everyone! Students also like taking advantage of various campus amenities such as "the pool, the rock wall, the indoor track, the gymnasium, and the pool table in the student center." Of course, similar to many undergraduate institutions, "social gatherings are huge here." Students "love inviting [their] friends and teammates over to get over a stressful week of studying and homework." However, these get-togethers don't tend to get too raucous. As an English major tells us, "Although fun is encouraged, we are often reminded of how to keep everyone safe. Underage drinking is NOT tolerated, and we take it seriously when rules are broken." Finally, when the weather permits, these undergrads flock to nearby Chick's Beach. And many can be found sampling the "delicious restaurants around Norfolk" and Virginia Beach.

Student Body

Undergrads at Virginia Wesleyan speak very highly of their peers. Granted, this isn't surprising given that the student body is comprised of "friendly and outgoing" individuals who are typically "laid back." A psychology major provides a little more insight by stating, "Students are generally pretty spirited and helpful, and most [people] seem to genuinely care about their academics." By and large, undergrads here are "open to new things." They also tend to be "very busy" since it's quite typical for students to be "involved in several different clubs and community service groups." Of course, though many VWU undergrads "join one of the [eight] Greek organizations available" or become "a member of a sports team" to "fit in," we're also told that it's by no means a necessity. A chemistry major assures us, "Whatever you are interested in, you can easily find a group of people that connect with you. Our school is so inviting that it's hard to not fit in somewhere." Finally, another psychology major boasts, "I feel like my school is extremely accepting, and we have events for all cultures, beliefs, and extracurricular [activities] all the time."

VIRGINIA WESLEYAN UNIVERSITY

Financial Aid: 757-455-3345 • E-Mail: admissions@vwu.edu • Website: www.vwu.edu

THE PRINCETON REVIEW SAYS

Admissions

Very important factors considered include: rigor of secondary school record, academic GPA, standardized test scores, level of applicant's interest. *Important factors considered include:* extracurricular activities. *Other factors considered include:* recommendation(s), interview, talent/ability, character/personal qualities, first generation, alumni/ae relation, volunteer work, work experience. ACT with or without writing accepted. SAT with or without Essay component accepted. High school diploma is required and GED is accepted. *Academic units required:* 4 English, 3 math, 2 science, 2 science labs, 2 foreign language, 1 history, 1 computer science. *Academic units recommended:* 4 English, 3 math, 2 science, 2 science labs, 2 foreign language, 1 history, 4 academic electives, 1 computer science.

Financial Aid

Students should submit: FAFSA; State aid form. Priority filing deadline is 3/1. The Princeton Review suggests that all financial aid forms be submitted as soon as possible after October 1. *Need-based scholarships/grants offered:* College/university scholarship or grant aid from institutional funds; Federal Pell; Private scholarships; SEOG; State scholarships/grants. *Loan aid offered:* Direct PLUS loans; Direct Subsidized Stafford Loans; Direct Unsubsidized Stafford Loans. Applicants will be notified of awards on a rolling basis beginning 10/15. Federal Work-Study Program available. Institutional employment available.

The Inside Word

As Virginia Wesleyan's profile rises, so too does the number of applications it receives. And each year, competition for admission increases. Therefore, to receive a coveted acceptance letter, applicants need to have earned strong grades in college prep courses. Additionally, given the college's small size, admissions officers are on the lookout for students who will contribute to campus life. Therefore, active and sustained participation in a handful of extracurricular activities helps candidates appear more attractive to the admissions committee.

THE SCHOOL SAYS "..."

From the Admissions Office

"Virginia Wesleyan University seeks to enroll qualified students from diverse social, religious, racial, economic, and geographic backgrounds. Admission is based solely on the applicant's academic and personal qualifications. Factors considered include grades, recommendations, standardized test scores, and extracurricular activities. Virginia Wesleyan requires either SAT or ACT scores. Although we do not require more than one SAT or ACT score, we do take the highest individual verbal and math scores from all of the tests taken. A high school diploma is required (GED accepted) and proof of English proficiency is required for all international applicants. Virginia Wesleyan considers applications on a rolling admissions basis. Applicants can typically expect notification within two to three weeks after we receive your completed application and supporting documents. Priority decisions for spring freshman applications is January 1; for fall freshman applications, March 1. Prospective students are encouraged to visit our beautiful 283-acre wooded campus for a tour and to meet with an enrollment counselor. Learn more about admissions at www.vwu.edu."

SELECTIVITY

Admissions Rating	79
# of applicants	2,200
% of applicants accepted	71
% of acceptees attending	27

FRESHMAN PROFILE

Range SAT EBRW	490–590
Range SAT Math	463–570
Range ACT Composite	19–25
# submitting SAT scores	378
% submitting SAT scores	89
# submitting ACT scores	60
% submitting ACT scores	14
Average HS GPA	3.2
% graduated top 10% of class	15
% graduated top 25% of class	33
% graduated top 50% of class	63

DEADLINES

Regular	
Priority	3/1
Notification	Rolling, 9/15
Nonfall registration?	Yes

APPLICANTS ALSO LOOK AT AND OFTEN PREFER
Old Dominion University

FINANCIAL FACTS

Financial Aid Rating	85
Annual tuition	$36,010
Room and board	$9,988
Required fees	$850
Books and supplies	$1,500
Average frosh need-based scholarship	$23,917
Average UG need-based scholarship	$22,042
% needy frosh rec. need-based scholarship or grant aid	100
% needy UG rec. need-based scholarship or grant aid	99
% needy frosh rec. non-need-based scholarship or grant aid	14
% needy UG rec. non-need-based scholarship or grant aid	17
% needy frosh rec. need-based self-help aid	79
% needy UG rec. need-based self-help aid	77
% frosh rec. any financial aid	99.3
% UG rec. any financial aid	97.6
% UG borrow to pay for school	86
Average cumulative indebtedness	$32,404
% frosh need fully met	11
% ugrads need fully met	13
Average % of frosh need met	65
Average % of ugrad need met	63

WABASH COLLEGE

P.O. Box 352, Crawfordsville, IN 47933-0352 • Admissions: 765-361-6225 • Fax: 765-361-6437

STUDENTS SAY ". . ."

Academics

Students live by "the Gentleman's Rule" at the all-male Wabash College in Crawfordsville, Indiana. Backed by an "exceptional" academic reputation and preparation for graduate professional schools ("Wabash's medical school acceptance rates are above 80 percent"), Wabash is "truly an A school for B students." Students say that Wabash "does a great job of making opportunity for students in the Rust Belt." "It opened the world up to me," says one student, "it changed the arc of my life." The school has a "great alumni base" that will help develop a student's "career while…in school and make it easier to get a job after you graduate." "Well-regarded," "outstanding," and "down-to-earth" professors "include students in research" (one student mentions being "published as the first author in a biochemistry journal soon"), "always have their doors open for questions," and "occasionally open up their home to students" for an "evening of dinner and discussion about an assignment or topic that is bothering you." The "classes are tough but rewarding" and require "lots of reading…and critical thinking." There is plenty of "opportunity for students to take leadership positions on campus," with students having "a lot of control over their budget," as one example. Students also praise Wabash's office of "career services" and "immersion learning." And not for nothing, students feel respected and heard: "I think that our school does a great job of…engaging with the students and allowing their voices to be heard equally with that of the professor in order to progress the narrative and enhance the learning process, rather than just dismissing student perspectives as background noise."

Life

"Our school spirit and tradition-oriented culture is second to none!" exclaims one student. Wabash is an "academically rigorous school," so weekdays are "devoted to studying," but "extracurriculars are easy to come by and active." Many students "compete in intramural sports." Students tend to be "very involved with extracurricular organizations," which include "jazz band, "dance marathon, "German club," and "College Mentors for Kids." The "surrounding area is very rural, so life is centered around the campus." Students attend class until "around 4:00 P.M. during the week." "Over half of the campus is in a fraternity," and on weekends, "a fraternity is almost always holding a party on Friday and Saturday nights." There are "campus unity tours (otherwise called TGIF)" where students "go to each fraternity house and living unit and socialize for fifteen minutes or so," a "great way to get to know people." The Wabash "brotherhood" also "love to support athletic teams." The football home section is "almost always sold out." About "half of the student body plays a sport," and the vast majority of the student body is "in a school-sponsored club or organization." On weekends, students are also down to take a "quick trip to Lafayette or Indianapolis to experience the bigger-city life."

Student Body

This "800-odd all male campus in rural western Indiana is more than just a brotherhood." "There is no doubt that any lack of success a student at Wabash experiences is a product of their own work ethic," says one student. Though the men generally hold each other in high esteem: "When I go out into the world, if I find another Wabash man, the connection we have is instantaneous," one student says. "Our experiences, while different, are rooted in the same traditions and ideals, and thus, we can share a bond, despite the other man being 10, 20, 30, 40, or even 50 years older." An "openly gay" student observes that the "overall atmosphere…is a welcoming and accepting one; I feared attending a small campus in Indiana, but, entering my last semester, I realize it is incredibly easy to find a loving group of individuals. I truly believe a great majority of Wabash's students embody the Gentleman's Rule and act accordingly." The student body is a "diverse melting pot of all kinds of students." From "rural Midwestern towns to rough inner city neighborhoods in Philly and Chicago, to affluent suburbs and many foreign countries, the student body at Wabash is home to a breathtakingly wide array of perspectives and beliefs." This amount of diversity "poses a positive challenge to Wabash men, as it gives us the ability to open our eyes to new ways of thinking and living … and also teaches how to go into a new and changing world."

WABASH COLLEGE

Financial Aid: 765-361-6375 • E-Mail: admissions@wabash.edu • Website: www.wabash.edu

THE PRINCETON REVIEW SAYS

Admissions

Very important factors considered include: rigor of secondary school record, class rank, academic GPA, level of applicant's interest. *Important factors considered include:* standardized test scores, interview, extracurricular activities, talent/ability. *Other factors considered include:* application essay, recommendation(s), character/personal qualities, first generation, alumni/ae relation, geographical residence, racial/ethnic status, volunteer work, work experience. ACT with Writing recommended. SAT with Essay component recommended. High school diploma is required and GED is accepted. *Academic units recommended:* 4 English, 4 math, 2 science, 2 science labs, 2 foreign language, 2 social studies, 2 history, 2 academic electives.

Financial Aid

Students should submit: FAFSA. Priority filing deadline is 1/15. The Princeton Review suggests that all financial aid forms be submitted as soon as possible after October 1. *Need-based scholarships/grants offered:* College/university scholarship or grant aid from institutional funds; Federal Pell; Private scholarships; SEOG; State scholarships/grants; United Negro College Fund. *Loan aid offered:* Direct PLUS loans; Direct Subsidized Stafford Loans; Direct Unsubsidized Stafford Loans. Applicants will be notified of awards on a rolling basis beginning 12/15. Federal Work-Study Program available. Institutional employment available.

The Inside Word

Because Wabash is so specific and unique, it self-selects a small but strong applicant pool. Don't let its relatively high acceptance rate deceive you: admitted students are in for four years of academic rigor, so don't apply if you're not ready to apply serious intellectual muscle and work ethic. Students must submit SAT/ACT scores. Although not a requirement, an applicant may also submit a written statement to include additional details about himself for consideration during the application review.

THE SCHOOL SAYS "..."

From the Admissions Office

"Wabash College is different—and distinctive—from other liberal arts colleges. Different in that Wabash is an outstanding college for men only. Distinctive in the quality and character of the faculty, in the demanding nature of the academic program, in the seriousness and maturity of the men who enroll, and in the richness of the traditions that have evolved throughout its 188-year history. Wabash is preeminently a teaching institution and the Princeton Review annually lauds the accessibility of the faculty and the classroom experience. Faculty and students talk to each other with mutual respect for the expression of informed opinion. Students who collaborate with faculty on research projects are considered their peers in the research—an esteem not usually extended to undergraduates—and are honored annually in a celebration of undergraduate research. Wabash also earns national recognition for its alumni network, internship program, and career services, all of which are critical to our graduates' success in every walk of life. But perhaps the single most striking aspect of student life at Wabash is personal freedom. The College has only one rule: 'The student is expected to conduct himself at all times, both on and off the campus, as a gentleman and a responsible citizen.' Wabash College treats students as adults, and such treatment attracts responsible freshmen and fosters their independence and maturity. For students seeking admission, Wabash places emphasis on high school GPA and difficulty of subjects, and will be SAT and ACT test optional in 2020–2021."

SELECTIVITY
Admissions Rating	86
# of applicants	1,307
% of applicants accepted	64
% of acceptees attending	27
# of early decision applicants	43
% accepted early decision	91

FRESHMAN PROFILE
Range SAT EBRW	560–650
Range SAT Math	560–670
Range SAT Composite	1120–1310
Range ACT Composite	23–29
# submitting SAT scores	188
% submitting SAT scores	82
# submitting ACT scores	128
% submitting ACT scores	56
Average HS GPA	3.8
% graduated top 10% of class	25
% graduated top 25% of class	60
% graduated top 50% of class	92

DEADLINES
Early decision	
Deadline	11/1
Notification	12/5
Early action	
Deadline	12/1
Notification	12/31
Regular	
Priority	12/1
Deadline	7/1
Notification	Rolling, 1/28
Nonfall registration?	Yes

APPLICANTS ALSO LOOK AT AND SOMETIMES PREFER
Indiana University Bloomington; Purdue University—West Lafayette; DePauw University

FINANCIAL FACTS
Financial Aid Rating	95
Annual tuition	$45,000
Room and board	$10,900
Required fees	$850
Books and supplies	$950
Average frosh need-based scholarship	$34,992
Average UG need-based scholarship	$34,377
% needy frosh rec. need-based scholarship or grant aid	99
% needy UG rec. need-based scholarship or grant aid	99
% needy frosh rec. non-need-based scholarship or grant aid	25
% needy UG rec. non-need-based scholarship or grant aid	16
% needy frosh rec. need-based self-help aid	75
% needy UG rec. need-based self-help aid	82
% frosh rec. any financial aid	100
% UG rec. any financial aid	99.9
% UG borrow to pay for school	72
Average cumulative indebtedness	$35,273
% frosh need fully met	77
% ugrads need fully met	78
Average % of frosh need met	95
Average % of ugrad need met	93

WAGNER COLLEGE

One Campus Road, Staten Island, NY 10301 • Admissions: 718-390-3411 • Fax: 718-390-3105

CAMPUS LIFE

Quality of Life Rating	81
Fire Safety Rating	98
Green Rating	60*
Type of school	Private
Environment	Metropolis

STUDENTS

Total undergrad enrollment	1,752
% male/female	35/65
% from out of state	46
% frosh from public high school	67
% frosh live on campus	73
% ugrads live on campus	63
# of fraternities	5
# of sororities	4
% African American	8
% Asian	5
% Caucasian	62
% Hispanic	13
% Native American	<1
% Pacific Islander	<1
% Two or more races	3
% Race and/or ethnicity unknown	5
% international	4

SURVEY SAYS . . .

Class discussions encouraged
Theater is popular
Everone loves the Seahawks

ACADEMICS

Academic Rating	80
% students returning for sophomore year	81
% students graduating within 4 years	63
% students graduating within 6 years	70
Calendar	Semester
Student/faculty ratio	13:1
Profs interesting rating	85
Profs accessible rating	90

Most classes have 10–19 students.
Most lab/discussion sessions have
10–19 students.

MOST POPULAR MAJORS

Visual and Performing Arts, General; Business/
Commerce, General; Nursing Science

STUDENTS SAY "..."

Academics

Wagner College, located on Staten Island, is a "tight-knit and fun, yet academically challenging," liberal arts school that operates under the Wagner Plan, combining a solid foundation in the liberal arts with practical and applied experiences like internships, with a commitment to service learning and community. The school is "in the perfect location with a surplus of unique resources" and is composed of "an excellent and vibrant community that supports its students every step of the way." The "commitment of the faculty and staff have for the student body is outstanding." Thanks to the plan, students are encouraged "to explore and reflect upon a myriad of subjects and issues." "Even though I am a biology major, I have the wonderful opportunity to explore interdisciplinary topics in the humanities and social sciences throughout my undergraduate career," says one student. The college's unique first-year program consists of a set of three classes with the same twenty-eight students, which "helps transition us from high school to college by progressively learning how to write college-level pieces as well as by engaging in a mandatory thirty-hour community service requirement." This "small, beautiful learning community" is guided by an "extremely attentive and competent" faculty. The professors "ask you to do your best and to push your limitations away" and are "extremely accessible outside of class." "The first time I was nervous about registration, my advisor sat down had lunch, and we registered together," says a student. "It is comforting that I can go to my professors whenever I need assistance with work." The school's science and physicians' assistant programs are notably strong, as are the "fantastic" theater and musical programs. Students all universally agree that Wagner "lets you experience all different types of subjects by following the concept: learning by doing."

Life

At Wagner, students are "mostly concerned about their careers, whether they want to make it on Broadway or find the cure for cancer." There's plenty of school-run activities "through co-curricular programs and various clubs," so there are "countless things to do." Beyond all doubt, "the best thing to do…is to take advantage of New York City." The campus is just "a ferry ride away from Manhattan," and the majority of people takes the Wagner shuttle to the S.I. ferry ("all for free!") and goes to the city, whether to shop, eat, or go to a Broadway show. On weekends, there are "parties run by organizations from time to time" or in dorm rooms, since "there is no off-campus housing." Every year, the school has an event called Wagner Stock, where a famous musician or group comes to play. Food is a huge pain point here: Students want "more access to the dining hall in the late hours of the night," "more food options," and just better food in general.

Student Body

The student body here celebrates its "diverse" makeup but Division I athletics and the "great theater program" are very visible in this "small close community." But a student not in either of these programs can find their group through clubs and the major that they are in." Many students have "one major and a minor," and "half of them might study abroad for a semester and or have one or two internships before they graduate." Everyone basically goes about their own business, but "is very approachable." No one seems to have any trouble finding their own crowd, but even once that occurs, "different crowds frequently mingle and almost everyone gets along." "People just talk to everyone," says a student.

WAGNER COLLEGE

Financial Aid: 718-390-3183 • E-Mail: adm@wagner.edu • Website: www.wagner.edu

THE PRINCETON REVIEW SAYS

Admissions

Very important factors considered include: rigor of secondary school record, class rank, academic GPA. *Important factors considered include:* application essay, recommendation(s), interview, extracurricular activities, talent/ability, character/personal qualities. *Other factors considered include:* standardized test scores, volunteer work, work experience, level of applicant's interest. ACT with or without writing accepted. SAT with or without Essay component accepted. High school diploma is required and GED is accepted. *Academic units required:* 4 English, 3 math, 2 science, 1 science lab, 2 foreign language, 3 history, 7 academic electives.

Financial Aid

Students should submit: FAFSA; State aid form. Priority filing deadline is 1/15. The Princeton Review suggests that all financial aid forms be submitted as soon as possible after October 1. *Need-based scholarships/grants offered:* College/university scholarship or grant aid from institutional funds; Federal Pell; Private scholarships; SEOG; State scholarships/grants. *Loan aid offered:* Direct PLUS loans; Direct Subsidized Stafford Loans; Direct Unsubsidized Stafford Loans. Applicants will be notified of awards on a rolling basis beginning 1/31. Federal Work-Study Program available. Institutional employment available.

The Inside Word

As far as grades and test scores, the profile of the average freshman class at Wagner is solid. Standardized tests are optional, and there is more value placed on the strength of your course work and your grades in those classes. The admissions staff here is dedicated to finding the right students for their school. Wagner is looking for students who like to be involved in community events, so make sure your application reflects your extracurriculars. An interview bodes well for serious applicants.

THE SCHOOL SAYS "..."

From the Admissions Office

"At Wagner College, we attract and develop active learners and future leaders. Wagner College has received national acclaim (*Time* magazine, American Association of Colleges and Universities) for its innovative curriculum, The Wagner Plan for the Practical Liberal Arts. At Wagner, we capitalize on our unique geography; we are a traditional, scenic, residential campus, which happens to sit atop a hill on an island overlooking lower Manhattan. Our location allows us to offer a program that couples required off-campus experiences (experiential learning), with 'learning community' clusters of courses. This program begins in the first semester and continues through the senior capstone experience in the major. Fieldwork and internships, writing-intensive reflective tutorials, connected learning, 'reading, writing, and doing': At Wagner College our students truly discover 'the practical liberal arts in New York City.'"

SELECTIVITY

Admissions Rating	83
# of applicants	2,898
% of applicants accepted	70
% of acceptees attending	21
# offered a place on the wait list	84
% accepting a place on wait list	77
% admitted from wait list	48

FRESHMAN PROFILE

Range SAT EBRW	540–640
Range SAT Math	530–630
Range ACT Composite	22–28
# submitting SAT scores	283
% submitting SAT scores	68
# submitting ACT scores	35
% submitting ACT scores	8
Average HS GPA	3.5
% graduated top 10% of class	20
% graduated top 25% of class	49
% graduated top 50% of class	80

DEADLINES

Early action	
Deadline	12/1
Notification	1/5
Regular	
Priority	12/1
Deadline	2/15
Notification	2/15
Nonfall registration?	Yes

APPLICANTS ALSO LOOK AT AND OFTEN PREFER
New York University; Northeastern University; Fordham University

AND SOMETIMES PREFER
Ithaca College; Muhlenberg College; Fairfield University

AND RARELY PREFER
Drew University; Manhattan College; Marist College; Quinnipiac University

FINANCIAL FACTS

Financial Aid Rating	86
Annual tuition	$47,300
Room and board	$14,575
Required fees	$950
Books and supplies	$850
Average frosh need-based scholarship	$17,851
Average UG need-based scholarship	$23,332
% needy frosh rec. need-based scholarship or grant aid	100
% needy UG rec. need-based scholarship or grant aid	100
% needy frosh rec. non-need-based scholarship or grant aid	0
% needy UG rec. non-need-based scholarship or grant aid	0
% needy frosh rec. need-based self-help aid	67
% needy UG rec. need-based self-help aid	78
% frosh rec. any financial aid	99
% UG rec. any financial aid	93
% frosh need fully met	24
% ugrads need fully met	22
Average % of frosh need met	73
Average % of ugrad need met	71

WAKE FOREST UNIVERSITY

P.O. Box 7305 Reynolda Station, Winston Salem, NC 27109 • Admissions: 336-758-5201 • Fax: 336-758-4324

STUDENTS SAY ". . ."

Academics

North Carolina's own Wake Forest University prepares students to lead lives that matter and has a reputation for quality that affords its students "excellent placement into jobs and graduate schools." Students come to Wake Forest for an education of the entire person, and the school "practices intentional interactions between professors and students, students with each other, and students and their larger community." This grand scale plan for well-rounded development includes "opportunities to serve, to become a leader, and to become part of initiatives that are larger than you." Professors "demand a lot of work but love teaching and students" and "ensure that students are comfortable with voicing their opinions." Classes "are not easy and good grades are tough to come by." "Professors often expect their class to be every student's focus, which is often very difficult," says one student. Fortunately, faculty "are extremely helpful and excited to be teaching or meeting with students one-on-one." In fact, 59 percent of the class of 2017 received academic credit for faculty-directed research. Indeed, "from the students to the faculty and staff to the administrators, everyone is open and greets everyone with a smile." "Overall I've had a fantastic academic experience with professors that have helped me discover my intellectual passions and have had a vested interest in my success," says a junior. The small school atmosphere matched with the large school resources, and reputation are "some of the greatest aspects of Wake Forest." "I feel that I could ask any professor I've had at Wake for a letter of recommendation, and they would know me personally enough to do so," says a student. There is a similarly "strong vision and support" from the administration and the alumni network, who back "crazy opportunities that meld ideas and people that just don't happen at other colleges." The school is committed to the teacher-scholar model, so not only do professors do cutting edge research, they let undergrads in on it. "Wake Forest is a campus where some of the most academically impressive and competitive students assemble, the community is an encouraging atmosphere evident to anyone who steps on the grounds, and the social life is unbeatable," says a student.

Life

Wake Forest students work extremely hard on weekdays, often spending hours in the library to complete work, but "absolutely let loose on weekends." The school's "vibrant social scene" and a schedule that is "always bustling with extracurricular activities" keep the candle burning at both ends, and "parties, going to bars downtown, concerts, game nights, and chill hang outs at friends' houses" are other methods of fun. The D1 athletics—perhaps you've heard of them?—lend Wake Forest a "big-school sports feel at a small school"; and many students play intramural sports or exercise fairly regularly as "people are very conscious of their image" at this health-conscious university. While Greek life is highly visible here, there are also organizations like the Student Union that "promote other fun aspects of campus life (i.e., Movie nights, guest speakers, campus carnivals)." Students take part in "lots of great traditions at Wake Forest, like our annual Shag on the Mag dance in the spring," "rolling the quad after a big athletic win," and dinner at the on-campus restaurant Shorty's. Philanthropy is a "HUGE part of the WFU experience," and there are several extremely large community service events that happen throughout the year, including the Project Pumpkin Halloween festival, the Hit the Bricks race to support cancer research, and many others.

Student Body

The university is steeped in Southern traditions and hospitality that "most students fit into or learn to adhere to in their tenure as Wake Students," but the school "is also home to students from around the country and the world." In this "tight-knit, supportive community" nearly everybody is "intelligent, ambitious, [and] highly involved." "It's like a living J.Crew magazine," says one student; it can seem like almost everyone here is "preppy, involved in greek life, [and] from the east coast (either north or south)." Thanks to a strong foundation of friendliness and acceptance among the student body, "people generally don't have any trouble fitting in here, and can usually easily find groups of people who share their interests." WFU students come from 49 states and more than 40 countries.

WAKE FOREST UNIVERSITY

Financial Aid: 336-758-5154 • E-Mail: admissions@wfu.edu • Website: www.wfu.edu

THE PRINCETON REVIEW SAYS

Admissions

Very important factors considered include: rigor of secondary school record, class rank, academic GPA, application essay, character/personal qualities. *Important factors considered include:* recommendation(s), interview, extracurricular activities, talent/ability. *Other factors considered include:* standardized test scores, first generation, alumni/ae relation, geographical residence, state residency, religious affiliation/commitment, racial/ethnic status, volunteer work, level of applicant's interest. ACT with or without writing accepted. SAT with or without Essay component accepted. High school diploma is required and GED is accepted. *Academic units required:* 4 English, 3 math, 1 science, 2 foreign language, 2 social studies. *Academic units recommended:* 4 English, 4 math, 4 science, 4 foreign language, 4 social studies.

Financial Aid

Students should submit: CSS/Financial Aid PROFILE; FAFSA; Noncustodial PROFILE; State aid form. Priority filing deadline is 1/1. The Princeton Review suggests that all financial aid forms be submitted as soon as possible after October 1. *Need-based scholarships/grants offered:* College/university scholarship or grant aid from institutional funds; Federal Pell; Private scholarships; SEOG; State scholarships/grants; United Negro College Fund. *Loan aid offered:* Direct PLUS loans; Direct Subsidized Stafford Loans; Direct Unsubsidized Stafford Loans. Applicants will be notified of awards on a rolling basis beginning 4/1. Federal Work-Study Program available. Institutional employment available.

The Inside Word

Wake Forest's considerable application numbers afford admissions officers the opportunity to be rather selective. In particular, admissions officers remain diligent in their matchmaking efforts—finding students who are good fits for the school—and their hard work is rewarded by a high graduation rate. Candidates will need to be impressive in all areas to gain admission, since all areas of their applications are considered carefully. A relatively large number of qualified students find themselves on Wake Forest's wait list.

THE SCHOOL SAYS "..."

From the Admissions Office

"Wake Forest University has been dedicated to the liberal arts for over a century and a half; this means education in the fundamental fields of human knowledge and achievement. It seeks to encourage habits of mind that ask why, that evaluate evidence, that are open to new ideas, that attempt to understand and appreciate the perspective of others, that accept complexity and grapple with it, that admit error, and that pursue truth. Wake Forest is among a small, elite group of American colleges and universities recognized for their outstanding academic quality. It offers small classes taught by full-time faculty—not graduate assistants—and a commitment to student interaction with those professors. Wake Forest balances the personal attention of a liberal arts college with the academic vitality and broad opportunities of a research university. Students are admitted based on the unique qualities they bring to our community. Wake Forest's generous financial aid program allows deserving students to enroll regardless of their financial circumstances.

"Wake Forest is the first top thirty national university in the United States to make standardized tests such as the SAT and ACT with writing optional in the admissions process. If applicants feel that their SAT or ACT with writing scores are a good indicator of their abilities, they may submit them and they will be considered in the admissions decision. If, however, a prospective student does not feel that their scores accurately represent their academic abilities, they do not need to submit them until after they have been accepted and choose to enroll. Wake Forest takes a holistic look at each applicant."

SELECTIVITY

Admissions Rating	96
# of applicants	12,559
% of applicants accepted	30
% of acceptees attending	37
# of early decision applicants	2,047
% accepted early decision	31

FRESHMAN PROFILE

Range SAT EBRW	650–720
Range SAT Math	670–770
Range SAT Composite	1340–1470
Range ACT Composite	30–33
# submitting SAT scores	604
% submitting SAT scores	44
# submitting ACT scores	617
% submitting ACT scores	45
% graduated top 10% of class	75
% graduated top 25% of class	92
% graduated top 50% of class	98

DEADLINES

Early decision	
Deadline	11/15
Notification	Rolling
Other ED Deadline	1/1
Other ED Notification	2/15
Regular	
Deadline	1/1
Notification	4/1
Nonfall registration?	No

FINANCIAL FACTS

Financial Aid Rating	97
Annual tuition	$56,722
Room and board	$17,334
Required fees	$1,038
Books and supplies	$1,500
Average frosh need-based scholarship	$52,729
Average UG need-based scholarship	$50,178
% needy frosh rec. need-based scholarship or grant aid	95
% needy UG rec. need-based scholarship or grant aid	97
% needy frosh rec. non-need-based scholarship or grant aid	86
% needy UG rec. non-need-based scholarship or grant aid	65
% needy frosh rec. need-based self-help aid	88
% needy UG rec. need-based self-help aid	92
% frosh rec. any financial aid	39
% UG rec. any financial aid	34
% UG borrow to pay for school	30
Average cumulative indebtedness	$34,053
% frosh need fully met	100
% ugrads need fully met	100
Average % of frosh need met	100
Average % of ugrad need met	100

WARREN WILSON COLLEGE

P.O. Box 9000, Asheville, NC 28815-9000 • Admissions: 828-771-2073 • Fax: 828-298-1440

CAMPUS LIFE

Quality of Life Rating	87
Fire Safety Rating	69
Green Rating	76
Type of school	Private
Environment	City

STUDENTS

Total undergrad enrollment	706
% male/female	33/67
% from out of state	63
% frosh from public high school	80
% frosh live on campus	99
% ugrads live on campus	87
# of fraternities	0
# of sororities	0
% African American	6
% Asian	1
% Caucasian	75
% Hispanic	8
% Native American	1
% Pacific Islander	0
% Two or more races	5
% Race and/or ethnicity unknown	1
% international	3
# of countries represented	14

SURVEY SAYS . . .

Lots of liberal students
Class discussions encouraged
Students aren't religious
Students involved in community service
Students environmentally aware
Students love Asheville, NC
Theater is popular

ACADEMICS

Academic Rating	81
% students returning for sophomore year	65
% students graduating within 4 years	49
% students graduating within 6 years	53
Calendar	Semester
Student/faculty ratio	10:1
Profs interesting rating	91
Profs accessible rating	92

Most classes have 10–19 students.

MOST POPULAR MAJORS

Environmental Studies; Biology/Biological Sciences, General; Psychology, General

STUDENTS SAY "..."

Academics

Everything at Warren Wilson College, a small liberal arts school outside Asheville, North Carolina, can be attributed to its unique approach to learning, where academics are combined with "work and service." As one student describes the College, it's "work for the hands, service for the heart, learning for the mind." Outside the classroom, "students are also required to work 10–15 hours a week on one of many work crews" around campus, and "are also required to fulfill a certain amount of community service work in coordination with one of many community partners." The "work program at Warren Wilson is one of the main reasons I chose the school," says one environmental science major, and another student adds that the "work program is [what's] truly interesting about this school. We run our own little country here basically." That doesn't mean academics get short shrift—as one history major points out, "We take as many credits as other college students and we work 10–15 hours a week." Professors at Warren Wilson earn mostly high praise from students: "They are great at both lectures and discussion, and are able to teach nuanced, complex ideas and concepts in interesting and concise ways." With the small size and strong sense of community, the faculty here is very involved and very accessible.

Life

With class work, community service, and time spent on one of the numerous campus work crews, students say "days are easily filled" and "weekdays tend to be very busy." When it's time to relax, "plenty of students spend as much time outside as possible hiking, swimming, skating, exploring the city of Asheville, and partying." "It's a very outdoorsy campus environment because we are in the middle of Appalachia" and "we have miles and miles of hiking trails that are campus property." Beyond the outdoors, "creative writing and coffee culture are a big part of Warren Wilson's culture," along with live music and "contra dancing on Thursdays." Some students say that the work crews are the closest thing the school has to fraternities and some of the more popular pastimes are "activities related to the crews—like blacksmithing workshops, beekeeping workshops, fabric workshops." With the school's appreciation of music, the "cafe is usually hosting shows that are a huge draw." In one student's estimation, "Everyone at the school loves the outdoors and has a healthy appreciation for taking an afternoon off to explore the river or trails." Warren Wilson is a place where politically-, socially-, and environmentally-focused "discussions are ubiquitous in and out of the classroom."

Student Body

"The student body at [Warren Wilson] is sustainable, eclectic, earthy, hard-working and very community oriented." As one photography major puts it, "If you're looking for someplace different, this is it." The school's former motto was "We're not for everyone, but maybe you're not everyone" and some students find that still holds true, though others note that "limited racial diversity" "does not create a welcoming environment to racial and ethnic minorities on the campus." At the same time, vocal students stress the school's accepting nature, underscoring that Warren Wilson "has a strong LGBTQ community that [faces] a far lesser level of discrimination at this school than at most colleges and universities." As an environmental science major puts it, "The environment and proximity to Asheville attract the typical tree-hugging hippie crowd, but there's really a place for everyone at the college" and nearly everyone is "actively engaged in issues of social justice." In short, Warren Wilson students are "fantastically talented, hardworking, and willing to think outside the box."

WARREN WILSON COLLEGE

Financial Aid: 828-771-2082 • E-Mail: admit@warren-wilson.edu • Website: www.warren-wilson.edu

THE PRINCETON REVIEW SAYS

Admissions

Very important factors considered include: rigor of secondary school record, recommendation(s). *Important factors considered include:* academic GPA, application essay, interview, volunteer work, work experience. *Other factors considered include:* class rank, standardized test scores, extracurricular activities, talent/ability, character/personal qualities, first generation. ACT with or without writing accepted. SAT with or without Essay component accepted. High school diploma is required and GED is accepted. *Academic units recommended:* 4 English, 3 math, 2 science, 2 science labs, 2 foreign language, 3 social studies.

Financial Aid

Students should submit: FAFSA; State aid form. Priority filing deadline is 2/1. The Princeton Review suggests that all financial aid forms be submitted as soon as possible after October 1. *Need-based scholarships/grants offered:* College/university scholarship or grant aid from institutional funds; Federal Pell; Private scholarships; SEOG; State scholarships/grants. *Loan aid offered:* Direct PLUS loans; Direct Subsidized Stafford Loans; Direct Unsubsidized Stafford Loans. Applicants will be notified of awards on a rolling basis beginning 3/1. Federal Work-Study Program available. Institutional employment available.

The Inside Word

In keeping with Warren Wilson College's mission of combining academics, work, and community service, prospective students should be aware that their efforts outside the classroom are as important as their performance in it. The admissions committee looks for signs of maturity, integrity, and a commitment to the mission of the college in each applicant. Warren Wilson accepts the Common Application, with their own writing supplement (not required, but strongly recommended), and standardized test scores are optional.

THE SCHOOL SAYS "..."

From the Admissions Office

"Warren Wilson College students think and act independently, actively participate in their education, and want a college that provides a sense of community. Consider joining us if you're looking for a rigorous liberal arts education that integrates applied learning throughout. Warren Wilson students use work, service, internships and research to round out their core academic program, developing into highly sought-after global citizens."

SELECTIVITY

Admissions Rating	75
# of applicants	1,013
% of applicants accepted	86
% of acceptees attending	29
# of early decision applicants	22
% accepted early decision	91

FRESHMAN PROFILE

Range ACT Composite	21–28
# submitting SAT scores	10
% submitting SAT scores	4
# submitting ACT scores	102
% submitting ACT scores	41

DEADLINES

Early decision	
Deadline	11/1
Notification	12/1
Early action	
Deadline	11/15
Notification	12/15
Regular	
Priority	2/1
Notification	Rolling, 12/1
Nonfall registration?	Yes

FINANCIAL FACTS

Financial Aid Rating	84
Annual tuition	$37,500
Room and board	$11,750
Required fees	$850
Books and supplies	$850
% frosh rec. any financial aid	100
% UG rec. any financial aid	95

WASHINGTON COLLEGE

300 Washington Avenue, Chestertown, MD 21620 • Admissions: 410-778-7700 • Fax: 410-778-7287

CAMPUS LIFE

Quality of Life Rating	90
Fire Safety Rating	94
Green Rating	63
Type of school	Private
Environment	Rural

STUDENTS

Total undergrad enrollment	1,266
% male/female	40/60
% from out of state	58
% frosh live on campus	100
% ugrads live on campus	80
# of fraternities (% ugrad men join)	4 (5)
# of sororities (% ugrad women join)	3 (12)
% African American	11
% Asian	3
% Caucasian	69
% Hispanic	6
% Native American	<1
% Pacific Islander	<1
% Two or more races	<1
% Race and/or ethnicity unknown	5
% international	5
# of countries represented	22

SURVEY SAYS . . .

Students are happy
Lab facilities are great
Career services are great
Internships are widely available
Class discussions encouraged
Easy to get around campus
Recreation facilities are great
Everyone loves the Sho'men & Sho'women
Theater is popular

ACADEMICS

Academic Rating	87
% students returning for sophomore year	81
% students graduating within 4 years	69
% students graduating within 6 years	73
Calendar	Semester
Student/faculty ratio	10:1
Profs interesting rating	93
Profs accessible rating	96

Most classes have 10–19 students.
Most lab/discussion sessions have
10–19 students.

MOST POPULAR MAJORS

Biology/Biological Sciences, General; Business
Administration and Management, General;
Psychology, General

STUDENTS SAY "..."

Academics

Washington College is all about "gaining a distinctive and strong education in the liberal arts through personalized programs and hands-on experience." Located in small-town Chestertown, Maryland, this "small, tight-knit" community fosters a "high level of education" and an "intimate and personalized education experience." Washington College is a place where "students learn to think outside of the box while becoming better people and having the time of their lives." Centrally located between "three major employment markets: Washington, D.C., Philadelphia, and Baltimore," this "beautiful campus" "provides the perfect setting for a learning environment." "There are not as many distractions, but there is enough to keep you busy." Professors here are "highly educated, very personal, and willing to bend over backwards to ensure your education." Unlike at large research universities, faculty at Washington College are "here to teach, and they love to teach." The "attention given to the students by faculty is undeniable." The English and creative writing programs are among "the best in the country," earning Washington College a reputation "as a writing school," with the famous "Rose O'Neill Literary House, and the Sophie Kerr Prize." Students say all in one breath, "The professors are world-class, and the campus is beautiful. Also the Eastern Shore of Maryland is an incredible place to be."

Life

Living at Washington College "is as good as a college experience can get." "No matter what your interests are, there is plenty to do." Some note that because of "the small-town environment, we have to make our own fun on weekends, but there's usually something on-campus to make it less of a challenge." "I personally love the environment and being outdoors. I spend a lot of time kayaking at our boat house on the Chester River, fishing on the Eastern Shore of Maryland, and supporting our athletic teams." "The school's rather small, so we know almost all of the athletes, so we're not only supporting a program, we're supporting our best friends." On campus, "there are plenty of student-run activities." When it comes to facilities, "the athletic department is great, and the dining hall is new and wonderful." For fun, students "often go to plays hosted by the drama department, attend interesting guest lectures, play [video games] in the dorm rooms, play Frisbee on the campus green, play pool in the student center, go to movies, or stroll around Chestertown and the waterfront." "We drink in the dorms and suites because almost everyone lives on campus." Washington College "is located within a rural town; however, we are not completely isolated. We are about forty minutes away from Annapolis." The school also offers weekend shuttles to off-campus hotspots like Annapolis, local transit stations, and shopping. Students do warn, "Being in a rural town was hard at first."

Student Body

A typical Washington College student "is preppy—from the way they dress to the way that they interact with each other and their professors." It's "an athletic campus, as even non-athletes...generally...participate in intramural sports." Most students "come from a somewhat affluent background, and the majority study and work very hard, but they also party very hard on the weekends." Though some note "there is very little diversity on campus," others say while the campus "might lack in racial diversity, people have diverse morals, values, and political views." There seem to be "two major, distinct campus cultures: the athletic/Greek life people and the English/drama people. People generally gravitate to one or the other." "It isn't hard to find your 'place,' though." Most students are "involved in several different types of activities." Students "usually fit in by playing a sport or joining Greek life, but there is always a club for everyone." Others concur, Washington College is a "melting pot of individuals from different backgrounds, but the typical student is open-minded, ambitious, and extremely innovative." Athletes and burgeoning writers alike "have strong pride and love for our school."

Financial Aid: 410-778-7214 • E-Mail: wc_admissions@washcoll.edu • Website: www.washcoll.edu

THE PRINCETON REVIEW SAYS

Admissions

Very important factors considered include: rigor of secondary school record, academic GPA, interview, level of applicant's interest. *Important factors considered include:* class rank, application essay, standardized test scores. *Other factors considered include:* recommendation(s), extracurricular activities, talent/ability, character/personal qualities, first generation, alumni/ae relation, geographical residence, state residency, racial/ethnic status, volunteer work, work experience. ACT with or without writing accepted. SAT with or without Essay component accepted. High school diploma is required and GED is accepted. *Academic units required:* 4 English, 3 math, 3 science, 2 science labs, 2 foreign language, 2 social studies, 2 history. *Academic units recommended:* 4 English, 4 math, 4 science, 3 science labs, 4 foreign language, 2 social studies, 2 history.

Financial Aid

Students should submit: FAFSA. Priority filing deadline is 3/1. The Princeton Review suggests that all financial aid forms be submitted as soon as possible after October 1. *Need-based scholarships/grants offered:* College/university scholarship or grant aid from institutional funds; Federal Pell; Private scholarships; SEOG; State scholarships/grants. *Loan aid offered:* Direct PLUS loans; Direct Subsidized Stafford Loans; Direct Unsubsidized Stafford Loans. Applicants will be notified of awards on a rolling basis beginning 2/1. Federal Work-Study Program available. Institutional employment available.

THE SCHOOL SAYS "..."

From the Admissions Office

"Founded in 1782, Washington College was the first college chartered in the sovereign United States of America. General George Washington lent us his name, donated 50 guineas to our founding, and served on our first Board of Visitors and Governors. Our goal back then was to cultivate responsible, educated citizen-leaders who could nurture the new democracy. It still is today.

"A Washington College education affords students unmatched opportunities to work closely with an exceptional faculty on projects they are passionate about. Whether they study the sciences or the liberal arts, our students have access to top-notch facilities and programs. Run experiments in our state-of-the-art Toll Science Center, print a book of poetry on our working antique letterpresses in the Rose O'Neill Literary House, or trek out to our 4,700-acre River and Field Campus to band birds or scan the Chester River on one of our research vessels.

"We believe that a diverse liberal arts education is both academically rewarding and the most effective way to prepare for a future in anything you want to do. Our students are driven to explore their interests, examine different perspectives, and challenge old ways of thinking. There is no one-size-fits-all education at Washington College: from double-majoring to internships to study abroad and semester-long interdisciplinary programs, students at Washington College get the chance to shape a college experience that is right for them.

"Admission to Washington College is selective; decisions are based primarily on a student's record of academic achievement. We strongly recommend visiting campus."

SELECTIVITY

Admissions Rating	81
# of applicants	2,224
% of applicants accepted	92
% of acceptees attending	16

FRESHMAN PROFILE

Range SAT EBRW	560–660
Range SAT Math	530–640
Range SAT Composite	1100–1280
Range ACT Composite	20–29
# submitting SAT scores	241
% submitting SAT scores	74
# submitting ACT scores	68
% submitting ACT scores	21
Average HS GPA	3.4
% graduated top 10% of class	28
% graduated top 25% of class	53
% graduated top 50% of class	83

DEADLINES

Early decision	
Deadline	11/15
Notification	12/15
Other ED Deadline	12/15
Other ED Notification	1/15
Early action	
Deadline	12/1
Notification	1/15
Regular	
Deadline	2/15
Notification	Rolling, 10/1
Nonfall registration?	Yes

FINANCIAL FACTS

Financial Aid Rating	88
Annual tuition	$48,678
Room and board	$13,038
Books and supplies	$1,400
Average frosh need-based scholarship	$36,444
Average UG need-based scholarship	$36,365
% needy frosh rec. need-based scholarship or grant aid	99
% needy UG rec. need-based scholarship or grant aid	100
% needy frosh rec. non-need-based scholarship or grant aid	18
% needy UG rec. non-need-based scholarship or grant aid	15
% needy frosh rec. need-based self-help aid	71
% needy UG rec. need-based self-help aid	72
% frosh rec. any financial aid	99.1
% UG rec. any financial aid	96.4
% UG borrow to pay for school	65
Average cumulative indebtedness	$34,903
% frosh need fully met	19
% ugrads need fully met	17
Average % of frosh need met	85
Average % of ugrad need met	85

WASHINGTON & JEFFERSON COLLEGE

60 South Lincoln Street, Washington, PA 15301 • Admissions: 724-223-6025 • Fax: 724-223-6534

CAMPUS LIFE

Quality of Life Rating	81
Fire Safety Rating	95
Green Rating	78
Type of school	Private
Environment	Village

STUDENTS

Total undergrad enrollment	1,246
% male/female	48/52
% from out of state	23
% frosh from public high school	81
% frosh live on campus	99
% ugrads live on campus	92
# of fraternities (% ugrad men join)	5 (31)
# of sororities (% ugrad women join)	4 (29)
% African American	7
% Asian	2
% Caucasian	74
% Hispanic	6
% Native American	<1
% Pacific Islander	0
% Two or more races	3
% Race and/or ethnicity unknown	6
% international	3
# of countries represented	29

SURVEY SAYS . . .

Lab facilities are great
Frats and sororities are popular
Everyone loves the Presidents

ACADEMICS

Academic Rating	83
% students returning for sophomore year	83
% students graduating within 4 years	69
% students graduating within 6 years	75
Calendar	4/1/4
Student/faculty ratio	10:1
Profs interesting rating	90
Profs accessible rating	94

Most classes have 10–19 students.
Most lab/discussion sessions have
  10–19 students.

MOST POPULAR MAJORS

Business/Commerce, General; Accounting;
Psychology, General

STUDENTS SAY " . . ."

Academics

Washington & Jefferson College is a small school known for its "academic rigor" and "prestigious reputation." In addition to two conventional semesters, the college also features a unique two-week intercession period in January, which allows for "focused learning on a topic that is often much different than something … offered during a semester, including travel and topics of specific interest to professors." Students feel that there is a very "open learning environment," and that "as the class levels increase, so does the amount of open discussion." The professors "want the students to learn" and "are willing to meet with students at any point to discuss how to better their education." "They are very knowledgeable and are very accessible outside of class," and personal connections with professors "oftentimes leads to internships or research projects" for undergraduate students. In general, the college is excellent at providing students with ample opportunities to prepare for their futures. It boasts "a great reputation for graduate school preparation" and has an "impeccable record at placing students in medical, graduate, and law schools." Additionally, there are "so many opportunities with alumni relations." The study abroad office is also excellent, and there are "tons of grants to do a research project abroad or to do internships across the U.S" or overseas with funding from the Magellan Project.

Life

Life at Washington & Jefferson College is a "good balance of schoolwork, athletics, and fun." The "beautiful, small campus" is home to a "friendly, warm," "family-like environment," where the emphasis is placed on the well-being of the students. It is "easy to get involved and be active in campus organizations." Students "study hard during the week, but party hard on the weekends," however, the school also "provides multiple activities over the weekends—especially for students who do not drink." "There are always music, art, speakers, and events" on campus. Some students complain, "There needs to be more to do on campus on the weekends"; and the school is trying to respond to this demand by "working hard to produce more student activities, such as bringing in great bands for concerts." A few students also feel that the Greek life on campus is a bit too prevalent. Some students suggest that Washington & Jefferson's home city of Washington "isn't ideal" for their desired getaways, but student services provides a shuttle to and from nearby Pittsburgh on the weekends, which can be "a great escape from the close-knit campus community."

Student Body

At Washington & Jefferson, "while every student is generally friendly and will help you, interaction between different kinds of people is still limited and at times, the student body can be cliquish," and some describe the average student as a "white upper middle class Republican Christian," although there is a "growing number of international students." While many students are "truly good, smart, open-minded people," there are "a few religious bigots who are rich and feel elite." Some feel that the overall vibe trends toward students who are "athletic, sporty, smart," "well-off financially," and "relatively preppy." However, students are also noted for being very social, as well as "extremely friendly and helpful." The typical student at W&J is focused on his or her course work; he or she is "also involved outside of the classroom in clubs, athletics, Greek Life, or one of a variety of other things the school has to offer." The students here "have a common goal to be successful in life," and with this goal in mind, everyone works together to form a tight-knit community and "gets along pretty well."

WASHINGTON & JEFFERSON COLLEGE

Financial Aid: 724-223-6019 • E-Mail: admission@washjeff.edu • Website: www.washjeff.edu

THE PRINCETON REVIEW SAYS

Admissions

Very important factors considered include: rigor of secondary school record, class rank, academic GPA, application essay, recommendation(s), interview, character/personal qualities. *Important factors considered include:* extracurricular activities. *Other factors considered include:* standardized test scores, talent/ability, alumni/ae relation, geographical residence, state residency, racial/ethnic status, volunteer work, work experience, level of applicant's interest. ACT with or without writing accepted. SAT with or without Essay component accepted. High school diploma is required and GED is accepted. *Academic units required:* 3 English, 3 math, 1 science, 1 science lab, 2 foreign language, 6 academic electives. *Academic units recommended:* 4 English, 4 math, 2 science, 2 science labs, 3 foreign language, 6 academic electives.

Financial Aid

Students should submit: FAFSA. The Princeton Review suggests that all financial aid forms be submitted as soon as possible after October 1. *Need-based scholarships/grants offered:* College/university scholarship or grant aid from institutional funds; Federal Pell; Private scholarships; SEOG; State scholarships/grants; United Negro College Fund. *Loan aid offered:* Direct PLUS loans; Direct Subsidized Stafford Loans; Direct Unsubsidized Stafford Loans. Applicants will be notified of awards on a rolling basis beginning 12/15. Federal Work-Study Program available. Institutional employment available.

The Inside Word

Washington & Jefferson College takes a well-rounded approach to admissions, reflecting the type of student the school aims to admit. Academic record, class rank, personal statement, and extracurricular activities are all thoroughly evaluated. Most prospective students work diligently to secure a spot at this prestigious institution. The lucky applicants who receive a fat letter in the mail are welcomed into a distinctive community that promises to broaden their horizons and to prepare them for a successful future.

THE SCHOOL SAYS "..."

From the Admissions Office

"At Washington & Jefferson College, the entire community is devoted to ensuring student success. In the last few years, 100 percent of W&J graduates taking the Pennsylvania bar exam passed, and we regularly see admission rates of 90 percent for graduates headed to medical and law school. The College has added $100 million in new facilities since 2002, including residence halls, a Recreation Center, tennis courts, a state-of-the-art technology center, the Burnett Center (housing accounting, business, economics, education, entrepreneurial studies, and modern languages), and the new Swanson Science Center (dedicated to the physical sciences, including physics, chemistry, and biochemistry). Unique to W&J, the Magellan Project provides funding to students to take advantage of challenging projects in international locations; prestigious internships in New York, Washington, or other cities; and research experiences in major laboratories. Alumni mentors help students attain valuable internships and, upon graduation, assist with career placement. You dream it; we help make it happen. Our students are balanced, goal oriented, active, engaged, and involved, and we look for applicants who demonstrate these qualities in every stage of the admissions process. If you are a student who thrives on academic rigor, wants a close personal relationship with top-notch faculty, and values being a member of a true college community, we encourage you to consider W&J. Finally, W&J recommends but does not require scores from the SAT (or ACT). If submitted, we will use the best scores from either test."

SELECTIVITY

Admissions Rating	76
# of applicants	2,722
% of applicants accepted	85
% of acceptees attending	13
# of early decision applicants	13
% accepted early decision	62

FRESHMAN PROFILE

Range SAT EBRW	550–640
Range SAT Math	540–640
Range SAT Composite	1100–1290
Range ACT Composite	22–28
# submitting SAT scores	174
% submitting SAT scores	60
# submitting ACT scores	61
% submitting ACT scores	21
Average HS GPA	3.7
% graduated top 10% of class	24
% graduated top 25% of class	48
% graduated top 50% of class	85

DEADLINES

Early decision	
Deadline	12/1
Notification	12/15
Early action	
Deadline	1/15
Notification	2/15
Regular	
Priority	1/15
Deadline	3/1
Notification	Rolling, 10/1
Nonfall registration?	Yes

FINANCIAL FACTS

Financial Aid Rating	87
Annual tuition	$48,758
Room and board	$13,044
Required fees	$550
Books and supplies	$1,000
Average frosh need-based scholarship	$38,477
Average UG need-based scholarship	$35,258
% needy frosh rec. need-based scholarship or grant aid	100
% needy UG rec. need-based scholarship or grant aid	97
% needy frosh rec. non-need-based scholarship or grant aid	10
% needy UG rec. non-need-based scholarship or grant aid	38
% needy frosh rec. need-based self-help aid	80
% needy UG rec. need-based self-help aid	80
% frosh rec. any financial aid	100
% UG rec. any financial aid	100
% UG borrow to pay for school	83
Average cumulative indebtedness	$48,582
% frosh need fully met	22
% ugrads need fully met	19
Average % of frosh need met	86
Average % of ugrad need met	83

WASHINGTON STATE UNIVERSITY

PO Box 641067, Pullman, WA 99164-1067 • Admissions: 509-335-5586 • Fax: 509-335-4902

STUDENTS SAY "..."

Academics

Located in the city of Pullman and home to over 18,000 undergrads and over 2,600 graduate and professional students, Washington State University is known for its friendly, spirited environment and its motivated student body. The WSU school spirit is evident across the campus "with a wave of a flag or a loud 'Go Cougs!'" "There is no other place that has ever made me feel so invited and generally concerned about my well-being both as a student and as a member of the Coug family," says a student. Faculty members are constantly doing "world changing research projects" and "love getting students involved"; instructors will often bring in "great information they have found while researching something applicable to your learning." This makes classes both "challenging and rewarding, offering many additional opportunities throughout the course." "I've never [come] across a WSU professor who was not extremely knowledgeable and prepared," says a student. Faculty members urge students to ask questions, which lead to "awesome discussions" that take classes "from a one-sided lecture to discussions that have deepened my understanding of material." The school also offers a university-wide Freshman Focus residential learning community program that allows students to take a general education class with other students who live near them in residence halls. There is a top-notch Junior Writing Portfolio program in place to determine if students' writing abilities are up to par, "numerous study-abroad opportunities," and classes that provide "a chance to be innovative while still teaching you the experiences to be a good candidate in prospective fields." This opens the door for students to receive hands-on experiences by "creating connections to job opportunities, life experiences, and internships." Academic benefits aside, in the end, Cougar pride trumps all: "Win or lose, we're die hard Cougs."

Life

WSU's location in southeast Washington "makes for a gorgeous campus" and there is a real "college town atmosphere" in Pullman. There are "so many great restaurants" that students frequent. Skiing, hiking, camping, and boating are nearby. Greek life is popular, and students "love giving back to the community": "In Pullman, we don't have hello or goodbye—we have GO COUGS." The campus is "safe to the greatest extent," but the school "provides free rides to those who do not feel safe." The student recreation center is known for its undeniable awesomeness: "We have a pool shaped like the state of Washington and a hot tub that can hold fifty people." The university does an excellent job of providing events, activities and performances to attend, ranging "from movies to restaurants to bowling." Football games are a must for this crimson and gray sporting group, and good old Netflix watching and socializing in the dorms is always in season.

Student Body

Most WSU students are "friendly, and an active member of the community." A lot of WSU students have jobs and are heavily involved in extracurriculars, and "students typically fit in with others in their department." "There is a sort of bond between classmates that can lead to friendships and study partners in other classes," says a student. Almost everyone here is "wearing Cougar gear at least three days a week" and "spends some time working out, studying, or hanging out with friends."

WASHINGTON STATE UNIVERSITY

Financial Aid: 509-335-9711 • E-Mail: admissions@wsu.edu • Website: www.wsu.edu

THE PRINCETON REVIEW SAYS

Admissions

Very important factors considered include: academic GPA, standardized test scores. Washington State University will not require SAT or ACT scores for applicants seeking to enter fall semester (August) 2021 or spring semester (January) 2022, and SAT/ACT scores will not be used as a factor in admission decisions for those terms. *Important factors considered include:* rigor of secondary school record, grade trends. High school diploma is required and GED is accepted. *Academic units required:* 4 English, 3 math, 2 science, 2 foreign language, 3 social studies, 1 visual/performing arts, 1 unit from above areas or other academic areas. *Academic units recommended:* 4 English, 4 math, 2 lab science, 2 foreign language, 3 social studies, 1 visual/performing arts or academic elective.

Financial Aid

Students should submit: FAFSA; State aid form. Priority filing deadline is 1/31. The Princeton Review suggests that all financial aid forms be submitted as soon as possible after October 1. *Need-based scholarships/grants offered:* College/university scholarship or grant aid from institutional funds; Federal Pell; Private scholarships; SEOG; State scholarships/grants. *Loan aid offered:* Direct PLUS loans; Federal Subsidized and Unsubsidized Loans. Applicants will be notified of awards on a rolling basis beginning mid-December. Federal and state work-study programs available. Institutional employment available.

The Inside Word

Admission to Washington State University requires successful completion of a college prep curriculum. Applicants who are either in the top 10 percent of their high school class or have a minimum cumulative GPA of 3.5 on a 4.0 scale are guaranteed admission. Depending on what your educational purpose is, the requirements and the application may vary.

THE SCHOOL SAYS " . . ."

From the Admissions Office

"One of America's leading public research institutions, Washington State University offers eager minds access to life-changing opportunity. Graduates benefit from an outstanding education, delivered affordably, with exceptionally high return on investment.

"As a student, you'll explore your interests with guidance from nationally recognized faculty. Academic programs are so strong that graduates become a top pick for employers in every sector: high-tech, healthcare, news media, energy, finance, and more. A worldwide network of alumni supports your transition from classroom to career.

"For 130 years, WSU has championed the greater good. Its research targets critical national and global challenges: resource sustainability, human/animal health, opportunity and equity, smart systems, and national security. The Elson S. Floyd College of Medicine trains physicians to serve Washington communities where they are needed most.

"WSU locations make degree programs accessible to all. Campuses in Pullman, Spokane, the Tri-Cities, Vancouver, Everett, and online (Global Campus) enroll undergraduate, graduate, and professional students from every state and 118 countries.

"Professors design online courses to deliver a compelling academic experience. The Global Campus shares its vast expertise in online teaching methods with faculty university-wide.

"To be considered for admission, complete the high school core curriculum. If you apply by the designated date and are among the top 10 percent of your high school class or have at least a 3.5 cumulative GPA on a 4.0 scale, you are assured admission. For priority dates and deadlines for admission, financial aid, and scholarship applications, check apply.wsu.edu."

SELECTIVITY

Admissions Rating	80
# of applicants	21,434
% of applicants accepted	76
% of acceptees attending	30

FRESHMAN PROFILE

Range SAT EBRW	510–620
Range SAT Math	510–610
Range SAT Composite	1030–1220
Range ACT Composite	20–26
# submitting SAT scores	4,106
% submitting SAT scores	85
# submitting ACT scores	1,169
% submitting ACT scores	24
Average HS GPA	3.5

DEADLINES

Regular	
Priority	1/31
Notification	Rolling, 11/1
Nonfall registration?	Yes

APPLICANTS ALSO LOOK AT AND OFTEN PREFER
Central Washington University; Eastern Washington University; University of Washington; Western Washington University

AND SOMETIMES PREFER
Gonzaga University; Oregon State University; Seattle University; University of Idaho; University of Oregon; University of Portland

AND RARELY PREFER
Arizona State University at the Tempe campus; Pacific Lutheran University; Seattle Pacific University

FINANCIAL FACTS

Financial Aid Rating	84
Annual in-state tuition	$9,953
Annual out-of-state tuition	$24,531
Room and board	$11,648
Required fees	$1,888
Books and supplies	$960
Average frosh need-based scholarship	$11,370
Average UG need-based scholarship	$11,416
% needy frosh rec. need-based scholarship or grant aid	92
% needy UG rec. need-based scholarship or grant aid	87
% needy frosh rec. non-need-based scholarship or grant aid	75
% needy UG rec. non-need-based scholarship or grant aid	50
% needy frosh rec. need-based self-help aid	62
% needy UG rec. need-based self-help aid	65
% frosh rec. any financial aid	86
% UG rec. any financial aid	76
% UG borrow to pay for school	57
Average cumulative indebtedness	$25,899
% frosh need fully met	14
% ugrads need fully met	11
Average % of frosh need met	64
Average % of ugrad need met	64

WASHINGTON UNIVERSITY IN ST. LOUIS

Campus Box 1089, St. Louis, MO 63130-4899 • Admissions: 314-935-6000 • Fax: 314-935-4290

CAMPUS LIFE

Quality of Life Rating	95
Fire Safety Rating	97
Green Rating	96
Type of school	Private
Environment	Metropolis

STUDENTS

Total undergrad enrollment	7,404
% male/female	47/53
% from out of state	89
% frosh from public high school	58
% frosh live on campus	100
% ugrads live on campus	72
# of fraternities (% ugrad men join)	15 (26)
# of sororities (% ugrad women join)	10 (39)
% African American	9
% Asian	16
% Caucasian	49
% Hispanic	10
% Native American	<1
% Pacific Islander	<1
% Two or more races	5
% Race and/or ethnicity unknown	2
% international	8
# of countries represented	47

SURVEY SAYS . . .

Students always studying
Students are happy
Classroom facilities are great
Lab facilities are great
Great library
Internships are widely available
School is well run
Great financial aid
Students are friendly
Great food on campus
Great off-campus food
Dorms are like palaces
Easy to get around campus
Recreation facilities are great
Frats and sororities are popular
Theater is popular
Active student government
Active minority support groups

ACADEMICS

Academic Rating	92
% students returning for sophomore year	97
% students graduating within 4 years	89
% students graduating within 6 years	95
Calendar	Semester
Student/faculty ratio	7:1
Profs interesting rating	90
Profs accessible rating	93

Most classes have 10–19 students.
Most lab/discussion sessions have
10–19 students.

MOST POPULAR MAJORS
Psychology, Computer Science, Biology/Biological Sciences, Econometrics and Quantitative Economics, Finance

STUDENTS SAY "..."

Academics

Wide-ranging exploration and customized learning are the driving forces at Washington University in St. Louis. There's an "academic flexibility" that allows undergrads to explore many different areas of study and find their passions. WashU focuses on the balanced student: "academically involved, part of many student groups, really immersed in the culture here." The "collaborative culture" is apparent in all aspects of the school, and because students here are so dedicated to their studies, there are "many clubs dedicated to specific areas" of academics, as well as research opportunities. The school's Center for Experiential Learning lets students put their learnings into practice and consult with actual companies or create mock business, and it is "easy to switch schools and majors" for students that find a new interest pulling them. Even first-year seminars "sometimes include out-of-class components like research or travel," and the school encourages civic engagement like local service projects, even building them into some classes. Additionally, around 40 percent of students study abroad during their time at WashU.

Academics are "great, but incredibly difficult," but the support systems in place for first-year students "help ease the college transition immensely," and the administration "deeply cares about the well-being of the students." For classes that need more resources (such as introductory courses like chemistry, biology, physics), there are "homework help sessions and tutoring groups that you can access easily." Professors are similarly "wonderful" and "encourage building personal relationships." Students particularly love the real-world applications of their classes: "We get to work with real companies, choose semester-long projects that interest our teams, and enjoy the humor that our professors bring to lectures." Best of all, for almost any program a student chooses to pursue, there is "flexibility so you can major or minor or take classes across schools without red tape."

Life

WashU is "the package deal. Great academics, amazing extracurricular activities, and the best people." There's "always funding for student groups, student initiatives, university-run activities, research, and the infrastructure is "unmatched": "Dorms are five-star hotels, food is delicious with tons of variety, [and] the buildings are gorgeous." The campus is also stunning, and "there is beautiful architecture, both historic and modern, and excellent maintenance of plant life." Campus life is "exciting and lively," and people are busy: "very few people do nothing for more than two hours per day." The "library is always filled, people are always playing Frisbee on the open fields," and "everyone is involved in multiple extracurricular activities." On the weekends students will go to the Loop (a stretch of restaurants near campus) for dinner with friends, or "older students go out to bars or clubs." The social scene is "largely Greek life-based," though big clubs or student groups also have "a very strong social aspect." The greater St. Louis area is a destination in itself, and people will often run in Forest Park or go exploring things "like music festivals or the local food scene." Brunch is a "super popular weekend option for getting off campus," and all students receive a free train and public transportation pass to make getting off campus possible.

Student Body

WashU's population is "small enough to walk around campus and say hi to a lot of people, but you can still meet new people every day." Everyone here is "passionate about something," and that passion is "contagious and highly motivating, especially at such a collaborative environment." There is a "diverse student body racially and religiously," and they are the most "genuine, down-to-earth, driven, non-competitive, outgoing student population" on top of being "intellectually curious, multi-talented, and engaged with the world around them." Above all, what really sets WashU apart is something called the "nice factor," where "students across all disciplines are collaborative in their work and kind to others." People "build each other up here and cheer each other on, and it really creates a community."

WASHINGTON UNIVERSITY IN ST. LOUIS

Financial Aid: 888-547-6670 • E-Mail: admissions@wustl.edu • Website: wustl.edu

THE PRINCETON REVIEW SAYS

Admissions

Very important factors considered include: rigor of secondary school record, class rank, academic GPA, application essay, standardized test scores, recommendation(s), extracurricular activities, talent/ability, character/personal qualities, volunteer work, work experience, level of applicant's interest. *Important factors considered include:* first generation. *Other factors considered include:* interview, alumni/ae relation, geographical residence, state residency, racial/ethnic status. ACT with or without writing accepted. SAT with or without Essay component accepted. High school diploma is required and GED is accepted. *Academic units required:* 4 English, 3 math, 3 science, 2 science labs, 2 foreign language, 2 social studies, 2 history. *Academic units recommended:* 4 English, 4 math, 4 science, 4 science labs, 4 foreign language, 4 social studies, 4 history.

Financial Aid

Students should submit: CSS/Financial Aid PROFILE; FAFSA; Noncustodial PROFILE. The Princeton Review suggests that all financial aid forms be submitted as soon as possible after October 1. *Need-based scholarships/grants offered:* College/university scholarship or grant aid from institutional funds; Federal Pell; Private scholarships; SEOG; State scholarships/grants; United Negro College Fund. *Loan aid offered:* Direct PLUS loans; Direct Subsidized Stafford Loans; Direct Unsubsidized Stafford Loans. Applicants will be notified of awards on or about 4/1. Federal Work-Study Program available. Institutional employment available.

The Inside Word

Washington University is highly selective, and competition for admission is fierce. A strong transcript and course selection will also be important. For example, it's highly recommended that business candidates take calculus, and all STEM candidates take calculus, chemistry, and physics. Finally, students applying to the College of Architecture are highly encouraged to submit a portfolio. Portfolios are required for applicants to the College of Art.

THE SCHOOL SAYS "..."

From the Admissions Office

"Nestled in the heart of St. Louis, Washington University offers a nurturing, yet intellectually rigorous, environment where students from all identities and backgrounds thrive. WashU's state-of-the-art buildings, laboratories, classrooms, and libraries foster a sense of community, creativity, and collaboration. On campus and across the world, you'll find talented, inspiring WashU students and faculty developing big ideas and pushing the boundaries on what it means to learn.

"WashU's undergraduate program is comprised of four undergraduate schools: the Sam Fox School of Design & Visual Arts, which houses both the College of Architecture and College of Art, College of Arts & Sciences, Olin Business School, and McKelvey School of Engineering. Offering more than 90 areas of study and 1,500 courses, students have the flexibility to explore multiple interests.

"Students can choose to join one of WashU's 380+ clubs and organizations, get involved in the St. Louis community, and have the opportunity to participate in cutting-edge research alongside professors who are leaders in their fields.

"WashU accepts Common Application and Coalition Application in Early Decision I, Early Decision II, and Regular Decision rounds, and requires a supplemental essay for scholarship consideration. Overall, the Admissions Committee reviews a large quantity of qualified and talented students each year. Each applicant is looked at individually with a holistic perspective. Once students are admitted, WashU commits to meeting 100 percent of demonstrated financial need, and counselors from Student Financial Services work with students and their families to ensure that a WashU education is not out of reach."

SELECTIVITY

Admissions Rating	99
# of applicants	25,426
% of applicants accepted	14
% of acceptees attending	49
# of early decision applicants	3,066
% accepted early decision	34

FRESHMAN PROFILE

Range SAT EBRW	720–760
Range SAT Math	760–800
Range SAT Composite	1480–1560
Range ACT Composite	33–35
# submitting SAT scores	646
% submitting SAT scores	37
# submitting ACT scores	1,173
% submitting ACT scores	68
Average HS GPA	4.2
% graduated top 10% of class	84
% graduated top 25% of class	96
% graduated top 50% of class	100

DEADLINES

Early decision	
Deadline	11/1
Notification	12/15
Other ED Deadline	1/2
Other ED Notification	2/15
Regular	
Deadline	1/2
Notification	4/1
Nonfall registration?	No

APPLICANTS ALSO LOOK AT AND OFTEN PREFER

Brown University; Duke University; Harvard College; Princeton University; Stanford University; University of Pennsylvania; Yale University

AND SOMETIMES PREFER

University of California—Berkeley; The University of Chicago; Northwestern University; Rice University; Cornell University; Vanderbilt University; Johns Hopkins University

AND RARELY PREFER

University of Michigan—Ann Arbor; University of California, Los Angeles; Emory University

FINANCIAL FACTS

Financial Aid Rating	99
Annual tuition	$56,300
Room and board	$17,402
Required fees	$1,086
Books and supplies	$1,144
Average frosh need-based scholarship	$51,449
Average UG need-based scholarship	$50,725
% needy frosh rec. need-based scholarship or grant aid	97
% needy UG rec. need-based scholarship or grant aid	98
% needy frosh rec. non-need-based scholarship or grant aid	9
% needy UG rec. non-need-based scholarship or grant aid	5
% needy frosh rec. need-based self-help aid	74
% needy UG rec. need-based self-help aid	67
% frosh rec. any financial aid	52
% UG rec. any financial aid	50
% UG borrow to pay for school	28
Average cumulative indebtedness	$24,247
% frosh need fully met	99
% ugrads need fully met	99
Average % of frosh need met	100
Average % of ugrad need met	100

WEBB INSTITUTE

298 Crescent Beach Road, Glen Cove, NY 11542-1398 • Admissions: 516-671-8355 • Fax: 516-674-9838

STUDENTS SAY "..."

Academics

As Webb Institute proudly boasts: "If you can design a ship, you can design anything." All graduates of this unique Long Island engineering school receive a full-tuition scholarship and leave with a dual degree in naval architecture and marine engineering, with paid internships required during every academic year. Grads have a 100 percent job placement rate. The curriculum is "intense," but the academics tie in well with the winter work terms: "Work terms give each student a feel for industry sectors and allow them to make improved career decisions when selecting a first job," says a student. "You'll learn something in the classroom and then see it in action." Students find this incredibly valuable; "not only do you know how things work, you understand why they work."

Students "are surrounded by ship models, half hulls on the walls, and people who are all interested in ships, boats, cutters, yachts, and anything else that goes in the water." The professors are "brilliant," and since they all have practical experience, they are "able to make our education applicable to what we'll be doing once we graduate." There are only four classrooms at Webb; desks are in the back, chairs for class are in the front. Students do their homework at their desk in the classroom, surrounded by classmates, and if help is needed on a problem, "all you have to do is look up and ask the room."

The specialized tools that are made available to students are what "most schools could only dream of buying," and the level of trust from the staff means students can freely take advantage of such resources as the towing tank and student garage. The student body at Webb functions based on an honor code, creating a "safe and supportive environment," which "allows our professors to give us take home tests knowing that no one will cheat." "I fully trust any individual at Webb," says a student. You also "cannot beat the alumni network here," which readily helps students find jobs, lodging, and anything else they need.

Life

All students live on campus during their time at Webb, and while "most of the day is devoted to work," there are several comfortable lounges with large television sets that are open 24/7 and a gym "not too far away." The campus has a pub that includes a pool table, darts, and a ping pong table, as well as a private beach for sailing, kitesurfing, waterskiing, and other water sports, which are predictably popular. Everyone participates in the student-run government, and extracurriculars are rampant; "if students want to do something, they take it upon themselves to make it happen" (no skill or prior experience is required to join any team at Webb). You "have to really push yourself to get work done to the point where you can leave on a weekend." However, students often tend to mix work and play in smaller increments, which is more doable. Proximity to New York City makes it easy for students to take day trips on weekends if they choose. In addition, "the school offers sponsored trips into the city to see cultural events like Broadway shows or symphony performances several times per semester."

Student Body

Given that there are only about a hundred students total, students "become best friends very quickly, giving everyone great support systems both academically and socially." "My classmates are like a family to me," says one. "They are all smart, capable people who work hard and play hard." As another person puts it, "You can tell people apart by the sound of their footsteps." Students come from around the country (and the world in some cases) which "brings different views together and creates a good mix within the student body." Though academic stress can arise, students find easy comfort in each other. "We have all come for the same reasons, and most of us enjoy the same stuff. Therefore, we all have similar quirks and use these to entertain ourselves."

Financial Aid: 516-403-5928 • E-Mail: admissions@webb.edu • Website: www.webb.edu

THE PRINCETON REVIEW SAYS

Admissions

Very important factors considered include: rigor of secondary school record, class rank, academic GPA, application essay, standardized test scores, recommendation(s), interview, character/personal qualities, level of applicant's interest. *Important factors considered include:* extracurricular activities, talent/ability. *Other factors considered include:* volunteer work, work experience. ACT with Writing recommended. SAT with Essay component recommended. High school diploma is required and GED is not accepted. *Academic units required:* 4 English, 4 math, 2 science, 2 science labs, 2 social studies, 4 academic electives.

Financial Aid

Students should submit: Business/Farm Supplement; FAFSA; Institution's own financial aid form. Priority filing deadline is 4/1. The Princeton Review suggests that all financial aid forms be submitted as soon as possible after October 1. *Need-based scholarships/grants offered:* College/university scholarship or grant aid from institutional funds; Federal Pell; Private scholarships; State scholarships/grants. *Loan aid offered:* Direct PLUS loans; Direct Subsidized Stafford Loans; Direct Unsubsidized Stafford Loans. Applicants will be notified of awards on or about 6/1.

The Inside Word

Although the applicant pool is highly self-selecting, admission to Webb is ultra-tough. The admissions committee is dedicated to finding students who will excel in the school's rigorous program. To apply, prospective students must submit high-school transcripts indicating rank in class, two letters of recommendation, and SAT or ACT scores, plus it is recommended that students submit SAT subject tests in mathematics level I or II and physics or chemistry. Applications and all supporting materials must be filed by October 15 for early decision and February 1 for regular decision.

THE SCHOOL SAYS "..."

From the Admissions Office

"Webb, the only college in the country that specializes in the engineering field of naval architecture and marine engineering, seeks young men and women of all races from all over the country who are interested in receiving an excellent engineering education with a full-tuition scholarship. Students don't have to know anything about ships, they just have to be motivated to study how mechanical, civil, structural, and electrical engineering come together with the design elements that make up a ship and all its systems. Being small and private has its major advantages. Every applicant is special and the President as well as a faculty member will interview all entering students personally. The student/faculty ratio is nine to one, and since there are no teaching assistants, interaction with the faculty occurs daily in class and labs at a level not found at most other colleges. The entire campus operates under the Student Organization's honor system that allows unsupervised exams and twenty-four-hour access to the library, every classroom and laboratory, and the shop and gymnasium. Despite a total enrollment of approximately one hundred students and a demanding workload, Webb manages to field five intercollegiate teams. Currently more than 60 percent of the members of the student body play on one or more intercollegiate teams. Work hard, play hard and the payoff is a job for every student upon graduation. The placement record of the college is 100 percent every year.

"Freshman applicants must take the SAT or ACT. We also recommend scores from two SAT Subject Tests in math level 1 or 2 and either physics or chemistry."

SELECTIVITY

Admissions Rating	97
# of applicants	129
% of applicants accepted	24
% of acceptees attending	84
# offered a place on the wait list	13
% accepting a place on wait list	100
% admitted from wait list	0
# of early decision applicants	42
% accepted early decision	19

FRESHMAN PROFILE

Range SAT EBRW	680–730
Range SAT Math	730–790
Range ACT Composite	31–34
# submitting SAT scores	20
% submitting SAT scores	77
# submitting ACT scores	6
% submitting ACT scores	23
Average HS GPA	4.0
% graduated top 10% of class	82
% graduated top 25% of class	100
% graduated top 50% of class	0

DEADLINES

Early decision	
Deadline	10/15
Notification	12/15
Regular	
Priority	10/15
Deadline	1/15
Notification	Rolling, 3/15
Nonfall registration?	No

APPLICANTS ALSO LOOK AT AND SOMETIMES PREFER

University of Michigan—Ann Arbor; United States Naval Academy; Massachusetts Institute of Technology

FINANCIAL FACTS

Financial Aid Rating	60*
Annual tuition	$0
Room and board	$15,750
Required fees	$460
Books and supplies	$700
Average frosh need-based scholarship	$52,810
Average UG need-based scholarship	$54,080
% needy frosh rec. need-based scholarship or grant aid	100
% needy UG rec. need-based scholarship or grant aid	100
% needy frosh rec. non-need-based scholarship or grant aid	100
% needy UG rec. non-need-based scholarship or grant aid	97
% needy frosh rec. need-based self-help aid	100
% needy UG rec. need-based self-help aid	100
% frosh rec. any financial aid	37
% UG rec. any financial aid	14
% UG borrow to pay for school	32
Average cumulative indebtedness	$25,270
Average % of frosh need met	95
Average % of ugrad need met	95

WELLESLEY COLLEGE

Admission Office, Wellesley, MA 02481-8203 • Admissions: 781-283-2270 • Fax: 781-283-3678

STUDENTS SAY "..."

Academics

For more than 150 years, Wellesley College has given ambitious young women an education in the liberal arts with a global perspective by offering more than fifty majors and hundreds of funded internships around the world. The school's financial support allows "students to pursue internships and research [opportunities] that they would otherwise not take because they are unpaid." The school stresses leadership, service, and the idea of Wellesley students contributing to the world both now and after graduation. To enhance that education even further, enrollees are able to cross-register (or even dual degree) with other nearby colleges. Students are "pushed to explore different departments through the distribution requirements, providing them with a liberal arts education that shapes their personhood and education." And each department is "provided with ample resources and handpicked professors" who "truly value building relationships with their students." It's not uncommon for faculty "to take their class out to a restaurant, or even invite students to their home for a meal." The First-Year Experience at Wellesley further helps ease students into college, including mentor groups, a required writing class, and First-Year Seminars where new students "have the chance to dive deep into a specific topic without feeling the pressure of having [senior students] dominate the conversation."

Academic opportunities extend beyond the classroom: The school's reputation and alumnae network "open so many doors for you in the future," and students can "take part from the moment [they] accept the enrollment offer, and for as long afterwards as [they] wish." Wellesley works to create an environment "where students can naturally progress through leadership positions on campus, whether that be through research, residential life, or student-run organizations." There are also "vast opportunities [for] study abroad programs in so many locations."

Life

While the average Wellesley "workload is not for the faint of heart," students find balance "with extracurricular activities, social life, and self-care." One student explains, "Even when classes are stressful, there is a beautiful campus that sparks happiness at random moments." That joy is apparent because almost everyone here is passionate about their extracurriculars, and "each organization at Wellesley is full of members who intensely love what they do." Outside of clubs or organizations, tons of students engage in "the weekly Thursday pub night" on campus, and Wellesley "usually has some cultural shows or lectures going on in the afternoon" which are well-attended. When they need a change of scenery, people often head to "neighboring universities to have fun on weekends" and "there is a bus that provides easy transportation" into Boston; many also "take advantage of [the] proximity to other east coast cities and states and take weekend trips." One student sums up the campus life at Wellesley: "Going to a party is just as acceptable as staying in and watching a movie or playing board games," and the school is "very much a choose your own adventure" environment.

Student Body

Among this "study-focused group of diverse people who hail from many countries and backgrounds," students "can be who [they] want and explore different identities." Thanks to that aspect of the student body, everyone is "exposed to countless cultures and viewpoints." These "intellectual, driven, [and] inclusive scholars" are "uplifting and kind to each other both in class and outside of class," and part of the campus culture "is the 'Why not?' attitude that we all share." "Everyone at Wellesley is nonjudgmental," says a student, and there's a "large feminist culture and LGBT population" on campus. Another student sums up the campus environment, saying Wellesley makes a huge effort "to cultivate and facilitate a strong support network for all."

WELLESLEY COLLEGE

Financial Aid: 781-283-2360 • E-Mail: admission@wellesley.edu • Website: www.wellesley.edu

THE PRINCETON REVIEW SAYS
Admissions
Very important factors considered include: rigor of secondary school record, academic GPA, recommendation(s), character/personal qualities. *Important factors considered include:* class rank, application essay, standardized test scores, extracurricular activities, talent/ability. *Other factors considered include:* interview, first generation, alumni/ae relation, geographical residence, state residency, racial/ethnic status, volunteer work, work experience, level of applicant's interest. ACT with Writing required. SAT with or without Essay component accepted. High school diploma or equivalent is not required. *Academic units recommended:* 4 English, 4 math, 3 science, 2 science labs, 4 foreign language, 4 social studies, 4 history.

Financial Aid
Students should submit: CSS/Financial Aid PROFILE; FAFSA; Noncustodial PROFILE. Priority filing deadline is 2/15. The Princeton Review suggests that all financial aid forms be submitted as soon as possible after October 1. *Need-based scholarships/grants offered:* College/university scholarship or grant aid from institutional funds; Federal Pell; Private scholarships; SEOG; State scholarships/grants; United Negro College Fund. *Loan aid offered:* Direct PLUS loans; Direct Subsidized Stafford Loans; Direct Unsubsidized Stafford Loans. Applicants will be notified of awards on or about 4/1. Federal Work-Study Program available. Institutional employment available.

The Inside Word
When making an admissions decision, Wellesley considers a broad range of factors, including a student's academic record, the difficulty of her high school curriculum, participation in extracurricular activities, class rank, recommendations, personal essay, standardized test scores, leadership, and special talents (students may submit art, music, or theater supplements along with their applications if they have a special talent in those areas). Personal interviews are highly recommended as they can be useful in standing out in Wellesley's extraordinary applicant pool, but they are not required.

THE SCHOOL SAYS "..."
From the Admissions Office
"Widely acknowledged as the nation's best women's college, Wellesley College provides students with numerous opportunities on campus and beyond. With a long-standing commitment to and established reputation for academic excellence, Wellesley offers more than 1,000 courses in more than fifty departmental and interdepartmental majors and supports more than 160 clubs, organizations, and activities for its students. The College is easily accessible to Boston, a great city in which to meet other college students and to experience theater, art, sports, and entertainment. Considered one of the most diverse colleges in the nation, Wellesley students hail from over eighty countries and all fifty states.

"As a community, we are looking for students who possess intellectual curiosity: the ability to think independently, ask challenging questions, and grapple with answers. Strong candidates demonstrate both academic achievement and an excitement for learning. They also display leadership, an appreciation for diverse perspectives, and an understanding of the College's mission to educate women who will make a difference in the world.

"The SAT or ACT are required. We strongly recommend that students planning to apply early decision complete the tests before the end of their junior year and no later than October of their senior year."

SELECTIVITY
Admissions Rating	97
# of applicants	6,631
% of applicants accepted	20
% of acceptees attending	47
# offered a place on the wait list	1,909
% accepting a place on wait list	65
% admitted from wait list	3
# of early decision applicants	802
% accepted early decision	31

FRESHMAN PROFILE
Range SAT EBRW	670–740
Range SAT Math	660–780
Range ACT Composite	30–34
# submitting SAT scores	404
% submitting SAT scores	66
# submitting ACT scores	292
% submitting ACT scores	47
% graduated top 10% of class	83
% graduated top 25% of class	96
% graduated top 50% of class	99

DEADLINES
Early decision	
Deadline	11/1
Notification	12/15
Other ED Deadline	1/1
Other ED Notification	2/28
Regular	
Deadline	1/15
Notification	4/1
Nonfall registration?	No

APPLICANTS ALSO LOOK AT AND OFTEN PREFER
Harvard College; Brown University

AND SOMETIMES PREFER
Columbia University; New York University; Barnard College; The University of Chicago; Cornell University

AND RARELY PREFER
Mount Holyoke College; Boston University; Smith College

FINANCIAL FACTS
Financial Aid Rating	97
Annual tuition	$53,408
Room and board	$16,468
Required fees	$324
Books and supplies	$800
Average frosh need-based scholarship	$52,881
Average UG need-based scholarship	$50,752
% needy frosh rec. need-based scholarship or grant aid	97
% needy UG rec. need-based scholarship or grant aid	95
% needy frosh rec. non-need-based scholarship or grant aid	8
% needy UG rec. non-need-based scholarship or grant aid	7
% needy frosh rec. need-based self-help aid	93
% needy UG rec. need-based self-help aid	94
% frosh rec. any financial aid	60
% UG rec. any financial aid	63
% UG borrow to pay for school	52
Average cumulative indebtedness	$16,122
% frosh need fully met	100
% ugrads need fully met	100
Average % of frosh need met	100
Average % of ugrad need met	100

WESLEYAN UNIVERSITY

70 Wyllys Avenue, Middletown, CT 06459 • Admissions: 860-685-3000 • Fax: 860-685-3001

STUDENTS SAY ". . ."

Academics

Wesleyan University is a liberal arts school in Middletown, Connecticut that "allows students to explore a broad spectrum of subjects" through an "open curriculum" without core requirements beyond your major. Classes are "challenging, but aren't so difficult that you don't have time for extracurriculars and friends." Plus, the small class sizes allow for connections and opportunity. One first-year student says they have already been "recommended as a TA to another professor." Faculty members are "experts in their field and make learning challenging, yet rewarding," and these "exceptional" professors "not only teach, but carry out their personal research as well, making sure to keep updated in this field." In particular, students "have raved about the college of social studies, the college of letters," and the "writing and the film" departments. Wesleyan also boasts the "highest STEM funding of any NESCAC school." In addition to career development through the Gordon Career Center, Wesleyan students benefit from an "altruistic alumni network that takes pride in school culture and the well-being of current students." And, students note, "because of Wesleyan's no loan/reduced-loan policy, the school is a very affordable option to students who come from a low income background."

Life

Wesleyan students are "committed to academics and many take more than a full course load," so studying is the common activity on weeknights. On the weekends, students tend to "sleep in, go to brunch, and then do some work in the afternoon." Wesleyan offers "theatrical or artistic performances throughout the semester," as well as "movies in the on-campus theater," where they show movies Wednesday to Saturday, and "a plethora of fun events like dance group performances, theater performances, athletic competitions, lecture series." There are "winter or Halloween festivals that go on in Middletown (about a ten to fifteen minute walk from campus)" and "Wes kids also love murder mystery parties." Sitting on Foss Hill when the weather is nice is the "most quintessential Wesleyan activity," and students praise the housing, where "you progress from dorms to apartment-style living to wood frame houses as seniors," along with "program houses." Wesleyan hosts the "most competitive athletic teams in NESCAC Division III sports," so "there are a lot of athletes on campus" and "many games students can attend, such as soccer, hockey, lacrosse, and football." Weekends bring a mix of people together at the parties thrown by "senior houses, frats, and program houses like Art House and Music House."

Student Body

The Wesleyan "unofficial motto is 'Keep Wes Weird,' and it's a credo students take seriously, whether it means playing their electric mandolin on Foss Hill or sleeping in the middle of the dining hall as their senior art thesis." Wesleyan offers a "mixed bag of athletes, artsy kids, and hardcore STEM kids," who "like to stay busy," which extends to the prominent "political and social activism" on campus. The size of the campus is "perfect for meeting new students (even in your third or fourth years) and this helps drive students toward classes and activities that may not be on their radar at first." The open curriculum means you'll find students "with an array of interests that may seem strange outside of the Wesleyan Bubble, such as a double major in Theater and Molecular Biology, or a varsity athlete who finds time to be heavily involved with dance and theater." "Wesleyan's greatest strengths are its diversity and its willingness to engage in the hard questions," one student remarks. It's a community of "individuals who aren't afraid to be themselves" and who "appreciate the differences in others." Students come from a diverse set of backgrounds, including "first-generation/low-income" students, some who report experiencing "a bit of culture shock," as first years, but stress that "most of the students here are friendly and easy to talk to." If you are "trying to find yourself (on a personal, spiritual, academic level), Wesleyan is a good place to do that." "It's truly amazing to me how such a small school can be so engaged, energetic, and exciting."

Financial Aid: 860-685-2800 • E-Mail: admission@wesleyan.edu • Website: www.wesleyan.edu

THE PRINCETON REVIEW SAYS

Admissions

Very important factors considered include: rigor of secondary school record. *Important factors considered include:* class rank, academic GPA, application essay, recommendation(s), talent/ability, character/personal qualities, first generation, racial/ethnic status. *Other factors considered include:* standardized test scores, interview, extracurricular activities, alumni/ae relation, geographical residence, volunteer work, work experience. ACT with or without writing accepted. SAT with or without Essay component accepted. High school diploma is required and GED is accepted. *Academic units recommended:* 4 English, 4 math, 4 science, 3 science labs, 4 foreign language, 4 social studies, 4 history.

Financial Aid

Students should submit: CSS/Financial Aid PROFILE; FAFSA; Noncustodial PROFILE. Priority filing deadline is 2/15. The Princeton Review suggests that all financial aid forms be submitted as soon as possible after October 1. *Need-based scholarships/grants offered:* College/university scholarship or grant aid from institutional funds; Federal Pell; Private scholarships; SEOG; State scholarships/grants. *Loan aid offered:* Direct PLUS loans; Direct Subsidized Stafford Loans; Direct Unsubsidized Stafford Loans. Applicants will be notified of awards on or about 4/1. Federal Work-Study Program available. Institutional employment available.

The Inside Word

Gaining acceptance to Wesleyan is no easy feat. A highly regarded institution, the university seeks candidates who demonstrate intellectual curiosity and a real thirst for knowledge. Certainly, a rigorous high school curriculum replete with advanced placement and honors courses is a must. Class rank and teacher recommendations are also heavily considered. But Wesleyan is a test optional school for most students, and while interviews are not required they are strongly recommended. Wesleyan's admissions page notes that in the face of "recent catastrophic events in the United States and around the world," and as an "institution and community that values access," they "want to be as flexible and accommodating as we can to offset barriers students are facing in the wake of these disruptions."

THE SCHOOL SAYS "..."

From the Admissions Office

"Wesleyan faculty believe in an education that is flexible and affords individual freedom and that a strong liberal arts education is the best foundation for success in any endeavor. The broad curriculum provides a rigorous education that values putting ideas into practice. Students have the opportunity to discover what they love to do, work at the highest level, and apply their knowledge in meaningful ways. As a result, Wesleyan students achieve a very personalized but broad education. Wesleyan's Vice President and Dean of Admission and Financial Aid, Amin Abdul-Malik Gonzalez, describes the qualities Wesleyan seeks in its students: 'Our holistic process, which carefully considers candidates in their respective contexts, aims to select high-achieving, intellectually engaged, broadly talented, and socially conscious students who will thrive in Wesleyan's vibrant academic environment. At Wesleyan, we value character and personal promise as much as impressive credentials and accomplishments. We seek students who will leverage our outstanding resources, realize their personal potentials, and make meaningful contributions to both our dynamically diverse community and wider world.'"

SELECTIVITY

Admissions Rating	97
# of applicants	13,264
% of applicants accepted	16
% of acceptees attending	35
# offered a place on the wait list	1,945
% accepting a place on wait list	55
% admitted from wait list	9
# of early decision applicants	1,102
% accepted early decision	37

FRESHMAN PROFILE

Range SAT EBRW	650–740
Range SAT Math	670–770
Range ACT Composite	31–34
# submitting SAT scores	487
% submitting SAT scores	63
# submitting ACT scores	303
% submitting ACT scores	39
% graduated top 10% of class	67
% graduated top 50% of class	94

DEADLINES

Early decision	
Deadline	11/15
Notification	12/15
Other ED Deadline	1/1
Other ED Notification	2/15
Regular	
Deadline	1/1
Notification	4/1
Nonfall registration?	No

FINANCIAL FACTS

Financial Aid Rating	97
Annual tuition	$59,086
Room and board	$16,384
Required fees	$300
Books and supplies	$1,200
Average frosh need-based scholarship	$52,149
Average UG need-based scholarship	$52,284
% needy frosh rec. need-based scholarship or grant aid	100
% needy UG rec. need-based scholarship or grant aid	99
% needy frosh rec. non-need-based scholarship or grant aid	4
% needy UG rec. non-need-based scholarship or grant aid	3
% needy frosh rec. need-based self-help aid	98
% needy UG rec. need-based self-help aid	99
% frosh rec. any financial aid	48
% UG rec. any financial aid	47
% UG borrow to pay for school	36
Average cumulative indebtedness	$26,016
% frosh need fully met	100
% ugrads need fully met	100
Average % of frosh need met	100
Average % of ugrad need met	100

West Virginia University

Admissions Office, Morgantown, WV 26506-6009 • Admissions: 304-293-2121 • Fax: 304-293-3080

CAMPUS LIFE
Quality of Life Rating	87
Fire Safety Rating	98
Green Rating	80
Type of school	Public
Environment	Town

STUDENTS
Total undergrad enrollment	20,499
% male/female	52/48
% from out of state	48
% frosh live on campus	92
% ugrads live on campus	22
# of fraternities	9
# of sororities	8
% African American	4
% Asian	2
% Caucasian	80
% Hispanic	4
% Native American	<1
% Pacific Islander	<1
% Two or more races	4
% Race and/or ethnicity unknown	<1
% international	6
# of countries represented	108

SURVEY SAYS . . .
Great library
Recreation facilities are great
Lots of beer drinking
Hard liquor is popular
Everyone loves the Mountaineers

ACADEMICS
Academic Rating	76
% students returning for sophomore year	76
% students graduating within 4 years	35
% students graduating within 6 years	58
Calendar	Semester
Student/faculty ratio	18:1
Profs interesting rating	86
Profs accessible rating	91

Most classes have 20–29 students.
Most lab/discussion sessions have
20–29 students.

MOST POPULAR MAJORS
Engineering, General; Business Administration
and Management, General; Journalism

STUDENTS SAY "..."

Academics

One student reports that West Virginia University boasts "a relaxed, social, and extremely school-spirited environment," and that WVU's academics "challenge students in the class-room" and prepare them "to be successful in the next step of life after college." Another student praises the engineering program, which offers "many opportunities for seniors looking for jobs. I also like the fact that it is a big university, but being in Morgantown gives it a homey feel." Students find a happy medium that combines studying and social-izing. "The school is all about connecting academics and leadership with incredible enthu-siasm for school activities." "A wonderful experience with a good balance of academics and fun opportunities." "Great academic experience wrapped up in a fun college atmosphere." For in-state undergraduates, affordability is the key to choosing WVU. Many students are drawn to the "diversity of programs" offered at West Virginia University. With this variety of programs comes a "diversified faculty who bring a wide range of knowledge and experi-ences." Some students would prefer smaller classes because, as one student put it, "The large classes make it difficult to form solid teacher-student relationships." But another student offers a different perspective, "If you put forth any type of effort, you'll get to know your professors at WVU. Of course, with some of the bigger classes, you can sit in the back and go unnoticed, but that's a personal choice."

Life

There is no escaping the "pride" West Virginia University students feel for their school, many of whom say they were "born to be a Mountaineer." Whether it's describing their majors, the marching band, alumni, or the football and basketball teams, it seems unani-mous that the "spirit of the university is outstanding." As one student states, "West Virginia University is all about combining such high academic standards with the atmo-sphere of Mountaineer pride, only something you can feel at a football game singing 'Country Roads' with 50,000 of your closest friends." "Fun" seems to best describe student life at WVU. Whether on campus at the "amazing student recreational center," which is "complete with weight room, indoor swimming pool, hot tubs, indoor track, indoor bas-ketball and racquetball courts, ping-pong tables, and boxing equipment," at the Mountainlair student union watching free movies, or off campus exploring Morgantown, everyone seems to be having a good time. "One of the best things about Morgantown is downtown High Street. People always ask, 'you goin downtown tonight?'" This is referring to the very wide selection of bars, clubs, lounges, and restaurants that are located down-town, most concentrated along High Street. High Street starts at the south end of down-town and travels all the way up through the downtown campus. Some students would like to see an improvement in both parking and transportation, but the beauty of the area and the level of student assistance "outside the classroom with learning centers, free tutors, [and] group work areas" all get high marks.

Student Body

Students describe themselves as "outgoing" as well as "relaxed and social." School spirit is evident. "The typical student always has some piece of WVU apparel on, and that's usu-ally sweatpants." "Students are very involved on campus with academics and various clubs and organizations. It is a very lively campus and there is always something going on. Although one student reports, "A lot of people here drink quite often," students also say that there is plenty to do on campus that doesn't include alcohol.

Financial Aid: 304-293-5242 • E-Mail: go2wvu@mail.wvu.edu • Website: www.wvu.edu

THE PRINCETON REVIEW SAYS

Admissions

Very important factors considered include: academic GPA, standardized test scores. *Important factors considered include:* rigor of secondary school record, state residency. *Other factors considered include:* extracurricular activities, talent/ability. ACT with Writing required. SAT with Essay component required. High school diploma is required and GED is accepted. *Academic units required:* 4 English, 4 math, 3 science, 3 science labs, 2 foreign language, 3 social studies, 1 visual/performing arts.

Financial Aid

Students should submit: FAFSA. Priority filing deadline is 3/1. The Princeton Review suggests that all financial aid forms be submitted as soon as possible after October 1. *Need-based scholarships/grants offered:* College/university scholarship or grant aid from institutional funds; Federal Nursing Scholarships; Federal Pell; Private scholarships; SEOG. *Loan aid offered:* Direct PLUS loans; Direct Subsidized Stafford Loans; Direct Unsubsidized Stafford Loans. Applicants will be notified of awards on a rolling basis beginning 12/1. Federal Work-Study Program available. Institutional employment available.

The Inside Word

While standards for general admission to WVU aren't especially rigorous, you'll find admission to its premier programs to be quite competitive. Admission to the College of Business and Economics, for example, requires a high school GPA of at least 3.75 and an SAT math score of at least 610. Programs in computer science, education, engineering, fine arts, forensics, journalism, medicine, and nursing all require fairly impressive credentials. If you're not admitted to the program of your choice, you may be able to transfer to it later if your grades are good enough, but it won't be easy.

THE SCHOOL SAYS "..."

From the Admissions Office

"From quality academic programs and outstanding, caring faculty, to incredible new facilities and a campus environment that focuses on students' needs, WVU is a place where dreams can come true. Our tradition of academic excellence attracts some of the region's best high school seniors. WVU has produced twenty-four Rhodes Scholars, thirty-five Goldwater Scholars, twenty-two Truman Scholars, six members of the *USA Today's* All-USA College Academic First Team, and two Udall Scholarship winners. Whether your goal is to be an aerospace engineer, reporter, physicist, athletic trainer, opera singer, forensic investigator, pharmacist, or CEO, WVU's 191 degree choices can make it happen. Unique student-centered initiatives help students experience true education beyond the classroom. The Mountaineer parents club connects more than 20,000 families, and a parents' helpline (800-WVU-0096) leads to a full-time parent advocate. A Student Recreation Center includes athletic courts, pools, weight/fitness equipment, and a fifty-foot indoor climbing wall. A major building program is creating new classrooms, labs, health-care facilities, an art museum, and a student wellness center. With programs for studying abroad, a Center from Black Culture and Research, and Office of Disability Services, and a student body that comes from every WV county, fifty states, and 108 different countries, WVU encourages diversity. WVU research funding has topped $174 million for the second consecutive year, making WVU a major research institution where undergraduates can participate. All applicants are required to take the ACT writing assessment as part of the ACT exam, or take the SAT to be considered for admission."

SELECTIVITY

Admissions Rating	77
# of applicants	18,639
% of applicants accepted	82
% of acceptees attending	31

FRESHMAN PROFILE

Range SAT EBRW	530–620
Range SAT Math	520–620
Range ACT Composite	21–27
# submitting SAT scores	2,688
% submitting SAT scores	57
# submitting ACT scores	3,088
% submitting ACT scores	65
Average HS GPA	3.5
% graduated top 10% of class	23
% graduated top 25% of class	48
% graduated top 50% of class	78

DEADLINES

Regular	
Priority	3/1
Deadline	8/1
Notification	Rolling, 9/15
Nonfall registration?	Yes

APPLICANTS ALSO LOOK AT AND OFTEN PREFER

Penn State University Park; University of Maryland, College Park; Virginia Polytechnic Institute and State University

AND SOMETIMES PREFER

James Madison University; University of Pittsburgh—Pittsburgh Campus; Towson University

AND RARELY PREFER

Fairmont State University, including Pierpont Community & Technical College

FINANCIAL FACTS

Financial Aid Rating	79
Annual in-state tuition	$8,976
Annual out-of-state tuition	$25,320
Room and board	$10,918
Books and supplies	$950
Average frosh need-based scholarship	$6,190
Average UG need-based scholarship	$5,812
% needy frosh rec. need-based scholarship or grant aid	81
% needy UG rec. need-based scholarship or grant aid	74
% needy frosh rec. non-need-based scholarship or grant aid	46
% needy UG rec. non-need-based scholarship or grant aid	39
% needy frosh rec. need-based self-help aid	69
% needy UG rec. need-based self-help aid	77
% frosh rec. any financial aid	72
% UG rec. any financial aid	75
% UG borrow to pay for school	61
Average cumulative indebtedness	$32,541
% frosh need fully met	13
% ugrads need fully met	11

WESTMINSTER COLLEGE (UT)

1840 South 1300 East, Salt Lake City, UT 54105 • Admissions: 801-832-2200 • Fax: 801-832-3101

CAMPUS LIFE
Quality of Life Rating	89
Fire Safety Rating	95
Green Rating	85
Type of school	Private
Environment	Metropolis

STUDENTS
Total undergrad enrollment	1,946
% male/female	40/60
% from out of state	36
% frosh live on campus	68
% ugrads live on campus	32
# of fraternities	0
# of sororities	0
% African American	2
% Asian	3
% Caucasian	70
% Hispanic	12
% Native American	<1
% Pacific Islander	<1
% Two or more races	5
% Race and/or ethnicity unknown	3
% international	4
# of countries represented	43

SURVEY SAYS . . .
Class discussions encouraged
Students environmentally aware
Students love Salt Lake City, UT
Easy to get around campus

ACADEMICS
Academic Rating	83
% students returning for sophomore year	82
% students graduating within 4 years	47
% students graduating within 6 years	62
Calendar	4/1/4
Student/faculty ratio	8:1
Profs interesting rating	91
Profs accessible rating	93

Most classes have 10–19 students.
Most lab/discussion sessions have
fewer than 10 students.

STUDENTS SAY "..."

Academics

Set amidst the spectacular peaks of the Wasatch Mountains, Westminster College is a quaint liberal arts college in a small neighborhood of Salt Lake City. Undergrads praise "a very rigorous academic load" and "a community that doesn't center around academic competition, but academic empowerment." This collaborative culture includes faculty that is "attentive and understanding." One undergrad says, "Professors are very accessible..., [and] if office hours don't work for you, they will make other times to meet." Students generally agree that professors are "experts in their fields [and] extremely knowledgeable." There are complaints, however, about adjunct professors who "seem to be less committed." The small campus and class sizes allow students "to communicate one-on-one with professors [and give students] the opportunity to get to know ... classmates better." Despite the size of Westminster, "resources are abundant at the college," and students have access to hands-on research opportunities, internships, study abroad programs, and conferences. Frequently mentioned majors include "a great nursing program," biology, and theater.

Life

Outdoor activities are a big draw to students at Westminster. And with six ski resorts within a half-hour drive, "a lot of people look forward to snowboarding and skiing." In fact, one student says that "Westminster has a core of people who like to ski and that is often all they do"—Griffins love their slopes! Others clarify that "there is more [to] Westminster than just skiing and snowboarding." Sure, "winter sports are popular here, but most of us are more concerned with our academics than the ski hill." A happy medium would be the on-campus clubs available to students, which "always try to provide activities or events." Something students are unanimous on is the food options, from on-campus student centers that "are great stops for a quick meal or coffee to recharge" to the restaurants in Salt Lake City, which has the added benefit of being "a very cool city."

Student Body

"The culture is welcoming and socially relaxed" at Westminster College. "There is a general mix of artistic and intellectual students who are driven by learning." Additionally, there is also an awareness of social issues, and "it's easy to strike up a conversation about gender bias or cultural inequality because our students are well educated and always up for challenging their thought process to make positive change happen," one undergrad reports. That said, some take issue with the common "liberal ideology." Moreover, while students may have a "diversity of interests," some find that "there is not much diversity in terms of race, gender, sexual orientation, and ability." The student body is predominantly "white and at least upper middle class." But while it might seem like a fairly uniform campus, "everyone you meet is open to every walk of life [and] accepting of differences."

WESTMINSTER COLLEGE (UT)

Financial Aid: 801-832-2502 • E-Mail: admission@westminstercollege.edu • Website: www.westminstercollege.edu

THE PRINCETON REVIEW SAYS

Admissions

Very important factors considered include: rigor of secondary school record, academic GPA, application essay, standardized test scores, recommendation(s). *Important factors considered include:* class rank, interview, extracurricular activities, talent/ability, character/personal qualities. *Other factors considered include:* first generation, alumni/ae relation, volunteer work, work experience. ACT with or without writing accepted. SAT with or without Essay component accepted. High school diploma is required and GED is accepted. *Academic units required:* 4 English, 2 math, 3 science, 2 foreign language, 2 social studies, 1 history, 2 academic electives. *Academic units recommended:* 4 English, 3 math, 3 science, 3 foreign language, 2 social studies, 1 history, 3 academic electives.

Financial Aid

Students should submit: FAFSA; Institution's own financial aid form. Priority filing deadline is 11/1. The Princeton Review suggests that all financial aid forms be submitted as soon as possible after October 1. *Need-based scholarships/grants offered:* College/university scholarship or grant aid from institutional funds; Federal Pell; Private scholarships; SEOG; State scholarships/grants. *Loan aid offered:* Direct PLUS loans; Direct Subsidized Stafford Loans; Direct Unsubsidized Stafford Loans. Applicants will be notified of awards on a rolling basis beginning 1/1. Federal Work-Study Program available. Institutional employment available.

The Inside Word

A strong academic record isn't the top priority at Westminster. With a 93 percent acceptance rate, considerations include the rigor of a student's high school transcript and test scores. Admitted students have average SAT scores of between 1080–1260 or an average ACT score of 21–27. A strong personal statement plays an important role in the admission decision and gives admissions officers an opportunity to get to know the person behind the transcript. A campus interview is encouraged, and admissions are rolling.

THE SCHOOL SAYS "..."

From the Admissions Office

"At Westminster, you'll spend less time with your nose in a textbook and more time engaged in lively discussion with your classmates. You'll be challenged to apply your knowledge in interesting, innovative ways, while learning from professors who are passionate about what they do. And with an average class size of 17, your teachers won't just know you by name, they'll know what drives you.

"Our new general education program, WCore, gives you the opportunity to explore new subjects through small, interdisciplinary courses, where you'll spend time engaging in and challenging ideas, rather than just memorizing facts. With specialized offerings like our Honors College, dedicated faculty mentors, and internship and professional connections throughout the community, you'll graduate prepared to take on whatever's next.

"Each application is read and reviewed individually by an admission committee that takes into account both level of challenge in coursework and grades received. Either the SAT or ACT exam is accepted. Westminster College has a rolling application deadline and will accept applications until the class is filled. To be eligible for the widest array of financial aid—more than 98 percent of first-year students receive scholarship or financial aid—April 15 is the priority consideration deadline for fall semester, and May 15 is the priority deadline for on-campus housing applications."

SELECTIVITY

Admissions Rating	75
# of applicants	1,864
% of applicants accepted	93
% of acceptees attending	25

FRESHMAN PROFILE

Range SAT EBRW	540–640
Range SAT Math	540–620
Range ACT Composite	21–27
# submitting SAT scores	118
% submitting SAT scores	27
# submitting ACT scores	362
% submitting ACT scores	83
Average HS GPA	3.6
% graduated top 10% of class	21
% graduated top 25% of class	44
% graduated top 50% of class	81

DEADLINES

Regular	
Notification	Rolling, 8/1
Nonfall registration?	Yes

APPLICANTS ALSO LOOK AT AND OFTEN PREFER
University of Utah; Utah State University

AND SOMETIMES PREFER
Brigham Young University (UT); Weber State University; Southern Utah University

AND RARELY PREFER
Idaho State University; Montana State University; Northern Arizona University; Boise State University; University of Portland

FINANCIAL FACTS

Financial Aid Rating	88
Annual tuition	$34,464
Room and board	$9,810
Required fees	$820
Books and supplies	$1,000
Average frosh need-based scholarship	$25,861
Average UG need-based scholarship	$23,545
% needy frosh rec. need-based scholarship or grant aid	100
% needy UG rec. need-based scholarship or grant aid	100
% needy frosh rec. non-need-based scholarship or grant aid	18
% needy UG rec. non-need-based scholarship or grant aid	17
% needy frosh rec. need-based self-help aid	85
% needy UG rec. need-based self-help aid	86
% frosh rec. any financial aid	98
% UG rec. any financial aid	97
% UG borrow to pay for school	60
Average cumulative indebtedness	$29,713
% frosh need fully met	24
% ugrads need fully met	23
Average % of frosh need met	83
Average % of ugrad need met	80

WHEATON COLLEGE (IL)

501 College Avenue, Wheaton, IL 60187 • Admissions: 630-752-5011 • Fax: 630-752-5285

STUDENTS SAY ". . ."

Academics

Wheaton College, located just outside of Chicago, Illinois, is a great option for students who want a school with a "phenomenal" sense of community and "exceptional liberal arts program." It's also an evangelical institution and undergrads here value "the college's commitment to providing a rigorous academic experience through a Christian worldview." As one undergrad explains, "I wanted to come to a school where my faith would be challenged and grown by those around me." Beyond religion, students love that class sizes are "relatively small" which "make it easier to develop relationships with professors and peers." The classroom experience consists of "uniformly fantastic" professors who care deeply and "genuinely want to know about their students' lives." Another incredulous undergrad shares, "They invest time and energy into their students and all are always available for office hours or meals." Wheaton professors also actively look to "involve students in research or mentoring." Just as crucial, they are "super knowledgeable and enthusiastic about the subject they teach." And they're "always open to questions/challenges and at the same time are willing to challenge and encourage students in a way that maximizes learning." It is truly evident that Wheaton professors "want their students to succeed."

Life

It's rather easy to lead a fun and fulfilling life at Wheaton. For starters, students have "chapel services every other day during the week, with worship and guest speakers who are simply amazing." Many people also "like to attend events put on by Wheaton's music conservatory." Additionally, the majority of students are rather "active" and a large number "participat[e] in intramural sports." Even if sports aren't your strong suit, the athletic program "encourages non-athletic people to get involved." Wheaton students are also quite adept at finding "creative ways to have fun." For example, "geocaching" is pretty popular. Once the weekend rolls around, lots of undergrads participate in "game night," "movie night," or "college events such as lip syncing competitions or an interactive art festival." It's also rather common for people to attend both "church and brunch." Of course, when students want a break from campus life, they can easily "take the train to Chicago to enjoy the sights and the lights." A student concludes, "There is never a dull moment here on campus, whether I'm studying or having fun with friends or attending special lectures, concerts, services, or just class. I love life at Wheaton!"

Student Body

Unsurprisingly, undergrads at Wheaton are "uniformly Christian" and "devoted to serving Christ and His kingdom." The student body is also "predominantly white" though many individuals insist, "diversity is a big part of the campus conversation." Thankfully, beyond these two facets, you'll find a variety of "background[s], opinion[s], and interests around Wheaton." As one student interjects, "Wheaton gets a bad rap for being really conservative, but that doesn't mean there's not a diversity of political and theological thought." What's more, students say that their peers comprise of a "caring group of individuals who have fun while living an upright lifestyle." The vast majority are also "hardworking" and "very, very driven." And they're fairly worldly since a good number "have traveled to participate in some type of missions or humanitarian work." Wheaton undergrads are impressed by their fellow students' intellect as well, reporting that they "are exceptionally versatile, excelling in music, art, athletics, and oftentimes speaking multiple languages." Finally, another student praises, "I am consistently blown away by the high intellectual capacity the students of Wheaton College possess, as well as their resolve to live selflessly, and use their education to create a better world."

WHEATON COLLEGE (IL)

Financial Aid: 630-752-5021 • E-Mail: admissions@wheaton.edu • Website: www.wheaton.edu

THE PRINCETON REVIEW SAYS

Admissions

Very important factors considered include: rigor of secondary school record, academic GPA, application essay, standardized test scores, recommendation(s), character/personal qualities, religious affiliation/commitment. *Important factors considered include:* interview, extracurricular activities, talent/ability. *Other factors considered include:* class rank, first generation, alumni/ae relation, geographical residence, state residency, racial/ethnic status, work experience, level of applicant's interest. ACT with or without writing accepted. SAT with or without Essay component accepted. High school diploma is required and GED is accepted. *Academic units required:* 4 English, 3 math, 3 science, 2 foreign language, 3 social studies. *Academic units recommended:* 4 English, 4 math, 4 science, 3 foreign language, 4 social studies.

Financial Aid

Students should submit: FAFSA. Priority filing deadline is 11/10. The Princeton Review suggests that all financial aid forms be submitted as soon as possible after October 1. *Need-based scholarships/grants offered:* College/university scholarship or grant aid from institutional funds; Federal Pell; Private scholarships; SEOG; State scholarships/grants. *Loan aid offered:* Direct PLUS loans; Direct Subsidized Stafford Loans; Direct Unsubsidized Stafford Loans. Applicants will be notified of awards on a rolling basis beginning 12/31. Federal Work-Study Program available. Institutional employment available.

The Inside Word

Wheaton College is on the hunt for applicants who display a thirst for knowledge. Therefore, admissions officers tend to favor students who have taken at least a handful of honors, advanced placement or IB classes. Given the school's evangelical association, students must also demonstrate a commitment to their faith. To that end, all applicants are required to submit a pastoral recommendation letter. It's also important to note that candidates can apply to either the College of Arts and Sciences or the Conservatory of Music, but not both.

THE SCHOOL SAYS "..."

From the Admissions Office

"At Wheaton, we're committed to being a community that fearlessly pursues truth, upholds an academically rigorous curriculum, and promotes virtue. The college takes seriously its impact on society. The influence of Wheaton is seen in fields ranging from government (congressmen, senator, U.S. ambassador, presidential speech writer) to sports (NBA managers and coaches) to business (former CEO of John Deere) to music (Metropolitan Opera National Competition winners) to education (over forty college presidents) to global ministry (Billy Graham). Wheaton seeks students who want to make a difference and are passionate about their Christian faith and rigorous academic pursuit.

"Every applicant to Wheaton is considered holistically for academic scholarships, based on standardized tests, GPA, academic rigor of curriculum, and class rank (if available). Students who qualify will receive their scholarship offer with their acceptance letter. Wheaton uses the highest critical reading and math scores from any sitting of the SAT test and/or the highest composite (super-scored) ACT scores."

SELECTIVITY

Admissions Rating	87
# of applicants	1,889
% of applicants accepted	85
% of acceptees attending	38
# offered a place on the wait list	258
% accepting a place on wait list	26
% admitted from wait list	60

FRESHMAN PROFILE

Range SAT EBRW	620–720
Range SAT Math	600–720
Range SAT Composite	1240–1430
Range ACT Composite	26–32
# submitting SAT scores	379
% submitting SAT scores	62
# submitting ACT scores	340
% submitting ACT scores	55
Average HS GPA	3.7
% graduated top 10% of class	49
% graduated top 25% of class	78
% graduated top 50% of class	92

DEADLINES

Early action	
Deadline	11/1
Notification	12/31
Regular	
Deadline	1/10
Notification	4/1
Nonfall registration?	Yes

APPLICANTS ALSO LOOK AT AND SOMETIMES PREFER
Calvin College; Taylor University

AND RARELY PREFER
Baylor University; Biola University; Covenant College; Gordon College; Grove City College; Hope College

FINANCIAL FACTS

Financial Aid Rating	84
Annual tuition	$39,100
Room and board	$10,990
Books and supplies	$800
Average frosh need-based scholarship	$26,088
Average UG need-based scholarship	$22,583
% needy frosh rec. need-based scholarship or grant aid	99
% needy UG rec. need-based scholarship or grant aid	97
% needy frosh rec. non-need-based scholarship or grant aid	10
% needy UG rec. non-need-based scholarship or grant aid	7
% needy frosh rec. need-based self-help aid	70
% needy UG rec. need-based self-help aid	71
% frosh rec. any financial aid	90
% UG rec. any financial aid	85
% UG borrow to pay for school	59
Average cumulative indebtedness	$29,555
% frosh need fully met	13
% ugrads need fully met	10
Average % of frosh need met	79
Average % of ugrad need met	71

WHEATON COLLEGE (MA)

26 East Main Street, Norton, MA 02766 • Admissions: 508-286-8251 • Fax: 508-286-8271

CAMPUS LIFE

Quality of Life Rating	88
Fire Safety Rating	95
Green Rating	73
Type of school	Private
Environment	Village

STUDENTS

Total undergrad enrollment	1,750
% male/female	39/61
% from out of state	61
% frosh from public high school	69
% frosh live on campus	98
% ugrads live on campus	96
# of fraternities	0
# of sororities	0
% African American	5
% Asian	5
% Caucasian	65
% Hispanic	8
% Native American	<1
% Pacific Islander	0
% Two or more races	4
% Race and/or ethnicity unknown	2
% international	10
# of countries represented	67

SURVEY SAYS . . .

Students are happy
Lab facilities are great
Students are friendly
Diverse student types interact on campus
Students environmentally aware
Easy to get around campus
Active student government
Active minority support groups

ACADEMICS

Academic Rating	89
% students returning for sophomore year	87
% students graduating within 4 years	72
% students graduating within 6 years	78
Calendar	Semester
Student/faculty ratio	11:1
Profs interesting rating	92
Profs accessible rating	95

Most classes have 10–19 students.
Most lab/discussion sessions have
10–19 students.

MOST POPULAR MAJORS

Psychology, General; Business Administration and
Management, General; Film/Cinema/Media Studies

STUDENTS SAY "..."

Academics

Armed with a "gorgeous" campus in Norton, Massachusetts and a "community" feel, Wheaton College aims to provide an "interdisciplinary" liberal arts education that "fosters appreciation for critical thinking, diversity, and civic engagement." Undergrads here particularly love that their school champions "diversity and multiculturalism." And, in doing so, Wheaton has created a "very progressive and forward-thinking environment." Students also greatly appreciate that their classes are chockfull of "active learning." Indeed, professors "encourage you to ask questions instead of quietly sitting in the back of the classroom." It also helps that instructors are "incredibly knowledgeable in their fields." More importantly, it's quite evident that professors "work really hard to put the student interests first." For example, "they love to discuss their areas of study with students and are accessible outside of class time." A junior explains, "I have made extremely close ties to many professors here at Wheaton. My art history professors have helped me get internships over the summer, given me research opportunities, and helped me with my transition to college. I honestly couldn't ask for a better support system." All in all, it is "obvious that everyone who works at Wheaton is passionate about the institution and care[s] about the student body."

Life

There's no denying that Wheaton undergrads love to stay busy. As such, they are "very committed to extracurricular activities." To begin with, "student musical groups are big on campus as well as other performing arts groups." Many Wheaton undergraduates are "involved in community service" as well. People frequently gather at the Lyons Den, a student-run coffee shop that's "open late and hosts open mics on Wednesdays." Once the weekend rolls around, you'll discover that "there are numerous events scheduled. Anything from a movie in one of the auditoriums to food trucks to dance and music performances." Wheaton also sponsors "special treats from time to time": During a recent exam week, students were able to enjoy and de-stress with "a little animal petting farm." As if that wasn't enough, "cupcakes were brought in [too]!" Additionally, plenty of students can also be found attending parties on "Thursday, Friday, and Saturday" at different theme houses, though there "is a definite sober population on campus." Unfortunately, there "is not much to do in Norton." But if students are looking for off-campus excitement, they can easily head into Providence or Boston (twenty minutes and forty minutes away, respectively).

Student Body

Undergraduates at Wheaton seem to agree that their peers are "creative, energetic, and have a love for academics." They also continually prove themselves to be "kind," "respectful," and "interested in being...genuinely good [people]." Moreover, students here do an admirable job of making sure they're conscious about what's happening "outside the Wheaton bubble." To that end, many are "very liberally minded and outspoken with those views." Undergrads also applaud the fact that their college "is home to a wide array of culturally-diverse and open-minded individuals." Indeed, "everybody is very welcoming and very willing to learn about new cultures and experiences." That's probably due in large part to the fact that Wheaton has "students from all over the country as well as the world, a prominent LGBTQ community, [and] students from all walks of life." Further, since the college "is able to offer financial aid to many [individuals], Wheaton students are not all just upper-class suburban kids like at other private colleges around the country." All of this helps to foster a "sense of community [that] runs deep throughout the student body." As one thankful student summarizes, "Unity is a trait that shines here...[and] something that we are all extremely proud of."

WHEATON COLLEGE (MA)

Financial Aid: 508-286-8232 • E-Mail: admission@wheatoncollege.edu • Website: www.wheatoncollege.edu

THE PRINCETON REVIEW SAYS

Admissions

Very important factors considered include: rigor of secondary school record, academic GPA, application essay, recommendation(s), character/personal qualities. *Important factors considered include:* extracurricular activities, talent/ability, alumni relation. *Other factors considered include:* optional portfolios, class rank, standardized test scores, interview, first generation, geographical residence, state residency, racial/ethnic status, volunteer work, work experience. ACT with or without writing accepted. SAT with or without Essay component accepted. High school diploma is required and GED is accepted. *Academic units required:* 4 English. *Academic units recommended:* 4 math, 4 science, 4 foreign language, 4 social studies, 4 history.

Financial Aid

Students should submit: CSS/Financial Aid PROFILE; FAFSA; Noncustodial PROFILE. The Princeton Review suggests that all financial aid forms be submitted as soon as possible after October 1. *Need-based scholarships/grants offered:* College/university scholarship or grant aid from institutional funds; Federal Pell; SEOG; State scholarships/grants. *Loan aid offered:* Direct Subsidized Loans; Direct Unsubsidized Loans. Applicants will be notified of awards on or about 3/15. Federal Work-Study Program available. Institutional employment available.

The Inside Word

Wheaton is a selective college so gaining admission won't be a cakewalk. The school takes a holistic approach when evaluating applicants meaning everything from the difficulty of your high school curriculum to your writing ability and extracurricular involvement will be considered. And if you're standardized test-averse, take heart; Wheaton is test optional. Finally, if you're confident that Wheaton is your first choice, the college highly recommends that you apply Early Decision.

THE SCHOOL SAYS "..."

From the Admissions Office

"We have been described as a place sparking possibilities and world-changing ideas. Our students come from all over the world, and they definitely stand out from the crowd. Since 2000, more than 250 Wheaton students have won national and international scholarships, including the Rhodes, Marshall, Fulbright, Truman, and Watson awards. Our faculty are world-class researchers, scholars, artists, teachers, and advisors, as well as involved and connected community members. They engage their students in original research and scholarship projects and build relationships that sustain and last a lifetime. Our Filene Center for Academic Advising and Career Services invests about $1.2 million in stipends annually as part of The Wheaton Edge, which provides access to funding for an internship or other experiential learning opportunity to every student before the start of their senior year. We also get our students connected to our passionate, worldwide alumni network, who advise graduates on career choices, internships and getting acclimated to their first jobs. The value of a Wheaton education is undeniable and success for Wheaton graduates starts early, with 97 percent of respondents to our First Destination survey over the past five years finding employment, graduate education or social change opportunities within six months after leaving our picturesque New England campus."

SELECTIVITY

Admissions Rating	85
# of applicants	3,673
% of applicants accepted	70
% of acceptees attending	19
# offered a place on the wait list	73
% accepting a place on wait list	49
% admitted from wait list	0
# of early decision applicants	147
% accepted early decision	73

FRESHMAN PROFILE

Range SAT EBRW	600–680
Range SAT Math	580–670
Range ACT Composite	27–31
# submitting SAT scores	230
% submitting SAT scores	46
# submitting ACT scores	49
% submitting ACT scores	10
Average HS GPA	3.4
% graduated top 10% of class	21
% graduated top 25% of class	52
% graduated top 50% of class	84

DEADLINES

Early decision	
Deadline	11/15
Notification	12/3
Other ED Deadline	1/1
Other ED Notification	2/1
Early action	
Deadline	11/15
Notification	12/21
Regular	
Priority	11/15
Deadline	1/15
Notification	3/15
Nonfall registration?	Yes

FINANCIAL FACTS

Financial Aid Rating	90
Annual tuition	$54,118
Room and board	$14,096
Required fees	$450
Books and supplies	$940
Average frosh need-based scholarship	$42,146
Average UG need-based scholarship	$38,800
% needy frosh rec. need-based scholarship or grant aid	100
% needy UG rec. need-based scholarship or grant aid	100
% needy frosh rec. non-need-based scholarship or grant aid	12
% needy UG rec. non-need-based scholarship or grant aid	8
% needy frosh rec. need-based self-help aid	76
% needy UG rec. need-based self-help aid	83
% frosh rec. any financial aid	99
% UG rec. any financial aid	97
% UG borrow to pay for school	69
Average cumulative indebtedness	$34,830
% frosh need fully met	53
% ugrads need fully met	41
Average % of frosh need met	91
Average % of ugrad need met	87

WHITMAN COLLEGE

345 Boyer Avenue, Walla Walla, WA 99362 • Admissions: 509-527-5176 • Fax: 509-527-4967

STUDENTS SAY ". . ."

Academics

If learning can be both rigorous and laid-back at the same time, it happens at Whitman College in Walla Walla, WA. The "challenging" academics here are coupled with a "relaxed attitude" in order to give students "the best education possible without sacrificing all the fun one expects of college." Populated mainly by "intelligent, ambitious liberals with far-reaching goals," this somewhat idealistic school seeks to build critical thinking skills through "an earnest discourse about 'life, the universe, and everything.'" So no one starts off with a blank slate, all first-year students are required to take a course referred to as "Encounters" which is a two semester introduction to the liberal arts and the academic construction of knowledge. Distribution requirements ensure that all students get a breadth of courses, and a lack of TAs ensures that they get all the attention they need. Although there's always a dud or two in the mix, professors are "genuinely brilliant and interesting people" and "love to spend time with students outside of class," whether it be for academic help or just conversation. "It is not uncommon to have potlucks, classes, or movie night over at your professor's house with your class," says one student.

On the administrative side of things, bureaucracy and red tape are kept to a minimum in this chill environment through "effortless use of the 'system'" and the administration gets raves all around for its devotion to "maintaining quality student life," which is something of a rarity. "I have never heard of *any* college being as supportive as this place has been to me in just the past two years," says a student. As one can imagine, all these things come together to form a student body that's "happy, well-balanced, and well-cared-for."

Life

Most people stay on campus for their fun, "especially first-years," and throughout this "bubble" the "sense of closeness and comradeship is very evident through attendance at student-run concerts, art shows, etc." Everything is within ten minutes' walking distance. Academics take precedence for almost everyone, but "most students find time to party on the weekends," due to a "lenient and fair" alcohol policy. Thanks to the campus activities board, "there's almost always something fun going on, whether or not a person chooses to drink," such as Drive-In Movie Night and Casino Night. With "four beautiful seasons," outdoor activities are also very popular, thanks to "a great gear rental program that gets people outside hiking, biking, kayaking, and rock-climbing," and "Frisbees are everywhere when it's warm." In fact, there's so much going on "if someone says they are bored, students laugh and wish they could relate."

Student Body

It's a sociable bunch at Whitman, where most students "are interested in trying new things and meeting new people" and "everyone seems to have a weird interest or talent or passion." The quirky Whitties "usually have a strong opinion about *something*," and one freshman refers to her classmates as "cool nerds." Diversity has risen steadily over the past several years, as the school has made an effort to recruit beyond the typical "mid- to upper-class and white" contingent. Everyone here is pretty outdoorsy and environmentally aware ("to the point where you almost feel guilty for printing an assignment"), and a significant number of students have won fellowships and scholarships such as the Fulbright, Watson, Truman, and Udall.

Financial Aid: 509-527-5178 • E-Mail: admission@whitman.edu • Website: https://www.whitman.edu

THE PRINCETON REVIEW SAYS

Admissions

Very important factors considered include: rigor of secondary school record, academic GPA, application essay. *Important factors considered include:* recommendation(s), extracurricular activities, talent/ability, character/personal qualities. *Other factors considered include:* class rank, standardized test scores, interview, first generation, alumni/ae relation, geographical residence, state residency, religious affiliation/commitment, racial/ethnic status, volunteer work, work experience, level of applicant's interest. ACT with or without writing accepted. SAT with or without Essay component accepted. High school diploma is required and GED is accepted. *Academic units recommended:* 4 English, 4 math, 3 science, 3 science labs, 2 foreign language, 2 social studies, 2 history.

Financial Aid

Students should submit: CSS/Financial Aid PROFILE; FAFSA; Noncustodial PROFILE. Priority filing deadline is 11/15. The Princeton Review suggests that all financial aid forms be submitted as soon as possible after October 1. *Need-based scholarships/grants offered:* College/university scholarship or grant aid from institutional funds; Federal Pell; Private scholarships; SEOG; State scholarships/grants. *Loan aid offered:* Direct PLUS loans; Direct Subsidized Stafford Loans; Direct Unsubsidized Stafford Loans. Applicants will be notified of awards on or about 4/1. Federal Work-Study Program available. Institutional employment available.

The Inside Word

Whitman's admissions committee emphasizes essays and extracurriculars more than standardized test scores, which are optional here. The college cares much more about who you are and what you have to offer if you enroll than it does about what your numbers will do for the freshman academic profile. Whitman is a mega-sleeper. Educators all over the country know it as an excellent institution, and the college's alums support it at one of the highest rates of giving at any college in the nation. Students seeking a top-quality liberal arts college owe it to themselves to take a look.

THE SCHOOL SAYS "..."

From the Admissions Office

"Whitman College offers a rigorous but collaborative academic environment, a down-to-earth Northwest culture, and a vibrant campus life. Whitman is also distinguished by the following:

- Capstone written and oral assessments in one's major field of study
- Numerous winners of Fulbright, Watson, Goldwater, National Science Foundation, Rhodes, Truman, Beinecke, and Udall fellowships and scholarships
- A Student Engagement Center which oversees internship and community service opportunities as well as graduate school and employment planning
- Science departments that have been recognized by the National Science Foundation as among the top fifty colleges per capita producing graduates who earn Ph.D.'s in science and engineering
- Eighty-eight off-campus study opportunities
- State of the art facilities including a library, computer labs and a health center open 24/7
- The Harper Joy Theatre, which hosts 8 productions a year open to all students
- An annual undergraduate research conference with over 200 students presenting their original research to the Whitman community
- Strong intramural, club and NCAA Division III sports programs
- A nationally renowned Outdoor Program
- Semester in the West, an experiential, on-the-road study of economic, cultural and environmental issues
- A 94 percent retention rate, 87 percent graduation rate, and a 70 percent graduate school rate."

SELECTIVITY

Admissions Rating	91
# of applicants	4,081
% of applicants accepted	52
% of acceptees attending	18
# offered a place on the wait list	998
% accepting a place on wait list	19
% admitted from wait list	41
# of early decision applicants	179
% accepted early decision	71

FRESHMAN PROFILE

Range SAT EBRW	510–690
Range SAT Math	510–680
Range ACT Composite	26–31
# submitting SAT scores	195
% submitting SAT scores	48
# submitting ACT scores	205
% submitting ACT scores	50
Average HS GPA	3.8
% graduated top 10% of class	59
% graduated top 25% of class	88
% graduated top 50% of class	98

DEADLINES

Early decision	
Deadline	11/15
Notification	12/20
Other ED Deadline	1/1
Other ED Notification	2/1
Regular	
Priority	11/15
Deadline	1/15
Notification	4/1
Nonfall registration?	No

APPLICANTS ALSO LOOK AT AND OFTEN PREFER

Bowdoin College; Brown University; Middlebury College; Pomona College; Stanford University; Macalester College; University of California—Berkeley; Carleton College

AND SOMETIMES PREFER

Colorado College; Reed College; University of Washington; University of Puget Sound; Western Washington University; University of California, Davis

FINANCIAL FACTS

Financial Aid Rating	87
Annual tuition	$53,420
Room and board	$13,512
Required fees	$400
Books and supplies	$1,400
Average frosh need-based scholarship	$36,323
Average UG need-based scholarship	$38,369
% needy frosh rec. need-based scholarship or grant aid	100
% needy UG rec. need-based scholarship or grant aid	100
% needy frosh rec. non-need-based scholarship or grant aid	48
% needy UG rec. non-need-based scholarship or grant aid	33
% needy frosh rec. need-based self-help aid	79
% needy UG rec. need-based self-help aid	79
% frosh rec. any financial aid	83
% UG rec. any financial aid	76
% UG borrow to pay for school	46
Average cumulative indebtedness	$23,254
% frosh need fully met	25
% ugrads need fully met	31
Average % of frosh need met	92
Average % of ugrad need met	94

WHITTIER COLLEGE

13406 E. Philadelphia Street, Whittier, CA 90608-0634 • Admissions: 562-907-4238 • Fax: 562-907-4870

CAMPUS LIFE

Quality of Life Rating	86
Fire Safety Rating	95
Green Rating	60*
Type of school	Private
Environment	City

STUDENTS

Total undergrad enrollment	1,664
% male/female	44/56
% from out of state	16
% frosh live on campus	75
% ugrads live on campus	50
# of fraternities	4
# of sororities	5
% African American	5
% Asian	7
% Caucasian	27
% Hispanic	50
% Native American	<1
% Pacific Islander	0
% Two or more races	7
% Race and/or ethnicity unknown	1
% international	3
# of countries represented	24

SURVEY SAYS . . .

Great library
Class discussions encouraged

ACADEMICS

Academic Rating	84
% students returning for sophomore year	78
% students graduating within 4 years	58
% students graduating within 6 years	63
Calendar	4/1/4
Student/faculty ratio	12:1
Profs interesting rating	92
Profs accessible rating	95

Most classes have 10–19 students.
Most lab/discussion sessions have
10–19 students.

MOST POPULAR MAJORS

Business Administration and Management,
General; Political Science and Government,
General; Psychology, General

STUDENTS SAY "..."

Academics

This tiny pearl of a liberal arts school is home to around 1,600 undergrads and focuses on an interdisciplinary education for all. Considering the small population, Whittier offers a relatively good breadth in classes and "is a great school for those who are trying to figure out what they want to do or those who want to create their own major." One-on-one interaction is quite prevalent among teachers and students, and everyone here is "passionate about the subject that they teach." It should be unsurprising that a school whose mascot is Johnny Poet provides "a nuanced literary foundation" for all students.

The faculty brings real-world and work experience to their various courses: "they're not just lifelong academics, most of them have had successful professional careers outside of teaching" and they "really make [Whittier] worthwhile." These professors are "engaged, love what they do," and "truly care about the success of their students, both academically and personally." Discussions are highly encouraged and interesting debates fostered, and assigned papers "always force you to stretch your knowledge." Teachers sometimes challenge the class's knowledge by "presenting a topic that can have pros and cons and by asking to prove where the idea came from." Classes are small, so professors know "know your strengths and weaknesses and try their best to help you out."

Life

The campus is small, so "it's easy to make friends" and there are typically "lots of events (academic or recreational) to go to." Different clubs run the gamut from Anime Club to Fun Night Club to a larping group, but marauders beware: "RAs are required to put on events such as Assassins." "There was once a Beowulf reading at night where you got a free dinner in addition," says a student. Whittier's version of Greek life comes in the form of the school's eleven "societies," and a majority of students have some form of involvement in a society or a sport. The school's size naturally leaves enough time to for extracurriculars and outside interests, as "it is difficult not to get involved when everyone is."

Whitter is relatively close to LA and the beach, so the weather is "mostly very nice" and students often "lounge around outside under trees and on the grass to do homework and socialize," "play Frisbee, walk on slack lines, and play soccer for fun in the courtyards." The pool facility is brand new and many "hang out on the decks to tan and cool off in the heat," and there are hills behind the campus that are good for hiking or running. There "is always something going on on-campus and that makes students even more involved."

Student Body

This is a "diverse community" that includes a sizeable number of non-Californians, and most people are "very friendly, respectful of others' different identities, and comfortable with people of different backgrounds." There is "a good meshing" of all the students regardless of what their involvements are, and a real "community-based feeling" abounds. Whittier sees a higher transfer rate than many similar schools, so "it is very easy to know at least ten or more students who transfer after a year or two." The majority of people here are involved in some form of sport, but are not looking to go beyond the collegiate or intramural level.

WHITTIER COLLEGE

Financial Aid: 562-907-4285 • E-Mail: admissions@whittier.edu • Website: www.whittier.edu

THE PRINCETON REVIEW SAYS

Admissions

Very important factors considered include: rigor of secondary school record, academic GPA, application essay, recommendation(s), character/personal qualities. *Important factors considered include:* interview, extracurricular activities, talent/ability. *Other factors considered include:* class rank, standardized test scores, first generation, alumni/ae relation, geographical residence, state residency, racial/ethnic status, work experience. ACT with or without writing accepted. SAT with or without Essay component accepted. High school diploma is required and GED is accepted. *Academic units required:* 3 English, 2 math, 1 science, 1 science lab, 2 foreign language, 1 social studies. *Academic units recommended:* 4 English, 3 math, 2 science, 3 foreign language, 2 social studies.

Financial Aid

Students should submit: FAFSA. Priority filing deadline is 3/1. The Princeton Review suggests that all financial aid forms be submitted as soon as possible after October 1. *Need-based scholarships/grants offered:* College/university scholarship or grant aid from institutional funds; Federal Pell; Private scholarships; SEOG; State scholarships/grants. *Loan aid offered:* Direct PLUS loans; Direct Subsidized Stafford Loans; Direct Unsubsidized Stafford Loans. Applicants will be notified of awards on a rolling basis beginning 2/15. Federal Work-Study Program available.

The Inside Word

Whittier is looking for well-rounded students, and so activities and recommendations are just as important as scores and grades—the admissions office hates to focus just on numbers. In fact, test scores are optional for students with a GPA of 3.0 or higher. Though 65 percent of students hail from California, no preference is given to state of origin. Through the Whittier Scholars program, students may construct a personalized major that fits academic and career goals.

THE SCHOOL SAYS "..."

From the Admissions Office

"Faculty and students at Whittier share a love of learning and delight in the life of the mind. They join in understanding the value of the intellectual quest, the use of reason, and a respect for values. They seek knowledge of their own culture and the informed appreciation of other traditions, and they explore the interrelatedness of knowledge and the connections among disciplines. An extraordinary community emerges from teachers and students representing a variety of academic pursuits, individuals who have come together at Whittier in the belief that study within the liberal arts forms the best foundation for rewarding endeavor throughout a lifetime.

"Whittier College is a vibrant, residential, four-year liberal arts institution where intellectual inquiry and experiential learning are fostered in a community that promotes respect for diversity of thought and culture. A Whittier College education produces enthusiastic, independent thinkers who flourish in graduate studies, the evolving global workplace, and life."

SELECTIVITY
Admissions Rating	74
# of applicants	4,585
% of applicants accepted	99
% of acceptees attending	11

FRESHMAN PROFILE
Range SAT EBRW	510–620
Range SAT Math	500–600
Range ACT Composite	21–27
# submitting SAT scores	372
% submitting SAT scores	72
# submitting ACT scores	209
% submitting ACT scores	40
Average HS GPA	3.5
% graduated top 10% of class	21
% graduated top 25% of class	63
% graduated top 50% of class	92

DEADLINES
Early action	
Deadline	11/15
Notification	12/30
Regular	
Priority	2/1
Notification	Rolling, 12/30
Nonfall registration?	Yes

APPLICANTS ALSO LOOK AT AND OFTEN PREFER
University of Redlands; Occidental College

AND SOMETIMES PREFER
Pitzer College; Loyola Marymount University

AND RARELY PREFER
Chapman University; Claremont McKenna College

FINANCIAL FACTS
Financial Aid Rating	86
Annual tuition	$47,496
Room and board	$13,742
Required fees	$590
Books and supplies	$800
Average frosh need-based scholarship	$38,039
Average UG need-based scholarship	$36,009
% needy frosh rec. need-based scholarship or grant aid	86
% needy UG rec. need-based scholarship or grant aid	89
% needy frosh rec. non-need-based scholarship or grant aid	14
% needy UG rec. non-need-based scholarship or grant aid	11
% needy frosh rec. need-based self-help aid	81
% needy UG rec. need-based self-help aid	82
% frosh rec. any financial aid	92
% UG rec. any financial aid	89
% UG borrow to pay for school	77
Average cumulative indebtedness	$32,167
% frosh need fully met	19
% ugrads need fully met	15
Average % of frosh need met	79
Average % of ugrad need met	77

WILLIAM & MARY

Office of Admissions, Williamsburg, VA 23187-8795 • Admissions: 757-221-4223 • Fax: 757-221-1242

CAMPUS LIFE

Quality of Life Rating	94
Fire Safety Rating	92
Green Rating	60*
Type of school	Public
Environment	Town

STUDENTS

Total undergrad enrollment	6,249
% male/female	43/57
% from out of state	31
% frosh from public high school	77
% frosh live on campus	100
% ugrads live on campus	71
# of fraternities (% ugrad men join)	19 (28)
# of sororities (% ugrad women join)	14 (29)
% African American	7
% Asian	8
% Caucasian	59
% Hispanic	9
% Native American	<1
% Pacific Islander	<1
% Two or more races	5
% Race and/or ethnicity unknown	6
% international	6
# of countries represented	84

SURVEY SAYS . . .

Students are happy
Lab facilities are great
Great library
Career services are great
Internships are widely available
No one cheats
Students are friendly
Diverse student types interact on campus
Students involved in community service
Students environmentally aware
Easy to get around campus
Frats and sororities are popular
Theater is popular
Active student government
Active minority support groups
Active student-run political groups

ACADEMICS

Academic Rating	92
% students returning for sophomore year	95
% students graduating within 4 years	85
% students graduating within 6 years	92
Calendar	Semester
Student/faculty ratio	12:1
Profs interesting rating	93
Profs accessible rating	97

Most classes have 10–19 students.
Most lab/discussion sessions have
   10–19 students.

MOST POPULAR MAJORS

Political Science and Government, General;
Biology/Biological Sciences, General; Psychology,
General

STUDENTS SAY "..."

Academics

This "Public Ivy" in Williamsburg, Virginia is the nation's second-oldest institution of higher education and one of the most selective public universities in the nation. Due to the rigorous curriculum (Phi Beta Kappa was founded here), everyone who joins the campus community, nicknamed the Tribe, are "academic and quick and dynamic." Across campus all students "can identify a tangible way William & Mary [has] made them a better version of themselves." Because the student body is very intelligent, "there is a certain competitive culture on campus" in which students are "very driven and determined to do well, which makes classes challenging in a good way." William & Mary "does a great job networking their students with alumni," which include such past and present reputable names as "Thomas Jefferson, James Monroe, John Tyler, [and] Jon Stewart." The Cohen Career Center "does a great job placing students" at internships and full-time work, and the school has "a powerful reputation" that "allows employers and graduate schools to feel comfortable with W&M student's abilities to perform in a real job situation."

Professors "love teaching here" and "even in the very few 100+ classes at W&M... [they] still try their very best to know your name," even taking photos to help them remember. The much more prevalent small class sizes help students bounce their ideas and opinions off not just the professor, but also off each other, and "minute interactions with professors and other students inspire and encourage students." "Sure, anyone can learn information from a textbook, but my professors have brought information to life and made an effort to get to know me as a person," says a student. The academic experience here "is shaped by your interests and is not limited to class itself." The resources available to students are undeniable, and "no matter what you want to do (even if that is creating your very own professional career field)," professors and staff are available "to help you succeed and find meaning in your work."

Life

William & Mary is a school where "you can map your interests across the board through multiple venues." Everyone stays pretty busy juggling academics, but most people are "pretty involved" with the more than 450 clubs on campus, which range from "the Quidditch team to the Exotic Cheese club." There is "always something going on," and campus life often involves guest speakers, who have in the past included the Dalai Lama and Condoleezza Rice. Students make their own fun during the day, from "frisbee with friends in the Sunken Gardens or [going] for a Cider Walk in Colonial Williamsburg." Then, at night, there are "tons of events" hosted by organizations, from Screen on the Green to "more interactive activities like Zombie Apocalypse during Halloween weekend where students volunteer to be zombies." Students are "constantly seen in neighboring Colonial Williamsburg at the famous Cheese Shop," as well as across the pond: Almost half of all students study abroad at some point in their academic careers.

Student Body

The community is "extremely close knit and supportive," and "everyone has something, usually obscure, that they're extremely passionate about," which everyone else "is really excited to hear about." Students can be "pretty nerdy," and the phrase TWAMP (Typical William & Mary Person) gets used "whenever someone does something nerdy like drop a Star Wars reference or talk about how long they've spent studying." These "quirky, fun" people are "inspiring in their choice to challenge themselves every day" and help make the W&M experience all about "learning not just for grades or jobs but [for] developing and satisfying your curiosity." "When we stress 'One Tribe, One Family,' we aren't just doing it for the postcards," says one student.

Financial Aid: 757-221-2420 • E-Mail: admission@wm.edu • Website: www.wm.edu

THE PRINCETON REVIEW SAYS

Admissions

Very important factors considered include: rigor of secondary school record, class rank, academic GPA, application essay, standardized test scores, recommendation(s), extracurricular activities, talent/ability, character/personal qualities, state residency, volunteer work, work experience. *Other factors considered include:* interview, first generation, alumni/ae relation, geographical residence, racial/ethnic status, level of applicant's interest. ACT with or without writing accepted. SAT with or without Essay component accepted. High school diploma or equivalent is not required. *Academic units recommended:* 4 English, 4 math, 4 science, 3 science labs, 4 foreign language, 4 social studies.

Financial Aid

Students should submit: CSS/Financial Aid PROFILE; FAFSA. Priority filing deadline is 3/1. The Princeton Review suggests that all financial aid forms be submitted as soon as possible after October 1. *Need-based scholarships/grants offered:* College/university scholarship or grant aid from institutional funds; Federal Pell; Private scholarships; SEOG; State scholarships/grants. *Loan aid offered:* Direct PLUS loans; Direct Subsidized Stafford Loans; Direct Unsubsidized Stafford Loans. Applicants will be notified of awards on or about 3/15. Federal Work-Study Program available. Institutional employment available.

The Inside Word

The volume of applications at William & Mary is extremely high; thus, admission is ultra competitive. Only very strong students from out-of-state should apply. The large applicant pool necessitates a labor-intensive evaluation process; each admissions officer reads roughly 150 application folders per week during the peak review season. But this is one admissions committee that moves fast without sacrificing a thorough holistic review. There probably isn't a tougher public college admission committee in the country.

THE SCHOOL SAYS "..."

From the Admissions Office

"Since our founding in 1693, William & Mary has established a legacy of distinction and excellence. Located in Williamsburg, VA, we combine the research and global opportunities of a larger research university with the close-knit and personal environment of a smaller liberal arts and sciences school. As a W&M student, you will be challenged daily both inside and outside the classroom by your world-class faculty and diverse classmates, all while being surrounded by the historic and aesthetic beauty of Williamsburg.

"With over 450 student organizations and more than 100 majors and minors, William & Mary students have no shortage of opportunities to explore their passions. As a member of our campus community you'll walk in the footsteps of alumni ranging from Thomas Jefferson and James Monroe to former *Daily Show* host Jon Stewart, comedians Patton Oswalt and Michelle Wolf, Hulu co-founder Beth Comstock, and Super Bowl-winning Pittsburgh Steeler's coach Mike Tomlin.

"In short, William & Mary provides a top-rated educational experience while being consistently recognized as one of the best values in the nation. If you are an academically strong, involved student looking for a challenge in a globally minded community, William & Mary may well be the place for you. Come learn for yourself what makes William & Mary so powerfully unique."

SELECTIVITY
Admissions Rating	95
# of applicants	14,644
% of applicants accepted	37
% of acceptees attending	29
# offered a place on the wait list	4,133
% accepting a place on wait list	53
% admitted from wait list	4
# of early decision applicants	922
% accepted early decision	58

FRESHMAN PROFILE
Range SAT EBRW	660–730
Range SAT Math	650–760
Range ACT Composite	30–33
# submitting SAT scores	1,202
% submitting SAT scores	78
# submitting ACT scores	597
% submitting ACT scores	39
Average HS GPA	4.2
% graduated top 10% of class	77
% graduated top 25% of class	95
% graduated top 50% of class	99

DEADLINES
Early decision	
Deadline	11/1
Notification	12/1
Other ED Deadline	1/1
Other ED Notification	2/1
Regular	
Deadline	1/1
Notification	4/1
Nonfall registration?	No

APPLICANTS ALSO LOOK AT AND SOMETIMES PREFER
University of Virginia; Virginia Polytechnic Institute and State University; The University of North Carolina at Chapel Hill; Cornell University; Wake Forest University; Georgetown University; University of Richmond; Boston College

FINANCIAL FACTS
Financial Aid Rating	86
Annual in-state tuition	$17,434
Annual out-of-state tuition	$40,089
Room and board	$12,926
Required fees	$6,194
Books and supplies	$1,000
Average frosh need-based scholarship	$19,108
Average UG need-based scholarship	$17,561
% needy frosh rec. need-based scholarship or grant aid	90
% needy UG rec. need-based scholarship or grant aid	89
% needy frosh rec. non-need-based scholarship or grant aid	42
% needy UG rec. non-need-based scholarship or grant aid	37
% needy frosh rec. need-based self-help aid	49
% needy UG rec. need-based self-help aid	58
% frosh rec. any financial aid	40
% UG rec. any financial aid	36
% UG borrow to pay for school	35
Average cumulative indebtedness	$25,409
% frosh need fully met	27
% ugrads need fully met	24
Average % of frosh need met	82
Average % of ugrad need met	81

WILLIAM JEWELL COLLEGE

500 College Hill, Liberty, MO 64068 • Admissions: 816-415-7511 • Fax: 816-415-5040

STUDENTS SAY ". . ."

Academics
The minute students step onto campus at William Jewell, they are welcomed into an "amazing community" replete with "top-notch academics." As one senior gushes, "Everyone on campus makes you feel at home and the faculty and staff are some of the most genuine people you will ever meet." Moreover, as a small liberal arts college, William Jewell "provides a superb education" that many undergrads here feel is "unmatched in the Midwest." After all, the college endeavors to transform undergrads into "critical thinkers" who are bound to achieve "success and find [their] passion." This is no doubt due in large part to the fact that "William Jewell provides a well-rounded education for its students and challenges them to step outside of their own perspectives." Though the college has many fantastic majors from which to choose, undergrads are especially quick to highlight "the strong science and pre-med program" along with the "well established" non-profit program. The nursing program also has a "great reputation." On the whole, undergrads speak very highly of their "amazingly dedicated" professors. Impressively, teachers here tend to be "great lecturers...who [also] excel in discussion formatted classes." Another senior adds, "The professors at William Jewell are very personable and willing to go the extra step to build a connection with each and every student. They are always finding the best way to reach out to their students and provide each student with the best chance of success." Overall, William Jewell offers a "rigorous set of programs that push you to the limits of your ability."

Life
Students here agree that "life at Jewell is a busy one." As one knowledgeable senior happily shares, "There are always campus activities going on whether that be sporting events or resident hall gatherings or even the occasional fraternity/sorority party." A junior specifies, "Student organizations often sponsor events like CU-At-the-Movies, Skate Night, [and] Bowling Night where we get discounted prices to go out and have fun. We also play 'Gotcha!' (an assassin game), on campus every year and Browning Hall is playing Humans vs. Zombies this year." Additionally, "a number of students...are active in Greek life." Fortunately, we're assured that there's no pressure to join, and independent students still feel included. Undergrads here also love to take advantage of the "Harriman-Jewell series [which] offers free tickets to students, and brings world-class arts and culture such as pianists (Emanuel Ax) and dance (Mark Morris Dance Group) to Kansas City." Speaking of KC, William Jewell is only a "twenty-minute drive away" from the heart of the city. As another senior brags, "Once downtown, you can do just about anything. There is the Power & Light District with the Sprint Center, the Kaufman Center and just a few miles south you get into Westport where you can find numerous college/young adult students at any given time."

Student Body
Undergrads at William Jewell are a "laid back but focused" lot. Indeed, students are quick to define their peers as "driven" and "intelligent" people who are "committed to their education and community." Of course, some see the typical Jewell student as "a white, Protestant, upper-middle class, girl who loves Pinterest." Although a junior cautions that, "the population isn't as diverse as other schools I have been to," he also counters that, "everyone is pretty open and accepting of just about anyone." Fortunately, many find that "students fit in very easily." Overall, "no one really is ever left out of anything as long as they're putting the effort in to have friends and be a part of an organization as well as the Jewell community as a whole." Another junior adds that, "While most [undergrads] attend college straight out of high school, there is a growing number of non-traditional students especially in the nursing program." Finally, as one satisfied political science student succinctly states, "We have a high retention rate, which tells me that students fit in well."

WILLIAM JEWELL COLLEGE

Financial Aid: 816-415-5973 • E-Mail: admission@william.jewell.edu • Website: www.jewell.edu

THE PRINCETON REVIEW SAYS

Admissions

Very important factors considered include: rigor of secondary school record, academic GPA. *Important factors considered include:* class rank, standardized test scores, recommendation(s), extracurricular activities, talent/ability, character/personal qualities. *Other factors considered include:* application essay, interview, first generation, alumni/ae relation, volunteer work, work experience. ACT with Writing recommended. SAT with Essay component recommended. High school diploma is required and GED is accepted. *Academic units required:* 4 English, 3 math, 3 science, 1 science lab, 2 foreign language, 3 social studies. *Academic units recommended:* 4 math, 3 foreign language, 2 academic electives.

Financial Aid

Students should submit: FAFSA. Priority filing deadline is 2/1. The Princeton Review suggests that all financial aid forms be submitted as soon as possible after October 1. *Need-based scholarships/grants offered:* College/university scholarship or grant aid from institutional funds; Federal Pell; Private scholarships; SEOG; State scholarships/grants; United Negro College Fund. *Loan aid offered:* Direct PLUS loans; Direct Subsidized Stafford Loans; Direct Unsubsidized Stafford Loans. Applicants will be notified of awards on a rolling basis beginning 11/1. Federal Work-Study Program available. Institutional employment available.

The Inside Word

Competition for admission is strong and candidates must demonstrate success with a rigorous course load. Of course, similar to most small colleges, Jewell is also looking for applicants who will complement the campus. Therefore, you can be assured that personal statements and recommendations will be closely assessed.

THE SCHOOL SAYS "..."

From the Admissions Office

"William Jewell College is a four-year, private liberal arts college in Liberty, Missouri. Jewell's commitment to cultivating critical thinkers in pursuit of meaningful lives is woven into the living and learning community and is the basis of the Critical Thought and Inquiry Core Curriculum. Our 30-plus majors include nursing, civil engineering, data science, business, music, psychological science and nonprofit leadership, with 99.6% of students employed or in graduate school within six months of graduation. Jewell's one to ten faculty-student ratio allows a personalized experience through numerous distinctive programs. The Oxbridge Honors Program, supported by the Hall Family Foundation, combines British tutorial methods of instruction with a year of study in Oxford, England. Students have traveled to 59 countries with their Journey Grants, a $2,000 minimum grant available for academic enrichment, leadership and service. Our Pryor Leadership Program is open to students from all disciplines, featuring an Outward Bound experience in the Florida Everglades and culminating in a class legacy project. Jewell's national award-winning Concert Choir has produced two CDs, and members go on a triennial concert tour in England and Scotland. A national champion debate team, the Harriman-Jewell premier performing arts series and the Idea Exchange Innovation Lab also demonstrate the depth of opportunities available to students."

SELECTIVITY

Admissions Rating	89
# of applicants	1,167
% of applicants accepted	46
% of acceptees attending	31

FRESHMAN PROFILE

Range SAT EBRW	540–650
Range SAT Math	540–650
Range ACT Composite	22–27
% submitting SAT scores	12
% submitting ACT scores	91
Average HS GPA	3.6
% graduated top 10% of class	34
% graduated top 25% of class	61
% graduated top 50% of class	86

DEADLINES

Regular	
Notification	Rolling, 9/15
Nonfall registration?	Yes

APPLICANTS ALSO LOOK AT AND OFTEN PREFER
University of Missouri; University of Missouri—Kansas City

AND SOMETIMES PREFER
Truman State University; University of Kansas

AND RARELY PREFER
Missouri State University; Rockhurst University

FINANCIAL FACTS

Financial Aid Rating	89
Annual tuition	$33,500
Room and board	$10,220
Required fees	$950
Books and supplies	$800
Average frosh need-based scholarship	$27,036
Average UG need-based scholarship	$26,204
% needy frosh rec. need-based scholarship or grant aid	100
% needy UG rec. need-based scholarship or grant aid	100
% needy frosh rec. non-need-based scholarship or grant aid	19
% needy UG rec. non-need-based scholarship or grant aid	20
% needy frosh rec. need-based self-help aid	78
% needy UG rec. need-based self-help aid	76
% frosh rec. any financial aid	100
% UG rec. any financial aid	99
% UG borrow to pay for school	59
Average cumulative indebtedness	$37,322
% frosh need fully met	35
% ugrads need fully met	35
Average % of frosh need met	88
Average % of ugrad need met	82

WILLIAMS COLLEGE

995 Main St., Williamstown, MA 01267 • Admissions: 413-597-2211 • Fax: 413-597-4052

STUDENTS SAY "..."

Academics

Tucked away in western Massachusetts, Williams College is a "top-notch" liberal arts college that is "committed to making all students' dreams a reality." Indeed, this highly-selective institution is an ideal place for people "who truly love to learn and explore new academic passions." And it offers the "perfect combination of...liberal arts and research opportunities; neither one has to be sacrificed here." Moreover, undergrads report that "the courses offered are diverse and interesting, while the divisional requirements mean that classes are more open to non-majors than at other schools." Of course, no matter what classes they take, students can rest assured that they'll be taught "how to think critically." Further, Williams' "small" size, with an enrollment of 2,025, also allows for "individualized attention." Undergrads also proudly proclaim that their professors are "the best in the nation, if not the world." Not only is each instructor "an expert in his or her field" but the vast majority have proven themselves to be "gifted teacher[s] as well." Even better, "they all make sure to be readily accessible and try to get to know every single student, even in a larger lecture class." And while they maintain "high expectations," courses are often "highly rewarding." What more could you hope for?

Life

Undergrads at Williams are "always busy, always a little bit stressed." This comes as no surprise given that there are so many activities hosted on campus. To begin with, "the college makes sure to offer a ton of lectures, performances, art exhibits, movie screenings, fun activities, etc. so that people feel fulfilled staying on campus." There are also numerous "student-led events." As one content undergrad explains, "On Wednesday nights, my friends and I [go] to Stressbusters where you get free treats and the student-run coffee bar has an open tab." Additionally, Williams undergrads are always game for sporting events. After all, "30 percent of the school are varsity athletes [and] almost everyone else either is on a club sport, plays intramural, or goes to the gym regularly." There are also plenty of "opportunities to explore the outdoors [including] hiking, skiing, running, biking, [and] swimming." And once the weekend hits, you can find "lots of different kinds of parties... all-campus parties that the college puts on, big parties sponsored by different clubs, smaller parties, and people just hanging out in dorms." Lastly, though Williamstown is pretty "rural" and "remote," there are "amazing art offerings in the area at the Clark Art Institute, Massachusetts Museum of Contemporary Art, and the Williams College Museum of Art." Overall, you're bound to find something that will pique your interest and keep you entertained at Williams.

Student Body

The student body at Williams College is comprised of "driven," "quirky," and "mostly type-A" individuals. Across the board, undergrads here stress that their peers are incredibly "intelligent." As one impressed student shares, "Williams is great because you never feel like the smartest one in the room, and you genuinely feel as though your classmates have valuable input in all scenarios." In addition, Williams students are "dedicated to pursuing their passions, which cover a diverse spectrum and often fall outside of what is typical." Indeed, "it's not unusual to find a football player who is deeply interested in experimental theatre or a computer science major who is also one of the friendliest people you know." While many Williams students categorize each other as "white, athlet[ic and] preppy," lots of undergrads assure us that "so many people fall outside of [these boxes]" as well. However, some do caution that "the average student is very socially and politically liberal, and conservative ideas (particularly socially conservative ideas) aren't welcome on campus." Nevertheless, most agree that the "sense of community is overwhelmingly strong and welcoming." After all, the students here "want to be surrounded by each other and learn from each other—otherwise they wouldn't have chosen to go to a school together in the middle of nowhere!"

WILLIAMS COLLEGE

Financial Aid: 413-597-4181 • E-Mail: admission@williams.edu • Website: www.williams.edu

THE PRINCETON REVIEW SAYS

Admissions

Very important factors considered include: rigor of secondary school record, class rank, academic GPA, standardized test scores, recommendation(s), character/personal qualities. *Important factors considered include:* application essay, extracurricular activities, talent/ability, first generation, alumni/ae relation, racial/ethnic status, volunteer work, work experience. *Other factors considered include:* geographical residence, religious affiliation/commitment. ACT with or without writing accepted. SAT with or without Essay component accepted. High school diploma or equivalent is not required. *Academic units recommended:* 4 English, 4 math, 4 science, 3 science labs, 4 foreign language, 4 social studies.

Financial Aid

Students should submit: CSS/Financial Aid PROFILE; FAFSA; Noncustodial PROFILE. The Princeton Review suggests that all financial aid forms be submitted as soon as possible after October 1. *Need-based scholarships/grants offered:* College/university scholarship or grant aid from institutional funds; Federal Pell; SEOG; State scholarships/grants. *Loan aid offered:* Direct PLUS loans; Direct Subsidized Stafford Loans; Direct Unsubsidized Stafford Loans. Applicants will be notified of awards on or about 4/1. Federal Work-Study Program available. Institutional employment available.

The Inside Word

Williams College is incredibly selective and earning a coveted acceptance letter will not be easy. Certainly, applicants will need to have earned top grades in a rigorous high school curriculum; advanced placement, honors and/or IB courses are a must. Beyond academic accolades, admissions officers are looking for students who demonstrate themselves to be creative thinkers and individuals who will bring diverse perspectives to campus life. To that end, personal statements, extracurricular involvement, and letters of recommendation also hold substantial weight.

THE SCHOOL SAYS "..."

From the Admissions Office

"In addition to all the things that make liberal arts colleges the global gold standard—small classes, attentive faculty, close-knit community—Williams offers unique opportunities like the renowned Oxford-tutorial program, where students (in pairs) research and defend ideas and engage in weekly debate with a professor. Half of Williams' students pursue study abroad, with about thirty students annually spending a year at Oxford. Four weeks of Winter Study each January provide time for individualized projects, research and novel fields of study. Students compete on 34 Division III athletic teams, perform in 25 musical groups, stage 10 theatrical productions and volunteer in 350 local organizations. The college receives several million dollars annually for undergraduate science research and is a leader in preparing its students for graduate study. The local community offers three distinguished art museums, the Williams College Museum of Art, the Clark Art Institute, the Massachusetts Museum of Contemporary Art, and 2,200 forest acres—complete with a treetop canopy walkway—for environmental research and recreation.

"In the 2020–2021 admission cycle only, students have the option of applying under a test-optional policy. For students who submit standardized test results, those results will be considered as part of a holistic, student-centered admission process. Williams maintains one of the lowest loan expectations of any college or university in the country. Often the aid packages of students whose families demonstrate high financial need are made up entirely of grants and a campus job—and do not include any loans."

SELECTIVITY

Admissions Rating	98
# of applicants	9,715
% of applicants accepted	13
% of acceptees attending	45
# offered a place on the wait list	1,857
% accepting a place on wait list	35
% admitted from wait list	4
# of early decision applicants	689
% accepted early decision	37

FRESHMAN PROFILE

Range SAT EBRW	700–760
Range SAT Math	710–790
Range SAT Composite	1420–1540
Range ACT Composite	32–35
# submitting SAT scores	362
% submitting SAT scores	66
# submitting ACT scores	259
% submitting ACT scores	47
% graduated top 10% of class	85
% graduated top 25% of class	98
% graduated top 50% of class	99

DEADLINES

Early decision	
Deadline	11/15
Notification	12/15
Regular	
Deadline	1/1
Notification	4/7
Nonfall registration?	No

APPLICANTS ALSO LOOK AT AND OFTEN PREFER
Harvard College; Stanford University; Yale University

AND SOMETIMES PREFER
Brown University; Princeton University; Columbia University

AND RARELY PREFER
Amherst College; Duke University; Middlebury College; Swarthmore College; Dartmouth College; The University of Chicago; University of Pennsylvania; Cornell University; Northwestern University

FINANCIAL FACTS

Financial Aid Rating	99
Annual tuition	$59,350
Room and board	$15,000
Required fees	$310
Books and supplies	$800
Average frosh need-based scholarship	$54,973
Average UG need-based scholarship	$56,788
% needy frosh rec. need-based scholarship or grant aid	100
% needy UG rec. need-based scholarship or grant aid	100
% needy frosh rec. non-need-based scholarship or grant aid	0
% needy UG rec. non-need-based scholarship or grant aid	0
% needy frosh rec. need-based self-help aid	87
% needy UG rec. need-based self-help aid	87
% frosh rec. any financial aid	52
% UG rec. any financial aid	52
% UG borrow to pay for school	33
Average cumulative indebtedness	$15,911
% frosh need fully met	100
% ugrads need fully met	100
Average % of frosh need met	100
Average % of ugrad need met	100

WITTENBERG UNIVERSITY

P.O. Box 720, Springfield, OH 45501 • Admissions: 937-327-6314 • Fax: 937-327-6379

STUDENTS SAY ". . ."

Academics

Located in Springfield, Ohio, Wittenberg combines a "small school atmosphere" with "a wide horizon of learning opportunities." The school offers "high academic standards and a dedication to research" that makes "an environment where students can excel in the classroom and out." This "friendly, athletic campus" "offers a close-knit community where professors and students build professional and personal relationships." The school's motto is "Having Light, We Pass It On To Others." This is taken seriously by the "extremely engaging" professors who are "committed to helping students both in and out of the classroom." The "fabulous" teachers at Wittenberg are "always accessible and willing to help" and really get to know students "on a personal level." "I feel like I am learning from my best friends," one happy student reports. An Environmental Science student agrees, saying, "I have become very close to a few of my professors and have really come to enjoy my classroom experience." Some students say that "communication with the student body" and "upper level administration" "is not always the best." Still, a Communications major lavishes praise on the entire staff, "not only just teachers, but I would go as far to say even down to the maintenance and janitor crew." Part of the reason students love classes at Wittenberg is the small class sizes. This "means excellent attention paid to students." "The class sizes and student-teacher ratio makes it an ideal place to develop professional relationships" and these relationships "really elevates the learning environment and makes classes far more interesting than large schools." The "open-minded and encouraging" faculty really pushes "students to build our own ideas and projects." All in all, "the people, the faculty and students are a very happy, connected, and welcoming community." This, combined with the "gorgeous campus" might explain the "high morale among the students." As a Psychology major explains, "Wittenberg is a place where students can develop themselves as a whole person—academically, professionally, and socially."

Life

Students are typically busy and even "often over-involved" at Wittenberg. Your average student might be "involved and overcommitted in at least two clubs and a sport or Greek life." "With over 100 student clubs and organizations, it is easy to find things to get involved in," one student explains. "Witt students generally know how to work hard and play hard" and "party every day." One student says that partying is so pervasive that "if you do not drink then you have no chance of fitting in." "The typical student is one who drinks constantly, and rarely ever gets in trouble for it," since, students say, the University is lax on enforcing drug and alcohol rules. Still, there are plenty of other activities to do on campus from "just hang[ing] out and spend[ing] time with each other" to "Witt Wednesday" in which "comedians or musicians come to entertain." "What don't we do?" one student says. One quirky, or even "downright surreal" part of campus life has to do with the crows. "Our crow-deterrent alarms, which are mounted on the roofs of every building, are triggered by students walking by," one student explains. "It's downright uncanny at night to hear crow death screams played from the rooftops as you walk back to your dorm." Students who love nature will enjoy "a reservoir to swim in, two playgrounds/parks, and three national parks for hiking."

Student Body

This "beautiful school" is filled with "friendly," "outgoing," and "quirky people." "It is hard to describe a typical student because we are very diverse, but with that diversity we all are able to get in," an Environmental Science student says. If you had to generalize, most students are "white, from Ohio, [and] middle class," but "Wittenberg has a wonderful variety of students." Students tend to be "fun personalities, engaged, curious and eager to learn, smart." "All types of students here are welcomed in with ease" and everyone can "find at least one friend group." One student elaborates that these groups "are like amoebas that are constantly shifting, made up of many different people." Overall Wittenberg is a "tight-knit community" where all you have to do to make a friend is "step out and say hello!"

WITTENBERG UNIVERSITY

Financial Aid: 937-327-7321 • E-Mail: admission@wittenberg.edu • Website: www.wittenberg.edu

THE PRINCETON REVIEW SAYS

Admissions

Very important factors considered include: rigor of secondary school record, class rank, academic GPA. *Important factors considered include:* application essay, recommendation(s), extracurricular activities, talent/ability, character/personal qualities, volunteer work. *Other factors considered include:* standardized test scores, interview, first generation, alumni/ae relation, work experience. ACT with or without writing accepted. SAT with or without Essay component accepted. High school diploma is required and GED is accepted. *Academic units required:* 4 English, 3 math, 3 science, 2 science labs, 2 foreign language, 2 history. *Academic units recommended:* 4 English, 4 math, 5 science, 2 science labs, 3 foreign language, 3 history.

Financial Aid

Students should submit: FAFSA. Priority filing deadline is 3/1. The Princeton Review suggests that all financial aid forms be submitted as soon as possible after October 1. *Need-based scholarships/grants offered:* College/university scholarship or grant aid from institutional funds; Federal Pell; Private scholarships; SEOG; State scholarships/grants; United Negro College Fund. *Loan aid offered:* Direct PLUS loans; Direct Subsidized Stafford Loans; Direct Unsubsidized Stafford Loans. Applicants will be notified of awards on a rolling basis beginning 3/1. Federal Work-Study Program available. Institutional employment available.

The Inside Word

Wittenberg accepts both its own application and the common application, and the application fee is waived if you apply online. The university only requires a short personal statement instead of the traditional formal essay. Wittenberg has a fairly high acceptance rate, but students will still want to make sure all parts of their application are the best they can be.

THE SCHOOL SAYS "..."

From the Admissions Office

"At Wittenberg, you will experience an active and engaged learning environment, a setting where you can refine your definition of self yet gain exposure to the varied kinds of knowledge, people, views, activities, options, and ideas that add richness to our lives. Wittenberg is a university where students are able to thrive in a small campus environment with many opportunities for intellectual and personal growth in and out of the classroom. Campus life is as diverse as the interests of our students. Wittenberg attracts students from all over the United States and from many other countries. Historically, the university has been committed to geographical, educational, cultural, and religious diversity. With their varied backgrounds and interests, Wittenberg students have helped initiate many of the more than 125 student organizations that are active on campus. The students will be the first to tell you there's never a lack of things to do on or near the campus any day of the week, if you're willing to get involved.

"Wittenberg University is test score optional. Freshman applicants can choose to submit either ACT (with or without writing component) or SAT scores."

SELECTIVITY

Admissions Rating	77
# of applicants	7,393
% of applicants accepted	74
% of acceptees attending	9
# of early decision applicants	955
% accepted early decision	89

FRESHMAN PROFILE

Range SAT EBRW	540–650
Range SAT Math	530–620
Range ACT Composite	22–28
# submitting SAT scores	80
% submitting SAT scores	17
# submitting ACT scores	269
% submitting ACT scores	56
Average HS GPA	3.5
% graduated top 10% of class	16
% graduated top 25% of class	40
% graduated top 50% of class	73

DEADLINES

Early decision	
Deadline	11/15
Notification	12/1
Early action	
Deadline	12/1
Notification	1/1
Regular	
Priority	3/15
Notification	Rolling, 1/1
Nonfall registration?	Yes

APPLICANTS ALSO LOOK AT AND SOMETIMES PREFER

Ohio University—Athens; Miami University; University of Dayton; University of Cincinnati; Otterbein College; Wright State University; Ohio Wesleyan University; Capital University; Xavier University; The Ohio State University—Columbus

FINANCIAL FACTS

Financial Aid Rating	89
Annual tuition	$39,450
Room and board	$10,564
Required fees	$890
Books and supplies	$1,000
Average frosh need-based scholarship	$31,156
Average UG need-based scholarship	$27,774
% needy frosh rec. need-based scholarship or grant aid	100
% needy UG rec. need-based scholarship or grant aid	99
% needy frosh rec. non-need-based scholarship or grant aid	0
% needy UG rec. non-need-based scholarship or grant aid	0
% needy frosh rec. need-based self-help aid	99
% needy UG rec. need-based self-help aid	92
% frosh rec. any financial aid	99
% UG rec. any financial aid	97
% UG borrow to pay for school	73
Average cumulative indebtedness	$37,154
% frosh need fully met	32
% ugrads need fully met	26
Average % of frosh need met	85
Average % of ugrad need met	81

WOFFORD COLLEGE

429 North Church Street, Spartanburg, SC 29303-3663 • Admissions: 864-597-4130 • Fax: 864-597-4147

STUDENTS SAY "..."

Academics

With a "family atmosphere and close-knit community," Wofford College in Spartanburg, South Carolina, is a fantastic option for students seeking a "rigorous" liberal arts experience. It also helps that the "campus is beautiful" and "the facilities are clean and up to date." More impressively, undergrads here have the opportunity to "network with highly influential people," and participate in "an outstanding study abroad program." And thanks to Wofford's "small" size, students are truly able to receive "an individualized education and personal attention." While coursework is "challenging," undergrads are appreciative, noting that their college "specializes in preparing students for graduate or professional school." For the most part, they also give their professors high marks. After all, Wofford instructors tend to be "extremely passionate about their fields and are very well educated." And they "frequently hold review sessions and are always available by email if they are not in their offices." Best of all, "each person, whether in the dining hall or the classroom, is there for your success. Knowing that we have these amazing adults there for us no matter what is something that allows us to thrive and become the best personal versions of ourselves."

Life

At Wofford College, dull moments are few and far between. Sure, students "work hard during the week" but they also manage to carve out time for some fun. For example, many undergrads "spend a lot of time at the gym, either working out, playing games or participating in classes such as yoga or Afro beat." Students also "love to hang out at Burwell, our main cafeteria, and grab a bite to eat." Once the weekend hits, you will find lots of undergrads "playing sand volleyball and dancing at the Greek Village with their friends to the live bands." Indeed, the college maintains six fraternities, four sororities, two historically African-American fraternities, and a multicultural house at the Greek Village and much of the social life revolves around them. However, there's still plenty to enjoy if Greek life isn't your scene. After all, Wofford sponsors a number of great events like "trivia nights," "cultural events" and concerts. Further, outdoor enthusiasts will be thrilled to learn that there are "countless hiking trails near campus, including those at Glendale Shoals," where Wofford's Goodall Environmental Studies Center with its vineyard garden and amphitheater is located. Lastly, though some individuals complain that the city of Spartanburg doesn't offer much to do for fun, heading "off-campus" for activities like "bowling, shopping, or movies are common."

Student Body

Wofford undergrads are "kind," "friendly" and often embody "Southern hospitality." They tend to view their peers as "family" rather than simply fellow students. And while people certainly "have friend groups that they commonly hang out with, [there are] no strict cliques like in high school." Just as critical, Wofford students are "hardworking" and "driven" and they "all take pride in their academic success." Undergrads do acknowledge, however, that the college is "predominantly white." Though they also insist "diversity has increased." And a handful of individuals argue that Wofford yields "many international students from various countries as well as American students from all across the country from all financial backgrounds." Regardless of where they come from, undergrads say it is very "easy to connect with most other students" and that everyone is "respectful and kind toward one another." After all, it is "a very open school and everyone says 'Hi' because you've most likely had a class with them before." One student points out, "you may not know everyone's name, but everyone has some common ground... no one feels left out."

WOFFORD COLLEGE

Financial Aid: 864-597-4160 • E-Mail: admission@wofford.edu • Website: www.wofford.edu

THE PRINCETON REVIEW SAYS

Admissions

Very important factors considered include: rigor of secondary school record, academic GPA. *Important factors considered include:* class rank, application essay, extracurricular activities, talent/ability, character/personal qualities. *Other factors considered include:* standardized test scores, recommendation(s), interview, first generation, alumni/ae relation, geographical residence, state residency, religious affiliation/commitment, racial/ethnic status, volunteer work, work experience, level of applicant's interest. ACT with or without writing accepted. SAT with or without Essay component accepted. High school diploma is required and GED is accepted. *Academic units required:* 4 English, 4 math, 3 science, 3 science labs, 3 foreign language, 3 social studies. *Academic units recommended:* 4 English, 4 math, 3 science, 3 science labs, 3 foreign language, 3 social studies, 1 history, 1 academic elective, 1 computer science, 1 visual/performing arts.

Financial Aid

Students should submit: FAFSA. Priority filing deadline is 1/1. The Princeton Review suggests that all financial aid forms be submitted as soon as possible after October 1. *Need-based scholarships/grants offered:* College/university scholarship or grant aid from institutional funds; Federal Pell; Private scholarships; SEOG; State scholarships/grants. *Loan aid offered:* Direct PLUS loans; Direct Subsidized Stafford Loans; Direct Unsubsidized Stafford Loans. Applicants will be notified of awards on or about 3/15. Federal Work-Study Program available. Institutional employment available.

The Inside Word

Wofford College aims to take a holistic approach to the admissions process. Therefore, students can expect all facets of their application will be closely scrutinized. Successful candidates typically have completed a rigorous high school curriculum, replete with a few honors or AP courses. They also present thoughtful personal statements and are active in their school and community. It's important to mention that Wofford is a test optional school. Students should only submit their scores if they feel that they adequately represent their academic abilities.

THE SCHOOL SAYS "..."

From the Admissions Office

"A century ago Wofford College athletics teams chose the Boston Terrier as the mascot. The small but tenacious and fierce dog is full of intelligence and energy making it an ideal mascot for the 1,725 undergraduates who call Wofford home. Nationally known for the strength of its academic program, outstanding faculty, study abroad participation and successful graduates, Wofford scores among the best in the country on the National Survey of Student Engagement, which measures high-impact, transformative learning experiences, and the college was ranked #8 in the nation by Open Doors (2019) for the percentage of students who study abroad for credit. A new strategic vision has Wofford reimagining what it means to be a premier, innovative and distinctive national liberal arts college that includes award-winning housing for seniors in The Village, exciting Division I athletics with student-athletes who excel both on the playing field and in the classroom, and opportunities to prepare for a future of lifelong learning, leadership, and citizenship. Wofford students, faculty and staff as well as the upstate South Carolina community are enjoying two new buildings on campus. The Rosalind Sallenger Richardson Center for the Arts and the Jerry Richardson Indoor Stadium, along with the new Stewart H. Johnson Greek Village, are game changers, offering exciting and diverse opportunities for academic and social enrichment."

SELECTIVITY

Admissions Rating	86
# of applicants	3,787
% of applicants accepted	60
% of acceptees attending	21
# offered a place on the wait list	666
% accepting a place on wait list	33
% admitted from wait list	16
# of early decision applicants	128
% accepted early decision	92

FRESHMAN PROFILE

Range SAT EBRW	600–680
Range SAT Math	590–670
Range ACT Composite	26–30
# submitting SAT scores	203
% submitting SAT scores	43
# submitting ACT scores	165
% submitting ACT scores	35
Average HS GPA	3.7
% graduated top 10% of class	39
% graduated top 25% of class	70
% graduated top 50% of class	94

DEADLINES

Early decision	
Deadline	11/1
Notification	12/1
Early action	
Deadline	11/15
Notification	2/1
Regular	
Deadline	1/15
Notification	3/1
Nonfall registration?	Yes

APPLICANTS ALSO LOOK AT AND SOMETIMES PREFER
Furman University

FINANCIAL FACTS

Financial Aid Rating	89
Annual tuition	$46,010
Room and board	$13,790
Required fees	$1,640
Books and supplies	$1,200
Average frosh need-based scholarship	$35,614
Average UG need-based scholarship	$35,045
% needy frosh rec. need-based scholarship or grant aid	100
% needy UG rec. need-based scholarship or grant aid	100
% needy frosh rec. non-need-based scholarship or grant aid	32
% needy UG rec. non-need-based scholarship or grant aid	31
% needy frosh rec. need-based self-help aid	53
% needy UG rec. need-based self-help aid	53
% frosh rec. any financial aid	97
% UG rec. any financial aid	95
% UG borrow to pay for school	53
Average cumulative indebtedness	$31,107
% frosh need fully met	40
% ugrads need fully met	39
Average % of frosh need met	84
Average % of ugrad need met	83

WORCESTER POLYTECHNIC INSTITUTE

Admissions Office, Bartlett Center, Worcester, MA 01609 • Admissions: 508-831-5286 • Fax: 508-831-5875

STUDENTS SAY ". . ."

Academics

Sometimes it can be challenging to understand how to apply your college coursework to your future career. But for the 4,600 undergraduates at Massachusetts' Worcester Polytechnic Institute, there's no doubt that their global, project-based STEM education gives them "a lot of necessary tools" to succeed. From the very first day of class, many students say the "unique quarter system" and "projects that are related to the real world" are foundational to their success. This program, known as the WPI Plan, is split into seven-week terms, each of which has three classes. A two-term Great Problems Seminar serves to ease students into university level research, and subsequent classes continue to emphasize the "learn by doing" method. Once settled into the WPI academic structure, many students take advantage of the "excellent resources for academics and future aspirations" by actively pursuing "personal engineering projects" and "opportunities for study abroad, co-ops, [and] internships." Of course, as an interdisciplinary and global institution with over fifty project centers around the world, most students rave about the "research opportunities. . . available for students who wish to have a larger role in the subject they enjoy." At the end of their academic career with WPI, not only do all students end up completing the equivalent of a minor in Humanities & Arts, but they know that their "hands-on learning, group work, and cool projects where you actually get to make something" are exactly what "employers love best about [them]."

Project-based learning is central to the academic experience at WPI, which involves an "incredibly supportive and collaborative" environment between students and faculty. A project often incorporates real world problems and "allows [students] to actually utilize the theoretical knowledge [they] are learning" via "lots of hands-on learning [where] students steer most projects themselves." There are "a plethora of projects…that reflect what can actually happen in the workplace." These ventures range from managing an "independent software startup" to completing a software engineering class that is "run like an internship." Many students say that for both their larger capstone projects and regular coursework, "professors are always available for office hours and meetings" to help. Instructors also "work hard to engage students in course material," so expect them to support all types of learners with lectures "reinforced with some kind of lab, project, practice, or interactive activity." Working closely with such "interested and engaged" educators has had a long-term impact on some undergrads. As one student notes, "My chemistry professor has inspired me to pursue a masters or PhD in renewable energy after I graduate from WPI."

Life

Academics are time-consuming, and everyone runs on a "very intense schedule," but students enjoy taking breaks with "school-sponsored events such as karaoke, Just Dance, and trivia" and there's "always time for socializing on the quad when it is nice out. Schedules "are filled to the brim with club involvements [and] sports." Activities range from "a lot of. . . intramural sports" to "theater and performance groups," and even an active "Greek life [that] is run very well and makes a large impact on the community." As one undergrad puts it, "We live by our Outlook calendars, and they fill up quickly with club meetings and sports." And if students are looking to get off campus, the hopping town of Worcester is just down the hill, filled with "so many good places to eat." Even with all the exciting activities on and off campus, "students manage their time extremely well and remain positive about their school life."

Student Body

WPI undergrads are "well-rounded students" who "are very involved on campus and live the campus life to the fullest." Many enrollees note that people are "extremely interested in their respective STEM fields but also have incredibly diverse extracurricular interests," which contributes to the "specific vibe" at WPI. That is, when you get on the WPI wavelength, "you feel as if you finally belong somewhere." Everyone "is so warm and inviting to anyone new" and "the sense of community is extremely strong, and students are very supportive and welcoming." And if you find yourself struggling, fellow students "are super willing to help you if you have a tough class." One student captures the spirit of the institution, saying, "The student body at WPI feels like a community of like-minded peers. It is exciting to see what other people achieve, both inside and outside the classroom. Even if you don't know someone, it feels like they're your friend because you know how much hard work they put in to reach their achievements."

WORCESTER POLYTECHNIC INSTITUTE

Financial Aid: 508-831-5469 • E-Mail: admissions@wpi.edu • Website: https://www.wpi.edu/

THE PRINCETON REVIEW SAYS

Admissions

Very important factors considered include: rigor of secondary school record, academic GPA. *Important factors considered include:* class rank, standardized test scores, recommendation(s), extracurricular activities, character/personal qualities. *Other factors considered include:* application essay, interview, talent/ability, first generation, alumni/ae relation, geographical residence, racial/ethnic status, volunteer work, work experience, level of applicant's interest. ACT with or without writing accepted. SAT with or without Essay component accepted. High school diploma is required and GED is accepted. *Academic units required:* 4 English, 4 math, 2 science, 2 science labs. *Academic units recommended:* 4 science, 2 foreign language, 2 social studies, 1 history, 1 computer science.

Financial Aid

Students should submit: CSS/Financial Aid PROFILE; FAFSA; Noncustodial PROFILE. Priority filing deadline is 2/1. The Princeton Review suggests that all financial aid forms be submitted as soon as possible after October 1. *Need-based scholarships/grants offered:* College/university scholarship or grant aid from institutional funds; Federal Pell; Private scholarships; SEOG; State scholarships/grants. *Loan aid offered:* Direct PLUS loans; Direct Subsidized Stafford Loans; Direct Unsubsidized Stafford Loans. Applicants will be notified of awards on a rolling basis beginning 12/16. Federal Work-Study Program available. Institutional employment available.

The Inside Word

The WPI applicant pool is both self-selective and competitive, due to its focused curriculum and solid reputation. Admissions officers tend to prioritize those interested in STEM fields and who show a fit with the campus vibe, but they are also looking for students who have interests that go beyond science and math. Consequently, it would be wise to emphasize your extracurricular passions on your applications along with your academic record. WPI is test optional.

THE SCHOOL SAYS ". . ."

From the Admissions Office

"WPI is a research university distinguished by an innovative project-based curriculum converting classroom concepts to real-world impact, empowering students to pursue their passions in solving critical problems and developing skills employers seek. By pairing together theory and practice, students receive a high-caliber education fused with hands-on solving of issues in the world.

"WPI's return on investment enables students to receive a strong starting salary and to ascend to high-income brackets over their lives. Students call WPI's project-based, global approach "life-changing." WPI works with more than 200 companies, government agencies, and private organizations each year, providing opportunities to work in real, professional settings. WPI also receives acclaim for professors who engage their students in research.

"WPI consistently achieves high rankings for academic reputation and student satisfaction. A majority of students travel to over 50 global project centers as part of their project work, leading to ranking No. 1 for the best study-abroad program in the nation (*Princeton Review*). WPI offers every student a Global Scholarship of up to $5,000 to help with travel costs."

SELECTIVITY

Admissions Rating	94
# of applicants	10,645
% of applicants accepted	49
% of acceptees attending	23
# offered a place on the wait list	2,559
% accepting a place on wait list	45
% admitted from wait list	39

FRESHMAN PROFILE

Range SAT EBRW	630–710
Range SAT Math	680–760
Range SAT Composite	1320–1450
Range ACT Composite	29–33
# submitting SAT scores	857
% submitting SAT scores	71
# submitting ACT scores	283
% submitting ACT scores	24
Average HS GPA	3.9
% graduated top 10% of class	63
% graduated top 25% of class	96
% graduated top 50% of class	100

DEADLINES

Early decision	
Deadline	11/1
Notification	12/15
Other ED Deadline	1/15
Other ED Notification	2/15
Early action	
Deadline	11/1
Notification	1/15
Regular	
Deadline	1/15
Notification	3/15
Nonfall registration?	No

FINANCIAL FACTS

Financial Aid Rating	89
Annual tuition	$51,604
Room and board	$15,292
Required fees	$916
Books and supplies	$1,000
Average frosh need-based scholarship	$28,153
Average UG need-based scholarship	$25,304
% needy frosh rec. need-based scholarship or grant aid	100
% needy UG rec. need-based scholarship or grant aid	97
% needy frosh rec. non-need-based scholarship or grant aid	99
% needy UG rec. non-need-based scholarship or grant aid	47
% needy frosh rec. need-based self-help aid	44
% needy UG rec. need-based self-help aid	45
% frosh rec. any financial aid	98.9
% UG rec. any financial aid	91
% frosh need fully met	65
% ugrads need fully met	47
Average % of frosh need met	91
Average % of ugrad need met	80

XAVIER UNIVERSITY OF LOUISIANA

1 Drexel Drive, New Orleans, LA 70125 • Admissions: 504-520-7388 • Fax: 504-520-7941

CAMPUS LIFE

Quality of Life Rating	79
Fire Safety Rating	99
Green Rating	60*
Type of school	Private
Affiliation	Roman Catholic
Environment	Metropolis

STUDENTS

Total undergrad enrollment	2,515
% male/female	24/76
% from out of state	62
% frosh live on campus	84
% ugrads live on campus	62
# of fraternities (% ugrad men join)	4 (1)
# of sororities (% ugrad women join)	4 (5)
% African American	79
% Asian	4
% Caucasian	2
% Hispanic	5
% Native American	<1
% Pacific Islander	0
% Two or more races	4
% Race and/or ethnicity unknown	5
% international	2
# of countries represented	13

SURVEY SAYS . . .

Lots of liberal students
Students involved in community service
Very little drug use

ACADEMICS

Academic Rating	78
% students returning for sophomore year	70
% students graduating within 4 years	38
% students graduating within 6 years	51
Calendar	Semester
Student/faculty ratio	15:1
Profs interesting rating	82
Profs accessible rating	88

Most classes have 20–29 students.
Most lab/discussion sessions have
20–29 students.

MOST POPULAR MAJORS

Pre-Medicine/Pre-Medical Studies; Pre-Pharmacy
Studies; Psychology, General

STUDENTS SAY ". . ."

Academics

Recognized for its "challenging classes" and "academic resources," Xavier University of Louisiana is a Catholic and historically black university that stresses a well-rounded curriculum within a nurturing learning environment. Students here can "be whoever they want to be," which is why the school's support extends beyond programs in STEM and health sciences to a required 40-hour credit core curriculum that focuses on Catholic tradition and contemporary learning. For many students, attending this "extremely academically focused" university pays off. Several undergrads cite that the university is "known for having successful graduates go on to complete medical and graduate school."

But don't let Xavier's strenuous curriculum intimidate you. Many students agree, "[Our] school's greatest strength is our sense of togetherness. We all want to see each other succeed and are willing to help each other along the way," professors included. Most students describe their professors as "kind, understanding and always willing to work with you to achieve a goal." Faculty at the university "value [their students'] education," as observed by students who find that their instructors go above and beyond conventional teaching methods and try to incorporate pedagogical innovation into classes: "Instead of a final exam, my professor is making us do a podcast project in the style of a Vanderbilt professor." Additionally, as a school that challenges its students to be their best, "there is always a resource center or a teacher offering their services" to offer additional guidance. Overall, students agree that Xavier "truly prepares students for experiences after they graduate."

Life

It's a life of books at this rigorously academic university, so "literally most of us are in the library most of the day if not in class," though you will find that "students congregate in their dorm rooms or in the lobby area of the cafeteria." A life of books, at least, until the weekend, at which point the bustle of the nearby city calls out: "There's always something to do in New Orleans." As far as clubs and organizations go, there is "something for everyone, and you even have the opportunity to start clubs of your own." Many enrollees enjoy the Peer Dean Association, which has select members "provide a family space for incoming students" and help them acclimate to life on campus." This is preceded by the Vanguard, in which student ambassadors "are seen as the faces of Xavier" and offer tours and host events for prospective undergrads. Additionally, basketball games are wildly popular, and there are some events thrown on campus, such as "live music [on] Fridays," which "includes free food, dancing, and fun."

Student Body

"Though Xavier University of Louisiana is a historically black university, the student body is very diverse," with notably "well-rounded" and "community-minded" individuals. Several students identify that "even though this is a small campus, the people can be so different." Since Xavierites come from so many different backgrounds and regions, "they bring unique elements such as regional dances, phrases, mannerisms, and recipes." Though some might worry about feeling isolated, Xavier is "one big family" where "no one feels unreachable or untouchable." Additionally, it's clear that Xavier students recognize how hard their classmates work and make the effort to lift one another up. As one student puts it best, "No one will allow you to fail" but they will "[give] you challenges to push yourself forward."

XAVIER UNIVERSITY OF LOUISIANA

Financial Aid: 504-520-7835 • E-Mail: apply@xula.edu • Website: www.xula.edu

THE PRINCETON REVIEW SAYS

Admissions

Very important factors considered include: rigor of secondary school record, academic GPA, standardized test scores, recommendation(s). *Important factors considered include:* class rank, application essay, *Other factors considered include:* interview, extracurricular activities, talent/ability, character/personal qualities, alumni/ae relation, volunteer work, work experience, level of applicant's interest. ACT with or without writing accepted. SAT with or without Essay component accepted. High school diploma is required and GED is accepted. *Academic units required:* 4 English, 2 math, 2 science, 1 social studies, 7 academic electives. *Academic units recommended:* 4 math, 3 science, 1 foreign language, 1 history.

Financial Aid

Students should submit: FAFSA. Priority filing deadline is 1/1. The Princeton Review suggests that all financial aid forms be submitted as soon as possible after October 1. *Need-based scholarships/grants offered:* College/university scholarship or grant aid from institutional funds; Federal Pell; SEOG; State scholarships/grants; United Negro College Fund. *Loan aid offered:* Direct PLUS loans; Direct Subsidized Stafford Loans; Direct Unsubsidized Stafford Loans. Federal Work-Study Program available. Institutional employment available.

The Inside Word

Gaining admission to Xavier University of Louisiana is competitive. Fortunately, admissions officers make every effort to take a holistic approach and strive to get to know each candidate as best as possible. To that end, the university considers everything from high school transcripts and standardized test scores to recommendations and extracurricular involvement. Xavier also makes a point of noting that it does not consider gender, race, religion, creed, color, national origin, or handicap when deciding who to admit.

THE SCHOOL SAYS " . . . "

From the Admissions Office

"You have made a great decision in planning to go to college. A college education will help you reach your greatest potential as an individual and as a contributing member of our society. You will make another important decision when you select Xavier for your college education. For more than 90 years, Xavier has been expanding horizons, opening new worlds, enriching lives, developing leaders, and sending graduates out to conquer their selected corner of the world. Xavier graduates have heeded the call of providing enlightened leadership in city government. Our graduates have served as mayors, headed municipal agencies, donned judicial robes and served in state legislatures. In the health professions, Xavier is a national leader in providing graduates for schools of medicine and dentistry, including the country's top-ranked schools. College of Pharmacy graduates can be found in almost every state, serving in neighborhood pharmacies, in hospitals, and in the pharmaceutical industry. Xavier graduates are vital members of health care teams, while others conduct biomedical research. Xavier-taught educators are found in classrooms of colleges and schools. They also serve as presidents, superintendents, and principals. Business graduates rise quickly in the world of business and industry. Xavier alumni report the news on network television and in leading national publications. They perform on opera and concert stages in the music centers of the world. As lawyers and social scientists, they help right some of the wrongs of our society. Xavier seeks students to keep that tradition alive—students with great potential, who will not settle for less than high achievement, who strive to make a difference in the lives they touch. You can join the ranks of our notable alums by joining the Xavier family today."

SELECTIVITY

Admissions Rating	85
# of applicants	9,291
% of applicants accepted	60
% of acceptees attending	15

FRESHMAN PROFILE

Range SAT EBRW	510–580
Range SAT Math	480–580
Range SAT Composite	980–1180
Range ACT Composite	20–26
# submitting SAT scores	377
% submitting SAT scores	45
# submitting ACT scores	581
% submitting ACT scores	70
Average HS GPA	3.7
% graduated top 10% of class	30
% graduated top 25% of class	59
% graduated top 50% of class	85

DEADLINES

Regular	
Priority	3/1
Deadline	7/1
Nonfall registration?	Yes

FINANCIAL FACTS

Financial Aid Rating	76
Annual tuition	$23,065
Room and board	$9,458
Required fees	$2,882
Books and supplies	$1,300
Average frosh need-based scholarship	$9,385
Average UG need-based scholarship	$8,570
% needy frosh rec. need-based scholarship or grant aid	79
% needy UG rec. need-based scholarship or grant aid	73
% needy frosh rec. non-need-based scholarship or grant aid	0
% needy UG rec. non-need-based scholarship or grant aid	0
% needy frosh rec. need-based self-help aid	96
% needy UG rec. need-based self-help aid	93
% frosh rec. any financial aid	78
% UG rec. any financial aid	73
Average cumulative indebtedness	$21,820
% frosh need fully met	38
% ugrads need fully met	38
Average % of frosh need met	83
Average % of ugrad need met	64

XAVIER UNIVERSITY (OH)

3800 Victory Parkway, Cincinnati, OH 45207-5311 • Admissions: 513-745-3301 • Fax: 513-745-4319

CAMPUS LIFE

Quality of Life Rating	85
Fire Safety Rating	87
Green Rating	76
Type of school	Private
Affiliation	Roman Catholic-Jesuit
Environment	Metropolis

STUDENTS

Total undergrad enrollment	5,047
% male/female	46/54
% from out of state	57
% frosh from public high school	51
% frosh live on campus	91
% ugrads live on campus	46
# of fraternities	0
# of sororities	0
% African American	9
% Asian	3
% Caucasian	75
% Hispanic	6
% Native American	<1
% Pacific Islander	<1
% Two or more races	4
% Race and/or ethnicity unknown	2
% international	1
# of countries represented	45

SURVEY SAYS . . .

Lots of conservative students
Everyone loves the Musketeers

ACADEMICS

Academic Rating	78
% students returning for sophomore year	83
% students graduating within 4 years	66
% students graduating within 6 years	73
Calendar	Semester
Student/faculty ratio	11:1
Profs interesting rating	87
Profs accessible rating	92

Most classes have 20–29 students.
Most lab/discussion sessions have 10–19 students.

STUDENTS SAY "..."

Academics

Xavier University is a Catholic college that prides itself on being a small community driven by Jesuit ideals, making "[all students] feel comfortable in every aspect over their four years." The school "focuses on how to make [its students] better people," and the school's connections throughout the city and state provide "post-graduate opportunities that involve careers [and] volunteer work," as well as access to the sprawling Jesuit alumni network. Study abroad, field work, and internship opportunities are plentiful, and many students also volunteer on campus, which brings to the school "an amazing atmosphere for any student regardless of … age, religion, or culture."

"Professors are more than enthusiastic about their students' success," says a student. Faculty members utilize their skills and resources to "challenge the minds of students in the best possible way," truly preparing them for the future "especially when it comes to critical thinking." Classes incorporate guest speakers who "share experiences and tips," projects utilize programs that are relevant to real world practices, such as Qualtrics and Nielsen, and many core classes are seminars where students "solely discuss as a class and engage with each other" rather than a traditional lecture. Although "exams can be difficult depending on the class," most professors will offer the opportunity "to earn points back or redo parts of [an] exam," and "smaller class sizes make it easy to get to know your professors and create a bond with many of them."

Life

"People at Xavier fill their days with clubs, activities, sports, … and studying," and "everyone here has so much school spirit." "Basketball season is the best time of year at Xavier," says a student. "Students … are very devoted to studying," so during the weekdays they are really focused on doing their schoolwork. "There is more time to go out and roam around off-campus [and] the Cincinnati area" on the weekends, so that's when social gatherings usually take place. The campus is "gorgeous and well-maintained," though students admit it "could use more on-campus dining options." Students love "the size of the university and … the general feel." It's "very easy to see the same people each and every day," which means "making friends [is] easy and fun." This is a social bunch, and students "truly like to be around others, since everyone is so nice." When not studying, many students "go grab coffee at Gallagher Student Center or hang out on the lawn if the weather is good."

Student Body

"Xavier students are well-rounded and highly involved individuals," which means "the campus feels like family." The small, tight-knit community here "brings a sense of intimacy." "If you're struggling with something, there will be someone to help you," says a student. People tend to be "laid-back and welcoming but are also a somewhat homogenous group," though everyone is "inclusive and supportive of different faiths [and] political views." Students note that the school is in the act of "becoming more diverse," which allows "for more discussion to learn new perspectives and … in turn to understand each other more deeply."

XAVIER UNIVERSITY (OH)

Financial Aid: 513-745-3142 • E-Mail: xuadmit@xavier.edu • Website: www.xavier.edu

THE PRINCETON REVIEW SAYS

Admissions

Very important factors considered include: rigor of secondary school record, academic GPA. *Important factors considered include:* application essay, standardized test scores, recommendation(s), extracurricular activities, character/personal qualities, volunteer work. *Other factors considered include:* class rank, talent/ability, first generation, alumni/ae relation, work experience, level of applicant's interest. ACT with or without writing accepted. SAT with or without Essay component accepted. High school diploma is required and GED is accepted. *Academic units recommended:* 4 English, 3 math, 3 science, 2 foreign language, 3 social studies, 5 academic electives, 1 unit from above areas or other academic areas.

Financial Aid

Students should submit: FAFSA. Priority filing deadline is 2/15. The Princeton Review suggests that all financial aid forms be submitted as soon as possible after October 1. *Need-based scholarships/grants offered:* College/university scholarship or grant aid from institutional funds; Federal Pell; Private scholarships; SEOG; State scholarships/grants; United Negro College Fund. *Loan aid offered:* Direct PLUS loans; Direct Subsidized Stafford Loans; Direct Unsubsidized Stafford Loans. Applicants will be notified of awards on a rolling basis beginning 12/15. Federal Work-Study Program available. Institutional employment available.

The Inside Word

There will be no major hurdles for above-average students when it comes to gaining admission to Xavier. For select schools within Xavier it will take a little more legwork; Music and Theatre students must audition, and Nursing students must indicate their intent to enroll in the nursing school on the initial application. Look to provide credible demonstrations of commitment to academics and Jesuit ideals of service if you want to win over admissions officers.

THE SCHOOL SAYS "..."

From the Admissions Office

"Founded in 1831, Xavier University is the fourth oldest of the twenty-eight Jesuit colleges and universities in the United States. The Jesuit tradition is evident in the university's core curriculum, degree programs, and involvement opportunities. Xavier is home to approximately 7,000 total students; 4,300 degree-seeking undergraduates. The student population represents more than forty-five states and forty-three foreign countries. Xavier offers more than eighty undergraduate academic majors and more than fifty minors in the College of Arts and Sciences; the Williams College of Business; and the College of Social Sciences, Health, and Education. Most popular majors include business, natural sciences, nursing, communication arts, education, psychology, biology, sport management/marketing, and pre-professional study. Other programs of note include University Scholars; Honors AB; Philosophy, Politics, and the Public; Army ROTC, study abroad, academic service-learning, and community engagement fellowship. There are more than 100 academic clubs, social and service organizations, and recreational sports activities on campus. Students participate in groups such as student government, campus ministry, performing arts, and intramural sports as well as one of the largest service-oriented Alternative Break clubs in the country. Xavier is a member of the Division I Big East Conference and fields teams in men's and women's basketball, cross-country, track, golf, soccer, swimming, and tennis, as well as men's baseball and women's volleyball. Xavier is situated on more than 180 acres in a residential area of Cincinnati, Ohio. The face of Xavier continues to change with the addition of the technology-based Conaton Learning Commons and Smith Hall, a new building for the Williams College of Business, both which opened in fall 2010, Fenwick Place which includes a 535-bed residence hall, a dining hall and offices that opened in fall 2011 and a new classroom building that opened in fall 2015. Xavier University offers test-optional admission. It is your choice to include ACT or SAT scores as part of your application."

SELECTIVITY

Admissions Rating	78
# of applicants	14,758
% of applicants accepted	76
% of acceptees attending	11
# offered a place on the wait list	366

FRESHMAN PROFILE

Range SAT EBRW	540–640
Range SAT Math	530–640
Range SAT Composite	1083–1270
Range ACT Composite	22–28
# submitting SAT scores	486
% submitting SAT scores	40
# submitting ACT scores	897
% submitting ACT scores	74
Average HS GPA	3.6
% graduated top 10% of class	23
% graduated top 25% of class	52
% graduated top 50% of class	82

DEADLINES

Regular	
Priority	2/1
Notification	Rolling, 10/15
Nonfall registration?	Yes

FINANCIAL FACTS

Financial Aid Rating	80
Annual tuition	$42,230
Room and board	$13,310
Required fees	$230
Books and supplies	$1,300
Average frosh need-based scholarship	$24,587
Average UG need-based scholarship	$23,327
% needy frosh rec. need-based scholarship or grant aid	60
% needy UG rec. need-based scholarship or grant aid	60
% needy frosh rec. non-need-based scholarship or grant aid	39
% needy UG rec. non-need-based scholarship or grant aid	31
% needy frosh rec. need-based self-help aid	55
% needy UG rec. need-based self-help aid	60
% frosh rec. any financial aid	99.7
% UG rec. any financial aid	89.3
% UG borrow to pay for school	53
Average cumulative indebtedness	$10,348
% frosh need fully met	10
% ugrads need fully met	6
Average % of frosh need met	66
Average % of ugrad need met	63

YALE UNIVERSITY

PO Box 208234, New Haven, CT 06520-8234 • Admissions: 203-432-9300 • Fax: 203-432-9392

STUDENTS SAY "..."

Academics

Listening to Yale students wax rhapsodic about their school, one can be forgiven for wondering whether they aren't actually describing the platonic form of the university. By their own account, students here benefit not only from "amazing academics and extensive resources" that provide "phenomenal in- and out-of-class education," but also from participation in "a student body that is committed to learning and to each other." Unlike some other prestigious, prominent research universities, Yale "places unparalleled focus on undergraduate education," requiring all professors to teach at least one undergraduate course each year. "[You know] the professors actually love teaching, because if they just wanted to do their research, they could have easily gone elsewhere." A residential college system further personalizes the experience. Each residential college "has a Dean and a [Head], each of which is only responsible for 300 to 500 students, so administrative attention is highly specialized and widely available." Students further enjoy access to "a seemingly never-ending supply of resources (they really just love throwing money at us)" that includes "the [13.8] million volumes in our libraries." In short, "the opportunities are truly endless." "The experiences you have here and the people that you meet will change your life and strengthen your dreams," says one student. Looking for the flip side to all this? "If the weather were a bit nicer, that would be excellent," one student offers. Guess that will have to do.

Life

Yale is, of course, extremely challenging academically, but students assure us that "aside from the stress of midterms and finals, life at Yale is relatively carefree." Work doesn't keep undergrads from participating in "a huge variety of activities for fun. There are more than 400 student groups, including singing, dancing, juggling fire, theater...the list goes on. Because of all of these groups, there are shows on-campus all the time, which are a lot of fun and usually free or less than five dollars. On top of that, there are parties and events on campus and off campus, as well as many subsidized trips to New York City and Boston." Many here "are politically active (or at least politically aware)" and "a very large number of students either volunteer or try to get involved in some sort of organization to make a difference in the world." When the weekend comes around, "there are always parties to go to, whether at the frats or in rooms, but there's definitely no pressure to drink if you don't want to. A good friend of mine pledged a frat without drinking and that's definitely not unheard of (but still not common)." The relationship between Yale and the city of New Haven "sometimes leaves a little to be desired, but overall it's a great place to be for four years."

Student Body

A typical Yalie is "tough to define because so much of what makes Yale special is the unique convergence of different students to form one cohesive entity. Nonetheless, the one common characteristic of Yale students is passion—each Yalie is driven and dedicated to what he or she loves most, and it creates a palpable atmosphere of enthusiasm on campus." True enough, the student body represents a wide variety of ethnic, religious, economic, and academic backgrounds, but they all "thrive on learning, whether in a class, from a book, or from a conversation with a new friend." Students here also "tend to do a lot." "Everyone has many activities that they are a part of, which in turn fosters the closely connected feel of the campus." Undergrads tend to lean to the left politically, but for "those whose political views aren't as liberal as the rest of the campus...there are several campus organizations that cater to them."

YALE UNIVERSITY

Financial Aid: 203-432-2700 • E-Mail: student.questions@yale.edu • Website: www.yale.edu

THE PRINCETON REVIEW SAYS

Admissions

Very important factors considered include: rigor of secondary school record, class rank, academic GPA, application essay, standardized test scores, recommendation(s), extracurricular activities, talent/ability, character/personal qualities. *Other factors considered include:* interview, first generation, alumni/ae relation, geographical residence, state residency, racial/ethnic status, volunteer work, work experience. ACT with or without writing accepted. SAT with or without Essay component accepted. High school diploma is required and GED is accepted.

Financial Aid

Students should submit: CSS/Financial Aid PROFILE; FAFSA; Institution's own financial aid form; Noncustodial PROFILE. Priority filing deadline is 3/1. The Princeton Review suggests that all financial aid forms be submitted as soon as possible after October 1. *Need-based scholarships/grants offered:* College/university scholarship or grant aid from institutional funds; Federal Pell; Private scholarships; SEOG; State scholarships/grants; United Negro College Fund. *Loan aid offered:* Direct PLUS loans; Direct Subsidized Stafford Loans; Direct Unsubsidized Stafford Loans. Applicants will be notified of awards on or about 4/1. Institutional employment available.

The Inside Word

Yale estimates that over three-quarters of all its applicants are qualified to attend the university, but less than 10 percent get in. That adds up to a lot of broken hearts among kids who, if admitted, could probably handle the academic program. With so many qualified applicants to choose from, Yale can winnow to build an incoming class that is balanced in terms of income level, racial/ethnic background, geographic origin, and academic interest. Legacies (descendants of Yale grads) gain some advantage—although they still need exceptionally strong credentials.

THE SCHOOL SAYS "..."

From the Admissions Office

"The most important questions the admissions committee must resolve are 'Who is likely to make the most of Yale's resources?' and 'Who will contribute significantly to the Yale community?' These questions suggest an approach to evaluating applicants that is more complex than whether Yale would rather admit well-rounded people or those with specialized talents. In selecting a class of 1,550 from roughly 30,000 applicants, the admissions committee looks for academic ability and achievement combined with such personal characteristics as motivation, curiosity, energy, and leadership ability. The nature of these qualities is such that there is no simple profile of grades, scores, interests, and activities that will assure admission. Diversity within the student population is important, and the admissions committee selects a class of able and contributing individuals from a variety of backgrounds and with a broad range of interests and skills."

SELECTIVITY

Admissions Rating	99
# of applicants	35,307
% of applicants accepted	6
% of acceptees attending	70

FRESHMAN PROFILE

Range SAT EBRW	720–770
Range SAT Math	730–790
Range ACT Composite	33–35
# submitting SAT scores	1,066
% submitting SAT scores	68
# submitting ACT scores	857
% submitting ACT scores	54
% graduated top 10% of class	95
% graduated top 25% of class	99
% graduated top 50% of class	100

DEADLINES

Early action	
Deadline	11/1
Notification	12/15
Regular	
Deadline	1/2
Notification	4/1
Nonfall registration?	No

FINANCIAL FACTS

Financial Aid Rating	99
Annual tuition	$55,500
Room and board	$16,600
Required fees	
Books and supplies	$3,670
Average frosh need-based scholarship	$57,954
Average UG need-based scholarship	$56,602
% needy frosh rec. need-based scholarship or grant aid	100
% needy UG rec. need-based scholarship or grant aid	100
% needy frosh rec. non-need-based scholarship or grant aid	0
% needy UG rec. non-need-based scholarship or grant aid	0
% needy frosh rec. need-based self-help aid	75
% needy UG rec. need-based self-help aid	85
% frosh rec. any financial aid	51
% UG rec. any financial aid	52
% UG borrow to pay for school	16
Average cumulative indebtedness	$14,575
% frosh need fully met	100
% ugrads need fully met	100
Average % of frosh need met	100
Average % of ugrad need met	100

2021 BEST REGIONAL COLLEGES

In addition to the 386 schools in this book, we salute the following 270 schools that we consider academically outstanding and well worth consideration in your college search. For more information on these schools, visit PrincetonReview.com to find admissions information, costs, and more.

MIDWEST

Illinois
Augustana College
Dominican University
Elmhurst College
Illinois College
Lewis University
Millikin University
Monmouth College
North Central College
Principia College
Rockford University
Southern Illinois University Carbondale
University of St. Francis
Western Illinois University

Indiana
Anderson University
Ball State University
Grace College and Seminary
Huntington University
Indiana State University
Manchester University
Saint Joseph's College
Saint Mary's College
Taylor University
Trine University
Valparaiso University

Iowa
Briar Cliff University
Clarke University
Dordt College
Drake University
Graceland University
Luther College
Morningside College
Northwestern College
St. Ambrose University
University of Northern Iowa
Wartburg College

Kansas
Baker University
Emporia State University
Pittsburg State University
Sterling College
University of Saint Mary

Michigan
Alma College
Eastern Michigan University
Grand Valley State University
Hope College
University of Michigan—Flint
Western Michigan University

Minnesota
Augsburg University
The College of Saint Scholastica
Gustavus Adolphus College
Saint Mary's University of Minnesota
St. Catherine University
University of Minnesota, Crookston
University of Saint Thomas
Winona State University

Missouri
Columbia College
Southeast Missouri State University
University of Central Missouri
University of Missouri—Kansas City
Westminster College

Nebraska
Doane University
Hastings College
Nebraska Wesleyan University
University of Nebraska Omaha

North Dakota
Mayville State University
University of Jamestown

Ohio
Ashland University
Baldwin Wallace University
Cedarville University
The Cleveland Institute of Art
Hiram College
John Carroll University
Lake Erie College
Lourdes University
Marietta College
The University of Akron
The University of Findlay
Wright State University

South Dakota
Augustana University

Wisconsin
Carthage College
Edgewood College
Milwaukee School of Engineering
Northland College
St. Norbert College
University of Wisconsin—Eau Claire
University of Wisconsin—Milwaukee
University of Wisconsin—River Falls

NORTHEAST

Connecticut
Central Connecticut State University
Eastern Connecticut State University

Maine
University of Maine—Fort Kent

Maryland
Hood College
Maryland Institute College of Art
Towson University

Massachusetts
Bard College at Simon's Rock
Hampshire College
Lesley University
Merrimack College
Nichols College
Regis College
University of Massachusetts Boston
Wentworth Institute of Technology
Worcester State University

New Hampshire
Keene State College

New Jersey
Ramapo College of New Jersey
Stockton University

New York
Adelphi University
Elmira College
Eugene Lang College of Liberal Arts
Hartwick College
Houghton College
Iona College
LIM College
Long Island University
Molloy College
Niagara University
Pratt Institute
Roberts Wesleyan College
St. John Fisher College
State University of New York—Alfred State University
State University of New York at Cortland
State University of New York at New Paltz
State University of New York—Fredonia
State University of New York—Maritime College
State University of New York—Oswego
State University of New York—The College at Brockport
State University of New York—University at Albany
State University of New York—University at Buffalo
Wells College

Pennsylvania
Albright College
Arcadia University
California University of Pennsylvania
Chatham University
Chestnut Hill College
Delaware Valley University
Elizabethtown College
King's College (PA)
Kutztown University of Pennsylvania
La Roche University
Lebanon Valley College
Messiah College
Misericordia University
Moore College of Art and Design
Neumann University
Robert Morris University
Rosemont College
Seton Hill University
Slippery Rock University of Pennsylvania
University of the Arts
University of Pittsburgh at Bradford
University of Pittsburgh at Johnstown
Westminster College (PA)
Wilkes University
York College of Pennsylvania

Rhode Island
Roger Williams University
Salve Regina University

SOUTHEAST

Alabama
Auburn University at Montgomery
Birmingham-Southern College
Huntingdon College
Samford University
Talladega College
Troy University—Troy

Arkansas
Arkansas State University
Harding University
Hendrix College
Lyon College

Florida
Florida Agriculture and Mechanical University
Florida Atlantic University
Florida Gulf Coast University
Palm Beach Atlantic University
University of North Florida
University of West Florida
Webber International University

Georgia
Brenau University
Clark Atlanta University
Covenant College
Georgia College & State University
Oglethorpe University
Savannah College of Art and Design
Shorter University
Toccoa Falls College
University of West Georgia
Wesleyan College

Kentucky
Brescia University
Kentucky State University
Kentucky Wesleyan College

Mississippi
Mississippi College

North Carolina
Appalachian State University
Barton College
Belmont Abbey College
Campbell University
Meredith College
University of North Carolina Wilmington

South Carolina
Anderson University
Coker College
Winthrop University

Tennessee
Belmont University
Carson-Newman University
Christian Brothers University
East Tennessee State University
Fisk University
King University
Lee University
Lipscomb University
Tennessee Technological University
Union University
The University of Tennessee at Martin

Virginia
Averett University
Bridgewater College
Longwood University
Mary Baldwin College
Old Dominion University
Radford University
Sweet Briar College

West Virginia
Bethany College (WV)
Concord University
Shepherd University
University of Charleston
Virginia Wesleyan University

WEST

Alaska
University of Alaska Fairbanks

Arizona
Prescott College

California
Azusa Pacific University
Biola University
California Institute of the Arts
California State Polytechnic University, Pomona
California State University, East Bay
California State University, Long Beach
California State University, San Bernardino
Hult International Business School

Humboldt State University
Menlo College
Otis College of Art and Design
University of California—Irvine
University of California—Merced
Westmont College

Colorado
Fort Lewis College

Hawaii
Hawaii Pacific University

Idaho
The College of Idaho
Northwest Nazarene University

New Mexico
New Mexico Institute of Mining and Technology
Santa Fe University of Art and Design

Oklahoma
Oklahoma Baptist University
Oklahoma Christian University
Oklahoma City University
Oklahoma State University
Oral Roberts University

Oregon
Corban University
George Fox University
Linfield College
Oregon State University
Pacific University
University of Portland

Texas
Abilene Christian University
Hardin-Simmons University
Schreiner University
St. Edward's University
Texas Lutheran University
Texas Tech University
University of North Texas
University of St. Thomas
The University of Texas at Arlington

Utah
Southern Utah University
Utah State University
Weber State University

Washington
Pacific Lutheran University
Seattle Pacific University
University of Washington—Bothell
Walla Walla University
Whitworth University

INTERNATIONAL
Canada
University of Toronto

Ireland
Maynooth University
Trinity College Dublin

PART 4

Indexes

INDEX OF SCHOOLS BY LOCATION

INDEX OF SCHOOLS BY TUITION

Price categories are based on figures the schools reported to us in early spring 2020 for tuition and required fees (in-state tuition for public schools) and do not include room, board, transportation, or other expenses.

DePaul University	210	Washington College	784
Drew University	216	Washington & Jefferson College	786
Duquesne University	224	Whittier College	808
Fordham College	228	Wittenberg University	810
Eckerd College	230	Wofford College	818
Emerson College	236	Xavier University (OH)	824
Fairfield University	242		
Gonzaga University	268	**OVER $50,000**	
Goucher College	272	Allegheny College	62
Hampden-Sydney College	282	American University	64
Hofstra University	300	Amherst College	66
Illinois Institute of Technology	306	Babson College	78
Illinois Wesleyan University	308	Bard College	80
Ithaca College	316	Barnard College	82
Juniata College	322	Bates College	84
Kettering University	330	Beloit College	92
Lake Forest College	336	Bennington College	94
Lawrence University	340	Bentley University	96
Loyola University of Chicago	352	Boston College	102
Loyola University New Orleans	356	Boston University	104
Lycoming College	358	Bowdoin College	106
Manhattan College	362	Brandeis University	110
Manhattanville College	364	Brown University	114
Marist College	366	Bryn Mawr College	118
Marquette University	368	Bucknell University	120
McDaniel College	372	California Institute of Technology	124
Millsaps College	390	Carleton College	130
Moravian College	398	Carnegie Mellon University	132
Ohio Wesleyan University	428	Case Western Reserve University	134
Pace University	432	Chapman University	146
Quinnipiac University	450	Claremont McKenna College	158
Randolph-Macon College	454	Clarkson University	160
Rhodes College	460	Colby College	168
Rice University	462	Colgate University	170
Rider University	464	College of the Holy Cross	180
Ripon College	466	The College of Wooster	184
Roanoke College	468	Colorado College	186
Rochester Institute of Technology	470	Columbia University	190
Rose-Hulman Institute of Technology	474	Connecticut College	192
Sacred Heart University	478	Cornell University	198
Saint Anselm College	480	Dartmouth College	202
St. John's University (NY)	488	Davidson College	204
Saint Joseph's University (PA)	490	Denison University	208
Saint Louis University	494	DePauw University	212
Saint Michael's College	500	Dickinson College	214
St. Olaf College	502	Drexel University	218
Seattle University	514	Duke University	222
Siena College	518	Emory University	238
Simmons University	520	Fordham University	250
Southwestern University	530	Franklin & Marshall College	252
Stetson University	548	Franklin W. Olin College of Engineering	254
Stonehill College	552	Furman University	256
Suffolk University	554	Georgetown University	260
Susquehanna University	556	The George Washington University	262
Texas Christian University	566	Gettysburg College	266
Transylvania University	572	Grinnell College	274
Trinity University	576	Hamilton College	280
University of Dallas	632	Harvard College	288
University of Dayton	634	Harvey Mudd College	290
University of New Haven	692	Haverford College	292
University of Redlands	718	Hobart and William Smith Colleges	298
The University of Scranton	730	Johns Hopkins University	320
The University of the South	732	Kalamazoo College	324
The University of Tulsa	750	Kenyon College	328
Wabash College	776	Knox College	332
Wagner College	778	Lafayette College	334

Lehigh University	342	Swarthmore College	558
Lewis & Clark College	346	Syracuse University	560
Loyola Marymount University	350	Trinity College (CT)	574
Loyola University Maryland	354	Tufts University	580
Macalester College	360	Tulane University	582
Massachusetts Institute of Technology	370	Union College (NY)	586
Middlebury College	384	The University of Chicago	624
Mount Holyoke College	400	University of Denver	638
Muhlenberg College	402	University of Miami	674
New York University	410	University of Notre Dame	706
Northeastern University	414	University of Pennsylvania	712
Northwestern University	416	University of Puget Sound	716
Oberlin College	418	University of Richmond	722
Occidental College	420	University of Rochester	724
Pepperdine University	436	University of San Diego	726
Pitzer College	438	University of San Francisco	728
Pomona College	440	University of Southern California	740
Princeton University	444	Ursinus College	764
Providence College	446	Vanderbilt University	766
Reed College	456	Vassar College	768
Rensselaer Polytechnic Institute	458	Villanova University	770
Rollins College	472	Wake Forest University	780
St. Lawrence University	492	Washington University in St. Louis	790
Saint Mary's College of California	496	Wellesley College	794
Santa Clara University	508	Wesleyan University	796
Sarah Lawrence College	510	Wheaton College (MA)	804
Scripps College	512	Whitman College	806
Skidmore College	522	Williams College	814
Smith College	524	Worcester Polytechnic Institute	820
Southern Methodist University	528	Yale University	826
Stanford University	534		
Stevens Institute of Technology	550		

THE PRINCETON REVIEW NATIONAL COLLEGE COUNSELOR ADVISORY BOARD, 2020–2021

We thank the members of this board for their careful and considered input.

Michael A. Acquilano, Director of College Guidance, Staten Island Academy, Staten Island, NY

Roland M. Allen, Director of College Counseling, St. Margaret's Episcopal School, San Juan Capistrano, CA

Lee Bierer, Weekly Countdown to College Syndicated Columnist and Independent College Counselor, College Admission Strategies, Charlotte, NC

Marianne M. Borgmann, College Advisor, St. Xavier High School, Cincinatti, OH

Henry DelAngelo, School Counselor, Joel Barlow High School, Redding, CT

Stacey Evert, Director of College Counseling, Brownell Talbot School, Omaha, NE

Judy S. Fairfull, Guidance Department Head, Doherty Memorial High School, Worcester, MA, Worcester Public School District, MA

Meghan Farley, Director of College Counseling, Pingree School, South Hamilton, MA

Deadra Faulkner, Director of Guidance, Westbury Public Schools, Old Westbury, NY

Maureen A. Ferrell, Director of College Counseling, The Summit Country Day School, Cincinnati, OH

Anne Gregory, Director of Guidance, Pope John XXIII High School, Sparta, NJ

Nancy Griesemer, MPA, Columnist for Examiner.com and Independent College Counsultant, College Explorations LLC, Oakton, VA

Troy B. Hammond, Director of University Counseling & Student Services Department Head, Bayview Glen Independent School, Toronto, Ontario, Canada

Robert Harry, Director of College Counseling, Saint James School, Hagerstown, MD

Ann Herbener, College Counselor, Waukegan High School, Waukegan, IL

William Hirt, College Counselor, Professional Children's School, New York, NY

Nikki Hostnik, Associate Director of College Counseling, Saint Louis Priory School, St. Louis, MO

Marilyn J. Kaufman, M.Ed., Independent College Counselor and Educational Consultant, (Professional Member, Independent Educational Consultants Association), President of College Admission Consultants, Inc., Dallas, Texas

Geri Kellogg, LPC Counselor, J. J. Pearce High School. Richardson, TX

Joanne Levy-Prewitt, Independent College Admissions Advisor; Get Going Workshops; Moraga, CA

Earl R. Macam, Ed.D., College Counselor, Mary Institute and St. Louis Country Day School (MICDS), St. Louis, MO

Susan Marrs, Director of College Counseling, Seven Hills School, Cincinnati, OH

Erin M. McElligott, Director of College Counseling, Prospect Hill Academy Charter School, Cambridge, MA

Moira McKinnon, Director of College Counseling, Berwick Academy, South Berrwick, ME

Ms. Kathy Morgan, Director of Guidance, Notre Dame Academy, Los Angeles, CA

Elizabeth A. Roper, MSEd, Director of College and Academic Guidance, The Ursuline School, New Rochelle, NY

Casey Rowley, College Counselor, Beverly Hills High School, Beverly Hills, CA

Kimberly Simpson, Educational Consultant, Collegiate Admissions Consulting Services, LLC, Covington, LA

Ed Stone, College & Career Specialist, Freehold Regional High School District, Englishtown, NJ

Chris Teare, Director of College Counseling, The Wardlaw+Hartridge School, Edison, NJ

Theresa Urist, Global Director of University Counseling, The Aga Khan Academies and Independent College Consultant, Boston, MA

Michael Wilner, Educational Consultant and Founder, Wilner Education, Putney, VT

SCHOOL SAYS . . .

In this section you'll find advertisements directly from colleges with information they'd like you to consider about their schools. The editorial in these pages is written by the schools, which pay a fee to offset the cost of printing their advertisements in this section.

The Princeton Review does not charge schools for inclusion in the School Profiles (pp 55–827) section in this book. The company has never required colleges, universities, or any institutions to pay a fee for their profiles or inclusions in our books.

For information about how we selected the 386 outstanding schools in this book, see page 19, "How We Produce This Book."

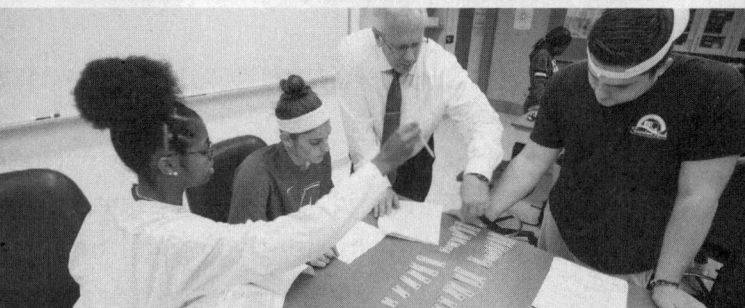

SEE YOURSELF HERE.

KNOW ANYTHING IS POSSIBLE.

You are wonderfully unique. Your education should be equally so.

HERE, you will be guided by trusted mentors who understand your goals and dreams, connect you with life-changing opportunities and consider your well-being as important as their own.

(Come see what's possible when people walking different paths come together with common purpose.)

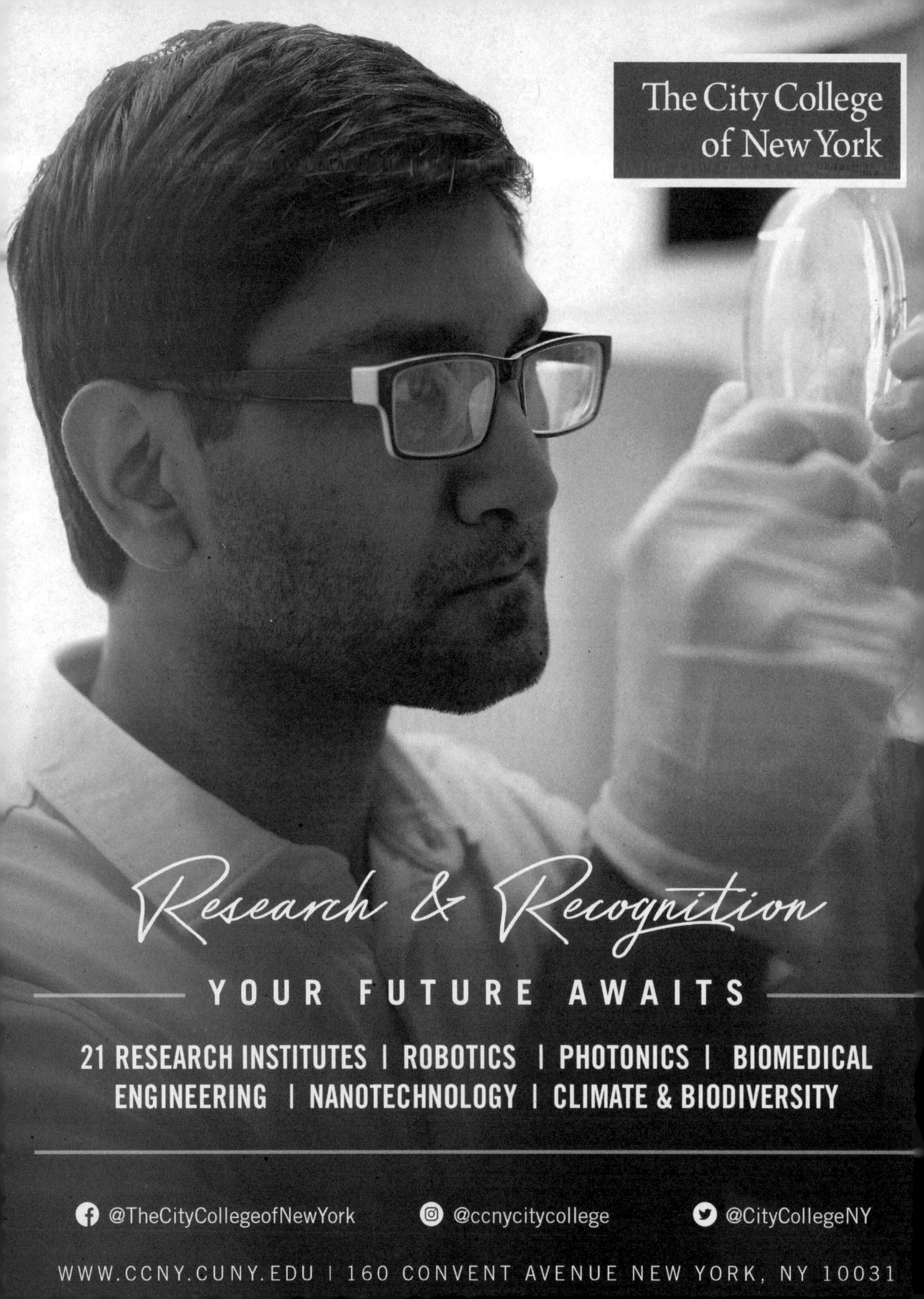
The City College of New York
Research & Recognition
YOUR FUTURE AWAITS
21 RESEARCH INSTITUTES | ROBOTICS | PHOTONICS | BIOMEDICAL ENGINEERING | NANOTECHNOLOGY | CLIMATE & BIODIVERSITY
@TheCityCollegeofNewYork
@ccnycitycollege
@CityCollegeNY
WWW.CCNY.CUNY.EDU | 160 CONVENT AVENUE NEW YORK, NY 10031

CLEMS☙N

clemson.edu/admissions

→ *Leading the way*

For 12 consecutive years, Clemson University has been a top-ranked national public university. And while we have a reputation for excellence that spans the globe, it's our commitment to community that sets us apart.

The 80+ undergraduate degrees in seven colleges take students from the classroom to a learning environment focused on hands-on experiences and one-on-one guidance. And our abundance of minors, concentrations and emphasis areas uniquely prepare students to follow their passions. Clemson students will be the ones who build the foundations, research the cures and create the technology that will impact their world, and ours, forever.

Discover all that Clemson has to offer at *clemson.edu*.

let's begin →

High Expectations?

Say <u>Hi</u> to The College of New Jersey.

PROFESSION ✦ PASSION

Fusion is the process that powers stars – and dreams.

Your Drury Fusion™ is our innovative academic program allowing you to fuse professional goals and personal passions. It's unlike anything you've ever done. **Yet.**

START YOUR FUSION AT **DRURY.EDU/APPLY**

OUR GUARANTEES

Florida Southern College goes beyond the conventional college experience, guaranteeing each student an internship, a travel-study experience, and graduation in four years. These signature opportunities, combined with our world-class faculty and stunning historic campus, create a college experience unlike any other.

FLORIDA SOUTHERN COLLEGE

flsouthern.edu/**guarantees**

WHATEVER IS
NEXT...

Everyone wonders what's next.
For Grand Valley students, next
is opportunity and innovation.
Next is global, connecting and
uniting us. It's local, shaping the
spaces in which we work and live.
It's a commitment to progress.
Next is where minds are free to
imagine what could be. At GVSU,
next is now. And whatever's next
for you, we will help you get there.

gvsu.edu/next

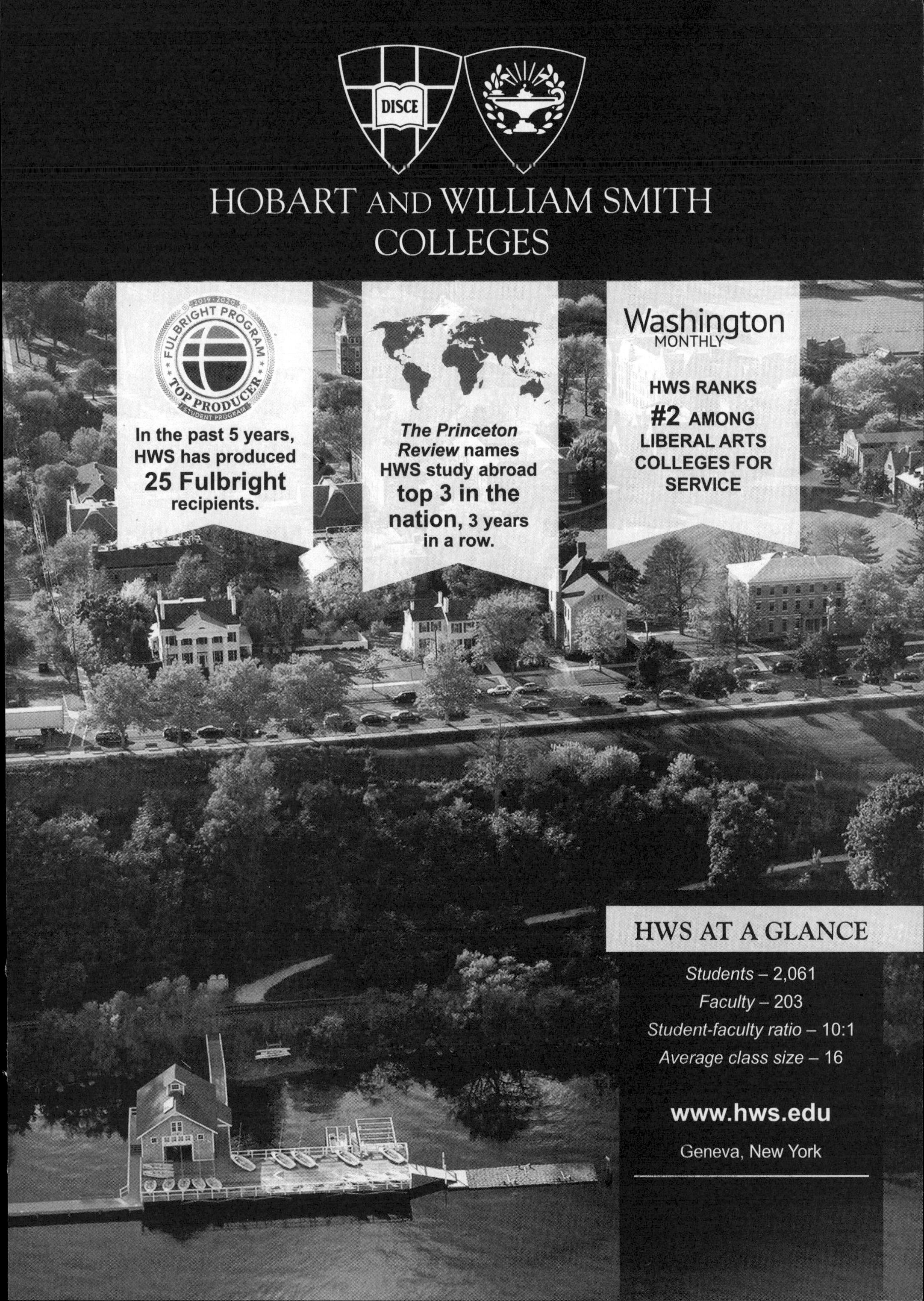

HOBART AND WILLIAM SMITH COLLEGES
DISCE
2019 · 2020 FULBRIGHT PROGRAM TOP PRODUCER STUDENT PROGRAM
In the past 5 years, HWS has produced 25 Fulbright recipients.
The Princeton Review names HWS study abroad top 3 in the nation, 3 years in a row.
Washington MONTHLY
HWS RANKS #2 AMONG LIBERAL ARTS COLLEGES FOR SERVICE
HWS AT A GLANCE
Students – 2,061
Faculty – 203
Student-faculty ratio – 10:1
Average class size – 16
www.hws.edu
Geneva, New York

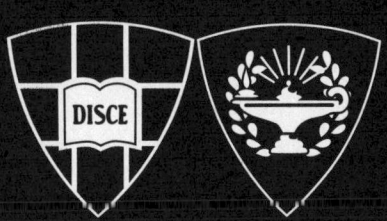

LIVE YOUR DREAMS.
LIVE YOUR STORY.

EXPLORE.
BUILD experiences.
Discover
what is **POSSIBLE**

Learn more at **naz.edu**

SALVE

REGINA UNIVERSITY

salve.edu

When your entire life is ahead of you, it can be hard to take a step in any one direction. Then you find an unparalleled opportunity to develop yourself in bold new ways, and suddenly your next steps become much clearer. At Salve, our community of active scholars prepares students for personal and professional journeys filled with creative ambition and fearless discovery. In an ever-changing world where standing still is not an option, Salve continues to evolve to meet the educational and spiritual needs of today's students and tomorrow's leaders. **Come here, work hard and go far.**

98%
of graduates are employed or pursuing advanced degrees within six months of Commencement

60
Undergraduate and graduate degree programs

BEST
U.S. News
RANKINGS

A Top Regional and Best Value School

99%
of students receive scholarships and/or financial aid

20 varsity level sports

Over **200**
study abroad programs in 45 countries

Salve graduates are in the **TOP 8%** of all colleges and universities for lifetime earnings. That is a real return on investment!

VISIT! Go to salve.edu/visit
to learn about all your options for experiencing campus.

There are Spiders everywhere.

AND THAT'S A GOOD THING.

The moment a new Spider's boundless ambition meets Richmond's programs, an incomparable partnership forms between student and University. Our faculty become accompanists, mentors, and confidants to you in your studies. And when you graduate, you join a global web of successful Spiders who are advancing in fields worldwide.

From here, you can go anywhere — and it all starts within you.

richmond.edu

Robert Franek, Editor-in-Chief at The Princeton Review, is the company's chief expert on education and college issues. Over his 25-year career, he has served as a college admissions administrator, test prep teacher, author, and lecturer. Rob visits more than 50 colleges a year and oversees the company's line of 150 titles from best-selling test-prep guides to college- and graduate school-related books. Prior to joining The Princeton Review in 1999, Rob served as a college admissions administrator at Wagner College (New York City) for six years. He earned his BA at Drew University in Political Science and History. Follow him on Twitter: @RobFranek.

David Soto, Director of Content Development, is a graduate of the Walter Cronkite School of Journalism at Arizona State University and Director of Content Development for The Princeton Review. He helps create a line of guidebook titles on various aspects of the admissions process, including college, graduate school, and career-related topics, as well as the company website which serves more than half of all college-bound students. Prior to joining The Princeton Review in 2001, David worked as a photojournalist at The Arizona Republic (Phoenix) for two years. He lives in Brooklyn, NY.

Stephen Koch, Student Survey Manager, received a BA from Wesleyan University in Middletown, Connecticut. He has been a member of The Princeton Review admissions content team since 2011. Stephen gathers and synthesizes all types of data The Princeton Review uses to create our guidebooks and website content. He lives in Brooklyn, NY. In his free time, he loves to travel (only sometimes to colleges) and performing with his improv team at the Upright Citizens Brigade, The People's Improv Theater, and all over the New York area.

Aaron Riccio, Senior Editor, earned a BA from Binghamton University in 2005. Since then, he has been working in various capacities within educational services, and has been with The Princeton Review's editorial department for the last five years. (He also moonlights as a TV, theater, and video game critic for Slant Magazine.)

College Hopes & Worries Survey 2021

Mail to The Princeton Review, 2021 College Hopes & Worries Survey, c/o Robert Franek, The Princeton Review, 110 E. 42nd Street, 7th Fl., New York, NY 10017. (mailed entries must be received by February 20, 2021) or fill out online (online entries can be submitted between January 20 and February 28, 2021) at www.Princeton-Review.com/go/survey.

TAKE 3 MINUTES FOR A CHANCE TO WIN OUR $2,000 SCHOLARSHIP!

Name

Address (optional) _____

City / State / ZIP _____

Daytime phone _____

E-mail address _____

I am a:

○ student applying to college

○ parent of a student applying to college

What year will you (your child) begin college?

○ 2019

○ 2020

○ 2021

○ 2022

○ Other (please specify) _____

1. **What would be your "dream" college? What college would you most like to attend (or see your child attend) if chance of being accepted or cost were not an issue? (Please write complete name of the school, e.g., "University of Oklahoma," not initials such as "OU" which could also be an abbreviation for Ohio University.)**

   _____

2. **How many colleges will you (your child) apply to?**

   ○ 1 to 4

   ○ 5 to 8

   ○ 9 to 12

   ○ 13 or more

3. **What is/will be the toughest part of your (your child's) college application experience?**

    ○ Researching colleges

    ○ Taking SAT®, ACT®, or AP® Exams

    ○ Completing applications for admission and financial aid

    ○ Waiting for the decision letters and choosing which college to attend

4. **Which college admission exam do you (your child) plan to (or have taken)?**

    ○ The ACT®

    ○ The SAT®

4a. **How likely is it that you (your child) will take both the ACT® and the SAT®?**

    ○ Extremely likely

    ○ Very likely

    ○ Somewhat likely

    ○ Not very likely

    ○ Not at all likely

5. **How would you rate the college application guidance and support you (your child) have (has) received from your (your child's) high school college advisor / guidance counselor?**

    ○ Excellent

    ○ Good

    ○ Fair

    ○ Poor

6. **What do you estimate your (or your child's) college degree will cost, including four years of tuition, room & board, fees, books and other expenses?**

    ○ More than $100,000

    ○ $75,000 to $100,000

    ○ $50,000 to $75,000

    ○ $25,000 to $50,000

    ○ More than $25,000

7. **How necessary will financial aid—education loans, scholarships or grants—be to pay for your (your child's) college education?**

    ○ Extremely

    ○ Very

    ○ Somewhat

    ○ Not at all

8. **What's your biggest concern about your (your child's) college applications?**

   ○ Won't get into first-choice college

   ○ Will get into first-choice college but won't be able to afford to attend

   ○ Level of debt I (my child) will take on to pay for the degree

   ○ Will attend a college I (my child) may regret

9. **How would you gauge your stress level about the college application process?**

   ○ Very High

   ○ High

   ○ Average

   ○ Low

   ○ Very Low

10. **Ideally, how far from home would you like the college you (your child) attend(s) to be?**

    ○ Less than 250 miles

    ○ 250 to 500 miles

    ○ 500 to 1,000 miles

    ○ More than 1,000 miles

11. **When it comes to choosing the college you (your child) will attend, which of the following do you think it is most likely to be?**

    ○ College with best academic reputation

    ○ College with best program for my (my child's) career interests

    ○ College that will be the most affordable

    ○ College that will be the best overall fit

12. **If you (your child) had a way to compare colleges based on their reputation with regard to their career services offerings, how much would this affect your (your child's) decision to apply to or attend a school?**

    ○ Strongly

    ○ Very much

    ○ Somewhat

    ○ Not much

    ○ Not at all

13. **If you (your child) had a way to compare colleges based on their commitment to environmental "green" issues (e.g., practices concerning energy use, recycling, etc. or academic offerings), how much would this affect your (your child's) decision to apply to or attend a school?**

   ○ Strongly

   ○ Very much

   ○ Somewhat

   ○ Not much

   ○ Not at all

14. **What will be the biggest benefit of your (your child) getting a college degree?**

   ○ The education overall

   ○ The exposure to new ideas, places, people

   ○ The potentially better job and higher income

15. **On the whole, do you believe college will be "worth it" for you (your child)?**

   ○ Yes

   ○ No

What advice would you give to college applicants or parents of applicants going through this experience next year?

_____

_____

_____

_____

_____

_____

_____

_____

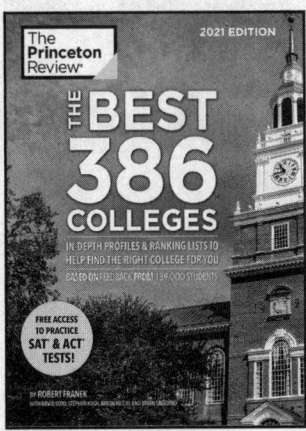